D0691178

Financial Aid
for Hispanic Americans
2017-2019

Gail Ann Schlachter
R. David Weber

A Listing of Scholarships, Fellowships, Grants, Awards, and
Other Sources of Free Money Available Primarily or
Exclusively to Hispanic Americans, Plus a Set of Six Indexes
(Program Title, Sponsoring Organization, Residency,
Tenability, Subject, and Deadline Date)

WALLA WALLA COMMUNITY
COLLEGE LIBRARY

AdmitHub
Boston, Massachusetts

© 2017 AdmitHub

All rights reserved. No part of this publication may be reproduced, stored in a retrieval system, or transmitted, in any form or by any means, electronic, mechanical, photocopying, recording, or otherwise, except for the inclusion of brief quotations in a review, without the prior permission in writing from the publisher. AdmitHub vigorously defends its copyrighted material.

AdmitHub
Harvard Innovation Launch Lab
114 Western Ave.
Boston, MA 02134
     (617) 575-9369
       E-mail: rsp@admithub.com
Visit our web site: www.admithub.com

Manufactured in the United States of America

Contents

Foreword

About Dr. Gail Schlachter and Reference Service Press

Dr. Gail Ann Schlachter (1943-2015), original founder of Reference Service Press, was working as a librarian in the mid-1970s when she recognized that women applying for college faced significant obstacles finding information about financial aid resources designed to help them. This challenge inspired her to publish her ground-breaking book, Directory of Financial Aids for Women, in 1977. The book's success prompted additional financial aid directories for other underserved communities, including the present volume for Hispanic Americans.

By 1985, the business had become so successful that she left her job as a publishing company executive to run her company, Reference Service Press, full-time. Over the years, the company's offerings expanded to over two dozen financial aid titles covering many different types of students—law students, business students, students studying abroad, and many more. The company's success was driven by its database of tens of thousands of financial aid programs, laboriously hand-built over the decades and kept current to exacting specifications. In 1995, Reference Service Press once again broke new ground by launching one of the first-ever searchable electronic databases of financial aid resources (initially through America Online). For more background about the founding and success of Reference Service Press, see Katina Strauch's 1997 "Against the Grain" interview with Dr. Schlachter, available at http://docs.lib.purdue.edu/cgi/viewcontent.cgi?article=2216&context=atg.

Dr. Schlachter was also a major figure in the library community for nearly five decades. She served: as reference book review editor for RQ (now Reference and User Services Quarterly) for 10 years; as president of the American Library Association's Reference and User Services Association; as editor of the Reference and User Services Association Quarterly; seven terms on the American Library Association's governing council; and as a member of the association's Executive Board at the time of her death. She was posthumously inducted into the California Library Association Hall of Fame. The University of Wisconsin School of Library and Information Studies named Dr. Schlachter an "Alumna of the Year," and she was recognized with both the Isadore Gilbert Mudge Citation and the Louis Shores/Oryx Press Award.

Dr. Schlachter will be remembered for how her financial aid directories helped thousands of students achieve their educational and professional dreams. She also will be remembered for her countless contributions to the library profession. And, as an American Library Association Executive Board resolution from June 2015 says, she will be remembered, "most importantly, for her mentorship, friendship, and infectious smile." Yet, despite her impressive lifetime of professional accomplishments, Dr. Schlachter always was most proud of her family, including her husband Stuart Hauser, her daughter Dr. Sandy Hirsh (and Jay Hirsh) and son Eric Goldman (and Lisa Goldman), and her grandchildren Hayley, Leah, Jacob, and Dina.

Introduction

WHY THIS DIRECTORY IS NEEDED

Despite our country's ongoing economic problems and increased college costs, the financial aid picture for minorities has never looked brighter. Currently, billions of dollars are set aside each year specifically for Hispanic Americans, African Americans, Asian Americans, and Native Americans. This funding is open to minorities at any level (high school through postdoctoral and professional) for a variety of activities, including study, research, travel, training, career development, and creative projects.

While numerous print and online listings have been prepared to identify and describe general financial aid opportunities (those open to all segments of society), those resources have never covered more than a small portion of the programs designed primarily or exclusively for minorities. As a result, many advisors, librarians, scholars, researchers, and students often have been unaware of the extensive funding available to Hispanic Americans and other minorities. But, with the ongoing publication of *Financial Aid for Hispanic Americans* that has all changed. Here, in just one place, Hispanic American students, professionals, and postdoctorates now have current and detailed information about the special resources set aside specifically for them.

Financial Aid for Hispanic Americans is prepared biennially as part of Reference Service Press' four-volume *Minority Funding Set* (the other volumes in the set cover funding for African Americans, Asian Americans, and Native Americans). Each of the volumes in this set is sold separately, or the complete set can be purchased at a discounted price.

No other source, in print or online, offers the extensive coverage of funding for minorities provided by these titles. That's why the Grantsmanship Center labeled the set "a must for every organization serving minorities," *Reference Sources for Small and Medium-Sized Libraries* called the titles "the absolute best guides for finding funding," and *Reference Books Bulletin* selected each of the volumes in the *Minority Funding Set* as their "Editor's Choice." *Financial Aid for Hispanic Americans,* itself, has also received rave reviews. The National Chicano Council on Higher Education called it "a most necessary publication," it was chosen as a "Recommended Resource" by the Ventures Scholars Program, and *Vista: The Hispanic Magazine* pronounced it a "very comprehensive work." Perhaps *Reference Books Bulletin* sums up best the critical reaction to *Financial Aid for Hispanic Americans:* "accurate, comprehensive financial aid information in an easy to use, well arranged format."

WHAT'S UPDATED?

The preparation of each new edition of *Financial Aid for Hispanic Americans* involves extensive updating and revision. To make sure that the information included here is both reliable and current, the editors at Reference Service Press 1) reviewed and updated all relevant programs covered in the previous edition of the directory, 2) collected information on all programs open to Hispanic Americans that were added to Reference Service Press' funding database since the last edition of the directory, and then 3) searched extensively for new program leads in a variety of sources, including printed directories, news reports, journals, newsletters, house organs, annual reports, and sites on the Internet. We only include program descriptions that are written directly from information supplied by the sponsoring organization in print or online (no information is ever taken from secondary sources). When that information could not be found, we sent up to four data collection letters (followed by up to three telephone or e-mail inquiries, if necessary) to those sponsors. Despite our best efforts, however, some sponsoring organizations still failed to respond and, as a result, their programs are not included in this edition of the directory.

The 2017-2019 edition of *Financial Aid for Hispanic Americans* completely revises and updates the previous (eighth) edition. Programs that have ceased operations have been dropped from the listing. Similarly, programs that have broadened their scope and no longer focus on Hispanic Americans have also been removed from the directory. Profiles of continuing programs have been rewritten to reflect current requirements; nearly 85 percent of the continuing programs reported substantive changes in their locations, requirements (particularly application deadline), benefits, or eligibility requirements since the 2014-2016 edition. In addition, hundreds of new entries have been added to the program section of the directory. The resulting listing describes the more than 1,200 biggest and best sources of free money available to Hispanic Americans, including scholarships, fellowships, grants, awards, and other funding opportunities.

WHAT MAKES THIS DIRECTORY UNIQUE?

The 2017-2019 edition of *Financial Aid for Hispanic Americans* will help Hispanic Americans (persons whose origins are from Mexico, Central America, Puerto Rico, Cuba, or other Latin American countries) tap into the billions of dollars available to them, as minorities, for study, research, creative activities, past accomplishments, future projects, professional development, and many other activities. The listings cover every major subject area, are sponsored by more than 900 different private and public agencies and organizations, and are open to Hispanic Americans at any level, from college-bound high school students through professionals and postdoctorates.

Not only does *Financial Aid for Hispanic Americans* provide the most comprehensive coverage of available funding (1,215 entries), but it also displays the most informative program descriptions (on the average, more than twice the detail found in any other listing). In addition to this extensive and focused coverage, *Financial Aid for Hispanic Americans* also offers several other unique features. First of all, hundreds of funding opportunities listed here have never been covered in any other source. So, even if you have checked elsewhere, you will want to look at *Financial Aid for Hispanic Americans* for additional leads. And, here's another plus: all of the funding programs in this edition of the directory offer "free" money; not one of the programs will ever require you to pay anything back (provided, of course, that you meet the program requirements).

Further, unlike other funding directories, which generally follow a straight alphabetical arrangement, *Financial Aid for Hispanic Americans* groups entries by intended recipients (undergraduates, graduate students, or professionals/postdoctorates), to make it easy for you to search for appropriate programs. This same convenience is offered in the indexes, where program title, sponsoring organization, geographic, subject, and deadline date entries are each subdivided by recipient group.

Finally, we have tried to anticipate all the ways you might wish to search for funding. The volume is organized so you can identify programs not only by intended recipient, but also by subject focus, sponsoring organization, program title, residency requirements, where the money can be spent, and even deadline date. Plus, we've included all the information you'll need to decide if a program is right for you: purpose, eligibility requirements, financial data, duration, special features, limitations, number awarded, and application date. You even get fax numbers, toll-free numbers, e-mail address, and web site (when available), along with complete contact information.

WHAT'S EXCLUDED?

While this book is intended to be the most comprehensive source of information on funding available to Hispanic Americans, there are some programs we've specifically excluded from the directory:

- *Programs that do not accept applications from U.S. citizens or residents.* If a program is open only to foreign nationals or excludes Americans from applying, it is not covered.

- *Programs that are open equally to all segments of the population.* Only funding opportunities set aside primarily or exclusively for Hispanic Americans are included here.

- *Money for study or research outside the United States.* Since there are comprehensive and up-to-date directories that describe the available funding for study and research abroad (see the list of Reference Service Press publications opposite the directory's title page), only programs that fund activities in the United States are covered here.

- *Very restrictive programs.* In general, programs are excluded if they are open only to a limited geographic area (less than a state) or offer limited financial support (less than $1,000). Note, however, that the vast majority of programs included here go way beyond that, paying up to full tuition or stipends that exceed $25,000 a year!

- *Programs administered by individual academic institutions solely for their own students.* The directory identifies "portable" programs—ones that can be used at any number of schools. Financial aid administered by individual schools specifically for their own students is not covered. Check directly with the schools you are considering to get information on their offerings.

- *Scholarships offered by individual law firms.* Many law firms attempt to promote diversity by offering scholarships to Hispanic American and other underrepresented students, but usually tie the stipend to employment at the firm.

- *Money that must be repaid.* Only "free money" is identified here. If a program requires repayment or charges interest, it's not listed. Now you can find out about billions of dollars in aid and know (if you meet the program requirements) that not one dollar of that will ever need to be repaid.

HOW THE DIRECTORY IS ORGANIZED

Financial Aid for Hispanic Americans is divided into two sections: 1) a detailed list of funding opportunities open to Hispanic Americans and 2) a set of six indexes to help you pinpoint appropriate funding programs.

Financial Aid Programs Open to Hispanic Americans. The first section of the directory describes 1,215 sources of free money available to Hispanic Americans. The focus is on financial aid aimed at American citizens or residents to support study, research, or other activities in the United States. The programs listed here are sponsored by more than 900 different government agencies, professional organizations, corporations, sororities and fraternities, foundations, religious groups, educational associations, and military/veterans organizations. All areas of the sciences, social sciences, and humanities are covered.

To help you focus your search, the entries in this section are grouped into the following three chapters:

- **Undergraduates:** Included here are 590 scholarships, grants, awards, and other sources of free money that support undergraduate study, training, research, or creative activities. These programs are open to high school seniors, high school graduates, currently-enrolled college students, and students returning to college after an absence. Money is available to support these students in any type of public or private postsecondary institution, ranging from technical schools and community colleges to major universities in the United States.

- **Graduate Students:** Described here are 463 fellowships, grants, awards, and other sources of free money that support post-baccalaureate study, training, research, and creative activities. These programs are open to students applying to, currently enrolled in, or returning to a master's, doctoral, professional, or specialist program in public or private graduate schools in the United States.

- **Professionals/Postdoctorates:** Included here are 162 funding programs for U.S. citizens or residents who 1) are in professional positions (e.g., artists, writers), whether or not they have an advanced degree; 2) are master's or professional degree recipients; 3) have earned a doctoral degree or its equivalent (e.g., Ph.D., Ed.D., M.D.); or 4) have recognized stature as established scientists, scholars, academicians, or researchers.

Within each of these three chapters, entries appear alphabetically by program title. Since some of the programs supply assistance to more than one specific group, those are listed in all relevant chapters. For example, the Association of Cuban Engineers Scholarships support students working on either a bachelor's or master's degree, so the program is described in both the Undergraduates *and* Graduate Students chapters.

Each program entry has been designed to give you a concise profile that, as the sample on page 7 illustrates, includes Information (when available) on organization address and telephone numbers (including toll-free and fax numbers), e-mail address and web site, purpose, eligibility, money awarded, duration, special features, limitations, number of awards, and application deadline.

The information reported for each of the programs in this section was gathered from research conducted through the middle of 2017. While the listing is intended to cover as comprehensively as possible the biggest and best sources of free money available to Hispanic Americans, some sponsoring organizations did not post information online or respond to our research inquiries and, consequently, are not included in this edition of the directory.

Indexes. To help you find the aid you need, we have constructed six indexes; these will let you access the listings by program title, sponsoring organization, residency, tenability, subject focus, and deadline date. These indexes use a word-by-word alphabetical arrangement. Note: numbers in the index refer to entry numbers, not to page numbers in the book.

Program Title Index. If you know the name of a particular funding program and want to find out where it is covered in the directory, use the Program Title Index. To assist you in your search, every program is listed by all its known names, former names, and abbreviations. Since one program can be included in more than one place (e.g., a program providing assistance to both undergraduate and graduate students is described in both the first and second chapters), each entry number in the index has been coded to indicate the intended recipient group ("U" = Undergraduates; "G" = Graduate Students; "P = Professionals/Postdoctorates). By using this coding system, you can avoid duplicate entries and turn directly to the programs that match your eligibility characteristics.

Sponsoring Organization Index. This index makes it easy to identify agencies that offer funding primarily or exclusively to Hispanic Americans. More than 900 organizations are indexed here. As in the Program Title Index, we've used a code to help you determine which organizations sponsor programs that match your educational level.

Residency Index. Some programs listed in this book are restricted to Hispanic Americans in a particular state or region. Others are open to Hispanic Americans wherever they live. This index helps you identify programs available only to residents in your area as well as programs that have no residency requirements. Further, to assist you in your search, we've also indicated the recipient level for the funding offered to residents in each of the areas listed in the index.

Tenability Index. This index identifies the geographic locations where the funding described in *Financial Aid for Hispanic Americans* may be used. Index entries (city, county, state, region) are arranged alphabetically (word by word) and subdivided by recipient group. Use this index when you are looking for money to support your activities in a particular geographic area.

Subject Index. This index allows you to identify the subject focus of each of the financial aid opportunities described in *Financial Aid for Hispanic Americans*. More than 250 different subject terms are listed. Extensive "see" and "see also" references, as well as recipient group subdivisions, will help you locate appropriate funding opportunities.

Calendar Index. Since most financial aid programs have specific deadline dates, some may have closed by the time you begin to look for funding. You can use the Calendar Index to determine which programs are still open. This index is arranged by recipient group (Undergraduates, Graduate Students, and Professionals/Postdoctorates) and subdivided by the month during which the deadline falls. Filing dates can and quite often do vary from year to year; consequently, this index should be used only as a guide for deadlines beyond 2016.

HOW TO USE THE DIRECTORY

Here are some tips to help you get the most out of the funding opportunities listed in *Financial Aid for Hispanic Americans.*

To Locate Funding by Recipient Group.   To bring together programs with a similar educational focus, this directory is divided into three chapters: Undergraduates, Graduate Students, and Professionals/Postdoctorates. If you want to get an overall picture of the sources of free money available to Hispanic Americans in any of these categories, turn to the appropriate chapter and then review the entries there. Since each of these chapters functions as a self-contained entity, you can browse through any of them without having to first consulting an index.

To Find Information on a Particular Financial Aid Program.   If you know the name of a particular financial aid program, and the group eligible for that award, then go directly to the appropriate chapter in the directory (e.g., Undergraduates, Graduate Students), where you will find the program profiles arranged alphabetically by title. To save time, though, you should always check the Program Title Index first if you know the name of a specific award but are not sure in which chapter it has been listed. Plus, since we index each program by all its known names and abbreviations, you'll also be able to track down a program there when you may not know its exact official title.

To Locate Programs Sponsored by a Particular Organization.   The Sponsoring Organization Index makes it easy to identify agencies that provide financial assistance to Hispanic Americans or to identify specific financial aid programs offered by a particular organization. Each entry number in the index is coded to identify recipient group (Undergraduates, Graduate Students, Professionals/Postdoctorates), so that you can easily target appropriate entries.

To Browse Quickly Through the Listings.   Look at the listings in the chapter that relates to you (Undergraduates, Graduate Students, or Professionals/Postdoctorates) and read the "Summary" paragraph in each entry. In seconds, you'll know if this is an opportunity that you might want to pursue. If it is, be sure to read the rest of the information in the entry, to make sure you meet all of the program requirements before writing or going online for an application form. Please save your time and energy. Don't apply if you don't qualify!

To Locate Funding Available to Hispanic Americans from or Tenable in a Particular City, County, or State.   The Residency Index identifies financial aid programs open to Hispanic Americans in a specific state, region, etc. The Tenability Index shows where the money can be spent. In both indexes, "see" and "see also" references are used liberally, and index entries for a particular geographic area are subdivided by recipient group (Undergraduates, Graduate Students, and Professionals/Postdoctorates) to help you identify the funding that's right for you. When using these indexes, always check the listings under the term "United States," since the programs indexed there have no geographic restrictions and can be used in any area.

To Locate Financial Aid Programs Open to Hispanic Americans in a Particular Subject Area.   Turn to the Subject Index first if you are interested in identifying funding programs for Hispanic Americans that are focused on a particular subject area. To make your search easier, the intended recipient groups (Undergraduates, Graduate Students, Professionals/Postdoctorates) are clearly labeled in the more than 250 subject listings. Extensive cross-references are also provided. Since a large number of programs are not restricted by subject, be sure to check the references listed under the "General programs" heading in the index, in addition to the specific terms that directly relate to your interest areas. The listings under "General programs" can be used to fund activities in any subject area (although the programs may be restricted in other ways).

To Locate Financial Aid Programs for Hispanic Americans by Deadline Date.   If you are working with specific time constraints and want to weed out the financial aid programs whose filing dates you won't be able to meet, turn first to the Calendar Index and check the program references listed under the appropriate recipient group and month. Note: not all sponsoring organizations supplied deadline information; those programs are listed under the "Deadline not specified" entries in the index. To identify every relevant financial aid program, regardless of filing date, go the appropriate chapter and read through all the entries there that match your educational level.

To Locate Financial Aid Programs Open to All Segments of the Population.   Only programs available to Hispanic Americans are listed in this publication. However, there are thousands of other programs that are open equally to all segments of the population. To identify these programs, talk to your local librarian, check with your financial aid office on campus, look at the list of RSP print resources on the page opposite the title page in this directory, or see if your library subscribes to Reference Service Press' interactive online funding database: *RSP FundingFinder.* For more information on that award-winning resource, go online to: www.rspfunding.com/esubscriptions.html.

PLANS TO UPDATE THE DIRECTORY

This volume, covering 2017-2019, is the ninth edition of *Financial Aid for Hispanic Americans.* The next biennial edition will cover the years 2019-2021 and will be issued by the beginning of 2019.

ACKNOWLEDGEMENTS

A debt of gratitude is owed all the organizations that contributed information to the 2017-2019 edition of *Financial Aid for Hispanic Americans.* Their generous cooperation has helped to make this publication a current and comprehensive survey of awards.

SAMPLE ENTRY

(1) **[68]**

(2) **BECAS UNIVISION SCHOLARSHIP PROGRAM**

(3) Hispanic Scholarship Fund
Attn: Selection Committee
1411 West 190th Street, Suite 700
Gardena, CA 90248
(310) 975-3700
(877) HSF-INFO
Fax: (310) 349-3328
E-mail: scholar1@hsf.net
Web: hsf.net/en/scholarships/programs/becas-univision-scholarship-program

(4) **Summary** To provide financial assistance for college or graduate school to Hispanic American students.

(5) **Eligibility** This program is open to U.S. citizens, permanent residents, Deferred Action for Childhood Arrival (DACA) students, and eligible non-citizens. Applicants must be of Hispanic heritage and enrolled or planning to enroll full time in a degree program at an accredited 4-year college or university as an undergraduate or graduate student (including GED recipients and community college transfers). High school seniors must have a GPA of 3.0 or higher; current undergraduate and graduate students must have a GPA of 2.5 or higher. Selection is based on merit; financial need is considered in determining the amount of the award.

(6) **Financial data** Stipends normally range from $500 to $5,000 per year.

(7) **Duration** 1 year; recipients may reapply.

(8) **Additional information** This program is sponsored by Becas Univision.

(9) **Number awarded** Varies each year.

(10) **Deadline** March of each year.

DEFINITION

(1) **Entry number:** The consecutive number that is given to each entry and used to identify the entry in the index.

(2) **Program title:** Title of scholarship, fellowship, grant, award, or other source of free money described in the directory.

(3) **Sponsoring organization:** Name, address, and telephone number, toll-free number, fax number, e-mail address, and/or web site (when information was available) for organization sponsoring the program.

(4) **Summary:** Identifies the major program requirements; read the rest of the entry for additional detail.

(5) **Eligibility:** Qualifications required of applicants, plus information on application procedure and selection process.

(6) **Financial data:** Financial details of the program, including fixed sum, average amount, or range of funds offered, expenses for which funds may and may not be applied, and cash-related benefits supplied (e.g., room and board).

(7) **Duration:** Period for which support is provided; renewal prospects.

(8) **Additional information:** Any unusual (generally nonmonetary) benefits, features, restrictions, or limitations associated with the program.

(9) **Number awarded:** Total number of recipients each year or other specified period.

(10) **Deadline:** The month by which applications must be submitted.

ABOUT THE AUTHORS

Dr. Gail Ann Schlachter (1943-2015) worked for more than three decades as a library manager, a library educator, and an administrator of library-related publishing companies. Among the reference books to her credit are the biennially-issued *Directory of Financial Aids for Women* and two award-winning bibliographic guides: *Minorities and Women: A Guide to Reference Literature in the Social Sciences* (which was chosen as an "outstanding reference book of the year" by *Choice)* and *Reference Sources in Library and Information Services* (which won the first Knowledge Industry Publications "Award for Library Literature"). She was the reference book review editor for *RQ* (now *Reference and User Services Quarterly)* for 10 years, was a past president of the American Library Association's Reference and User Services Association, was the editor-in-chief of the *Reference and User Services Association Quarterly,* and was serving her sixth term on the American Library Association's governing council at the time of her death. In recognition of her outstanding contributions to reference service, Dr. Schlachter was named the University of Wisconsin School of Library and Information Studies "Alumna of the Year" and was awarded both the Isadore Gilbert Mudge Citation and the Louis Shores/Oryx Press Award.

Dr. R. David Weber taught history and economics at Los Angeles Harbor College (in Wilmington, California) for many years and continues to teach history there as an emeritus professor. During his years at Harbor College, and earlier at East Los College, he directed the Honors Program and was frequently chosen the "Teacher of the Year." He has written a number of critically-acclaimed reference works, including *Dissertations in Urban History* and the three-volume *Energy Information Guide.* With Gail Schlachter, he is the author of Reference Service Press' *Financial Aid for Persons with Disabilities and Their Families,* which was selected by *Library Journal* as one of the "best reference books of the year," and a number of other financial aid titles, including the *College Student's Guide to Merit and Other No-Need Funding,* which was chosen as one of the "outstanding reference books of the year" by *Choice.*

Financial Aid Programs
Open to Hispanic Americans

Undergraduates ●

Graduate Students ●

Professionals/Postdoctorates ●

Undergraduates

Listed alphabetically by program title and described in detail here are 590 scholarships, forgivable loans, grants, awards, and other sources of "free money" set aside for Hispanic Americans who are college-bound high school seniors or continuing and returning undergraduate students. This funding is available to support study, training, research, and/or creative activities in the United States.

[1]
21ST CENTURY LEADERS SUMMER INTERNSHIP PROGRAM

United States Hispanic Leadership Institute
431 South Dearborn Street, Suite 1203
Chicago, IL 60605
(312) 427-8683   Toll Free: (800) 959-5151
Fax: (312) 427-5183   E-mail: acalderon@ushli.org
Web: www.ushli.org/summer_internship.html

Summary To provide summer work experience at the United States Hispanic Leadership Institute (USHLI) to high school graduates and college students.

Eligibility This program is open to high school graduates and college students enrolled or planning to enroll at an accredited 2- or 4-year college or university. Applicants must be interested in working during the summer at USHLI on a project involving registering Latino voters. They must be able to demonstrate involvement in campus or community organizations. Along with their application, they must submit a 2-page essay about their past leadership experience and community involvement. An interview is required.

Financial Data Interns receive a stipend of $5.00 per registration.

Duration 10 weeks during the summer.

Additional data This program began in 1994.

Number awarded 1 or more each year.

Deadline May of each year.

[2]
AAPT-ALPHA AWARD

American Association of Physics Teachers
Attn: Awards Committee
One Physics Ellipse
College Park, MD 20740-3845
(301) 209-3311   Fax: (301) 209-0845
E-mail: awards@aapt.org
Web: www.aapt.org

Summary To recognize and reward undergraduate students, especially Hispanics and other minorities, who build and develop an advanced laboratory experiment for their school's advanced laboratory program.

Eligibility This award is available to undergraduate students, acting individually or in a group, who have built (and possibly developed) an advanced laboratory experiment that will become a new part of their school's program. The experiment must be new to the home department, either based on the literature or being used at other institutions. It may have been carried out as a senior project, senior thesis, or equivalent. Nominations of women and members of underrepresented minority groups are especially encouraged.

Financial Data The award includes an honorarium of $4,000, a citation, reimbursement of travel expenses to the meeting of the American Association of Physics Teachers (AAPT) at which the award is presented, and the opportunity to present a talk at that meeting. The faculty supervisor receives a citation and travel expenses to the same AAPT meeting. For groups of students, the honorarium is shared among all those involved.

Duration The award is presented annually.

Additional data This program began in 2014 with support from TeachSpin, Inc. It is jointly administered by AAPT and the Advanced Laboratory Physics Association (ALPhA).

Number awarded 1 each year.

Deadline August of each year.

[3]
AAUW CAREER DEVELOPMENT GRANTS

American Association of University Women
Attn: AAUW Educational Foundation
1111 16th Street, N.W.
Washington, DC 20036-4873
(202) 785-7700   Toll Free: (800) 326-AAUW
Fax: (202) 872-1425   TDD: (202) 785-7777
E-mail: aauw@applyists.com
Web: www.aauw.org

Summary To provide financial assistance to women who are seeking career advancement, career change, or reentry into the workforce, especially Hispanics and other women of color.

Eligibility This program is open to women who are U.S. citizens or permanent residents, have earned a bachelor's degree, received their most recent degree more than 4 years ago, and are making career changes, seeking to advance in current careers, or reentering the workforce. Applicants must be interested in working toward a master's degree, second bachelor's or associate degree, professional degree (e.g., M.D., J.D.), certification program, or technical school certificate. They must be planning to undertake course work at an accredited 2- or 4-year college or university (or a technical school that is licensed, accredited, or approved by the U.S. Department of Education). Primary consideration is given to women of color and women pursuing their first advanced degree or credentials in nontraditional fields. Support is not provided for prerequisite course work or for Ph.D. course work or dissertations. Selection is based on demonstrated commitment to education and equity for women and girls, reason for seeking higher education or technical training, degree to which study plan is consistent with career objectives, potential for success in chosen field, documentation of opportunities in chosen field, feasibility of study plans and proposed time schedule, validity of proposed budget and budget narrative (including sufficient outside support), and quality of written proposal.

Financial Data Grants range from $2,000 to $12,000. Funds may be used for tuition, fees, books, supplies, local transportation, dependent child care, or purchase of a computer required for the study program.

Duration 1 year, beginning in July; nonrenewable.

Additional data The filing fee is $35.

Number awarded Varies each year; recently, 63 of these grants, with a value of $670,000, were awarded.

Deadline December of each year.

[4]
ABC LATINO MINISTRIES SCHOLARSHIP

American Baptist Churches USA
Attn: American Baptist Home Mission Societies
National Coordinator for Intercultural Ministries
P.O. Box 851
Valley Forge, PA 19482-0851
(610) 768-2421   Toll Free: (800) ABC-3USA, ext. 2421
Fax: (610) 768-2453
E-mail: Salvador.Orellana@abhms.org
Web: abhms.org

Summary   To provide financial assistance to Latinos who are interested in preparing for or furthering a church career in the American Baptist Church (ABC).

Eligibility   This program is open to Latino members of the ABC or its recognized institutions who demonstrate financial need. They must be enrolled full time at an accredited institution, working on an undergraduate degree or first professional degree in a seminary. Applicants must be currently serving or planning to serve in a vocation with the church or with its recognized institutions. They must be U.S. citizens who have been a member of an American Baptist Church for at least 1 year.

Financial Data   The stipends range from $500 to $3,000 per year.

Duration   1 year; may be renewed.

Number awarded   Varies each year.

Deadline   May of each year.

[5]
ACADEMY OF NUTRITION AND DIETETICS BACCALAUREATE (DIDACTIC OR COORDINATED PROGRAM) SCHOLARSHIPS

Academy of Nutrition and Dietetics
Attn: Foundation
120 South Riverside Plaza, Suite 2000
Chicago, IL 60606-6995
(312) 899-4821   Toll Free: (800) 877-1600, ext. 4821
Fax: (312) 899-4796   E-mail: scholarship@eatright.org
Web: www.eatrightacend.org

Summary   To provide financial assistance to undergraduate student members of the Academy of Nutrition and Dietetics, especially Hispanics and other underrepresented minorities.

Eligibility   This program is open to ADA members enrolled at a CADE-accredited/approved college or university program for at least junior status in the dietetics program. Applicants must be U.S. citizens or permanent residents and show promise of being a valuable, contributing member of the profession. Some scholarships require membership in a specific dietetic practice group, residency in a specific state, or underrepresented minority group status. The same application form can be used for all categories.

Financial Data   Stipends range from $500 to $10,000 but most are for $1,000.

Duration   1 year.

Additional data   The Academy of Nutrition and Dietetics was formerly the American Dietetic Association.

Number awarded   Between 30 and 35 each year.

Deadline   February of each year.

[6]
ACCELERATOR APPLICATIONS DIVISION SCHOLARSHIP

American Nuclear Society
Attn: Scholarship Coordinator
555 North Kensington Avenue
La Grange Park, IL 60526-5535
(708) 352-6611   Toll Free: (800) 323-3044
Fax: (708) 352-0499   E-mail: outreach@ans.org
Web: www.ans.org/honors/scholarships/aad

Summary   To provide financial assistance to undergraduate students, especially Hispanics and other minorities who are interested in preparing for a career dealing with accelerator applications aspects of nuclear science or nuclear engineering.

Eligibility   This program is open to students entering their junior year in physics, engineering, or materials science at an accredited institution in the United States. Applicants must submit a description of their long- and short-term professional objectives, including their research interests related to accelerator aspects of nuclear science and engineering. Selection is based on that statement, faculty recommendations, and academic performance. Special consideration is given to members of underrepresented groups (women and minorities), students who can demonstrate financial need, and applicants who have a record of service to the American Nuclear Society (ANS).

Financial Data   The stipend is $1,000 per year.

Duration   1 year (the junior year); may be renewed for the senior year.

Additional data   This program is offered by the Accelerator Applications Division (AAD) of the ANS.

Number awarded   1 each year.

Deadline   January of each year.

[7]
ACCOUNTANCY BOARD OF OHIO EDUCATION ASSISTANCE PROGRAM

Accountancy Board of Ohio
Attn: Executive Director
77 South High Street, Suite 1802
Columbus, OH 43215-6128
(614) 466-4135   Fax: (614) 466-2628
E-mail: john.e.patterson@acc.ohio.gov
Web: www.acc.ohio.gov

Summary   To provide financial assistance to Hispanic and other minority or financially disadvantaged students enrolled in an accounting education program at Ohio academic institutions approved by the Accountancy Board of Ohio.

Eligibility   This program is open to minority and financially disadvantaged Ohio residents who apply as full-time juniors or seniors in an accounting program at an accredited college or university in the state. Students who remain in good standing at their institutions and who enter a qualified fifth-year program are then eligible to receive these funds. Minority is defined as Hispanics, Blacks, Native Americans, and Asians. Financial disadvantage is defined according to information provided on the Free Application for Federal Student Aid (FAFSA). U.S. citizenship or permanent resident status is required.

Financial Data The amount of the stipend is determined annually but does not exceed the in-state tuition at Ohio public universities (currently, $13,067).

Duration 1 year (the fifth year of an accounting program). Funds committed to students who apply as juniors must be used within 4 years and funds committed to students who apply as seniors must be used within 3 years. The award is nonrenewable and may only be used when the student enrolls in the fifth year of a program.

Number awarded Several each year.

Deadline Applications may be submitted at any time.

[8]
ACT SIX SCHOLARSHIPS

Act Six
c/o Degrees of Change
1109 A Street, Suite 101
P.O. Box 1573
Tacoma, WA 98401
(253) 642-6712   E-mail: tim.herron@actsix.org
Web: www.actsix.org

Summary To provide financial assistance to residents of Washington and Oregon who are Hispanics or come from other diverse backgrounds and are interested in attending designated private faith-based universities in those states.

Eligibility This program is open to high school seniors or recent graduates and planning to enter college as freshmen who come from diverse, multicultural backgrounds. Applicants must be residents of the following regions and interested in attending designated colleges for that region: Portland: George Fox University or Warner Pacific College; Spokane: Gonzaga University or Whitworth University; Tacoma-Seattle: Gonzaga University, Northwest University, Pacific Lutheran University, or Whitworth University; or Yakima Valley: Heritage University. Students are not required to make a faith commitment, but they must be willing to explore Christian spirituality as it relates to service and leadership. Ethnicity and family income are considered as factors in selecting an intentionally diverse group of scholars, but there are no income restrictions and students from all ethnic backgrounds are encouraged to apply.

Financial Data The program makes up the difference between any other assistance the student receives and full tuition. For recipients who demonstrate financial need in excess of tuition, awards cover some or all of the cost of room and board, books, travel, and personal expenses.

Duration 1 year; may be renewed.

Number awarded Varies each year; recently, 56 were awarded.

Deadline November of each year.

[9]
ACTUARIAL DIVERSITY SCHOLARSHIPS

Actuarial Foundation
Attn: Actuarial Education and Research Fund Committee
475 North Martingale Road, Suite 600
Schaumburg, IL 60173-2226
(847) 706-3535   Fax: (847) 706-3599
E-mail: scholarships@actfnd.org
Web: www.actuarialfoundation.org

Summary To provide financial assistance to Hispanic and other minority undergraduate students who are preparing for a career in actuarial science.

Eligibility This program is open to members of minority groups, defined as having at least 1 birth parent who is Hispanic, Black/African American, Native North American, or Pacific Islander. Applicants must be graduating high school seniors or current full-time undergraduate students working on or planning to work on a degree at an accredited 2- or 4-year college or university that may lead to a career in the actuarial profession. They must have a GPA of 3.0 or higher; high school seniors must also have a minimum score of 28 on the ACT mathematics examination or 600 on the SAT mathematics examination. Along with their application, they must submit a 1- or 2-page personal statement that covers why they are interested in becoming an actuary, the steps they are taking to enter the actuarial profession, participation in actuarial internships, and participation in extracurricular activities. Financial need is not considered in the selection process.

Financial Data Annual stipends are $1,000 for high school seniors applying for freshman year, $2,000 for college freshmen applying for sophomore year, $3,000 for college sophomores applying for junior year, or $4,000 for college juniors applying for senior year.

Duration 1 year; may be renewed, provided the recipient remains enrolled full time, in good academic standing, in a course of study that may lead to a career in the actuarial profession, and (for college juniors and higher) passes actuarial examinations.

Additional data This program began in 1977 by the Casualty Actuarial Society and the Society of Actuaries. In 2008, it was transferred to the Actuarial Foundation.

Number awarded Varies each year; recently, 40 were awarded.

Deadline April of each year.

[10]
ACXIOM DIVERSITY SCHOLARSHIP PROGRAM

Acxiom Corporation
601 East Third Street
P.O. Box 8190
Little Rock, AR 72203-8190
(501) 342-1000   Toll Free: (877) 314-2049
E-mail: Candice.Davis@acxiom.com
Web: www.acxiom.com/about-acxiom/careers

Summary To provide financial assistance and possible work experience to upper-division and graduate students who are Hispanics or members of other diverse populations that historically have been underrepresented in the information technology work force.

Eligibility This program is open to juniors, seniors, and graduate students who are working full time on a degree in a field of information technology, including computer science, computer information systems, management information systems, information quality, information systems, engineering, mathematics, statistics, or related areas of study. Women, veterans, minorities, and individuals with disabilities are encouraged to apply. Applicants must have a GPA of 3.0 or higher. Along with their application, they must submit a 500-word essay describing how the scholarship will help them achieve their academic, professional, and personal goals. Selection is based on academic achievement, relationship of field of study to information technology, and relationship of areas of professional interest to the sponsor's business needs.

Financial Data   The stipend is $5,000 per year.

Duration   1 year; may be renewed 1 additional year, provided the recipient remains enrolled full time, maintains a GPA of 3.0 or higher, and (if offered an internship) continues to meet internship expectations.

Additional data   Recipients may be offered an internship (fall, spring, summer, year-round) at 1 of the sponsor's offices in Austin (Texas), Conway (Arkansas), Downers Grove (Illinois), Little Rock (Arkansas), Nashville (Tennessee), New York (New York), or Redwood City (California).

Number awarded   Up to 5 each year.

Deadline   December of each year.

[11]
A.D. OSHERMAN SCHOLARSHIP FUND

Greater Houston Community Foundation
Attn: Scholarships Assistant
5120 Woodway Drive, Suite 6000
Houston, TX 77056
(713) 333-2236   Fax: (713) 333-2220
E-mail: jlauver@ghcf.org
Web: www.ghcfscholar.org

Summary   To provide financial assistance to residents of Texas who are Hispanics members of other designated underrepresented groups and are interested in attending college in any state.

Eligibility   This program is open to Texas residents who are graduating high school seniors or full-time freshmen, sophomores, or juniors at an accredited public 2- or 4-year college or university in any state. Applicants must qualify as a member of a recognized minority group, the first in their family to attend college, or a veteran with active service, particularly service in Iraq or Afghanistan. They must have a GPA of 2.75 or higher and a history of community service. Financial need is considered in the selection process.

Financial Data   The stipend is $2,500 per year for students at 4-year universities or $1,500 per year for students at 2-year colleges.

Duration   1 year; recipients may reapply.

Number awarded   2 each year.

Deadline   March of each year.

[12]
ADDIE B. MORRIS SCHOLARSHIP

American Association of Railroad Superintendents
P.O. Box 200
La Fox, IL 60147
(331) 643-3369   E-mail: aars@supt.org
Web: www.railroadsuperintendents.org/Scholarships

Summary   To provide financial assistance to undergraduate and graduate students, especially Hispanics and other minorities, who are working on a degree in transportation.

Eligibility   This program is open to full-time undergraduate and graduate students enrolled at accredited colleges and universities in Canada or the United States. Applicants must have completed enough credits to have standing as a sophomore and must have a GPA of 2.75 or higher. Preference is

given to minority students enrolled in the transportation field who can demonstrate financial need.

Financial Data   The stipend is $1,000. Funds are sent directly to the recipient's institution.

Duration   1 year.

Number awarded   1 or more each year.

Deadline   June of each year.

[13]
AFSCME UNION SCHOLARSHIPS OF THE THURGOOD MARSHALL COLLEGE FUND

Thurgood Marshall College Fund
Attn: Senior Manager of Scholarship Programs
901 F Street, N.W., Suite 300
Washington, DC 20004
(202) 507-4851   Fax: (202) 652-2934
E-mail: deshuandra.walker@tmcfund.org
Web: www.tmcf.org

Summary   To provide financial assistance and work experience with the American Federation of State, County and Municipal Employees (AFSCME) to Latino and other students of color interested in preparing for a career in the labor union movement.

Eligibility   This program is open to students of color (Latino American, African American, American Indian/Alaskan Native, and Asian Pacific Islander American) who are currently enrolled as sophomores or juniors at a college or university in any state. Applicants must be interested in participating in a summer field placement in a union organizing campaign at 1 of several locations across the country followed by a year of academic study at their college or university. They must have a current GPA of 2.5 or higher and a demonstrated interest in working through the union labor movement. Along with their application, they must submit a personal statement on an assigned topic, a letter of recommendation, and their current academic transcript.

Financial Data   The program provides 1) a stipend of up to $4,000 (provided by AFSCME) and on-site housing for the summer field placement; and 2) an academic scholarship of up to $6,300 for the school year, based on successful completion of the summer program and financial need.

Duration   10 weeks for the summer field placement; students who enter the program as sophomores are eligible for a second placement at AFSCME headquarters in Washington, D.C.; 1 year for the academic scholarship.

Additional data   This program is sponsored by AFSCME.

Number awarded   Varies each year.

Deadline   February of each year.

[14]
AGA INVESTING IN THE FUTURE STUDENT RESEARCH FELLOWSHIPS

American Gastroenterological Association
Attn: AGA Research Foundation
Research Awards Manager
4930 Del Ray Avenue
Bethesda, MD 20814-2512
(301) 222-4012   Fax: (301) 654-5920
E-mail: awards@gastro.org
Web: www.gastro.org

Summary To provide funding for research on digestive diseases or nutrition to undergraduate and medical students who are Hispanics/Latinos or members of ther underrepresented minority groups.

Eligibility This program is open to undergraduate and medical students at accredited U.S. institutions who are African Americans, Hispanic/Latino Americans, Alaska Natives, American Indians, or Natives of the U.S. Pacific Islands. Applicants must be interested in conducting research on digestive diseases or nutrition. They may not hold similar salary support awards from other agencies (e.g., American Liver Foundation, Crohn's and Colitis Foundation). Research must be conducted under the supervision of a preceptor who is a full-time faculty member at an institution in a state other than the student's, directing a research project in a gastroenterology-related area, and a member of the American Gastroenterological Association (AGA).

Financial Data Fellowships provide payment of housing, travel, and a stipend of $5,000.

Duration 8 to 10 weeks. The work may take place at any time during the year.

Additional data This program is supported by the National Institute of Diabetes and Digestive and Kidney Diseases (NIDDKD) of the U.S. National Institutes of Health (NIH).

Number awarded 12 each year.

Deadline February of each year.

[15]
AHIMA FOUNDATION DIVERSITY SCHOLARSHIPS

American Health Information Management Association
Attn: AHIMA Foundation
233 North Michigan Avenue, 21st Floor
Chicago, IL 60601-5809
(312) 233-1137　　　　　　　Fax: (312) 233-1537
E-mail: info@ahimafoundation.org
Web: www.ahimafoundation.org

Summary To provide financial assistance to Hispanic and other members of the American Health Information Management Association (AHIMA) who are interested in working on an undergraduate or graduate degree in health information management (HIM) or health information technology (HIT) and will contribute to diversity in the profession in other ways.

Eligibility This program is open to AHIMA members who are enrolled at least half time in an accredited program. Applicants must be working on a degree in HIM or HIT at the associate, bachelor's, post-baccalaureate, master's, or doctoral level. They must have a GPA of 3.5 or higher and at least 6 credit hours remaining after the date of the award. To qualify for this support, applicants must demonstrate how they will contribute to diversity in the health information management profession; diversity is defined as differences in race, ethnicity, nationality, gender, sexual orientation, socioeconomic status, age, physical capabilities, or religious beliefs. Along with their application, they must submit essays on assigned topics related to their involvement in the HIM profession. Selection is based on the clarity and completeness of thought in the essays; cumulative GPA; volunteer, work, and/or leadership experience; honors, awards, or recognitions; commitment to the HIM profession; and references.

Financial Data Stipends are $1,000 for associate degree students, $1,500 for bachelor's degree or post-baccalaureate

certificate students, $2,000 for master's degree students, or $2,500 for doctoral degree students.

Duration 1 year.

Number awarded 1 or more each year.

Deadline September of each year.

[16]
AIA/F DIVERSITY ADVANCEMENT SCHOLARSHIP

American Institute of Architects
Attn: AIA Foundation
1799 New York Avenue, N.W.
Washington, DC 20006-5292
(202) 626-7511　　　　　　　Fax: (202) 626-7420
E-mail: divscholarship@aia.org
Web: www.aia.org/about/initiatives/AIAB101856

Summary To provide financial assistance to Hispanic and other high school and college students from diverse backgrounds who are interested in studying architecture in college.

Eligibility This program is open to students from minority and/or financially disadvantaged backgrounds who are high school seniors, students in a community college or technical school transferring to an accredited architectural program, or college freshmen entering a professional degree program at an accredited program of architecture. Students who have completed 1 or more years of a 4-year college curriculum are not eligible. Applicants must submit 2 or 3 drawings, including 1 freehand sketch of any real life object (e.g., buildings, people, objects, self-portrait) and 1 or 2 additional images of drawings or drafted floor plans or drawings using computer-aided design (CAD). Selection is based on those drawings and financial need.

Financial Data Stipends range from $3,000 to $4,000 per year, depending upon individual need. Students must apply for supplementary funds from other sources.

Duration 1 year; may be renewed for up to 4 additional years or until completion of a degree.

Additional data This program was established in 1970 as the AIA/AAF Minority Disadvantaged Scholarship Program.

Number awarded 2 each year.

Deadline April of each year.

[17]
AICPA SCHOLARSHIPS FOR MINORITY ACCOUNTING STUDENTS

American Institute of Certified Public Accountants
Attn: Academic and Career Development Division
220 Leigh Farm Road
Durham, NC 27707-8110
(919) 402-4500　　　　　　　Fax: (919) 402-4505
E-mail: scholarships@aicpa.org
Web: www.aicpa.org

Summary To provide financial assistance to Hispanics and other minorities interested in studying accounting at the undergraduate or graduate school level.

Eligibility This program is open to minority undergraduate and graduate students, enrolled full time, who have a GPA of 3.3 or higher (both cumulatively and in their major) and intend to pursue a C.P.A. credential. The program defines minority students as those whose heritage is Hispanic or Latino, Black or African American, Native American, or Asian American. Undergraduates must have completed at least 30 semester hours, including at least 6 semester hours of a major in accounting. Graduate students must be working on a master's degree in accounting, finance, taxation, or a related program. Applicants must be U.S. citizens or permanent residents and student affiliate members of the American Institute of Certified Public Accountants (AICPA). Along with their application, they must submit 500-word essays on 1) why they want to become a C.P.A. and how attaining that licensure will contribute to their goals; and 2) how they would spread the message about accounting and the C.P.A. profession in their community and school. In the selection process, some consideration is given to financial need.

Financial Data Stipends range up to $5,000 per year. Funds are disbursed directly to the recipient's school.

Duration 1 year; may be renewed up to 3 additional years or until completion of a bachelor's or master's degree, whichever is earlier.

Additional data This program began in 1969. Additional support is provided by the Accounting Education Foundation of the Texas Society of Certified Public Accountants, the New Jersey Society of Certified Public Accountants, Robert Half International, and the Virgin Islands Society of Certified Public Accountants.

Number awarded Varies each year; recently, 94 students received funding through this program.

Deadline March of each year.

[18]
AIET MINORITIES AND WOMEN EDUCATIONAL SCHOLARSHIP PROGRAM

Appraisal Institute
Attn: Appraisal Institute Education Trust
200 West Madison Street, Suite 1500
Chicago, IL 60606
(312) 335-4133   Fax: (312) 335-4134
E-mail: educationtrust@appraisalinstitute.org
Web: www.appraisalinstitute.org

Summary To provide financial assistance to Hispanic and other minority undergraduate students majoring in real estate or allied fields.

Eligibility This program is open to members of groups underrepresented in the real estate appraisal profession. Those groups include Hispanics, American Indians, Alaska Natives, Asians and Pacific Islanders, Blacks or African Americans, and women. Applicants must be full- or part-time students enrolled in real estate courses within a degree-granting college, university, or junior college. They must have a GPA of 2.5 or higher and be able to demonstrate financial need. U.S. citizenship is required.

Financial Data The stipend is $1,000. Funds are paid directly to the recipient's institution to be used for tuition and fees.

Duration 1 year.

Number awarded At least 1 each year.

Deadline April of each year.

[19]
ALAN COMPTON AND BOB STANLEY MINORITY AND INTERNATIONAL SCHOLARSHIP

Baptist Communicators Association
Attn: Scholarship Committee
4519 Lashley Court
Marietta, GA 30068
(678) 641-4457   E-mail: margaretcolson@bellsouth.net
Web: www.baptistcommunicators.org/about/scholarship.cfm

Summary To provide financial assistance to Hispanic and other minority students who are working on an undergraduate degree to prepare for a career in Baptist communications.

Eligibility This program is open to undergraduate students of minority or international origin. Applicants must be majoring in communications, English, journalism, or public relations and have a GPA of 2.5 or higher. Their vocational objective must be in Baptist communications. Along with their application, they must submit a statement explaining why they want to receive this scholarship.

Financial Data The stipend is $1,000.

Duration 1 year; recipients may reapply.

Additional data This program began in 1996.

Number awarded 1 each year.

Deadline March of each year.

[20]
ALBERT LEE WRIGHT, JR. MEMORIAL MIGRANT SCHOLARSHIP

National Association of State Directors of Migrant Education
Attn: Samantha Murray
1001 Connecticut Avenue, N.W., Suite 915
Washington, DC 20036
(202) 775-7780   Fax: (202) 775-7784
E-mail: mlap@mlap.org
Web: www.nasdme.org

Summary To provide financial assistance for college to Hispanic and other high school seniors who qualify as migrant students.

Eligibility This program is open to graduating high school seniors who have been accepted, or are awaiting acceptance, at a postsecondary degree-granting institution. Applicants must have attended more than 1 school in a year and/or have traveled on their own or with a parent or guardian in pursuit of agricultural, agriculture-related, timber, or fishing work in the summer or regular school term. Along with their application, they must submit a 500-word essay describing their background (including information about disrupted schooling and barriers presented because of agriculture/fishing-related mobility), career and personal goals, and why they should receive this assistance. Students who demonstrate a strong interest in science, technology, engineering, or mathematics (STEM) are especially encouraged to apply. Financial need is considered in the selection process.

Financial Data The stipend is at least $3,000.

Duration 1 year.

Number awarded 1 or more each year.

Deadline February of each year.

[21]
ALBUQUERQUE HISPANO CHAMBER OF COMMERCE OPPORTUNITY SCHOLARSHIP

Albuquerque Hispano Chamber of Commerce
Attn: Scholarship Coordinator
1309 Fourth Street, S.W.
Albuquerque, NM 87102
(505) 842-9003   Fax: (505) 764-9664
Web: www.ahcnm.org/Scholarship_Applications.aspx

Summary   To provide financial assistance to Hispanic residents of New Mexico who have been out of school for at least 1 year and are interested in returning to college in the state.

Eligibility   This program is open to Hispanic residents of New Mexico who are at least 19 years of age. Applicants must have earned their high school diploma or GED at least 1 year previously and be interested in continuing their postsecondary education at a New Mexico institution. Along with their application, they must submit an essay of 300 to 500 words on their financial need, educational and career goals, how those goals relate to their ethnic background, and their philosophy toward their Hispanic heritage.

Financial Data   A stipend is awarded (amount not specified).

Duration   1 year.

Number awarded   1 or more each year.

Deadline   March of each year.

[22]
ALMA EXLEY SCHOLARSHIP

Community Foundation of Greater New Britain
Attn: Scholarship Manager
74A Vine Street
New Britain, CT 06052-1431
(860) 229-6018, ext. 305   Fax: (860) 225-2666
E-mail: cfarmer@cfgnb.org
Web: www.cfgnb.org

Summary   To provide financial assistance to Hispanic and other minority college students in Connecticut who are interested in preparing for a teaching career.

Eligibility   This program is open to students of color (Hispanic Americans, African Americans, Asian Americans, and Native Americans) enrolled in a teacher preparation program in Connecticut. Applicant must 1) have been admitted to a traditional teacher preparation program at an accredited 4-year college or university in the state; or 2) be participating in the Alternate Route to Certification (ARC) program sponsored by the Connecticut Department of Higher Education.

Financial Data   The stipend is $1,500 per year for students at a 4-year college or university or $500 for a student in the ARC program.

Duration   2 years for students at 4-year colleges or universities; 1 year for students in the ARC program.

Number awarded   2 each year: 1 to a 4-year student and 1 to an ARC student.

Deadline   October of each year.

[23]
AMAC MEMBER AWARD

Airport Minority Advisory Council
Attn: AMAC Foundation
2001 Jefferson Davis Highway, Suite 500
Arlington, VA 22202
(703) 414-2622   Fax: (703) 414-2686
E-mail: terrifrierson@palladiumholdingsco.com
Web: amac-org.com/amac-foundation/scholarships

Summary   To provide financial assistance to Hispanic and other minority high school seniors and undergraduates who are preparing for a career in the aviation industry and are connected to the Airport Minority Advisory Council (AMAC).

Eligibility   This program is open to minority and female high school seniors and current undergraduates who have a GPA of 2.5 or higher and a record of involvement in community and extracurricular activities. Applicants must be interested in working on a bachelor's degree in accounting, architecture, aviation, business administration, engineering, or finance as preparation for a career in the aviation or airport industry. They must be AMAC members, family of members, or mentees of member. Along with their application, they must submit a 750-word essay on how they have overcome barriers in life to achieve their academic and/or career goals; their dedication to succeed in the aviation industry and how AMAC can help them achieve their goal; and the most important issues that the aviation industry is facing today and how they see themselves changing those. Financial need is not considered in the selection process. U.S. citizenship is required.

Financial Data   The stipend is $2,000 per year.

Duration   1 year; recipients may reapply.

Number awarded   4 each year.

Deadline   May of each year.

[24]
AMELIA KEMP MEMORIAL SCHOLARSHIP

Women of the Evangelical Lutheran Church in America
Attn: Scholarships
8765 West Higgins Road
Chicago, IL 60631-4101
(773) 380-2741   Toll Free: (800) 638-3522, ext. 2741
Fax: (773) 380-2419   E-mail: valora.starr@elca.org
Web: www.womenoftheelca.org

Summary   To provide financial assistance to Hispanic and other lay women of color who are members of Evangelical Lutheran Church of America (ELCA) congregations and who wish to study on the undergraduate, graduate, professional, or vocational school level.

Eligibility   This program is open to ELCA lay women of color who are at least 21 years of age and have experienced an interruption of at least 2 years in their education since high school. Applicants must have been admitted to an educational institution to prepare for a career in other than ordained ministry. U.S. citizenship is required.

Financial Data   The maximum stipend is $1,000 per year.

Duration   1 year; recipients may reapply for 1 additional year.

Number awarded   1 or more each year.

Deadline   February of each year.

[25]
AMERICAN ASSOCIATION OF BLACKS IN ENERGY NATIONAL SCHOLARSHIPS

American Association of Blacks in Energy
Attn: Scholarship Committee
1625 K Street, N.W., Suite 405
Washington, DC 20006
(202) 371-9530   Fax: (202) 371-9218
E-mail: info@aabe.org
Web: www.aabe.org/index.php?component=pages&id=4

Summary To provide financial assistance to Hispanic and other underrepresented minority high school seniors who are interested in preparing for a career in a field related to energy in college.

Eligibility This program is open to members of minority groups underrepresented in energy-related fields (Hispanics, African Americans, and Native Americans) who are graduating high school seniors. Applicants must have a GPA of 3.0 or higher and have taken the SAT and/or ACT test. They must be planning to attend an accredited college or university to major in business, engineering, mathematics, technology, or the physical sciences. Along with their application, they must submit a 350-word essay that includes 1) when they discovered their interest in the field of energy and what sparked their interest; and 2) either what excites them about the field of energy or how they expect their education to prepare them for the field of energy. Financial need is not considered in the selection process. All applications must be submitted to the local office of the sponsoring organization in the student's state. For a list of local offices, contact the scholarship committee at the national office. The highest-ranked applicant receives the Rufus D. Gladney Premier Award.

Financial Data The stipends are $3,000. The Rufus D. Gladney Premier Award is $5,000. All funds are paid directly to the students upon proof of enrollment at an accredited college or university.

Duration 1 year; nonrenewable.

Number awarded 6 each year (1 in each of the organization's regions); of those 6 winners, 1 is chosen to receive the Rufus D. Gladney Premier Award.

Deadline March of each year.

[26]
AMERICAN ASSOCIATION OF PHYSICISTS IN MEDICINE DIVERSITY RECRUITMENT THROUGH EDUCATION AND MENTORING (DREAM) PROGRAM

American Association of Physicists in Medicine
Attn: AAPM Education and Research Fund
One Physics Ellipse
College Park, MD 20740
(301) 209-3350   Fax: (301) 209-0862
E-mail: jackie@aapm.org
Web: www.aapm.org/education/GrantsFellowships.asp

Summary To provide an opportunity for Hispanic and other minority upper-division students to gain summer work experience performing research in a medical physics laboratory or assisting with clinical service at a clinical facility.

Eligibility This program is open to minority undergraduates who are entering their junior or senior year at an Historically Black College or University (HBCU), Minority Serving Institution (MSI), or non-Minority Serving Institution. Applicants must be interested in gaining experience in medical physics by performing research in a laboratory or assisting with clinical service at a clinical facility. Preference is given to those who have declared a major in physics, engineering, or other science that requires mathematics at least through differential equations and junior-level courses in modern physics or quantum mechanics and electricity and magnetism or equivalent courses in engineering sciences. They must be U.S. citizens, U.S. permanent residents, or Canadian citizens. Work must be conducted under the supervision of a mentor who is a member of the American Association of Physicists in Medicine (AAPM) employed by a university, hospital, clinical facility, or radiological industry within the United States.

Financial Data The stipend is $5,000.

Duration 10 weeks during the summer.

Additional data This program was formerly known as the American Association of Physicists in Medicine Minority Undergraduate Experience Program.

Number awarded Varies each year; recently, 9 were awarded.

Deadline February of each year.

[27]
AMERICAN BUS ASSOCIATION DIVERSITY SCHOLARSHIPS

American Bus Association
Attn: ABA Foundation
111 K Street, N.E., Ninth Floor
Washington, DC 20002
(202) 842-1645   Toll Free: (800) 283-2877
Fax: (202) 842-0850   E-mail: abainfo@buses.org
Web: www.buses.org/aba-foundation/scholarships/diversity

Summary To provide financial assistance for college to Hispanics and members of other traditionally underrepresented groups who are preparing for a career in the transportation, travel, hospitality, and tourism industry.

Eligibility This program is open to members of traditionally underrepresented groups who have completed at least 1 year of study at a 2- or 4-year college or university. Applicants must be working on a degree in a course of study related to the transportation, travel, hospitality, and tourism industry. They must have a GPA of 3.0 or higher. Along with their application, they must submit a 500-word essay on the role they hope to play in advancing the future of the transportation, travel, hospitality, and tourism industry. Selection is based on academic achievement, character, leadership, financial need, and commitment to advancing the transportation, travel, hospitality, and tourism industry. Additional consideration is given to applicants who are affiliated with a company that is a member of the American Bus Association (ABA).

Financial Data The stipend is $2,500.

Duration 1 or more each year.

Deadline April of each year.

[28]
AMERICAN CHEMICAL SOCIETY SCHOLARS PROGRAM

American Chemical Society
Attn: Scholars Program
1155 16th Street, N.W.
Washington, DC 20036
(202) 872-6250   Toll Free: (800) 227-5558, ext. 6250
Fax: (202) 872-4361   E-mail: scholars@acs.org
Web: www.acs.org

Summary To provide financial assistance to Hispanic and other underrepresented minority students who have a strong interest in chemistry and a desire to prepare for a career in a chemically-related science.

Eligibility This program is open to 1) college-bound high school seniors; 2) freshmen, sophomores, and juniors enrolled full time at an accredited college or university; 3) community college students planning to transfer to a 4-year school; and 4) community college students working on a 2-year degree. Applicants must be African American, Hispanic/ Latino, or Native American. They must be majoring or planning to major in chemistry, biochemistry, chemical engineering, or other chemically-related fields, such as environmental science, materials science, or toxicology, in preparation for a career in the chemical sciences or chemical technology. Students planning careers in medicine or pharmacy are not eligible. U.S. citizenship or permanent resident status is required. Selection is based on academic record (GPA of 3.0 or higher), career objective, leadership ability, participation in school activities, community service, and financial need.

Financial Data Stipends range up to $5,000 per year, depending on the availability of funding, the number of scholarships awarded, and the need of the recipient. Funds are sent directly to the recipient's college or university.

Duration 1 year, may be renewed.

Additional data This program began in 1994.

Number awarded Varies each year; recently, 309 students received these awards.

Deadline February of each year.

[29]
AMERICAN GI FORUM OF KANSAS EDUCATIONAL FUND SCHOLARSHIP

American GI Forum of Kansas
Attn: Educational Fund
c/o Barbara Olivas
1000 North Cheyenne
Ulysses, KS 67880

Summary To provide financial assistance to Hispanic and other residents of Kansas who are interested in attending college or graduate school in any state.

Eligibility This program is open to Hispanic and other residents of Kansas who are currently enrolled as undergraduate, vocational/technical, or graduate students at a school in any state. Preference is given to members of the American GI Forum of Kansas. Applicants must submit a 1-page personal statement on their career goals, academic and personal achievements, how they plan to help the American GI Forum of Kansas help others like themselves in the future, and their involvement with their chapter. Selection is based on that

statement, academic achievement, 2 letters of recommendation, and financial need.

Financial Data Stipends range from $200 to $1,000.

Duration 1 year.

Number awarded 1 or more each year.

Deadline March of each year.

[30]
AMGEN SCHOLARS PROGRAM AT NIH

National Institutes of Health
Attn: Office of Intramural Training and Education
2 Center Drive
Building 2, Second Floor
Bethesda, MD 20892-0230
(301) 594-2053   Fax: (301) 594-9606
TDD: (888) 352-3001   E-mail: NIH-Amgen@od.nih.gov
Web: www.training.nih.gov/amgenscholars

Summary To provide an opportunity for undergraduates, especially Hispanics and other underrepresented groups, to participate in summer research projects in intramural biomedical science laboratories of the National Institutes of Health (NIH).

Eligibility This program is open to rising juniors and seniors at 4-year colleges and universities in the United States, Puerto Rico, and other U.S. territories. Applicants must be U.S. citizens or permanent residents who have a cumulative GPA of 3.2 or higher and an interest in continuing on for a Ph.D. or other combined degree program in the sciences. Students with experience in health disparities and a keen interest in learning more about the biological, environmental, social, and genetic causes of health disparities are especially encouraged to apply. Preference is given to students who lack opportunities to perform independent research during the school year. NIH welcomes applications from students in all science disciplines and encourages students from diverse backgrounds to apply.

Financial Data The stipend is $2,140 per month for rising juniors or $2,240 per month for rising seniors.

Duration 10 weeks during the summer.

Additional data This program serves as the NIH component of the Amgen Scholars Program, which also operates at 9 U.S. universities and is funded by the Amgen Foundation.

Number awarded Approximately 20 each year.

Deadline January of each year.

[31]
AMS MINORITY SCHOLARSHIPS

American Meteorological Society
Attn: Development and Student Program Manager
45 Beacon Street
Boston, MA 02108-3693
(617) 227-2426, ext. 3907   Fax: (617) 742-8718
E-mail: dFernandez@ametsoc.org
Web: www2.ametsoc.org

Summary To provide financial assistance to Hispanic and other underrepresented minority students entering college and planning to major in meteorology or an aspect of atmospheric sciences.

Eligibility This program is open to members of minority groups traditionally underrepresented in the sciences (especially Hispanics, Native Americans, and Blacks/African Americans) who are entering their freshman year at a college or university and planning to work on a degree in the atmospheric or related oceanic and hydrologic sciences. Applicants must submit an official high school transcript showing grades from the past 3 years, a letter of recommendation from a high school teacher or guidance counselor, a copy of scores from an SAT or similar national entrance exam, and a 500-word essay on a topic that changes annually; recently, applicants were invited to write on global change and how they would use their college education in atmospheric science (or a closely-related field) to make their community a better place in which to live. Selection is based on the essay and academic performance in high school.

Financial Data   The stipend is $3,000 per year.

Duration   1 year; may be renewed for the second year of college study.

Additional data   This program is funded by grants from industry and by donations to the American Meteorological Society (AMS) 21st Century Campaign. Requests for an application must be accompanied by a self-addressed stamped envelope.

Number awarded   Varies each year; recently, 3 were awarded.

Deadline   February of each year.

[32]
ANA MULTICULTURAL EXCELLENCE SCHOLARSHIP

American Association of Advertising Agencies
Attn: AAAA Foundation
1065 Avenue of the Americas, 16th Floor
New York, NY 10018
(212) 262-2500   E-mail: ameadows@aaaa.org
Web: www.aaaa.org

Summary   To provide financial assistance to Hispanic and other multicultural students who are working on an undergraduate degree in advertising.

Eligibility   This program is open to undergraduate students who are U.S. citizens of proven multicultural heritage and have at least 1 grandparent of multicultural heritage. Applicants must be participating in the Multicultural Advertising Intern Program (MAIP). They must be entering their senior year at an accredited college or university in the United States and have a GPA of 3.0 or higher. Selection is based on academic ability.

Financial Data   The stipend is $2,500.

Duration   1 year.

Additional data   This program was established by the Association of National Advertisers (ANA) in 2001. The American Association of Advertising Agencies (AAAA) assumed administration in 2003.

Number awarded   2 each year.

Deadline   Deadline not specified.

[33]
ANAC STUDENT DIVERSITY MENTORSHIP SCHOLARSHIP

Association of Nurses in AIDS Care
Attn: Awards Committee
3538 Ridgewood Road
Akron, OH 44333-3122
(330) 670-0101   Toll Free: (800) 260-6780
Fax: (330) 670-0109   E-mail: anac@anacnet.org
Web: www.nursesinaidscare.org

Summary   To provide financial assistance to student nurses from Hispanic and other minority groups who are interested in HIV/AIDS nursing and in attending the national conference of the Association of Nurses in AIDS Care (ANAC).

Eligibility   This program is open to student nurses from a diverse racial or ethnic background, defined to include Hispanics/Latinos, African Americans, Asians/Pacific Islanders, and American Indians/Alaskan Natives. Candidates must have a genuine interest in HIV/AIDS nursing, be interested in attending the ANAC national conference, and desire to develop a mentorship relationship with a member of the ANAC Diversity Specialty Committee. They may be 1) pre-licensure students enrolled in an initial R.N. or L.P.N./L.V.N. program (i.e. L.P.N./L.V.N., A.D.N., diploma, B.S./B.S.N.); or 2) current licensed R.N. students with an associate or diploma degree who are enrolled in a bachelor's degree program. Nominees may be recommended by themselves, nursing faculty members, or ANAC members, but their nomination must be supported by an ANAC member. Along with their nomination form, they must submit a 2,000-character essay describing their interest or experience in HIV/AIDS care and why they want to attend the ANAC conference.

Financial Data   Recipients are awarded a $1,000 scholarship (paid directly to the school), up to $599 in reimbursement of travel expenses to attend the ANAC annual conference, free conference registration, an award plaque, a free ticket to the awards ceremony at the conference, and a 2-year ANAC membership.

Duration   1 year.

Additional data   The mentor will be assigned at the conference and will maintain contact during the period of study.

Number awarded   1 each year.

Deadline   August of each year.

[34]
ANHELO PROJECT DREAM SCHOLARSHIP

Anhelo Project
c/o Joana Maravilla-Cano
P.O. Box 08290
Chicago, IL 60608
(773) 609-4252
E-mail: dreamscholarshipchicago@gmail.com
Web: www.theanheloproject.org/dream-scholarship

Summary   To provide financial assistance to undocumented students in Illinois who are interested in attending college or graduate school in the state.

Eligibility   This program is open to residents of Illinois who are undocumented students. Applicants must be enrolled full time at a college or university in the state. They must have a GPA of 2.5 or higher and be able to demonstrate financial need, community involvement, and ineligibility for federal financial assistance. DACA students are eligible, but international students with F-1 visas are not.

Financial Data A stipend is awarded (amount not specified).

Duration 1 year.

Number awarded Varies each year.

Deadline January of each year.

[35]
ANN SEKI MEMORIAL SCHOLARSHIPS

Great Minds in STEM
Attn: HENAAC Scholars Program
602 Monterey Pass Road
Monterey Park, CA 91754
(323) 262-0997   Fax: (323) 262-0946
E-mail: scholars@greatmindsinstem.org
Web: www.greatmindsinstem.org

Summary To provide financial assistance to Hispanic undergraduate students interested in working on a degree in designated fields of engineering at a university in any state.

Eligibility This program is open to students who are entering their sophomore, junior, or senior year in a field of STEM at a 4-year college or university in any state. Applicants must be of Hispanic origin and/or must significantly participate in and promote organizations and activities in the Hispanic community. They must have a GPA of 3.3 or higher and a major in engineering (chemical, civil, electrical, facilities, mechanical, or petroleum). Along with their application, they must submit a 700-word essay on a topic that changes annually. Selection is based on leadership, academic achievements, and campus and community activities; financial need is not considered. U.S. citizenship or permanent resident status is required.

Financial Data The stipend is $1,000.

Duration 1 year.

Additional data The Hispanic Engineer National Achievement Awards Conference (HENAAC) was established in 1989 and initiated a scholarship program in 2000. In 2010, the sponsoring organization officially adopted its current name, but it continues to hold the annual HENAAC conference, at which the scholarships are presented. This program, which began in 2010, is sponsored by Chevron. Recipients must attend the conference to accept their scholarship. The sponsor subsidizes the cost of travel, 3 nights of lodging, and meals.

Number awarded Varies each year; recently, 7 were awarded.

Deadline April of each year.

[36]
ANNE SHEN SMITH ENDOWED SCHOLARSHIP

Society of Women Engineers
Attn: Scholarship Selection Committee
203 North LaSalle Street, Suite 1675
Chicago, IL 60601-1269
(312) 596-5223   Toll Free: (877) SWE-INFO
Fax: (312) 644-8557   E-mail: scholarships@swe.org
Web: societyofwomenengineers.swe.org

Summary To provide financial assistance to women, especially Hispanics and members of other underrepresented groups, working on an undergraduate degree in engineering at colleges in California.

Eligibility This program is open to women who are entering their sophomore, junior, or senior year at a 4-year ABET-accredited college or university in California. Applicants must be working full time on a degree in computer science or any field of engineering. Preference is given to members of groups underrepresented in engineering. U.S. citizenship is required. Selection is based on merit.

Financial Data The stipend is $1,000.

Duration 1 year.

Additional data This program began in 2015.

Number awarded 1 each year.

Deadline February of each year.

[37]
ANTHEM BLUE CROSS BLUE SHIELD OF WISCONSIN NURSING SCHOLARSHIPS

Wisconsin League for Nursing
Attn: Scholarship Chair
P.O. Box 653
Germantown, WI 53022
(414) 454-9561   E-mail: info@wisconsinwln.org
Web: www.wisconsinwln.org/t/Scholarships

Summary To provide financial assistance to residents of Wisconsin, especially Hispanics and other minorities, attending a school of nursing in the state.

Eligibility This program is open to residents of Wisconsin who are enrolled at an accredited school of nursing in the state in an L.P.N., A.D.N., B.S.N., M.S.N., D.N.P., or Ph.D. program. Applicants must have completed at least half the credits needed for graduation. Ethnic minority students are especially encouraged to apply. Students must submit their applications to their school, not directly to the sponsor. Each school may nominate 4 graduate students, 6 students in an R.N. program, and 2 L.P.N. students. Selection is based on scholastic ability, professional abilities and/or community service, understanding of the nursing profession, goals upon graduation, and financial need.

Financial Data Stipends are $500 for L.P.N. students or $1,000 for all other students.

Duration 1 year.

Additional data This program is sponsored by Anthem Blue Cross Blue Shield of Wisconsin.

Number awarded Varies each year; recently, the program awarded 31 scholarships, including 2 L.P.N. awards, 10 associate degree awards, 16 B.S.N. awards, and 3 graduate awards.

Deadline April of each year.

[38]
APAPRO SCHOLARSHIP

Association of Peruvian American Professionals
Attn: Scholarships
593 Farmington Avenue
Hartford, CT 06105
(860) 830-3827   E-mail: info@apapro.org
Web: www.apapro.org/pages/education_scholarship.asp

Summary To provide financial assistance to Latino residents of Connecticut who are interested in attending college in the state.

Eligibility This program is open to seniors and graduates of public high schools in Connecticut who are of Latino descent. Applicants must be between 16 and 21 years of age and enrolled or planning to enroll at a 2- or 4-year college or university in Connecticut. Selection is based on achievement, potential, commitment to pursuing higher education, and financial need.

Financial Data The stipend is $1,000 per year. Funds are disbursed directly to the educational institution.

Duration 1 year; recipients may reapply.

Number awarded 3 each year.

Deadline June of each year.

[39]
APS/IBM RESEARCH INTERNSHIP FOR UNDERREPRESENTED MINORITY STUDENTS

American Physical Society
Attn: Committee on Minorities
One Physics Ellipse
College Park, MD 20740-3844
(301) 209-3232   Fax: (301) 209-0865
E-mail: apsibmin@us.ibm.com
Web: www.aps.org

Summary To provide an opportunity for Hispanic and other underrepresented minority students to participate in a summer research internship in science or engineering at facilities of IBM.

Eligibility This program is open to members of underrepresented minority groups currently enrolled as sophomores or juniors and majoring in biology, chemistry, chemical engineering, computer science or engineering, electrical engineering, materials science or engineering, mechanical engineering, or physics. Applicants are not required to be U.S. citizens, but they must be enrolled at a college or university in the United States. They must be interested in working as a research intern at a participating IBM laboratory. A GPA of at least 3.0 is required. Selection is based on commitment to and interest in their major field of study.

Financial Data Interns receive a competitive salary of approximately $8,000 for the summer.

Duration 10 weeks during the summer.

Additional data Participating IBM laboratories are the Almaden Research Center in San Jose, California, the Watson Research Center in Yorktown Heights, New York, or the Austin Research Laboratory in Austin, Texas.

Number awarded 1 each year.

Deadline February of each year.

[40]
ARCELORMITTAL EMERGING LEADER SCHOLARSHIPS

Society of Women Engineers
Attn: Scholarship Selection Committee
203 North LaSalle Street, Suite 1675
Chicago, IL 60601-1269
(312) 596-5223   Toll Free: (877) SWE-INFO
Fax: (312) 644-8557   E-mail: scholarships@swe.org
Web: societyofwomenengineers.swe.org

Summary To provide financial assistance to members of the Society of Women Engineers (SWE), especially Hispanics and other underrepresented minorities, who are inter-

ested in studying specified fields of engineering at designated universities.

Eligibility This program is open to SWE members who are entering their junior year at Ohio State University, Indiana University, Purdue University, Michigan State University, Michigan Technological University, Pennsylvania State University, Rose-Hulman Institute of Technology, Purdue University Northwest (formerly Purdue University-Calumet), Missouri University of Science and Technology, Iowa State University, or University of Illinois at Urbana-Champaign. Applicants must be enrolled full time and majoring in computer science or computer, electrical, or materials engineering. They must be U.S. citizens. Preference is given to members of underrepresented groups, including veterans. Selection is based on merit and financial need.

Financial Data The stipend is $1,000.

Duration 1 year.

Additional data This program is sponsored by ArcelorMittal.

Number awarded 1 each year.

Deadline February of each year.

[41]
ARIZONA HISPANIC CHAMBER OF COMMERCE SCHOLARSHIP

Arizona Community Foundation
Attn: Director of Scholarships
2201 East Camelback Road, Suite 405B
Phoenix, AZ 85016
(602) 381-1400   Toll Free: (800) 222-8221
Fax: (602) 381-1575
E-mail: scholarship@azfoundation.org
Web: azfoundation.academicworks.com/opportunities/2511

Summary To provide financial assistance to upper-division students of Hispanic heritage working on a bachelor's degree in business at a college in Arizona.

Eligibility This program is open to students entering their junior or senior year in a business degree program at an accredited college or university in Arizona. Applicants must have at least 1 parent of Hispanic heritage. They must be enrolled full time and have a GPA of 3.0 or higher. Preference is given to applicants who have a recognized physical disability or are dependents of or employees of a company that is a member of the Arizona Hispanic Chamber of Commerce.

Financial Data The stipend is $5,000 per year.

Duration 1 year; may be renewed 1 additional year.

Additional data This program is sponsored by the Arizona Hispanic Chamber of Commerce. Recipients are paired with a mentor from the chamber.

Number awarded Varies each year.

Deadline April of each year.

[42]
ARKANSAS CONFERENCE ETHNIC AND LANGUAGE CONCERNS COMMITTEE SCHOLARSHIPS

United Methodist Church-Arkansas Conference
Attn: Committee on Ethnic and Language Concerns
800 Daisy Bates Drive
Little Rock, AR 72202
(501) 324-8045   Toll Free: (877) 646-1816
Fax: (501) 324-8018   E-mail: mallen@arumc.org
Web: www.arumc.org/docs-and-forms

Summary To provide financial assistance to Hispanic and other ethnic minority Methodist students from Arkansas who are interested in attending college or graduate school in any state.

Eligibility This program is open to ethnic minority undergraduate and graduate students who are active members of local congregations affiliated with the Arkansas Conference of the United Methodist Church (UMC). Applicants must be currently enrolled in an accredited institution of higher education in any state. Along with their application, they must submit an essay explaining how this scholarship will make them a leader in the UMC. Preference is given to students attending a UMC-affiliated college or university.

Financial Data The stipend is $500 per semester ($1,000 per year) for undergraduates or $1,000 per semester ($2,000 per year) for graduate students.

Duration 1 year; may be renewed.

Number awarded 5 each year: 1 in each UMC Arkansas district.

Deadline February or September of each year.

[43]
ARTHUR H. GOODMAN MEMORIAL SCHOLARSHIP

San Diego Foundation
Attn: Community Scholarships
2508 Historic Decatur Road, Suite 200
San Diego, CA 92106
(619) 814-1343   Fax: (619) 239-1710
E-mail: scholarships@sdfoundation.org
Web: www.sdfoundation.org

Summary To provide financial assistance to Hispanic and other minority community college students in California or Arizona planning to transfer to a 4-year school in any state to prepare for a career in economic development.

Eligibility This program is open to women and minorities currently enrolled at a community college in California or Arizona and planning to transfer as a full- or part-time student at a 4-year school in any state. Applicants must submit information on their long-term career goal, a list of volunteer and extracurricular activities, documentation of financial need, and a 3-page personal statement on their commitment to community involvement and desire to prepare for a career in the field of economic development.

Financial Data Stipends range from $1,500 to $3,000.

Duration 1 year.

Additional data This program was established in 1998 by the CDC Small Business Finance Corporation.

Number awarded Varies each year; recently, 5 were awarded.

Deadline April of each year.

[44]
ARTTABLE MENTORED INTERNSHIPS FOR DIVERSITY IN THE VISUAL ARTS PROFESSIONS

ArtTable Inc.
1 East 53rd Street, Fifth Floor
New York, NY 10022
(212) 343-1735   Fax: (866) 363-4188
E-mail: info@arttable.org
Web: www.arttable.org/summermentoredinternship

Summary To provide an opportunity for women who are Hispanics or from other diverse backgrounds to gain mentored work experience during the summer and to prepare for a career as an art professional.

Eligibility This program is open to women who are college seniors, recent graduates, or graduate students and interested in preparing for a career as a visual arts professional (including administrative director, art adviser, art appraiser, art critic, art dealer, art librarian, arts funder, arts lawyer, conservator, curator, editor, educator, fundraiser, management consultant, public relations consultant, writer). Applicants must be from a cultural or ethnic background that is underrepresented in the field. They must be interested in working during the summer with a mentor at an art museum or similar facility. U.S. citizenship or permanent resident status is required.

Financial Data The stipend is $3,000. The hosting institution or mentor receives $500 for administrative and other costs.

Duration 8 weeks during the summer.

Additional data This program began in 2000. Support is provided by the Samuel H. Kress Foundation.

Number awarded Varies each year; recently, 5 of these internships were awarded.

Deadline February of each year.

[45]
ASCPA EDUCATIONAL FOUNDATION DIVERSITY SCHOLARSHIPS

Alabama Society of Certified Public Accountants
Attn: ASCPA Educational Foundation
1041 Longfield Court
P.O. Box 242987
Montgomery, AL 36124-2987
(334) 834-7650   Toll Free: (800) 227-1711 (within AL)
Fax: (334) 834-7603
Web: www.ascpa.org

Summary To provide financial assistance to Hispanic and other minority accounting students at colleges and universities in Alabama.

Eligibility This program is open to minority (Hispanic or Latino, Black or African American, Native American, or Asian) residents of any state enrolled at least half time at colleges and universities in Alabama with at least 1 full year of school remaining. Applicants must have declared a major in accounting and have completed intermediate accounting courses. They must have a GPA of 3.0 or higher overall and in all accounting classes. Along with their application, they must submit a 25-word essay on why the scholarship is important to them. Financial need is not considered in the selection process. Preference is given to students who have a strong interest in a career as a C.P.A. in Alabama. U.S. citizenship or permanent resident status is required.

Financial Data   The stipend is $2,500.

Duration   1 year.

Additional data   This program began in 2012.

Number awarded   5 each year.

Deadline   March of each year.

[46]
ASLA COUNCIL OF FELLOWS SCHOLARSHIPS

Landscape Architecture Foundation
Attn: Leadership in Landscape Scholarship Program
1129 20th Street, N.W., Suite 202
Washington, DC 20036
(202) 331-7070   Fax: (202) 331-7079
E-mail: scholarships@lafoundation.org
Web: www.lafoundation.org

Summary   To provide financial assistance to upper-division students, especially Hispanics and those from other disadvantaged and underrepresented groups, working on a degree in landscape architecture.

Eligibility   This program is open to landscape architecture students in the third, fourth, or fifth year of undergraduate work. Preference is given to, and 1 scholarship is reserved for, members of underrepresented ethnic or cultural groups. Applicants must submit a 500-word essay on how they envision themselves contributing to the profession of landscape architecture, 2 letters of recommendation, documentation of financial need, and (for students applying for the scholarship reserved for underrepresented groups) a statement identifying their association with a specific ethnic or cultural group. U.S. citizenship or permanent resident status is required.

Financial Data   The stipend is $4,000. Students also receive a 1-year membership in the American Society of Landscape Architects (ASLA), general registration fees for the ASLA annual meeting, and a travel stipend to attend the meeting.

Duration   1 year.

Additional data   This program is sponsored by ASLA and administered by the Landscape Architecture Foundation.

Number awarded   3 each year, of which 1 is reserved for a member of an underrepresented group.

Deadline   February of each year.

[47]
ASSE DIVERSITY COMMITTEE UNDERGRADUATE SCHOLARSHIP

American Society of Safety Engineers
Attn: ASSE Foundation
Scholarship Award Program
520 North Northwest Highway
Park Ridge, IL 60068-2538
(847) 699-2929   Fax: (847) 296-3769
E-mail: assefoundation@asse.org
Web: foundation.asse.org/scholarships-and-grants

Summary   To provide financial assistance to upper-division students who are Hispanics or come from diverse groups and are working on a degree related to occupational safety.

Eligibility   This program is open to students who are working on an undergraduate degree in occupational safety, health, environment, industrial hygiene, occupational health nursing, or a closely-related field (e.g., industrial or environmental engineering). Applicants must be full-time students who have completed at least 60 semester hours and have a GPA of 3.0 or higher. A goal of this program is to support individuals regardless of race, ethnicity, gender, religion, personal beliefs, age, sexual orientation, physical challenges, geographic location, university, or specific area of study. U.S. citizenship is not required. Membership in the American Society of Safety Engineers (ASSE) is not required, but preference is given to members.

Financial Data   The stipend is $1,000 per year.

Duration   1 year; recipients may reapply.

Number awarded   1 each year.

Deadline   November of each year.

[48]
ASSOCIATED FOOD AND PETROLEUM DEALERS MINORITY SCHOLARSHIPS

Associated Food and Petroleum Dealers
Attn: AFPD Foundation
5779 West Maple Road
West Bloomfield, MI 48322
(248) 671-9600   Toll Free: (800) 666-6233
Fax: (866) 601-9610   E-mail: info@afpdonline.org
Web: www.afpdonline.org/michigan-scholarship.php

Summary   To provide financial assistance to Hispanic and other minority high school seniors and current college students from Michigan who are enrolled or planning to enroll at a college in any state.

Eligibility   This program is open to Michigan residents who are high school seniors or college freshmen, sophomores, or juniors. Applicants must be members of 1 of the following minority groups: Hispanic, African American, Asian, Native American, or Arab/Chaldean. They must be enrolled or planning to enroll full time at a college or university in any state. Preferential consideration is given to applicants with a membership affiliation in the Associated Food and Petroleum Dealers (AFPD), although membership is not required. Selection is based on academic performance, leadership, and participation in school and community activities; college grades are considered if the applicant is already enrolled in college.

Financial Data   The stipend is $1,500 per year.

Duration   1 year; may be renewed 1 additional year.

Additional data   This program is administered by International Scholarship and Tuition Services, Inc. The AFPD was formed in 2006 by a merger of the Associated Food Dealers of Michigan and the Great Lakes Petroleum Retailers and Allied Trades Association.

Number awarded   At least 10 each year, of which at least 3 must be awarded to member customers.

Deadline   March of each year.

[49]
ASSOCIATION FOR WOMEN GEOSCIENTISTS MINORITY SCHOLARSHIP

Association for Women Geoscientists
Attn: AWG Foundation
12000 North Washington Street, Suite 285
Thornton, CO 80241
(303) 412-6219   Fax: (303) 253-9220
E-mail: office@awg.org
Web: www.awg.org/eas/minority.htm

Summary To provide financial assistance to Hispanic and other underrepresented minority women who are interested in working on an undergraduate degree in the geosciences.

Eligibility This program is open to women who are Hispanic, African American, or Native American (including Eskimo, Hawaiian, Samoan, or American Indian). Applicants must be full-time students working on, or planning to work on, an undergraduate degree in the geosciences (including geology, geophysics, geochemistry, hydrology, meteorology, physical oceanography, planetary geology, or earth science education). They must submit a 500-word essay on their academic and career goals, 2 letters of recommendation, high school and/or college transcripts, and SAT or ACT scores. Financial need is not considered in the selection process. U.S. citizenship is required.

Financial Data A total of $6,000 is available for this program each year.

Duration 1 year; may be renewed.

Additional data This program, first offered in 2004, is supported by ExxonMobil Foundation.

Number awarded 1 or more each year.

Deadline June of each year.

[50]
ASSOCIATION OF CUBAN ENGINEERS SCHOLARSHIPS

Association of Cuban Engineers
P.O. Box 941436
Miami, FL 33194-1436
Web: www.aic-ace.com/?q=node/27

Summary To provide financial assistance to undergraduate and graduate students of Cuban American heritage who are interested in preparing for a career in engineering.

Eligibility This program is open to U.S. citizens and legal residents who have completed at least 30 units of college work in the United States and are working on an undergraduate or graduate degree in engineering. Applicants must be attending an ABET-accredited college or university within the United States or Puerto Rico as a full-time student and have a GPA of 3.0 or higher. They must be of Cuban or other Hispanic heritage (at least 1 grandparent Cuban or other Hispanic nationality). Along with their application, they must submit brief essays on their family history, professional goals, extracurricular activities, work experience, and how they will help other Cuban and Hispanic engineering students in the future. Financial need is not considered in the selection process.

Financial Data Stipends range from $500 to $2,000.

Duration 1 year; may be renewed.

Additional data This program also includes the Pedro O. Martinez Scholarship and the Luciano de Goicochea Award

(for students at the University of Miami), the Antonio Choy Award (for a student at the University of Florida), and the Noel Betancourt Award (for a student at Florida International University).

Number awarded Varies each year; recently, 11 were awarded.

Deadline November of each year.

[51]
ASSOCIATION OF LATINO PROFESSIONALS FOR AMERICA SCHOLARSHIP PROGRAM

Association of Latino Professionals For America
Attn: Scholarships
801 South Grand Avenue, Suite 400
Los Angeles, CA 90017
(714) 757-6133   E-mail: scholarships@national.alpfa.org
Web: www.alpfa.fluidreview.com

Summary To provide financial assistance to members of the Association of Latino Professionals For America (ALPFA) who are working on an undergraduate or master's degree in a field related to business.

Eligibility This competition is open to members of ALPFA who are full-time sophomores, juniors, seniors, or master's degree students at colleges and universities in the United States, Puerto Rico, U.S. Virgin Islands, or Guam. Students enrolled at community colleges and planning to transfer to 4-year institutions are also eligible. Applicants must be working on a degree in accounting, business administration, economics, finance, information systems, information technology, management, marketing, or other business-related field. They must be U.S. citizens or permanent residents and have a GPA of 3.0 or higher. Along with their application, they must submit a resume, official transcript, and proof of full-time enrollment.

Financial Data Stipends range from $2,000 to $10,000.

Duration 1 year.

Additional data This program began in 2005 when the sponsor was named the Association of Latino Professionals in Finance and Accounting.

Number awarded Varies each year. Since the program was established, it has awarded 578 scholarships worth $1.14 million.

Deadline May of each year.

[52]
ATKINS NORTH AMERICA ACHIEVEMENT COLLEGE SCHOLARSHIP

Conference of Minority Transportation Officials
Attn: National Scholarship Program
100 M Street, S.E., Suite 917
Washington, DC 20003
(202) 506-2917   E-mail: info@comto.org
Web: www.comto.org/page/scholarships

Summary To provide financial assistance to Hispanic and other minority undergraduates interested in working on a degree in transportation or a related field.

Eligibility This program is open to minority students who have completed at least 12 semester hours as full-time undergraduates. Applicants must be studying transportation, engineering, planning, or a related discipline. Along with their application they must submit a cover letter on their transportation-related career goals and life aspirations. Financial need is not considered in the selection process.

Financial Data The stipend is $2,000. Funds are paid directly to the recipient's college or university.

Duration 1 year.

Additional data This program is sponsored by Atkins North America.

Number awarded 1 each year.

Deadline April of each year.

[53]
ATKINS NORTH AMERICA ACHIEVEMENT HIGH SCHOOL SCHOLARSHIP

Conference of Minority Transportation Officials
Attn: National Scholarship Program
100 M Street, S.E., Suite 917
Washington, DC 20003
(202) 506-2917   E-mail: info@comto.org
Web: www.comto.org/page/scholarships

Summary To provide financial assistance to Hispanic and other minority high school seniors interested in working on a degree in transportation or a related field.

Eligibility This program is open to minority seniors graduating from high school with a GPA of 3.0 or higher. Applicants must be planning to study aspects of transportation, including technology, engineering, planning, or management. Along with their application they must submit a cover letter on their transportation-related career goals and life aspirations. Financial need is not considered in the selection process.

Financial Data The stipend is $2,000. Funds are paid directly to the recipient's college or university.

Duration 1 year.

Additional data This program is sponsored by Atkins North America.

Number awarded 1 each year.

Deadline April of each year.

[54]
ATKINS NORTH AMERICA LEADERSHIP SCHOLARSHIP

Conference of Minority Transportation Officials
Attn: National Scholarship Program
100 M Street, S.E., Suite 917
Washington, DC 20003
(202) 506-2917   E-mail: info@comto.org
Web: www.comto.org/page/scholarships

Summary To provide financial assistance to Hispanic and other minority undergraduate and graduate students interested in working on a degree in transportation or a related field.

Eligibility This program is open to minority 1) undergraduates who have completed at least 12 semester hours of study; and 2) graduate students. Applicants must be studying transportation, engineering, planning, or a related discipline. Along with their application they must submit a cover letter on their transportation-related career goals and life aspirations. Financial need is not considered in the selection process.

Financial Data The stipend is $3,000. Funds are paid directly to the recipient's college or university.

Duration 1 year.

Additional data This program is sponsored by Atkins North America.

Number awarded 1 each year.

Deadline April of each year.

[55]
ATLANTA CHAPTER AABE SCHOLARSHIPS

American Association of Blacks in Energy-Atlanta Chapter
Attn: Scholarship Committee
P.O. Box 55216
Atlanta, GA 30308-5216
(404) 506-6756
E-mail: G2AABEATCHAP@southernco.com
Web: www.aabe.org/atlanta

Summary To provide financial assistance to Hispanics and members of other underrepresented minority groups who are high school seniors in Georgia and planning to major in an energy-related field at a college in any state.

Eligibility This program is open to seniors graduating from high schools in Georgia and planning to attend a college or university in any state. Applicants must be Hispanics, African Americans, or Native Americans who have a GPA of 3.0 or higher and who have taken the ACT and/or SAT test. Their intended major must be business, engineering, technology, mathematics, the physical sciences, or other energy-related field. Along with their application, they must submit a 350-word essay that includes 1) when they discovered their interest in the field of energy and what sparked their interest; and 2) either what excites them about the field of energy or how they expect their education to prepare them for the field of energy. Financial need is not considered in the selection process.

Financial Data Stipends of varying amounts are awarded.

Duration 1 year; may be renewed at the rate of $500 per year, provided the recipient remains enrolled full time and maintains a GPA of 3.0 or higher.

Additional data The winners are eligible to compete for regional and national scholarships.

Number awarded 1 or more each year.

Deadline March of each year.

[56]
AURELIO "LARRY" JAZO MIGRANT SCHOLARSHIP

Geneseo Migrant Center
Attn: Scholarship Funds
3 Mt. Morris-Leicester Road
Leicester, NY 14481
(585) 658-7960   Toll Free: (800) 245-5681
Fax: (585) 658-7969   E-mail: mreho@gvboces.org
Web: www.migrant.net/migrant/scholarships/jazo.htm

Summary To provide financial assistance for college to migrant farmworker high school seniors from Illinois.

Eligibility This program is open to migrant farmworker students with a history of migration to and/or within Illinois. Applicants must have senior status in high school and plans to attend a postsecondary institution or other advanced training. Along with their application, they must submit a statement of 250 to 300 words on their experience as a migrant farmworker, their educational goals, why they are deserving of this scholarship, and a situation or obstacle they have faced in their life that has an important lesson in their development; 2 letters of recommendation; transcripts; and a copy of their current Migrant Certificate of Eligibility (COE). Selection is based on demonstrated commitment to educational goals, participation in school and Migrant Education Outreach Program (MEOP) activities, participation in community and/or non-school activities, citizenship, evidence of high mobility (interstate or intrastate), record of overcoming unusual obstacles, and financial need.

Financial Data   The stipend is $1,000.

Duration   1 year.

Number awarded   1 or more each year.

Deadline   May of each year.

[57]
AVIATION AND PROFESSIONAL DEVELOPMENT SCHOLARSHIP

Airport Minority Advisory Council
Attn: AMAC Foundation
2001 Jefferson Davis Highway, Suite 500
Arlington, VA 22202
(703) 414-2622   Fax: (703) 414-2686
E-mail: terrifrierson@palladiumholdingsco.com
Web: amac-org.com/amac-foundation/scholarships

Summary   To provide financial assistance to Hispanic and other minority high school seniors and undergraduates who are preparing for a career in the aviation industry and interested in participating in activities of the Airport Minority Advisory Council (AMAC).

Eligibility   This program is open to minority and female high school seniors and current undergraduates who have a GPA of 2.5 or higher and a record of involvement in community and extracurricular activities. Applicants must be interested in working on a bachelor's degree in accounting, architecture, aviation, business administration, engineering, or finance as preparation for a career in the aviation or airport industry. They must be interested in participating in the AMAC program, including becoming a member if they are awarded a scholarship, and communicating with AMAC once each semester during the term of the scholarship. Along with their application, they must submit a 750-word essay on how they have overcome barriers in life to achieve their academic and/or career goals; their dedication to succeed in the aviation industry and how AMAC can help them achieve their goal; and the most important issues that the aviation industry is facing today and how they see themselves changing those. Financial need is not considered in the selection process. U.S. citizenship is required.

Financial Data   The stipend is $2,000 per year.

Duration   1 year; recipients may reapply.

Number awarded   4 each year.

Deadline   May of each year.

[58]
AWS FOX VALLEY SECTION SCHOLARSHIP

American Welding Society-Fox Valley Section
c/o AWS Foundation, Inc.
8669 N.W. 36th Street, Suite 130
Doral, FL 33166-6672
(305) 443-9353   Toll Free: (800) 443-9353, ext. 250
Fax: (305) 443-7559   E-mail: nprado-pulido@aws.org
Web: www.awssection.org/foxvalley/scholarship

Summary   To provide financial assistance to residents of Wisconsin and the Upper Peninsula of Michigan, especially Hispanics and other underrepresented minorities, who are interested in working on a certificate or degree in a welding-related field at a school in any state.

Eligibility   This program is open to residents of Wisconsin and the Upper Peninsula of Michigan who are U.S. citizens and either high school seniors or current undergraduate students. Applicants must be working or planning to work full or part time (preferable full time) on a welding program certificate or college degree focused on welding at a school in any state. They must have a GPA of 2.5 or higher. Financial need is not considered in the selection process. Preference is given to members of groups underrepresented in the welding industry.

Financial Data   The stipend is $1,500 per year; funds are paid directly to the educational institution.

Duration   1 year; may be renewed for 1 additional year.

Number awarded   1 each year.

Deadline   February of each year.

[59]
AWS TIDEWATER VIRGINIA SECTION SCHOLARSHIP

American Welding Society-Tidewater Section
c/o Jackie Phillips, Section Chair
Newport News Shipbuilding
4101 Washington Avenue
Newport News, VA 23607
(757) 688-4469 E-mail: jacqueline.a.phillips@hii-nns.com
Web: www.awssection.org/tidewater/scholarship

Summary   To provide financial assistance to residents of Virginia, especially Hispanics and other underrepresented minorities, who are interested in working on an undergraduate degree in designated fields related to welding.

Eligibility   This program is open to students working on an associated or bachelor's degree in welding engineering, materials joining engineering, welding engineering technology, or materials joining engineering technology. Priority is given in the following order: first to residents of the Tidewater region of Virginia; second to residents of Virginia; and third to students at LeTourneau University. High school seniors must have a GPA of 2.4 or higher; students already enrolled in college must have a GPA of at least 2.1 overall and 2.3 in their major. Preference is given to full-time students, but part-time students are encouraged to apply if they are also working at a job or have other circumstances that prevent them from enrolling full time. U.S. citizenship is required. Financial need is considered in the selection process. Special consideration is given to applicants who are enrolled in an ABET-accredited program, have a documented working history that includes hands-on welding experience, have successfully completed a high school welding curriculum, or are from a group under-represented in the welding industry.

Financial Data The stipend is $1,000 per year.

Duration 1 year; may be renewed up to 2 additional years upon reapplication.

Number awarded 1 or more each year.

Deadline April of each year.

[60]
AZALAS HIGH SCHOOL SENIOR SCHOLARSHIPS

Arizona Association of Latino Administrators and
  Superintendents
Attn: Scholarship Committee
P.O. Box 18271
Phoenix, AZ 85005
(480) 753-3542
Web: azalas.org

Summary To provide financial assistance to Latino high school seniors in Arizona who plan to attend college in any state.

Eligibility This program is open to seniors graduating from high schools in Arizona who have at least 1 parent of Hispanic heritage. Applicants must have a GPA of 2.5 or higher. Along with their application, they must submit a 500-word essay on how their Latino heritage has influenced their life goals, mission, and desire to make a positive impact in their environment. Selection is based on the essay, academic achievement, and extracurricular activities.

Financial Data The stipend is $1,000.

Duration 1 year.

Additional data The sponsoring organization, the Arizona Association of Latino Administrators and Superintendents (AZALAS), was formerly named the Arizona Hispanic School Administrators Association.

Number awarded 5 each year.

Deadline April of each year.

[61]
BALTIMORE CHAPTER AABE SCHOLARSHIPS

American Association of Blacks in Energy-Baltimore
  Chapter
Attn: Scholarship Committee
P.O. Box 1903
Baltimore, MD 21203
E-mail: aabe.baltimore@gmail.com
Web: www.aabe.org

Summary To provide financial assistance to Hispanics and members of other underrepresented minority groups who are high school seniors in Maryland and planning to major in an energy-related field at a college in any state.

Eligibility This program is open to seniors graduating from high schools in Maryland and planning to attend a college or university in any state. Applicants must be Hispanics, African Americans, or Native Americans who have a GPA of 3.0 or higher and who have taken the ACT and/or SAT test. Their intended major must be business, engineering, technology, mathematics, the physical sciences, or other energy-related field. Along with their application, they must submit a 350-word essay that includes 1) when they discovered their interest in the field of energy and what sparked their interest; and 2) either what excites them about the field of energy or how

they expect their education to prepare them for the field of energy. Financial need is not considered in the selection process.

Financial Data The stipend is $1,000.

Duration 1 year.

Additional data The winners are eligible to compete for regional and national scholarships.

Number awarded 2 each year.

Deadline March of each year.

[62]
BARRIENTOS SCHOLARSHIP FOUNDATION ARTS SCHOLARSHIPS

Barrientos Scholarship Foundation
Attn: Scholarship Chair
P.O. Box 7173
Omaha, NE 68107
(402) 215-5106   E-mail: info@barrientosscholarship.org
Web: barrientosscholarship.org

Summary To provide financial assistance to Latino students who are interested in attending college in Nebraska or western Iowa to study designated fields of the arts.

Eligibility This program is open to students of Latino heritage enrolled or planning to enroll at colleges and universities in Nebraska or western Iowa. Applicants must be graduating high school seniors or current college students and have a GPA of 3.0 or higher. They must have a strong interest in studying music, visual arts, theater, or dance. Along with their application, they must submit a personal essay of 250 to 500 words on their educational and career goals, what inspired them to pursue your chosen field of study, how their Latino culture has influenced their life, how they see themselves making a difference in the Latino community in their future, and how this scholarship will assist them in their pursuit of a higher education.

Financial Data The stipend is $2,500.

Duration 1 year.

Additional data This foundation was established in 2005.

Number awarded 1 or more each year. Since this foundation was established, it has awarded a total of $80,000 to 121 students.

Deadline April of each year.

[63]
BARRIENTOS SCHOLARSHIP FOUNDATION EDUCATION SCHOLARSHIPS

Barrientos Scholarship Foundation
Attn: Scholarship Chair
P.O. Box 7173
Omaha, NE 68107
(402) 215-5106   E-mail: info@barrientosscholarship.org
Web: barrientosscholarship.org

Summary To provide financial assistance to Latino students who are interested in attending college in Nebraska or western Iowa to study education.

Eligibility This program is open to students of Latino heritage enrolled or planning to enroll at colleges and universities in Nebraska or western Iowa. Applicants must be graduating high school seniors or current college students and have a GPA of 3.0 or higher. They must be interested in studying education, including counseling and education. Along with their application, they must submit a personal essay of 250 to 500 words on their educational and career goals, what inspired them to pursue your chosen field of study, how their Latino culture has influenced their life, how they see themselves making a difference in the Latino community in their future, and how this scholarship will assist them in their pursuit of a higher education.

Financial Data The stipend is $2,500.

Duration 1 year.

Additional data This foundation was established in 2005.

Number awarded 1 or more each year. Since this foundation was established, it has awarded a total of $80,000 to 121 students.

Deadline April of each year.

[64]
BARRIENTOS SCHOLARSHIP FOUNDATION ENGINEERING/TECHNOLOGY SCHOLARSHIPS

Barrientos Scholarship Foundation
Attn: Scholarship Chair
P.O. Box 7173
Omaha, NE 68107
(402) 215-5106   E-mail: info@barrientosscholarship.org
Web: barrientosscholarship.org

Summary To provide financial assistance to Latino students who are interested in attending college in Nebraska or western Iowa to study engineering or technology.

Eligibility This program is open to students of Latino heritage enrolled or planning to enroll at colleges and universities in Nebraska or western Iowa. Applicants must be graduating high school seniors or current college students and have a GPA of 3.0 or higher. They must be interested in studying engineering or technology. Along with their application, they must submit a personal essay of 250 to 500 words on their educational and career goals, what inspired them to pursue your chosen field of study, how their Latino culture has influenced their life, how they see themselves making a difference in the Latino community in their future, and how this scholarship will assist them in their pursuit of a higher education.

Financial Data The stipend is $2,500.

Duration 1 year.

Additional data This foundation was established in 2005.

Number awarded 1 or more each year. Since this foundation was established, it has awarded a total of $80,000 to 121 students.

Deadline April of each year.

[65]
BARRIENTOS SCHOLARSHIP FOUNDATION HEALTH SCHOLARSHIPS

Barrientos Scholarship Foundation
Attn: Scholarship Chair
P.O. Box 7173
Omaha, NE 68107
(402) 215-5106   E-mail: info@barrientosscholarship.org
Web: barrientosscholarship.org

Summary To provide financial assistance to Latino students who are interested in attending college in Nebraska or western Iowa to study designated health-related fields.

Eligibility This program is open to students of Latino heritage enrolled or planning to enroll at colleges and universities

in Nebraska or western Iowa. Applicants must be graduating high school seniors or current college students and have a GPA of 3.0 or higher. They must have a strong interest in studying nursing, therapy, medical research, or other fields of medical practice. Along with their application, they must submit a personal essay of 250 to 500 words on their educational and career goals, what inspired them to pursue your chosen field of study, how their Latino culture has influenced their life, how they see themselves making a difference in the Latino community in their future, and how this scholarship will assist them in their pursuit of a higher education.

Financial Data The stipend is $2,500.

Duration 1 year.

Additional data This foundation was established in 2005.

Number awarded 1 or more each year. Since this foundation was established, it has awarded a total of $80,000 to 121 students.

Deadline April of each year.

[66]
BAYER SCHOLARSHIPS

Society of Women Engineers
Attn: Scholarship Selection Committee
203 North LaSalle Street, Suite 1675
Chicago, IL 60601-1269
(312) 596-5223   Toll Free: (877) SWE-INFO
Fax: (312) 644-8557   E-mail: scholarships@swe.org
Web: societyofwomenengineers.swe.org

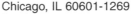

Summary To provide financial assistance to women, especially Hispanics and members of other underrepresented groups, working on an undergraduate degree in designated fields of engineering at colleges in Pennsylvania and Texas.

Eligibility This program is open to women who are entering their sophomore, junior, or senior year at a 4-year ABET-accredited college or university in Pennsylvania or Texas. Applicants must be working full time on a degree in computer science or chemical, electrical, materials, or mechanical engineering. Preference is given to members of groups underrepresented in engineering, including veterans. Selection is based on financial need and merit.

Financial Data The stipend is $2,500.

Duration 1 year.

Additional data This program, which began in 2015, is sponsored by Bayer.

Number awarded 2 each year.

Deadline February of each year.

[67]
BEAUTIFUL MINDS SCHOLARSHIP

RentDeals.com
Attn: Scholarships
14173 Northwest Freeway, Suite 190
Houston, TX 77040
Toll Free: (800) 644-5012
Web: www.rentdeals.com/scholarship.php

Summary To provide financial assistance to Hispanics and other minority high school seniors who submit outstanding essays on finding their purpose and plan to attend college.

Eligibility This program is open to graduating high school seniors who are members of minority groups and have a GPA of 3.0 or higher. Applicants must be planning to enroll at an accredited postsecondary institution and major in any field. Selection is based primarily on an essay on the topic, "Finding My Purpose."

Financial Data The stipend is $1,000.

Duration 1 year.

Number awarded 1 each year.

Deadline March of each year.

[68]
BECAS UNIVISION SCHOLARSHIP PROGRAM

Hispanic Scholarship Fund
Attn: Selection Committee
1411 West 190th Street, Suite 700
Gardena, CA 90248
(310) 975-3700   Toll Free: (877) HSF-INFO
Fax: (310) 349-3328   E-mail: scholar1@hsf.net
Web: hsf.net

Summary To provide financial assistance for college or graduate school to Hispanic American students.

Eligibility This program is open to U.S. citizens, permanent residents, Deferred Action for Childhood Arrival (DACA) students, and eligible non-citizens. Applicants must be of Hispanic heritage and enrolled or planning to enroll full time in a degree program at an accredited 4-year college or university as an undergraduate or graduate student (including GED recipients and community college transfers). High school seniors must have a GPA of 3.0 or higher; current undergraduate and graduate students must have a GPA of 2.5 or higher. Selection is based on merit; financial need is considered in determining the amount of the award.

Financial Data Stipends normally range from $500 to $5,000 per year.

Duration 1 year; recipients may reapply.

Additional data This program is sponsored by Becas Univision.

Number awarded Varies each year.

Deadline March of each year.

[69]
BECHTEL UNDERGRADUATE FELLOWSHIP AWARD

National Action Council for Minorities in Engineering
Attn: Director, Scholarships and University Relations
440 Hamilton Avenue, Suite 302
White Plains, NY 10601-1813
(914) 539-4316   Fax: (914) 539-4032
E-mail: scholars@nacme.org
Web: www.nacme.org/scholarships

Summary To provide financial assistance to Latino and other underrepresented minority college juniors majoring in construction engineering.

Eligibility This program is open to Latino, American Indian, and African American college juniors who have a GPA of 3.0 or higher and have demonstrated academic excellence, leadership skills, and a commitment to science and engineering as a career. Applicants must be enrolled full time at an ABET-accredited engineering program and preparing for a career in a construction-related engineering discipline.

Financial Data The stipend is $2,500 per year. Funds are sent directly to the recipient's university.

Duration Up to 2 years.

Additional data This program was established by the Bechtel Group Foundation.

Number awarded 2 each year.

Deadline April of each year.

[70]
BEN AND DELIA SIFUENTES SCHOLARSHIPS

Hispanic Scholarship Consortium
Attn: Scholarship Selection Committee
7703 North Lamar Boulevard, Suite 310
Austin, TX 78752
(512) 368-2956   Fax: (512) 692-1831
E-mail: scholarships@hispanicscholar.org
Web: hispanicscholar.academicworks.com

Summary To provide financial assistance to high school seniors of Hispanic heritage in Texas who plan to attend a college in any state.

Eligibility This program is open to seniors of Hispanic heritage graduating from high schools in Texas and planning to enroll full time at a 2- or 4-year college or university in any state. Applicants must have a GPA of 3.0 or higher. Selection is based on academic achievement, community service, personal strengths, leadership, and financial need. U.S. citizenship is not required; students may qualify under Texas Senate Bill 1528.

Financial Data A stipend is awarded (amount not specified).

Duration 1 year; may be renewed up to 3 additional years, provided the recipient remains enrolled full time, maintains a GPA of 3.0 or higher, and participates in at least 25 hours of community service per semester.

Number awarded Varies each year; recently, 6 were awarded.

Deadline April of each year.

[71]
BILL BERNBACH DIVERSITY SCHOLARSHIPS

American Association of Advertising Agencies
Attn: AAAA Foundation
1065 Avenue of the Americas, 16th Floor
New York, NY 10018
(212) 262-2500   E-mail: bbscholarship@ddb.com
Web: www.aaaa.org

Summary To provide financial assistance to Hispanics and other multicultural students interested in working on an undergraduate or graduate degree in advertising at designated schools.

Eligibility This program is open to Hispanic Americans, African Americans, Asian Americans, and Native Americans (including American Indians, Alaska Natives, Native Hawaiians, and other Pacific Islanders) who are interested in studying the advertising creative arts at designated institutions as a full-time student. Applicants must be working on or have already received an undergraduate degree and be able to demonstrate creative talent and promise. They must be U.S. citizens, nationals, or permanent residents. Along with their application, they must submit 10 samples of creative work in their respective field of expertise.

Financial Data The stipend is $5,000.

Duration 1 year.

Additional data This program, which began in 1998, is currently sponsored by DDB Worldwide. The participating schools are the Art Center College of Design (Pasadena, California), Creative Circus (Atlanta, Georgia), Miami Ad School (Miami Beach, Florida), University of Oklahoma (Norman, Oklahoma), University of Texas at Austin, VCU Brandcenter (Richmond, Virginia), Savannah College of Art and Design (Savannah, Georgia), University of Oregon (Eugene), City College of New York, School of Visual Arts (New York, New York), Fashion Institute of Technology (New York, New York), and Howard University (Washington, D.C.).

Number awarded 3 each year.

Deadline May of each year.

[72]
BILL DICKEY GOLF SCHOLARSHIPS

Bill Dickey Scholarship Association
Attn: Scholarship Committee
1241 East Washington Street, Suite 101
Phoenix, AZ 85034
(602) 258-7851   Fax: (602) 258-3412
E-mail: andrea@bdscholar.org
Web: www.nmjgsa.org/scholarships.php

Summary To provide financial assistance to Hispanic and other minority high school seniors and undergraduate students who excel at golf.

Eligibility This program is open to graduating high school seniors and current undergraduate students who are members of minority groups (Hispanic, African American, Asian/Pacific Islander, or American Indian/Alaskan Native). Applicants must submit a 500-word essay on a topic that changes annually but relates to minorities and golf. Selection is based on academic achievement, leadership, evidence of community service, golfing ability, and financial need.

Financial Data Stipends range from 1-time awards of $1,000 to 4-year awards of $3,500 per year. Funds are paid directly to the recipient's college.

Duration 1 year or longer.

Additional data This sponsor was established in 1984 as the National Minority Junior Golf Association and given its current name in 2006. Support is provided by the Jackie Robinson Foundation, PGA of America, Anheuser-Busch, the Tiger Woods Foundation, and other cooperating organizations.

Number awarded Varies; generally 80 or more each year.

Deadline May of each year.

[73]
BIRMINGHAM CHAPTER AABE SCHOLARSHIPS

American Association of Blacks in Energy-Birmingham
   Chapter
Attn: Scholarship Committee
P.O. Box 3035
Birmingham, AL 35202
(205) 325-3578   E-mail: larringt@southernco.com
Web: www.aabe.org/index.php?component=pages&id=161

Summary To provide financial assistance to Hispanics and members of other underrepresented minority groups who are high school seniors in Alabama and planning to major in an energy-related field at a college in any state.

Eligibility This program is open to seniors graduating from high schools in Alabama and planning to attend a college or university in any state. Applicants must be Hispanics, African Americans, or Native Americans who have a GPA of 3.0 or higher and who have taken the ACT and/or SAT test. Their intended major must be business, engineering, technology, mathematics, the physical sciences, or other energy-related field. Along with their application, they must submit a 350-word essay that includes 1) when they discovered their interest in the field of energy and what sparked their interest; and 2) either what excites them about the field of energy or how they expect their education to prepare them for the field of energy. Financial need is not considered in the selection process.

Financial Data The stipend is $5,000.

Duration 1 year.

Additional data The winner is eligible to compete for regional and national scholarships.

Number awarded 1 each year.

Deadline March of each year.

[74]
BLANDY EXPERIMENTAL FARM RESEARCH EXPERIENCES FOR UNDERGRADUATES PROGRAM

University of Virginia
Attn: Blandy Experimental Farm
400 Blandy Farm Lane
Boyce, VA 22620
(540) 837-1758, ext. 292   Fax: (540) 837-1523
E-mail: blandy@virginia.edu
Web: sites.google.com/site/blandyreu

Summary To provide an opportunity for undergraduates, especially Hispanics and other underrepresented minorities, to conduct ecological and evolutionary research during the summer at the Blandy Experimental Farm in Clarke County, Virginia.

Eligibility This program is open to undergraduate students interested in ecological and evolutionary biology. Applicants must submit a proposal for a research project at the farm under the mentorship of a professional staff member. Current research interests of the staff include plant reproductive ecology, aquatic community ecology, biological invasions, plant population biology, conservation biology, pollination, and plant succession. Interested students should submit, along with their application, a current transcript, 2 letters of recommendation, a statement describing how this program would contribute to their education and career goals, and the names of the mentors whose research areas interest them. They must be U.S. citizens or permanent residents. Applications are especially encouraged from underrepresented minorities, persons with disabilities, and women.

Financial Data Students receive a $5,775 stipend, an additional meal budget, free housing, and a modest budget for supplies and travel.

Duration 11 weeks, from late May through mid-August.

Additional data This program, established in 1993, receives funding support from the Research Experiences for Undergraduates (REU) program of the National Science Foundation.

Number awarded   10 each year.
Deadline   February of each year.

[75]
BLUECROSS BLUESHIELD OF TENNESSEE COMMUNITY TRUST DIVERSITY SCHOLARSHIP

National Association of Health Services Executives-
  Memphis Chapter
Attn: Selection Committee
P.O. Box 40051
Memphis, TN 38174-0051
E-mail: nahsememphis@gmail.com
Web: www.bcbst.com

Summary   This program is open to Hispanic and other minority students who are residents of Tennessee working on an undergraduate degree in a field of health care at a college in the state.

Eligibility   This program is open to minority residents of Tennessee who are currently enrolled as full-time sophomores or juniors at an accredited college or university in the state. Applicants must be working on a degree in a field of health care and have a GPA of 2.5 or higher. They must be U.S. citizens between 18 and 23 years of age. Along with their application, they must submit a 500-word essay on their particular field of study, why they chose to prepare for a career in health care, and how they plan to use their skills or knowledge to help raise awareness of health issues in their community.

Financial Data   The stipend is $10,000. Funds are paid directly to the recipient's university.

Duration   1 year.

Additional data   This program is sponsored by BlueCross BlueShield of Tennessee in collaboration with the Memphis Chapter of the National Association of Health Services Executives (NAHSE).

Number awarded   3 each year: 1 each for the west, middle, and east region of Tennessee.

Deadline   March of each year.

[76]
BOEING SCHOLARSHIP OF THE SOCIETY OF HISPANIC PROFESSIONAL ENGINEERS

Society of Hispanic Professional Engineers
Attn: Scholarships
13181 Crossroads Parkway North, Suite 450
City of Industry, CA 91715
(323) 725-3970, ext. 108   Fax: (323) 725-0316
E-mail: scholarships@shpe.org
Web: shpe.awardspring.com

Summary   To provide financial assistance to Hispanic undergraduate students who are working on a degree in a field of science, technoloogy, engineering, or mathematics.

Eligibility   This program is open to U.S. citizens and permanent residents of Hispanic descent who are enrolled full time at a college or university in the United States or Puerto Rico. Applicants must be working on an undergraduate degree in a field of STEM and have a GPA of 3.0 or higher. Selection is based on academic standing and financial need.

Financial Data   The stipend is $1,820.

Duration   1 year.

Additional data   This program is sponsored by the Boeing Company. Recipients must attend the annual conference of the Society of Hispanic Professional Engineers.

Number awarded   1 or more each year.

Deadline   July of each year.

[77]
BOX ENGINEERING DIVERSITY SCHOLARSHIP

Box, Inc.
Attn: Scholarship
4440 El Camino Real
Los Altos, CA 94022
Toll Free: (877) 729-4269   E-mail: scholarship@box.com
Web: www.boxdiversityscholarship.com

Summary   To provide financial assistance to Hispanics and other underrepresented minority college students majoring in designated fields of technology.

Eligibility   This program is open to U.S. citizens currently enrolled as sophomores or juniors at a 4-year college or university who are majoring in science, engineering, information technology, mathematics, or a related field. Applicants must identify with an underrepresented minority (e.g., female, LGBT, Hispanic, African American, or Native American). Finalists are invited to the sponsor's headquarters in Los Altos, California.

Financial Data   Stipends are $20,000 or $4,000.

Duration   1 year.

Number awarded   1 at $20,000 and 4 at $4,000 each year.

Deadline   October of each year.

[78]
BREAKTHROUGH TO NURSING SCHOLARSHIPS

National Student Nurses' Association
Attn: Foundation
45 Main Street, Suite 606
Brooklyn, NY 11201
(718) 210-0705   Fax: (718) 210-0710
E-mail: nsna@nsna.org
Web: www.nsna.org

Summary   To provide financial assistance to Hispanic and other minority undergraduate and graduate students who wish to prepare for careers in nursing.

Eligibility   This program is open to students currently enrolled in state-approved schools of nursing or pre-nursing associate degree, baccalaureate, diploma, generic master's, generic doctoral, R.N. to B.S.N., R.N. to M.S.N., or L.P.N./ L.V.N. to R.N. programs. Graduating high school seniors are not eligible. Support for graduate education is provided only for a first degree in nursing. Applicants must be members of a racial or ethnic minority underrepresented among registered nurses (Hispanic, Native Hawaiian or other Pacific Islander, American Indian or Alaska Native, Black or African American, or Asian). They must be committed to providing quality health care services to underserved populations. Along with their application, they must submit a 200-word description of their professional and educational goals and how this scholarship will help them achieve those goals. Selection is based on academic achievement, financial need, and involvement in student nursing organizations and community health activities. U.S. citizenship or permanent resident status is required.

Financial Data   Stipends range from $1,000 to $2,000.

Duration 1 year.

Additional data Applications must be accompanied by a $10 processing fee.

Number awarded Varies each year; recently, 13 were awarded: 10 sponsored by the American Association of Critical-Care Nurses and 3 sponsored by the Mayo Clinic.

Deadline January of each year.

[79]
BRONSON T.J. TREMBLAY MEMORIAL SCHOLARSHIP

Colorado Nurses Foundation
Attn: Scholarships
P.O. Box 3406
Englewood, CO 80155
(303) 694-4728   Toll Free: (800) 205-6655
Fax: (303) 200-7099   E-mail: mail@cnfound.org
Web: www.coloradonursesfoundation.com/?page_id=1087

Summary To provide financial assistance to Hispanic and other non-white male undergraduate and graduate nursing students in Colorado.

Eligibility This program is open to non-white male Colorado residents who have been accepted as a student in an approved nursing program in the state. Applicants may be 1) second-year students in an associate degree program; 2) junior or senior level B.S.N. undergraduate students; 3) R.N.s enrolled in a baccalaureate or higher degree program in a school of nursing; 4) R.N.s with a master's degree in nursing, currently practicing in Colorado and enrolled in a doctoral program; or 5) students in the second or third year of a Doctorate Nursing Practice (D.N.P.) or Ph.D. program. Undergraduates must have a GPA of 3.25 or higher and graduate students must have a GPA of 3.5 or higher. Selection is based on professional philosophy and goals, dedication to the improvement of patient care in Colorado, demonstrated commitment to nursing, potential for leadership, involvement in community and professional organizations, recommendations, GPA, and financial need.

Financial Data The stipend is $1,000.

Duration 1 year.

Number awarded 1 each year.

Deadline October of each year.

[80]
BROWN AND CALDWELL MINORITY SCHOLARSHIP

Brown and Caldwell
Attn: HR/Scholarship Program
1527 Cole Boulevard, Suite 300
Lakewood, CO 80401
(303) 239-5400   Fax: (303) 239-5454
E-mail: scholarships@brwncald.com
Web: www.brownandcaldwell.com/Scholarships.asp?id=1

Summary To provide financial assistance to Hispanic and other minority students working on an undergraduate or graduate degree in an environmental or engineering field.

Eligibility This program is open to members of minority groups (Hispanics, African Americans, Hispanics, Asians, Pacific Islanders, Native Americans, or Alaska Natives) who are full-time juniors, seniors, or graduate students at an accredited 4-year college or university. Applicants must have

a GPA of 3.0 or higher and a declared major in civil, chemical, or environmental engineering or an environmental science (e.g., biology, ecology, geology, hydrogeology). They must be U.S. citizens or permanent residents. Along with their application, they must submit an essay (up to 250 words) on a topic that changes annually but relates to their personal development. Financial need is not considered in the selection process.

Financial Data The stipend is $5,000.

Duration 1 year.

Number awarded 1 each year.

Deadline May of each year.

[81]
BUENAS OPINIONES SCHOLARSHIP FOR LATINO STUDENTS

Buenas Opiniones
120 Flower Street
Los Angeles, CA 90071
(213) 293-4312
E-mail: scholarships@buenasopiniones.com
Web: www.buenasopiniones.com/scholarship

Summary To provide financial assistance to Latino students interested in working on an undergraduate or graduate degree in any field.

Eligibility This program is open to Latino high school seniors, community college students, undergraduates, and graduate students. Applicants may study any academic field, but they must have a GPA of 3.0 or higher. Along with their application, they must submit an essay of 500 to 1,000 words on their struggles as a Latino student. Selection is based on merit.

Financial Data The stipend is $2,500 per year.

Duration Up to 4 years.

Number awarded 1 or more each semester.

Deadline August of each year for fall semester; January of each year for spring semester.

[82]
CAFE BUSTELO EL CAFE DEL FUTURO SCHOLARSHIP ESSAY CONTEST

Hispanic Association of Colleges and Universities
Attn: National Scholarship Program
8415 Datapoint Drive, Suite 400
San Antonio, TX 78229
(210) 692-3805   Fax: (210) 692-0823
TDD: (800) 855-2880   E-mail: scholarship@hacu.net
Web: www.hacu.net/hacu/Scholarships.asp

Summary To recognize and reward, with scholarships, students at member institutions of the Hispanic Association of Colleges and Universities (HACU) who submit outstanding essays on their Latino heritage.

Eligibility This program is open to full-time undergraduate students at HACU member institutions who are legal residents of the United States or Puerto Rico of Latino descent. Applicants must submit an 800-word essay on how their Latino heritage, family, and the community in which they grew up have impacted their desire and motivation to obtain a college degree, including what they intend to accomplish with their degree and how they will give back to their community. Selection is based entirely on the essay.

Financial Data   The award is a $5,000 scholarship sent directly to the winner's college or university.

Duration   1 year.

Additional data   This program is sponsored by Rowland Coffee Roasters.

Number awarded   9 each year.

Deadline   May of each year.

[83]
CALDER SUMMER UNDERGRADUATE RESEARCH PROGRAM

Fordham University
Attn: Louis Calder Center Biological Field Station
53 Whippoorwill Road
P.O. Box 887
Armonk, NY 10504
(914) 273-3078, ext. 10   Fax: (914) 273-2167
E-mail: REUatCalder@fordham.edu
Web: www.fordham.edu

Summary   To provide an opportunity for undergraduates, especially Hispanics and other underrepresented minorities, to pursue summer research activities in biology at Fordham University's Louis Calder Center Biological Field Station.

Eligibility   This program is open to undergraduates interested in conducting a summer research project of their own design at the center. Applicants must be U.S. citizens, nationals, or permanent residents. Fields of interest must relate to the activities of staff who will serve as mentors on the projects; those include forest ecology, limnology, wildlife ecology, microbial ecology, Lyme disease, insect-plant interactions, evolutionary ecology, and the effects of urbanization on ecosystem processes. Applications from underrepresented minorities and women are especially encouraged.

Financial Data   The program provides a stipend of $5,000, housing on the site, and support for research supplies and local travel.

Duration   10 weeks during the summer.

Additional data   This program has operated since 1967 with support from the Research Experiences for Undergraduates (REU) program of the National Science Foundation.

Number awarded   Up to 10 each year.

Deadline   January of each year.

[84]
CALIFORNIA PLANNING FOUNDATION DIVERSITY IN PLANNING SCHOLARSHIP

American Planning Association-California Chapter
Attn: California Planning Foundation
c/o Kelly Main
California Polytechnic State University at San Luis Obispo
City and Regional Planning Department
Office 21-116B
San Luis Obispo, CA 93407-0283
(805) 756-2285   Fax: (805) 756-1340
E-mail: cpfapplications@gmail.com
Web: www.californiaplanningfoundation.org

Summary   To provide financial assistance to undergraduate and graduate students in accredited planning programs at California universities, especially Hispanics and others who will increase diversity in the profession.

Eligibility   This program is open to students entering their final year for an undergraduate or master's degree in an accredited planning program at a university in California. Applicants must be students who will increase diversity in the planning profession. Along with their application, they must submit 1) a 500-word personal statement explaining why planning is important to them, their potential contribution to the profession of planning in California, and how this scholarship would help them to complete their degree; 2) a 500-word description of their experience in planning (e.g., internships, volunteer experiences, employment); and 3) a 500-word essay on what they consider to be 1 of the greatest planning challenges in California today. Selection is based on academic performance, increasing diversity in the planning profession, commitment to serve the planning profession in California, and financial need.

Financial Data   The stipend is $3,000. The award includes a 1-year student membership in the American Planning Association (APA) and payment of registration for the APA California Conference.

Duration   1 year.

Additional data   The accredited planning programs are at 3 campuses of the California State University system (California State Polytechnic University at Pomona, California Polytechnic State University at San Luis Obispo, and San Jose State University), 3 campuses of the University of California (Berkeley, Irvine, and Los Angeles), and the University of Southern California.

Number awarded   1 each year.

Deadline   March of each year.

[85]
CALIFORNIA TABLE GRAPE WORKER SCHOLARSHIPS

California Table Grape Commission
Attn: Scholarship Committee
392 West Fallbrook, Suite 101
Fresno, CA 93711-6150
(559) 447-8350   Toll Free: (800) 813-8478
Fax: (559) 447-9184
E-mail: scholarship@grapesfromcalifornia.com
Web: www.grapesfromcalifornia.com/scholarships.php

Summary   To provide financial assistance to the children of California table grape field workers who are interested in attending a college in the state.

Eligibility   This program is open to high school graduates or seniors graduating in June. They, or their parents, must have worked in either of the 2 previous California table grape harvests. Farmers and their families, raisin and wine grape workers, students currently enrolled in college, permanent staff and members of the California Table Grape Commission and their families, and commission suppliers are not eligible. Applicants must intend to attend a 2- or 4-year college or university in California as a full-time student. Selection is based on academic performance, financial need, obstacles overcome, leadership ability and/or community service, and ability to succeed.

Financial Data   The stipend is $5,000 per year for students at 4-year universities or $1,750 per year for students at 2-year colleges.

Duration 4 years for students at 4-year universities or 2 years for students at 2-year colleges, provided the recipient remains enrolled full time with a GPA of 2.0 or higher.

Additional data This program began in 1984.

Number awarded 7 each year: 3 to students at 4-year universities and 4 to students at 2-year colleges.

Deadline January of each year.

[86]
CALIFORNIA WINE GRAPE GROWERS FOUNDATION SCHOLARSHIPS

California Association of Winegrape Growers
Attn: California Wine Grape Growers Foundation
1121 L Street, Suite 304
Sacramento, CA 95814
(916) 379-8995   Toll Free: (800) 241-1800
Fax: (916) 379-8999   E-mail: info@cawg.org
Web: www.cawgfoundation.org/apply-now

Summary To provide financial assistance for college to high school seniors in California whose parent(s) work in the grape wine vineyards.

Eligibility This program is open to high school seniors in California who plan to attend a branch of the University of California, a branch of the California State University system, or a community college in the state. Applicants must have a parent or legal guardian who was employed as a vineyard worker by a winegrape grower during either or both of the 2 preceding seasons. Along with their application, they must submit a high school transcript, a copy of their SAT or ACT scores (if they are planning to attend a 4-year university), a letter of recommendation from a school official, and a 500-word essay on themselves and their career goals. Applications are available in both English and Spanish. Selection is based on that essay, demonstrated academic ability, community involvement and leadership, work history, determination to succeed, and financial need.

Financial Data The stipend is $2,000 per year at a 4-year university or $1,000 per year at a community college.

Duration 4 years at branches of the University of California or California State University system; 2 years at community colleges.

Additional data Recipients must enroll in 12 college units each semester while receiving scholarship money.

Number awarded At least 6 each year: 2 at 4-year universities and 4 at community colleges.

Deadline March of each year.

[87]
CALSA STUDENT SCHOLARSHIPS

California Association of Latino Superintendents and
  Administrators
Attn: Executive Assistant
1029 J Street, Suite 500
Sacramento, CA 95814
(916) 329-3847   E-mail: awyatt@calsa.org
Web: www.calsa.org/scholarships

Summary To provide financial assistance to Latino/a high school seniors in California who plan to attend college in any state.

Eligibility This program is open to Latino/a seniors graduating from public high schools in California in a district of a member of the Association of Latino Superintendents and Administrators (CALSA). Applicants must be planning to enroll at a 4-year university in any state and be sponsored by the CALSA member. Along with their application, they must submit an essay of 400 to 500 words on where they plan to attend college, their proposed major, the most significant challenge they have faced, steps they have taken to address that challenge, how a college degree will assist them in making a contribution to themselves and their community, and why they should be granted a CALSA scholarship.

Financial Data The stipend is $1,000.

Duration 1 year.

Additional data This program began in 2006.

Number awarded 11 each year.

Deadline May of each year.

[88]
CALTECH AMGEN SCHOLARS PROGRAM

California Institute of Technology
Attn: Student-Faculty Programs
1200 East California Boulevard
MailCode 330-87
Pasadena, CA 91125
(626) 395-2885   Fax: (626) 389-5467
E-mail: sfp@clatech.edu
Web: sfp.caltech.edu/programs/amgen_scholars

Summary To provide an opportunity for undergraduate students, especially Hispanics and those from other diverse populations, to participate in biological and chemical summer research at the California Institute of Technology (Caltech).

Eligibility This program is open to sophomores, juniors, and non-graduating seniors at 4-year colleges and universities in the United States, Puerto Rico, and other U.S. territories. Applicants must be U.S. citizens or permanent residents who have a cumulative GPA of 3.2 or higher and an interest in preparing for a Ph.D. or M.D./Ph.D. They must be interested in working on a summer research project at Caltech in biology, chemistry, or biotechnical-related fields. Applications are encouraged from, but not limited to, underrepresented minorities, women, first-generation college students, geographically underrepresented students, educationally and financially disadvantaged students, and students with disabilities.

Financial Data Scholars receive a stipend of $6,000, campus housing, a modest board allowance, and travel to and from Pasadena.

Duration 10 weeks during the summer.

Additional data This program serves as the Cal Tech component of the Amgen Scholars Program, which operates at 8 other U.S. universities (and the National Institutes of Health) and is funded by the Amgen Foundation.

Number awarded Varies each year.

Deadline February of each year.

[89]
CAMMER-HILL GRANT

Wisconsin Women of Color Network, Inc.
c/o P.E. Kiram
756 North 35th Street, Suite 101
Milwaukee, WI 53208
(414) 899-2329   E-mail: pekiram64@gmail.com

Summary To provide financial assistance for vocational/technical school or community college to Hispanics or other adult women of color from Wisconsin.

Eligibility This program is open to residents of Wisconsin who are adult women of color planning to continue their education at a vocational/technical school or community college in any state. Applicants must be a member of 1 of the following groups: African American, Asian, American Indian, or Hispanic. They must be able to demonstrate financial need. Along with their application, they must submit a 1-page essay on how this scholarship will help them accomplish their educational goal. U.S. citizenship is required.

Financial Data A stipend is awarded (amount not specified).

Duration 1 year.

Additional data This program began in 1994.

Number awarded 1 each year.

Deadline May of each year.

[90]
CAMP SCHOLARSHIPS

Migrant Students Foundation
305 Prospect Avenue, Suite 4
Lewiston, ID 83501
(509) 368-7132   E-mail: support@migrantstudents.org
Web: www.migrantstudents.org

Summary To provide financial assistance for college to high school seniors from migrant or seasonal farmworker families.

Eligibility This program is open to migrant and seasonal farmworkers and their families working in agricultural activities directly related to the production of crops, dairy products, poultry, or livestock; the cultivation or harvesting of trees; or fish farms. Applicants must plan to enroll as a freshman at a 4-year college or university that participates in the College Assistance Migrant Program (CAMP) of the U.S. Department of Education to complete a bachelor's degree, be a U.S. citizen or permanent resident, and be able to document financial need.

Financial Data The stipends range from $750 to $4,000, depending on the need of the recipients and the school they attend.

Duration 1 year.

Additional data Currently, nearly 40 colleges and universities participate in the CAMP program, including schools in Arizona, California, Colorado, Florida, Georgia, Idaho, Kansas, Michigan, Missouri, New Mexico, New York, Oregon, Texas, and Washington.

Number awarded Approximately 2,000 each year.

Deadline Each participating college or university sets its own deadline.

[91]
CANCER RESEARCH SUMMER FELLOWSHIP

University of Colorado Cancer Center
Attn: Cancer Research Summer Fellowship
13001 East 17th Place
Building 500, Sixth Floor
Mailstop F434
Aurora, CO 80045
(303) 724-3174   Fax: (303) 724-3163
E-mail: jill.penafiel@ucdenver.edu
Web: www.ucdenver.edu

Summary To provide an opportunity for high school seniors and college undergraduates, especially Hispanics and other minorities, to work during the summer on a cancer research project in Colorado.

Eligibility This program is open to high school seniors and college undergraduates who are interested in working on a cancer research project at the University of Colorado Anschutz Medical Center, the Boulder campus of the University of Colorado, or other institutions in the Denver area. Along with their application, they must submit a 2-page essay explaining why they wish to apply for this fellowship, school transcripts, and 2 letters of recommendation. Minority students are particularly encouraged to apply.

Financial Data The stipend is $2,000 for high school seniors or $3,000 for college undergraduates.

Duration 10 weeks during the summer.

Additional data Funding for this program is provided by a grant from the National Cancer Institute.

Number awarded Varies each year; recently, 41 students participated in this project.

Deadline January of each year.

[92]
CANFIT PROGRAM CULINARY ARTS SCHOLARSHIPS

Communities-Adolescents-Nutrition-Fitness
Attn: Scholarship Program
P.O. Box 3989
Berkeley, CA 94703
(510) 644-1533, ext. 112   Toll Free: (800) 200-3131
Fax: (510) 843-9705   E-mail: info@canfit.org
Web: www.canfit.org/scholarships

Summary To provide financial assistance to Hispanic and other minority culinary arts students in California.

Eligibility This program is open to Latinos/Hispanics, American Indians, Alaska Natives, African Americans, Asian Americans, and Pacific Islanders from California who are enrolled at a culinary arts college in the state. Applicants are not required to have completed any college units. Along with their application, they must submit 1) documentation of financial need; 2) letters of recommendation from 2 individuals; 3) a 1-to 2-page letter describing their academic goals and involvement in community nutrition and/or physical education activities; and 4) an essay of 500 to 1,000 words on a topic related to healthy foods for youth from low-income communities of color.

Financial Data A stipend is awarded (amount not specified).

Number awarded 1 or more each year.

Deadline March of each year.

[93]
CANFIT PROGRAM UNDERGRADUATE SCHOLARSHIPS

Communities-Adolescents-Nutrition-Fitness
Attn: Scholarship Program
P.O. Box 3989
Berkeley, CA 94703
(510) 644-1533, ext. 112   Toll Free: (800) 200-3131
Fax: (510) 843-9705   E-mail: info@canfit.org
Web: www.canfit.org/scholarships

Summary To provide financial assistance to Hispanic and other minority undergraduate students who are working on a degree in nutrition, culinary arts, or physical education in California.

Eligibility This program is open to Latinos/Hispanics, American Indians, Alaska Natives, African Americans, Asian Americans, and Pacific Islanders from California who are enrolled in an approved bachelor's degree program in nutrition, culinary arts, or physical education in the state. Applicants must have completed at least 50 semester units and have a GPA of 2.5 or higher. Along with their application, they must submit 1) documentation of financial need; 2) letters of recommendation from 2 individuals; 3) a 1-to 2-page letter describing their academic goals and involvement in community nutrition and/or physical education activities; and 4) an essay of 500 to 1,000 words on a topic related to healthy foods for youth from low-income communities of color.

Financial Data A stipend is awarded (amount not specified).

Number awarded 1 or more each year.

Deadline March of each year.

[94]
CAPT CYNTHIA I. MACRI SCHOLARSHIP

National Naval Officers Association-Washington, D.C.
  Chapter
c/o LCDR Stephen Williams
P.O. Box 30784
Alexandria, VA 22310
(703) 644-2605   Fax: (703) 644-8503
E-mail: Stephen.Williams@navy.mil
Web: www.dcnnoa.org/dcnnoa-scholarship

Summary To provide financial assistance to Hispanic and other minority high school seniors from the Washington, D.C. area who are interested in majoring in a field of science, technology, engineering, or mathematics (STEM) at a college in any state.

Eligibility This program is open to minority seniors graduating from high schools in the Washington, D.C. metropolitan area who plan to enroll full time and major in a STEM discipline at an accredited 2- or 4-year college or university in any state. Applicants must have a GPA of 3.0 or higher and be U.S. citizens or permanent residents. Selection is based on academic achievement, community involvement, and financial need.

Financial Data The stipend is $1,000.

Duration 1 year; nonrenewable.

Additional data This program is sponsored by the Washington D.C. Chapter of the National Naval Officers Association (DCNNOA), an organization of African American naval officers, but all minorities are eligible and recipients are not required to join or affiliate with the military in any way.

Number awarded 1 each year.

Deadline February of each year.

[95]
CAREERS IN TRANSPORTATION FOR YOUTH (CITY) INTERNSHIP PROGRAM

Conference of Minority Transportation Officials
Attn: Internship Program
100 M Street, S.E., Suite 917
Washington, DC 20003
(202) 506-2917   E-mail: bwilliams@comto.org
Web: www.comto.org/page/internship

Summary To provide summer work experience in transportation-related fields to Hispanics and other underrepresented upper-division students.

Eligibility This program is open to full-time minority or underrepresented students entering their junior or senior year with a GPA of 2.5 or higher. Applicants must be working on a degree related to public transportation. They must be interested in a summer internship with transit firms or agencies in Chicago, Dallas, Detroit, Jacksonville, New York, Oakland, Philadelphia, San Antonio, Seattle, southern California, Tampa, or Washington, D.C. Along with their application, they must submit a 1-page essay on their transportation interests, including how participation in this internship will enhance their educational plan, their mid- and long-term professional goals, their specific transportation-related goal, the issues of interest to them, their plans to further their education and assist in making future contributions to their field of study, and their expectations for this internship experience. U.S. citizenship is required.

Financial Data The stipend recently was $15 per hour.

Duration 10 weeks during the summer.

Additional data This program is managed by the Conference of Minority Transportation Officials (COMTO), with funding provided by the Federal Transit Administration. Interns work at transit agencies, private transit-related consulting firms, transportation service providers, manufacturers, and suppliers.

Number awarded Varies each year; recently, internships were awarded to 30 students.

Deadline April of each year.

[96]
CARMEN E. TURNER SCHOLARSHIPS

Conference of Minority Transportation Officials
Attn: National Scholarship Program
100 M Street, S.E., Suite 917
Washington, DC 20003
(202) 506-2917   E-mail: info@comto.org
Web: www.comto.org/page/scholarships

Summary To provide financial assistance for college or graduate school to Hispanic and other members of the Conference of Minority Transportation Officials (COMTO) and their families.

Eligibility This program is open to undergraduate and graduate students who have been members or whose parents, guardians, or grandparents have been members of COMTO for at least 1 year. Applicants must be working on a degree in a field related to transportation and have a GPA of 2.5 or higher. Along with their application they must submit a cover letter on their transportation-related career goals and life aspirations. Financial need is not considered in the selection process.

Financial Data　The stipend is $3,500. Funds are paid directly to the recipient's college or university.

Duration　1 year.

Number awarded　1 each year.

Deadline　April of each year.

[97]
CAROLE SIMPSON RTDNF SCHOLARSHIP

Radio Television Digital News Foundation
Attn: Membership and Programs Manager
529 14th Street, N.W., Suite 1240
Washington, DC 20045
(202) 662-7257　　　　　　　　Fax: (202) 223-4007
E-mail: karenh@rtdna.org
Web: www.rtdna.org/content/carole_simpson_scholarship

Summary　To provide financial assistance to Hispanic and other minority undergraduate students who are interested in preparing for a career in electronic journalism.

Eligibility　This program is open to sophomore or more advanced minority undergraduate students enrolled in a radio, television, or digital journalism sequence at an accredited or nationally-recognized college or university. Applicants must submit a cover letter that discusses their current and past journalism experience, describes how they would use the funds if they were to receive the scholarship, discusses their reasons for preparing for a career in electronic journalism, and includes 3 to 5 links to their best and most relevant work samples.

Financial Data　The stipend is $2,000, paid in semiannual installments of $1,000 each.

Duration　1 year.

Additional data　The Radio Television Digital News Foundation (RTDNF) also provides an all-expense paid trip to the Excellence in Journalism conference held that year. The RTDNF was formerly the Radio and Television News Directors Foundation (RTNDF).

Number awarded　1 each year.

Deadline　May of each year.

[98]
CARY INSTITUTE OF ECOSYSTEM STUDIES RESEARCH EXPERIENCES FOR UNDERGRADUATES PROGRAM

Cary Institute of Ecosystem Studies
Attn: Undergraduate Research Program
2801 Sharon Turnpike
P.O. Box AB
Millbrook, NY 12545
(845) 677-7600, ext. 326　　　　　Fax: (845) 677-5976
E-mail: caryreu@caryinstitute.org
Web: www.caryinstitute.org/students/reu-program

Summary　To provide undergraduate students, especially Hispanics and members of other diverse groups, with an opportunity to conduct research on translational ecology during the summer at the Cary Institute of Ecosystem Studies (IES) at Millbrook, New York.

Eligibility　This program is open to undergraduate freshmen, sophomores, juniors, and first semester seniors. Applicants must be interested in conducting an independent research project of their own design under the guidance of a mentor scientist. They must identify their interest in ecological research, their current career plans, and how participating in this program could help them in their degree program and their future pursuits. Recently, research topics focused on translational ecology. The program welcomes applications from students of diverse backgrounds at schools in all parts of the country. U.S. citizenship or permanent resident status is required.

Financial Data　The stipend is $6,300. Housing and a $900 allowance for food are also provided.

Duration　12 weeks during the summer.

Additional data　This program is supported by the National Science Foundation as part of its Research Experiences for Undergraduates (REU) program.

Number awarded　8 to 12 each year.

Deadline　February of each year.

[99]
CCNMA SCHOLARSHIPS

CCNMA: Latino Journalists of California
c/o ASU Cronkite School of Journalism
725 Arizona Avenue, Suite 206
Santa Monica, CA 90401-1734
(424) 229-9482　　　　　E-mail: ccnmainfo@ccnma.org
Web: www.ccnma.org

Summary　To provide financial assistance to Latino students from California interested in preparing for a career in journalism.

Eligibility　This program is open to high school seniors and college students of Latino descent who are California residents attending a college or university in any state or students from other states attending a college or university in California. Applicants may major in any field, but they must enroll full time and be able to prove a sincere interest in preparing for a career in journalism. They must submit 1) an autobiographical essay of 300 to 500 words, including their family background, any hardships they have experienced, why they want to be a journalist, and what they believe is the role of Latino journalists in the news media; 2) samples of their journalism-related work (e.g., newspaper articles, photographs, or TV or radio audition tapes); 3) transcripts; and 4) letters of reference. Finalists are interviewed. Selection is based on academic achievement, commitment to the journalism field, awareness of Latino issues, and financial need.

Financial Data　Stipends range from $500 to $1,000.

Duration　1 year.

Additional data　This program includes the Joel Garcia Memorial Scholarship, the George Ramos Memorial Scholarship, and the Frank del Olmo Memorial Scholarship. The sponsor was formerly named the California Chicano News Media Association.

Number awarded　Varies each year; recently, 7 were awarded.

Deadline　March of each year.

[100]
CESDA DIVERSITY SCHOLARSHIPS

Colorado Educational Services and Development
Association
P.O. Box 40214
Denver, CO 80204
(303) 492-2178   E-mail: Maria.Barajas@colorado.edu
Web: www.cesda.org/#!scholarships/crq5

Summary To provide financial assistance to high school seniors in Colorado who are planning to attend college in the state and are either first-generation college students or members of underrepresented ethnic or racial minorities (such as Hispanics).

Eligibility This program is open to seniors graduating from high schools in Colorado who are 1) the first member of their family to attend college; 2) a member of an underrepresented ethnic or racial minority (Hispanic/Chicano/Latino, African American, Asian/Pacific Islander, or American Indian); and/or 3) able to demonstrate financial need. Applicants must have a GPA of 2.8 or higher and be planning to enroll at a 2- or 4-year college or university in Colorado. U.S. citizenship or permanent resident status is required. Selection is based on leadership and community service (particularly within minority communities), past academic performance, personal and professional accomplishments, personal attributes, special abilities, academic goals, and financial need.

Financial Data The stipend is $1,000.

Duration 1 year; nonrenewable.

Number awarded Varies each year.

Deadline March of each year.

[101]
CFA HEA/SSP SOLAR SUMMER INTERN PROGRAM

Harvard-Smithsonian Center for Astrophysics
Attn: Solar REU Program
60 Garden Street, Mail Stop 58
Cambridge, MA 02138
(617) 496-7703   E-mail: sdaly@cfa.harvard.edu
Web: www.cfa.harvard.edu

Summary To enable undergraduates, especially Hispanics and other underrepresented minorities, to participate in a summer research program at the Harvard-Smithsonian Center for Astrophysics (CfA).

Eligibility This program is open to U.S. citizens, nationals, and permanent residents who are full-time undergraduates, preferably those entering their junior or senior year. Applicants must be interested in working during the summer on a project in either of 2 CfA divisions: high energy astrophysics (HEA), which focuses on X-ray astronomy, or solar, stellar, and planetary (SSP) group, which focuses on understanding star and planet formation and the physical processes in the Sun, stars, and stellar systems. Applications from underrepresented minorities, persons with disabilities, and women are encouraged.

Financial Data The stipend is $5,000. Housing and travel expenses are also covered.

Duration 10 weeks during the summer.

Additional data This program is supported by the National Science Foundation as part of its Research Experiences for Undergraduates (REU) Program and by the U.S. National Aeronautics and Space Administration (NASA).

Number awarded 8 each year.

Deadline February of each year.

[102]
CH2M HILL INDUSTRY PARTNER SCHOLARSHIP

Conference of Minority Transportation Officials
Attn: National Scholarship Program
100 M Street, S.E., Suite 917
Washington, DC 20003
(202) 506-2917   E-mail: info@comto.org
Web: www.comto.org/page/scholarships

Summary To provide financial assistance to Hispanic and other minority high school and college students interested in working on a degree in a field related to transportation.

Eligibility This program is open to minority high school seniors and current undergraduates who have a GPA of 3.0 or higher. Applicants must be working on or planning to work on a degree in engineering with a focus on the field of transportation. Along with their application they must submit a cover letter on their transportation-related career goals and life aspirations. Financial need is not considered in the selection process.

Financial Data The stipend is $3,000. Funds are paid directly to the recipient's college or university.

Duration 1 year.

Additional data This program is sponsored by CH2M Hill.

Number awarded 1 each year.

Deadline April of each year.

[103]
CHARLES L. WARREN MEMORIAL HERITAGE SCHOLARSHIP

Ohio Association for College Admission Counseling
Attn: Inclusion, Access and Success Committee
P.O. Box 959
Marysville, OH 43040
(937) 642-1234   E-mail: execadmin@oacac.org
Web: www.oacac.org/student-scholarships

Summary To provide financial assistance for college in Ohio to seniors at high schools that are members of the Ohio Association for College Admission Counseling (OACAC), especially Hispanics and other underrepresented minorities.

Eligibility This program is open to seniors graduating from high schools that are members of OACAC and planning to attend a college or university in the state. Members of underrepresented populations are encouraged to apply. Applicants must have a GPA of 3.0 or higher and be able to show a continued commitment to cultural and intellectual diversity. Along with their application, they must submit a 500-word essay that includes a description of the environment (family, community, or school) from which they came and how it has influenced what they value most about their heritage, how they have contributed to the intellectual and cultural diversity of their high school or community and how they plan to continue their commitment at their college or university, and why they are deserving of this scholarship.

Financial Data The stipend is $1,000.

Duration 1 year; nonrenewable.

Number awarded   Several each year.

Deadline   January of each year.

[104]
CHCI-SHRM SCHOLAR INTERN PROGRAM

Congressional Hispanic Caucus Institute, Inc.
911 Second Street, N.E.
Washington, DC 20002
(202) 543-1771   Toll Free: (800) EXCEL-DC
Fax: (202) 546-2143   E-mail: chci@chci.org
Web: www.chci.org

Summary   To provide financial assistance and work experience at designated member organizations of the Society for Human Resource Management (SHRM) to undergraduate and graduate students of Hispanic descent.

Eligibility   This program is open to U.S. citizens, asylees, valid visa holders, and permanent residents who are of Hispanic descent and currently enrolled full time at an accredited 4-year university in the United States or Puerto Rico as undergraduates of at least sophomore standing or graduate students. They must have at least 1 year of study remaining until graduation. Students registered in the DACA program must possess an Employment Authorization Document. Applicants must be working on a degree in business or human resources. They must be interested in a paid summer internship in SHRM member organizations in Chicago, Dallas, or Los Angeles County/Orange County. Financial need is considered in the selection process.

Financial Data   For the scholarship component of this program, the stipend is $2,500. For the internship component, undergraduates receive a salary of $15 per hour and graduate students receive a salary of $19 per hour.

Duration   1 year; nonrenewable.

Additional data   Funding for this program is provided by SHRM.

Number awarded   Up to 5 each year.

Deadline   February of each year.

[105]
CHCI-UNITED HEALTH FOUNDATION SCHOLAR INTERN PROGRAM

Congressional Hispanic Caucus Institute, Inc.
911 Second Street, N.E.
Washington, DC 20002
(202) 543-1771   Toll Free: (800) EXCEL-DC
Fax: (202) 546-2143   E-mail: chci@chci.org
Web: www.chci.org

Summary   To provide financial assistance and work experience at community health organizations to undergraduate and graduate students of Hispanic descent.

Eligibility   This program is open to U.S. citizens, asylees, valid visa holders, and permanent residents who are of Hispanic descent and currently enrolled full time at an accredited community college, 4-year university, or graduate/professional program with a GPA of 3.0 or higher. Applicants must be preparing for a career as a primary care health professional, defined to include general practitioners, internists, family practitioners, OB/GYNs, pediatricians, dentists, public health professionals, mental health professionals, nurses (including advanced practice nurses, and nurse practitioners), physician assistants, and pharmacists. They must

obtain a paid internship at a community-based health organization that will require a total of at least 80 hours of service. Financial need is considered in the selection process.

Financial Data   For the scholarship component of the program, the stipend is $2,500 for students at community colleges or $5,000 per year for undergraduate and graduate students. For the internship component, participants receive a salary from the health organization where they work; upon verification of completion of 80 hours of paid employment, they also receive an educational stipend of $1,000 from the Congressional Hispanic Caucus Institute (CHCI).

Duration   The stipend supports 1 year of study. The award is nonrenewable for community college students but may be renewed for up to 2 additional years by undergraduates or up to 1 additional year by graduate students.

Additional data   Funding for this program is provided by United Health Foundation.

Number awarded   Varies each year; recently, 18 of these scholarship/internships were awarded: 14 to undergraduates, and 4 to graduate students.

Deadline   March of each year.

[106]
CHCI-WYNDHAM WORLDWIDE SCHOLAR INTERN PROGRAM

Congressional Hispanic Caucus Institute, Inc.
911 Second Street, N.E.
Washington, DC 20002
(202) 543-1771   Toll Free: (800) EXCEL-DC
Fax: (202) 546-2143   E-mail: chci@chci.org
Web: www.chci.org

Summary   To provide financial assistance and work experience at offices of Wyndham Worldwide in Parsippany, New Jersey to undergraduate and graduate students of Hispanic descent.

Eligibility   This program is open to U.S. citizens, asylees, valid visa holders, and permanent residents who are of Hispanic descent and currently enrolled full time at an accredited 4-year university in the United States or Puerto Rico as undergraduates of at least sophomore standing or graduate students. They must have at least 1 year of study remaining until graduation. Students registered in the DACA program must possess an Employment Authorization Document. Applicants must be working on a degree in accounting, communications, computer science, journalism, marketing, media, public relations, or other fields of interest to Wyndham. They must be interested in a paid summer internship of 10 weeks at Wyndham's offices in Parsippany. Financial need is considered in the selection process.

Financial Data   For the scholarship component of this program, the stipend is $2,500. For the internship component, participants receive a competitive salary from Wyndham. A housing allowance may also be available.

Duration   1 year; nonrenewable.

Additional data   Funding for this program is provided by Wyndham Worldwide.

Number awarded   Up to 5 each year.

Deadline   December of each year for the first priority deadline; January of each year for the second priority deadline; February of each year for the final deadline.

[107]
CHCI-ZGS COMMUNICATIONS SCHOLAR INTERN PROGRAM

Congressional Hispanic Caucus Institute, Inc.
911 Second Street, N.E.
Washington, DC 20002
(202) 543-1771   Toll Free: (800) EXCEL-DC
Fax: (202) 546-2143   E-mail: chci@chci.org
Web: www.chci.org

Summary To provide financial assistance and work experience at radio and television stations of ZGS Communications in Florida to undergraduate students of Hispanic descent.

Eligibility This program is open to U.S. citizens, asylees, valid visa holders, and permanent residents who are of Hispanic descent and currently enrolled full time at an accredited 4-year university in the United States or Puerto Rico as juniors. Students registered in the DACA program must possess an Employment Authorization Document. Applicants must be working on a media-related degree, including consumer marketing, journalism, communications, digital or social media, news, radio and television broadcasting, research, sourcing, or sports. They must be interested in a paid summer internship at ZGS Communications radio and television stations in Miami or Tampa. Financial need is considered in the selection process.

Financial Data For the scholarship component of this program, the stipend is $2,500. For the internship component, the salary is $12 per hour.

Duration 1 year (including 8 weeks for the internship); nonrenewable.

Additional data Funding for this program is provided by ZGS Communications.

Number awarded 4 each year: 2 for internships in Miami and 2 for internships in Tampa.

Deadline February of each year.

[108]
CHICANO/LATINO COMMUNITY COLLEGE SCHOLARSHIP

Scholarship Administrative Services, Inc.
Attn: MEFUSA Program
13730 Loumont Street
Whittier, CA 90601

Summary To provide financial assistance to Chicano/Latino high school seniors who are interested in attending a community college.

Eligibility This program is open to Chicano/Latino seniors graduating from high schools anywhere in the United States. Applicants must be planning to attend a community college on a full-time basis. Along with their application, they must submit a 1,000-word essay on their educational and career goals, how a community college education will help them to achieve those goals, and how they plan to serve the Chicano/Latino community after completing their education. Selection is based on the essay, high school GPA (2.5 or higher), SAT or ACT scores, involvement in the Chicano/Latino community, and financial need.

Financial Data The stipend is $5,000 per year.

Duration 1 year; may be renewed 1 additional year if the recipient maintains full-time enrollment and a GPA of 2.5 or higher.

Additional data This program is sponsored by the Minority Educational Foundation of the United States of America (MEFUSA) and administered by Scholarship Administrative Services, Inc. MEFUSA was established in 2001 to meet the needs of minority students who "show a determination to get a college degree," but who, for financial or other personal reasons, are not able to attend a 4-year college or university. Requests for applications should be accompanied by a self-addressed stamped envelope, the student's e-mail address, and the name of the source where they found the scholarship information.

Number awarded Up to 100 each year.

Deadline April of each year.

[109]
CHILDREN'S MERCY HOSPITALS AND CLINICS PEDIATRIC NURSING SCHOLARSHIP

National Association of Hispanic Nurses
Attn: Scholarships
1500 Sunday Drive, Suite 102
Raleigh, NC 27607
(919) 787-5181, ext. 1255   Fax: (919) 787-4916
E-mail: director@thehispanicnurses.org
Web: www.nahnnet.org/NAHNScholarships.html

Summary To provide financial assistance to members of the National Association of Hispanic Nurses (NAHN) who are interested in preparing for a career in pediatric nursing.

Eligibility Eligible are members of the association enrolled in associate, diploma, baccalaureate, graduate, or practical/vocational nursing programs in pediatric nursing. Applicants must have a GPA of 3.0 or higher. Along with their application, they must submit a letter of recommendation; a 300-word essay that reflects their qualifications and potential for leadership in nursing in the Hispanic community; a resume that includes earned certificates, awards, and special honors; information on their financial status; and an official transcript. U.S. citizenship or permanent resident status is required.

Financial Data The stipend is $2,000.

Duration 1 year.

Additional data Support for this program, which began in 2013, is provided by Children's Mercy Hospitals of Kansas City, Missouri.

Number awarded 1 each year.

Deadline June of each year.

[110]
CHIPS QUINN SCHOLARS PROGRAM

Newseum Institute
Attn: Chips Quinn Scholars Program
555 Pennsylvania Avenue, N.W.
Washington, DC 20001
(202) 292-6271   Fax: (202) 292-6275
E-mail: kcatone@freedomforum.org
Web: www.newseuminstitute.org

Summary To provide work experience to Hispanic and other minority college students and recent graduates who are majoring in journalism.

Eligibility This program is open to students of color who are college juniors, seniors, graduate students, or recent graduates with journalism majors or career goals in newspapers. Candidates must be nominated or endorsed by journalism faculty, campus media advisers, editors of newspapers, or leaders of minority journalism associations. Along with their application, they must submit a resume, transcripts, 2 letters of recommendation, and an essay of 200 to 400 words on why they want to be a Chips Quinn Scholar. Reporters and copy editors must also submit 6 samples of published articles they have written; photographers must submit 15 to 25 photographs on a DVD; multimedia journalists and graphic designers should submit 6 to 10 samples of their work on a DVD. Applicants must have a car and be available to work as a full-time intern during the spring or summer. U.S. citizenship or permanent resident status is required. Campus newspaper experience is strongly encouraged.

Financial Data   Students chosen for this program receive a travel stipend to attend a Multimedia training program in Nashville, Tennessee prior to reporting for their internship, a $500 housing allowance from the Freedom Forum, and a competitive salary during their internship.

Duration   Internships are for 10 to 12 weeks, in spring or summer.

Additional data   This program began in 1991 in memory of the late John D. Quinn Jr., managing editor of the *Poughkeepsie Journal.* Funding is provided by the Freedom Forum, formerly the Gannett Foundation. After graduating from college and obtaining employment with a newspaper, alumni of this program are eligible to apply for fellowship support to attend professional journalism development activities.

Number awarded   Approximately 70 each year. Since the program began, more than 1,300 scholars have been selected.

Deadline   September of each year.

[111]
CHRISTIAN COLLEGE LEADERS SCHOLARSHIPS

Foundation for College Christian Leaders
2658 Del Mar Heights Road
PMB 266
Del Mar, CA 92014
(858) 481-0848   E-mail: LMHays@aol.com
Web: www.collegechristianleader.com

Summary   To provide financial assistance for college to Christian students from California, Oregon, and Washington, especially Hispanics and other minorities.

Eligibility   This program is open to entering or continuing undergraduate students who reside or attend college in California, Oregon, or Washington. Applicants must have a GPA of 3.0 or higher, be able to document financial need (parents must have a combined income of less than $75,000), and be able to demonstrate Christian testimony and Christian leadership. Selection is based on identified leadership history, academic achievement, financial need, and demonstrated academic, vocational, and ministry training to further the Kingdom of Jesus Christ. Special consideration is given to minority students.

Financial Data   A stipend is awarded (amount not specified).

Duration   1 year; may be renewed.

Additional data   The foundation, formerly known as the Eckmann Foundation, was founded in 1988.

Number awarded   Varies each year.
Deadline   May of each year.

[112]
CINTHYA FELIX SCHOLARSHIP

Latino Medical Student Association-West Region
c/o Susie Sandoval, Scholarship Vice President
USC Keck School of Medicine
1975 Zonal Avenue
Los Angeles, CA 90033
E-mail: vp_scholarship@lmsa.net
Web: www.lmsa.net

Summary   To provide financial assistance to undergraduate and postbaccalaureate Latino students in designated western states who are planning to prepare for a career in medicine.

Eligibility   This program is open to Latino students at the sophomore or higher or postbaccalaureate level who are planning to attend medical school. Applicants should be able to demonstrate a desire to advance the state of health care and education in Latino communities through extracurricular activities and/or membership in civic organizations. They must be committed to preparing for a professional career in medicine and dedicated to serving the Latino and underserved communities. Membership in the Latino Medical Student Association (LMSA) in western states (Arizona, California, Oregon, Utah, Washington) is required. There are no citizenship requirements. Along with their application, they must submit a 1-page personal statement describing their family and personal background, educational objectives, community involvement, financial need, and how they would assist the sponsoring organization in its mission to provide health care to the Latino and underserved communities.

Financial Data   A stipend is awarded (amount not specified).

Duration   1 year.

Additional data   Until 2002, this organization was known as the Chicano/Latino Medical Student Association of California. It established this program in 2011.

Number awarded   Varies each year.

Deadline   January of each year.

[113]
CLARKE WATSON SCHOLARSHIPS

American Association of Blacks in Energy-Denver Area
   Chapter
Attn: Scholarship Committee
18601 Green Valley Ranch Boulevard, 108-264
Denver, CO 80249
E-mail: Denver@aabe.org
Web: www.aabe.org/index.php?component=pages&id=270

Summary   To provide financial assistance to Hispanics and members of other underrepresented minority groups who are high school seniors in Colorado and planning to major in an energy-related field at a college in any state.

Eligibility   This program is open to seniors graduating from high schools in Colorado who are planning to work on a bachelor's degree at a college or university in any state. Applicants must be Hispanics, African Americans, or Native Americans who have a GPA of 3.0 or higher and have taken the ACT and/or SAT test. They must be planning to major in a field of business, engineering, technology, physical science, or mathematics related to energy. Along with their application, they must submit a 350-word essay that includes 1) when they discovered their interest in the field of energy and what sparked their interest; and 2) either what excites them about the field of energy or how they expect their education to prepare them for the field of energy. Financial need is not considered in the selection process.

Financial Data The stipend is $1,000. Funds are disbursed directly to the recipient's college or university.

Duration 1 year; may be renewed.

Additional data Winners are eligible to compete for regional and national scholarships.

Number awarded 1 or more each year.

Deadline February of each year.

[114]
CLAY FORD MINORITY SCHOLARSHIPS

Florida Board of Accountancy
Florida Department of Business and Professional
 Regulation
Attn: Division of Certified Public Accounting
240 N.W. 76th Drive, Suite A
Gainesville, FL 32607-6656
(352) 333-2505   Fax: (352) 333-2508
E-mail: CPA.Applications@dbpr.state.fl.us
Web: www.myfloridalicense.com

Summary To provide financial assistance to Hispanic and other minority residents of Florida who are entering the fifth year of an accounting program.

Eligibility This program is open to Florida residents who have completed at least 120 credit hours at a college or university in the state and have a GPA of 2.5 or higher. Applicants must be planning to remain in school as a full-time student for the fifth year required to sit for the C.P.A. examination. They must be members of a minority group, defined to include African Americans, Hispanic Americans, Asian Americans, Native Americans, or women. Selection is based on scholastic ability and performance and financial need.

Financial Data Stipends range from $3,000 to $6,000 per semester.

Duration 1 semester; may be renewed 1 additional semester.

Number awarded Varies each year; a total of $200,000 is available for this program annually.

Deadline May of each year.

[115]
COLGATE "BRIGHT SMILES, BRIGHT FUTURES" MINORITY SCHOLARSHIPS

American Dental Hygienists' Association
Attn: Institute for Oral Health
444 North Michigan Avenue, Suite 3400
Chicago, IL 60611-3980
(312) 440-8900, ext. 244   Fax: (312) 440-6726
E-mail: institute@adha.net
Web: www.adha.org/ioh-associate-certificate-scholarships

Summary To provide financial assistance to Hispanic and other minority students who are members of the American Dental Hygienists' Association (ADHA) and enrolled in certificate programs in dental hygiene.

Eligibility This program is open to members of groups currently underrepresented in the dental hygiene profession (Hispanics, Native Americans, Hispanics, African Americans, Hispanics, Asians, and males) who are student or active members of the ADHA. Applicants must have a GPA of 3.5 or higher and have completed at least 1 year of full-time enrollment in an accredited dental hygiene certificate or associate degree program in the United States.

Financial Data The stipend is $1,250.

Duration 1 year; nonrenewable.

Additional data These scholarships are sponsored by the Colgate-Palmolive Company.

Number awarded 2 each year.

Deadline January of each year.

[116]
COLLABORATIVE RESEARCH EXPERIENCES FOR UNDERGRADUATES

Computing Research Association
1828 L Street, N.W., Suite 800
Washington, DC 20036-4632
(202) 234-2111   Fax: (202) 667-1066
E-mail: creu@cra.org
Web: www.cra.org/cra-w/creu

Summary To provide funding to Hispanic and other underrepresented undergraduate students who are interested in conducting a research project in computer science or engineering.

Eligibility This program is open to teams of 2 or 4 undergraduates who have completed 2 years of study, including at least 4 courses in computer science or computer engineering, at a college or university in the United States. Applicants must be interested in conducting a research project directly related to computer science or computer engineering. They must apply jointly with 1 or 2 sponsoring faculty members. Teams consisting of underrepresented groups (Mexican-Americans, mainland Puerto Ricans, African Americans, American Indians, Alaska Natives, Native Hawaiians, Pacific Islanders, women, individuals who identify as part of the LGBTQI community, and persons with disabilities) are especially encouraged to apply; teams may also include students from non-underrepresented groups, but financial support is available only to underrepresented students. U.S. citizenship or permanent resident status is required.

Financial Data The program provides a stipend of $3,000 for the academic year. Students who wish to participate in an optional summer extension receive an additional stipend of $4,000. Additional funding up to $1,500 per team may be available for purchase of supporting materials and/or travel to conferences to present the work.

Duration 1 academic year plus an optional summer extension.

Additional data This program is sponsored by the Computing Research Association's Committee on the Status of Women in Computing Research (CRA-W) and the Coalition to Diversify Computing (CDC) in cooperation with the National Science Foundation.

Number awarded Varies each year; recently, 14 teams of students received support from this program.

Deadline May of each year.

[117]
COLLEGE STUDENT PRE-COMMISSIONING INITIATIVE

U.S. Coast Guard
Attn: Recruiting Command
2703 Martin Luther King, Jr. Avenue, S.E., Stop 7419
Washington, DC 20593-7200
(202) 795-6864
Web: www.gocoastguard.com

Summary To provide financial assistance to college students at Hispanid Serving or other designated institutions who are willing to serve in the Coast Guard following graduation.

Eligibility This program is open to students entering their junior or senior year at a college or university designated as an Hispanic Serving Institution (HSI), Historically Black College or University (HBCU), Predominantly Black Institution (PBI), Asian American and Native American Pacific Islander-Serving Institution, American Indian Tribally Controlled College or University (TCU), Alaska Native Serving Institution (ANSI), or Native American Serving, Non-Tribal Institution. Applicants must be U.S. citizens; have a GPA of 2.5 or higher; have scores of 1100 or higher on the critical reading and mathematics SAT, 23 or higher on the ACT, or 109 or higher technical score on the ASVAB; be between 19 and 27 years of age; and meet all physical requirements for a Coast Guard commission. They must agree to attend the Coast Guard Officer Candidate School following graduation and serve on active duty as an officer for at least 3 years.

Financial Data Those selected to participate receive full payment of tuition, books, and fees; monthly housing and food allowances; medical and life insurance; special training in leadership, management, law enforcement, navigation, and marine science; 30 days of paid vacation per year; and a Coast Guard monthly salary of approximately $1,800.

Duration Up to 2 years.

Number awarded Varies each year; recently, 38 were awarded.

Deadline September or January of each year.

[118]
COLOMBIAN EDUCATION FUND SCHOLARSHIPS

Colombian Education Fund
Attn: Kimberley Rodriguez, Director of Educational Programs
5-11 47th Avenue, Suite 8C
Long Island City, NY 11101
E-mail: info@colombianscholarshipfund.org
Web: www.colombianeducationfund.org/scholarship

Summary To provide financial assistance to residents of New York who are of Colombian origin and interested in attending college in any state.

Eligibility This program is open to residents of New York who are of Columbian origin or descent. Applicants must be 1) high school or home-schooled seniors, graduates, or recipients of a GED diploma planning to enroll at an accredited U.S. college or university; or 2) currently enrolled full time as sophomores at an accredited 2- or 4-year college or university. They must have a GPA of 3.0 or higher in high school or college. Students attending or planning to attend a technical college, vocational program, or for-profit college are not eligi-

ble. U.S. citizenship or permanent resident status is not required. Along with their application, they must submit a 1-page personal statement describing their involvement with the immigrant community, how they plan to give back to the Colombian community when they accomplish their professional goals, their commitment to community advancement, any obstacles they have faced in their educational career, and what this scholarship would mean to them. In the selection process, primary consideration is given to financial need.

Financial Data The stipend is $2,000.

Duration 1 year; nonrenewable.

Additional data This program began in 2013. Recipients are expected to complete 200 hours of combined community service, internships, or scholarship-related activities during their year as a scholar.

Number awarded 5 each year.

Deadline March of each year.

[119]
COLORADO EDUCATION ASSOCIATION MINORITY STUDENT SCHOLARSHIPS

Colorado Education Association
Attn: Ethnic Minority Advisory Council
1500 Grant Street
Denver, CO 80203
(303) 837-1500   Toll Free: (800) 332-5939
Web: www.coloradoea.org

Summary To provide financial assistance to Hispanic and other minority high school seniors in Colorado who are children of members of the Colorado Education Association (CEA) and planning to attend college in any state.

Eligibility This program is open to seniors graduating from high schools in Colorado who are members of a minority ethnic group, defined to include Hispanics, American Indians/Alaska Natives, Asians, Blacks, Native Hawaiians/Pacific Islanders, and multi-ethnic. Applicants must be the dependent child of an active, retired, or deceased CEA member. They must be planning to attend an accredited institution of higher education in any state. Along with their application, they must submit brief statements on 1) their need for this scholarship; and 2) why they plan to pursue a college education.

Financial Data The stipend is $1,000.

Duration 1 year; nonrenewable.

Number awarded 4 each year.

Deadline April of each year.

[120]
COLORADO FIESTA PAGEANT QUEEN

Colorado State Fair
Attn: Fiesta Committee
c/o Brian Montez
1001 Beulah Avenue
Pueblo, CO 81004
(719) 778-4350   E-mail: pageant@fiestacommittee.org
Web: sites.google.com

Summary To recognize and reward, with college scholarships, Hispanic women who participate in the Colorado State Fair Fiesta Pageant.

Eligibility This competition is open to women of Hispanic descent who have been residents of Colorado for at least 6 months and are U.S. citizens or eligible non-citizens. Applicants must be between 18 and 22 years of age and enrolled or planning to enroll full time at a college or university in Colorado. They must have a GPA of 3.0 or higher. During the Colorado State Fair Fiesta in June, they participate in the Queen Pageant, with the Queen and Attendants selected on the basis of personal interviews (30%), a 3- to 5-minute speech (30%), talent (20%), evening gown (10%), and an impromptu question (10%).

Financial Data Awards are $2,500 for the Fiesta Queen, $1,500 to the First Attendant, $1,250 to the Second Attendant, and $1,000 to the Third Attendant. Funds are disbursed directly to the college each recipient attends, upon proof of full-time enrollment.

Duration The competition is held annually.

Number awarded 4 each year.

Deadline May of each year.

[121]
COLUMBIA UNIVERSITY/BARNARD COLLEGE AMGEN SCHOLARS SUMMER RESEARCH PROGRAM

Columbia University
Attn: Biological Sciences
1212 Amsterdam Avenue
MC2454
New York, NY 10027
(212) 854-2262   E-mail: amgen@biology.columbia.edu
Web: www.columbia.edu/cu/biology/ug/amgen

Summary To provide an opportunity for undergraduates, especially Hispanics and other underrepresented minorities, to participate in summer research projects in the biological sciences at Columbia University.

Eligibility This program is open to sophomores, juniors, and non-graduating seniors at 4-year colleges and universities in the United States, Puerto Rico, and other U.S. territories. Applicants must be U.S. citizens or permanent residents who have a cumulative GPA of 3.2 or higher. They must be interested in working on a summer research project at Columbia University in the following laboratory programs: biochemistry and molecular biophysics, biological sciences, biomedical engineering, genetics and development, microbiology and immunology, pathology and cell biology, physiology and cell biophysics, or psychiatry. The Amgen Scholars Program encourages applications from students who are members of groups underrepresented in the biological sciences.

Financial Data Scholars receive a stipend of $4,000, a flex meal plan of $500, transportation to and from New York, and housing on the Morningside campus of Columbia.

Duration 10 weeks during the summer.

Additional data This program serves as the Columbia component of the Amgen Scholars Program, which operates at 8 other U.S. universities (and the National Institutes of Health) and is funded by the Amgen Foundation.

Number awarded Up to 30 each year, of whom half are from Columbia or Barnard and half from other universities.

Deadline January of each year.

[122]
COMMISSION ON DIETETIC REGISTRATION DIVERSITY SCHOLARSHIPS

Academy of Nutrition and Dietetics
Attn: Foundation
120 South Riverside Plaza, Suite 2000
Chicago, IL 60606-6995
(312) 899-4821   Toll Free: (800) 877-1600, ext. 4821
Fax: (312) 899-4796   E-mail: blabrador@eatright.org
Web: www.eatrightfoundation.org/foundation/scholarships

Summary To provide financial assistance to Hispanics and members of other underrepresented minority groups who are enrolled in an undergraduate or graduate program in dietetics.

Eligibility This program is open to students enrolled at a CADE-accredited/approved college or university in the undergraduate coordinated dietetics program, the undergraduate didactic program in dietetics, a dietetic internship program, a dietetic technician program, or a dietetic graduate program. Applicants must be members of underrepresented minority groups (Hispanic, African American, Native American). They must be U.S. citizens or permanent residents and show promise of being a valuable, contributing member of the profession. Membership in the Academy of Nutrition and Dietetics is encouraged but not required.

Financial Data The stipend is $5,000.

Duration 1 year.

Number awarded 20 each year.

Deadline March of each year.

[123]
COMMUNICATIONS INTERNSHIP AWARD FOR STUDENTS OF COLOR

College and University Public Relations and Allied
  Professionals
237 South Fraser Street
P.O. Box 10034
State College, PA 16805-0034
Fax: (814) 863-3428   E-mail: ehanson@cuprap.org
Web: www.cuprap.org/awards/communications-internships

Summary To provide an opportunity for Hispanics and other students of color at institutions that are members of the College and University Public Relations and Allied Professionals (CUPRAP) to complete an internship in communications.

Eligibility This program is open to students of color (i.e., African Americans, Asian/Pacific Islanders, Hispanics/Latinos, and Native Americans) who have completed the first year of college and are enrolled as a degree candidate in the second year or higher. Applicants must obtain and complete a verifiable internship of at least 150 hours in a communications-related field (e.g., print media, radio, television, public relations, advertising, graphic/web design). They must be enrolled full time at an accredited 2- or 4-year college or university that is a member of CUPRAP. Selection is based on financial need, academic ability, communication skills, and creativity as demonstrated through work samples.

Financial Data The stipend is $2,000, paid upon confirmation of employment in an internship position.

Duration The internship award is presented annually; recipients may reapply.

Additional data This internship award was first presented in 1983.

Number awarded 1 each year.

Deadline January of each year.

[124]
COMMUNITY COUNCIL OF IDAHO HISPANIC STUDENT SCHOLARSHIP PROGRAM

Community Council of Idaho, Inc.
Attn: Hispanic Student Scholarship Program
317 Happy Day Boulevard, Suite 250
Caldwell, ID 83607
(208) 454-1652   Fax: (208) 459-0448
E-mail: info@ccimail.org
Web: www.communitycouncilofidaho.org

Summary To provide financial assistance to Hispanic high school seniors in Idaho who plan to attend college in the state.

Eligibility This program is open to residents of Idaho who are of Latino origin. Applicants must be planning to enter college in Idaho as freshmen in the following fall. They must have a GPA of 2.5 or higher. Selection is based on a 1-page statement on educational goals, high school transcripts, 3 letters of recommendation, and financial need.

Financial Data The stipend is $1,000.

Duration 1 year; nonrenewable.

Additional data This organization was formerly known as the Idaho Migrant Council, Inc. and designated its scholarship program the Idaho Migrant Council Latino Scholarship Fund. Recipients are expected to attend the sponsor's annual meeting in September to accept their award.

Number awarded Varies each year; recently, 11 were awarded.

Deadline April of each year.

[125]
COMTO COLORADO SCHOLARSHIPS

Conference of Minority Transportation Officials-Colorado
   Chapter
Attn: Scholarship Committee
1114 West Seventh Avenue
P.O. Box 13582
Denver, CO 80201
E-mail: DrMaryDavis@aol.com
Web: www.comtocolorado.org/scholarship-program

Summary To provide financial assistance to Hispanic and other minority high school seniors in Colorado who are interested in studying a transportation-related field at a college or university in any state.

Eligibility This program is open to minority seniors graduating from high schools in Colorado with a GPA of 2.5 or higher. Applicants must be planning to attend an accredited college, university, or trade school in any state. They must be planning to major in archaeology and/or cultural resources, architecture, aviation, engineering (chemical, civil, electrical, mechanical, or structural), computer aided design, computer science, construction engineering technology, construction and/or construction management, diesel mechanics, electrical, electronics, environmental science and related fields, geology and/or geotechnical engineering, heating and air conditioning, hydraulic and/or elevator mechanics, public

information and outreach programs, security systems, urban planning, or vehicle design and maintenance. Along with their application, they must submit an essay of 500 to 700 words on why they chose their planned field of study, how they think their course work and life experiences have helped them prepare for their college studies and the future, and why they are an excellent candidate for this scholarship. Selection is based on that essay (20%), GPA (15%), participation in career-related activities (10%), letters of recommendation (15%), high school citizenship (15%), and an interview (25%).

Financial Data A stipend is awarded (amount not specified). Funds may be used for tuition, books, and/or room and board expenses.

Duration 1 year.

Number awarded Up to 10 each year.

Deadline March of each year.

[126]
CONGRESO COLLEGE SCHOLARSHIPS

Baptist General Convention of Texas
Attn: Hispanic Evangelism Director
7557 Rambler Road, Suite 1200
Dallas, TX 75231-2388
(214) 828-5266   Toll Free: (888) 244-9400
Fax: (214) 828-5261
E-mail: joshua.delrisco@texasbaptists.org
Web: www.texasbaptists.org

Summary To provide financial assistance for college to Hispanic residents of Texas who attend the Congreso of the Baptist General Convention of Texas (BGCT).

Eligibility This program is open to active members of a BGCT affiliated congregation who currently participate in Hispanic-related ministry and are active in their youth, college, and/or singles group. Applicants must be enrolled full time at an accredited college or university in any state; high school and vocational students are not eligible. Applicants must also be U.S. citizens and have a GPA of 3.0 or higher. They must be a registered participant of Congreso and attend all of its activities; applications, including a 1-page essay on why they deserve to be a recipient of this scholarship, must be presented in person at Congreso.

Financial Data The stipend is $1,000. Funds must be used for college expenses, not for Congreso expenses.

Duration 1 year; nonrenewable.

Number awarded Approximately 30 each year.

Deadline April of each year.

[127]
CONGRESSIONAL HISPANIC CAUCUS INSTITUTE CONGRESSIONAL INTERNSHIP PROGRAM

Congressional Hispanic Caucus Institute, Inc.
911 Second Street, N.E.
Washington, DC 20002
(202) 543-1771   Toll Free: (800) EXCEL-DC
Fax: (202) 546-2143   E-mail: chci@chci.org
Web: www.chci.org

Summary To provide Latino undergraduates with an opportunity to work directly with Congress or federal agencies.

Eligibility This program is open to full-time Latino undergraduate students who have completed at least 1 year of college and are interested in an internship in a Congressional office or federal agency. College seniors graduating before the program begins are ineligible. Applicants must be U.S. citizens, asylees, valid visa holders, and permanent residents who are of Hispanic descent. They must be able to demonstrate 1) high academic achievement (preference is given to those with a GPA of 3.0 or higher); 2) commitment to public service activities; 3) leadership skills and potential for leadership growth; 4) superior analytical skills; and 5) outstanding oral and written communication skills. Students registered in the DACA program must possess an Employment Authorization Document.

Financial Data The stipend is $3,750 during the fall or spring or $2,500 during the summer. The program also provides round-trip transportation to Washington and housing in university dormitories.

Duration 12 weeks during the fall or spring or 8 weeks during the summer.

Additional data In addition to their internship, participants attend seminars and lectures that offer exposure to critical components of policy-making.

Number awarded Approximately 32 each year.

Deadline January of each year for summer; April of each year for fall; November of each year for spring.

[128]
CONNECTICUT ASSOCIATION OF LATINOS IN HIGHER EDUCATION SCHOLARSHIPS

Connecticut Association of Latinos in Higher Education, Inc.
CCSU-1615 Stanley Street
Clarence Carroll Hall 035 06
New Britain, CT 06050
Web: www.calahe.org/scholarships

Summary To provide financial assistance to Latino residents of Connecticut who are interested in attending college in any state.

Eligibility This program is open to graduating high school seniors, GED recipients, and current college students who have been residents of Connecticut during the preceding 12 months. Applicants must come from a Latino background and have a GPA of 2.75 or higher. They must be enrolled or planning to enroll full time at an accredited institution of higher education in any state. U.S. citizenship or permanent resident status is required. Selection is based on academic achievement, financial need, community service, and an essay on "How do you feel education is going to impact your ability to continue assisting others to pursue an education?"

Financial Data The stipend is $1,000.

Duration 1 year.

Number awarded Varies each year; recently, 20 were awarded.

Deadline April of each year.

[129]
CONNECTICUT CHAPTER AABE SCHOLARSHIPS

American Association of Blacks in Energy-Connecticut Chapter
Attn: Scholarship Committee
P.O. Box 1898
Hartford, CT 06144
(203) 499-2418   E-mail: presctchapter@gmail.com
Web: www.aabe.org/index.php?component=pages&id=827

Summary To provide financial assistance to Hispanics and members of other underrepresented minority groups who are high school seniors in Connecticut and western Massachusetts and planning to major in an energy-related field at a college in any state.

Eligibility This program is open to seniors graduating from high schools in Connecticut or western Massachusetts and planning to work on a bachelor's degree at a college or university in any state. Applicants must be Hispanics, African Americans, or Native Americans who have a GPA of 3.0 or higher and have taken the SAT and/or ACT test. Their intended major must be a field of business, engineering, mathematics, or science (e.g., chemistry, geology, meteorology, physics) related to energy. Along with their application, they must submit a 350-word essay that includes 1) when they discovered their interest in the field of energy and what sparked their interest; and 2) either what excites them about the field of energy or how they expect their education to prepare them for the field of energy. Financial need is not considered in the selection process.

Financial Data The stipend is $2,500. Funds are disbursed directly to the students.

Duration 1 year; nonrenewable.

Additional data Winners are eligible to compete for regional and national scholarships. This program began in 2003.

Number awarded 4 or 5 each year. Since this program began, it has awarded 45 scholarships with a total value of $109,000.

Deadline April of each year.

[130]
CONNECTICUT EDUCATION FOUNDATION SCHOLARSHIPS FOR MINORITY HIGH SCHOOL STUDENTS

Connecticut Education Association
Attn: Connecticut Education Foundation, Inc.
21 Oak Street, Suite 500
Hartford, CT 06106-8001
(860) 525-5641   Toll Free: (800) 842-4316
Fax: (860) 725-6323   E-mail: jeffl@cea.org
Web: www.cea.org/cef/ethnic-minority-scholarship-fund

Summary To provide financial assistance to Hispanic and other minority high school seniors in Connecticut who are interested in attending college in the state to prepare for a teaching career.

Eligibility This program is open to minority seniors (Hispanics or Latinos, Blacks, Native Americans or Alaskan Natives, and Asians or Pacific Islanders) graduating from high schools in Connecticut. Applicants have been accepted at an accredited 2- or 4-year college or university in the state and be planning to enter the teaching profession. They must have a GPA of 2.75 or higher. Finalists may be interviewed. Financial need is considered in the selection process.

Financial Data   The stipend is $2,000 per year.

Duration   1 year; may be renewed.

Number awarded   At least 1 each year.

Deadline   April of each year.

[131]
CONNECTICUT MINORITY TEACHER INCENTIVE GRANTS

Connecticut Office of Higher Education
Attn: Minority Teacher Incentive Grant Program
450 Columbus Boulevard, Suite 510
Hartford, CT 06103-1841
(860) 947-1855   Toll Free: (800) 842-0229 (within CT)
Fax: (860) 947-1311   E-mail: mtip@ctohe.org
Web: www.ctohe.org/sfa/sfa.shtml

Summary   To provide financial assistance and loan repayment to Hispanic and other minority upper-division college students in Connecticut who are interested in teaching at public schools in the state.

Eligibility   This program is open to juniors and seniors enrolled full time in Connecticut college and university teacher preparation programs. Applicants must be members of a minority group, defined as Hispanic/Latino, African American, Asian American, or Native American. They must be nominated by the education dean at their institution.

Financial Data   The maximum stipend is $5,000 per year. In addition, if recipients complete a credential and begin teaching at a public school in Connecticut within 16 months of graduation, they may receive up to $2,500 per year, for up to 4 years, to help pay off college loans.

Duration   Up to 2 years.

Number awarded   Varies each year.

Deadline   October of each year.

[132]
CONNTESOL SCHOLARSHIPS

Connecticut Teachers of English to Speakers of Other
  Languages
P.O. Box 4108
Hamden, CT 06514
E-mail: ConnTESOL@gmail.com
Web: www.conntesol.org

Summary   To provide financial assistance to Connecticut residents whose native language is not English and who are attending or planning to attend college in any state.

Eligibility   This program is open to residents of Connecticut whose first language is not English. Awards are presented in 4 categories: 1) high school seniors entering a 2-year college; 2) high school seniors entering a 4-year college or university; 3) high school seniors who are presently or were previously enrolled in English Language Learning (ELL) or bilingual education classes and entering a 2- or 4-year college or university (designated the CAPELL Scholarship for its sponsor, the Connecticut Administrators of Programs for English Language Learners); and 4) adult education students entering a college or university. Applicants must submit an essay of 250 to 500 words on how the education they are receiving in the United States is influencing their life.

Financial Data   The stipend is $1,000.

Duration   1 year.

Number awarded   At least 4 each year (1 in each category).

Deadline   May of each year.

[133]
CORNELL UNIVERSITY SUMMER PROGRAM IN ASTRONOMY AND ASTROPHYSICS

Cornell University
Department of Astronomy
Attn: REU Astronomy Coordinator
510 Space Sciences Building
Ithaca, NY 14853-6801
(607) 255-0288   Fax: (607) 255-1767
E-mail: reu@astro.cornell.edu
Web: astro.cornell.edu/specialprograms/reu

Summary   To provide an opportunity for undergraduate students, especially Hispanics and other underrepresented minorities, to work as student assistants on astronomy research projects at Cornell University during the summer.

Eligibility   This program is open to undergraduate students who have completed 1 to 3 years of academic training. Applicants must be interested in working with Cornell University faculty and research staff on projects covering a wide range of disciplines in planetary science, astronomical instrumentation, astrophysics, general relativity, and cosmology. They must be U.S. citizens or permanent residents. Applications are especially encouraged from underrepresented minorities, persons with disabilities, and women.

Financial Data   The stipend is $6,800. Other support includes $1,000 for relocation and housing and up to $1,000 for travel to a scientific meeting to present the results of the research.

Duration   10 weeks during the summer.

Additional data   This program is funded by the National Science Foundation as part of its Research Experiences for Undergraduates (REU) Program.

Number awarded   8 each year.

Deadline   February of each year.

[134]
COY AND MAE DELL YOUNG SCHOLARSHIP

National Naval Officers Association-Washington, D.C.
  Chapter
c/o LCDR Stephen Williams
P.O. Box 30784
Alexandria, VA 22310
(703) 644-2605   Fax: (703) 644-8503
E-mail: Stephen.Williams@navy.mil
Web: www.dcnnoa.org/dcnnoa-scholarship

Summary   To provide financial assistance to Hispanic and other minority high school seniors from the Washington, D.C. area who are interested in attending college in any state.

Eligibility   This program is open to minority seniors graduating from high schools in the Washington, D.C. metropolitan area who plan to enroll full time at an accredited 2- or 4-year college or university in any state. Applicants must have a GPA of 2.7 or higher and be U.S. citizens or permanent residents. Selection is based on academic achievement, community involvement, and financial need.

Financial Data   The stipend is $1,000.

Duration   1 year; nonrenewable.

Additional data   This program is sponsored by the Washington D.C. Chapter of the National Naval Officers Association (DCNNOA), an organization of African American naval officers, but all minorities are eligible and recipients are not required to join or affiliate with the military in any way.

Number awarded   1 each year.

Deadline   February of each year.

[135]
CUBA WADLINGTON, JR. AND MICHAEL P. JOHNSON SCHOLARSHIP

Tulsa Community Foundation
Attn: Scholarships
7030 South Yale Avenue, Suite 600
Tulsa, OK 74136
(918) 494-8823   Fax: (918) 494-9826
E-mail: scholarships@tulsacf.org
Web: www.tulsacf.org/whatwedo/education/scholarships

Summary   To provide financial assistance to upper-division students at colleges in any state who are Hispanics or members of another underrepresented group in the energy industry.

Eligibility   This program is open to students entering their junior or senior year at a college or university in any state and preparing for a career in the energy industry with a major in accounting, engineering, finance, or technology. Applicants must be members of a group underrepresented in the energy industry (women and ethnic minorities). They must have a GPA of 3.0 or higher. Along with their application, they must submit a 2-page personal essay that includes their future or academic career goals, any adversity or challenge they have overcome or anticipate in pursuit of their educational goals, and the importance of diversity in the workplace and how dealing with diversity in their own life has shaped them. Financial need is not considered in the selection process.

Financial Data   The stipend is $2,000. Funds are paid directly to the university.

Duration   1 year; nonrenewable.

Additional data   This program is supported by the Williams Companies of Tulsa, Oklahoma.

Number awarded   Varies each year.

Deadline   June of each year.

[136]
CUMMINS SCHOLARSHIPS

Society of Women Engineers
Attn: Scholarship Selection Committee
203 North LaSalle Street, Suite 1675
Chicago, IL 60601-1269
(312) 596-5223   Toll Free: (877) SWE-INFO
Fax: (312) 644-8557   E-mail: scholarships@swe.org
Web: societyofwomenengineers.swe.org

Summary   To provide financial assistance to women, especially Hispanics and members of other underrepresented groups, who are working on an undergraduate degree in computer science or designated engineering specialties.

Eligibility   This program is open to women who are sophomores, re-entry, or nontraditional students at 4-year ABET-accredited colleges and universities. Applicants must be working full time on a degree in computer science, industrial systems, metrology, metallurgy, or automotive, chemical, computer, electrical, industrial, manufacturing, materials, or mechanical engineering and have a GPA of 3.0 or higher. Preference is given to members of groups underrepresented in engineering or computer science and to students interested in an internship with the sponsor. Selection is based on merit.

Financial Data   The stipend is $2,500.

Duration   1 year.

Additional data   This program is sponsored by Cummins, Inc.

Number awarded   2 each year.

Deadline   February of each year.

[137]
DAMON P. MOORE SCHOLARSHIP

Indiana State Teachers Association
Attn: ISTA Foundation for the Improvement of Education
150 West Market Street, Suite 900
Indianapolis, IN 46204-2814
(317) 263-3306   Toll Free: (800) 382-4037, ext. 3306
Fax: (800) 777-6128   E-mail: ccherry@ista-in.org
Web: www.ista-in.org/our-profession/scholarships-awards

Summary   To provide financial assistance to Hispanic and other ethnic minority high school seniors in Indiana who are interested in studying education at a college in any state.

Eligibility   This program is open to ethnic minority public high school seniors in Indiana who are interested in studying education in college. Selection is based on academic achievement, leadership ability as expressed through co-curricular activities and community involvement, recommendations, and a 300-word essay on their educational goals and how they plan to use this scholarship.

Financial Data   The stipend is $1,000.

Duration   1 year; may be renewed for 3 additional years if the recipient maintains at least a "C+" average and continues to pursue a teaching credential.

Additional data   This program began in 1987.

Number awarded   1 each year.

Deadline   February of each year.

[138]
DANIELLA ALTFELD-MORENO SCHOLARSHIP

Pride Foundation
Attn: Educational Programs Director
2014 East Madison Street, Suite 300
Seattle, WA 98122
(206) 323-3318   Toll Free: (800) 735-7287
Fax: (206) 323-1017
E-mail: scholarships@pridefoundation.org
Web: www.pridefoundation.org

Summary   To provide financial assistance to Latino/a lesbian, gay, bisexual, transgender, or queer (LGBTQ) residents of the Northwest who are interested in attending college in any state, especially those involved in athletics.

Eligibility   This program is open to LGBTQ residents of Alaska, Idaho, Montana, Oregon, or Washington who are Latinos or Latinas and attending or planning to attend a college, university, or vocational school in any state. Applicants must be younger than 25 years of age. Preference is given to students who are involved in athletics. Selection is based on demonstrated commitment to social justice and LGBTQ concerns, leadership in their communities, the ability to be academically and personally successful, and (to some extent) financial need.

Financial Data   Recently, the average stipend for all scholarships awarded by the foundation was approximately $3,400. Funds are paid directly to the recipient's school.

Duration   1 year; recipients may reapply.

Number awarded   1 each year. Since it began offering scholarships in 1993, the foundation has awarded a total of more than $3.5 million to nearly 1,400 recipients.

Deadline   January of each year.

[139]
DANNY GUTIERREZ MEMORIAL SCHOLARSHIP

National Hispanic Coalition of Federal Aviation
  Employees
Attn: Scholarship Selection Committee
P.O. Box 23276
Washington, DC 20026-3276
E-mail: doe@nhcfae.org
Web: www.nhcfae.org

Summary   To provide financial assistance to Hispanic and other minorities who are interested in working on a degree in electronics or engineering.

Eligibility   This program is open to female and minority U.S. citizens and permanent residents residing in the United States or Puerto Rico. Applicants must be accepted to or attending an accredited college, university, or vocational/trade school with a major in electronics or engineering. Selection is based on academic achievement, community involvement, honors and awards, leadership, personal qualities and strengths, student activities, and financial need.

Financial Data   A stipend is awarded (amount not specified).

Duration   1 year; may be renewed.

Additional data   The National Hispanic Coalition of Federal Aviation Employees, established in 1978, is a nonprofit organization comprised mainly of Hispanics who are employed at the Federal Aviation Administration.

Number awarded   1 each year.

Deadline   April of each year.

[140]
DAVID SANKEY MINORITY SCHOLARSHIP IN METEOROLOGY

National Weather Association
Attn: Executive Director
3100 Monitor Avenue, Suite 123
Norman, OK 73072
(405) 701-5167   Fax: (405) 701-5227
E-mail: exdir@nwas.org
Web: www.nwas.org

Summary   To provide financial assistance to Hispanics and members of other underrepresented groups working on an undergraduate or graduate degree in meteorology.

Eligibility   This program is open to members of underrepresented ethnic groups who are either entering their sophomore or higher year of undergraduate study or enrolled as graduate students. Applicants must be working on a degree

in meteorology. Along with their application, they must submit a 1-page statement explaining why they are applying for this scholarship. Selection is based on that statement, academic achievement, and 2 letters of recommendation.

Financial Data   The stipend is $1,000.

Duration   1 year.

Additional data   This program began in 2002.

Number awarded   1 each year.

Deadline   April of each year.

[141]
DAVILA/TREVINO MEMORIAL SCHOLARSHIPS

Great Minds in STEM
Attn: HENAAC Scholars Program
602 Monterey Pass Road
Monterey Park, CA 91754
(323) 262-0997   Fax: (323) 262-0946
E-mail: scholars@greatmindsinstem.org
Web: www.greatmindsinstem.org

Summary   To provide financial assistance to Hispanic undergraduate students interested in working on a degree in a field of science, technology, engineering, or mathematics (STEM) at a university in Texas.

Eligibility   This program is open to students who are entering their junior or senior year in a field of STEM at a 4-year college or university in Texas. Applicants must be of Hispanic origin and/or must significantly participate in and promote organizations and activities in the Hispanic community. They must have a GPA of 3.0 or higher. Along with their application, they must submit a 700-word essay on a topic that changes annually. Selection is based on leadership, academic achievements, and campus and community activities; financial need is not considered. U.S. citizenship is required.

Financial Data   The stipend is $1,000.

Duration   1 year; recipients may reapply.

Additional data   The Hispanic Engineer National Achievement Awards Conference (HENAAC) was established in 1989 and initiated a scholarship program in 2000. In 2010, the sponsoring organization officially adopted its current name, but it continues to hold the annual HENAAC conference, at which the scholarships are presented. This program began in 2013. Recipients must attend the conference to accept their scholarship. The sponsor subsidizes the cost of travel, 3 nights of lodging, and meals.

Number awarded   Varies each year; recently, 10 were awarded.

Deadline   April of each year.

[142]
DELAWARE ATHLETIC TRAINERS' ASSOCIATION ETHNIC DIVERSITY ADVISORY COMMITTEE SCHOLARSHIP

Delaware Athletic Trainers' Association
c/o Education Committee Chair
University of Delaware
159 Fred Rust Ice Arena
Newark, DE 19716
(302) 831-6402   E-mail: kaminski@udel.edu
Web: www.delata.org/scholarship-applications.html

Summary   To provide financial assistance to Hispanic and other ethnic minority members of the National Athletic Trainers' Association (NATA) from Delaware who are working on an undergraduate or graduate degree in the field.

Eligibility   This program is open to NATA members who are members of ethnic diversity groups and residents of Delaware or attending college in that state. Applicants must be enrolled full time in an undergraduate athletic training education program or a graduate athletic training program and have a GPA of 2.5 or higher. They must intend to prepare for the profession of athletic training. Along with their application, they must submit an 800-word statement on their athletic training background, experience, philosophy, and goals. Selection is based equally on academic performance and athletic training clinical achievement.

Financial Data   A stipend is awarded (amount not specified).

Duration   1 year.

Number awarded   1 or more each year.

Deadline   February of each year.

[143]
DIETETIC TECHNICIAN PROGRAM SCHOLARSHIPS

Academy of Nutrition and Dietetics
Attn: Foundation
120 South Riverside Plaza, Suite 2000
Chicago, IL 60606-6995
(312) 899-4821   Toll Free: (800) 877-1600, ext. 4821
Fax: (312) 899-4796   E-mail: scholarship@eatright.org
Web: www.eatrightacend.org

Summary   To provide financial assistance to student members of the Academy of Nutrition and Dietetics, especially Hispanics and other underrepresented minorities, who are in the second year of a dietetic technician program.

Eligibility   This program is open to ADA student members entering the second year of study in an accredited dietetic technician program. Applicants must be U.S. citizens or permanent residents and show evidence of leadership and academic ability. Some scholarships require membership in a specific dietetic practice group, residency in a specific state, or underrepresented minority group status. The same application form can be used for all categories.

Financial Data   Stipends range from $500 to $10,000 but most are for $1,000.

Duration   1 year.

Additional data   The Academy of Nutrition and Dietetics was formerly the American Dietetic Association.

Number awarded   Varies each year.

Deadline   February of each year.

[144]
DIGITASLBI MULTICULTURAL SCHOLARSHIP

American Association of Advertising Agencies
Attn: AAAA Foundation
1065 Avenue of the Americas, 16th Floor
New York, NY 10018
(212) 262-2500   E-mail: ameadows@aaaa.org
Web: www.aaaa.org

Summary   To provide financial assistance to Hispanic and other multicultural students who are working on an undergraduate degree in advertising.

Eligibility   This program is open to undergraduate students of proven multicultural heritage. Applicants must be participating in the Multicultural Advertising Intern Program (MAIP). They must be enrolled at an accredited college or university in the United States and be able to demonstrate financial need.

Financial Data   The stipend is $5,000.

Duration   1 year.

Additional data   This program is funded by DigitasLBi.

Number awarded   1 each year.

Deadline   July of each year.

[145]
DISTRIBUTED RESEARCH EXPERIENCES FOR UNDERGRADUATES

Computing Research Association
1828 L Street, N.W., Suite 800
Washington, DC 20036-4632
(202) 234-2111   Fax: (202) 667-1066
E-mail: dreu@cra.org
Web: www.cra.org/cra-w/dreu

Summary   To provide an opportunity for Hispanic and other underrepresented undergraduate students to work on a summer research project in computer science or engineering.

Eligibility   This program is open to members of underrepresented groups (Hispanics, African Americans, American Indians, women, students with disabilities) who are entering their junior or senior year of college. Applicants must be interested in conducting a summer research project directly related to computer science or computer engineering under the mentorship of a faculty member at the mentor's home university. They must be U.S. citizens or permanent residents. Selection is based on the student's potential for success in graduate school, the extent of the student's experience and skills, the student's potential gain from the experience, and the potential that the student's participation will advance the goals of the program.

Financial Data   Students receive a stipend of $7,000 plus relocation travel assistance up to $500 if appropriate.

Duration   10 weeks during the summer.

Additional data   This program began in 1994 as the Distributed Mentor Project (DMP) by the Computing Research Association's Committee on the Status of Women in Computing Research (CRA-W). In 2007, the Coalition to Diversify Computing (CDC) became a cosponsor of the program and in 2009 it was given its current name. From the beginning, funding has been provided by the National Science Foundation.

Number awarded   Varies each year; recently, 46 students were selected to participate in this program.

Deadline   February of each year.

[146]
DIVERSITY SCHOLARSHIP FOR ENTRY-LEVEL ATHLETIC TRAINING STUDENTS

Indiana Athletic Trainers' Association
Attn: Scholarship Committee
125 West Market Street, Suite 300
Indianapolis, IN 46204
(317) 396-0002, ext. 2   Fax: (317) 634-5964
E-mail: jillewing@thecorydongroup.com
Web: www.iata-usa.org/page-1462928

Summary　To provide financial assistance to undergraduate and graduate student members of the Indiana Athletic Trainers' Association (IATA) who are Hispanics or from another ethnic or social diverse background.

Eligibility　This program is open to members of IATA who are from an ethnic or social diverse background and enrolled as full-time juniors, seniors, or graduate students at a college or university in Indiana. Undergraduates must have been an athletic training student for at least 1 year in a CAATE-accredited program; graduate students must be in the second semester of such a program. All applicants must have a GPA of 3.0 or higher and a sponsor who is a full-time member of the athletic training education program faculty or a full-time member of the athletic training staff. Along with their application, they must submit a brief personal statement on why they chose athletic training as a career and their future plans in the field. Financial need is not considered in the selection process.

Financial Data　The stipend is $1,000.

Duration　1 year.

Number awarded　1 each year.

Deadline　September of each year.

[147]
DIVERSITY SUMMER HEALTH-RELATED RESEARCH EDUCATION PROGRAM

Medical College of Wisconsin
Attn: Office of Student Diversity Affairs
8701 Watertown Plank Road
Milwaukee, WI 53226
(414) 955-8735　　　　　　　　Fax: (414) 955-0129
E-mail: studentdiversity@mcw.edu
Web: www.mcw.edu/Diversity-Programs.htm

Summary　To provide an opportunity for undergraduate residents of any state who are Hispanics or come from other diverse backgrounds to participate in a summer research training experience at the Medical College of Wisconsin.

Eligibility　This program is open to U.S. citizens and permanent residents who come from an ethnically, economically, and/or educationally disadvantaged backgrounds. The program targets African Americans, Mexican-Americans, Native Americans (American Indians, Alaska Natives, and Native Hawaiians), Pacific Islanders, Hmong, mainland Puerto Ricans, and individuals with disabilities. Applicants must be interested in participating in a summer research training program at the Medical College of Wisconsin. They must have completed at least 1 year of undergraduate study at an accredited college or university (or be a community college student enrolled in at least 3 courses per academic term) and have a GPA of 3.4 or higher.

Financial Data　The stipend is $10 per hour for a 40-hour week. Housing is provided for students who live outside Milwaukee County and travel expenses are paid for those who live outside Wisconsin.

Duration　10 weeks during the summer.

Additional data　Students are "matched" with a full-time faculty investigator to participate in a research project addressing the causes, prevention, and treatment of cardiovascular, pulmonary, or hematological diseases. This program is funded by the National Heart, Lung, and Blood Institute (NHLBI) of the National Institutes of Health (NIH). Partic-

ipants are required to prepare an abstract of their research and make a brief oral presentation of their project at the conclusion of the summer.

Number awarded　Approximately 12 each year.

Deadline　January of each year.

[148]
DIVISION OF PHYSICAL SCIENCES RESEARCH EXPERIENCE FOR UNDERGRADUATES

American Museum of Natural History
Attn: Division of Physical Sciences
Central Park West at 79th Street
New York, NY 10024-5192
(212) 769-5055　　　　　E-mail: Fellowships-rggs@amnh.org
Web: www.amnh.org

Summary　To provide an opportunity for undergraduate students, especially those from Hispanic or other Minority Serving Institutions, to gain research experience in designated physical sciences during the summer at the American Museum of Natural History in New York City.

Eligibility　This program is open to U.S. citizens and permanent residents who are currently working on a bachelor's degree. Applicants must be interested in participating in a research project at the American Museum of Natural History in the fields of earth and planetary sciences or astrophysics. Applications are especially encouraged from students who attend minority-serving institutions.

Financial Data　Participants receive a stipend of approximately $5,100, dormitory housing on a nearby university campus or an equivalent housing stipend, a subsistence allowance, and (depending on need) reimbursement of travel costs to and from New York.

Duration　Approximately 10 weeks during the summer.

Additional data　This program is sponsored by the National Science Foundation as part of its Research Experiences for Undergraduates (REU) program.

Number awarded　Approximately 8 each year.

Deadline　January of each year.

[149]
DOLLARS FOR SCHOLARS PROGRAM

United Methodist Higher Education Foundation
Attn: Scholarships Administrator
60 Music Square East, Suite 350
P.O. Box 340005
Nashville, TN 37203-0005
(615) 649-3990　　　　　　　Toll Free: (800) 811-8110
Fax: (615) 649-3980
E-mail: umhefscholarships@umhef.org
Web: www.umhef.org/online_applications/umdfs

Summary　To provide financial assistance to students, especially Hispanics and other minorities, at Methodist colleges, universities, and seminaries whose home churches agree to contribute to their support.

Eligibility　The Double Your Dollars for Scholars program is open to students attending or planning to attend a United Methodist-related college, university, or seminary as a full-time student. Applicants must have been an active, full member of a United Methodist Church for at least 1 year prior to applying. Their home church must nominate them and agree to contribute to their support. Many of the United Methodist colleges and universities have also agreed to contribute matching funds for a Triple Your Dollars for Scholars Program, and a few United Methodist conference foundations have agreed to contribute additional matching funds for a Quadruple Your Dollars for Scholars Program. Awards are granted on a first-come, first-served basis. Some of the awards are designated for Hispanic, Asian, and Native American (HANA) students funded by the General Board of Higher Education and Ministry.

Financial Data The sponsoring church contributes $1,000 and the United Methodist Higher Education Foundation (UMHEF) contributes a matching $1,000. Students who attend a participating United Methodist college or university receive an additional $1,000 for the Triple Your Dollars for Scholars Program, and those from a participating conference receive a fourth $1,000 increment for the Quadruple Your Dollars for Scholars Program.

Duration 1 year; may be renewed as long as the recipients maintain satisfactory academic progress as defined by their institution.

Additional data Currently, participants in the Double Your Dollars for Scholars program include 1 United Methodist seminary and theological school, 1 professional school, and 21 senior colleges and universities. The Triple Your Dollars for Scholars program includes a total of 13 United Methodist seminaries and theological schools, 70 senior colleges and universities, and 4 2-year colleges (for a complete list, consult the UMHEF). A total of 16 conference foundations participate in the Quadruple Your Dollars for Scholars Program.

Number awarded 600 each year, including 25 designated for HANA students.

Deadline Local churches must submit applications in February of each year for senior colleges, universities, and seminaries or May of each year for 2-year colleges.

[150]
DOMINION DIVERSITY SCHOLARSHIP PROGRAM

Dominion Resources Inc.
Attn: Diversity Team
701 East Cary Street, 13th Floor
Richmond, VA 23219
(804) 819-2000   E-mail: diversity@dom.com
Web: www.dom.com

Summary To provide financial assistance and work experience to high school seniors and college students who are Hispanics or will contribute to the diversity of the sponsor in other ways.

Eligibility This program is open to high school seniors and current college students who will not graduate for at least 2 years. Community college students must be enrolled in a program that will prepare them to transfer to a 4-year institution. Applicants must commit to a paid intern work session during the summer following their first year of scholarship support. Along with their application, they must submit an essay of 1,000 to 1,250 words that 1) describes the experiences or ideas they would bring to the diversity of the sponsor; 2) includes the new perspectives or new talents they will contribute to the sponsor; and 3) describes how this diversity scholarship program will help them achieve their career goals. The sponsor defines diversity to include minorities, women, protected veterans, and individuals with disabilities.

Financial Data The scholarship stipend is $5,000. A competitive salary is paid for the internship.

Duration 1 year for the scholarship; 10 to 12 weeks during the summer for the internship.

Additional data The sponsor operates electric distribution and transmission companies in North Carolina and Virginia and natural gas distribution companies in Ohio and West Virginia.

Number awarded 30 each year.

Deadline May of each year.

[151]
DON SAHLI–KATHY WOODALL MINORITY STUDENT SCHOLARSHIP

Tennessee Education Association
Attn: Sahli-Woodall Scholarship Fund
801 Second Avenue North
Nashville, TN 37201-1099
(615) 242-8392   Toll Free: (800) 342-8367
Fax: (615) 259-4581   E-mail: jdemain@tea.nea.org
Web: www.teateachers.org

Summary To provide financial assistance to Hispanic and other minority high school seniors in Tennessee who are interested in majoring in education at a college or university in the state.

Eligibility This program is open to minority high school seniors in Tennessee who are planning to attend a college or university in the state and major in education. Application must be made either by a Future Teachers of America chapter affiliated with the Tennessee Education Association (TEA) or by the student with the recommendation of an active TEA member. Selection is based on academic record, leadership ability, financial need, and demonstrated interest in becoming a teacher.

Financial Data The stipend is $1,000.

Duration 1 year.

Number awarded 1 each year.

Deadline February of each year.

[152]
DONALD AND ITASKER THORNTON MEMORIAL SCHOLARSHIP

Thornton Sisters Foundation
P.O. Box 21
Atlantic Highlands, NJ 07716-0021
(732) 872-1353   E-mail: tsfoundation2001@yahoo.com
Web: www.thornton-sisters.com/ttsf.htm

Summary To provide financial assistance for college to Latino and other women of color in New Jersey.

Eligibility This program is open to women of color (defined as Latino Americans, African Americans, Caribbean Americans, and Native Americans) who are graduating from high schools in New Jersey. Applicants must have a grade average of "C+" or higher and be able to document financial need. They must be planning to attend an accredited 4-year college or university. Along with their application, they must submit a 500-word essay describing their family background, personal and financial hardships, honors or academic distinctions, and community involvement and activities.

Financial Data A stipend is awarded (amount not specified). Funds are to be used for tuition and/or books.

Duration 1 year; nonrenewable.
Number awarded 1 or more each year.
Deadline May of each year.

[153]
DR. AMANDA PEREZ SCHOLARSHIP

Latino Medical Student Association-West Region
c/o Susie Sandoval, Scholarship Vice President
USC Keck School of Medicine
1975 Zonal Avenue
Los Angeles, CA 90033
E-mail: vp_scholarship@lmsa.net
Web: www.lmsa.net

Summary To provide financial assistance to high school seniors and college freshmen who are pre-medical student members of the Latino Medical Student Association (LMSA) in its western region and planning to attend medical school.

Eligibility This program is open to high school seniors and college freshmen who are LMSA members, residents of its western region (Arizona, California, Oregon, Utah, and Washington), and enrolled or planning to enroll in a pre-medical program at a 4-year university in any state. Applicants should be able to demonstrate a desire to advance the state of health care and education in Latino communities through extracurricular activities and/or membership in civic organizations. They must be committed to preparing for a professional career in medicine and dedicated to serving the Latino and underserved communities. Along with their application, they must submit a 1-page personal statement describing their family and personal background, educational objectives, community involvement, financial need, and how they would assist LMSA in its mission to provide health care to the Latino and underserved communities.

Financial Data A stipend is awarded (amount not specified).

Duration 1 year.

Additional data Until 2002, this organization was known as the Chicano/Latino Medical Student Association of California. This program was established in 2008.

Number awarded Varies each year.

Deadline May of each year.

[154]
DR. JO ANN OTA FUJIOKA SCHOLARSHIP

Phi Delta Kappa International
Attn: PDK Educational Foundation
320 West Eighth Street, Suite 216
P.O. Box 7888
Bloomington, IN 47407-7888
(812) 339-1156   Toll Free: (800) 766-1156
Fax: (812) 339-0018   E-mail: scholarships@pdkintl.org
Web: www.pdkintl.org

Summary To provide financial assistance to Hispanic high school seniors and other undergraduates of color who plan to study education at a college in any state and have a connection to Phi Delta Kappa (PDK).

Eligibility This program is open to high school seniors and undergraduates of color who are majoring or planning to major in education and can meet 1 of the following criteria: 1) is a member of Educators Rising (formerly the Future Educators Association); 2) is the child or grandchild of a PDK mem-

ber; or 3) has a reference letter written by a PDK member. Also eligible are undergraduate members of PDK or Educators Rising who are enrolled in a college education program. Applicants must submit a 500-word essay on a topic related to education that changes annually. Selection is based on the essay, academic standing, letters of recommendation, service activities, educational activities, and leadership activities; financial need is not considered.

Financial Data The stipend is $2,000.

Duration 1 year.

Additional data This program began in 2006.

Number awarded 1 each year.

Deadline March of each year.

[155]
DR. JUAN ANDRADE, JR. SCHOLARSHIP FOR YOUNG HISPANIC LEADERS

United States Hispanic Leadership Institute
Attn: Scholarship Committee
431 South Dearborn Street, Suite 1203
Chicago, IL 60605
(312) 427-8683   Toll Free: (800) 959-5151
Fax: (312) 427-5183   E-mail: acalderon@ushli.org
Web: www.ushli.org

Summary To provide financial assistance for college to Hispanic students in the United States.

Eligibility This program is open to residents of the United States and its territories who are enrolled or accepted for enrollment as full-time students at a 2- or 4-year college or university in the United States. Non-citizens (DACA or undocumented) are eligible. Applicants must have at least 1 parent of Hispanic ancestry. They must be able to demonstrate financial need. Along with their application, they must submit essays of 500 to 1,000 words on 1) a self-description that includes their family history, life and/or work experiences that have influenced them, and pertinent extracurricular and community involvement activities; and 2) the most pervasive issue in their community, how they will address it, and how their education and career experience will help them address that issue.

Financial Data The stipend is $1,000 for students at 4-year institutions or $500 for students at 2-year institutions.

Duration 1 year; nonrenewable.

Additional data This program began in 1994. Recipients are expected to pay for their own travel expenses to Chicago to attend a luncheon of the sponsor where they are introduced. Expenses for lodging and meals are covered by the sponsor.

Number awarded Varies each year; recently, 20 were awarded.

Deadline December of each year.

[156]
DR. JUAN D. VILLARREAL SCHOLARSHIPS

Hispanic Dental Association
Attn: HDA Foundation
3910 South IH-35, Suite 245
Austin, TX 78704
(512) 904-0252   E-mail: jessicac@hdassoc.org
Web: www.hdassoc.org

Summary To provide financial assistance to members of the Hispanic Dental Association (HDA) interested in studying dentistry or dental hygiene at institutions in Texas.

Eligibility This program is open to HDA members who have been accepted or are currently enrolled at an accredited dental school or dental hygiene program in Texas as a full-time student. Applicants must have a GPA of 3.0 or higher, an interest in improving the health of the Hispanic community, and a demonstrated commitment and dedication to serving the Hispanic community. Along with their application, they must submit a 250-word essay on their career goals, including how they were inspired to become a dentist or dental hygienist. Selection is based on academic achievement, leadership skills, community service, and commitment and dedication to improving the oral health of the Hispanic community.

Financial Data Stipends are $1,000 for dental students or $500 for dental hygiene students. An additional grant of $200 is provided for travel reimbursement and complimentary registration to the HDA annual meeting.

Duration 1 year.

Additional data This program began in 1995.

Number awarded 2 each year.

Deadline May of each year.

[157]
DR. MARTIN LUTHER KING, JR. SCHOLARSHIP

North Carolina Association of Educators, Inc.
Attn: Human and Civil Rights Commission
700 South Salisbury Street
P.O. Box 27347
Raleigh, NC 27611-7347
(919) 832-3000, ext. 203
Toll Free: (800) 662-7924, ext. 203
Fax: (919) 839-8229   E mail: derevana.leach@ncae.org
Web: www.ncae.org/get-involved/awards

Summary To provide financial assistance to Hispanic and other minority high school seniors in North Carolina who plan to attend college in any state.

Eligibility This program is open to seniors graduating from high schools in North Carolina who plan to attend a college or university in any state. They must have a GPA of 2.5 or higher. Along with their application, they must submit 1-page essays on 1) how the philosophies and ideals of Dr. Martin Luther King influenced their life; and 2) why they feel they deserve this scholarship and their need for financial assistance. Selection is based on those essays; academic record; a resume of accomplishments, extracurricular activities, scholarships, affiliations, and organizations; and 2 letters of recommendation.

Financial Data A stipend is awarded (amount not specified).

Duration 1 year.

Additional data This program was established in 1992 by the Minority Affairs Commission of the North Carolina Association of Educators (NCAE). It currently operates in partnership with the North Carolina Foundation for Public School Children.

Number awarded 1 or more each year.

Deadline January of each year.

[158]
DR. ROLANDO ANDRADE SCHOLARSHIPS

Educators and Community Helping Hispanics Onward
c/o Dean Altstaetter, Scholarship Committee
Ohio Northern University
Office of Admissions
Weber Hall 111
525 South Main Street
Ada, OH 45810
(419) 772-2274   E-mail: president@echho.org
Web: www.echho.org/scholarships.html

Summary To provide financial assistance to Hispanic Americans in Ohio who are interested in attending college in the state.

Eligibility This program is open to residents of Ohio who are of Hispanic origin and graduating high school seniors, GED recipients, current undergraduate students, or nontraditional (over 23 years of age) students. Applicants must be attending or planning to attend a postsecondary institution in Ohio that is a member of Educators and Community Helping Hispanics Onward (ECHHO). They must have a GPA of 2.5 or higher or a GED score of at least 450. Along with their application, they must submit a 500-word essay describing themselves; their abilities, interests, academic and professional goals, and experiences; and how those relate to their Hispanic heritage. Financial need is not considered in the selection process.

Financial Data The stipend is $1,000.

Duration 1 year.

Number awarded Varies each year; recently, 6 were awarded.

Deadline May of each year.

[159]
DUKE ENERGY HISPANICS IN ENGINEERING SCHOLARSHIP

North Carolina Society of Hispanic Professionals
Attn: North Carolina Hispanic College Fund
8450 Chapel Hill Road, Suite 209
Cary, NC 27513
(919) 467-8424   Fax: (919) 469-1785
E-mail: mailbox@thencshp.org
Web: www.thencshp.org/programs/nc-hispanic-college-fund

Summary To provide financial assistance to Hispanic residents of North Carolina who are interested in majoring in specified fields of engineering at colleges in the state.

Eligibility This program is open to residents of North Carolina who are of Hispanic background (both parents are at least half Hispanic or 1 parent is fully Hispanic) and either 1) are graduating high school seniors; or 2) graduated from high school within the past 2 years. Applicants must be enrolled or planning to enroll at a university or community college in the state and study chemical, civil, electrical, mechanical, or nuclear engineering. They must have a high school GPA of 2.5 or higher. Along with their application, they must submit a 500-word essay on why their Hispanic parentage and family background are important to them, personal and/or academic achievements, academic plans and career goals, and past and current efforts (as well as future plans) towards making a difference in their community. Preference is given to foreign-born applicants and the native-born children of foreign-born parents. Selection is based on academic achievement, community involvement, volunteerism, leadership, and family economic need.

Financial Data Stipends range from $500 to $2,500 per year. Funds are paid directly to the college or university.

Duration 1 year; may be renewed up to 3 additional years.

Additional data This program is sponsored by Duke Energy Foundation.

Number awarded 1 or more each year.

Deadline January of each year.

[160]
DWIGHT DAVID EISENHOWER TRANSPORTATION FELLOWSHIP PROGRAM FOR HISPANIC SERVING INSTITUTIONS

Department of Transportation
Federal Highway Administration
Attn: Universities and Grants Programs
4600 North Fairfax Drive, Suite 800
Arlington, VA 22203-1553
(703) 235-0538   Toll Free: (877) 558-6873
Fax: (703) 235-0593   E-mail: transportationedu@dot.gov
Web: www.fhwa.dot.gov/tpp/ddetfp.htm

Summary To provide financial assistance to undergraduate and graduate students working on a degree in a transportation-related field at an Hispanic Serving Institution (HSI).

Eligibility This program is open to students working on a bachelor's, master's, or doctoral degree at a federally-designated 4-year HSI. Applicants must be working on a degree in a transportation-related field (e.g., engineering, business, aviation, architecture, public policy and analysis, urban and regional planning). They must be U.S. citizens or have an I-20 (foreign student) or I-551 (permanent resident) identification card. Undergraduates must be entering at least their junior year and have a GPA of 3.0 or higher. Graduate students must have a GPA of at least 3.25. Selection is based on their proposed plan of study, academic achievement (based on class standing, GPA, and transcripts), transportation work experience, and letters of recommendation.

Financial Data Fellows receive payment of full tuition and fees (to a maximum of $10,000) and a monthly stipend of $1,450 for undergraduates, $1,700 for master's students, or $2,000 for doctoral students. They are also provided with a 1-time allowance of up to $1,500 to attend the annual Transportation Research Board (TRB) meeting.

Duration 1 year.

Additional data This program is administered by the participating HSIs: California State University at Fullerton, California State University at Los Angeles, City College of New York, Florida International University, Texas A&M University at Kingsville, the University of Puerto Rico at Mayaguez, the University of Texas at El Paso, the University of Texas at San Antonio, or Washington State University Tri Cities.

Number awarded Varies each year; recently, 28 were awarded.

Deadline January of each year.

[161]
DWIGHT MOSLEY SCHOLARSHIPS

United States Tennis Association
Attn: USTA Foundation
70 West Red Oak Lane
White Plains, NY 10604
(914) 696-7223   Fax: (914) 697-2307
E-mail: foundation@usta.com
Web: www.ustafoundation.com

Summary To provide financial assistance to female and male high school seniors (judged separately) who are Hispanics or from other diverse ethnic backgrounds, have participated in an organized community tennis program, and plan to attend college in any state.

Eligibility This program is open to high school seniors from diverse ethnic backgrounds who have excelled academically, demonstrated achievements in leadership, and participated extensively in an organized community tennis program. Applicants must be planning to enroll as a full-time undergraduate student at a 4-year college or university. They must have a GPA of 3.0 or higher and be able to demonstrate financial need and sportsmanship. Along with their application, they must submit an essay of 1 to 2 pages about how their participation in a tennis and education program has influenced their life, including examples of special mentors, volunteer service, and future goals. Females and males are considered separately.

Financial Data The stipend is $2,500 per year. Funds are paid directly to the recipient's college or university.

Duration 4 years.

Number awarded 2 each year: 1 female and 1 male.

Deadline February of each year.

[162]
EARLINE S. ROGERS STUDENT TEACHING STIPEND FOR MINORITIES

Indiana Commission for Higher Education
Attn: Financial Aid and Student Support Services
101 West Ohio Street, Suite 300
Indianapolis, IN 46204-4206
(317) 232-1023   Toll Free: (888) 528-4719 (within IN)
Fax: (317) 232-3260   E-mail: Scholars@che.in.gov
Web: www.in.gov/che/4511.htm

Summary To provide scholarship/loans to Hispanic and Black undergraduate students in Indiana interested in participating in student teaching at a college in the state.

Eligibility This program is open to Hispanic and Black students seeking certification in order to teach at an accredited elementary or secondary school in Indiana. Applicants must be Indiana residents and U.S. citizens or permanent residents who are enrolled as full-time students at an academic institution in Indiana. They must be entering a student teaching program or a school administration internship. Their GPA must qualify them for admission to their college's school of education.

Financial Data For students whose GPA is greater than 3.5, the stipend is $5,000. For students whose GPA is greater than 3.0 but less than 3.5, the stipend is $4,000. Recipients must agree in writing to apply for a teaching or administration position at an accredited school in Indiana following certification and, if hired, to teach or work as an administrator for at least 3 years.

Duration 1 year.

Additional data This program began in 2013 and was given its current name in 2016. Participating colleges in Indiana select the recipients. Students must submit their application to the financial aid office of the college they attend.

Number awarded Varies each year.

Deadline October of each year for students who begin student teaching in the fall; January of each year for students who begin student teaching in the spring.

[163]
EAST TENNESSEE CHAPTER AABE SCHOLARSHIPS

American Association of Blacks in Energy-East
  Tennessee Chapter
Attn: Chair of Scholarship and Fundraising Committee
P.O. Box 11446
Chattanooga, TN 37401
E-mail: irvinjo@epb.net
Web: www.aabe.org

Summary To provide financial assistance to Hispanics and members of other underrepresented minority groups who are high school seniors in Tennessee and planning to major in an energy-related field at a college in any state.

Eligibility This program is open to seniors graduating from high schools in Tennessee and planning to attend a college or university in any state. Applicants must be Hispanics, African Americans, or Native Americans who have a GPA of 3.0 or higher and can demonstrate financial need. Their intended major must be business, engineering, technology, mathematics, the physical sciences, or other energy-related field. Along with their application, they must submit a description of why they need this scholarship and how the money will aid them in reaching their educational and/or career goals. U.S. citizenship is required.

Financial Data The stipend is $1,500.

Duration 1 year.

Additional data Winners are eligible to compete for regional and national scholarships. This program is supported by the Tennessee Valley Authority (TVA).

Number awarded 2 each year.

Deadline April of each year.

[164]
EASTMAN SCHOLARSHIP OF THE SOCIETY OF HISPANIC PROFESSIONAL ENGINEERS

Society of Hispanic Professional Engineers
Attn: Scholarships
13181 Crossroads Parkway North, Suite 450
City of Industry, CA 91715
(323) 725-3970, ext. 108   Fax: (323) 725-0316
E-mail: scholarships@shpe.org
Web: shpe.awardspring.com

Summary To provide financial assistance to Hispanic undergraduate students who are working on a degree in specified fields of engineering.

Eligibility This program is open to U.S. citizens and permanent residents of Hispanic descent who are enrolled full time at a college or university in the United States or Puerto

Rico. Applicants must be sophomores, juniors, or seniors majoring in chemical, electrical, or mechanical engineering. They must be members of the Society of Hispanic Professional Engineers (SHPE) and have a GPA of 3.0 or higher. Selection is based on academic standing and financial need.

Financial Data The stipend is $5,000.

Duration 1 year.

Additional data This program is sponsored by Eastman Chemical Company.

Number awarded 1 or more each year.

Deadline July of each year.

[165]
ED BRADLEY SCHOLARSHIP

Radio Television Digital News Foundation
Attn: Membership and Programs Manager
529 14th Street, N.W., Suite 1240
Washington, DC 20045
(202) 662-7257   Fax: (202) 223-4007
E-mail: karenh@rtdna.org
Web: www.rtdna.org/content/ed_bradley_scholarship

Summary To provide financial assistance to Hispanic and other minority undergraduate students who are preparing for a career in electronic journalism.

Eligibility This program is open to sophomore or more advanced minority undergraduate students enrolled in an electronic journalism sequence at an accredited or nationally-recognized college or university. Applicants must submit a cover letter that discusses their current and past journalism experience, describes how they would use the funds if they were to receive the scholarship, discusses their reasons for preparing for a career in electronic journalism, and includes 3 to 5 links to their best and most relevant work samples.

Financial Data The stipend is $10,000, paid in semiannual installments of $5,000 each.

Duration 1 year.

Additional data The Radio Television Digital News Foundation (RTDNF) was formerly the Radio and Television News Directors Foundation (RTNDF).

Number awarded 1 each year.

Deadline May of each year.

[166]
EDSA MINORITY SCHOLARSHIP

Landscape Architecture Foundation
Attn: Leadership in Landscape Scholarship Program
1129 20th Street, N.W., Suite 202
Washington, DC 20036
(202) 331-7070   Fax: (202) 331-7079
E-mail: scholarships@lafoundation.org
Web: www.lafoundation.org

Summary To provide financial assistance to Hispanic and other minority college students who are interested in studying landscape architecture.

Eligibility This program is open to Hispanic, African American, Native American, and minority college students of other cultural and ethnic backgrounds. Applicants must be entering their final 2 years of undergraduate study in landscape architecture or working on a graduate degree in that field. Along with their application, they must submit a 500-word essay on a design or research effort they plan to pursue (explaining how it will contribute to the advancement of the profession and to their ethnic heritage), 3 work samples, and 2 letters of recommendation. Selection is based on professional experience, community involvement, extracurricular activities, and financial need.

Financial Data The stipend is $5,000.

Additional data This scholarship was formerly designated the Edward D. Stone, Jr. and Associates Minority Scholarship.

Number awarded 1 each year.

Deadline February of each year.

[167]
EDUCATIONAL FOUNDATION OF THE COLORADO SOCIETY OF CERTIFIED PUBLIC ACCOUNTANTS MINORITY SCHOLARSHIPS

Colorado Society of Certified Public Accountants
Attn: Educational Foundation
7887 East Belleview Avenue, Suite 200
Englewood, CO 80111
(303) 773-2877   Toll Free: (800) 523-9082 (within CO)
Fax: (303) 773-6344
Web: www.cocpa.org

Summary To provide financial assistance to Hispanic and other minority upper-division and graduate students in Colorado who are majoring in accounting.

Eligibility This program is open to Colorado minority residents (Hispanic or Latino, Black or African American, Native American, Asian American) who are upper-division or graduate students at colleges and universities in the state and have completed at least 6 semester hours of accounting courses. Applicants must have a GPA of at least 3.0 overall and 3.25 in accounting classes. They must be U.S. citizens or noncitizens legally living and studying in Colorado with a valid visa that enables them to become employed. Financial need is not considered in the selection process.

Financial Data The stipend is $2,500. Funds are paid directly to the recipient's school to be used for books, C.P.A. review materials, tuition, fees, and dormitory room and board.

Duration 1 year; recipients may reapply.

Number awarded 1 or more each year.

Deadline May of each year for fall semester or quarter; November of each year for winter quarter or spring semester.

[168]
EDWARD S. ROTH SCHOLARSHIP

Society of Manufacturing Engineers
Attn: SME Education Foundation
One SME Drive
P.O. Box 930
Dearborn, MI 48121-0930
(313) 425-3300   Toll Free: (866) 547-6333
Fax: (313) 425-3411   E-mail: foundation@sme.org
Web: www.smeef.org

Summary To provide financial assistance to students, especially Hispanics and other minorities, who are working on or planning to work on a bachelor's or master's degree in manufacturing engineering at selected universities.

Eligibility This program is open to U.S. citizens who are graduating high school seniors or currently-enrolled undergraduate or graduate students. Applicants must be enrolled or planning to enroll as a full-time student at 1 of 13 selected 4-year universities to work on a bachelor's or master's degree in manufacturing engineering. They must have a GPA of 3.0 or higher. Preference is given to 1) students demonstrating financial need; 2) minority students; and 3) students participating in a co-op program. Along with their application, they must submit a brief statement about why they chose their major, their career and educational objectives, and how this scholarship will help them attain those objectives.

Financial Data Stipends range from $1,000 to $6,000 and recently averaged approximately $2,000.

Duration 1 year; may be renewed.

Additional data The eligible institutions are California Polytechnic State University at San Luis Obispo, California State Polytechnic State University at Pomona, University of Miami (Florida), Bradley University (Illinois), Central State University (Ohio), Miami University (Ohio), Boston University, Worcester Polytechnic Institute (Massachusetts), University of Massachusetts, St. Cloud State University (Minnesota), University of Texas at Rio Grande Valley, Brigham Young University (Utah), and Utah State University.

Number awarded 2 each year.

Deadline January of each year.

[169]
ELAINE REIKO AKAGI SCHOLARSHIP

Japanese American Citizens League-Seattle Chapter
P.O. Box 18558
Seattle, WA 98118
(253) 256-2204   E-mail: bcaldwell44@yahoo.com
Web: www.jaclseattle.org

Summary To provide financial assistance to Hispanics and other people of color who are working on a degree in special education at a school in any state.

Eligibility This program is open to people of color who are enrolled at a college or university in any state. Applicants must have a declared major in special education and a GPA of 2.5 or higher. Along with their application, they must submit a list of extracurricular and community activities, 2 letters of recommendation, a list of awards or recognitions they have earned, and a 500-word essay on the importance of increasing the number of teachers of color in special education classrooms. In the selection process, consideration is given to how the applicants plan to give back to the education community, the reasons they wish to prepare for the field of education, their experiences in working with children with disabilities, their experience working with children of color, and the teaching field in which they are specializing; financial need is not considered.

Financial Data The stipend is $3,000.

Duration 1 year.

Additional data This program began in 2011.

Number awarded 1 each year.

Deadline March of each year.

[170]
EMERGING ARCHIVAL SCHOLARS PROGRAM

Archival Education and Research Institute
Center for Information as Evidence
c/o UCLA Graduate School of Education and Information Studies
Office of External Relations
2043 Moore Hall
Los Angeles, CA 90095-1521
(310) 206-0375   Fax: (310) 794-5324
Web: aeri.gseis.ucla.edu/fellowships.htm

Summary To provide an opportunity for Hispanic and other minority undergraduate and graduate students to learn more about the field of archival studies and to be exposed to research in the field.

Eligibility This program is open to undergraduates who have completed their junior year and to students who have completed the first year of a master's degree program. Applicants must be African American, Hispanic/Latino, Asian/Pacific Islander, Native American, Puerto Rican, or any other person who will add diversity to the field of archival studies. They must have a GPA of 3.0 or higher, but they may be working on a degree in any field and are not required to have prior knowledge of or experience in archival studies. U.S. citizenship or permanent resident status is required. Applicants must be interested in attending the week-long Archival Education and Research Institute (AERI), held at a different university each summer, where they are assigned both a faculty research mentor and a Ph.D. student mentor who introduce them to doctoral research and careers in archival studies.

Financial Data Grants provide payment of round-trip travel, accommodation, and most meals.

Duration These grants are offered annually.

Additional data This program, first offered in 2009, is supported by the Institute of Museum and Library Services. Scholars who indicate an interest in continuing on to a doctoral program in archival studies after completing the AERI may be invited to participate in a supervised research project that will last up to 1 year and to present results of their research in a poster session at the AERI of the following year.

Number awarded Up to 7 each year.

Deadline April of each year.

[171]
EMMA L. BOWEN FOUNDATION INTERNSHIPS

Emma L. Bowen Foundation
Attn: Senior Vice President, Eastern Region and National Recruitment
30 Rockefeller Plaza
(Campus 1221 Avenue of the Americas #28A41)
New York, NY 10112
(212) 975-2545   E-mail: sdrice@cbs.com
Web: www.emmabowenfoundation.com

Summary To provide financial assistance and work experience to Hispanic and other minority students interested in preparing for a career in the media industry.

Eligibility This program is open to minority students who are rising high school seniors, graduating high school seniors, or college freshmen. Applicants must be interested in working at a media company during the summer and school breaks until they graduate from college. They must

have a GPA of 3.0 or higher, plans to attend an accredited 4-year college or university, and an interest in the media industry as a career. Along with their application, they must submit an essay of 500 to 1,000 words on how the media industry helps to create the images that influence our decisions and perceptions on a daily basis. U.S. citizenship or permanent resident status is required.

Financial Data Interns receive a stipend of $2,500 to $3,000 and matching compensation of $2,500 to $3,000 to help pay for college tuition and other expenses.

Duration 1 summer for the internship; 1 academic year for the educational support; may be renewed until the intern graduates from college if he or she maintains a GPA of 3.0 or higher.

Additional data This program began in 1989. The sponsoring companies have included Broadcast Music Inc., CBS Incorporated, Charter Communications, Comcast NBC Universal, C-SPAN, Cox Communications, Fox Television Stations, Inc., Gannett Television, National Association of Broadcasters Educational Foundation, Turner Entertainment Networks.

Number awarded Approximately 60 to 70 new interns are selected each year.

Deadline Applications may be submitted at any time.

[172]
EMPIRE STATE DIVERSITY HONORS SCHOLARSHIP PROGRAM

State University of New York
Attn: Office of Diversity, Equity and Inclusion
State University Plaza, T1000A
353 Broadway
Albany, NY 12246
(518) 320-1189   E-mail: carlos.medina@suny.edu
Web: system.suny.edu/odei/diversity-programs

Summary To provide financial assistance to residents of New York who are attending campuses of the State University of New York (SUNY) who are Hispanics or will contribute to the diversity of the student body in other ways.

Eligibility This program is open to U.S. citizens and permanent residents who are New York residents and enrolled as undergraduate students at any of the participating SUNY colleges. Applicants must be able to demonstrate 1) how they will contribute to the diversity of the student body, primarily by having overcome a disadvantage or other impediment to success in higher education; and 2) high academic achievement. Economic disadvantage, although not a requirement, may be the basis for eligibility. Membership in a racial or ethnic group that is underrepresented at the applicant's school or program may serve as a plus factor in making awards, but may not form the sole basis of selection.

Financial Data The maximum stipend provided by the SUNY system is half the student's cost of attendance or $3,000, whichever is less. The individual campus must match the SUNY award in an equal amount.

Duration 1 year; renewable.

Number awarded Varies each year; recently, 929 students at 41 SUNY institutions received support from this program.

Deadline Deadline not specified.

[173]
EMPOWER BOOK SCHOLARSHIPS

Greater Washington Urban League
Attn: Thursday Network
Kristin Shymoniak
P.O. Box 73203
Washington, DC 20056-3202
E-mail: scholarship@thursdaynetwork.org
Web: www.thursdaynetwork.org/signature-programs

Summary To provide financial assistance to Hispanic and African American high school seniors in the service area of the Greater Washington Urban League (GWUL) who plan to attend college in any state.

Eligibility This program is open to Hispanic/Latino and African American seniors graduating from high schools in Washington, D.C., Prince George's County (Maryland), or Montgomery County (Maryland) and planning to enroll at a 4-year college or university in any state. Applicants must have a GPA of 2.5 or higher. Along with their application, they must submit copies of their SAT or ACT scores, documentation of financial need, and 2 essays of up to 500 words each on topics that change annually but relate to their community service. U.S. citizenship is required.

Financial Data Stipends are $500 or $1,000. Funds are paid directly to the recipient's institution to assist in the purchase of books.

Duration 1 year.

Additional data This program is operated by the Thursday Network, the young professionals' auxiliary of the GWUL, as part of its Young Blacks Give Back (YBGB) Month.

Number awarded Varies each year; recently, 3 at $1,000 and 4 at $500 were awarded.

Deadline January of each year.

[174]
ENCOURAGE MINORITY PARTICIPATION IN OCCUPATIONS WITH EMPHASIS ON REHABILITATION

Allina Health System
Courage Kenny Rehabilitation Institute-Volunteer
  Services
Attn: EMPOWER Scholarship Committee
3915 Golden Valley Road
Minneapolis, MN 55422
(612) 775-2728   E-mail: ckriempower@allina.com
Web: www.allinahealth.org

Summary To provide financial assistance to Hispanics and other students of color from Minnesota and western Wisconsin interested in attending college in any state to prepare for a career in the medical rehabilitation field.

Eligibility This program is open to ethnically diverse students accepted at or enrolled in an institution of higher learning in any state. Applicants must be residents of Minnesota or western Wisconsin (Burnett, Pierce, Polk, and St. Croix counties). They must be able to demonstrate a career interest in the medical rehabilitation field by a record of volunteer involvement related to health care and must have a GPA of 2.0 or higher. Along with their application, they must submit a 1-page essay that covers their medical/rehabilitation career-related volunteer service, including detailed information about patients or clients with whom they worked, what they

did, what they think they accomplished and gained from their experience and how it will assist them in your future endeavors. Financial need is considered in the selection process.

Financial Data The stipend is $1,500.

Duration 1 year.

Additional data This program, established in 1995 by the Courage Center, is also identified by its acronym as the EMPOWER Scholarship Award. The Courage Kenny Rehabilitation Institute was established in 2013 when Courage Center merged with the Sister Kenny Rehabilitation Institute and became part of Allina Health.

Number awarded 2 each year.

Deadline May of each year.

[175]
ENDOCRINE SOCIETY SUMMER RESEARCH FELLOWSHIPS

Endocrine Society
Attn: Summer Research Fellowships
2055 L Street, N.W., Suite 600
Washington, DC 20036
(202) 971-3636   Toll Free: (888) 363-6274
Fax: (202) 736-9705   E-mail: awards@endo-society.org
Web: www.endocrine.org

Summary To provide funding to undergraduate, medical, and graduate students, especially Hispanics and other underrepresented minorities, who are interested in conducting a summer research project in endocrinology.

Eligibility This program is open to full-time students who are undergraduates in the third year of study or higher, medical students beyond their first year of study, and first-year graduate students. Applicants must be interested in participating in a research project under the supervision of a mentor. The mentor must be an active member of the Endocrine Society. Each member may sponsor only 1 student. Projects must be relevant to an aspect of endocrinology and are expected to have clearly defined research goals; students should not function as aides or general research assistants. Applications on behalf of underrepresented minority students are especially encouraged.

Financial Data The grant of $4,000 provides funding for a stipend, fringe benefits, and indirect costs.

Duration 10 to 12 weeks during the summer.

Additional data At the conclusion of the fellowship period, students must submit a 1-page summary of their research project explaining how the fellowship affected their consideration of a career in endocrinology.

Number awarded Varies each year; recently, 12 were awarded.

Deadline January of each year.

[176]
EPISCOPALES ANONIMOS SCHOLARSHIP

Hispanic Scholarship Consortium
Attn: Scholarship Selection Committee
7703 North Lamar Boulevard, Suite 310
Austin, TX 78752
(512) 368-2956   Fax: (512) 692-1831
E-mail: scholarships@hispanicscholar.org
Web: hispanicscholar.academicworks.com

Summary To provide financial assistance to high school seniors of Hispanic heritage in Texas who are members of Episcopal churches and plan to attend a college in any state.

Eligibility This program is open to seniors of Hispanic heritage graduating from high schools in Texas and planning to enroll full time at a 2- or 4-year college or university in any state. Applicants be active members of an Episcopal church and submit a letter of recommendation from the priest serving the church where they are a member. They must have a GPA of 3.0 or higher. Selection is based on academic achievement, community service, personal strengths, leadership, and financial need. U.S. citizenship is not required; students may qualify under Texas Senate Bill 1528.

Financial Data A stipend is awarded (amount not specified).

Duration 1 year; may be renewed up to 3 additional years, provided the recipient remains enrolled full time, maintains a GPA of 3.0 or higher, and participates in at least 25 hours of community service per semester.

Number awarded 1 or more each year.

Deadline April of each year.

[177] ESA FOUNDATION SCHOLARSHIP PROGRAM

Entertainment Software Association
Attn: ESA Foundation
317 Madison Avenue, 22nd Floor
New York, NY 10017
(917) 522-3250
Web: www.esafoundation.org/scholarship.asp

Summary To provide financial assistance to Hispanics and members of other minority groups who are interested in attending college to prepare for a career in computer and video game arts.

Eligibility This program is open to women and members of minority groups who are high school seniors or undergraduates currently enrolled full time at an accredited 4-year college or university. Applicants must be interested in working on a degree leading to a career in computer and video game arts. They must be U.S. citizens and have a GPA of 2.75 or higher.

Financial Data The stipend is $3,000.

Duration 1 year; nonrenewable.

Additional data This program began in 2007.

Number awarded Up to 30 each year: 15 to graduating high school seniors and 15 to current undergraduates.

Deadline March of each year.

[178] ESPERANZA SCHOLARSHIP

New York Women in Communications, Inc.
Attn: NYWICI Foundation
355 Lexington Avenue, 15th Floor
New York, NY 10017-6603
(212) 297-2133   Fax: (212) 370-9047
E-mail: nywicipr@nywici.org
Web: www.nywici.org/foundation/scholarships

Summary To provide financial assistance to Hispanic women who are residents of designated eastern states and interested in preparing for a career in communications at a college or graduate school in any state.

Eligibility This program is open to Hispanic women who are seniors graduating from high schools in New York, New Jersey, Connecticut, or Pennsylvania or undergraduate or graduate students who are permanent residents of those states; they must be attending or planning to attend a college or university in any state. Graduate students must be members of New York Women in Communications, Inc. (NYWICI). Also eligible are Hispanic women who reside outside the 4 states but are currently enrolled at a college or university within 1 of the 5 boroughs of New York City. All applicants must be working on a degree in a communications-related field (e.g., advertising, broadcasting, communications, digital media, English, film, journalism, marketing, public relations, publishing) and have a GPA of 3.2 or higher. Along with their application, they must submit a 2-page resume; a personal essay of 300 words on an assigned topic that changes annually; 2 letters of recommendation; and an official transcript. Selection is based on academic record, need, demonstrated leadership, participation in school and community activities, honors and other awards or recognition, work experience, goals and aspirations, and unusual personal and/or family circumstances. U.S. citizenship or permanent resident status is required.

Financial Data The stipend ranges up to $10,000.

Duration 1 year.

Additional data This program is funded by Macy's and Bloomingdale's.

Number awarded 1 each year.

Deadline January of each year.

[179] EXELON SCHOLARSHIPS

Society of Women Engineers
Attn: Scholarship Selection Committee
203 North LaSalle Street, Suite 1675
Chicago, IL 60601-1269
(312) 596-5223   Toll Free: (877) SWE-INFO
Fax: (312) 644-8557   E-mail: scholarships@swe.org
Web: societyofwomenengineers.swe.org

Summary To provide financial assistance to women, especially Hispanics and other underrepresented minorities, who will be entering their freshman, sophomore, or junior year and are interested in studying engineering or computer science.

Eligibility This program is open to women who are enrolling full time in their freshman, sophomore, or junior year at an ABET-accredited 4-year college or university. Preference is given to students at Bradley University, Illinois Institute of Technology, University of Illinois at Chicago, University of Illinois at Urbana-Champaign, University of Maryland-Baltimore County, University of Maryland at College Park, Morgan State University, Pennsylvania State University, or Purdue University. Applicants must be planning to major in computer science or computer, electrical, or mechanical engineering. U.S. citizenship is required. Preference is given to members of groups underrepresented in engineering and computer science, including ethnic and racial minorities, persons with disabilities, and veterans. Selection is based on merit.

Financial Data The stipend is $1,000.

Duration 1 year.

Additional data This program is sponsored by Exelon Corporation, parent of ComEd and PECO, the electric utilities for northern Illinois and southeastern Pennsylvania, respectively.

Number awarded   5 each year.

Deadline   May of each year for entering freshmen; February of each year for continuing sophomores and juniors.

[180]
EXXONMOBIL BERNARD HARRIS MATH AND SCIENCE SCHOLARSHIPS

Council of the Great City Schools
1301 Pennsylvania Avenue, N.W., Suite 702
Washington, DC 20004
(202) 393-2427   Fax: (202) 393-2400
Web: www.cgcs.org/Page/47

Summary   To provide financial assistance to Hispanic and African American high school seniors interested in studying science, technology, engineering, or mathematics (STEM) in college.

Eligibility   This program is open to Hispanic and African American seniors graduating from high schools in a district that is a member of the Council of the Great City Schools, a coalition of 67 of the nation's largest urban public school systems. Applicants must be planning to enroll full time at a 4-year college or university and major in a STEM field of study. They must have a GPA of 3.0 or higher. Along with their application, they must submit 1-page essays on 1) how mathematics and science education has impacted their lives so far; and 2) why they have chosen to prepare for a career in a STEM field. Selection is based on those essays; academic achievement; extracurricular activities, community service, or other experiences that demonstrate commitment to a career in a STEM field; and 3 letters of recommendation. Financial need is not considered. Males and females are judged separately.

Financial Data   The stipend is $5,000.

Duration   1 year; nonrenewable.

Additional data   This program, which began in 2010, is sponsored by the ExxonMobil Corporation and The Harris Foundation.

Number awarded   4 each year: an African American male and female and an Hispanic male and female.

Deadline   May of each year.

[181]
EXXONMOBIL/LNESC SCHOLARSHIPS

League of United Latin American Citizens
Attn: LULAC National Education Service Centers
1133 19th Street, N.W., Suite 1000
Washington, DC 20036
(202) 835-9646   Fax: (202) 835-9685
E-mail: scholarships@lnesc.org
Web: www.lnesc.org/#!exxonmobillnesc-scholarship/c1m36

Summary   To provide financial assistance to Latino high school seniors in designated communities who plan to working on a bachelor's degree in engineering.

Eligibility   This program is open to Latino seniors graduating from high schools in Albuquerque, Bayamon (Puerto Rico), Colorado Springs, Corpus Christi, Dallas, El Paso, Houston, Kansas City (Missouri), Miami, Philadelphia, Pueblo (Colorado), or San Antonio. Applicants must be planning to work full time on a bachelor's degree in engineering at a colleges or university in the United States. They must have

a GPA of 3.5 or higher and have scored at least 29 on the ACT or 1350 on the critical reading and mathematics SAT. Along with their application, they must submit a 300-word essay on their professional and career goals. U.S. citizenship or permanent resident status is required.

Financial Data   The stipend is $3,000 per year for a national scholarship or $2,000 for a local scholarship in each of the designated communities. Funds are to be used to pay for tuition, required fees, room and board, and required educational materials and books; they are sent directly to the college or university and deposited in the scholarship recipient's name.

Duration   1 year; the national scholarship may be renewed 3 additional years but the local scholarships are nonrenewable.

Additional data   Funding for this program is provided by the ExxonMobil Corporation. The League of United Latin American Citizens (LULAC) began in 1929 and it established the LULAC National Education Service Centers (LNESC) in 1973 to support the educational activities of Hispanics.

Number awarded   1 national and 12 local (1 in each designated community) each year.

Deadline   July of each year.

[182]
EXXONMOBIL LOFT FELLOWSHIPS

Hispanic Heritage Foundation
1001 Pennsylvania Avenue, N.W.
Washington, DC 20004
(202) 558-9473   E-mail: Julian@hispanicheritage.org
Web: www.hispanicheritage.org

Summary   To provide financial assistance to Hispanic undergraduate and graduate students who participate in the Latinos on Fast Track (LOFT) program.

Eligibility   This program is open to Hispanic sophomores, juniors, seniors, and graduate students at 4-year colleges and universities who are U.S. citizens or permanent residents and fluent in English. Applicants must be working on a degree and preparing for a career in chemistry, engineering (chemical, civil, computer, electrical, environmental, industrial, materials, mechanical, or petroleum), geology, material sciences, mathematics, or physics. Their GPA must be at least 3.5. They must be participating in the LOFT program with an ExxonMobil engineer or scientist as mentor. Along with their application, they must submit an essay of 500 to 700 words that covers why they chose their major, how they intend to prepare for an active career related to their major, and why they should be considered for this program.

Financial Data   Selected LOFT participants receive $1,000 scholarships.

Duration   The scholarships are presented annually and are nonrenewable.

Additional data   The LOFT program involves 5 meetings of 1 hour each with the mentor (virtually or in person), participation in an online ExxonMobil mentee program that introduces them to career opportunities with the company, the possibility to interview for ExxonMobil internships or full-time positions upon successful completion of the program, and the possibility of these scholarships.

Number awarded   20 each year.

Deadline   April of each year.

[183]
FARM CREDIT EAST SCHOLARSHIPS

Farm Credit East
Attn: Scholarship Program
240 South Road
Enfield, CT 06082
(860) 741-4380   Toll Free: (800) 562-2235
Fax: (860) 741-4389
E-mail: specialoffers@famcrediteast.com
Web: www.farmcrediteast.com

Summary   To provide financial assistance to Hispanic and other minority residents of designated northeastern states who plan to attend school in any state to work on an undergraduate or graduate degree in a field related to agriculture, forestry, or fishing.

Eligibility   This program is open to residents of Connecticut, Maine, Massachusetts, New Jersey, Rhode Island, and portions of New York and New Hampshire. Applicants must be working on or planning to work on an associate, bachelor's, or graduate degree in production agriculture, agribusiness, the forest products industry, or commercial fishing at a college or university in any state. They must submit a 200-word essay on why they wish to prepare for a career in agriculture, forestry, or fishing. Selection is based on the essay, extracurricular activities (especially farm work experience and activities indicative of an interest in preparing for a career in agriculture or agribusiness), and interest in agriculture. The program includes diversity scholarships reserved for members of minority groups (Hispanic or Latino, Black or African American, American Indian or Alaska Native, Asian, or Native Hawaiian or other Pacific Islander).

Financial Data   The stipend is $1,500. Funds are paid directly to the student to be used for tuition, room and board, books, and other academic charges.

Duration   1 year; nonrenewable.

Additional data   Recipients are given priority for an internship with the sponsor in the summer following their junior year. Farm Credit East was formerly named First Pioneer Farm Credit.

Number awarded   Varies each year; recently, 32, including several diversity scholarships, were awarded.

Deadline   April of each year.

[184]
FIRST TRANSIT SCHOLARSHIP

Conference of Minority Transportation Officials
Attn: National Scholarship Program
100 M Street, S.E., Suite 917
Washington, DC 20003
(202) 506-2917   E-mail: info@comto.org
Web: www.comto.org/page/scholarships

Summary   To provide financial assistance to Hispanic and other minority upper-division and graduate students in engineering or other field related to transportation.

Eligibility   This program is open to minority juniors, seniors, and graduate students in transporation, planning, engineering or other technical transportation-related disciplines. Applicants must submit a cover letter on their transportation-related career goals and life aspirations. Financial need is not considered in the selection process.

Financial Data   The stipend is $6,000. Funds are paid directly to the recipient's college or university.

Duration   1 year.

Additional data   This program is sponsored by First Transit Inc.

Number awarded   1 each year.

Deadline   April of each year.

[185]
FIU-AEJMC LATINO/LATIN AMERICAN COMMUNICATION RESEARCH AWARD

Association for Education in Journalism and Mass
   Communication
Attn: International Communication Division
234 Outlet Pointe Boulevard, Suite A
Columbia, SC 29210-5667
(803) 798-0271   Fax: (803) 772-3509
E-mail: aejmc@aejmc.org
Web: www.aejmc.us/icd

Summary   To recognize and reward Latino and Latin American student and faculty members who submit outstanding research papers relevant to journalism and mass media in their communities for presentation at the annual conference of the Association for Education in Journalism and Mass Communication (AEJMC).

Eligibility   This competition is open to AEJMC members and non-members, students, and faculty who regard themselves as members of the Latino, Hispanic, or Latin American community. Applicants must submit papers for presentation at the AEJMC annual conference either for the International Communication Division or the Minorities in Communication Division. Eligible topics include matters of Inter-American or Iberian-American communication, new media flow, media theory, media technology or new media, communication for development and social change, media law and ethics, media education, ethnic or gender media and integration, media economics, media and the environment, political communication, critical media studies, popular culture, or cultural studies. All research methodologies are welcome.

Financial Data   Cash prizes are awarded.

Duration   The prizes are presented annually.

Additional data   This program began in 2014 with support from Florida International University's School of Journalism and Mass Communications.

Number awarded   1 each year.

Deadline   March of each year.

[186]
FLEMING/BLASZCAK SCHOLARSHIP

Society of Plastics Engineers
Attn: SPE Foundation
6 Berkshire Boulevard, Suite 306
Bethel, CT 06801
(203) 740-5457   Fax: (203) 775-8490
E-mail: foundation@4spe.org
Web: old.4spe.org/forms/spe-foundation-scholarship-form

Summary   To provide financial assistance to Mexican American undergraduate and graduate students who have a career interest in the plastics industry.

Eligibility   This program is open to full-time undergraduate and graduate students of Mexican descent who are enrolled at a 4-year college or university. Applicants must be U.S. citizens or legal residents. They must be majoring in or taking courses that would be beneficial to a career in the plastics or polymer industry (e.g., plastics engineering, polymer sciences, chemistry, physics, chemical engineering, mechanical engineering, industrial engineering). Along with their application, they must submit 3 letters of recommendation; a high school and/or college transcript; a 1- to 2-page statement telling why they are applying for the scholarship, their qualifications, and their educational and career goals in the plastics industry; their employment history; a list of current and past school activities and community activities and honors; and documentation of their Mexican heritage. Financial need is considered in the selection process.

Financial Data The stipend is $2,000. Funds are paid directly to the recipient's school.

Duration 1 year.

Number awarded 1 each year.

Deadline April of each year.

[187]
FLORIDA CHAPTER AABE SCHOLARSHIPS

American Association of Blacks in Energy-Florida
  Chapter
c/o Atanya Lewis, Scholarship Committee
700 Universe Boulevard, JNE/JB
Juno Beach, FL 33408
E-mail: Atanya.Lewis@fpl.com
Web: www.aabe.org/index.php?component=pages&id=811

Summary To provide financial assistance to Hispanic and members of other underrepresented minority groups who are high school seniors in Florida and planning to major in an energy-related field at a college in the state.

Eligibility This program is open to seniors graduating from high schools in Florida and planning to attend an accredited college or university in Florida. Applicants must be Hispanics, African Americans, or Native Americans who have a GPA of 3.0 or higher and have taken the SAT and/or ACT test. Their intended major must be business (business administration, accounting, finance); engineering (agricultural/biological, chemical, civil, computer, electrical, environmental, industrial, materials, mechanical, nuclear); technology (computer science); mathematics (applied or any other branch); the physical sciences (astronomy, chemistry, physics, or energy-related non-medical biology); or other energy-related field. Along with their application, they must submit a 350-word essay that includes 1) when they discovered their interest in the field of energy and what sparked their interest; and 2) either what excites them about the field of energy or how they expect their education to prepare them for the field of energy. The program includes both need-based and no-need scholarships.

Financial Data A stipend is awarded (amount not specified).

Duration 1 year.

Additional data Winners are eligible to compete for regional and national scholarships.

Number awarded Varies each year.

Deadline March of each year.

[188]
FORUM FOR CONCERNS OF MINORITIES SCHOLARSHIPS

American Society for Clinical Laboratory Science
Attn: Forum for Concerns of Minorities
1861 International Drive, Suite 200
McLean, VA 22102
(571) 748-3770   E-mail: ascls@ascls.org
Web: www.ascls.org/forum-for-concerns-of-minorities

Summary To provide financial assistance to Hispanic and other minority students in clinical laboratory scientist and clinical laboratory technician programs.

Eligibility This program is open to minority students who are enrolled in a program in clinical laboratory science, including clinical laboratory science/medical technology (CLS/MT) and clinical laboratory technician/medical laboratory technician (CLT/MLT). Applicants must be able to demonstrate financial need. Membership in the American Society for Clinical Laboratory Science is encouraged but not required.

Financial Data Stipends depend on the need of the recipients and the availability of funds.

Duration 1 year.

Number awarded 2 each year: 1 to a CLS/MT student and 1 to a CLT/MLT student.

Deadline March of each year.

[189]
FRAMELINE COMPLETION FUND

Frameline
Attn: Completion Fund
145 Ninth Street, Suite 300
San Francisco, CA 94103
(415) 703-8650   Fax: (415) 861-1404
E-mail: info@frameline.org
Web: frameline.org

Summary To provide funding to lesbian, gay, bisexual, and transgender (LGBT) film/video artists, including Hispanics and other people of color.

Eligibility This program is open to LGBT artists who are in the last stages of the production of documentary, educational, narrative, animated, or experimental projects about or of interest to LGBT people and their communities. Applicants may be independent artists, students, producers, or nonprofit corporations. They must be interested in completion work and must have 90% of the production completed; projects in development, script-development, pre-production, or production are not eligible. Student projects are eligible only if the student maintains artistic and financial control of the project. Women and people of color are especially encouraged to apply. Selection is based on financial need, the contribution the grant will make to completing the project, assurances that the project will be completed, and the statement the project makes about LGBT people and/or issues of concern to them and their communities.

Financial Data Grants range from $1,000 to $5,000.

Duration These are 1-time grants.

Additional data This program began in 1990.

Number awarded Varies each year; recently, 5 were awarded. Since this program was established, it has provided $464,200 in support to 136 films.

Deadline October of each year.

[190]
FRANCIS M. KEVILLE MEMORIAL SCHOLARSHIP

Construction Management Association of America
Attn: CMAA Foundation
7926 Jones Branch Drive, Suite 800
McLean, VA 22101-3303
(703) 677-3361   E-mail: foundation@cmaanet.org
Web: www.cmaafoundation.org

Summary To provide financial assistance to Hispanic and other minority undergraduate and graduate students working on a degree in construction management.

Eligibility This program is open to women and members of minority groups who are enrolled as full-time undergraduate or graduate students. Applicants must have completed at least 1 year of study and have at least 1 full year remaining for a bachelor's or master's degree in construction management or a related field. Along with their application, they must submit essays on why they are interested in a career in construction management and why they should be awarded this scholarship. Selection is based on that essay (20%), academic performance (40%), recommendation of the faculty adviser (15%), and extracurricular activities (25%); a bonus of 5% is given to student members of the Construction Management Association of America (CMAA).

Financial Data The stipend is $5,000. Funds are disbursed directly to the student's university.

Duration 1 year.

Number awarded 1 each year.

Deadline April of each year.

[191]
FRANK GILBERT MEMORIAL SCHOLARSHIP

South Carolina Professional Association for Access and
   Equity
Attn: Financial Secretary
P.O. Box 71297
North Charleston, SC 29415
(843) 670-4890   E-mail: anderson4569@bellsouth.net
Web: www.scpaae.org/#!scholarships/c11tv

Summary To provide financial assistance to undergraduate students at colleges and universities in South Carolina who are recognized as underrepresented minorities on their campus and have been involved in public service.

Eligibility This program is open to residents of any state who have completed at least 12 semester hours at a college or university in South Carolina. Applicants must be recognized as an underrepresented ethnic minority on their campus. They must have a GPA of 3.5 or higher. Along with their application, they must submit 1) a personal letter on their public service, academic and career goals, honors and awards, leadership skills and organization participation, community service, and a statement of why they would like to receive this scholarship; and 2) a paragraph defining access and equity and describing how they can assist in achieving access and

equity within South Carolina. Financial need is not considered in the selection process.

Financial Data The stipend is $1,500.

Duration 1 year.

Number awarded 1 or more each year.

Deadline February of each year.

[192]
FRANK KAZMIERCZAK MEMORIAL MIGRANT SCHOLARSHIP

Geneseo Migrant Center
Attn: Scholarship Funds
3 Mt. Morris-Leicester Road
Leicester, NY 14481
(585) 658-7960   Toll Free: (800) 245-5681
Fax: (585) 658-7969   E-mail: mreho@gvboces.org
Web: www.migrant.net

Summary To provide financial assistance for college to students from migrant farmworker families who are interested in preparing for a career in teaching.

Eligibility This program is open to migrant farmworkers and their children who are interested in preparing for a career as a teacher. Priority is given to applicants who have experienced mobility within the past 3 years. They must submit a personal essay of 300 to 500 words on their reasons for wanting to become a teacher, 2 letters of recommendation, and an official school transcript. Selection is based on financial need, academic achievement, and history of migration for agricultural employment.

Financial Data The stipend is $1,000.

Duration 1 year.

Number awarded 1 each year.

Deadline January of each year.

[193]
FREDDY MIRANDA ACCESS SCHOLARSHIP

Iowa Association for College Admission Counseling
c/o Lauren Garcia, Inclusion, Access and Success Chair
University of Iowa
Center for Diversity and Enrichment
24 Philips Hall
16 North Clinton Street
Iowa City, IA 52242-1323
(319) 335-3555   Fax: (319) 353-2537
E-mail: info@iowaacac.org
Web: www.iowaacac.com/resources-schol-

Summary To provide financial assistance to seniors, especially Hispanics and members of othr underrepresented groups, at high schools that are members of the Iowa Association for College Admission Counseling (ACAC) and planning to attend college in Iowa or nearby states.

Eligibility This program is open to seniors graduating from Iowa ACAC member high schools and planning to enroll full time at a postsecondary Iowa ACAC member institution (including those in Illinois, Kansas, Minnesota, Missouri, Nebraska, Ohio, South Dakota, and Wisconsin). Special consideration is given to those who are from underrepresented populations, first generation, or able to demonstrate financial need. Students must be nominated by a high school counselor, teaching, administrator, or board member. They must exhibit a commitment to learning and have demonstrated involvement and leadership in their schools, the community, and or service to others with a desire to complete their educational program. Letters of nomination must include a 300-word statement on why the student should receive the scholarship.

Financial Data   The stipend is $1,000.

Duration   1 year.

Additional data   Contact Iowa ACAC for a list of its high school and college members.

Number awarded   2 each year.

Deadline   March of each year.

[194]
FRIENDS OF SENATOR JACK PERRY MIGRANT SCHOLARSHIP

Geneseo Migrant Center
Attn: Scholarship Funds
3 Mt. Morris-Leicester Road
Leicester, NY 14481
(585) 658-7960   Toll Free: (800) 245-5681
Fax: (585) 658-7969   E-mail: mreho@gvboces.org
Web: www.migrant.net/migrant/scholarships/perry.htm

Summary   To provide financial assistance for college to migrant farmworker high school seniors with a history of involvement in New York.

Eligibility   This program is open to students from migrant farmworker families who have a history of migration to and/or within New York. Applicants must have senior status in high school and plans to attend a postsecondary institution or other advanced training, preferably in New York. Seniors at high schools outside New York are eligible if they have a history of movement to the state. If no eligible high school seniors apply, current college students may be considered. Along with their application, they must submit a statement of at least 250 words on their background and interest in higher education, at least 1 letter of recommendation, and a copy of their current Migrant Certificate of Eligibility (COE). Selection is based on demonstrated commitment to educational goals, participation in school and Migrant Education Outreach Program (MEOP) activities, participation in community and/or non-school activities, citizenship, evidence of high mobility (interstate or intrastate), record of overcoming unusual obstacles, and financial need.

Financial Data   A stipend is awarded (amount not specified).

Duration   1 year.

Number awarded   1 or more each year.

Deadline   April of each year.

[195]
GARRETT A. MORGAN TRANSPORTATION ACHIEVEMENT SCHOLARSHIP

Conference of Minority Transportation Officials-Michigan
   Chapter
Attn: President
P.O. Box 32439
Detroit, MI 48232
(269) 491-7279   E-mail: averyk@michigan.gov
Web: www.comtomichigan.org/scholarships.html

Summary   To provide financial assistance to Hispanic and other minority high school seniors in Michigan who plan to attend college in any state to major in a transportation-related field.

Eligibility   This program is open to seniors graduating from high schools in Michigan who are members of minority groups. Applicants must be planning to attend an accredited college, university, or vocational/technical institute and major in the field of transportation or a transportation-related discipline. They must have a GPA of 2.5 or higher. U.S. citizenship or legal resident status is required.

Financial Data   The stipend ranges from $500 to $3,000. Funds are paid directly to the student.

Duration   1 year.

Number awarded   1 or more each year.

Deadline   April of each year.

[196]
GATES MILLENNIUM SCHOLARS PROGRAM

Bill and Melinda Gates Foundation
P.O. Box 10500
Fairfax, VA 22031-8044
Toll Free: (877) 690-GMSP   Fax: (703) 205-2079
Web: www.gmsp.org

Summary   To provide financial assistance to Hispanic and other low-income minority students, particularly those interested in majoring in specific fields in college.

Eligibility   This program is open to African Americans, Alaska Natives, American Indians, Hispanic Americans, and Asian Pacific Islander Americans who are graduating high school seniors with a GPA of 3.3 or higher. Principals, teachers, guidance counselors, tribal higher education representatives, and other professional educators are invited to nominate students with outstanding academic qualifications, particularly those likely to succeed in the fields of computer science, education, engineering, library science, mathematics, public health, or science. Nominees should have significant financial need and have demonstrated leadership abilities through participation in community service, extracurricular, or other activities. U.S. citizenship, nationality, or permanent resident status is required. Nominees must be planning to enter an accredited college or university as a full-time, degree-seeking freshman in the following fall.

Financial Data   The program covers the cost of tuition, fees, books, and living expenses not paid for by grants and scholarships already committed as part of the recipient's financial aid package.

Duration   4 years or the completion of the undergraduate degree, if the recipient maintains at least a 3.0 GPA.

Additional data   This program, established in 1999, is funded by the Bill and Melinda Gates Foundation and administered by the United Negro College Fund with support from the American Indian Graduate Center, the Hispanic Scholarship Fund, and the Asian & Pacific Islander American Scholarship Fund.

Number awarded   1,000 new scholarships are awarded each year.

Deadline   January of each year.

[197]
GATEWAYS TO THE LABORATORY PROGRAM

Cornell University
Attn: Weill Cornell/Rockefeller/Sloan-Kettering Tri-
    Institutional MD-PhD Program
Gateways to the Laboratory Program
1300 York Avenue, Room C-103
New York, NY 10065-4805
(212) 746-6023   Fax: (212) 746-8678
E-mail: mdphd@med.cornell.edu
Web: weill.cornell.edu/mdphd/summerprogram

Summary To provide Hispanic and other underrepresented minority or disadvantaged college freshmen and sophomores with an opportunity to participate in a summer research internship in New York City through the Tri-Institutional MD-PhD Program of Weill Cornell Medical College, Rockefeller University, and Sloan-Kettering Institute.

Eligibility This program is open to college freshmen and sophomores who are defined by the National Institutes of Health (NIH) as in need of special recruitment and retention, i.e., members of racial and ethnic groups underrepresented in health-related sciences (American Indians or Alaska Natives, Blacks or African Americans, Hispanics or Latinos, and Native Hawaiians or Other Pacific Islanders), persons with disabilities, and individuals from disadvantaged backgrounds (low-income or from a rural or inner-city environment). Applicants must be interested in continuing on to a combined M.D./Ph.D. program following completion of their undergraduate degree. They should have a GPA of 3.0 or higher and have completed a college level calculus class. Along with their application, they must submit an essay summarizing their laboratory experience, research interests, and goals. U.S. citizenship or permanent resident status is required.

Financial Data Students receive a stipend of $4,300 and reimbursement of travel expenses. At the end of the summer, 1 family member receives airfare and hotel accommodations to come to New York for the final presentations.

Duration 10 weeks, during the summer.

Additional data Interns work independently on a research project at Weill Cornell Medical College, Rockefeller University, or Memorial Sloan-Kettering Cancer Center, all located across the street from each other on the Upper East Side of New York City.

Number awarded 15 each year.

Deadline January of each year.

[198]
GE/LNESC SCHOLARSHIPS

League of United Latin American Citizens
Attn: LULAC National Education Service Centers
1133 19th Street, N.W., Suite 1000
Washington, DC 20036
(202) 835-9646   Fax: (202) 835-9685
E-mail: scholarships@lnesc.org
Web: www.lnesc.org/#!gelnesc-scholarship/c15js

Summary To provide financial assistance to Latino and other minority students who are studying engineering or business in college.

Eligibility This program is open to minority students who will be enrolled as college sophomores and working full time on a baccalaureate degree in engineering or business at colleges or universities in the United States approved by the League of United Latin American Citizens (LULAC) and General Electric. Applicants must have a GPA of 3.25 or higher and be U.S. citizens or legal residents. Selection is based on academic performance, likelihood of preparing for a career in business or engineering, performance in business or engineering subjects, writing ability, extracurricular activities, and community involvement.

Financial Data The stipend is $5,000 per year. Funds are to be used to pay for tuition, required fees, room and board, and required educational materials and books; they are sent directly to the college or university and deposited in the scholarship recipient's name.

Duration 1 year; may be renewed if the recipient maintains a GPA of 3.0 or higher.

Additional data Funding for this program is provided by the GE Foundation. The League of United Latin American Citizens (LULAC) began in 1929 and it established the LULAC National Education Service Centers (LNESC) in 1973 to support the educational activities of Hispanics.

Number awarded Varies each year; recently, 7 were awarded.

Deadline August of each year.

[199]
GENERAL PEDRO DEL VALLE LEADERSHIP SCHOLARSHIPS

U.S. Navy
Attn: Naval Service Training Command Officer
    Development
NAS Pensacola
250 Dallas Street
Pensacola, FL 32508-5220
(850) 452-4941, ext. 29395
Toll Free: (800) NAV-ROTC, ext. 29395
Fax: (850) 452-2486
E-mail: pnsc_nrotc.scholarship@navy.mil
Web: www.marines.com

Summary To provide financial assistance to students who are entering or enrolled at specified Hispanic Serving Institutions (HSIs) and interested in joining Navy ROTC to prepare for service as an officer in the U.S. Marine Corps.

Eligibility This program is open to students attending or planning to attend 1 of 3 specified HSIs with a Navy ROTC unit on campus. Applicants may either apply through their local Marine recruiter for a 4-year scholarship or be nominated by the professor of naval science at their institution and meet academic requirements set by each school for 2- or 3-year scholarships. They must be U.S. citizens between 17 and 23 years of age who are willing to serve for 4 years as active-duty Marine Corps officers following graduation from college. They must not have reached their 27th birthday by the time of college graduation and commissioning; applicants who have prior active-duty military service may be eligible for age adjustments for the amount of time equal to their prior service, up to a maximum of 36 months. The qualifying scores are 1000 composite on the SAT or 22 composite on the ACT. Current enlisted and former military personnel are also eligible if they will complete the program by the age of 30.

Financial Data These scholarships provide payment of full tuition and required educational fees, as well as a specified amount for textbooks, supplies, and equipment. The program also provides a stipend for 10 months of the year that is $250 per month as a freshman, $300 per month as a sophomore, $350 per month as a junior, and $400 per month as a senior.

Duration Scholarships are available for 2-, 3-, or 4-year terms.

Additional data Recipients must complete 4 years of study in naval science classes as students at 1 of the following HSIs: California State University at San Marcos, University of New Mexico, or San Diego State University. After completing the program, all participants are commissioned as second lieutenants in the Marine Corps Reserve with an 8-year service obligation, including 4 years of active duty. Current military personnel who are accepted into this program are released from active duty and are not eligible for active-duty pay and allowances, medical benefits, or other active-duty entitlements.

Number awarded Varies each year.

Deadline January of each year for students applying for a 4-year scholarship through their local Marine recruiter; July of each year if applying for a 2- or 3-year scholarship through the Navy ROTC unit at their institution.

[200]
GENERATION GOOGLE SCHOLARSHIPS FOR CURRENT UNIVERSITY STUDENTS

Google Inc.
Attn: Scholarships
1600 Amphitheatre Parkway
Mountain View, CA 94043-8303
(650) 253-0000   Fax: (650) 253-0001
E-mail: generationgoogle@google.com
Web: www.google.com

Summary To provide financial assistance to Hispanics and members of other underrepresented groups enrolled as undergraduate or graduate students in a computer-related field.

Eligibility This program is open to students enrolled as full-time undergraduate or graduate students at a college or university in the United States or Canada. Applicants must be members of a group underrepresented in computer science: African Americans, Hispanics, American Indians, or Filipinos/Native Hawaiians/Pacific Islanders. They must be working on a degree in computer science, computer engineering, or a closely-related field. Selection is based on academic achievement, leadership, and passion for computer science and technology.

Financial Data The stipend is $10,000 per year for U.S. students or $C5,000 for Canadian students.

Duration 1 year; may be renewed.

Additional data Recipients are also invited to attend Google's Computer Science Summer Institute at Mountain View, California, Seattle, Washington, or Cambridge, Massachusetts in the summer.

Number awarded Varies each year.

Deadline February of each year.

[201]
GENERATION GOOGLE SCHOLARSHIPS FOR HIGH SCHOOL SENIORS

Google Inc.
Attn: Scholarships
1600 Amphitheatre Parkway
Mountain View, CA 94043-8303
(650) 253-0000   Fax: (650) 253-0001
E-mail: generationgoogle@google.com
Web: www.google.com

Summary To provide financial assistance to Hispanics and members of other underrepresented groups planning to work on a bachelor's degree in a computer-related field.

Eligibility This program is open to high school seniors planning to enroll full time at a college or university in the United States or Canada. Applicants must be members of a group underrepresented in computer science: African Americans, Hispanics, American Indians, Filipinos/Native Hawaiians/Pacific Islanders, women, or people with a disability. They must be interested in working on a bachelor's degree in computer science, computer engineering, or a closely-related field. Selection is based on academic achievement, leadership, and passion for computer science and technology.

Financial Data The stipend is $10,000 per year for U.S. students or $C5,000 for Canadian students.

Duration 1 year; may be renewed for up to 3 additional years or until graduation, whichever comes first.

Additional data Recipients are required to attend Google's Computer Science Summer Institute at Mountain View, California, Seattle, Washington, or Cambridge, Massachusetts in the summer.

Number awarded Varies each year.

Deadline February of each year.

[202]
GEOCORPS AMERICA DIVERSITY INTERNSHIPS

Geological Society of America
Attn: Program Officer, GeoCorps America
3300 Penrose Place
P.O. Box 9140
Boulder, CO 80301-9140
(303) 357-1025   Toll Free: (800) 472-1988, ext. 1025
Fax: (303) 357-1070   E-mail: mdawson@geosociety.org
Web: rock.geosociety.org

Summary To provide work experience at national parks to student members of the Geological Society of America (GSA) who are Hispanics or members of other underrepresented groups.

Eligibility This program is open to all GSA members, but applications are especially encouraged from groups historically underrepresented in the sciences (African Americans, American Indians, Alaska Natives, Hispanics, Native Hawaiians, other Pacific Islanders, and persons with disabilities). Applicants must be interested in a short-term work experience in facilities of the U.S. government. Geoscience knowledge and skills are a significant requirement for most positions, but students from diverse disciplines (e.g., chemistry, physics, engineering, mathematics, computer science, ecology, hydrology, meteorology, the social sciences, and the humanities) are also invited to apply. Activities involve research; interpretation and education; inventory and monitoring; or mapping, surveying, and GIS. Prior interns are not eligible. U.S. citizenship or possession of a proper visa is required.

Financial Data Each internship provides a $2,750 stipend. Also provided are free housing or a housing allowance of $1,500 to $2,000.

Duration 3 months during the spring, summer, fall, or winter.

Additional data This program is offered by the GSA in partnership with the National Park Service, the U.S. Forest Service, and the Bureau of Land Management.

Number awarded Varies each year.

Deadline March of each year for spring or summer positions; June of each year for fall or winter positions.

[203]
GEOLOGICAL SOCIETY OF AMERICA MINORITY STUDENT SCHOLARSHIP PROGRAM

Geological Society of America
Attn: Program Officer-Grants, Awards and Recognition
3300 Penrose Place
P.O. Box 9140
Boulder, CO 80301-9140
(303) 357-1060   Toll Free: (888) 443-4472, ext. 1060
Fax: (303) 357-1070   E-mail: awards@geosociety.org
Web: www.geosociety.org

Summary To provide financial assistance to Hispanic and other minority undergraduate student members of the Geological Society of America (GSA) working on a degree in geoscience.

Eligibility This program is open to GSA members who are U.S. citizens and members of a minority group working on an undergraduate degree. Applicants must have taken at least 2 introductory geoscience courses and be enrolled in additional geoscience courses for the upcoming academic year. Selection is based on the scientific merits of the proposal, the capability of the investigator, and the reasonableness of the budget.

Financial Data The stipend is $1,500. Funds may be used to pay college fees, purchase text books, or attend GSA field courses or conferences. Winners also receive meeting registration for the GSA annual meeting where the awards are presented and a complimentary GSA membership for the following year.

Duration 1 year.

Additional data This program is sponsored by ExxonMobil.

Number awarded 6 each year: 1 in each GSA geographic section.

Deadline January of each year.

[204]
GEORGE CAMPBELL, JR. FELLOWSHIP IN ENGINEERING

National Action Council for Minorities in Engineering
Attn: Director, Scholarships and University Relations
440 Hamilton Avenue, Suite 302
White Plains, NY 10601-1813
(914) 539-4316   Fax: (914) 539-4032
E-mail: scholars@nacme.org
Web: www.nacme.org/scholarships

Summary To provide financial assistance to Latino and other underrepresented minority college sophomores majoring in engineering or related fields.

Eligibility This program is open to Latino, African American, and American Indian college sophomores who have a GPA of 3.0 or higher and have demonstrated academic excellence, leadership skills, and a commitment to science and engineering as a career. Applicants must be enrolled full time at an ABET-accredited engineering program. Fields of study include all areas of engineering as well as computer science, materials science, mathematics, operations research, or physics.

Financial Data The stipend is $5,000 per year. Funds are sent directly to the recipient's university.

Duration Up to 3 years.

Number awarded 1 each year.

Deadline April of each year.

[205]
GEORGIA SCHOLARSHIP FOR ENGINEERING EDUCATION FOR MINORITIES

Georgia Student Finance Commission
Attn: Scholarships and Grants Division
2082 East Exchange Place, Suite 200
Tucker, GA 30084-5305
(770) 724-9249   Toll Free: (800) 505-GSFC
Fax: (770) 724-9089   E-mail: GAfutures@gsfc.org
Web: www.gafutures.org

Summary To provide scholarship/loans to Hispanic and other minority residents of Georgia who are interested in working on a degree in engineering at specified institutions in the state.

Eligibility This program is open to Georgia residents who are Hispanic, American Indian or Alaska Native, Native Hawaiian or other Pacific Islander, Asian American, or female. Applicants must be enrolled full time in an ABET-accredited engineering program at specified universities in Georgia. They must have completed at least 60 hours of study and have a GPA of 2.5 or higher. U.S. citizenship or eligible noncitizen status is required.

Financial Data The award is $5,250 per year, to a maximum of $15,750. This is a scholarship/loan program; recipients must agree to work in an engineering-related field in Georgia after graduation or repay the loan at an interest rate 1% over the prime rate. For each year of work as an engineer, the loan balance is reduced by $3,500.

Duration Up to 9 semesters.

Additional data The specified universities are Georgia Institute of Technology, Georgia Southern University, Kennesaw State University, Mercer University, and University of Georgia.

Number awarded Varies each year.

Deadline Applications must be submitted on or before the last day of the academic term.

[206]
GERRY VANDAVEER SCHOLARSHIP

Kansas Association of Migrant Directors
c/o Cynthia Adcock
USD 305
P.O. Box 797
Salina, KS 67402
(785) 309-4718   E-mail: Cynthia.Adcock@usd305.com

Summary To provide financial assistance for college to current or former migrants graduating from high schools in Kansas.

Eligibility This program is open to seniors graduating from high schools in Kansas and GED recipients who are current or former migrants. Applicants must be planning to attend a college or university in Kansas as a full-time student. Along with their application, they must submit a paragraph about their educational goals, explaining why they want to go to college and describing their plans after graduation. Selection is based on the essay, GPA, school performance, and financial need.

Financial Data A stipend is awarded (amount not specified).

Duration 4 semesters (2 years).

Number awarded Varies each year; recently, 2 were awarded.

Deadline March of each year.

[207]
GILBERT G. POMPA MEMORIAL ENDOWED SCHOLARSHIP

¡Adelante! U.S. Education Leadership Fund
8415 Datapoint Drive, Suite 400
San Antonio, TX 78229
(210) 692-1971   Toll Free: (877) 692-1971
Fax: (210) 692-1951   E-mail: info@adelantefund.org
Web: www.adelantefund.org/#!scholarships/cee5

Summary To proviial assistance to Hispanic undergraduates at colleges in Texas who are enrolled in a pre-law program.

Eligibility This program is open to full-time students of Hispanic descent who have completed at least 90 credit hours at an accredited college or university in Texas. Applicants may be majoring in any field, but they must be enrolled in a pre-law program and/or planning to attend law school. They must be U.S. citizens or permanent residents and have a GPA of 2.7 or higher.

Financial Data The stipend is $1,000.

Duration 1 year.

Additional data This fund was established by the Hispanic Association of Colleges and Universities in 1997 and became a separate organization in 1999.

Number awarded 1 each year.

Deadline July of each year.

[208]
GMIS STEM SHOWDOWN SCHOLARSHIPS

Great Minds in STEM
Attn: HENAAC Scholars Program
602 Monterey Pass Road
Monterey Park, CA 91754
(323) 262-0997   Fax: (323) 262-0946
E-mail: scholars@greatmindsinstem.org
Web: www.greatmindsinstem.org

Summary To recognize and reward Hispanic college students who achieve top scores in the Great Minds in STEM Showdown (GMiS Showdown) competition.

Eligibility This program is open to Hispanic students at the University of Houston, University of Texas at Austin, Rice University, and the University of St. Thomas who were college participants in the GMiS STEM Showdown. That competition involves teams of students from those universities working with seniors at high schools in Houston and Fort Worth in a variety of activities designed to foster career awareness and build skills in the applications of technology. College winners in those competitions receive these scholarships.

Financial Data The awards are $1,000 scholarships.

Duration 1 year.

Additional data The Hispanic Engineer National Achievement Awards Conference (HENAAC) was established in 1989 and initiated a scholarship program in 2000. In 2010, the sponsoring organization officially adopted its current name, but it continues to hold the annual HENAAC conference, at which the scholarships are presented. The GMiS STEM Showdown is sponsored by Shell Oil. It began in 2011 in Louisiana and moved to Texas in 2014.

Number awarded 2 each year.

Deadline April of each year.

[209]
GO RED MULTICULTURAL SCHOLARSHIP FUND

American Heart Association
Attn: Go Red for Women
7272 Greenville Avenue
Dallas, TX 75231-4596
Toll Free: (800) AHA-USA1
E-mail: GoRedScholarship@heart.org
Web: www.goredforwomen.org

Summary To provide financial assistance to women from Hispanic and other multicultural backgrounds who are preparing for a career in a field of health care.

Eligibility This program is open to women who are currently enrolled at an accredited college, university, health care institution, or program and have a GPA of 3.0 or higher. Applicants must be U.S. citizens or permanent residents of Hispanic, African American, Asian/Pacific Islander, or other minority origin. They must be working on an undergraduate or graduate degree as preparation for a career as a nurse, physician, or allied health care worker. Selection is based on community involvement, a personal essay, transcripts, and 2 letters of recommendation.

Financial Data The stipend is $2,500.

Duration 1 year.

Additional data This program, which began in 2012, is supported by Macy's.

Number awarded 16 each year.
Deadline December of each year.

[210]
GOLDEN DOOR SCHOLARS PROGRAM

Golden Door Scholars
c/o Red Ventures
1101 521 Corporate Center Drive
Fort Mill, SC 29707
E-mail: info@goldendoorscholars.org
Web: www.goldendoorscholars.org/apply-now.html

Summary To provide financial assistance for college to undocumented students, especially those from designated states.

Eligibility This program is open to undocumented students who are high school seniors or high school graduates who have not yet entered a 4-year college (including students currently attending a community college). Applicants must be planning to work on a 4-year degree. They must be eligible for Deferred Action for Childhood Arrivals (DACA). Along with their application, they must submit brief statements on their intended field of concentration, why they are choosing it, and why they should be selected as a recipient of this scholarship. Strong preference is given to applicants from Georgia, North Carolina, South Carolina, and Tennessee.

Financial Data The program provides funding to cover tuition (less other scholarships), room, and board. The program cooperates with participating colleges and universities in the preferred states that have agreed to provide recipients with substantial scholarship support or reduced tuition.

Duration Until completion of a 4-year degree.

Additional data This program began in 2012.

Number awarded Varies each year, recently, 13 were awarded.

Deadline October of each year.

[211]
GOLDMAN SACHS SCHOLARSHIP FOR EXCELLENCE

Goldman Sachs
Attn: Human Capital Management
200 West Street, 25th Floor
New York, NY 10282
E-mail: Iris.Birungi@gs.com
Web: www.goldmansachs.com

Summary To provide financial assistance and work experience to Latino and other underrepresented minority students preparing for a career in the financial services industry.

Eligibility This program is open to undergraduate students of Latino, Black, or Native American heritage. Applicants must be entering their sophomore or junior year and have a GPA of 3.4 or higher. Students with all majors and disciplines are encouraged to apply, but they must be able to demonstrate an interest in the financial services industry. Along with their application, they must submit 2 essays on the following topics: 1) the business principle of the sponsoring firm that resonates most with them personally, professionally or academically, and how they have exemplified this principle through their experiences; and 2) how they will embody the business principle they selected throughout their summer internship and as a campus ambassador of the firm. Selection is based on academic achievement, interest in the financial services industry, community involvement, and demonstrated leadership and teamwork capabilities.

Financial Data Sophomores receive a stipend of $10,000, a summer internship at Goldman Sachs, an opportunity to receive a second award upon successful completion of the internship, and an offer to return for a second summer internship. Juniors receive a stipend of $15,000 and a summer internship at Goldman Sachs.

Duration Up to 2 years.

Additional data This program was initiated in 1994 when it served only students at 4 designated Historically Black Colleges and Universities: Florida A&M University, Howard University, Morehouse College, and Spelman College. It has since been expanded to serve underrepresented minority students in all states.

Number awarded 1 or more each year.

Deadline December of each year.

[212]
GORDON STAFFORD SCHOLARSHIP IN ARCHITECTURE

Stafford King Wiese Architects
Attn: Scholarship Selection Committee
622 20th Street
Sacramento, CA 95811
(916) 930-5900   Fax: (916) 290-0100
E-mail: info@skwaia.com
Web: www.skwarchitects.com/about/scholarship

Summary To provide financial assistance to Hispanics and members of other minority groups from California interested in studying architecture at a college in any state.

Eligibility This program is open to California residents currently enrolled at accredited schools of architecture in any state as first-year new or first-year transfer students and working on a bachelor's or 5-year master's degree. Applicants must be able to demonstrate minority status (defined as Hispanic, Black, Native American, Pacific Asian, or Asian Indian). They must submit a 500-word statement expressing their desire to prepare for a career in architecture. Finalists are interviewed and must travel to Sacramento, California at their own expense for the interview.

Financial Data The stipend is $3,000 per year. That includes $1,500 deposited in the recipient's school account and $1,500 paid to the recipient directly.

Duration 1 year; may be renewed up to 4 additional years.

Additional data This program began in 1995.

Number awarded Up to 5 each year.

Deadline June of each year.

[213]
GREAT LAKES SECTION IFT DIVERSITY SCHOLARSHIP

Institute of Food Technologists-Great Lakes Section
c/o Andrea Kirk, Scholarship Chair
Post Foods, LLC
275 Cliff Street
Battle Creek, MI 49014
E-mail: greatlakesift@gmail.com
Web: www.greatlakesift.org/student-scholarships

Summary To provide financial assistance to Hispanic and other minority members of the Great Lakes Section of the Institute of Food Technologists (IFT) from any state who are working on an undergraduate or graduate degree related to food technology at a college in Michigan.

Eligibility This program is open to minority residents of any state who are members of the IFT Great Lakes Section (GLS) and working full time on an undergraduate or graduate degree in food science, nutrition, food engineering, food packaging, or related fields at a college or university in Michigan. Applicants must have a GPA of 3.0 or higher and plans for a career in the food industry. Along with their application, they must submit a 1-page personal statement that covers their academic program, future plans and career goals, extracurricular activities (including involvement in community, university, GLS, or national IFT activities), and work experience. Financial need is not considered in the selection process.

Financial Data The stipend is $1,000.

Duration 1 year; nonrenewable.

Number awarded 1 each year.

Deadline February of each year.

[214]
GREAT MINDS IN STEM TECHNICAL PAPERS AND POSTERS COMPETITION

Great Minds in STEM
Attn: Academic Affairs Specialist
602 Monterey Pass Road
Monterey Park, CA 91754
(323) 262-0997   Fax: (323) 262-0946
E-mail: gmontoya@greatmindsinstem.org
Web: www.greatmindsinstem.org

Summary To recognize and reward undergraduate and graduate students who present outstanding papers and posters at the annual Hispanic Engineer National Achievement Awards Conference (HENAAC).

Eligibility This competition is open to full-time undergraduate and graduate students in science, technology, engineering, mathematics, or health (STEM) disciplines. Applicants must prepare a technical paper or poster and submit an abstract of 600 to 800 words. Based on those abstracts, finalists are invited to present at HENAAC. Awards are presented in 5 categories: 1) graduate student technical papers; 2) graduate student engineering/technology posters; 3) graduate student science/mathematics posters; 4) undergraduate student engineering/technology posters; and 5) undergraduate science/mathematics posters.

Financial Data Awards for graduate student technical papers are $1,500 for first, $1,200 for second, and $1,000 for third. For both categories of graduate student posters, awards are $800 for first, $700 for second, and $600 for third. For both categories of undergraduate student posters, awards are $600 for first, $400 for second, and $200 for third.

Duration The competition is held annually.

Additional data Finalists are reimbursed for travel costs to attend the conference, but they must pay their own conference registration fee, which includes hotel and most meals. Recipients must attend the conference to accept their scholarship.

Number awarded 15 each year: 3 in each of the 5 categories.

Deadline Abstracts must be submitted by August of each year.

[215]
GREATER CINCINNATI SCHOLARSHIP

Hispanic Scholarship Fund
Attn: Selection Committee
1411 West 190th Street, Suite 700
Gardena, CA 90248
(310) 975-3700   Toll Free: (877) HSF-INFO
Fax: (310) 349-3328   E-mail: scholar1@hsf.net
Web: www.hsf.net

Summary To provide financial assistance for college or graduate school to Hispanic American students in Indiana, Kentucky, and Ohio.

Eligibility This program is open to U.S. citizens, permanent residents, Deferred Action for Childhood Arrival (DACA) students, and eligible non-citizens. Applicants must be of Hispanic heritage and enrolled or planning to enroll full time in a degree program at an accredited 4-year college or university as an undergraduate or graduate student (including GED recipients and community college transfers). High school seniors must reside in Indiana, Kentucky, or Ohio and have a GPA of 3.0 or higher. Current undergraduate and graduate students must reside or attend school in those states and have a GPA of 2.5 or higher. Selection is based on merit; financial need is considered in determining the amount of the award.

Financial Data Stipends normally range from $500 to $5,000 per year.

Duration 1 year; recipients may reapply.

Number awarded 1 or more each year.

Deadline March of each year.

[216]
HACEMOS SCHOLARSHIP PROGRAM

Scholarship America
Attn: Scholarship Management Services
One Scholarship Way
P.O. Box 297
St. Peter, MN 56082
(507) 931-1682   Toll Free: (844) 402-0357
Fax: (507) 931-9168
E-mail: hacemos@scholarshipamerica.org
Web: www.scholarsapply.org/hacemos

Summary To provide financial assistance to Hispanic students who are interested in working on an undergraduate degree at a college in any state.

Eligibility This program is open to high school seniors and graduates who are enrolled or planning to enroll full time at an accredited 2- or 4-year college or university in the United States or its territories. Applicants must be children of Hispanic origin or dependent children younger than 25 years of age of HACEMOS members and residing in an area with an active HACEMOS chapter. They may be planning to major in any field, but they must have a GPA of 3.0 or higher. Selection is based on academic record, demonstrated leadership and participation in school and community activities, honors, work experience, a statement of goals and aspirations, unusual personal or family circumstances, an outside appraisal, and financial need.

Financial Data The stipend is $2,500 for students at 4-year institutions or $1,500 for students at 2-year colleges.

Duration 1 year; nonrenewable.

Additional data This program is provided by the HAC-EMOS Scholarship Foundation, an organization of Hispanic AT&T employees. The name of the organization is derived from its slogan, "¡Juntos hacemos más!" (Together we can do more). It has 41 chapters that cover most of the United States. This program is administered by Scholarship Management Services of Scholarship America.

Number awarded 1 or more each year.

Deadline February of each year.

[217]
HANA SCHOLARSHIPS

United Methodist Church
Attn: General Board of Higher Education and Ministry
Office of Loans and Scholarships
1001 19th Avenue South
P.O. Box 340007
Nashville, TN 37203-0007
(615) 340-7342   Fax: (615) 340-7367
E-mail: umscholar@gbhem.org
Web: www.gbhem.org

Summary To provide financial assistance to upper-division and graduate Methodist students who are of Hispanic, Asian, Native American, or Pacific Islander ancestry.

Eligibility This program is open to full-time juniors, seniors, and graduate students at accredited colleges and universities in the United States who have been active, full members of a United Methodist Church (UMC) for at least 3 years prior to applying. Applicants must have at least 1 parent who is Hispanic, Asian, or Native American. They must be able to demonstrate involvement in their Hispanic, Asian, or Native American (HANA) community in the UMC. Selection is based on that involvement, academic ability (GPA of at least 2.85), and financial need. U.S. citizenship or permanent resident status is required.

Financial Data Stipends range from $1,000 to $3,000.

Duration 1 year; recipients may reapply.

Number awarded 50 each year.

Deadline February of each year.

[218]
HAPCOA SCHOLARSHIP

Hispanic American Police Command Officers Association
Attn: Scholarship Committee
P.O. Box 29626
Washington, DC 20017
(202) 664-4461   Fax: (202) 641-1304
E-mail: achapa@hapcoa.org
Web: www.hapcoa.org/hapcoa-scholarship

Summary To provide financial assistance to Hispanic undergraduate and graduate students who are preparing for a career in law enforcement.

Eligibility This program is open to Hispanic Americans currently working on an undergraduate or graduate degree in law enforcement. Along with their application, they must submit a 1-page essay on their long- and short-term career

goals, including academic goals, career goals, life goals, importance of education, achievements, and financial need. Selection is based on the essay, GPA, extracurricular activities, and honors and awards.

Financial Data The stipend is $2,500.

Duration 1 year.

Number awarded 1 or more each year.

Deadline July of each year.

[219]
HAPCOA SCHOLARSHIP AWARD FOR LAW ENFORCEMENT EXPLORERS

Boy Scouts of America
Attn: Learning for Life
1329 West Walnut Hill Lane
P.O. Box 152079
Irving, TX 75015-2079
(972) 580-2241   Toll Free: (855) 806-9992
Fax: (972) 580-2137   E-mail: exploring@lflmail.org
Web: www.exploring.org/exploring/safety/scholarships

Summary To provide financial assistance for college to Explorer Scouts of Hispanic or Latino heritage who plan a career in law enforcement.

Eligibility This program is open to Explorer Scouts who are of Hispanic or Latino ancestry and seniors in high school or current undergraduate students. Applicants must be active members of a Law Enforcement Explorer post registered with Boy Scouts of America and working on or planning to work on a college degree in law enforcement or criminal justice. They must have a GPA of 3.0 or higher and a record of demonstrated leadership and volunteer service experience. Along with their application, they must submit a 750-word essay on why they want to prepare for a career in the law enforcement or criminal justice profession. Selection is based on that essay, academic record, ability to make a meaningful contribution to society in present and future, character and ethics, and leadership abilities in Law Enforcement Exploring and their community.

Financial Data The stipend is $1,000. Funds are disbursed directly to the recipient's college or university.

Duration 1 year; nonrenewable.

Additional data This program is sponsored by the Hispanic American Police Command Officers Association (HAPCOA).

Number awarded 1 each year.

Deadline April of each year.

[220]
HARVARD AMGEN SCHOLARS PROGRAM

Harvard College
Attn: Office of Undergraduate Research and Fellowships
77 Dunster Street, Second Floor
Cambridge, MA 02138
(617) 496-6220   E-mail: amgenscholars@harvard.edu
Web: uraf.harvard.edu/amgen-scholars

Summary To provide an opportunity for undergraduates, especially Hispanics and members of other underrepresented groups, to participate in summer research projects in the biological sciences at Harvard University.

Eligibility This program is open to sophomores, juniors, and non-graduating seniors at 4-year colleges and universities in the United States, Puerto Rico, and other U.S. territories. Applicants must be U.S. citizens or permanent residents who have a cumulative GPA of 3.2 or higher and an interest in preparing for a Ph.D. or M.D./Ph.D. They must be interested in working on a summer research project at Harvard in fields of biotechnology. Applications are encouraged from members of groups traditionally underrepresented in fields of biotechnology: African American/Black, Chicano/Latino/Hispanic, Puerto Rican, American Indian/Alaskan Native, Pacific Islander, women, and those with disabilities, as well as students who come from rural or inner-city areas and individuals whose backgrounds and experiences would bring diversity to the biotechnology fields.

Financial Data Scholars receive a stipend of $4,000, a meal allowance of $500, housing in a residential River House of Harvard, and, for non-Harvard students, travel to and from Boston.

Duration 10 weeks during the summer.

Additional data This program serves as the Harvard component of the Amgen Scholars Program, which operates at 8 other U.S. universities (and the National Institutes of Health) and is funded by the Amgen Foundation.

Number awarded Approximately 20 each year.

Deadline January of each year.

[221]
HARVARD SCHOOL OF PUBLIC HEALTH SUMMER INTERNSHIPS IN BIOLOGICAL SCIENCES IN PUBLIC HEALTH

Harvard T.H. Chan School of Public Health
Attn: Summer Program Coordinator
677 Huntington Avenue, SPH2-119
Boston, MA 02115
(617) 432-4397   Fax: (617) 432-0433
E-mail: BPH@hsph.harvard.edu
Web: www.hsph.harvard.edu

Summary To enable Hispanic and other minority or disadvantaged college science students to participate in a summer research internship in biological sciences at Harvard School of Public Health.

Eligibility This program is open to U.S. citizens, nationals, and permanent residents who are 1) members of ethnic groups underrepresented in graduate education (African Americans, Hispanics/Latinos, American Indians, Alaskan Natives, Pacific Islanders, and Native Hawaiians); 2) first-generation college students; and 3) students from an economically disadvantaged background. Applicants must be entering their junior or senior year with a GPA of 3.0 or higher and be interested in preparing for a research career in the biological sciences. They must be interested in participating in a summer research project related to biological science questions that are important to the prevention of disease, especially such public health questions as cancer, infections (malaria, tuberculosis, parasites), lung diseases, common diseases of aging, diabetes, and obesity.

Financial Data The program provides a stipend of at least $3,600, a travel allowance of up to $500, and free dormitory housing.

Duration 8 weeks, beginning in mid-June.

Additional data Interns conduct research under the mentorship of Harvard faculty members who are specialists in cancer cell biology, immunology and infectious diseases,

molecular and cellular toxicology, environmental health sciences, nutrition, and cardiovascular research. Funding for this program is provided by the National Institutes of Health.

Number awarded Up to 10 each year.

Deadline January of each year.

[222]
HATTIE J. HILLIARD SCHOLARSHIP

Wisconsin Women of Color Network, Inc.
c/o P.E. Kiram
756 North 35th Street, Suite 101
Milwaukee, WI 53208
(414) 899-2329   E-mail: pekiram64@gmail.com

Summary To provide financial assistance to Hispanic and other women of color from Wisconsin who are interested in studying art at a school in any state.

Eligibility This program is open to residents of Wisconsin who are women of color enrolled or planning to enroll at a college, university, or vocational/technical school in any state. Applicants must be a member of 1 of the following groups: African American, Asian, American Indian, or Hispanic. Their field of study must be art, graphic art, commercial art, or a related area. They must be able to demonstrate financial need. Along with their application, they must submit a 1-page essay on how this scholarship will help them accomplish their educational goal. U.S. citizenship is required.

Financial Data A stipend is awarded (amount not specified).

Duration 1 year.

Additional data This program began in 1995.

Number awarded 1 each year.

Deadline May of each year.

[223]
HDAF SCHOLARSHIPS

Hispanic Dental Association
Attn: HDA Foundation
3910 South IH-35, Suite 245
Austin, TX 78704
(512) 904-0252   E-mail: jessicac@hdassoc.org
Web: www.hdassoc.org

Summary To provide financial assistance to members of the Hispanic Dental Association (HDA) interested in preparing for a career in a dental profession.

Eligibility This program is open to HDA members who are entering their first through fourth year of dental school or first or second year at an accredited dental hygiene, dental assisting, or dental technician program in the United States or Puerto Rico. Applicants must have a GPA of 3.0 or higher, an interest in improving the health of the Hispanic community, and a demonstrated commitment and dedication to serving the Hispanic community. They must be enrolled full time. Along with their application, they must submit a 250-word essay on their career goals, including how they were inspired to become a dentist, dental hygienist, dental assistant, or dental technician. Selection is based on academic achievement, leadership skills, community service, and commitment and dedication to improving the oral health of the Hispanic community.

Financial Data The stipend is $1,500 for dental students or $750 for dental hygiene, dental assisting, or dental technician students. An additional grant of $500 is provided for travel reimbursement and complimentary registration to the HDA annual meeting.

Duration 1 year.

Additional data This program is sponsored by the Hispanic Dental Association Foundation (HDAF).

Number awarded 6 each year.

Deadline May of each year.

[224]
HEALTH HISPANIC LEADERSHIP DEVELOPMENT FUND

United Methodist Church
General Board of Global Ministries
Attn: United Methodist Committee on Relief
Health and Welfare Ministries
475 Riverside Drive, Room 330
New York, NY 10115
(212) 870-3871 Toll Free: (800) UMC-GBGM
E-mail: jyoung@gbgm-umc.org
Web: umc-gbcs.org/conference-connections/grants

Summary To provide financial assistance to Methodists and other Christians of Hispanic descent who are preparing for a career in a health-related field.

Eligibility This program is open to undergraduate and graduate students who are U.S. citizens or permanent residents of Hispanic descent. Applicants must be professed Christians, preferably United Methodists. They must be working on an undergraduate or graduate degree to enter or continue in a health-related field. Financial need is considered in the selection process.

Financial Data The stipend is $2,000.

Duration 1 year.

Additional data This program began in 1986.

Number awarded Varies each year.

Deadline June of each year.

[225]
HEALTH RESEARCH AND EDUCATIONAL TRUST SCHOLARSHIPS

New Jersey Hospital Association
Attn: Health Research and Educational Trust
760 Alexander Road
P.O. Box 1
Princeton, NJ 08543-0001
(609) 275-4224 Fax: (609) 452-8097
E-mail: jhritz@njha.com
Web: www.njha.com/education/scholarships

Summary To provide financial assistance to New Jersey residents, especially Hispanics and other minorities, who are working on an undergraduate or graduate degree in a field related to health care administration at a school in any state.

Eligibility This program is open to residents of New Jersey enrolled in an upper-division or graduate program in hospital or health care administration, public administration, nursing, or other allied health profession at a school in any state. Graduate students working on an advanced degree to prepare to teach nursing are also eligible. Applicants must have a GPA of 3.0 or higher and be able to demonstrate financial need. Along with their application, they must submit a 2-page essay (on which 50% of the selection is based) describing

their academic plans for the future. Minorities and women are especially encouraged to apply.

Financial Data The stipend is $2,000.

Duration 1 year.

Additional data This program began in 1983.

Number awarded Varies each year; recently, 3 were awarded.

Deadline June of each year.

[226]
HENAAC CORPORATE/GOVERNMENT SPONSORED SCHOLARSHIPS

Great Minds in STEM
Attn: HENAAC Scholars Program
602 Monterey Pass Road
Monterey Park, CA 91754
(323) 262-0997 Fax: (323) 262-0946
E-mail: scholars@greatmindsinstem.org
Web: www.greatmindsinstem.org

Summary To provide financial assistance to Hispanic undergraduate and graduate students interested in working on a degree in a field of science, technology, engineering, or mathematics (STEM).

Eligibility This program is open to students who are working on or planning to work on an undergraduate or graduate degree in a field of STEM. Applicants must be of Hispanic origin and/or must significantly participate in and promote organizations and activities in the Hispanic community. They must have a GPA of 3.0 or higher. Along with their application, they must submit a 700-word essay on a topic that changes annually. Selection is based on leadership, academic achievements, and campus and community activities; financial need is not considered. U.S. citizenship or permanent resident status is required.

Financial Data Stipends range from $500 to $10,000.

Duration 1 year; recipients may reapply.

Additional data The Hispanic Engineer National Achievement Awards Conference (HENAAC) was established in 1989 and initiated a scholarship program in 2000. In 2010, the sponsoring organization officially adopted its current name, but it continues to hold the annual HENAAC conference, at which the scholarships are presented. Corporate sponsors include Boeing Company, Booz Allen Hamilton, Chevron, Chrysler Foundation, Cummins, Dell, Dow Chemical, Edison International, Leidos, Lemus Medical, Lockheed Martin Corporation, Northrop Grumman Foundation, Oracle, Rackspace, and The Gas Company. Government sponsors include NASA Langley. Recipients must attend the conference to accept their scholarship. The sponsor subsidizes the cost of travel, 3 nights of lodging, and meals.

Number awarded Varies each year; recently, 78 were awarded.

Deadline April of each year.

[227]
HENAAC STUDENT LEADERSHIP AWARDS

Great Minds in STEM
Attn: HENAAC Scholars Program
602 Monterey Pass Road
Monterey Park, CA 91754
(323) 262-0997   Fax: (323) 262-0946
E-mail: scholars@greatmindsinstem.org
Web: www.greatmindsinstem.org

Summary To provide financial assistance to Hispanic undergraduate and graduate students working on a degree in fields of science, technology, engineering, or mathematics (STEM).

Eligibility This program is open to undergraduate and graduate students who are enrolled at a college or university and working on a degree in a STEM field. Applicants must be of Hispanic origin and/or must significantly participate in and promote organizations and activities in the Hispanic community. They must have a GPA of 3.0 or higher. Along with their application, they must submit a 700-word essay on a topic that changes annually; recently, students were asked to write on how they see their academic major contributing to global efforts and technology and how they, in their field of study, will contribute to global progress as well as actively contribute to their local communities. Selection is based on leadership, academic achievements, and campus and community activities; financial need is not considered.

Financial Data The stipend is $1,000.

Duration 1 year.

Additional data The Hispanic Engineer National Achievement Awards Conference (HENAAC) was established in 1989 and initiated a scholarship program in 2000. In 2010, the sponsoring organization officially adopted its current name, but it continues to hold the annual HENAAC conference, at which the scholarships are presented. Recipients must attend the conference to accept their scholarship. The sponsor subsidizes the cost of travel, 3 nights of lodging, and meals.

Number awarded 2 each year: 1 undergraduate and 1 graduate student.

Deadline April of each year.

[228]
HENRY W. BRADY MEMORIAL SCHOLARSHIP

Great Minds in STEM
Attn: HENAAC Scholars Program
602 Monterey Pass Road
Monterey Park, CA 91754
(323) 262-0997   Fax: (323) 262-0946
E-mail: scholars@greatmindsinstem.org
Web: www.greatmindsinstem.org

Summary To provide financial assistance to Hispanic undergraduate students who are enrolled at universities in any state and majoring in engineering.

Eligibility This program is open to Hispanic undergraduate students who are majoring in engineering at a college or university in any state. Applicants must be of Hispanic origin and/or must significantly participate in and promote organizations and activities in the Hispanic community. They must have a GPA of 3.0 or higher. Along with their application, they must submit a 700-word essay on a topic that changes annually. Selection is based on leadership, academic achieve-ments, and campus and community activities; financial need is not considered. U.S. citizenship is required.

Financial Data The stipend is $1,000.

Duration 1 year; recipients may reapply.

Additional data The Hispanic Engineer National Achievement Awards Conference (HENAAC) was established in 1989 and initiated a scholarship program in 2000. In 2010, the sponsoring organization officially adopted its current name, but it continues to hold the annual HENAAC conference, at which the scholarships are presented. Recipients must attend the conference to accept their scholarship. The sponsor subsidizes the cost of travel, 3 nights of lodging, and meals.

Number awarded 1 each year.

Deadline April of each year.

[229]
HILDA SANCHEZ-HENKE MEMORIAL SCHOLARSHIP

Minnesota Association of Administrators of State and
  Federal Education Programs
c/o Matthew Mohs, Treasurer
2140 Timmy Street
St. Paul, MN 55120
(651) 632-3787   E-mail: matthew.mohs@spps.org
Web: www.maasfep.org/scholarships.shtml

Summary To provide financial assistance to Hispanic high school seniors in Minnesota who have participated in a Title I or Migrant Education Program and plan to attend college in any state.

Eligibility This program is open to Hispanic seniors gradu-ating from high schools in Minnesota who have participated in a Title I or Migrant Education Program while in high school. Applicants must be planning to attend a 2- or 4-year college, university, or vocational/technical school in any state. They must have a GPA of 2.5 or higher. Along with their application, they must submit 1) a 100-word essay on how the Title I or Migrant Education Program helped them with their education; 2) a 100-word essay on their plans for the future; and 3) a 250-word essay on a challenging experience they have had in their life and how they overcame it. Selection is based on those essays, desire for education beyond high school, study habits, positive attitude, and interest in school, community, and/or work-related activities.

Financial Data The stipend is $2,000.

Duration 1 year.

Number awarded 1 each year.

Deadline January of each year.

[230]
HISPANIC AMERICAN COMMITMENT TO EDUCATIONAL RESOURCES (HACER) SCHOLARSHIP PROGRAM

Ronald McDonald House Charities
Attn: U.S. Scholarship Program
One Kroc Drive
Oak Brook, IL 60523
(630) 623-7048   Fax: (630) 623-7488
E-mail: info@rmhc.org
Web: www.rmhc.org/rmhc-us-scholarships

Summary To provide financial assistance for college to Hispanic high school seniors in specified geographic areas.

Eligibility This program is open to high school seniors in designated McDonald's market areas who are legal residents of the United States and have at least 1 parent of Hispanic heritage. Applicants must be planning to enroll full time at an accredited 2- or 4-year college, university, or vocational/technical school. They must have a GPA of 2.7 or higher. Along with their application, they must submit a personal statement, up to 2 pages in length, on their Hispanic background, career goals, and desire to contribute to their community; information about unique, personal, or financial circumstances may be added. Selection is based on that statement, high school transcripts, a letter of recommendation, and financial need.

Financial Data Stipends are determined by participating McDonald's areas, but most are $1,000 per year. Funds are paid directly to the recipient's school.

Duration 1 year; nonrenewable.

Additional data This program is a component of the Ronald McDonald House Charities U.S. Scholarship Program, which began in 1985. It is administered by International Scholarship and Tuition Services, Inc. For a list of participating McDonald's market areas, contact Ronald McDonald House Charities (RMHC).

Number awarded Varies each year; since RMHC began this program, it has awarded more than $60 million in scholarships.

Deadline January of each year.

[231]
HISPANIC ANNUAL SALUTE SCHOLARSHIPS

Hispanic Annual Salute
Attn: Ray Hurtado
P.O. Box 40720
Denver, CO 80204
(303) 699-0715   Fax: (303) 577-8111
E-mail: rhurtado@danielsfund.org
Web: www.hispanicannualsalute.org/scholarships

Summary To provide financial assistance to Hispanic high school seniors in Colorado who have been active in community service and plan to attend college in any state.

Eligibility This program is open to seniors graduating from high schools in Colorado and planning to enroll at a college or university in any state. Applicants must have made notable volunteer contributions to the Hispanic community, especially in unpaid volunteer activities not related to fulfilling a requirement for a school activity. They must have a cumulative GPA of 2.5 or higher. Along with their application, they must submit a 300-word essay on what motivates them to volunteer and how their volunteer activities affect the community. Selection is based on that essay, letters of recommendation, and academic achievement.

Financial Data The stipend is $2,000.

Duration 1 year.

Additional data Recipients are required to attend the Annual Salute gala in February.

Number awarded Varies each year; recently, 10 were awarded.

Deadline April of each year.

[232]
HISPANIC ASSOCIATION OF COLLEGES AND UNIVERSITIES/DENNY'S HUNGRY FOR EDUCATION SCHOLARSHIPS

Hispanic Association of Colleges and Universities
Attn: National Scholarship Program
8415 Datapoint Drive, Suite 400
San Antonio, TX 78229
(210) 692-3805   Fax: (210) 692-0823
TDD: (800) 855-2880   E-mail: scholarship@hacu.net
Web: www.hacu.net/hacu/Scholarships.asp

Summary To provide financial assistance to undergraduate and graduate students at member institutions of the Hispanic Association of Colleges and Universities (HACU) who submit outstanding essays on childhood hunger.

Eligibility This program is open to full- and part-time undergraduate and graduate students at 2- and 4-year HACU member institutions. Applicants must have a GPA of 2.5 or higher. Along with their application, they must submit a 500-word essay on how Denny's can help in the fight against childhood hunger in the United States.

Financial Data The stipend is $1,000.

Duration 1 year.

Additional data This program is sponsored by Denny's as 1 of its Hungry for Education activities.

Number awarded 5 each year.

Deadline April of each year.

[233]
HISPANIC BUSINESS COUNCIL SCHOLARSHIPS

Hispanic Business Council Scholarship Foundation of
    New Jersey, Inc.
492-C Cedar Lane, Suite 313
Teaneck, NJ 07666
E-mail: hbcscholarship@aol.com
Web: hbcsf.fluidreview.com

Summary To provide financial assistance to Hispanic high school seniors in New Jersey who plan to attend college in any state.

Eligibility This program is open to seniors graduating from high schools in New Jersey who are of Hispanic heritage. Applicants must be planning to enroll full time at an accredited college, university, community college, or technical school in any state. They must have a GPA of 3.0 or higher and be able to demonstrate financial need. Along with their application, they must submit a 250-word essay on 1 of the following topics: 1) how their academic studies will impact their future; or 2) a significant experience, achievement, or ethical dilemma they faced and its impact on them.

Financial Data Stipends range from $1,000 to $4,000. Funds are paid directly to the recipient's college.

Duration 1 year; may be renewed, provided the recipient maintains a GPA of 3.0 or higher and completes at least 80 hours of community service.

Additional data This program began in 1993 under the auspices of the Bergen County Hispanic-American Chamber of Commerce. The current name was adopted in 2004 when the program was expanded to include all New Jersey counties.

Number awarded Varies each year. Since the program began, it has awarded $485,000 in scholarships to more than 190 students.

Deadline March of each year.

[234]
HISPANIC HERITAGE YOUTH AWARDS

Hispanic Heritage Foundation
1001 Pennsylvania Avenue, N.W.
Washington, DC 20004
(202) 558-9473 E-mail: info@hispanicheritage.org
Web: www.hispanicheritage.org

Summary To recognize and reward, with college scholarships or grants for community service projects, Hispanic high school juniors from selected metropolitan areas throughout the country who have excelled in various areas of activity.

Eligibility This program is open to high school juniors who are U.S. citizens or permanent residents and of Hispanic heritage (at least 1 parent must be able to trace family origins to Spain, Portugal, Brazil, Latin America, or the Spanish-speaking Caribbean). Recently, awards were available to students in 10 metropolitan regions: Atlanta, Chicago, Dallas, Houston, Los Angeles, Miami, New York, Phoenix, San Jose/San Francisco Bay area, and Washington, D.C. Applicants competed in the following 6 categories: business and entrepreneurship, education, engineering, mathematics, health care and science, and community service. They must have a GPA of 3.0 or higher. Along with their application, they must submit an essay that describes their personal qualities and strengths, dedication to community service and the impact it has had on their life, future career goals, areas of interest, and significance of heritage and/or family in their life. Selection criteria include, but are not limited to, the following: academic achievement, compelling essay responses, meritorious achievements in the applicant's chosen category, contribution to the community, overall character as a role model, and letters of recommendation.

Financial Data In each category and each city, regional winners receive $1,000. Awards are in the form of educational grants that recipients may use for their college education or to fund a community service project that they will plan, oversee, and sustain. The regional winners then advance to a national competition. National winners receive a state-of-the-art laptop computer and an all-expense paid trip to the national awards ceremony.

Duration The awards are presented annually and are non-renewable.

Additional data This program began in 1998 with sponsorship by the Fannie Mae Foundation for 5 cities and 1 category. As the program has gained additional sponsors, it has expanded to additional categories and cities. Recent sponsors have included BBVA for business, Southwest Airlines for education, ExxonMobil for engineering, PriceWaterhouseCoopers (PwC) for mathematics, CVS Caremark for health care and science, and Colgate-Palmolive for community service. Awardees must attend, at their own expense, a local awards ceremony for the region they have selected.

Number awarded Recently, 60 regional winners were selected: 1 in each of the 6 categories from each of the 10 cities. From those, 6 national winners were chosen: 1 in each of the categories.

Deadline September of each year.

[235]
HISPANIC METROPOLITAN CHAMBER SCHOLARSHIPS

Hispanic Metropolitan Chamber
Attn: Scholarship Committee
333 S.W. Fifth Avenue, Suite 100
P.O. Box 1837
Portland, OR 97207
(503) 222-0280 Fax: (503) 243-5597
E-mail: info@hmccoregon.com
Web: www.hmccoregon.com/scholarship.html

Summary To provide financial assistance to Hispanic residents of Oregon and Clark County, Washington who are interested in attending college or graduate school in any state.

Eligibility This program is open to residents of Oregon and Clark County, Washington who are of Hispanic ancestry. Applicants must have a GPA of 3.0 or higher and be enrolled or planning to enroll in an accredited community college, 4-year university, or graduate school in any state. Along with their application, they must submit 250-word essays on how their heritage has influenced their life and long-term goals, and either why they should be selected to receive another scholarship (for renewal applicants) or a community activity in which they have participated and how it has benefited the Latino community in the past year (for first-time applicants). Selection is based on the essays, academics, extra-curricular activities, community service, extracurricular activities, community service, and letters of recommendation. If they wish to be considered for a scholarship for low-income families, they may also submit documentation of financial need. U.S. citizenship or permanent resident status is required.

Financial Data Stipends range from $2,000 to $10,000.

Duration 1 year; may be renewed.

Additional data Matching funds are provided to students who choose to attend George Fox University, Lewis and Clark College, Linfield College, Oregon State University, Portland State University, University of Oregon, University of Portland, Western Oregon University, Whitman College, or Willamette University.

Number awarded Varies each year; recently, 50 were awarded: 1 at $10,000, 1 at $6,000, 3 at $5,000, 2 at $4,500, 1 at $4,000, 1 at $3,600, 12 at $3,500, 11 at $3,000, 3 at $2,500, and 15 at $2,000.

Deadline January of each year.

[236]
HISPANIC PROFESSIONALS OF GREATER MILWAUKEE UNDERGRADUATE SCHOLARSHIPS

Hispanic Professionals of Greater Milwaukee
Attn: Kim Schultz, Scholarship Program
759 North Milwaukee Street, Suite 322
Milwaukee, WI 53202
(414) 223-4611 Fax: (414) 223-45613
E-mail: Kim.Schultz@hpgm.org
Web: www.hpgm.org/scholarships

Summary To provide financial assistance to residents of Wisconsin who are of Hispanic heritage and working on an undergraduate degree in any state.

Eligibility This program is open to residents of Wisconsin who are U.S. citizens of Hispanic heritage. Applicants must be enrolled full time at an accredited college or university in any state at least as sophomores. They must have a GPA of 3.0 or higher. Along with their application, they must submit transcripts, a 2-page resume, their community service history, 2 essays of 1,000 to 1,500 words each on an assigned topic, and 2 letters of recommendation.

Financial Data The stipend is $10,000. Recipients who attend the University of Wisconsin at Milwaukee or Marquette University are eligible for a matching grant of an additional $10,000.

Duration 1 year.

Additional data This program began in 2016.

Number awarded Varies each year; recently, 4 were awarded.

Deadline June of each year.

[237]
HISPANIC PUBLIC RELATIONS ASSOCIATION SCHOLARSHIP PROGRAM

Hispanic Public Relations Association-Los Angeles
 Chapter
Attn: Scholarship Program Director
P.O. Box 86760
Los Angeles, CA 90086-0760
(323) 359-8869   E-mail: info@hpra-usa.org
Web: www.hpra-usa.org/laR/scholarship-program

Summary To provide financial assistance to Hispanic undergraduate students from California who are attending college in the state and preparing for a career in public relations.

Eligibility This program is open to residents of California who are of at least 25% Hispanic descent and entering the sophomore, junior, or senior year at a 4-year college or university or enrolling as a graduate student in the state. Applicants must have a GPA of 2.7 or higher cumulatively and 3.0 or higher in their major subject. They must be majoring in public relations, communications, journalism, advertising, and/or marketing. Students majoring in other disciplines but planning to work in the public relations industry are also eligible. Along with their application, they must submit a letter of recommendation, official university transcripts, a 1- to 2-page personal statement explaining their career and educational aspirations as well as their involvement in the Hispanic community, a 1-page resume, documentation of financial need, and writing samples. Any materials submitted in Spanish must include an English translation. The applicant whose contributions to the community are judged most outstanding receives the Esther Renteria Community Service Scholarship.

Financial Data The stipend is $2,000. The student selected as the winner of the Esther Renteria Community Service Scholarship receives an additional $1,000.

Duration 1 year; may be renewed 1 additional year.

Additional data Recipients are expected to attend the sponsor's Premio Awards dinner in October.

Number awarded 6 each year: 4 undergraduates and 2 graduate students (of whom 1 of the 6 receives the Esther Renteria Community Service Scholarship).

Deadline August of each year.

[238]
HISPANIC SCHOLARSHIP FUND GENERAL COLLEGE SCHOLARSHIPS

Hispanic Scholarship Fund
Attn: Selection Committee
1411 West 190th Street, Suite 700
Gardena, CA 90248
(310) 975-3700   Toll Free: (877) HSF-INFO
Fax: (310) 349-3328   E-mail: scholar1@hsf.net
Web: www.hsf.net

Summary To provide financial assistance for college or graduate school to Hispanic American students.

Eligibility This program is open to U.S. citizens, permanent residents, Deferred Action for Childhood Arrival (DACA) students, and eligible non-citizens. Applicants must be of Hispanic heritage and enrolled or planning to enroll full time in a degree program at an accredited 4-year college or university as an undergraduate or graduate student (including GED recipients and community college transfers). High school seniors must have a GPA of 3.0 or higher; current undergraduate and graduate students must have a GPA of 2.5 or higher. All academic majors are eligible, but emphasis is placed on students in fields of science, technology, engineering, and mathematics (STEM). Selection is based on merit; financial need is considered in determining the amount of the award.

Financial Data Stipends normally range from $500 to $5,000 per year.

Duration 1 year; recipients may reapply.

Additional data Since this program began in 1975, more than $470 million has been awarded to more than 100,000 Hispanic students.

Number awarded Varies each year; recently, this program awarded more than 5,100 scholarships.

Deadline March of each year.

[239]
HISPANIC-SERVING HEALTH PROFESSIONS SCHOOLS/DEPARTMENT OF VETERANS AFFAIRS GRADUATE FELLOWSHIP TRAINING PROGRAM

Hispanic-Serving Health Professions Schools
Attn: Graduate Fellowship Training Program
2639 Connecticut Avenue, N.W., Suite 203
Washington, DC 20008
(202) 290-1186   E-mail: hshps@hshps.org
Web: www.hshps.org/programs/gftp

Summary To provide an opportunity for Hispanic undergraduate and graduate students to obtain research experience at facilities of the U.S. Department of Veterans Affairs (VA) in the United States and Puerto Rico.

Eligibility This program is geared to graduate students in public health, but undergraduate juniors and seniors may also apply; individuals with 5 or more years of professional experience in the health field are not eligible. Applicants must be interested in participating in a research program conducted at a VA health care facility in the United States or Puerto Rico where they are matched with a mentor whom they assist with various aspects of a research project. They must be U.S. citizens or permanent residents and have working proficiency in English; some positions require Spanish fluency. Available assignments include hospital administration, nursing administration, program administration, patient safety/satisfaction, secondary data analysis, knowledge management/workforce, women's health, and health promotion/education. A GPA of 2.7 or higher is required.

Financial Data Grants provide a stipend of $300 per week, housing accommodations, reimbursement of up to $500 in transportation to the program site, and $30 per week for local transportation.

Duration 10 weeks during the summer.

Number awarded Varies each year.

Deadline March of each year.

[240]
HNTB SCHOLARSHIP

Conference of Minority Transportation Officials
Attn: National Scholarship Program
100 M Street, S.E., Suite 917
Washington, DC 20003
(202) 506-2917   E-mail: info@comto.org
Web: www.comto.org/page/scholarships

Summary To provide financial assistance to Hispanic and other minority high school seniors interested in working on a degree in transportation or a related field.

Eligibility This program is open to minority seniors graduating from high school with a GPA of 3.0 or higher. Applicants must have been accepted at an accredited university or technical college with the intent to study transportation or a transportation-related discipline. They must be able to demonstrate leadership skills and activities. Along with their application they must submit a cover letter on their transportation-related career goals and life aspirations. Financial need is not considered in the selection process.

Financial Data The stipend is $5,000. Funds are paid directly to the recipient's college or university.

Duration 1 year.

Additional data This program is sponsored by HNTB Corporation.

Number awarded 1 each year.

Deadline April of each year.

[241]
HOB SCHOLARSHIP PROGRAM

House of Blahnik
2939 Turner Street
Philadelphia, PA 19121
(215) 431-1790   E-mail: info@houseofblahnik.org
Web: houseofblahnik.org

Summary To provide financial assistance for college to Hispanic and other lesbian, gay, bisexual, and transgender (LBGT) people of color who are members of the house/ballroom community.

Eligibility This program is open to members of the house/ballroom community who are enrolled or applying to a college, university, or vocational program. Applicants must submit a personal statement regarding their work and aspirations, unofficial transcripts or a letter of acceptance to the institution they are planning to attend, and 2 letters of reference. The program includes scholarships for formal members of the House of Blahnik and for non-members who have demonstrated outstanding contributions to their local community and to their own personal and professional development.

Financial Data The stipend normally is $1,000.

Duration 1 year.

Additional data The House of Blahnik was founded in 2000 by African American and Latino gay and transgender persons to provide support to the ballroom community. This program began in 2008.

Number awarded 2 each year: 1 to a formal member of the House of Blahnik and 1 to a non-member.

Deadline December of each year.

[242]
HONDA SWE SCHOLARSHIPS

Society of Women Engineers
Attn: Scholarship Selection Committee
203 North LaSalle Street, Suite 1675
Chicago, IL 60601-1269
(312) 596-5223   Toll Free: (877) SWE-INFO
Fax: (312) 644-8557   E-mail: scholarships@swe.org
Web: societyofwomenengineers.swe.org

Summary To provide financial assistance to undergraduate women from designated states, especially Hispanics and members of other underrepresented groups, who are majoring in designated engineering specialties.

Eligibility This program is open to SWE members who are entering their junior or senior year at a 4-year ABET-accredited college or university. Preference is given to members of underrepresented ethnic or racial groups, candidates with disabilities, and veterans. Applicants must be U.S. citizens working full time on a degree in automotive engineering, chemical engineering, computer science, electrical engineering, engineering technology, manufacturing engineering, materials science and engineering, or mechanical engineering. They must be residents of or attending college in Illinois, Indiana, Michigan, Ohio, Pennsylvania, or Wisconsin. Financial need is considered in the selection process.

Financial Data The stipend is $1,000.

Duration 1 year.

Additional data This program is sponsored by American Honda Motor Company.

Number awarded 5 each year.

Deadline February of each year.

[243]
HONEYWELL SCHOLARSHIPS

Society of Women Engineers
Attn: Scholarship Selection Committee
203 North LaSalle Street, Suite 1675
Chicago, IL 60601-1269
(312) 596-5223   Toll Free: (877) SWE-INFO
Fax: (312) 644-8557   E-mail: scholarships@swe.org
Web: societyofwomenengineers.swe.org

Summary To provide financial assistance to members of the Society of Women Engineers (SWE) from designated states, especially Hispanics and members of other underrepresented groups, interested in studying specified fields of engineering in college.

Eligibility This program is open to SWE members who are rising college sophomores, juniors, or seniors and have a GPA of 3.5 or higher. Applicants must be enrolled full time at an ABET-accredited 4-year college or university and major in computer science or aerospace, automotive, chemical, computer, electrical, industrial, manufacturing, materials, mechanical, or petroleum engineering. They must reside or attend college in Arizona, California, Florida, Indiana, Kansas, Minnesota, New Mexico, Puerto Rico, Texas, or Washington. Preference is given to members of groups underrepresented in computer science and engineering who can demonstrate financial need. U.S. citizenship is required.

Financial Data   The stipend is $5,000.

Duration   1 year.

Additional data   This program is sponsored by Honeywell International Inc.

Number awarded   3 each year.

Deadline   February of each year for current college students; May of each year for high school seniors.

[244]
HORACE AND SUSIE REVELS CAYTON SCHOLARSHIP

Public Relations Society of America-Puget Sound
  Chapter
Attn: Diane Bevins
1006 Industry Drive
P.O. Box 58530
Seattle, WA 98138-1530
(206) 623-8632   Fax: (206) 575-9255
E-mail: prsascholarship@asi-seattle.net
Web: www.prsapugetsound.org/Page.aspx?nid=73

Summary   To provide financial assistance to Hispanic and other minority upperclassmen from Washington who are interested in preparing for a career in public relations.

Eligibility   This program is open to U.S. citizens who are members of minority groups, defined as Hispanic/Latino Americans, African Americans, Asian Americans, Native Americans, and Pacific Islanders. Applicants must be full-time juniors or seniors attending a college in Washington or Washington students (who graduated from a Washington high school or whose parents live in the state year-round) attending college elsewhere. They must have overcome barriers in pursuit of personal or academic goals. Selection is based on academic achievement, financial need, and demonstrated aptitude in public relations and related courses, activities, and/or internships.

Financial Data   The stipend is $3,500.

Duration   1 year.

Additional data   This program began in 1992.

Number awarded   1 each year.

Deadline   May of each year.

[245]
HOUSTON CHAPTER AABE SCHOLARSHIPS

American Association of Blacks in Energy-Houston
  Chapter
Attn: Scholarship Committee
P.O. Box 132723
Spring, TX 77393-2723
E-mail: scholarships@aabehouston.org
Web: www.aabe.org/index.php?component=pages&id=335

Summary   To provide financial assistance to Hispanics and members of other underrepresented minority groups who are high school seniors in Texas and planning to major in an energy-related field at a college in any state.

Eligibility   This program is open to seniors graduating from high schools in Texas and planning to attend a college or university in any state. Applicants must be Hispanics, African Americans, or Native Americans who have a GPA of 3.0 or higher and who have taken the ACT and/or SAT test. Their intended major must be business, engineering, technology, mathematics, the physical sciences, or other energy-related field. Along with their application, they must submit a 350-word essay that includes 1) when they discovered their interest in the field of energy and what sparked their interest; and 2) either what excites them about the field of energy or how they expect their education to prepare them for the field of energy. Financial need is not considered in the selection process.

Financial Data   Stipend amounts vary; a total of $10,000 is available for this program each year.

Duration   1 year.

Additional data   Winners are eligible to compete for regional and national scholarships.

Number awarded   3 or more each year.

Deadline   March of each year.

[246]
HWNT AUSTIN SCHOLARSHIP

Hispanic Scholarship Consortium
Attn: Scholarship Selection Committee
7703 North Lamar Boulevard, Suite 310
Austin, TX 78752
(512) 368-2956   Fax: (512) 692-1831
E-mail: scholarships@hispanicscholar.org
Web: hispanicscholar.academicworks.com

Summary   To provide financial assistance and work experience to female high school seniors and college seniors of Hispanic heritage from Texas who plan to attend college or graduate school in any state.

Eligibility   This program is open to female residents of Texas of Hispanic heritage who are either 1) seniors graduating from high schools in Texas; or 2) seniors graduating from colleges in any state. High school seniors must be planning to enroll full time at an accredited 2- or 4-year college or university in any state; college seniors must be planning to enroll in graduate school. Applicants must have a GPA of 3.0 or higher. Selection is based on academic achievement, community service, personal strengths, leadership, and financial need. U.S. citizenship is not required; students may qualify under Texas Senate Bill 1528.

Financial Data   The stipend is $2,000 per year.

Duration   1 year; may be renewed up to 3 additional years, provided the recipient remains enrolled full time, maintains a GPA of 3.0 or higher, and participates in at least 25 hours of community service per semester.

Additional data   This program is sponsored by the Austin chapter of Hispanic Women's Network of Texas (HWNT). Scholarship winners must also participate in a year-long internship with the magazine.

Number awarded   Varies each year; recently, 2 were awarded.

Deadline   April of each year.

[247]
HYATT HOTELS FUND FOR MINORITY LODGING MANAGEMENT STUDENTS

American Hotel & Lodging Educational Foundation
Attn: Manager of Foundation Programs
1250 I Street, N.W., Suite 1100
Washington, DC 20005-5904
(202) 289-3180   Fax: (202) 289-3199
E-mail: foundation@ahlef.org
Web: www.ahlef.org

Summary   To provide financial assistance to Hispanic and other minority college students working on a degree in hotel management.

Eligibility   This program is open to students majoring in hospitality management at a 4-year college or university as at least a junior. Applicants must be members of a minority group (Hispanic, African American, American Indian, Alaskan Native, Asian, or Pacific Islander). They must be enrolled full time. Along with their application, they must submit a 500-word essay on their personal background, including when they became interested in the hospitality field, the traits they possess or will need to succeed in the industry, and their plans as related to their educational and career objectives and future goals. Selection is based on industry-related work experience; financial need; academic record and educational qualifications; professional, community, and extracurricular activities; personal attributes, including career goals; the essay; and neatness and completeness of the application. U.S. citizenship or permanent resident status is required.

Financial Data   The stipend is $2,000.

Duration   1 year.

Additional data   Funding for this program, established in 1988, is provided by Hyatt Hotels & Resorts.

Number awarded   Varies each year; recently, 18 were awarded. Since this program was established, it has awarded scholarships worth $702,000 to 351 minority students.

Deadline   April of each year.

[248]
I EMPOWER SCHOLARSHIP

Greater Washington Urban League
Attn: Thursday Network
Kristin Shymoniak
P.O. Box 73203
Washington, DC 20056-3202
E-mail: scholarship@thursdaynetwork.org
Web: www.thursdaynetwork.org/signature-programs

Summary   To provide financial assistance to Hispanic and African American high school seniors in the service area of the Greater Washington Urban League (GWUL) who plan to attend college in any state.

Eligibility   This program is open to Hispanic/Latino and African American seniors graduating from high schools in Washington, D.C., Prince George's County (Maryland), or Montgomery County (Maryland) and planning to enroll at a 4-year college or university in any state. Applicants must have a GPA of 2.5 or higher. Along with their application, they must submit copies of their SAT or ACT scores, documentation of financial need, and 2 essays of up to 500 words each on topics that change annually but relate to their community service. U.S. citizenship is required.

Financial Data   Stipends range from $500 to $3,000. Funds are paid directly to the recipient's institution.

Duration   1 year.

Additional data   This program, which began in 1992, is operated by the Thursday Network, the young professionals' auxiliary of the GWUL, as part of its Young Blacks Give Back (YBGB) Month.

Number awarded   2 each year. Since the program began, it has awarded more than $158,000 in scholarships.

Deadline   January of each year.

[249]
IDAHO LATINO SCHOLARSHIPS

Idaho Latino Scholarship Foundation
c/o Luis Caloca, Scholarship Committee Chair
P.O. Box 9918
Boise, ID 83708
E-mail: info@idaholsf.org
Web: www.idaholsf.org/scholarships

Summary   To provide financial assistance to Latino residents of Idaho who are interested in attending a public college or university in the state.

Eligibility   This program is open to residents of Idaho who are of Hispanic/Latino descent. Applicants must be high school seniors or undergraduates currently enrolled at a public college, university, vocational/technical school, or other postsecondary institution in the state. They must have a GPA of 2.5 or higher. Along with their application, they must submit an essay of 3 to 5 pages on their choice of 4 topics that related to Latinos and higher education. Selection is based on that essay; academic achievement; demonstrated leadership qualities; involvement in service to school, community, and family; and financial need.

Financial Data   Scholarships provide full payment of tuition at a public postsecondary institution in Idaho, to a maximum of $5,000.

Duration   1 year.

Number awarded   Varies each year; recently, 14 were awarded.

Deadline   March of each year.

[250]
IDAHO STATE BROADCASTERS ASSOCIATION SCHOLARSHIPS

Idaho State Broadcasters Association
1674 Hill Road, Suite 3
Boise, ID 83702
(208) 345-3072   Fax: (208) 343-8046
E-mail: isba@qwestoffice.net
Web: www.idahobroadcasters.org/index.php/scholarships

Summary   To provide financial assistance to students at Idaho colleges and universities, especially Hispanics and members of other diverse groups, who are preparing for a career in the broadcasting field.

Eligibility   This program is open to full-time students at Idaho schools who are preparing for a career in broadcasting, including business administration, sales, journalism, or engineering. Applicants must have a GPA of at least 2.0 for the first 2 years of school or 2.5 for the last 2 years. Along with their application, they must submit a letter of recommendation from the general manager of a broadcasting station that is a member of the Idaho State Broadcasters Association and a 1-page essay describing their career plans and why they want the scholarship. Applications are encouraged from a broad and diverse student population. Financial need is not considered in the selection process.

Financial Data   The stipend is $1,000.

Duration   1 year.

Number awarded   At least 2 each year.

Deadline   March of each year.

[251]
ILACHE SCHOLARSHIPS

Illinois Latino Council on Higher Education
Attn: Scholarship Committee
P.O. Box 409368
Chicago, IL 60640
E-mail: ilache.scholarship@gmail.com
Web: www.ilache.com/scholarship

Summary   To provide financial assistance to Latino students in Illinois who are interested in attending college in the state.

Eligibility   This program is open to Latino residents of Illinois who are graduating high school seniors or students currently enrolled full time at 2- or 4-year colleges and universities in the state. Applicants must submit a 500-word essay on their Latino ancestry and how the receipt of this scholarship will help them achieve their educational and career goals. Selection is based on academic achievement, goals, campus involvement, community involvement, and career aspirations.

Financial Data   The stipend is #1,000.

Duration   1 year.

Number awarded   2 of each year.

Deadline   May of each year.

[252]
ILLINOIS BROADCASTERS ASSOCIATION MULTICULTURAL INTERNSHIPS

Illinois Broadcasters Association
Attn: MIP Coordinator
200 Missouri Avenue
Carterville, IL 62918
(618) 985-5555   Fax: (618) 985-6070
E-mail: iba@ilba.org
Web: www.ilba.org/careers/internship-program

Summary   To provide funding to Hispanic and other minority college students in Illinois who are majoring in broadcasting and interested in interning at a radio or television station in the state.

Eligibility   This program is open to currently-enrolled minority students majoring in broadcasting at a college or university in Illinois. Applicants must be interested in a fall, spring, or summer internship at a radio or television station that is a member of the Illinois Broadcasters Association. Along with their application, they must submit 1) a 250-word essay on how they expect to benefit from a grant through this program; and 2) at least 2 letters of recommendation from a broadcasting faculty member or professional familiar with their career potential and 1 other letter. The internship coordinator of the sponsoring organization selects those students nominated by their schools who have the best opportunity to

make it in the world of broadcasting and matches them with internship opportunities that would otherwise be unpaid.

Financial Data   This program provides a grant to pay the living expenses for the interns in the Illinois communities where they are assigned. The amount of the grant depends on the length of the internship.

Duration   16 weeks in the fall and spring terms or 12 weeks in the summer.

Number awarded   12 each year: 4 in each of the 3 terms.

Deadline   Deadline not specified.

[253]
ILLINOIS DREAM FUND SCHOLARSHIPS

Illinois Dream Fund
c/o Chicago Community Trust
225 North Michigan Avenue, Suite 2200
Chicago, IL 60601
(312) 616-8000   Fax: (312) 616-7955
E-mail: info@illinoisdreamfund.org
Web: www.illinoisdreamfund.org

Summary   To provide financial assistance to undocumented residents of Illinois who are interested in attending college in any state.

Eligibility   This program is open to undocumented immigrants who are incoming freshmen, current undergraduates, or transfer students. Applicants must have resided with their parents or guardians while attending high school in Illinois and have graduated (or be graduating) from a high school or received a GED in Illinois after attending an Illinois high school for at least 3 years. They must have a GPA of 2.5 or higher and be attending or planning to attend a college or university in any state. Financial need is considered in the selection process.

Financial Data   The stipend is $6,000 for students at 4-year institutions or $2,000 for students at 2-year colleges. Funds are paid directly to the recipient's school.

Duration   1 year.

Number awarded   Varies each year.

Deadline   March of each year.

[254]
ILLINOIS LEGISLATIVE LATINO CAUCUS FOUNDATION SCHOLARSHIPS

Illinois Legislative Latino Caucus Foundation
c/o Jesse H. Ruiz
Drinker Biddle Reath LLP
191 North Wacker Drive, Suite 3700
Chicago, IL 60606-1615
(312) 569-1135   E-mail: illcfchicago@gmail.com
Web: www.illcf.org

Summary   To provide financial assistance to Latino residents of Illinois attending college in any state.

Eligibility   This program is open to residents of Illinois who are of Latino ancestry and currently enrolled as an undergraduate at a 2- or 4-year college or university in any state. Applicants must submit a 250-word statement explaining why receipt of this scholarship will help them achieve their educational and career goals. Financial need is considered in the selection process.

Financial Data   The stipend is $2,000.

Duration   1 year.

Number awarded Approximately 25 each year.

Deadline September of each year.

[255]
ILLINOIS MIGRANT COUNCIL POSTSECONDARY SCHOLARSHIPS

Illinois Migrant Council
Attn: Director of Migrant Education Services
118 South Clinton Street, Suite 500
Chicago, IL 60661
(312) 663-1522   Fax: (312) 663-1994
E-mail: bpessin@illinoismigrant.org
Web: www.illinoismigrant.org

Summary To provide financial assistance for college to Hispanic and other minority migrant and seasonal farmworkers and their families in Illinois.

Eligibility This program is open to Illinois residents who are Hispanic or other minority migrant or seasonal farmworkers and their families. Applicants must have been accepted by an Illinois vocational institute or 2- or 4-year college or university. They must have a high school diploma or GED and be able to meet low income guidelines.

Financial Data Stipends cover school fees, tuition, and books.

Duration 1 year.

Number awarded Varies each year.

Deadline Applications may be submitted at any time.

[256]
ILLINOIS MIGRANT COUNCIL SCHOLARSHIPS FOR OCCUPATIONAL SKILLS TRAINING

Illinois Migrant Council
Attn: Director of Migrant Education Services
118 South Clinton Street, Suite 500
Chicago, IL 60661
(312) 663-1522   Fax: (312) 663-1994
E-mail: bpessin@illinoismigrant.org
Web: www.illinoismigrant.org

Summary To provide financial assistance for college to Hispanic and other minority migrant and seasonal farmworkers and their families in Illinois.

Eligibility This program is open to Illinois residents who are Hispanic or other minority migrant or seasonal farmworkers and their families. Applicants must meet the eligibility criteria of the National Farmworker Jobs Program by depending on employment in agricultural labor that is characterized by chronic unemployment or underemployment. They must have been accepted by an Illinois vocational institute or community college for a program that leads to licensing or credentialing in a specific occupation or career.

Financial Data Stipends cover school fees, tuition, books, transportation assistance, training/work clothing and tools, and job placement assistance.

Duration 1 year.

Additional data This program is funded through the National Farmworker Jobs Program of the Employment and Training Administration within the U.S. Department of Labor.

Number awarded Varies each year.

Deadline Applications may be submitted at any time.

[257]
ILLINOIS NURSES FOUNDATION CENTENNIAL SCHOLARSHIP

Illinois Nurses Association
Attn: Illinois Nurses Foundation
P.O. Box 636
Manteno, IL 60950
(815) 468-8804   Fax: (773) 304-1419
E-mail: info@ana-illinois.org
Web: www.ana-illinois.org

Summary To provide financial assistance to nursing undergraduate and graduate students who are Hispanics or members of other underrepresented groups.

Eligibility This program is open to students working on an associate, bachelor's, or master's degree at an accredited NLNAC or CCNE school of nursing. Applicants must be members of a group underrepresented in nursing (Hispanics, African Americans, American Indians, Asians, and males). Undergraduates must have earned a passing grade in all nursing courses taken to date and have a GPA of 2.85 or higher. Graduate students must have completed at least 12 semester hours of graduate work and have a GPA of 3.0 or higher. All applicants must be willing to 1) act as a spokesperson to other student groups on the value of the scholarship to continuing their nursing education; and 2) be profiled in any media or marketing materials developed by the Illinois Nurses Foundation. Along with their application, they must submit a narrative of 250 to 500 words on how they, as nurses, plan to affect policy at either the state or national level that impacts on nursing or health care generally, or how they believe they will impact the nursing profession in general.

Financial Data A stipend is awarded (amount not specified).

Duration 1 year.

Number awarded 1 or more each year.

Deadline March of each year.

[258]
ILUMINA SCHOLARSHIP PROGRAM

Comite Pro Bolivia
P.O. Box 41267
Arlington, VA 22204
(571) 234-7354   E-mail: iluminascholarship@gmail.com
Web: www.proboliviausa.org/ilumina-scholarship

Summary To provide financial assistance to residents of California, Maryland, Virginia, and Washington D.C. who are of Bolivian descent and interested in attending college in any state.

Eligibility This program is open to residents of California, Maryland, Virginia, and Washington, D.C. who are graduating high school seniors or undergraduates currently enrolled at an accredited postsecondary institution in any state. Applicants must be Bolivian or of Bolivian descent (either parent born in Bolivia). They must have a GPA of 2.8 or higher. Along with their application, they must submit a 300-word essay on how they have contributed to the betterment of their Bolivian community. Selection is based that essay, academic achievement, extracurricular activities, leadership positions in the community, and financial need.

Financial Data The stipend is $2,000 or $1,000.

Duration 1 year; nonrenewable.

Number awarded 2 at $2,000 and 5 at $1,000 are awarded each year.

Deadline June of each year.

[259]
INDIANA CHAPTER AABE SCHOLARSHIPS

American Association of Blacks in Energy-Indiana
  Chapter
c/o Tawana Tucker, Scholarship Committee Chair
801 East 86th Avenue
Merrillville, IN 46410
E-mail: tawanatucker@nisource.com
Web: www.aabe.org/index.php?component=pages&id=348

Summary To provide financial assistance to Hispanics and members of other underrepresented minority groups who are high school seniors in Indiana and planning to major in an energy-related field at a college in any state.

Eligibility This program is open to seniors graduating from high schools in Indiana and planning to work on a bachelor's degree at a college or university in any state. Applicants must be Hispanics, African Americans, or Native Americans who have a GPA of 3.0 or higher and have taken the ACT and/or SAT test. Their intended major must be a field of business, engineering, physical science, mathematics, or technology related to energy. Along with their application, they must submit a 350-word essay that includes 1) when they discovered their interest in the field of energy and what sparked their interest; and 2) either what excites them about the field of energy or how they expect their education to prepare them for the field of energy. Financial need is not considered in the selection process.

Financial Data The stipend is $2,000 or $1,000.

Duration 1 year; nonrenewable.

Additional data Winners are eligible to compete for regional and national scholarships.

Number awarded 3 each year: 1 at $2,000 and 2 at $1,000.

Deadline March of each year.

[260]
INDIANA INDUSTRY LIAISON GROUP SCHOLARSHIP

Indiana Industry Liaison Group
c/o Candee Chambers, Vice Chair
DirectEmployers Association
9002 North Purdue Road, Suite 100
Indianapolis, IN 46268
(317) 874-9000   Toll Free: (866) 268-6202
E-mail: vchair@indianailg.org
Web: www.indianailg.org

Summary To provide financial assistance to students from any state enrolled at colleges and universities in Indiana who are Hispanics or have been involved in other activities to promote diversity.

Eligibility This program is open to residents of any state currently enrolled at an accredited college or university in Indiana. Applicants must either 1) be enrolled in programs or classes related to diversity/Affirmative Action (AA)/Equal Employment Opportunity (EEO); or 2) have work or volunteer experience with diversity/AA/EEO organizations. Along with their application, they must submit an essay of 400 to 500 words on 1 of the following topics: 1) their personal commitment to diversity/AA/EEO within their community or business; 2) a time or situation in which they were able to establish and/or sustain a commitment to diversity; 3) a time when they have taken a position in favor of affirmative action and/or diversity; or 4) activities in which they have participated within their community that demonstrate their personal commitment to moving the community's diversity agenda forward. Financial need is not considered in the selection process.

Financial Data The stipend is $1,000.

Duration 1 year.

Number awarded 1 each year.

Deadline January of each year.

[261]
INFRASTRUCTURE ENGINEERING SCHOLARSHIP

Conference of Minority Transportation Officials
Attn: National Scholarship Program
100 M Street, S.E., Suite 917
Washington, DC 20003
(202) 506-2917   E-mail: info@comto.org
Web: www.comto.org/page/scholarships

Summary To provide financial assistance to Hispanic and other minority upper-division and graduate students interested in working on a degree in transportation or a related field.

Eligibility This program is open to minority juniors, seniors, and graduate student at an accredited college, university, or vocational/technical school. Applicants must be studying transportation, engineering, planning, or a related discipline. They must have a GPA of 2.5 or higher. Along with their application they must submit a cover letter on their transportation-related career goals and life aspirations. Financial need is not considered in the selection process. Membership in the Conference of Minority Transportation Officials is considered a plus but is not required.

Financial Data The stipend is $2,500. Funds are paid directly to the recipient's college or university.

Duration 1 year.

Additional data This program is sponsored by Infrastructure Engineering Inc.

Number awarded 1 each year.

Deadline April of each year.

[262]
INROADS NATIONAL COLLEGE INTERNSHIPS

INROADS, Inc.
10 South Broadway, Suite 300
St. Louis, MO 63102
(314) 241-7488   Fax: (314) 241-9325
E-mail: info@inroads.org
Web: www.inroads.org

Summary To provide an opportunity for Hispanic and other young people of color to gain work experience in business or industry.

Eligibility This program is open to Hispanics, African Americans, and Native Americans who reside in the areas served by INROADS. Applicants must be interested in preparing for a career in accounting, business, computer sciences, economics. engineering, finance, health care, management information systems, retail store management, or supply chain management. They must be high school seniors or freshmen or sophomores in 4-year colleges and universities and have a GPA of 3.0 or higher. International students may apply if they have appropriate visas.

Financial Data Salaries vary, depending upon the specific internship assigned; recently, the range was from $170 to $750 per week.

Duration Up to 4 years.

Additional data INROADS places interns in Fortune 1000 companies, where training focuses on preparing them for corporate and community leadership. The INROADS organization offers internship opportunities through 35 local affiliates in 26 states, Canada, and Mexico.

Number awarded Approximately 2,000 high school and college students are currently working for more than 200 corporate sponsors nationwide.

Deadline March of each year.

[263]
INTERMOUNTAIN SECTION AWWA DIVERSITY SCHOLARSHIP

American Water Works Association-Intermountain
  Section
Attn: Member Services Coordinator
3430 East Danish Road
Sandy, UT 84093
(801) 712-1619, ext. 2   Fax: (801) 487-6699
E-mail: nicoleb@ims-awwa.org
Web: ims-awwa.site-ym.com/group/StudentPO

Summary To provide financial assistance to Hispanic and other minority undergraduate and graduate students working on a degree in the field of water quality, supply, and treatment at a university in the Intermountain West.

Eligibility This program is open to 1) women; and 2) students who identify as Hispanic or Latino, Black or African American, Native Hawaiian or other Pacific Islander, Asian, or American Indian or Alaska Native. Applicants must be entering or enrolled in an undergraduate or graduate program at a college or university in the Intermountain West (defined to include all or portions of Arizona, Colorado, Idaho, Montana, Nevada, New Mexico, Utah, or Wyoming) that relates to water quality, supply, or treatment. Along with their application, they must submit a 2-page essay on their academic interests and career goals and how those relate to water quality, supply, or treatment. Selection is based on that essay, letters of recommendation, and potential to contribute to the field of water quality, supply, and treatment in the Intermountain West.

Financial Data The stipend is $1,000. The winner also receives a 1-year student membership in the Intermountain Section of the American Water Works Association (AWWA).

Duration 1 year; nonrenewable.

Number awarded 1 each year.

Deadline November of each year.

[264]
INTERPUBLIC GROUP SCHOLARSHIP AND INTERNSHIP

New York Women in Communications, Inc.
Attn: NYWICI Foundation
355 Lexington Avenue, 15th Floor
New York, NY 10017-6603
(212) 297-2133   Fax: (212) 370-9047
E-mail: nywicipr@nywici.org
Web: www.nywici.org/foundation/scholarships

Summary To provide financial assistance and work experience to Hispanic and other women from ethnically diverse groups who are residents of designated eastern states and enrolled as juniors at a college in any state to prepare for a career in advertising or public relations.

Eligibility This program is open to female residents of New York, New Jersey, Connecticut, or Pennsylvania who are from ethnically diverse groups and currently enrolled as juniors at a college or university in any state. Also eligible are women who reside outside the 4 states but are currently enrolled at a college or university within 1 of the 5 boroughs of New York City. Applicants must be preparing for a career in advertising or public relations and have a GPA of 3.2 or higher. They must be available for a summer internship with Interpublic Group (IPG) in New York City. Along with their application, they must submit a 2-page resume; a personal essay of 300 words on an assigned topic that changes annually; 2 letters of recommendation; and an official transcript. Selection is based on academic record, need, demonstrated leadership, participation in school and community activities, honors and other awards or recognition, work experience, goals and aspirations, and unusual personal and/or family circumstances. U.S. citizenship or permanent status is required.

Financial Data The scholarship stipend ranges up to $10,000; the internship is salaried (amount not specified).

Duration 1 year.

Additional data This program is sponsored by IPG, a holding company for a large number of firms in the advertising industry.

Number awarded 2 each year.

Deadline January of each year.

[265]
IRTS SUMMER FELLOWSHIP PROGRAM

International Radio and Television Society Foundation
Attn: Director, Special Projects
420 Lexington Avenue, Suite 1601
New York, NY 10170-0101
(212) 867-6650   Toll Free: (888) 627-1266
Fax: (212) 867-6653   E-mail: apply@irts.org
Web: irtsfoundation.org/summer-fellowship-program

Summary To provide summer work experience to upper-division and graduate students, especially minorities and other Hispanics, who are interested in working during the summer in broadcasting and related fields in the New York City area.

Eligibility This program is open to juniors, seniors, and graduate students at 4-year colleges and universities. Applicants must either be a communications major or have demonstrated a strong interest in the field through extracurricular activities or other practical experience. Minority (Hispanic/

Latino, African American, Asian/Pacific Islander, American Indian/Alaskan Native) students are especially encouraged to apply.

Financial Data Travel, housing, and a living allowance are provided.

Duration 9 weeks during the summer.

Additional data The first week consists of a comprehensive orientation to broadcasting, cable, advertising, and new media. Then, the participants are assigned an 8-week fellowship. This full-time "real world" experience in a New York-based corporation allows them to reinforce or redefine specific career goals before settling into a permanent job. Fellows have worked at all 4 major networks, at local New York City radio and television stations, and at national rep firms, advertising agencies, and cable operations. This program includes fellowships reserved for students at designated universities (University of Pennsylvania, Brooklyn College, City College of New York, College of the Holy Cross) and the following named awards: the Thomas S. Murphy Fellowship (sponsored by ABC National Television Sales), the Helen Karas Memorial Fellowship, the Mel Karmazin Fellowship, the Neil Postman Memorial Summer Fellowship, the Ari Bluman Memorial Summer Fellowship (sponsored by Group M), the Thom Casadonte Memorial Fellowship (sponsored by Bloomberg), the Joanne Mercado Memorial Fellowship (sponsored by Nielsen), the Donald V. West Fellowship (sponsored by the Library of American Broadcasting Foundation), the Leslie Moonves Fellowship (sponsored by CBS Television Station Sales, and the Sumner M. Redstone Fellowship (sponsored by CBS Television Station Sales). Other sponsors include the National Academy of Television Arts & Sciences, Fox Networks, NBCUniversal, and Unilever.

Number awarded Varies; recently, 30 were awarded.

Deadline November of each year.

[266]
ITW SCHOLARSHIPS

Society of Women Engineers
Attn: Scholarship Selection Committee
203 North LaSalle Street, Suite 1675
Chicago, IL 60601-1269
(312) 596-5223   Toll Free: (877) SWE-INFO
Fax: (312) 644-8557   E-mail: scholarships@swe.org
Web: societyofwomenengineers.swe.org

Summary To provide financial assistance to undergraduate women, especially Hispanics and other underrepresented minorities, who are majoring in designated engineering specialties.

Eligibility This program is open to women who are entering their junior year at a 4-year ABET-accredited college or university. Applicants must be working full time on a degree in computer science, electrical or mechanical engineering, or polymer science. Preference is given to 1) members of groups underrepresented in engineering or computer science; 2) students interested in an internship with the sponsor; 3) residents of Illinois, Ohio, Texas, or Wisconsin; and 4) students attending the University of Illinois at Chicago, Georgia Institute of Technology, Ohio State University, Northwestern University, or Pennsylvania State University. Selection is based on merit. U.S. citizenship is required.

Financial Data The stipend is $2,500 per year.

Duration 1 year; may be renewed 1 additional year.

Additional data This program is sponsored by Illinois Tool Works, Inc.

Number awarded 2 each year.

Deadline February of each year.

[267]
J. PARIS MOSLEY SCHOLARSHIP

Cleveland Foundation
Attn: Scholarship Processing
1422 Euclid Avenue, Suite 1300
Cleveland, OH 44115-2001
(216) 861-3810   Fax: (216) 861-1729
E-mail: mbaker@clevefdn.org
Web: www.clevelandfoundation.org

Summary To provide financial assistance for college to high school seniors in any state who are deaf or whose primary caregivers are deaf, especially Latinos and other minorities.

Eligibility This program is open to high school seniors in any state who are deaf or hard of hearing or the children or grandchildren of deaf or hard of hearing parents or grandparents. Applicants must be planning to attend a college, university, vocational school, or other postsecondary program in any state. They must use some form of sign language, have a GPA of 2.5 or higher, and be able to demonstrate financial need. Preference is given to students of African American, Latino American, or Native American descent.

Financial Data The stipend ranges from $500 to $1,000.

Duration 1 year.

Number awarded 1 or more each year.

Deadline March of each year.

[268]
JACOBS ENGINEERING SCHOLARSHIP

Conference of Minority Transportation Officials
Attn: National Scholarship Program
100 M Street, S.E., Suite 917
Washington, DC 20003
(202) 506-2917   E-mail: info@comto.org
Web: www.comto.org/page/scholarships

Summary To provide financial assistance to Hispanic and other minority upper-division and graduate student members of the Conference of Minority Transportation Officials (COMTO) working on a degree in transportation or a related field.

Eligibility This program is open to minority juniors, seniors, and graduate student who are COMTO members. Applicants must be studying transportation, engineering (civil, construction, or environmental), safety, urban planning, or a related discipline. They must have a GPA of 3.0 or higher. Along with their application they must submit a cover letter on their transportation-related career goals and life aspirations. Financial need is not considered in the selection process. Membership in the Conference of Minority Transportation Officials is considered a plus but is not required.

Financial Data The stipend is $2,500. Funds are paid directly to the recipient's college or university.

Duration 1 year.

Additional data This program is sponsored by Jacobs Engineering Group.

Number awarded 1 or more each year.

Deadline April of each year.

[269]
JACOBS ENGINEERING TRANSPORTATION SCHOLARSHIP

Conference of Minority Transportation Officials
Attn: National Scholarship Program
100 M Street, S.E., Suite 917
Washington, DC 20003
(202) 506-2917   E-mail: info@comto.org
Web: www.comto.org/page/scholarships

Summary To provide financial assistance to Hispanic and other minority upper-division and graduate student members of the Conference of Minority Transportation Officials (COMTO) and family of members working on a degree in transportation or a related field.

Eligibility This program is open to minority juniors, seniors, and graduate student who are COMTO members or whose parents, guardians, or grandparents are members. Applicants must be studying transportation, engineering (civil, construction, or environmental), safety, urban planning, or a related discipline. They must have a GPA of 3.0 or higher. Along with their application they must submit a cover letter on their transportation-related career goals and life aspirations. Financial need is not considered in the selection process.

Financial Data The stipend is $2,500. Funds are paid directly to the recipient's college or university.

Duration 1 year.

Additional data This program is sponsored by Jacobs Engineering Group.

Number awarded 1 or more each year.

Deadline April of each year.

[270]
JAMES B. MORRIS SCHOLARSHIPS

James B. Morris Scholarship Fund
Attn: Scholarship Selection Committee
P.O. Box 12145
Des Moines, IA 50312
(515) 864-0922
Web: www.morrisscholarship.org

Summary To provide financial assistance to Hispanic and other minority undergraduate, graduate, and law students from Iowa.

Eligibility This program is open to minority students (Hispanics, African Americans, Asian/Pacific Islanders, or Native Americans) who are interested in working on an undergraduate or graduate degree. Applicants must be either Iowa residents attending a college or university anywhere in the United States or non-Iowa residents who are attending a college or university in Iowa. Along with their application, they must submit an essay of 250 to 500 words on why they are applying for this scholarship, activities or organizations in which they are involved, and their future plans. Selection is based on the essay, academic achievement (GPA of 2.5 or higher), community service, and financial need. U.S. citizenship is required.

Financial Data The stipend ranges from $1,000 to $2,500 per year.

Duration 1 year; may be renewed.

Additional data This fund was established in 1978 in honor of the J.B. Morris family, who founded the Iowa branch of the National Association for the Advancement of Colored People and published the *Iowa Bystander* newspaper. The program includes the Ann Chapman Scholarships, the Vincent Chapman, Sr. Scholarships, the Catherine Williams Scholarships, and the Brittany Hall Memorial Scholarships. Support for additional scholarships is provided by EMC Insurance Group and Wells Fargo Bank.

Number awarded Varies each year; recently, 22 were awarded.

Deadline February of each year.

[271]
JAMES CARLSON MEMORIAL SCHOLARSHIP

Oregon Office of Student Access and Completion
Attn: Scholarship Processing Coordinator
1500 Valley River Drive, Suite 100
Eugene, OR 97401-2146
(541) 687-7422   Toll Free: (800) 452-8807, ext. 7422
Fax: (541) 687-7414   TDD: (800) 735-2900
E-mail: cheryl.a.connolly@state.or.us
Web: app.oregonstudentaid.gov/Catalog/Default.aspx

Summary To provide financial assistance to Oregon residents, especially Hispanics and members of other diverse groups, who are majoring in education on the undergraduate or graduate school level at a school in any state.

Eligibility This program is open to residents of Oregon who are U.S. citizens or permanent residents and enrolled at a college or university in any state. Applicants must be either 1) college seniors or fifth-year students majoring in elementary or secondary education; or 2) graduate students working on an elementary or secondary certificate. Full-time enrollment and financial need are required. Priority is given to 1) students who come from diverse environments and submit an essay of 250 to 350 words on their experience living or working in diverse environments; 2) dependents of members of the Oregon Education Association; and 3) applicants committed to teaching autistic children.

Financial Data Stipends for scholarships offered by the Oregon Office of Student Access and Completion (OSAC) range from $1,000 to $10,000 but recently averaged $4,368.

Duration 1 year; nonrenewable.

Additional data This program is administered by the OSAC with funds provided by the Oregon Community Foundation.

Number awarded Varies each year; recently, 3 were awarded.

Deadline February of each year.

[272]
JAMES E. WEBB INTERNSHIPS

Smithsonian Institution
Attn: Office of Fellowships and Internships
470 L'Enfant Plaza, Suite 7102
P.O. Box 37012, MRC 902
Washington, DC 20013-7012
(202) 633-7070   Fax: (202) 633-7069
E-mail: siofi@si.edu
Web: www.smithsonianofi.com

Summary To provide internship opportunities throughout the Smithsonian Institution to Hispanic and other minority upper-division and graduate students in business or public administration.

Eligibility This program is open to minorities who are juniors, seniors, or graduate students majoring in areas of business or public administration (finance, human resource management, accounting, or general business administration). Applicants must have a GPA of 3.0 or higher. They must seek placement in offices, museums, and research institutes within the Smithsonian Institution.

Financial Data Interns receive a stipend of $600 per week and a travel allowance.

Duration 10 weeks during the summer, fall, or spring.

Number awarded Varies each year; recently, 8 of these internships were awarded.

Deadline January of each year for summer or fall; September of each year for spring.

[273]
JAMES ECHOLS SCHOLARSHIP

California Association for Health, Physical Education,
  Recreation and Dance
Attn: Chair, Scholarship Committee
1501 El Camino Avenue, Suite 3
Sacramento, CA 95815-2748
(916) 922-3596   Toll Free: (800) 499-3596 (within CA)
Fax: (916) 922-0133   E-mail: reception@cahperd.org
Web: www.cahperd.org

Summary To provide financial assistance to Hispanic and other minority student members of the California Association for Health, Physical Education, Recreation and Dance.

Eligibility This program is open to California residents who have been members of the association for at least 60 days and are attending a 2- or 4-year college or university in the state. Applicants must be undergraduate or graduate students working on a degree in health education, physical education, recreation, or dance and have completed at least 60 semester hours of college work. Selection is based on scholastic proficiency (a GPA of 3.0 or higher); leadership ability in school, community, and professional activities; and personal qualities of enthusiasm, cooperativeness, responsibility, initiative, and ability to work with others. This scholarship is awarded to the highest-ranked minority (Asian, African American, Latino, or Native American) applicant.

Financial Data The stipend is $1,000.

Duration 1 year.

Number awarded 1 each year.

Deadline November of each year.

[274]
JAMES J. WYCHOR SCHOLARSHIPS

Minnesota Broadcasters Association
Attn: Scholarship Program
3033 Excelsior Boulevard, Suite 440
Minneapolis, MN 55416
(612) 926-8123   Toll Free: (800) 245-5838
Fax: (612) 926-9761
E-mail: llasere@minnesotabroadcasters.com
Web: www.minnesotabroadcasters.com/career-prep

Summary To provide financial assistance to Minnesota residents, including Hispanics and other minorities, who are interested in studying broadcasting at a college in any state.

Eligibility This program is open to residents of Minnesota who are accepted or enrolled at an accredited postsecondary institution in any state offering a broadcast-related curriculum. Applicants must have a high school or college GPA of 2.5 or higher and must submit a 500-word essay on why they wish to prepare for a career in broadcasting or electronic media. Employment in the broadcasting industry is not required, but students who are employed must include a letter from their general manager describing the duties they have performed as a radio or television station employee and evaluating their potential for success in the industry. Financial need is not considered in the selection process. Some of the scholarships are awarded only to minority or women candidates.

Financial Data The stipend is $1,500.

Duration 1 year; recipients who are college seniors may reapply for an additional 1-year renewal as a graduate student.

Number awarded 10 each year, distributed as follows: 3 within the 7-county metro area, 5 allocated geographically throughout the state (northeast, northwest, central, southeast, southwest), and 2 reserved specifically for women and minority applicants.

Deadline June of each year.

[275]
JANE C. WALDBAUM ARCHAEOLOGICAL FIELD SCHOOL SCHOLARSHIP

Archaeological Institute of America
c/o Boston University
656 Beacon Street, Sixth Floor
Boston, MA 02215-2006
(617) 358-4184   Fax: (617) 353-6550
E-mail: fellowships@aia.bu.edu
Web: www.archaeological.org/grants/708

Summary To provide funding to upper-division and graduate students, especially Hispanics and other minorities, who are interested in participating in an archaeological field project in the United States or any other country.

Eligibility This program is open to junior and senior undergraduates and first-year graduate students who are currently enrolled at a college or university in the United States or Canada. Minority and disadvantaged students are encouraged to apply. Applicants must be interested in participating in an archaeological excavation or survey project in any country. They may not have previously participated in an archaeological excavation. Students majoring in archaeology or related disciplines are especially encouraged to apply.

Financial Data The grant is $1,000.

Duration At least 1 month during the summer.

Additional data These scholarships were first awarded in 2007.

Number awarded Varies each year; recently, 15 were awarded.

Deadline February of each year.

[276]
JIMMY A. YOUNG MEMORIAL EDUCATION RECOGNITION AWARD

American Association for Respiratory Care
Attn: American Respiratory Care Foundation
9425 North MacArthur Boulevard, Suite 100
Irving, TX 75063-4706
(972) 243-2272　　　　　　　　Fax: (972) 484-2720
E-mail: info@arcfoundation.org
Web: www.arcfoundation.org

Summary To provide financial assistance to college students, especially Hispanics and other minorities, interested in becoming respiratory therapists.

Eligibility Candidates must be enrolled in an accredited respiratory therapy program, have completed at least 1 semester/quarter of the program, and have a GPA of 3.0 or higher. Preference is given to nominees of minority origin. Applications must include 6 copies of an original referenced paper on some aspect of respiratory care and letters of recommendation. The foundation prefers that the candidates be nominated by a school or program, but any student may initiate a request for sponsorship by a school (in order that a deserving candidate is not denied the opportunity to compete simply because the school does not initiate the application).

Financial Data The stipend is $1,000. The award also provides airfare, 1 night's lodging, and registration for the association's international congress.

Duration 1 year.

Number awarded 1 each year.

Deadline June of each year.

[277]
JOANN JETER MEMORIAL DIVERSITY SCHOLARSHIP

Associates Foundation
Attn: Claudia Perot, Scholarship Committee Chair
JCD 6
P.O. Box 3621
Portland, OR 97208-3621
(503) 230-3754
Web: www.theassociatesonline.org

Summary To provide financial assistance to students who are Hispanics or reflect other elements of diversity and are interested in working on an undergraduate or graduate degree in any field.

Eligibility This program is open to students who are enrolled or planning to enroll as a full-time undergraduate or graduate student at an accredited 4-year college or university or a full-time student at a 2-year college enrolled in a program leading to an academic degree. Applicants must be from a diverse background, including first-generation college student, cultural and/or ethnic minority background, low-income, or other clearly articulated aspects of diversity as presented in an essay.

Financial Data The stipend ranges from $500 to $1,000.

Duration 1 year.

Number awarded Varies each year; recently, 3 were awarded.

Deadline April of each year.

[278]
JOHN AND MURIEL LANDIS SCHOLARSHIPS

American Nuclear Society
Attn: Scholarship Coordinator
555 North Kensington Avenue
La Grange Park, IL 60526-5535
(708) 352-6611　　　　　Toll Free: (800) 323-3044
Fax: (708) 352-0499　　　　E-mail: outreach@ans.org
Web: committees.ans.org/need/apply.html

Summary To provide financial assistance to undergraduate or graduate students, especially Hispanics and other minorities, who are interested in preparing for a career in nuclear-related fields and can demonstrate financial need.

Eligibility This program is open to undergraduate and graduate students at colleges or universities located in the United States who are preparing for, or planning to prepare for, a career in nuclear science, nuclear engineering, or a nuclear-related field. Qualified high school seniors are also eligible. Applicants must have greater than average financial need and have experienced circumstances that render them disadvantaged. Along with their application, they must submit an essay on their academic and professional goals, experiences that have affected those goals, etc. Selection is based on that essay, academic achievement, letters of recommendation, and financial need. Women and members of minority groups are especially urged to apply. U.S. citizenship is not required.

Financial Data The stipend is $5,000, to be used to cover tuition, books, fees, room, and board.

Duration 1 year; nonrenewable.

Number awarded Up to 9 each year.

Deadline January of each year.

[279]
JOHN DEERE SCHOLARSHIP FOR FEMALE AND MINORITY STUDENTS

American Welding Society
Attn: AWS Foundation, Inc.
8669 N.W. 36th Street, Suite 130
Doral, FL 33166-6672
(305) 443-9353　　　Toll Free: (800) 443-9353, ext. 250
Fax: (305) 443-7559　　　E-mail: nprado-pulido@aws.org
Web: www.aws.org/foundation/page/john-deere-scholarship

Summary To provide financial assistance to Hispanic and other minority undergraduate students, especially those from designated states, who are working on a degree in welding engineering or welding engineering technology at a university in any state.

Eligibility This award is available to U.S. citizens who are women or members of minority groups. Preference is given to residents of Illinois, Iowa, Kansas Minnesota, Missouri, Nebraska, North Dakota, South Dakota, or Wisconsin. Applicants must have completed at least 1 semester of full-time study in a 4-year undergraduate program of welding engineering, welding engineering technology, or mechanical or manufacturing engineering with a welding emphasis. They must have a GPA of 3.0 or higher. Along with their application, they must submit a statement of unmet financial need (although financial need is not required to apply), transcripts, 2 letters of recommendation, and a personal statement that provides their personal objectives and values, their career objectives with a statement of why they want to prepare for a career in welding, participation and leadership in campus and outside organizations, participation in American Welding Society (AWS) student and section activities, and general background information.

Financial Data The stipend is $2,500.

Duration 1 year; nonrenewable.

Additional data This program is sponsored by John Deere.

Number awarded 1 each year.

Deadline February of each year.

[280]
JOHN DEERE SCHOLARSHIP OF THE SOCIETY OF HISPANIC PROFESSIONAL ENGINEERS

Society of Hispanic Professional Engineers
Attn: Scholarships
13181 Crossroads Parkway North, Suite 450
City of Industry, CA 91715
(323) 725-3970, ext. 108   Fax: (323) 725-0316
E-mail: scholarships@shpe.org
Web: shpe.awardspring.com

Summary To provide financial assistance to Hispanic undergraduate and graduate students who are working on a degree in specified fields of science, technology, engineering, or matheamtics (STEM).

Eligibility This program is open to U.S. citizens and permanent residents of Hispanic descent who are enrolled full time at a college or university in the United States or Puerto Rico. Applicants must be sophomores, juniors, or first-year graduate students working on a bachelor's or master's degree in engineering (aerospace, agricultural, computer, electrical, environmental, manufacturing, materials, mechanical, systems, or welding), computer science, management information systems, or technology management. They must be members of the Society of Hispanic Professional Engineers (SHPE) and have a GPA of 3.0 or higher. Selection is based on academic standing and financial need.

Financial Data The stipend is $2,000.

Duration 1 year.

Additional data This program is sponsored by John Deere.

Number awarded 1 or more each year.

Deadline July of each year.

[281]
JOHN S. MARTINEZ LEADERSHIP SCHOLARSHIP

National Hispanic Caucus of State Legislators
Attn: Scholarship Applications
444 North Capitol Street, N.W., Suite 404
Washington, DC 20001
(202) 434-8070   Fax: (202) 434-8072
E-mail: rhina@nhcsl.org
Web: www.nhcsl.org/scholarship.php

Summary To provide financial assistance for college to Hispanic high school students in states that have an Hispanic member of the state legislature.

Eligibility This program is open to juniors and seniors at public high schools in any of the 38 states that have an Hispanic member of the state legislature. Candidates must be nominated by a school official or an Hispanic legislator. Nom-

inees must be of Hispanic descent, have a GPA of 3.0 or higher, be U.S. citizens, and be planning to enroll full time at a college or university in any state. Financial need is considered in the selection process.

Financial Data The stipend is $3,000.

Duration 1 year; nonrenewable.

Additional data This program began in 2012 with support from Comcast.

Number awarded Varies each year; recently, 11 were awarded.

Deadline March of each year.

[282]
JOSE A. VILA SCHOLARSHIP

Cuban-American Association of Civil Engineers
Attn: Nominating Committee
Robyana and Associates, Inc.
5829 N.W. 158 Street
Miami Lakes, FL 33014
(305) 823-9516   Fax: (305) 823-1569
E-mail: info@robayna.com
Web: www.c-aace.org/scholarship-awards/premio-vila

Summary To provide financial assistance to Cuban American undergraduates from any state who are studying civil engineering at a college in Florida.

Eligibility This program is open to students from any state who have completed at least 80 credits in a civil engineering program at a college or university in Florida. Applicants must be Cuban, of Cuban descent, or of Hispanic heritage and able to speak, read, and write Spanish fluently. They must have a GPA of 3.0 or higher and be able to demonstrate financial need. Along with their application, they must submit a 500-word essay on why they think they deserve this scholarship.

Financial Data The stipend is $1,000.

Duration 1 year.

Number awarded 3 each year.

Deadline November of each year.

[283]
JOSE MARTI SCHOLARSHIP CHALLENGE GRANT FUND

Florida Department of Education
Attn: Office of Student Financial Assistance
State Scholarship and Grant Programs
325 West Gaines Street, Suite 1314
Tallahassee, FL 32399-0400
(850) 410-5160   Toll Free: (888) 827-2004
Fax: (850) 487-1809   E-mail: osfa@fldoe.org
Web: www.floridastudentfinancialaid.org

Summary To provide financial assistance to Hispanic American high school seniors and graduate students in Florida.

Eligibility This program is open to Florida residents of Spanish culture who were born in, or whose natural parent was born in, Mexico or a Hispanic country of the Caribbean, Central America, or South America. Applicants must be citizens or eligible noncitizens of the United States, be enrolled or planning to enroll as full-time undergraduate or graduate students at an eligible postsecondary school in Florida, be able to demonstrate financial need as determined by a nationally-recognized needs analysis service, and have earned a cumulative GPA of 3.0 or higher in high school or, if a graduate school applicant, in undergraduate course work.

Financial Data The maximum grant is $2,000 per academic year. Available funds are contingent upon matching contributions from private sources.

Duration 1 year; may be renewed if the student maintains full-time enrollment and a GPA of 3.0 or higher and continues to demonstrate financial need.

Number awarded Varies each year; recently, this program awarded 13 new and 26 renewal grants.

Deadline March of each year.

[284]
JOSEPHINE AND BENJAMIN WEBBER TRUST SCHOLARSHIPS

Arizona Association of Family and Consumer Sciences
Attn: Webber Trusts Committee
Julie Villaverde, Committee Chair
University of Arizona
Financial Services Office
Tucson, AZ 85719-0521
(502) 626-3094   Fax: (502) 621-7078
E-mail: webbertrusts@gmail.com
Web: cals.arizona.edu/webbertrusts

Summary To provide financial assistance to Hispanic women from mining towns in Arizona who are interested in working on an undergraduate or graduate degree in a field related to family and consumer sciences at a school in the state.

Eligibility This program is open to Hispanic women who reside in the following Arizona mining towns: Ajo, Arizona City, Bisbee, Clifton, Douglas, Duncan, Globe, Green Valley, Hayden, Kingman, Kearny, Mammoth, Morenci, Prescott, Safford, Sahuarita, San Manuel, Seligman, Superior, or Winkelman. If too few female Hispanic residents of those towns apply, the program may be open to 1) non-Hispanic women who live in those towns; and/or 2) Hispanic women who currently live elsewhere in Arizona and whose parents or grandparents had lived or continue to live in those communities. Applicants must be enrolled or planning to enroll at a college or university in Arizona to work on an undergraduate or graduate degree. Eligible fields of study include those in the following categories: foods, nutrition, and/or dietetics; restaurant and food service management; culinary arts; family studies; interior design; family and consumer science education; dietetic education; early childhood education; or apparel and clothing. Financial need is considered in the selection process.

Financial Data Funding at public colleges and universities provides for payment of tuition and fees, books, educational supplies, housing, food, and transportation to and from campus. At private institutions, stipend amounts are equivalent to those at public schools.

Duration 1 year; may be renewed for a total of 8 semesters and 2 summers of undergraduate study or 4 semesters and 2 summers of graduate study.

Additional data This program began in 1980.

Number awarded Varies each year; recently, 5 were awarded.

Deadline March of each year.

[285]
JOSIE K. CLAIBORNE MEMORIAL SCHOLARSHIPS

American Association of Blacks in Energy-South Carolina Chapter
Attn: Scholarship Committee
P.O. Box 7696
Columbia, SC 29202
(803) 933-7252   E-mail: mpriester-clarke@scana.com
Web: www.aabe.org/index.php?component=pages&id=920

Summary To provide financial assistance to Hispanics and members of other underrepresented minority groups who are high school seniors in South Carolina and planning to major in an energy-related field at a college in any state.

Eligibility This program is open to seniors graduating from high schools in South Carolina and planning to work on a bachelor's degree at a college or university in any state. Applicants must be Hispanics, African Americans, or Native Americans who have a GPA of 3.0 or higher and have taken the ACT and/or SAT test. Their intended major must be a field of business, engineering, physical sciences, mathematics, or technology related to energy. Along with their application, they must submit a 350-word essay that includes 1) when they discovered their interest in the field of energy and what sparked their interest; and 2) either what excites them about the field of energy or how they expect their education to prepare them for the field of energy. Financial need is not considered in the selection process.

Financial Data The stipend is $1,000.

Duration 1 year; nonrenewable.

Additional data Winners are eligible to compete for regional and national scholarships.

Number awarded Up to 2 each year.

Deadline March of each year.

[286]
JUDITH MCMANUS PRICE SCHOLARSHIPS

American Planning Association
Attn: Leadership Affairs Associate
205 North Michigan Avenue, Suite 1200
Chicago, IL 60601
(312) 431-9100   Fax: (312) 786-6700
E-mail: mgroh@planning.org
Web: www.planning.org/scholarships/apa

Summary To provide financial assistance to Hispanic and other underrepresented minority students enrolled in undergraduate or graduate degree programs at recognized planning schools.

Eligibility This program is open to undergraduate and graduate students in urban and regional planning who are women or members of the following minority groups: Hispanic American, African American, Native American, or female. Applicants must be citizens of the United States and able to document financial need. They must intend to work as practicing planners in the public sector. Along with their application, they must submit a 2-page personal and background statement describing how their education will be applied to career goals and why they chose planning as a career path. Selection is based (in order of importance), on: 1) commitment to planning as reflected in their personal statement and on their resume; 2) academic achievement and/or improvement during the past 2 years; 3) letters of recommendation; 4) financial need; and 5) professional presentation.

Financial Data Stipends range from $2,000 to $4,000 per year. The money may be applied to tuition and living expenses only. Payment is made to the recipient's university and divided by terms in the school year.

Duration 1 year; recipients may reapply.

Additional data This program began in 2002.

Number awarded Varies each year; recently, 3 were awarded.

Deadline April of each year.

[287]
JULIA E. MENDEZ/HPRA-NY SCHOLARSHIP PROGRAM

Hispanic Public Relations Association-New York Chapter
c/o Melissa Carrion, President
Cohn & Wolfe
200 Fifth Avenue
New York, NY 10010
(212) 798-9700   E-mail: info@ny.npra-usa.org
Web: www.hpra-usa.org

Summary To provide financial assistance to Hispanic undergraduate and graduate students from Connecticut, New Jersey, and New York who are attending college in those states and preparing for a career in public relations.

Eligibility This program is open to residents of Connecticut, New Jersey, and New York who are of Hispanic descent and enrolled as sophomores, juniors, or graduate students at a 4-year college or university in those states. Applicants must have a GPA of 2.7 or higher cumulatively and 3.0 or higher in their major subject. They must be majoring in public relations, communications, journalism, advertising, and/or marketing. Along with their application, they must submit a letter of recommendation, official university transcripts, a 1-page personal statement explaining their career and educational aspirations as well as their involvement in the Hispanic community, and a 1-page resume.

Financial Data The stipend is $1,000.

Duration 1 year.

Additional data This program began in 2013 and was given its current name in 2016. Recipients are invited to attend the sponsor's Premio Awards dinner in Los Angeles in October.

Number awarded 2 each year.

Deadline June of each year.

[288]
JUSTINE E. GRANNER MEMORIAL SCHOLARSHIP

Iowa United Methodist Foundation
2301 Rittenhouse Street
Des Moines, IA 50321
(515) 974-8927
Web: www.iumf.org/scholarships/general

Summary To provide financial assistance to members of United Methodist churches in Iowa who are Hispanics or other ethnic minorities interested in majoring in a health-related field.

Eligibility This program is open to ethnic minority students who are members of United Methodist churches and prepar-

ing for a career in nursing, public health, or a related field at a college or school of nursing in Iowa. Preference is given to graduates of Iowa high schools. Applicants must have a GPA of 3.0 or higher. They must submit transcripts, 3 letters of recommendation, ACT and/or SAT scores, and documentation of financial need.

Financial Data The stipend is $1,000.

Duration 1 year.

Number awarded 1 each year.

Deadline February of each year.

[289]
KAISER PERMANENTE COLORADO DIVERSITY SCHOLARSHIP PROGRAM

Kaiser Permanente
Attn: Diversity Development Department
10065 East Harvard Avenue, Suite 400
Denver, CO 80231
Toll Free: (877) 457-4772
E-mail: co-diversitydevelopment@kp.org

Summary To provide financial assistance to Colorado residents who are Latinos or come from other diverse backgrounds and are interested in working on an undergraduate or graduate degree in a health care field at a public college in the state.

Eligibility This program is open to all residents of Colorado, including those who identify as 1 or more of the following: Latino, African American, Asian Pacific, Native American, lesbian, gay, bisexual, transgender, intersex, U.S. veteran, and/or a person with a disability. Applicants must be enrolled or planning to enroll full time at a publicly-funded college, university, or technical school in Colorado as 1) a graduating high school senior with a GPA of 2.7 or higher; 2) a GED recipient with a GED score of 520 or higher; 3) an undergraduate student; or 4) a graduate or doctoral student. They must be preparing for a career in health care (e.g., athletic training, audiology, cardiovascular perfusion technology, clinical medical assisting, cytotechnology, dental assisting, dental hygiene, diagnostic medicine, dietetics, emergency medical technology, medicine, nursing, occupational therapy, pharmacy, phlebotomy, physical therapy, physician assistant, radiology, respiratory therapy, social work, sports medicine, surgical technology). Selection is based on academic achievement, character qualities, community outreach and volunteering, and financial need.

Financial Data Stipends range from $1,400 to $2,600 per year.

Duration 1 year; may be renewed.

Number awarded Varies each year; recently, 17 were awarded.

Deadline March of each year.

[290]
KAISER PERMANENTE NORTHWEST HEALTH CARE CAREER SCHOLARSHIPS

Kaiser Permanente Northwest
Attn: Community Health Careers Coordinator
500 N.E. Multnomah Street, Suite 100
Portland, OR 97232
(503) 813-4478   E-mail: kpnwscholarship@gmail.com
Web: www.kpnwscholarship.scholarsapply.org/Awards

Summary To provide financial assistance to seniors at designated high schools in Oregon and southwestern Washington, especially Hispanics and other minorities, who plan to attend college in any state to prepare for a career as a health care professional.

Eligibility This program is open to seniors graduating from 106 approved high schools in Oregon and 26 in southwestern Washington. Applicants must be planning to enroll full time at a college or university in any state to prepare for a career as a medical or dental health care professional. They must have a GPA of 2.5 or higher. Proof of U.S. citizenship or permanent resident status is not required; undocumented students and those with Deferred Action for Childhood Arrival (DACA) status are eligible. Preference is given to students who 1) can demonstrate financial need; 2) are the first member of their family to attend college; 3) speak English plus a second language fluently; 4) are a member of a diverse population, including an ethnic or racial group underrepresented in the health professions (Black or African American, Hispanic or Latino, Native American, Asian or Pacific Islander), LGBTQ, and those with a disability; 5) engage in organized health and wellness activities at school and/or school-based health center activities; or 6) regularly volunteer or work in a public health setting such as a free clinic or health education organization.

Financial Data Most stipends are $2,000 per year. Some awards are for $10,000 or $5,000 ($5,000 or $2,500 per year).

Duration 1 year (the freshman year of college) for the $2,000 awards or 2 years (the freshmen and sophomore years) for the $10,000 and $5,000 students; recipients may apply for 1 additional year (the junior year of college) of funding at $2,000.

Additional data This program began in 2008.

Number awarded At least 1 at each of the 132 approved high schools plus 24 to former recipients entering their junior year of college.

Deadline January of each year.

[291]
KANSAS ETHNIC MINORITY SCHOLARSHIP PROGRAM

Kansas Board of Regents
Attn: Student Financial Assistance
1000 S.W. Jackson Street, Suite 520
Topeka, KS 66612-1368
(785) 296-3518   Fax: (785) 296-0983
E-mail: loldhamburns@ksbor.org
Web: www.kansasregents.org/scholarships_and_grants

Summary To provide financial assistance to Hispanics and other minority students in Kansas who are interested in attending college in the state.

Eligibility Eligible to apply are Kansas residents who fall into 1 of these minority groups: Hispanic, American Indian, Alaskan Native, African American, Asian, or Pacific Islander. Applicants may be current college students (enrolled in community colleges, colleges, or universities in Kansas), but high school seniors graduating in the current year receive priority consideration. Minimum academic requirements include 1 of the following: 1) ACT score of 21 or higher or combined mathematics and critical reading SAT score of 990 or higher; 2) cumulative GPA of 3.0 or higher; 3) high school rank in upper 33%; 4) completion of the Kansas Scholars Curriculum (4 years of English, 4 years of mathematics, 3 years of science, 3 years of social studies, and 2 years of foreign language); 5) selection by the National Merit Corporation in any category; or 6) selection by the College Board as a Hispanic Scholar. Selection is based primarily on financial need.

Financial Data A stipend of up to $1,850 is provided, depending on financial need and availability of state funds.

Duration 1 year; may be renewed for up to 3 additional years (4 additional years for designated 5-year programs), provided the recipient maintains a 2.0 cumulative GPA and has financial need.

Number awarded Approximately 200 each year.

Deadline April of each year.

[292]
KANSAS SPJ MINORITY STUDENT SCHOLARSHIP

Society of Professional Journalists-Kansas Professional Chapter
c/o Denise Neil, Scholarship Committee
Wichita Eagle
825 East Douglas Avenue
P.O. Box 820
Wichita, KS 67201-0820
(316) 268-6327   E-mail: dneil@wichitaeagle.com

Summary To provide financial assistance to residents of any state enrolled at colleges and universities in Kansas who are Hispanics or members of other racial or ethnic minority groups and interested in a career in journalism.

Eligibility This program is open to residents of any state who are members of a racial or ethnic minority group and entering their junior or senior year at colleges and universities in Kansas. Applicants must be seriously considering a career in journalism. They must be enrolled at least half time and have a GPA of 2.5 or higher. Along with their application, they must submit a professional resume, 4 to 6 examples of their best work (clips or stories, copies of photographs, tapes or transcripts of broadcasts, printouts of web pages) and a 1-page cover letter about themselves, how they came to be interested in journalism, their professional goals, and (if appropriate) their financial need for this scholarship.

Financial Data The stipend is $1,000.

Duration 1 year.

Number awarded 1 each year.

Deadline March of each year.

[293]
KATHY MANN MEMORIAL SCHOLARSHIP

Wisconsin Education Association Council
Attn: Scholarship Committee
33 Nob Hill Drive
P.O. Box 8003
Madison, WI 53708-8003
(608) 276-7711   Toll Free: (800) 362-8034, ext. 278
Fax: (608) 276-8203   E-mail: BrisackM@weac.org
Web: www.weac.org

Summary To provide financial assistance to Hispanic and other minority high school seniors whose parent is a member of the Wisconsin Education Association Council (WEAC) and who plan to study education at a college in any state.

Eligibility This program is open to high school seniors whose parent is an active WEAC member, an active retired member, or a person who died while holding a WEAC membership. Applicants must be members of a minority group (Hispanic, American Indian, Eskimo or Aleut, Asian or Pacific Islander, or Black). They must rank in the top 25% of their graduating class or have a GPA of 3.0 or higher, plan to major or minor in education at a college in any state, and intend to teach in Wisconsin. Selection is based on an essay on why they want to enter the education profession and what they hope to accomplish, GPA, letters of recommendation, school and community activities, and financial need.

Financial Data The stipend is $1,450 per year.

Duration 4 years, provided the recipient maintains a GPA of 3.0 or higher.

Number awarded 1 each year.

Deadline February of each year.

[294]
KAY LONGCOPE SCHOLARSHIP AWARD

National Lesbian & Gay Journalists Association
2120 L Street, N.W., Suite 850
Washington, DC 20037
(202) 588-9888   Fax: (202) 588-1818
E-mail: info@nlgfa.org
Web: www.nlgja.org/resources/longcope

Summary To provide financial assistance to Hispanic and other lesbian, gay, bisexual, and transgender (LGBT) undergraduate and graduate students of color who are interested in preparing for a career in journalism.

Eligibility This program is open to LGBT students of color who are current or incoming undergraduate or graduate students at a college, university, or community college. Applicants must be planning a career in journalism and be committed to furthering the sponsoring organization's mission of fair and accurate coverage of the LGBT community. They must demonstrate an awareness of the issues facing the LGBT community and the importance of fair and accurate news coverage. For undergraduates, a declared major in journalism and/or communications is desirable but not required; non-journalism majors may demonstrate their commitment to a journalism career through work samples, internships, and work on a school news publication, online news service, or broadcast affiliate. Graduate students must be enrolled in a journalism program. Along with their application, they must submit a 1-page resume, 5 work samples, official transcripts, 3 letters of recommendation, and a 750-word news story on a designated subject involving the LGBT community. U.S. citizenship or permanent resident status is required. Selection is based on journalistic and scholastic ability.

Financial Data The stipend is $3,000.

Duration 1 year.

Additional data This program began in 2008.

Number awarded 1 each year.

Deadline May of each year.

[295]
KCACTF LATINIDAD PLAYWRITING AWARD

John F. Kennedy Center for the Performing Arts
Education Department
Attn: Kennedy Center American College Theater Festival
2700 F Street, N.W.
Washington, DC 20566
(202) 416-8864   Fax: (202) 416-8860
E-mail: ghenry@kennedy-center.org
Web: web.kennedy-center.org

Summary To recognize and reward outstanding plays by Latino student playwrights.

Eligibility Latino students at any accredited junior or senior college in the United States are eligible to compete, provided their college agrees to participate in the Kennedy Center American College Theater Festival (KCACTF). Undergraduate students must be carrying at least 6 semester hours, graduate students must be enrolled in at least 3 semester hours, and continuing part-time students must be enrolled in a regular degree or certificate program. This award is presented to the best student-written play by a Latino.

Financial Data The prizes are $1,000 for first place and $500 for second place. Other benefits include appropriate membership in the Dramatists Guild and an all-expense paid professional development opportunity.

Duration The award is presented annually.

Additional data This award, first presented in 2000, is part of the Michael Kanin Playwriting Awards Program. The sponsoring college or university must pay a registration fee of $275 for each production.

Number awarded 2 each year.

Deadline November of each year.

[296]
KENTUCKY LIBRARY ASSOCIATION SCHOLARSHIP FOR MINORITY STUDENTS

Kentucky Library Association
c/o Executive Director
5932 Timber Ridge Drive, Suite 101
Prospect, KY 40059
(502) 223-5322   Fax: (502) 223-4937
E-mail: info@kylibasn.org
Web: www.klaonline.org/scholarships965.cfm

Summary To provide financial assistance to Hispanics and members of other minority groups who are residents of Kentucky or attending school there and are working on an undergraduate or graduate degree in library science.

Eligibility This program is open to members of minority groups (defined as Hispanic, American Indian, Alaskan Native, Black, Pacific Islander, or other ethnic group) who are entering or continuing at a graduate library school accredited by the American Library Association (ALA) or an undergraduate library program accredited by the National Council for Teacher Education (NCATE). Applicants must be residents of Kentucky or a student in a library program in the state. Along with their application, they must submit a statement of their career objectives, why they have chosen librarianship as a career, and their reasons for applying for this scholarship. Selection is based on that statement, cumulative undergraduate and graduate GPA (if applicable), academic merit and potential, and letters of recommendation. U.S. citizenship or permanent resident status is required.

Financial Data   The stipend is $1,000.

Duration   1 year; nonrenewable.

Number awarded   1 or more each year.

Deadline   June of each year.

[297]
KENTUCKY MINORITY EDUCATOR RECRUITMENT AND RETENTION SCHOLARSHIPS

Kentucky Department of Education
Attn: Office of Next-Generation Learners
500 Mero Street, 19th Floor
Frankfort, KY 40601
(502) 564-1479   Fax: (502) 564-4007
TDD: (502) 564-4970
E-mail: jennifer.baker@education.ky.gov
Web: www.education.ky.gov

Summary   To provide forgivable loans to Hispanic and other minority undergraduate and graduate students enrolled in Kentucky public institutions who want to become teachers.

Eligibility   This program is open to residents of Kentucky who are undergraduate or graduate students pursuing initial teacher certification at a public university or community college in the state. Applicants must have a GPA of 2.75 or higher and either maintain full-time enrollment or be a part-time student within 18 semester hours of receiving a teacher education degree. They must be U.S. citizens and meet the Kentucky definition of a minority student.

Financial Data   Stipends are $5,000 per year at the 8 state universities in Kentucky or $2,000 per year at community and technical colleges. This is a scholarship/loan program. Recipients are required to teach 1 semester in Kentucky for each semester or summer term the scholarship is received. If they fail to fulfill that requirement, the scholarship converts to a loan payable at 6% annually.

Duration   1 year; may be renewed up to 3 additional years.

Additional data   The Kentucky General Assembly established this program in 1992.

Number awarded   Varies each year.

Deadline   Each state college of teacher education sets its own deadline.

[298]
KIA MOTORS AMERICA SCHOLARSHIP

Hispanic Association of Colleges and Universities
Attn: National Scholarship Program
8415 Datapoint Drive, Suite 400
San Antonio, TX 78229
(210) 692-3805   Fax: (210) 692-0823
TDD: (800) 855-2880   E-mail: scholarship@hacu.net
Web: www.hacu.net/hacu/Scholarships.asp

Summary   To provide financial assistance to undergraduate and students at member institutions of the Hispanic Association of Colleges and Universities (HACU) who are studying any field.

Eligibility   This program is open to full-time sophomores, juniors, and graduate students at HACU member 4-year institutions in the United States or Puerto Rico. Applicants may be working on a degree in any field, but they must have a GPA of 3.0 or higher. First generation college students are strongly encouraged to apply.

Financial Data   The stipend is $4,000.

Duration   1 year.

Additional data   This program is sponsored by KIA Motors America.

Number awarded   16 each year.

Deadline   May of each year.

[299]
KINESIS SCHOLARSHIPS

Kinesis Foundation
89 de Diego Avenue
PMB 607, Suite 105
San Juan, PR 00927
(787) 772-8269   E-mail: info@kinesispr.org
Web: www.kinesispr.org/beca-kinesis

Summary   To provide financial assistance to residents of Puerto Rico who are entering an undergraduate or graduate program at a college outside the Commonwealth.

Eligibility   This program is open to high school seniors and graduates who have been residents of Puerto Rico for at least 2 years. Applicants must be entering a bachelor's, master's, or doctoral degree program at a university on the mainland or in another country. They must have a GPA of 3.5 or higher and be able to demonstrate financial need. Along with their application, they must submit a 200-word essay on their academic goals and how they can contribute to the future of Puerto Rico.

Financial Data   Stipends average $5,000. Funds are disbursed directly to the recipient's university.

Duration   1 year; may be renewed, provided the recipient continues to meet eligibility requirements.

Number awarded   Approximately 100 each year.

Deadline   February of each year.

[300]
LA PLAZA SCHOLARSHIP FUND

Central Indiana Community Foundation
Attn: Scholarship Program
615 North Alabama Street, Suite 119
Indianapolis, IN 46204-1498
(317) 634-2423   Fax: (317) 684-0943
E-mail: scholarships@cicf.org
Web: www.cicf.org/grantseekers/scholarships

Summary   To provide financial assistance to residents of Indiana, especially Hispanics, who are interested in attending college in the state.

Eligibility   This program is open to seniors graduating from high schools in Indiana and students already enrolled at a college or university in the state. Preference is given to students of Hispanic descent. Applicants must have a GPA of 2.7 or higher. Along with their application, they must submit 1-page essays on 1) their desire to further their education and their career goals; and 2) their current involvement in the Hispanic community and why it is important to them. Selection is based on academic promise, determination and/or self-motivation, and financial need.

Financial Data   The stipend is at least $1,000.

Duration   1 year.

Additional data This program began in 1997.

Number awarded Varies each year; recently, 7 were awarded.

Deadline February of each year.

[301]
LA UNIDAD LATINA SCHOLARSHIPS

La Unidad Latina Foundation, Inc.
132 East 43rd Street, Suite 358
New York, NY 10017
E-mail: info@lulfoundation.org
Web: www.lulf.org/apply

Summary To provide financial assistance to Hispanic students who are working on a bachelor's or master's degree in any field.

Eligibility This program is open to students of Hispanic background who have completed at least 1 year of full-time undergraduate study or 1 semester of full-time graduate work. Undergraduates must have a GPA of 2.8 or higher. Applicants must be enrolled at an accredited 4-year college or university in the United States and working on a bachelor's or master's degree. Along with their application, they must submit brief essays on their financial need, their academic plans and career goals, an instance in which they have demonstrated exceptional leadership during their college or graduate experience, the impact they have had or plan to have on improving or supporting their Latino/Hispanic community, their extracurricular activities, any honors or awards they have received, and their special interests or hobbies.

Financial Data Stipends range from $500 to $1,000.

Duration 1 year.

Number awarded Varies each year; recently, 9 were awarded.

Deadline February of each year for spring semester; October of each year for fall semester.

[302]
LAGRANT FOUNDATION UNDERGRADUATE SCHOLARSHIPS

Lagrant Foundation
Attn: Senior Talent Acquisition and Fundraising Manager
633 West Fifth Street, 48th Floor
Los Angeles, CA 90071
(323) 469-8680, ext. 223   Fax: (323) 469-8683
E-mail: erickainiguez@lagrant.com
Web: www.lagrantfoundation.org/Scholarship%20Program

Summary To provide financial assistance to Hispanic and other minority college students who are interested in majoring in advertising, public relations, or marketing.

Eligibility This program is open to Hispanics/Latinos, African Americans, Asian Americans/Pacific Islanders, and Native Americans/American Indians who are full-time students at a 4-year accredited institution. Applicants must have a GPA of 2.75 or higher and be either majoring in advertising, marketing, or public relations or minoring in communications with plans to prepare for a career in advertising, marketing, or public relations. Along with their application, they must submit 1) a 1- to 2-page essay outlining their career goals; what steps they will take to increase ethnic representation in the fields of advertising, marketing, and public relations; and the role of an advertising, marketing, or public relations practitio-

ner; 2) a paragraph describing the college and/or community activities in which they are involved; 3) a brief paragraph describing any honors and awards they have received; 4) a letter of reference; 5) a resume; and 6) an official transcript. U.S. citizenship or permanent resident status is required.

Financial Data The stipend is $2,500.

Duration 1 year.

Number awarded Varies each year; recently, 22 were awarded.

Deadline February of each year.

[303]
LAMBDA THETA NU SORORITY LATINA SCHOLARSHIP PROGRAM

Lambda Theta Nu Sorority, Inc.
Attn: Director of Community Service
1220 Rosecrans, Suite 543
San Diego, CA 92106
E-mail: community@lambdathetanu.org
Web: www.lambdathetanu.org/community-service

Summary To provide financial assistance for college to female high school seniors with a connection to the Latino community.

Eligibility This program is open to female graduating high school seniors who are either of Latino heritage or able to demonstrate dedication to community service and empowerment of the Latino community. Applicants must be planning to attend an accredited community college, university, or vocational/technical school. Along with their application, they must submit a personal statement that covers their family background, academic achievements, educational and career goals, commitment to the Latino community, and financial need.

Financial Data A stipend is awarded (amount not specified).

Duration 1 year.

Number awarded Approximately 35 each year (1 selected by each chapter of the sorority).

Deadline April of each year.

[304]
LAPIZ FAMILY SCHOLARSHIP

Asian Pacific Fund
Attn: Scholarship Coordinator
465 California Street, Suite 809
San Francisco, CA 94104
(415) 395-9985 E-mail: scholarship@asianpacificfund.org
Web: www.asianpacificfund.org

Summary To provide financial assistance to students enrolled at campuses of the University of California (UC) who are children of farm workers.

Eligibility This program is open to residents of California who will be enrolled as a full time undergraduate at a UC campus in the following fall. Preference is given to students at UC Davis and UC Santa Cruz. Applicants may be of any ethnic or racial background but they must be a farm worker or the child of farm or migrant workers. They must have a GPA of 3.0 or higher and be able to demonstrate financial need. Along with their application, they must submit essays of 250 to 500 words each on 1) their experience as a farm worker or child of a farm worker and how that experience relates to their educational and career goals; 2) a project, experience, or person related to their academic and career goals that inspired them; and 3) their academic and career goals, hopes, and dreams for the future. U.S. citizenship or permanent resident status is required. Selection is based on personal strengths (responsibility, maturity, motivation, ability to overcome hardships); potential to succeed, including time management skills and realistic goals; and academic achievement.

Financial Data   The stipend is $2,000 per year.

Duration   1 year; may be renewed 1 additional year.

Number awarded   1 each year.

Deadline   February of each year.

[305]
LATIN AMERICAN EDUCATIONAL FOUNDATION SCHOLARSHIPS

Latin American Educational Foundation
Attn: Scholarship Selection Committee
561 Santa Fe Drive
Denver, CO 80204
(303) 446-0541   Fax: (303) 446-0526
E-mail: info@laef.org
Web: www.laef.org/Scholarship

Summary   To provide financial assistance to Hispanic American undergraduate students in Colorado who plan to attend college in any state.

Eligibility   This program is open to Colorado residents who are of Hispanic heritage and/or actively involved in the Hispanic community. Applicants must be attending or accepted at an accredited college, university, or vocational school in any state. They must have a cumulative GPA of 3.0 or higher. Along with their application, they must submit a 1-page essay on their interests and career goals, how they anticipate achieving their goals, and what has motivated them to pursue higher education; their essay must demonstrate how their Hispanic heritage or involvement in their community has influenced their life. Selection is based on the essay, community service and extracurricular activities, academic achievement, letters of recommendation, and financial need.

Financial Data   The amount of the award depends on the need of the recipient, ranging from $500 to $3,000 and averaging nearly $2,000. Scholarships may be used at Colorado colleges and universities or at out-of-state institutions. Most colleges and universities within Colorado participate in the Colorado Higher Education Partnership; member institutions provide additional funds to match the award granted by this foundation.

Duration   1 year; recipients may reapply.

Additional data   This program began in 1949. Recipients are required to perform 10 hours of community service during the academic year.

Number awarded   Varies each year; recently, more than 100 of these scholarships, with a value of nearly $200,000, were awarded.

Deadline   February of each year.

[306]
LATINOS AND PLANNING DIVISION SCHOLARSHIP

American Planning Association
Attn: Planning and the Black Community Division
205 North Michigan Avenue, Suite 1200
Chicago, IL 60601
(312) 431-9100   Fax: (312) 786-6700
Web: www.planning.org/divisions/latinos/scholarships

Summary   To provide financial assistance to Latinos interested in working on an undergraduate or graduate degree in planning.

Eligibility   This program is open to Latinos who are 1) undergraduate students in the third or fourth year of an accredited planning program; or 2) graduate students in the first or second year of an accredited planning program. Applicants must submit a 1- to 2-page personal statement on their interest in a career in planning and the impact they want to make on planning in Latino communities. Selection is based on that statement, a letter of recommendation, academic achievement, and/or service or impacts made in the Latino community or the planning profession.

Financial Data   The stipend is $500 per semester.

Duration   1 year.

Number awarded   1 each year.

Deadline   February of each year.

[307]
LAUNCHING LEADERS UNDERGRADUATE SCHOLARSHIP

JPMorgan Chase
Campus Recruiting
Attn: Launching Leaders
277 Park Avenue, Second Floor
New York, NY 10172
(212) 270-6000
E-mail: bronwen.x.baumgardner@jpmorgan.com
Web: careers.jpmorgan.com

Summary   To provide financial assistance and work experience to Hispanic and other underrepresented minority undergraduate students interested in a career in financial services.

Eligibility   This program is open to Hispanic, Black, and Native American students enrolled as sophomores or juniors and interested in financial services. Applicants must have a GPA of 3.5 or higher. Along with their application, they must submit 500-word essays on 1) why they should be considered potential candidates for CEO of the sponsoring bank in 2020; and 2) the special background and attributes they would contribute to the sponsor's diversity agenda. They must be interested in a summer associate position in the sponsor's investment banking, sales and trading, or research divisions.

Financial Data   The stipend is $5,000 for recipients accepted as sophomores or $10,000 for recipients accepted as juniors. For students accepted as sophomores and whose scholarship is renewed for a second year, the stipend is $15,000. The summer internship is a paid position.

Duration   1 year; may be renewed 1 additional year if the recipient successfully completes the 10-week summer intern program and maintains a GPA of 3.5 or higher.

Number awarded   Approximately 12 each year.

Deadline   October of each year.

[308]
LAURENCE R. FOSTER MEMORIAL SCHOLARSHIPS

Oregon Office of Student Access and Completion
Attn: Scholarship Processing Coordinator
1500 Valley River Drive, Suite 100
Eugene, OR 97401-2146
(541) 687-7422   Toll Free: (800) 452-8807, ext. 7422
Fax: (541) 687-7414   TDD: (800) 735-2900
E-mail: cheryl.a.connolly@state.or.us
Web: app.oregonstudentaid.gov/Catalog/Default.aspx

Summary   To provide financial assistance to residents of Oregon, especially Hispanics and members of other diverse groups, who are enrolled at a college or graduate school in any state to prepare for a public health career.

Eligibility   This program is open to residents of Oregon who are enrolled at least half time at a 4-year college or university in any state to prepare for a career in public health (not private practice). Preference is given first to applicants from diverse environments; second to persons employed in, or graduate students working on a degree in, public health; and third to juniors and seniors majoring in a health program (e.g., nursing, medical technology, physician assistant). Applicants must be able to demonstrate financial need. Along with their application, they must submit essays of 250 to 350 words on 1) what public health means to them; 2) the public health aspect they intend to practice and the health and population issues impacted by that aspect; and 3) their experience living or working in diverse environments.

Financial Data   Stipends for scholarships offered by the Oregon Office of Student Access and Completion (OSAC) range from $1,000 to $10,000 but recently averaged $4,368.

Duration   1 year.

Additional data   This program is administered by the OSAC with funds provided by the Oregon Community Foundation.

Number awarded   Varies each year; recently, 6 were awarded.

Deadline   February of each year.

[309]
LCDR JANET COCHRAN AND CDR CONNIE GREENE SCHOLARSHIP

National Naval Officers Association-Washington, D.C.
   Chapter
c/o LCDR Stephen Williams
P.O. Box 30784
Alexandria, VA 22310
(703) 644-2605   Fax: (703) 644-8503
E-mail: Stephen.Williams@navy.mil
Web: www.dcnnoa.org/dcnnoa-scholarship

Summary   To provide financial assistance to Hispanic and other female minority high school seniors from the Washington, D.C. area who are interested in attending college in any state.

Eligibility   This program is open to female minority seniors graduating from high schools in the Washington, D.C. metropolitan area who plan to enroll full time at an accredited 2- or 4-year college or university in any state. Applicants must have a GPA of 2.5 or higher and be U.S. citizens or permanent res-

idents. Selection is based on academic achievement, community involvement, and financial need.

Financial Data   The stipend is $1,500.

Duration   1 year; nonrenewable.

Additional data   This program is sponsored by the Washington D.C. Chapter of the National Naval Officers Association (DCNNOA), an organization of African American naval officers, but all minorities are eligible and recipients are not required to join or affiliate with the military in any way.

Number awarded   1 each year.

Deadline   February of each year.

[310]
LEADERSHIP FOR DIVERSITY SCHOLARSHIP

California School Library Association
Attn: CSL Foundation
6444 East Spring Street, Number 237
Long Beach, CA 90815-1553
Toll Free: (888) 655-8480   Fax: (888) 655-8480
E-mail: info@csla.net
Web: www.csla.net/awards-2/scholarships

Summary   To provide financial assistance to Hispanics and other students who reflect the diversity of California's population and are interested in earning a credential as a library media teacher in the state.

Eligibility   This program is open to students who are members of a traditionally underrepresented group enrolled in a college or university library media teacher credential program in California. Applicants must intend to work as a library media teacher in a California school library media center for a minimum of 3 years. Along with their application, they must submit a 250-word statement on what they can contribute to the profession, their commitment to serving the needs of multicultural and multilingual students, and their financial need.

Financial Data   The stipend is $1,500.

Duration   1 year.

Number awarded   1 each year.

Deadline   September of each year.

[311]
LEAGUE OF MEXICAN AMERICAN WOMEN SCHOLARSHIP

League of Mexican American Women
Attn: Scholarship Chair
P.O. Box 26522
Tucson, AZ 85726-6522
(520) 884-8538   E-mail: kennedypfcu@gmail.com
Web: www.leagueofmexicanamericanwomen.org/id8.html

Summary   To provide financial assistance to Mexican American and other students interested in attending a college or university in Arizona.

Eligibility   Applicants must be U.S. citizens and entering or continuing at a college or university in Arizona as a full-time student. Preference is given to Mexican American applicants. The immediate family of the League of Mexican American Women members are not eligible to apply. Financial need is considered in the selection process.

Financial Data   A stipend is awarded (amount not specified).

Duration   1 year.

Number awarded   Varies each year.

Deadline   April for the summer session; May for the fall or spring sessions.

[312]
LEDC LATINO SCHOLARSHIP

Latino Economic Development Center
Attn: Membership Services Coordinator
1501 East Lake Street, Lower Level
Minneapolis, MN 55407
(612) 724-5332   Fax: (612) 729-5342
E-mail: info@ledc-mn.org
Web: www.ledc-mn.org/scholarships.php

Summary   To provide financial assistance to Latino high school seniors in Minnesota who are interested in attending college in the state.

Eligibility   This program is open to seniors of Latino descent (either or both parents must have been born outside of the United States in a Latin American country and immigrated to the United States) graduating from high schools in Minnesota and planning to attend a college or university in the state. Applicants must have a GPA of 2.5 or higher. Selection is based on academic performance, educational goals, leadership in the Latino community, and financial need. Preference is given to students who are ineligible for local or federal government funds for college.

Financial Data   The stipend is $3,000.

Duration   1 year; nonrenewable.

Additional data   This program, which began in 2006, includes the George W. Linares Scholarship, the Garcia-Urzua Scholarship, the Los Ocampo Scholarship, and the Ramiro Hernández Márquez Scholarship.

Number awarded   Varies each year; recently, 8 were awarded.

Deadline   March of each year.

[313]
LEDGENT DIVERSITY UNDERGRADUATE SCHOLARSHIPS

Accounting and Financial Women's Alliance
Attn: Educational Foundation
2365 Harrodsburg Road, A325
Lexington, KY 40504
(859) 219-3532   Toll Free: (800) 326-2163
Fax: (859) 219-3577   E-mail: foundation@afwa.org
Web: www.afwa.org/foundation/scholarships

Summary   To provide financial assistance to Hispanic and other minority undergraduates interested in preparing for a career in accounting or finance.

Eligibility   This program is open to members of minority groups (Hispanic Americans, African Americans, Native Americans, or Asian Americans) who are entering their third, fourth, or fifth year of undergraduate study at a college, university, or professional school of accounting. Applicants must have completed at least 60 semester hours with a declared major in accounting or finance and a GPA of 3.0 or higher. Along with their application, they must submit an essay of 150 to 250 words on their career goals and objectives, the impact they want to have on the accounting world, community involvement, and leadership examples. Selection is based on leadership, character, communication skills, scholastic aver-

age, and financial need. Membership in the Accounting and Financial Women's Alliance (AFWA) is not required. Applications must be submitted to a local ASWA chapter.

Financial Data   A stipend is awarded (amount not specified).

Duration   1 year; recipients may reapply.

Additional data   This program is sponsored by Ledgent.

Number awarded   1 each year.

Deadline   Local chapters must submit their candidates to the national office by September of each year.

[314]
LEON BRADLEY SCHOLARSHIPS

American Association of School Personnel Administrators
Attn: Scholarship Program
11863 West 112th Street, Suite 100
Overland Park, KS 66210
(913) 327-1222   Fax: (913) 327-1223
E-mail: aaspa@aaspa.org
Web: www.aaspa.org/leon-bradley-scholarship

Summary   To provide financial assistance to Hispanic and other minority undergraduates, paraprofessionals, and graduate students preparing for a career in teaching and school leadership at colleges in designated southeastern states.

Eligibility   This program is open to members of minority groups (Hispanic, American Indian, Alaskan Native, Asian, Pacific Islander, Black, Middle Easterner) currently enrolled full time at a college or university in Alabama, Florida, Georgia, Kentucky, North Carolina, South Carolina, Tennessee, or Virginia. Applicants must be 1) undergraduates in their final year (including student teaching) of an initial teaching certification program; 2) paraprofessional career-changers in their final year (including student teaching) of an initial teaching certification program; or 3) graduate students who have served as a licensed teacher and are working on a school administrator credential. They must have an overall GPA of 3.0 or higher. Priority is given to applicants who 1) can demonstrate work experience that has been applied to college expenses; 2) have received other scholarship or financial aid support; or 3) are seeking initial certification and/or endorsement in a state-identified critical area.

Financial Data   Stipends are $2,500 for undergraduates in their final year, $1,500 for paraprofessionals in their final year, and $1,500 for graduate students.

Duration   1 year.

Number awarded   4 each year: 1 undergraduate, 1 paraprofessional, and 2 graduate students.

Deadline   May of each year.

[315]
LEONARD M. PERRYMAN COMMUNICATIONS SCHOLARSHIP FOR ETHNIC MINORITY STUDENTS

United Methodist Communications
Attn: Communications Ministry Team
810 12th Avenue South
P.O. Box 320
Nashville, TN 37202-0320
(615) 742-5481   Toll Free: (888) CRT-4UMC
Fax: (615) 742-5485   E-mail: scholarships@umcom.org
Web: www.umcom.org

Summary To provide financial assistance to Hispanic and other minority United Methodist college students who are interested in careers in religious communications.

Eligibility This program is open to United Methodist ethnic minority students enrolled in accredited institutions of higher education as juniors or seniors. Applicants must be interested in preparing for a career in religious communications. For the purposes of this program, "communications" is meant to cover audiovisual, electronic, and print journalism. Selection is based on Christian commitment and involvement in the life of the United Methodist church, academic achievement, journalistic experience, clarity of purpose, and professional potential as a religion communicator.

Financial Data The stipend is $2,500 per year.

Duration 1 year.

Additional data The scholarship may be used at any accredited institution of higher education.

Number awarded 1 each year.

Deadline March of each year.

[316]
LEROY APKER AWARD

American Physical Society
Attn: Honors Program
One Physics Ellipse
College Park, MD 20740-3844
(301) 209-3268   Fax: (301) 209-0865
E-mail: honors@aps.org
Web: www.aps.org/programs/honors/awards/apker.cfm

Summary To recognize and reward undergraduate students, especially Hispanics and other minorities, for outstanding work in physics.

Eligibility This program is open to undergraduate students at colleges and universities in the United States. Nominees should have completed or be completing the requirements for an undergraduate degree with an excellent academic record and should have demonstrated exceptional potential for scientific research by making an original contribution to physics. Each department of physics in the United States may nominate only 1 student. Each nomination packet should include the student's academic transcript, a description of the original contribution written by the student (such as a manuscript or reprint of a research publication or senior thesis), a 1,000-word summary, and 2 letters of recommendation. Nominations of qualified women and members of underrepresented minority groups are especially encouraged.

Financial Data The award consists of a $5,000 honorarium for the student, a certificate citing the work and school of the recipient, and an allowance for travel expenses to the meeting of the American Physical Society (APS) at which the prize is presented. Each of the finalists receives an honorarium of $2,000 and a certificate. Each of the physics departments whose nominees are selected as recipients and finalists receives a certificate and an award; the departmental award is $5,000 for recipients and $1,000 for finalists.

Duration The award is presented annually.

Additional data This award was established in 1978.

Number awarded 6 finalists are selected each year, of whom 2 receive awards: 1 to a student at a Ph.D. granting institution and 1 at a non-Ph.D. granting institution.

Deadline June of each year.

[317]
LEROY C. SCHMIDT, CPA MINORITY 150-HOUR ACCOUNTING SCHOLARSHIPS

Wisconsin Institute of Certified Public Accountants
Attn: WICPA Educational Foundation
W233N2080 Ridgeview Parkway, Suite 201
Waukesha, WI 53188
(262) 785-0445, ext. 3025
Toll Free: (800) 772-6939 (within WI)
Fax: (262) 785-0838   E-mail: jessica@wicpa.org
Web: www.wicpa.org

Summary To provide financial assistance to Hispanic and other underrepresented minority residents of Wisconsin enrolled at a college or university in the state and working to meet the requirements to sit for the Certified Public Accountant (C.P.A.) examination.

Eligibility This program is open to minority residents of Wisconsin (Hispanic, African American, Native American/Alaska Native, or Pacific Islander who have completed 120 credit hours at a college or university in the state in a degree program that qualifies them to sit for the Uniform C.P.A. Examination. Applicants must be entering their fifth-year requirement and eligible to receive a master's degree in business, a double major/minor, or additional courses for credit to satisfy the 150-hour requirement. They must be enrolled full time, have a GPA of 3.0 or higher, and be U.S. citizens.

Financial Data The stipend is $5,000 or $2,500.

Duration 1 year.

Number awarded Varies each year; recently, 2 were awarded: 1 at $5,000 and 1 at $2,500.

Deadline February of each year.

[318]
LIBERTY POWER BRIGHT HORIZONS SCHOLARSHIPS

United States Hispanic Chamber of Commerce
Attn: Foundation
1424 K Street, N.W., Suite 401
Washington, DC 20005-2404
(202) 842-1212   E-mail: ehernandez@ushccf.org
Web: www.ushccfoundation.org

Summary To provide financial assistance to Hispanic and other undergraduate and graduate students who are committed to diversity and are working on a degree in a field of science, technology, engineering, or mathematics (STEM).

Eligibility This program is open to U.S. citizens and permanent residents working on an undergraduate or graduate degree in a field of STEM to prepare for a career in energy or environment. Applicants must have completed at least 1 semester of college and have a GPA of 3.0 or higher. They must share the sponsor's goal of advocating on behalf of Hispanic-owned businesses. Along with their application, they must submit brief essays on 1) their interest in energy and/or the environment as a career; 2) why they chose that field of study; 3) why they should be selected as a recipient of this scholarship; 4) how this scholarship will help them achieve their educational/career goals; and 5) the positive impact they hope to have on society and/or the environment. They must also submit Tweets on why diversity is important in education, what Powerful Together means to them, and why living sustainably is so important to them.

Financial Data Stipends are $10,000, $6,000, or $4,000.

Duration 1 year.

Additional data This program, which began in 2013, is sponsored by Liberty Power of Fort Lauderdale, Florida.

Number awarded 1 at $10,000, 1 at $6,000, and 1 at $4,000 each year.

Deadline July of each year.

[319]
LOS HERMANOS DE STANFORD SCHOLARSHIPS

Los Hermanos de Stanford
Haas Center for Public Service
562 Salvatierra Walkway
Stanford, CA 94305
E-mail: loshermanosscholarship@gmail.com
Web: web.stanford.edu

Summary To provide financial assistance to Latino high school seniors who wish to attend college in any state.

Eligibility This program is open to Latino seniors graduating from high schools in any state and planning to enroll at any 2- or 4-year college, university, or community college. Applicants must submit essays of 1,000 words each on 1) how the challenges and adversity they have faced have influenced their actions and goals; and 2) how they incorporate the sponsor's guiding principles of cultural awareness, academic excellence, and community service into their everyday life and how those shape them as a person. Essays may be submitted in Spanish, and U.S. citizenship is not required. They must also submit document evidence of financial need and proof that they have applied for at least 1 other scholarship.

Financial Data The stipend is $1,000.

Duration 1 year.

Additional data Although this sponsoring organization is based at Stanford University, recipients are free to attend any college or university of their choice.

Number awarded 2 each year.

Deadline May of each year.

[320]
LOUIS B. RUSSELL, JR. MEMORIAL SCHOLARSHIP

Indiana State Teachers Association
Attn: ISTA Foundation for the Improvement of Education
150 West Market Street, Suite 900
Indianapolis, IN 46204-2814
(317) 263-3306   Toll Free: (800) 382-4037, ext. 3306
Fax: (800) 777-6128   E-mail: ccherry@ista-in.org
Web: www.ista-in.org/our-profession/scholarships-awards

Summary To provide financial assistance to Hispanic and other ethnic minority high school seniors in Indiana who are interested in attending vocational school in any state.

Eligibility This program is open to ethnic minority high school seniors in Indiana who are interested in continuing their education in the area of industrial arts, vocational education, or technical preparation at an accredited postsecondary institution in any state. Selection is based on academic achievement, leadership ability as expressed through co-curricular activities and community involvement, recommenda-

tions, and a 300-word essay on their educational goals and how they plan to achieve those goals.

Financial Data The stipend is $1,000.

Duration 1 year; may be renewed for 1 additional year, provided the recipient maintains a GPA of "C+" or higher.

Number awarded 1 each year.

Deadline February of each year.

[321]
LOUISE MORITZ MOLITORIS LEADERSHIP AWARD

Women's Transportation Seminar
Attn: WTS Foundation
1701 K Street, N.W., Suite 800
Washington, DC 20006
(202) 955-5085   Fax: (202) 955-5088
E-mail: wts@wtsinternational.org
Web: www.wtsinternational.org/education/scholarships

Summary To provide financial assistance to undergraduate women, especially Hispanics and other minorities, who are interested in a career in transportation.

Eligibility This program is open to women who are working on an undergraduate degree in transportation or a transportation-related field (e.g., transportation engineering, planning, finance, or logistics). Applicants must have a GPA of 3.0 or higher. Along with their application, they must submit a 500-word statement about their career goals after graduation and why they think they should receive the scholarship award; their statement should specifically address the issue of leadership. Applications must be submitted first to a local chapter; the chapters forward selected applications for consideration on the national level. Minority women are especially encouraged to apply. Selection is based on transportation involvement and goals, job skills, academic record, and leadership potential; financial need is not considered.

Financial Data The stipend is $5,000.

Duration 1 year.

Additional data Local chapters may also award additional funding to winners for their area.

Number awarded 1 each year.

Deadline Applications must be submitted by November to a local WTS chapter.

[322]
LOVE SCHOLARSHIP FOR DIVERSITY

International Council of Shopping Centers
Attn: ICSC Foundation
1221 Avenue of the Americas, 41st Floor
New York, NY 10020-1099
(646) 728-3628   Fax: (732) 694-1690
E-mail: foundation@icsc.org
Web: www.icsc.org

Summary To provide financial assistance to Hispanic and other minority undergraduate students who are preparing for a career as a retail real estate professional.

Eligibility This program is open to U.S. citizens who are full-time juniors or seniors working on a degree related to the retail real estate profession. Applicants must be a member of an underrepresented ethnic minority group (Hispanic, Caribbean, American Indian or Alaskan Native, Asian or Pacific

Islander, or African American). They must have a GPA of 3.0 or higher.

Financial Data The stipend is $1,000.

Duration 1 year.

Number awarded 1 or more each year.

Deadline January of each year.

[323]
LSAMP UNDERGRADUATE SUMMER RESEARCH PROGRAM

Cornell University
College of Engineering
Attn: Diversity Programs in Engineering
146 Olin Hall
Ithaca, NY 14853-5201
(607) 255-6403   Fax: (607) 255-2834
E-mail: dpeng@cornell.edu
Web: www.engineering.cornell.edu

Summary To provide an opportunity for Hispanic and other traditionally underrepresented minority groups in the sciences and engineering to participate in a summer research program in a field of science, technology, engineering, or mathematics (STEM) at Cornell University.

Eligibility This program is open to members of minority groups traditionally underrepresented in the sciences and engineering who are entering their sophomore, junior, or senior year at a college or university anywhere in the country. Applicants must be interested in working on a research project in a field of STEM under the guidance of a faculty or research mentor at Cornell University. They must have a GPA of 3.0 or higher and be U.S. citizens or permanent residents.

Financial Data Participating students receive a stipend of $4,000, a round-trip travel stipend of up to $300, a double room in a campus residential hall, and access to laboratories, libraries, computer facilities, and study lounges.

Duration 10 weeks during the summer.

Additional data This program is part of the Louis Stokes Alliance for Minority Participation (LSAMP), supported by the National Science Foundation as part of its Research Experiences for Undergraduates (REU) program. Students are encouraged to enter and present their research at their affiliated National Society of Black Engineers (NSBE), Society of Hispanic Professional Engineers (SHPE), or American Indian Science and Engineering Society (AISES) or professional conference.

Number awarded Varies each year; recently, 9 were accepted.

Deadline February of each year.

[324]
LTK ENGINEERING SCHOLARSHIP

Conference of Minority Transportation Officials
Attn: National Scholarship Program
100 M Street, S.E., Suite 917
Washington, DC 20003
(202) 506-2917   E-mail: info@comto.org
Web: www.comto.org/page/scholarships

Summary To provide financial assistance to Hispanic and other minority upper-division and graduate students in engineering or other field related to transportation.

Eligibility This program is open to full-time minority juniors, seniors, and graduate students in engineering or other technical transportation-related disciplines. Applicants must have a GPA of 3.0 or higher. Along with their application they must submit a cover letter on their transportation-related career goals and life aspirations. Financial need is not considered in the selection process.

Financial Data The stipend is $6,000. Funds are paid directly to the recipient's college or university.

Duration 1 year.

Additional data This program is sponsored by LTK Engineering Services.

Number awarded 1 each year.

Deadline April of each year.

[325]
LTK ENGINEERING TRANSPORTATION PLANNING SCHOLARSHIP

Conference of Minority Transportation Officials
Attn: National Scholarship Program
100 M Street, S.E., Suite 917
Washington, DC 20003
(202) 506-2917   E-mail: info@comto.org
Web: www.comto.org/page/scholarships

Summary To provide financial assistance to Hispanic and other minority upper-division and graduate students in planning or other field related to transportation.

Eligibility This program is open to full-time minority juniors, seniors, and graduate students in planning of other technical transportation-related disciplines. Applicants must have a GPA of 3.0 or higher. Along with their application they must submit a cover letter on their transportation-related career goals and life aspirations. Financial need is not considered in the selection process.

Financial Data The stipend is $5,000. Funds are paid directly to the recipient's college or university.

Duration 1 year.

Additional data This program is sponsored by LTK Engineering Services.

Number awarded 1 each year.

Deadline April of each year.

[326]
LUCY MORA BARRIENTOS SCHOLARSHIP

Barrientos Scholarship Foundation
Attn: Scholarship Chair
P.O. Box 7173
Omaha, NE 68107
(402) 215-5106   E-mail: info@barrientosscholarship.org
Web: barrientosscholarship.org

Summary To provide financial assistance to Latino students who are interested in studying any field at a college in Nebraska or western Iowa.

Eligibility This program is open to students of Latino heritage enrolled or planning to enroll at colleges and universities in Nebraska or western Iowa. Applicants must be graduating high school seniors or current college students and have a GPA of 2.8 or higher. They may be interested in studying any field. Along with their application, they must submit a personal essay of 250 to 500 words on their educational and career goals, what inspired them to pursue your chosen field of study, how their Latino culture has influenced their life, how they see themselves making a difference in the Latino community in their future, and how this scholarship will assist them in their pursuit of a higher education.

Financial Data   The stipend is $2,500.

Duration   1 year.

Additional data   This foundation was established in 2005.

Number awarded   1 or more each year. Since this foundation was established, it has awarded a total of $80,000 to 121 students.

Deadline   April of each year.

[327]
LULAC GENERAL AWARDS

League of United Latin American Citizens
Attn: LULAC National Education Service Centers
1133 19th Street, N.W., Suite 1000
Washington, DC 20036
(202) 835-9646   Fax: (202) 835-9685
E-mail: scholarships@lnesc.org
Web: www.lnesc.org/#!lnsf/c17bl

Summary   To provide financial assistance to Hispanic American undergraduate and graduate students.

Eligibility   This program is open to Hispanic Americans who are U.S. citizens, permanent residents, or Deferred Action for Childhood Arrivals (DACA) students currently enrolled or planning to enroll at an accredited college or university as a graduate or undergraduate student. Although grades are considered in the selection process, emphasis is placed on the applicant's motivation, sincerity, and integrity, as revealed through a personal interview and in a 300-word essay on their personal and professional goals. Need, community involvement, and leadership activities are also considered. Candidates must live near a participating local council of the League of United Latin American Citizens (LULAC) and must apply directly to that council.

Financial Data   The stipend ranges from $250 to $1,000 per year, depending on the need of the recipient.

Duration   1 year.

Additional data   This program represents an attempt to forge a partnership between the corporate world and the community. Under its fundsharing concept, LULAC's National Education Service Center gathers contributions nationally from corporations, while LULAC councils raise money locally. The total corporate donations are then apportioned back to the councils according to effort. Applications must be obtained directly from participating LULAC councils; for a list, contact the sponsor.

Number awarded   Varies; approximately 500 each year.

Deadline   March of each year.

[328]
LULAC HONORS AWARDS

League of United Latin American Citizens
Attn: LULAC National Education Service Centers
1133 19th Street, N.W., Suite 1000
Washington, DC 20036
(202) 835-9646   Fax: (202) 835-9685
E-mail: scholarships@lnesc.org
Web: www.lnesc.org/#!lnsf/c17bl

Summary   To provide financial assistance to Hispanic American undergraduate and graduate students who are doing well in school.

Eligibility   This program is open to Hispanic Americans who are U.S. citizens, permanent residents, or Deferred Action for Childhood Arrivals (DACA) students currently enrolled or planning to enroll at an accredited college or university as a graduate or undergraduate student. Applicants who are already in college must have a GPA of 3.0 or higher. Entering freshmen must have ACT scores of 23 or higher or SAT scores of 1100 or higher. In addition, applicants must demonstrate motivation, sincerity, and integrity through a personal interview and in a 300-word essay on their personal and professional goals. Need, community involvement, and leadership activities are also considered. Candidates must live near a participating local council of the League of United Latin American Citizens (LULAC) and must apply directly to that council.

Financial Data   The stipend ranges from $500 to $2,000 per year, depending on the need of the recipient.

Duration   1 year.

Additional data   This program represents an attempt to forge a partnership between the corporate world and the community. Under its fundsharing concept, LULAC's National Education Service Center gathers contributions nationally from corporations, while LULAC councils raise money locally. The total corporate donations are then apportioned back to the councils according to effort. Applications must be obtained directly from participating LULAC councils; for a list, send a self-addressed stamped envelope to the sponsor.

Number awarded   Varies each year.

Deadline   March of each year.

[329]
LULAC NATIONAL SCHOLASTIC ACHIEVEMENT AWARDS

League of United Latin American Citizens
Attn: LULAC National Education Service Centers
1133 19th Street, N.W., Suite 1000
Washington, DC 20036
(202) 835-9646   Fax: (202) 835-9685
E-mail: scholarships@lnesc.org
Web: www.lnesc.org/#!lnsf/c17bl

Summary   To provide financial assistance to academically outstanding Hispanic American undergraduate and graduate students.

Eligibility   This program is open to Hispanic Americans who are U.S. citizens, permanent residents, or Deferred Action for Childhood Arrivals (DACA) students currently enrolled or planning to enroll at an accredited college or university as a graduate or undergraduate student. Applicants who are already in college must have a GPA of 3.5 or higher. Entering freshmen must have ACT scores of 29 or higher or SAT scores of 1350 or higher. In addition, applicants must demonstrate motivation, sincerity, and community involvement through a personal interview and in a 300-word essay on their personal and professional goals. Need, community involvement, and leadership activities are also considered. Candidates must live near a participating local council of the League of United Latin American Citizens (LULAC) and must apply directly to that council.

Financial Data   Stipends are at least $2,000 per year.

Duration 1 year.

Additional data This program represents an attempt to forge a partnership between the corporate world and the community. Under its fundsharing concept, LULAC's National Education Service Center gathers contributions nationally from corporations, while LULAC councils raise money locally. The total corporate donations are then apportioned back to the councils according to effort. Applications must be obtained directly from participating LULAC councils; for a list, send a self-addressed stamped envelope to the sponsor.

Number awarded Varies each year.

Deadline March of each year.

[330]
LYDIA CRUZ AND SANDRA MARIE RAMOS SCHOLARSHIP

Delta Tau Lambda Sorority
P.O. Box 7714
Ann Arbor, MI 48107
E-mail: DTL-info@deltataulambda.org
Web: www.deltataulambda.org/dtl_scholarship.html

Summary To provide financial assistance for college to Latina high school seniors.

Eligibility This program is open to Latinas who are graduating from high schools in any state and planning to enroll at a 2- or 4-year college or university. Applicants must submit 500-word essays on 1) the extracurricular activities with which they have been involved; and 2) the social or personal issue about which they are most passionate and how earning a higher education degree will help them resolve those issues or bring awareness to them. Selection is based on academic excellence and community service.

Financial Data A stipend is awarded (amount not specified).

Duration 1 year.

Additional data Delta Tau Lambda was established in 1994 as a social sorority for Latinas. It established this scholarship in 1995.

Number awarded 1 or more each year.

Deadline Deadline not specified.

[331]
MABEL SMITH MEMORIAL SCHOLARSHIP

Wisconsin Women of Color Network, Inc.
c/o P.E. Kiram
756 North 35th Street, Suite 101
Milwaukee, WI 53208
(414) 899-2329   E-mail: pekiram64@gmail.com

Summary To provide financial assistance for vocation/technical school or community college to Hispanic and other minority residents of Wisconsin.

Eligibility This program is open to residents of Wisconsin who are high school or GED-equivalent graduating seniors planning to continue their education at a vocational/technical school or community college in any state. Applicants must be a member of 1 of the following groups: Latina, African American, Asian, American Indian, or biracial. They must have a GPA of 2.0 or higher and be able to demonstrate financial need. Along with their application, they must submit a 1-page essay on how this scholarship will help them accomplish their educational goal. U.S. citizenship is required.

Financial Data A stipend is awarded (amount not specified).

Duration 1 year.

Additional data This program began in 1990.

Number awarded 1 each year.

Deadline May of each year.

[332]
MAES SCHOLARSHIP

Hispanic Scholarship Consortium
Attn: Scholarship Selection Committee
7703 North Lamar Boulevard, Suite 310
Austin, TX 78752
(512) 368-2956   Fax: (512) 692-1831
E-mail: scholarships@hispanicscholar.org
Web: hispanicscholar.academicworks.com

Summary To provide financial assistance to residents of Texas of Hispanic heritage who plan to major in a field of science, technology, engineering, or mathematics (STEM) at a college in the Austin area.

Eligibility This program is open to residents of Texas who are of Hispanic heritage and entering their freshman or sophomore year at a 2- or 4-year college or university in the Austin area. Applicants must be planning to enroll full time and major in a field of STEM. They must have a GPA of 3.0 or higher Selection is based on academic achievement, community service, personal strengths, leadership, and financial need. U.S. citizenship is not required; students may qualify under Texas Senate Bill 1528.

Financial Data The stipend is $1,500 per year.

Duration 1 year; may be renewed up to 3 additional years, provided the recipient remains enrolled full time, maintains a GPA of 3.0 or higher, and participates in at least 25 hours of community service per semester.

Additional data This program is sponsored by the Society of Mexican American Engineers and Scientists (MAES).

Number awarded 1 or more each year.

Deadline April of each year.

[333]
MAINE SECTION ASCE HIGH SCHOOL SCHOLARSHIP

American Society of Civil Engineers-Maine Section
c/o Leslie L. Corrow, Scholarship Chair
Kleinschmidt Associates
141 Main Street
P.O. Box 650
Pittsfield, ME 04967
(207) 487-3328   Fax: (207) 487-3124
E-mail: scholarships@maineasce.org
Web: www.facebook.com/maineasce

Summary To provide financial assistance to high school seniors in Maine, especially Hispanics and other minorities, who are interested in studying civil engineering in college.

Eligibility This program is open to graduating high school seniors who are Maine residents and who intend to study civil engineering in college. Women and minorities are especially encouraged to apply. Applicants must submit a 200-word statement describing why they have chosen civil engineering as a career and what they hope to accomplish by being a civil engineer. Selection is based on the statement, academic performance, extracurricular activities, and letters of recommendation.

Financial Data A total of $4,000 is available for this program each year.

Duration 1 year; nonrenewable.

Number awarded Several each year.

Deadline January of each year.

[334]
MANUEL AND JANE ZUNIGA SCHOLARSHIPS

Hispanic Scholarship Consortium
Attn: Scholarship Selection Committee
7703 North Lamar Boulevard, Suite 310
Austin, TX 78752
(512) 368-2956   Fax: (512) 692-1831
E-mail: scholarships@hispanicscholar.org
Web: hispanicscholar.academicworks.com

Summary To provide financial assistance to high school seniors of Hispanic heritage in Texas who plan to attend a college in any state.

Eligibility This program is open to seniors of Hispanic heritage graduating from high schools in Texas and planning to enroll full time at a 2- or 4-year college or university in any state. Applicants must have a GPA of 3.0 or higher. Selection is based on academic achievement, community service, personal strengths, leadership, and financial need. U.S. citizenship is not required; students may qualify under Texas Senate Bill 1528.

Financial Data The stipend is $4,000 per year.

Duration 1 year; may be renewed up to 3 additional years, provided the recipient remains enrolled full time, maintains a GPA of 3.0 or higher, and participates in at least 25 hours of community service per semester.

Number awarded Varies each year; recently, 3 were awarded.

Deadline April of each year.

[335]
MANUELA NEHLS RE-ENTRY SCHOLARSHIPS

American GI Forum Colorado State Women
Attn: Kathleen Clenin, Scholarship Committee Chair
P.O. Box 11784
Denver, CO 80211
(303) 458-1700   Toll Free: (866) 244-3628
Fax: (303) 458-1634   E-mail: kathyclenin@comcast.net
Web: www.agifusa.org/women

Summary To provide financial assistance to Hispanic and other women from Colorado who are members of the American GI Forum and interested in attending college.

Eligibility This program is open to female residents of Colorado who have been members of the American GI Forum for at least 18 months. Applicants must be enrolled or planning to enroll in a certificate, vocational, or degree program at a school in any state. Along with their application, they must submit an essay of 250 to 500 words on their educational and career goals, why they should be selected to receive this award, and what they know about the American GI Forum. Selection is based on that essay, academic goals, extracurricular activities, and community service.

Financial Data A stipend is awarded (amount not specified).

Duration 1 year; recipients may reapply.

Additional data The American GI Forum is the largest federally-chartered Hispanic veterans' organization in the United States.

Number awarded 1 or more each year.

Deadline April of each year.

[336]
MARCIA SILVERMAN MINORITY STUDENT AWARD

Public Relations Student Society of America
Attn: Vice President of Member Services
33 Maiden Lane, 11th Floor
New York, NY 10038-5150
(212) 460-1474   Fax: (212) 995-0757
E-mail: prssa@prsa.org
Web: www.prssa.prsa.org

Summary To provide financial assistance to Hispanic and other minority college seniors who are interested in preparing for a career in public relations.

Eligibility This program is open to minotino, African American/Black, Asian, Native American, Alaskan Native, or Pacific Islander) students who are entering their senior year at an accredited 4-year college or university. Applicants must have a GPA of 3.0 or higher and be working on a degree in public relations, journalism, or other field to prepare for a career in public relations. Along with their application, they must submit an essay on their view of the public relations profession and their public relations career goals. Selection is based on academic achievement, demonstrated leadership, practical experience, commitment to public relations, writing skills, and letters of recommendation.

Financial Data The stipend is $5,000.

Duration 1 year.

Additional data This program began in 2010.

Number awarded 1 each year.

Deadline June of each year.

[337]
MARJORIE BOWENS-WHEATLEY SCHOLARSHIPS

Unitarian Universalist Association
Attn: UU Women's Federation
258 Harvard Street
Brookline, MA 02446
(617) 838-6989   E-mail: uuwf@uua.org
Web: www.uuwf.org

Summary To provide financial assistance to Hispanic and other women of color who are working on an undergraduate or graduate degree to prepare for Unitarian Universalist ministry or service.

Eligibility This program is open to women of color who are either 1) aspirants or candidates for the Unitarian Universalist ministry; or 2) candidates in the Unitarian Universalist Association's professional religious education or music leadership credentialing programs. Applicants must submit a 1- to 2-page narrative that covers their call to UU ministry, religious education, or music leadership; their passions; how their racial/ethnic/cultural background influences their goals for their calling; and how the work of the program's namesake relates to their dreams and plans for their UU service.

Financial Data The stipend is $1,500.

Duration 1 year.

Additional data This program began in 2009.

Number awarded Varies each year; recently, 2 were awarded.

Deadline March of each year.

[338]
MARTHA GUERRA-ARTEAGA SCHOLARSHIP

National Organization of Professional Hispanic Natural Resources Conservation Service Employees
c/o Angel M. Domenech, Scholarship Committee Co-Chair
Natural Resources Conservation Service
Soil Survey Office
3100 Alvey Park Drive West
Owensboro, KY 42303-2191
(270) 685-1707, ext. 118
E-mail: scholarships@nophnrcse.org
Web: www.nophnrcse.org

Summary To provide financial assistance to Hispanic women interested in working on a bachelor's degree in a field related to public affairs or natural resources conservation.

Eligibility This program is open to Hispanic women who are graduating high school seniors or current full-time college students with at least 1 year remaining before graduation. Applicants must be interested in working on a bachelor's degree in public affairs, communications, or natural resources conservation. They must have a GPA of 2.75 or higher. Along with their application, they must submit a personal statement (in English) of 350 to 500 words on their background, name of school they attend or plan to attend, personal and career goals, extracurricular activities, and interest in preparing for a career related to natural resources conservation. Financial need is not considered in the selection process. U.S. citizenship is required.

Financial Data The stipend is $1,000.

Duration 1 year.

Additional data The National Organization of Professional Hispanic Natural Resources Conservation Service Employees (NOPRNRCSE) is comprised of Hispanic employees of the Natural Resources Conservation Service of the U.S. Department of Agriculture (USDA-NRCS).

Number awarded 1 each year.

Deadline May of each year.

[339]
MARTIN LUTHER KING, JR. MEMORIAL SCHOLARSHIP FUND

California Teachers Association
Attn: CTA Foundation for Teaching and Learning
1705 Murchison Drive
P.O. Box 921
Burlingame, CA 94011-0921
(650) 697-1400   E-mail: scholarships@cta.org
Web: www.cta.org

Summary To provide financial assistance for college or graduate school to Hispanic and other racial and ethnic minorities who are members of the California Teachers Association (CTA), children of members, or members of the Student CTA.

Eligibility This program is open to members of racial or ethnic minority groups (Hispanics, African Americans, American Indians/Alaska Natives, and Asians/Pacific Islanders) who are 1) active CTA members; 2) dependent children of active, retired, or deceased CTA members; or 3) members of Student CTA. Applicants must be interested in preparing for a teaching career in public education or already engaged in such a career.

Financial Data Stipends vary each year; recently, they ranged up to $6,000.

Duration 1 year.

Number awarded Varies each year; recently, 24 were awarded: 1 to a CTA member, 10 to children of CTA members, and 13 to Student CTA members.

Deadline February of each year.

[340]
MARTIN LUTHER KING JR. SCHOLARSHIP AWARDS

American Correctional Association
Attn: Scholarship Award Committee
206 North Washington Street, Suite 200
Alexandria, VA 22314
(703) 224-0000   Toll Free: (800) ACA-JOIN
Fax: (703) 224-0179   E-mail: execoffice@aca.org
Web: www.aca.org

Summary To provide financial assistance for undergraduate or graduate study to Hispanics and other minorities interested in a career in the criminal justice field.

Eligibility Members of the American Correctional Association (ACA) may nominate a minority person for these awards. Nominees do not need to be ACA members, but they must have been accepted to or be enrolled in an undergraduate or graduate program in criminal justice at a 4-year college or university. Along with the nomination package, they must submit a 250-word essay describing their reflections on the ideals and philosophies of Dr. Martin Luther King and how they have attempted to emulate those qualities in their lives. They must provide documentation of financial need, academic achievement, and commitment to the principles of Dr. King.

Financial Data A stipend is awarded (amount not specified). Funds are paid directly to the recipient's college or university.

Duration 1 year.

Number awarded 1 each year.

Deadline May of each year.

[341]
MARY E. BORDER SCHOLARSHIP

Kansas 4-H
c/o K-State Research and Extension
201 Umberger Hall
Manhattan, KS 66506-3404
(785) 532-5800   Fax: (785) 532-5981
Web: www.kansas4-h.org/p.aspx?tabid=479

Summary To provide financial assistance to members of Kansas 4-H who are Hispanic or other minority or economically-disadvantaged high school seniors or returning adults planning to enroll at a college in any state and major in any field.

Eligibility This program is open to residents of Kansas who have completed at least 1 year of 4-H work and are planning to enroll at a college in any state and major in any field. Applicants may be 1) economically-disadvantaged high school seniors; 2) high school seniors who are members of minority groups (African American, Asian/Pacific Islander, American Indian/Alaska Native, Hispanic/Latino); or 3) adults returning to college. Along with their application, they must submit a 1-page summary of 4-H leadership, community service, participation, and recognition; a 1-page essay on how 4-H has impacted them; and a 1-page summary of non-4-H leadership, community service, participation, and recognition in school and community. Selection is based on 4-H leadership (40%), 4-H citizenship and community service (30%), 4-H participation and recognition (20%), and non-4-H leadership, citizenship, and recognition (10%).

Financial Data The stipend is $1,500.

Duration 1 year.

Number awarded 1 each year.

Deadline January of each year.

[342]
MARY HILL DAVIS ETHNIC/MINORITY SCHOLARSHIP PROGRAM

Baptist General Convention of Texas
Attn: Theological Education
7557 Rambler Road, Suite 1200
Dallas, TX 75231-2388
(214) 828-5252   Toll Free: (888) 244-9400
Fax: (214) 828-5261   E-mail: institutions@bgct.org
Web: www.texasbaptists.org

Summary To provide financial assistance for college to Hispanic and other ethnic minority residents of Texas who are members of Texas Baptist congregations.

Eligibility This program is open to members of Texas Baptist congregations who are of Hispanic, African American, Native American, or other intercultural heritage. Applicants must be attending or planning to attend a university affiliated with the Baptist General Convention of Texas to work on a bachelor's degree as preparation for service as a future lay or vocational ministry leader in a Texas Baptist ethnic/minority church. They must have been active in their respective ethnic/minority community. Along with their application, they must submit a letter of recommendation from their pastor and transcripts. Students still in high school must have a GPA of at least 3.0; students previously enrolled in a college must have at least a 2.0 GPA. U.S. citizenship or permanent resident status is required.

Financial Data Stipends are $800 per semester ($1,600 per year) for full-time students or $400 per semester ($800 per year) for part-time students.

Duration 1 semester; may be renewed up to 7 additional semesters.

Additional data The scholarships are funded through the Week of Prayer and the Mary Hill Davis Offering for state missions sponsored annually by Women's Missionary Union of Texas. The eligible institutions are Baptist University of The Americas, Baylor University, Dallas Baptist University, East Texas Baptist University, Hardin Simmons University, Houston Baptist University, Howard Payne University, University of Mary Hardin Baylor, and Wayland Baptist University.

Number awarded Varies each year.

Deadline April of each year.

[343]
MARY WOLFSKILL TRUST FUND INTERNSHIP

Library of Congress
Library Services
Attn: Junior Fellows Program Coordinator
101 Independence Avenue, S.E., Room LM-642
Washington, DC 20540-4600
(202) 707-9929   Fax: (202) 707-6269
E-mail: jfla@loc.gov
Web: www.loc.gov

Summary To provide summer work experience in the Manuscript Division of the Library of Congress (LC) to upper-division and graduate students, especially Hispanics and other minorities.

Eligibility This program is open to undergraduate and graduate students who have expertise in library science or collections conservation and preservation. Applicants must be interested in gaining an introductory knowledge of the principles, concepts, and techniques of archival management through a summer internship in the LC Manuscript Division. They should be able to demonstrate an ability to communicate effectively in writing and have knowledge of integrated library systems, basic library applications, and other information technologies. Knowledge of American history is beneficial. Applications from minorities and students at smaller and lesser-known schools are particularly encouraged. U.S. citizenship is required.

Financial Data The stipend is $3,000.

Duration 10 weeks during the summer. Fellows work a 40-hour week.

Number awarded 1 each year.

Deadline January of each year.

[344]
MARYLAND HISPANIC ACHIEVEMENT SCHOLARSHIP

Montgomery County Executive Hispanic Gala
c/o Lorna Virgili
P.O. Box 4162
Rockville, MD 20849
(240) 277-8072
E-mail: scholarships@montgomeryhispanicgala.org
Web: www.montgomeryhispanicgala.org/scholarship.html

Summary To provide financial assistance to Hispanic residents of Maryland who are interested in attending college in the state.

Eligibility This program is open to Hispanic high school seniors and current undergraduates who have graduate from a high school in Maryland or obtained a GED in that state within the past 4 years. Applicants must be enrolled or planning to enroll full or part time at an accredited postsecondary institution in the state. They must have a GPA of 2.5 or higher, have made a significant contribution of voluntary community service within the past 12 months, and be able to demonstrate financial need. Along with their application, they must submit a 500-word essay on how growing up in a diverse community influenced their life and how it will affect their career choices in the future. They must be a U.S. citizen, resident, or Dreamer.

Financial Data The stipend is $2,000. Funds are sent directly to the recipient's college or university.

Duration 1 year; nonrenewable.

Number awarded Multiple scholarships are awarded each year.

Deadline June of each year.

[345]
MARYLAND SEA GRANT RESEARCH EXPERIENCES FOR UNDERGRADUATES PROGRAM

Maryland Sea Grant
Attn: Associate Director for Research and Administration
University of Maryland
4321 Hartwick Road, Suite 300
College Park, MD 20740
(301) 405-7500   Fax: (301) 405-5780
E-mail: mallen@mdsg.umd.edu
Web: www.mdsg.umd.edu/reu

Summary To provide an opportunity for undergraduates, especially Hispanics and members of other underrepresented groups, to conduct summer research related to the mission of Maryland Sea Grant.

Eligibility This program is open to U.S. citizens and permanent residents who have completed at least 2 years of undergraduate work on a bachelor's degree but have not yet completed that degree; preference is given to rising seniors. Students from underrepresented groups and institutions with limited research opportunities are especially encouraged to apply. Applicants must be majoring in marine science, ecology, environmental science, biology, chemistry, engineering, physics, or mathematics. They must be interested in working on a summer research project at either of the research laboratories of the University of Maryland Center for Environmental Sciences on Chesapeake Bay: the Chesapeake Biological Laboratory in Solomons, Maryland or the Horn Point Laboratory in Cambridge, Maryland.

Financial Data Fellows receive a stipend of $6,000, housing costs, and round-trip travel expenses.

Duration 12 weeks during the summer.

Additional data This program is supported by the National Science Foundation through its Research Experiences for Undergraduates program.

Number awarded 15 each year.

Deadline February of each year.

[346]
MAS FAMILY SCHOLARSHIPS

Jorge Mas Canosa Freedom Foundation
Attn: Scholarship Coordinator
P.O. Box 14-1898
Coral Gables, FL 33114
(305) 507-7323   E-mail: info@canf.org
Web: www.masscholarships.org

Summary To provide financial assistance to students of Cuban descent who are interested in working on an undergraduate degree in selected subject areas.

Eligibility This program is open to students who were born in Cuba or are of direct Cuban descent. Applicants must have

a GPA of 3.5 or higher and be able to demonstrate financial need. They must be interested in working on a degree in 1 of the following subjects: engineering, business, international relations, economics, communications, or journalism. Along with their application, they must submit transcripts that include SAT and/or ACT scores and an essay up to 1,000 words in length on a topic related to liberty. Selection is based on academic performance, leadership qualities, potential to contribute to the advancement of a free society, and likelihood of succeeding in their chosen field. Finalists may be interviewed.

Financial Data The stipend ranges up to $8,000 per year.

Duration 1 year; may be renewed up to 3 additional years.

Additional data This program, established in 1997, was previously offered by the Cuban American National Foundation.

Number awarded Varies each year; since this program was established, it has provided support to more than 100 students.

Deadline January of each year.

[347]
MASSMUTUAL SCHOLARS PROGRAM

Massachusetts Mutual Life Insurance Company
1295 State Street
Springfield, MA 01111-0001
Toll Free: (800) 542-6767
Web: www.massmutual.scholarsapply.org

Summary To provide financial assistance to Hispanics and other undergraduates who reflect the diversity of the country and are preparing for a career in the insurance and financial services industry.

Eligibility This program is open to full-time students from diverse backgrounds who are entering their sophomore, junior, senior, or fifth-year senior year at an accredited college or university in the United States, Puerto Rico, U.S. Virgin Islands, or Guam. Applicants must be U.S. citizens or permanent residents and have a GPA of 3.0 or higher. They may be majoring in any field, but preference is given to students who demonstrate 1) an interest in preparing for a career in the insurance and financial services industry; and 2) leadership and participation in extracurricular activities. Financial need is considered in the selection process.

Financial Data The stipend is $2,500 for students at 2-year colleges or $5,000 for students at 4-year institutions.

Duration 1 year.

Number awarded 30 each year.

Deadline March of each year.

[348]
MAUREEN L. AND HOWARD N. BLITMAN, P.E. SCHOLARSHIP TO PROMOTE DIVERSITY IN ENGINEERING

National Society of Professional Engineers
Attn: NSPE Educational Foundation
1420 King Street
Alexandria, VA 22314-2794
(703) 684-2833   Toll Free: (888) 285-NSPE
Fax: (703) 684-2821   E-mail: education@nspe.org
Web: www.nspe.org

Summary To provide financial assistance for college to Hispanics and members of other underrepresented ethnic minority groups who are interested in preparing for a career in engineering.

Eligibility This program is open to members of underrepresented ethnic minorities (Hispanics, African Americans, or Native Americans) who are high school seniors accepted into an ABET-accredited engineering program at a 4-year college or university. Applicants must have a GPA of 3.5 or higher, verbal SAT score of 600 or higher, and math SAT score of 700 or higher (or English ACT score of 29 or higher and math ACT score of 29 or higher). They must submit brief essays on 4 assigned topics. Selection is based on those essays, GPA, internship/co-op experience and community involvement, 2 faculty recommendations, and honors/scholarships/awards. U.S. citizenship is required.

Financial Data The stipend is $5,000 per year; funds are paid directly to the recipient's institution.

Duration 1 year; nonrenewable.

Number awarded 1 each year.

Deadline February of each year.

[349]
MCKINNEY FAMILY FUND SCHOLARSHIP

Cleveland Foundation
Attn: Scholarship Processing
1422 Euclid Avenue, Suite 1300
Cleveland, OH 44115-2001
(216) 861-3810   Fax: (216) 861-1729
E-mail: mbaker@clevefdn.org
Web: www.clevelandfoundation.org

Summary To provide financial assistance to residents of Ohio, especially Hispanics and members of other minority groups, who are interested in attending college or graduate school in any state.

Eligibility This program is open to U.S. citizens who have been residents of Ohio for at least 2 years. Applicants must be high school seniors or graduate students and interested in working full or part time on an associate, bachelor's, master's, or doctoral degree at an accredited college or university in any state. They must have a GPA of 2.5 or higher. Preference is given to applicants of minority descent. Selection is based on evidence of sincerity toward obtaining an academic credential. Financial need may be used as a tiebreaker.

Financial Data The stipend is $2,000 per year. Funds are paid directly to the school and must be applied to tuition, fees, books, supplies, and equipment required for course work.

Duration 1 year; may be renewed up to 3 additional.

Number awarded 1 or more each year.

Deadline March of each year.

[350]
MEDIA GENERAL MINORITY SCHOLARSHIP AND TRAINING PROGRAM

Media General
Attn: Angie Cartwright, Human Resources
9101 Burnet Road
Austin, TX 78758
(512) 380-4400
Web: www.mediageneral.com/careers/scholarship.html

Summary To provide scholarship/loans to Hispanic and other minority undergraduates interested in earning a degree in a field related to broadcast journalism and working at a station owned by LIN Television Corporation.

Eligibility This program is open to U.S. citizens and permanent residents of non-white origin who are enrolled as a sophomore or junior at a college or university. Applicants must have a declared major in broadcast journalism, digital multimedia, mass/speech/digital communication, television production, or marketing and a GPA of 3.0 or higher. Along with their application, they must submit a list of organizations and activities in which they have held leadership positions, 3 references, a 50-word description of their career goals, a list of personal achievements and honors, and a 500-word essay about themselves. Financial need is not considered in the selection process.

Financial Data The program pays for tuition and fees, books, and room and board, to a maximum of $10,000 per year. Recipients must sign an employment agreement that guarantees them part-time employment as an intern during school and a 2-year regular position at a television station owned by Media General following graduation. If they fail to honor the employment agreement, they must repay all scholarship funds received.

Duration 2 years.

Additional data This program began in 1998 under LIN Television Corporation, which was acquired by Media General in 2014. Media General owns 71 television stations in 48 media markets in the United States. Recipients of these scholarships must work at a station selected by Media General management.

Number awarded 2 each year: 1 for a student in broadcast television and 1 for a student in digital media.

Deadline January of each year.

[351]
MELLON UNDERGRADUATE CURATORIAL FELLOWSHIP PROGRAM

Art Institute of Chicago
Attn: Coordinator, Andrew W. Mellon Academic Programs
111 South Michigan Avenue
Chicago, IL 60603
(312) 443-3581   E-mail: fmings@artic.edu
Web: www.artic.edu/mellon

Summary To provide an opportunity for undergraduates who are Hispanics or members of other groups historically underrepresented in the curatorial field to gain academic training and work experience to prepare for a career as an art curator.

Eligibility This program is open to undergraduates (typically freshmen or sophomores) who can commit 2 years to a program of preparation for a career as an art curator. Applicants must be studying art history, art, or the museum field at a college or university in the vicinity of 5 designated art museums. They must be members of groups historically underrepresented in the curatorial field and interested in continuing on to graduate school for advanced study in a relevant academic discipline. They must also be available to work with a mentor at the museum during the academic year to gain experience with curators and staff on exhibitions, collections, and programs and to participate in a summer internship. Interested students first apply to participate in a Summer Academy at the museum in their area. Selection for the Academy is based on academic record, extracurricular activities, background or other experiences, and expected contribution to the program. Based on performance during the Academy and personal interviews, Curatorial Fellows are selected at each of the 5 museums.

Financial Data Students selected for the Summer Academies receive a per diem allowance. Students selected as fellows receive an academic stipend of $4,000 per year and a grant of $6,000 for the summer internship.

Duration The Summer Academy lasts 1 week. The fellowship is 2 years, including 10-week summer internships.

Additional data The Andrew W. Mellon Foundation established this program in 2013. In addition to the Art Institute of Chicago, it also operates at the High Museum of Art in Atlanta, the Los Angeles County Museum of Art, the Museum of Fine Arts, Houston, and the Nelson-Atkins Museum of Art in Kansas City. Students who attend college in the vicinity of those museums should contact them about this program.

Number awarded 15 students at each of the 5 museums are selected each year to participate in the Summer Academy. Of those, 2 are selected at each museum to receive the Curatorial Fellowship.

Deadline February of each year.

[352]
MEXICAN AMERICAN ENGINEERS AND SCIENTISTS SCHOLARSHIP PROGRAM

Society of Mexican American Engineers and Scientists
Attn: Scholarship Program
2437 Bay Area Boulevard, Suite 100
Houston, TX 77058
(281) 557-3677   Fax: (281) 715-5100
E-mail: questions@mymaes.org
Web: www.mymaes.org/student

Summary To provide financial assistance to undergraduate and graduate student members of the Society of Mexican American Engineers and Scientists (MAES).

Eligibility This program is open to MAES student members who are full-time undergraduate or graduate students at a college or university in the United States and have a GPA of 2.0 or higher. Community college students must be enrolled in majors that can transfer to a 4-year institution offering a baccalaureate degree. All applicants must be majoring in a field of science, technology, engineering, or mathematics (STEM). U.S. citizenship or permanent resident status is required. Along with their application, they must submit a personal statement that includes information on their family background, involvement in school and community activities, MAES involvement, and financial need.

Financial Data Stipends range from $1,000 to $4,000.

Duration 1 year.

Additional data This program includes Padrino/Madrina Scholarships at $4,000, the Founder's Scholarship at $2,500, the Presidential Scholarship at $2,500, and general scholarships at $1,000 or $2,000. The Padrino/Madrina Scholarships are sponsored by ExxonMobil and Lockheed Martin; the Presidential Scholarship is sponsored by ExxonMobil; other scholarships are sponsored by Applied Materials, General Motors, Lockheed Martin, and various professional chapters

of MAES. Recipients must attend the MAES International Symposium's Medalla de Oro Banquet in December.

Number awarded Varies each year; recently, available scholarships included 2 Padrino/Madrina Scholarships, 1 Founder's Scholarship, 1 Presidential Scholarship, and 13 general scholarships.

Deadline September of each year.

[353]
MEXICAN FIESTA SCHOLARSHIPS

Wisconsin Hispanic Scholarship Foundation, Inc.
2997 South 20th Street
Milwaukee, WI 53215
(414) 383-7066   Fax: (414) 383-6677
E-mail: info@mexicanfiesta.org
Web: www.mexicanfiesta.org/scholarships.php

Summary To provide financial assistance to Hispanic American students in Wisconsin who are interested in attending college or graduate school in the state.

Eligibility This program is open to Wisconsin residents who are of at least 25% Hispanic descent and entering or enrolled at a 2- or 4-year college or university or graduate school in the state. Applicants must complete at least 20 hours of volunteer service during the Mexican Fiesta festival in Milwaukee during August of each year. They must have a GPA of 2.5 or higher. Along with their application, they must submit an essay on how they plan to assist or help the Hispanic community after their receive their degree. U.S. citizenship or permanent resident status is required.

Financial Data Stipends range from $250 to $2,000.

Duration 1 year; recipients may reapply.

Additional data The sponsor is an affiliate of the League of United Latin American Citizens (LULAC) Wisconsin Councils 319 and 322.

Number awarded More than 100 each year.

Deadline March of each year.

[354]
MEXICAN SCHOLARSHIP FUND

Central Indiana Community Foundation
Attn: Scholarship Program
615 North Alabama Street, Suite 119
Indianapolis, IN 46204-1498
(317) 634-2423   Fax: (317) 684-0943
E-mail: scholarships@cicf.org
Web: www.cicf.org/grantseekers/scholarships

Summary To provide financial assistance to residents of Indiana, especially Mexican Americans, who are interested in attending college in any state.

Eligibility This program is open to residents of Indiana who are enrolled or planning to enroll at a college, university, or vocational/technical school in any state. Preference is given to students of Mexican descent. Applicants must have a GPA of 3.0 or higher. Along with their application, they must submit a 1-page essay either on what their Mexican heritage means to them or on their involvement with the Hispanic community. Financial need is considered in the selection process.

Financial Data The stipend is $2,000.

Duration 1 year.

Additional data The Consulate General of Mexico in Indianapolis established this program in 2005. The program includes an award funded by the Ambassador Randall L. Tobias and Dr. Marianne W. Tobias Endowed Scholarship Fund. The Tobias Scholars are expected to submit semi-annual letters written in Spanish about their academic progress.

Number awarded Varies each year; recently, 10 were awarded.

Deadline February of each year.

[355]
MICHAEL BAKER SCHOLARSHIP FOR DIVERSITY IN ENGINEERING

Association of Independent Colleges and Universities of Pennsylvania
101 North Front Street
Harrisburg, PA 17101-1404
(717) 232-8649   Fax: (717) 233-8574
E-mail: info@aicup.org
Web: www.aicup.org/Foundation-Scholarships

Summary To provide financial assistance to Hispanics and other minority students from any state enrolled at member institutions of the Association of Independent Colleges and Universities of Pennsylvania (AICUP) who are majoring in designated fields of engineering.

Eligibility This program is open to full-time undergraduate students from any state enrolled at designated AICUP colleges and universities who are women and/or members of the following minority groups: Hispanics/Latinos, American Indians, Alaska Natives, Asians, Blacks/African Americans, Native Hawaiians, or Pacific Islanders. Applicants must be juniors majoring in architectural, civil, or environmental engineering with a GPA of 3.0 or higher. Along with their application, they must submit a 2-page essay on what they believe will be the greatest challenge facing the engineering profession over the next decade, and why.

Financial Data The stipend is $2,500 per year.

Duration 1 year; may be renewed 1 additional year if the recipient maintains appropriate academic standards.

Additional data This program, sponsored by the Michael Baker Corporation, is available at the 88 private colleges and universities in Pennsylvania that comprise the AICUP.

Number awarded 1 each year.

Deadline April of each year.

[356]
MICHIGAN ACCOUNTANCY FOUNDATION FIFTH/ GRADUATE YEAR SCHOLARSHIP PROGRAM

Michigan Association of Certified Public Accountants
Attn: Michigan Accountancy Foundation
5480 Corporate Drive, Suite 200
P.O. Box 5068
Troy, MI 48007-5068
(248) 267-3680   Toll Free: (888) 877-4CPE (within MI)
Fax: (248) 267-3737   E-mail: MAF@micpa.org
Web: www.mafonline.org/?page_id=35

Summary To provide financial assistance to students at Michigan colleges and universities, especially Hispanics and members of other underrepresented groups, who are working on a degree in accounting.

Eligibility This program is open to students enrolled full time at accredited Michigan colleges and universities with a declared concentration in accounting. Applicants must be seniors planning to enter the fifth or graduate year of their school's program. They must intend to or have successfully passed the Michigan C.P.A. examination and intend to practice public accounting in the state. Along with their application, they must submit 500-word statements about 1) examples of their leadership roles and extracurricular activities, community involvement and volunteerism, how they are financing their education, and the accomplishments of which they are most proud; and 2) their professional goals for the next 5 years and any special circumstances they wish to have considered. Special consideration is given to applicants who are single parents, physically challenged, minority, or self-supporting. U.S. citizenship or eligibility for permanent employment in the United States is required.

Financial Data The stipend is $3,000; funds are disbursed directly to the recipient's college or university.

Duration 1 year.

Additional data This program includes the William E. Balhoff Leadership Scholarship, the Jeff Bergeron Leadership Scholarship, the Robert A. Bogan Scholarship (limited to a student from the metropolitan Detroit area), the Kenneth Bouyer Leadership Scholarship, the Peggy A. Dzierzawski Leadership Scholarship, the George Johnson Leadership Scholarship, the Thomas McTavish Leadership Scholarship, the Randy Paschke Leadership Scholarship, and the Governor Rick Snyder Leadership Scholarship.

Number awarded 15 to 20 each year.

Deadline January of each year.

[357]
MICHIGAN CHAPTER AABE SCHOLARSHIPS

American Association of Blacks in Energy-Michigan Chapter
Attn: Scholarship Committee
37637 Five Mile Road, Suite 405
Livonia, MI 48154
(810) 760-3465   E-mail: aaron.parket@cmsenergy.com
Web: www.aabe.org/index.php?component=pages&id=582

Summary To provide financial assistance to Hispanic and members of other underrepresented minority groups who are high school seniors in Michigan and planning to major in an energy-related field at a college in any state.

Eligibility This program is open to seniors graduating from high schools in Michigan and planning to work on a bachelor's degree at a college or university in any state. Applicants must be Hispanics, African Americans, or Native Americans who have a GPA of 3.0 or higher and have taken the ACT and/or SAT test. Their intended major must be a field of business, engineering, physical science, mathematics, or technology related to energy. Along with their application, they must submit a 350-word essay that includes 1) when they discovered their interest in the field of energy and what sparked their interest; and 2) either what excites them about the field of energy or how they expect their education to prepare them for the field of energy. Financial need is not considered in the selection process.

Financial Data A stipend is awarded (amount not specified).

Duration 1 year; nonrenewable.

Additional data Winners are eligible to compete for regional and national scholarships.

Number awarded At least 1 each year.

Deadline March of each year.

[358]
MICHIGAN CHAPTER COMTO SCHOLARSHIPS

Conference of Minority Transportation Officials-Michigan Chapter
Attn: President
P.O. Box 32439
Detroit, MI 48232
(269) 491-7279   E-mail: averyk@michigan.gov
Web: www.comtomichigan.org/scholarships.html

Summary To provide financial assistance to Hispanics and other minority undergraduate and graduate students in Michigan who are working on a degree in a transportation-related field.

Eligibility This program is open to members of minority groups enrolled full time as sophomores, juniors, seniors, or graduate students at colleges or universities in Michigan. Applicants must be working on a degree in engineering, planning, or other transportation-related discipline. Graduate students must be members of the Conference of Minority Transportation Officials (COMTO); if undergraduates are not already members, they must become a member within 30 days of the scholarship award. U.S. citizenship or legal resident status is required.

Financial Data The stipend ranges from $500 to $3,000. Funds are paid directly to the student.

Duration 1 year.

Number awarded Varies each year; recently, 7 were awarded: 1 at $3,000, 1 at $2,000, 2 at $1,000, and 3 at $500.

Deadline April of each year.

[359]
MICKEY LELAND ENERGY FELLOWSHIPS

Oak Ridge Institute for Science and Education
Attn: MLEF Fellowship Program
1299 Bethel Valley Road, Building SC-200
P.O. Box 117, MS 36
Oak Ridge, TN 37831-0117
(865) 574-6440   Fax: (865) 576-0734
E-mail: barbara.dunkin@orau.org
Web: orise.orau.gov/mlef/index.html

Summary To provide summer work experience at fossil energy sites of the Department of Energy (DOE) to Hispanic and other underrepresented minority and female students or postdoctorates.

Eligibility This program is open to U.S. citizens currently enrolled full time at an accredited college or university. Applicants must be undergraduate, graduate, or postdoctoral students in fields of science, technology (IT), engineering, or mathematics (STEM) and have a GPA of 3.0 or higher. They must be interested in a summer work experience at a DOE fossil energy research facility. Along with their application, they must submit a 100-word statement on why they want to participate in this program. A goal of the program is to recruit women and underrepresented minorities into careers related to fossil energy, although all qualified students are encouraged to apply.

Financial Data Weekly stipends are $600 for undergraduates, $750 for master's degree students, or $850 for doctoral and postdoctoral students. Travel costs for a round trip to and from the site and for a trip to a designated place for technical presentations are also paid.

Duration 10 weeks during the summer.

Additional data This program began as 3 separate activities: the Historically Black Colleges and Universities Internship Program established in 1995, the Hispanic Internship Program established in 1998, and the Tribal Colleges and Universities Internship Program, established in 2000. Those 3 programs were merged into the Fossil Energy Minority Education Initiative, renamed the Mickey Leland Energy Fellowship Program in 2000. Sites to which interns may be assigned include the National Energy Technology Laboratory (Morgantown, West Virginia, Albany, Oregon and Pittsburgh, Pennsylvania), Pacific Northwest National Laboratory (Richland, Washington), Sandia National Laboratory (Livermore, California), Lawrence Berkeley National Laboratory (Berkeley, California), Los Alamos National Laboratory (Los Alamos, New Mexico), Strategic Petroleum Reserve Project Management Office (New Orleans, Louisiana), or U.S. Department of Energy Headquarters (Washington, D.C.).

Number awarded Varies each year; recently, 30 students participated in this program.

Deadline December of each year.

[360]
MIDWIVES OF COLOR-WATSON MIDWIFERY STUDENT SCHOLARSHIP

American College of Nurse-Midwives
Attn: ACNM Foundation, Inc.
8403 Colesville Road, Suite 1550
Silver Spring, MD 20910-6374
(240) 485-1850   Fax: (240) 485-1818
E-mail: foundation@acnmf.org
Web: www.midwife.org

Summary To provide financial assistance for midwifery education to Hispanic and other students of color who belong to the American College of Nurse-Midwives (ACNM).

Eligibility This program is open to ACNM members of color who are currently enrolled in an accredited basic midwife education program and have successfully completed 1 academic or clinical semester/quarter or clinical module. Applicants must submit they must submit a 150-word essay on their 5-year midwifery career plans; a 150-word essay on their intended future participation in the local, regional, and/or national activities of the ACNM; a 150-word essay on their need for financial assistance; and a 100-word statement on how they would use the funds if they receive the scholarship. Selection is based on academic excellence, leadership potential, and financial need.

Financial Data The stipend is $3,000.

Duration 1 year.

Number awarded Varies each year; recently, 3 were awarded.

Deadline February of each year.

[361]
MIGRANT FARMWORKER BACCALAUREATE SCHOLARSHIP

Geneseo Migrant Center
Attn: Scholarship Funds
3 Mt. Morris-Leicester Road
Leicester, NY 14481
(585) 658-7960   Toll Free: (800) 245-5681
Fax: (585) 658-7969   E-mail: mreho@gvboces.org
Web: www.migrant.net/migrant/scholarships/mfb.htm

Summary   To provide financial assistance to migrant farmworkers who are currently enrolled in college.

Eligibility   This program is open to migrant farmworker students with a history of migrating for employment in agriculture. Applicants must have completed at least 1 year of college. Along with their application, they must submit a personal essay of at least 500 words on their background, career and personal goals, and why they should receive this assistance; 3 letters of recommendation; a college transcript; a copy of their Migrant Education Certificate of Eligibility (COE), and documentation of financial need.

Financial Data   The stipend is $20,000 per year. These funds are intended to be in addition to any that the student receives through federal, state, or other scholarship assistance as an undergraduate. The same annual amount is available for graduate study or loan repayment.

Duration   1 year; may be renewed for an additional 2 years of undergraduate study. Recipients also have the option of an additional 2 years of graduate support or 3 years of loan repayment.

Additional data   Following completion of their baccalaureate degree, recipients may apply for additional support as a graduate student or for assistance in repayment of educational loans.

Number awarded   1 each year.

Deadline   June of each year.

[362]
MIGRANT HEALTH SCHOLARSHIPS

National Center for Farmworker Health, Inc.
Attn: Migrant Health Scholarship
1770 FM 967
Buda, TX 78610
(512) 312-2700   Toll Free: (800) 531-5120
Fax: (512) 312-2600   E-mail: favre@ncfh.org
Web: www.ncfh.org/scholarships.html

Summary   To provide financial assistance to people working in the migrant health field, especially those with a farmworker background, who are interested in additional education.

Eligibility   This program is open to staff in clinical, administrative, and support positions at community and migrant health centers who are interested in obtaining additional education at the undergraduate or graduate level. Applicants must submit a 1-page personal statement discussing such issues as why they are interested in migrant health, personal experiences and achievements, future career goals, commitment to migrant health, and financial need. Preference is given to applicants with a farmworker background.

Financial Data   The stipend is $1,000.

Duration   1 year.

Additional data   This program began in 1984.

Number awarded   Varies each year; recently, 6 were awarded. Since the program was established, it has awarded 210 of these scholarships.

Deadline   March of each year.

[363]
MIGRANT STUDENT LEADERSHIP AND ACADEMIC SCHOLARSHIPS

Washington Apple Education Foundation
Attn: Scholarship Committee
2900 Euclid Avenue
Wenatchee, WA 98801
(509) 663-7713   Fax: (509) 663-7469
E-mail: scholarships@waef.org
Web: www.waef.org/scholarships

Summary   To provide financial assistance to residents of Washington whose families engage in migrant labor and who are interested in attending college in any state.

Eligibility   This program is open to residents of Washington who are current or former high school seniors or students already enrolled at a 2- or 4-year college, university, or trade/technical school in any state. Applicants must have moved across school boundaries for family employment in agriculture or fishing seasonal work, meeting federal eligibility criteria of the Title 1 Migrant Education Program. They must be able to demonstrate a high degree of community service involvement or an ability to be a positive role model for migrant youth. Along with their application, they must submit an official transcript, their SAT or ACT scores, 2 letters of reference, and an essay on an assigned topic. Financial need is also considered in the selection process.

Financial Data   The stipend is $1,000.

Duration   1 year.

Number awarded   2 each year.

Deadline   February of each year.

[364]
MILE HIGH CHAPTER SCHOLARSHIP AWARDS PROGRAM

American GI Forum-Mile High Chapter
Attn: Education Committee
1717 Federal Boulevard
Denver, CO 80204
(303) 455-3304
Web: www.agifmilehigh.org/EduComm.html

Summary   To provide financial assistance to Hispanic residents of Colorado who are attending or planning to attend college in any state.

Eligibility   This program is open to Colorado residents who are high school seniors, high school graduates, GED recipients, or continuing college students. Applicants must be of Hispanic background or involved with the Hispanic community or veteran's organizations. They must have a GPA of 2.0 or higher and be attending or planning to attend college in any state. Along with their application, they must submit an essay of 250 to 500 words on their educational and career goals, their financial need, and why they should be selected to receive a scholarship award. Selection is based on that essay, academic potential, community service and extracurricular activities, and financial need. Preference is given to applicants who have an association with the Mile High Chapter of the American GI Forum.

Financial Data A stipend is awarded (amount not specified).

Duration 1 year.

Additional data Recipients must provide 4 hours of volunteer service to the Mile High Chapter during the year they receive the award.

Number awarded Up to 10 each year.

Deadline July of each year.

[365]
MILLERCOORS CHICAGO SCHOLARSHIP

¡Adelante! U.S. Education Leadership Fund
8415 Datapoint Drive, Suite 400
San Antonio, TX 78229
(210) 692-1971   Toll Free: (877) 692-1971
Fax: (210) 692-1951   E-mail: info@adelantefund.org
Web: www.adelantefund.org/#!scholarships/cee5

Summary To provide financial assistance to Hispanic upper-division students enrolled at a college in the Chicago metropolitan area and majoring in designated fields of business or engineering.

Eligibility This program is open to full-time incoming juniors and seniors at colleges and universities in the Chicago metropolitan area, especially designated partner universities. Applicants may be studying any field of business or engineering, but preference is given to those majoring in accounting, biochemistry, communications, computer information systems, computer science, electrical engineering, finance, international business, marketing, management, mechanical engineering, public relations, sales, or supply chain management. They must be of Hispanic descent, have a GPA of 3.0 or higher, be U.S. citizens or permanent residents, agree to attend the Adelante Leadership Institute, and provide 2 letters of recommendation.

Financial Data The stipend is $3,000.

Duration 1 year.

Additional data This fund was established by the Hispanic Association of Colleges and Universities in 1997 and became a separate organization in 1999. This program is sponsored by MillerCoors. The Chicago area partner universities are Columbia College, DePaul University, Loyola University, Northeastern Illinois University, Roosevelt University, and University of Illinois at Chicago.

Number awarded Several each year.

Deadline July of each year.

[366]
MILLERCOORS COLORADO SCHOLARSHIP

¡Adelante! U.S. Education Leadership Fund
8415 Datapoint Drive, Suite 400
San Antonio, TX 78229
(210) 692-1971   Toll Free: (877) 692-1971
Fax: (210) 692-1951   E-mail: info@adelantefund.org
Web: www.adelantefund.org/#!scholarships/cee5

Summary To provide financial assistance to Hispanic upper-division students enrolled at a college in Colorado and majoring in designated fields of business or engineering.

Eligibility This program is open to full-time incoming juniors and seniors at colleges and universities in Colorado.

Applicants may be studying any field of business or engineering, but preference is given to those majoring in accounting, biochemistry, communications, computer information systems, computer science, electrical engineering, finance, international business, marketing, management, mechanical engineering, public relations, sales, or supply chain management. They must be of Hispanic descent, have a GPA of 3.0 or higher, be U.S. citizens or permanent residents, agree to attend the Adelante Leadership Institute, and provide 2 letters of recommendation.

Financial Data The stipend is $3,000.

Duration 1 year.

Additional data This fund was established by the Hispanic Association of Colleges and Universities in 1997 and became a separate organization in 1999. This program is sponsored by MillerCoors.

Number awarded Several each year.

Deadline July of each year.

[367]
MILLERCOORS ENGINEERING AND SCIENCE SCHOLARSHIP

¡Adelante! U.S. Education Leadership Fund
8415 Datapoint Drive, Suite 400
San Antonio, TX 78229
(210) 692-1971   Toll Free: (877) 692-1971
Fax: (210) 692-1951   E-mail: info@adelantefund.org
Web: www.adelantefund.org/#!scholarships/cee5

Summary To provide financial assistance to upper-division Hispanic students majoring in fields of science, technology, engineering, and mathematics (STEM) at designated universities.

Eligibility This program is open to Hispanic students entering their junior or senior year as full-time students at any of 91 designated partner colleges and universities. Applicants must be working on a degree in a field of STEM. They must have a GPA of 3.0 or higher, be U.S. citizens or permanent residents, agree to attend the Adelante Leadership Institute, and provide 2 letters of recommendation.

Financial Data The stipend is $3,000.

Duration 1 year.

Additional data This fund was established by the Hispanic Association of Colleges and Universities in 1997 and became a separate organization in 1999. For a list of the 91 partner institutions, contact the fund. This program is sponsored by MillerCoors.

Number awarded Several each year.

Deadline July of each year.

[368]
MILLERCOORS NATIONAL SCHOLARSHIP

¡Adelante! U.S. Education Leadership Fund
8415 Datapoint Drive, Suite 400
San Antonio, TX 78229
(210) 692-1971   Toll Free: (877) 692-1971
Fax: (210) 692-1951   E-mail: info@adelantefund.org
Web: www.adelantefund.org/#!scholarships/cee5

Summary To provide financial assistance to upper-division Hispanic students majoring in fields related to business at designated universities.

Eligibility This program is open to Hispanic students entering their junior or senior year as full-time students at any of 91 designated partner colleges and universities. Applicants must be working on a degree in accounting, communications, computer information systems, computer science, finance, international business, marketing, management, public relations, sales, or supply chain management. They must have a GPA of 3.0 or higher, be U.S. citizens or permanent residents, agree to attend the Adelante Leadership Institute, and provide 2 letters of recommendation.

Financial Data The stipend is $3,000.

Duration 1 year.

Additional data This fund was established by the Hispanic Association of Colleges and Universities in 1997 and became a separate organization in 1999. For a list of the 91 partner institutions, contact the fund. This program is sponsored by MillerCoors.

Number awarded Several each year.

Deadline July of each year.

[369]
MINNESOTA SOCIAL SERVICE ASSOCIATION DIVERSITY SCHOLARSHIP

Minnesota Social Service Association
Attn: Membership and Diversity Committee
125 Charles Avenue
St. Paul, MN 55103
(651) 644-0556   Fax: (651) 224-6540
E-mail: ajorgensen@mnssa.org
Web: www.mnssa.org

Summary To provide financial assistance to Hispanic and other students from a diverse background who are enrolled in an undergraduate program in the health and human services field at a college in the upper Midwest.

Eligibility This program is open to residents of any state entering their junior or senior year at a college or university in Iowa, Minnesota, North Dakota, South Dakota, or Wisconsin. Applicants must be working full time on a degree in the health and human services field and have a GPA of 3.0 or higher. They must be from a diverse background, which may be along the dimensions of race, ethnicity, gender, sexual orientation, socioeconomic status, age, physical ability, religion, or other ideology. Financial need is considered in the selection process.

Financial Data The stipend is $1,000.

Duration 1 year.

Number awarded 1 each year.

Deadline May of each year.

[370]
MINORITIES IN GOVERNMENT FINANCE SCHOLARSHIP

Government Finance Officers Association
Attn: Scholarship Committee
203 North LaSalle Street, Suite 2700
Chicago, IL 60601-1210
(312) 977-9700   Fax: (312) 977-4806
Web: www.gfoa.org

Summary To provide financial assistance to Hispanic and other minority upper-division and graduate students who are preparing for a career in state and local government finance.

Eligibility This program is open to upper-division and graduate students who are preparing for a career in public finance by working on a degree in public administration, accounting, finance, political science, economics, or business administration (with a specific focus on government or nonprofit management). Applicants must be members of a minority group, citizens or permanent residents of the United States or Canada, and able to provide a letter of recommendation from a representative of their school. The program defines minorities as Hispanics or Latinos, Blacks or African Americans, American Indians or Alaskan Natives, Native Hawaiians or other Pacific Islanders, or Asians. Selection is based on career plans, academic record, plan of study, letters of recommendation, and GPA. Financial need is not considered.

Financial Data The stipend is $6,000.

Duration 1 year.

Number awarded 1 each year.

Deadline February of each year.

[371]
MINORITY AFFAIRS COMMITTEE'S AWARD FOR OUTSTANDING SCHOLASTIC ACHIEVEMENT

American Institute of Chemical Engineers
Attn: Minority Affairs Committee
120 Wall Street, FL 23
New York, NY 10005-4020
Toll Free: (800) 242-4363   Fax: (203) 775-5177
E-mail: awards@aiche.org
Web: www.aiche.org

Summary To recognize and reward Hispanic and other underrepresented minority students majoring in chemical engineering who serve as role models for other minority students.

Eligibility Members of the American Institute of Chemical Engineers (AIChE) may nominate any chemical engineering student who serves as a role model for minority students in that field. Nominees must be members of a minority group that is underrepresented in chemical engineering (i.e., Hispanic, African American, Native American, Alaskan Native). They must have a GPA of 3.0 or higher. Along with their application, they must submit a 300-word essay on their immediate plans after graduation, areas of chemical engineering of most interest, and long-range career plans. Selection is based on that essay, academic record, participation in AIChE student chapter and professional or civic activities, and financial need.

Financial Data The award consists of a plaque and a $1,500 honorarium.

Duration The award is presented annually.

Additional data This award was first presented in 1996.

Number awarded 1 each year.

Deadline Nominations must be submitted by May of each year.

[372]
MINORITY AND UNDERREPRESENTED ENVIRONMENTAL LITERACY PROGRAM

Missouri Department of Higher Education
Attn: Student Financial Assistance
205 Jefferson Street
P.O. Box 1469
Jefferson City, MO 65102-1469
(573) 751-2361   Toll Free: (800) 473-6757
Fax: (573) 751-6635   E-mail: info@dhe.mo.gov
Web: www.dhe.mo.gov/ppc/grants/muelp_0310_final.php

Summary To provide financial assistance to Hispanic and other underrepresented and minority students from Missouri who are or will be working on a bachelor's or master's degree in an environmental field.

Eligibility This program is open to residents of Missouri who are high school seniors or current undergraduate or graduate students enrolled or planning to enroll full time at a college or university in the state. Priority is given to members of the following underrepresented minority ethnic groups: Hispanic or Latino Americans, African Americans, Native Americans and Alaska Natives, and Native Hawaiians and Pacific Islanders. Applicants must be working on or planning to work on a bachelor's or master's degree in 1) engineering (civil, chemical, environmental, mechanical, or agricultural); 2) environmental studies (geology, biology, wildlife management, natural resource planning, natural resources, or a closely-related course of study); 3) environmental chemistry; or 4) environmental law enforcement. They must be U.S. citizens or permanent residents or otherwise lawfully present in the United States. Graduating high school seniors must have a GPA of 3.0 or higher; students currently enrolled in college or graduate school must have a GPA of 2.5 or higher. Along with their application, they must submit a 1-page essay on why they are applying for this scholarship, 3 letters of recommendation, a resume of school and community activities, and transcripts that include SAT or ACT scores. Financial need is not considered in the selection process.

Financial Data Stipends vary each year; recently, they averaged approximately $3,045 per year.

Duration 1 year; may be renewed if the recipient maintains a GPA of 2.5 or higher and full-time enrollment.

Additional data This program was established by the Missouri Department of Natural Resources but transferred to the Department of Higher Education in 2009.

Number awarded Varies each year.

Deadline May of each year.

[373]
MINORITY COMMUNITY COLLEGE TRANSFER SCHOLARSHIPS

State University System of Florida
Attn: Board of Governors
325 West Gaines Street
Tallahassee, FL 32399-0400
(850) 245-0466   Fax: (850) 245-9685
E-mail: info@flbog.org

Summary To provide financial assistance to Hispanic and other minority community college students in Florida who are interested in transferring to a school within the State University System of Florida (SUS).

Eligibility This program is open to minority community college students who complete A.A. or A.S. degrees from an accredited Florida community college between December and August of the current year. Applicants must have been admitted as degree-seeking junior-level students at an SUS institution. All recipients must have participated in, received a waiver for, or passed the College-Level Academic Skills Test program. In addition, male applicants must have complied with the Selective Service System registration requirements. Students may apply for need awards, merit/need awards, or merit awards. The minimum cumulative GPA on postsecondary credits is 2.0 for need-based applicants or 3.0 for merit/need and merit applicants.

Financial Data The stipend is $800 per semester ($1,600 per year).

Duration Up to 6 semesters, provided need recipients maintain at least a 2.0 GPA and need/merit or merit recipients maintain at least a 3.0 average.

Additional data This program is administered by the equal opportunity program at each of the 12 SUS 4-year institutions. Contact that office for further information.

Number awarded Varies each year.

Deadline Each participating university sets its own deadline.

[374]
MINORITY SCHOLARSHIP AWARD FOR ACADEMIC EXCELLENCE IN PHYSICAL THERAPY

American Physical Therapy Association
Attn: Honors and Awards Program
1111 North Fairfax Street
Alexandria, VA 22314-1488
(703) 684-APTA   Toll Free: (800) 999-APTA, ext. 8082
Fax: (703) 684-7343   TDD: (703) 683-6748
E-mail: honorsandawards@apta.org
Web: www.apta.org

Summary To provide financial assistance to Hispanic and other minority students who are interested in becoming a physical therapist or physical therapy assistant.

Eligibility This program is open to U.S. citizens and permanent residents who are members of the following minority groups: Hispanic/Latino, African American or Black, Asian, Native Hawaiian or other Pacific Islander, American Indian, or Alaska Native. Applicants must be in the final year of a professional physical therapy or physical therapy assistant education program. They must submit a personal essay outlining their professional goals and minority service. U.S. citizenship or permanent resident status is required. Selection is based on 1) demonstrated evidence of contributions in the area of minority affairs and services with an emphasis on contributions made while enrolled in a physical therapy program; 2) potential to contribute to the profession of physical therapy; and 3) scholastic achievement. Preference is given to members of the American Physical Therapy Association (APTA).

Financial Data The stipend varies; recently, stipends were $5,000 for physical therapy professional education students or $2,000 for physical therapy assistant students.

Duration 1 year.

Number awarded Varies each year; recently, 7 professional education students and 1 physical therapy assistant student received awards.

Deadline November of each year.

[375]
MINORITY SCHOLARSHIP AWARDS FOR COLLEGE STUDENTS IN CHEMICAL ENGINEERING

American Institute of Chemical Engineers
Attn: Minority Affairs Committee
120 Wall Street, FL 23
New York, NY 10005-4020
Toll Free: (800) 242-4363   Fax: (203) 775-5177
E-mail: awards@aiche.org
Web: www.aiche.org

Summary To provide financial assistance for the undergraduate study of chemical engineering to Hispanic and other underrepresented minority college student members of the American Institute of Chemical Engineers (AIChE).

Eligibility This program is open to undergraduate student AIChE members who are also members of a minority group that is underrepresented in chemical engineering (Hispanics, African Americans, Native Americans, Alaskan Natives, and Pacific Islanders). They must have a GPA of 3.0 or higher. Along with their application, they must submit a 300-word essay on their immediate plans after graduation, areas of chemical engineering of most interest, and long-range career plans. Selection is based on that essay, academic record, participation in AIChE student chapter and professional or civic activities, and financial need.

Financial Data The stipend is $1,000.

Duration 1 year; nonrenewable.

Number awarded Varies each year; recently, 16 were awarded.

Deadline June of each year.

[376]
MINORITY SCHOLARSHIP AWARDS FOR INCOMING COLLEGE FRESHMEN IN CHEMICAL ENGINEERING

American Institute of Chemical Engineers
Attn: Minority Affairs Committee
120 Wall Street, FL 23
New York, NY 10005-4020
Toll Free: (800) 242-4363   Fax: (203) 775-5177
E-mail: awards@aiche.org
Web: www.aiche.org

Summary To provide financial assistance to incoming Hispanic and other minority freshmen interested in studying science or engineering in college.

Eligibility Eligible are members of a minority group that is underrepresented in chemical engineering (Hispanics, African Americans, Native Americans, Alaskan Natives, and Pacific Islanders). Applicants must be graduating high school seniors planning to enroll at a 4-year university with a major in science or engineering. They must be nominated by an American Institute of Chemical Engineers (AIChE) local section. Selection is based on academic record (including a GPA of 3.0 or higher), participation in school and work activities, a

300-word letter outlining the reasons for choosing science or engineering, and financial need.

Financial Data The stipend is $1,000.

Duration 1 year; nonrenewable.

Number awarded Approximately 10 each year.

Deadline Nominations must be submitted by June of each year.

[377]
MINORITY SCHOLARSHIP IN CLASSICS AND CLASSICAL ARCHAEOLOGY

Society for Classical Studies
Attn: Executive Director
New York University
20 Cooper Square
New York, NY 10003
(212) 992-7828   Fax: (212) 995-3531
E-mail: xd@classicalstudies.org
Web: www.classicalstudies.org

Summary To provide Hispanic and other minority undergraduates with summer training as preparation for advanced work in the classics or classical archaeology.

Eligibility Eligible to apply are minority (Hispanic American, African American, Asian American, and Native American) undergraduate students who wish to engage in summer study as preparation for graduate work in the classics or classical archaeology. Applicants may propose participation in summer programs in Italy, Greece, Egypt, or other classical centers; language training at institutions in the United States, Canada, or Europe; or other relevant courses of study. Selection is based on academic qualifications, especially in classics; demonstrated ability in at least 1 classical language; quality of the proposal for study with respect to preparation for a career in classics; and financial need.

Financial Data The maximum award is $4,500.

Duration 1 summer.

Additional data This program includes 1 scholarship supported by the Gladys Krieble Delmas Foundation.

Number awarded 2 each year.

Deadline December of each year.

[378]
MINORITY SERVING INSTITUTION SCHOLARSHIP PROGRAM

U.S. Navy
Attn: Naval Service Training Command Officer
  Development
NAS Pensacola
250 Dallas Street
Pensacola, FL 32508-5220
(850) 452-4941, ext. 29395
Toll Free: (800) NAV-ROTC, ext. 29395
Fax: (850) 452-2486
E-mail: pnsc_nrotc.scholarship@navy.mil
Web: www.nrotc.navy.mil/MSI.html

Summary To provide financial assistance to students at specified Hispanic and other minority institutions who are interested in joining Navy ROTC to prepare for service as an officer in the U.S. Navy.

Eligibility This program is open to students attending or planning to attend 1 of 3 High Hispanic Enrollment (HHE)

schools, 1 of 17 specified Historically Black Colleges or Universities (HBCUs), or 1 other minority institution, all of which have a Navy ROTC unit on campus. Applicants must be nominated by the professor of naval science at their institution and meet academic requirements set by each school. They must be U.S. citizens between 17 and 23 years of age who are willing to serve for 4 years as active-duty Navy officers following graduation from college. They must not have reached their 27th birthday by the time of college graduation and commissioning; applicants who have prior active-duty military service may be eligible for age adjustments for the amount of time equal to their prior service, up to a maximum of 36 months. The qualifying scores are 550 critical reading and 540 mathematics on the SAT or 22 on English and 21 on mathematics on the ACT. Current enlisted and former military personnel are also eligible if they will complete the program by the age of 30.

Financial Data These scholarships provide payment of full tuition and required educational fees, as well as a specified amount for textbooks, supplies, and equipment. The program also provides a stipend for 10 months of the year that is $250 per month as a freshman, $300 per month as a sophomore, $350 per month as a junior, and $400 per month as a senior.

Duration Up to 4 years.

Additional data The eligible HHEs are Central New Mexico Community College, Pima Community College, and the University of New Mexico. The eligible HBCUs are Allen University, Clark Atlanta University, Dillard University, Florida A&M University, Hampton University, Howard University, Huston-Tillotson University, Morehouse College, Norfolk State University, Prairie View A&M University, Savannah State University, Southern University and A&M College, Spelman College, Tennessee State University, Texas Southern University, Tuskegee University, and Xavier University. The other minority institution is Kennedy King College. After completing the program, all participants are commissioned as ensigns in the Naval Reserve with an 8-year service obligation, including 4 years of active duty. Current military personnel who are accepted into this program are released from active duty and are not eligible for active-duty pay and allowances, medical benefits, or other active-duty entitlements.

Number awarded Varies each year.

Deadline January of each year.

[379]
MINORITY TEACHER EDUCATION SCHOLARSHIPS

Florida Fund for Minority Teachers, Inc.
Attn: Executive Director
G415 Norman Hall
618 S.W. 12th Street
P.O. Box 117045
Gainesville, FL 32611-7045
(352) 392-9196   Fax: (352) 846-3011
E-mail: info@ffmt.org
Web: www.ffmt.org/mtes-application-active

Summary To provide scholarship/loans to Florida residents who are Hispanics or members of other minority groups preparing for a career as a teacher.

Eligibility This program is open to Florida residents who are Hispanic/Latino, African American/Black, Asian American/Pacific Islander, or American Indian/Alaskan Native.

Applicants must be entering their junior year in a teacher education program at a participating college or university in Florida. Along with their application, they must submit an essay of 100 to 300 words on how their life experiences have impacted them to go into the field of education. Special consideration is given to community college graduates. Selection is based on writing ability, communication skills, overall academic performance, and evidence of commitment to the youth of America (preferably demonstrated through volunteer activities).

Financial Data The stipend is $4,000 per year. Recipients are required to teach 1 year in a Florida public school for each year they receive the scholarship. If they fail to teach in a public school, they are required to repay the total amount of support received at an annual interest rate of 8%.

Duration Up to 2 consecutive years, provided the recipient remains enrolled full time with a GPA of 2.5 or higher.

Additional data For a list of the 22 participating public institutions and the 16 participating private institutions, contact the Florida Fund for Minority Teachers (FFMT). Recipients are also required to attend the annual (FFMT) recruitment and retention conference.

Number awarded Varies each year.

Deadline June of each year for fall semester; October of each year for spring semester.

[380]
MINORITY TEACHERS OF ILLINOIS SCHOLARSHIP PROGRAM

Illinois Student Assistance Commission
Attn: Scholarship and Grant Services
1755 Lake Cook Road
Deerfield, IL 60015-5209
(847) 948-8550   Toll Free: (800) 899-ISAC
Fax: (847) 831-8549   TDD: (800) 526-0844
E-mail: isac.studentservices@isac.illinois.gov
Web: www.isac.org

Summary To provide scholarship/loans to Hispanic and other minority students in Illinois who plan to become teachers at the preschool, elementary, or secondary level.

Eligibility Applicants must be Illinois residents, U.S. citizens or eligible noncitizens, members of a minority group (Hispanic American, African American/Black, Asian American, or Native American), and high school graduates or holders of a General Educational Development (GED) certificate. They must be enrolled at least half time as an undergraduate or graduate student, have a GPA of 2.5 or higher, not be in default on any student loan, and be enrolled or accepted for enrollment in a teacher education program.

Financial Data Grants up to $5,000 per year are awarded. This is a scholarship/loan program. Recipients must agree to teach full time 1 year for each year of support received. The teaching agreement may be fulfilled at a public, private, or parochial preschool, elementary school, or secondary school in Illinois; at least 30% of the student body at those schools must be minority. It must be fulfilled within the 5-year period following the completion of the undergraduate program for which the scholarship was awarded. The time period may be extended if the recipient serves in the U.S. armed forces, enrolls full time in a graduate program related to teaching, becomes temporarily disabled, is unable to find employment as a teacher at a qualifying school, or takes additional courses on at least a half-time basis to obtain certification as a teacher in Illinois. Recipients who fail to honor this work obligation must repay the award with 5% interest.

Duration 1 year; may be renewed for a total of 8 semesters or 12 quarters.

Number awarded Varies each year.

Deadline Priority consideration is given to applications received by February of each year.

[381]
MINORITY TEACHING FELLOWS PROGRAM OF TENNESSEE

Tennessee Student Assistance Corporation
Parkway Towers
404 James Robertson Parkway, Suite 1510
Nashville, TN 37243-0820
(615) 741-1346   Toll Free: (800) 342-1663
Fax: (615) 741-6101   E-mail: TSAC.Aidinfo@tn.gov
Web: www.tn.gov

Summary To provide scholarship/loans to Hispanic and other minority residents of Tennessee who wish to attend college in the state to prepare for a career in the teaching field.

Eligibility This program is open to minority residents of Tennessee who are either high school seniors planning to enroll full time at a college or university in the state or continuing college students at a Tennessee college or university. High school seniors must have a GPA of 2.75 or higher and an ACT score of at least 18 or an equivalent SAT score. Continuing college students must have a college GPA of 2.5 or higher. All applicants must agree to teach at the K-12 level in a Tennessee public school following graduation from college. Along with their application, they must submit a 250-word essay on why they chose teaching as a profession. U.S. citizenship is required.

Financial Data The scholarship/loan is $5,000 per year. Recipients incur an obligation to teach at the preK-12 level in a Tennessee public school 1 year for each year the award is received.

Duration 1 year; may be renewed for up to 3 additional years, provided the recipient maintains full-time enrollment and a cumulative GPA of 2.5 or higher.

Additional data This program began in 1989.

Number awarded Varies each year; recently, 62 fellows received $287,000 in support through this program.

Deadline April of each year.

[382]
MIRIAM WEINSTEIN PEACE AND JUSTICE EDUCATION AWARD

Philanthrofund Foundation
Attn: Scholarship Committee
1409 Willow Street, Suite 109
Minneapolis, MN 55403-2241
(612) 870-1806   Toll Free: (800) 435-1402
Fax: (612) 871-6587   E-mail: info@PfundOnline.org
Web: www.pfundonline.org/scholarships.html

Summary To provide financial assistance to Hispanic and other minority students from Minnesota who have supported gay, lesbian, bisexual, and transgender (GLBT) activities and are interested in working on a degree in education.

Eligibility This program is open to residents of Minnesota and students attending a Minnesota educational institution who are members of a religious, racial, or ethnic minority. Applicants must be self-identified as GLBT or from a GLBT family and have demonstrated a commitment to peace and justice issues. They may be attending or planning to attend trade school, technical college, college, or university (as an undergraduate or graduate student). Preference is given to students who have completed at least 2 years of college and are working on a degree in education. Selection is based on the applicant's 1) affirmation of GLBT or allied identity; 2) evidence of experience and skills in service and leadership; and 3) evidence of service, leading, and working for change in GLBT communities, including serving as a role model, mentor, and/or adviser.

Financial Data The stipend is $3,000. Funds must be used for tuition, books, fees, or dissertation expenses.

Duration 1 year.

Number awarded 1 each year.

Deadline January of each year.

[383]
MISSISSIPPI CHAPTER AABE SCHOLARSHIPS

American Association of Blacks in Energy-Mississippi
   Chapter
Attn: Scholarship Committee Chair
P.O. Box 986
Jackson, MS 39205
(601) 969-2326   E-mail: aabems1990@yahoo.com
Web: www.aabe.org/index.php?component=pages&id=387

Summary To provide financial assistance to Hispanic and members of other underrepresented minority groups who are high school seniors in Mississippi and planning to major in an energy-related field at a college in any state.

Eligibility This program is open to seniors graduating from high schools in Mississippi and planning to attend a 4-year college or university in any state. Applicants must be Hispanics, African Americans, or Native Americans who have a GPA of 3.0 or higher and have taken the ACT and/or SAT test. Their intended major must be a field of business, engineering, physical science, mathematics, or technology related to energy. Along with their application, they must submit a 350-word essay that includes 1) when they discovered their interest in the field of energy and what sparked their interest; and 2) either what excites them about the field of energy or how they expect their education to prepare them for the field of energy. Financial need is not considered in the selection process.

Financial Data Stipends are $2,000 or $1,000.

Duration 1 year.

Additional data Winners are eligible to compete for regional and national scholarships.

Number awarded Varies each year; recently, 5 were awarded.

Deadline March of each year.

[384]
MISSOURI MINORITY TEACHING SCHOLARSHIP PROGRAM

Missouri Department of Higher Education
Attn: Student Financial Assistance
205 Jefferson Street
P.O. Box 1469
Jefferson City, MO 65102-1469
(573) 751-2361   Toll Free: (800) 473-6757
Fax: (573) 751-6635   E-mail: info@dhe.mo.gov
Web: www.dhe.mo.gov/ppc/grants/minorityteaching.php

Summary   To provide scholarships and forgivable loans to Hispanic and other minority high school seniors, high school graduates, and college students in Missouri who are interested in preparing for a teaching career in mathematics or science.

Eligibility   This program is open to Missouri residents who are Hispanic American, African American, Asian American, or Native American. Applicants must be 1) high school seniors, college students, or returning adults (without a degree) who rank in the top 25% of their high school class and have scores in the top 25% of the ACT or SAT examination (recently, that meant a composite score of 24 or higher on the ACT or 1360 or higher on the composite critical reading and mathematics SAT); or 2) baccalaureate degree-holders who are returning to an approved mathematics or science teacher education program. They must be a U.S. citizen or permanent resident or otherwise lawfully present in the United States. All applicants must be enrolled full time in an approved teacher education program at a community college, 4-year college, or university in Missouri. Selection is based on high school class rank, ACT or SAT scores, school and community activities, career interest in teaching, leadership skills, employment experience, and recommendations.

Financial Data   The stipend is $3,000 per year, of which $2,000 is provided by the state as a forgivable loan and $1,000 is provided by the school as a scholarship. Recipients must commit to teaching in a Missouri public elementary or secondary school for 5 years following graduation. If they fail to fulfill that obligation, they must repay the state portion of the scholarship with interest at 9.5%.

Duration   Up to 4 years.

Number awarded   Up to 100 each year.

Deadline   May of each year.

[385]
MIT AMGEN-UROP SCHOLARS PROGRAM

Massachusetts Institute of Technology
Attn: Undergraduate Research Opportunities Program
Office of Undergraduate Advising and Academic
  Programming
77 Massachusetts Avenue, Room 7-104
Cambridge, MA 02139
(617) 253-7306   E-mail: mit-amgenscholars@mit.edu
Web: web.mit.edu/urop/amgenscholars

Summary   To provide an opportunity for undergraduates, especially Hispanics and members of other underrepresented groups, to participate in summer research projects in biotechnology at Massachusetts Institute of Technology (MIT).

Eligibility   This program is open to sophomores, juniors, and non-graduating seniors at 4-year colleges and universities in the United States, Puerto Rico, and other U.S. territories. Applicants must be U.S. citizens or permanent residents who have a cumulative GPA of 3.2 or higher and an interest in preparing for a Ph.D. or M.D./Ph.D. They must be interested in working on a summer research project at MIT in the following laboratory programs: biological engineering; biology, brain, and cognitive sciences; environmental health; chemistry; chemical engineering; health sciences and technology; or mechanical engineering (for bioengineering or biotechnology only). The Amgen Scholars Program encourages applications from students who are members of groups underrepresented in fields of biotechnology.

Financial Data   Scholars receive a stipend of $4,320, a meal allowance of $800, housing in a designated MIT residence hall, and, for non-MIT students, travel to and from Boston.

Duration   9 weeks during the summer.

Additional data   This program serves as the MIT component of the Amgen Scholars Program, which operates at 8 other U.S. universities (and the National Institutes of Health) and is funded by the Amgen Foundation.

Number awarded   Up to 20 each year.

Deadline   January of each year.

[386]
MNACC STUDENT OF COLOR SCHOLARSHIP

Minnesota Association of Counselors of Color
c/o Cristina Montañez, Scholarship Committee
University of Minnesota at Morris
600 East Fourth Street
Morris, MN 56267
E-mail: scholarships@mnacc.org
Web: www.mnacc.org

Summary   To provide financial assistance to Hispanic and other high school seniors of color in Minnesota who plan to attend college in the area.

Eligibility   This program is open to seniors graduating from public and private high schools in Minnesota who are students of color. Applicants must be planning to enroll full time at a 4-year college or university, a 2-year college, or a trade or technical college that is a member of the Minnesota Association of Counselors of Color (MnACC). Along with their application, they must submit an essay, up to 500 words in length, on their choice of assigned topics.

Financial Data   Stipends are $1,000 or $500.

Duration   1 year; nonrenewable.

Additional data   These scholarships may be used at approximately 67 MnACC member institutions, including colleges, universities, and technical schools in Minnesota as well as selected schools in Iowa, Michigan, North Dakota, South Dakota, and Wisconsin.

Number awarded   Varies each year; recently, 26 were awarded.

Deadline   March of each year.

[387]
MONSIGNOR PHILIP KENNEY SCHOLARSHIP FUND

New Hampshire Charitable Foundation
37 Pleasant Street
Concord, NH 03301-4005
(603) 225-6641   Toll Free: (800) 464-6641
Fax: (603) 225-1700   E-mail: info@nhcf.org
Web: www.nhcf.org/page.aspx?pid=482

Summary To provide financial assistance for college to minority students from New Hampshire, especially Hispanics.

Eligibility This program is open to all minority residents of New Hampshire, but first preference is given to Hispanics. Applicants may be planning to attend a local community college, enroll in a 4-year degree program, or study part time, but they must be in a degree or recognized certification program. Both traditional college-age and adult students are eligible. Their family income must be less than $27,930 for a family of 1, rising to $94,710 for a family of 8. Selection is based on academic achievement, involvement in school and community activities, work experience, and financial need.

Financial Data The stipend ranges from $500 to $2,500 per year.

Duration 1 year; recipients may reapply.

Additional data This program was established by Monsignor Philip Kenney in 1986 with the award funds he received as Manchester's Citizen of the Year.

Number awarded 8 to 10 each year.

Deadline April of each year.

[388]
MONTGOMERY SUMMER RESEARCH DIVERSITY FELLOWSHIPS

American Bar Foundation
Attn: Summer Research Diversity Fellowship
750 North Lake Shore Drive
Chicago, IL 60611-4403
(312) 988-6515   Fax: (312) 988-6579
E-mail: fellowships@abfn.org
Web: www.americanbarfoundation.org

Summary To provide an opportunity for Hispanic and other undergraduate students from diverse backgrounds to work on a summer research project in the field of law and social science.

Eligibility This program is open to U.S. citizens and permanent residents who are Hispanic/Latinos, African Americans, Asians, Puerto Ricans, Native Americans, or other individuals who will add diversity to the field of law and social science (e.g., persons with disabilities and LGBTQ individuals). Applicants must be sophomores or juniors in college, have a GPA of 3.0 or higher, be majoring in the social sciences or humanities, and be willing to consider an academic or research career. Along with their application, they must submit a 200-word essay on their future plans and why this fellowship would contribute to them, another essay on an assigned topic, official transcripts, and a letter of recommendation from a faculty member familiar with their work.

Financial Data Participants receive a stipend of $3,600.

Duration 35 hours per week for 8 weeks during the summer.

Additional data Students are assigned to an American Bar Foundation Research Professor who involves the student in the design and conduct of the professor's research project and who acts as mentor during the student's tenure.

Number awarded 4 each year.

Deadline February of each year.

[389]
MORENO/RANGEL LEGISLATIVE LEADERSHIP PROGRAM

Mexican American Legislative Leadership Foundation
Attn: Legislative Leadership Program
202 West 13th Street
Austin, TX 78701
(512) 499-0804   Fax: (512) 480-8313
E-mail: director@mallfoundation.org
Web: mallfoundation.org

Summary To provide an opportunity for undergraduate and graduate students in Texas to gain work experience on the staff of members of the Mexican American Legislative Caucus of the Texas state legislature.

Eligibility This program is open to undergraduate and graduate students who are enrolled at 2- and 4-year colleges and universities in Texas and have completed at least 60 credit hours of work; recent graduates are also welcome to apply. Applicants must be interested in working full time on the staff of a Latino member of the Texas House of Representatives. They must be at least 21 years of age, have a record of community and extracurricular involvement, be able to demonstrate excellent composition and communication skills, and have a GPA of 2.5 or higher. Along with their application, they must submit an essay of 500 to 750 words in which they describe the family, work, educational, and community experiences that led them to apply for this program; they should also explain how those experiences relate to their long-term personal goals and how this legislative experience will contribute to their future leadership within the Latino community.

Financial Data Participants receive a monthly stipend (amount not specified) to assist with living expenses.

Duration 5 months, beginning in January.

Additional data This program is named after Paul C. Moreno (the longest-serving Hispanic member of the Texas House of Representatives) and Irma Rangel (the first Mexican American woman to serve in the Texas Legislature).

Number awarded Varies each year; recently, 6 of these internships/fellowships were awarded.

Deadline November of each year.

[390]
MOSS ADAMS FOUNDATION SCHOLARSHIP

Educational Foundation for Women in Accounting
Attn: Foundation Administrator
136 South Keowee Street
Dayton, OH 45402
(937) 424-3391   Fax: (937) 222-5749
E-mail: info@efwa.org
Web: www.efwa.org/scholarships_graduate.php

Summary To provide financial support to women, including Hispanic and other minority women, who are working on an accounting degree.

Eligibility This program is open to women who are enrolled in an accounting degree program at an accredited college or university. Applicants must meet 1 of the following criteria: 1) women pursuing a fifth-year requirement either through general studies or within a graduate program; 2) women returning to school as current or reentry juniors or seniors; or 3) minority women. Selection is based on aptitude for accounting and business, commitment to the goal of working on a degree in accounting (including evidence of continued commitment after receiving this award), clear evidence that the candidate has established goals and a plan for achieving those goals (both personal and professional), financial need, and a demonstration of how the scholarship will impact her life. U.S. citizenship is required.

Financial Data The stipend is $1,000.

Duration 1 year.

Additional data This program was established by Rowling, Dold & Associates LLP, a woman-owned C.P.A. firm based in San Diego. It was renamed when that firm merged with Moss Adams LLP.

Number awarded 2 each year: 1 to an undergraduate and 1 to a graduate student.

Deadline April of each year.

[391]
MR. CHARLIE TOMPKINS SCHOLARSHIP

National Naval Officers Association-Washington, D.C.
   Chapter
c/o LCDR Stephen Williams
P.O. Box 30784
Alexandria, VA 22310
(703) 566-3840   Fax: (703) 566-3813
E-mail: Stephen.Williams@navy.mil
Web: dcnnoa.memberlodge.com/page-309002

Summary To provide financial assistance to Hispanic and other minority high school seniors from the Washington, D.C. area who are interested in attending college in any state.

Eligibility This program is open to minority seniors graduating from high schools in the Washington, D.C. metropolitan area who plan to enroll full time at an accredited 2- or 4-year college or university in any state. Applicants must have a GPA of 2.5 or higher and be U.S. citizens or permanent residents. Selection is based on academic achievement, community involvement, and financial need.

Financial Data The stipend is $2,000.

Duration 1 year; nonrenewable.

Additional data This program is sponsored by the Washington D.C. Chapter of the National Naval Officers Association (DCNNOA), an organization of African American naval officers, but all minorities are eligible and recipients are not required to join or affiliate with the military in any way.

Number awarded 1 each year.

Deadline February of each year.

[392]
MSCPA/ALPFA SCHOLARSHIPS

Massachusetts Society of Certified Public Accountants
Attn: MSCPA Educational Foundation
105 Chauncy Street, Tenth Floor
Boston, MA 02111
(617) 556-4000   Toll Free: (800) 392-6145
Fax: (617) 556-4126   E-mail: info@mscpaonline.org
Web: www.cpatrack.com/scholarships

Summary To provide financial assistance to members of the Association of Latino Professionals For America (ALPFA) from Massachusetts working on an undergraduate degree in accounting at a college or university in the state.

Eligibility This program is open to student members of the Boston chapter of ALPFA who are enrolled at a college or university in Massachusetts. Applicants must have completed at least the first semester of their sophomore year and be able to demonstrate financial need, academic excellence, and an intention to prepare for a career as a Certified Public Accountant (C.P.A.) at a firm in Massachusetts.

Financial Data The stipend is $2,500.

Duration 1 year.

Additional data This program is sponsored by ALPFA-Boston and the Massachusetts Society of Certified Public Accountants (MSCPA).

Number awarded 2 each year.

Deadline March of each year.

[393]
MSCPA MINORITY SCHOLARSHIPS

Missouri Society of Certified Public Accountants
Attn: MSCPA Educational Foundation
540 Maryville Centre Drive, Suite 200
P.O. Box 958868
St. Louis, MO 63195-8868
(314) 997-7966   Toll Free: (800) 264-7966 (within MO)
Fax: (314) 997-2592   E-mail: dhull@mocpa.org
Web: www.mocpa.org/students/scholarships

Summary To provide financial assistance to Hispanic and other minority residents of Missouri who are working on an undergraduate or graduate degree in accounting at a university in the state.

Eligibility This program is open to members of minority groups underrepresented in the accounting profession (Hispanic/Latino, Black/African American, Native American, Asian American) who are currently working full time on an undergraduate or graduate degree in accounting at a college or university in Missouri. Applicants must either be residents of Missouri or the children of members of the Missouri Society of Certified Public Accountants (MSCPA). They must be U.S. citizens, have completed at least 30 semester hours of college work, have a GPA of 3.3 or higher, and be student members of the MSCPA. Selection is based on the GPA, involvement in MSCPA, educator recommendations, and leadership potential. Financial need is not considered.

Financial Data The stipend is $1,250 per year.

Duration 1 year; may be renewed.

Number awarded Varies each year; recently, 3 were awarded.

Deadline February of each year.

[394]
MSIPP INTERNSHIPS

Department of Energy
Office of Environmental Management
Savannah River National Laboratory
Attn: MSIPP Program Manager
Building 773-41A, 232
Aiken, SC 29808
(803) 725-9032   E-mail: connie.yung@srnl.doe.gov
Web: srnl.doe.gov/msipp/internships.htm

Summary   To provide an opportunity for undergraduate and graduate students at Hispanic and other Minority Serving Institutions (MSIs) to work on a summer research project at designated National Laboratories of the U.S. Department of Energy (DOE).

Eligibility   This program is open to full-time undergraduate and graduate students enrolled at an accredited MSI. Applicants must be interested in working during the summer on a research project at a participating DOE National Laboratory. They must be working on a degree in a field of science, technology, engineering, or mathematics (STEM); the specific field depends on the particular project on which they wish to work. Their GPA must be 3.0 or higher. U.S. citizenship is required.

Financial Data   The stipend depends on the cost of living at the location of the host laboratory.

Duration   10 weeks during the summer.

Additional data   This program is administered at the Savannah River National Laboratory (SRNL) in Aiken, South Carolina, which serves as the National Laboratory for the DOE Office of Environmental Management. The other participating National Laboratories are Argonne National Laboratory (ANL) in Argonne, Illinois, Idaho National Laboratory (INL) in Idaho Falls, Idaho, Los Alamos National Laboratory (LANL) in Los Alamos, New Mexico, Oak Ridge National Laboratory (ORNL) in Oak Ridge, Tennessee, and Pacific Northwest National Laboratory (PNNL) in Richland, Washington. The program began in 2016.

Number awarded   Varies each year. Recently, the program offered 11 research projects at SRNL, 12 at ANL, 1 at INL, 7 at LANL, 4 at ORNL, and 7 at PNNL.

Deadline   March of each year.

[395]
MULTICULTURAL AUDIENCE DEVELOPMENT INITIATIVE INTERNSHIPS

Metropolitan Museum of Art
Attn: Internship Programs
1000 Fifth Avenue
New York, NY 10028-0198
(212) 570-3710   Fax: (212) 570-3782
E-mail: mmainterns@metmuseum.org
Web: www.metmuseum.org

Summary   To provide summer work experience at the Metropolitan Museum of Art to Hispanic and other college undergraduates, graduate students, and recent graduates from diverse backgrounds.

Eligibility   This program is open to members of diverse groups who are undergraduate juniors and seniors, students currently working on a master's degree, or individuals who completed a bachelor's or master's degree within the past year. Ph.D. students may be eligible to apply during the first 12 months of their program, provided they have not yet achieved candidacy. Students from various academic backgrounds are encouraged to apply, but they must be interested in preparing for a career in the arts and museum fields. Freshmen and sophomores are not eligible.

Financial Data   The stipend is $3,750.

Duration   10 weeks, beginning in June.

Additional data   Interns are assigned to departmental projects (curatorial, administration, or education) at the Metropolitan Museum of Art; other assignments may include giving gallery talks and working at the Visitor Information Center. The assignment is for 35 hours a week. The internships are funded by the Multicultural Audience Initiative at the museum.

Number awarded   1 or more each year.

Deadline   January of each year.

[396]
MUTUAL OF OMAHA ACTUARIAL SCHOLARSHIP FOR MINORITY STUDENTS

Mutual of Omaha
Attn: Strategic Staffing-Actuarial Recruitment
3300 Mutual of Omaha Plaza
Omaha, NE 68175
Toll Free: (800) 365-1405
E-mail: diversity@mutualofomaha.com
Web: www.mutualofomaha.com

Summary   To provide financial assistance and work experience to Hispanic and other minority undergraduate students who are preparing for an actuarial career.

Eligibility   This program is open to members of minority groups (Hispanic, African American, Native American, Asian or Pacific Islander, or Alaskan Eskimo) who have completed at least 24 semester hours of full-time study. Applicants must be working on an actuarial or mathematics-related degree with the goal of preparing for an actuarial career. They must have a GPA of 3.4 or higher and have passed at least 1 actuarial examination. Prior to accepting the award, they must be available to complete a summer internship at the sponsor's home office in Omaha, Nebraska. Along with their application, they must submit a 1-page personal statement on why they are interested in becoming an actuary and how they are preparing themselves for an actuarial career. Status as a U.S. citizen, permanent resident, asylee, or refugee must be established.

Financial Data   The scholarship stipend is $5,000 per year. Funds are paid directly to the student. For the internship, students receive an hourly rate of pay, subsidized housing, and financial incentives for successful examination results received during the internship period.

Duration   1 year. Recipients may reapply if they maintain a cumulative GPA of 3.4 or higher.

Number awarded   Varies each year.

Deadline   October of each year.

[397]
MV TRANSIT COLLEGE SCHOLARSHIP

Conference of Minority Transportation Officials
Attn: National Scholarship Program
100 M Street, S.E., Suite 917
Washington, DC 20003
(202) 506-2917   E-mail: info@comto.org
Web: www.comto.org/page/scholarships

Summary To provide financial assistance to Hispanic and other minority college student members of the Conference of Minority Transportation Officials (COMTO) and family of members working on a degree in transportation or a related field.

Eligibility This program is open to minority undergraduate students who have been COMTO members or whose parents, guardians, or grandparents have been members for at least 1 year. Applicants must be majoring in transportation, engineering, planning, or a related discipline. They must have a GPA of 2.0 or higher. Along with their application they must submit a cover letter on their transportation-related career goals and life aspirations. Financial need is not considered in the selection process.

Financial Data The stipend is $4,000. Funds are paid directly to the recipient's college or university.

Duration 1 year.

Additional data This program is sponsored by MV Transportation, Inc.

Number awarded 1 or more each year.

Deadline April of each year.

[398]
MV TRANSIT HIGH SCHOOL SENIOR SCHOLARSHIP

Conference of Minority Transportation Officials
Attn: National Scholarship Program
100 M Street, S.E., Suite 917
Washington, DC 20003
(202) 506-2917   E-mail: info@comto.org
Web: www.comto.org/page/scholarships

Summary To provide financial assistance to Hispanic and other minority high school seniors who are members of the Conference of Minority Transportation Officials (COMTO) or family of members and interested in working on a degree in transportation or a related field.

Eligibility This program is open to minority high school seniors who have been COMTO members or whose parents, guardians, or grandparents have been members for at least 1 year. Applicants must be planning to enroll at an accredited college, university, or vocational/technical institute and major in a transportation-related field. They must have a GPA of 2.0 or higher. Along with their application they must submit a cover letter on their transportation-related career goals and life aspirations. Financial need is not considered in the selection process.

Financial Data The stipend is $3,500. Funds are paid directly to the recipient's college or university.

Duration 1 year.

Additional data This program is sponsored by MV Transportation, Inc.

Number awarded 1 or more each year.

Deadline April of each year.

[399]
NACOPRW NY SCHOLARSHIP

National Conference of Puerto Rican Women-New York
   Chapter
Attn: Scholarship Chair
P.O. Box 469 Lenox Hill Station
New York, NY 10021
(276) 690-9196
E-mail: scholarshipchair@nacoprwnewyork.org
Web: www.nacoprwnewyork.org/scholarships

Summary To provide financial assistance to Puerto Rican women who are residents of New York and interested in attending college in any state.

Eligibility This program is open to women who are residents of New York and of Puerto Rican heritage by birth or descent through maternal lineage. Applicants must be enrolled or planning to enroll at a college, university, or trade/vocational school in any state. They must have a GPA of at least 3.0 in high school, college, or university or 2.5 in trade/vocational school. Along with their application, they must submit a 250-word essay describing their career goals and explaining what this award means to them.

Financial Data The stipend is $1,500.

Duration 1 year.

Additional data Recipients must commit to up to 10 hours of community service during the academic year.

Number awarded 1 or more each year.

Deadline June of each year.

[400]
NACOPRW SCHOLARSHIP AWARD

National Conference of Puerto Rican Women-Miami
   Chapter
c/o Zoraida Sequinot, President
1506 East Mowry Drive
Homestead, FL 33033
(305) 247-9925   E-mail: NACOPRW.MIAMI@gmail.com
Web: www.nacoprwmiami.org/category/scholarship-awards

Summary To provide financial assistance for college to Puerto Rican women.

Eligibility This program is open to women who are Puerto Rican by birth or descent. Applicants must have been admitted to an accredited college or university in the United States or Puerto Rico. They must have a GPA of 3.0 or higher and be able to demonstrate financial need.

Financial Data The stipend is approximately $1,000.

Duration 1 year.

Additional data The National Conference of Puerto Rican Women (NACOPRW) "promotes the full participation of Puerto Rican and other Hispanic women in the economic, social and political life of the United States and Puerto Rico."

Number awarded 2 each year.

Deadline April of each year.

[401]
NAHN PAST PRESIDENTS SCHOLARSHIP FUND

National Association of Hispanic Nurses
Attn: Scholarships
1500 Sunday Drive, Suite 102
Raleigh, NC 27607
(919) 787-5181, ext. 1255   Fax: (919) 787-4916
E-mail: director@thehispanicnurses.org
Web: www.nahnnet.org/NAHNScholarships.html

Summary   To provide financial assistance for nursing education to members of the National Association of Hispanic Nurses (NAHN).

Eligibility   Eligible are members of the association enrolled in associate, diploma, baccalaureate, graduate, or practical/vocational nursing programs at NLN-accredited schools of nursing. Applicants must have a GPA of 3.0 or higher. Along with their application, they must submit a letter of recommendation; a 300-word essay that reflects their qualifications and potential for leadership in nursing in the Hispanic community; a resume that includes earned certificates, awards, and special honors; information on their financial status; and an official transcript. U.S. citizenship or permanent resident status is required.

Financial Data   Stipends recently averaged $1,125.

Duration   1 year.

Number awarded   Varies each year; recently, 4 were awarded.

Deadline   June of each year.

[402]
NASA SCHOLARSHIP AND RESEARCH OPPORTUNITIES (SRO) MINORITY UNIVERSITY RESEARCH AND EDUCATION PROJECT (MUREP) SCHOLARSHIPS

National Aeronautics and Space Administration
Attn: National Scholarship Deputy Program Manager
Office of Education and Public Outreach
Ames Research Center
Moffett Field, CA 94035
(650) 604-6958   E-mail: elizabeth.a.cartier@nasa.gov
Web: intern.nasa.gov

Summary   To provide financial assistance and summer research experience at National Aeronautics and Space Administration (NASA) facilities to undergraduate students majoring in designated fields of science, technology, engineering, or mathematics (STEM) at an Hispanic or other Minority Serving Institution (MSI).

Eligibility   This program is open to U.S. citizens and nationals who are working on an undergraduate degree at an MSI and have a GPA of 3.0 or higher with at least 2 years of full-time study remaining. Applicants must be majoring in chemistry, computer and information science and engineering, engineering (aeronautical and aerospace, biomedical, chemical, civil, computer, electrical and electronic, environmental, industrial and operations research, materials, mechanical, nuclear, ocean, optical, polymer, or systems) geosciences (including geophysics, hydrology, physical and dynamic meteorology, physical oceanography, planetary science), life sciences (including biochemistry, cell biology, developmental biology, evolutionary biology, genetics, physiology), materials research, mathematical sciences, or physics and astronomy.

They must be available for an internship at a NASA center performing aeronautical research during the summer between their junior and senior years. Along with their application, they must submit a 1,000-word essay on 1) their professional goals and what attracted them to their intended STEM field of study; 2) the events and individuals that have been critical in influencing their academic and career decisions; and 3) how receiving the MUREP scholarship would help them accomplish their professional goals. Financial need is not considered in the selection process.

Financial Data   Students receive 75% of their tuition and education-related costs, up to $9,000 per academic year. The stipend for the summer internship is $6,000.

Duration   2 years.

Number awarded   Up to 20 each year.

Deadline   March of each year.

[403]
NATIONAL ASSOCIATION OF HISPANIC JOURNALISTS SCHOLARSHIPS

National Association of Hispanic Journalists
Attn: Scholarship Committee
1050 Connecticut Avenue, N.W., Fifth Floor
Washington, DC 20036
(202) 853-7760   E-mail: nahj@nahj.org
Web: www.nahj.org/nahj-scholarships

Summary   To provide financial assistance to undergraduate and graduate student members of the National Association of Hispanic Journalists (NAHJ) who are interested in preparing for careers in the media.

Eligibility   This program is open to Hispanic American high school seniors, undergraduates, and graduate students who are interested in preparing for a career in English- or Spanish-language print, broadcast (radio or television), online, or photojournalism; students majoring in other fields must be able to demonstrate a strong interest in preparing for a career in journalism. Applicants must be enrolled full time at a college or university in the United States or Puerto Rico. They must be NAHJ members. Along with their application, they must submit transcripts, a 1-page resume, 2 letters of recommendation, work samples, and a 1,000-word autobiographical essay that includes why they are interested in a career in journalism, what inspired them to prepare for a career in the field, what hardships or obstacles they have experienced while trying to realize their goal of becoming a journalist, and the role Latino journalists play in the news industry. Selection is based on commitment to the field of journalism, academic achievement, awareness of the Latino community, and financial need.

Financial Data   Stipends range from $2,000 to $5,000.

Duration   1 year.

Additional data   This program consists of the Rubén Salazar Scholarships (established in 1986), the Maria Elena Salinas Scholarships (established in 2002), and the Hortencia Zavala Scholarship (established in 2016).

Number awarded   Varies each year.

Deadline   February of each year.

[404]
NATIONAL ASSOCIATION OF HISPANIC NURSES MICHIGAN CHAPTER SCHOLARSHIPS

National Association of Hispanic Nurses-Michigan
  Chapter
c/o Dottie Rodriquez, Scholarship Committee
769 Fox River Drive
Bloomfield Township, MI 48304
(313) 282-8471   E-mail: dottierodr@aol.com
Web: michiganhispanicnurses.org/scholarships.html

Summary To provide financial assistance to undergraduate and graduate nursing students who are members of the National Association of Hispanic Nurses (NAHN) enrolled in a program in Michigan or Ohio.

Eligibility This program is open to members of NAHN and its Michigan chapter who have completed at least 1 semester of a generic nursing degree or certificate (L.P.N., A.D.N., B.S.N., M.S., M.S.N., Ph.D., or D.N.P.) at a school in Michigan or Ohio; R.N. to B.S.N. students are not eligible. Undergraduates must have a GPA of 2.75 or higher and graduate students 3.0 or higher. Applicants must submit a 2-page essay that includes personal background information, school involvement, community service, goals after graduation, and how they plan to serve the NAHN Michigan chapter. Financial need is not considered in the selection process.

Financial Data The stipend is $1,000.

Duration 1 year; nonrenewable.

Additional data Recipients must agree to perform 10 to 20 hours of volunteer service to the sponsor within 1 year of receipt of this scholarship.

Number awarded Varies each year; recently, 4 were awarded.

Deadline October of each year.

[405]
NATIONAL CO-OP SCHOLARSHIP PROGRAM

World Association for Cooperative Education (WACE)
600 Suffolk Street, Suite 125
Lowell, MA 01854
(978) 934-1870   E-mail: Marty_ford@uml.edu
Web: www.waceinc.org/scholarship/index.html

Summary To provide financial assistance to students, especially Hispanics and other minorities, who are participating or planning to participate in cooperative education projects at designated colleges and universities.

Eligibility This program is open to high school seniors and community college transfer students entering 1 of the 11 partner colleges and universities. Applicants must be planning to participate in college cooperative education. They must have a GPA of 3.5 or higher. Along with their application, they must submit a 1-page essay describing why they have chosen to enter a college cooperative education program. Applications are especially encouraged from minorities, women, and students interested in science, mathematics, engineering, and technology. Selection is based on merit; financial need is not considered.

Financial Data The stipend is $6,000 per year.

Duration 1 year; may be renewed up to 3 additional years or (for some programs) up to 4 additional years.

Additional data The schools recently participating in this program were Clarkson University (Potsdam, New York),

Drexel University (Philadelphia, Pennsylvania), Johnson & Wales University (Providence, Rhode Island; Charleston, South Carolina; Norfolk, Virginia; North Miami, Florida; Denver, Colorado; and Charlotte, North Carolina), Kettering University (Flint, Michigan), Rochester Institute of Technology (Rochester, New York), State University of New York at Oswego (Oswego, New York), University of Cincinnati (Cincinnati, Ohio), University of Massachusetts at Lowell, University of Toledo (Toledo, Ohio), Merrimack College (North Andover, Massachusetts), and Wentworth Institute of Technology (Boston, Massachusetts). Applications must be sent directly to the college or university.

Number awarded Varies each year; recently, 195 were awarded: 10 at Clarkson, 30 at Drexel, 15 at Johnson & Wales, 20 at Kettering, 15 at Rochester Tech, 15 at SUNY Oswego, 15 at Cincinnati, 15 at UM Lowell, 15 at Toledo, 15 at Merrimack, and 30 at Wentworth Tech.

Deadline February of each year.

[406]
NATIONAL HISPANIC HEALTH PROFESSIONAL SCHOLARSHIPS

National Hispanic Medical Association
Attn: National Hispanic Health Foundation
1216 Fifth Avenue, Room 457
New York, NY 10029
(212) 419-3686   Toll Free: (866) 628-6462
E-mail: scholarship@nhmafoundation.org
Web: www.nhmafoundation.org

Summary To provide financial assistance to Hispanic students working on a health-related degree at the graduate level.

Eligibility This program is open to U.S. citizens, permanent residents, and Deferred Action for Childhood Arrivals (DACA) students. Applicants must be currently enrolled full time at a graduate dental, medical (allopathic or osteopathic), nursing, pharmacy, public health, or health policy school in any state and have a GPA of 3.0 or higher. They are not required to be Hispanic, but they must be able to demonstrate an affinity for the health of Hispanic communities. Along with their application, they must submit a letter of recommendation, transcripts, a personal statement that includes their career goals, and a current curriculum vitae. Students in prehealth professional program are not eligible. The only eligible undergraduates are nursing students who have completed at least 60 sememster hours of a B.S.N. program. Selection is based on academic performance, leadership, and commitment to their Hispanic community.

Financial Data Stipends are $5,000 or $2,000.

Duration 1 year; the $5,000 awards may be renewed 1 additional year.

Additional data This program began in 2005 in affiliation with the Robert F. Wagner Graduate School of Public Service at New York University.

Number awarded Varies each year; recently, 21 were awarded: 11 at $5,000 per year for 2 years and 10 for 1 year at $2,000.

Deadline September of each year.

[407]
NATIONAL INSTITUTES OF HEALTH UNDERGRADUATE SCHOLARSHIP PROGRAM

National Institutes of Health
Attn: Office of Intramural Training and Education
2 Center Drive
Building 2, Room 2E24
Bethesda, MD 20892-0230
(301) 594-2222   Fax: (301) 594-9606
TDD: (888) 352-3001   E-mail: ugsp@nih.gov
Web: www.training.nih.gov/programs/ugsp

Summary   To provide loans-for-service for undergraduate education in the life sciences to Hispanics and other under-reprsented students from disadvantaged backgrounds.

Eligibility   This program is open to U.S. citizens, nationals, and permanent residents who are enrolled or accepted for enrollment as full-time students at accredited 4-year institutions of higher education and committed to careers in biomedical, behavioral, and social science health-related research. Applicants must come from a family that meets federal standards of low income, currently defined as a family with an annual income below $23,540 for a 1-person family, ranging to below $81,780 for families of 8 or more. They must have a GPA of 3.3 or higher or be in the top 5% of their class. Selection is based on commitment to a career in biomedical, behavioral, or social science health-related research as an employee of the National Institutes of Health (NIH); academic achievements; recommendations and evaluations of skills, abilities, and goals; and relevant extracurricular activities. Applicants are ranked according to the following priorities: first, juniors and seniors who have completed 2 years of undergraduate course work including 4 core science courses in biology, chemistry, physics, and calculus; second, other undergraduates who have completed those 4 core science courses; third, freshmen and sophomores at accredited undergraduate institutions; and fourth, high school seniors who have been accepted for enrollment as full-time students at accredited undergraduate institutions. The sponsor especially encourages applications from underrepresented minorities, women, and individuals with disabilities.

Financial Data   Stipends are available up to $20,000 per year, to be used for tuition, educational expenses (such as books and lab fees), and qualified living expenses while attending a college or university. Recipients incur a service obligation to work as an employee of the NIH in Bethesda, Maryland for 10 consecutive weeks (during the summer) during the sponsored year and, upon graduation, for 52 weeks for each academic year of scholarship support. The NIH 52-week employment obligation may be deferred if the recipient goes to graduate or medical school.

Duration   1 year; may be renewed for up to 3 additional years.

Number awarded   15 each year.

Deadline   March of each year.

[408]
NATIONAL OCEANIC AND ATMOSPHERIC ADMINISTRATION EDUCATIONAL PARTNERSHIP PROGRAM WITH MINORITY SERVING INSTITUTIONS UNDERGRADUATE SCHOLARSHIPS

National Oceanic and Atmospheric Administration
Attn: Office of Education
1315 East-West Highway
SSMC3, Room 10600
Silver Spring, MD 20910-6233
(301) 628-2900   E-mail: EPP.USP@noaa.gov
Web: www.noaa.gov

Summary   To provide financial assistance and research experience to undergraduate students at Hispanic and other Minority Serving Institutions who are majoring in scientific fields of interest to the National Oceanic and Atmospheric Administration (NOAA).

Eligibility   This program is open to full-time juniors at Minority Serving Institutions, including Hispanic Serving Institutions (HSIs), Historically Black Colleges and Universities (HBCUs), Tribal Colleges and Universities (TCUs), Alaskan Native Serving Institutions, and Native Hawaiian Serving Institutions. Applicants must have a GPA of 3.2 or higher and a major in atmospheric science, biology, computer science, engineering, environmental science, geography, hydrology, mathematics, oceanography, physical science, physics, remote sensing, social science, or other field that supports NOAA's programs and mission. They must also be interested in participating in a research internship at an NOAA site. Selection is based on relevant course work (30%), education plan and statement of career interest (40%), recommendations (20%), and additional experience related to diversity of education, extracurricular activities, honors and awards, non-academic and volunteer work, and communication skills (10%). U.S. citizenship is required.

Financial Data   Total support for 2 academic years and 2 summer internships is $45,000.

Duration   2 academic years and 2 summer internships.

Number awarded   Up to 15 each year.

Deadline   February of each year.

[409]
NATIONAL ORGANIZATION OF PROFESSIONAL HISPANIC NATURAL RESOURCES CONSERVATION SERVICE EMPLOYEES SCHOLARSHIPS

National Organization of Professional Hispanic Natural
   Resources Conservation Service Employees
c/o Angel M. Domenech, Scholarship Committee Co-
   Chair
Natural Resources Conservation Service
Soil Survey Office
3100 Alvey Park Drive West
Owensboro, KY 42303-2191
(270) 685-1707, ext. 118
E-mail: scholarships@nophnrcse.org
Web: www.nophnrcse.org

Summary   To provide financial assistance to Hispanic high seniors and college students interested in working on a bachelor's degree in a field related to natural resources or conservation.

Eligibility This program is open to Hispanic high school seniors and full-time college students who are attending or planning to attend an accredited 4-year college or university. Applicants must be planning to work on a bachelor's degree in an agricultural, natural resources, or natural resources conservation-related field of study. They must have a GPA of 2.75 or higher. Along with their application, they must submit a personal statement (in English) of 350 to 500 words on their background, name of school they attend or plan to attend, personal and career goals, extracurricular activities, and interest in preparing for a career related to natural resources conservation. Financial need is not considered in the selection process. U.S. citizenship is required.

Financial Data The stipend is $1,000.

Duration 1 year.

Additional data The National Organization of Professional Hispanic Natural Resources Conservation Service Employees (NOPRNRCSE) is comprised of Hispanic employees of the Natural Resources Conservation Service of the U.S. Department of Agriculture (USDA-NRCS).

Number awarded Varies each year; recently, 3 were awarded.

Deadline May of each year.

[410]
NATIONAL PRESS CLUB SCHOLARSHIP FOR JOURNALISM DIVERSITY

National Press Club
Attn: Executive Director's Office
529 14th Street, N.W., 13th Floor
Washington, DC 20045
(202) 662-7599
Web: www.press.org/about/scholarships/diversity

Summary To provide funding to high school seniors who are planning to major in journalism in college and are Hispanics or others who will bring diversity to the field.

Eligibility This program is open to high school seniors who have been accepted to college and plan to prepare for a career in journalism. Applicants must submit 1) a 500-word essay explaining how they would add diversity to U.S. journalism; 2) up to 5 work samples demonstrating an ongoing interest in journalism through work on a high school newspaper or other media; 3) letters of recommendation from 3 people; 4) a copy of their high school transcript; 5) documentation of financial need; 6) a letter of acceptance from the college or university of their choice; and 7) a brief description of how they have pursued journalism in high school.

Financial Data The stipend is $2,000 for the first year and $2,500 for each subsequent year. The program also provides an additional $500 book stipend, designated the Ellen Masin Persina Scholarship, for the first year.

Duration 4 years.

Additional data The program began in 1990.

Number awarded 1 each year.

Deadline February of each year.

[411]
NATIONAL SPACE GRANT COLLEGE AND FELLOWSHIP PROGRAM

National Aeronautics and Space Administration
Attn: Office of Education
300 E Street, S.W.
Mail Suite 6M35
Washington, DC 20546-0001
(202) 358-1069   Fax: (202) 358-7097
E-mail: aleksandra.korobov@nasa.gov
Web: www.nasa.gov

Summary To provide financial assistance to undergraduate and graduate students, especially Hispanics and members of other underrepresented groups, who are interested in preparing for a career in a space-related field.

Eligibility This program is open to undergraduate and graduate students at colleges and universities that participate in the National Space Grant program of the U.S. National Aeronautics and Space Administration (NASA) through their state consortium. Applicants must be interested in a program of study and/or research in a field of science, technology, engineering, or mathematics (STEM) related to space. A specific goal of the program is to recruit and train U.S. citizens, especially underrepresented minorities, women, and persons with disabilities, for careers in aerospace science and technology. Financial need is not considered in the selection process.

Financial Data Each consortium establishes the terms of the fellowship program in its state.

Additional data NASA established the Space Grant program in 1989. It operates through 52 consortia in each state, the District of Columbia, and Puerto Rico. Each consortium includes selected colleges and universities in that state as well as other affiliates from industry, museums, science centers, and state and local agencies.

Number awarded Varies each year.

Deadline Each consortium sets its own deadlines.

[412]
NATIONWIDE HISPANIC SCHOLARSHIPS OF THE INDEPENDENT COLLEGE FUND OF MARYLAND

Independent College Fund of Maryland
Attn: Director of Programs and Scholarships
3225 Ellerslie Avenue, Suite C-160
Baltimore, MD 21218-3519
(443) 997-5700   Fax: (443) 997-2740
E-mail: lfund@jhu.edu
Web: www.i-fundinfo.org

Summary To provide financial assistance to upper-division Hispanic students from any state at member institutions of the Independent College Fund of Maryland who are majoring in business.

Eligibility This program is open to Hispanic students from any state currently entering their junior, or senior year at member institutions. Applicants must be enrolled full time and majoring in or be able to demonstrate a career interest in business, particularly financial services. They must have a GPA of 3.0 or higher.

Financial Data The stipend is $2,000.

Duration 1 year.

Additional data The member institutions are Notre Dame of Maryland University, Goucher College, Hood College, Johns Hopkins University, Loyola University of Maryland, McDaniel College, Mount St. Mary's University, St. John's College, Stevenson University, and Washington College.

Number awarded 1 or more each year.

Deadline Deadline not specified.

[413]
NBCUNIVERSAL/LNESC SCHOLARSHIPS

League of United Latin American Citizens
Attn: LULAC National Education Service Centers
1133 19th Street, N.W., Suite 1000
Washington, DC 20036
(202) 835-9646   Fax: (202) 835-9685
E-mail: scholarships@lnesc.org
Web: www.lnesc.org/#!nbcuniversal-scholarship/cun4

Summary To provide financial assistance to Latino students who are working on a bachelor's degree in any field.

Eligibility This program is open to Latino high school seniors and current undergraduates working full time on a bachelor's degree in any field at colleges or universities in the United States. Applicants must have a GPA of 3.0 or higher and be U.S. citizens or legal residents. High school seniors must have scored at least 26 on the ACT or 1770 on the SAT. Selection is based on academic performance, likelihood of preparing for a career in business or engineering, performance in business or engineering subjects, writing ability, extracurricular activities, and community involvement.

Financial Data The stipend is $5,000. Funds are to be used to pay for tuition, required fees, room and board, and required educational materials and books; they are sent directly to the college or university and deposited in the scholarship recipient's name.

Duration 1 year; nonrenewable.

Additional data Funding for this program is provided by NBCUniversal. The League of United Latin American Citizens (LULAC) began in 1929 and it established the LULAC National Education Service Centers (LNESC) in 1973 to support the educational activities of Hispanics.

Number awarded 10 each year.

Deadline July of each year.

[414]
NELLIE STONE JOHNSON SCHOLARSHIP

Nellie Stone Johnson Scholarship Program
P.O. Box 40309
St. Paul, MN 55104
(651) 738-1404   Toll Free: (866) 738-5238
E-mail: info@nelliestone.org
Web: www.nelliestone.org/scholarship-program

Summary To provide financial assistance to Hispanic and other racial minority union members and their families who are interested in working on an undergraduate or graduate degree in any field at a Minnesota state college or university.

Eligibility This program is open to students in undergraduate and graduate programs at a 2- or 4-year institution that is a component of Minnesota State Colleges and Universities (MnSCU). Applicants must be a minority (Chicano(a) or Latino(a), Asian, American Indian, Alaska Native, Black/African American, Native Hawaiian, or Pacific Islander) and a union member or the child, grandchild, or spouse of a minority union member. They must submit a 2-page essay about their background, educational goals, career goals, and commitment to the causes of human or civil rights. Undergraduates must have a GPA of 2.0 or higher; graduate students must have a GPA of 3.0 or higher. Preference is given to Minnesota residents. Selection is based on the essay, commitment to human or civil rights, extracurricular activities, volunteer activities, community involvement, academic standing, and union verification.

Financial Data Stipends are $1,200 per year for full-time students or $500 per year for part-time students.

Duration 1 year; may be renewed up to 3 additional years for students working on a bachelor's degree, 1 additional year for students working on a master's degree, or 1 additional year for students in a community or technical college program.

Number awarded Varies each year; recently, 18 were awarded.

Deadline May of each year.

[415]
NEW JERSEY CHAPTER AABE SCHOLARSHIPS

American Association of Blacks in Energy-New Jersey
   Chapter
Attn: Scholarship Committee
P.O. Box 32578
Newark, NJ 07102
E-mail: NewJersey@aabe.org
Web: www.aabe.org/index.php?component=pages&id=692

Summary To provide financial assistance to Hispanic and members of other underrepresented minority groups who are high school seniors in New Jersey and planning to major in an energy-related field at a college in any state.

Eligibility This program is open to seniors graduating from high schools in New Jersey and planning to attend a college or university in any state. Applicants must be Hispanics, African Americans, or Native Americans who have a GPA of 3.0 or higher and who have taken the ACT and/or SAT test. Their intended major must be business, engineering, technology, mathematics, the physical sciences, or other energy-related field. Along with their application, they must submit a 350-word essay that includes 1) when they discovered their interest in the field of energy and what sparked their interest; and 2) either what excites them about the field of energy or how they expect their education to prepare them for the field of energy. Financial need is not considered in the selection process.

Financial Data The stipend is $1,000.

Duration 1 year.

Additional data The winner is eligible to compete for regional and national scholarships.

Number awarded 1 each year.

Deadline March of each year.

[416]
NEW MEXICO ALLIANCE FOR HISPANIC EDUCATION SCHOLARSHIPS

New Mexico Alliance for Hispanic Education
Attn: Program Director
P.O. Box 25806
Albuquerque, NM 87125
(505) 342-3504
Web: www.nmalliance.org/home/scholarships

Summary To provide financial assistance to Hispanic residents of New Mexico who are interested in attending college or graduate school in any state.

Eligibility This program is open to residents of New Mexico who are of Hispanic heritage and interested enrolling full time at an accredited 2- or 4-year college or university in the United States, Puerto Rico, the U.S. Virgin Islands, or Guam. Applicants must have a GPA of 3.0 or higher and be working on or planning to work on an undergraduate or graduate degree. They must be U.S. citizens, permanent residents, or visitors with a passport stamped I-551. In addition to submitting the application, they must apply for federal financial aid by completing the Free Application for Federal Student Aid (FAFSA).

Financial Data Stipends range from $1,000 to $2,500.

Duration 1 year.

Number awarded Varies each year.

Deadline February of each year.

[417]
NEW YORK EXCEPTIONAL UNDERGRADUATE/ GRADUATE STUDENT SCHOLARSHIP

Conference of Minority Transportation Officials
Attn: National Scholarship Program
100 M Street, S.E., Suite 917
Washington, DC 20003
(202) 506-2917   E-mail: info@comto.org
Web: www.comto.org/page/scholarships

Summary To provide financial assistance to Hispanic and other minority students who are members or relatives of members of the Conference of Minority Transportation Officials (COMTO) in New York and working on an undergraduate or graduate degree in transportation.

Eligibility This program is open to minorities who have been members or relatives of members of COMTO in New York for at least 1 year. Applicants must be enrolled full time at an accredited college, university, or vocational/technical institute and working on an undergraduate or graduate degree in a transportation-related discipline. They must have a GPA of 3.5 or higher. Along with their application they must submit a cover letter on their transportation-related career goals and life aspirations. Financial need is not considered in the selection process.

Financial Data The stipend is $5,000. Funds are paid directly to the recipient's college or university.

Duration 1 year.

Number awarded 1 each year.

Deadline April of each year.

[418]
NJUA EXCELLENCE IN DIVERSITY SCHOLARSHIP

New Jersey Utilities Association
50 West State Street, Suite 1117
Trenton, NJ 08608
(609) 392-1000   Fax: (609) 396-4231
E-mail: info@njua.com
Web: www.njua.com/excellence_in_diversity_scholarship

Summary To provide financial assistance to Hispanic and other underrepresented high school seniors in New Jersey interested in attending college in any state.

Eligibility This program is open to seniors graduating from high schools in New Jersey who are women, minorities (Hispanic or Latino, Black or African American, American Indian or Alaska Native, Asian, Native Hawaiian or Pacific Islander, or 2 or more races), and persons with disabilities. Applicants must be planning to work on a bachelor's degree at a college or university in any state. Along with their application, they must submit a 500-word essay explaining their career ambition and why they have chosen that career. Children of employees of any New Jersey Utilities Association-member company are ineligible. Selection is based on overall academic excellence and demonstrated financial need. U.S. citizenship or permanent resident status is required.

Financial Data The stipend is $1,500 per year. Funds are paid to the recipient's college or university.

Duration 4 years.

Number awarded 1 each year.

Deadline April of each year.

[419]
NOKIA BELL LABORATORIES INTERN PROGRAM

Nokia Bell Laboratories
Attn: Special Programs Manager
600-700 Mountain Avenue
Murray Hill, NJ 07974
(908) 582-3000   E-mail: info@bell-labs.com
Web: www.bell-labs.com/connect/internships

Summary To provide technical work experience at facilities of Nokia Bell Laboratories during the summer to Hispanic and other underrepresented minority undergraduate students.

Eligibility This program is open to women and members of minority groups (Hispanics, African Americans, and Native American Indians) who are underrepresented in the sciences. Applicants must be interested in pursuing technical employment experience in research and development facilities of Nokia Bell Laboratories. The program is primarily directed at undergraduate students who have completed their second or third year of college. Emphasis is placed on the following disciplines: business modeling, chemical engineering, chemistry, computer science and engineering, economics, electrical engineering, engineering mechanics, industrial engineering, manufacturing engineering, mathematics, mechanical engineering, operations research, physics, statistics, systems engineering, and telecommunications. U.S. citizenship or permanent resident status is required. Selection is based on academic achievement, personal motivation, and compatibility of student interests with current Nokia Bell Laboratories activities.

Financial Data   Salaries are commensurate with those of regular Nokia Bell Laboratories employees with comparable education. Interns are reimbursed for travel expenses up to the cost of round-trip economy-class airfare.

Duration   10 weeks during the summer.

Additional data   Nokia Bell Laboratories facilities are located in central and northern New Jersey and in Naperville, Illinois.

Number awarded   Varies each year.

Deadline   November of each year.

[420]
NORA STONE SMITH SCHOLARSHIP

Seattle Foundation
Attn: Scholarship Administrator
1200 Fifth Avenue, Suite 1300
Seattle, WA 98101-3151
(206) 515-2119   Fax: (206) 622-7673
E-mail: scholarships@seattlefoundation.org
Web: www.washboard.org

Summary   To provide financial assistance for college to high school seniors who have been enrolled in English as a Second Language/English Language Learners (ESL/ELL) programs.

Eligibility   This program is open to seniors graduating from high schools who are current or former ESL/ELL students, regardless of their citizenship status. Applicants must be planning to enroll full time at a 2- or 4-year college, university, or vocational/trade school. Along with their application, they must submit a 250-word essay about themselves, where they are from, how they came to be here, their educational achievements, and their future goals. Financial need is considered in the selection process.

Financial Data   The maximum stipend is $2,000 per year.

Duration   1 year; may be renewed up to 3 additional years.

Number awarded   10 each year.

Deadline   March of each year.

[421]
NORMA KORNEGAY CLARKE SCHOLARSHIP

Northeast Human Resources Association
Attn: Director of Professional Development
490 Virginia Road, Suite 32
Concord, MA 01742-2747
(781) 239-8718   Fax: (781) 237-8745
E-mail: nreiser@nehra.com
Web: www.nehra.com/?page=DIScholarshipApp

Summary   To provide financial assistance for college to Hispanic and other high school seniors from the New England states who have promoted diversity.

Eligibility   This program is open to seniors who are graduating from high schools in New England and planning to attend a college or university. Applicants should have demonstrated academic responsibility, performed community service, offered a helping hand to fellow students, and promoted harmony among diverse groups. They must have a GPA of 3.0 or higher and be able to demonstrate financial need. Along with their application, they must submit a 750-word personal statement explaining what diversity means to them, how they promote diversity in their community or school, and how they propose to promote diversity in the future.

Financial Data   The stipend is $5,000.

Duration   1 year.

Additional data   The sponsor is an affiliate of the Society for Human Resource Management (SHRM). Its Diversity and Inclusion Committee focuses on veterans, the GLBT community, people with disabilities, gender equity, and race/ethnicity. The Back Bay Staffing Group established this program in 1998.

Number awarded   1 each year.

Deadline   February of each year.

[422]
NORTH CAROLINA CHAPTER AABE SCHOLARSHIPS

American Association of Blacks in Energy-North Carolina Chapter
Attn: Scholarship Committee
P.O. Box 207
Raleigh, NC 27602-0207
E-mail: northcarolina@aabe.org
Web: www.aabe.org

Summary   To provide financial assistance to Hispanics and members of other underrepresented minority groups who are high school seniors in North Carolina and planning to major in an energy-related field at a college in any state.

Eligibility   This program is open to seniors graduating from high schools in North Carolina and planning to work on a bachelor's degree at a college or university in any state. Applicants must be Hispanics, African Americans, or Native Americans who have a GPA of 3.0 or higher and have taken the ACT and/or SAT test. Their intended major must be a field of business, engineering, physical science, mathematics, or technology related to energy. Along with their application, they must submit a 350-word essay that includes 1) when they discovered their interest in the field of energy and what sparked their interest; and 2) either what excites them about the field of energy or how they expect their education to prepare them for the field of energy. Financial need is not considered in the selection process.

Financial Data   The stipend is $1,000.

Duration   1 year; nonrenewable.

Additional data   Winners are eligible to compete for regional and national scholarships.

Number awarded   1 or more each year.

Deadline   March of each year.

[423]
NORTH CAROLINA CPA FOUNDATION OUTSTANDING MINORITY ACCOUNTING STUDENT SCHOLARSHIPS

North Carolina Association of Certified Public Accountants
Attn: North Carolina CPA Foundation, Inc.
P.O. Box 80188
Raleigh, NC 27623-0188
(919) 469-1040, ext. 130   Toll Free: (800) 722-2836
Fax: (919) 378-2000   E-mail: nccpafound@ncacpa.org
Web: www.ncacpa.org/scholarship-recipients

Summary   To provide financial assistance to Hispanic and other minority undergraduate students working on a degree in accounting at colleges and universities in North Carolina.

Eligibility This program is open to North Carolina residents who are members of a minority group, defined as Hispanic, Black, Native American/Alaskan Native, Middle-Eastern, or Asian or Pacific Islander and enrolled full time in an accounting program at a college or university in the state. Applicants must have completed at least 36 semester hours, including at least 1 college or university-level accounting course, and have a GPA of 3.0 or higher. They must be sponsored by an accounting faculty member. Selection is based on the content of an essay on a topic related to the public accounting profession (35%), essay grammar (35%), and extracurricular activities (30%).

Financial Data Stipends are $2,000 or $1,000.

Duration 1 year; may be renewed up to 2 additional years.

Number awarded 2 each year: 1 at $2,000 and 1 at $1,000.

Deadline February of each year.

[424]
NORTH CAROLINA HISPANIC COLLEGE FUND SCHOLARSHIPS

North Carolina Society of Hispanic Professionals
Attn: North Carolina Hispanic College Fund
8450 Chapel Hill Road, Suite 209
Cary, NC 27513
(919) 467-8424   Fax: (919) 469-1785
E-mail: mailbox@thencshp.org
Web: www.thencshp.org/programs/nc-hispanic-college-fund

Summary To provide financial assistance to Hispanic students from North Carolina who are interested in attending college in any state.

Eligibility This program is open to residents of North Carolina who are of Hispanic background (both parents are at least half Hispanic or 1 parent is fully Hispanic) and either 1) are graduating high school seniors; or 2) graduated from high school within the past 2 years. Applicants must be enrolled or planning to enroll at a 2- or 4-year college or university in any state and be committed to public service and community development. They must have a high school GPA of 2.5 or higher. Along with their application, they must submit a 500-word essay on why their Hispanic parentage and family background are important to them, personal and/or academic achievements, academic plans and career goals, and past and current efforts (as well as future plans) towards making a difference in their community. Preference is given to foreign-born applicants and the native-born children of foreign-born parents. Selection is based on academic achievement, community involvement, volunteerism, leadership, and family economic need.

Financial Data Stipends range from $500 to $2,500 per year. Funds are paid directly to the college or university.

Duration 1 year; may be renewed up to 3 additional years.

Number awarded Varies each year; recently 15 were awarded.

Deadline January of each year.

[425]
NORTH DAKOTA DEPARTMENT OF TRANSPORTATION EDUCATIONAL GRANT PROGRAM

North Dakota Department of Transportation
608 East Boulevard Avenue
Bismarck, ND 58505-0700
(701) 328-2550   Toll Free: (855) ND-ROADS
Fax: (701) 328-0319   TDD: (800) 366-6888
E-mail: dot@nd.gov
Web: www.dot.nd.gov/dotnet2/view/careers.aspx

Summary To provide forgivable loans to undergraduates in North Dakota colleges and universities, especially Hispanics and other minorities, who are majoring in fields related to the needs and missions of the North Dakota Department of Transportation.

Eligibility This program is open to students who are attending an institution of higher learning in North Dakota, have completed 1 year of study, and are majoring in civil engineering, construction engineering, diesel technology, engineering technology, or other field that meets the needs and missions of the department. Current department employees are also eligible for aid if they have completed 1 year of study or have worked for the department as a classified employee for at least 2 years. All applicants must be attending a college or university in North Dakota. Priority is given to students who are available for summer employment with the department. Women and minorities are particularly encouraged to apply. Selection is based on: potential to contribute to the department's program, financial need, academic achievement, and relevant experience.

Financial Data The maximum stipend is $2,000 per year. These are forgivable loans. Recipients who fail to honor their work obligation must repay the grant on a prorated basis at 6% interest. Funds must be used only for educational expenses, including tuition, required fees, books, materials, and necessary personal expenses while attending college.

Duration 1 year; may be renewed up to 2 additional years.

Additional data Upon graduation, recipients must agree to work for the department for a period of time at least equal to the grant study period.

Number awarded Varies each year; recently, 14 of these grants were awarded.

Deadline Deadline not specified.

[426]
NORTH TEXAS EXCEPTIONAL HIGH SCHOOL STUDENT SCHOLARSHIP

Conference of Minority Transportation Officials
Attn: National Scholarship Program
100 M Street, S.E., Suite 917
Washington, DC 20003
(202) 506-2917   E-mail: info@comto.org
Web: www.comto.org/page/scholarships

Summary To provide financial assistance to Hispanic and other minority high school seniors who are members or family of members of the Conference of Minority Transportation Officials (COMTO) in Texas and planning to work on a degree in transportation.

Eligibility This program is open to minority residents of Texas who have been members or whose parents, guardians, or grandparents have been members of COMTO for at least 1 year. Applicants must be high school seniors who have been accepted at an accredited college, university, or vocational/technical institute and planning to work on a degree in a transportation-related discipline. They must have a GPA of 2.0 or higher. Along with their application they must submit a cover letter on their transportation-related career goals and life aspirations. Financial need is not considered in the selection process.

Financial Data The stipend is $3,000. Funds are paid directly to the recipient's college or university.

Duration 1 year.

Number awarded 1 each year.

Deadline April of each year.

[427]
NORTH TEXAS EXCEPTIONAL UNDERGRADUATE/GRADUATE STUDENT SCHOLARSHIP

Conference of Minority Transportation Officials
Attn: National Scholarship Program
100 M Street, S.E., Suite 917
Washington, DC 20003
(202) 506-2917   E-mail: info@comto.org
Web: www.comto.org/page/scholarships

Summary To provide financial assistance to Hispanic and other minority residents of Texas who are working on an undergraduate or graduate degree in transportation.

Eligibility This program is open to minorities who are residents of Texas enrolled at an accredited college, university, or vocational/technical institute and working on an undergraduate or graduate degree in a transportation-related discipline. Applicants must have a GPA of 2.5 or higher. Along with their application they must submit a cover letter on their transportation-related career goals and life aspirations. Financial need is not considered in the selection process. Membership in the Conference of Minority Transportation Officials (COMTO) is considered a plus but is not required.

Financial Data The stipend is $4,500. Funds are paid directly to the recipient's college or university.

Duration 1 year.

Number awarded 1 each year.

Deadline April of each year.

[428]
NORTHWEST FARM CREDIT SERVICES MINORITY SCHOLARSHIPS

Northwest Farm Credit Services
Attn: Public Relations and Events Manager
P.O. Box 2515
Spokane, WA 99220-2515
(509) 340-5467   Toll Free: (800) 743-2125
Fax: (800) 255-1789
E-mail: heidi.whitman@northwestfcs.com
Web: www.northwestfcs.com

Summary To provide financial assistance to Hispanic and other minority students who are majoring in a field related to agricultural business at universities in designated northwestern states.

Eligibility This program is open to members of minority ethnic groups (Latino/Hispanic, African American or Black,

American Indian or Alaska Native, Asian, Latino/Hispanic, or Pacific Islander) currently enrolled as full-time sophomores or higher at 4-year universities in Alaska, Idaho, Montana, Oregon, Utah, or Washington. Applicants must be studying accounting, business, finance, agricultural business, or economics. They must have a GPA of 3.0 or higher and be U.S. citizens or legal residents. Along with their application, they must submit a 1-page essay on how they will use their education and degree to make a positive impact. Selection is based on that essay (20%), academic achievement (20%), leadership (25%), participation in extracurricular activities (25%), and letters of recommendation (10%).

Financial Data The stipend is $2,000.

Duration 1 year; nonrenewable.

Number awarded 4 each year.

Deadline February of each year.

[429]
NORTHWEST JOURNALISTS OF COLOR SCHOLARSHIP AWARDS

Northwest Journalists of Color
c/o Anika Anand
The Evergrey
P.O. Box 30854
Seattle, WA 98113
E-mail: anikaanand00@gmail.com
Web: www.aajaseattle.org/scholarships

Summary To provide financial assistance to students from Washington state who are Hispanic or others who demonstrate a commitment to the importance of diverse cultural backgrounds and are interested in careers in journalism.

Eligibility This program is open to students who are 1) current high school juniors or seniors in Washington; 2) residents of any state attending a 2- or 4-year college, university, or vocational school in Washington; or 3) seniors graduating from Washington high schools and planning to attend a 2- or 4-year college, university, or vocational school in any state. Applicants must be preparing for a career in broadcast, photo, or print journalism. They do not need to identify as a student of color, but strong preference is given to applicants who demonstrate an understanding of and commitment to the importance of diverse cultural backgrounds and experiences in newsrooms. Along with their application, they must submit 1) a 500-word essay about their interest in a career as a journalist; 2) link to a resume; 3) up to 3 work samples; and 4) a 250-word statement of financial need.

Financial Data Stipends range up to $2,500 per year.

Duration 1 year; may be renewed.

Additional data This program, established in 1986, is sponsored by local chapters of the Asian American Journalists Association, the Native American Journalists Association, the Black Journalists Association of Seattle, and the National Association of Hispanic Journalists.

Number awarded Varies each year.

Deadline April of each year.

[430]
NPM LA BECA JUAN XXIII

National Association of Pastoral Musicians
Attn: NPM Scholarships
962 Wayne Avenue, Suite 210
Silver Spring, MD 20910-4461
(240) 247-3000   Toll Free: (855) 207-0293
Fax: (240) 247-3001   E-mail: npmsing@npm.org
Web: www.npm.org/Membership/scholarship.htm

Summary To provide financial assistance to Latino/a undergraduate or graduate student members of the National Association of Pastoral Musicians.

Eligibility This program is open to Latino/a members of the association who are enrolled part or full time in an undergraduate or graduate degree program. They must be studying in a field related to pastoral music, be able to demonstrate financial need, and be intending to work for at least 2 years in the field of pastoral music following graduation. Applicants must submit 1) documentation of financial need; and 2) a 5-minute performance CD of themselves or the choir-ensemble they direct.

Financial Data The stipend is $3,000 per year. Funds must be used to pay for tuition, registration, fees, or books.

Duration 1 year; recipients may reapply.

Number awarded 1 each year.

Deadline April of each year.

[431]
NSCA MINORITY SCHOLARSHIPS

National Strength and Conditioning Association
Attn: NSCA Foundation
1885 Bob Johnson Drive
Colorado Springs, CO 80906-4000
(719) 632-6722, ext. 152   Toll Free: (800) 815-6826
Fax: (719) 632-6367   E-mail: foundation@nsca.org
Web: www.nsca.com/foundation/nsca-scholarships

Summary To provide financial assistance to Hispanics and other minorities who are interested in working on an undergraduate or graduate degree in strength training and conditioning.

Eligibility This program is open to Hispanics, Blacks, Asian Americans, and Native Americans who are 17 years of age and older. Applicants must have been accepted into an accredited postsecondary institution to work on an undergraduate or graduate degree in the strength and conditioning field. Along with their application, they must submit a 500-word essay on their personal and professional goals and how receiving this scholarship will assist them in achieving those goals. Selection is based on that essay, academic achievement, strength and conditioning experience, honors and awards, community involvement, letters of recommendation, and involvement in the National Strength and Conditioning Association (NSCA).

Financial Data The stipend is $1,500.

Duration 1 year.

Additional data The NSCA is a nonprofit organization of strength and conditioning professionals, including coaches, athletic trainers, physical therapists, educators, researchers, and physicians. This program was first offered in 2003.

Number awarded Varies each year; recently, 5 were awarded.

Deadline March of each year.

[432]
NYSACAC SCHOLARSHIP

New York State Association for College Admission Counseling
Attn: Scholarship Committee
P.O. Box 28
Red Hook, NY 12571
(845) 389-1300   Fax: (866) 370-1008
E-mail: Scholarship@nysacad.org
Web: www.nysacac.org/nysacac-scholarship

Summary To provide financial assistance to residents of New York, especially Hispanics and other underrepresented minorities, who are nominated by a member of the New York State Association for College Admission Counseling (NYSACAC) and plan to attend a NYSACAC member college.

Eligibility This program is open to residents of New York who are graduating from a public or private secondary school in the state, are completing a home school program in the state, or obtained a GED. Applicants must have overcome barriers, have succeeded with limited resources; or be a member of an underrepresented group. They must be entering freshmen at a 2- or 4-year college or university that is a NYSACAC member. A NYSACAC individual member must nominate them. Along with their application, they must submit a 500-word essay on 1 of the following topics: 1) how they have overcome barriers; 2) how they have applied the sponsor's motto of Leading the Way; or 3) the person who has influenced them the most through the college admission process.

Financial Data The stipend is $1,000.

Duration 1 year.

Number awarded 4 each year.

Deadline May of each year.

[433]
OHIO HIGH SCHOOL ATHLETIC ASSOCIATION MINORITY SCHOLAR ATHLETE SCHOLARSHIPS

Ohio High School Athletic Association
Attn: Foundation
4080 Roselea Place
Columbus, OH 43214
(614) 267-2502   Fax: (614) 267-1677
Web: www.ohsaa.org/School-Resources

Summary To provide financial assistance to Hispanic and other minority high school seniors in Ohio who have participated in athletics and plan to attend college in any state.

Eligibility This program is open to minority seniors graduating from high schools in Ohio that are members of the Ohio High School Athletic Association (OHSAA). Applicants must have received at least 3 varsity letters in 1 sport or 4 letters in 2 sports and have a GPA of 3.25 or higher. They must be planning to attend a college or university in any state. Along with their application, they must submit a 1-page essay on the role that interscholastic athletics has played in their life and how such participation will benefit them in the future. Selection is based on that essay, GPA, ACT and SAT scores, varsity letters earned, and athletic honors.

Financial Data   The stipend is $1,000.

Duration   1 year.

Number awarded   6 each year: 1 in each OHSSA District.

Deadline   April of each year.

[434]
OHIO NEWSPAPERS FOUNDATION MINORITY SCHOLARSHIPS

Ohio Newspaper Association
Attn: Foundation
1335 Dublin Road, Suite 216-B
Columbus, OH 43215-7038
(614) 486-6677, ext. 1010   Fax: (614) 486-6373
E-mail: ariggs@ohionews.org
Web: www.ohionews.org/aws/ONA/pt/sp/scholarships

Summary   To provide financial assistance to Hispanic and other minority high school seniors in Ohio planning to attend college in any state to prepare for a career in the newspaper industry.

Eligibility   This program is open to high school seniors in Ohio who are members of minority groups (African American, Hispanic, Asian American, or American Indian) and planning to prepare for a career in the newspaper industry, especially advertising, communications, journalism, or marketing. Applicants must have a high school GPA of 2.5 or higher and demonstrate writing ability in an autobiography of 750 to 1,000 words that describes their academic and career interests, awards, extracurricular activities, and journalism-related activities. They must be planning to attend a college or university in Ohio.

Financial Data   The stipend is $1,500.

Duration   1 year; nonrenewable.

Additional data   This program began in 1990.

Number awarded   1 each year.

Deadline   March of each year.

[435]
OHIO NURSES FOUNDATION MINORITY STUDENT SCHOLARSHIP

Ohio Nurses Association
Attn: Ohio Nurses Foundation
4000 East Main Street
Columbus, OH 43213-2983
(614) 237-5414   Fax: (614) 237-6081
E-mail: info@ohionursesfoundation.org
Web: www.ohionursesfoundation.org

Summary   To provide financial assistance to Hispanic and other minority residents of Ohio who are interested in working on a degree in nursing at a school in any state.

Eligibility   This program is open to residents of Ohio who are members of a minority group and interested in attending college in any state to prepare for a career as a nurse. Applicants must be attending or have attended a high school in the state. If still in high school, they must have a cumulative GPA of 3.5 or higher at the end of their junior year. If out of high school, they may not have had a break of more than 2 years between high school and enrollment in a nursing program. Selection is based on a personal statement, high school or

college academic records, school activities, and community services.

Financial Data   The stipend is $1,000.

Duration   1 year; recipients may reapply for 1 additional year if they remain enrolled full time and maintain a cumulative GPA of 2.5 or higher.

Number awarded   1 or more each year.

Deadline   January of each year.

[436]
OHIO SOCIETY OF CPAS COLLEGE SCHOLARSHIP PROGRAM

Ohio Society of CPAs
Attn: Ohio CPA Foundation
535 Metro Place South
P.O. Box 1810
Dublin, OH 43017-7810
(614) 764-2727, ext. 344
Toll Free: (800) 686-2727, ext. 344
Fax: (614) 764-5880   E-mail: oscpa@ohio-cpa.com
Web: www.ohiocpa.com

Summary   To provide financial assistance to undergraduate and graduate student members of the Ohio Society of CPAs, especially Hispanics and members of other underrepresented groups, who are working on a degree in accounting at colleges and universities in the state.

Eligibility   This program is open to U.S. citizens who are Ohio residents working on undergraduate or graduate degrees in accounting at colleges and universities in the state in order to complete the 150 hours required for the C.P.A. examination. Applicants must have completed at least 30 hours of college credit and have a GPA of 3.0 or higher. Awards are available to 3 categories of students: 1) 2-year awards, for students at community colleges or other 2-year institutions; 2) 4-year awards, for students at 4-year colleges and universities; and 3) diversity awards, for students from underrepresented ethnic, racial, or cultural groups.

Financial Data   The stipend is $2,000.

Duration   1 year; nonrenewable.

Number awarded   Varies each year; recently, 20 were awarded.

Deadline   November of each year.

[437]
OKLAHOMA CAREERTECH FOUNDATION TEACHER RECRUITMENT/RETENTION SCHOLARSHIP FOR STUDENTS

Oklahoma CareerTech Foundation
Attn: Administrator
1500 West Seventh Avenue
Stillwater, OK 74074-4364
(405) 743-5453   Fax: (405) 743-5541
E-mail: leden@careertech.ok.gov
Web: www.okcareertech.org

Summary   To provide financial assistance to residents of Oklahoma who are Hispanics or other students reflecting the diversity of the state and attending a college or university in the state to prepare for a career in the Oklahoma CareerTech system.

Eligibility   This program is open to residents of Oklahoma who are juniors or seniors at an institution of higher education in the state. Applicants must be working on a bachelor's degree and teacher certification in Oklahoma's CareerTech system. They must reflect the ethnic diversity of the state. Along with their application, they must submit brief statements on their interest and commitment to the CareerTech teaching profession and their financial need.

Financial Data   The stipend ranges from $500 per semester to $1,500 per year.

Duration   1 semester; may be renewed, provided the recipient maintains a GPA of 2.5 or higher.

Number awarded   1 or more each year.

Deadline   May of each year.

[438]
OLFIELD DUKES MULTICULTURAL STUDENT AWARD

Public Relations Student Society of America
Attn: Vice President of Member Services
33 Maiden Lane, 11th Floor
New York, NY 10038-5150
(212) 460-1474   Fax: (212) 995-0757
E-mail: DukesScholarship@prsa.org
Web: www.prssa.prsa.org

Summary   To provide financial assistance to Hispanic and other multicultural college seniors who are interested in preparing for a career in public relations.

Eligibility   This program is open to multicultural (Hispanic/Latino, African American/Black, Asian, Native American, Alaskan Native, or Pacific Islander) students who are entering their junior year at an accredited 4-year college or university. Applicants must have a GPA of 3.0 or higher and be working on a degree in public relations, journalism, or other field to prepare for a career in public relations. Selection is based on academic achievement, specific examples of commitment to service and social responsibility, awards and honors received for academic or extracurricular achievements, writing skills, and letters of recommendation.

Financial Data   The stipend is $1,000.

Duration   1 year.

Additional data   This program began in 2013 with support from Prudential Financial and Weber Shandwick.

Number awarded   1 each year.

Deadline   June of each year.

[439]
ONEONTA TRADING CORPORATION/ COOPRIDER SCHOLARSHIPS

Washington Apple Education Foundation
Attn: Scholarship Committee
2900 Euclid Avenue
Wenatchee, WA 98801
(509) 663-7713   Fax: (509) 663-7469
E-mail: scholarships@waef.org
Web: www.waef.org/scholarships

Summary   To provide financial assistance to Hispanics whose parents are employed within the Washington tree fruit industry and who are interested in attending a public college in the state and participating in college sports.

Eligibility   This program is open to Hispanic students who are enrolled or entering college and whose parents are involved in Washington's tree fruit industry. Applicants must

be interested in participating in college sports at a Washington state public college or university. Along with their application, they must submit an official transcript, their SAT or ACT scores, 2 letters of reference, and an essay on an assigned topic. Financial need is also considered in the selection process. Preference is given to students at Wenatchee Valley College.

Financial Data   The stipend is $3,000.

Duration   1 year.

Additional data   This program is sponsored by Oneonta Trading Corporation to honor Sandy Cooprider, a physical education instructor at Wenatchee Valley College.

Number awarded   Up to 4 each year.

Deadline   February of each year.

[440]
OPERATION JUMP START III SCHOLARSHIPS

American Association of Advertising Agencies
Attn: AAAA Foundation
1065 Avenue of the Americas, 16th Floor
New York, NY 10018
(212) 262-2500   E-mail: ameadows@aaaa.org
Web: www.aaaa.org

Summary   To provide financial assistance to Hispanic and other multicultural art directors and copywriters interested in working on an undergraduate or graduate degree in advertising.

Eligibility   This program is open to Hispanic Americans, African Americans, Asian Americans, and Native Americans who are U.S. citizens or permanent residents. Applicants must be incoming graduate students at 1 of 6 designated portfolio schools or full-time juniors at 1 of 2 designated colleges. They must be able to demonstrate extreme financial need, creative talent, and promise. Along with their application, they must submit 10 samples of creative work in their respective field of expertise.

Financial Data   The stipend is $5,000 per year.

Duration   Most awards are for 2 years.

Additional data   Operation Jump Start began in 1997 and was followed by Operation Jump Start II in 2002. The current program began in 2006. The 6 designated portfolio schools are the AdCenter at Virginia Commonwealth University, the Creative Circus in Atlanta, the Portfolio Center in Atlanta, the Miami Ad School, the University of Texas at Austin, and Pratt Institute. The 2 designated colleges are the Minneapolis College of Art and Design and the Art Center College of Design at Pasadena, California.

Number awarded   20 each year.

Deadline   Deadline not specified.

[441]
OREGON ALLIANCE OF INDEPENDENT COLLEGES AND UNIVERSITIES NAMED SCHOLARSHIP FOR UNDERREPRESENTED POPULATIONS

Oregon Alliance of Independent Colleges and Universities
Attn: Vice President
16101 S.W. 72nd Avenue, Suite 100
Portland, OR 97224
(503) 639-4541   Fax: (503) 639-4851
E-mail: brent@oaicu.org
Web: www.oaicu.org

Summary To provide financial assistance to residents of Oregon who are Hispanics or members of another underrepresented population and interested in studying at an independent college in the state.

Eligibility This program is open to Oregon residents who are members of underrepresented populations and are enrolled or planning to enroll full time at a college or university that is a member of the Oregon Alliance of Independent Colleges and Universities (OAICU). Applicants must be planning to major in a field related to the business focus of designated sponsors. Selection is based on academic record in high school, achievements in school or community activities, financial need, and a written statement, up to 500 words, on the meaning of good citizenship and how the fulfillment of their personal goals will help applicants live up to that definition.

Financial Data Stipends awarded by OAICU normally average approximately $2,500.

Duration 1 year.

Additional data The OAICU member institutions are Concordia University, Corban University, George Fox University, Lewis and Clark College, Linfield College, Marylhurst University, Northwest Christian University, Pacific University, Reed College, University of Portland, Warner Pacific College, and Willamette University. Recent sponsors included the BNSF Railway Foundation, Costco Wholesale, KeyBank, NW Natural, UPS Foundation, and Wells Fargo Bank.

Number awarded Varies each year.

Deadline March of each year.

[442]
OREGON ASSOCIATION OF LATINO ADMINISTRATORS SCHOLARSHIP

Confederation of Oregon School Administrators
Attn: Youth Development Program
707 13th Street, S.E., Suite 100
Salem, OR 97301-4035
(503) 581-3141   Fax: (503) 581-9840
Web: www.cosa.k12.or.us/members/scholarships

Summary To provide financial assistance to Latino high school seniors in Oregon who are interested in attending a community college, college, or university in the state.

Eligibility This program is open to seniors graduating from public high schools in Oregon who are of Latino descent. Applicants must be interested in attending a community college, college, or university in the state. They must have been active in community and school affairs, have at least a 3.5 GPA, and be able to enroll in the fall term after graduating from high school. Along with their application, they must sub-

mit a 1-page statement on their background, influences, and goals and the endorsement of a member of the Confederation of Oregon School Administrators (COSA). Financial need is not considered in the selection process.

Financial Data The stipend is $1,000. Funds are paid directly to the recipient.

Duration 1 year; nonrenewable.

Number awarded 1 each year.

Deadline February of each year.

[443]
PA STUDENT SCHOLARSHIPS

American Academy of Physician Assistants
Attn: Physician Assistant Foundation
2318 Mill Road, Suite 1300
Alexandria, VA 22314-6868
(703) 836-2272   Fax: (703) 684-1924
E-mail: pafoundation@aapa.org
Web: www.pa-foundation.org

Summary To provide financial assistance to student members of the American Academy of Physician Assistants (AAPA) who are Hispanics, other underrepresented minorities, or economically and/or educationally disadvantaged.

Eligibility This program is open to AAPA student members attending a physician assistant program accredited by the Commission on Accreditation of Allied Health Education Programs. Applicants must qualify as 1) an underrepresented minority (American Indian, Alaska Native, Black or African American, Hispanic or Latino, Native Hawaiian or other Pacific Islander, or Asian other than Chinese, Filipino, Japanese, Korean, Asian Indian, or Thai); 2) economically disadvantaged (with income below a specified level); or 3) educationally disadvantaged (from a high school with low SAT scores, from a school district in which less than half of graduates go on to college, has a diagnosed physical or mental impairment, English is not their primary language, the first member of their family to attend college). They must have completed at least 1 semester of PA studies.

Financial Data Stipends are $2,500, $2,000, or $1,000.

Duration 1 year; nonrenewable.

Additional data This program includes the AAPA Past Presidents Scholarship, the Bristol-Myers Squibb Endowed Scholarship, the National Commission on Certification of Physician Assistants Endowed Scholarships, the Procter & Gamble Endowed Scholarship, and the PA Foundation Scholarships.

Number awarded Varies each year; recently, 32 were awarded: 3 at $2,500, 27 at $2,000, and 2 at $1,000.

Deadline January of each year.

[444]
PAGE EDUCATION FOUNDATION GRANTS

Page Education Foundation
901 North Third Street, Suite 355
P.O. Box 581254
Minneapolis, MN 55458-1254
(612) 332-0406   Fax: (612) 332-0403
E-mail: info@page-ed.org
Web: www.page-ed.org

Summary To provide funding to Hispanics and other high school seniors of color in Minnesota who plan to attend college in the state.

Eligibility This program is open to students of color who are graduating from high schools in Minnesota and planning to enroll full time at a postsecondary school in the state. Applicants must submit a 500-word essay that deals with why they believe education is important, their plans for the future, and the service-to-children project they would like to complete in the coming school year. Selection is based on the essay, 3 letters of recommendation, and financial need.

Financial Data Stipends range from $1,000 to $2,500 per year.

Duration 1 year; may be renewed up to 3 additional years.

Additional data This program was founded in 1988 by Alan Page, a former football player for the Minnesota Vikings. While attending college, the Page Scholars fulfill a 50-hour service-to-children contract that brings them into contact with K-8 students of color.

Number awarded Varies each year; recently, 503 Page Scholars (210 new recipients and 293 renewals) were enrolled, of whom 260 were African American, 141 Asian American, 70 Chicano/Latino, 13 American Indian, and 19 biracial or multiracial.

Deadline April of each year.

[445]
PCMA EDUCATION FOUNDATION DIVERSITY SCHOLARSHIP

Professional Convention Management Association
Attn: PCMA Education Foundation
35 East Wacker Drive, Suite 500
Chicago, IL 60601
(312) 423-7262   Toll Free: (877) 827-7262
Fax: (312) 423-7222   E-mail: foundation@pcma.org
Web: www.pcma.org

Summary To provide financial assistance to student members of the Professional Convention Management Association (PCMA) who are Hispanics or members of other underrepresented groups and majoring in a field related to the meetings or hospitality industry.

Eligibility This program is open to PCMA members who are currently enrolled in at least 6 credit hours with a major directly related to the meetings or hospitality industry. Applicants must be students traditionally underrepresented in the industry, including (but not limited to) those identifying by a certain race, sex, color, religion, creed, sexual orientation, gender identity or expression, or disability, as well as those with a history of overcoming adversity. They must have a GPA of 2.75 or higher. Along with their application, they must submit a 750-word essay that details how they became interested in the meetings and events industry and a short paragraph describing the potential impact receiving this scholarship would have for them. Selection is based on that essay, academic record, meetings industry experience, and a letter of recommendation.

Financial Data The stipend is $2,500.

Duration 1 year.

Number awarded 1 each year.

Deadline March of each year.

[446]
PDEF MICKEY WILLIAMS MINORITY SCHOLARSHIPS

Society of Nuclear Medicine and Molecular Imaging
Attn: Grants and Awards
1850 Samuel Morse Drive
Reston, VA 20190-5316
(703) 708-9000, ext. 1255   Fax: (703) 708-9015
E-mail: grantinfo@snm.org
Web: www.snmmi.org

Summary To provide financial support to Hispanics and other minority students working on an associate or bachelor's degree in nuclear medicine technology.

Eligibility This program is open to members of the Technologist Section of the Society of Nuclear Medicine and Molecular Imaging (SNMMI-TS) who are accepted or enrolled in a baccalaureate or associate degree program in nuclear medicine technology. Applicants must be members of a minority group: Hispanic American, African American, Native American (including American Indian, Eskimo, Hawaiian, and Samoan), Asian American, or Pacific Islander. They must have a cumulative GPA of 2.5 or higher and be able to demonstrate financial need. Along with their application, they must submit an essay on their reasons for entering the nuclear medicine technology field, their career goals, and their financial need. U.S. citizenship or permanent resident status is required.

Financial Data The stipend is $2,500.

Duration 1 year; may be renewed for 1 additional year.

Additional data This program is supported by corporate sponsors of the Professional Development and Education Fund (PDEF) of the SNMMI-TS.

Number awarded Varies each year; recently, 2 were awarded.

Deadline December of each year.

[447]
PEERMUSIC LATIN SCHOLARSHIP

Broadcast Music Inc.
Attn: BMI Foundation, Inc.
7 World Trade Center
250 Greenwich Street
New York, NY 10007-0030
(212) 220-3103   E-mail: info@bmifoundation.org
Web: www.bmifoundation.org

Summary To recognize and reward students at colleges and universities who submit outstanding songs or instrumental works in a Latin genre.

Eligibility This competition is open to students between 16 and 24 years of age enrolled at colleges and universities in the United States and Puerto Rico. Applicants may not have had any musical work commercially recorded or distributed. They must submit an original song or instrumental work in a Latin genre. The entry must be submitted as an MP3 or MP4a, accompanied by a typed copy of the lyric as a PDF.

Financial Data The award is $5,000.

Duration The award is presented annually.

Additional data This award, first presented in 2003, is sponsored by peermusic Companies.

Number awarded 1 each year.

Deadline January of each year.

[448]
PEGGY PETERMAN SCHOLARSHIP

Tampa Bay Times
Attn: Director of Corporate Giving
490 First Avenue South
St. Petersburg, FL 33701
(727) 893-8780   Toll Free: (800) 333-7505, ext. 8780
Fax: (727) 892-2257   E-mail: waclawek@tampabay.com
Web: www.tampabay.com

Summary   To provide financial assistance to Hispanic and other minority undergraduate and graduate students who are interested in preparing for a career in the newspaper industry and who accept an internship at the *Tampa Bay Times.*

Eligibility   This program is open to minority college sophomores, juniors, seniors, and graduate students from any state who are interested in preparing for a career in the newspaper industry. Applicants must be interested in an internship at the *Tampa Bay Times* and must apply for that at the same time as they apply for this scholarship. They should have experience working on a college publication and at least 1 professional internship.

Financial Data   The stipend is $5,000.

Duration   Internships are for 12 weeks during the summer. Scholarships are for 1 year.

Number awarded   1 each year.

Deadline   October of each year.

[449]
PENNSYLVANIA ACADEMY OF NUTRITION AND DIETETICS FOUNDATION DIVERSITY SCHOLARSHIP

Pennsylvania Academy of Nutrition and Dietetics
Attn: Foundation
96 Northwoods Boulevard, Suite B2
Columbus, OH 43235
(614) 436-6136   Fax: (614) 436-6181
E-mail: padafoundation@eatrightpa.org
Web: www.eatrightpa.org/scholarshipapp.cfm

Summary   To provide financial assistance to members of the Pennsylvania Academy of Nutrition and Dietetics who are Hispanics or members of other minority groups and working on an associate or bachelor's degree in dietetics.

Eligibility   This program is open to academy members who are Hispanic, Black, Asian or Pacific Islander, or Native American (Alaskan Native, American Indian, or Hawaiian Native). Applicants must be 1) enrolled in the first year of study in an accredited dietetic technology program; or 2) enrolled in the third year of study in an accredited undergraduate or coordinated program in dietetics. They must have a GPA of 2.5 or higher. Along with their application, they must submit a letter indicating their intent and the reason they are applying for the scholarship, including a description of their personal financial situation. Selection is based on academic achievement (20%), commitment to the dietetic profession (30%), leadership ability (30%), and financial need (20%).

Financial Data   The stipend is $1,000.

Duration   1 year.

Additional data   The Pennsylvania Academy of Nutrition and Dietetics is the Pennsylvania affiliate of the Academy of Nutrition and Dietetics.

Number awarded   1 or more each year.

Deadline   April of each year.

[450]
PFATS-NFL CHARITIES MINORITY SCHOLARSHIPS

Professional Football Athletic Trainers Society
c/o Britt Brown, ATC, Associate Athletic Trainer
Dallas Cowboys
One Cowboys Parkway
Irving, TX 75063
(972) 497-4992   E-mail: bbrown@dallascowboys.net
Web: www.pfats.com/about/scholarships

Summary   To provide financial assistance to Hispanic and other ethnic minority undergraduate and graduate students working on a degree in athletic training.

Eligibility   This program is open to ethnic minority students who are working on an undergraduate or graduate degree in athletic training. Applicants must have a GPA of 2.5 or higher. Along with their application, they must submit a cover letter, a curriculum vitae, and a letter of recommendation from their supervising athletic trainer. Female athletic training students are encouraged to apply.

Financial Data   A stipend is awarded (amount not specified).

Duration   1 year.

Additional data   Recipients also have an opportunity to work at summer training camp of a National Football League (NFL) team. Support for this program, which began in 1993, is provided by NFL Charities.

Number awarded   1 or more each year.

Deadline   March of each year.

[451]
PGA OF AMERICA DIVERSITY SCHOLARSHIP PROGRAM

Professional Golfers' Association of America
Attn: PGA Foundation
100 Avenue of the Champions
Palm Beach Gardens, FL 33418
Toll Free: (888) 532-6662   E-mail: sjubb@pgahq.com
Web: www.pgafoundation.com

Summary   To provide financial assistance to Hispanics and other minorities interested in attending a designated college or university to prepare for a career as a golf professional.

Eligibility   This program is open to women and minorities interested in becoming a licensed PGA Professional. Applicants must be interested in attending 1 of 20 colleges and universities that offer the Professional Golf Management (PGM) curriculum sanctioned by the PGA.

Financial Data   The stipend is $3,000 per year.

Duration   1 year; may be renewed.

Additional data   This program began in 1993. Programs are offered at the following universities: Arizona State University (Tempe), Campbell University (Buies Creek, North Carolina), Clemson University (Clemson, South Carolina), Coastal Carolina University (Conway, South Carolina), Eastern Kentucky University (Richmond), Ferris State University (Big Rapids, Michigan), Florida State University (Tallahassee), Florida Gulf Coast University (Fort Myers), Methodist University (Fayetteville, North Carolina), Mississippi State University

(Mississippi State), New Mexico State University (Las Cruces), North Carolina State University (Raleigh), Pennsylvania State University (University Park), Sam Houston State University (Huntsville), University of Central Oklahoma (Edmond), University of Colorado at Colorado Springs, University of Idaho (Moscow), University of Maryland Eastern Shore (Princess Anne), University of Nebraska at Lincoln, and University of Nevada at Las Vegas.

Number awarded Varies each year; recently, 20 were awarded.

Deadline Deadline not specified.

[452]
PHILADELPHIA CHAPTER AABE SCHOLARSHIPS

American Association of Blacks in Energy-Philadelphia Chapter
Attn: Scholarship Committee
P.O. Box 34282
Philadelphia, PA 19104
(267) 882-7385 E-mail: Sherri.Pennington@pgworks.com
Web: www.aabe.org/index.php?component=pages&id=706

Summary To provide financial assistance to Hispanics and members of other underrepresented minority groups who are high school seniors in Delaware and Pennsylvania and planning to major in an energy-related field at a college in any state.

Eligibility This program is open to seniors graduating from high schools in Delaware or Pennsylvania and planning to work on a bachelor's degree at a college or university in any state. Applicants must be Hispanics, African Americans, or Native Americans who have a GPA of 3.0 or higher and have taken the ACT and/or SAT test. Their intended major must be a field of business, engineering, physical sciences, mathematics, or technology related to energy. Along with their application, they must submit a 350-word essay that includes 1) when they discovered their interest in the field of energy and what sparked their interest; and 2) either what excites them about the field of energy or how they expect their education to prepare them for the field of energy. Financial need is not considered in the selection process.

Financial Data The stipend is $2,000.

Duration 1 year; nonrenewable.

Additional data Winners are eligible to compete for regional and national scholarships.

Number awarded 6 each year.

Deadline March of each year.

[453]
PHILIP ARREOLA RETURNING STUDENT SCHOLARSHIPS

Hispanic Chamber of Commerce-Wisconsin
Attn: Scholarship Committee
1021 West National Avenue
Milwaukee, WI 53204
(414) 643-6963   Fax: (414) 643-6994
E-mail: Pamela@hccw.org
Web: www.hccw.org/scholarships

Summary To provide financial assistance to Hispanic students who are reentering colleges and universities in Wisconsin after a lapse of time.

Eligibility This program is open to Hispanic students currently enrolled full or part time at a college or university in Wisconsin after at least a 1-year lapse in their undergraduate education. Applicants must be residents of Wisconsin, have a high school diploma or GED, be able to demonstrate financial need, be able to demonstrate life experiences and/or participation in school and/or community activities, and be U.S. citizens or legal residents (although DACA-approved students are eligible). Along with their application, they must submit a 1-page essay covering their strengths that should be considered for this scholarship, career plans, current and future commitment to the Hispanic community, and financial need.

Financial Data The stipend is $1,000.

Duration 1 year; nonrenewable.

Number awarded Varies each year; recently, 2 were awarded.

Deadline May of each year.

[454]
PHILIP ARREOLA SCHOLARSHIPS

Hispanic Chamber of Commerce-Wisconsin
Attn: Scholarship Committee
1021 West National Avenue
Milwaukee, WI 53204
(414) 643-6963   Fax: (414) 643-6994
E-mail: Pamela@hccw.org
Web: www.hccw.org/scholarships

Summary To provide financial assistance to Hispanic high school seniors in Wisconsin who plan to attend college in the state.

Eligibility This program is open to Hispanic students graduating from high schools in Wisconsin and planning to enroll full time at an accredited college or university in the state. Applicants must be residents of Wisconsin; have a history of academic achievement, participation in school activities, and involvement in community activities; be able to demonstrate financial need; and be U.S. citizens or permanent residents. They must have a GPA of 3.3 or higher and satisfactory SAT/ACT scores. Along with their application, they must submit a 3-page essay covering their strengths that should be considered for this scholarship, career plans, current and future commitment to the Hispanic community, and financial need.

Financial Data The stipend is $2,500 per year.

Duration 4 years, provided the recipient remains enrolled full time with a GPA of 2.5 or higher and volunteers for 20 hours of community service work annually.

Number awarded Varies each year; recently, 3 were awarded.

Deadline May of each year.

[455]
PHILLIP D. REED UNDERGRADUATE ENDOWMENT FELLOWSHIP

National Action Council for Minorities in Engineering
Attn: Director, Scholarships and University Relations
440 Hamilton Avenue, Suite 302
White Plains, NY 10601-1813
(914) 539-4316   Fax: (914) 539-4032
E-mail: scholars@nacme.org
Web: www.nacme.org/scholarships

Summary To provide financial assistance to Latino and other underrepresented minority college sophomores majoring in engineering or related fields.
Eligibility This program is open to Latino, African American, and American Indian college sophomores who have a GPA of 3.0 or higher and have demonstrated academic excellence, leadership skills, and a commitment to science and engineering as a career. Applicants must be enrolled full time at an ABET-accredited engineering program. Fields of study include all areas of engineering as well as computer science, materials science, mathematics, operations research, or physics.
Financial Data The stipend is $5,000 per year. Funds are sent directly to the recipient's university.
Duration Up to 3 years.
Number awarded 1 each year.
Deadline April of each year.

[456]
PHYLLIS G. MEEKINS SCHOLARSHIP

Ladies Professional Golf Association
Attn: LPGA Foundation
100 International Golf Drive
Daytona Beach, FL 32124-1082
(386) 274-6200   Fax: (386) 274-1099
E-mail: foundation.scholarships@lpga.com
Web: www.lpga.com

Summary To provide financial assistance to Hispanic and other minority female graduating high school seniors who played golf in high school and plan to continue to play in college.
Eligibility This program is open to female high school seniors who are members of a recognized minority group. Applicants must have a GPA of 3.0 or higher and a background in golf. They must be planning to enroll full time at a college or university in the United States and play competitive golf. Along with their application, they must submit a letter that describes how golf has been an integral part of their lives and includes their personal, academic, and professional goals; their chosen discipline of study; and how this scholarship will be of assistance. Financial need is considered in the selection process. U.S. citizenship or legal resident status is required.
Financial Data The stipend is $1,250.
Duration 1 year.
Additional data This program began in 2006.
Number awarded 1 each year.
Deadline May of each year.

[457]
P.O. PISTILLI SCHOLARSHIPS

Design Automation Conference
c/o Andrew B. Kahng, Scholarship Director
University of California at San Diego-Jacobs School of
   Engineering
Jacobs Hall, EBU3B, Rpp, 2134
9500 Gilman Drive
La Jolla, CA 92093-0404
(858) 822-4884   Fax: (858) 534-7029
E-mail: abk@cs.ucsd.edu
Web: www.dac.com

Summary To provide financial assistance to Hispanic and other underrepresented high school seniors who are interested in preparing for a career in computer science or electrical engineering.
Eligibility This program is open to graduating high school seniors who are members of underrepresented groups: Hispanics, African Americans, Native Americans, and students with disabilities. Applicants must be interested in preparing for a career in electrical engineering, computer engineering, or computer science. They must have at least a 3.0 GPA, have demonstrated high achievements in math and science courses, have demonstrated involvement in activities associated with the underrepresented group they represent, and be able to demonstrate significant financial need. U.S. citizenship is not required, but applicants must be U.S. residents when they apply and must plan to attend an accredited U.S. college or university. Along with their application, they must submit 3 letters of recommendation, official transcripts, ACT/SAT and/or PSAT scores, a personal statement outlining future goals and why they think they should receive this scholarship, and documentation of financial need.
Financial Data Stipends are $4,000 per year. Awards are paid each year in 2 equal installments.
Duration 1 year; may be renewed up to 4 additional years.
Additional data This program is funded by the Design Automation Conference of the Association for Computing Machinery's Special Interest Group on Design Automation.
Number awarded 2 to 7 each year.
Deadline January of each year.

[458]
PORTLAND LATINO GAY PRIDE SCHOLARSHIP

Equity Foundation
Attn: Programs and Office Administrator
221 N.W. Fifth Avenue, Suite 208
P.O. Box 5696
Portland, OR 97228-5696
(503) 231-5759, ext. 522   Fax: (503) 231-5793
E-mail: danib@equityfoundation.org
Web: www.equityfoundation.org

Summary To provide financial assistance to gays, lesbians, bisexuals, transgenders, and their children in Oregon and Clark County, Washington, especially Latinos, who plan to attend college in any state.
Eligibility This program is open to residents of Oregon and Clark County, Washington. Applicants must be either 1) gay, lesbian, bisexual, or transgender; or 2) the child of a gay, lesbian, bisexual, or transgender parent. They must be attending or entering a college, university, or trade or vocational school in any state. Financial need is considered in the selection process. Preference is given to Latino candidate.
Financial Data A stipend is awarded (amount not specified).
Duration 1 year.
Additional data This program began in 2012.
Number awarded Varies each year.
Deadline June of each year.

[459]
PRAXAIR LIMITED SCHOLARSHIPS

American Welding Society
Attn: AWS Foundation, Inc.
8669 N.W. 36th Street, Suite 130
Doral, FL 33166-6672
(305) 443-9353   Toll Free: (800) 443-9353, ext. 212
Fax: (305) 443-7559   E-mail: vpinsky@aws.org
Web: app.aws.org/foundation/scholarships/praxair.html

Summary To provide financial assistance to students, especially Hispanics and other underrepresented minorities, who are interested in working on a degree or certificate in welding at colleges within designated sections of the American Welding Society.

Eligibility This program is open to high school seniors who are planning to enroll full or part time (full time is preferred) in a degree or certificate welding program at a 2- or 4-year college or university. Applicants must be entering an academic institution located within 1 of 13 AWS sections and be residents of the state in which the section is located. They must be U.S. citizens and have a GPA of 2.5 or higher. Along with their application, they must submit a personal statement that covers their demonstrated timeliness and completion of assignments; creativity in solving problems; demonstrated responsibility on own initiative; ability to work well with others; organizational skills; participation in class, and outside organizations; participation in student and section activities; general background; and career objectives. Preference is given to applicants from groups underrepresented in the welding industry. Financial need is not required.

Financial Data The stipend is $2,000 per year; funds are paid directly to the educational institution.

Duration 1 year; may be renewed for 1 additional year.

Additional data This program is supported by Praxair, Inc. The participating sections are Chicago, Cleveland, Dallas (for North Texas), Detroit, Fox Valley (for Wisconsin and the Upper Peninsula of Michigan), Houston, Kansas City (for 18 counties of eastern Kansas or 41 counties of western Missouri), Los Angeles, North Dakota, Portland, Utah, Tulsa, and North Carolina (divided between Charlotte and Research Triangle Park).

Number awarded 26 each year: 2 in each of the participating sections.

Deadline March of each year.

[460]
PRINCETON SUMMER UNDERGRADUATE RESEARCH EXPERIENCE

Princeton University
Attn: Graduate School
Office of Academic Affairs and Diversity
Clio Hall
Princeton, NJ 08544-0255
(609) 258-2066   E-mail: diverse@princeton.edu
Web: gradschool.princeton.edu

Summary To provide an opportunity for Hispanic and other minority or disadvantaged students to assist Princeton faculty in any area during the summer.

Eligibility This program is open to full-time sophomores and juniors at all colleges and universities in the United States who are majoring in any academic discipline and have a GPA of 3.5 or higher in their major. Current college freshmen and graduating seniors are not eligible. Applicants must be interested in working during the summer with a Princeton faculty member. They should have a goal of continuing on for a Ph.D. and preparing for a career in college or university teaching and research. Students in the sciences and engineering normally work in a laboratory group on an aspect of the faculty member's current research. Students in the humanities and social sciences might assist a faculty member engaged in a particular research, editing, bibliographical, or course-preparation project; alternatively, they may work on a research paper under faculty supervision. Members of racial and ethnic minority groups underrepresented in doctoral research programs, students from socioeconomically disadvantaged backgrounds, and students at small liberal arts colleges are especially encouraged to apply.

Financial Data Participants receive a stipend of $3,750, housing in a campus dormitory, a $150 meal card, and up to $500 in reimbursement of travel costs.

Duration 8 weeks during the summer.

Number awarded Up to 20 each year.

Deadline January of each year.

[461]
PROCTER & GAMBLE DENTAL AND DENTAL AUXILIARY SCHOLARSHIPS

Hispanic Dental Association
Attn: HDA Foundation
3910 South IH-35, Suite 245
Austin, TX 78704
(512) 904-0252   E-mail: jessicac@hdassoc.org
Web: www.hdassoc.org

Summary To provide financial assistance to members of the Hispanic Dental Association (HDA) interested in preparing for a career in a dental profession.

Eligibility This program is open to HDA members who are entering their first through fourth year of dental school or first or second year at an accredited dental hygiene, dental assisting, or dental technician program in the United States or Puerto Rico. Applicants must have a GPA of 3.0 or higher, an interest in improving the health of the Hispanic community, and a demonstrated commitment and dedication to serving the Hispanic community. They must be enrolled full time Along with their application, they must submit a 250-word essay on their career goals, including how they were inspired to become a dentist, dental hygienist, dental assistant, or dental technician. Selection is based on academic achievement, leadership skills, community service, and commitment and dedication to improving the oral health of the Hispanic community.

Financial Data The stipend is $2,000 for dental students or $1,000 for dental hygiene, dental assisting, or dental technician students. An additional grant of $500 is provided for travel reimbursement and complimentary registration to the HDA annual meeting.

Duration 1 year.

Additional data This program, which began in 1994, is sponsored by Procter & Gamble Company.

Number awarded 6 each year.

Deadline May of each year.

[462]
PROFESSIONAL STAFFING GROUP SCHOLARSHIP

Northeast Human Resources Association
Attn: Director of Professional Development
490 Virginia Road, Suite 32
Concord, MA 01742-2747
(781) 239-8718   Fax: (781) 237-8745
E-mail: nreiser@nehra.com
Web: www.nehra.com/?page=DIScholarshipApp

Summary   To provide financial assistance for college to high school seniors from the New England states who are Hispanics or have promoted diversity in other ways.

Eligibility   This program is open to seniors who are graduating from high schools in New England and planning to attend a college or university. Applicants should have exemplified living an inclusive life and promoting diversity through education. They must have a GPA of 3.0 or higher and be able to demonstrate financial need. Along with their application, they must submit a 750-word personal statement explaining what diversity means to them, how they promote diversity in their community or school, and how they propose to promote diversity in the future.

Financial Data   The stipend is $5,000.

Duration   1 year.

Additional data   The sponsor is an affiliate of the Society for Human Resource Management (SHRM). Its Diversity and Inclusion Committee focuses on veterans, the GLBT community, people with disabilities, gender equity, and race/ethnicity. The Professional Staffing Group established this program in 2004.

Number awarded   1 each year.

Deadline   February of each year.

[463]
PRSA DIVERSITY MULTICULTURAL SCHOLARSHIPS

Public Relations Student Society of America
Attn: Vice President of Member Services
33 Maiden Lane, 11th Floor
New York, NY 10038-5150
(212) 460-1474   Fax: (212) 995-0757
E-mail: prssa@prsa.org
Web: www.prssa.prsa.org

Summary   To provide financial assistance to Hispanic and other minority college students who are interested in preparing for a career in public relations.

Eligibility   This program is open to minority (Hispanic/Latino, African American/Black, Asian, Native American, Alaskan Native, or Pacific Islander) students who are at least juniors at an accredited 4-year college or university. Applicants must be enrolled full time, be able to demonstrate financial need, and have a GPA of 3.0 or higher. Membership in the Public Relations Student Society of America is preferred but not required. A major or minor in public relations is preferred; students who attend a school that does not offer a public relations degree or program must be enrolled in a communications degree program (e.g., journalism, mass communications).

Financial Data   The stipend is $1,500.

Duration   1 year.

Additional data   This program began in 1989.

Number awarded   2 each year.

Deadline   May of each year.

[464]
QUE LLUEVA CAFE SCHOLARSHIPS

Chicano Organizing & Research in Education
P.O. Box 160144
Sacramento, CA 95816
E-mail: information@ca-core.org
Web: www.ca-core.org

Summary   To provide financial assistance to undocumented Latino students who are interested in attending college.

Eligibility   This program is open to undocumented Latino students in the United States and Puerto Rico. Applicants must be high school or GED graduates planning to enroll for the first time at an accredited college or university in the United States or Puerto Rico. Along with their application, they must submit a 1,000-word personal statement that focuses on their financial need. Selection is based on that statement, academic promise, and extracurricular involvement.

Financial Data   The stipend ranges from $500 to $1,000.

Duration   1 year.

Additional data   This program began in 2009.

Number awarded   Varies each year; recently, 30 were awarded.

Deadline   February of each year.

[465]
RACE RELATIONS MULTIRACIAL STUDENT SCHOLARSHIP

Christian Reformed Church
Attn: Office of Race Relations
1700 28th Street, S.E.
Grand Rapids, MI 49508
(616) 224-5883   Toll Free: (877) 864-3977
Fax: (616) 224-0834   E-mail: elugo@crcna.org
Web: www.crcna.org/race/scholarships

Summary   To provide financial assistance to Hispanic and other minority undergraduate and graduate students interested in attending colleges related to the Christian Reformed Church in North America (CRCNA).

Eligibility   This program is open to students of color in the United States and Canada. Normally, applicants are expected to be members of CRCNA congregations who plan to pursue their educational goals at Calvin Theological Seminary or any of the colleges affiliated with the CRCNA. They must be interested in training for the ministry of racial reconciliation in church and/or in society. Along with their application, they must submit paragraphs about their personal history and family, Christian faith, and Christian leadership goals. Students who have no prior history with the CRCNA must attend a CRCNA-related college or seminary for a full academic year before they are eligible to apply for this program. Students entering their sophomore year must have earned a GPA of 2.0 or higher as freshmen; students entering their junior year must have earned a GPA of 2.3 or higher as sophomores; students entering their senior year must have earned a GPA of 2.6 or higher as juniors.

Financial Data First-year students receive $500 per semester. Other levels of students may receive up to $2,000 per academic year.

Duration 1 year.

Additional data This program was first established in 1971 and revised in 1991. Recipients are expected to train to engage actively in the ministry of racial reconciliation in church and in society. They must be able to work in the United States or Canada upon graduating and must consider working for 1 of the agencies of the CRCNA.

Number awarded Varies each year; recently, 31 students received a total of $21,000 in support.

Deadline March of each year.

[466]
RALPH BUNCHE SUMMER INSTITUTE

American Political Science Association
Attn: Diversity and Inclusion Programs
1527 New Hampshire Avenue, N.W.
Washington, DC 20036-1206
(202) 349-9362   Fax: (202) 483-2657
E-mail: kmealy@apsanet.org
Web: www.apsanet.org/rbsi

Summary To introduce Latino and other underrepresented minority undergraduate students to the world of graduate study and to encourage their eventual application to a Ph.D. program in political science.

Eligibility This program is open to Latino(a), African American, Native American, and Pacific Islander college students completing their junior year. Applicants must be interested in attending graduate school and working on a degree in a field related to political science. Along with their application, they must submit a 2-page personal statement on their reasons for wanting to participate in this program and their future academic and professional plans. U.S. citizenship is required.

Financial Data Participants receive a stipend of $200 per week plus full support of tuition, transportation, room, board, books, and instructional materials.

Duration 5 weeks during the summer.

Additional data The institute includes 2 transferable credit courses (1 in quantitative analysis and the other on race and American politics). In addition, guest lecturers and recruiters from Ph.D. programs visit the students. Classes are held on the campus of Duke University. Most students who attend the institute excel in their senior year and go on to graduate school, many with full graduate fellowships and teaching assistantships. This program is funded by the National Science Foundation.

Number awarded 20 each year.

Deadline January of each year.

[467]
RAUL YZAGUIRRE SCHOLARSHIP

Adelante
c/o Frito-Lay, Inc.
Attn: M. Ochoa-Dennis
7701 Legacy Drive
Mail drop 4A-197
Plano, TX 75024-4099

Summary To provide financial assistance for college to Hispanic students who have been activists for their community.

Eligibility This program is open to Hispanic students who are entering or enrolled at a 2- or 4-year college or university. Applicants must have an activist vision of equality that advances the inclusion and progress of the Hispanic community. They must have a GPA of 2.5 or higher. Along with their application, they must submit an essay of 1 to 2 pages that answers 1 of the following questions: what person or circumstance has most impacted their life, what legacy do they wish to leave behind, or what have they done to make a difference in their community.

Financial Data Stipends are $6,000, $3,000, or $1,000.

Duration 1 year.

Additional data The sponsoring organization is the Latino/Hispanic employee resource group of PepsiCo.

Number awarded 3 each year: 1 each at $6,000, $3,000, and $1,000.

Deadline May of each year.

[468]
RAY AND CARMELLA MELLADO SCHOLARSHIP

Great Minds in STEM
Attn: HENAAC Scholars Program
602 Monterey Pass Road
Monterey Park, CA 91754
(323) 262-0997   Fax: (323) 262-0946
E-mail: scholars@greatmindsinstem.org
Web: www.greatmindsinstem.org

Summary To provide financial assistance to Hispanic undergraduate and graduate students who are enrolled at a university in any state and working on a degree in a field of science, technology, engineering, or mathematics (STEM).

Eligibility This program is open to undergraduate and graduate students who are working on a degree in a field of STEM at colleges and universities in any state. Applicants must be of Hispanic origin and/or must significantly participate in and promote organizations and activities in the Hispanic community. They must have a GPA of 3.0 or higher. There is no citizenship requirement. Along with their application, they must submit a 700-word essay on a topic that changes annually. Selection is based on leadership, academic achievements, and campus and community activities; financial need is not considered.

Financial Data Stipends range from $500 to $10,000.

Duration 1 year; recipients may reapply.

Additional data The Hispanic Engineer National Achievement Awards Conference (HENAAC) was established in 1989 and initiated a scholarship program in 2000. In 2010, the sponsoring organization officially adopted its current name, but it continues to hold the annual HENAAC conference, at which the scholarships are presented. Recipients must attend the conference to accept their scholarship. The sponsor subsidizes the cost of travel, 3 nights of lodging, and meals.

Number awarded 4 each year: 2 to undergraduates and 2 to graduate students.

Deadline April of each year.

[469]
RDW GROUP, INC. MINORITY SCHOLARSHIP FOR COMMUNICATIONS

Rhode Island Foundation
Attn: Donor Services Administrator
One Union Station
Providence, RI 02903
(401) 427-4011   Fax: (401) 331-8085
E-mail: rbogert@rifoundation.org
Web: www.rifoundation.org

Summary   To provide financial assistance to Hispanic and other undergraduate and graduate students of color from Rhode Island who are interested in preparing for a career in communications at a school in any state.

Eligibility   This program is open to undergraduate and graduate students at colleges and universities in any state who are Rhode Island residents of color. Applicants must intend to work on a degree in communications (including computer graphics, art, cinematography, or other fields that would prepare them for a career in advertising). They must be able to demonstrate financial need and a commitment to a career in communications. Along with their application, they must submit an essay (up to 300 words) on the impact they would like to have on the communications field.

Financial Data   The stipend is approximately $2,000 per year.

Duration   1 year; recipients may reapply.

Additional data   This program is sponsored by the RDW Group, Inc.

Number awarded   1 each year.

Deadline   April of each year.

[470]
RENAE WASHINGTON-LORINE DUBOSE MEMORIAL SCHOLARSHIPS

Oklahoma CareerTech Foundation
Attn: Oklahoma Association of Minorities in Career and
  Technology Education
c/o Patti Pouncil, Scholarship Committee Chair
3 CT Circle
Drumright, OK 74030
918) 352-2551, ext. 285
Web: www.okcareertech.org

Summary   To provide financial assistance to Hispanic and other minority students enrolled at Oklahoma Career and Technology Education (CTE) centers.

Eligibility   This program is open to residents of Oklahoma who are members of an ethnic minority group (Hispanic, American Indian/Alaskan, Asian, African American, Native Hawaiian/Pacific Islander). Applicants must be enrolled full time at a CTE center in the state. Along with their application, they must submit a 100-word essay on why they have applied for this scholarship. Financial need is considered in the selection process.

Financial Data   The stipend is $1,000.

Duration   1 year.

Number awarded   2 each year.

Deadline   May of each year.

[471]
RENE MATOS SCHOLARSHIP

National Hispanic Coalition of Federal Aviation
  Employees
Attn: Scholarship Selection Committee
P.O. Box 23276
Washington, DC 20026-3276
E-mail: doe@nhcfae.org
Web: www.nhcfae.org/rene-matos-scholarship-program

Summary   To provide financial assistance to students of Hispanic descent who are working on an undergraduate or graduate degree.

Eligibility   This program is open to U.S. citizens and permanent residents of Hispanic descent who reside in the United States or Puerto Rico. Applicants must be accepted to or attending an accredited college, university, or vocational/trade school as an undergraduate or graduate student. Selection is based on academic achievement, community involvement, honors and awards, leadership, personal qualities and strengths, student activities, and financial need.

Financial Data   A stipend is awarded (amount not specified).

Duration   1 year; may be renewed.

Additional data   The National Hispanic Coalition of Federal Aviation Employees, established in 1978, is a nonprofit organization comprised mainly of Hispanics who are employed at the Federal Aviation Administration.

Number awarded   1 or more each year.

Deadline   April of each year.

[472]
RESEARCH AND ENGINEERING APPRENTICESHIP PROGRAM

Academy of Applied Science
Attn: REAP
24 Warren Street
Concord, NH 03301
(603) 228-4530   Fax: (603) 228-4730
E-mail: phampton@aas-world.org
Web: www.usaeop.com/programs/apprenticeships/reap

Summary   To provide an opportunity for high school students from Hispanic or other groups historically underrepresented in science, technology, engineering, or mathematics (STEM) to engage in a summer research apprenticeship.

Eligibility   This program is open to high school students who meet at least 2 of the following requirements: 1) qualifies for free or reduced lunch; 2) is a member of a group historically underrepresented in STEM, including Hispanics, Blacks/African Americans, Native Americans, Alaskan Natives, Native Hawaiians, or other Pacific Islanders; 3) is a woman in physical science, computer science, mathematics, or engineering; 4) receives special education services; 5) has a disability; 6) speaks English as a second language; or 7) has parents who did not attend college. Applicants must be interested in working as an apprentice on a research project in the laboratory of a mentor scientist at a college or university near their home. Selection is based on demonstrated interests in STEM research and demonstrated potential for a successful career in STEM. They must be at least 16 years of age.

Financial Data   The stipend is $1,300.

Duration   5 to 8 weeks during the summer.

Additional data The program provides intensive summer training for high school students in the laboratories of scientists. The program, established in 1980, is funded by a grant from the U.S. Army Educational Outreach Program. Students must live at home while they participate in the program and must live in the area of an approved college or university. The program does not exist in every state.

Number awarded Varies; recently, approximately 120 students were funded at more than 50 universities nationwide.

Deadline February of each year.

[473]
RESEARCH EXPERIENCES FOR UNDERGRADUATES PROGRAM IN SOLAR AND SPACE PHYSICS

University of Colorado
Attn: Laboratory for Atmospheric and Space Physics
1234 Innovation Drive
Boulder, CO 80303-7814
(303) 735-2143   E-mail: martin.snow@lasp.colorado.edu
Web: lasp.colorado.edu/home/education/reu

Summary To provide an opportunity for upper-division students, especially Hispanics and other underrepresented minorities, to work on research projects related to solar and space physics at laboratories in Boulder, Colorado during the summer.

Eligibility This program is open to students currently enrolled as sophomores and juniors at colleges and universities in any state. Applicants must be interested in participating on a research project related to solar and space physics at a participating laboratory in Boulder, Colorado. They must be U.S. citizens, nationals, or permanent residents. Applications are especially encouraged from underrepresented minorities, persons with disabilities, and women.

Financial Data The stipend is $500 per week. Students also receive dormitory housing, a food allowance, and a travel stipend of $500.

Duration 8 weeks, starting in June.

Additional data The participating laboratories are the Laboratory for Atmospheric and Space Physics (LASP) of the University of Colorado, the High Altitude Observatory (HAO) of the National Center for Atmospheric Research (NCAR), the Space Weather Prediction Center (SWPC) of the National Oceanic and Atmospheric Administration (NOAA), the Planetary Science Directorate of the Southwest Research Institute (SwRI), NorthWest Research Associates (NWRA), Atmospheric and Environmental Research (AER), or Atmospheric and Space Technology Research Associates (ASTRA). This program is funded by the National Science Foundation as part of its Research Experiences for Undergraduates (REU) Program.

Number awarded Varies each year; recently, 17 of these internships were awarded.

Deadline February of each year.

[474]
RESEARCH IN SCIENCE AND ENGINEERING PROGRAM

Rutgers University
Attn: Graduate School
25 Bishop Place
New Brunswick, NJ 08901-1181
(848) 932-6584   Fax: (732) 932-7407
E-mail: rise@rci.rutgers.edu
Web: rise.rutgers.edu/index.php

Summary To provide an opportunity for undergraduate students from any state, especially Hispanics and members of other underrepresented minorities, to work on a summer research project in science, mathematics, or engineering at Rutgers University in New Jersey.

Eligibility This program is open to undergraduates majoring in science (especially the biomedical sciences), mathematics, or engineering at a college or university in any state. Applicants must be interested in participating in a summer research project under the guidance of a faculty member at the graduate school of Rutgers University in New Brunswick. They should have completed at least the sophomore year and have a GPA of 3.0 or higher. Applications are especially encouraged from groups underrepresented in the sciences, math, or engineering; students from economically/educationally disadvantaged backgrounds; first generation to attend college; students attending predominantly undergraduate institutions that do not offer opportunities for independent, cutting-edge research; nontraditional students; and individuals who have faced life challenges. U.S. citizenship or permanent resident status is required.

Financial Data The program provides a stipend of up to $5,000, free housing, and up to $500 of reimbursement for travel expenses.

Duration 8 or 10 weeks during the summer.

Additional data This program is administered by the Rutgers University Graduate School. Support is provided by many sponsors, including the National Science Foundation, the Federation of American Societies for Experimental Biology, Merck Research Laboratories, Public Service Electric and Gas, the New Jersey Space Grant Consortium, the New Jersey Commission on Cancer Research, and the McNair Scholars Program.

Number awarded 20 to 25 each year.

Deadline Applications are accepted on a rolling basis; selection begins in January and continues until all places are filled.

[475]
RESOURCES FOR THE FUTURE SUMMER INTERNSHIPS

Resources for the Future
Attn: Internship Coordinator
1616 P Street, N.W., Suite 600
Washington, DC 20036-1400
(202) 328-5020   Fax: (202) 939-3460
E-mail: IC@rff.org
Web: www.rff.org

Summary To provide internships to undergraduate and graduate students, especially Hispanics and other minorities, who are interested in working on research projects in public policy during the summer.

Eligibility This program is open to undergraduate and graduate students (with priority to graduate students) interested in an internship at Resources for the Future (RFF). Applicants must be working on a degree in the social and natural sciences and have training in economics and quantitative methods or an interest in public policy. They should display strong writing skills and a desire to analyze complex environmental policy problems amenable to interdisciplinary methods. The ability to work without supervision in a careful and conscientious manner is essential. Women and minority candidates are strongly encouraged to apply. Both U.S. and non-U.S. citizens are eligible, if the latter have proper work and residency documentation.

Financial Data The stipend is $375 per week for graduate students or $350 per week for undergraduates. Housing assistance is not provided.

Duration 10 weeks during the summer; beginning and ending dates can be adjusted to meet particular student needs.

Number awarded Varies each year.

Deadline March of each year.

[476]
RHODE ISLAND LATINO DOLLARS SCHOLARSHIPS

Latino Dollars for Scholars of Rhode Island
P.O. Box 6764
Providence, RI 02940
(401) 495-5052   E-mail: ladori.dfs@gmail.com
Web: latino-rhodeisland.dollarsforscholars.org

Summary To provide financial assistance to Latino residents of Rhode Island who are interested in attending college in any state.

Eligibility This program is open to Latino residents (at least 1 parent must be of Latino descent) of Rhode Island who are enrolled or planning to enroll at a college or university in any state. Applicants must be able to demonstrate financial need. Selection is based on academic excellence and commitment to improving the community.

Financial Data A stipend is awarded (amount not specified).

Duration 1 year.

Additional data This program began in 1993.

Number awarded Varies each year; recently, 20 were awarded. Since the program was established, it has awarded more than $250,000 in scholarships.

Deadline March of each year.

[477]
RICHARD B. FISHER SCHOLARSHIP

Morgan Stanley
Attn: Diversity Recruiting
1585 Broadway
New York, NY 10036
(212) 762-0211   Toll Free: (888) 454-3965
Fax: (212) 507-4972
E-mail: richardbfisherprogram@morganstanley.com
Web: www.morganstanley.com

Summary To provide financial assistance and work experience to Hispanics and members of other underrepresented groups who are preparing for a career in technology within the financial services industry.

Eligibility This program is open to Hispanic, African American, Native American and lesbian/gay/bisexual/transgender students who are enrolled in their sophomore or junior year of college (or the third or fourth year of a 5-year program). Applicants must be enrolled full time and have a GPA of 3.4 or higher. They must be willing to commit to a paid summer internship in the Morgan Stanley Information Technology Division. All majors and disciplines are eligible, but preference is given to students preparing for a career in technology within the financial services industry. Along with their application, they must submit 1-page essays on 1) why they are applying for this scholarship and why they should be selected as a recipient; 2) a technical project on which they worked, either through a university course or previous work experience, their role in the project, and how they contributed to the end result; and 3) a software, hardware, or new innovative application of existing technology that they would create if they could and the impact it would have. Financial need is not considered in the selection process.

Financial Data The stipend is $7,500 per year.

Duration 1 year (the junior year); may be renewed for the senior year.

Additional data The program, established in 1993, includes a paid summer internship in the Morgan Stanley Information Technology Division in the summer following the time of application.

Number awarded 1 or more each year.

Deadline December of each year.

[478]
RICHARD GILDER GRADUATE SCHOOL REU BIOLOGY PROGRAM

American Museum of Natural History
Attn: Richard Gilder Graduate School
Central Park West at 79th Street
New York, NY 10024-5192
(212) 769-5055   E-mail: Fellowships-rggs@amnh.org
Web: www.amnh.org

Summary To provide an opportunity for undergraduate students, especially those at Hispanic Serving and other Minority Serving Institutions, to gain research experience in biology during the summer at the American Museum of Natural History in New York City.

Eligibility This program is open to U.S. citizens, nationals, and permanent residents who are currently working on an associate or bachelor's degree. Applicants must be interested in participating in a research project at the American Museum of Natural History under the mentorship of its curators, faculty, and postdoctoral fellows. Research projects involve diverse fields of comparative biology, including paleontology, genomics, population biology, conservation biology, phylogenetics, and taxonomy. Applications are especially encouraged from students who attend community colleges, undergraduate-only institutions, and minority-serving institutions.

Financial Data Participants receive a stipend of $5,000, per diem costs for housing and meals, relocation expenses, and transportation subsidies.

Duration 10 weeks during the summer.

Additional data This program is sponsored by the National Science Foundation as part of its Research Experiences for Undergraduates (REU) program.

Number awarded Approximately 8 each year.

Deadline February of each year.

[479]
RICHARD L. HOLMES COMMUNITY SERVICE AWARD

American Association of Blacks in Energy-Atlanta
  Chapter
Attn: Scholarship Committee
P.O. Box 55216
Atlanta, GA 30308-5216
(404) 506-6756
E-mail: G2AABEATCHAP@southernco.com
Web: www.aabe.org/atlanta

Summary To provide financial assistance to high school senior Hispanics and members of other underrepresented minority groups in Georgia who have demonstrated outstanding community service and are planning to major in an energy-related field at a college in any state.

Eligibility This program is open to seniors graduating from high schools in Georgia and planning to attend a college or university in any state. Applicants must be Hispanics, African Americans, or Native Americans who have a GPA of 3.0 or higher and who have taken the ACT and/or SAT test. They must be able to demonstrate exceptional responsibility to give back to their community and/or to help others. Their intended major must be business, engineering, technology, mathematics, the physical sciences, or other energy-related field. Along with their application, they must submit a 350-word essay that includes 1) when they discovered their interest in the field of energy and what sparked their interest; and 2) either what excites them about the field of energy or how they expect their education to prepare them for the field of energy. Financial need is not considered in the selection process.

Financial Data A stipend is awarded; amount not specified.

Duration 1 year.

Number awarded 1 each year.

Deadline March of each year.

[480]
RICHARD S. SMITH SCHOLARSHIP

United Methodist Church
Attn: General Board of Discipleship
Young People's Ministries
P.O. Box 340003
Nashville, TN 37203-0003
(615) 340-7184   Toll Free: (877) 899-2780, ext. 7184
Fax: (615) 340-7063
E-mail: youngpeople@umcdiscipleship.org
Web: www.umcyoungpeople.org/grants-scholarships

Summary To provide financial assistance to Hispanic and other minority high school seniors who wish to prepare for a Methodist church-related career.

Eligibility This program is open to graduating high school seniors who are members of racial/ethnic minority groups and have been active members of a United Methodist Church for at least 1 year. Applicants must have been admitted to an accredited college or university to prepare for a church-related career. They must have maintained at least a "C" average throughout high school and be able to demonstrate financial need. Along with their application, they must submit brief essays on their participation in church projects and activities, a leadership experience, the role their faith plays in their life, the church-related vocation to which God is calling them, and their extracurricular interests and activities. U.S. citizenship or permanent resident status is required.

Financial Data The stipend is $1,000.

Duration 1 year; nonrenewable.

Additional data This program began in 1997. Recipients must enroll full time in their first year of undergraduate study.

Number awarded 2 each year.

Deadline May of each year.

[481]
RIXIO MEDINA & ASSOCIATES HISPANICS IN SAFETY UNDERGRADUATE SCHOLARSHIP

American Society of Safety Engineers
Attn: ASSE Foundation
Scholarship Award Program
520 North Northwest Highway
Park Ridge, IL 60068-2538
(847) 699-2929   Fax: (847) 296-3769
E-mail: assefoundation@asse.org
Web: foundation.asse.org/scholarships-and-grants

Summary To provide financial assistance to Hispanic upper-division students working on a degree related to occupational safety.

Eligibility This program is open to students who are working on an undergraduate degree in occupational safety, health, environment, industrial hygiene, occupational health nursing, or a closely-related field (e.g., industrial or environmental engineering). Applicants must be bilingual (Spanish-English); Hispanic ethnicity is preferred. Students enrolled in an ASAC/ABET-accredited safety program also receive preference. They must be full-time students who have completed at least 60 semester hours and have a GPA of 3.0 or higher. U.S. citizenship is not required. Membership in the American Society of Safety Engineers (ASSE) is not required, but preference is given to members.

Financial Data The stipend is $4,000 per year.

Duration 1 year; recipients may reapply.

Additional data This program began in 2005.

Number awarded 1 each year.

Deadline November of each year.

[482]
ROBERT T. CHAPA SR. MEMORIAL SCHOLARSHIPS

Hispanic Scholarship Consortium
Attn: Scholarship Selection Committee
7703 North Lamar Boulevard, Suite 310
Austin, TX 78752
(512) 368-2956   Fax: (512) 692-1831
E-mail: scholarships@hispanicscholar.org
Web: hispanicscholar.academicworks.com

Summary To provide financial assistance to high school seniors of Hispanic heritage from Texas who plan to attend college in any state.

Eligibility This program is open to seniors graduating from high schools in Texas who are of Hispanic heritage and have a GPA of 3.0 or higher. Applicants must be planning to enroll full time at an accredited 2- or 4-year college or university in the United States. Selection is based on academic achievement, community service, personal strengths, leadership, and financial need. U.S. citizenship is not required; students may qualify under Texas Senate Bill 1528.

Financial Data The stipend is $2,000 per year.

Duration 1 year; may be renewed up to 3 additional years, provided the recipient remains enrolled full time, maintains a GPA of 3.0 or higher, and participates in at least 25 hours of community service per semester.

Additional data This program is sponsored by the Fiesta de Independencia Foundation.

Number awarded Varies each year; recently, 4 were awarded.

Deadline April of each year.

[483]
ROBERTA BANASZAK GLEITER—ENGINEERING ENDEAVOR SCHOLARSHIP

Society of Women Engineers
Attn: Scholarship Selection Committee
203 North LaSalle Street, Suite 1675
Chicago, IL 60601-1269
(312) 596-5223   Toll Free: (877) SWE-INFO
Fax: (312) 644-8557   E-mail: scholarships@swe.org
Web: societyofwomenengineers.swe.org

Summary To provide financial assistance to members of the Society of Women Engineers (SWE), especially Hispanics and members of other underrepresented groups, who will be entering their sophomore or junior year of a program in aeronautical or chemical engineering.

Eligibility This program is open to SWE members who are U.S. citizens entering their sophomore or junior year of full-time study at an ABET-accredited 4-year college or university. Applicants must be studying aeronautical or chemical engineering. Preference is given to members of underrepresented groups, reentry candidates, and students who can demonstrate financial need.

Financial Data The stipend is $1,250 per year.

Duration 1 year; may be renewed, provided the recipient continues to meet eligibility requirements.

Additional data This program began in 2013.

Number awarded 1 each year.

Deadline February of each year.

[484]
ROSA L. PARKS COLLEGE SCHOLARSHIP

Conference of Minority Transportation Officials
Attn: National Scholarship Program
100 M Street, S.E., Suite 917
Washington, DC 20003
(202) 506-2917   E-mail: info@comto.org
Web: www.comto.org/page/scholarships

Summary To provide financial assistance to Hispanic and other students who have a tie to the Conference of Minority Transportation Officials (COMTO) and are interested in working on an undergraduate or master's degree in transportation.

Eligibility This program is open to 1) undergraduates who have completed at least 60 semester credit hours in a transportation discipline; and 2) students working on a master's degree in transportation who have completed at least 15 credits. Applicants must be or have a parent, guardian, or grandparent who has been a COMTO member for at least 1 year. They must have a GPA of 3.0 or higher. Along with their application they must submit a cover letter on their transportation-related career goals and life aspirations. Financial need is not considered in the selection process.

Financial Data The stipend is $4,500. Funds are paid directly to the recipient's college or university.

Duration 1 year.

Number awarded 1 each year.

Deadline April of each year.

[485]
ROSA L. PARKS HIGH SCHOOL SCHOLARSHIP

Conference of Minority Transportation Officials
Attn: National Scholarship Program
100 M Street, S.E., Suite 917
Washington, DC 20003
(202) 506-2917   E-mail: info@comto.org
Web: www.comto.org/page/scholarships

Summary To provide financial assistance for college to Hispanic and other children and grandchildren of members of the Conference of Minority Transportation Officials (COMTO) who are interested in studying any field.

Eligibility This program is open to high school seniors who are members or whose parent, guardian, or grandparent has been a COMTO member for at least 1 year and who have been accepted at an accredited college, university, or vocational/technical institution. Applicants must have a GPA of 3.0 or higher. Along with their application they must submit a cover letter on their transportation-related career goals and life aspirations. Financial need is not considered in the selection process.

Financial Data The stipend is $4,500. Funds are paid directly to the recipient's college or university.

Duration 1 year.

Number awarded 1 each year.

Deadline April of each year.

[486]
ROYCE OSBORN MINORITY STUDENT SCHOLARSHIPS

American Society of Radiologic Technologists
Attn: ASRT Foundation
15000 Central Avenue, S.E.
Albuquerque, NM 87123-3909
(505) 298-4500, ext. 1392
Toll Free: (800) 444-2778, ext. 1392
Fax: (505) 298-5063   E-mail: foundation@asrt.org
Web: foundation.asrt.org/what-we-do/scholarships

Summary To provide financial assistance to Hispanic and other minority students enrolled in entry-level radiologic sciences programs.

Eligibility This program is open to Hispanics or Latinos, Blacks or African Americans, American Indians or Alaska Natives, Asians, and Native Hawaiians or other Pacific Islanders who are enrolled in an accredited entry-level program in radiography, sonography, magnetic resonance, or nuclear medicine. Applicants must be able to finish their degree or certificate in the year for which they are applying. They must be U.S. citizens, nationals, or permanent residents have a GPA of 3.0 or higher. Along with their application, they must submit 9 essays of 200 words each on assigned topics related to their personal situation and interest in a career in radiologic science. Selection is based on those essays, academic and professional achievements, recommendations, and financial need.

Financial Data The stipend is $4,000. Funds are paid directly to the recipient's institution.

Duration 1 year.

Number awarded 5 each year.

Deadline January of each year.

[487]
RUBINOS-MESIA SCHOLARSHIP

Structural Engineers Association of Illinois
Attn: Structural Engineers Foundation
134 North LaSalle Street, Suite 1910
Chicago, IL 60602
(312) 726-4165   Fax: (312) 277-1991
E-mail: eoconnor@seaol.org
Web: www.seaoi.org/sef.htm

Summary To provide financial assistance to upper-division and graduate students of Hispanic descent interested in a career in structural engineering.

Eligibility This program is open to students of Hispanic descent who are 1) entering their third or higher year of an undergraduate program; or 2) entering or continuing a graduate program. Applicants must be enrolled in a civil or architectural engineering program and planning to continue with a structural engineering specialization. Students enrolled in structural engineering technology programs are also eligible if they are qualified to take the Fundamentals of Engineering and Principles and Practice licensure examinations in their home state upon graduation. U.S. citizenship or permanent resident status is required. Students enrolled in military academies or ROTC programs are not eligible. Selection is based on a statement giving reasons why the applicant should receive the award (including plans for continued formal education), academic performance, and potential for development and leadership. Financial need is not considered.

Financial Data The stipend is $2,000.

Duration 1 year; nonrenewable.

Number awarded 1 each year.

Deadline April of each year.

[488]
RUDY AND MICAELA CAMACHO SCHOLARSHIP

Baptist General Convention of Texas
Attn: Office of Hispanic Ministries
7557 Rambler Road, Suite 1200
Dallas, TX 75231-2388
(214) 887-5425   Toll Free: (888) 244-9400
Fax: (214) 828-5261
E-mail: rolando.rodriguez@texasbaptists.org
Web: www.texasbaptists.org

Summary To provide financial assistance for college to Hispanic residents of Texas who are members of Texas Baptist congregations.

Eligibility This program is open to residents of Texas who are enrolled or planning to enroll at a 4-year college or university in the state. Applicants must be Christians and members of a Hispanic Baptist church that contributes to the Cooperative Program through the Baptist General Convention of Texas.

Financial Data The stipend is $1,000 per year.

Duration 1 year; may be renewed up to 3 additional years.

Number awarded 1 or 2 each year.

Deadline April of each year.

[489]
RUTH WEBB MINORITY SCHOLARSHIP

California Academy of Physician Assistants
2318 South Fairview Street
Santa Ana, CA 92704-4938
(714) 427-0321   Fax: (714) 427-0324
E-mail: capa@capanet.org
Web: www.capanet.org

Summary To provide financial assistance to Hispanic and other minority student members of the California Academy of Physician Assistants (CAPA) enrolled in physician assistant programs in California.

Eligibility This program is open to student members of CAPA enrolled in primary care physician assistant programs in California. Applicants must be members of a minority group (Hispanic, African American, Asian/Pacific Islander, or Native American/Alaskan Native). They must have maintained good academic standing and conducted activities to promote the physician assistant profession. Along with their application, they must submit an essay describing the activities they have performed to promote the physician assistant profession, the importance of representing minorities in their community, and why they should be awarded this scholarship. Financial need is considered in the selection process.

Financial Data The stipend is $2,000.

Duration 1 year.

Number awarded 1 each year.

Deadline December of each year.

[490]
SADCO SCHOLARSHIP PROGRAM

Sociedad Amigos de Colombia
Attn: Scholarship Selection Committee
P.O. Box 1141
Carmel, IN 46082
(317) 767-7927   E-mail: information@sadco.org
Web: www.sadco.org/sadco-scholarship-program

Summary To provide financial assistance to Hispanic residents of Indiana who are attending or planning to attend college in any state.

Eligibility This program is open to high school seniors and college freshmen, sophomores, and juniors who are Indiana residents and Hispanics of first, second, or third generation. Applicants must be attending or planning to attend an accredited college or university in any state to work on an associate or bachelor's degree. Achievement awards are available to students who have a GPA of 3.6 or higher and a record of positive leadership ability, community service, and demonstrated responsibility. Need awards are available to students who have a GPA of 3.0 or higher and are able to demonstrate financial need or verifiable, unique, unusual, or mitigating circumstances.

Financial Data   Stipends vary but recently were $2,000 for awards based on need or $1,000 for awards based on achievement.

Duration   1 year.

Additional data   Sponsors of this program include Lumina Foundation for Education, Dow AgroSciences, Cummins, USA Funds, and Key Bank.

Number awarded   Varies each year; recently, 20 were awarded.

Deadline   April of each year.

[491]
SANDISK SCHOLARS PROGRAM

SanDisk Foundation
951 SanDisk Drive
Milpitas, CA 97034-7933
(408) 801-1240   Fax: (408) 801-8657
E-mail: Mike.wong@sandisk.com
Web: www.sandisk.com

Summary   To provide financial assistance to Hispanic and other high school seniors and lower-division college students who are interested in studying computer science or engineering in college.

Eligibility   This program is open to U.S. citizens and legal residents who are high school seniors or college freshmen or sophomores enrolled or planning to enroll full time at a 4-year college or university in the United States, Puerto Rico, the U.S. Virgin Islands, or Guam. Applicants must be interested in majoring in computer science or engineering and have a GPA of 3.0 or higher. Selection is based on academic excellence, demonstrated leadership in extracurricular and/or community activities, a personal statement, and financial need. Some scholarships are reserved for dependents of SanDisk employees, participants in the Center for Talented Youth at Johns Hopkins University, Hispanic students, and African American students.

Financial Data   The stipend is $2,500 per year.

Duration   1 year; may be renewed up to 3 additional years.

Additional data   This program, which began in 2012, is offered in partnership with the United Negro College Fund (UNCF), the Silicon Valley Community Foundation (SVCF), and International Scholarship and Tuition Services (ISTS).

Number awarded   40 each year, including 8 awarded to the general public, 3 to dependents of SanDisk employees, 2 to participants or alumni of the Center for Talented Youth at Johns Hopkins University, 13 to Hispanic students through the Silicon Valley Community Foundation, and 14 to African American students through the United Negro College Fund.

Deadline   March of each year.

[492]
SAO REU SUMMER INTERN PROGRAM

Harvard-Smithsonian Center for Astrophysics
Attn: Summer Intern Program
60 Garden Street, Mail Stop 70
Cambridge, MA 02138
(617) 496-7063   E-mail: intern@cfa.harvard.edu
Web: www.cfa.harvard.edu/opportunities/reu//REU.html

Summary   To enable undergraduates, especially Hispanics and other underrepresented minorities, who are interested in a physical science career or science education to obtain summer research experience at the Smithsonian Astrophysical Observatory (SAO) at Harvard University.

Eligibility   This program is open to U.S. citizens, nationals, and permanent residents enrolled in a program leading to a bachelor's degree. Applicants must be interested in a career in astronomy, astrophysics, physics, or related physical sciences. Along with their application, they must submit an essay of 600 to 800 words describing academic and career goals, scientific interests, relevant work experience, why they would like to be in the program, and why they would be a good candidate. Graduating seniors are not eligible. Applications are especially encouraged from underrepresented minorities, persons with disabilities, and women.

Financial Data   The stipend is $5,000. Housing and travel expenses are provided.

Duration   10 weeks during the summer.

Additional data   Each intern works with a scientist on an individual research project. Potential areas of research include observational and theoretical cosmology, extragalactic and galactic astronomy, interstellar medium and star formation, laboratory astrophysics, supernovae and supernova remnants, planetary science, and solar and stellar astrophysics. Also included in the program are weekly lectures, field trips, and workshops specifically designed for the participants. This program is supported by the National Science Foundation as part of its Research Experiences for Undergraduates (REU) Program.

Number awarded   10 each year.

Deadline   January of each year.

[493]
SCHOLARSHIPS FOR RACIAL JUSTICE

Higher Education Consortium for Urban Affairs
Attn: Student Services
2233 University Avenue West, Suite 210
St. Paul, MN 55114-1698
(651) 287-3300   Toll Free: (800) 554-1089
Fax: (651) 659-9421   E-mail: hecua@hecua.org
Web: www.hecua.org

Summary   To provide financial assistance to Hispanics and other students of color who are enrolled in programs of the Higher Education Consortium for Urban Affairs (HECUA) at participating colleges and universities and are committed to undoing institutionalized racism.

Eligibility   This program is open to students at member colleges and universities who are participating in HECUA programs. Applicants must be a student of color who can demonstrate a commitment to undoing institutionalized racism. Along with their application, they must submit a reflective essay of 550 to 1,700 words on the personal, social, or political influences in their lifetime that have motivated them to work on racial justice issues.

Financial Data The stipend is $4,000.

Duration 1 semester.

Additional data This program began in 2012. Consortium members include Augsburg College (Minneapolis, Minnesota), Augustana College (Sioux Falls, South Dakota), Carleton College (Northfield, Minnesota), College of Saint Scholastica (Duluth, Minnesota), Colorado College (Colorado Springs, Colorado), Denison University (Granville, Ohio), Gustavus Adolphus College (St. Peter, Minnesota), Hamline University (St. Paul, Minnesota), Macalester College (St. Paul, Minnesota), Northland College (Ashland, Wisconsin), Saint Mary's University (Winona, Minnesota), Saint Catherine University (St. Paul, Minnesota), Saint Olaf College (Northfield, Minnesota), Swarthmore College (Swarthmore, Pennsylvania), University of Minnesota (Twin Cities, Duluth, Morris, Crookston, Rochester), and University of Saint Thomas (St. Paul, Minnesota).

Number awarded Several each year.

Deadline April of each year for summer and fall programs; November of each year for January and spring programs.

[494]
SCHOLARSHIPS FOR SOCIAL JUSTICE

Higher Education Consortium for Urban Affairs
Attn: Student Services
2233 University Avenue West, Suite 210
St. Paul, MN 55114-1698
(651) 287-3300   Toll Free: (800) 554-1089
Fax: (651) 659-9421   E-mail: hecua@hecua.org
Web: www.hecua.org

Summary To provide financial assistance to Hispanics and students from other targeted groups who are enrolled in programs of the Higher Education Consortium for Urban Affairs (HECUA) at participating colleges and universities.

Eligibility This program is open to students at member colleges and universities who are participating in HECUA programs. Applicants must be a first-generation college student, from a low-income family, and/or a student of color. Along with their application, they must submit a reflective essay of 500 to 1,700 words, drawing on their life experiences and their personal and academic goals, on what they believe they can contribute to the mission of HECUA to equip students with the knowledge, experiences, tools, and passion to address issues of social justice and social change. The essay should also explain how the HECUA program will benefit them and the people, issues, and communities they care about.

Financial Data The stipend is $1,500. Funds are applied as a credit to the student's HECUA program fees for the semester.

Duration 1 semester.

Additional data This program began in 2006. Consortium members include Augsburg College (Minneapolis, Minnesota), Augustana College (Sioux Falls, South Dakota), Carleton College (Northfield, Minnesota), College of Saint Scholastica (Duluth, Minnesota), Colorado College (Colorado Springs, Colorado), Denison University (Granville, Ohio), Gustavus Adolphus College (St. Peter, Minnesota), Hamline University (St. Paul, Minnesota), Macalester College (St. Paul, Minnesota), Northland College (Ashland, Wisconsin), Saint Mary's University (Winona, Minnesota), Saint Catherine

University (St. Paul, Minnesota), Saint Olaf College (Northfield, Minnesota), Swarthmore College (Swarthmore, Pennsylvania), University of Minnesota (Twin Cities, Duluth, Morris, Crookston, Rochester), and University of Saint Thomas (St. Paul, Minnesota).

Number awarded Several each year.

Deadline April of each year for summer and fall programs; November of each year for January and spring programs.

[495]
SCIENCE AND ENGINEERING APPRENTICE PROGRAM

American Society for Engineering Education
Attn: Army SEAP Help-Desk
1818 N Street, N.W., Suite 600
Washington, DC 20036-2479
Toll Free: (855) 592-3556   E-mail: armyseap@asee.org
Web: www.usaeop.com/programs/apprenticeships/seap

Summary To provide an opportunity for high school students (especially Hispanics, African Americans, and women) to work during the summer on research projects at selected Department of Defense laboratories.

Eligibility This program is open to high school students interested in careers in science and engineering. A goal of the program is to encourage Hispanics, African Americans, and women to expand their interest in science and engineering careers. Applicants must submit a 1-page statement on their personal goals and why they want to participate in a research project at a Department of Defense laboratory, 1 or 2 letters of recommendation, and a transcript. Most laboratories require U.S. citizenship, although some accept permanent residents. In a few laboratories, security clearance is required. Selection is based on grades, science and mathematics courses taken, scores on national standardized tests, areas of interest, teacher recommendations, and the personal statement.

Financial Data The stipend is $2,000. Students are responsible for transportation to and from the laboratory site.

Duration 8 weeks during the summer.

Additional data This program was previously administered by George Washington University. Funding is provided by the U.S. Department of Defense. Participating laboratories include the Army Engineer Research and Development Center, Geospatial Research Laboratory (Alexandria, Virginia); Army Center for Environmental Health Medicine (Fort Detrick, Maryland); Army Medical Research Institute of Chemical Defense (Aberdeen Proving Ground, Maryland); Army Research Institute of Infectious Diseases (Fort Detrick, Maryland); Army Medical Research and Materiel Command, Walter Reed Army Institute of Research (Silver Spring, Maryland); Army Research Laboratory (Aberdeen Proving Ground, Maryland and Adelphi, Maryland); Army Aviation and Missile Research, Development and Engineering Center (Redstone Arsenal, Alabama); Army Engineer Research and Development Center, Construction Engineering Research Laboratory (Champaign, Illinois); Night Vision and Electronic Sensors Directorate (Fort Belvoir, Virginia); and Army Engineer Research and Development Center (Vicksburg, Mississippi).

Number awarded Varies each year.

Deadline February of each year.

[496]
SCIENCE AND ENGINEERING PROGRAMS FOR WOMEN AND MINORITIES AT BROOKHAVEN NATIONAL LABORATORY

Brookhaven National Laboratory
Attn: Diversity Office, Human Resources Division
Building 400B
P.O. Box 5000
Upton, New York 11973-5000
(631) 344-2703   Fax: (631) 344-5305
E-mail: palmore@bnl.gov
Web: www.bnl.gov/diversity/programs.asp

Summary   To provide on-the-job training in scientific areas at Brookhaven National Laboratory (BNL) during the summer to Hispanics and other underrepresented minority students.

Eligibility   This program at BNL is open to women and underrepresented minority (Hispanic, African American/Black, Native American, or Pacific Islander) students who have completed their freshman, sophomore, or junior year of college. Applicants must be U.S. citizens or permanent residents, at least 18 years of age, and majoring in applied mathematics, biology, chemistry, computer science, engineering, high and low energy particle accelerators, nuclear medicine, physics, or scientific writing. Since no transportation or housing allowance is provided, preference is given to students who reside in the BNL area.

Financial Data   Participants receive a competitive stipend.

Duration   10 to 12 weeks during the summer.

Additional data   Students work with members of the scientific, technical, and professional staff of BNL in an educational training program developed to give research experience.

Number awarded   Varies each year.

Deadline   April of each year.

[497]
SC-PAAE SCHOLARSHIPS

South Carolina Professional Association for Access and
    Equity
Attn: Financial Secretary
P.O. Box 71297
North Charleston, SC 29415
(843) 670-4890   E-mail: anderson4569@bellsouth.net
Web: www.scpaae.org/#!scholarships/c11tv

Summary   To provide financial assistance to undergraduate students at colleges and universities in South Carolina who are recognized as underrepresented minorities on their campus.

Eligibility   This program is open to residents of any state who have completed at least 12 semester hours at a college or university in South Carolina. Applicants must be recognized as an underrepresented ethnic minority on their campus. They must have a GPA of 2.75 or higher. Along with their application, they must submit 1) a personal letter on their academic and career goals, honors and awards, leadership skills and organization participation, community service, and a statement of why they would like to receive this scholarship; and 2) a paragraph defining access and equity and describing how they can assist in achieving access and equity within South Carolina. Financial need is not considered in the selection process.

Financial Data   Stipends are $750 for students at 2-year institutions or $1,000 for students at 4-year institutions.

Duration   1 year.

Number awarded   Varies each year.

Deadline   February of each year.

[498]
SEA MAR FARM WORKER SCHOLARSHIP

Sea Mar Community Health Centers
Attn: Scholarship Committee
113 23rd Avenue South
Seattle, WA 98144
(206) 965-1057   E-mail: scholarships@seamarchc.org
Web: www.seamar.org

Summary   To provide financial assistance to residents of Washington who are the children of farm workers and interested in attending college in any state.

Eligibility   This program is open to residents of Washington who are high school seniors or current undergraduates at a college or university in any state. Applicants must work or have worked or have parents who work or have worked as a farm worker. Eligibility includes HB 1079 (undocumented) students because they are considered Washington residents.

Financial Data   The stipend is $1,000.

Duration   1 year; nonrenewable.

Number awarded   Approximately 100 each year.

Deadline   March of each year.

[499]
SEATTLE CHAPTER AWIS SCHOLARSHIPS

Association for Women in Science-Seattle Chapter
c/o Fran Solomon, Scholarship Committee Chair
5805 16th Avenue, N.E.
Seattle, WA 98105
(206) 522-6441   E-mail: scholarship@seattleawis.org
Web: www.seattleawis.org/award/scholarships

Summary   To provide financial assistance to women undergraduates from any state, especially Hispanics and other minorities, who are majoring in science, mathematics, or engineering at colleges and universities in Washington.

Eligibility   This program is open to women from any state entering their junior or senior year at a 4-year college or university in Washington. Applicants must have a declared major in science (e.g., biological sciences, environmental science, biochemistry, chemistry, pharmacy, geology, computer science, physics), mathematics, or engineering. Along with their application, they must submit essays on the events that led to their choice of a major, their current career plans and long-term goals, and their volunteer and community activities. Selection is based on academic excellence, motivation to prepare for a science-based career, record of giving back to their communities, and financial need. At least 1 scholarship is reserved for a woman from a group that is underrepresented in science, mathematics, and engineering careers, including Mexican Americans/Chicanas/Latinas, Native American Indians and Alaska Natives, Black/African Americans, Native Pacific Islanders (Polynesians, Melanesians, and Micronesians), adult learners (returning students), and women with disabilities.

Financial Data   Stipends range from $1,000 to $5,000.

Duration   1 year.

Additional data This program includes the following named awards: the Virginia Badger Scholarship, the Angela Paez Memorial Scholarship, and the Fran Solomon Scholarship. Support for the program is provided by several sponsors, including the American Chemical Society, Iota Sigma Pi, Rosetta Inpharmatics, and ZymoGenetics, Inc.

Number awarded Varies each year; recently 2 at $5,000, 1 at $1,500, and 1 at $1,000 were awarded.

Deadline March of each year.

[500]
SENATOR GREGORY LUNA LEGISLATIVE SCHOLARS AND FELLOWS PROGRAM

Senate Hispanic Research Council, Inc.
Attn: Executive Director
1001 Congress Avenue, Suite 100
Austin, TX 78701
(512) 499-8606   Fax: (512) 499-8607
E-mail: sarah@tshrc.org
Web: www.tshrc.org/luna-scholars-fellows-program

Summary To provide Hispanic undergraduate and graduate students at colleges and universities in Texas with an opportunity to gain work experience at the Texas Senate.

Eligibility This program is open to undergraduate and graduate students who have completed at least 60 semester hours at an accredited 2- or 4-year educational institution in Texas; recent graduates are also eligible. Applicants must demonstrate academic achievement; leadership qualities; potential for further growth; exceptional writing, comprehension, and analytical skills; and an interest in government and public policy through active participation in community service activities. Along with their application, they must submit a personal statement on the experiences or activities that led to their interest in government and this internship program, a sample of their writing of a policy analysis on an issue affecting the state of Texas, and 2 letters of recommendation.

Financial Data Interns receive a stipend of $2,000 per month to help cover the expense of living and working in Austin.

Duration Approximately 5 months, during the term of the Texas Senate, beginning in mid-January of odd-numbered years.

Additional data This program began in 2001. Interns are assigned to the office of a state senator to perform a variety of legislative tasks, including drafting legislation, floor statements, articles, press releases, legislative research summaries, and hearing agendas. The Senate Hispanic Research Council was established in 1993 to provide educational and leadership opportunities to all segments of the Hispanic community in Texas.

Number awarded Up to 16 each odd-numbered year.

Deadline November of each even-numbered year.

[501]
SEO UNDERGRADUATE CAREER PROGRAM

Sponsors for Educational Opportunity
Attn: Career Program
55 Exchange Place
New York, NY 10005
(212) 979-2040   Toll Free: (800) 462-2332
Fax: (646) 706-7113
E-mail: careerprogram@seo-usa.org
Web: www.seocareer.org

Summary To provide Hispanic and other undergraduate students of color with an opportunity to gain summer work experience in selected fields.

Eligibility This program is open to students of color at colleges and universities in the United States. Applicants must be interested in a summer internship in 1 of the following fields: asset management, consulting, engineering, finance and accounting, human resources, investment banking, investment research, marketing and sales, nonprofit sector, private equity, sales and trading, technology with banks, technology with global companies, or transaction services. Freshmen are not eligible. Sophomores are eligible for asset management, finance and accounting, investment banking, sales and trading, technology with banks, and transaction services. Juniors are eligible for all fields. Seniors and current graduate students are not eligible. All applicants must have a cumulative GPA of 3.0 or higher. Personal interviews are required.

Financial Data Interns receive a competitive stipend of up to $1,300 per week.

Duration 10 weeks during the summer.

Additional data This program began in 1980. Corporate leadership internships are in the New York metro area, New Jersey, Connecticut, Iowa, Massachusetts, North Carolina, Ohio, California, and other areas; banking and private equity internships are in New York City with limited opportunities in New Jersey, Connecticut and possibly Miami or Houston; nonprofit internships are in New York City.

Number awarded Approximately 300 to 400 each year.

Deadline December of each year for sales and trading; January of each year for asset management, consulting, investment banking, investment research, nonprofit sector, private equity, and transaction services; February of each year for engineering, finance and accounting, human resources, marketing and sales, and technology.

[502]
SHARON D. BANKS MEMORIAL UNDERGRADUATE SCHOLARSHIP

Women's Transportation Seminar
Attn: WTS Foundation
1701 K Street, N.W., Suite 800
Washington, DC 20006
(202) 955-5085   Fax: (202) 955-5088
E-mail: wts@wtsinternational.org
Web: www.wtsinternational.org/education/scholarships

Summary To provide financial assistance to undergraduate women, especially Hispanics and other minorities, who are interested in a career in transportation.

Eligibility This program is open to women who are working on an undergraduate degree in transportation or a transportation-related field (e.g., transportation engineering, planning, finance, or logistics). Applicants must have a GPA of 3.0 or higher and be interested in a career in transportation. Along with their application, they must submit a 500-word statement about their career goals after graduation and why they think they should receive the scholarship award. Applications must be submitted first to a local chapter; the chapters forward selected applications for consideration on the national level. Minority women are especially encouraged to apply. Selection is based on transportation involvement and goals, job skills, and academic record; financial need is not considered.

Financial Data   The stipend is $5,000.

Duration   1 year.

Additional data   This program began in 1992. Local chapters may also award additional funding to winners in their area.

Number awarded   1 each year.

Deadline   Applications must be submitted by November to a local WTS chapter.

[503]
SHELL INCENTIVE FUND SCHOLARSHIPS FOR HIGH SCHOOL SENIORS

Shell Oil Company
Attn: Scholarship Administrator
910 Louisiana, Suite 4476C
Houston, TX 77002
(713) 718-6379
E-mail: SI-Shell-US-Recruitment-Scholarships@shell.
   com
Web: www.shell.us

Summary   To provide financial assistance to Hispanic and other minority high school seniors planning to major in specified engineering and geosciences fields in college.

Eligibility   This program is open to graduating high school seniors who are members of underrepresented minority groups (Hispanic/Latino, Black, American Indian, Alaskan Native) and planning to enroll full time at 22 participating universities. Applicants must be planning to major in engineering (chemical, civil, electrical, geological, geophysical, mechanical, or petroleum) or geosciences (geology, geophysics, or physics). They must be U.S. citizens or authorized to work in the United States. Along with their application, they must submit a 100-word essay on the kind of work they plan to be doing in 10 years, both in their career and in their community; they should comment specifically on how they could potentially contribute to the petrochemical industry. Financial need is not considered in the selection process.

Financial Data   The stipend is $2,500.

Duration   1 year; nonrenewable, although recipients may apply for a Shell Incentive Fund Scholarship for Undergraduate Students to cover the remaining years of their undergraduate program.

Additional data   This program is managed by International Scholarship and Tuition Services, Inc. The participating institutions are Colorado School of Mines, Cornell University, Florida A&M University, Georgia Institute of Technology, Louisiana State University, Massachusetts Institute of Technology, Michigan State University, North Carolina A&T State University, Ohio State University, Pennsylvania State University, Prairie View A&M University, Purdue University, Rice University, Stanford University, Texas A&M University, University of Colorado at Boulder, University of Houston, University of Illi-

nois at Urbana-Champaign, University of Michigan, University of Oklahoma, University of Texas at Austin, and University of Texas at El Paso.

Number awarded   Up to 20 each year.

Deadline   February of each year.

[504]
SHELL INCENTIVE FUND SCHOLARSHIPS FOR UNDERGRADUATE STUDENTS

Shell Oil Company
Attn: Scholarship Administrator
910 Louisiana, Suite 4476C
Houston, TX 77002
(713) 718-6379
E-mail: SI-Shell-US-Recruitment-Scholarships@shell.
   com
Web: www.shell.us

Summary   To provide financial assistance to Hispanic and other underrepresented minority students majoring in specified engineering and geosciences fields at designated universities.

Eligibility   This program is open to students enrolled full time as sophomores, juniors, or seniors at 22 participating universities. Applicants must be U.S. citizens or authorized to work in the United States and members of a race or ethnicity underrepresented in the technical and scientific academic areas (Hispanic/Latino, Black, American Indian, or Alaskan Native). They must have a GPA of 3.2 or higher with a major in engineering (chemical, civil, electrical, geological, geophysical, mechanical, or petroleum) or geosciences (geology, geophysics, or physics). Along with their application, they must submit a 100-word essay on the kind of work they plan to be doing in 10 years, both in their career and in their community. Financial need is not considered in the selection process.

Financial Data   The stipend is $5,000 per year.

Duration   1 year; may be renewed up to 3 additional years, provided the recipient remains qualified and accepts a Shell Oil Company internship (if offered).

Additional data   This program is managed by International Scholarship and Tuition Services Inc. The participating institutions are Colorado School of Mines, Cornell University, Florida A&M University, Georgia Institute of Technology, Louisiana State University, Massachusetts Institute of Technology, Michigan State University, North Carolina A&T State University, Ohio State University, Pennsylvania State University, Prairie View A&M University, Purdue University, Rice University, Stanford University, Texas A&M University, University of Colorado at Boulder, University of Houston, University of Illinois at Urbana-Champaign, University of Michigan, University of Oklahoma, University of Texas at Austin, and University of Texas at El Paso.

Number awarded   Up to 20 each year.

Deadline   January of each year.

[505]
SHPE AUSTIN SCHOLARSHIP

Austin Community Foundation
4315 Guadalupe Street, Suite 300
Austin, TX 78751
(512) 472-4483   Fax: (512) 472-4486
E-mail: info@austincf.org
Web: www.austincf.academicworks.com/opportunities/216

Summary   To provide financial assistance for students of Hispanic heritage who are studying a field of science, technology, engineering, or mathematics (STEM) at a university in the Austin area of Texas.

Eligibility   This program is open to students of Hispanic heritage who reside in any state. Applicants must be enrolled full time at a 4-year college or university in the Austin area (Hays, Travis, or Williamson counties) area of Texas. They must be working on a degree in a field of STEM and have a GPA of 2.5 or higher. Along with their application, they must submit a 100-word essay about themselves, including their community involvement and all prior and current work experience. Preference is given to members of the Society of Hispanic Professional Engineers (SHPE).

Financial Data   The stipend is $1,000.

Duration   1 year.

Additional data   This program is sponsored by the Austin Chapter of SHPE.

Number awarded   1 each year.

Deadline   March of each year.

[506]
SHPE CHEVRON SCHOLARSHIP

Society of Hispanic Professional Engineers
Attn: Scholarships
13181 Crossroads Parkway North, Suite 450
City of Industry, CA 91715
(323) 725-3970, ext. 108   Fax: (323) 725-0316
E-mail: scholarships@shpe.org
Web: shpe.awardspring.com

Summary   To provide financial assistance to Hispanic undergraduate students who are majoring in designated fields of engineering at selected universities.

Eligibility   This program is open to Hispanic students who are enrolled full time in an undergraduate engineering program at the University of California at Davis, the University of Houston, the University of Puerto Rico at Mayaguez, the University of Southern California, or the University of Texas at Austin. First priority is given to sophomores and second to juniors. Applicants must be U.S. citizens or permanent residents and have a GPA of at least 3.0. They must be members of a professional society or engaged in an extracurricular activity. Preference is given to students majoring in the following rank order mechanical engineering, chemical engineering, electrical engineering, civil engineering, and computer science. Selection is based on academic standing, leadership potential, and financial need.

Financial Data   The stipend is $5,000.

Duration   1 year.

Additional data   This program is sponsored by Chevron.

Number awarded   1 or more each year.

Deadline   July of each year.

[507]
SHPE GRADUATING HIGH SCHOOL SENIOR SCHOLARSHIP

Society of Hispanic Professional Engineers
Attn: Scholarships
13181 Crossroads Parkway North, Suite 450
City of Industry, CA 91715
(323) 725-3970, ext. 108   Fax: (323) 725-0316
E-mail: scholarships@shpe.org
Web: shpe.awardspring.com

Summary   To provide financial assistance to graduating high school seniors of Hispanic descent who are planning to prepare for a career in science, technology, engineering, mathematics (STEM), or a related field in college.

Eligibility   This program is open to graduating high school seniors of Hispanic descent who are planning to attend an accredited 2- or 4-year college or university in the United States or Puerto Rico and are junior members of the Society of Hispanic Professional Engineers (SHPE). Applicants must intend to work full time on an undergraduate degree in a STEM or related field. They must have a GPA of 2.75 or higher and be able to demonstrate financial need. Along with their application, they must submit a 500-word personal statement covering their community involvement, leadership, academic achievements, research internship and co-op experiences, and short-term and long-term goals and aspirations.

Financial Data   The stipend is $1,000.

Duration   1 year.

Number awarded   1 or more each year.

Deadline   July of each year.

[508]
SHPE NORTHROP GRUMMAN SCHOLARSHIP

Society of Hispanic Professional Engineers
Attn: Scholarships
13181 Crossroads Parkway North, Suite 450
City of Industry, CA 91715
(323) 725-3970, ext. 108   Fax: (323) 725-0316
E-mail: scholarships@shpe.org
Web: shpe.awardspring.com

Summary   To provide financial assistance to Hispanic undergraduate students who are majoring in designated fields of engineering.

Eligibility   This program is open to U.S. citizens of Hispanic descent who are enrolled full time at a college or university in the United States or Puerto Rico. Applicants must be majoring in computer science or computer, electrical, software, or systems engineering. They must have a GPA of 3.0 or higher. Selection is based on academic standing and financial need.

Financial Data   A stipend is awarded (amount not specified).

Duration   1 year.

Additional data   This program is sponsored by Northrop Grumman.

Number awarded   1 or more each year.

Deadline   July of each year.

[509]
SHPE UNDERGRADUATE SCHOLARSHIP

Society of Hispanic Professional Engineers
Attn: Scholarships
13181 Crossroads Parkway North, Suite 450
City of Industry, CA 91715
(323) 725-3970, ext. 108   Fax: (323) 725-0316
E-mail: scholarships@shpe.org
Web: shpe.awardspring.com

Summary To provide financial assistance to undergraduate students of Hispanic descent who are preparing for a career in science, technology, engineering, mathematics (STEM), or a related field.

Eligibility This program is open to students of Hispanic descent who are attending an accredited 2- or 4-year college or university in the United States or Puerto Rico and are members of the Society of Hispanic Professional Engineers (SHPE). Applicants must be working full time on an undergraduate degree in a STEM or related field. They must have a GPA of 2.75 or higher and be able to demonstrate financial need. Along with their application, they must submit a 500-word personal statement covering their community involvement, leadership, academic achievements, research internship and co-op experiences, and short-term and long-term goals and aspirations.

Financial Data The stipend is $2,000.

Duration 1 year.

Number awarded 1 or more each year.

Deadline July of each year.

[510]
SHPE-TC SCHOLARSHIPS

Society of Hispanic Professional Engineers-Twin Cities
   Chapter
Attn: Education Chair
P.O. Box 6196
Minneapolis, MN 55406-0196
(612) 618-7807   E-mail: education@shpetwincities.org
Web: www.shpetwincities.org/scholarships.html

Summary To provide financial assistance to Hispanic students who have a tie to Minnesota and are interested in working on a degree in a field of science, technology, engineering, or mathematics (STEM).

Eligibility This program is open to Hispanic or Latino students who reside or attend a college, university, or community college in Minnesota. Applicants must be working on or planning to work on a degree in a field of STEM and have a GPA of 3.0 or higher. Along with their application, they must submit a personal statement and documentation of financial need.

Financial Data The stipend is at least $1,000.

Duration 1 year.

Additional data Corporate sponsors of this program include Hormel, Medtronic, 3M, Xcel Energy, and Mortenson.

Number awarded Varies each year; recently, 8 were awarded.

Deadline Deadline not specified.

[511]
SIGNIFICANT OPPORTUNITIES IN ATMOSPHERIC RESEARCH AND SCIENCE (SOARS) PROGRAM

University Corporation for Atmospheric Research
Attn: SOARS Program Manager
3090 Center Green Drive
P.O. Box 3000
Boulder, CO 80307-3000
(303) 497-8622   Fax: (303) 497-8629
E-mail: soars@ucar.edu
Web: www.soars.ucar.edu

Summary To provide summer work experience to undergraduate or graduate students, especially Hispanics and members of other underrepresented groups, who are interested in preparing for a career in atmospheric or a related science.

Eligibility This program is open to U.S. citizens or permanent residents who have completed their sophomore year of college and are majoring in atmospheric science or a related field (e.g., biology, chemistry, computer science, earth science, engineering, environmental science, the geosciences, mathematics, meteorology, oceanography, physics, or social science). Applicants must have a GPA of 3.0 or higher and be planning to prepare for a career in the field of atmospheric or a related science. The program especially encourages applications from members of groups that are historically underrepresented in the atmospheric and related sciences, including Blacks/African Americans, Hispanics/Latinos, American Indians/Alaskan Natives, women, first-generation college students, and students with disabilities. It also welcomes applications from students who are gay, lesbian, bisexual, or transgender; have experienced, and worked to overcome, educational or economic disadvantage; or have personal or family circumstances that may complicate their continued progress in research careers.

Financial Data Participants receive a competitive stipend and a housing allowance. Round-trip travel between Boulder and any 1 location within the continental United States is also provided. Students who are accepted into a graduate program receive full scholarships (with SOARS and the participating universities each sharing the costs).

Duration 10 weeks during the summer. Students are encouraged to continue for 4 subsequent summers.

Additional data This program began in 1996. Students are assigned positions with a research project. They are exposed to the research facilities at the National Center for Atmospheric Research (NCAR), including computers, libraries, laboratories, and aircraft. NCAR is operated by the University Corporation for Atmospheric Research (a consortium of more than 100 North American universities) with primary support from the National Science Foundation (NSF); other sponsors include the Department of Energy, the Department of Defense, the National Aeronautics and Space Administration (NASA), the Environmental Protection Agency (EPA), the Federal Aviation Administration (FAA), and the National Oceanic and Atmospheric Administration (NOAA). Before completing their senior years, students are encouraged to apply to a master's or doctoral degree program at 1 of the participating universities.

Number awarded Varies each year; recently, 17 were awarded.

Deadline January of each year.

[512]
SINCLAIR BROADCAST DIVERSITY SCHOLARSHIP

Sinclair Broadcast Group, Inc.
10706 Beaver Dam Road
Hunt Valley, MD 21030
(410) 568-1500 E-mail: scholarshipquestions@sbgtv.com
Web: www.sbgi.net/scholarship

Summary To provide financial assistance to college students who are Hispanics or members of other underrepresented minority groups and working on a degree in broadcasting, journalism, or marketing.

Eligibility This program is open to students currently enrolled as sophomores or juniors at a 4-year college or university in any state. Applicants must be members of an underrepresented minority group (Hispanic/Latino, Asian/Pacific Islander, African American/Black, or Native American/Alaskan) and taking classes in broadcasting, journalism, or media marketing (although they are not required to be majoring in those fields). They must have a GPA of 3.0 or higher and be able to demonstrate a genuine interest in broadcasting and broadcast journalism. Along with their application, they must submit 1) a 300-word cover letter that explains their personal background, career goals, and financial need; 2) work samples; and 3) a 500-word essay on either the role of journalism in a democracy or why they want a career in broadcasting. In the selection process, consideration is given to academic achievement and work experience, but scholarships are presented only to students who can demonstrate financial need.

Financial Data The stipend is $5,000.

Duration 1 year.

Additional data This program began in 2016.

Number awarded Up to 10 each year.

Deadline March of each year.

[513]
SMITHSONIAN LATINO CENTER YOUNG AMBASSADORS PROGRAM

Smithsonian Latino Center
Attn: Young Ambassadors Program
600 Maryland Avenue, S.W., Suite 7042
MRC 512
P.O. Box 37012
Washington, DC 20013-7012
(202) 633-1240   Fax: (202) 633-1132
E-mail: SLCEducation@si.edu
Web: www.latino.si.edu/Education/YAP

Summary To provide high school seniors with an opportunity to participate in a summer arts, sciences, and humanities internship program affiliated with the Smithsonian Latino Center.

Eligibility This program is open to graduating high school seniors who are interested in learning more about the arts (e.g., film, visual, performing, design), the sciences (e.g., natural, biological, chemical, planetary), or the humanities (e.g., language, literature, social sciences, business) at those pertain to Latino communities and cultures. Applicants must

have a GPA of 3.25 or higher and be U.S. citizens or permanent residents (DACA students are eligible if they have proof of DACA status, a valid work authorization permit, and a valid Social Security number), fluent in English, and accepted for full-time enrollment at a 2- or 4-year college or university in the following fall. They must be interested in spending a week during the summer at the Smithsonian Latino Center in Washington, D.C. for a training seminar and then participating in an internship at their choice of 26 museums, galleries, or other cultural institutions in 17 cities in the United States and Puerto Rico. If they complete the internship, they receive a stipend for tuition in the following fall. Selection is based on excellence in the arts, sciences, or humanities; academic record; leadership experience; commitment to education; and service learning and engagement with the Latino community.

Financial Data For the training seminar, interns receive round-trip travel costs to Washington, D.C. and a program stipend. They are responsible for all expenses during the internship, including transportation, accommodations, and meals; students are advised to select an internship at a site where they can live with family or friends. The stipend for college study is $2,000.

Duration 1 week for the seminar (the first week of July) followed by 4 weeks for the internship.

Additional data This program, which began in 2006, is supported by the Ford Motor Company Fund. For a list of the available internships, contact the sponsor.

Number awarded Up to 24 each year.

Deadline April of each year.

[514]
SMITHSONIAN MINORITY AWARDS PROGRAM

Smithsonian Institution
Attn: Office of Fellowships and Internships
470 L'Enfant Plaza, Suite 7102
P.O. Box 37012, MRC 902
Washington, DC 20013-7012
(202) 633-7070   Fax: (202) 633-7069
E-mail: siofi@si.edu
Web: www.smithsonianofi.com

Summary To provide funding to Hispanic and other minority undergraduate and graduate students interested in conducting research at the Smithsonian Institution.

Eligibility This program is open to members of U.S. minority groups underrepresented in the Smithsonian's scholarly programs. Applicants must be undergraduates or beginning graduate students interested in conducting research in the Institution's disciplines and in the museum field. They must be U.S. citizens or permanent residents and have a GPA of 3.0 or higher.

Financial Data Students receive a grant of $600 per week.

Duration Up to 10 weeks.

Additional data Recipients must carry out independent research projects in association with the Smithsonian's research staff. Eligible fields of study currently include animal behavior, ecology, and environmental science (including an emphasis on the tropics); anthropology (including archaeology); astrophysics and astronomy; earth sciences and paleobiology; evolutionary and systematic biology; history of science and technology; history of art (especially American, contemporary, African, Asian, and 20th-century art); American crafts and decorative arts; social and cultural history of the United States; and folklife. Students are required to be in residence at the Smithsonian for the duration of the fellowship.

Number awarded Varies each year; recently, 25 were granted: 2 for fall, 19 for summer, and 4 for spring.

Deadline January of each year for summer and fall residency; September of each year for spring residency.

[515]
SOMOS SCHOLARSHIPS

Somos Foundation
c/o Utah Hispanic Chamber of Commerce
1635 South, Redwood Road
Salt Lake City, UT 84104
(801) 532-3308   Fax: (801) 532-3309
E-mail: gala@utahhcc.com
Web: somosfoundationutah.org/hispanic-scholarships

Summary To provide financial assistance to Hispanic residents of Utah who are interested in attending college in the state.

Eligibility This program is open to residents of Utah who are of Hispanic/Latino descent. Applicants must be enrolled as a senior in high school or a student at a college, university, or vocational school in the state. They must be able to demonstrate academic and vocational achievement, financial need, and leadership in school, community, and/or other service organizations that promote, enhance, or strengthen diversity.

Financial Data Stipends vary; recently, they averaged approximately $4,500.

Duration 1 year.

Number awarded Varies each year; recently, approximately 400 were awarded.

Deadline September of each year.

[516]
SPANISH BAPTIST CONVENTION OF NEW MEXICO SCHOLARSHIP

Baptist Convention of New Mexico
Attn: Missions Mobilization Team
5325 Wyoming Boulevard, N.E.
P.O. Box 94485
Albuquerque, NM 87199-4485
(505) 924-2315   Toll Free: (800) 898-8544
Fax: (505) 924-2320   E-mail: cpairett@bcnm.com
Web: www.bcnm.com/scholarships

Summary To provide financial assistance to Hispanic Baptist students from New Mexico interested in attending college or seminary in any state.

Eligibility This program is open to college and seminary students who are active members of churches affiliated with the Baptist Convention of New Mexico. Applicants must be of Hispanic background and committed to full-time Christian service. They must be attending college or seminary in any state.

Financial Data A stipend is awarded (amount not specified).

Duration 1 year; may be renewed.

Number awarded 1 or more each year.

Deadline April of each year.

[517]
SPHINX COMPETITION AWARDS

Sphinx Organization
Attn: Screening Committee
400 Renaissance Center, Suite 2550
Detroit, MI 48243
(313) 877-9100   Fax: (313) 877-0164
E-mail: Competition@sphinxmusic.org
Web: www.sphinxmusic.org/sphinx-competition

Summary To recognize and reward outstanding junior high, high school, and college-age Latino and Black string instrumentalists.

Eligibility This competition is open to Latino and Black instrumentalists in 2 divisions: junior, for participants who are 17 years of age or younger, and senior, for participants who are between 18 and 30 years of age. All entrants must be current U.S. residents who can compete in the instrumental categories of violin, viola, cello, and double bass. Along with their applications, they must submit a preliminary audition tape that includes all of the required preliminary repertoire for their instrument category. Based on those tapes, qualifiers are invited to participate in the semifinals and finals competitions, held at sites in Detroit and Ann Arbor, Michigan.

Financial Data In the senior division, the first-place winner receives the Robert Frederick Smith Prize of $50,000, solo appearances with major orchestras, and a performance with the Sphinx Symphony; the second-place winner receives a $20,000 cash prize and a performance with the Sphinx Symphony; and the third-place winner receives a $10,000 cash prize and a performance with the Sphinx Symphony. In the junior division, the first-place winner receives a $10,000 cash prize, solo appearances with major orchestras, a national radio debut, and performances with the Sphinx Symphony; the second-place winner receives a $5,000 cash prize and a performance with the Sphinx Symphony; the third-place winner receives a $3,000 cash prize and a performance with the Sphinx Symphony. All semifinalists receive scholarships to attend designated summer programs. They also receive full tuition scholarships for their instrumental studies at selected colleges and universities from the Sphinx Music Assistance Fund (MAF) of the League of American Orchestras.

Duration The competition is held annually.

Additional data The sponsoring organization was incorporated in 1996 to hold this competition, first conducted in 1998. The Sphinx Symphony is an all African American and Latino orchestra that performs at Orchestra Hall in Detroit. The MAF program was established by the New York Philharmonic in 1965, transferred to the American Symphony Orchestra League in 1994, and to the League of American Orchestras in 2001. In 2002, it partnered with the Sphinx Organization to provide scholarships to all 18 semifinalists. Applications must be accompanied by a $35 fee. That fee may be waived from both divisions and all instrumental categories if demonstrable need is shown.

Number awarded 18 semifinalists (9 from each age division) are selected each year. Of those, 3 junior and 3 senior competitors win cash prizes.

Deadline November of each year.

[518]
SSRP-AMGEN SCHOLARS PROGRAM

Stanford University
School of Medicine
Attn: Office of Graduate Education
MSOB X1C20
1265 Welch Road
Stanford, CA 94305-5421
(650) 725-8791 Fax: (650) 725-3867
E-mail: ssrpmail@stanford.edu
Web: biosciences.stanford.edu/prospective/diversity/ssrp

Summary To provide Hispanic and other underrepresented minority undergraduate students with a summer research experience at Stanford University in biological and biomedical sciences.

Eligibility This program is open to sophomores, juniors, and non-graduating seniors at 4-year colleges and universities in the United States, Puerto Rico, and U.S. territories. Students from all ethnic backgrounds are eligible, but the program especially encourages applications from Latino/Hispanic Americans, African Americans, Native Americans, Pacific Islanders, and other undergraduates who, by reason of their culture, class, race, ethnicity, background, work and life experiences, skills, and interests would bring diversity to graduate study in the biological and biomedical sciences (biochemistry, bioengineering, biology, biomedical informatics, biophysics, cancer biology, chemical and systems biology, developmental biology, genetics, immunology, microbiology, molecular and cellular physiology, neurosciences, stem cell and regenerative medicine, and structural biology). Applicants must have at least 1 year of undergraduate education remaining before graduation and should be planning to prepare for and enter a Ph.D. program in the biological or biomedical sciences. They must have a GPA of 3.2 or higher. U.S. citizenship or permanent resident status is required.

Financial Data The program provides a stipend of $3,500, housing, meals, and transportation to and from the San Francisco Bay area.

Duration 9 weeks during the summer.

Additional data This program encompasses 1) the Stanford component of the Amgen Scholars Program, which operates at 8 other U.S. universities (and the National Institutes of Health) and is funded by the Amgen Foundation; 2) Genetics Department Funding; and 3) Stanford Medicine Dean's Funding.

Number awarded 30 to 35 each year.

Deadline January of each year.

[519]
STATE COUNCIL ON ADAPTED PHYSICAL EDUCATION CULTURAL DIVERSITY STUDENT SCHOLARSHIP

California Association for Health, Physical Education, Recreation and Dance
Attn: State Council on Adapted Physical Education
1501 El Camino Avenue, Suite 3
Sacramento, CA 95815-2748
(916) 922-3596 Toll Free: (800) 499-3596 (within CA)
Fax: (916) 922-0133
E-mail: califstatecouncilape@gmail.com
Web: www.califstatecouncilape.org

Summary To provide financial assistance to Hispanics and other culturally diverse members of the California Association for Health, Physical Education, Recreation and Dance (CAHPERD) who are preparing to become a student teacher in the field of adapted physical education.

Eligibility This program is open to CAHPERD members who are attending a California college or university and specializing in the field of adapted physical education. Applicants must be members of an ethnic or cultural minority group (e.g., Mexican American, other Latino, African American, American Indian/Native American, Asian American, Filipino, Pacific Islander). They must be planning to become a student teacher during the following academic year. Along with their application, they must submit a 300-word statement of their professional goals and philosophy of physical education for individuals with disabilities. Selection is based on academic proficiency; leadership ability; personal qualities; school, community, and professional activities; and experience and interest in working with individuals with disabilities.

Financial Data The stipend is $1,000.

Duration 1 year.

Number awarded 1 each year.

Deadline January of each year.

[520]
STATE REPRESENTATIVE IRMA RANGEL MEMORIAL SCHOLARSHIPS

Hispanic Scholarship Consortium
Attn: Scholarship Selection Committee
7703 North Lamar Boulevard, Suite 310
Austin, TX 78752
(512) 368-2956 Fax: (512) 692-1831
E-mail: scholarships@hispanicscholar.org
Web: hispanicscholar.academicworks.com

Summary To provide financial assistance to Hispanic residents of Texas who are pre-law students at universities in designated counties.

Eligibility This program is open to residents of Texas who are of Hispanic heritage and enrolled full time at a 4-year college or university in Hays, Travis, or Williamson counties. Applicants must be rising juniors or seniors and planning to take the LSAT examination in the current or following academic year. They must have a GPA of 3.0 or higher. Along with their application, they must submit a 500-word essay on why they would like to become an attorney. Selection is based on academic achievement, community service, personal strengths, leadership, and financial need. U.S. citizenship is not required; students may qualify under Texas Senate Bill 1528.

Financial Data A stipend is awarded (amount not specified).

Duration 1 year.

Additional data This program is sponsored by the Hispanic Bar Association of Austin College Fund.

Number awarded Varies each year; recently, 9 were awarded.

Deadline April of each year.

[521]
STEPS TO SUCCESS-THE DOUG PAUL SCHOLARSHIP PROGRAM

Credit Suisse
Attn: Diversity and Inclusion Programs
Eleven Madison Avenue
New York, NY 10010-3629
(212) 325-2000   Fax: (212) 325-6665
E-mail: campus.diversity@credit-suisse.com
Web: www.credit-suisse.com

Summary To provide financial assistance and work experience at Credit Suisse in New York to Hispanic and other underrepresented minority undergraduate students interested in a career in financial services.

Eligibility This program is open to college students entering their junior year who are Hispanic/Latino, Black/African American, or Native American. Applicants must be preparing for a career in financial services by studying such fields as asset management, equity research, finance, investment banking, information technology, operations, and sales and trading. They must be interested in an internship in New York with Credit Suisse. Selection is based on academic excellence, leadership ability, and interest in the financial services industry.

Financial Data Students who complete the summer internship receive a stipend of $5,000 for the following year of academic study.

Duration The internship is 10 weeks during the summer, followed by a year of academic study (the junior year) and a possible renewal of the internship the following summer.

Number awarded 1 or more each year.

Deadline June of each year.

[522]
STUDENT OPPORTUNITY SCHOLARSHIPS OF THE PRESBYTERIAN CHURCH (USA)

Presbyterian Church (USA)
Attn: Office of Financial Aid for Service
100 Witherspoon Street
Louisville, KY 40202-1396
(502) 569-5224   Toll Free: (888) 728-7228, ext. 5224
Fax: (502) 569-8766   TDD: (800) 833-5955
E-mail: finaid@pcusa.org
Web: www.presbyterianmission.org

Summary To provide financial assistance to Presbyterian college students, especially Hispanics and those of other racial/ethnic minority heritage.

Eligibility This program is open to active members of the Presbyterian Church (USA) who are entering their sophomore, junior, or senior year of college as full-time students in a bachelor's degree program. Preference is given to applicants who are members of racial/ethnic minority groups (Hispanic American, Asian American, African American, Native American, Alaska Native). Applicants must have a GPA of 2.5 or higher and be able to demonstrate financial need.

Financial Data Stipends range up to $2,000 per year, depending upon the financial need of the recipient.

Duration 1 year; may be renewed if the recipient continues to need financial assistance and demonstrates satisfactory academic progress.

Number awarded Approximately 80 each year.

Deadline May of each year.

[523]
SUMMER CLINICAL AND TRANSLATIONAL RESEARCH PROGRAM

Harvard Medical School
Office for Diversity Inclusion and Community Partnership
Attn: Program for Faculty Development and Diversity Inclusion
164 Longwood Avenue, Second Floor
Boston, MA 02115-5810
(617) 432-1892   Fax: (617) 432-3834
E-mail: pfdd_dcp@hms.harvard.edu
Web: mfdp.med.harvard.edu

Summary To provide an opportunity for undergraduate students, especially Hispanics and other underrepresented minorities, to engage in research at Harvard Medical School during the summer.

Eligibility This program is open to undergraduate sophomores, juniors, and seniors who are preparing for a career in medical research. Priority is given to students at schools that receive funding from the Minority Biomedical Research Support (MBRS) or Minority Access to Research Careers (MARC) programs of the National Institute of Health (NIH), Hispanic Serving Institutions (HSIs), Historically Black Colleges and Universities (HBCUs), or Tribal Colleges and Universities (TCUs). Applicants must be interested in working on a summer research program at Harvard Medical School under the mentorship of a faculty advisor. They must be interested in a research and health-related career, especially in clinical or translational research or research that transforms scientific discoveries arising from laboratory, clinical, or population studies into clinical or population-based applications to improve health. U.S. citizenship, nationality, or permanent resident status is required.

Financial Data Participants receive a stipend (amount not specified), housing, and reimbursement of transportation costs to Boston up to $400.

Duration 10 weeks during the summer.

Additional data This program, established in 2008, is funded by the National Center for Research Resources of the NIH. It is a joint enterprise of Harvard University, its 10 schools, its 17 Academic Healthcare Centers, Boston College School of Nursing, MIT, the Cambridge Health Alliance, and other community partners. Interns attend weekly seminars with Harvard faculty focusing on such topics as research methodology, health disparities, ethics, and career paths. They also have the opportunity to participate in offerings of other Harvard Medical School programs, such a career development seminars and networking dinners.

Number awarded Varies each year; recently, 10 college students were admitted to this program.

Deadline December of each year.

[524]
SUMMER HONORS UNDERGRADUATE RESEARCH PROGRAM

Harvard Medical School
Attn: Division of Medical Sciences
Diversity Programs Office
260 Longwood Avenue, T-MEC 335
Boston, MA 02115-5720
(617) 432-4980   Toll Free: (800) 367-9019
Fax: (617) 432-2644   E-mail: shurp@hms.harvard.edu
Web: www.hms.harvard.edu/dms/diversity/shurp

Summary   To provide an opportunity for Hispanic and other underrepresented minority students to engage in research at Harvard Medical School during the summer.

Eligibility   This program at Harvard Medical School is open to undergraduate students belonging to minority groups that are underrepresented in the sciences. Applicants must have had at least 1 summer (or equivalent) of experience in a research laboratory and have taken at least 1 upper-level biology course that includes molecular biology. They should be considering a career in biological or biomedical research. U.S. citizenship or permanent resident status is required.

Financial Data   The program provides a stipend of $450 per week, dormitory housing, travel costs, a meal card, and health insurance if it is needed.

Duration   10 weeks during the summer.

Number awarded   Varies each year.

Deadline   January of each year.

[525]
SUMMER PROGRAM IN BIOSTATISTICS AND COMPUTATIONAL BIOLOGY

Harvard T.H. Chan School of Public Health
Department of Biostatistics
Attn: Diversity Coordinator
677 Huntington Avenue, SPH2, Fourth Floor
Boston, MA 02115
(617) 432-3175   Fax: (617) 432-5619
E-mail: biostat_diversity@hsph.harvard.edu
Web: www.hsph.harvard.edu

Summary   To enable Hispanic and other underrepresented minority or disadvantaged science undergraduates to participate in a summer research internship at Harvard T.H. Chan School of Public Health that focuses on biostatistics, epidemiology, and public health.

Eligibility   This program is open to 1) members of ethnic groups underrepresented in graduate education (African Americans, Hispanic/Latinos, Native Americans, Pacific Islanders, biracial/multiracial); 2) first-generation college students; 3) low-income students; or 4) individuals with a disability. Applicants must be current undergraduates interested in participating in a summer program on the use of quantitative methods for biological, environmental, and medical research as preparation for graduate studies in biostatistics or computational biology. They must have a strong GPA, including course work in calculus, and a strong interest in mathematics, statistics, computer science, and other quantitative subjects. U.S. citizenship or permanent resident status is required.

Financial Data   Funding covers travel, housing, course materials, and a stipend to cover meals and incidentals.

Duration   6 weeks, starting in June.

Additional data   Interns take non-credit classes in biostatistics and epidemiology, participate in a collaborative research project, and travel to local laboratories and research centers to observe public health research in action.

Number awarded   Normally 12 each year.

Deadline   January of each year.

[526]
SUMMER PROGRAM IN EPIDEMIOLOGY

Harvard T.H. Chan School of Public Health
Department of Epidemiology
655 Huntington Avenue
Boston, MA 02115
(617) 432-1050   Fax: (617) 566-7805
E-mail: edigiova@hsph.harvard.edu
Web: www.hsph.harvard.edu

Summary   To enable Hispanic and other underrepresented minority or disadvantaged undergraduates to participate in a summer research program in epidemiology at Harvard T.H. Chan School of Public Health.

Eligibility   This program is open to undergraduate students who 1) are U.S. citizens, nationals, or permanent residents; 2) have a GPA of 3.0 or higher; 3) have a quantitative science background or have taken several quantitative classes beyond introductory level courses; 4) can demonstrate an interest in public health; and 5) are from at least 1 underrepresented group in biomedical research, including people with disabilities, members of minority racial and ethnic groups (African Americans, Hispanic/Latinos, Native Americans, Pacific Islanders), people of disadvantaged and low socioeconomic status, members of families with annual income below established thresholds, and people from a rural, inner-city, or other environment that has inhibited them from getting the knowledge, skills, and abilities needed for a research career. They must be planning to apply to a graduate program to work on a master's or doctoral degree in epidemiology; students planning to apply to medical school and students already accepted to graduate school are not eligible.

Financial Data   Interns receive a salary (amount not specified) and support for travel.

Duration   5 weeks, during the summer.

Additional data   The program includes introductory course work in epidemiology and biostatistics, formal lectures by faculty at the Harvard T.H. Chan School of Public Health, a group research project, and a Kaplan GRE course.

Number awarded   Varies each year; recently, 8 were awarded.

Deadline   February of each year.

[527]
SUMMER RESEARCH OPPORTUNITIES PROGRAM (SROP)

Committee on Institutional Cooperation
Attn: Academic and International Programs
1819 South Neil Street, Suite D
Champaign, IL 61820-7271
(217) 333-8475   Fax: (217) 244-7127
E-mail: cic@staff.cic.net
Web: www.cic.net/students/srop/introduction

Summary   To provide an opportunity for Hispanics and other undergraduates from diverse backgrounds to gain research experience at member institutions of the Committee on Institutional Cooperation (CIC) during the summer.

Eligibility This program is open to students currently enrolled in a degree-granting program at a college or university who have a GPA of 3.0 or higher and an interest in continuing on to graduate school. Applicants must be interested in conducting a summer research project under the supervision of a faculty mentor at a CIC member institution. The program is designed to increase educational access for students from diverse backgrounds; members of racial and ethnic minority groups and low-income first-generation students are especially encouraged to apply. U.S. citizenship or permanent resident status is required.

Financial Data Participants are paid a stipend that depends on the participating CIC member institution, but ranges from $3,000 to $6,000. Faculty mentors receive a $500 research allowance for the cost of materials.

Duration 8 to 10 weeks during the summer.

Additional data Participants work directly with faculty mentors at the institution of their choice and engage in other enrichment activities, such as workshops and social gatherings. In July, all participants come together at 1 of the CIC campuses for the annual SROP conference. The participating CIC member institutions are University of Illinois at Urbana-Champaign, University of Iowa, University of Michigan, University of Minnesota, University of Nebraska at Lincoln, University of Wisconsin at Madison, Michigan State University, Northwestern University, Ohio State University, Pennsylvania State University, Purdue University, and Rutgers University. Students are required to write a paper and an abstract describing their projects and to present the results of their work at a campus symposium.

Number awarded Varies each year.

Deadline February of each year.

[528]
SUMMER RESEARCH PROGRAM IN ECOLOGY

Harvard University
Harvard Forest
324 North Main Street
Petersham, MA 01366
(978) 724-3302   Fax: (978) 724-3595
E-mail: hfapps@fas.harvard.edu
Web: harvardforest.fas.harvard.edu/other-tags/reu

Summary To provide an opportunity for undergraduate students and recent graduates, especially Hispanics and members of other diverse groups, to participate in a summer ecological research project at Harvard Forest in Petersham, Massachusetts.

Eligibility This program is open to undergraduate students and recent graduates interested in participating in a mentored research project at the Forest. The research may relate to the effects of natural and human disturbances on forest ecosystems, including global climate change, hurricanes, forest harvest, changing wildlife dynamics, or invasive species. Investigators come from many disciplines, and specific projects center on population and community ecology, paleoecology, land use history, aquatic ecology, biochemistry, soil science, ecophysiology, and atmosphere-biosphere exchanges. Students from diverse backgrounds are strongly encouraged to apply.

Financial Data The stipend is $5,775. Free housing, meals, and travel reimbursement for 1 round trip are also provided.

Duration 11 weeks during the summer.

Additional data Funding for this program is provided by the National Science Foundation (as part of its Research Experience for Undergraduates program).

Number awarded Up to 25 each year.

Deadline February of each year.

[529]
SUMMER TRANSPORTATION INTERNSHIP PROGRAM FOR DIVERSE GROUPS

Department of Transportation
Attn: Summer Transportation Internship Program for
  Diverse Groups
Eighth Floor E81-105
1200 New Jersey Avenue, S.E.
Washington, DC 20590
(202) 366-2907   E-mail: Crystal.Taylor@dot.gov
Web: www.fhwa.dot.gov/education/stipdg.cfm

Summary To enable Hispanic and other undergraduate, graduate, and law students from diverse groups to gain work experience during the summer at facilities of the U.S. Department of Transportation (DOT).

Eligibility This program is open to all qualified applicants, but it is designed to provide women, persons with disabilities, and members of diverse social and ethnic groups with summer opportunities in transportation. Applicants must be U.S. citizens currently enrolled in a degree-granting program of study at an accredited institution of higher learning at the undergraduate (community or junior college, university, college, or Tribal College or University) or graduate level. Undergraduates must be entering their junior or senior year; students attending a Tribal or community college must have completed their first year of school; law students must be entering their second or third year of school. Students who will graduate during the spring or summer are not eligible unless they have been accepted for enrollment in graduate school. The program accepts applications from students in all majors who are interested in working on transportation-related topics and issues. Preference is given to students with a GPA of 3.0 or higher. Undergraduates must submit a 1-page essay on their transportation interests and how participation in this program will enhance their educational and career plans and goals. Graduate students must submit a writing sample representing their educational and career plans and goals. Law students must submit a legal writing sample.

Financial Data The stipend is $4,000 for undergraduates or $5,000 for graduate and law students. The program also provides housing and reimbursement of travel expenses from interns' homes to their assignment location.

Duration 10 weeks during the summer.

Additional data Assignments are at the DOT headquarters in Washington, D.C., a selected modal administration, or selected field offices around the country.

Number awarded 80 to 100 each year.

Deadline January of each year.

[530]
SUMMER UNDERGRADUATE RESEARCH FELLOW (SURF) INDIVIDUAL AWARDS

American Society for Pharmacology and Experimental
Therapeutics
9650 Rockville Pike
Bethesda, MD 20814-3995
(301) 634-7060   Fax: (301) 634-7061
E-mail: cfry@aspet.org
Web: www.aspet.org/awards/SURF

Summary To provide funding to undergraduate students, especially Hispanics and other underrepresented minorities, who are interested in participating in a summer research project at a laboratory affiliated with the American Society for Pharmacology and Experimental Therapeutics (ASPET).

Eligibility This program is open to undergraduate students interested in working during the summer in the laboratory of a society member who must agree to act as a mentor. Fields of study include pharmacology, toxicology, pharmaceutical sciences, and/or biological chemistry. Applications must be submitted jointly by the student and the mentor, and they must include 1) a letter from the mentor with a brief description of the proposed research, a statement of the qualifications of the student, the degree of independence the student will have, a description of enrichment activities available to the student, and a description of how the student will report on the research results; 2) a 500-word statement from the student indicating the nature of their interest in the research project and how participation would contribute to their career goals; 3) a copy of the sponsor's updated curriculum vitae; and 4) copies of all the student's undergraduate transcripts. Selection is based on the nature of the research opportunities provided, student and sponsor qualifications, and the likelihood the student will prepare for a career in pharmacology. Applications from those traditionally underrepresented in the biomedical sciences are particularly encouraged.

Financial Data The stipend is $2,800. Funds are paid directly to the institution but may be used only for student stipends.

Duration 10 weeks during the summer.

Additional data Some of these awards are funded through the Glenn E. Ullyot Fund; those recipients are designated as the Ullyot Fellows.

Number awarded Varies each year; recently, 4 were awarded.

Deadline February of each year.

[531]
SUMMER UNDERGRADUATE RESEARCH FELLOWSHIPS IN ORGANIC CHEMISTRY

American Chemical Society
Division of Organic Chemistry
1155 16th Street, N.W.
Washington, DC 20036
(202) 872-4401   Toll Free: (800) 227-5558, ext. 4401
E-mail: division@acs.org
Web: www.organicdivision.org/?nd=p_surf_program

Summary To provide an opportunity for college juniors, especially Hispanics and other minorities, to work on a research project in organic chemistry during the summer.

Eligibility This program is open to students who are currently enrolled as juniors at a college or university in the United States and are nominated by their school. Nominees must be interested in conducting a research project in organic chemistry at their home institution during the following summer. The project must be mentored by a member of the Organic Division of the American Chemical Society. Along with their application, students must submit brief statements on the project they propose to undertake, their background that has prepared them to do this work, their proposed methodology, and how a summer research project fits into their long-range plans. U.S. citizenship or permanent resident status is required. Selection is based on demonstrated interest and talent in organic chemistry, merit and feasibility of the research project, commitment of a faculty mentor to support the student, academic record (particularly in organic chemistry and related sciences), and importance of the award in facilitating the personal and career plans of the student. Applications from minorities are especially encouraged.

Financial Data Grants range up to $5,000. The program also covers the costs of a trip by all participants to an industrial campus in the fall for a dinner, award session, scientific talks, a tour of the campus, and a poster session where the results of the summer research investigations are presented.

Duration Summer months.

Additional data Current corporate sponsors of this program include Pfizer and Cubist Pharmaceuticals.

Number awarded Up to 12 each year.

Deadline January of each year.

[532]
SURETY AND FIDELITY INDUSTRY SCHOLARSHIP PROGRAM

The Surety Foundation
Attn: Scholarship Program for Minority Students
1101 Connecticut Avenue, N.W., Suite 800
Washington, DC 20036
(202) 463-0600, ext. 638   Fax: (202) 463-0606
E-mail: scarradine@surety.org
Web: www.thesuretyfoundation.org

Summary To provide financial assistance to Hispanic and other minority undergraduates working on a degree in a field related to insurance.

Eligibility This program is open to full-time undergraduates who are U.S. citizens and members of a minority group (Hispanic, Black, Native American/Alaskan Native, and Asian/Pacific Islander). Applicants must have completed at least 30 semester hours of study at an accredited 4-year college or university and have a declared major in insurance/risk management, accounting, business, or finance. They must have a GPA of 3.0 or higher and be able to demonstrate financial need.

Financial Data The stipend is $5,000 per year.

Duration 1 year; recipients may reapply.

Additional data This program, established in 2003 by The Surety & Fidelity Association of America, includes the Adrienne Alexander Scholarship and the George W. McClellan Scholarship.

Number awarded Varies each year; recently, 3 were awarded.

Deadline January of each year.

[533]
SYNOD OF LAKES AND PRAIRIES RACIAL ETHNIC SCHOLARSHIPS

Synod of Lakes and Prairies
Attn: Committee on Racial Ethnic Ministry
2115 Cliff Drive
Eagen, MN 55122-3327
(651) 357-1140   Toll Free: (800) 328-1880, ext. 202
Fax: (651) 357-1141   E-mail: mkes@lakesandprairies.org
Web: www.lakesandprairies.org

Summary To provide financial assistance to Hispanic and other minority residents of the Presbyterian Church (USA) Synod of Lakes and Prairies who are working on an undergraduate or graduate degree at a college or seminary in any state as preparation for service to the church.

Eligibility This program is open to members of Presbyterian churches who reside within the Synod of Lakes and Prairies (Iowa, Minnesota, Nebraska, North Dakota, South Dakota, and Wisconsin). Applicants must be members of ethnic minority groups studying at least half time for service in the Presbyterian Church (USA) as a teaching elder, ordained minister, commissioned ruling elder, lay professional, or volunteer. They must be in good academic standing, making progress toward an undergraduate or graduate degree, and able to demonstrate financial need. Along with their application, they must submit essays of 200 to 500 words on 1) what the church needs to do to be faithful to its mission in the world today; and 2) the people, practices, or events that influence their commitment to Christ in ways that renew their fair and strengthen their service.

Financial Data Stipends range from $850 to $3,500.

Duration 1 year.

Number awarded Varies each year; recently, 9 were awarded.

Deadline September of each year.

[534]
TELACU ARTS AWARD

TELACU Education Foundation
Attn: College Success Program
5400 East Olympic Boulevard, Suite 300
Los Angeles, CA 90022
(323) 721-1655   Fax: (323) 721-3560
E-mail: collegesuccess@telacu.com
Web: www.telacu.com

Summary To provide financial assistance to Latino students from eligible communities in California, Texas, Illinois, and New York who are interested in studying the arts at a college or university in any state.

Eligibility This program is open to Latino residents of selected communities in southern California, selected cities in Texas, the Greater Chicagoland area of Illinois, or the state of New York. Applicants must 1) be a first-generation college student; 2) be from a low-income family; and 3) have a GPA of 2.5 or higher. They must be enrolled or planning to enroll full time at a college or university in any state and major in fine arts, music, dance, drama, or theater. Selection is based on leadership potential, professional and extracurricular achievement, commitment to the development and economic empowerment of communities, and financial need. Priority is given to students attending institutions that provide matching funds (for a list, contact the sponsor).

Financial Data Stipends range from $500 to $5,000 per year.

Duration 1 year; may be renewed up to 3 additional years, provided the recipient remains enrolled full time, maintains a GPA of 2.75 or higher, and volunteers for at least 20 hours of community service.

Additional data The eligible areas in California include underserved communities in Los Angeles, Orange, and San Bernardino counties such as unincorporated areas of east Los Angeles and the cities of Baldwin Park, Bell Gardens, Commerce, Huntington Park, Los Angeles, Montebello, Ontario, Pico Rivera, Pomona, San Bernardino, Santa Ana, and South Gate. The cities in Texas are Austin, Edinburg, Laredo, Rio Grande City, and San Antonio.

Number awarded 1 or more each year.

Deadline February of each year.

[535]
TELACU BUSINESS AWARD

TELACU Education Foundation
Attn: College Success Program
5400 East Olympic Boulevard, Suite 300
Los Angeles, CA 90022
(323) 721-1655   Fax: (323) 721-3560
E-mail: collegesuccess@telacu.com
Web: www.telacu.com

Summary To provide financial assistance to Latino students from eligible communities in California, Texas, Illinois, and New York who are interested in studying business at a college or university in any state.

Eligibility This program is open to Latino residents of selected communities in southern California, selected cities in Texas, the Greater Chicagoland area of Illinois, or the state of New York. Applicants must 1) be a first-generation college student; 2) be from a low-income family; and 3) have a GPA of 2.5 or higher. They must be enrolled or planning to enroll full time at a college or university in any state and major in business. Selection is based on leadership potential, professional and extracurricular achievement, commitment to the development and economic empowerment of communities, and financial need. Priority is given to students attending institutions that provide matching funds (for a list, contact the sponsor).

Financial Data Stipends range from $500 to $5,000 per year.

Duration 1 year; may be renewed up to 3 additional years, provided the recipient remains enrolled full time, maintains a GPA of 2.75 or higher, and volunteers for at least 20 hours of community service.

Additional data The eligible areas in California include underserved communities in Los Angeles, Orange, and San Bernardino counties such as unincorporated areas of east Los Angeles and the cities of Baldwin Park, Bell Gardens, Commerce, Huntington Park, Los Angeles, Montebello, Ontario, Pico Rivera, Pomona, San Bernardino, Santa Ana, and South Gate. The cities in Texas are Austin, Edinburg, Laredo, Rio Grande City, and San Antonio.

Number awarded 1 or more each year.

Deadline February of each year.

[536]
TELACU COMMUNITY LEADERSHIP AWARD

TELACU Education Foundation
Attn: College Success Program
5400 East Olympic Boulevard, Suite 300
Los Angeles, CA 90022
(323) 721-1655   Fax: (323) 721-3560
E-mail: collegesuccess@telacu.com
Web: www.telacu.com

Summary To provide financial assistance to Latino students from eligible communities in California, Texas, Illinois, and New York who can demonstrate outstanding leadership abilities and are interested in attending college in any state.

Eligibility This program is open to Latino residents of selected communities in southern California, selected cities in Texas, the Greater Chicagoland area of Illinois, or the state of New York. Applicants must 1) be a first-generation college student; 2) be from a low-income family; 3) have a GPA of 2.5 or higher; and 4) be able to demonstrate outstanding leadership abilities. They must be enrolled or planning to enroll full time at a college or university in any state. Selection is based on leadership potential, professional and extracurricular achievement, commitment to the development and economic empowerment of communities, and financial need. Priority is given to students attending institutions that provide matching funds (for a list, contact the sponsor).

Financial Data The stipend is $2,500.

Duration 1 year.

Additional data The eligible areas in California include underserved communities in Los Angeles, Orange, and San Bernardino counties such as unincorporated areas of east Los Angeles and the cities of Baldwin Park, Bell Gardens, Commerce, Huntington Park, Los Angeles, Montebello, Ontario, Pico Rivera, Pomona, San Bernardino, Santa Ana, and South Gate. The cities in Texas are Austin, Edinburg, Laredo, Rio Grande City, and San Antonio.

Number awarded 1 each year.

Deadline February of each year.

[537]
TELACU EDUCATION AWARD

TELACU Education Foundation
Attn: College Success Program
5400 East Olympic Boulevard, Suite 300
Los Angeles, CA 90022
(323) 721-1655   Fax: (323) 721-3560
E-mail: collegesuccess@telacu.com
Web: www.telacu.com

Summary To provide financial assistance to Latino students from eligible communities in California, Texas, Illinois, and New York who are interested in attending college in any state to prepare for a career as a teacher.

Eligibility This program is open to Latino residents of selected communities in southern California, selected cities in Texas, the Greater Chicagoland area of Illinois, or the state of New York. Applicants must 1) be a first-generation college student; 2) be from a low-income family; and 3) have a GPA of 2.5 or higher. They must be enrolled or planning to enroll full time at a college or university in any state and preparing for a career as a teacher. Selection is based on leadership potential, professional and extracurricular achievement, commitment to the development and economic empowerment of

communities, and financial need. Priority is given to students attending institutions that provide matching funds (for a list, contact the sponsor).

Financial Data Stipends range from $500 to $5,000 per year.

Duration 1 year; may be renewed up to 3 additional years, provided the recipient remains enrolled full time, maintains a GPA of 2.75 or higher, and volunteers for at least 20 hours of community service.

Additional data The eligible areas in California include underserved communities in Los Angeles, Orange, and San Bernardino counties such as unincorporated areas of east Los Angeles and the cities of Baldwin Park, Bell Gardens, Commerce, Huntington Park, Los Angeles, Montebello, Ontario, Pico Rivera, Pomona, San Bernardino, Santa Ana, and South Gate. The cities in Texas are Austin, Edinburg, Laredo, Rio Grande City, and San Antonio.

Number awarded 1 or more each year.

Deadline February of each year.

[538]
TELACU SCHOLARSHIPS

TELACU Education Foundation
Attn: College Success Program
5400 East Olympic Boulevard, Suite 300
Los Angeles, CA 90022
(323) 721-1655   Fax: (323) 721-3560
E-mail: collegesuccess@telacu.com
Web: www.telacu.com

Summary To provide financial assistance to Latino students from eligible communities in California, Texas, Illinois, and New York who are interested in attending college in any state.

Eligibility This program is open to Latino residents of selected communities in southern California, selected cities in Texas, the Greater Chicagoland area of Illinois, or the state of New York. Applicants must 1) be a first-generation college student; 2) be from a low-income family; and 3) have a GPA of 2.5 or higher. They must be enrolled or planning to enroll full time at a college or university in any state. Selection is based on leadership potential, professional and extracurricular achievement, commitment to the development and economic empowerment of communities, and financial need. Priority is given to students attending institutions that provide matching funds (for a list, contact the sponsor).

Financial Data Stipends range from $500 to $5,000 per year.

Duration Both 1-year and continuing scholarships are available. Continuing scholarships may be renewed for a total of 4 years, provided the recipient attends all sessions of the College Advisement and Leadership Program each year, maintains a GPA of 2.75 or higher, and volunteers 20 hours of service annually to the TELACU Education Foundation or other community organization.

Additional data The eligible areas in California include underserved communities in Los Angeles, Orange, and San Bernardino counties such as unincorporated areas of east Los Angeles and the cities of Baldwin Park, Bell Gardens, Commerce, Huntington Park, Los Angeles, Montebello, Ontario, Pico Rivera, Pomona, San Bernardino, Santa Ana, and South Gate. The cities in Texas are Austin, Edinburg, Laredo, Rio Grande City, and San Antonio.

Number awarded Varies each year; the program supports approximately 500 students annually.
Deadline February of each year.

[539]
TELACU STEM AWARD

TELACU Education Foundation
Attn: College Success Program
5400 East Olympic Boulevard, Suite 300
Los Angeles, CA 90022
(323) 721-1655 Fax: (323) 721-3560
E-mail: collegesuccess@telacu.com
Web: www.telacu.com

Summary To provide financial assistance to Latino students from eligible communities in California, Texas, Illinois, and New York who are interested in studying fields of science, technology, engineering, or mathematics (STEM) at colleges and universities in any state.

Eligibility This program is open to Latino residents of selected communities in southern California, selected cities in Texas, the Greater Chicagoland area of Illinois, or the state of New York. Applicants must 1) be a first-generation college student; 2) be from a low-income family; and 3) have a GPA of 2.5 or higher. They must be enrolled or planning to enroll full time at a college or university in any state and major in a field of STEM. Selection is based on leadership potential, professional and extracurricular achievement, commitment to the development and economic empowerment of communities, and financial need. Priority is given to students attending institutions that provide matching funds (for a list, contact the sponsor).

Financial Data Stipends range from $500 to $5,000 per year.

Duration 1 year; may be renewed up to 3 additional years, provided the recipient remains enrolled full time, maintains a GPA of 2.75 or higher, and volunteers for at least 20 hours of community service.

Additional data The eligible areas in California include underserved communities in Los Angeles, Orange, and San Bernardino counties such as unincorporated areas of east Los Angeles and the cities of Baldwin Park, Bell Gardens, Commerce, Huntington Park, Los Angeles, Montebello, Ontario, Pico Rivera, Pomona, San Bernardino, Santa Ana, and South Gate. The cities in Texas are Austin, Edinburg, Laredo, Rio Grande City, and San Antonio.

Number awarded 1 or more each year.
Deadline February of each year.

[540]
TELEMUNDO EL PODER EN TI SCHOLARSHIP

Society of Hispanic Professional Engineers
Attn: Scholarships
13181 Crossroads Parkway North, Suite 450
City of Industry, CA 91715
(323) 725-3970, ext. 108 Fax: (323) 725-0316
E-mail: scholarships@shpe.org
Web: shpe.awardspring.com

Summary To provide financial assistance to Hispanic undergraduate students who are working on a degree in a field of science, technology, engineering, or matheamtics (STEM) at a college in designated cities.

Eligibility This program is open to full-time undergraduates of Hispanic descent who are enrolled at a college or university in Chicago, Los Angeles, Miami, New York, or Phoenix. Applicants must be majoring in a field of STEM and be members of the Society of Hispanic Professional Engineers (SHPE). They must have a GPA of 3.0 or higher. Selection is based on academic standing and financial need.

Financial Data The stipend is $2,000.
Duration 1 year.
Additional data This program is sponsored by NBCUniversal Telemundo Enterprises.
Number awarded 1 or more each year.
Deadline July of each year.

[541]
THE ANHELO PROJECT DREAM SCHOLARSHIP

The Anhelo Project
c/o Joanna Maravilla-Cano
P.O. Box 08290
Chicago, IL 60608
(773) 609-4252
E-mail: dreamscholarshipchicago@gmail.com
Web: theanheloproject.org/dream-scholarship

Summary To provide financial assistance to undocumented residents of Illinois who are attending college in Chicago.

Eligibility This program is open to undocumented students who are residents of Illinois. Applicants must be enrolled full time at an accredited college or university in Chicago and have completed at least 12 credit hours with a cumulative GPA of 2.75 or higher. They must be able to demonstrate leadership through community involvement (on and/or off campus) and financial need. Holders of F-1 student visas and international students are not eligible.

Financial Data A stipend is awarded (amount not specified).

Duration 1 year.
Additional data Recipients must commit 20 hours of volunteer time to The Anhelo Project events during the following academic year.

Number awarded Varies each year.
Deadline March of each year.

[542]
THEDREAM.US NATIONAL SCHOLARSHIP PROGRAM

TheDream.US
c/o International Scholarship and Tuition Services, Inc.
1321 Murfreesboro Road, Suite 800
Nashville, TN 37217
Toll Free: (855) 670-ISTS
E-mail: TheDream.US@applyists.com
Web: thedream.us/scholarships/national-scholarship

Summary To provide financial assistance to students who qualify for the U.S. Citizenship and Immigration Services (USCIS) Deferred Action for Childhood Arrivals (DACA) program or Temporary Protected Status (TPS) and are interested in attending specified colleges.

Eligibility This program is open to 1) high school seniors and graduates who are entering college as first-time students to work on an associate or bachelor's degree; and 2) students about to graduate from a community college and planning to transfer to a 4-year university. Students currently enrolled in a bachelor's degree program are not eligible. Applicants must meet DACA or TPS eligibility criteria and have applied for or received notification of DACA or TPS approval. They must have a GPA of 2.5 or higher or an equivalent GED score and be able to demonstrate significant financial need. Along with their application, they must submit 750-word essays on 1) their educational and career goals, who or what has inspired or helped shape those goals, and the most significant challenges they expect to face to complete college; and 2) a challenging family or personal circumstance that has affected their achievement or participation in school, work, or community activities and how they overcame that challenge.

Financial Data Funding covers tuition and fees (but not room and board, supplies, or transportation) to a maximum of $12,500 for an associate degree or $25,000 for a bachelor's degree.

Duration Up to 3 years or until completion of an associate degree (whichever occurs first); up to 6 years or until completion of a bachelor's degree (whichever occurs first). Students remain eligible for continuing support only if they maintain a GPA of 3.0 or higher, full-time enrollment, DACA or TPS eligibility, and good status in their college accounts and charges.

Additional data This program, which began in 2014, is sponsored by TheDream.US and managed by International Scholarship and Tuition Services. For a list of the more than 75 current participating partner colleges and universities in 14 states, contact the sponsor.

Number awarded Varies each year.

Deadline March of each year.

[543]
THEDREAM.US OPPORTUNITY SCHOLARSHIP PROGRAM

TheDream.US
c/o International Scholarship and Tuition Services, Inc.
1321 Murfreesboro Road, Suite 800
Nashville, TN 37217
Toll Free: (855) 670-ISTS
E-mail: TheDream.US@applyists.com
Web: thedream.us/scholarships/opportunity-scholarship

Summary To provide financial assistance to students who qualify for the U.S. Citizenship and Immigration Services (USCIS) Deferred Action for Childhood Arrivals (DACA) program or Temporary Protected Status (TPS) but cannot attend college in their home state and are interested in attending specified universities.

Eligibility This program is open to high school seniors and graduates who are seeking attend to college as first-time students to work on a bachelor's degree at designated partner universities (Delaware State University, Eastern Connecticut State University, Western Oregon University, Christian Brothers University, or Trinity Washington University). Applicants must meet DACA or TPS eligibility criteria and have applied for or received notification of DACA or TPS approval, but live in a state that does not recognize DACA status. They must have a GPA of 2.5 or higher or an equivalent GED score and be able to demonstrate significant financial need. Along with their application, they must submit 750-word essays on 1) their educational and career goals, who or what has inspired or helped shape those goals, and the most significant chal-

lenges they expect to face to complete college; and 2) a challenging family or personal circumstance that has affected their achievement or participation in school, work, or community activities and how they overcame that challenge.

Financial Data Funding covers tuition, fees, and on-campus housing and fees to a maximum of $80,000 for a bachelor's degree.

Duration Up to 6 years or until completion of a bachelor's degree (whichever occurs first). Students remain eligible for continuing support only if they maintain a GPA of 3.0 or higher, full-time enrollment, DACA or TPS eligibility, and good status in their college accounts and charges.

Additional data The states that do not recognize DACA status are Alaska, Arkansas, Georgia, Idaho, Indiana, Iowa, Louisiana, Mississippi, Missouri, North Carolina, North Dakota, South Carolina, South Dakota, West Virginia, and Wisconsin.

Number awarded Varies each year.

Deadline January of each year.

[544]
THEDREAM.US SCHOLARSHIPS

TheDream.US
c/o International Scholarship and Tuition Services, Inc.
1321 Murfreesboro Road, Suite 800
Nashville, TN 37217
Toll Free: (855) 670-ISTS
E-mail: contactus@applyists.com
Web: www.thedream.us/scholars

Summary To provide financial assistance to students from any state who qualify for Deferred Action for Childhood Arrivals (DACA) or Temporary Protected Status (TPS) and wish to attend designated partner colleges in designated states.

Eligibility This program is open to students who came to the United States prior to their 16th birthday, are DACA or TPS eligible, and have applied for or received DACA or TPS approval. Applicants may reside in any state but they must be interested in working full time on an associate or bachelor's degree at an approved partner college in Arizona, California, Florida, Illinois, New York, Texas, Virginia, or Washington, D.C. and be eligible for in-state tuition (if applicable). They may be 1) first-time college students who are graduating from high school, earning a GED diploma, or have already graduated or earned a GED diploma; have an unweighted high school GPA of 2.5 or higher; and demonstrate significant unmet financial need; or 2) community college graduates who are earning an associate degree or have earned an associate degree; have not yet enrolled in a bachelor's degree program; have a college GPA of 3.0 or higher; and demonstrate significant unmet financial need. Along with their application, they must submit 200-word essays on 1) their educational and career goals; and 2) a challenging family or personal circumstance that affected their achievement or participation in school, work, or community activities and how they overcame it.

Financial Data Support is provided up to a total of $12,500 for an associate degree or $25,000 for a bachelor's degree.

Duration 1 year; may be renewed until completion of an associate or bachelor's degree, provided the recipient maintains a GPA of 3.0 or higher, remains enrolled full time, continues to qualify for DACA or TPS, and remains current on all their college accounts and charged.

Additional data For a list of partner colleges, contact The-Dream.US. Scholarship America is the fiscal sponsor for this program. International Scholarship and Tuition Services administers it.

Number awarded Varies each year.

Deadline March of each year.

[545]
THOMAS DARGAN MINORITY SCHOLARSHIP

KATU-TV
Attn: Human Resources
2153 N.E. Sandy Boulevard
P.O. Box 2
Portland, OR 97207-0002
(503) 231-4222
Web: www.katu.com

Summary To provide financial assistance to Hispanic and other minority students from Oregon and Washington who are studying broadcasting or communications in college.

Eligibility This program is open to minority (Hispanic or Latino, Asian, Black/African American, Native Hawaiian or Pacific Islander, American Indian or Alaska Native) U.S. citizens, currently enrolled as a sophomore or higher at a 4-year college or university or an accredited community college in Oregon or Washington. Residents of Oregon or Washington enrolled at a school in any state are also eligible. Applicants must be majoring in broadcasting or communications and have a GPA of 3.0 or higher. Community college students must be enrolled in a broadcast curriculum that is transferable to a 4-year accredited university. Finalists are interviewed. Selection is based on financial need, academic achievement, and an essay on personal and professional goals.

Financial Data The stipend is $6,000. Funds are sent directly to the recipient's school.

Duration 1 year; recipients may reapply if they have maintained a GPA of 3.0 or higher.

Additional data Winners are also eligible for a paid internship in selected departments at Fisher Broadcasting/KATU in Portland, Oregon.

Number awarded 1 each year.

Deadline April of each year.

[546]
THOMAS G. NEUSOM SCHOLARSHIPS

Conference of Minority Transportation Officials
Attn: National Scholarship Program
100 M Street, S.E., Suite 917
Washington, DC 20003
(202) 506-2917   E-mail: info@comto.org
Web: www.comto.org/page/scholarships

Summary To provide financial assistance for college or graduate school to Hispanic and other minority members of the Conference of Minority Transportation Officials (COMTO) and their families.

Eligibility This program is open to undergraduate and graduate students who have been members of COMTO or whose parents, guardians, or grandparents have been members for at least 1 year. Applicants must be working (either full or part time) on a degree in a field related to transportation

and have a GPA of 2.5 or higher. Along with their application they must submit a cover letter on their transportation-related career goals and life aspirations. Financial need is not considered in the selection process.

Financial Data The stipend is $5,500. Funds are paid directly to the recipient's college or university.

Duration 1 year.

Number awarded 1 each year.

Deadline April of each year.

[547]
TRAILBLAZER SCHOLARSHIP

Conference of Minority Transportation Officials
Attn: National Scholarship Program
100 M Street, S.E., Suite 917
Washington, DC 20003
(202) 506-2917   E-mail: info@comto.org
Web: www.comto.org/page/scholarships

Summary To provide financial assistance for college or graduate school to Hispanic and other minority members of the Conference of Minority Transportation Officials (COMTO) and their families.

Eligibility This program is open to undergraduate and graduate students who have been members of COMTO or whose parents, guardians, or grandparents have been members for at least 1 year. Applicants must be working (either full or part time) on a degree in a field related to transportation and have a GPA of 2.5 or higher. Along with their application they must submit a cover letter on their transportation-related career goals and life aspirations. Financial need is not considered in the selection process.

Financial Data The stipend is $2,500. Funds are paid directly to the recipient's college or university.

Duration 1 year.

Number awarded 1 each year.

Deadline April of each year.

[548]
TRANSPORTATION INDUSTRY COLLEGE SCHOLARSHIP

Conference of Minority Transportation Officials-Fort
   Lauderdale Chapter
Attn: Scholarship Committee
Victor Garcia, South Florida Regional Transportation
   Authority
801 N.W. 33rd Street
Pompano Beach, FL 33064
(954) 788-7925   Toll Free: (800) GO-SFRTA
Fax: (854) 788-7961   TDD: (800) 273-7545
E-mail: victorgarcia@comtoftlauderdale.org
Web: www.comtoftlauderdale.org/scholarship-program

Summary To provide financial assistance to Hispanic and other minority students working on a transportation-related undergraduate degree at a college in Florida.

Eligibility This program is open to minority students currently enrolled at accredited colleges and universities in Florida. Applicants must be majoring in a transportation-related field and have a GPA of 2.5 or higher. They must be U.S. citizens or permanent residents. Along with their application, they must submit an essay of 500 to 750 words on their transportation-related career goals and life aspirations. Financial need is not considered in the selection process.

Financial Data   The stipend is $1,500.

Duration   1 year; nonrenewable.

Additional data   This program began in 2015.

Number awarded   1 each year.

Deadline   April of each year.

[549]
TYLER J. VINEY MEMORIAL SCHOLARSHIP

Texas Society of Architects
Attn: Texas Architectural Foundation
500 Chicon Street
Austin, TX 78702
(512) 478-7386   Fax: (512) 478-0528
E-mail: foundation@texasarchitect.org
Web: www.texasarchitects.org/v/scholarships

Summary   To provide financial assistance to residents of any state, especially Hispanics and other minorities, who are entering their fourth or fifth year of study at a school of architecture in Texas.

Eligibility   This program is open to residents of any state who are entering their fourth or fifth year of study at 1 of the 8 schools of architecture in Texas. Applicants must submit their application to the office of the dean of their school. Along with their application, they must submit essays on 1) the principal architectural areas or practice categories in which they are most interested, excel, or desire to develop their proficiency; and 2) career plans, short/long-range goals, vision, or other topic about which they are passionate. Selection is based on potential architectural talent, demonstrated interest in photography, and financial need. Priority is given to female and minority students.

Financial Data   The stipend ranges up to $2,000.

Duration   1 year.

Number awarded   1 each year.

Deadline   February of each year.

[550]
UCSD MSTP SUMMER UNDERGRADUATE RESEARCH FELLOWSHIP PROGRAM

University of California at San Diego
Attn: School of Medicine
Medical Scientist Training Program
9500 Gilman Drive, MC 0661
La Jolla, CA 92093-0661
(858) 822-5631   Toll Free: (800) 925-8704
Fax: (858) 822-3067   E-mail: mstp@ucsd.edu
Web: mstp.ucsd.edu/surf/Pages/default.aspx

Summary   To provide an opportunity for Hispanics and undergraduate students from other underrepresented groups to work during the summer on a research project in the biomedical sciences at the University of California at San Diego (UCSD).

Eligibility   This program is open to undergraduate students at colleges in any state who are members of an underrepresented group (racial and ethnic groups that have been shown to be underrepresented in health-related sciences, individuals with disabilities, or individuals from a disadvantaged background). Applicants must be interested in working on a research project in the laboratory of a UCSD faculty member

in the biomedical sciences. They must be U.S. citizens, permanent residents, or nationals. Along with their application, they must submit brief essays on 1) why they consider themselves an individual from a disadvantaged ethnicity or background or are underrepresented in the biomedical sciences; 2) their past research experiences; 3) the areas of research they wish to pursue in the program; 4) their educational and career plans and how this program will advance them towards their goals; and 5) anything else that might help to evaluate their application.

Financial Data   The program provides a stipend of $1,600 per month, room (but not board), and a $500 travel allowance.

Duration   8 weeks during the summer.

Additional data   This program is sponsored by the National Heart, Lung, and Blood Institute (NHLBI) of the National Institutes of Health (NIH).

Number awarded   Varies each year; recently, 11 students participated in this program.

Deadline   February of each year.

[551]
UNITED HEALTH FOUNDATION NATIONAL ASSOCIATION OF HISPANIC NURSES SCHOLARSHIP AWARDS

National Association of Hispanic Nurses
Attn: Scholarships
1500 Sunday Drive, Suite 102
Raleigh, NC 27607
(919) 787-5181, ext. 1255   Fax: (919) 787-4916
E-mail: director@thehispanicnurses.org
Web: www.nahnnet.org/NAHNScholarships.html

Summary   To provide financial assistance for nursing education to members of the National Association of Hispanic Nurses (NAHN).

Eligibility   Eligible are members of the association enrolled in associate, diploma, baccalaureate, graduate, or practical/vocational nursing programs at NLN-accredited schools of nursing. Applicants must have a GPA of 3.0 or higher. Along with their application, they must submit a letter of recommendation; a 300-word essay that reflects their qualifications and potential for leadership in nursing in the Hispanic community; a resume that includes earned certificates, awards, and special honors; information on their financial status; and an official transcript. U.S. citizenship or permanent resident status is required.

Financial Data   The stipend is $5,000.

Duration   1 year; may be renewed.

Additional data   This program is sponsored by United Health Foundation as part of its Latino Health Scholars Program.

Number awarded   Varies each year; recently, 8 new and 8 renewal scholarships were awarded.

Deadline   June of each year.

[552]
UNITED METHODIST FOUNDATION COLLEGE AND UNIVERSITY MERIT SCHOLARS PROGRAM

United Methodist Higher Education Foundation
Attn: Scholarships Administrator
60 Music Square East, Suite 350
P.O. Box 340005
Nashville, TN 37203-0005
(615) 649-3974   Toll Free: (800) 811-8110
Fax: (615) 649-3980
E-mail: umhefscholarships@umhef.org
Web: www.umhef.org

Summary To provide financial assistance to Hispanic and other minority undergraduate students attending colleges and universities affiliated with the United Methodist Church.

Eligibility This program is open to freshmen, sophomores, juniors, and seniors at United Methodist-related 4-year colleges and universities and to freshmen and sophomores at 2-year colleges. Nominees must have been active members of the United Methodist Church for at least 1 year prior to application. They must be planning to enroll full time and have a GPA of 3.0 or higher. Preference is given to ethnic minority and first generation college students. Financial need is considered in the selection process. U.S. citizenship or permanent resident status is required.

Financial Data The stipend is $2,000.

Duration 1 year; nonrenewable.

Additional data Students may obtain applications from their school.

Number awarded 420 each year: 1 to a member of each class at each school.

Deadline Nominations from schools must be received by September of each year.

[553]
UNITED PARCEL SERVICE SCHOLARSHIP FOR MINORITY STUDENTS

Institute of Industrial and Systems Engineers
Attn: Scholarship Coordinator
3577 Parkway Lane, Suite 200
Norcross, GA 30092
(770) 449-0461, ext. 105   Toll Free: (800) 494-0460
Fax: (770) 441-3295   E-mail: bcameron@iisenet.org
Web: www.iienet2.org/Details.aspx?id=857

Summary To provide financial assistance to Hispanic and other minority undergraduates who are studying industrial engineering at a school in the United States, Canada, or Mexico.

Eligibility Eligible to be nominated are minority undergraduate students enrolled at any school in the United States or its territories, Canada, or Mexico, provided the school's engineering program is accredited by an agency recognized by the Institute of Industrial and Systems Engineers (IISE) and the student is pursuing a full-time course of study in industrial engineering with a GPA of at least 3.4. Nominees must have at least 5 full quarters or 3 full semesters remaining until graduation. Students may not apply directly for these awards; they must be nominated by the head of their industrial engineering department. Nominees must be IISE members. Selection is based on scholastic ability, character, leadership, and potential service to the industrial engineering profession.

Financial Data The stipend is $4,000.

Duration 1 year.

Additional data Funding for this program is provided by the UPS Foundation.

Number awarded 1 each year.

Deadline Schools must submit nominations by November of each year.

[554]
UNITED STATES HISPANIC LEADERSHIP INSTITUTE/DENNY'S HUNGRY FOR EDUCATION SCHOLARSHIP

United States Hispanic Leadership Institute
Attn: Scholarship Committee
431 South Dearborn Street, Suite 1203
Chicago, IL 60605
(312) 427-8683   Toll Free: (800) 959-5151
Fax: (312) 427-5183   E-mail: acalderon@ushli.org
Web: www.ushli.org

Summary To provide financial assistance for college to Hispanic students in the United States who submit outstanding essays on hunger.

Eligibility This program is open to students enrolled as undergraduates at colleges and universities in the United States. Applicants must be U.S. citizens, lawful permanent residents, or individuals authorized to work full-time without restriction for U.S. employers. Along with their application, they must submit a 500-word essay on how Denny's can impact childhood hunger in their community. In the selection process, some consideration is given to grades and academic performance as indicators of potential, but emphasis is placed on the essay.

Financial Data The stipend is $1,000.

Duration 1 year; nonrenewable.

Additional data This program is sponsored by Denny's as 1 of its Hungry for Education scholarship activities.

Number awarded 5 each year.

Deadline April of each year.

[555]
UNIVERSITY OF CALIFORNIA AT BERKELEY AMGEN SCHOLARS PROGRAM

University of California at Berkeley
Attn: Amgen Scholars Program
158 Barrows Hall
MC 2990
Berkeley, CA 94720-2990
(510) 642-0280   Fax: (510) 643-6762
E-mail: amgenscholars@berkeley.edu
Web: amgenscholars.berkeley.edu

Summary To provide undergraduate students, especially Hispanics and members of other diverse groups, with a summer research experience at the University of California at Berkeley in biological and biomedical sciences.

Eligibility This program is open to sophomores, juniors, and non-graduating seniors at 4-year colleges and universities in the United States, Puerto Rico, and U.S. territories. Applicants must be interested in a summer research experience at UC Berkeley in biochemistry, bioengineering, biophysics, cell and developmental biology, chemical biology, chemical and biomedical engineering, chemistry, computational biology, genetics, genomics and development, immunology, integrative biology, metabolic biology, microbiology, molecular and cell biology, molecular toxicology, neurobiology, neuroscience, pathogenesis, plant and microbial biology, RNA systems biology, structural biology, or synthetic biology. They must have a GPA of 3.2 or higher and an interest in continuing on to a Ph.D. or M.D./Ph.D. (but not M.D.) program. Applications are especially encouraged from students from diverse populations and backgrounds. U.S. citizenship or permanent resident status is required.

Financial Data Housing, travel to and from Berkeley, meals, and a stipend of $5,000 are provided.

Duration 10 weeks during the summer.

Additional data This program serves as the UC Berkeley component of the Amgen Scholars Program, which operates at 8 other U.S. universities (and the National Institutes of Health) and is funded by the Amgen Foundation.

Number awarded 25 each year.

Deadline January of each year.

[556]
UNIVERSITY OF CALIFORNIA AT LOS ANGELES AMGEN SCHOLARS PROGRAM

University of California at Los Angeles
Attn: URC-Sciences
2121 Life Sciences Building
621 Charles E. Young Drive
Los Angeles, CA 90095-1606
(310) 206-2182   Fax: (310) 267-2219
E-mail: amgensch@lifesci.ucla.edu
Web: www.ugresearchsci.ucla.edu/amgenscholars.htm

Summary To provide undergraduate students, especially Hispanics and members of other diverse groups, with a summer research experience at the University of California at Los Angeles in biological and biomedical sciences.

Eligibility This program is open to sophomores, juniors, and non-graduating seniors at 4-year colleges and universities in the United States, Puerto Rico, and U.S. territories. Applicants must be interested in a summer research experience at UCLA in biomedical science, chemistry, bioengineering, or chemical engineering. They must have a GPA of 3.2 or higher and an interest in continuing on to a Ph.D. or M.D./Ph.D. (but not M.D.) program. Applications are especially encouraged from students from diverse populations and backgrounds. U.S. citizenship or permanent resident status is required.

Financial Data The program provides a stipend of $3,600, on-campus housing, some meals, and a travel allowance for non-UCLA students of $250 for those from California or $500 for students from other states.

Duration 10 weeks during the summer.

Additional data This program serves as the UCLA component of the Amgen Scholars Program, which operates at 8 other U.S. universities (and the National Institutes of Health) and is funded by the Amgen Foundation.

Number awarded 20 each year, including 5 undergraduates from UCLA and 15 from other colleges and universities.

Deadline January of each year.

[557]
UNIVERSITY OF CALIFORNIA AT SAN FRANCISCO SUMMER RESEARCH PROGRAMS

University of California at San Francisco
Office of Graduate Outreach
Attn: Outreach and Student Programs Coordinator
1675 Owens Street, Room 310
Box 0523
San Francisco, CA 94143-0523
(415) 514-3510   Fax: (415) 514-0844
E-mail: julia.clark@ucsf.edu
Web: graduate.ucsf.edu/srtp

Summary To provide undergraduate students, especially Hispanic and other underrepresented minorities, with a summer research experience at the University of California at San Francisco in biological and biomedical sciences.

Eligibility This activity consists of 5 separate programs, but they operate together and have a common application and requirements. The 5 programs are the Amgen Scholars Program, the Molecular Biosciences Research Experiences for Undergraduates (REU), the Summer Research Training Program (SRTP), the graduate group in biophysics, and the graduate group in pharmaceutical sciences and pharmacogenomics. The activity is open to sophomores, juniors, and non-graduating seniors at 4-year colleges and universities in the United States, Puerto Rico, and U.S. territories. Applicants must be interested in a summer research experience at UC San Francisco in biochemistry, bioengineering, biological and biomedical informatics, biology (molecular, cell, and developmental), biomedical sciences, biophysics, chemical biology, chemistry, epidemiology and translational research, genetics, neuroscience, oral and craniofacial sciences, or pharmaceutical sciences and pharmacogenomics. They must be U.S. citizens or permanent residents. The Amgen Scholars Program requires a GPA of 3.2 or higher but the other 2 components have no minimum GPA requirement; all programs require an interest in continuing on to a Ph.D. or M.D./Ph.D. (but not M.D.) program. Applications are especially encouraged from underrepresented minority, socioeconomically disadvantaged, and first-generation college students and from students with limited access to research laboratories.

Financial Data The program provides a stipend of $4,000, a $500 allowance for travel to and from San Francisco, housing in the city, health insurance, and a public transportation pass.

Duration 10 weeks during the summer.

Additional data This program is comprised of 1) the UC San Francisco component of the Amgen Scholars Program, which operates at 8 other U.S. universities (and the National Institutes of Health) and is funded by the Amgen Foundation; 2) the REU program, funded by the National Science Foundation; 3) the SRTP, which is a UCSF program with supplemental funding from Genentech and the Howard Hughes Medical Institute; 4) the graduate group in biophysics, (a component of the SRTP); and 5) the graduate group in pharmaceutical sciences and pharmacogenomics (a component of the SRTP).

Number awarded Approximately 60 each year.

Deadline January of each year.

[558]
UPS/CIC FOUNDATION SCHOLARSHIPS

Wisconsin Association of Independent Colleges and
Universities
Attn: Senior Vice President for Educational Services
122 West Washington Avenue, Suite 700
Madison, WI 53703-2723
(608) 256-7761, ext. 223   Fax: (608) 256-7065
E-mail: carole.trone@waicu.org
Web: www.waicu.org

Summary To provide financial assistance to students at
member institution of the Wisconsin Association of Independent Colleges and Universities (WAICU) who are Hispanics
or members of other designated target populations.

Eligibility This program is open to students enrolled full
time at WAICU member colleges or universities. The background of applicants must reflect 1 or more of the components of the target population for the UPS Foundation and the
First Opportunity Program of the Council of Independent Colleges (CIC): first generation, low-income, minority, or new
American students.

Financial Data The stipend is $2,600.

Duration 1 year.

Additional data The WAICU member schools are Alverno
College, Bellin College, Beloit College, Cardinal Stritch University, Carroll College, Carthage College, Columbia College
of Nursing, Concordia University of Wisconsin, Edgewood
College, Lakeland College, Lawrence University, Marian College, Marquette University, Medical College of Wisconsin,
Milwaukee Institute of Art & Design, Milwaukee School of
Engineering, Mount Mary College, Nashotah House Theological Seminary, Northland College, Ripon College, St. Norbert
College, Silver Lake College of the Holy Family, Viterbo University, and Wisconsin Lutheran College. This program is
supported by the UPS Foundation and administered nationally through CIC.

Number awarded Up to 24 each year: 1 at each of the
member schools.

Deadline Each participating college sets its own deadline.

[559]
UPS DIVERSITY SCHOLARSHIPS OF THE AMERICAN SOCIETY OF SAFETY ENGINEERS

American Society of Safety Engineers
Attn: ASSE Foundation
Scholarship Award Program
520 North Northwest Highway
Park Ridge, IL 60068-2538
(847) 699-2929   Fax: (847) 296-3769
E-mail: assefoundation@asse.org
Web: foundation.asse.org/scholarships-and-grants

Summary To provide financial assistance to Hispanic and
other minority upper-division students working on a degree
related to occupational safety.

Eligibility This program is open to students who are U.S.
citizens and members of minority ethnic or racial groups.
Applicants must be majoring in occupational safety, health,
environment, industrial hygiene, occupational health nursing,
or a closely-related field (e.g., industrial or environmental
engineering). They must be full-time students who have completed at least 60 semester hours and have a GPA of 3.0 or

higher. Membership in the American Society of Safety Engineers (ASSE) is not required, but preference is given to members.

Financial Data The stipend is $5,250 per year.

Duration 1 year; recipients may reapply.

Additional data Funding for this program is provided by
the UPS Foundation. Recipients may also be provided with
the opportunity to attend a professional development conference related to safety.

Number awarded 3 each year.

Deadline November of each year.

[560]
U.S. NAVY STEM SCHOLARSHIPS

Great Minds in STEM
Attn: HENAAC Scholars Program
602 Monterey Pass Road
Monterey Park, CA 91754
(323) 262-0997   Fax: (323) 262-0946
E-mail: scholars@greatmindsinstem.org
Web: www.greatmindsinstem.org

Summary To provide financial assistance to Hispanic high
school seniors majoring in a field of science, technology,
engineering, or mathematics (STEM) at an Hispanic Serving
Institution (HSI).

Eligibility This program is open to high school seniors who
plan to enroll at an HSI and work on an undergraduate
degree in a field of STEM. Applicants must be of Hispanic origin and/or must significantly participate in and promote organizations and activities in the Hispanic community. They must
have a GPA of 3.0 or higher and a record of activity in school
and community organizations. Along with their application,
they must submit a 700-word essay on a topic that changes
annually. Selection is based on leadership, academic
achievements, campus and community activities, and financial need. U.S. citizenship is required.

Financial Data The stipend is $10,000.

Duration 1 year; recipients may reapply.

Additional data The Hispanic Engineer National Achievement Awards Conference (HENAAC) was established in 1989
and initiated a scholarship program in 2000. In 2010, the
sponsoring organization officially adopted its current name,
but it continues to hold the annual HENAAC conference, at
which the scholarships are presented. This program is sponsored by the Naval Sea Systems Command (NAVSEA) of the
U.S. Navy. Recipients must attend the conference to accept
their scholarship. The sponsor subsidizes the cost of travel, 3
nights of lodging, and meals.

Number awarded Varies each year; recently, 14 were
awarded.

Deadline April of each year.

[561]
VILLA ESPERANZA SCHOLARSHIP

Hispanic Scholarship Consortium
Attn: Scholarship Selection Committee
7703 North Lamar Boulevard, Suite 310
Austin, TX 78752
(512) 368-2956   Fax: (512) 692-1831
E-mail: scholarships@hispanicscholar.org
Web: hispanicscholar.academicworks.com

Summary To provide financial assistance to high school seniors of Hispanic heritage in Texas who plan to attend a college in the Austin area.

Eligibility This program is open to seniors of Hispanic heritage graduating from high schools in Texas and planning to enroll full time at a designated college or university in the Austin area. Applicants must be immigrants and first-generation college students. They must have a GPA of 3.0 or higher Selection is based on academic achievement, community service, personal strengths, leadership, and financial need. U.S. citizenship is not required; students may qualify under Texas Senate Bill 1528.

Financial Data The stipend is $2,000 per year.

Duration 1 year; may be renewed up to 3 additional years, provided the recipient remains enrolled full time, maintains a GPA of 3.0 or higher, and participates in at least 25 hours of community service per semester.

Additional data Eligible schools are Austin Community College, University of Texas at Austin, St. Edward's University, Concordia University, Huston-Tillotson, Texas State University, and Southwestern University.

Number awarded Varies each year; recently, 3 were awarded.

Deadline April of each year.

[562]
VIRGINIA CHAPTER AABE SCHOLARSHIPS

American Association of Blacks in Energy-Virginia
  Chapter
c/o Teresa Vaughan, Scholarship Committee Chair
701 East Cary Street, Seventh Floor
Richmond, VA 23218
E-mail: Virginia@aabe.org
Web: www.aabe.org

Summary To provide financial assistance to Hispanics and members of other underrepresented minority groups who are high school seniors in Virginia and planning to major in an energy-related field at a college in any state.

Eligibility This program is open to seniors graduating from high schools in Virginia and planning to attend a college or university in any state. Applicants must be Hispanics, African Americans, or Native Americans who have a GPA of 3.0 or higher and who have taken the ACT and/or SAT test. Their intended major must be business, engineering, technology, mathematics, the physical sciences, or other energy-related field. Along with their application, they must submit a 350-word essay that includes 1) when they discovered their interest in the field of energy and what sparked their interest; and 2) either what excites them about the field of energy or how they expect their education to prepare them for the field of energy. Financial need is not considered in the selection process.

Financial Data Stipends range from $1,000 to $3,000.

Duration 1 year.

Additional data The winner is eligible to compete for regional and national scholarships.

Number awarded 4 each year: 1 at $3,000, 1 at $2,000, and 2 at $1,000.

Deadline March of each year.

[563]
VIRGINIA LATINO HIGHER EDUCATION NETWORK SCHOLARSHIP

Virginia Latino Higher Education Network
c/o Monica Gomez, Scholarship Co-Chair
Northern Virginia Community College
Loudon/Reston Center, Room 332
1831 Wiehle Avenue
Reston, VA 20190
(703) 948-7583   E-mail: scholarships@valhen.org
Web: www.valhen.org/scholarship

Summary To provide financial assistance to Latino residents of Virginia who are interested in attending college in the state.

Eligibility This program is open to residents of Virginia who are of Latino/Hispanic heritage and either high school seniors or students currently enrolled full time at an institution of higher education in the state. Applicants must have a GPA of 2.5 or higher and be able to demonstrate financial need. Along with their application, they must submit a 500-word essay on what being Latino in America means to them.

Financial Data Stipends are $1,000 or $1,700.

Duration 1 year.

Additional data This program includes the Rivadeneira Memorial Scholarship Award and the CVC Campaign Scholarship Award.

Number awarded Varies each year; recently, 3 were awarded: 1 at $1,700 and 2 at $1,000.

Deadline October of each year.

[564]
VIRGINIA TEACHING SCHOLARSHIP LOAN PROGRAM

Virginia Department of Education
Division of Teacher Education and Licensure
Attn: Director of Teacher Education
P.O. Box 2120
Richmond, VA 23218-2120
(804) 371-2475   Toll Free: (800) 292-3820
Fax: (804) 786-6759
E-mail: JoAnne.Carver@doe.virginia.gov
Web: www.doe.virginia.gov

Summary To provide scholarship/loans to Hispanic and other minority undergraduate and graduate students in Virginia who are interested in a career in teaching.

Eligibility This program is open to Virginia residents who are enrolled full or part time as a sophomore, junior, senior, or graduate student in a state-approved teacher preparation program in Virginia, who were in the top 10% of their high school class, and have a GPA of 2.7 or higher. Applicants must meet 1 or more of the following criteria: 1) are enrolled in a program leading to endorsement in a critical shortage area; 2) are a male in an elementary or middle school education program; 3) are a minority teaching candidate in any endorsement area; or 4) are a student in an approved teacher education program leading to an endorsement in career and technical education. They must agree to engage in full-time teaching following graduation in 1) designated teacher shortage areas within Virginia; 2) a school with a high concentration of students eligible for free or reduced lunch; 3) within a school division with a shortage of teachers; or 4) in a rural or urban region of the state with a teacher shortage.

Financial Data   The maximum scholarship/loan is $10,000 per year for full-time students or a prorated amount for part-time students. Loans are forgiven by qualified teaching of 1 year for each year of support received. If the recipient fails to fulfill the teaching service requirement, the loan must be repaid with interest.

Duration   1 year; may be renewed.

Additional data   Critical shortage teaching areas in Virginia are currently identified as special education, career and technical education (including technology education, trade and industrial education, business education, and family and consumer sciences), mathematics (6-12), foreign language (preK-12), English, middle school (6-8), elementary education (preK-6), history and social sciences, health and physical education (preK-12), and school counselor (preK-12).

Number awarded   Varies each year.

Deadline   Deadline not specified.

[565]
VSCPA MINORITY ACCOUNTING SCHOLARSHIPS

Virginia Society of Certified Public Accountants
Attn: Educational Foundation
4309 Cox Road
Glen Allen, VA 23060
(804) 612-9417   Toll Free: (800) 733-8272
Fax: (804) 273-1741   E-mail: foundation@vscpa.com
Web: www.vscpa.com

Summary   To provide financial assistance to Hispanic and other minority students enrolled in an undergraduate accounting program in Virginia.

Eligibility   Applicants must be minority students (Hispanic or Latino, African American or Black, American Indian or Native Alaskan, Asian, Native Hawaiian or other Pacific Islander) currently enrolled in a Virginia college or university undergraduate accounting program. They must be U.S. citizens, be majoring in accounting, have completed at least 3 hours of accounting, be currently registered for 3 more credit hours of accounting, and have a GPA of 3.0 or higher. Selection is based on an essay, transcripts, a current resume, a faculty letter of recommendation, and financial need.

Financial Data   The stipend is $1,000.

Duration   1 year.

Number awarded   Normally 3 each year.

Deadline   March of each year.

[566]
WARNER NORCROSS & JUDD PARALEGAL AND LEGAL SECRETARIAL SCHOLARSHIP

Grand Rapids Community Foundation
Attn: Education Program Officer
185 Oakes Street S.W.
Grand Rapids, MI 49503-4008
(616) 454-1751, ext. 103   Fax: (616) 454-6455
E-mail: rbishop@grfoundation.org
Web: www.grfoundation.org/scholarshipslist

Summary   To provide financial assistance to Hispanic and other minority residents of Michigan who are interested in

working on a paralegal or legal secretarial studies degree at an institution in the state.

Eligibility   This program is open to residents of Michigan who are students of color attending or planning to attend an accredited public or private 2- or 4-year college or university in the state. Applicants must have a declared major in paralegal or legal secretarial studies. They must be U.S. citizens or permanent residents and have a GPA of 2.5 or higher. Financial need is considered in the selection process.

Financial Data   The stipend is $2,000. Funds are paid directly to the recipient's institution.

Duration   1 year.

Additional data   Funding for this program is provided by the law firm Warner Norcross & Judd LLP.

Number awarded   1 each year.

Deadline   March of each year.

[567]
WARREN G. MAGNUSON EDUCATIONAL SUPPORT PERSONNEL SCHOLARSHIP GRANT

Washington Education Association
32032 Weyerhaeuser Way South
P.O. Box 9100
Federal Way, WA 98063-9100
(253) 765-7056   Toll Free: (800) 622-3393, ext. 7056
E-mail: Janna.Connor@Washingtonea.org
Web: www.washingtonea.org

Summary   To provide funding to Educational Support Personnel (ESP) members of the Washington Education Association (WEA), especially Hispanics and other minorities, who are interested in taking classes to obtain an initial teaching certificate.

Eligibility   This program is open to WEA/ESP members who are engaged in course work related to obtaining an initial teaching certificate. Applicants must submit a plan for obtaining an initial certificate, a letter describing their passion to become a teacher, evidence of activities and/or leadership in the association, and 3 to 5 letters of reference. Minority members of the association are especially encouraged to apply; 1 of the scholarships is reserved for them.

Financial Data   The stipend is $1,500.

Duration   These are 1-time grants.

Number awarded   3 each year, including 1 reserved for a minority member.

Deadline   June of each year.

[568]
WASHINGTON ADMIRAL'S FUND SCHOLARSHIP

National Naval Officers Association-Washington, D.C.
  Chapter
c/o LCDR Stephen Williams
P.O. Box 30784
Alexandria, VA 22310
(703) 644-2605   Fax: (703) 644-8503
E-mail: Stephen.Williams@navy.mil
Web: www.dcnnoa.org/dcnnoa-scholarship

Summary   To provide financial assistance to Hispanic and other minority high school seniors from the Washington, D.C. area who are interested in attending a college or university in any state and enrolling in the Navy Reserve Officers Training Corps (NROTC) program.

Eligibility This program is open to minority seniors graduating from high schools in the Washington, D.C. metropolitan area who plan to enroll full time at an accredited 2- or 4-year college or university in any state. Applicants must be planning to enroll in the NROTC program. They must have a GPA of 2.5 or higher and be U.S. citizens or permanent residents. Selection is based on academic achievement, community involvement, and financial need.

Financial Data The stipend is $1,000.

Duration 1 year; nonrenewable.

Additional data This program is sponsored by the Washington D.C. Chapter of the National Naval Officers Association (DCNNOA), an organization of African American naval officers, but all minorities are eligible and recipients are not required to join or affiliate with the military in any way. If the recipient fails to enroll in the NROTC unit, all scholarship funds must be returned.

Number awarded 1 each year.

Deadline February of each year.

[569]
WASHINGTON D.C. AREA SUPPLY OFFICERS SCHOLARSHIP

National Naval Officers Association-Washington, D.C.
 Chapter
c/o LCDR Stephen Williams
P.O. Box 30784
Alexandria, VA 22310
(703) 644-2605   Fax: (703) 644-8503
E-mail: Stephen.Williams@navy.mil
Web: www.dcnnoa.org/dcnnoa-scholarship

Summary To provide financial assistance to Hispanic and other minority high school seniors from the Washington, D.C. area who are interested in attending college in any state.

Eligibility This program is open to minority seniors graduating from high schools in the Washington, D.C. metropolitan area who plan to enroll full time at an accredited 2- or 4-year college or university in any state. Applicants must have a GPA of 3.0 or higher and be U.S. citizens or permanent residents. Selection is based on academic achievement, community involvement, and financial need.

Financial Data The stipend is $3,000.

Duration 1 year; nonrenewable.

Additional data This program is sponsored by the Washington D.C. Chapter of the National Naval Officers Association (DCNNOA), an organization of African American naval officers, but all minorities are eligible and recipients are not required to join or affiliate with the military in any way.

Number awarded 1 each year.

Deadline February of each year.

[570]
WASHINGTON DC METROPOLITAN AREA CHAPTER AABE SCHOLARSHIPS

American Association of Blacks in Energy-Washington
 DC Metropolitan Area Chapter
Attn: Scholarship Committee
P.O. Box 77263
Washington, DC 20013
E-mail: aabedc.scholarshipchair@gmail.com
Web: www.aabe.org

Summary To provide financial assistance to Hispanics and members of other underrepresented minority groups who are high school seniors in the Washington, D.C. metropolitan area and planning to major in an energy-related field at a college in any state.

Eligibility This program is open to seniors graduating from high schools in the Washington, D.C. metropolitan area who are planning to work on a bachelor's degree at a college or university in any state. Applicants must be Hispanics, African Americans, or Native Americans who have a GPA of 3.0 or higher and have taken the ACT and/or SAT test. Their intended major must be a field of business, engineering, physical science, mathematics, or technology related to energy. Along with their application, they must submit a 350-word essay that includes 1) when they discovered their interest in the field of energy and what sparked their interest; and 2) either what excites them about the field of energy or how they expect their education to prepare them for the field of energy. Financial need is not considered in the selection process.

Financial Data Stipends range from $1,500 to $2,500.

Duration 1 year; nonrenewable.

Additional data Winners are eligible to compete for regional and national scholarships.

Number awarded 3 each year: 1 each at $2,500, $2,000, and $1,500.

Deadline April of each year.

[571]
WASHINGTON SCIENCE TEACHERS ASSOCIATION SCIENCE LEADERSHIP SCHOLARSHIPS

Washington Science Teachers Association
Attn: Andy Boyd, President
2911 88th Street S.E.
Everett, WA 98109
(425) 337-5552   E-mail: boydscience@gmail.com
Web: www.wsta.net/WSTALeadershipScholarship

Summary To provide financial assistance to upper-division students and teachers in Washington, especially Hispanics and other minorities, who are interested in training in science education.

Eligibility This program is open to juniors and seniors at colleges and universities in Washington who are working on certification in science education or in elementary education with an emphasis on science. Preference is given to Hispanics, African Americans, Native Americans, Asian and Pacific Islanders, and women.

Financial Data The stipend is $2,000.

Duration 1 year; nonrenewable.

Additional data This program began in 2003 as the Peggy Vatter Memorial Scholarships.

Number awarded 1 or more each year.

Deadline June of each year.

[572]
WASHINGTON UNIVERSITY AMGEN SCHOLARS PROGRAM

Washington University
Division of Biology and Biomedical Sciences
Attn: Summer Research Admissions
660 South Euclid Avenue
Campus Box 8226
St. Louis, MO 63110-1093
(314) 362-7963   Toll Free: (800) 852-9074
E-mail: DBBS-summerresearch@wusm.wustl.edu
Web: dbbs.wustl.edu

Summary   To provide Hispanic and other underrepresented minority undergraduate students with a summer research experience at Washington University in St. Louis in biological and biomedical sciences.

Eligibility   This program is open to sophomores, juniors, and non-graduating seniors at 4-year colleges and universities in the United States, Puerto Rico, and U.S. territories. Applicants must be interested in a summer research experience at Washington University in biochemistry, bioengineering, bioinformatics, biology (molecular, cell, and developmental), biopsychology, biotechnology, chemical and biomedical engineering, chemistry, immunology, medical pharmacology, microbiology, molecular genetics, molecular medicine, molecular pharmacology, neurobiology, neuroscience, pathology, physiological psychology, physiological science, statistics, or toxicology. They must have a GPA of 3.2 or higher and an interest in continuing on to a Ph.D. or M.D./Ph.D. (but not M.D.) program. Applications are especially encouraged from students from economically disadvantaged backgrounds, those who attend small liberal arts colleges, and from members of groups traditionally underrepresented in biomedical research (African Americans, Hispanic Americans, Native Americans, Pacific Islanders, women, and people with disabilities). U.S. citizenship or permanent resident status is required.

Financial Data   Housing, travel to and from St. Louis, meals, and a stipend of $4,000 are provided.

Duration   10 weeks during the summer.

Additional data   This program serves as the Washington University component of the Amgen Scholars Program, which operates at 8 other U.S. universities (and the National Institutes of Health) and is funded by the Amgen Foundation.

Number awarded   20 each year.

Deadline   January of each year.

[573]
WAVE FELLOWS PROGRAM

California Institute of Technology
Student-Faculty Programs
1200 East California Boulevard
Mail Code 33-087
Pasadena, CA 91125
(626) 395-2885   Fax: (626) 389-5467
E-mail: sfp@caltech.edu
Web: sfp.caltech.edu/programs/wavefellows

Summary   To provide an opportunity for Hispanic and other underrepresented college students to work in a research laboratory at California Institute of Technology (Caltech) during the summer.

Eligibility   This program is open to underrepresented minorities, women, first-generation college students, geographically underrepresented students, educationally and financially disadvantaged students, and students with disabilities. Applicants must be interested in working during the summer in a modern academic research laboratory at Caltech under the guidance of experienced scientists and engineers. They must be undergraduate sophomores, juniors, or non-graduating seniors who have a GPA of 3.2 or higher and a major in a field of science, technology, engineering, or mathematics (STEM). U.S. citizenship or permanent resident status is required.

Financial Data   The stipend is $600 per week. A $500 housing allowance is also provided.

Duration   8 to 10 weeks during the summer, beginning in June.

Additional data   Support for this program is provided by Edison International and the Genentech Foundation.

Number awarded   Varies each year.

Deadline   January of each year.

[574]
WAYNE D. CORNILS SCHOLARSHIP

Idaho State Broadcasters Association
1674 Hill Road, Suite 3
Boise, ID 83702
(208) 345-3072   Fax: (208) 343-8046
E-mail: isba@qwestoffice.net
Web: www.idahobroadcasters.org/index.php/scholarships

Summary   To provide financial assistance to Hispanic and other less advantaged students at Idaho colleges and universities who are preparing for a career in the broadcasting field.

Eligibility   This program is open to full-time students at Idaho schools who are preparing for a career in broadcasting, including business administration, sales, journalism, or engineering. Applicants must have a GPA of at least 2.0 for the first 2 years of school or 2.5 for the last 2 years. Along with their application, they must submit a letter of recommendation from the general manager of a broadcasting station that is a member of the Idaho State Broadcasters Association and a 1-page essay describing their career plans and why they want the scholarship. Applications are encouraged from a broad and diverse student population. This scholarship is reserved for a less advantaged applicant.

Financial Data   The stipend depends on the need of the recipient.

Duration   1 year.

Number awarded   1 each year.

Deadline   March of each year.

[575]
WESTERN UNION FOUNDATION FAMILY SCHOLARSHIP PROGRAM

Western Union Foundation
c/o Institute of International Education
1400 K Street, N.W., Suite 700
Washington, DC 20005
(202) 686-8652   E-mail: wufoundaton@iie.org
Web: foundation.westernunion.com

Summary To provide financial assistance to pairs of students from the same family of immigrants, both of whom wish to attend college in any state.

Eligibility Applications to this program must be submitted jointly by 2 students who are members of the same family (parent and child, siblings). Both applicants must be 18 years of age or older, have been born outside of the United States, have been in this country for 7 years or less, and be planning to attend an accredited institution of higher education or non-profit training institute in any state. Funding is available for college or university tuition, language acquisition classes, technical or skill training, and/or financial literacy; graduate study is not supported.

Financial Data Stipends range from $1,000 to $5,000 per family. Funds are paid directly to the educational institution.

Duration 1 year.

Additional data This program began in 2009.

Number awarded Varies each year.

Deadline May of each year.

[576]
WILLIAM A. CRAWFORD MINORITY TEACHER SCHOLARSHIP

Indiana Commission for Higher Education
Attn: Financial Aid and Student Support Services
101 West Ohio Street, Suite 300
Indianapolis, IN 46204-4206
(317) 232-1023   Toll Free: (888) 528-4719 (within IN)
Fax: (317) 232-3260   E-mail: Scholars@che.in.gov
Web: www.in.gov/che/4507.htm

Summary To provide scholarship/loans to Hispanic and Black undergraduate students in Indiana interested in preparing for a teaching career at a school in the state.

Eligibility This program is open to Hispanic and Black students seeking certification in order to teach at an accredited elementary or secondary school in Indiana. Applicants must be Indiana residents and U.S. citizens or permanent residents who are enrolled or accepted for enrollment as full-time students at an academic institution in Indiana. Students who are already enrolled in college must have a GPA of 2.0 or higher. Financial need may be considered, but it is not a requirement.

Financial Data Minority students demonstrating financial need may receive up to $4,000 per year. They must agree in writing to apply for a teaching position at an accredited school in Indiana following certification and, if hired, to teach for at least 3 years.

Duration 1 year; may be renewed up to 3 additional years if recipients maintain a 2.0 GPA. They may, however, take up to 6 years to complete the program from the start of receiving the first scholarship.

Additional data This program began in 1988 to address the critical shortage of Black and Hispanic teachers in Indiana. It was given its current name in 2016. Participating colleges in Indiana select the recipients. Students must submit their application to the financial aid office of the college they plan to attend.

Number awarded Varies each year.

Deadline September of each year.

[577]
WILLIAM K. SCHUBERT M.D. MINORITY NURSING SCHOLARSHIP

Cincinnati Children's Hospital Medical Center
Attn: Office of Diversity and Inclusion, MLC 9008
3333 Burnet Avenue
Cincinnati, OH 45229-3026
(513) 803-6416   Toll Free: (800) 344-2462
Fax: (513) 636-5643   TDD: (513) 636-4900
E-mail: diversity@cchmc.org
Web: www.cincinnatichildrens.org

Summary To provide financial assistance to Hispanics and members of other underrepresented groups interested in working on a bachelor's or master's degree in nursing to prepare for licensure in Ohio.

Eligibility This program is open to members of groups underrepresented in the nursing profession (males, American Indians or Alaska Natives, Blacks or African Americans, Hawaiian Natives or other Pacific Islanders, Hispanics or Latinos, or Asians). Applicants must be enrolled or accepted in a professional bachelor's or master's registered nurse program at an accredited school of nursing to prepare for initial licensure in Ohio. They must have a GPA of 2.75 or higher. Along with their application, they must submit a 750-word essay that covers 1) their long-range personal, educational, and professional goals; 2) why they chose nursing as a profession; 3) how their experience as a member of an underrepresented group has influenced a major professional and/or personal decision in their life; 4) any unique qualifications, experiences, or special talents that demonstrate their creativity; and 5) how their work experience has contributed to their personal development.

Financial Data The stipend is $2,750 per year.

Duration 1 year. May be renewed up to 3 additional years for students working on a bachelor's degree or 1 additional year for students working on a master's degree; renewal requires that students maintain a GPA of 2.75 or higher.

Number awarded 1 or more each year.

Deadline April of each year.

[578]
WILLIAM RANDOLPH HEARST ENDOWMENT SCHOLARSHIPS

National Action Council for Minorities in Engineering
Attn: Director, Scholarships and University Relations
440 Hamilton Avenue, Suite 302
White Plains, NY 10601-1813
(914) 539-4316   Fax: (914) 539-4032
E-mail: scholars@nacme.org
Web: www.nacme.org/scholarships

Summary To provide financial assistance to Latino and other underrepresented minority college freshmen or sophomores majoring in engineering or related fields.

Eligibility This program is open to Latino, African American, and American Indian college freshmen and sophomores who have a GPA of 2.8 or higher and have demonstrated academic excellence, leadership skills, and a commitment to science and engineering as a career. Applicants must be enrolled full time at an ABET-accredited engineering program. Fields of study include all areas of engineering as well as computer science, materials science, mathematics, operations research, or physics.

Financial Data   The stipend is $2,500 per year. Funds are sent directly to the recipient's university.
Duration   Up to 4 years.
Additional data   This program was established by the William Randolph Hearst Foundation.
Number awarded   2 each year.
Deadline   April of each year.

[579]
WILLIAM RUCKER GREENWOOD SCHOLARSHIP

Association for Women Geoscientists-Potomac Chapter
Attn: Scholarships
P.O. Box 6644
Arlington, VA 22206-0644
E-mail: awgpotomacschol@hotmail.com
Web: www.awg.org/members/po_scholarships.htm

Summary   To provide financial assistance to Hispanic and other minority women from any state working on an undergraduate or graduate degree in the geosciences at a college in the Potomac Bay region.
Eligibility   This program is open to minority women who are residents of any state and currently enrolled as full-time undergraduate or graduate geoscience majors at an accredited, degree-granting college or university in Delaware, the District of Columbia, Maryland, Virginia, or West Virginia. Selection is based on the applicant's 1) participation in geoscience or earth science educational activities; and 2) potential for leadership as a future geoscience professional.
Financial Data   The stipend is $1,000. The recipient also is granted a 1-year membership in the Association for Women Geoscientists (AWG).
Duration   1 year.
Number awarded   1 each year.
Deadline   April of each year.

[580]
WILLIE BRADSHAW MEMORIAL ENDOWED SCHOLARSHIPS

North Carolina High School Athletic Association
Attn: Director of Grants and Fundraising
222 Finley Golf Course Road
P.O. Box 3216
Chapel Hill, NC 27515-3216
(919) 240-7371   Fax: (919) 240-7399
E-mail: mary@nchsaa.org
Web: www.nchsaa.org

Summary   To provide financial assistance to Hispanic and other minority seniors (males and females considered separately) at high schools in North Carolina who have participated in lacrosse and plan to attend college in any state.
Eligibility   This program is open to Hispanic American, American Indian/Alaska Native, African American, and Asian Pacific Islander American seniors graduating from high schools that are members of the North Carolina High School Athletic Association (NCHSAA). Applicants must be U.S. citizens, nationals, or permanent residents planning to attend college in any state. They must have participated in a sanctioned varsity sport, demonstrate leadership abilities through participation in community service and extracurricular or other activities, have clean school and athletic disciplinary records, and have adjusted gross family income between

$30,000 and $75,000 per year. Males and females are considered separately.
Financial Data   The stipend is $750 for regional winners; state winners receive an additional $1,000.
Duration   1 year; nonrenewable.
Number awarded   16 regional winners (1 male and 1 female in each of 8 regions) are selected each year; from those winners, 1 male and 1 female are selected as state winners.
Deadline   February of each year.

[581]
WISCONSIN CHAPTER AABE SCHOLARSHIPS

American Association of Blacks in Energy-Wisconsin
   Chapter
Attn: Scholarship Committee
P.O. Box 1907
Milwaukee, WI 53203
E-mail: aabe-wi@we-energies.com
Web: www.aabe.org/index.php?component=pages&id=627

Summary   To provide financial assistance to Hispanics and members of other underrepresented minority groups who are high school seniors in Wisconsin and planning to major in an energy-related field at a college in any state.
Eligibility   This program is open to seniors graduating from high schools in Tennessee and planning to attend a college or university in any state. Applicants must be Hispanics, African Americans, or Native Americans who have a GPA of 3.0 or higher and have taken the ACT and/or SAT test. Their intended major must be business, engineering, technology, mathematics, the physical sciences, or other energy-related field. Along with their application, they must submit a 350-word essay that includes 1) when they discovered their interest in the field of energy and what sparked their interest; and 2) either what excites them about the field of energy or how they expect their education to prepare them for the field of energy. Financial need is not considered in the selection process.
Financial Data   The stipend is $1,000 for academic scholarships and $250 for book awards.
Duration   1 year.
Additional data   Winners are eligible to compete for regional and national scholarships.
Number awarded   1 academic scholarships and 2 book awards are presented each year.
Deadline   March of each year.

[582]
WISCONSIN MINORITY UNDERGRADUATE RETENTION GRANTS

Wisconsin Higher Educational Aids Board
131 West Wilson Street, Suite 902
P.O. Box 7885
Madison, WI 53707-7885
(608) 267-2212   Fax: (608) 267-2808
E-mail: deanna.schulz@wi.gov
Web: www.heab.state.wi.us/programs.html

Summary   To provide financial assistance to Hispanics and other minorities in Wisconsin who are currently enrolled at a college in the state.

Eligibility This program is open to residents of Wisconsin who are Hispanic Americans, African Americans, American Indians, or southeast Asians (students who were admitted to the United States after December 31, 1975 and who are a former citizen of Laos, Vietnam, or Cambodia or whose ancestor was a citizen of 1 of those countries). Applicants must be enrolled at least half time as sophomores, juniors, seniors, or fifth-year undergraduates at a Wisconsin technical college, tribal college, or independent college or university in the state. They must be nominated by their institution and be able to demonstrate financial need.

Financial Data Stipends range from $250 to $2,500 per year, depending on the need of the recipient.

Duration Up to 4 years.

Additional data The Wisconsin Higher Educational Aids Board administers this program for students at private non-profit institutions, technical colleges, and tribal colleges. The University of Wisconsin has a similar program for students attending any of the branches of that system. Eligible students should apply through their school's financial aid office.

Number awarded Varies each year.

Deadline Deadline dates vary by institution; check with your school's financial aid office.

[583]
WOMAN WHO MOVES THE NATION SCHOLARSHIP

Conference of Minority Transportation Officials
Attn: National Scholarship Program
100 M Street, S.E., Suite 917
Washington, DC 20003
(202) 506-2917   E-mail: info@comto.org
Web: www.comto.org/page/scholarships

Summary To provide financial assistance to Hispanic and other minority women who are working on an undergraduate or graduate degree in specified fields to prepare for a management career in a transportation-related organization.

Eligibility This program is open to minority women who are working on an undergraduate or graduate degree with intent to lead in some capacity as a supervisor, manager, director, or other position in transit or a transportation-related organization. Applicants may be studying business, entrepreneurship, political science, or other specialized area. They must have a GPA of 3.0 or higher. Along with their application they must submit a cover letter on their transportation-related career goals and life aspirations. Financial need is not considered in the selection process.

Financial Data The stipend is $5,000. Funds are paid directly to the recipient's college or university.

Duration 1 year.

Number awarded 1 each year.

Deadline April of each year.

[584]
WOMEN'S TRANSPORTATION SEMINAR JUNIOR COLLEGE SCHOLARSHIP

Women's Transportation Seminar
Attn: WTS Foundation
1701 K Street, N.W., Suite 800
Washington, DC 20006
(202) 955-5085   Fax: (202) 955-5088
E-mail: wts@wtsinternational.org
Web: www.wtsinternational.org/education/scholarships

Summary To provide financial assistance to women, especially Hispanics and other minorities, who are enrolled at a community college or trade school to prepare for a career in transportation.

Eligibility This program is open to women who are working on an associate or technical degree in transportation or a transportation-related field (e.g., transportation engineering, planning, finance, or logistics). Applicants must have a GPA of 3.0 or higher. Along with their application, they must submit a 500-word statement about their career goals after graduation and why they think they should receive the scholarship award. Applications must be submitted first to a local chapter; the chapters forward selected applications for consideration on the national level. Minority women are especially encouraged to apply. Selection is based on transportation involvement and goals, job skills, academic record, and leadership potential; financial need is not considered.

Financial Data The stipend is $1,000.

Duration 1 year.

Additional data Local chapters may also award additional funding to winners for their area.

Number awarded 1 each year.

Deadline Applications must be submitted by November to a local WTS chapter.

[585]
WOODS HOLE OCEANOGRAPHIC INSTITUTION MINORITY FELLOWSHIPS

Woods Hole Oceanographic Institution
Attn: Academic Programs Office
Clark Laboratory 223, MS 31
360 Woods Hole Road
Woods Hole, MA 02543-1541
(508) 289-2219   Fax: (508) 457-2188
E-mail: education@whoi.edu
Web: www.whoi.edu/page.do?pid=9377

Summary To provide work experience to Hispanic and other minority group members who are interested in preparing for careers in the marine sciences, oceanographic engineering, or marine policy.

Eligibility This program is open to ethnic minority undergraduates enrolled in U.S. colleges or universities who have completed at least 1 year of study and who are interested in the physical or natural sciences, mathematics, engineering, or marine policy. Applicants must be U.S. citizens or permanent residents and Chicano, Mexican American, Puerto Rican or other Hispanic; African American or Black; Asian American; or Native American, Alaska Native, or Native Hawaiian. They must be interested in participating in a program of study and research at Woods Hole Oceanographic Institution. Selection is based on previous academic and scientific achievements and promise as future ocean scientists or ocean engineers.

Financial Data The stipend is $500 per week; trainees also receive free housing and additional support for travel to Woods Hole.

Duration 10 to 12 weeks during the summer or 1 semester during the academic year; renewable.

Additional data Trainees are assigned advisers who supervise their research programs and supplementary study activities. Some traineeships involve field work or research cruises. This program is conducted as part of the Research Experiences for Undergraduates (REU) Program of the National Science Foundation.

Number awarded 4 to 5 each year.

Deadline February of each year.

[586]
WORLDSTUDIO AIGA SCHOLARSHIPS

AIGA, the professional association for design
Attn: Scholarships
233 Broadway, 17th floor
New York, NY 10279
(212) 710-3111   E-mail: scholarship@aiga.org
Web: www.aiga.org/worldstudio-scholarship

Summary To provide financial assistance to Hispanic and other minority or economically disadvantaged students who are interested in working on an undergraduate or graduate degree in specified fields of the arts.

Eligibility This program is open to undergraduate and graduate students who are currently enrolled or planning to enroll full time at an accredited college or university and work on a degree in 1 of the following areas: fine art, graphic design (including visual design), illustration (including animation), interactive design (including UI/UX, motion, digital, and web design), or photography. Other fields of the arts, (e.g., industrial design, interior design, film, architecture, landscape design, theater design, fashion design) are not eligible. Although not required, minority status is a significant factor in the selection process. U.S. citizenship or permanent resident status is required. Applicants must have a GPA of 2.0 or higher. Along with their application, they must submit a 600-word statement of purpose that includes a brief autobiography, an explanation of how their experiences have influenced their creative work and/or their career plans, and how they see themselves contributing to the community at large in the future. Selection is based on that statement, the quality of submitted work, financial need, minority status, recommendations, and academic record.

Financial Data Basic stipends range from $2,000 to $3,000, but awards up to $5,000 are also presented at the discretion of the jury. Honorable mentions are $500. Funds are paid directly to the recipient's school.

Duration 1 academic year. Recipients may reapply.

Additional data This program is offered by AIGA, founded in 1914 as the American Institute of Graphic Arts, in cooperation with the Worldstudio Foundation.

Number awarded Varies each year; recently, 16 scholarships and 2 honorable mentions were awarded.

Deadline April of each year.

[587]
WSP/PARSONS BRINCKERHOFF ENGINEERING SCHOLARSHIP

Conference of Minority Transportation Officials
Attn: National Scholarship Program
100 M Street, S.E., Suite 917
Washington, DC 20003
(202) 506-2917   E-mail: info@comto.org
Web: www.comto.org/page/scholarships

Summary To provide financial assistance to Hispanics and other members of the Conference of Minority Transportation Officials (COMTO) and their families who are working on an undergraduate degree in engineering.

Eligibility This program is open to undergraduate students who are members and their parents, guardians, or grandparents who have been members of COMTO for at least 1 year. Applicants must be working on a degree in engineering and have a GPA of 3.0 or higher. Along with their application they must submit a cover letter on their transportation-related career goals and life aspirations. Financial need is not considered in the selection process.

Financial Data The stipend is $2,500. Funds are paid directly to the recipient's college or university.

Duration 1 year.

Additional data This program is sponsored by WSP USA, formerly Parsons Brinckerhoff, Inc.

Number awarded 2 each year.

Deadline April of each year.

[588]
WSP/PARSONS BRINCKERHOFF GOLDEN APPLE SCHOLARSHIP

Conference of Minority Transportation Officials
Attn: National Scholarship Program
100 M Street, S.E., Suite 917
Washington, DC 20003
(202) 506-2917   E-mail: info@comto.org
Web: www.comto.org/page/scholarships

Summary To provide financial assistance to Hispanics and other members of the Conference of Minority Transportation Officials (COMTO) and their children who are high school seniors planning to attend college to prepare for a career in transportation.

Eligibility This program is open to graduating high school seniors who are members of COMTO or whose parents are members. Applicants must be planning to attend an accredited college, university, or vocational/technical institution to prepare for a career in transportation. They must have a GPA of 2.0 or higher. Along with their application they must submit a cover letter on their transportation-related career goals and life aspirations. Financial need is not considered in the selection process.

Financial Data The stipend is $2,500. Funds are paid directly to the recipient's college or university.

Duration 1 year.

Additional data This program is sponsored by WSP USA, formerly Parsons Brinckerhoff, Inc.

Number awarded 2 each year.

Deadline April of each year.

[589]
WTS TRANSPORTATION YOU HIGH SCHOOL SCHOLARSHIP

Women's Transportation Seminar
Attn: WTS Foundation
1701 K Street, N.W., Suite 800
Washington, DC 20006
(202) 955-5085   Fax: (202) 955-5088
E-mail: wts@wtsinternational.org
Web: www.wtsinternational.org/education/scholarships

Summary   To provide financial assistance to female high school seniors, especially Hispanics and other minorities, who are studying fields of science, technology, engineering, or mathematics (STEM) and planning to attend college to prepare for a career in transportation.

Eligibility   This program is open to women who are high school seniors with a GPA of 3.0 or higher. Applicants must be studying STEM fields in high school and be planning to attend college to prepare for a career in transportation (e.g., civil engineering, city planning, logistics, automotive engineering, truck repair). Along with their application, they must submit a 500-word statement about their career goals after graduation and why they think they should receive the scholarship. Applications must be submitted first to a local chapter; the chapters forward selected applications for consideration on the national level. Minority women are especially encouraged to apply. Selection is based on transportation involvement and goals, job skills, academic record, and leadership potential; financial need is not considered.

Financial Data   The stipend is $1,000.

Duration   1 year.

Additional data   Local chapters may also award additional funding to winners for their area.

Number awarded   1 each year.

Deadline   Applications must be submitted by November to a local WTS chapter.

[590]
XEROX TECHNICAL MINORITY SCHOLARSHIP PROGRAM

Xerox Corporation
Attn: Technical Minority Scholarship Program
150 State Street, Fourth Floor
Rochester, NY 14614
Toll Free: (877) 747-3625   E-mail: xtmsp@rballiance.com
Web: www.xerox.com/jobs/minority-scholarships/enus.html

Summary   To provide financial assistance to Hispanics and other minorities interested in undergraduate or graduate education in the sciences and/or engineering.

Eligibility   This program is open to minorities (people of Hispanic, African American, Asian, Pacific Islander, Native American, or Native Alaskan descent) working full time on a bachelor's, master's, or doctoral degree in chemistry, computing and software systems, engineering (chemical, computer, electrical, imaging, manufacturing, mechanical, optical, or software), information management, laser optics, materials science, physics, or printing management science. Applicants must be U.S. citizens or permanent residents with a GPA of 3.0 or higher and attending a 4-year college or university.

Financial Data   Stipends range from $1,000 to $10,000.

Duration   1 year.

Number awarded   Varies each year, recently, 128 were awarded.

Deadline   September of each year.

Graduate Students

Listed alphabetically by program title and described in detail here are 463 fellowships, forgivable loans, grants, awards, and other sources of "free money" set aside for Hispanic Americans who are incoming, continuing, or returning graduate students working on a master's, doctoral, or professional degree. This funding is available to support study, training, research, and/or creative activities in the United States.

[591]
AAUW CAREER DEVELOPMENT GRANTS

American Association of University Women
Attn: AAUW Educational Foundation
1111 16th Street, N.W.
Washington, DC 20036-4873
(202) 785-7700   Toll Free: (800) 326-AAUW
Fax: (202) 872-1425   TDD: (202) 785-7777
E-mail: aauw@applyists.com
Web: www.aauw.org

Summary   To provide financial assistance to women who are seeking career advancement, career change, or reentry into the workforce, especially Hispanics and other women of color.

Eligibility   This program is open to women who are U.S. citizens or permanent residents, have earned a bachelor's degree, received their most recent degree more than 4 years ago, and are making career changes, seeking to advance in current careers, or reentering the workforce. Applicants must be interested in working toward a master's degree, second bachelor's or associate degree, professional degree (e.g., M.D., J.D.), certification program, or technical school certificate. They must be planning to undertake course work at an accredited 2- or 4-year college or university (or a technical school that is licensed, accredited, or approved by the U.S. Department of Education). Primary consideration is given to women of color and women pursuing their first advanced degree or credentials in nontraditional fields. Support is not provided for prerequisite course work or for Ph.D. course work or dissertations. Selection is based on demonstrated commitment to education and equity for women and girls, reason for seeking higher education or technical training, degree to which study plan is consistent with career objectives, potential for success in chosen field, documentation of opportunities in chosen field, feasibility of study plans and proposed time schedule, validity of proposed budget and budget narrative (including sufficient outside support), and quality of written proposal.

Financial Data   Grants range from $2,000 to $12,000. Funds may be used for tuition, fees, books, supplies, local transportation, dependent child care, or purchase of a computer required for the study program.

Duration   1 year, beginning in July; nonrenewable.

Additional data   The filing fee is $35.

Number awarded   Varies each year; recently, 63 of these grants, with a value of $670,000, were awarded.

Deadline   December of each year.

[592]
ABC LATINO MINISTRIES SCHOLARSHIP

American Baptist Churches USA
Attn: American Baptist Home Mission Societies
National Coordinator for Intercultural Ministries
P.O. Box 851
Valley Forge, PA 19482-0851
(610) 768-2421   Toll Free: (800) ABC-3USA, ext. 2421
Fax: (610) 768-2453
E-mail: Salvador.Orellana@abhms.org
Web: abhms.org

Summary   To provide financial assistance to Latinos who are interested in preparing for or furthering a church career in the American Baptist Church (ABC).

Eligibility   This program is open to Latino members of the ABC or its recognized institutions who demonstrate financial need. They must be enrolled full time at an accredited institution, working on an undergraduate degree or first professional degree in a seminary. Applicants must be currently serving or planning to serve in a vocation with the church or with its recognized institutions. They must be U.S. citizens who have been a member of an American Baptist Church for at least 1 year.

Financial Data   The stipends range from $500 to $3,000 per year.

Duration   1 year; may be renewed.

Number awarded   Varies each year.

Deadline   May of each year.

[593]
ACADEMIC LIBRARY ASSOCIATION OF OHIO DIVERSITY SCHOLARSHIP

Academic Library Association of Ohio
c/o Eileen Theodore-Shusta, Diversity Committee Chair
Ohio University
Library Administrative Services
422 Alden
30 Park Place
Athens, OH 45701
(740) 593-2989   E-mail: theodore@ohio.edu
Web: www.alaoweb.org/procmanual/policies.html#diversity

Summary   To provide financial assistance to residents of Ohio, especially Hispanics and members of other underrepresented groups, who are working on a master's degree in library science at a school in any state and will contribute to diversity in the profession.

Eligibility   This program is open to residents of Ohio who are enrolled or entering an ALA-accredited program for a master's degree in library science, either on campus or via distance education. Applicants must be able to demonstrate how they will contribute to diversity in the profession, including (but not limited to) race or ethnicity, sexual orientation, life experience, physical ability, and a sense of commitment to those and other diversity issues. Along with their application, they must submit 1) a list of participation in honor societies or professional organizations, awards, scholarships, prizes, honors, or class offices; 2) a list of their community, civic, organizational, or volunteer experiences; and 3) an essay on their understanding of and commitment to diversity in libraries, including how they, as library school students and future professionals, might address the issue.

Financial Data   The stipend is $1,500.

Duration   1 year.

Number awarded   2 each year.

Deadline   March of each year.

[594]
ACADEMY OF NUTRITION AND DIETETICS GRADUATE SCHOLARSHIPS

Academy of Nutrition and Dietetics
Attn: Foundation
120 South Riverside Plaza, Suite 2000
Chicago, IL 60606-6995
(312) 899-4821   Toll Free: (800) 877-1600, ext. 4821
Fax: (312) 899-4796   E-mail: scholarship@eatright.org
Web: www.eatrightacend.org

Summary   To provide financial assistance to graduate student members of the Academy of Nutrition and Dietetics, especially Hispanics and members of other underrepresented groups.

Eligibility   This program is open to members of the academy who are enrolled in the second year of a master's or doctoral degree program in dietetics. Applicants who are currently completing a dietetic internship or pre-professional practice program that is combined with a graduate program may also apply. The graduate scholarships are available only to U.S. citizens and permanent residents. Applicants should intend to practice in the field of dietetics. Some scholarships require specific areas of study (e.g., public health nutrition, food service administration) and status as a registered dietitian. Others may require membership in a specific dietetic practice group, residency in a specific state, or underrepresented minority group status. The same application form can be used for all categories.

Financial Data   Stipends range from $500 to $10,000.

Duration   1 year.

Additional data   The Academy of Nutrition and Dietetics was formerly the American Dietetic Association.

Number awarded   Approximately 60 each year.

Deadline   February of each year.

[595]
ACC GREATER PHILADELPHIA DIVERSITY CORPORATE SUMMER INTERNSHIP

Association of Corporate Counsel-Greater Philadelphia
  Chapter
c/o Anne Bancroft, Diversity Committee Co-Chair
Exelon Business Services Company
2301 Market Street, Suite 23
Philadelphia, PA 19103
Toll Free: (800) 494-4000
E-mail: anne.bancroft@exeloncorp.com
Web: www.acc.com

Summary   To provide an opportunity for law students from diverse backgrounds, including Hispanics, to gain summer work experience in corporate law at firms in the Philadelphia area.

Eligibility   This program is open to students who are members of minority groups traditionally underrepresented in the legal profession (Hispanic, Asian/Pacific Islander, African American, American Indian/Alaska Native). Applications are solicited from law schools in the Philadelphia area, but students at all other law schools may be eligible if they are interested in a summer internship in corporate law at a firm in that area. Interested students must submit information about their financial status, a list of extracurricular activities, any relevant legal experience, a legal writing sample, and an essay of 250

to 500 words explaining why they qualify for this internship and what they hope to gain from the experience.

Financial Data   The stipend is $7,500.

Duration   Summer months.

Number awarded   Approximately 15 each year.

Deadline   January of each year.

[596]
ACC NATIONAL CAPITAL REGION CORPORATE SCHOLARS PROGRAM

Association of Corporate Counsel-National Capital
  Region
Attn: Executive Director
P.O. Box 2147
Rockville, MD 20847-2147
(301) 881-3018   E-mail: Ilene.Reid-NCR@accglobal.com
Web: m.acc.com/chapters/ncr/scholars.cfm

Summary   To provide an opportunity for summer work experience in the metropolitan Washington, D.C. area to students at law schools in the area who will contribute to the diversity of the profession, such as Hispanics.

Eligibility   This program is open to students entering their second or third year of part- or full-time study at law schools in the Washington, D.C. metropolitan area (including suburban Maryland and all of Virginia). Applicants must be able to demonstrate how they contribute to diversity in the legal profession, based not only on ideas about gender, race, and ethnicity, but also concepts of socioeconomic background and their individual educational and career path. They must be interested in working during the summer at a sponsoring private corporation and nonprofit organizations in the Washington, D.C. area. Along with their application, they must submit a personal statement of 250 to 500 words explaining why they qualify for this program, a writing sample, their law school transcript, and a resume.

Financial Data   The stipend is at least $9,000.

Duration   10 weeks during the summer.

Additional data   The sponsor is the local chapter of the Association of Corporate Counsel (ACC). It established this program in 2004 with support from the Minority Corporate Counsel Association (MCCA).

Number awarded   Varies each year; recently, 13 of these internships were awarded.

Deadline   January of each year.

[597]
ACCESS TO JUSTICE FELLOWSHIPS OF THE OREGON STATE BAR

Oregon State Bar
Attn: Diversity and Inclusion Department
16037 S.W. Upper Boones Ferry Road
P.O. Box 231935
Tigard, OR 97281-1935
(503) 620-0222
Toll Free: (800) 452-8260, ext. 338 (within OR)
Fax: (503) 684-1366   TDD: (503) 684-7416
E-mail: cling@osbar.org
Web: www.osbar.org/diversity/programs.html#access

Summary   To provide summer work experience to Hispanic and other minority law students in Oregon who have encountered barriers and will help the Oregon State Bar achieve its diversity and inclusion objectives.

Eligibility This program is open to students at law schools in Oregon who have experienced economic, social, or other barriers; who have a demonstrated commitment to increasing access to justice; who have personally experienced discrimination or oppression; and who will contribute to the Oregon State Bar's diversity and inclusion program, defined to include age, culture, disability, ethnicity, gender and gender identity or expression, geographic location, national origin, race, religion, sex, sexual orientation, and socio-economic status. They must be interested in working for a public employer or nonprofit organization in Oregon during the summer. Preference is given to students who indicate an intention to practice in Oregon. Along with their application, they must submit a 500-word personal statement on either 1) how their status as a person of diversity has influenced their decision to become a lawyer and how will it influence them throughout their legal professional career; or 2) a challenge they have faced, how they met the challenge, and how that experience will affect the decisions they will make as a legal professional. They must also submit a sample of their legal writing. Selection is based on the personal statement (35%), legal writing ability (25%), academic achievement (15%), work experience and honors (10%), and financial need (15%).

Financial Data Fellows receive a stipend of $5,000.

Duration 3 months during the summer.

Number awarded 2 each year.

Deadline January of each year.

[598]
ACM/IEEE-CS GEORGE MICHAEL MEMORIAL HPC FELLOWSHIPS

Association for Computing Machinery
Attn: Awards Committee Liaison
2 Penn Plaza, Suite 701
New York, NY 10121-0701
(212) 626-0561　　　　　Toll Free: (800) 342-6626
Fax: (212) 944-1318　　　E-mail: acm-awards@acm.org
Web: awards.acm.org/hpcfell/nominations.cfm

Summary To provide financial assistance to Hispanic and other minority doctoral students from any country who are working on a degree in high performance computing (HPC) and will contribute to diversity in the field.

Eligibility This program is open to students from any country who have completed at least 1 year full-time study in a Ph.D. program in HPC and have at least 1 year remaining before graduating. Applications from women, minorities, international students, and all who contribute to diversity are especially encouraged. Selection is based on overall potential for research excellence, degree to which technical interests align with those of the HPC community, demonstration of current and planned future use of HPC resources, evidence of a plan of student to enhance HPC-related skills, evidence of academic progress to date (including presentations and publications), and recommendation by faculty adviser.

Financial Data The stipend is $5,000. Fellows also receive reimbursement of travel expenses to attend the conference of the Association for Computing Machinery (ACM).

Duration 1 year.

Additional data This program, which began in 2007, is sponsored by the IEEE Computer Society.

Number awarded Up to 6 each year.

Deadline April of each year.

[599]
ACM SIGHPC/INTEL COMPUTATIONAL AND DATA SCIENCE FELLOWSHIPS

Association for Computing Machinery
Attn: Special Interest Group on High Performance
　Computing (SIGHPC)
Office of SIG Services
2 Penn Plaza, Suite 701
New York, NY 10121-0701
(212) 626-0606　　　　　Toll Free: (800) 342-6626
Fax: (212) 944-1318　　　E-mail: cappo@hq.acm.org
Web: www.sighpc.org/fellowships

Summary To provide financial assistance to Hispanic and other underrepresented minority graduate students in any country who are working on a degree in computational or data science.

Eligibility This program is open to women and members of racial or ethnic backgrounds that have not traditionally participated in the computing field. Applicants must be enrolled as graduate students at a college or university in any country and working on a graduate degree in computational or data science. They must have completed less than half of their planning program of study; preference is given to students who are still early in their studies. Selection is based on overall potential for excellence in data science and/or computational science, likelihood of successfully completing a graduate degree, and extent to which applicants will increase diversity in the workplace.

Financial Data The stipend is $15,000.

Duration 1 year.

Additional data This program was established in 2016 by Intel Corporation.

Number awarded Varies each year; recently, 14 were presented.

Deadline April of each year.

[600]
ACOUSTICAL SOCIETY OF AMERICA MINORITY FELLOWSHIP

Acoustical Society of America
Attn: Office Manager
1305 Walt Whitman Road, Suite 300
Melville, NY 11747-4300
(516) 576-2360　　　　　Fax: (631) 923-2875
E-mail: asa@acousticalsociety.org
Web: www.acousticalsociety.org

Summary To provide financial assistance to Hispanics and other underrepresented minorities who are working on a graduate degree involving acoustics.

Eligibility This program is open to U.S. and Canadian citizens and permanent residents who are members of a minority group that is underrepresented in the sciences (Hispanic, African American, or Native American). Applicants must be enrolled in or accepted to a graduate degree program as a full-time student. Their program of study may be in any field of pure or applied science and engineering directly related to acoustics, including acoustical oceanography, architectural acoustics, animal bioacoustics, biomedical ultrasound, bioresponse to vibration, engineering acoustics, musical acoustics, noise, physical acoustics, psychological acoustics, physiological acoustics, signal processing in acoustics, speech communication, structural acoustics and vibration, and underwater acoustics. Along with their application, student must submit a statement on why they are enrolled in their present academic program, including how they intend to use their graduate education to develop a career and how the study of acoustics is relevant to their career objectives.

Financial Data   The stipend is $20,000 per year. The sponsor strongly encourages the host educational institution to waive all tuition costs and assessed fees. Fellows also receive $1,000 for travel to attend a national meeting of the sponsor.

Duration   1 year; may be renewed for 1 additional year if the recipient is making normal progress toward a degree and is enrolled full time.

Additional data   This program began in 1992.

Number awarded   1 each year.

Deadline   March of each year.

[601]
ACXIOM DIVERSITY SCHOLARSHIP PROGRAM

Acxiom Corporation
601 East Third Street
P.O. Box 8190
Little Rock, AR 72203-8190
(501) 342-1000   Toll Free: (877) 314-2049
E-mail: Candice.Davis@acxiom.com
Web: www.acxiom.com/about-acxiom/careers

Summary   To provide financial assistance and possible work experience to upper-division and graduate students who are Hispanics or members of other diverse populations that historically have been underrepresented in the information technology work force.

Eligibility   This program is open to juniors, seniors, and graduate students who are working full time on a degree in a field of information technology, including computer science, computer information systems, management information systems, information quality, information systems, engineering, mathematics, statistics, or related areas of study. Women, veterans, minorities, and individuals with disabilities are encouraged to apply. Applicants must have a GPA of 3.0 or higher. Along with their application, they must submit a 500-word essay describing how the scholarship will help them achieve their academic, professional, and personal goals. Selection is based on academic achievement, relationship of field of study to information technology, and relationship of areas of professional interest to the sponsor's business needs.

Financial Data   The stipend is $5,000 per year.

Duration   1 year; may be renewed 1 additional year, provided the recipient remains enrolled full time, maintains a GPA of 3.0 or higher, and (if offered an internship) continues to meet internship expectations.

Additional data   Recipients may be offered an internship (fall, spring, summer, year-round) at 1 of the sponsor's offices in Austin (Texas), Conway (Arkansas), Downers Grove (Illinois), Little Rock (Arkansas), Nashville (Tennessee), New York (New York), or Redwood City (California).

Number awarded   Up to 5 each year.

Deadline   December of each year.

[602]
ADDIE B. MORRIS SCHOLARSHIP

American Association of Railroad Superintendents
P.O. Box 200
La Fox, IL 60147
(331) 643-3369   E-mail: aars@supt.org
Web: www.railroadsuperintendents.org/Scholarships

Summary   To provide financial assistance to undergraduate and graduate students, especially Hispanics and other minorities, who are working on a degree in transportation.

Eligibility   This program is open to full-time undergraduate and graduate students enrolled at accredited colleges and universities in Canada or the United States. Applicants must have completed enough credits to have standing as a sophomore and must have a GPA of 2.75 or higher. Preference is given to minority students enrolled in the transportation field who can demonstrate financial need.

Financial Data   The stipend is $1,000. Funds are sent directly to the recipient's institution.

Duration   1 year.

Number awarded   1 or more each year.

Deadline   June of each year.

[603]
A-DEC SCHOLARSHIPS

Hispanic Dental Association
Attn: HDA Foundation
3910 South IH-35, Suite 245
Austin, TX 78704
(512) 904-0252   E-mail: jessicac@hdassoc.org
Web: www.hdassoc.org

Summary   To provide financial assistance to members of the Hispanic Dental Association (HDA) who are entering their third or fourth year of dental school.

Eligibility   This program is open to HDA members who are entering their third or fourth year at an accredited dental school in the United States or Puerto Rico. Applicants must have a GPA of 3.0 or higher, an interest in improving the health of the Hispanic community, and a demonstrated commitment and dedication to serving the Hispanic community. They must be enrolled full time. Along with their application, they must submit a 250-word essay on their career goals, including how they were inspired to become a dentist. Selection is based on academic achievement, leadership skills, community service, and commitment and dedication to improving the oral health of the Hispanic community.

Financial Data   The stipend is $2,000. An additional grant of $500 is provided for travel reimbursement and complimentary registration to the HDA annual meeting.

Duration   1 year.

Additional data   This program is sponsored by A-dec.

Number awarded   2 each year.

Deadline   May of each year.

[604]
ADRIENNE M. AND CHARLES SHELBY ROOKS FELLOWSHIP FOR RACIAL AND ETHNIC THEOLOGICAL STUDENTS

United Church of Christ
Attn: Associate Director, Grant and Scholarship
 Administration
700 Prospect Avenue East
Cleveland, OH 44115-1100
(216) 736-2166   Toll Free: (866) 822-8224, ext. 2166
Fax: (216) 736-3783   E-mail: scholarships@ucc.org
Web: www.ucc.org/ministry_education_scholarships

Summary To provide financial assistance to Hispanic and other minority students who are either enrolled at an accredited seminary preparing for a career of service in the United Church of Christ (UCC) or working on a doctoral degree in the field of religion.

Eligibility This program is open to members of underrepresented ethnic groups (African American, Hispanic American, Asian American, Native American Indian, or Pacific Islander) who have been a member of a UCC congregation for at least 1 year. Applicants must be either 1) enrolled in an accredited school of theology in the United States or Canada and working on an M.Div. degree with the intent of becoming a pastor or teacher within the UCC; or 2) doctoral (Ph.D., Th.D., or Ed.D.) students preparing for a scholarly teaching vocation in the field of religion. Seminary students must have a GPA in all postsecondary work of 3.0 or higher and must have begun the in-care process; preference is given to students who have demonstrated leadership (through a history of service to the church) and scholarship (through exceptional academic performance). For doctoral students, preference is given to applicants who have demonstrated academic excellence, teaching effectiveness, and commitment to the UCC and who intend to become professors in colleges, seminaries, or graduate schools.

Financial Data Grants range from $500 to $5,000 per year.

Duration 1 year; may be renewed.

Number awarded Varies each year; recently, 12 of these scholarships, including 8 for M.Div. students and 4 for doctoral students, were awarded.

Deadline February of each year.

[605]
AERA-MET DISSERTATION FELLOWSHIP PROGRAM

American Educational Research Association
Attn: Fellowships Program
1430 K Street, N.W., Suite 1200
Washington, DC 20005
(202) 238-3200   Fax: (202) 238-3250
E-mail: fellowships@aera.net
Web: www.aera.net

Summary To provide funding to doctoral candidates in the field of education, especially Hispanics and other underrepresented minorities, who are interested in conducting dissertation research using the Measures of Effective Teaching (MET) database.

Eligibility This program is open to doctoral candidates who are at the dissertation stage of their program in a field of edu-

cation or related social or behavioral science field (e.g., economics, political science, psychology, sociology). Applicants must be interested in conducting dissertation research utilizing the Measures of Effective Teaching (MET) Longitudinal Database collected by the Inter-university Consortium for Political and Social Research (ICPSR) of the University of Michigan. Selection is based on potential for the study to advance knowledge and understanding with the discipline and/or the education field; what is already known on the issue; appropriateness of the MET database to address the research questions; qualifications of the applicant to carry out the proposed study; and relationship of the methodology to the policy question. Underrepresented racial and ethnic minority researchers and women and strongly encouraged to apply. U.S. citizenship or permanent resident status is required.

Financial Data Fellows receive a stipend of $20,000 plus full payment of expenses to attend the fall research conference of the American Educational Research Association (AERA) in Washington, D.C.

Duration 1 year.

Additional data This program is jointly administered by the AERA and the IPCSR with funding provided by the Bill and Melinda Gates Foundation.

Number awarded Several each year.

Deadline May of each year.

[606]
AFPE UNDERREPRESENTED MINORITY PRE-DOCTORAL FELLOWSHIP

American Foundation for Pharmaceutical Education
Attn: Grants Manager
6076 Franconia Road, Suite C
Alexandria, VA 22310-1758
(703) 875-3006   Toll Free: (055) 024-9520
Fax: (703) 875-3098   E-mail: info@afpenet.org
Web: www.afpenet.org

Summary To provide funding for dissertation research to Hispanic/Latino and other underrepresented minority graduate students working on a Ph.D. in pharmaceutical science.

Eligibility This program is open to Hispanic/Latino, African American/Black, and Native American students who have completed at least 3 semesters of full-time graduate study and have no more than 3 and a half years remaining to complete a Ph.D. in pharmaceutical science at a U.S. school or college of pharmacy. Students enrolled in joint Pharm.D./Ph.D. programs are eligible if they have completed 3 full semesters of graduate credit toward the Ph.D. and if the Ph.D. degree will be awarded within 3 additional years. Applicants must be U.S. citizens or permanent residents. Selection is based on research plan and experience (50%), academic performance (35%), and leadership and character (15%).

Financial Data The grant is $10,000 per year. Funds must be used to enable the students to make progress on their Ph.D. (e.g., student stipend, laboratory supplies, books, materials, travel) but not for indirect costs for the institution.

Duration 1 year; may be renewed 1 additional year.

Number awarded Up to 5 each year.

Deadline December of each year.

[607]
AGA INVESTING IN THE FUTURE STUDENT RESEARCH FELLOWSHIPS

American Gastroenterological Association
Attn: AGA Research Foundation
Research Awards Manager
4930 Del Ray Avenue
Bethesda, MD 20814-2512
(301) 222-4012   Fax: (301) 654-5920
E-mail: awards@gastro.org
Web: www.gastro.org

Summary   To provide funding for research on digestive diseases or nutrition to undergraduate and medical students who are Hispanics/Latinos or members of ther underrepresented minority groups.

Eligibility   This program is open to undergraduate and medical students at accredited U.S. institutions who are African Americans, Hispanic/Latino Americans, Alaska Natives, American Indians, or Natives of the U.S. Pacific Islands. Applicants must be interested in conducting research on digestive diseases or nutrition. They may not hold similar salary support awards from other agencies (e.g., American Liver Foundation, Crohn's and Colitis Foundation). Research must be conducted under the supervision of a preceptor who is a full-time faculty member at an institution in a state other than the student's, directing a research project in a gastroenterology-related area, and a member of the American Gastroenterological Association (AGA).

Financial Data   Fellowships provide payment of housing, travel, and a stipend of $5,000.

Duration   8 to 10 weeks. The work may take place at any time during the year.

Additional data   This program is supported by the National Institute of Diabetes and Digestive and Kidney Diseases (NIDDKD) of the U.S. National Institutes of Health (NIH).

Number awarded   12 each year.

Deadline   February of each year.

[608]
AGING RESEARCH DISSERTATION AWARDS TO INCREASE DIVERSITY

National Institute on Aging
Attn: Office of Extramural Affairs
7201 Wisconsin Avenue, Suite 2C-218
Bethesda, MD 20814
(301) 402-4158   Fax: (301) 402-2945
TDD: (301) 451-0088   E-mail: hunterc@nia.nih.gov
Web: www.grants.nih.gov

Summary   To provide financial assistance to doctoral candidates who are Hispanics or members of underrepresented groups and wish to conduct research on aging.

Eligibility   This program is open to doctoral candidates conducting research on a dissertation with an aging-related focus, including the basic biology of aging; chronic, disabling, and degenerative diseases of aging, with a particular focus on Alzheimer's Disease; multiple morbidities; individual behavioral and social changes with aging; caregiving; longevity; and the consequences for society of an aging population. Applicants must be 1) members of an ethnic or racial group underrepresented in biomedical or behavioral research (Hispanics or Latinos, Blacks or African Americans, American Indians, Alaska Natives, Native Hawaiians, and other Pacific Islanders); 2) individuals with disabilities; or 3) individuals from socially, culturally, economically, or educationally disadvantaged backgrounds that have inhibited their ability to prepare for a career in health-related research. They must be U.S. citizens, nationals, or permanent residents.

Financial Data   Grants provide $23,376 per year for stipend and up to $20,000 for additional expenses. No funds may be used to pay for tuition or fees associated with completion of doctoral studies. The institution may receive up to 8% of direct costs as facilities and administrative costs per year.

Duration   Up to 2 years.

Number awarded   Up to 5 each year.

Deadline   Applications must be submitted by February, June, or October of each year.

[609]
AHIMA FOUNDATION DIVERSITY SCHOLARSHIPS

American Health Information Management Association
Attn: AHIMA Foundation
233 North Michigan Avenue, 21st Floor
Chicago, IL 60601-5809
(312) 233-1137   Fax: (312) 233-1537
E-mail: info@ahimafoundation.org
Web: www.ahimafoundation.org

Summary   To provide financial assistance to Hispanic and other members of the American Health Information Management Association (AHIMA) who are interested in working on an undergraduate or graduate degree in health information management (HIM) or health information technology (HIT) and will contribute to diversity in the profession in other ways.

Eligibility   This program is open to AHIMA members who are enrolled at least half time in an accredited program. Applicants must be working on a degree in HIM or HIT at the associate, bachelor's, post-baccalaureate, master's, or doctoral level. They must have a GPA of 3.5 or higher and at least 6 credit hours remaining after the date of the award. To qualify for this support, applicants must demonstrate how they will contribute to diversity in the health information management profession; diversity is defined as differences in race, ethnicity, nationality, gender, sexual orientation, socioeconomic status, age, physical capabilities, or religious beliefs. Along with their application, they must submit essays on assigned topics related to their involvement in the HIM profession. Selection is based on the clarity and completeness of thought in the essays; cumulative GPA; volunteer, work, and/or leadership experience; honors, awards, or recognitions; commitment to the HIM profession; and references.

Financial Data   Stipends are $1,000 for associate degree students, $1,500 for bachelor's degree or post-baccalaureate certificate students, $2,000 for master's degree students, or $2,500 for doctoral degree students.

Duration   1 year.

Number awarded   1 or more each year.

Deadline   September of each year.

[610]
AICPA FELLOWSHIPS FOR MINORITY DOCTORAL STUDENTS

American Institute of Certified Public Accountants
Attn: Academic and Career Development Division
220 Leigh Farm Road
Durham, NC 27707-8110
(919) 402-4500   Fax: (919) 402-4505
E-mail: scholarships@aicpa.org
Web: www.aicpa.org

Summary To provide financial assistance to Hispanic and other underrepresented minority doctoral students who wish to prepare for a career teaching accounting at the college level.

Eligibility This program is open to underrepresented minority students who have applied to and/or been accepted into a doctoral program with a concentration in accounting. Applicants must have earned a master's degree or completed a minimum of 3 years of full-time work in accounting. They must be attending or planning to attend school full time and agree not to work full time in a paid position, teach more than 1 course as a teaching assistant, or work more than 25% as a research assistant. U.S. citizenship or permanent resident status is required. Preference is given to applicants who have attained a C.P.A. designation and/or are members of the American Institute of Certified Public Accountants (AICPA) and those who perform AICPA committee service. For purposes of this program, the AICPA defines minority students as those whose heritage is Hispanic or Latino, Black or African American, or Native American. Selection is based on academic and professional achievement, commitment to earning an accounting doctoral degree, and financial need.

Financial Data The stipend is $12,000 per year.

Duration 1 year; may be renewed up to 4 additional years.

Number awarded Varies each year; recently, 25 were awarded.

Deadline May of each year.

[611]
AICPA SCHOLARSHIPS FOR MINORITY ACCOUNTING STUDENTS

American Institute of Certified Public Accountants
Attn: Academic and Career Development Division
220 Leigh Farm Road
Durham, NC 27707-8110
(919) 402-4500   Fax: (919) 402-4505
E-mail: scholarships@aicpa.org
Web: www.aicpa.org

Summary To provide financial assistance to Hispanics and other minorities interested in studying accounting at the undergraduate or graduate school level.

Eligibility This program is open to minority undergraduate and graduate students, enrolled full time, who have a GPA of 3.3 or higher (both cumulatively and in their major) and intend to pursue a C.P.A. credential. The program defines minority students as those whose heritage is Hispanic or Latino, Black or African American, Native American, or Asian American. Undergraduates must have completed at least 30 semester hours, including at least 6 semester hours of a major in accounting. Graduate students must be working on a master's degree in accounting, finance, taxation, or a related program. Applicants must be U.S. citizens or permanent resi-

dents and student affiliate members of the American Institute of Certified Public Accountants (AICPA). Along with their application, they must submit 500-word essays on 1) why they want to become a C.P.A. and how attaining that licensure will contribute to their goals; and 2) how they would spread the message about accounting and the C.P.A. profession in their community and school. In the selection process, some consideration is given to financial need.

Financial Data Stipends range up to $5,000 per year. Funds are disbursed directly to the recipient's school.

Duration 1 year; may be renewed up to 3 additional years or until completion of a bachelor's or master's degree, whichever is earlier.

Additional data This program began in 1969. Additional support is provided by the Accounting Education Foundation of the Texas Society of Certified Public Accountants, the New Jersey Society of Certified Public Accountants, Robert Half International, and the Virgin Islands Society of Certified Public Accountants.

Number awarded Varies each year; recently, 94 students received funding through this program.

Deadline March of each year.

[612]
AIR FORCE SUMMER FACULTY FELLOWSHIP PROGRAM

Systems Plus, Inc.
Attn: AFSFF Program
One Research Court, Suite 360
Rockville, MD 20850
(301) 948-4232   Fax: (301) 948-3918
E-mail: afsffp.pmo@sysplus.com
Web: afsffp.sysplus.com

Summary To provide funding to science and engineering faculty and graduate students interested in conducting summer research at Air Force facilities, especially those teaching at Hispanic and other minority institutions.

Eligibility This program is open to U.S. citizens and permanent residents who have a full-time faculty appointment at a U.S. college or university in a field of engineering, mathematics, or science of interest to the Air Force. Applicants must be interested in conducting a research project, under the direction of an Air Force research adviser, at an Air Force Research Laboratory, Air Force Test Center, the U.S. Air Force Academy, or the Air Force Institute of Technology. A graduate student may accompany the faculty member. Faculty and students at Historically Black Colleges and Universities ((HBCUs), Minority Institutions (MIs), American Indian Tribal Colleges and Universities (TCUs), and Hispanic Serving Institutions (HSIs) are especially encouraged to apply.

Financial Data Stipends depend on academic rank or position. Relocation reimbursement and a weekly expense allowance of $350 (for fellows with a commute distance greater than 50 miles) are also available.

Duration 8 to 12 weeks during the summer. May be renewed for a second and third summer, but recipients may not reapply for 2 years after completing a third summer.

Additional data This program first operated in 2005. Research must be conducted in residence at an Air Force facility.

Number awarded Approximately 100 each year.
Deadline December of each year.

[613]
ALAS/HOUGHTON MIFFLIN HARCOURT SCHOLARSHIP

Association of Latino Administrators & Superintendents
P.O. Box 65204
Washington, DC 20035
(202) 466-0808   E-mail: contact@alasedu.org
Web: www.alasedu.org/Scholarships.aspx

Summary To provide financial assistance to members of the Association of Latino Administrators & Superintendents (ALAS) who are interested in working on an advanced degree in educational administration.

Eligibility This program is open to members of ALAS who are interested in working on an advanced degree in education with the goal of becoming a superintendent. Applicants must submit a 500-word essay on how an advanced degree will help them achieve their goals and further the goals of ALAS.

Financial Data The stipend is $10,000. An honorable mention scholarship of $1,000 may also be awarded.

Duration 1 year.

Additional data This scholarship, first awarded in 2006, is supported by Houghton Mifflin Harcourt.

Number awarded 1 or 2 each year.

Deadline September of each year.

[614]
ALBERT W. DENT STUDENT SCHOLARSHIP

American College of Healthcare Executives
Attn: Scholarship Committee
One North Franklin Street, Suite 1700
Chicago, IL 60606-3529
(312) 424-2800   Fax: (312) 424-0023
E-mail: contact@ache.org
Web: www.ache.org

Summary To provide financial assistance to Hispanic and other minority graduate student members of the American College of Healthcare Executives (ACHE).

Eligibility This program is open to ACHE student associates entering their final year of classroom work in a health care management master's degree program. Applicants must be minority students, enrolled full time, able to demonstrate financial need, and U.S. or Canadian citizens. Along with their application, they must submit a 1- to 2-page essay describing their leadership abilities and experiences, their community and volunteer involvement, their goals as a health care executive, and how this scholarship can help them achieve their career goals.

Financial Data The stipend is $5,000.

Duration 1 year.

Additional data The program was established and named in honor of Dr. Albert W. Dent, the foundation's first African American fellow and president emeritus of Dillard University.

Number awarded Varies each year; the sponsor awards up to 20 scholarships through this and its other scholarship program.

Deadline March of each year.

[615]
AMA FOUNDATION MINORITY SCHOLARS AWARDS

American Medical Association
Attn: AMA Foundation
330 North Wabash Avenue, Suite 39300
Chicago, IL 60611-5885
(312) 464-5019   Fax: (312) 464-4142
E-mail: amafoundation@ama-assn.org
Web: www.ama-assn.org

Summary To provide financial assistance to medical school students who are Hispanics or members of other underrepresented minority groups.

Eligibility This program is open to first- and second-year medical students who are members of the following traditionally underrepresented groups in the medical profession: Hispanic, African American, American Indian, Native Hawaiian, or Alaska Native. Only nominations are accepted. Each medical school is invited to submit 2 nominees. U.S. citizenship or permanent resident status is required.

Financial Data The stipend is $10,000.

Duration 1 year.

Additional data This program is offered by the AMA Foundation of the American Medical Association in collaboration with the Minority Affairs Consortium (MAC) and with support from the Pfizer Medical Humanities Initiative.

Number awarded Varies each year; recently, 20 were awarded.

Deadline March of each year.

[616]
AMAF VALUING DIVERSITY PH.D. SCHOLARSHIPS

American Marketing Association Foundation
Attn: Foundation Manager
311 South Wacker Drive, Suite 5800
Chicago, IL 60606
(312) 542-9015   Fax: (312) 542-9001
E-mail: jschnidman@ama.org
Web: www.themarketingfoundation.org

Summary To provide financial assistance to Hispanics and members of other underrepresented minority groups working on a doctoral degree in advertising or marketing.

Eligibility This program is open to African Americans, Hispanics, and Native Americans who have completed at least 1 year of a full-time Ph.D. program in advertising or marketing. Applicants must submit an essay that explains how receiving this scholarship will help them further their research efforts, including information on 1 of the following: 1) how their dissertation research incorporates conceptual, design, or methods issues related to diversity; 2) how their dissertation research contributes to advancing the field of marketing; or 3) how their dissertation research incorporates any innovative theories or advanced, cutting-edge designs, methods, or approaches. They must be U.S. citizens or permanent residents.

Financial Data The stipend is $1,000.

Duration 1 year; recipients may reapply.

Additional data This program began in 2003.

Number awarded Varies each year; recently, 5 were awarded.

Deadline April of each year.

[617]
AMELIA KEMP MEMORIAL SCHOLARSHIP

Women of the Evangelical Lutheran Church in America
Attn: Scholarships
8765 West Higgins Road
Chicago, IL 60631-4101
(773) 380-2741   Toll Free: (800) 638-3522, ext. 2741
Fax: (773) 380-2419   E-mail: valora.starr@elca.org
Web: www.womenoftheelca.org

Summary To provide financial assistance to Hispanic and other lay women of color who are members of Evangelical Lutheran Church of America (ELCA) congregations and who wish to study on the undergraduate, graduate, professional, or vocational school level.

Eligibility This program is open to ELCA lay women of color who are at least 21 years of age and have experienced an interruption of at least 2 years in their education since high school. Applicants must have been admitted to an educational institution to prepare for a career in other than ordained ministry. U.S. citizenship is required.

Financial Data The maximum stipend is $1,000 per year.

Duration 1 year; recipients may reapply for 1 additional year.

Number awarded 1 or more each year.

Deadline February of each year.

[618]
AMERICAN ANTHROPOLOGICAL ASSOCIATION MINORITY DISSERTATION FELLOWSHIP PROGRAM

American Anthropological Association
Attn: Committee on Minority Issues in Anthropology
2300 Clarendon Boulevard, Suite 1301
Arlington, VA 22201
(703) 528-1902   Fax: (703) 528-3546
E-mail: arussell@aaanet.org
Web: www.aaanet.org/cmtes/minority/Minfellow.cfm

Summary To provide funding to Latinos and other minorities who are working on a Ph.D. dissertation in anthropology.

Eligibility This program is open to Latino(a), Native American, African American, Pacific Islander, and Asian American doctoral students who have been admitted to degree candidacy in anthropology. Applicants must be U.S. citizens, enrolled in a full-time academic program leading to a doctoral degree in anthropology, and members of the American Anthropological Association. They must have a record of outstanding academic success, have had their dissertation proposal approved by their dissertation committee prior to application, be writing a dissertation in an area of anthropological research, and need funding to complete the dissertation. Along with their application, they must submit a cover letter, a research plan summary, a curriculum vitae, a statement regarding employment, a disclosure statement providing information about other sources of available and pending financial support, 3 letters of recommendation, and an official transcript from their doctoral program. Selection is based on the quality of the submitted information and the judged likelihood that the applicant will have a good chance of completing the dissertation.

Financial Data The grant is $10,000. Funds are sent in 2 installments (in September and in January) directly to the recipient.

Duration 1 year; nonrenewable.

Number awarded 1 each year.

Deadline February of each year.

[619]
AMERICAN BAR ASSOCIATION LEGAL OPPORTUNITY SCHOLARSHIP

American Bar Association
Attn: Fund for Justice and Education
321 North Clark Street, 21st Floor
Chicago, IL 60654-7598
(312) 988-5927   Fax: (312) 988-6392
E-mail: legalosf@staff.abanet.org
Web: www.americanbar.org

Summary To provide financial assistance to Hispanic and other racial and ethnic minority students who are interested in attending law school.

Eligibility This program is open to racial and ethnic minority college graduates who are interested in attending an ABA-accredited law school. Only students beginning law school may apply; students who have completed 1 or more semesters of law school are not eligible. Applicants must have a cumulative GPA of 2.5 or higher and be citizens or permanent residents of the United States. Along with their application, they must submit a 1,000-word statement describing their personal and family background, community service activities, and other connections to their racial and ethnic minority community. Financial need is also considered in the selection process.

Financial Data The stipend is $5,000 per year.

Duration 1 year; may be renewed for 2 additional years if satisfactory performance in law school has been achieved.

Additional data This program began in the 2000-01 academic year.

Number awarded Approximately 20 each year.

Deadline February of each year.

[620]
AMERICAN EDUCATIONAL RESEARCH ASSOCIATION MINORITY FELLOWSHIPS IN EDUCATION RESEARCH

American Educational Research Association
Attn: Fellowships Program
1430 K Street, N.W., Suite 1200
Washington, DC 20005
(202) 238-3200   Fax: (202) 238-3250
E-mail: fellowships@aera.net
Web: www.aera.net

Summary To provide funding to Hispanic and other minority doctoral students writing their dissertation on educational research.

Eligibility This program is open to U.S. citizens and permanent residents who have advanced to candidacy and successfully defended their Ph.D./Ed.D. dissertation research proposal. Applicants must plan to work full time on their dissertation in educational research, the humanities, or social or behavioral science disciplinary or interdisciplinary fields, such as economics, political science, psychology, or sociology.

This program is targeted for members of groups historically underrepresented in higher education (Hispanics or Latinos, African Americans, American Indians, Alaskan Natives, Asian Americans, and Native Hawaiians or other Pacific Islanders). Selection is based on scholarly achievements and publications, letters of recommendation, quality and significance of the proposed research, and commitment of the applicant's faculty mentor to the goals of the program.

Financial Data The grant is $20,000, including up to $1,000 for travel to the sponsor's annual conference.

Duration 1 year; nonrenewable.

Additional data This program began in 1991.

Number awarded Up to 3 each year.

Deadline October of each year.

[621]
AMERICAN EPILEPSY SOCIETY PREDOCTORAL RESEARCH FELLOWSHIPS

American Epilepsy Society
135 South LaSalle Street, Suite 2850
Chicago, IL 60603
(312) 883-3800　　　　　　　　　Fax: (312) 896-5784
E-mail: info@aesnet.org
Web: www.aesnet.org

Summary To provide funding to doctoral candidates who are interested in conducting dissertation research related to epilepsy, especially Hispanics and members of other underrepresented groups.

Eligibility This program is open full-time doctoral students conducting dissertation research with an epilepsy-related theme under the guidance of a mentor with expertise in epilepsy research. Applicants must have a defined research plan and access to institutional resources to conduct the proposed project. Selection is based on the applicant's potential and commitment to develop as an independent and productive epilepsy researcher, academic record, and research experience; the mentor's research qualifications; the research training plan; and the quality of the research facilities, resources, and training opportunities. Applications are especially encouraged from women, members of minority groups, and people with disabilities. U.S. citizenship is not required, but all research must be conducted in the United States.

Financial Data Grants range up $30,000, including $29,000 as stipend and $1,000 for travel support and complimentary registration to attend the sponsor's annual meeting.

Duration 1 year; nonrenewable.

Additional data In addition to the funding provided by the American Epilepsy Society, support is available from the TESS Research Foundation for applications focused on epilepsy due to SLC13A5 mutations; the LGS Foundation for applications focused on Lennox-Gastaut-Syndrome; the PCDH19 Alliance for applications focused on epilepsy due to PCDH19 mutations; the Dravet Syndrome Foundation for applications focused on Dravet Syndrome; Wishes for Elliott for applications focused on epilepsy due to SCN8A mutations; and the TS Alliance for applications focused on epilepsy associated with tuberous sclerosis complex (TSC).

Number awarded Varies each year.

Deadline Letters of intent must be submitted by October of each year; final proposals are due in January.

[622]
AMERICAN GEOGRAPHICAL SOCIETY LIBRARY FELLOWSHIP FOR MSI SCHOLARS

University of Wisconsin at Milwaukee
Attn: Libraries
American Geographical Society Library
2311 East Hartford Avenue
P.O. Box 399,
Milwaukee, WI 53201-0399
(414) 229-6282　　　　　　　Toll Free: (800) 558-8993
Fax: (414) 229-3624　　　　　　E-mail: agsl@uwm.edu
Web: www.uwm.edu/libraries/agsl/fellowshipdescriptions

Summary To provide funding to pre- and postdoctoral scholars at Minority Serving Institutions (MSIs) interested in conducting research at the American Geographical Society Library (AGSL) of the University of Wisconsin at Milwaukee (UWM) Libraries.

Eligibility This program is open to established scholars and doctoral students who are affiliated with an MSI. Doctoral students must have completed their course work and be writing their dissertations. Individuals with a record of publication relevant to this program and those with government or business ties who could use the library's resources to further policy studies are also eligible. Applicants' research must benefit from extensive use of the AGSL, including (but not limited to) area studies, history of cartography, history of geographic thought, discovery and exploration, historical geography, other geographic themes with a significant historical component, or any topic that has policy, business, or similar applications.

Financial Data The grant is $600 per week. Funds must be used to help pay travel and living expenses related to the residency.

Duration Up to 4 weeks.

Additional data Funding for this program is provided by a U.S. Department of Education National Resource Center grant.

Number awarded 1 or more each year.

Deadline November of each year.

[623]
AMERICAN GI FORUM OF KANSAS EDUCATIONAL FUND SCHOLARSHIP

American GI Forum of Kansas
Attn: Educational Fund
c/o Barbara Olivas
1000 North Cheyenne
Ulysses, KS 67880

Summary To provide financial assistance to Hispanic and other residents of Kansas who are interested in attending college or graduate school in any state.

Eligibility This program is open to Hispanic and other residents of Kansas who are currently enrolled as undergraduate, vocational/technical, or graduate students at a school in any state. Preference is given to members of the American GI Forum of Kansas. Applicants must submit a 1-page personal statement on their career goals, academic and personal achievements, how they plan to help the American GI Forum of Kansas help others like themselves in the future, and their involvement with their chapter. Selection is based on that statement, academic achievement, 2 letters of recommendation, and financial need.

Financial Data Stipends range from $200 to $1,000.

Duration 1 year.

Number awarded 1 or more each year.

Deadline March of each year.

[624]
AMERICAN NURSES ASSOCIATION MINORITY FELLOWSHIP PROGRAM

American Nurses Association
Attn: SAMHSA Minority Fellowship Programs
8515 Georgia Avenue, Suite 400
Silver Spring, MD 20910-3492
(301) 628-5247   Toll Free: (800) 274-4ANA
Fax: (301) 628-5339   E-mail: janet.jackson@ana.org
Web: www.emfp.org

Summary To provide financial assistance to Hispanic and other minority nurses who are doctoral candidates interested in psychiatric, mental health, and substance abuse issues that impact the lives of ethnic minority people.

Eligibility This program is open to nurses who have a master's degree and are members of an ethnic or racial minority group, including but not limited to Hispanics or Latinos, Blacks or African Americans, American Indians and Alaska Natives, Asians and Asian Americans, and Native Hawaiians and other Pacific Islanders. Applicants must be enrolled full time in an accredited doctoral nursing program. They must be certified as a Mental Health Nurse Practitioner, Mental Health Clinical Nurse Specialist, or Mental Health Nurse. U.S. citizenship or permanent resident status and membership in the American Nurses Association are required. Selection is based on commitment to a career in substance abuse in psychiatric/mental health issues affecting minority populations.

Financial Data The program provides an annual stipend of $22,476 and tuition assistance up to $5,000.

Duration 3 to 5 years.

Additional data Funds for this program are provided by the Substance Abuse and Mental Health Services Administration (SAMHSA).

Number awarded 1 or more each year.

Deadline March of each year.

[625]
AMERICAN NURSES ASSOCIATION MINORITY FELLOWSHIP PROGRAM YOUTH

American Nurses Association
Attn: SAMHSA Minority Fellowship Programs
8515 Georgia Avenue, Suite 400
Silver Spring, MD 20910-3492
(301) 628-5247   Toll Free: (800) 274-4ANA
Fax: (301) 628-5339   E-mail: janet.jackson@ana.org
Web: www.emfp.org

Summary To provide financial assistance to Hispanic and other minority nurses who are interested in working on a master's degree in psychiatric/mental health nursing for service to young people.

Eligibility This program is open to nurses who are members of the American Nurses Association and members of an ethnic or racial minority group, including but not limited to Blacks or African Americans, Hispanics or Latinos, American Indians and Alaska Natives, Asians and Asian Americans, and Native Hawaiians and other Pacific Islanders. Applicants must be enrolled full time in an accredited master's degree behavioral health (psychiatric/mental health/substance abuse) nursing program. They must intend to apply for certification to become a Psychiatric Mental Health Nurse Practitioners, a fellowship-approved certification in substance abuse, or another sub-specialty that is associated with behavioral health services for children, adolescents, and youth transitioning into adulthood (ages 16 through 25). U.S. citizenship or permanent resident status is required. Selection is based on commitment to a career that provides behavioral health services to young people.

Financial Data The stipend is $11,500 per year. Funds are disbursed directly to the fellow.

Duration 1 year; may be renewed.

Additional data Funds for this program are provided by the Substance Abuse and Mental Health Services Administration (SAMHSA).

Number awarded 1 or more each year.

Deadline March of each year.

[626]
AMERICAN POLITICAL SCIENCE ASSOCIATION MINORITY FELLOWS PROGRAM

American Political Science Association
Attn: Diversity and Inclusion Programs
1527 New Hampshire Avenue, N.W.
Washington, DC 20036-1206
(202) 349-9362   Fax: (202) 483-2657
E-mail: kmealy@apsanet.org
Web: www.apsanet.org/mfp

Summary To provide financial assistance to Latinos and other underrepresented minorities interested in working on a doctoral degree in political science.

Eligibility This program is open to Latino(a)s, African Americans, Asian Pacific Americans, and Native Americans who are in their senior year at a college or university or currently enrolled in a master's degree program. Applicants must be planning to enroll in a doctoral program in political science to prepare for a career in teaching and research. They must be U.S. citizens and able to demonstrate financial need. Along with their application, they must submit a 500-word personal statement that includes why they are interested in attending graduate school in political science, what specific fields within the discipline they plan to study, and how they intend to contribute to research within the discipline. Selection is based on interest in teaching and potential for research in political science.

Financial Data The stipend is $2,000 per year.

Duration 2 years.

Additional data In addition to the fellows who receive stipends from this program, students who are selected as fellows without stipend are recommended for admission and financial support to every doctoral political science program in the country. This program was established in 1969.

Number awarded Up to 12 fellows receive stipends each year.

Deadline March or October of each year.

[627]
AMERICAN SOCIETY OF HEMATOLOGY MINORITY GRADUATE STUDENT ABSTRACT ACHIEVEMENT AWARD

American Society of Hematology
Attn: Awards Manager
2021 L Street, N.W., Suite 900
Washington, DC 20036
(202) 776-0544   Fax: (202) 776-0545
E-mail: awards@hematology.org
Web: www.hematology.org

Summary To recognize and reward Hispanic and other underrepresented minority graduate students who present outstanding abstracts at the annual meeting of the American Society of Hematology (ASH).

Eligibility This award is available to students who are enrolled in the first 3 years of work on a Ph.D. in the field of hematology and submit an abstract to the annual ASH meeting that is accepted for oral or poster presentation. Applicants must be a member of a racial or ethnic group that has been shown to be underrepresented in health-related sciences in the United States and Canada, including Hispanics or Latinos, American Indians, Alaska Natives, Blacks or African Americans, Native Hawaiians, other Pacific Islanders, African Canadians, Inuit, and First Nation Peoples. They must be working under the direction of an ASH member.

Financial Data The award is $1,500.

Duration The award is presented annually.

Number awarded Varies each year; recently, 4 were presented.

Deadline The deadline for applying for these awards is the same as that for submitting abstracts for the annual meeting. Usually, that date is in early August.

[628]
AMERICAN SPEECH-LANGUAGE-HEARING FOUNDATION SCHOLARSHIP FOR MINORITY STUDENTS

American Speech-Language-Hearing Foundation
Attn: Programs Administrator
2200 Research Boulevard
Rockville, MD 20850-3289
(301) 296-8703   Toll Free: (800) 498-2071, ext. 8703
Fax: (301) 296-8567
E-mail: foundationprograms@asha.org
Web: www.ashfoundation.org

Summary To provide financial assistance to Hispanic and other minority graduate students in communication sciences and disorders programs.

Eligibility This program is open to full-time graduate students who are enrolled in communication sciences and disorders programs, with preference given to U.S. citizens who are members of a racial or ethnic minority group. Applicants must submit an essay, up to 5 pages in length, on a topic that relates to the future of leadership in the discipline. Selection is based on academic promise and outstanding academic achievement.

Financial Data The stipend is $5,000. Funds must be used for educational support (e.g., tuition, books, school living expenses), not for personal or conference travel.

Duration 1 year.

Number awarded Up to 3 each year.

Deadline May of each year.

[629]
AMERICAN THEOLOGICAL LIBRARY ASSOCIATION DIVERSITY SCHOLARSHIP

American Theological Library Association
Attn: Diversity Committee
300 South Wacker Drive, Suite 2100
Chicago, IL 60606-6701
(312) 454-5100   Toll Free: (888) 665-ATLA
Fax: (312) 454-5505   E-mail: memberrep@atla.com
Web: www.atla.com

Summary To provide funding to Hispanic library students and members of other underrepresented groups who are members of the American Theological Library Association (ATLA) interested in working on a master's degree in theological librarianship.

Eligibility This program is open to ATLA members from underrepresented groups (religious, racial, ethnic, or gender) who are enrolled at an ALA-accredited master's degree program in library and information studies. Applicants must submit personal statements on what diversity means to them, why their voice has not yet been heard, how they will increase diversity in their immediate context, and how they plan to increase diversity and participate fully in the ATLA.

Financial Data The stipend is $2,400.

Duration 1 year.

Number awarded 1 each year.

Deadline April of each year.

[630]
ANHELO PROJECT DREAM SCHOLARSHIP

Anhelo Project
c/o Joana Maravilla-Cano
P.O. Box 08290
Chicago, IL 60608
(773) 609-4252
E-mail: dreamscholarshipchicago@gmail.com
Web: www.theanheloproject.org/dream-scholarship

Summary To provide financial assistance to undocumented students in Illinois who are interested in attending college or graduate school in the state.

Eligibility This program is open to residents of Illinois who are undocumented students. Applicants must be enrolled full time at a college or university in the state. They must have a GPA of 2.5 or higher and be able to demonstrate financial need, community involvement, and ineligibility for federal financial assistance. DACA students are eligible, but international students with F-1 visas are not.

Financial Data A stipend is awarded (amount not specified).

Duration 1 year.

Number awarded Varies each year.

Deadline January of each year.

[631]
ANL LABORATORY–GRADUATE RESEARCH APPOINTMENTS

Argonne National Laboratory
Division of Educational Programs
Attn: Graduate Student Program Office
9700 South Cass Avenue/DEP 223
Argonne, IL 60439-4845
(630) 252-3366   Fax: (630) 252-3193
E-mail: education@anl.gov
Web: www.anl.gov

Summary To offer opportunities for qualified graduate students, especially Hispanics and other underrepresented minorities, to carry out their master's or doctoral thesis research at the Argonne National Laboratory (ANL).

Eligibility Appointments are available for graduate students at U.S. universities who wish to carry out their thesis research under the co-sponsorship of an Argonne National Laboratory staff member and a faculty member. Research may be conducted in the basic physical and life sciences, mathematics, computer science, and engineering, as well as in a variety of applied areas relating to energy, conservation, environmental impact and technology, nanomaterials, and advanced nuclear energy systems. Applicants must be U.S. citizens or permanent residents. The laboratory encourages applications from all qualified persons, especially women and members of underrepresented minority groups.

Financial Data Support consists of a stipend, tuition payments up to $5,000 per year, and payment of certain travel expenses. In addition, the student's faculty sponsor may receive payment for limited travel expenses.

Duration 1 year; may be renewed.

Additional data This program, which is also referred to as the Lab–Grad Program, is sponsored by the U.S. Department of Energy. In certain cases, students may be awarded support for pre-thesis studies on campus, provided that they intend to carry out their thesis research at Argonne.

Number awarded Varies each year.

Deadline Applications may be submitted at any time, but a complete application should be submitted at least 2 months prior to the proposed starting date.

[632]
ANTHEM BLUE CROSS BLUE SHIELD OF WISCONSIN NURSING SCHOLARSHIPS

Wisconsin League for Nursing
Attn: Scholarship Chair
P.O. Box 653
Germantown, WI 53022
(414) 454-9561   E-mail: info@wisconsinwln.org
Web: www.wisconsinwln.org/t/Scholarships

Summary To provide financial assistance to residents of Wisconsin, especially Hispanics and other minorities, attending a school of nursing in the state.

Eligibility This program is open to residents of Wisconsin who are enrolled at an accredited school of nursing in the state in an L.P.N., A.D.N., B.S.N., M.S.N., D.N.P., or Ph.D. program. Applicants must have completed at least half the credits needed for graduation. Ethnic minority students are especially encouraged to apply. Students must submit their applications to their school, not directly to the sponsor. Each school may nominate 4 graduate students, 6 students in an R.N. program, and 2 L.P.N. students. Selection is based on scholastic ability, professional abilities and/or community service, understanding of the nursing profession, goals upon graduation, and financial need.

Financial Data Stipends are $500 for L.P.N. students or $1,000 for all other students.

Duration 1 year.

Additional data This program is sponsored by Anthem Blue Cross Blue Shield of Wisconsin.

Number awarded Varies each year; recently, the program awarded 31 scholarships, including 2 L.P.N. awards, 10 associate degree awards, 16 B.S.N. awards, and 3 graduate awards.

Deadline April of each year.

[633]
APA MINORITY MEDICAL STUDENT SUMMER MENTORING PROGRAM

American Psychiatric Association
Attn: Division of Diversity and Health Equity
1000 Wilson Boulevard, Suite 1825
Arlington, VA 22209-3901
(703) 907-8653   Toll Free: (888) 35-PSYCH
Fax: (703) 907-7852   E-mail: mking@psych.org
Web: www.psychiatry.org/minority-fellowship

Summary To provide funding to Hispanic and other minority medical students who are interested in working on a summer project with a psychiatrist mentor.

Eligibility This program is open to minority medical students who are interested in psychiatric issues. Minorities include Hispanic/Latinos, American Indians, Alaska Natives, Native Hawaiians, Asian Americans, and African Americans. Applicants must be interested in working with a psychiatrist mentor, primarily on clinical work with underserved minority populations and mental health care disparities. Work settings may be in a research, academic, or clinical environment. Most of them are inner-city or rural and deal with psychiatric subspecialties, particularly substance abuse and geriatrics. Selection is based on interest of the medical student and specialty of the mentor, practice setting, and geographic proximity of the mentor to the student. U.S. citizenship or permanent resident status is required.

Financial Data Fellowships provide $1,500 for living and out-of-pocket expenses directly related to the conduct of the fellowship.

Duration Summer months.

Additional data This program is funded by the Substance Abuse and Mental Health Services Administration.

Number awarded Varies each year.

Deadline March of each year.

[634]
APAGS COMMITTEE FOR THE ADVANCEMENT OF RACIAL AND ETHNIC DIVERSITY (CARED) GRANT PROGRAM

American Psychological Association
Attn: American Psychological Association of Graduate
  Students
750 First Street, N.E.
Washington, DC 20002-4242
(202) 336-6014   Fax: (202) 336-5694
E-mail: apags@apa.org
Web: www.apa.org/about/awards/apags-cema.aspx

Summary   To provide funding to graduate students who are members of the American Psychological Association of Graduate Students (APAGS) and who wish to develop a project that increases membership and participation of Hispanics and other ethnic minority students within the association.

Eligibility   This program is open to members of APAGS who are enrolled at least half time in a master's or doctoral program at an accredited university. Applicants must be interested in developing a project to increase the membership and participation of ethnic minority graduate students within APAGS, advertise education and training opportunities for ethnic minorities, and enhance the recruitment and retention efforts for ethnic minority students in psychology. Examples include, but are not limited to, workshops, conferences, speaker series, mentorship programs, and the development of student organizations with a focus on multiculturalism or ethnic minority concerns.

Financial Data   The grant is $1,000.

Duration   The grant is presented annually.

Additional data   This grant was first awarded in 1997.

Number awarded   4 each year.

Deadline   November of each year.

[635]
APF GRADUATE STUDENT SCHOLARSHIPS

American Psychological Foundation
750 First Street, N.E.
Washington, DC 20002-4242
(202) 336-5843   Fax: (202) 336-5812
E-mail: foundation@apa.org
Web: www.apa.org/apf/funding/cogdop.aspx

Summary   To provide funding for research to graduate students in psychology, especially Hispanics and members of other diverse groups.

Eligibility   Each department of psychology that is a member in good standing of the Council of Graduate Departments of Psychology (COGDOP) may nominate up to 3 candidates for these scholarships. Nominations must include a completed application form, a letter of nomination from the department chair or director of graduate studies, a letter of recommendation from the nominee's graduate research adviser, a transcript of all graduate course work completed by the nominee, a curriculum vitae, and a brief outline of the nominee's thesis or dissertation research project. Selection is based on the context for the research, the clarity and comprehensibility of the research question, the appropriateness of the research design, the general importance of the research, and the use of requested funds. The sponsor encourages applications from individuals who represent diversity in race, ethnicity, gender, age, disability, and sexual orientation.

Financial Data   Awards range from $1,000 to $5,000 per year. A total of $28,000 is available for these scholarships each year.

Duration   1 year.

Additional data   The highest rated nominees receive the Charles and Carol Spielberger Scholarship of $5,000, the Harry and Miriam Levinson Scholarship of $5,000 and the William and Dorothy Bevan Scholarship of $5,000. The next highest rated nominee receives the Ruth G. and Joseph D. Matarazzo Scholarship of $3,000. The next highest rated nominee receives the Clarence J. Rosecrans Scholarship of $2,000. The next highest rated nominees receive the William C. Howell Scholarship, the Dr. Judy Kuriansky Scholarship, and the Peter and Malina James and Dr. Louis P. James Legacy Scholarship of $1,000 each. Another 8 scholarships of $1,000 each, offered by the COGDOP, are also awarded.

Number awarded   16 each year: 3 at $5,000, 1 at $3,000, 1 at $2,000, and 11 at $1,000.

Deadline   June of each year.

[636]
ARKANSAS CONFERENCE ETHNIC AND LANGUAGE CONCERNS COMMITTEE SCHOLARSHIPS

United Methodist Church-Arkansas Conference
Attn: Committee on Ethnic and Language Concerns
800 Daisy Bates Drive
Little Rock, AR 72202
(501) 324-8045   Toll Free: (877) 646-1816
Fax: (501) 324-8018   E-mail: mallen@arumc.org
Web: www.arumc.org/docs-and-forms

Summary   To provide financial assistance to Hispanic and other ethnic minority Methodist students from Arkansas who are interested in attending college or graduate school in any state.

Eligibility   This program is open to ethnic minority undergraduate and graduate students who are active members of local congregations affiliated with the Arkansas Conference of the United Methodist Church (UMC). Applicants must be currently enrolled in an accredited institution of higher education in any state. Along with their application, they must submit an essay explaining how this scholarship will make them a leader in the UMC. Preference is given to students attending a UMC-affiliated college or university.

Financial Data   The stipend is $500 per semester ($1,000 per year) for undergraduates or $1,000 per semester ($2,000 per year) for graduate students.

Duration   1 year; may be renewed.

Number awarded   5 each year: 1 in each UMC Arkansas district.

Deadline   February or September of each year.

[637]
ARL CAREER ENHANCEMENT PROGRAM

Association of Research Libraries
Attn: Director of Diversity Programs
21 Dupont Circle, N.W., Suite 800
Washington, DC 20036
(202) 296-2296   Fax: (202) 872-0884
E-mail: mpuente@arl.org
Web: www.arl.org

Summary To provide an opportunity for Hispanics and members of other minority racial and ethnic groups to gain work experience at a library that is a member of the Association of Research Libraries (ARL).

Eligibility This program is open to members of racial and ethnic minority groups that are underrepresented as professionals in academic and research libraries (American Indian or Alaska Native, Asian, Black or African American, Native Hawaiian or other Pacific Islander, or Hispanic or Latino). Applicants must have completed at least 12 credit hours of an M.L.I.S. degree program at an ALA-accredited institution. They must be interested in an internship at 1 of 7 ARL member institutions. Along with their application, they must submit a 500-word essay on what attracts them to an internship opportunity in an ARL library, their professional interests as related to the internship, and their goals for the internship.

Financial Data Fellows receive a stipend of $4,800 for the internship, housing reimbursement up to $2,500, relocation assistance up to $1,000, and financial support (approximately $1,400) to attend the annual ARL Leadership Institute.

Duration The internship lasts 6 to 12 weeks (or 240 hours).

Additional data This program is funded by the Institute of Museum and Library Services. Recently, the 7 participating ARL institutions were the University of Arizona, University of California at San Diego, University of Kentucky, University of Michigan, University of Washington, National Library of Medicine, and North Carolina State University.

Number awarded Varies each year; recently, 13 of these fellows were selected.

Deadline October of each year.

[638]
ARL INITIATIVE TO RECRUIT A DIVERSE WORKFORCE

Association of Research Libraries
Attn: Director of Diversity Programs
21 Dupont Circle, N.W., Suite 800
Washington, DC 20036
(202) 296-2296   Fax: (202) 872-0884
E-mail: mpuente@arl.org
Web: www.arl.org

Summary To provide financial assistance to Hispanics and members of other minority racial and ethnic groups who are interested in preparing for a career as an academic or research librarian.

Eligibility This program is open to members of racial and ethnic minority groups that are underrepresented as professionals in academic and research libraries (American Indian or Alaska Native, Asian, Black or African American, Native Hawaiian or other Pacific Islander, or Hispanic or Latino). Applicants must be interested in working on an M.L.I.S. degree at an ALA-accredited program. They must be citizens or permanent residents of the United States (including Puerto Rico) or Canada.

Financial Data The stipend is $5,000 per year.

Duration 2 years.

Additional data This program began in 2000. Funding is currently provided by the Institute of Museum and Library Services and by the contributions of 52 libraries that are members of the Association of Research Libraries (ARL).

Number awarded Varies each year; recently, 15 were awarded.

Deadline April of each year.

[639]
ARL/SAA MOSAIC SCHOLARSHIPS

Society of American Archivists
Attn: Chair, Awards Committee
17 North State Street, Suite 1425
Chicago, IL 60602-4061
(312) 606-0722   Toll Free: (866) 722-7858
Fax: (312) 606-0728   E-mail: info@archivists.org
Web: www2.archivists.org

Summary To provide financial assistance to Hispanic and other minority students who are working on a graduate degree in archival science.

Eligibility This program is open to minority graduate students, defined as those of Hispanic/Latino, American Indian/Alaska Native, Asian, Black/African American, or Native Hawaiian/other Pacific Islander descent. Applicants must be enrolled or planning to enroll full or part time in a master's degree program or a multi-course program in archival science, archival management, digital archives, special collections, or a related program. They may have completed no more than half of the credit requirements for a degree. Along with their application, they must submit a 500-word essay outlining their interests and future goals in the archives profession. U.S. or Canadian citizenship or permanent resident status is required.

Financial Data The stipend is $10,000.

Duration 1 year.

Additional data This program began in 2009. A second iteration of the program began in 2013 in partnership with the Association of Research Libraries (ARL) and financial support provided by the Institute of Museum and Library Sciences (IMLS).

Number awarded 1 or 2 each year.

Deadline June of each year.

[640]
ARRASTIA, CAPOTE & PHANG SCHOLARSHIP

Hispanic National Bar Association
Attn: HNBA Legal Education Fund
1020 19th Street, N.W., Suite 505
Washington, DC 20036
(202) 223-4777   Fax: (202) 503-3403
E-mail: ovargas@hnbafund.org
Web: www.hnbafund.org/Scholarships.aspx

Summary To provide financial assistance to Hispanic law students.

Eligibility This program is open to Hispanic students who are enrolled full or part time as first-year students at an ABA-accredited law school. Selection is based on GPA, class rank, and demonstrated financial need.

Financial Data　The stipend is $1,500.

Duration　1 year.

Additional data　This program, sponsored by the law firm Arrastia, Capote & Phang, began in 2014.

Number awarded　1 each year.

Deadline　February of each year.

[641]
ARTTABLE MENTORED INTERNSHIPS FOR DIVERSITY IN THE VISUAL ARTS PROFESSIONS

ArtTable Inc.
1 East 53rd Street, Fifth Floor
New York, NY 10022
(212) 343-1735　　　　　　　　Fax: (866) 363-4188
E-mail: info@arttable.org
Web: www.arttable.org/summermentoredinternship

Summary　To provide an opportunity for women who are Hispanics or from other diverse backgrounds to gain mentored work experience during the summer and to prepare for a career as an art professional.

Eligibility　This program is open to women who are college seniors, recent graduates, or graduate students and interested in preparing for a career as a visual arts professional (including administrative director, art adviser, art appraiser, art critic, art dealer, art librarian, arts funder, arts lawyer, conservator, curator, editor, educator, fundraiser, management consultant, public relations consultant, writer). Applicants must be from a cultural or ethnic background that is underrepresented in the field. They must be interested in working during the summer with a mentor at an art museum or similar facility. U.S. citizenship or permanent resident status is required.

Financial Data　The stipend is $3,000. The hosting institution or mentor receives $500 for administrative and other costs.

Duration　8 weeks during the summer.

Additional data　This program began in 2000. Support is provided by the Samuel H. Kress Foundation.

Number awarded　Varies each year; recently, 5 of these internships were awarded.

Deadline　February of each year.

[642]
ASA MINORITY FELLOWSHIP PROGRAM GENERAL FELLOWSHIP

American Sociological Association
Attn: Minority Affairs Program
1430 K Street, N.W., Suite 600
Washington, DC 20005-2504
(202) 383-9005, ext. 322　　　　　Fax: (202) 638-0882
TDD: (202) 638-0981　E-mail: minority.affairs@asanet.org
Web: www.asanet.org

Summary　To provide financial assistance to doctoral students in sociology who are Hispanics or members of other minority groups.

Eligibility　This program is open to U.S. citizens, permanent residents, and noncitizen nationals who are Latinos (e.g., Mexican Americans, Puerto Ricans, Cubans), Blacks/African Americans, American Indians or Alaskan Natives, Asian Americans (e.g., southeast Asians, Japanese, Chinese, Koreans), or Pacific Islanders (e.g., Filipinos, Samoans, Hawaiians, Guamanians). Applicants must be entering or continuing students in sociology at the doctoral level. Along with their application, they must submit 3-page essays on 1) the reasons why they decided to undertake graduate study in sociology, their primary research interests, and why they hope to do with a Ph.D. in sociology; and 2) what led them to select the doctoral program they attend or hope to attend and how they see that doctoral program preparing them for a professional career in sociology. Selection is based on commitment to research, focus of research experience, academic achievement, writing ability, research potential, and financial need.

Financial Data　The stipend is $18,000 per year.

Duration　1 year; may be renewed up to 2 additional years.

Additional data　This program, which began in 1974, is supported by individual members of the American Sociological Association (ASA) and by several affiliated organizations (Alpha Kappa Delta, Sociologists for Women in Society, the Association of Black Sociologists, the Midwest Sociological Society, and the Southwestern Sociological Association).

Number awarded　Varies each year; since the program began, more than 500 of these fellowships have been awarded.

Deadline　January of each year.

[643]
ASCO MEDICAL STUDENT ROTATION FOR UNDERREPRESENTED POPULATIONS

American Society of Clinical Oncology
Attn: Conquer Cancer Foundation of ASCO
2318 Mill Road, Suite 800
Alexandria, VA 22314
(571) 483-1700
E-mail: grants@conquercancerfoundation.org
Web: www.conquercancerfoundation.org

Summary　To provide funding to medical students who are Hispanics or members of other underrepresented groups and interested in a clinical research oncology rotation.

Eligibility　This program is open to U.S. citizens, nationals, and permanent residents who are currently enrolled at a U.S. medical school. Applicants must be a member of a group currently underrepresented in medicine, defined as American Indian/Alaska Native, Black/African American, Hispanic/Latino, or Native Hawaiian/Pacific Islander. They must be interested in a rotation either in a cancer patient care setting or a cancer clinical research setting; the rotation may take place either at their own school or another institution but must have a faculty member who belongs to the American Society of Clinical Oncology (ASCO) and is willing to serve as a mentor. Selection is based on interest in preparing for a career in oncology; demonstration of leadership, volunteerism and/ or commitment to underserved populations or heath disparities; letters of recommendation; and overall academic record.

Financial Data　Students receive a stipend of $5,000 plus $1,500 for future travel to the annual meeting of the American Society of Clinical Oncology (ASCO). Their mentor receives a grant of $2,000.

Duration　8 to 10 weeks.

Additional data　This program, which began in 2009, is currently sponsored by Lilly and Genentech BioOncology.

Number awarded Varies each year; recently, 4 were awarded.

Deadline January of each year.

[644]
ASME GRADUATE TEACHING FELLOWSHIP

ASME International
Attn: Education Manager
Two Park Avenue, Floor 7
New York, NY 10016-5618
(212) 591-7559   Toll Free: (800) THE-ASME
Fax: (212) 591-7856   E-mail: lawreya@asme.org
Web: www.asme.org

Summary To provide funding to members of the American Society of Mechanical Engineers (ASME), especially Hispanics and other minorites, who are working on a doctorate in mechanical engineering.

Eligibility This program is open to U.S. citizens or permanent residents who have an undergraduate degree from an ABET-accredited program, belong to the society as a student member, are currently employed as a teaching assistant with lecture responsibility, and are working on a Ph.D. in mechanical engineering. Along with their application, they must submit a statement about their interest in a faculty career. Applications from women and minorities are particularly encouraged.

Financial Data Fellowship stipends are $5,000 per year.

Duration Up to 2 years.

Additional data Recipients must teach at least 1 lecture course.

Number awarded Up to 4 each year.

Deadline February of each year.

[645]
ASP GRADUATE STUDENT VISITOR PROGRAM

National Center for Atmospheric Research
Attn: Advanced Study Program
3090 Center Green Drive
P.O. Box 3000
Boulder, CO 80307-3000
(303) 497-1328   Fax: (303) 497-1646
E-mail: paulad@ucar.edu
Web: www.asp.ucar.edu/graduate/graduate_visitor.php

Summary To provide an opportunity for graduate students, especially Hispanics and other underrepresented minorities, to conduct research at the National Center for Atmospheric Research (NCAR) in Boulder, Colorado under the supervision of a staff member.

Eligibility This program is open to advanced M.S. and Ph.D. students in the atmospheric and related sciences, engineering, and scientific computing. Interdisciplinary studies utilizing the NCAR resources in climate, weather, and related disciplines are also welcome. Applicants should consult with an NCAR staff member who will agree to serve as a host for the research project. Students may not apply directly for this program; the application must be submitted by the NCAR staff member in collaboration with the student's thesis adviser. Selection is based on 1) the programmatic fit and need to visit NCAR as part of the thesis or final project work; and 2) the commitment to student mentoring by the NCAR host and the student's adviser. The program encourages applications from members of groups historically underrepresented in the atmospheric and related sciences, including Hispanics or Latinos, American Indians and Alaska Natives, Blacks or African Americans, women, first-generation college students, LGBT students, and students with disabilities.

Financial Data Support is limited to travel expenses for the student and a per diem allowance of $2,000 per month. Travel expenses are also supported for the student's thesis adviser for visits up to 2 weeks. The student's university must provide all support for the student's salary and benefits.

Duration Visits may extend from a few months to a year, but most are 3 to 6 months.

Additional data NCAR is operated by the University Corporation for Atmospheric Research (a consortium of more than 100 North American universities and research institutes) and sponsored by the National Science Foundation. This program was established in 2006.

Number awarded Varies each year; recently, 24 students received support from this program.

Deadline October of each year.

[646]
ASSE DIVERSITY COMMITTEE GRADUATE SCHOLARSHIP

American Society of Safety Engineers
Attn: ASSE Foundation
Scholarship Award Program
520 North Northwest Highway
Park Ridge, IL 60068-2538
(847) 699-2929   Fax: (847) 296-3769
E-mail: assefoundation@asse.org
Web: foundation.asse.org/scholarships-and-grants

Summary To provide financial assistance to graduate students who are Hispanics or come from other diverse groups and are working on a degree related to occupational safety.

Eligibility This program is open to students who are working on a graduate degree in occupational safety, health, environment, industrial hygiene, occupational health nursing, or a closely-related field (e.g., industrial or environmental engineering). Applicants must be full- or part-time students who have completed at least 9 semester hours and have a GPA of 3.5 or higher. A goal of this program is to support individuals regardless of race, ethnicity, gender, religion, personal beliefs, age, sexual orientation, physical challenges, geographic location, university, or specific area of study. U.S. citizenship is not required. Membership in the American Society of Safety Engineers (ASSE) is not required, but preference is given to members.

Financial Data The stipend is $1,000 per year.

Duration 1 year; recipients may reapply.

Number awarded 1 each year.

Deadline November of each year.

[647]
ASSOCIATION OF CUBAN ENGINEERS SCHOLARSHIPS

Association of Cuban Engineers
P.O. Box 941436
Miami, FL 33194-1436
Web: www.aic-ace.com/?q=node/27

Summary To provide financial assistance to undergraduate and graduate students of Cuban American heritage who are interested in preparing for a career in engineering.

Eligibility This program is open to U.S. citizens and legal residents who have completed at least 30 units of college work in the United States and are working on an undergraduate or graduate degree in engineering. Applicants must be attending an ABET-accredited college or university within the United States or Puerto Rico as a full-time student and have a GPA of 3.0 or higher. They must be of Cuban or other Hispanic heritage (at least 1 grandparent Cuban or other Hispanic nationality). Along with their application, they must submit brief essays on their family history, professional goals, extracurricular activities, work experience, and how they will help other Cuban and Hispanic engineering students in the future. Financial need is not considered in the selection process.

Financial Data Stipends range from $500 to $2,000.

Duration 1 year; may be renewed.

Additional data This program also includes the Pedro O. Martinez Scholarship and the Luciano de Goicochea Award (for students at the University of Miami), the Antonio Choy Award (for a student at the University of Florida), and the Noel Betancourt Award (for a student at Florida International University).

Number awarded Varies each year; recently, 11 were awarded.

Deadline November of each year.

[648]
ASSOCIATION OF LATINO PROFESSIONALS FOR AMERICA SCHOLARSHIP PROGRAM

Association of Latino Professionals For America
Attn: Scholarships
801 South Grand Avenue, Suite 400
Los Angeles, CA 90017
(714) 757-6133   E-mail: scholarships@national.alpfa.org
Web: www.alpfa.fluidreview.com

Summary To provide financial assistance to members of the Association of Latino Professionals For America (ALPFA) who are working on an undergraduate or master's degree in a field related to business.

Eligibility This competition is open to members of ALPFA who are full-time sophomores, juniors, seniors, or master's degree students at colleges and universities in the United States, Puerto Rico, U.S. Virgin Islands, or Guam. Students enrolled at community colleges and planning to transfer to 4-year institutions are also eligible. Applicants must be working on a degree in accounting, business administration, economics, finance, information systems, information technology, management, marketing, or other business-related field. They must be U.S. citizens or permanent residents and have a GPA of 3.0 or higher. Along with their application, they must submit a resume, official transcript, and proof of full-time enrollment.

Financial Data Stipends range from $2,000 to $10,000.

Duration 1 year.

Additional data This program began in 2005 when the sponsor was named the Association of Latino Professionals in Finance and Accounting.

Number awarded Varies each year. Since the program was established, it has awarded 578 scholarships worth $1.14 million.

Deadline May of each year.

[649]
ATKINS NORTH AMERICA LEADERSHIP SCHOLARSHIP

Conference of Minority Transportation Officials
Attn: National Scholarship Program
100 M Street, S.E., Suite 917
Washington, DC 20003
(202) 506-2917   E-mail: info@comto.org
Web: www.comto.org/page/scholarships

Summary To provide financial assistance to Hispanic and other minority undergraduate and graduate students interested in working on a degree in transportation or a related field.

Eligibility This program is open to minority 1) undergraduates who have completed at least 12 semester hours of study; and 2) graduate students. Applicants must be studying transportation, engineering, planning, or a related discipline. Along with their application they must submit a cover letter on their transportation-related career goals and life aspirations. Financial need is not considered in the selection process.

Financial Data The stipend is $3,000. Funds are paid directly to the recipient's college or university.

Duration 1 year.

Additional data This program is sponsored by Atkins North America.

Number awarded 1 each year.

Deadline April of each year.

[650]
BALFOUR PHI DELTA PHI MINORITY SCHOLARSHIP AWARD

Phi Delta Phi International Legal Fraternity
Attn: Executive Director
P.O. Box 11570
Fort Lauderdale, FL 33339
(202) 223-6801   Toll Free: (800) 368-5606
Fax: (202) 223-6808   E-mail: info@phideltaphi.org
Web: www.phideltaphi.org/?page=BalfourMinorityGuide

Summary To provide financial assistance to Hispanics and other minorities who are members of Phi Delta Phi International Legal Fraternity.

Eligibility This program is open to law students who have been members of the legal fraternity for at least 1 year. Applicants must be minorities, defined to include Hispanic, African Americans, Asian/Pacific Islanders, American Indians/Alaskan Natives, or LGBT students. They must affirm that they intend to practice law in inner-cities of the United States, especially in New England. Along with their application, they must submit a 750-word essay on why they consider themselves qualified to serve as role models for minority youth. Priority is given to students at law schools in New England, especially Massachusetts.

Financial Data The stipend is $3,000.

Duration 1 year.

Additional data This program began in 1997 with funding from the Lloyd G. Balfour Foundation.

Number awarded 1 each year.

Deadline October of each year.

[651]
BASIC PSYCHOLOGICAL SCIENCE RESEARCH GRANT

American Psychological Association
Attn: American Psychological Association of Graduate
  Students
750 First Street, N.E.
Washington, DC 20002-4242
(202) 336-6014   E-mail: apags@apa.org
Web: www.apa.org/about/awards/apags-science.aspx

Summary To provide funding to members of the American Psychological Association of Graduate Students (APAGS) who are interested in conducting graduate research in psychological science, including those dealing specifically with diversity issues.

Eligibility This program is open to members of the association who are enrolled at least half time in a psychology or neuroscience graduate program at an accredited university. Applicants must be interested in conducting thesis, dissertation, or other research in psychological science. Along with their application, they must submit a curriculum vitae, letter of recommendation, and 3-page research proposal. The program includes grants specifically reserved for research focused on diversity, defined to include issues of age, sexual orientation, physical disability, socioeconomic status, race/ethnicity, workplace role/position, religious and spiritual orientation, and work/family concerns. Applicants for diversity grants must also submit a 250-word statement that explains 1) how this research applies to one or more areas of diversity; and 2) how the overall merit and broader implications of this study contribute to our psychological understanding of diversity.

Financial Data The stipend is $1,000.

Duration 1 year.

Additional data These grants were first awarded in 2009; the diversity component began in 2014.

Number awarded Approximately 12 each year, of which up to 3 are reserved for researchers specifically focusing on diversity issues.

Deadline November of each year.

[652]
BECAS UNIVISION SCHOLARSHIP PROGRAM

Hispanic Scholarship Fund
Attn: Selection Committee
1411 West 190th Street, Suite 700
Gardena, CA 90248
(310) 975-3700   Toll Free: (877) HSF-INFO
Fax: (310) 349-3328   E-mail: scholar1@hsf.net
Web: hsf.net

Summary To provide financial assistance for college or graduate school to Hispanic American students.

Eligibility This program is open to U.S. citizens, permanent residents, Deferred Action for Childhood Arrival (DACA) students, and eligible non-citizens. Applicants must be of Hispanic heritage and enrolled or planning to enroll full time in a degree program at an accredited 4-year college or university as an undergraduate or graduate student (including GED recipients and community college transfers). High school seniors must have a GPA of 3.0 or higher; current undergraduate and graduate students must have a GPA of 2.5 or higher. Selection is based on merit; financial need is considered in determining the amount of the award.

Financial Data Stipends normally range from $500 to $5,000 per year.

Duration 1 year; recipients may reapply.

Additional data This program is sponsored by Becas Univision.

Number awarded Varies each year.

Deadline March of each year.

[653]
BETTY LEA STONE RESEARCH FELLOWSHIP

American Cancer Society-New England Division
30 Speen Street
Framingham, MA 01701
(508) 270-4645   Toll Free: (800) 952-7664, ext. 4645
Fax: (508) 393-8607 E-mail: maureen.morse@cancer.org
Web: www.cancer.org

Summary To provide funding for summer cancer research to medical students in New England, especially Hispanics and other minorities.

Eligibility This program is open to first-year students at medical schools in New England. Applicants must be interested in working on a summer research project under the supervision of a faculty sponsor. Minority students and those with American Cancer Society volunteer experience are encouraged to apply.

Financial Data The grant is $5,000.

Duration 10 weeks during the summer.

Number awarded 1 or more each year.

Deadline January of each year.

[654]
BILL BERNBACH DIVERSITY SCHOLARSHIPS

American Association of Advertising Agencies
Attn: AAAA Foundation
1065 Avenue of the Americas, 16th Floor
New York, NY 10018
(212) 262-2500   E-mail: bbscholarship@ddb.com
Web: www.aaaa.org

Summary To provide financial assistance to Hispanics and other multicultural students interested in working on an undergraduate or graduate degree in advertising at designated schools.

Eligibility This program is open to Hispanic Americans, African Americans, Asian Americans, and Native Americans (including American Indians, Alaska Natives, Native Hawaiians, and other Pacific Islanders) who are interested in studying the advertising creative arts at designated institutions as a full-time student. Applicants must be working on or have already received an undergraduate degree and be able to demonstrate creative talent and promise. They must be U.S. citizens, nationals, or permanent residents. Along with their application, they must submit 10 samples of creative work in their respective field of expertise.

Financial Data The stipend is $5,000.

Duration 1 year.

Additional data This program, which began in 1998, is currently sponsored by DDB Worldwide. The participating schools are the Art Center College of Design (Pasadena, California), Creative Circus (Atlanta, Georgia), Miami Ad School (Miami Beach, Florida), University of Oklahoma (Norman, Oklahoma), University of Texas at Austin, VCU Brandcenter (Richmond, Virginia), Savannah College of Art and Design (Savannah, Georgia), University of Oregon (Eugene), City College of New York, School of Visual Arts (New York, New York), Fashion Institute of Technology (New York, New York), and Howard University (Washington, D.C.).

Number awarded 3 each year.

Deadline May of each year.

[655]
BISHOP THOMAS HOYT, JR. FELLOWSHIP

St. John's University
Attn: Collegeville Institute for Ecumenical and Cultural
  Research
2475 Ecumenical Drive
P.O. Box 2000
Collegeville, MN 56321-2000
(320) 363-3366   Fax: (320) 363-3313
E-mail: staff@CollegevilleInstitute.org
Web: www.collegevilleinstitute.org

Summary To provide funding to Hispanic and other students of color who wish to complete their doctoral dissertation while in residence at the Collegeville Institute for Ecumenical and Cultural Research of St. John's University in Collegeville, Minnesota.

Eligibility This program is open to people of color completing a doctoral dissertation in ecumenical and cultural research. Applicants must be interested in a residency at the Collegeville Institute for Ecumenical and Cultural Research of St. John's University. Along with their application, they must submit a 1,000-word description of the research project they plan to complete while in residence at the Institute.

Financial Data The stipend covers the residency fee of $2,500, which includes housing and utilities.

Duration 1 year.

Additional data Residents at the Institute engage in research, publication, and education on the important intersections between faith and culture. They seek to discern and communicate the meaning of Christian identity and unity in a religiously and culturally diverse world.

Number awarded 1 each year.

Deadline January of each year.

[656]
BREAKTHROUGH TO NURSING SCHOLARSHIPS

National Student Nurses' Association
Attn: Foundation
45 Main Street, Suite 606
Brooklyn, NY 11201
(718) 210-0705   Fax: (718) 210-0710
E-mail: nsna@nsna.org
Web: www.nsna.org

Summary To provide financial assistance to Hispanic and other minority undergraduate and graduate students who wish to prepare for careers in nursing.

Eligibility This program is open to students currently enrolled in state-approved schools of nursing or pre-nursing associate degree, baccalaureate, diploma, generic master's, generic doctoral, R.N. to B.S.N., R.N. to M.S.N., or L.P.N./L.V.N. to R.N. programs. Graduating high school seniors are not eligible. Support for graduate education is provided only for a first degree in nursing. Applicants must be members of a racial or ethnic minority underrepresented among registered nurses (Hispanic, Native Hawaiian or other Pacific Islander, American Indian or Alaska Native, Black or African American, or Asian). They must be committed to providing quality health care services to underserved populations. Along with their application, they must submit a 200-word description of their professional and educational goals and how this scholarship will help them achieve those goals. Selection is based on academic achievement, financial need, and involvement in student nursing organizations and community health activities. U.S. citizenship or permanent resident status is required.

Financial Data Stipends range from $1,000 to $2,000.

Duration 1 year.

Additional data Applications must be accompanied by a $10 processing fee.

Number awarded Varies each year; recently, 13 were awarded: 10 sponsored by the American Association of Critical-Care Nurses and 3 sponsored by the Mayo Clinic.

Deadline January of each year.

[657]
BRONSON T.J. TREMBLAY MEMORIAL SCHOLARSHIP

Colorado Nurses Foundation
Attn: Scholarships
P.O. Box 3406
Englewood, CO 80155
(303) 694-4728   Toll Free: (800) 205-6655
Fax: (303) 200-7099   E-mail: mail@cnfound.org
Web: www.coloradonursesfoundation.com/?page_id=1087

Summary To provide financial assistance to Hispanic and other non-white male undergraduate and graduate nursing students in Colorado.

Eligibility This program is open to non-white male Colorado residents who have been accepted as a student in an approved nursing program in the state. Applicants may be 1) second-year students in an associate degree program; 2) junior or senior level B.S.N. undergraduate students; 3) R.N.s enrolled in a baccalaureate or higher degree program in a school of nursing; 4) R.N.s with a master's degree in nursing, currently practicing in Colorado and enrolled in a doctoral program; or 5) students in the second or third year of a Doctorate Nursing Practice (D.N.P.) or Ph.D. program. Undergraduates must have a GPA of 3.25 or higher and graduate students must have a GPA of 3.5 or higher. Selection is based on professional philosophy and goals, dedication to the improvement of patient care in Colorado, demonstrated commitment to nursing, potential for leadership, involvement in community and professional organizations, recommendations, GPA, and financial need.

Financial Data The stipend is $1,000.

Duration 1 year.

Number awarded 1 each year.

Deadline October of each year.

[658]
BROWN AND CALDWELL MINORITY SCHOLARSHIP

Brown and Caldwell
Attn: HR/Scholarship Program
1527 Cole Boulevard, Suite 300
Lakewood, CO 80401
(303) 239-5400   Fax: (303) 239-5454
E-mail: scholarships@brwncald.com
Web: www.brownandcaldwell.com/Scholarships.asp?id=1

Summary   To provide financial assistance to Hispanic and other minority students working on an undergraduate or graduate degree in an environmental or engineering field.

Eligibility   This program is open to members of minority groups (Hispanics, African Americans, Hispanics, Asians, Pacific Islanders, Native Americans, or Alaska Natives) who are full-time juniors, seniors, or graduate students at an accredited 4-year college or university. Applicants must have a GPA of 3.0 or higher and a declared major in civil, chemical, or environmental engineering or an environmental science (e.g., biology, ecology, geology, hydrogeology). They must be U.S. citizens or permanent residents. Along with their application, they must submit an essay (up to 250 words) on a topic that changes annually but relates to their personal development. Financial need is not considered in the selection process.

Financial Data   The stipend is $5,000.

Duration   1 year.

Number awarded   1 each year.

Deadline   May of each year.

[659]
BUCKFIRE & BUCKFIRE MEDICAL SCHOOL DIVERSITY SCHOLARSHIP

Buckfire & Buckfire, P.C.
Attn: Scholarships
25800 Northwestern Highway, Suite 890
Southfield, MI 48075
(248) 569-4646   Toll Free: (800) 606-1717
Fax: (248) 569-6737 E-mail: marketing@buckfirelaw.com
Web: www.buckfirelaw.com/library/general

Summary   To provide financial assistance to medical students who are Hispanics, come from a minority background, or have a commitment to diversity.

Eligibility   This program is open to U.S. citizens who are members of an ethnic, racial, or other minority or who demonstrate a defined commitment to issues of diversity within their academic career. Applicants must have completed at least 1 semester at an accredited medical school and have a GPA of 3.0 or higher. Selection is based on academic achievement and an essay on how they will utilize their medical degree to promote diversity.

Financial Data   The stipend is $2,000.

Duration   1 year.

Additional data   This program began in 2014.

Number awarded   1 each year.

Deadline   May of each year.

[660]
BUENAS OPINIONES SCHOLARSHIP FOR LATINO STUDENTS

Buenas Opiniones
120 Flower Street
Los Angeles, CA 90071
(213) 293-4312
E-mail: scholarships@buenasopiniones.com
Web: www.buenasopiniones.com/scholarship

Summary   To provide financial assistance to Latino students interested in working on an undergraduate or graduate degree in any field.

Eligibility   This program is open to Latino high school seniors, community college students, undergraduates, and graduate students. Applicants may study any academic field, but they must have a GPA of 3.0 or higher. Along with their application, they must submit an essay of 500 to 1,000 words on their struggles as a Latino student. Selection is based on merit.

Financial Data   The stipend is $2,500 per year.

Duration   Up to 4 years.

Number awarded   1 or more each semester.

Deadline   August of each year for fall semester; January of each year for spring semester.

[661]
CALIFORNIA BAR FOUNDATION 1L DIVERSITY SCHOLARSHIPS

State Bar of California
Attn: California Bar Foundation
180 Howard Street
San Francisco, CA 94105-1639
(415) 856-0780   Fax: (415) 856-0788
E-mail: scholarships@calbarfoundation.org
Web: www.calbarfoundation.org

Summary   To provide financial assistance to residents of any state who are Hispanics or members of other groups historically underrepresented in the legal profession and entering law school in California.

Eligibility   This program to open to residents of any state who are entering their first year at a law school in California. Applicants must be able to contribute to greater diversity in the legal profession. Diversity includes a broad array of backgrounds and life experiences, including students from groups or with skills or attributes that are underrepresented in the legal profession. Students from socially and economically disadvantaged backgrounds are especially encouraged to apply. Along with their application, they must submit a 500-word essay describing their commitment to serving the community and, if applicable, any significant obstacles or hurdles they have overcome to attend law school. Financial need is considered in the selection process.

Financial Data   The stipend is $7,500.

Duration   1 year.

Additional data   This program began in 2008. Each year, the foundation grants awards named after sponsors that donate funding for the scholarships.

Number awarded   Varies each year; recently, 33 were awarded.

Deadline   May of each year.

[662]
CALIFORNIA COMMUNITY SERVICE-LEARNING PROGRAM

National Medical Fellowships, Inc.
Attn: Scholarship Program
347 Fifth Avenue, Suite 510
New York, NY 10016
(212) 483-8880   Toll Free: (877) NMF-1DOC
Fax: (212) 483-8897 E-mail: scholarships@nmfonline.org
Web: www.nmfonline.org

Summary   To provide funding to Hispanic and other underrepresented medical students in California who wish to participate in a community service program for underserved areas of the state.

Eligibility   This program is open to members of underrepresented minority groups (African American, Hispanic/Latino, Native American, Vietnamese, or Cambodian) who are U.S. citizens or DACA certified. Applicants must be currently enrolled in an accredited medical school in California. They must be interested in a self-directed service-learning experience that provides 200 hours of community service in medically-underserved areas of the state. Selection is based on demonstrated leadership early in career and commitment to serving medically underserved communities.

Financial Data   The stipend is $5,000.

Additional data   Funding for this program, which began in 2013 and is administered by National Medical Fellowships (NMF), is provided by the California Wellness Foundation.

Number awarded   10 each year.

Deadline   March of each year.

[663]
CALIFORNIA PLANNING FOUNDATION DIVERSITY IN PLANNING SCHOLARSHIP

American Planning Association-California Chapter
Attn: California Planning Foundation
c/o Kelly Main
California Polytechnic State University at San Luis Obispo
City and Regional Planning Department
Office 21-116B
San Luis Obispo, CA 93407-0283
(805) 756-2285   Fax: (805) 756-1340
E-mail: cpfapplications@gmail.com
Web: www.californiaplanningfoundation.org

Summary   To provide financial assistance to undergraduate and graduate students in accredited planning programs at California universities, especially Hispanics and others who will increase diversity in the profession.

Eligibility   This program is open to students entering their final year for an undergraduate or master's degree in an accredited planning program at a university in California. Applicants must be students who will increase diversity in the planning profession. Along with their application, they must submit 1) a 500-word personal statement explaining why planning is important to them, their potential contribution to the profession of planning in California, and how this scholarship would help them to complete their degree; 2) a 500-word description of their experience in planning (e.g., internships, volunteer experiences, employment); and 3) a 500-word essay on what they consider to be 1 of the greatest planning challenges in California today. Selection is based on academic performance, increasing diversity in the planning pro-fession, commitment to serve the planning profession in California, and financial need.

Financial Data   The stipend is $3,000. The award includes a 1-year student membership in the American Planning Association (APA) and payment of registration for the APA California Conference.

Duration   1 year.

Additional data   The accredited planning programs are at 3 campuses of the California State University system (California State Polytechnic University at Pomona, California Polytechnic State University at San Luis Obispo, and San Jose State University), 3 campuses of the University of California (Berkeley, Irvine, and Los Angeles), and the University of Southern California.

Number awarded   1 each year.

Deadline   March of each year.

[664]
CALSA MEMBER SCHOLARSHIP FOR EXTENDED EDUCATION

California Association of Latino Superintendents and
  Administrators
Attn: Executive Assistant
1029 J Street, Suite 500
Sacramento, CA 95814
(916) 329-3847   E-mail: awyatt@calsa.org
Web: www.calsa.org/scholarships

Summary   To provide financial assistance to members of the California Association of Latino Superintendents and Administrators (CALSA) who are interested in working on an advanced degree to become a superintendent.

Eligibility   This program is open to CALSA members who are aspiring superintendents. Applicants must submit a 500-word essay on how an advanced degree will help them achieve their goals and further the goals of CALSA.

Financial Data   The stipend is $5,000.

Duration   1 year.

Additional data   This program is sponsored by Curriculum Associates.

Number awarded   1 each year.

Deadline   June of each year.

[665]
CANFIT PROGRAM GRADUATE SCHOLARSHIPS

Communities-Adolescents-Nutrition-Fitness
Attn: Scholarship Program
P.O. Box 3989
Berkeley, CA 94703
(510) 644-1533, ext. 112   Toll Free: (800) 200-3131
Fax: (510) 843-9705   E-mail: info@canfit.org
Web: www.canfit.org/scholarships

Summary   To provide financial assistance to Hispanic and other minority graduate students who are working on a degree in nutrition, physical education, or public health in California.

Eligibility   This program is open to Latinos/Hispanics, American Indians, Alaska Natives, African Americans, Asian Americans, and Pacific Islanders from California who are enrolled in 1) an approved master's or doctoral program in nutrition, public health, or physical education in the state; or 2) a pre-professional practice program approved by the

American Dietetic Association at an accredited university in the state. Applicants must have completed 12 to 15 units of graduate course work and have a cumulative GPA of 3.0 or higher. Along with their application, they must submit 1) documentation of financial need; 2) letters of recommendation from 2 individuals; 3) a 1- to 2-page letter describing their academic goals and involvement in community nutrition and/or physical education activities; and 4) an essay of 500 to 1,000 words on a topic related to healthy foods for youth from low-income communities of color.

Financial Data A stipend is awarded (amount not specified).

Number awarded 1 or more each year.

Deadline March of each year.

[666]
CARLOS M. CASTANEDA JOURNALISM SCHOLARSHIP

Carlos M. Castañeda Educational Foundation
Attn: FECMC Journalism Scholarship
1925 Brickell Avenue, Suite D-1108
Miami, FL 33129
(305) 283-4963   E-mail: fecmc@me.com
Web: fecmc.tripod.com

Summary To provide financial assistance to Spanish-speaking graduate students and journalists working on a master's degree in journalism.

Eligibility This program is open to Spanish-speaking students and journalists from any country (including the United States) who have been accepted into a graduate program in journalism at a university in the United States. Applicants must have completed a 4-year undergraduate degree with a GPA of 3.0 or higher. They are not required to have majored in journalism as an undergraduate, but their curriculum must have included courses in history and liberal arts. A knowledge of and interest in Hispanic culture and an awareness of current events in Latin America are also required. Along with their application, they must submit a curriculum vitae, a cover letter, 3 reference letters, a portfolio with 3 stories published by professional or school publications in Spanish, and a 2,000-word essay (in Spanish) on the work of Carlos M. Castañeda as a champion of freedom of the press and human rights. Financial need is considered in the selection process.

Financial Data The stipend is $7,000.

Duration 1 year; may be renewed 1 additional year if the recipient maintains a GPA of 3.0 or higher.

Additional data This program began in 2005.

Number awarded 1 or more each year.

Deadline April of each year.

[667]
CARMEN E. TURNER SCHOLARSHIPS

Conference of Minority Transportation Officials
Attn: National Scholarship Program
100 M Street, S.E., Suite 917
Washington, DC 20003
(202) 506-2917   E-mail: info@comto.org
Web: www.comto.org/page/scholarships

Summary To provide financial assistance for college or graduate school to Hispanic and other members of the Conference of Minority Transportation Officials (COMTO) and their families.

Eligibility This program is open to undergraduate and graduate students who have been members or whose parents, guardians, or grandparents have been members of COMTO for at least 1 year. Applicants must be working on a degree in a field related to transportation and have a GPA of 2.5 or higher. Along with their application they must submit a cover letter on their transportation-related career goals and life aspirations. Financial need is not considered in the selection process.

Financial Data The stipend is $3,500. Funds are paid directly to the recipient's college or university.

Duration 1 year.

Number awarded 1 each year.

Deadline April of each year.

[668]
CARRINGTON-HSIA-NIEVES SCHOLARSHIP FOR MIDWIVES OF COLOR

American College of Nurse-Midwives
Attn: ACNM Foundation, Inc.
8403 Colesville Road, Suite 1550
Silver Spring, MD 20910-6374
(240) 485-1850   Fax: (240) 485-1818
E-mail: foundation@acnmf.org
Web: www.midwife.org

Summary To provide financial assistance to Hispanic and other midwives of color who are members of the American College of Nurse-Midwives (ACNM) and engaged in doctoral or postdoctoral study.

Eligibility This program is open to ACNM members of color who are certified nurse midwives (CNM) or certified midwives (CM). Applicants must be enrolled in a program of doctoral or postdoctoral education. Along with their application, they must submit brief statements on their 5-year academic career plans, their intended use of the funds, and their intended future participation in the local, regional, and/or national activities of the ACNM and in activities that otherwise contribute substantially to midwifery research, education, or practice.

Financial Data The stipend is $5,000.

Duration 1 year.

Number awarded 1 each year.

Deadline October of each year.

[669]
CATHY L. BROCK SCHOLARSHIP

Institute for Diversity in Health Management
Attn: Membership and Education Specialist
155 North Wacker Avenue
Chicago, IL 60606
(312) 422-2658   E-mail: cbiddle@aha.org
Web: www.diversityconnection.org

Summary To provide financial assistance to graduate students in health care management, especially financial operations, who are Hispanics or will contribute to ethnic diversity in the profession in other ways.

Eligibility This program is open to U.S. citizens who represent ethnically diverse cultural backgrounds. Applicants must be enrolled in the first or second year of a master's degree program in health administration or a comparable program and have a GPA of 3.0 or higher. Along with their application, they must submit 1) a personal statement of 1 to 2 pages on their interest in health care management and their career goals; 2) an essay on what they see as the most challenging issue facing America's hospitals and health systems; and 3) a 500-word essay on their interest and background in health care finance. Selection is based on academic achievement, commitment to a career in health care finance, and financial need.

Financial Data　The stipend is $1,000.

Duration　1 year.

Number awarded　1 each year.

Deadline　January of each year.

[670]
CENTER FOR U.S.-MEXICAN STUDIES SCHOLARS PROGRAM

University of California at San Diego
Attn: Center for U.S.-Mexican Studies
School of Global Policy and Strategy
9500 Gilman Drive, 519
La Jolla, CA 92093-0519
(858) 534-0192　　　　　E-mail: usmex@ucsd.edu
Web: usmex.ucsd.edu/scholars/application-process.html

Summary　To provide funding to doctoral candidates interested in conducting dissertation research on topics related to Mexico.

Eligibility　This program is open to Ph.D. candidates who have completed all requirements for their degree except the dissertation and have completed a substantial portion of research for the dissertation. Applicants must be interested in conducting research on contemporary Mexico, Mexican history, or U.S.-Mexico relations. Comparative studies with a substantial Mexico component are also encouraged. Priority is given to proposals that are relevant to public policy. Proposals from Mexican scholars are particularly encouraged.

Financial Data　Stipends average $22,500.

Duration　From 4 to 9 months (not over the summer months).

Number awarded　Varies each year; recently, 5 were awarded.

Deadline　January of each year.

[671]
CH2M HILL PARTNERSHIP SCHOLARSHIP

Women's Transportation Seminar
Attn: WTS Foundation
1701 K Street, N.W., Suite 800
Washington, DC 20006
(202) 955-5085　　　　　Fax: (202) 955-5088
E-mail: wts@wtsinternational.org
Web: www.wtsinternational.org/education/scholarships

Summary　To provide financial assistance to women graduate students, especially Hispanics and other minorities, who are interested in preparing for a career in transportation.

Eligibility　This program is open to women who are enrolled in a graduate degree program in a transportation-related field (e.g., transportation engineering, planning, finance, or logistics). Applicants must have at least a 3.0 GPA and be interested in a career in transportation. Along with

their application, they must submit a 750-word statement about their career goals after graduation and why they think they should receive the scholarship award. Applications must be submitted first to a local chapter; the chapters forward selected applications for consideration on the national level. Minority women are particularly encouraged to apply. Selection is based on transportation involvement and goals, job skills, and academic record.

Financial Data　The stipend is $10,000.

Duration　1 year.

Additional data　This program is sponsored by CH2M Hill. Local chapters may also award additional funding to winners in their area.

Number awarded　1 each year.

Deadline　Applications must be submitted by November to a local WTS chapter.

[672]
CHARLES B. RANGEL GRADUATE FELLOWSHIP PROGRAM

Howard University
Attn: Ralph J. Bunche International Affairs Center
2218 Sixth Street, N.W.
Washington, DC 20059
(202) 806-4367　　　　　Toll Free: (877) 633-0002
Fax: (202) 806-5424　E-mail: rangelprogram@howard.edu
Web: www.rangelprogram.org

Summary　To provide financial assistance for graduate study in a field related to the work of the Foreign Service, especially to Hispanics and members of other underrepresented minority groups.

Eligibility　This program is open to U.S. citizens who are either graduating college seniors or recipients of an undergraduate degree. Applicants must be planning to enter graduate school to work on a master's degree in international affairs or other area of interest to the Foreign Service of the U.S. Department of State (e.g., public administration, public policy, business administration, foreign languages, economics, political science, or communications). They must have a GPA of 3.2 or higher. The program encourages applications from members of minority groups historically underrepresented in the Foreign Service and those who can demonstrate financial need.

Financial Data　The program provides a stipend of $20,000 per year for tuition and fees, $15,000 per year for room, board, books, and other education-related expenses, and a stipend of $10,000 per year for housing, transportation, and related expenses for summer internships.

Duration　2 years.

Additional data　This program is offered jointly by Howard University and the U.S. Department of State. Fellows are provided an internship working on international issues for members of Congress during the summer after they are selected and before they begin graduate study. They are provided a second internship at a U.S. embassy overseas during the summer before their second year of graduate study. Fellows who complete the program and Foreign Service entry requirements receive appointments as Foreign Service Officers. Each fellow who obtains a master's degree is committed to at least 5 years of service as a Foreign Service Officer. If recipients do not complete the program successfully or do not fulfill the 3-year service obligation, they may be subject to a reimbursement obligation.

Number awarded 20 each year.

Deadline January of each year.

[673]
CHARLOTTE LEGAL DIVERSITY CLERKSHIP

Mecklenburg County Bar
Attn: Diversity and Inclusion Committee
2850 Zebulon Avenue
Charlotte, NC 28208
(704) 375-8624, ext. 127   Fax: (704) 333-6209
E-mail: adeburst@meckbar.org
Web: www.meckbar.org

Summary To provide summer work experience with a law firm and corporate legal department in Charlotte, North Carolina to law students from any state who are Hispanics or will advance the diversity of the local legal community in other ways.

Eligibility This program is open to first-year law students who represent diverse groups. Applicants must be interested in a summer clerkship in Charlotte, North Carolina that includes work with a law firm in the downtown area and with a corporate legal department in the general area. Along with their application, they must submit a 1- to 2-page statement explaining how they would contribute to the goal of creating a more diverse legal community in Charlotte and why they would like to practice in Charlotte.

Financial Data Participating law firms pay the same salary as for all of their summer law associates. Participating corporate legal departments jointly determine the compensation for their portion of the program.

Duration 12 weeks during the summer: 6 weeks with a law firm and 6 weeks with a corporate legal department.

Additional data This program began in 2008.

Number awarded 8 each year.

Deadline January of each year.

[674]
CHCI-SHRM SCHOLAR INTERN PROGRAM

Congressional Hispanic Caucus Institute, Inc.
911 Second Street, N.E.
Washington, DC 20002
(202) 543-1771   Toll Free: (800) EXCEL-DC
Fax: (202) 546-2143   E-mail: chci@chci.org
Web: www.chci.org

Summary To provide financial assistance and work experience at designated member organizations of the Society for Human Resource Management (SHRM) to undergraduate and graduate students of Hispanic descent.

Eligibility This program is open to U.S. citizens, asylees, valid visa holders, and permanent residents who are of Hispanic descent and currently enrolled full time at an accredited 4-year university in the United States or Puerto Rico as undergraduates of at least sophomore standing or graduate students. They must have at least 1 year of study remaining until graduation. Students registered in the DACA program must possess an Employment Authorization Document. Applicants must be working on a degree in business or human resources. They must be interested in a paid summer internship in SHRM member organizations in Chicago, Dal-

las, or Los Angeles County/Orange County. Financial need is considered in the selection process.

Financial Data For the scholarship component of this program, the stipend is $2,500. For the internship component, undergraduates receive a salary of $15 per hour and graduate students receive a salary of $19 per hour.

Duration 1 year; nonrenewable.

Additional data Funding for this program is provided by SHRM.

Number awarded Up to 5 each year.

Deadline February of each year.

[675]
CHCI-UNITED HEALTH FOUNDATION SCHOLAR INTERN PROGRAM

Congressional Hispanic Caucus Institute, Inc.
911 Second Street, N.E.
Washington, DC 20002
(202) 543-1771   Toll Free: (800) EXCEL-DC
Fax: (202) 546-2143   E-mail: chci@chci.org
Web: www.chci.org

Summary To provide financial assistance and work experience at community health organizations to undergraduate and graduate students of Hispanic descent.

Eligibility This program is open to U.S. citizens, asylees, valid visa holders, and permanent residents who are of Hispanic descent and currently enrolled full time at an accredited community college, 4-year university, or graduate/professional program with a GPA of 3.0 or higher. Applicants must be preparing for a career as a primary care health professional, defined to include general practitioners, internists, family practitioners, OB/GYNs, pediatricians, dentists, public health professionals, mental health professionals, nurses (including advanced practice nurses, and nurse practitioners), physician assistants, and pharmacists. They must obtain a paid internship at a community-based health organization that will require a total of at least 80 hours of service. Financial need is considered in the selection process.

Financial Data For the scholarship component of the program, the stipend is $2,500 for students at community colleges or $5,000 per year for undergraduate and graduate students. For the internship component, participants receive a salary from the health organization where they work; upon verification of completion of 80 hours of paid employment, they also receive an educational stipend of $1,000 from the Congressional Hispanic Caucus Institute (CHCI).

Duration The stipend supports 1 year of study. The award is nonrenewable for community college students but may be renewed for up to 2 additional years by undergraduates or up to 1 additional year by graduate students.

Additional data Funding for this program is provided by United Health Foundation.

Number awarded Varies each year; recently, 18 of these scholarship/internships were awarded: 14 to undergraduates, and 4 to graduate students.

Deadline March of each year.

[676]
CHCI-WYNDHAM WORLDWIDE SCHOLAR INTERN PROGRAM

Congressional Hispanic Caucus Institute, Inc.
911 Second Street, N.E.
Washington, DC 20002
(202) 543-1771   Toll Free: (800) EXCEL-DC
Fax: (202) 546-2143   E-mail: chci@chci.org
Web: www.chci.org

Summary   To provide financial assistance and work experience at offices of Wyndham Worldwide in Parsippany, New Jersey to undergraduate and graduate students of Hispanic descent.

Eligibility   This program is open to U.S. citizens, asylees, valid visa holders, and permanent residents who are of Hispanic descent and currently enrolled full time at an accredited 4-year university in the United States or Puerto Rico as undergraduates of at least sophomore standing or graduate students. They must have at least 1 year of study remaining until graduation. Students registered in the DACA program must possess an Employment Authorization Document. Applicants must be working on a degree in accounting, communications, computer science, journalism, marketing, media, public relations, or other fields of interest to Wyndham. They must be interested in a paid summer internship of 10 weeks at Wyndham's offices in Parsippany. Financial need is considered in the selection process.

Financial Data   For the scholarship component of this program, the stipend is $2,500. For the internship component, participants receive a competitive salary from Wyndham. A housing allowance may also be available.

Duration   1 year; nonrenewable.

Additional data   Funding for this program is provided by Wyndham Worldwide.

Number awarded   Up to 5 each year.

Deadline   December of each year for the first priority deadline; January of each year for the second priority deadline; February of each year for the final deadline.

[677]
CHILDREN'S MERCY HOSPITALS AND CLINICS PEDIATRIC NURSING SCHOLARSHIP

National Association of Hispanic Nurses
Attn: Scholarships
1500 Sunday Drive, Suite 102
Raleigh, NC 27607
(919) 787-5181, ext. 1255   Fax: (919) 787-4916
E-mail: director@thehispanicnurses.org
Web: www.nahnnet.org/NAHNScholarships.html

Summary   To provide financial assistance to members of the National Association of Hispanic Nurses (NAHN) who are interested in preparing for a career in pediatric nursing.

Eligibility   Eligible are members of the association enrolled in associate, diploma, baccalaureate, graduate, or practical/vocational nursing programs in pediatric nursing. Applicants must have a GPA of 3.0 or higher. Along with their application, they must submit a letter of recommendation; a 300-word essay that reflects their qualifications and potential for leadership in nursing in the Hispanic community; a resume that includes earned certificates, awards, and special honors;

information on their financial status; and an official transcript. U.S. citizenship or permanent resident status is required.

Financial Data   The stipend is $2,000.

Duration   1 year.

Additional data   Support for this program, which began in 2013, is provided by Children's Mercy Hospitals of Kansas City, Missouri.

Number awarded   1 each year.

Deadline   June of each year.

[678]
CHIPS QUINN SCHOLARS PROGRAM

Newseum Institute
Attn: Chips Quinn Scholars Program
555 Pennsylvania Avenue, N.W.
Washington, DC 20001
(202) 292-6271   Fax: (202) 292-6275
E-mail: kcatone@freedomforum.org
Web: www.newseuminstitute.org

Summary   To provide work experience to Hispanic and other minority college students and recent graduates who are majoring in journalism.

Eligibility   This program is open to students of color who are college juniors, seniors, graduate students, or recent graduates with journalism majors or career goals in newspapers. Candidates must be nominated or endorsed by journalism faculty, campus media advisers, editors of newspapers, or leaders of minority journalism associations. Along with their application, they must submit a resume, transcripts, 2 letters of recommendation, and an essay of 200 to 400 words on why they want to be a Chips Quinn Scholar. Reporters and copy editors must also submit 6 samples of published articles they have written; photographers must submit 15 to 25 photographs on a DVD; multimedia journalists and graphic designers should submit 6 to 10 samples of their work on a DVD. Applicants must have a car and be available to work as a full-time intern during the spring or summer. U.S. citizenship or permanent resident status is required. Campus newspaper experience is strongly encouraged.

Financial Data   Students chosen for this program receive a travel stipend to attend a Multimedia training program in Nashville, Tennessee prior to reporting for their internship, a $500 housing allowance from the Freedom Forum, and a competitive salary during their internship.

Duration   Internships are for 10 to 12 weeks, in spring or summer.

Additional data   This program began in 1991 in memory of the late John D. Quinn Jr., managing editor of the *Poughkeepsie Journal*. Funding is provided by the Freedom Forum, formerly the Gannett Foundation. After graduating from college and obtaining employment with a newspaper, alumni of this program are eligible to apply for fellowship support to attend professional journalism development activities.

Number awarded   Approximately 70 each year. Since the program began, more than 1,300 scholars have been selected.

Deadline   September of each year.

[679]
CLA SCHOLARSHIP FOR MINORITY STUDENTS IN MEMORY OF EDNA YELLAND

California Library Association
1055 East Colorado Boulevard, Fifth Floor
Pasadena, CA 91106
(626) 204-4071   E-mail: info@cla-net.org
Web: www.cla-net.org/?page=110

Summary   To provide financial assistance to Hispanics and other students of ethnic minority origin in California who are attending graduate school in any state to prepare for a career in library or information science.

Eligibility   This program is open to California residents who are members of ethnic minority groups (Latino/Hispanic, American Indian/Alaska Native, African American/Black, Asian American, or Pacific Islander). Applicants must have completed at least 1 course in a master's program at an accredited graduate library school in any state. Evidence of financial need and U.S. citizenship or permanent resident status must be submitted. Finalists are interviewed.

Financial Data   The stipend is $2,500.

Duration   1 academic year.

Additional data   This fellowship is named for the executive secretary of the California Library Association from 1947 to 1963 who worked to promote the goals of the California Library Association and the profession. Until 1985, it was named the Edna Yelland Memorial Scholarship.

Number awarded   3 each year.

Deadline   July of each year.

[680]
COLGATE-PALMOLIVE DENTAL RESIDENCY OR SPECIALTY PROGRAM SCHOLARSHIPS

Hispanic Dental Association
Attn: HDA Foundation
3910 South IH-35, Suite 245
Austin, TX 78704
(512) 904-0252   E-mail: jessicac@hdassoc.org
Web: www.hdassoc.org

Summary   To provide financial assistance to members of the Hispanic Dental Association (HDA) interested in enrolling in a dental residency or a dental specialty program.

Eligibility   This program is open to HDA members who are accepted or enrolled full time in a dental program in the United States or Puerto Rico. Applicants must be seeking support for training in an accredited dental residency or dental specialty program, including dental public health, oral surgery, orthodontics, endodontics, pediatric dentistry, prosthodontics, periodontics, pathology, or radiology. They must have a GPA of 3.0 or higher, an interest in improving the health of the Hispanic community, and a demonstrated commitment and dedication to serving the Hispanic community. Along with their application, they must submit a 250-word essay on their career goals, including how they were inspired to become a dentist. Selection is based on academic achievement, leadership skills, community service, and commitment and dedication to improving the oral health of the Hispanic community.

Financial Data   The stipend is $4,000. An additional grant of $500 is provided for travel reimbursement and complimentary registration to the HDA annual meeting.

Duration   1 year.

Additional data   This program, which began in 2005, is sponsored by the Colgate-Palmolive Company.

Number awarded   Varies each year; recently, 4 were awarded.

Deadline   May of each year.

[681]
COMMERCIAL AND FEDERAL LITIGATION SECTION DIVERSITY FELLOWSHIP

The New York Bar Foundation
One Elk Street
Albany, NY 12207
(518) 487-5651   Fax: (518) 487-5699
E-mail: moclair@tnybf.org
Web: www.tnybf.org/fellandschol

Summary   To provide an opportunity for residents of any state who are Hispanics or from other diverse backgrounds and attending law school in New York to gain summer work experience in a litigation position in the public sector in the state.

Eligibility   This program is open to Black/African American, Latino/a, Native American or Alaskan Native, or Asian/Pacific Islander students from any state who are enrolled in the first year at a law school in New York. Applicants must have demonstrated an interest in commercial and federal litigation. They must be interested in working in a litigation position during the summer in the public sector in New York. Selection is based on content and quality of application materials, demonstrated interest in litigation, work experience, academic record, leadership experience, extracurricular activities, community service, quality of written expression, maturity, integrity, and professionalism.

Financial Data   The stipend is $6,000.

Duration   10 weeks during the summer.

Additional data   This program began in 2007 with support from the Commercial and Federal Litigation Section of the New York State Bar Association. It is administered by The New York Bar Foundation.

Number awarded   1 each year.

Deadline   January of each year.

[682]
COMMISSION ON DIETETIC REGISTRATION DIVERSITY SCHOLARSHIPS

Academy of Nutrition and Dietetics
Attn: Foundation
120 South Riverside Plaza, Suite 2000
Chicago, IL 60606-6995
(312) 899-4821   Toll Free: (800) 877-1600, ext. 4821
Fax: (312) 899-4796   E-mail: blabrador@eatright.org
Web: www.eatrightfoundation.org/foundation/scholarships

Summary   To provide financial assistance to Hispanics and members of other underrepresented minority groups who are enrolled in an undergraduate or graduate program in dietetics.

Eligibility   This program is open to students enrolled at a CADE-accredited/approved college or university in the undergraduate coordinated dietetics program, the undergraduate didactic program in dietetics, a dietetic internship program, a dietetic technician program, or a dietetic graduate program.

Applicants must be members of underrepresented minority groups (Hispanic, African American, Native American). They must be U.S. citizens or permanent residents and show promise of being a valuable, contributing member of the profession. Membership in the Academy of Nutrition and Dietetics is encouraged but not required.

Financial Data   The stipend is $5,000.

Duration   1 year.

Number awarded   20 each year.

Deadline   March of each year.

[683]
COMMITTEE ON ETHNIC MINORITY RECRUITMENT SCHOLARSHIP

United Methodist Church-California-Pacific Annual
  Conference
Attn: Board of Ordained Ministry
1720 East Linfield Street
Glendora, CA 91740
(626) 824-2284   E-mail: admin@bom.calpacumc.org
Web: www.calpacumc.org/ordainedministry/scholarships

Summary   To provide financial assistance to Hispanics and members of other ethnic minority groups in the California-Pacific Annual Conference of the United Methodist Church (UMC) who are attending a seminary in any state to qualify for ordination as an elder or deacon.

Eligibility   This program is open to members of ethnic minority groups in the UMC California-Pacific Annual Conference who are enrolled at a seminary in any state approved by the UMC University Senate. Applicants must have been approved as certified candidates by their district committee and be seeking Probationary Deacon or Elder's Orders. They may apply for 1 or more types of assistance: tuition scholarships, grants for books and school supplies (including computers), or emergency living expense grants.

Financial Data   Tuition stipends are $1,000 per year; books and supplies grants range up to $1,000 per year; emergency living expense grants depend on need and the availability of funds.

Duration   1 year; may be renewed up to 2 additional years.

Additional data   The California-Pacific Annual Conference includes churches in southern California, Hawaii, Guam, and Saipan.

Number awarded   Varies each year.

Deadline   August of each year for fall term; December of each year for spring term.

[684]
COMPUTATIONAL CHEMISTRY AND MATERIALS SCIENCE SUMMER INSTITUTE

Lawrence Livermore National Laboratory
Physical and Life Sciences Directorate
Attn: Director of Student Programs
7000 East Avenue, L-452
Livermore, CA 94550
(925) 422-6351   E-mail: kulp2@llnl.gov
Web: www-pls.llnl.gov

Summary   To provide an opportunity for doctoral students, especially Hispanics and other minorities, to work on summer research projects on computational materials science and chemistry at Lawrence Livermore National Laboratory (LLNL).

Eligibility   This program is open to full-time doctoral students who are interested in working on research projects involving computational materials and chemistry. Applicants must be interested in working at LLNL as a guest of an LLNL host scientist on a computational project. They must be enrolled in a Ph.D. program at a U.S. or foreign university. U.S. citizenship is not required. Selection is based on academic record, aptitude, research interests, and recommendations of instructors. Strong preference is given to students with exceptional academic records and potential for making outstanding contributions to applied science. Women and minorities are encouraged to apply.

Financial Data   The stipend ranges from $4,100 to $4,900 per month, depending on number of school years completed. Living accommodations and arrangements are the responsibility of the intern.

Duration   8 to 10 weeks, during the summer.

Number awarded   10 to 15 each year.

Deadline   February of each year.

[685]
CONNECTICUT HISPANIC BAR ASSOCIATION SCHOLARSHIPS

Connecticut Hispanic Bar Association
Attn: Scholarships
P.O. Box 230869
Hartford, CT 06123-0869
E-mail: info@ct-hbe.org
Web: www.ct-hba.org/for-students

Summary   To provide financial assistance to students who are enrolled at law schools in Connecticut and have a connection to the Latino community.

Eligibility   This program is open to students currently enrolled at law schools in Connecticut who have a strong connection to the Latino community. Applicants must submit a personal statement of 500 to 1,000 words discussing what they hope to achieve as a lawyer and their commitment to the Latino community, particularly in Connecticut. They must be able to demonstrate financial need.

Financial Data   A stipend is awarded (amount not specified).

Duration   1 year.

Additional data   This program, established in 1997, is offered through the Hartford Foundation for Public Giving.

Number awarded   Varies each year; recently, 5 were awarded.

Deadline   September of each year.

[686]
CONSORTIUM FOR GRADUATE STUDY IN MANAGEMENT FELLOWSHIPS

Consortium for Graduate Study in Management
229 Chesterfield Business Parkway
Chesterfield, MO 63005
(636) 681-5553   Fax: (636) 681-5499
E-mail: recruiting@cgsm.org
Web: www.cgsm.org

Summary   To provide financial assistance and work experience to Hispanics and other underrepresented racial minorities interested in preparing for a management career in business.

Eligibility This program is open to Hispanic Americans (Chicanos, Cubans, Dominicans, and Puerto Ricans), African Americans, and Native Americans who have graduated from college and are interested in preparing for a career in business. Other U.S. citizens and permanent residents who can demonstrate a commitment to the sponsor's mission of enhancing diversity in business education are also eligible. An undergraduate degree in business or economics is not required. Applicants must be planning to work on an M.B.A. degree at 1 of the consortium's 18 schools.

Financial Data The fellowship pays full tuition and required fees. Summer internships with the consortium's cooperative sponsors, providing paid practical experience, are also offered.

Duration Up to 4 semesters.

Additional data This program began in 1966. The participating schools are Carnegie Mellon University, Cornell University, Dartmouth College, Emory University, Georgetown University, Indiana University, University of Michigan, New York University, University of California at Berkeley, University of California at Los Angeles, University of North Carolina at Chapel Hill, University of Rochester, University of Southern California, University of Texas at Austin, University of Virginia, Washington University, University of Wisconsin at Madison, and Yale University. Fellowships are tenable at member schools only. Application fees are $150 for students applying to 1 or 2 schools, $200 for 3 schools, $240 for 4 schools, $275 for 5 schools, or $300 for 6 schools.

Number awarded Varies each year; recently, 420 were awarded.

Deadline January of each year.

[687]
CONSUELO W. GOSNELL MEMORIAL SCHOLARSHIPS

National Association of Social Workers
Attn: NASW Foundation
750 First Street, N.E., Suite 800
Washington, DC 20002-4241
(202) 408-8600, ext. 298   Fax: (202) 336-8292
E-mail: naswfoundation@naswdc.org
Web: www.naswfoundation.org/gosnell.asp

Summary To provide financial assistance to Hispanic American and other minority students interested in working on a master's degree in social work.

Eligibility This program is open to students who have applied to or been accepted into an accredited M.S.W. program. Applicants must have demonstrated a commitment to work with, or have a special affinity with, American Indian, Alaska Native, or Hispanic/Latino populations in the United States. They must be members of the National Association of Social Workers (NASW), have the potential for completing an M.S.W. program, and have a GPA of 3.0 or higher. Applicants who have demonstrated a commitment to working with public or voluntary nonprofit agencies or with local grassroots groups in the United States are also eligible. Financial need is considered in the selection process.

Financial Data The stipends range up to $4,000 per year.

Duration Up to 1 year; may be renewed for 1 additional year.

Number awarded Up to 10 each year.

Deadline February of each year.

[688]
CORRIS BOYD SCHOLARS PROGRAM

Association of University Programs in Health Administration
Attn: Prizes, Fellowships and Scholarships
2000 14th Street North, Suite 780
Arlington, VA 22201
(703) 894-0940, ext. 122   Fax: (703) 894-0941
E-mail: lmeckley@aupha.org
Web: www.aupha.org

Summary To provide financial assistance to Hispanic and other minority students entering graduate schools affiliated with the Association of University Programs in Health Administration (AUPHA).

Eligibility This program is open to students of color (Latino/Hispanics, African Americans, American Indians, Alaska Natives, Asian Americans, Native Hawaiians, Pacific Islanders) who have been accepted to a master's degree program in health care management at an AUPHA member institution. Applicants must be U.S. citizens or permanent residents and have a GPA of 3.0 or higher. Along with their application, they must submit a personal statement explaining why they are choosing to prepare for a career in health administration. Selection is based on leadership qualities, academic achievement, community involvement, and commitment to health care and health care management as a career path; financial need may be considered if all other factors are equal.

Financial Data The stipend is $40,000.

Duration 1 year.

Additional data This program began in 2006.

Number awarded 2 each year.

Deadline April of each year.

[689]
CREDIT SUISSE MBA FELLOWSHIP

Credit Suisse
Attn: Diversity and Inclusion Programs
Eleven Madison Avenue
New York, NY 10010-3629
(212) 325-2000   Fax: (212) 325-6665
E-mail: campus.diversity@credit-suisse.com
Web: www.credit-suisse.com

Summary To provide financial assistance and work experience at offices of Credit Suisse to Hispanic and other underrepresented minority graduate students working on a master's degree as preparation for a career in investment banking.

Eligibility This program is open to students entering their first year of a full-time M.B.A. program who are Hispanic/Latino, Black/African American, Native American, or female. Applicants must be able to demonstrate a strong interest in a career in investment banking. Selection is based on academic excellence, leadership ability, and interest in the financial services industry.

Financial Data   The stipend is $15,000 for the first year; for the second year, students may elect to have $30,000 paid directly to their university or to have $15,000 paid to them for tuition and for academic and living expenses.

Duration   1 year (the first year of graduate school), followed by a summer internship at 1 of the offices of Credit Suisse. Students who successfully complete the internship and accept an office of full-time employment with the firm are eligible for a second year of funding.

Additional data   Offices of Credit Suisse are located in Chicago, Houston, Los Angeles, New York, and San Francisco.

Number awarded   1 or more each year.

Deadline   November of each year.

[690]
CUBAN AMERICAN BAR ASSOCIATION SCHOLARSHIPS

Cuban American Bar Association
Attn: Foundation
c/o Manuel L. Crespo
Greenspoor Marder
600 Brickell Avenue, Suite 3600
Miami, FL 33131
(305) 789-2770   Fax: (305) 537-3900
E-mail: manny.crespo@gmlaw.com
Web: www.cabaonline.com/foundation/scholarships

Summary   To provide financial assistance to law students who have a connection with the Cuban American community.

Eligibility   This program is open to students currently enrolled at an accredited law school who 1) are Cuban Americans with a distinguished record of academic achievement and/or service-oriented activities; or 2) have distinguished themselves in research, writing, community services, and/or activities of importance to the Cuban American community. Applicants must submit a 1,000-word essay focusing on and describing in detail the activities and achievements that qualify them for the award.

Financial Data   The stipend is $2,500.

Duration   1 year.

Additional data   This program includes the Osvaldo Soto Scholarship and the Judge Margarita Esquiroz Scholarship.

Number awarded   Varies each year; recently, 4 were awarded.

Deadline   August of each year.

[691]
DALLAS HISPANIC LAW FOUNDATION SCHOLARSHIPS

Dallas Hispanic Law Foundation
c/o Chris Luna, President
P.O. Box 1523
Dallas, TX 75221
E-mail: dhlf.scholarships@gmail.com
Web: www.dallashispaniclawfoundation.com

Summary   To provide financial assistance to residents of Texas attending law school in the state and planning to serve the Hispanic community.

Eligibility   This program is open to residents of Texas attending law school in the state. Applicants must submit a 1-page statement on their career aspirations and how they

intend to use their law degree to benefit the Hispanic community in Texas. Financial need is considered in the selection process.

Financial Data   The stipend is at least $1,000.

Duration   1 year.

Additional data   This program began in 2006.

Number awarded   Varies each year; recently, 15 were awarded.

Deadline   March of each year.

[692]
DALMAS A. TAYLOR MEMORIAL SUMMER MINORITY POLICY FELLOWSHIP

Society for the Psychological Study of Social Issues
208 I Street, N.E.
Washington, DC 20002-4340
(202) 675-6956   Toll Free: (877) 310-7778
Fax: (202) 675-6902   E-mail: awards@spssi.org
Web: www.spssi.org

Summary   To enable Hispanic and other graduate students of color to be involved in the public policy activities of the American Psychological Association (APA) during the summer.

Eligibility   This program is open to graduate students who are members of an ethnic minority group (including, but not limited to, Hispanic, African American, Alaskan Native, American Indian, Asian American, and Pacific Islander) and/or have demonstrated a commitment to a career in psychology or a related field with a focus on ethnic minority issues. Applicants must be interested in spending a summer in Washington, D.C. to work on public policy issues in conjunction with the Minority Fellowship Program of the APA. Their application must indicate why they are interested in the fellowship, their previous and current research experiences, their interest and involvement in ethnic minority psychological issues, and how the fellowship would contribute to their career goals.

Financial Data   The stipend is $3,000. The sponsor also provides travel expenses and up to $1,500 for living expenses.

Duration   8 to 12 weeks.

Additional data   This program began in 2000. The sponsor is Division 9 of the APA.

Number awarded   1 each year.

Deadline   February of each year.

[693]
DAVE CALDWELL SCHOLARSHIP

American Water Works Association
Attn: Scholarship Coordinator
6666 West Quincy Avenue
Denver, CO 80235-3098
(303) 794-7771   Toll Free: (800) 926-7337
Fax: (303) 347-0804   E-mail: scholarships@awwa.org
Web: www.awwa.org

Summary   To provide financial assistance to Hispanic and other minority students interested in working on a graduate degree in the field of water supply and treatment.

Eligibility   This program is open to minority and female students working on a graduate degree in the field of water supply and treatment at a college or university in Canada, Guam, Mexico, Puerto Rico, or the United States. Students who have been accepted into graduate school but have not yet begun graduate study are encouraged to apply. Applicants must submit a 2-page resume, official transcripts, 3 letters of recommendation, a proposed curriculum of study, a 1-page statement of educational plans and career objectives demonstrating an interest in the drinking water field, and a 3-page proposed plan of research. Selection is based on academic record and potential to provide leadership in applied research and consulting in the drinking water field.

Financial Data The stipend is $10,000.

Duration 1 year; nonrenewable.

Additional data Funding for this program comes from the engineering firm Brown and Caldwell.

Number awarded 1 each year.

Deadline January of each year.

[694]
DAVID C. LIZARRAGA GRADUATE FELLOWSHIPS

TELACU Education Foundation
Attn: David Lizárraga Fellowship Program
5400 East Olympic Boulevard, Suite 300
Los Angeles, CA 90022
(323) 721-1655   Fax: (323) 721-3560
E-mail: jogarcia@telacu.com
Web: www.telacu.com

Summary To provide financial assistance to Latino students from designated communities who are working on a master's degree in business or engineering at a school in any state.

Eligibility This program is open to Latino residents of selected communities in southern California, selected cities in Texas, the Greater Chicagoland area of Illinois, or the state of New York. Applicants must be working full time on a master's degree in business administration or engineering at a university in any state; students working on other graduate degrees may be considered at the discretion of the sponsor. Priority is given to students in their last year of graduate study, although first-year graduate students may be considered. They must be a first-generation college student and have a GPA of 2.5 or higher. Selection is based on leadership potential, professional and extracurricular achievement, commitment to the development and economic empowerment of communities, and financial need.

Financial Data The stipend ranges from $500 to $5,000.

Duration 1 year.

Additional data This program is sponsored by Toyota. The eligible areas in California include underserved communities in Los Angeles, Orange, and San Bernardino counties such as unincorporated areas of east Los Angeles and the cities of Baldwin Park, Bell Gardens, Commerce, Huntington Park, Los Angeles, Montebello, Ontario, Pico Rivera, Pomona, San Bernardino, Santa Ana, and South Gate. The cities in Texas are Austin, Edinburg, Laredo, Rio Grande City, and San Antonio.

Number awarded Up to 6 each year.

Deadline February of each year.

[695]
DAVID EATON SCHOLARSHIP

Unitarian Universalist Association
Attn: Ministerial Credentialing Office
24 Farnsworth Street
Boston, MA 02210-1409
(617) 948-6403   Fax: (617) 742-2875
E-mail: mcoadministrator@uua.org
Web: www.uua.org

Summary To provide financial assistance to Hispanic and other minority women preparing for the Unitarian Universalist (UU) ministry.

Eligibility This program is open to women from historically marginalized groups who are currently enrolled or planning to enroll full or at least half time in a UU ministerial training program with aspirant or candidate status. Applicants must be citizens of the United States or Canada. Priority is given first to those who have demonstrated outstanding ministerial ability and secondarily to students with the greatest financial need (especially persons of color).

Financial Data The stipend ranges from $1,000 to $15,000 per year.

Duration 1 year.

Number awarded 1 or 2 each year.

Deadline April of each year.

[696]
DAVID POHL SCHOLARSHIP

Unitarian Universalist Association
Attn: Ministerial Credentialing Office
24 Farnsworth Street
Boston, MA 02210-1409
(617) 948-6403   Fax: (617) 742-2875
E-mail: mcoadministrator@uua.org
Web: www.uua.org

Summary To provide financial assistance to seminary students, especially Hispanics and other persons of color, who are preparing for the Unitarian Universalist (UU) ministry.

Eligibility This program is open to seminary students who are enrolled full or at least half time in a UU ministerial training program with candidate status. Applicants must be citizens of the United States or Canada. Priority is given first to those who have demonstrated outstanding ministerial ability and secondarily to students with the greatest financial need (especially persons of color).

Financial Data The stipend ranges from $1,000 to $15,000 per year.

Duration 1 year.

Number awarded 1 each year.

Deadline April of each year.

[697]
DAVID SANKEY MINORITY SCHOLARSHIP IN METEOROLOGY

National Weather Association
Attn: Executive Director
3100 Monitor Avenue, Suite 123
Norman, OK 73072
(405) 701-5167   Fax: (405) 701-5227
E-mail: exdir@nwas.org
Web: www.nwas.org

Summary To provide financial assistance to Hispanics and members of other underrepresented groups working on an undergraduate or graduate degree in meteorology.

Eligibility This program is open to members of underrepresented ethnic groups who are either entering their sophomore or higher year of undergraduate study or enrolled as graduate students. Applicants must be working on a degree in meteorology. Along with their application, they must submit a 1-page statement explaining why they are applying for this scholarship. Selection is based on that statement, academic achievement, and 2 letters of recommendation.

Financial Data The stipend is $1,000.

Duration 1 year.

Additional data This program began in 2002.

Number awarded 1 each year.

Deadline April of each year.

[698]
DEEP CARBON OBSERVATORY DIVERSITY GRANTS

American Geosciences Institute
Attn: Grant Coordinator
4220 King Street
Alexandria, VA 22302-1502
(703) 379-2480   Fax: (703) 379-7563
E-mail: hrhp@agiweb.org
Web: www.americangeosciences.org

Summary To provide funding to geoscientists who are Hispanics or members of other underrepresented ethnic groups and interested in participating in research and other activities of the Deep Carbon Observatory (DCO) project.

Eligibility This program is open to traditionally underrepresented geoscientists (e.g., African Americans, Native Americans, Native Alaskans, Hispanics, Latinos, Latinas, Native Hawaiians, Native Pacific Islanders, Filipinos, of mixed racial/ethnic backgrounds) who are U.S. citizens or permanent residents. Applicants must be interested in participating in the DCO, a global research program focused on understanding carbon in Earth, and must have research interests that are aligned with its mission. They may be doctoral students, postdoctoral researchers, or early-career faculty members or research staff.

Financial Data Grants average $5,000.

Duration 1 year.

Additional data This program is funded by the Alfred P. Sloan Foundation.

Number awarded 4 or 5 each year.

Deadline April of each year.

[699]
DELAWARE ATHLETIC TRAINERS' ASSOCIATION ETHNIC DIVERSITY ADVISORY COMMITTEE SCHOLARSHIP

Delaware Athletic Trainers' Association
c/o Education Committee Chair
University of Delaware
159 Fred Rust Ice Arena
Newark, DE 19716
(302) 831-6402   E-mail: kaminski@udel.edu
Web: www.delata.org/scholarship-applications.html

Summary To provide financial assistance to Hispanic and other ethnic minority members of the National Athletic Trainers' Association (NATA) from Delaware who are working on an undergraduate or graduate degree in the field.

Eligibility This program is open to NATA members who are members of ethnic diversity groups and residents of Delaware or attending college in that state. Applicants must be enrolled full time in an undergraduate athletic training education program or a graduate athletic training program and have a GPA of 2.5 or higher. They must intend to prepare for the profession of athletic training. Along with their application, they must submit an 800-word statement on their athletic training background, experience, philosophy, and goals. Selection is based equally on academic performance and athletic training clinical achievement.

Financial Data A stipend is awarded (amount not specified).

Duration 1 year.

Number awarded 1 or more each year.

Deadline February of each year.

[700]
DELORES A. AUZENNE FELLOWSHIP FOR GRADUATE STUDY

State University System of Florida
Attn: Board of Governors
325 West Gaines Street
Tallahassee, FL 32399-0400
(850) 245-0466   Fax: (850) 245-9685
E-mail: info@flbog.org

Summary To provide financial assistance to Hispanic and other minority students in Florida working on a graduate degree in an underrepresented discipline.

Eligibility This program is open to members of minority groups working full time on a graduate degree in a discipline in which there is an underrepresentation of the minority group to which they belong. Applicants must have been residents of Florida for at least 2 years and be enrolled at a public institution in the state. A GPA of 3.0 or higher and U.S. citizenship or permanent resident status are required.

Financial Data The stipend is $5,000 per year.

Duration 1 year; may be renewed if the recipient maintains full-time enrollment and at least a 3.0 GPA.

Additional data This program is administered by the equal opportunity program at each of the 12 State University System of Florida 4-year institutions. Contact that office for further information.

Number awarded Varies each year.

Deadline Each participating university sets its own deadline.

[701]
DIETETIC INTERNSHIP SCHOLARSHIPS

Academy of Nutrition and Dietetics
Attn: Foundation
120 South Riverside Plaza, Suite 2000
Chicago, IL 60606-6995
(312) 899-4821   Toll Free: (800) 877-1600, ext. 4821
Fax: (312) 899-4796   E-mail: scholarship@eatright.org
Web: www.eatrightacend.org

Summary To provide financial assistance to student members of the Academy of Nutrition and Dietetics who have applied for a dietetic internship, especially Hispanics and other underrepresented minorities.

Eligibility This program is open to student members who have applied for an accredited dietetic internship. Applicants must be participating in the computer-matching process, be U.S. citizens or permanent residents, and show promise of being a valuable, contributing member of the profession. Some scholarships require membership in a specific dietetic practice group, residency in a specific state, or underrepresented minority group status. The same application form can be used for all categories. Students who are currently completing the internship component of a combined graduate/dietetic internship should apply for the Academy of Nutrition and Dietetics' Graduate Scholarship.

Financial Data Stipends range from $500 to $10,000 but most are for $1,000.

Duration 1 year.

Additional data The Academy of Nutrition and Dietetics was formerly the American Dietetic Association.

Number awarded Approximately 40 each year.

Deadline February of each year.

[702]
DISSERTATION FELLOWSHIPS OF THE CONSORTIUM FOR FACULTY DIVERSITY

Consortium for Faculty Diversity at Liberal Arts Colleges
c/o Gettysburg College
Provost's Office
300 North Washington Street
Campus Box 410
Gettysburg, PA 17325
(717) 337-6796   E-mail: sgockows@gettysburg.edu
Web: www.gettysburg.edu

Summary To provide an opportunity for doctoral candidates who are Hispanics or will promote diversity in other ways to work on their dissertation while in residence at selected liberal arts colleges.

Eligibility This program is open to U.S. citizens and permanent residents who have completed all the requirements for the Ph.D. or M.F.A. except the dissertation. Applicants must be interested in a residency at a member institution of the Consortium for Faculty Diversity at Liberal Arts Colleges during which they will complete their dissertation. They must be able to contribute to diversity at the institution.

Financial Data Dissertation fellows receive a stipend based on the average salary paid to instructors at the participating college. Modest funds are made available to finance the fellow's proposed research, subject to the usual institutional procedures.

Duration 1 year.

Additional data The following schools are participating in the program: Allegheny College, Amherst College, Bard College, Bowdoin College, Bryn Mawr College, Bucknell University, Carleton College, Centenary College of Louisiana, Centre College, College of the Holy Cross, Colorado College, Denison University, DePauw University, Dickinson College, Gettysburg College, Grinnell College, Gustavus Adolphus College, Hamilton College, Haverford College, Hobart and William Smith Colleges, Juniata College, Lafayette College, Lawrence University, Luther College, Macalester College, Mount Holyoke College, Muhlenberg College, Oberlin College, Pitzer College, Pomona College, Reed College, Scripps College, Skidmore College, Smith College, Southwestern University, St. Lawrence University, St. Olaf College, Swarthmore College, The College of Wooster, Trinity College, University of Richmond, Vassar College, and Wellesley College. Fellows are expected to teach at least 1 course in each academic term of residency, participate in departmental seminars, and interact with students.

Number awarded Varies each year.

Deadline October of each year.

[703]
DISSERTATION FELLOWSHIPS OF THE FORD FOUNDATION DIVERSITY FELLOWSHIP PROGRAM

The National Academies of Sciences, Engineering, and Medicine
Attn: Fellowships Office
500 Fifth Street, N.W.
Washington, DC 20001
(202) 334-2872   Fax: (202) 334-3419
E-mail: FordApplications@nas.edu
Web: sites.nationalacademies.org

Summary To provide funding for dissertation research to Hispanic and other graduate students whose success will increase the racial and ethnic diversity of U.S. colleges and universities.

Eligibility This program is open to citizens, permanent residents, and nationals of the United States who are Ph.D. or Sc.D. degree candidates committed to a career in teaching and research at the college or university level. Applicants must be completing a degree in 1 of the following fields: American studies, anthropology, archaeology, art and theater history, astronomy, chemistry, communications, computer science, cultural studies, earth sciences, economics, education, engineering, ethnic studies, ethnomusicology, geography, history, international relations, language, life sciences, linguistics, literature, mathematics, performance study, philosophy, physics, political science, psychology, religious studies, sociology, urban planning, and women's studies. Also eligible are interdisciplinary programs such as African American studies, Native American studies, area studies, peace studies, and social justice. Students in practice-oriented areas, terminal master's degrees, other doctoral degrees (e.g., Ed.D., D.F.A., Psy.D.), professional degrees (e.g., medicine, law, public health), or joint degrees (e.g., M.D./Ph.D., J.D./Ph.D., M.F.A./Ph.D.) are not eligible. The following are considered as positive factors in the selection process: evidence of superior academic achievement; promise of continuing achievement as scholars and teachers; membership in a group whose underrepresentation in the American professoriate has been severe and longstanding, including Puerto Ricans, Mexican Americans/Chicanos/Chicanas, Black/African Americans, Native American Indians, Alaska Natives (Eskimos, Aleuts, and other indigenous people of Alaska), and Native Pacific Islanders (Hawaiians, Micronesians, or Polynesians); capacity to respond in pedagogically productive ways to the learning needs of students from diverse backgrounds; sustained personal engagement with communities that are underrepresented in the academy and an ability to bring this asset to learning, teaching, and scholarship at the college and university level; and likelihood of using the diversity of human experience as an educational resource in teaching and scholarship.

Financial Data   The stipend is $25,000; stipend payments are made through fellowship institutions.

Duration   9 to 12 months.

Additional data   The competition for this program is conducted by the National Research Council on behalf of the Ford Foundation. Fellows may not accept remuneration from another fellowship or similar external award while supported by this program; however, supplementation from institutional funds, educational benefits from the Department of Veterans Affairs, or educational incentive funds may be received concurrently with Ford Foundation support. Dissertation fellows are required to submit an interim progress report 6 months after the start of the fellowship and a final report at the end of the 12 month tenure.

Number awarded   Approximately 36 each year.

Deadline   November of each year.

[704]
DIVERSIFYING HIGHER EDUCATION FACULTY IN ILLINOIS

Illinois Board of Higher Education
Attn: DFI Program
431 East Adams Street, Second Floor
Springfield, IL 62701-1404
(217) 782-2551   Fax: (217) 782-8548
TDD: (888) 261-2881   E-mail: DFI@ibhe.org
Web: www.ibhe.state.il.us/DFI/default.htm

Summary   To provide fellowship/loans to Hispanic and other minority students interested in enrolling in graduate school programs in Illinois to prepare for a career in higher education.

Eligibility   This program is open to U.S. citizens and permanent residents who 1) are residents of Illinois and have received a baccalaureate degree from an educational institution in the state; or 2) have received a baccalaureate degree from an accredited educational institution in any state and have lived in Illinois for at least the 3 previous years. Applicants must be members of a minority group traditionally underrepresented in graduate school enrollment in Illinois (Hispanic Americans, African Americans, Alaskan Natives, Asian Americans, American Indians, Native Alaskans, Native Hawaiians, or other Pacific Islanders) and have been admitted to a graduate program in the state to work on a doctoral or master's degree and prepare for a career in teaching or administration at an Illinois postsecondary institution or Illinois higher education governing board. They must have a GPA of 2.75 or higher in the last 60 hours of undergraduate work or 3.2 or higher in at least 9 hours of graduate study. Along with their application, they must submit statements on 1) their professional goals (including their intended employment setting, intended position in Illinois higher education, plans for achieving their intended goals, and current and/or past experiences that would be helpful in achieving their intended goals; and 2) their underrepresented status (including how their underrepresented status influenced their personal and academic development and why they should be awarded a fellowship designated specifically for underrepre-

sented groups in higher education). Financial need is considered in the selection process.

Financial Data   Stipends are $10,000 for new fellows or $13,000 per year for renewal fellows. Some participating institutions also provide a tuition waiver or scholarship. This is a fellowship/loan program. Recipients must agree to accept a position, in teaching or administration, at an Illinois postsecondary educational institution, on an Illinois higher education governing or coordinating board, or at a state agency in an education-related position. Recipients failing to fulfill the conditions of the award are required to repay 20% of the total award.

Duration   Up to 2 years for master's degree students; up to 4 years for doctoral students.

Additional data   The Illinois General Assembly established this program in 2004 as a successor to 2 earlier programs (both established in 1985); the Illinois Consortium for Educational Opportunity Program (ICEOP) and the Illinois Minority Graduate Incentive Program (IMGIP).

Number awarded   Varies each year; recently, 111 new and renewal fellows were receiving support through this program.

Deadline   February of each year.

[705]
DIVERSITY SCHOLARSHIP FOR ENTRY-LEVEL ATHLETIC TRAINING STUDENTS

Indiana Athletic Trainers' Association
Attn: Scholarship Committee
125 West Market Street, Suite 300
Indianapolis, IN 46204
(317) 396-0002, ext. 2   Fax: (317) 634-5964
E-mail: jillewing@thecorydongroup.com
Web: www.iata-usa.org/page-1462928

Summary   To provide financial assistance to undergraduate and graduate student members of the Indiana Athletic Trainers' Association (IATA) who are Hispanics or from another ethnic or social diverse background.

Eligibility   This program is open to members of IATA who are from an ethnic or social diverse background and enrolled as full-time juniors, seniors, or graduate students at a college or university in Indiana. Undergraduates must have been an athletic training student for at least 1 year in a CAATE-accredited program; graduate students must be in the second semester of such a program. All applicants must have a GPA of 3.0 or higher and a sponsor who is a full-time member of the athletic training education program faculty or a full-time member of the athletic training staff. Along with their application, they must submit a brief personal statement on why they chose athletic training as a career and their future plans in the field. Financial need is not considered in the selection process.

Financial Data   The stipend is $1,000.

Duration   1 year.

Number awarded   1 each year.

Deadline   September of each year.

[706]
DIVERSITY SUMMER FELLOWSHIP IN HEALTH LAW

The New York Bar Foundation
One Elk Street
Albany, NY 12207
(518) 487-5651   Fax: (518) 487-5699
E-mail: moclair@tnybf.org
Web: www.tnybf.org/fellandschol

Summary To provide an opportunity for Hispanics and other diverse residents of any state attending law school in New York to gain work experience in health law with an attorney or facility in the state.

Eligibility This program is open to diverse students from any state who are enrolled at a law school in New York. They must be interested in working on health law with a health care attorney or facility in New York. Along with their application, they must submit a writing sample on any topic, preferably health law. Selection is based on content and quality of application materials, demonstrated interest in health law, work experience, academic record, leadership experience, extracurricular activities, community service, quality of written expression, maturity, integrity, and professionalism.

Financial Data The stipend is $5,000.

Duration 8 weeks during the summer.

Additional data This program began in 2011 by the Health Law Section of the New York State Bar Association. It is administered by The New York Bar Foundation.

Number awarded 2 each year.

Deadline December of each year.

[707]
DOCTORAL DISSERTATION IMPROVEMENT GRANTS IN THE DIRECTORATE FOR BIOLOGICAL SCIENCES

National Science Foundation
Directorate for Biological Sciences
Attn: Division of Environmental Biology
4201 Wilson Boulevard
Arlington, VA 22230
(703) 292-8480   TDD: (800) 281-8749
E-mail: ddig-deb@nsf.gov
Web: www.nsf.gov

Summary To provide partial support to doctoral canddi-dates, especially Hispanics and other underrepresented minorities, interested in conducting dissertation research in selected areas supported by the National Science Foundation (NSF) Directorate for Biological Sciences (DBS).

Eligibility Applications may be submitted through regular university channels by dissertation advisers on behalf of graduate students who have advanced to candidacy and have begun or are about to begin dissertation research. Students must be enrolled at U.S. institutions but need not be U.S. citizens. Proposals should focus on the ecology, ecosystems, systematics, or population biology programs in the DBS Division of Environmental Biology, or the animal behavior programs in the DBS Division of Integrative Organismal Systems. In the selection process, consideration is given to the achievement of societally relevant outcomes, including full participation of women, persons with disabilities, and underrepresented minorities.

Financial Data Grants range up to $13,000; funds may be used for travel to specialized facilities or field research locations, specialized research equipment, purchase of supplies and services not otherwise available, fees for computerized or other forms of data, and rental of environmental chambers or other research facilities. Funding is not provided for stipends, tuition, textbooks, journals, allowances for dependents, travel to scientific meetings, publication costs, dissertation preparation or reproduction, or indirect costs.

Duration Normally 2 years.

Number awarded 100 to 120 each year; approximately $1,600,000 is available for this program each year.

Deadline October of each year.

[708]
DOCTORAL DIVERSITY FELLOWSHIPS IN SCIENCE, TECHNOLOGY, ENGINEERING, AND MATHEMATICS

State University of New York
Attn: Office of Diversity, Equity and Inclusion
State University Plaza, T1000A
353 Broadway
Albany, NY 12246
(518) 320-1189   E-mail: carlos.medina@suny.edu
Web: system.suny.edu/odei/diversity-programs

Summary To provide financial assistance to residents of any state who are working on a doctoral degree in a field of science, technology, engineering, or mathematics (STEM) at campuses of the State University of New York (SUNY) and contribute to the diversity of the student body.

Eligibility This program is open to U.S. citizens and permanent residents who are residents of any state and enrolled as doctoral students at any of the participating SUNY institutions. Applicants must be working on a degree in a field of STEM. They must be able to demonstrate how they will contribute to the diversity of the student body, primarily by having overcome a disadvantage or other impediment to success in higher education. Economic disadvantage, although not a requirement, may be the basis for eligibility. Membership in a racial or ethnic group that is underrepresented at the applicant's school or program may serve as a plus factor in making awards, but may not form the sole basis of selection.

Financial Data The stipend is $20,000 per year. A grant of $2,000 to support research and professional development is also provided.

Duration 3 years; may be renewed for up to 2 additional years.

Number awarded 2 each year.

Deadline March of each year.

[709]
DOCTORAL/POST-DOCTORAL FELLOWSHIP PROGRAM IN LAW AND SOCIAL SCIENCE

American Bar Foundation
Attn: Administrative Assistant for Academic Affairs and Research Administration
750 North Lake Shore Drive
Chicago, IL 60611-4403
(312) 988-6517   Fax: (312) 988-6579
E-mail: aehrhardt@abfn.org
Web: www.americanbarfoundation.org

Summary To provide research funding to scholars, especially Hispanics and other minorities, who are completing or have completed doctoral degrees in fields related to law, the legal profession, and legal institutions.

Eligibility This program is open to Ph.D. candidates in the social sciences who have completed all doctoral requirements except the dissertation. Applicants who have completed the dissertation are also eligible. Doctoral and proposed research must be in the general area of sociolegal studies or in social scientific approaches to law, the legal profession, or legal institutions and legal processes. Applications must include 1) a dissertation abstract or proposal with an outline of the substance and methods of the research; 2) 2 letters of recommendation; and 3) a curriculum vitae. Minority candidates are especially encouraged to apply.

Financial Data The stipend is $30,000. Fellows may request up to $1,500 to reimburse expenses associated with research, travel to meet with advisers, or travel to conferences at which papers are presented. Relocation expenses of up to $2,500 may be reimbursed on application.

Duration 12 months, beginning in September.

Additional data Fellows are offered access to the computing and word processing facilities of the American Bar Foundation and the libraries of Northwestern University and the University of Chicago. This program was established in 1996. Fellowships must be held in residence at the American Bar Foundation. Appointments to the fellowship are full time; fellows are not permitted to undertake other work.

Number awarded 1 or more each year.

Deadline December of each year.

[710]
DOLLARS FOR SCHOLARS PROGRAM

United Methodist Higher Education Foundation
Attn: Scholarships Administrator
60 Music Square East, Suite 350
P.O. Box 340005
Nashville, TN 37203-0005
(615) 649-3990   Toll Free: (800) 811-8110
Fax: (615) 649-3980
E-mail: umhefscholarships@umhef.org
Web: www.umhef.org/online_applications/umdfs

Summary To provide financial assistance to students, especially Hispanics and other minorities, at Methodist colleges, universities, and seminaries whose home churches agree to contribute to their support.

Eligibility The Double Your Dollars for Scholars program is open to students attending or planning to attend a United Methodist-related college, university, or seminary as a full-time student. Applicants must have been an active, full member of a United Methodist Church for at least 1 year prior to applying. Their home church must nominate them and agree to contribute to their support. Many of the United Methodist colleges and universities have also agreed to contribute matching funds for a Triple Your Dollars for Scholars Program, and a few United Methodist conference foundations have agreed to contribute additional matching funds for a Quadruple Your Dollars for Scholars Program. Awards are granted on a first-come, first-served basis. Some of the awards are designated for Hispanic, Asian, and Native American (HANA) students funded by the General Board of Higher Education and Ministry.

Financial Data The sponsoring church contributes $1,000 and the United Methodist Higher Education Foundation (UMHEF) contributes a matching $1,000. Students who attend a participating United Methodist college or university receive an additional $1,000 for the Triple Your Dollars for Scholars Program, and those from a participating conference receive a fourth $1,000 increment for the Quadruple Your Dollars for Scholars Program.

Duration 1 year; may be renewed as long as the recipients maintain satisfactory academic progress as defined by their institution.

Additional data Currently, participants in the Double Your Dollars for Scholars program include 1 United Methodist seminary and theological school, 1 professional school, and 21 senior colleges and universities. The Triple Your Dollars for Scholars program includes a total of 13 United Methodist seminaries and theological schools, 70 senior colleges and universities, and 4 2-year colleges (for a complete list, consult the UMHEF). A total of 16 conference foundations participate in the Quadruple Your Dollars for Scholars Program.

Number awarded 600 each year, including 25 designated for HANA students.

Deadline Local churches must submit applications in February of each year for senior colleges, universities, and seminaries or May of each year for 2-year colleges.

[711]
DOMINICAN BAR ASSOCIATION LAW SCHOOL SCHOLARSHIPS

Dominican Bar Association
Attn: Law School Scholarship Program
Canal Street Station
P.O. Box 203
New York, NY 10013
(917) 953-1285   E-mail: dominicanbarassoc@gmail.com
Web: www.dominicanbarassociation.org/Scholarship

Summary To provide financial assistance to Latino law students.

Eligibility This program is open to Latino students currently enrolled in their first, second, or third year of law school. Applicants must submit a personal statement that addresses 2 of the following questions: 1) why they attended law school; 2) their biggest challenge and how they were able to overcome it; 3) their commitment to serve the Latino community; or 4) their community involvement and/or commitment to the public interest. Selection is based on academic and personal achievement, demonstrated involvement in and commitment to serve the Latino community through the legal profession, and financial need.

Financial Data The stipend is $3,000.

Duration 1 year.

Additional data This program began in 2003.

Number awarded 3 each year.

Deadline July of each year.

[712]
DR. DAVID K. MCDONOUGH SCHOLARSHIP IN OPHTHALMOLOGY/ENT

National Medical Fellowships, Inc.
Attn: Scholarship Program
347 Fifth Avenue, Suite 510
New York, NY 10016
(212) 483-8880   Toll Free: (877) NMF-1DOC
Fax: (212) 483-8897 E-mail: scholarships@nmfonline.org
Web: www.nmfonline.org

Summary To provide financial assistance to Latino and other underrepresented minority students specializing in ophthalmology or ear, nose, and throat (ENT) specialties at medical schools in New York City.

Eligibility This program is open to Afro-Latino, African American, and Native American medical students enrolled at a school in New York City. Applicants must be preparing for a career in ophthalmology or ENT specialties. They must be U.S. citizens or DACA students. Selection is based on leadership, commitment to serving medically underserved communities, and financial need.

Financial Data The stipend is $5,000.

Duration 1 year.

Number awarded 1 each year.

Deadline September of each year.

[713]
DR. DAVID MONASH/HARRY LLOYD AND ELIZABETH PAWLETTE MARSHALL MEDICAL STUDENT SERVICE SCHOLARSHIPS

National Medical Fellowships, Inc.
Attn: Scholarship Program
347 Fifth Avenue, Suite 510
New York, NY 10016
(212) 483-8880   Toll Free: (877) NMF-1DOC
Fax: (212) 483-8897 E-mail: scholarships@nmfonline.org
Web: www.nmfonline.org

Summary To provide funding for a community health project to Hispanic and other underrepresented medical students in Chicago who are committed to remaining in the area and working to reduce health disparities.

Eligibility This program is open to residents of any state who are currently enrolled in their second through fourth year at a medical school in Chicago. U.S. citizenship is required. Applicants must be interested in conducting a community health project in an underserved community. They must identify as an underrepresented minority student in health care (defined as African American, Hispanic/Latino, American Indian, Alaska Native, Native Hawaiian, Vietnamese, Cambodian, or Pacific Islander) and/or socioeconomically disadvantaged student. Along with their application, they must submit documentation of financial status; a short biography; a resume; 2 letters of recommendation; a personal statement of 500 to 1,000 words on their personal and professional motivation for a medical career, their commitment to primary care and service in a health and/or community setting, their motivation for working to reduce health disparities, and their commitment to improving health care; a personal statement of 500 to 1,000 words on the experiences that are preparing them to practice in an underserved community; and a 150- to 350-word description of their proposed community service project. Selection is based on demonstrated leadership early in career and commitment to serving medically underserved communities in Chicago.

Financial Data The stipend is $5,000.

Duration 1 year.

Additional data This program began in 2010 with support from the Chicago Community Trust.

Number awarded 6 each year.

Deadline May of each year.

[714]
DR. ESPERANZA RODRIGUEZ SCHOLARSHIP

Hispanic Dental Association
Attn: HDA Foundation
3910 South IH-35, Suite 245
Austin, TX 78704
(512) 904-0252   E-mail: jessicac@hdassoc.org
Web: www.hdassoc.org

Summary To provide financial assistance to members of the Hispanic Dental Association (HDA) who are entering their second or third year of dental school.

Eligibility This program is open to HDA members who are entering their second or third year at an accredited dental school in the United States or Puerto Rico. Applicants must have a GPA of 3.0 or higher, an interest in improving the health of the Hispanic community, and a demonstrated commitment and dedication to serving the Hispanic community. They must be enrolled full time. Along with their application, they must submit a 250-word essay on their career goals, including how they were inspired to become a dentist. Selection is based on academic achievement, leadership skills, community service, and commitment and dedication to improving the oral health of the Hispanic community.

Financial Data The stipend is $1,000. An additional grant of $500 is provided for travel reimbursement and complimentary registration to the HDA annual meeting.

Duration 1 year.

Number awarded 1 each year.

Deadline May of each year.

[715]
DR. JUAN D. VILLARREAL SCHOLARSHIPS

Hispanic Dental Association
Attn: HDA Foundation
3910 South IH-35, Suite 245
Austin, TX 78704
(512) 904-0252   E-mail: jessicac@hdassoc.org
Web: www.hdassoc.org

Summary To provide financial assistance to members of the Hispanic Dental Association (HDA) interested in studying dentistry or dental hygiene at institutions in Texas.

Eligibility This program is open to HDA members who have been accepted or are currently enrolled at an accredited dental school or dental hygiene program in Texas as a full-time student. Applicants must have a GPA of 3.0 or higher, an interest in improving the health of the Hispanic community, and a demonstrated commitment and dedication to serving the Hispanic community. Along with their application, they must submit a 250-word essay on their career goals, including how they were inspired to become a dentist or dental hygienist. Selection is based on academic achievement, leadership skills, community service, and commitment and dedication to improving the oral health of the Hispanic community.

Financial Data Stipends are $1,000 for dental students or $500 for dental hygiene students. An additional grant of $200 is provided for travel reimbursement and complimentary registration to the HDA annual meeting.

Duration 1 year.

Additional data This program began in 1995.

Number awarded 2 each year.

Deadline May of each year.

[716]
DR. NANCY FOSTER SCHOLARSHIP PROGRAM

National Oceanic and Atmospheric Administration
Attn: Office of National Marine Sanctuaries
1305 East-West Highway
N/ORM 6 SSMC4, Room 11146
Silver Spring, MD 20910
(301) 713-7245   Fax: (301) 713-9465
E-mail: fosterscholars@noaa.gov
Web: fosterscholars.noaa.gov/aboutscholarship.html

Summary To provide financial assistance to graduate students, especially Hispanics and other minorities, who are interested in working on a degree in fields related to marine sciences.

Eligibility This program is open to U.S. citizens, particularly women and members of minority groups, currently working on or intending to work on a master's or doctoral degree in oceanography, marine biology, or maritime archaeology, including all science, engineering, and resource management of ocean and coastal areas. Applicants must submit a description of their academic, research, and career goals, and how their proposed course of study or research will help them to achieve those goals. They must be enrolled full time and have a GPA of 3.3 or higher. As part of their program, they must be interested in participating in a summer research collaboration at a facility of the National Oceanic and Atmospheric Administration (NOAA). Selection is based on academic record and a statement of career goals and objectives (20%); quality of project and applicability to program priorities (30%); recommendations and/or endorsements (15%); additional relevant experience related to diversity of education, extracurricular activities, honors and awards, written and oral communication skills, and interpersonal skills (20%); and financial need (15%).

Financial Data The program provides a stipend of $30,000 per academic year, a tuition allowance of up to $12,000 per academic year, and up to $10,000 of support for a 4- to 6-week research collaboration at a NOAA facility is provided.

Duration Master's degree students may receive up to 2 years of stipend and tuition support and 1 research collaboration (for a total of $94,000). Doctoral students may receive up to 4 years of stipend and tuition support and 2 research collaborations (for a total of $188,000).

Additional data This program began in 2001.

Number awarded Varies each year; recently, 3 were awarded.

Deadline December of each year.

[717]
DR. ROSE M. GREEN THOMAS ACADEMIC MEDICINE SCHOLARSHIP AWARD

Black Women Physicians Educational and Research
  Foundation
Attn: Scholars Fund
P.O. Box 4502
Gary, IN 46404
(219) 616-3912
Web: www.aacom.org

Summary To provide financial assistance to Hispanic and other minority female medical students interested in a career in academic medicine.

Eligibility This program is open to minority women currently enrolled at an accredited medical school in any state. Applicants must submit an essay of 500 to 650 words on their career goals in academic medicine. Selection is based on academic achievement, motivation for a career in academic medicine, leadership activities, and community involvement.

Financial Data The stipend is $1,000.

Duration 1 year.

Number awarded 1 each year.

Deadline May of each year.

[718]
DRI LAW STUDENT DIVERSITY SCHOLARSHIP

DRI-The Voice of the Defense Bar
Attn: Deputy Executive Director
55 West Monroe Street, Suite 2000
Chicago, IL 60603
(312) 795-1101   Fax: (312) 795-0747
E-mail: dri@dri.org
Web: www.dri.org/About

Summary To provide financial assistance to Hispanic and other minority law students.

Eligibility This program is open to full-time students entering their second or third year of law school who are Hispanic, African American, Asian, Native American, women, or other students who will come from backgrounds that would add to the cause of diversity, including sexual orientation. Applicants must submit an essay, up to 1,000 words, on a topic that changes annually but relates to the work of defense attorneys. Selection is based on that essay, demonstrated academic excellence, service to the profession, service to the community, and service to the cause of diversity. Students affiliated with the American Association for Justice as members, student members, or employees are not eligible. Finalists are invited to participate in personal interviews.

Financial Data The stipend is $10,000.

Duration 1 year.

Additional data This program began in 2004.

Number awarded 2 each year.

Deadline May of each year.

[719]
DRUG ABUSE DISSERTATION RESEARCH

National Institute on Drug Abuse
Attn: Division of Clinical Neuroscience and Behavioral
   Research
6101 Executive Boulevard, Suite 3154
Bethesda, MD 20892-9593
(301) 443-3207   Fax: (301) 443-6814
E-mail: aklinwm@mail.nih.gov
Web: www.grants.nih.gov

Summary To provide financial assistance to Hispanic and other underrepresented doctoral candidates interested in conducting dissertation research on drug abuse treatment and health services.

Eligibility This program is open to doctoral candidates who are conducting dissertation research in a field of the behavioral, biomedical, or social sciences related to drug abuse treatment, including research in epidemiology, prevention, treatment, services, and women and sex/gender differences. Students working on an M.D., D.O., D.D.S., or similar professional degree are not eligible. Applicants must be U.S. citizens, nationals, or permanent residents and must have completed all requirements for the doctoral degree except the dissertation. Special attention is paid to recruiting members of racial and ethnic groups underrepresented in the biomedical and behavioral sciences (Hispanic Americans, African Americans, Native Americans, Alaskan Natives, and Pacific Islanders), persons with disabilities, and individuals from disadvantaged backgrounds.

Financial Data The maximum grant is $50,000 per year, including support for the recipient's salary (up to $21,180 per year), research assistant's salary and direct research project expenses. Funding may not be used for tuition, alterations or renovations, faculty salary, contracting costs, or space rental. The recipient's institution may receive facilities and administrative costs of up to 8% of total direct costs.

Duration Up to 2 years; may be extended for 1 additional year.

Number awarded Varies each year, depending on the availability of funds.

Deadline February, June, or October of each year.

[720]
DWIGHT DAVID EISENHOWER
TRANSPORTATION FELLOWSHIP PROGRAM

Department of Transportation
Federal Highway Administration
Attn: Universities and Grants Programs
4600 North Fairfax Drive, Suite 800
Arlington, VA 22203-1553
(703) 235-0538   Toll Free: (877) 558-6873
Fax: (703) 235-0593   E-mail: transportationedu@dot.gov
Web: www.fhwa.dot.gov/tpp/ddetfp.htm

Summary To provide financial assistance to graduate students, especially those at Hispanic and other Minority Serving Institutions who are working on a master's or doctoral degree in transportation-related fields.

Eligibility This program is open to students enrolled or planning to enroll full time to work on a master's or doctoral degree in a field of study directly related to transportation. Applicants must be planning to enter the transportation profession after completing their higher-level education. They

must be U.S. citizens or have an I-20 (foreign student) or I-551 (permanent resident) identification card. Selection is based on the proposed plan of study, academic records (class standing, GPA, and official transcripts), transportation work experience (including employer's endorsement), and recommendations. Students at Historically Black Colleges and Universities (HBCUs), Hispanic Serving Institutions (HSIs), and Tribal Colleges and Universities (TCUs) are especially encouraged to apply.

Financial Data Fellows receive tuition and fees (to a maximum of $10,000 per year), monthly stipends of $1,700 for master's degree students or $2,000 for doctoral students, and a 1-time allowance of up to $1,500 for travel to an annual meeting of the Transportation Research Board.

Duration For master's degree students, 24 months, and the degree must be completed within 3 years; for doctoral students, 36 months, and the degree must be completed within 5 years.

Number awarded Varies each year; recently, 59 were awarded.

Deadline March of each year.

[721]
DWIGHT DAVID EISENHOWER
TRANSPORTATION FELLOWSHIP PROGRAM
FOR HISPANIC SERVING INSTITUTIONS

Department of Transportation
Federal Highway Administration
Attn: Universities and Grants Programs
4600 North Fairfax Drive, Suite 800
Arlington, VA 22203-1553
(703) 235-0538   Toll Free: (877) 558-6873
Fax: (703) 235-0593   E-mail: transportationedu@dot.gov
Web: www.fhwa.dot.gov/tpp/ddetfp.htm

Summary To provide financial assistance to undergraduate and graduate students working on a degree in a transportation-related field at an Hispanic Serving Institution (HSI).

Eligibility This program is open to students working on a bachelor's, master's, or doctoral degree at a federally-designated 4-year HSI. Applicants must be working on a degree in a transportation-related field (e.g., engineering, business, aviation, architecture, public policy and analysis, urban and regional planning). They must be U.S. citizens or have an I-20 (foreign student) or I-551 (permanent resident) identification card. Undergraduates must be entering at least their junior year and have a GPA of 3.0 or higher. Graduate students must have a GPA of at least 3.25. Selection is based on their proposed plan of study, academic achievement (based on class standing, GPA, and transcripts), transportation work experience, and letters of recommendation.

Financial Data Fellows receive payment of full tuition and fees (to a maximum of $10,000) and a monthly stipend of $1,450 for undergraduates, $1,700 for master's students, or $2,000 for doctoral students. They are also provided with a 1-time allowance of up to $1,500 to attend the annual Transportation Research Board (TRB) meeting.

Duration 1 year.

Additional data This program is administered by the participating HSIs: California State University at Fullerton, California State University at Los Angeles, City College of New York, Florida International University, Texas A&M University at Kingsville, the University of Puerto Rico at Mayaguez, the

University of Texas at El Paso, the University of Texas at San Antonio, or Washington State University Tri Cities.

Number awarded Varies each year; recently, 28 were awarded.

Deadline January of each year.

[722]
EDSA MINORITY SCHOLARSHIP

Landscape Architecture Foundation
Attn: Leadership in Landscape Scholarship Program
1129 20th Street, N.W., Suite 202
Washington, DC 20036
(202) 331-7070   Fax: (202) 331-7079
E-mail: scholarships@lafoundation.org
Web: www.lafoundation.org

Summary To provide financial assistance to Hispanic and other minority college students who are interested in studying landscape architecture.

Eligibility This program is open to Hispanic, African American, Native American, and minority college students of other cultural and ethnic backgrounds. Applicants must be entering their final 2 years of undergraduate study in landscape architecture or working on a graduate degree in that field. Along with their application, they must submit a 500-word essay on a design or research effort they plan to pursue (explaining how it will contribute to the advancement of the profession and to their ethnic heritage), 3 work samples, and 2 letters of recommendation. Selection is based on professional experience, community involvement, extracurricular activities, and financial need.

Financial Data The stipend is $5,000.

Additional data This scholarship was formerly designated the Edward D. Stone, Jr. and Associates Minority Scholarship.

Number awarded 1 each year.

Deadline February of each year.

[723]
EDUCATIONAL FOUNDATION OF THE COLORADO SOCIETY OF CERTIFIED PUBLIC ACCOUNTANTS MINORITY SCHOLARSHIPS

Colorado Society of Certified Public Accountants
Attn: Educational Foundation
7887 East Belleview Avenue, Suite 200
Englewood, CO 80111
(303) 773-2877   Toll Free: (800) 523-9082 (within CO)
Fax: (303) 773-6344
Web: www.cocpa.org

Summary To provide financial assistance to Hispanic and other minority upper-division and graduate students in Colorado who are majoring in accounting.

Eligibility This program is open to Colorado minority residents (Hispanic or Latino, Black or African American, Native American, Asian American) who are upper-division or graduate students at colleges and universities in the state and have completed at least 6 semester hours of accounting courses. Applicants must have a GPA of at least 3.0 overall and 3.25 in accounting classes. They must be U.S. citizens or noncitizens legally living and studying in Colorado with a valid visa that enables them to become employed. Financial need is not considered in the selection process.

Financial Data The stipend is $2,500. Funds are paid directly to the recipient's school to be used for books, C.P.A. review materials, tuition, fees, and dormitory room and board.

Duration 1 year; recipients may reapply.

Number awarded 1 or more each year.

Deadline May of each year for fall semester or quarter; November of each year for winter quarter or spring semester.

[724]
EDWARD S. ROTH SCHOLARSHIP

Society of Manufacturing Engineers
Attn: SME Education Foundation
One SME Drive
P.O. Box 930
Dearborn, MI 48121-0930
(313) 425-3300   Toll Free: (866) 547-6333
Fax: (313) 425-3411   E-mail: foundation@sme.org
Web: www.smeef.org

Summary To provide financial assistance to students, especially Hispanics and other minorities, who are working on or planning to work on a bachelor's or master's degree in manufacturing engineering at selected universities.

Eligibility This program is open to U.S. citizens who are graduating high school seniors or currently-enrolled undergraduate or graduate students. Applicants must be enrolled or planning to enroll as a full-time student at 1 of 13 selected 4-year universities to work on a bachelor's or master's degree in manufacturing engineering. They must have a GPA of 3.0 or higher. Preference is given to 1) students demonstrating financial need; 2) minority students; and 3) students participating in a co-op program. Along with their application, they must submit a brief statement about why they chose their major, their career and educational objectives, and how this scholarship will help them attain those objectives.

Financial Data Stipends range from $1,000 to $6,000 and recently averaged approximately $2,000.

Duration 1 year; may be renewed.

Additional data The eligible institutions are California Polytechnic State University at San Luis Obispo, California State Polytechnic State University at Pomona, University of Miami (Florida), Bradley University (Illinois), Central State University (Ohio), Miami University (Ohio), Boston University, Worcester Polytechnic Institute (Massachusetts), University of Massachusetts, St. Cloud State University (Minnesota), University of Texas at Rio Grande Valley, Brigham Young University (Utah), and Utah State University.

Number awarded 2 each year.

Deadline January of each year.

[725]
ELLIOTT C. ROBERTS SCHOLARSHIP

Institute for Diversity in Health Management
Attn: Membership and Education Specialist
155 North Wacker Avenue
Chicago, IL 60606
(312) 422-2658   E-mail: cbiddle@aha.org
Web: www.diversityconnection.org

Summary To provide financial assistance to graduate students in health care management who are Hispanices or will contribute to ethnic diversity in the profession in other ways.

Eligibility This program is open to U.S. citizens who represent ethnically diverse cultural backgrounds. Applicants must be enrolled in the second year of a master's degree program in health administration or a comparable program and have a GPA of 3.0 or higher. Along with their application, they must submit 1) a personal statement of 1 to 2 pages on their interest in health care management and their career goals; 2) an essay on what they see as the most challenging issue facing America's hospitals and health systems; and 3) a 500-word essay on their interest and background in health care finance. Selection is based on academic achievement, commitment to community service, and financial need.

Financial Data The stipend is $1,000.

Duration 1 year.

Number awarded 1 each year.

Deadline January of each year.

[726]
EMERGING ARCHIVAL SCHOLARS PROGRAM

Archival Education and Research Institute
Center for Information as Evidence
c/o UCLA Graduate School of Education and Information
  Studies
Office of External Relations
2043 Moore Hall
Los Angeles, CA 90095-1521
(310) 206-0375   Fax: (310) 794-5324
Web: aeri.gseis.ucla.edu/fellowships.htm

Summary To provide an opportunity for Hispanic and other minority undergraduate and graduate students to learn more about the field of archival studies and to be exposed to research in the field.

Eligibility This program is open to undergraduates who have completed their junior year and to students who have completed the first year of a master's degree program. Applicants must be African American, Hispanic/Latino, Asian/Pacific Islander, Native American, Puerto Rican, or any other person who will add diversity to the field of archival studies. They must have a GPA of 3.0 or higher, but they may be working on a degree in any field and are not required to have prior knowledge of or experience in archival studies. U.S. citizenship or permanent resident status is required. Applicants must be interested in attending the week-long Archival Education and Research Institute (AERI), held at a different university each summer, where they are assigned both a faculty research mentor and a Ph.D. student mentor who introduce them to doctoral research and careers in archival studies.

Financial Data Grants provide payment of round-trip travel, accommodation, and most meals.

Duration These grants are offered annually.

Additional data This program, first offered in 2009, is supported by the Institute of Museum and Library Services. Scholars who indicate an interest in continuing on to a doctoral program in archival studies after completing the AERI may be invited to participate in a supervised research project that will last up to 1 year and to present results of their research in a poster session at the AERI of the following year.

Number awarded Up to 7 each year.

Deadline April of each year.

[727]
ENDOCRINE SOCIETY SUMMER RESEARCH FELLOWSHIPS

Endocrine Society
Attn: Summer Research Fellowships
2055 L Street, N.W., Suite 600
Washington, DC 20036
(202) 971-3636   Toll Free: (888) 363-6274
Fax: (202) 736-9705   E-mail: awards@endo-society.org
Web: www.endocrine.org

Summary To provide funding to undergraduate, medical, and graduate students, especially Hispanics and other underrepresented minorities, who are interested in conducting a summer research project in endocrinology.

Eligibility This program is open to full-time students who are undergraduates in the third year of study or higher, medical students beyond their first year of study, and first-year graduate students. Applicants must be interested in participating in a research project under the supervision of a mentor. The mentor must be an active member of the Endocrine Society. Each member may sponsor only 1 student. Projects must be relevant to an aspect of endocrinology and are expected to have clearly defined research goals; students should not function as aides or general research assistants. Applications on behalf of underrepresented minority students are especially encouraged.

Financial Data The grant of $4,000 provides funding for a stipend, fringe benefits, and indirect costs.

Duration 10 to 12 weeks during the summer.

Additional data At the conclusion of the fellowship period, students must submit a 1-page summary of their research project explaining how the fellowship affected their consideration of a career in endocrinology.

Number awarded Varies each year; recently, 12 were awarded.

Deadline January of each year.

[728]
ENVIRONMENT AND NATURAL RESOURCES FELLOWSHIPS

Harvard University
John F. Kennedy School of Government
Belfer Center for Science and International Affairs
Attn: STPP Fellowship Coordinator
79 John F. Kennedy Street, Mailbox 53
Cambridge, MA 02138
(617) 495-1498   Fax: (617) 495-8963
E-mail: patricia_mclaughlin@hks.harvard.edu
Web: belfercenter.ksg.harvard.edu

Summary To provide funding to professionals, postdoctorates, and doctoral students, especially Hispanics and other minorities, who are interested in conducting research on environmental and natural resource issues at the Belfer Center for Science and International Affairs at Harvard University in Cambridge, Massachusetts.

Eligibility The postdoctoral fellowship is open to recent recipients of the Ph.D. or equivalent degree, university faculty members, and employees of government, military, international, humanitarian, and private research institutions who have appropriate professional experience. Applicants for predoctoral fellowships must have passed their general examinations. Scholars from a wide range of disciplinary and multi-disciplinary fields and those holding a Ph.D. in engineering or in the natural sciences are strongly encouraged to apply. The program especially encourages applications from women, minorities, and citizens of all countries. All applicants must be interested in conducting research on projects of the Environment and Natural Resources (ENRP) Program. Recently, those included projects on energy technology innovation, sustainable energy development in China, managing the atom, and the geopolitics of energy.

Financial Data   The stipend is $37,500 for postdoctoral research fellows or $25,000 for predoctoral research fellows. Fellows who renew their grant receive a monthly stipend of $3,750 for postdoctoral fellows or $2,500 for predoctoral fellows. Stipends for advanced research fellows vary. Health insurance is also provided.

Duration   10 months; may be renewed on a month-by-month basis.

Additional data   Fellows are expected to devote some portion of their time to collaborative endeavors, as arranged by the appropriate program or project director. Predoctoral fellows are expected to contribute to the program's research activities, as well as work on (and ideally complete) their dissertations. Postdoctoral research fellows are also expected to complete a book, monograph, or other significant publication during their period of residence.

Number awarded   A limited number each year.

Deadline   January of each year.

[729]
EPISCOPAL HISPANIC MINISTRIES THEOLOGICAL EDUCATION SCHOLARSHIPS

Episcopal Church Center
Attn: Domestic and Foreign Missionary Society
Scholarship Committee
815 Second Avenue, Fifth Floor
New York, NY 10017-4503
(212) 716-6168   Toll Free: (800) 334-7626
Fax: (212) 867-0395
E-mail: ahercules@episcopalchurch.org
Web: www.episcopalchurch.org

Summary   To provide financial assistance to Hispanic Americans interested in seeking ordination and serving in a ministry involving African Americans in the Episcopal Church.

Eligibility   This program is open to Hispanic American students pursuing theological education, including diocesan programs as well as seminary education. Applicants must be a member of an Hispanic constituency in the Episcopal Church and have begun the process of seeking ordination through a local Episcopal diocese. Scholarships are presented only for full-time study.

Financial Data   The maximum stipend is $10,000 per year.

Duration   1 year; may be renewed up to 3 additional years.

Additional data   This program began in 1982.

Number awarded   Varies each year; recently, 7 of these scholarships, with a value of $32,000, were awarded.

Deadline   April of each year.

[730]
ESPERANZA SCHOLARSHIP

New York Women in Communications, Inc.
Attn: NYWICI Foundation
355 Lexington Avenue, 15th Floor
New York, NY 10017-6603
(212) 297-2133   Fax: (212) 370-9047
E-mail: nywicipr@nywici.org
Web: www.nywici.org/foundation/scholarships

Summary   To provide financial assistance to Hispanic women who are residents of designated eastern states and interested in preparing for a career in communications at a college or graduate school in any state.

Eligibility   This program is open to Hispanic women who are seniors graduating from high schools in New York, New Jersey, Connecticut, or Pennsylvania or undergraduate or graduate students who are permanent residents of those states; they must be attending or planning to attend a college or university in any state. Graduate students must be members of New York Women in Communications, Inc. (NYWICI). Also eligible are Hispanic women who reside outside the 4 states but are currently enrolled at a college or university within 1 of the 5 boroughs of New York City. All applicants must be working on a degree in a communications-related field (e.g., advertising, broadcasting, communications, digital media, English, film, journalism, marketing, public relations, publishing) and have a GPA of 3.2 or higher. Along with their application, they must submit a 2-page resume; a personal essay of 300 words on an assigned topic that changes annually; 2 letters of recommendation; and an official transcript. Selection is based on academic record, need, demonstrated leadership, participation in school and community activities, honors and other awards or recognition, work experience, goals and aspirations, and unusual personal and/or family circumstances. U.S. citizenship or permanent resident status is required.

Financial Data   The stipend ranges up to $10,000.

Duration   1 year.

Additional data   This program is funded by Macy's and Bloomingdale's.

Number awarded   1 each year.

Deadline   January of each year.

[731]
ESTHER NGAN-LING CHOW AND MAREYJOYCE GREEN SCHOLARSHIP

Sociologists for Women in Society
Attn: Administrative Officer
University of Kansas
Department of Sociology
1415 Jayhawk Boulevard, Room 716
Lawrence, KS 66045
(785) 864-9405   E-mail: swsao@outlook.com
Web: www.socwomen.org

Summary   To provide funding to Hispanic and other women of color who are conducting dissertation research in sociology.

Eligibility   This program is open to women from a racial/ethnic group that faces discrimination in the United States. Applicants must be in the early stages of writing a doctoral dissertation in sociology on a topic relating to the concerns that women of color face domestically and/or internationally. They must be able to demonstrate financial need. Both domestic and international students are eligible to apply. Along with their application, they must submit a personal statement that details their short- and long-term career and research goals; a resume or curriculum vitae; 2 letters of recommendation; and a 5-page dissertation proposal that includes the purpose of the research, the work to be accomplished through support from this scholarship, and a time line for completion.

Financial Data The stipend is $15,000. An additional grant of $500 is provided to enable the recipient to attend the winter meeting of Sociologists for Women in Society (SWS), and travel expenses to attend the summer meeting are reimbursed.

Duration 1 year.

Additional data This program began in 2007 and was originally named the Women of Color Dissertation Scholarship.

Number awarded 1 each year.

Deadline March of each year.

[732]
ETHNIC IN-SERVICE TRAINING FUND FOR CLINICAL PASTORAL EDUCATION (EIST-CPE)

United Methodist Church
Attn: General Board of Higher Education and Ministry
Office of Loans and Scholarships
1001 19th Avenue South
P.O. Box 340007
Nashville, TN 37203-0007
(615) 340-7342   Fax: (615) 340-7367
E-mail: umscholar@gbhem.org
Web: www.gbhem.org

Summary To provide financial assistance to United Methodist Church clergy and candidates for ministry who are Hispanics or members of other minority groups interested in preparing for a career as a clinical pastor.

Eligibility This program is open to U.S. citizens and permanent residents who are members of ethnic or racial minority groups and have been active, full members of a United Methodist Church for at least 1 year prior to applying. Applicants must be United Methodist clergy, certified candidates for ministry, or seminary students accepted into an accredited Clinical Pastor Education (CPE) or an accredited American Association of Pastoral Counselors (AAPC) program. They must be preparing for a career as a chaplain, pastoral counselor, or in pastoral care.

Financial Data Grants range up to $2,000.

Duration 1 year.

Number awarded 1 each year.

Deadline February of each year.

[733]
EXTERNSHIP IN ADDICTION PSYCHIATRY

American Psychiatric Association
Attn: Minority Medical Student Awards
1000 Wilson Boulevard, Suite 1825
Arlington, VA 22209-3901
(703) 907-7894   Toll Free: (888) 357-7849
Fax: (703) 907-1087   E-mail: Mfpstudents@psych.org
Web: www.psychiatry.org

Summary To provide an opportunity for Hispanic and other minority medical students to spend an elective residency learning about substance abuse disorders, prevention, and early intervention.

Eligibility This program is open to student members of the American Psychiatric Association (APA) who come from racial/ethnic minorities and are currently enrolled at accredited U.S. medical school. Applicants must be interested in working with a mentor at a designated site to gain exposure to how psychiatrists treat patients with substance abuse disorders and participate in an interactive didactic experiential learning program. Mentors and sites are selected where there is an approved substance abuse training program and a significant number of substance abuse disorder patients from minority and underserved populations. U.S. citizenship or permanent resident status is required.

Financial Data The program provides a stipend of $1,500 for living expenses and funding for travel to and from the mentoring site.

Duration 1 month during the summer.

Number awarded 6 each year.

Deadline March of each year.

[734]
EXXONMOBIL LOFT FELLOWSHIPS

Hispanic Heritage Foundation
1001 Pennsylvania Avenue, N.W.
Washington, DC 20004
(202) 558-9473   E-mail: Julian@hispanicheritage.org
Web: www.hispanicheritage.org

Summary To provide financial assistance to Hispanic undergraduate and graduate students who participate in the Latinos on Fast Track (LOFT) program.

Eligibility This program is open to Hispanic sophomores, juniors, seniors, and graduate students at 4-year colleges and universities who are U.S. citizens or permanent residents and fluent in English. Applicants must be working on a degree and preparing for a career in chemistry, engineering (chemical, civil, computer, electrical, environmental, industrial, materials, mechanical, or petroleum), geology, material sciences, mathematics, or physics. Their GPA must be at least 3.5. They must be participating in the LOFT program with an ExxonMobil engineer or scientist as mentor. Along with their application, they must submit an essay of 500 to 700 words that covers why they chose their major, how they intend to prepare for an active career related to their major, and why they should be considered for this program.

Financial Data Selected LOFT participants receive $1,000 scholarships.

Duration The scholarships are presented annually and are nonrenewable.

Additional data   The LOFT program involves 5 meetings of 1 hour each with the mentor (virtually or in person), participation in an online ExxonMobil mentee program that introduces them to career opportunities with the company, the possibility to interview for ExxonMobil internships or full-time positions upon successful completion of the program, and the possibility of these scholarships.

Number awarded   20 each year.

Deadline   April of each year.

[735]
FACS GRADUATE FELLOWSHIPS

National Association of Teacher Educators for Family and
  Consumer Sciences
c/o Debra Price, Fellowship Committee Chair
116 East Summit Street
Bolivar, MO 65613
(417) 327-6636   E-mail: debraprice81@gmail.com
Web: www.natefacs.org/Pages/awards.html

Summary   To provide financial assistance to graduate students, especially Hispanics and other minorities, in family and consumer science education.

Eligibility   This program is open to graduate students working on a master's or doctoral degree in family and consumer sciences education. Applicants must submit an autobiographical sketch (up to 3 pages in length) presenting their professional goals, including information on the institution where they are studying or planning to study, areas or emphases of study, possible research topic, and other pertinent information regarding their plans. Selection is based on likelihood of completing the degree, likelihood of contribution to family and consumer sciences education, previous academic work, professional association involvement, professional experience (including scholarly work), and references. At least 1 fellowship is reserved for a minority (Hispanic American, African American, Native American, or Asian American) candidate.

Financial Data   Stipends range from $2,000 to $4,000.

Duration   1 year.

Additional data   The sponsor is an affiliate of the Family and Consumer Sciences (FACS) Division of the Association for Career and Technical Education (ACTE).

Number awarded   Varies each year.

Deadline   September of each year.

[736]
FARM CREDIT EAST SCHOLARSHIPS

Farm Credit East
Attn: Scholarship Program
240 South Road
Enfield, CT 06082
(860) 741-4380   Toll Free: (800) 562-2235
Fax: (860) 741-4389
E-mail: specialoffers@famcrediteast.com
Web: www.farmcrediteast.com

Summary   To provide financial assistance to Hispanic and other minority residents of designated northeastern states who plan to attend school in any state to work on an undergraduate or graduate degree in a field related to agriculture, forestry, or fishing.

Eligibility   This program is open to residents of Connecticut, Maine, Massachusetts, New Jersey, Rhode Island, and portions of New York and New Hampshire. Applicants must be working on or planning to work on an associate, bachelor's, or graduate degree in production agriculture, agribusiness, the forest products industry, or commercial fishing at a college or university in any state. They must submit a 200-word essay on why they wish to prepare for a career in agriculture, forestry, or fishing. Selection is based on the essay, extracurricular activities (especially farm work experience and activities indicative of an interest in preparing for a career in agriculture or agribusiness), and interest in agriculture. The program includes diversity scholarships reserved for members of minority groups (Hispanic or Latino, Black or African American, American Indian or Alaska Native, Asian, or Native Hawaiian or other Pacific Islander).

Financial Data   The stipend is $1,500. Funds are paid directly to the student to be used for tuition, room and board, books, and other academic charges.

Duration   1 year; nonrenewable.

Additional data   Recipients are given priority for an internship with the sponsor in the summer following their junior year. Farm Credit East was formerly named First Pioneer Farm Credit.

Number awarded   Varies each year; recently, 32, including several diversity scholarships, were awarded.

Deadline   April of each year.

[737]
FELLOWSHIPS FOR LATINO/A, ASIAN AND FIRST NATIONS DOCTORAL STUDENTS

Forum for Theological Exploration
Attn: Fellowship Program
160 Clairemont Avenue, Suite 300
Decatur, GA 30030
(678) 369-6755   Fax: (678) 369-6757
E-mail: dhutto@fteleaders.org
Web: www.fteleaders.org

Summary   To provide funding to Latino/as, Asians, and members of First Nations who are working on a doctoral degree in religious, theological, or biblical studies.

Eligibility   This program is open to students of Latino/a, Asian, or First Nations descent who are U.S. or Canadian citizens or permanent residents working full time on a Ph.D. or Th.D. degree. Applicants must be past the course work stage; they are not required to have been advanced to candidacy, but they must have had their dissertation topic approved and be in a position to devote full time to writing. Students who are working on a Doctor of Ministry (D.Min.) degree are not eligible.

Financial Data   The stipend is $25,000.

Duration   1 year.

Additional data   Fellows also receive reimbursement of expenses to attend the sponsor's Christian Leadership Forum. This sponsor was formerly named the The Fund for Theological Education, Inc.

Number awarded   Varies each year; recently, 12 were awarded.

Deadline   January of each year.

[738]
FIRST TRANSIT SCHOLARSHIP

Conference of Minority Transportation Officials
Attn: National Scholarship Program
100 M Street, S.E., Suite 917
Washington, DC 20003
(202) 506-2917   E-mail: info@comto.org
Web: www.comto.org/page/scholarships

Summary To provide financial assistance to Hispanic and other minority upper-division and graduate students in engineering or other field related to transportation.

Eligibility This program is open to minority juniors, seniors, and graduate students in transpoation, planning, engineering or other technical transportation-related disciplines. Applicants must submit a cover letter on their transportation-related career goals and life aspirations. Financial need is not considered in the selection process.

Financial Data The stipend is $6,000. Funds are paid directly to the recipient's college or university.

Duration 1 year.

Additional data This program is sponsored by First Transit Inc.

Number awarded 1 each year.

Deadline April of each year.

[739]
FIU-AEJMC LATINO/LATIN AMERICAN COMMUNICATION RESEARCH AWARD

Association for Education in Journalism and Mass
  Communication
Attn: International Communication Division
234 Outlet Pointe Boulevard, Suite A
Columbia, SC 29210-5667
(803) 798-0271   Fax: (803) 772-3509
E-mail: aejmc@aejmc.org
Web: www.aejmc.us/icd

Summary To recognize and reward Latino and Latin American student and faculty members who submit outstanding research papers relevant to journalism and mass media in their communities for presentation at the annual conference of the Association for Education in Journalism and Mass Communication (AEJMC).

Eligibility This competition is open to AEJMC members and non-members, students, and faculty who regard themselves as members of the Latino, Hispanic, or Latin American community. Applicants must submit papers for presentation at the AEJMC annual conference either for the International Communication Division or the Minorities in Communication Division. Eligible topics include matters of Inter-American or Iberian-American communication, new media flow, media theory, media technology or new media, communication for development and social change, media law and ethics, media education, ethnic or gender media and integration, media economics, media and the environment, political communication, critical media studies, popular culture, or cultural studies. All research methodologies are welcome.

Financial Data Cash prizes are awarded.

Duration The prizes are presented annually.

Additional data This program began in 2014 with support from Florida International University's School of Journalism and Mass Communications.

Number awarded 1 each year.

Deadline March of each year.

[740]
FLEMING/BLASZCAK SCHOLARSHIP

Society of Plastics Engineers
Attn: SPE Foundation
6 Berkshire Boulevard, Suite 306
Bethel, CT 06801
(203) 740-5457   Fax: (203) 775-8490
E-mail: foundation@4spe.org
Web: old.4spe.org/forms/spe-foundation-scholarship-form

Summary To provide financial assistance to Mexican American undergraduate and graduate students who have a career interest in the plastics industry.

Eligibility This program is open to full-time undergraduate and graduate students of Mexican descent who are enrolled at a 4-year college or university. Applicants must be U.S. citizens or legal residents. They must be majoring in or taking courses that would be beneficial to a career in the plastics or polymer industry (e.g., plastics engineering, polymer sciences, chemistry, physics, chemical engineering, mechanical engineering, industrial engineering). Along with their application, they must submit 3 letters of recommendation; a high school and/or college transcript; a 1- to 2-page statement telling why they are applying for the scholarship, their qualifications, and their educational and career goals in the plastics industry; their employment history; a list of current and past school activities and community activities and honors; and documentation of their Mexican heritage. Financial need is considered in the selection process.

Financial Data The stipend is $2,000. Funds are paid directly to the recipient's school.

Duration 1 year.

Number awarded 1 each year.

Deadline April of each year.

[741]
FLORIDA LIBRARY ASSOCIATION MINORITY SCHOLARSHIPS

Florida Library Association
541 East Tennessee Street, Suite 103
Tallahassee, FL 32308
(850) 270-9205   Fax: (850) 270-9405
E-mail: flaexecutivedirector@comcast.net
Web: www.flalib.org/scholarships.php

Summary To provide financial assistance to Hispanic and other minority students working on a graduate degree in library and information science in Florida.

Eligibility This program is open to residents of Florida who are working on a graduate degree in library and information science at schools in the state. Applicants must be members of a minority group: Black/African American, American Indian/Alaska Native, Asian/Pacific Islander, or Hispanic/Latino. They must have some experience in a Florida library, must be a member of the Florida Library Association, and must commit to working in a Florida library for at least 1 year after graduation. Along with their application, they must submit 1) a list of activities, honors, awards, and/or offices held during college and outside college; 2) an essay of 1 to 2 pages on why they are entering librarianship; and 3) an essay of 1 to 2 pages on their career goals with respect to Florida libraries. Financial need is considered in the selection process.

Financial Data   The stipend is $2,000.

Duration   1 year.

Number awarded   1 each year.

Deadline   January of each year.

[742]
FRAMELINE COMPLETION FUND

Frameline
Attn: Completion Fund
145 Ninth Street, Suite 300
San Francisco, CA 94103
(415) 703-8650   Fax: (415) 861-1404
E-mail: info@frameline.org
Web: frameline.org

Summary   To provide funding to lesbian, gay, bisexual, and transgender (LGBT) film/video artists, including Hispanics and other people of color.

Eligibility   This program is open to LGBT artists who are in the last stages of the production of documentary, educational, narrative, animated, or experimental projects about or of interest to LGBT people and their communities. Applicants may be independent artists, students, producers, or nonprofit corporations. They must be interested in completion work and must have 90% of the production completed; projects in development, script-development, pre-production, or production are not eligible. Student projects are eligible only if the student maintains artistic and financial control of the project. Women and people of color are especially encouraged to apply. Selection is based on financial need, the contribution the grant will make to completing the project, assurances that the project will be completed, and the statement the project makes about LGBT people and/or issues of concern to them and their communities.

Financial Data   Grants range from $1,000 to $5,000.

Duration   These are 1-time grants.

Additional data   This program began in 1990.

Number awarded   Varies each year; recently, 5 were awarded. Since this program was established, it has provided $464,200 in support to 136 films.

Deadline   October of each year.

[743]
FRANCIS M. KEVILLE MEMORIAL SCHOLARSHIP

Construction Management Association of America
Attn: CMAA Foundation
7926 Jones Branch Drive, Suite 800
McLean, VA 22101-3303
(703) 677-3361   E-mail: foundation@cmaanet.org
Web: www.cmaafoundation.org

Summary   To provide financial assistance to Hispanic and other minority undergraduate and graduate students working on a degree in construction management.

Eligibility   This program is open to women and members of minority groups who are enrolled as full-time undergraduate or graduate students. Applicants must have completed at least 1 year of study and have at least 1 full year remaining for a bachelor's or master's degree in construction management

or a related field. Along with their application, they must submit essays on why they are interested in a career in construction management and why they should be awarded this scholarship. Selection is based on that essay (20%), academic performance (40%), recommendation of the faculty adviser (15%), and extracurricular activities (25%); a bonus of 5% is given to student members of the Construction Management Association of America (CMAA).

Financial Data   The stipend is $5,000. Funds are disbursed directly to the student's university.

Duration   1 year.

Number awarded   1 each year.

Deadline   April of each year.

[744]
FRANKLIN C. MCLEAN AWARD

National Medical Fellowships, Inc.
Attn: Scholarship Program
347 Fifth Avenue, Suite 510
New York, NY 10016
(212) 483-8880   Toll Free: (877) NMF-1DOC
Fax: (212) 483-8897   E-mail: scholarships@nmfonline.org
Web: www.nmfonline.org

Summary   To provide financial assistance to Hispanic and othr underrepresented minority medical students who demonstrate academic achievement.

Eligibility   This program is open to Hispanics/Latinos, African Americans, Native Americans, Vietnamese, Cambodians, and Pacific Islanders who are entering their senior year of medical school. They must be U.S. citizens or DACA students. Selection is based on academic achievement, leadership, and community service.

Financial Data   The stipend is $5,000.

Duration   1 year.

Additional data   This program began in 1968.

Number awarded   1 each year.

Deadline   September of each year.

[745]
FUND FOR LATINO SCHOLARSHIP

American Political Science Association
Attn: Diversity and Inclusion Programs
1527 New Hampshire Avenue, N.W.
Washington, DC 20036-1206
(202) 349-9362   Fax: (202) 483-2657
E-mail: kmealy@apsanet.org
Web: www.apsanet.org

Summary   To provide funding for travel or research to members of the American Political Science Association (APSA) and other students and scholars who are involved with Latinos.

Eligibility   Applications for this assistance should involve activities that 1) provide professional opportunities and financial assistance to Latino/a graduate students in political science programs; 2) support the teaching, research, and publishing activities of junior-level, tenure-track Latino/a political science faculty; or 3) support activities that advance our knowledge of Latino/a politics. Latino/a scholars (whatever their research field) and all scholars (including non-Latinos/as) who are studying Latino politics in the United States are eligible.

Financial Data Travel grants and most research grants are $500. Under exceptional circumstances, a grant of up to $1,000 may be awarded. Funding is intended for travel assistance to attend the APSA annual meeting, conduct field research, attend another scholarly conference, or participate in a program at the APSA Centennial Center for Political Science and Public Affairs.

Duration These are 1-time grants.

Number awarded 1 or more each year.

Deadline June of each year.

[746]
GAIUS CHARLES BOLIN DISSERTATION AND POST-MFA FELLOWSHIPS

Williams College
Attn: Dean of the Faculty
880 Main Street
Hopkins Hall, Third Floor
P.O. Box 141
Williamstown, MA 01267
(413) 597-4351   Fax: (413) 597-3553
E-mail: gburda@williams.edu
Web: faculty.williams.edu

Summary To provide financial assistance to Hispanics and members of other underrepresented groups who are interested in teaching courses at Williams College while working on their doctoral dissertation or building their post-M.F.A. professional portfolio.

Eligibility This program is open to members of underrepresented groups, including ethnic minorities, first-generation college students, women in predominantly male fields, and scholars with disabilities. Applicants must be 1) doctoral candidates in any field who have completed all work for a Ph.D. except for the dissertation; or 2) artists who completed an M.F.A. degree within the past 2 years and are building their professional portfolio. They must be willing to teach a course at Williams College. Along with their application, they must submit a full curriculum vitae, a graduate school transcript, 3 letters of recommendation, a copy of their dissertation prospectus or samples of their artistic work, and a description of their teaching interests within a department or program at Williams College. U.S. citizenship or permanent resident status is required.

Financial Data Fellows receive $38,000 for the academic year, plus housing assistance, office space, computer and library privileges, and a research allowance of up to $4,000.

Duration 2 years.

Additional data Bolin fellows are assigned a faculty adviser in the appropriate department. This program was established in 1985. Fellows are expected to teach a 1-semester course each year. They must be in residence at Williams College for the duration of the fellowship.

Number awarded 2 each year.

Deadline November of each year.

[747]
GEM M.S. ENGINEERING FELLOWSHIP PROGRAM

National Consortium for Graduate Degrees for Minorities in Engineering and Science (GEM)
Attn: Manager, Fellowships Administration
1430 Duke Street
Alexandria, VA 22314
(703) 562-3646   Fax: (202) 207-3518
E-mail: info@gemfellowship.org
Web: www.gemfellowship.org

Summary To provide financial assistance and summer work experience to Hispanic and other underrepresented minority students interested in working on a master's degree in engineering or computer science.

Eligibility This program is open to U.S. citizens and permanent residents who are members of ethnic groups underrepresented in engineering: American Indians/Native Americans, Blacks/African Americans, or Latinos/Hispanic Americans. Applicants must be a senior or graduate of an ABET-accredited engineering or computer science program and have an academic record that indicates the ability to pursue graduate studies in engineering (including a GPA of 2.8 or higher). They must agree to apply to at least 3 of the 106 GEM member universities that offer a master's degree and to intern during summers with a sponsoring GEM employer.

Financial Data Full fellows receive 1) a stipend of $4,000 per semester; 2) full tuition and fees at the GEM member university; and 3) a salary during the summer work assignment as a GEM summer intern. Associate fellows receive the stipend and payment of tuition and fees, but are not offered a summer salary. University fellows receive only payment of tuition from a participating university.

Duration Up to 4 semesters; full fellows also receive summer work internships lasting 10 to 14 weeks for up to 2 summers.

Additional data During the summer internship, each fellow is assigned an engineering project in a research setting. Each project is based on the fellow's interest and background and is carried out under the supervision of an experienced engineer. At the conclusion of the internship, each fellow writes a project report. Recipients must work on a master's degree in the same engineering discipline as their baccalaureate degree.

Number awarded Varies each year; recently, 48 full fellowships, 6 associate fellowships, and 11 university fellowships were awarded.

Deadline November of each year.

[748]
GEM PH.D. ENGINEERING FELLOWSHIP PROGRAM

National Consortium for Graduate Degrees for Minorities in Engineering and Science (GEM)
Attn: Manager, Fellowships Administration
1430 Duke Street
Alexandria, VA 22314
(703) 562-3646   Fax: (202) 207-3518
E-mail: info@gemfellowship.org
Web: www.gemfellowship.org

Summary To provide financial assistance and summer work experience to Hispanic and other underrepresented minority students interested in obtaining a Ph.D. degree in engineering.

Eligibility This program is open to U.S. citizens and permanent residents who are members of ethnic groups underrepresented in engineering: American Indians/Native Americans, Blacks/African Americans, and Latinos/Hispanic Americans. Applicants must be college seniors, master's degree students, or graduates of an ABET-accredited program in engineering and have an academic record that indicates the ability to work on a doctoral degree in engineering (including a GPA of 3.0 or higher). They must agree to apply to at least 3 of the 102 GEM member universities that offer a doctoral degree in engineering and to intern during summer with a sponsoring GEM employer.

Financial Data For full fellows, the stipend is $16,000 for the first year; in subsequent years, fellows receive full payment of tuition and fees plus an additional stipend and assistantship from their university that is equivalent to funding received by other doctoral students in their department. They also receive a paid internship during the summer following their first year of study. Associate fellows receive the same first-year stipend and payment of tuition and fees for subsequent years, but the additional stipend paid by the university is optional.

Duration 3 to 5 years for the fellowship; 12 weeks during the summer immediately after sponsorship for the internship.

Additional data This program is valid only at 1 of the 106 participating GEM member universities; contact GEM for a list. The fellowship award is designed to support the student in the first year of the doctoral program without working. Subsequent years may be subsidized by the respective universities and will usually include either a teaching or research assistantship. Recipients must participate in the GEM summer internship; failure to agree to accept the internship cancels the fellowship.

Number awarded Varies each year; recently, 26 full fellowships and 15 associate fellowships were awarded.

Deadline November of each year.

[749]
GEM PH.D. SCIENCE FELLOWSHIP PROGRAM

National Consortium for Graduate Degrees for Minorities in Engineering and Science (GEM)
Attn: Manager, Fellowships Administration
1430 Duke Street
Alexandria, VA 22314
(703) 562-3646   Fax: (202) 207-3518
E-mail: info@gemfellowship.org
Web: www.gemfellowship.org

Summary To provide financial assistance and summer work experience to Hispanic and other underrepresented minority students interested in working on a Ph.D. degree in the life sciences, mathematics, or physical sciences.

Eligibility This program is open to U.S. citizens and permanent residents who are members of ethnic groups underrepresented in the natural sciences: American Indians/Native Americans, Blacks/African Americans, and Latinos/Hispanic Americans. Applicants must be college seniors, master's degree students, or recent graduates in the biological sciences, mathematics, or physical sciences (chemistry, computer science, environmental sciences, and physics) with an academic record that indicates the ability to pursue doctoral

studies (including a GPA of 3.0 or higher). They must agree to apply to at least 3 of the 106 GEM member universities that offer a doctoral degree in science and to intern during summer with a sponsoring GEM employer.

Financial Data For full fellows, the stipend is $16,000 for the first year; in subsequent years, fellows receive full payment of tuition and fees plus an additional stipend and assistantship from their university that is equivalent to funding received by other doctoral students in their department. They also receive a paid internship during the summer following their first year of study. Associate fellows receive the same first-year stipend and payment of tuition and fees for subsequent years, but the additional stipend paid by the university is optional.

Duration 3 to 5 years for the fellowship; 12 weeks during the summer immediately after sponsorship for the internship.

Additional data This program is valid only at 1 of 106 participating GEM member universities; contact GEM for a list. The fellowship award is designed to support the student in the first year of the doctoral program without working. Subsequent years are subsidized by the respective university and will usually include either a teaching or research assistantship. Recipients must participate in the GEM summer internship; failure to agree to accept the internship cancels the fellowship. Recipients must enroll in the same scientific discipline as their undergraduate major.

Number awarded Varies each year; recently, 28 full fellowships and 14 associate fellowships were awarded.

Deadline November of each year.

[750]
GENERATION GOOGLE SCHOLARSHIPS FOR CURRENT UNIVERSITY STUDENTS

Google Inc.
Attn: Scholarships
1600 Amphitheatre Parkway
Mountain View, CA 94043-8303
(650) 253-0000   Fax: (650) 253-0001
E-mail: generationgoogle@google.com
Web: www.google.com

Summary To provide financial assistance to Hispanics and members of other underrepresented groups enrolled as undergraduate or graduate students in a computer-related field.

Eligibility This program is open to students enrolled as full-time undergraduate or graduate students at a college or university in the United States or Canada. Applicants must be members of a group underrepresented in computer science: African Americans, Hispanics, American Indians, or Filipinos/Native Hawaiians/Pacific Islanders. They must be working on a degree in computer science, computer engineering, or a closely-related field. Selection is based on academic achievement, leadership, and passion for computer science and technology.

Financial Data The stipend is $10,000 per year for U.S. students or $C5,000 for Canadian students.

Duration 1 year; may be renewed.

Additional data Recipients are also invited to attend Google's Computer Science Summer Institute at Mountain View, California, Seattle, Washington, or Cambridge, Massachusetts in the summer.

Number awarded Varies each year.
Deadline February of each year.

[751]
GE-NMF PRIMARY CARE LEADERSHIP PROGRAM

National Medical Fellowships, Inc.
Attn: Scholarship Program
347 Fifth Avenue, Suite 510
New York, NY 10016
(212) 483-8880   Toll Free: (877) NMF-1DOC
Fax: (212) 483-8897   E-mail: pclpinfo@nmfonline.org
Web: www.nmfonline.org

Summary To provide funding to Hispanic and other underrepresented medical and nursing students who wish to participate in a summer mentored clinical experience in selected communities.

Eligibility This program is open to members of underrepresented minority groups (Hispanic/Latino, African American, American Indian, Native Hawaiian, Alaska Native, Vietnamese, Cambodian, or Native Pacific Islander) and/or socioeconomically disadvantaged students. U.S. citizenship is required. Applicants must be currently enrolled in an accredited medical school or graduate-level nursing degree program. They must be interested in a mentored clinical service-learning experience that includes a site-specific independent project at a community health center in Atlanta, Boston/Lynn, Chicago, Houston, Los Angeles, Miami, Mound Bayou (Mississippi), New York, Phoenix, Rochester (New York), or Seattle. Along with their application, they must submit documentation of financial status; a short biography; a resume; 2 letters of recommendation; and a 500-word personal statement on their experiences working in or being part of a medically underserved population and how those experiences have impacted their educational path, professional aspirations, and decision to apply to this program.

Financial Data The stipend is $5,000. Funds are expected to cover travel, living, and lodging expenses.

Duration Scholars are required to complete 200 clinical service-learning hours within a 6- to 8-week period during the summer following receipt of the award.

Additional data Funding for this program, which began in 2012 and is administered by National Medical Fellowships (NMF), is provided by the GE Foundation.

Number awarded Varies each year, recently, 59 were granted: 2 in Atlanta, 2 in Boston/Lynn, 8 in Chicago, 5 in Houston, 12 in Los Angeles, 8 in Miami, 2 in Bound Bayou, 2 in New York, 8 in Phoenix, 4 in Rochester, and 6 in Seattle.

Deadline March of each year.

[752]
GEOCORPS AMERICA DIVERSITY INTERNSHIPS

Geological Society of America
Attn: Program Officer, GeoCorps America
3300 Penrose Place
P.O. Box 9140
Boulder, CO 80301-9140
(303) 357-1025   Toll Free: (800) 472-1988, ext. 1025
Fax: (303) 357-1070   E-mail: mdawson@geosociety.org
Web: rock.geosociety.org

Summary To provide work experience at national parks to student members of the Geological Society of America (GSA) who are Hispanics or members of other underrepresented groups.

Eligibility This program is open to all GSA members, but applications are especially encouraged from groups historically underrepresented in the sciences (African Americans, American Indians, Alaska Natives, Hispanics, Native Hawaiians, other Pacific Islanders, and persons with disabilities). Applicants must be interested in a short-term work experience in facilities of the U.S. government. Geoscience knowledge and skills are a significant requirement for most positions, but students from diverse disciplines (e.g., chemistry, physics, engineering, mathematics, computer science, ecology, hydrology, meteorology, the social sciences, and the humanities) are also invited to apply. Activities involve research; interpretation and education; inventory and monitoring; or mapping, surveying, and GIS. Prior interns are not eligible. U.S. citizenship or possession of a proper visa is required.

Financial Data Each internship provides a $2,750 stipend. Also provided are free housing or a housing allowance of $1,500 to $2,000.

Duration 3 months during the spring, summer, fall, or winter.

Additional data This program is offered by the GSA in partnership with the National Park Service, the U.S. Forest Service, and the Bureau of Land Management.

Number awarded Varies each year.

Deadline March of each year for spring or summer positions; June of each year for fall or winter positions.

[753]
GEOGRAPHY AND SPATIAL SCIENCES DOCTORAL DISSERTATION RESEARCH IMPROVEMENT AWARDS

National Science Foundation
Directorate for Social, Behavioral, and Economic
  Sciences
Attn: Geography and Spatial Sciences Program
4201 Wilson Boulevard
Arlington, VA 22230
(703) 292-7301   TDD: (800) 281-8749
E-mail: tbaerwal@nsf.gov
Web: www.nsf.gov

Summary To provide funding for dissertation research to doctoral candidates in geography and spatial sciences.

Eligibility This program is open to doctoral candidates at U.S. universities in fields related to geography and spatial sciences, especially Hispanics and othr underrepresented minorities, who are conducting dissertation research. Applicants are encouraged to propose plans for research about the nature, causes, and consequences of human activity and natural environmental processes across a range of scales. Proposals should offer promise of contributing to scholarship by enhancing geographical knowledge, concepts, theories, methods, and their application to societal problems and concerns. In the selection process, the sponsor values the advancement of scientific knowledge and activities that contribute to societally relevant outcomes, such as full participation of women, persons with disabilities, and underrepresented minorities in science, technology, engineering, or mathematics (STEM).

Financial Data Grants are $16,000, including both direct and indirect costs. Funds may be used only for research and related costs; support is not provided for a stipend or salary for the student or for tuition.

Duration 1 year.

Number awarded 30 to 40 each year.

Deadline February or August of each year.

[754]
GEOLOGICAL SOCIETY OF AMERICA GRADUATE STUDENT RESEARCH GRANTS

Geological Society of America
Attn: Program Officer-Grants, Awards and Recognition
3300 Penrose Place
P.O. Box 9140
Boulder, CO 80301-9140
(303) 357-1060   Toll Free: (888) 443-4472, ext. 1060
Fax: (303) 357-1070   E-mail: awards@geosociety.org
Web: www.geosociety.org/grants/gradgrants.htm

Summary To provide funding to graduate student members of the Geological Society of America (GSA), especially Hispanics and other underrepresented minorities, who are interested in conducting research at universities in the United States, Canada, Mexico, or Central America.

Eligibility This program is open to GSA members working on a master's or doctoral degree at a university in the United States, Canada, Mexico, or Central America. Applicants must be interested in conducting geological research. Minorities, women, and persons with disabilities are strongly encouraged to apply. Selection is based on the scientific merits of the proposal, the capability of the investigator, and the reasonableness of the budget.

Financial Data Grants range up to $2,500 and recently averaged $1,851. Funds can be used for the cost of travel, room and board in the field, services of a technician or field assistant, funding of chemical and isotope analyses, or other expenses directly related to the fulfillment of the research contract. Support is not provided for the purchase of ordinary field equipment, for maintenance of the families of the grantees and their assistants, as reimbursement for work already accomplished, for institutional overhead, for adviser participation, or for tuition costs.

Duration 1 year.

Additional data In addition to general grants, GSA awards a number of specialized grants.

Number awarded Varies each year; recently, the society awarded nearly 400 grants worth more than $723,000 through this and all of its specialized programs.

Deadline January of each year.

[755]
GEORGE A. STRAIT MINORITY SCHOLARSHIP ENDOWMENT

American Association of Law Libraries
Attn: Chair, Scholarships Committee
105 West Adams Street, Suite 3300
Chicago, IL 60603
(312) 939-4764   Fax: (312) 431-1097
E-mail: scholarships@aall.org
Web: www.aallnet.org

Summary To provide financial assistance to Hispanic and other minority college seniors or college graduates who are interested in becoming law librarians.

Eligibility This program is open to college graduates with meaningful law library experience who are members of minority groups and intend to have a career in law librarianship. Applicants must be degree candidates at an ALA-accredited library school or an ABA-accredited law school. Along with their application, they must submit a personal statement that discusses their interest in law librarianship, reason for applying for this scholarship, career goals as a law librarian, and any other pertinent information.

Financial Data The stipend is $3,500.

Duration 1 year.

Additional data This program, established in 1990, is currently supported by Thomson Reuters.

Number awarded Varies each year; recently, 6 were awarded.

Deadline March of each year.

[756]
GERBER SCHOLARSHIP IN PEDIATRICS

National Medical Fellowships, Inc.
Attn: Scholarship Program
347 Fifth Avenue, Suite 510
New York, NY 10016
(212) 483-8880   Toll Free: (877) NMF-1DOC
Fax: (212) 483-8897   E-mail: scholarships@nmfonline.org
Web: www.nmfonline.org

Summary To provide financial assistance to Hispanic and other underrepresented minority medical students who are interested in pediatrics.

Eligibility This program is open to Hispanics/Latinos, African Americans, Native Americans, Vietnamese, Cambodians, and Pacific Islanders who are enrolled in medical school. Applicants must be interested in pediatrics with an emphasis on nutrition. They must be U.S. citizens or DACA students. Selection is based on leadership, commitment to serving medically underserved communities, and financial need.

Financial Data The stipend is $5,000.

Duration 1 year.

Additional data This program, which began in 1997, is supported by Gerber.

Number awarded 2 each year.

Deadline September of each year.

[757]
GILBERT RIOS MEMORIAL AWARD

Los Padres Foundation
P.O. Box 305
Nassau, DE 19969
(302) 644-1124　　　　　Toll Free: (800) 528-4105
Fax: (866) 810-1361
E-mail: lpfadmin@lospadresfoundation.com
Web: www.lospadresfoundation.com

Summary To provide financial assistance to low-income Puerto Rican/Latino family members working on a graduate degree at a college in the New York City/New Jersey metropolitan area.

Eligibility This program is open to graduate students who are the first in their family to attend college and whose family meets the federal low-income guidelines. Applicants must be U.S. citizens or permanent residents of Puerto Rican/Latino origin planning to attend an accredited college or university in the New York City/New Jersey metropolitan area. They must have a GPA of 3.0 or higher and a record of at least 100 hours of non-faith based volunteer community service each year they were enrolled in undergraduate school. Along with their application, they must submit 250-word personal essays on 1) their future objectives and goals; 2) the volunteer community service projects which with they have been involved as an undergraduate; 3) the issue or problem that was the focus of each organization with which they were a volunteer; 4) the influence or impact of this activity or program on their community; and 5) what they consider to be the major issue affecting their community. Males and females are considered separately.

Financial Data The stipend is $5,000.

Duration 1 year.

Additional data This program began in 2005.

Number awarded 2 each year: 1 to a male and 1 to a female.

Deadline May of each year.

[758]
GO RED MULTICULTURAL SCHOLARSHIP FUND

American Heart Association
Attn: Go Red for Women
7272 Greenville Avenue
Dallas, TX 75231-4596
Toll Free: (800) AHA-USA1
E-mail: GoRedScholarship@heart.org
Web: www.goredforwomen.org

Summary To provide financial assistance to women from Hispanic and other multicultural backgrounds who are preparing for a career in a field of health care.

Eligibility This program is open to women who are currently enrolled at an accredited college, university, health care institution, or program and have a GPA of 3.0 or higher. Applicants must be U.S. citizens or permanent residents of Hispanic, African American, Asian/Pacific Islander, or other minority origin. They must be working on an undergraduate or graduate degree as preparation for a career as a nurse, physician, or allied health care worker. Selection is based on community involvement, a personal essay, transcripts, and 2 letters of recommendation.

Financial Data The stipend is $2,500.

Duration 1 year.

Additional data This program, which began in 2012, is supported by Macy's.

Number awarded 16 each year.

Deadline December of each year.

[759]
GOLDMAN SACHS MBA FELLOWSHIP

Goldman Sachs
Attn: Human Capital Management
200 West Street, 25th Floor
New York, NY 10282
E-mail: Iris.Birungi@gs.com
Web: www.goldmansachs.com

Summary To provide financial assistance and work experience to Hispanic and other underrepresented minority students interested in working on an M.B.A. degree.

Eligibility This program is open to graduate students of Black, Hispanic, or Native American descent who are interested in working on an M.B.A. degree. Applicants must be preparing for a career in the financial services industry. Along with their application, they must submit 2 essays of 500 words or less on the following topics: 1) why they are preparing for a career in the financial services industry; and 2) their current involvement with a community-based organization. Selection is based on analytical skills and the ability to identify significant problems, gather facts, and analyze situations in depth; interpersonal skills, including, but not limited to, poise, confidence, and professionalism; academic record; evidence of hard work and commitment; ability to work well with others; and commitment to community involvement.

Financial Data Fellows receive $25,000 toward payment of tuition and living expenses for the first year of business school; an internship at a domestic office of Goldman Sachs during the summer after the first year of business school; and (after successful completion of the summer internship and acceptance of an offer to return to the firm after graduation as a full-time regular employee) either payment of tuition costs for the second year of business school or an additional $25,000 toward tuition and living costs.

Duration Up to 2 years.

Additional data This program was initiated in 1997.

Number awarded 1 or more each year.

Deadline November of each year.

[760]
GOLDSTEIN AND SCHNEIDER SCHOLARSHIPS BY THE MACEY FUND

Society for Industrial and Organizational Psychology Inc.
Attn: SIOP Foundation
440 East Poe Road, Suite 101
Bowling Green, OH 43402
(419) 353-0032　　　　　Fax: (419) 352-2645
E-mail: siopfoundation@siop.org
Web: www.siop.org/SIOPAwards/thornton.aspx

Summary To provide funding to Hispanic and other minority student members of the Society for Industrial and Organizational Psychology (SIOP) who are conducting doctoral research.

Eligibility This program is open to student affiliate members of SIOP who are enrolled full time in a doctoral program in industrial and organizational (I/O) psychology or a closely-related field at an accredited college or university. Applicants must be members of an ethnic minority group (Native American/Alaskan Native, Asian/Pacific American, African/Caribbean American, or Latino/Hispanic American). They must have an approved dissertation plan that has potential to make significant theoretical and application contributions to the field of I/O psychology.

Financial Data   The stipend is $3,000. Students may elect to have the funds paid to them directly or to be deposited into a "professional development" account at their university.

Duration   1 academic year.

Additional data   The SIOP is Division 14 of the American Psychological Association. This program consists of the Benjamin Schneider Scholarship (offered in odd-numbered years) and the Irwin L. Goldstein Scholarship (offered in even-numbered years).

Number awarded   1 each year.

Deadline   October of each year.

[761]
GORDON STAFFORD SCHOLARSHIP IN ARCHITECTURE

Stafford King Wiese Architects
Attn: Scholarship Selection Committee
622 20th Street
Sacramento, CA 95811
(916) 930-5900   Fax: (916) 290-0100
E-mail: info@skwaia.com
Web: www.skwarchitects.com/about/scholarship

Summary   To provide financial assistance to Hispanics and members of other minority groups from California interested in studying architecture at a college in any state.

Eligibility   This program is open to California residents currently enrolled at accredited schools of architecture in any state as first-year new or first-year transfer students and working on a bachelor's or 5-year master's degree. Applicants must be able to demonstrate minority status (defined as Hispanic, Black, Native American, Pacific Asian, or Asian Indian). They must submit a 500-word statement expressing their desire to prepare for a career in architecture. Finalists are interviewed and must travel to Sacramento, California at their own expense for the interview.

Financial Data   The stipend is $3,000 per year. That includes $1,500 deposited in the recipient's school account and $1,500 paid to the recipient directly.

Duration   1 year; may be renewed up to 4 additional years.

Additional data   This program began in 1995.

Number awarded   Up to 5 each year.

Deadline   June of each year.

[762]
GRADUATE FELLOWSHIP IN THE HISTORY OF SCIENCE

American Geophysical Union
Attn: History of Geophysics
2000 Florida Avenue, N.W.
Washington, DC 20009-1277
(202) 777-7522   Toll Free: (800) 966-2481
Fax: (202) 328-0566
E-mail: HistoryofGeophysics@agu.org
Web: education.agu.org

Summary   To provide funding to doctoral candidates, especially Hispanics and members of other underrepresented groups, who are conducting dissertation research in the history of geophysics.

Eligibility   This program is open to doctoral candidates at U.S. institutions who have passed all preliminary examinations. Applicants must be completing a dissertation in the history of the geophysical sciences, including topics related to atmospheric sciences, biogeosciences, geodesy, geomagnetism and paleomagnetism, hydrology, ocean sciences, planetary sciences, seismology, space physics, aeronomy, tectonophysics, volcanology, geochemistry, and petrology. They must submit a cover letter with a curriculum vitae, undergraduate and graduate transcripts, a 10-page description of the dissertation topic and proposed research plan, and 3 letters of recommendation. U.S. citizenship or permanent resident status is required. Applications are encouraged from women, minorities, and students with disabilities who are traditionally underrepresented in the geophysical sciences.

Financial Data   The grant is $5,000; funds are to be used to assist with the costs of travel to obtain archival or research materials.

Duration   1 year.

Number awarded   1 each year.

Deadline   September of each year.

[763]
GRADUATE RESEARCH FELLOWSHIP PROGRAM OF THE NATIONAL SCIENCE FOUNDATION

National Science Foundation
Directorate for Education and Human Resources
Attn: Division of Graduate Education
4201 Wilson Boulevard, Room 875S
Arlington, VA 22230
(703) 331-3542   Toll Free: (866) NSF-GRFP
Fax: (703) 292-9048   E-mail: info@nsfgrfp.org
Web: www.nsf.gov/funding/pgm_summ.jsp?pims_id=6201

Summary   To provide financial assistance to Hispanic and other underrepresented graduate students interested in working on a master's or doctoral degree in fields supported by the National Science Foundation (NSF).

Eligibility   This program is open to U.S. citizens, nationals, and permanent residents who wish to work on research-based master's or doctoral degrees in a field of science, technology, engineering, or mathematics (STEM) supported by NSF (including astronomy, chemistry, computer and information sciences and engineering, geosciences, engineering, life sciences, materials research, mathematical sciences, physics, psychology, social sciences, or STEM education and learning). Other work in medical, dental, law, public health, or practice-oriented professional degree programs, or in joint science-professional degree programs, such as M.D./Ph.D. and J.D./Ph.D. programs, is not eligible. Applications normally should be submitted during the senior year in college or in the first year of graduate study; eligibility is limited to those who have completed no more than 12 months of graduate study since completion of a baccalaureate degree. Applicants who have already earned an advanced degree in science, engineering, or medicine (including an M.D., D.D.S., or D.V.M.) are ineligible. Selection is based on 1) intellectual merit of the proposed activity: strength of the academic record, proposed plan of research, previous research experience, references, appropriateness of the choice of institution; and 2) broader impacts of the proposed activity: how well does the activity advance discovery and understanding, how well does it broaden the participation of underrepresented groups (e.g., women, minorities, persons with disabilities, veterans), to what extent will it enhance the infrastructure for research and education, will the results be disseminated broadly to enhance scientific and technological understanding, what may be the benefits of the proposed activity to society).

Financial Data The stipend is $32,000 per year; an additional $12,000 cost-of-education allowance is provided to the recipient's institution.

Duration Up to 3 years, usable over a 5-year period.

Number awarded Approximately 2,000 each year.

Deadline October of each year.

[764]
GREAT LAKES SECTION IFT DIVERSITY SCHOLARSHIP

Institute of Food Technologists-Great Lakes Section
c/o Andrea Kirk, Scholarship Chair
Post Foods, LLC
275 Cliff Street
Battle Creek, MI 49014
E-mail: greatlakesift@gmail.com
Web: www.greatlakesift.org/student-scholarships

Summary To provide financial assistance to Hispanic and other minority members of the Great Lakes Section of the Institute of Food Technologists (IFT) from any state who are working on an undergraduate or graduate degree related to food technology at a college in Michigan.

Eligibility This program is open to minority residents of any state who are members of the IFT Great Lakes Section (GLS) and working full time on an undergraduate or graduate degree in food science, nutrition, food engineering, food packaging, or related fields at a college or university in Michigan. Applicants must have a GPA of 3.0 or higher and plans for a career in the food industry. Along with their application, they must submit a 1-page personal statement that covers their academic program, future plans and career goals, extracurricular activities (including involvement in community, university, GLS, or national IFT activities), and work experience. Financial need is not considered in the selection process.

Financial Data The stipend is $1,000.

Duration 1 year; nonrenewable.

Number awarded 1 each year.

Deadline February of each year.

[765]
GREAT MINDS IN STEM TECHNICAL PAPERS AND POSTERS COMPETITION

Great Minds in STEM
Attn: Academic Affairs Specialist
602 Monterey Pass Road
Monterey Park, CA 91754
(323) 262-0997   Fax: (323) 262-0946
E-mail: gmontoya@greatmindsinstem.org
Web: www.greatmindsinstem.org

Summary To recognize and reward undergraduate and graduate students who present outstanding papers and posters at the annual Hispanic Engineer National Achievement Awards Conference (HENAAC).

Eligibility This competition is open to full-time undergraduate and graduate students in science, technology, engineering, mathematics, or health (STEM) disciplines. Applicants must prepare a technical paper or poster and submit an abstract of 600 to 800 words. Based on those abstracts, finalists are invited to present at HENAAC. Awards are presented in 5 categories: 1) graduate student technical papers; 2) graduate student engineering/technology posters; 3) graduate student science/mathematics posters; 4) undergraduate student engineering/technology posters; and 5) undergraduate science/mathematics posters.

Financial Data Awards for graduate student technical papers are $1,500 for first, $1,200 for second, and $1,000 for third. For both categories of graduate student posters, awards are $800 for first, $700 for second, and $600 for third. For both categories of undergraduate student posters, awards are $600 for first, $400 for second, and $200 for third.

Duration The competition is held annually.

Additional data Finalists are reimbursed for travel costs to attend the conference, but they must pay their own conference registration fee, which includes hotel and most meals. Recipients must attend the conference to accept their scholarship.

Number awarded 15 each year: 3 in each of the 5 categories.

Deadline Abstracts must be submitted by August of each year.

[766]
GREATER CINCINNATI SCHOLARSHIP

Hispanic Scholarship Fund
Attn: Selection Committee
1411 West 190th Street, Suite 700
Gardena, CA 90248
(310) 975-3700   Toll Free: (877) HSF-INFO
Fax: (310) 349-3328   E-mail: scholar1@hsf.net
Web: www.hsf.net

Summary To provide financial assistance for college or graduate school to Hispanic American students in Indiana, Kentucky, and Ohio.

Eligibility This program is open to U.S. citizens, permanent residents, Deferred Action for Childhood Arrival (DACA) students, and eligible non-citizens. Applicants must be of Hispanic heritage and enrolled or planning to enroll full time in a degree program at an accredited 4-year college or university as an undergraduate or graduate student (including GED recipients and community college transfers). High school seniors must reside in Indiana, Kentucky, or Ohio and have a

GPA of 3.0 or higher. Current undergraduate and graduate students must reside or attend school in those states and have a GPA of 2.5 or higher. Selection is based on merit; financial need is considered in determining the amount of the award.

Financial Data Stipends normally range from $500 to $5,000 per year.

Duration 1 year; recipients may reapply.

Number awarded 1 or more each year.

Deadline March of each year.

[767]
GREENSPOON MARDER DIVERSITY SCHOLARSHIP PROGRAM FOR LAW STUDENTS

Community Foundation of Sarasota County
Attn: Grants and Scholarships Coordinator
2635 Fruitville Road
P.O. Box 49587
Sarasota, FL 34230-6587
(941) 556-7114   Fax: (941) 952-7115
E-mail: eyoung@cfsarasota.org
Web: www.cfsarasota.org

Summary To provide financial assistance to Hispanic and other minority students from any state attending designated law schools (most of which are in Florida).

Eligibility This program is open to racial and ethnic minority students from any state who are members of groups traditionally underrepresented in the legal profession. Applicants must be entering their second year of full-time study at the University of Florida Levin College of Law, Florida State University College of Law, Stetson University College of Law, Nova Southeastern University Shepard Broad Law Center, St. Thomas University School of Law, Howard University College of Law, Texas Southern University Thurgood Marshall School of Law, Florida Coastal School of Law, or Florida International University College of Law. They must have a GPA of 2.6 or higher. Along with their application, they must submit a 1,000-word personal statement that describes their personal strengths, their contributions through community service, any special or unusual circumstances that may have affected their academic performance, or their personal and family history of educational or socioeconomic disadvantage; it should include aspects of their minority racial or ethnic identity that are relevant to their application. Applicants may also include information about their financial circumstances if they wish to have those considered in the selection process. U.S. citizenship or permanent resident status is required.

Financial Data The stipend is $2,500 per semester.

Duration 1 semester (the spring semester of the second year of law school); may be renewed 1 additional semester (the fall semester of the third year).

Additional data This program was established by the Florida law firm Ruden McClosky, which was acquired by the firm Greenspoon Marder in 2011. It is administered by the Community Foundation of Sarasota County, but the law firm selects the recipients.

Number awarded 1 or more each year.

Deadline July of each year.

[768]
HANA SCHOLARSHIPS

United Methodist Church
Attn: General Board of Higher Education and Ministry
Office of Loans and Scholarships
1001 19th Avenue South
P.O. Box 340007
Nashville, TN 37203-0007
(615) 340-7342   Fax: (615) 340-7367
E-mail: umscholar@gbhem.org
Web: www.gbhem.org

Summary To provide financial assistance to upper-division and graduate Methodist students who are of Hispanic, Asian, Native American, or Pacific Islander ancestry.

Eligibility This program is open to full-time juniors, seniors, and graduate students at accredited colleges and universities in the United States who have been active, full members of a United Methodist Church (UMC) for at least 3 years prior to applying. Applicants must have at least 1 parent who is Hispanic, Asian, or Native American. They must be able to demonstrate involvement in their Hispanic, Asian, or Native American (HANA) community in the UMC. Selection is based on that involvement, academic ability (GPA of at least 2.85), and financial need. U.S. citizenship or permanent resident status is required.

Financial Data Stipends range from $1,000 to $3,000.

Duration 1 year; recipients may reapply.

Number awarded 50 each year.

Deadline February of each year.

[769]
HAPCOA SCHOLARSHIP

Hispanic American Police Command Officers Association
Attn: Scholarship Committee
P.O. Box 29626
Washington, DC 20017
(202) 664-4461   Fax: (202) 641-1304
E-mail: achapa@hapcoa.org
Web: www.hapcoa.org/hapcoa-scholarship

Summary To provide financial assistance to Hispanic undergraduate and graduate students who are preparing for a career in law enforcement.

Eligibility This program is open to Hispanic Americans currently working on an undergraduate or graduate degree in law enforcement. Along with their application, they must submit a 1-page essay on their long- and short-term career goals, including academic goals, career goals, life goals, importance of education, achievements, and financial need. Selection is based on the essay, GPA, extracurricular activities, and honors and awards.

Financial Data The stipend is $2,500.

Duration 1 year.

Number awarded 1 or more each year.

Deadline July of each year.

[770]
HAZEL D. COLE FELLOWSHIP

University of Washington
Attn: Stroum Center for Jewish Studies
Henry M. Jackson School of International Studies
Thomson Hall
Box 353650
Seattle, WA 98195-3650
(206) 543-0138   Fax: (206) 685-0668
E-mail: jewishst@uw.edu
Web: www.jewishstudies.washington.edu

Summary To provide funding to pre- and postdoctoral scholars in Jewish studies, including Hispanics and other underrepresented minorities, who are interested in conducting research at the University of Washington.

Eligibility This program is open to postdoctoral scholars who completed their Ph.D. within the past 3 years and to doctoral candidates working on a dissertation. Applicants must be interested in conducting research in a field of Jewish studies while in residence at the University of Washington for the tenure of their fellowship. They may be from any American or foreign university. Along with their application, they must submit a current curriculum vitae, a description of their scholarly interests and their proposed research project, a proposal for a course they would like to teach (including a prospective syllabus), 2 letters of recommendation, and an academic writing sample. The program encourages applications from women, minorities, individuals with disabilities, and covered veterans.

Financial Data The fellowship provides a stipend of $50,000 plus benefits.

Duration 1 year.

Additional data The fellow also offers an undergraduate seminar or lecture course and makes a public presentation.

Number awarded 1 each year.

Deadline October of each year.

[771]
HBA-DC FOUNDATION FELLOWSHIPS

Hispanic Bar Association of the District of Columbia
Attn: Foundation
P.O. Box 1011
Washington, DC 20013-1011
E-mail: fellowships@hbadc.org
Web: www.hbadc.org/?page=foundation

Summary To provide funding to Hispanic law students in Washington, D.C. who wish to gain work experience in public interest law during the summer.

Eligibility This program is open to first- and second-year Hispanic students from any state who are enrolled at law schools in the District of Columbia metropolitan area. Applicants must be interested in working in the area of public interest law at a nonprofit, non-governmental organization in Washington or the surrounding region that provides legal services at low or no cost to clients. Along with their application, they must submit a 300-word personal statement on their reasons for seeking a position with their proposed sponsoring organization and how their Latino heritage is important to that choice. Preference is given to students working with organizations serving the District of Columbia Latino community among its client base. Financial need is considered in the selection process.

Financial Data The stipend is $5,000.

Duration 8 weeks during the summer.

Number awarded Varies each year; recently, 6 were awarded.

Deadline April of each year.

[772]
HBA-DC FOUNDATION SCHOLARSHIPS

Hispanic Bar Association of the District of Columbia
Attn: Foundation
P.O. Box 1011
Washington, DC 20013-1011
E-mail: fellowships@hbadc.org
Web: www.hbadc.org/?page=foundation

Summary To provide financial assistance to Hispanic students at law schools in Washington, D.C.

Eligibility This program is open to Hispanic students from any state who are enrolled in their final year of studies at ABA-accredited law schools in Washington, D.C. Applicants must be able to demonstrate commitment to the advancement of the Hispanic community and financial need. Along with their application, they must submit an essay on their recent community and law school activities and how, as a future lawyer, they intend to contribute to the advancement of the community and the Hispanic bar.

Financial Data The stipend is $2,500.

Duration 1 year.

Number awarded 2 each year.

Deadline October of each year.

[773]
HBALEF SCHOLARSHIPS

Hispanic Bar Association of Pennsylvania
Attn: Legal Education Fund
P.O. Box 59106
Philadelphia, PA 19102-9106
(215) 707-1986   E-mail: pahbanews@gmail.com
Web: www.hbapa.net/lef-info

Summary To provide financial assistance to Hispanic residents of any state attending law school in Pennsylvania or the Delaware Valley.

Eligibility This program is open to students of Hispanic background from any state who are currently enrolled at a law school located in Pennsylvania or the Delaware Valley (defined to include Burlington, Camden, Cumberland, Gloucester, and Salem counties in New Jersey; New Castle County in Delaware; and Cecil County in Maryland). Applicants must submit a personal statement of 1 to 3 pages that covers their background, achievements, career goals, geographic area where they will consider practicing, involvement in community activities, involvement in law school organizations and/or activities, and financial need.

Financial Data The stipend is normally $2,000.

Duration 1 year.

Number awarded 1 or more each year.

Deadline September of each year.

[774]
HDAF SCHOLARSHIPS

Hispanic Dental Association
Attn: HDA Foundation
3910 South IH-35, Suite 245
Austin, TX 78704
(512) 904-0252   E-mail: jessicac@hdassoc.org
Web: www.hdassoc.org

Summary   To provide financial assistance to members of the Hispanic Dental Association (HDA) interested in preparing for a career in a dental profession.

Eligibility   This program is open to HDA members who are entering their first through fourth year of dental school or first or second year at an accredited dental hygiene, dental assisting, or dental technician program in the United States or Puerto Rico. Applicants must have a GPA of 3.0 or higher, an interest in improving the health of the Hispanic community, and a demonstrated commitment and dedication to serving the Hispanic community. They must be enrolled full time. Along with their application, they must submit a 250-word essay on their career goals, including how they were inspired to become a dentist, dental hygienist, dental assistant, or dental technician. Selection is based on academic achievement, leadership skills, community service, and commitment and dedication to improving the oral health of the Hispanic community.

Financial Data   The stipend is $1,500 for dental students or $750 for dental hygiene, dental assisting, or dental technician students. An additional grant of $500 is provided for travel reimbursement and complimentary registration to the HDA annual meeting.

Duration   1 year.

Additional data   This program is sponsored by the Hispanic Dental Association Foundation (HDAF).

Number awarded   6 each year.

Deadline   May of each year.

[775]
HEALTH HISPANIC LEADERSHIP DEVELOPMENT FUND

United Methodist Church
General Board of Global Ministries
Attn: United Methodist Committee on Relief
Health and Welfare Ministries
475 Riverside Drive, Room 330
New York, NY 10115
(212) 870-3871   Toll Free: (800) UMC-GBGM
E-mail: jyoung@gbgm-umc.org
Web: umc-gbcs.org/conference-connections/grants

Summary   To provide financial assistance to Methodists and other Christians of Hispanic descent who are preparing for a career in a health-related field.

Eligibility   This program is open to undergraduate and graduate students who are U.S. citizens or permanent residents of Hispanic descent. Applicants must be professed Christians, preferably United Methodists. They must be working on an undergraduate or graduate degree to enter or continue in a health-related field. Financial need is considered in the selection process.

Financial Data   The stipend is $2,000.

Duration   1 year.

Additional data   This program began in 1986.

Number awarded   Varies each year.

Deadline   June of each year.

[776]
HEALTH POLICY RESEARCH SCHOLARS

Robert Wood Johnson Foundation
50 College Road East
Princeton, NJ 08540-6614
Toll Free: (877) 843-RWJF   E-mail: mail@rwjf.org
Web: www.rwjf.org

Summary   To provide funding to doctoral students who are Hispanics or from other diverse backgrounds and interested in working on a degree related to health policy.

Eligibility   This program is open to full-time doctoral students in the first or second year of their program. Applicants must be from underrepresented populations or disadvantaged backgrounds (e.g., first-generation college students, individuals from lower socioeconomic backgrounds, members of racial and ethnic groups underrepresented in doctoral programs, people with disabilities). They must be working on a degree in a field related to health policy, such as urban planning, political science, economics, ethnography, education, social work, or sociology; the program is not intended for students working on a clinical doctorate without a research focus. Prior experience or knowledge in health policy is neither required nor expected.

Financial Data   The stipend is $30,000 per year. Scholars are also eligible for $10,000 research grants if their dissertation is related to health policy.

Duration   Up to 4 years. Participants may continue in the program without the annual stipend for a fifth year or until they complete their doctoral program, whichever occurs first.

Number awarded   Up to 50 each year.

Deadline   March of each year.

[777]
HEALTH RESEARCH AND EDUCATIONAL TRUST SCHOLARSHIPS

New Jersey Hospital Association
Attn: Health Research and Educational Trust
760 Alexander Road
P.O. Box 1
Princeton, NJ 08543-0001
(609) 275-4224   Fax: (609) 452-8097
E-mail: jhritz@njha.com
Web: www.njha.com/education/scholarships

Summary   To provide financial assistance to New Jersey residents, especially Hispanics and other minorities, who are working on an undergraduate or graduate degree in a field related to health care administration at a school in any state.

Eligibility   This program is open to residents of New Jersey enrolled in an upper-division or graduate program in hospital or health care administration, public administration, nursing, or other allied health profession at a school in any state. Graduate students working on an advanced degree to prepare to teach nursing are also eligible. Applicants must have a GPA of 3.0 or higher and be able to demonstrate financial need. Along with their application, they must submit a 2-page essay (on which 50% of the selection is based) describing their academic plans for the future. Minorities and women are especially encouraged to apply.

Financial Data The stipend is $2,000.

Duration 1 year.

Additional data This program began in 1983.

Number awarded Varies each year; recently, 3 were awarded.

Deadline June of each year.

[778]
HELENE M. OVERLY MEMORIAL GRADUATE SCHOLARSHIP

Women's Transportation Seminar
Attn: WTS Foundation
1701 K Street, N.W., Suite 800
Washington, DC 20006
(202) 955-5085   Fax: (202) 955-5088
E-mail: wts@wtsinternational.org
Web: www.wtsinternational.org/education/scholarships

Summary To provide financial assistance to women graduate students, especially Hispanics and other minorities, who are interested in preparing for a career in transportation.

Eligibility This program is open to women who are enrolled in a graduate degree program in a transportation-related field (e.g., transportation engineering, planning, finance, or logistics). Applicants must have at least a 3.0 GPA and be interested in a career in transportation. Along with their application, they must submit a 750-word statement about their career goals after graduation and why they think they should receive the scholarship award. Applications must be submitted first to a local chapter; the chapters forward selected applications for consideration on the national level. Minority women are particularly encouraged to apply. Selection is based on transportation involvement and goals, job skills, and academic record.

Financial Data The stipend is $10,000.

Duration 1 year.

Additional data This program began in 1981. Local chapters may also award additional funding to winners in their area.

Number awarded 1 each year.

Deadline Applications must be submitted by November to a local WTS chapter.

[779]
HENAAC CORPORATE/GOVERNMENT SPONSORED SCHOLARSHIPS

Great Minds in STEM
Attn: HENAAC Scholars Program
602 Monterey Pass Road
Monterey Park, CA 91754
(323) 262-0997   Fax: (323) 262-0946
E-mail: scholars@greatmindsinstem.org
Web: www.greatmindsinstem.org

Summary To provide financial assistance to Hispanic undergraduate and graduate students interested in working on a degree in a field of science, technology, engineering, or mathematics (STEM).

Eligibility This program is open to students who are working on or planning to work on an undergraduate or graduate degree in a field of STEM. Applicants must be of Hispanic origin and/or must significantly participate in and promote organizations and activities in the Hispanic community. They must have a GPA of 3.0 or higher. Along with their application, they must submit a 700-word essay on a topic that changes annually. Selection is based on leadership, academic achievements, and campus and community activities; financial need is not considered. U.S. citizenship or permanent resident status is required.

Financial Data Stipends range from $500 to $10,000.

Duration 1 year; recipients may reapply.

Additional data The Hispanic Engineer National Achievement Awards Conference (HENAAC) was established in 1989 and initiated a scholarship program in 2000. In 2010, the sponsoring organization officially adopted its current name, but it continues to hold the annual HENAAC conference, at which the scholarships are presented. Corporate sponsors include Boeing Company, Booz Allen Hamilton, Chevron, Chrysler Foundation, Cummins, Dell, Dow Chemical, Edison International, Leidos, Lemus Medical, Lockheed Martin Corporation, Northrop Grumman Foundation, Oracle, Rackspace, and The Gas Company. Government sponsors include NASA Langley. Recipients must attend the conference to accept their scholarship. The sponsor subsidizes the cost of travel, 3 nights of lodging, and meals.

Number awarded Varies each year; recently, 78 were awarded.

Deadline April of each year.

[780]
HENAAC STUDENT LEADERSHIP AWARDS

Great Minds in STEM
Attn: HENAAC Scholars Program
602 Monterey Pass Road
Monterey Park, CA 91754
(323) 262-0997   Fax: (323) 262-0946
E-mail: scholars@greatmindsinstem.org
Web: www.greatmindsinstem.org

Summary To provide financial assistance to Hispanic undergraduate and graduate students working on a degree in fields of science, technology, engineering, or mathematics (STEM).

Eligibility This program is open to undergraduate and graduate students who are enrolled at a college or university and working on a degree in a STEM field. Applicants must be of Hispanic origin and/or must significantly participate in and promote organizations and activities in the Hispanic community. They must have a GPA of 3.0 or higher. Along with their application, they must submit a 700-word essay on a topic that changes annually; recently, students were asked to write on how they see their academic major contributing to global efforts and technology and how they, in their field of study, will contribute to global progress as well as actively contribute to their local communities. Selection is based on leadership, academic achievements, and campus and community activities; financial need is not considered.

Financial Data The stipend is $1,000.

Duration 1 year.

Additional data The Hispanic Engineer National Achievement Awards Conference (HENAAC) was established in 1989 and initiated a scholarship program in 2000. In 2010, the sponsoring organization officially adopted its current name, but it continues to hold the annual HENAAC conference, at which the scholarships are presented. Recipients must attend the conference to accept their scholarship. The sponsor subsidizes the cost of travel, 3 nights of lodging, and meals.

Number awarded   2 each year: 1 undergraduate and 1 graduate student.

Deadline   April of each year.

[781]
HENRY L. DIAMOND B&D LAW CLERK

Environmental Law Institute
2000 L Street, N.W., Suite 620
Washington, DC 20036
(202) 939-380037   Fax: (202) 939-3868
E-mail: law@eli.org
Web: www.eli.org/jobs/beveridge-diamond-acoel-law-clerks

Summary   To provide law students, especially Hispanics and other minorities, with summer work experience at the Environmental Law Institute (ELI) in Washington, D.C.

Eligibility   This program is open to law students, especially first-year students, who have an interest in environmental law. Applicants must be interested in working during the summer at ELI on its domestic and international projects and publications (such as the *Environmental Law Reporter*). Along with their application they must submit a resume (including college and law school transcripts), references, transcripts, a writing sample, and a cover letter that explains how the applicant will contribute to the diversity of environmental law, management, and policy. Minority candidates are encouraged to apply.

Financial Data   The stipend is $5,000.

Duration   At least 10 weeks during the summer.

Additional data   This program is supported by the law firm Beveridge & Diamond, P.C.

Number awarded   1 each year.

Deadline   Applications may be submitted at any time.

[782]
HERBERT W. NICKENS MEDICAL STUDENT SCHOLARSHIPS

Association of American Medical Colleges
Attn: Division of Diversity Policy and Programs
655 K Street, N.W., Suite 100
Washington, DC 20001-2399
(202) 862-6203   Fax: (202) 828-1125
E-mail: nickensawards@aamc.org
Web: www.aamc.org/initiatives/awards/nickens-student

Summary   To provide financial assistance to medical students who have demonstrated efforts to address the health-care needs of Hispanics and other minorities.

Eligibility   This program is open to U.S. citizens and permanent residents entering their third year of study at a U.S. allopathic medical school. Each medical school may nominate 1 student for these awards. The letter must describe the nominee's 1) academic achievement through the first and second year, including special awards and honors, clerkships or special research projects, and extracurricular activities in which the student has shown leadership abilities; 2) leadership efforts to eliminate inequities in medical education and health care; 3) demonstrated leadership efforts in addressing the educational, societal, and health-care needs of minorities; and 4) awards and honors, special research projects, and extracurricular activities in which the student has shown leadership abilities. Nominees must submit a curriculum vitae and a 2-page essay that discusses their leadership efforts in eliminating inequities in medical education and health care for minorities.

Financial Data   The stipend is $5,000.

Duration   1 year.

Number awarded   5 each year.

Deadline   April of each year.

[783]
HERMAN G. GREEN, PHD MEMORIAL SCHOLARSHIP

South Carolina Professional Association for Access and
  Equity
Attn: Financial Secretary
P.O. Box 71297
North Charleston, SC 29415
(843) 670-4890   E-mail: anderson4569@bellsouth.net
Web: www.scpaae.org/#!scholarships/c11tv

Summary   To provide financial assistance to graduate students at colleges and universities in South Carolina who are recognized as underrepresented minorities on their campus.

Eligibility   This program is open to residents of any state who have completed at least 9 semester hours of graduate study at a college or university in South Carolina. Applicants must be recognized as an underrepresented ethnic minority on their campus. They must have a GPA of 3.5 or higher. Along with their application, they must submit 1) a personal letter on their public service, academic and career goals, honors and awards, leadership skills and organization participation, community service, and a statement of why they would like to receive this scholarship; and 2) a paragraph defining access and equity and describing how they can assist in achieving access and equity within South Carolina. Financial need is not considered in the selection process.

Financial Data   The stipend is $1,200.

Duration   1 year.

Number awarded   1 or more each year.

Deadline   February of each year.

[784]
HISPANIC ASSOCIATION OF COLLEGES AND UNIVERSITIES/DENNY'S HUNGRY FOR EDUCATION SCHOLARSHIPS

Hispanic Association of Colleges and Universities
Attn: National Scholarship Program
8415 Datapoint Drive, Suite 400
San Antonio, TX 78229
(210) 692-3805   Fax: (210) 692-0823
TDD: (800) 855-2880   E-mail: scholarship@hacu.net
Web: www.hacu.net/hacu/Scholarships.asp

Summary   To provide financial assistance to undergraduate and graduate students at member institutions of the Hispanic Association of Colleges and Universities (HACU) who submit outstanding essays on childhood hunger.

Eligibility   This program is open to full- and part-time undergraduate and graduate students at 2- and 4-year HACU member institutions. Applicants must have a GPA of 2.5 or higher. Along with their application, they must submit a 500-

word essay on how Denny's can help in the fight against childhood hunger in the United States.

Financial Data   The stipend is $1,000.

Duration   1 year.

Additional data   This program is sponsored by Denny's as 1 of its Hungry for Education activities.

Number awarded   5 each year.

Deadline   April of each year.

[785]
HISPANIC BAR ASSOCIATION OF NEW JERSEY SCHOLARSHIP

Hispanic Bar Association of New Jersey
Attn: Scholarship Committee Chair
P.O. Box 25562
Newark, NJ 07101
E-mail: jacky.pena@gmail.com
Web: www.njhba.org/scholarship

Summary   To provide financial assistance to Hispanic law students from New Jersey.

Eligibility   This program is open to students of Hispanic ancestry (at least 1 parent of Hispanic descent) who are enrolled in the first, second, or third year of study at an ABA-approved law school in the United States. Applicants must be or have been residents of New Jersey. Along with their application, they must submit a statement describing their recent community and/or law school activities and how they, after graduating as a lawyer, intend to contribute to the advancement of the Hispanic community and Bar. Financial need is considered in the selection process.

Financial Data   The stipend is $3,000. Funds are paid directly to the student.

Duration   1 year.

Number awarded   1 or more each year.

Deadline   May of each year.

[786]
HISPANIC HIGHER EDUCATION SCHOLARSHIP FUND

New Jersey Mental Health Institute
Attn: Debra Wentz, Executive Director
The Neuman Building
3575 Quakerbridge Road, Suite 102
Mercerville, NJ 08619
(609) 838-5488, ext. 292   Fax: (609) 838-5480
E-mail: dwentz@njmhi.org
Web: www.njmhi.org/scholarshipfunds.html

Summary   To provide financial assistance to Hispanic students working on a master's degree in social work at New Jersey universities.

Eligibility   This program is open to U.S. citizens and permanent residents of Hispanic background who have a baccalaureate degree. Applicants must be interested in working on a master's degree in social work at a university in New Jersey. They must be bilingual (English and Spanish) in both their verbal and written communications. Along with their application, they must submit a brief personal statement explaining why they believe they should receive this scholarship and a 1-page essay on why they are entering the field of social work and how they plan to contribute to the field. Selection is based

on information in the application, a personal interview, and an in-person written and verbal communications skills test.

Financial Data   A stipend is awarded (amount not specified).

Duration   1 year.

Additional data   This program began in 2002.

Number awarded   1 each year.

Deadline   April of each year.

[787]
HISPANIC METROPOLITAN CHAMBER SCHOLARSHIPS

Hispanic Metropolitan Chamber
Attn: Scholarship Committee
333 S.W. Fifth Avenue, Suite 100
P.O. Box 1837
Portland, OR 97207
(503) 222-0280   Fax: (503) 243-5597
E-mail: info@hmccoregon.com
Web: www.hmccoregon.com/scholarship.html

Summary   To provide financial assistance to Hispanic residents of Oregon and Clark County, Washington who are interested in attending college or graduate school in any state.

Eligibility   This program is open to residents of Oregon and Clark County, Washington who are of Hispanic ancestry. Applicants must have a GPA of 3.0 or higher and be enrolled or planning to enroll in an accredited community college, 4-year university, or graduate school in any state. Along with their application, they must submit 250-word essays on how their heritage has influenced their life and long-term goals, and either why they should be selected to receive another scholarship (for renewal applicants) or a community activity in which they have participated and how it has benefited the Latino community in the past year (for first-time applicants). Selection is based on the essays, academics, extra-curricular activities, community service, extracurricular activities, community service, and letters of recommendation. If they wish to be considered for a scholarship for low-income families, they may also submit documentation of financial need. U.S. citizenship or permanent resident status is required.

Financial Data   Stipends range from $2,000 to $10,000.

Duration   1 year; may be renewed.

Additional data   Matching funds are provided to students who choose to attend George Fox University, Lewis and Clark College, Linfield College, Oregon State University, Portland State University, University of Oregon, University of Portland, Western Oregon University, Whitman College, or Willamette University.

Number awarded   Varies each year; recently, 50 were awarded: 1 at $10,000, 1 at $6,000, 3 at $5,000, 2 at $4,500, 1 at $4,000, 1 at $3,600, 12 at $3,500, 11 at $3,000, 3 at $2,500, and 15 at $2,000.

Deadline   January of each year.

[788]
HISPANIC PROFESSIONALS OF GREATER MILWAUKEE ADVANCED DEGREE SCHOLARSHIPS

Hispanic Professionals of Greater Milwaukee
Attn: Kim Schultz, Scholarship Program
759 North Milwaukee Street, Suite 322
Milwaukee, WI 53202
(414) 223-4611   Fax: (414) 223-45613
E-mail: Kim.Schultz@hpgm.org
Web: www.hpgm.org/scholarships

Summary   To provide financial assistance to residents of Wisconsin who are of Hispanic heritage and working on an advanced degree in any state.

Eligibility   This program is open to residents of Wisconsin who are U.S. citizens of Hispanic heritage. Applicants must be enrolled at least half time at an accredited college or institute in any state and working on an advanced degree (e.g., M.B.A., M.A., M.S., Ph.D., J.D.). Along with their application, they must submit transcripts with a GPA of 3.0 or higher, a 2-page resume, their community service history, an essay of 1,000 to 1,500 words on an assigned topic, and a letter of recommendation. Students who have a GPA of 3.2 or higher are eligible for a larger stipend if they submit an additional essay. Students who have a GPA of 3.5 or higher are eligible for an even larger stipend is they submit an additional essay, submit an additional letter of recommendation, and are available for a personal interview.

Financial Data   Stipends are $2,500 for students who have a GPA of 3.0 or higher, $5,000 for students who have a GPA of 3.2 or higher, or $10,000 if their GPA is 3.5 or higher.

Duration   1 year.

Additional data   This program began in 2004.

Number awarded   7 each year: 1 at $10,000, 2 at $5,000, and 4 at $2,500.

Deadline   June of each year.

[789]
HISPANIC PUBLIC RELATIONS ASSOCIATION SCHOLARSHIP PROGRAM

Hispanic Public Relations Association-Los Angeles
    Chapter
Attn: Scholarship Program Director
P.O. Box 86760
Los Angeles, CA 90086-0760
(323) 359-8869   E-mail: info@hpra-usa.org
Web: www.hpra-usa.org/laR/scholarship-program

Summary   To provide financial assistance to Hispanic undergraduate students from California who are attending college in the state and preparing for a career in public relations.

Eligibility   This program is open to residents of California who are of at least 25% Hispanic descent and entering the sophomore, junior, or senior year at a 4-year college or university or enrolling as a graduate student in the state. Applicants must have a GPA of 2.7 or higher cumulatively and 3.0 or higher in their major subject. They must be majoring in public relations, communications, journalism, advertising, and/or marketing. Students majoring in other disciplines but planning to work in the public relations industry are also eligible. Along with their application, they must submit a letter of recommendation, official university transcripts, a 1- to 2-page personal statement explaining their career and educational aspirations as well as their involvement in the Hispanic community, a 1-page resume, documentation of financial need, and writing samples. Any materials submitted in Spanish must include an English translation. The applicant whose contributions to the community are judged most outstanding receives the Esther Renteria Community Service Scholarship.

Financial Data   The stipend is $2,000. The student selected as the winner of the Esther Renteria Community Service Scholarship receives an additional $1,000.

Duration   1 year; may be renewed 1 additional year.

Additional data   Recipients are expected to attend the sponsor's Premio Awards dinner in October.

Number awarded   6 each year: 4 undergraduates and 2 graduate students (of whom 1 of the 6 receives the Esther Renteria Community Service Scholarship).

Deadline   August of each year.

[790]
HISPANIC SCHOLARSHIP FUND GENERAL COLLEGE SCHOLARSHIPS

Hispanic Scholarship Fund
Attn: Selection Committee
1411 West 190th Street, Suite 700
Gardena, CA 90248
(310) 975-3700   Toll Free: (877) HSF-INFO
Fax: (310) 349-3328   E-mail: scholar1@hsf.net
Web: www.hsf.net

Summary   To provide financial assistance for college or graduate school to Hispanic American students.

Eligibility   This program is open to U.S. citizens, permanent residents, Deferred Action for Childhood Arrival (DACA) students, and eligible non-citizens. Applicants must be of Hispanic heritage and enrolled or planning to enroll full time in a degree program at an accredited 4-year college or university as an undergraduate or graduate student (including GED recipients and community college transfers). High school seniors must have a GPA of 3.0 or higher; current undergraduate and graduate students must have a GPA of 2.5 or higher. All academic majors are eligible, but emphasis is placed on students in fields of science, technology, engineering, and mathematics (STEM). Selection is based on merit; financial need is considered in determining the amount of the award.

Financial Data   Stipends normally range from $500 to $5,000 per year.

Duration   1 year; recipients may reapply.

Additional data   Since this program began in 1975, more than $470 million has been awarded to more than 100,000 Hispanic students.

Number awarded   Varies each year; recently, this program awarded more than 5,100 scholarships.

Deadline   March of each year.

[791]
HISPANIC-SERVING HEALTH PROFESSIONS SCHOOLS/DEPARTMENT OF VETERANS AFFAIRS GRADUATE FELLOWSHIP TRAINING PROGRAM

Hispanic-Serving Health Professions Schools
Attn: Graduate Fellowship Training Program
2639 Connecticut Avenue, N.W., Suite 203
Washington, DC 20008
(202) 290-1186   E-mail: hshps@hshps.org
Web: www.hshps.org/programs/gftp

Summary To provide an opportunity for Hispanic undergraduate and graduate students to obtain research experience at facilities of the U.S. Department of Veterans Affairs (VA) in the United States and Puerto Rico.

Eligibility This program is geared to graduate students in public health, but undergraduate juniors and seniors may also apply; individuals with 5 or more years of professional experience in the health field are not eligible. Applicants must be interested in participating in a research program conducted at a VA health care facility in the United States or Puerto Rico where they are matched with a mentor whom they assist with various aspects of a research project. They must be U.S. citizens or permanent residents and have working proficiency in English; some positions require Spanish fluency. Available assignments include hospital administration, nursing administration, program administration, patient safety/satisfaction, secondary data analysis, knowledge management/workforce, women's health, and health promotion/education. A GPA of 2.7 or higher is required.

Financial Data Grants provide a stipend of $300 per week, housing accommodations, reimbursement of up to $500 in transportation to the program site, and $30 per week for local transportation.

Duration 10 weeks during the summer.

Number awarded Varies each year.

Deadline March of each year.

[792]
HOLLY A. CORNELL SCHOLARSHIP

American Water Works Association
Attn: Scholarship Coordinator
6666 West Quincy Avenue
Denver, CO 80235-3098
(303) 794-7771   Toll Free: (800) 926-7337
Fax: (303) 347-0804   E-mail: scholarships@awwa.org
Web: www.awwa.org

Summary To provide financial assistance to Hispanic and other minority students interested in working on an master's degree in the field of water supply and treatment.

Eligibility This program is open to minority and female students working on a master's degree in the field of water supply and treatment at a college or university in Canada, Guam, Mexico, Puerto Rico, or the United States. Students who have been accepted into graduate school but have not yet begun graduate study are encouraged to apply. Applicants must submit a 2-page resume, official transcripts, 3 letters of recommendation, a proposed curriculum of study, a 1-page statement of educational plans and career objectives demonstrating an interest in the drinking water field, and a 3-page proposed plan of research. Selection is based on academic

record and potential to provide leadership in the field of water supply and treatment.

Financial Data The stipend is $7,500.

Duration 1 year; nonrenewable.

Additional data Funding for this program, which began in 1990, comes from the consulting firm CH2M Hill.

Number awarded 1 each year.

Deadline January of each year.

[793]
HOWARD MAYER BROWN FELLOWSHIP

American Musicological Society
6010 College Station
Brunswick, ME 04011-8451
(207) 798-4243   Toll Free: (877) 679-7648
Fax: (207) 798-4254   E-mail: ams@ams-net.org
Web: www.ams-net.org/fellowships/hmb.php

Summary To provide financial assistance to Hispanic and other minority students who are working on a doctoral degree in the field of musicology.

Eligibility This program is open to members of minority groups historically underrepresented in the field of musicology. In the United States, that includes Hispanic Americans, African Americans, Native Americans, and Asian Americans. In Canada, it refers to aboriginal people and visible minorities. Applicants must have completed at least 1 year of full-time academic work at an institution with a graduate program in musicology and be planning to complete a Ph.D. degree in the field. There are no restrictions on research area, age, or sex. U.S. or Canadian citizenship or permanent resident status is required.

Financial Data The stipend is $20,000.

Duration 1 year; nonrenewable.

Additional data This fellowship was first awarded in 1995.

Number awarded 1 each year.

Deadline December of each year.

[794]
HUGGINS-QUARLES AWARD

Organization of American Historians
Attn: Award and Committee Coordinator
112 North Bryan Street
Bloomington, IN 47408-4141
(812) 855-7311   Fax: (812) 855-0696
E-mail: khamm@oah.org
Web: www.oah.org

Summary To provide funding to Hispanic and other minority graduate students who are completing dissertations in American history.

Eligibility This program is open to graduate students of color (Latino(a), African American, Asian American, Native American) at the dissertation research stage of their Ph.D. programs. Their dissertation must deal with a topic related to American history. Along with their application, they must submit a cover letter that also indicates their progress on the dissertation, a curriculum vitae, a 5-page dissertation proposal (including an explanation of the project's significance and contribution to the field and a description of the most important primary sources) and a 1-page itemized budget explaining travel and research plans.

Financial Data   The grant is $1,500 (if 1 is presented) or $750 (if 2 are presented). Funds are to be used to assist with costs of travel to collections to complete research on the dissertation.

Additional data   This program was established in honor of Benjamin Quarles and the late Nathan Huggins, both outstanding historians of the African American past.

Number awarded   1 or 2 each year.

Deadline   November of each year.

[795]
HUGH J. ANDERSEN MEMORIAL SCHOLARSHIPS

National Medical Fellowships, Inc.
Attn: Scholarship Program
347 Fifth Avenue, Suite 510
New York, NY 10016
(212) 483-8880   Toll Free: (877) NMF-1DOC
Fax: (212) 483-8897 E-mail: scholarships@nmfonline.org
Web: www.nmfonline.org

Summary   To provide financial assistance to Hispanic and other underrepresented minority medical students at schools in Minnesota.

Eligibility   This program is open to Hispanics/Latinos, African Americans, Native Americans, Vietnamese, Cambodians, and Pacific Islanders who are entering the second or third year of medical school. Applicants must be Minnesota residents enrolled at an accredited medical school in Minnesota. They must be U.S. citizens or DACA students. Selection is based on leadership, commitment to serving medically underserved communities, and financial need.

Financial Data   The stipend is $5,000.

Duration   1 year.

Additional data   This program began in 1982.

Number awarded   2 each year.

Deadline   September of each year.

[796]
HWNT AUSTIN SCHOLARSHIP

Hispanic Scholarship Consortium
Attn: Scholarship Selection Committee
7703 North Lamar Boulevard, Suite 310
Austin, TX 78752
(512) 368-2956   Fax: (512) 692-1831
E-mail: scholarships@hispanicscholar.org
Web: hispanicscholar.academicworks.com

Summary   To provide financial assistance and work experience to female high school seniors and college seniors of Hispanic heritage from Texas who plan to attend college or graduate school in any state.

Eligibility   This program is open to female residents of Texas of Hispanic heritage who are either 1) seniors graduating from high schools in Texas; or 2) seniors graduating from colleges in any state. High school seniors must be planning to enroll full time at an accredited 2- or 4-year college or university in any state; college seniors must be planning to enroll in graduate school. Applicants must have a GPA of 3.0 or higher. Selection is based on academic achievement, community service, personal strengths, leadership, and financial need. U.S. citizenship is not required; students may qualify under Texas Senate Bill 1528.

Financial Data   The stipend is $2,000 per year.

Duration   1 year; may be renewed up to 3 additional years, provided the recipient remains enrolled full time, maintains a GPA of 3.0 or higher, and participates in at least 25 hours of community service per semester.

Additional data   This program is sponsored by the Austin chapter of Hispanic Women's Network of Texas (HWNT). Scholarship winners must also participate in a year-long internship with the magazine.

Number awarded   Varies each year; recently, 2 were awarded.

Deadline   April of each year.

[797]
IBM PHD FELLOWSHIP PROGRAM

IBM Corporation
Attn: University Relations
1133 Westchester Avenue
White Plains, NY 10604
Toll Free: (800) IBM-4YOU   TDD: (800) IBM-3383
E-mail: phdfellow@us.ibm.com
Web: www.research.ibm.com

Summary   To provide funding and work experience to students from any country, especially Hispanics and other minorities, who are working on a Ph.D. in a research area of broad interest to IBM.

Eligibility   Students nominated for this fellowship should be enrolled full time at an accredited college or university in any country and should have completed at least 1 year of graduate study in computer science or engineering, electrical or mechanical engineering, physical sciences (chemistry, material sciences, physics), mathematical sciences, public sector and business sciences, or service science, management, and engineering (SSME). Focus areas that receive special consideration include technology that creates new business or social value, cognitive computing research, cloud and distributed computing technology and solutions, or fundamental science and technology. Applicants should be planning a career in research. Nominations must be made by a faculty member and endorsed by the department head. The program values diversity, and encourages nominations of women, minorities, and others who contribute to that diversity. Selection is based on the applicants' potential for research excellence, the degree to which their technical interests align with those of IBM, and academic progress to date. Preference is given to students who have had an IBM internship or have closely collaborated with technical or services people from IBM.

Financial Data   Fellowships pay tuition, fees, and a stipend of $17,500 per year.

Duration   1 year; may be renewed up to 2 additional years, provided the recipient is renominated, interacts with IBM's technical community, and demonstrates continued progress and achievement.

Additional data   Recipients are offered an internship at 1 of the IBM Research Division laboratories and are given an IBM computer.

Number awarded   Varies each year; recently, 57 were awarded.

Deadline   October of each year.

[798]
ILLINOIS NURSES FOUNDATION CENTENNIAL SCHOLARSHIP

Illinois Nurses Association
Attn: Illinois Nurses Foundation
P.O. Box 636
Manteno, IL 60950
(815) 468-8804   Fax: (773) 304-1419
E-mail: info@ana-illinois.org
Web: www.ana-illinois.org

Summary   To provide financial assistance to nursing undergraduate and graduate students who are Hispanics or members of other underrepresented groups.

Eligibility   This program is open to students working on an associate, bachelor's, or master's degree at an accredited NLNAC or CCNE school of nursing. Applicants must be members of a group underrepresented in nursing (Hispanics, African Americans, American Indians, Asians, and males). Undergraduates must have earned a passing grade in all nursing courses taken to date and have a GPA of 2.85 or higher. Graduate students must have completed at least 12 semester hours of graduate work and have a GPA of 3.0 or higher. All applicants must be willing to 1) act as a spokesperson to other student groups on the value of the scholarship to continuing their nursing education; and 2) be profiled in any media or marketing materials developed by the Illinois Nurses Foundation. Along with their application, they must submit a narrative of 250 to 500 words on how they, as nurses, plan to affect policy at either the state or national level that impacts on nursing or health care generally, or how they believe they will impact the nursing profession in general.

Financial Data   A stipend is awarded (amount not specified).

Duration   1 year.

Number awarded   1 or more each year.

Deadline   March of each year.

[799]
INDIANA CLEO FELLOWSHIPS

Indiana Supreme Court
Attn: Division of State Court Administration
30 South Meridian Street, Suite 500
Indianapolis, IN 46204
(317) 232-2542   Toll Free: (800) 452-9963
Fax: (317) 233-6586   E-mail: ashley.rozier@courts.in.gov
Web: www.in.gov/judiciary/cleo/2402.htm

Summary   To provide financial assistance to Hispanic and other minority or disadvantaged college seniors from any state interested in attending law school in Indiana.

Eligibility   This program is open to residents of Indiana who attend college in the state or attend college out of state and are recommended by the admissions officer at a law school in the state. Applicants must be minority, low income, first-generation college, or limited English proficiency college seniors who have applied to an Indiana law school. Selected applicants are invited to participate in the Indiana Conference for Legal Education Opportunity (Indiana CLEO) Summer Institute, held at a law school in the state. Admission to that program is based on GPA, LSAT scores, 3 letters of recommendation, a resume, a personal statement, and financial need. Students who successfully complete the Institute and are admitted to an Indiana law school receive these fellowships.

Financial Data   All expenses for the Indiana CLEO Summer Institute are paid. The fellowship stipend is $9,000 per year.

Duration   The Indiana CLEO Summer Institute lasts 6 weeks. Fellowships are for 1 year and may be renewed up to 2 additional years.

Additional data   The first Summer Institute was held in 1997.

Number awarded   30 students are invited to participate in the summer institute; the number of those selected to receive a fellowship varies each year.

Deadline   February of each year.

[800]
INTEL FOUNDATION GRADUATE SCHOLARSHIPS

Great Minds in STEM
Attn: HENAAC Scholars Program
602 Monterey Pass Road
Monterey Park, CA 91754
(323) 262-0997   Fax: (323) 262-0946
E-mail: scholars@greatmindsinstem.org
Web: www.greatmindsinstem.org

Summary   To provide financial assistance to Hispanic graduate students in fields of interest to Intel.

Eligibility   This program is open to graduate students in computer science, computer engineering, electrical engineering, or other computer-related fields. Applicants must be of Hispanic origin and/or must significantly participate in and promote organizations and activities in the Hispanic community. They must have a GPA of 3.0 or higher. Along with their application, they must submit a 700-word essay on a topic that changes annually. Selection is based on leadership, academic achievements, and campus and community activities; financial need is not considered. U.S. citizenship or permanent resident status is required.

Financial Data   The stipend is $10,000.

Duration   1 year.

Additional data   The Hispanic Engineer National Achievement Awards Conference (HENAAC) was established in 1989 and initiated a scholarship program in 2000. In 2010, the sponsoring organization officially adopted its current name, but it continues to hold the annual HENAAC conference, at which the scholarships are presented. This program is sponsored by the Intel Foundation.

Number awarded   8 each year.

Deadline   April of each year.

[801]
INTELLECTUAL PROPERTY LAW SECTION WOMEN AND MINORITY SCHOLARSHIP

State Bar of Texas
Attn: Intellectual Property Law Section
c/o Bhaveeni D. Parmar, Scholarship Selection
   Committee
Law Office of Bhaveeni Parmar PLLC
4447 North Central Expressway, Suite 110-295
Dallas, Texas 75205
E-mail: bhaveeni@parmarlawoffice.com
Web: www.texasbariplaw.org

Summary To provide financial assistance to Hispanic and other minority students at law schools in Texas who plan to practice intellectual property law.

Eligibility This program is open to women and members of minority groups (Hispanics, African Americans, Asian Americans, and Native Americans) from any state who are currently enrolled at an ABA-accredited law school in Texas. Applicants must be planning to practice intellectual property law in Texas. Along with their application, they must submit a 2-page essay explaining why they plan to prepare for a career in intellectual property law in Texas, any qualifications they believe are relevant for their consideration for this scholarship, and (optionally) any issues of financial need they wish to have considered.

Financial Data The stipend is $5,000.

Duration 1 year.

Number awarded 2 each year: 1 to a women and 1 to a minority.

Deadline May of each year.

[802]
INTERFAITH SPIRITUALITY SCHOLARSHIP

Unitarian Universalist Association
Attn: Ministerial Credentialing Office
24 Farnsworth Street
Boston, MA 02210-1409
(617) 948-6403   Fax: (617) 742-2875
E-mail: mcoadministrator@uua.org
Web: www.uua.org

Summary To provide financial assistance to seminary students, especially Hispanics and other persons of color, who are preparing for the Unitarian Universalist (UU) ministry and are interested in interfaith understanding.

Eligibility This program is open to seminary students who are enrolled full or at least half time in a UU ministerial training program with candidate status. Applicants must have demonstrated 1) an interest in and desire to integrate interfaith understanding into their ministry; and 2) a commitment to guiding others on their own spiritual path. They must be citizens of the United States or Canada. Priority is given first to those who have demonstrated outstanding ministerial ability and secondarily to students with the greatest financial need (especially persons of color).

Financial Data The stipend ranges from $1,000 to $15,000 per year.

Duration 1 year.

Number awarded 1 each year.

Deadline April of each year.

[803]
INTERMOUNTAIN SECTION AWWA DIVERSITY SCHOLARSHIP

American Water Works Association-Intermountain
  Section
Attn: Member Services Coordinator
3430 East Danish Road
Sandy, UT 84093
(801) 712-1619, ext. 2   Fax: (801) 487-6699
E-mail: nicoleb@ims-awwa.org
Web: ims-awwa.site-ym.com/group/StudentPO

Summary To provide financial assistance to Hispanic and other minority undergraduate and graduate students working on a degree in the field of water quality, supply, and treatment at a university in the Intermountain West.

Eligibility This program is open to 1) women; and 2) students who identify as Hispanic or Latino, Black or African American, Native Hawaiian or other Pacific Islander, Asian, or American Indian or Alaska Native. Applicants must be entering or enrolled in an undergraduate or graduate program at a college or university in the Intermountain West (defined to include all or portions of Arizona, Colorado, Idaho, Montana, Nevada, New Mexico, Utah, or Wyoming) that relates to water quality, supply, or treatment. Along with their application, they must submit a 2-page essay on their academic interests and career goals and how those relate to water quality, supply, or treatment. Selection is based on that essay, letters of recommendation, and potential to contribute to the field of water quality, supply, and treatment in the Intermountain West.

Financial Data The stipend is $1,000. The winner also receives a 1-year student membership in the Intermountain Section of the American Water Works Association (AWWA).

Duration 1 year; nonrenewable.

Number awarded 1 each year.

Deadline November of each year.

[804]
INTERNATIONAL SECURITY AND COOPERATION PREDOCTORAL FELLOWSHIPS

Stanford University
Center for International Security and Cooperation
Attn: Fellowships Coordinator
Encina Hall, Room C206-10
616 Serra Street
Stanford, CA 94305-6165
(650) 723-9625   Fax: (650) 724-5683
E-mail: CISACfellowship@stanford.edu
Web: cisac.fsi.stanford.edu/docs/cisac_fellowship_program

Summary To provide funding to doctoral students, especially Hispanics and other minorities, who are interested in working on a dissertation on international security problems at Stanford University's Center for International Security and Cooperation.

Eligibility This program is open to students currently enrolled in doctoral programs at academic institutions in the United States who would benefit from access to the facilities offered by the center. Applicants may be working in any discipline of the social sciences, humanities, natural sciences, law, or engineering that relates to international security problems. Relevant topics include nuclear weapons policy and nonproliferation; nuclear energy; cybersecurity, cyberwarfare, and the future of the Internet; war and civil conflict; global governance, migration and transnational flows, from norms to criminal trafficking; biosecurity and global health; implications of geostrategic shifts; insurgency, terrorism, and homeland security; and consolidating peace after conflict. The sponsor welcomes applications from women, minorities, and citizens of all countries.

Financial Data The stipend ranges from $25,000 to $28,000. Medical insurance is available for those who do not have coverage.

Duration 9 to 11 months.

Additional data Fellows are expected to complete dissertation chapters or their dissertation during their fellowship. They should not plan to spend any time conducting research abroad or in other parts of the country.

Number awarded Varies each year; recently, 9 were awarded.

Deadline January of each year.

[805]
IRTS BROADCAST SALES ASSOCIATE PROGRAM

International Radio and Television Society Foundation
Attn: Director, Special Projects
1697 Broadway, 10th Floor
New York, NY 10019
(212) 867-6650   Toll Free: (888) 627-1266
Fax: (212) 867-6653   E-mail: submit@irts.org
Web: 406.144.myftpupload.com

Summary To provide summer work experience to Hispanic and other minority graduate students interested in working in broadcast sales in the New York City area.

Eligibility This program is open to graduating college seniors and students already enrolled in graduate school who are members of a minority (Hispanic/Latino, African American, Asian/Pacific Islander, American Indian/Alaskan Native) group. Applicants must be interested in working during the summer in a sales training program traditionally reserved for actual station group employees. They must be a communications major or have demonstrated a strong interest in the field through extracurricular activities or other practical experience, but they are not required to have experience in broadcast sales.

Financial Data Travel, housing, and a living allowance are provided.

Duration 9 weeks during the summer.

Additional data The program consists of a 1-week orientation to the media and entertainment business, followed by an 8-week internship experience in the sales division of a network stations group.

Number awarded Varies each year.

Deadline February of each year.

[806]
IRTS SUMMER FELLOWSHIP PROGRAM

International Radio and Television Society Foundation
Attn: Director, Special Projects
420 Lexington Avenue, Suite 1601
New York, NY 10170-0101
(212) 867-6650   Toll Free: (888) 627-1266
Fax: (212) 867-6653   E-mail: apply@irts.org
Web: irtsfoundation.org/summer-fellowship-program

Summary To provide summer work experience to upper-division and graduate students, especially minorities and other Hispanics, who are interested in working during the summer in broadcasting and related fields in the New York City area.

Eligibility This program is open to juniors, seniors, and graduate students at 4-year colleges and universities. Applicants must either be a communications major or have demonstrated a strong interest in the field through extracurricular activities or other practical experience. Minority (Hispanic/Latino, African American, Asian/Pacific Islander, American Indian/Alaskan Native) students are especially encouraged to apply.

Financial Data Travel, housing, and a living allowance are provided.

Duration 9 weeks during the summer.

Additional data The first week consists of a comprehensive orientation to broadcasting, cable, advertising, and new media. Then, the participants are assigned an 8-week fellowship. This full-time "real world" experience in a New York-based corporation allows them to reinforce or redefine specific career goals before settling into a permanent job. Fellows have worked at all 4 major networks, at local New York City radio and television stations, and at national rep firms, advertising agencies, and cable operations. This program includes fellowships reserved for students at designated universities (University of Pennsylvania, Brooklyn College, City College of New York, College of the Holy Cross) and the following named awards: the Thomas S. Murphy Fellowship (sponsored by ABC National Television Sales), the Helen Karas Memorial Fellowship, the Mel Karmazin Fellowship, the Neil Postman Memorial Summer Fellowship, the Ari Bluman Memorial Summer Fellowship (sponsored by Group M), the Thom Casadonte Memorial Fellowship (sponsored by Bloomberg), the Joanne Mercado Memorial Fellowship (sponsored by Nielsen), the Donald V. West Fellowship (sponsored by the Library of American Broadcasting Foundation), the Leslie Moonves Fellowship (sponsored by CBS Television Station Sales, and the Sumner M. Redstone Fellowship (sponsored by CBS Television Station Sales). Other sponsors include the National Academy of Television Arts & Sciences, Fox Networks, NBCUniversal, and Unilever.

Number awarded Varies; recently, 30 were awarded.

Deadline November of each year.

[807]
ISAAC J. "IKE" CRUMBLY MINORITIES IN ENERGY GRANT

American Association of Petroleum Geologists
    Foundation
Attn: Grants-in-Aid Program
1444 South Boulder Avenue
P.O. Box 979
Tulsa, OK 74101-0979
(918) 560-2644   Toll Free: (855) 302-2743
Fax: (918) 560-2642   E-mail: foundation@aapg.org
Web: foundation.aapg.org

Summary To provide funding to Hispanic and other minority graduate students who are interested in conducting research related to earth science aspects of the petroleum industry.

Eligibility This program is open to women and ethnic minorities (Hispanic, Black, Asian, or Native American, including American Indian, Eskimo, Hawaiian, or Samoan) who are working on a master's or doctoral degree. Applicants must be interested in conducting research related to the search for and development of petroleum and energy-minerals resources and to related environmental geology issues. Selection is based on student's academic and employment history (10 points), scientific merit of proposal (30 points), suitability to program objectives (30 points), financial merit of proposal (20 points), and endorsement by faculty or department adviser (10 points).

Financial Data Grants range from $500 to $3,000. Funds are to be applied to research-related expenses (e.g., a summer of field work). They may not be used to purchase capital equipment or to pay salaries, tuition, room, or board.

Duration 1 year. Doctoral candidates may receive a 1-year renewal.

Number awarded 1 each year.

Deadline February of each year.

[808]
JACK L. STEPHENS GRADUATE SCHOLARSHIP

Conference of Minority Transportation Officials-Fort Lauderdale Chapter
Attn: Scholarship Committee
Victor Garcia, South Florida Regional Transportation Authority
801 N.W. 33rd Street
Pompano Beach, FL 33064
(954) 788-7925   Toll Free: (800) GO-SFRTA
Fax: (854) 788-7961   TDD: (800) 273-7545
E-mail: victorgarcia@comtoftlauderdale.org
Web: www.comtoftlauderdale.org/scholarship-program

Summary To provide financial assistance to Hispanic and other minority students working on a transportation-related graduate degree at a college in Florida.

Eligibility This program is open to minority students currently enrolled at accredited colleges and universities in Florida. Applicants must be working on a master's or doctoral degree in a transportation-related field and have a GPA of 2.5 or higher. They must be U.S. citizens or permanent residents. Along with their application, they must submit an essay of 500 to 750 words on their transportation-related career goals and life aspirations. Financial need is not considered in the selection process.

Financial Data The stipend is $2,500.

Duration 1 year; nonrenewable.

Additional data This program began in 2015.

Number awarded 1 each year.

Deadline April of each year.

[809]
JACOB WILLIAMS SCHOLARSHIP

United Methodist Foundation of Indiana
8401 Fishers Center Drive
Fishers, IN 46038-2318
(317) 788-7879   Toll Free: (877) 391-8811
Fax: (317) 788-0089
E-mail: foundation@UMFIndiana.org
Web: www.umfindiana.org/endowments

Summary To provide financial assistance to Hispanic and other ethnic minority ministerial students from Indiana who are attending a seminary in any state that is approved by the United Methodist Church (UMC).

Eligibility This program is open to members of ethnic minority groups who are candidates for ordination and certified by a District Committee of the Indiana Conference of the UMC. Applicants must be enrolled full time at an approved seminary in any state. They must be seeking ordination as a deacon or elder. Along with their application, they must sub-

mit documentation of financial need and a statement of their vocational goals.

Financial Data Stipends are awarded at the rate of $100 per credit hour (per semester) and $200 per projected decade of service remaining (per semester).

Duration 1 year; may be renewed.

Number awarded 1 or more each year.

Deadline May of each year for fall semester; October of each year for spring semester.

[810]
JAMES B. MORRIS SCHOLARSHIPS

James B. Morris Scholarship Fund
Attn: Scholarship Selection Committee
P.O. Box 12145
Des Moines, IA 50312
(515) 864-0922
Web: www.morrisscholarship.org

Summary To provide financial assistance to Hispanic and other minority undergraduate, graduate, and law students from Iowa.

Eligibility This program is open to minority students (Hispanics, African Americans, Asian/Pacific Islanders, or Native Americans) who are interested in working on an undergraduate or graduate degree. Applicants must be either Iowa residents attending a college or university anywhere in the United States or non-Iowa residents who are attending a college or university in Iowa. Along with their application, they must submit an essay of 250 to 500 words on why they are applying for this scholarship, activities or organizations in which they are involved, and their future plans. Selection is based on the essay, academic achievement (GPA of 2.5 or higher), community service, and financial need. U.S. citizenship is required.

Financial Data The stipend ranges from $1,000 to $2,500 per year.

Duration 1 year; may be renewed.

Additional data This fund was established in 1978 in honor of the J.B. Morris family, who founded the Iowa branch of the National Association for the Advancement of Colored People and published the *Iowa Bystander* newspaper. The program includes the Ann Chapman Scholarships, the Vincent Chapman, Sr. Scholarships, the Catherine Williams Scholarships, and the Brittany Hall Memorial Scholarships. Support for additional scholarships is provided by EMC Insurance Group and Wells Fargo Bank.

Number awarded Varies each year; recently, 22 were awarded.

Deadline February of each year.

[811]
JAMES CARLSON MEMORIAL SCHOLARSHIP

Oregon Office of Student Access and Completion
Attn: Scholarship Processing Coordinator
1500 Valley River Drive, Suite 100
Eugene, OR 97401-2146
(541) 687-7422   Toll Free: (800) 452-8807, ext. 7422
Fax: (541) 687-7414   TDD: (800) 735-2900
E-mail: cheryl.a.connolly@state.or.us
Web: app.oregonstudentaid.gov/Catalog/Default.aspx

Summary To provide financial assistance to Oregon residents, especially Hispanics and members of other diverse groups, who are majoring in education on the undergraduate or graduate school level at a school in any state.

Eligibility This program is open to residents of Oregon who are U.S. citizens or permanent residents and enrolled at a college or university in any state. Applicants must be either 1) college seniors or fifth-year students majoring in elementary or secondary education; or 2) graduate students working on an elementary or secondary certificate. Full-time enrollment and financial need are required. Priority is given to 1) students who come from diverse environments and submit an essay of 250 to 350 words on their experience living or working in diverse environments; 2) dependents of members of the Oregon Education Association; and 3) applicants committed to teaching autistic children.

Financial Data Stipends for scholarships offered by the Oregon Office of Student Access and Completion (OSAC) range from $1,000 to $10,000 but recently averaged $4,368.

Duration 1 year; nonrenewable.

Additional data This program is administered by the OSAC with funds provided by the Oregon Community Foundation.

Number awarded Varies each year; recently, 3 were awarded.

Deadline February of each year.

[812]
JAMES E. WEBB INTERNSHIPS

Smithsonian Institution
Attn: Office of Fellowships and Internships
470 L'Enfant Plaza, Suite 7102
P.O. Box 37012, MRC 902
Washington, DC 20013-7012
(202) 633-7070   Fax: (202) 633-7069
E-mail: siofi@si.edu
Web: www.smithsonianofi.com

Summary To provide internship opportunities throughout the Smithsonian Institution to Hispanic and other minority upper-division and graduate students in business or public administration.

Eligibility This program is open to minorities who are juniors, seniors, or graduate students majoring in areas of business or public administration (finance, human resource management, accounting, or general business administration). Applicants must have a GPA of 3.0 or higher. They must seek placement in offices, museums, and research institutes within the Smithsonian Institution.

Financial Data Interns receive a stipend of $600 per week and a travel allowance.

Duration 10 weeks during the summer, fall, or spring.

Number awarded Varies each year; recently, 8 of these internships were awarded.

Deadline January of each year for summer or fall; September of each year for spring.

[813]
JAMES ECHOLS SCHOLARSHIP

California Association for Health, Physical Education,
  Recreation and Dance
Attn: Chair, Scholarship Committee
1501 El Camino Avenue, Suite 3
Sacramento, CA 95815-2748
(916) 922-3596   Toll Free: (800) 499-3596 (within CA)
Fax: (916) 922-0133   E-mail: reception@cahperd.org
Web: www.cahperd.org

Summary To provide financial assistance to Hispanic and other minority student members of the California Association for Health, Physical Education, Recreation and Dance.

Eligibility This program is open to California residents who have been members of the association for at least 60 days and are attending a 2- or 4-year college or university in the state. Applicants must be undergraduate or graduate students working on a degree in health education, physical education, recreation, or dance and have completed at least 60 semester hours of college work. Selection is based on scholastic proficiency (a GPA of 3.0 or higher); leadership ability in school, community, and professional activities; and personal qualities of enthusiasm, cooperativeness, responsibility, initiative, and ability to work with others. This scholarship is awarded to the highest-ranked minority (Asian, African American, Latino, or Native American) applicant.

Financial Data The stipend is $1,000.

Duration 1 year.

Number awarded 1 each year.

Deadline November of each year.

[814]
JAMES W. STOUDT SCHOLARSHIPS

Pennsylvania Bar Association
Attn: Foundation
100 South Street
P.O. Box 186
Harrisburg, PA 17108-0186
(717) 213-2501   Toll Free: (888) 238-3036
Fax: (717) 213-2548   E-mail: info@pabarfoundation.org
Web: www.pabarfoundation.org

Summary To provide financial assistance to residents of Pennsylvania, especially Hispanics and other underrepresented minorities, who are attending law school in the state.

Eligibility This program is open to residents of Pennsylvania who are currently enrolled in the second year (or third year of a 4- or 5-year law school program) at a law school in the state. Applicants must be members of the Pennsylvania Bar Association student division. Some of the awards are reserved for students who are members of groups historically underrepresented in the legal profession (Hispanic Americans, African Americans, and Native Americans). Along with their application, they must submit a 500-word essay explaining how they plan to demonstrate their potential for making a contribution to society and the legal profession. Selection is based on that essay, academic achievement, and financial need.

Financial Data The stipend is $3,000.

Duration 1 year.

Number awarded　3 each year, of which 2 are reserved for underrepresented minority students.

Deadline　November of each year.

[815]
JANE C. WALDBAUM ARCHAEOLOGICAL FIELD SCHOOL SCHOLARSHIP

Archaeological Institute of America
c/o Boston University
656 Beacon Street, Sixth Floor
Boston, MA 02215-2006
(617) 358-4184　　　　　　　　Fax: (617) 353-6550
E-mail: fellowships@aia.bu.edu
Web: www.archaeological.org/grants/708

Summary　To provide funding to upper-division and graduate students, especially Hispanics and other minorities, who are interested in participating in an archaeological field project in the United States or any other country.

Eligibility　This program is open to junior and senior undergraduates and first-year graduate students who are currently enrolled at a college or university in the United States or Canada. Minority and disadvantaged students are encouraged to apply. Applicants must be interested in participating in an archaeological excavation or survey project in any country. They may not have previously participated in an archaeological excavation. Students majoring in archaeology or related disciplines are especially encouraged to apply.

Financial Data　The grant is $1,000.

Duration　At least 1 month during the summer.

Additional data　These scholarships were first awarded in 2007.

Number awarded　Varies each year; recently, 15 were awarded.

Deadline　February of each year.

[816]
JEANNE SPURLOCK RESEARCH FELLOWSHIP IN SUBSTANCE ABUSE AND ADDICTION FOR MINORITY MEDICAL STUDENTS

American Academy of Child and Adolescent Psychiatry
Attn: Department of Research, Training, and Education
3615 Wisconsin Avenue, N.W.
Washington, DC 20016-3007
(202) 587-9663　　　　　　　　Fax: (202) 966-5894
E-mail: training@aacap.org
Web: www.aacap.org

Summary　To provide funding to Hispanic and other minority medical students who are interested in working during the summer on the topics of drug abuse and addiction with a child and adolescent psychiatrist researcher-mentor.

Eligibility　This program is open to Hispanic, African American, Asian American, Native American, Alaska Native, Mexican American, and Pacific Islander students in accredited U.S. medical schools. Applicants must present a plan for a program of research training in drug abuse and addiction that involves significant contact with a mentor who is an experienced child and adolescent psychiatrist researcher. The plan should include program planning discussions; instruction in research planning and implementation; regular meetings with the mentor, laboratory director, and research group; and assigned readings. The mentor must be a member of the

American Academy of Child and Adolescent Psychiatry (AACAP). Research assignments may include responsibility for part of the observation or evaluation, developing specific aspects of the research mechanisms, conducting interviews or tests, using rating scales, and psychological or cognitive testing of subjects. The training plan also should include discussion of ethical issues in research, such as protocol development, informed consent, collection and storage of raw data, safeguarding data, bias in analyzing data, plagiarism, protection of patients, and ethical treatment of animals. U.S. citizenship or permanent resident status is required.

Financial Data　The stipend is $4,000. Fellows also receive reimbursement of travel expenses to attend the annual meeting of the American Academy of Child and Adolescent Psychiatry.

Duration　12 weeks during the summer.

Additional data　Upon completion of the training program, the student is required to submit a brief paper summarizing the research experience. The fellowship pays expenses for the fellow to attend the academy's annual meeting and present this paper. This program is co-sponsored by the National Institute on Drug Abuse.

Number awarded　Up to 5 each year.

Deadline　February of each year.

[817]
JIM MCKAY SCHOLARSHIP PROGRAM

National Collegiate Athletic Association
Attn: Jim McKay Scholarship Program Staff Liaison
700 West Washington Street
P.O. Box 6222
Indianapolis, IN 46206-6222
(317) 917-6683　　　　　　　　Fax: (317) 917-6888
E-mail: lthomas@ncaa.org
Web: www.ncaa.org/jim-mckay-scholarship-program

Summary　To provide financial assistance to student-athletes, especially Hispanics and other minorities, who are interested in attending graduate school to prepare for a career in sports communications.

Eligibility　This program is open to college seniors planning to enroll full time in a graduate degree program and to students already enrolled full time in graduate study at an institution that is a member of the National Collegiate Athletic Association (NCAA). Applicants must have competed in intercollegiate athletics as a member of a varsity team at an NCAA member institution and have an overall undergraduate cumulative GPA of 3.5 or higher. They must be preparing for a career in the sports communications industry. Women and minorities are especially encouraged to apply. Neither financial need nor U.S. citizenship are required. Nominations must be submitted by the faculty athletics representative or chief academic officer at the institution in which the student is or was an undergraduate.

Financial Data　The stipend is $10,000.

Duration　1 year; nonrenewable.

Additional data　This program began in 2008.

Number awarded　2 each year: 1 female and 1 male.

Deadline　January of each year.

[818]
JOANN JETER MEMORIAL DIVERSITY SCHOLARSHIP

Associates Foundation
Attn: Claudia Perot, Scholarship Committee Chair
JCD 6
P.O. Box 3621
Portland, OR 97208-3621
(503) 230-3754
Web: www.theassociatesonline.org

Summary To provide financial assistance to students who are Hispanics or reflect other elements of diversity and are interested in working on an undergraduate or graduate degree in any field.

Eligibility This program is open to students who are enrolled or planning to enroll as a full-time undergraduate or graduate student at an accredited 4-year college or university or a full-time student at a 2-year college enrolled in a program leading to an academic degree. Applicants must be from a diverse background, including first-generation college student, cultural and/or ethnic minority background, low-income, or other clearly articulated aspects of diversity as presented in an essay.

Financial Data The stipend ranges from $500 to $1,000.

Duration 1 year.

Number awarded Varies each year; recently, 3 were awarded.

Deadline April of each year.

[819]
JOHN A. MAYES EDAC SCHOLARSHIP

National Athletic Trainers' Association
Attn: Ethnic Diversity Advisory Committee
1620 Valwood Parkway, Suite 115
Carrollton, TX 75006
(214) 637-6282   Toll Free: (800) 879-6282
Fax: (214) 637-2206
Web: www.nata.org

Summary To provide financial aid to Hispanics and other ethnically diverse graduate students who are preparing for a career as an athletic trainer.

Eligibility This program is open to members of ethnically diverse groups who have been accepted into an entry-level master's athletic training degree program or into a doctoral-level athletic training and/or sports medicine degree program. Applicants must be sponsored by a certified athletic trainer who is a member of the National Athletic Trainers' Association (NATA). They must have a cumulative undergraduate GPA of 3.2 or higher. First priority is given to a student working on an entry-level athletic training master's degree; second priority is given to a student entering the second year of an athletic training master's degree program; third priority is given to a student working on a doctoral degree in athletic training or sports medicine. Special consideration is given to applicants who have been members of NATA for at least 2 years.

Financial Data The stipend is $2,300.

Duration 1 year.

Additional data This program began in 2009.

Number awarded 1 each year.

Deadline February of each year.

[820]
JOHN AND MURIEL LANDIS SCHOLARSHIPS

American Nuclear Society
Attn: Scholarship Coordinator
555 North Kensington Avenue
La Grange Park, IL 60526-5535
(708) 352-6611   Toll Free: (800) 323-3044
Fax: (708) 352-0499   E-mail: outreach@ans.org
Web: committees.ans.org/need/apply.html

Summary To provide financial assistance to undergraduate or graduate students, especially Hispanics and other minorities, who are interested in preparing for a career in nuclear-related fields and can demonstrate financial need.

Eligibility This program is open to undergraduate and graduate students at colleges or universities located in the United States who are preparing for, or planning to prepare for, a career in nuclear science, nuclear engineering, or a nuclear-related field. Qualified high school seniors are also eligible. Applicants must have greater than average financial need and have experienced circumstances that render them disadvantaged. Along with their application, they must submit an essay on their academic and professional goals, experiences that have affected those goals, etc. Selection is based on that essay, academic achievement, letters of recommendation, and financial need. Women and members of minority groups are especially urged to apply. U.S. citizenship is not required.

Financial Data The stipend is $5,000, to be used to cover tuition, books, fees, room, and board.

Duration 1 year; nonrenewable.

Number awarded Up to 9 each year.

Deadline January of each year.

[821]
JOHN DEERE SCHOLARSHIP OF THE SOCIETY OF HISPANIC PROFESSIONAL ENGINEERS

Society of Hispanic Professional Engineers
Attn: Scholarships
13181 Crossroads Parkway North, Suite 450
City of Industry, CA 91715
(323) 725-3970, ext. 108   Fax: (323) 725-0316
E-mail: scholarships@shpe.org
Web: shpe.awardspring.com

Summary To provide financial assistance to Hispanic undergraduate and graduate students who are working on a degree in specified fields of science, technology, engineering, or matheamtics (STEM).

Eligibility This program is open to U.S. citizens and permanent residents of Hispanic descent who are enrolled full time at a college or university in the United States or Puerto Rico. Applicants must be sophomores, juniors, or first-year graduate students working on a bachelor's or master's degree in engineering (aerospace, agricultural, computer, electrical, environmental, manufacturing, materials, mechanical, systems, or welding), computer science, management information systems, or technology management. They must be members of the Society of Hispanic Professional Engineers (SHPE) and have a GPA of 3.0 or higher. Selection is based on academic standing and financial need.

Financial Data The stipend is $2,000.

Duration 1 year.

Additional data This program is sponsored by John Deere.

Number awarded 1 or more each year.

Deadline July of each year.

[822]
JOHN HOPE FRANKLIN DISSERTATION FELLOWSHIP

American Philosophical Society
Attn: Director of Grants and Fellowships
104 South Fifth Street
Philadelphia, PA 19106-3387
(215) 440-3429   Fax: (215) 440-3436
E-mail: LMusumeci@amphilsoc.org
Web: amphilsoc.org/grants/johnhopefranklin

Summary To provide funding to Hispanic and other under-represented minority graduate students conducting research for a doctoral dissertation.

Eligibility This program is open to Hispanic American, African American, and Native American graduate students working on a degree at a Ph.D. granting institution in the United States. Other talented students who have a demonstrated commitment to eradicating racial disparities and enlarging minority representation in academia are also eligible. Applicants must have completed all course work and examinations preliminary to the doctoral dissertation and be able to devote full-time effort, with no teaching obligations, to researching or writing their dissertation. The proposed research should relate to a topic in which the holdings of the Library of the American Philosophical Society (APS) are particularly strong: quantum mechanics, nuclear physics, computer development, the history of genetics and eugenics, the history of medicine, Early American political and cultural history, natural history in the 18th and 19th centuries, the development of cultural anthropology, or American Indian culture and linguistics.

Financial Data The grant is $25,000; an additional grant of $5,000 is provided to support the cost of residency in Philadelphia.

Duration 12 months, to begin at the discretion of the grantee.

Additional data This program began in 2005. Recipients are expected to spend a significant amount of time in residence at the APS Library.

Number awarded 1 each year.

Deadline March of each year.

[823]
JOHN MCLENDON MEMORIAL MINORITY POSTGRADUATE SCHOLARSHIP AWARD

National Association of Collegiate Directors of Athletics
Attn: NACDA Foundation
24651 Detroit Road
Westlake, OH 44145
(440) 788-7474   Fax: (440) 892-4007
E-mail: knewman@nacda.com
Web: www.nacda.com/mclendon/scholarship.html

Summary To provide financial assistance to Hispanic and other minority college seniors who are interested in working on a graduate degree in athletics administration.

Eligibility This program is open to minority college students who are seniors, are attending school on a full-time basis, have a GPA of 3.2 or higher, intend to attend graduate school to earn a degree in athletics administration, and are involved in college or community activities. Also eligible are college graduates who have at least 2 years' experience in an athletics administration position. Candidates must be nominated by an official of a member institution of the National Association of Collegiate Directors of Athletics (NACDA) or (for college graduates) a supervisor.

Financial Data The stipend is $10,000.

Duration 1 year.

Additional data Recipients must maintain full-time status during the senior year to retain their eligibility. They must attend NACDA-member institutions.

Number awarded 5 each year.

Deadline Nominations must be submitted by April of each year.

[824]
JOHN STANFORD MEMORIAL WLMA SCHOLARSHIP

Washington Library Association-School Library Division
c/o Susan Kaphammer, Scholarship Chair
521 North 24th Avenue
Yakima, WA 98902
(509) 972-5999   E-mail: scholarships@wlma.org
Web: www.wla.org/school-scholarships

Summary To provide financial assistance to Hispanic and other ethnic minorities in Washington who are interested in attending a school in any state to prepare for a library media career.

Eligibility This program is open to residents of Washington who are working toward a library media endorsement or graduate degree in the field at a school in any state. Applicants must be members of an ethnic minority group. They must be working or planning to work in a school library. Along with their application, they must submit a 3-page letter that includes a description of themselves and their achievements to date, their interest and work in the library field, their personal and professional activities, their goals and plans for further education and professional development, how they expect the studies funded by this award to impact their professional practice and contributions to the Washington school library community, and their financial need.

Financial Data The stipend is $1,000.

Duration 1 year.

Additional data The School Library Division of the Washington Library Association was formerly the Washington Library Media Association (WLMA).

Number awarded 1 each year.

Deadline May of each year.

[825]
JOHNSON & JOHNSON/AACN MINORITY NURSE FACULTY SCHOLARS PROGRAM

American Association of Colleges of Nursing
One Dupont Circle, N.W., Suite 530
Washington, DC 20036
(202) 463-6930   Fax: (202) 785-8320
E-mail: scholarship@aacn.nche.edu
Web: www.aacn.nche.edu/students/scholarships/minority

Summary To provide fellowship/loans to Hispanic and other minority students who are working on a graduate degree in nursing to prepare for a career as a faculty member.

Eligibility This program is open to members of racial and ethnic minority groups (Hispanic or Latino, Alaska Native, American Indian, Black or African American, Native Hawaiian or other Pacific Islander, or Asian American) who are enrolled full time at a school of nursing. Applicants must be working on 1) a doctoral nursing degree (e.g., Ph.D., D.N.P.); or 2) a clinically-focused master's degree in nursing (e.g., M.S.N., M.S.). They must commit to 1) serve in a teaching capacity at a nursing school for a minimum of 1 year for each year of support they receive; 2) provide 6-month progress reports to the American Association of Colleges of Nursing (AACN) throughout the entire funding process and during the payback period; 3) agree to work with an assigned mentor throughout the period of the scholarship grant; and 4) attend an annual leadership training conference to connect with their mentor, fellow scholars, and colleagues. Selection is based on ability to contribute to nursing education; leadership potential; development of goals reflecting education, research, and professional involvement; ability to work with a mentor/adviser throughout the award period; proposed research and/or practice projects that are significant and show commitment to improving nursing education and clinical nursing practice in the United States; proposed research and/or clinical education professional development plan that exhibits quality, feasibility, and innovativeness; and evidence of commitment to a career in nursing education and to recruiting, mentoring, and retaining other underrepresented minority nurses. Preference is given to students enrolled in doctoral nursing programs. Applicants must be U.S. citizens, permanent residents, refugees, or qualified immigrants.

Financial Data The stipend is $18,000 per year. The award includes $1,500 that is held in escrow to cover the costs for the recipient to attend the leadership training conference. Recipients are required to sign a letter of commitment that they will provide 1 year of service in a teaching capacity at a nursing school in the United States for each year of support received; if they fail to complete that service requirement, they must repay all funds received.

Duration 1 year; may be renewed 1 additional year.

Additional data This program, established in 2007, is sponsored by the Johnson & Johnson Campaign for Nursing's Future.

Number awarded 5 each year.

Deadline April of each year.

[826]
JOSE MARTI SCHOLARSHIP CHALLENGE GRANT FUND

Florida Department of Education
Attn: Office of Student Financial Assistance
State Scholarship and Grant Programs
325 West Gaines Street, Suite 1314
Tallahassee, FL 32399-0400
(850) 410-5160   Toll Free: (888) 827-2004
Fax: (850) 487-1809   E-mail: osfa@fldoe.org
Web: www.floridastudentfinancialaid.org

Summary To provide financial assistance to Hispanic American high school seniors and graduate students in Florida.

Eligibility This program is open to Florida residents of Spanish culture who were born in, or whose natural parent was born in, Mexico or a Hispanic country of the Caribbean, Central America, or South America. Applicants must be citizens or eligible noncitizens of the United States, be enrolled or planning to enroll as full-time undergraduate or graduate students at an eligible postsecondary school in Florida, be able to demonstrate financial need as determined by a nationally-recognized needs analysis service, and have earned a cumulative GPA of 3.0 or higher in high school or, if a graduate school applicant, in undergraduate course work.

Financial Data The maximum grant is $2,000 per academic year. Available funds are contingent upon matching contributions from private sources.

Duration 1 year; may be renewed if the student maintains full-time enrollment and a GPA of 3.0 or higher and continues to demonstrate financial need.

Number awarded Varies each year; recently, this program awarded 13 new and 26 renewal grants.

Deadline March of each year.

[827]
JOSEPHINE AND BENJAMIN WEBBER TRUST SCHOLARSHIPS

Arizona Association of Family and Consumer Sciences
Attn: Webber Trusts Committee
Julie Villaverde, Committee Chair
University of Arizona
Financial Services Office
Tucson, AZ 85719-0521
(502) 626-3094   Fax: (502) 621-7078
E-mail: webbertrusts@gmail.com
Web: cals.arizona.edu/webbertrusts

Summary To provide financial assistance to Hispanic women from mining towns in Arizona who are interested in working on an undergraduate or graduate degree in a field related to family and consumer sciences at a school in the state.

Eligibility This program is open to Hispanic women who reside in the following Arizona mining towns: Ajo, Arizona City, Bisbee, Clifton, Douglas, Duncan, Globe, Green Valley, Hayden, Kingman, Kearny, Mammoth, Morenci, Prescott, Safford, Sahuarita, San Manuel, Seligman, Superior, or Winkelman. If too few female Hispanic residents of those towns apply, the program may be open to 1) non-Hispanic women who live in those towns; and/or 2) Hispanic women who currently live elsewhere in Arizona and whose parents or grandparents had lived or continue to live in those communities. Applicants must be enrolled or planning to enroll at a college or university in Arizona to work on an undergraduate or graduate degree. Eligible fields of study include those in the following categories: foods, nutrition, and/or dietetics; restaurant and food service management; culinary arts; family studies; interior design; family and consumer science education; dietetic education; early childhood education; or apparel and clothing. Financial need is considered in the selection process.

Financial Data Funding at public colleges and universities provides for payment of tuition and fees, books, educational supplies, housing, food, and transportation to and from campus. At private institutions, stipend amounts are equivalent to those at public schools.

Duration 1 year; may be renewed for a total of 8 semesters and 2 summers of undergraduate study or 4 semesters and 2 summers of graduate study.

Additional data This program began in 1980.

Number awarded Varies each year; recently, 5 were awarded.

Deadline March of each year.

[828]
JOSEPHINE FORMAN SCHOLARSHIP

Society of American Archivists
Attn: Chair, Awards Committee
17 North State Street, Suite 1425
Chicago, IL 60602-4061
(312) 606-0722   Toll Free: (866) 722-7858
Fax: (312) 606-0728   E-mail: info@archivists.org
Web: www2.archivists.org

Summary To provide financial assistance to Hispanic and other minority graduate students working on a degree in archival science.

Eligibility This program is open to members of minority groups (Hispanic/Latino, American Indian/Alaska Native, Asian, Black/African American, or Native Hawaiian/other Pacific Islander) currently enrolled in or accepted to a graduate program or a multi-course program in archival administration. The program must offer at least 3 courses in archival science and students may have completed no more than half of the credit requirements toward their graduate degree. Selection is based on potential for scholastic and personal achievement and commitment both to the archives profession and to advancing diversity concerns within it. U.S. citizenship or permanent resident status is required.

Financial Data The stipend is $10,000.

Duration 1 year.

Additional data Funding for this program, established in 2011, is provided by the General Commission on Archives and History of the United Methodist Church.

Number awarded 1 each year.

Deadline February of each year.

[829]
JOSIAH MACY JR. FOUNDATION SCHOLARSHIPS

National Medical Fellowships, Inc.
Attn: Scholarship Program
347 Fifth Avenue, Suite 510
New York, NY 10016
(212) 483-8880   Toll Free: (877) NMF-1DOC
Fax: (212) 483-8897 E-mail: scholarships@nmfonline.org
Web: www.nmfonline.org

Summary To provide financial assistance to Hispanic and other underrepresented minority medical students who demonstrate financial need.

Eligibility This program is open to Hispanics/Latinos, African Americans, Native Americans, Vietnamese, Cambodians, and Pacific Islanders who are entering their second or third year of medical school. They must be U.S. citizens or DACA students. Selection is based on leadership, commitment to serving medically underserved communities, and financial need.

Financial Data A stipend is awarded (amount not specified).

Duration 1 year.

Additional data This program is sponsored by the Josiah Macy Jr. Foundation.

Number awarded 4 each year.

Deadline September of each year.

[830]
JOURNEY TOWARD ORDAINED MINISTRY SCHOLARSHIP

United Methodist Church
Attn: General Board of Higher Education and Ministry
Office of Loans and Scholarships
1001 19th Avenue South
P.O. Box 340007
Nashville, TN 37203-0007
(615) 340-7344   Fax: (615) 340-7367
E-mail: umscholar@gbhem.org
Web: www.gbhem.org

Summary To provide financial assistance to Hispanic and other minority United Methodist students preparing for ministry at a Methodist-related institution.

Eligibility This program is open to members of racial or ethnic minority groups who are 30 years of age or younger and have been active, full members of a United Methodist Church for at least 2 years prior to applying. Applicants must be enrolled as full-time undergraduate or graduate students at a United Methodist-related institution in a program that leads to ordained ministry. Undergraduates must have a GPA of 2.85 or higher and graduate students must have a GPA of 3.0 or higher.

Financial Data The stipend is $5,000.

Duration 1 year.

Number awarded 1 or more each year.

Deadline February of each year.

[831]
JTBF SUMMER JUDICIAL INTERNSHIP PROGRAM

Just the Beginning Foundation
c/o Maria Shade Harris, Chief Operating Officer
233 South Wacker Drive, Suite 6600
Chicago, IL 60606
(312) 258-5930   E-mail: mharris@jtb.org
Web: www.jtb.org/about/our-programs

Summary To provide work experience to Hispanic or other minority or economically disadvantaged law students who plan to seek judicial clerkships after graduation.

Eligibility This program is open to students currently enrolled in their second or third year of law school who are members of minority or economically disadvantaged groups. Applicants must intend to work as a clerk in the federal or state judiciary upon graduation or within 5 years of graduation.

Financial Data Program externs receive a summer stipend in an amount determined by the sponsor.

Duration Students must perform at least 35 hours per week of work for at least 8 weeks during the summer.

Additional data This program began in 2005. Law students are matched with federal and state judges across the country who provide assignments to the participants that will enhance their legal research, writing, and analytical skills (e.g., drafting memoranda). Students are expected to complete at least 1 memorandum of law or other key legal document each semester of the externship. Course credit may be offered, but students may not receive academic credit and a stipend simultaneously.

Number awarded Varies each year.

Deadline January of each year.

[832]
JUDICIAL INTERN OPPORTUNITY PROGRAM

American Bar Association
Attn: Section of Litigation
321 North Clark Street
Chicago, IL 60654-7598
(312) 988-6348   Fax: (312) 988-6234
E-mail: Gail.Howard@americanbar.org
Web: www.americanbar.org

Summary To provide an opportunity for Hispanic and other minority or economically disadvantaged law students to gain experience as judicial interns in selected courts during the summer.

Eligibility This program is open to first- and second-year students at ABA-accredited law schools who are 1) members of racial or ethnic groups that are traditionally underrepresented in the legal profession (Hispanics/Latinos, African Americans, Asians, Native Americans); 2) students with disabilities; 3) students who are economically disadvantaged; or 4) students who identify themselves as lesbian, gay, bisexual, or transgender. Applicants must be interested in a judicial internship at courts in selected areas and communities. They may indicate a preference for the area in which they wish to work, but they may not specify a court or a judge. Along with their application, they must submit a current resume, a 10-page legal writing sample, and a 2-page statement of interest that outlines their qualifications for the internship. Screening interviews are conducted by staff of the American Bar Association, either in person or by telephone. Final interviews are conducted by the judges with whom the interns will work. Some spots are reserved for students with an interest in intellectual property law.

Financial Data The stipend is $2,000.

Duration 6 weeks during the summer.

Additional data Recently, internships were available in the following locations: Chicago along with surrounding cities and circuits throughout Illinois; Houston, Dallas, and the southern and eastern districts of Texas; Miami, Florida; Phoenix, Arizona; Los Angeles, California; New York City; Philadelphia, Pennsylvania; San Francisco, California; Seattle, Washington; and Washington, D.C. Some internships in Chicago, Los Angeles, Texas, and Washington, D.C. are reserved for students with an interest in intellectual property law.

Number awarded Varies each year; recently, 194 of these internships were awarded, including 31 at courts in Illinois, 17 in Dallas, 14 in Houston, 14 in Miami, 17 in Phoenix, 23 in Los Angeles, 30 in San Francisco, 10 in New York, 12 in Philadelphia, 8 in Seattle, and 18 in Washington, D.C.

Deadline January of each year.

[833]
JUDITH MCMANUS PRICE SCHOLARSHIPS

American Planning Association
Attn: Leadership Affairs Associate
205 North Michigan Avenue, Suite 1200
Chicago, IL 60601
(312) 431-9100   Fax: (312) 786-6700
E-mail: mgroh@planning.org
Web: www.planning.org/scholarships/apa

Summary To provide financial assistance to Hispanic and other underrepresented minority students enrolled in undergraduate or graduate degree programs at recognized planning schools.

Eligibility This program is open to undergraduate and graduate students in urban and regional planning who are women or members of the following minority groups: Hispanic American, African American, Native American, or female. Applicants must be citizens of the United States and able to document financial need. They must intend to work as practicing planners in the public sector. Along with their application, they must submit a 2-page personal and background statement describing how their education will be applied to career goals and why they chose planning as a career path. Selection is based (in order of importance), on: 1) commitment to planning as reflected in their personal statement and on their resume; 2) academic achievement and/or improvement during the past 2 years; 3) letters of recommendation; 4) financial need; and 5) professional presentation.

Financial Data Stipends range from $2,000 to $4,000 per year. The money may be applied to tuition and living expenses only. Payment is made to the recipient's university and divided by terms in the school year.

Duration 1 year; recipients may reapply.

Additional data This program began in 2002.

Number awarded Varies each year; recently, 3 were awarded.

Deadline April of each year.

[834]
JULIA E. MENDEZ/HPRA-NY SCHOLARSHIP PROGRAM

Hispanic Public Relations Association-New York Chapter
c/o Melissa Carrion, President
Cohn & Wolfe
200 Fifth Avenue
New York, NY 10010
(212) 798-9700   E-mail: info@ny.npra-usa.org
Web: www.hpra-usa.org

Summary To provide financial assistance to Hispanic undergraduate and graduate students from Connecticut, New Jersey, and New York who are attending college in those states and preparing for a career in public relations.

Eligibility This program is open to residents of Connecticut, New Jersey, and New York who are of Hispanic descent and enrolled as sophomores, juniors, or graduate students at a 4-year college or university in those states. Applicants must have a GPA of 2.7 or higher cumulatively and 3.0 or higher in their major subject. They must be majoring in public relations, communications, journalism, advertising, and/or marketing. Along with their application, they must submit a letter of recommendation, official university transcripts, a 1-page personal statement explaining their career and educational aspirations as well as their involvement in the Hispanic community, and a 1-page resume.

Financial Data   The stipend is $1,000.

Duration   1 year.

Additional data   This program began in 2013 and was given its current name in 2016. Recipients are invited to attend the sponsor's Premio Awards dinner in Los Angeles in October.

Number awarded   2 each year.

Deadline   June of each year.

[835]
JULIE CUNNINGHAM LEGACY SCHOLARSHIP

Conference of Minority Transportation Officials
Attn: National Scholarship Program
100 M Street, S.E., Suite 917
Washington, DC 20003
(202) 506-2917   E-mail: info@comto.org
Web: www.comto.org/page/scholarships

Summary   To provide financial assistance to Hispanic and other minority graduate students who are working on a degree in transportation to prepare for a leadership role in that industry.

Eligibility   This program is open to minorities who are working on a graduate degree with an interest in leadership in transportation. Applicants must have a GPA of 3.0 or higher. They must be able to demonstrate strong leadership skills, active commitment to community service and diversity, and a commitment to the Conference of Minority Transportation Officials (COMTO) on a local or national level. Along with their application they must submit a cover letter on their transportation-related career goals and life aspirations. Financial need is not considered in the selection process.

Financial Data   The stipend is $7,500. Funds are paid directly to the recipient's college or university.

Duration   1 year.

Number awarded   1 each year.

Deadline   April of each year.

[836]
KAISER PERMANENTE COLORADO DIVERSITY SCHOLARSHIP PROGRAM

Kaiser Permanente
Attn: Diversity Development Department
10065 East Harvard Avenue, Suite 400
Denver, CO 80231
Toll Free: (877) 457-4772
E-mail: co-diversitydevelopment@kp.org

Summary   To provide financial assistance to Colorado residents who are Latinos or come from other diverse backgrounds and are interested in working on an undergraduate or graduate degree in a health care field at a public college in the state.

Eligibility   This program is open to all residents of Colorado, including those who identify as 1 or more of the following: Latino, African American, Asian Pacific, Native American, lesbian, gay, bisexual, transgender, intersex, U.S. veteran, and/or a person with a disability. Applicants must be enrolled or planning to enroll full time at a publicly-funded college, university, or technical school in Colorado as 1) a graduating

high school senior with a GPA of 2.7 or higher; 2) a GED recipient with a GED score of 520 or higher; 3) an undergraduate student; or 4) a graduate or doctoral student. They must be preparing for a career in health care (e.g., athletic training, audiology, cardiovascular perfusion technology, clinical medical assisting, cytotechnology, dental assisting, dental hygiene, diagnostic medicine, dietetics, emergency medical technology, medicine, nursing, occupational therapy, pharmacy, phlebotomy, physical therapy, physician assistant, radiology, respiratory therapy, social work, sports medicine, surgical technology). Selection is based on academic achievement, character qualities, community outreach and volunteering, and financial need.

Financial Data   Stipends range from $1,400 to $2,600 per year.

Duration   1 year; may be renewed.

Number awarded   Varies each year; recently, 17 were awarded.

Deadline   March of each year.

[837]
KAY LONGCOPE SCHOLARSHIP AWARD

National Lesbian & Gay Journalists Association
2120 L Street, N.W., Suite 850
Washington, DC 20037
(202) 588-9888   Fax: (202) 588-1818
E-mail: info@nlgfa.org
Web: www.nlgja.org/resources/longcope

Summary   To provide financial assistance to Hispanic and other lesbian, gay, bisexual, and transgender (LGBT) undergraduate and graduate students of color who are interested in preparing for a career in journalism.

Eligibility   This program is open to LGBT students of color who are current or incoming undergraduate or graduate students at a college, university, or community college. Applicants must be planning a career in journalism and be committed to furthering the sponsoring organization's mission of fair and accurate coverage of the LGBT community. They must demonstrate an awareness of the issues facing the LGBT community and the importance of fair and accurate news coverage. For undergraduates, a declared major in journalism and/or communications is desirable but not required; non-journalism majors may demonstrate their commitment to a journalism career through work samples, internships, and work on a school news publication, online news service, or broadcast affiliate. Graduate students must be enrolled in a journalism program. Along with their application, they must submit a 1-page resume, 5 work samples, official transcripts, 3 letters of recommendation, and a 750-word news story on a designated subject involving the LGBT community. U.S. citizenship or permanent resident status is required. Selection is based on journalistic and scholastic ability.

Financial Data   The stipend is $3,000.

Duration   1 year.

Additional data   This program began in 2008.

Number awarded   1 each year.

Deadline   May of each year.

[838]
KCACTF LATINIDAD PLAYWRITING AWARD

John F. Kennedy Center for the Performing Arts
Education Department
Attn: Kennedy Center American College Theater Festival
2700 F Street, N.W.
Washington, DC 20566
(202) 416-8864   Fax: (202) 416-8860
E-mail: ghenry@kennedy-center.org
Web: web.kennedy-center.org

Summary To recognize and reward outstanding plays by Latino student playwrights.

Eligibility Latino students at any accredited junior or senior college in the United States are eligible to compete, provided their college agrees to participate in the Kennedy Center American College Theater Festival (KCACTF). Undergraduate students must be carrying at least 6 semester hours, graduate students must be enrolled in at least 3 semester hours, and continuing part-time students must be enrolled in a regular degree or certificate program. This award is presented to the best student-written play by a Latino.

Financial Data The prizes are $1,000 for first place and $500 for second place. Other benefits include appropriate membership in the Dramatists Guild and an all-expense paid professional development opportunity.

Duration The award is presented annually.

Additional data This award, first presented in 2000, is part of the Michael Kanin Playwriting Awards Program. The sponsoring college or university must pay a registration fee of $275 for each production.

Number awarded 2 each year.

Deadline November of each year.

[839]
KENTUCKY LIBRARY ASSOCIATION SCHOLARSHIP FOR MINORITY STUDENTS

Kentucky Library Association
c/o Executive Director
5932 Timber Ridge Drive, Suite 101
Prospect, KY 40059
(502) 223-5322   Fax: (502) 223-4937
E-mail: info@kylibasn.org
Web: www.klaonline.org/scholarships965.cfm

Summary To provide financial assistance to Hispanics and members of other minority groups who are residents of Kentucky or attending school there and are working on an undergraduate or graduate degree in library science.

Eligibility This program is open to members of minority groups (defined as Hispanic, American Indian, Alaskan Native, Black, Pacific Islander, or other ethnic group) who are entering or continuing at a graduate library school accredited by the American Library Association (ALA) or an undergraduate library program accredited by the National Council for Teacher Education (NCATE). Applicants must be residents of Kentucky or a student in a library program in the state. Along with their application, they must submit a statement of their career objectives, why they have chosen librarianship as a career, and their reasons for applying for this scholarship. Selection is based on that statement, cumulative undergraduate and graduate GPA (if applicable), academic merit and

potential, and letters of recommendation. U.S. citizenship or permanent resident status is required.

Financial Data The stipend is $1,000.

Duration 1 year; nonrenewable.

Number awarded 1 or more each year.

Deadline June of each year.

[840]
KENTUCKY MINORITY EDUCATOR RECRUITMENT AND RETENTION SCHOLARSHIPS

Kentucky Department of Education
Attn: Office of Next-Generation Learners
500 Mero Street, 19th Floor
Frankfort, KY 40601
(502) 564-1479   Fax: (502) 564-4007
TDD: (502) 564-4970
E-mail: jennifer.baker@education.ky.gov
Web: www.education.ky.gov

Summary To provide forgivable loans to Hispanic and other minority undergraduate and graduate students enrolled in Kentucky public institutions who want to become teachers.

Eligibility This program is open to residents of Kentucky who are undergraduate or graduate students pursuing initial teacher certification at a public university or community college in the state. Applicants must have a GPA of 2.75 or higher and either maintain full-time enrollment or be a part-time student within 18 semester hours of receiving a teacher education degree. They must be U.S. citizens and meet the Kentucky definition of a minority student.

Financial Data Stipends are $5,000 per year at the 8 state universities in Kentucky or $2,000 per year at community and technical colleges. This is a scholarship/loan program. Recipients are required to teach 1 semester in Kentucky for each semester or summer term the scholarship is received. If they fail to fulfill that requirement, the scholarship converts to a loan payable at 6% annually.

Duration 1 year; may be renewed up to 3 additional years.

Additional data The Kentucky General Assembly established this program in 1992.

Number awarded Varies each year.

Deadline Each state college of teacher education sets its own deadline.

[841]
KIA MOTORS AMERICA SCHOLARSHIP

Hispanic Association of Colleges and Universities
Attn: National Scholarship Program
8415 Datapoint Drive, Suite 400
San Antonio, TX 78229
(210) 692-3805   Fax: (210) 692-0823
TDD: (800) 855-2880   E-mail: scholarship@hacu.net
Web: www.hacu.net/hacu/Scholarships.asp

Summary To provide financial assistance to undergraduate and students at member institutions of the Hispanic Association of Colleges and Universities (HACU) who are studying any field.

Eligibility This program is open to full-time sophomores, juniors, and graduate students at HACU member 4-year institutions in the United States or Puerto Rico. Applicants may be working on a degree in any field, but they must have a GPA of

3.0 or higher. First generation college students are strongly encouraged to apply.

Financial Data   The stipend is $4,000.

Duration   1 year.

Additional data   This program is sponsored by KIA Motors America.

Number awarded   16 each year.

Deadline   May of each year.

[842]
KINESIS SCHOLARSHIPS

Kinesis Foundation
89 de Diego Avenue
PMB 607, Suite 105
San Juan, PR 00927
(787) 772-8269   E-mail: info@kinesispr.org
Web: www.kinesispr.org/beca-kinesis

Summary   To provide financial assistance to residents of Puerto Rico who are entering an undergraduate or graduate program at a college outside the Commonwealth.

Eligibility   This program is open to high school seniors and graduates who have been residents of Puerto Rico for at least 2 years. Applicants must be entering a bachelor's, master's, or doctoral degree program at a university on the mainland or in another country. They must have a GPA of 3.5 or higher and be able to demonstrate financial need. Along with their application, they must submit a 200-word essay on their academic goals and how they can contribute to the future of Puerto Rico.

Financial Data   Stipends average $5,000. Funds are disbursed directly to the recipient's university.

Duration   1 year; may be renewed, provided the recipient continues to meet eligibility requirements.

Number awarded   Approximately 100 each year.

Deadline   February of each year.

[843]
KPMG MINORITY ACCOUNTING DOCTORAL SCHOLARSHIPS

KPMG Foundation
Attn: Scholarship Administrator
Three Chestnut Ridge Road
Montvale, NJ 07645-0435
(201) 307-7161   Fax: (201) 624-7763
E-mail: us-kpmgfoundation@kpmg.com
Web: www.kpmgfoundation.org

Summary   To provide funding to Hispanic and other underrepresented minority students working on a doctoral degree in accounting.

Eligibility   Applicants must be Hispanic Americans, African Americans, or Native Americans. They must be U.S. citizens or permanent residents and accepted or enrolled in a full-time accounting doctoral program. Along with their application, they must submit a brief letter explaining their reason for working on a Ph.D. in accounting.

Financial Data   The stipend is $10,000 per year.

Duration   1 year; may be renewed up to 4 additional years.

Additional data   These funds are not intended to replace funds normally made available by the recipient's institution. The foundation recommends that the recipient's institution

also award, to the recipient, a $5,000 annual stipend, a teaching or research assistantship, and a waiver of tuition and fees.

Number awarded   Approximately 12 each year.

Deadline   April of each year.

[844]
LA UNIDAD LATINA SCHOLARSHIPS

La Unidad Latina Foundation, Inc.
132 East 43rd Street, Suite 358
New York, NY 10017
E-mail: info@lulfoundation.org
Web: www.lulf.org/apply

Summary   To provide financial assistance to Hispanic students who are working on a bachelor's or master's degree in any field.

Eligibility   This program is open to students of Hispanic background who have completed at least 1 year of full-time undergraduate study or 1 semester of full-time graduate work. Undergraduates must have a GPA of 2.8 or higher. Applicants must be enrolled at an accredited 4-year college or university in the United States and working on a bachelor's or master's degree. Along with their application, they must submit brief essays on their financial need, their academic plans and career goals, an instance in which they have demonstrated exceptional leadership during their college or graduate experience, the impact they have had or plan to have on improving or supporting their Latino/Hispanic community, their extracurricular activities, any honors or awards they have received, and their special interests or hobbies.

Financial Data   Stipends range from $500 to $1,000.

Duration   1 year.

Number awarded   Varies each year; recently, 9 were awarded.

Deadline   February of each year for spring semester; October of each year for fall semester.

[845]
LAGRANT FOUNDATION GRADUATE SCHOLARSHIPS

Lagrant Foundation
Attn: Senior Talent Acquisition and Fundraising Manager
633 West Fifth Street, 48th Floor
Los Angeles, CA 90071
(323) 469-8680, ext. 223   Fax: (323) 469-8683
E-mail: erickainiguez@lagrant.com
Web: www.lagrantfoundation.org

Summary   To provide financial assistance to Hispanic and other minority graduate students who are working on a degree in advertising, public relations, or marketing.

Eligibility   This program is open to Hispanics/Latinos, African Americans, Asian American/Pacific Islanders, and Native Americans/American Indians who are full-time graduate students at an accredited institution. Applicants must have a GPA of 3.2 or higher and be working on a master's degree in advertising, marketing, or public relations. They must have at least 2 academic semesters remaining to complete their degree. Along with their application, they must submit 1) a 1- to 2-page essay outlining their career goals; why it is important to increase ethnic representation in the fields of advertising, marketing, and public relations; and the role of an advertising, marketing, or public relations practitioner; 2) a paragraph describing the graduate school and/or community activities in which they are involved; 3) a brief paragraph describing any honors and awards they have received; 4) a letter of reference; 5) a resume; and 6) an official transcript. U.S. citizenship or permanent resident status is required.

Financial Data The stipend is $5,000.

Duration 1 year.

Number awarded Varies each year; recently, 19 were awarded.

Deadline February of each year.

[846]
LATINA LAWYERS BAR ASSOCIATION SCHOLARSHIPS

Latina Lawyers Bar Association
Attn: Scholarship Committee
P.O. Box 86488
Los Angeles, CA 90086
E-mail: scholarships@llbalaw.org
Web: www.llbalaw.org/content/scholarship

Summary To provide financial assistance for tuition or bar review courses to students, especially Latinas, currently enrolled at law schools in California or preparing for the state bar examination.

Eligibility This program is open to students currently enrolled at California law schools and current candidates for the California State Bar examination. Preference is given to Latina law students. Applicants must be able to demonstrate community service, commitment to the Latina community, potential to succeed, and financial need. Along with their application, they must submit a 1,000-word statement that includes information regarding their background, reasons for pursuing further education, challenges they face outside of school, legal field of interest, career goals, special circumstances, and financial need.

Financial Data A stipend is awarded (amount not specified).

Duration Funds provide 1 year of support at a California law school or a 1-time grant for bar examination assistance.

Number awarded 1 or more each year.

Deadline July of each year.

[847]
LATINO MEDICAL STUDENT ASSOCIATION MIDWEST REGION SCHOLARSHIP

Latino Medical Student Association-Midwest
c/o Michelle Estrada, Parliamentarian
University of Cincinnati College of Medicine
3230 Eden Avenue
Cincinnati, OH 45267
(513) 558-7333   Fax: (513) 558-3512
E-mail: parliamentarian.midwest@lmsa.net
Web: www.lmsa.net

Summary To provide financial assistance to members of the Latino Medical Student Association (LMSA) at medical schools in the Midwest.

Eligibility This program is open to LMSA members currently enrolled or accepted for enrollment at allopathic or osteopathic medical schools in Illinois, Indiana, Iowa, Kansas, Michigan, Minnesota, Missouri, Nebraska, North Dakota, Ohio, South Dakota, or Wisconsin. Applicants must be able to

demonstrate a desire to advance the state of health care and education in Latino and underserved communities through leadership in extracurricular activities and/or membership in civic organizations. Along with their application, they must submit a personal financial statement and a 500-word essay describing their family and personal background, professional goals, involvement and contributions to the Latino community, and how they would assist LMSA Midwest in its mission. There are no citizenship requirements.

Financial Data The stipend is $1,000.

Duration 1 year.

Number awarded 1 each year.

Deadline April of each year.

[848]
LATINOS AND PLANNING DIVISION SCHOLARSHIP

American Planning Association
Attn: Planning and the Black Community Division
205 North Michigan Avenue, Suite 1200
Chicago, IL 60601
(312) 431-9100   Fax: (312) 786-6700
Web: www.planning.org/divisions/latinos/scholarships

Summary To provide financial assistance to Latinos interested in working on an undergraduate or graduate degree in planning.

Eligibility This program is open to Latinos who are 1) undergraduate students in the third or fourth year of an accredited planning program; or 2) graduate students in the first or second year of an accredited planning program. Applicants must submit a 1- to 2-page personal statement on their interest in a career in planning and the impact they want to make on planning in Latino communities. Selection is based on that statement, a letter of recommendation, academic achievement, and/or service or impacts made in the Latino community or the planning profession.

Financial Data The stipend is $500 per semester.

Duration 1 year.

Number awarded 1 each year.

Deadline February of each year.

[849]
LAUNCHING LEADERS MBA SCHOLARSHIP

JPMorgan Chase
Campus Recruiting
Attn: Launching Leaders
277 Park Avenue, Second Floor
New York, NY 10172
(212) 270-6000
E-mail: bronwen.x.baumgardner@jpmorgan.com
Web: careers.jpmorgan.com

Summary To provide financial assistance and work experience to Hispanic and other underrepresented minority students enrolled in the first year of an M.B.A. program.

Eligibility This program is open to Hispanic, Black, and Native American students enrolled in the first year of an M.B.A. program. Applicants must have a demonstrated commitment to working in financial services. Along with their application, they must submit essays on 1) a hypothetical proposal on how to use $50 million from a donor to their school to benefit all of its students; and 2) the special background and attributes they would contribute to the sponsor's diversity agenda and their motivation for applying to this scholarship program. They must be interested in a summer associate position in the sponsor's investment banking, sales and trading, or research divisions.

Financial Data The stipend is $40,000 for the first year of study; a paid summer associate position is also provided.

Duration 1 year; may be renewed 1 additional year if the recipient successfully completes the 10-week summer associate program.

Number awarded Varies each year.

Deadline October of each year.

[850]
LAURENCE R. FOSTER MEMORIAL SCHOLARSHIPS

Oregon Office of Student Access and Completion
Attn: Scholarship Processing Coordinator
1500 Valley River Drive, Suite 100
Eugene, OR 97401-2146
(541) 687-7422   Toll Free: (800) 452-8807, ext. 7422
Fax: (541) 687-7414   TDD: (800) 735-2900
E-mail: cheryl.a.connolly@state.or.us
Web: app.oregonstudentaid.gov/Catalog/Default.aspx

Summary To provide financial assistance to residents of Oregon, especially Hispanics and members of other diverse groups, who are enrolled at a college or graduate school in any state to prepare for a public health career.

Eligibility This program is open to residents of Oregon who are enrolled at least half time at a 4-year college or university in any state to prepare for a career in public health (not private practice). Preference is given first to applicants from diverse environments; second to persons employed in, or graduate students working on a degree in, public health; and third to juniors and seniors majoring in a health program (e.g., nursing, medical technology, physician assistant). Applicants must be able to demonstrate financial need. Along with their application, they must submit essays of 250 to 350 words on 1) what public health means to them; 2) the public health aspect they intend to practice and the health and population issues impacted by that aspect; and 3) their experience living or working in diverse environments.

Financial Data Stipends for scholarships offered by the Oregon Office of Student Access and Completion (OSAC) range from $1,000 to $10,000 but recently averaged $4,368.

Duration 1 year.

Additional data This program is administered by the OSAC with funds provided by the Oregon Community Foundation.

Number awarded Varies each year; recently, 6 were awarded.

Deadline February of each year.

[851]
LAW AND SOCIAL SCIENCES DOCTORAL DISSERTATION RESEARCH IMPROVEMENT GRANTS

National Science Foundation
Attn: Directorate for Social, Behavioral, and Economic Sciences
Division of Social and Economic Sciences
4201 Wilson Boulevard, Room 995N
Arlington, VA 22230
(703) 292-7023   Fax: (703) 292-9083
TDD: (800) 281-8749   E-mail: hsilvers@nsf.gov
Web: www.nsf.gov

Summary To provide funding for dissertation research to doctoral candidates, especially Hispanics and other underrepresented minorities, in fields related to law and social sciences.

Eligibility This program is open to doctoral candidates who have passed their qualifying examinations, completed all course work required for the degree, and had their dissertation topic approved. Fields of study including crime, violence, and punishment; economic issues; governance; legal decision making; legal mobilization and conceptions of justice; and litigation and the legal profession. Applicants must submit a project description that includes the scientific significance of the work, its relationship to other current research, and the design of the project in sufficient detail to permit evaluation. In the selection process, consideration is given to the project's broader impact of contributing to societally relevant outcomes, including full participation of women, persons with disabilities, and underrepresented minorities in science, technology, engineering, and mathematics (STEM).

Financial Data Grants range up to $20,000. Funds may be used only for costs directly associated with the conduct of dissertation research.

Duration Up to 12 months.

Number awarded Varies each year.

Deadline January of each year.

[852]
LEADERSHIP FOR DIVERSITY SCHOLARSHIP

California School Library Association
Attn: CSL Foundation
6444 East Spring Street, Number 237
Long Beach, CA 90815-1553
Toll Free: (888) 655-8480   Fax: (888) 655-8480
E-mail: info@csla.net
Web: www.csla.net/awards-2/scholarships

Summary To provide financial assistance to Hispanics and other students who reflect the diversity of California's population and are interested in earning a credential as a library media teacher in the state.

Eligibility This program is open to students who are members of a traditionally underrepresented group enrolled in a college or university library media teacher credential program in California. Applicants must intend to work as a library media teacher in a California school library media center for a minimum of 3 years. Along with their application, they must submit a 250-word statement on what they can contribute to the profession, their commitment to serving the needs of multicultural and multilingual students, and their financial need.

Financial Data The stipend is $1,500.

Duration 1 year.

Number awarded 1 each year.

Deadline September of each year.

[853]
LEADERSHIP LEGACY SCHOLARSHIP FOR GRADUATES

Women's Transportation Seminar
Attn: WTS Foundation
1701 K Street, N.W., Suite 800
Washington, DC 20006
(202) 955-5085　　　　　　　　Fax: (202) 955-5088
E-mail: wts@wtsinternational.org
Web: www.wtsinternational.org/education/scholarships

Summary To provide financial assistance to graduate women, especially Hispanics and other minorities, who are interested in a career in transportation.

Eligibility This program is open to women who are working on a graduate degree in transportation or a transportation-related field (e.g., transportation engineering, planning, business management, finance, or logistics). Applicants must have a GPA of 3.0 or higher and be interested in a career in transportation. Along with their application, they must submit a 1,000-word statement about their vision of how their education will give them the tools to better serve their community's needs and transportation issues. Applications must be submitted first to a local chapter; the chapters forward selected applications for consideration on the national level. Minority women are especially encouraged to apply. Selection is based on transportation involvement and goals, job skills, and academic record; financial need is not considered.

Financial Data The stipend is $5,000.

Duration 1 year.

Additional data This program began in 2008. Each year, it focuses on women with a special interest; recently, it was reserved for women who have a specific interest in addressing the impact of transportation on sustainability, land use, environmental impact, security, and quality of life issues internationally.

Number awarded 1 each year.

Deadline Applications must be submitted by November to a local WTS chapter.

[854]
LEON BRADLEY SCHOLARSHIPS

American Association of School Personnel Administrators
Attn: Scholarship Program
11863 West 112th Street, Suite 100
Overland Park, KS 66210
(913) 327-1222　　　　　　　　Fax: (913) 327-1223
E-mail: aaspa@aaspa.org
Web: www.aaspa.org/leon-bradley-scholarship

Summary To provide financial assistance to Hispanic and other minority undergraduates, paraprofessionals, and graduate students preparing for a career in teaching and school leadership at colleges in designated southeastern states.

Eligibility This program is open to members of minority groups (Hispanic, American Indian, Alaskan Native, Asian, Pacific Islander, Black, Middle Easterner) currently enrolled full time at a college or university in Alabama, Florida, Geor-

gia, Kentucky, North Carolina, South Carolina, Tennessee, or Virginia. Applicants must be 1) undergraduates in their final year (including student teaching) of an initial teaching certification program; 2) paraprofessional career-changers in their final year (including student teaching) of an initial teaching certification program; or 3) graduate students who have served as a licensed teacher and are working on a school administrator credential. They must have an overall GPA of 3.0 or higher. Priority is given to applicants who 1) can demonstrate work experience that has been applied to college expenses; 2) have received other scholarship or financial aid support; or 3) are seeking initial certification and/or endorsement in a state-identified critical area.

Financial Data Stipends are $2,500 for undergraduates in their final year, $1,500 for paraprofessionals in their final year, and $1,500 for graduate students.

Duration 1 year.

Number awarded 4 each year: 1 undergraduate, 1 paraprofessional, and 2 graduate students.

Deadline May of each year.

[855]
LEONARD AND HELEN R. STULMAN ENDOWED SCHOLARS GRANTS

Central Scholarship Bureau
6 Park Center Court, Suite 221
Owings Mills, MD 21117
(410) 415-5558　　　　　　　　Toll Free: (855) 276-0239
Fax: (410) 415-5501
E-mail: gohigher@central-scholarship.org
Web: www.central-scholarship.org/scholarships/overview

Summary To provide financial assistance to bilingual residents of any state working on a graduate degree in mental health or social work.

Eligibility This program is open to residents of any state who are bilingual; strong preference is given to Spanish speakers. Applicants must be enrolled in a graduate program in mental health or social work. They must be able to demonstrate financial need (family income less than $90,000). Along with their application, they must submit a 500-word essay on their achievements, career and educational goals, and personal or family circumstances demonstrating exceptional merit or need. U.S. citizenship or permanent resident status is required.

Financial Data The stipend is $5,000 per year.

Duration 1 year; may be renewed.

Number awarded 1 or more each year.

Deadline March of each year.

[856]
LIBERTY POWER BRIGHT HORIZONS SCHOLARSHIPS

United States Hispanic Chamber of Commerce
Attn: Foundation
1424 K Street, N.W., Suite 401
Washington, DC 20005-2404
(202) 842-1212　　　　　　　　E-mail: ehernandez@ushccf.org
Web: www.ushccfoundation.org

Summary To provide financial assistance to Hispanic and other undergraduate and graduate students who are committed to diversity and are working on a degree in a field of science, technology, engineering, or mathematics (STEM).

Eligibility This program is open to U.S. citizens and permanent residents working on an undergraduate or graduate degree in a field of STEM to prepare for a career in energy or environment. Applicants must have completed at least 1 semester of college and have a GPA of 3.0 or higher. They must share the sponsor's goal of advocating on behalf of Hispanic-owned businesses. Along with their application, they must submit brief essays on 1) their interest in energy and/or the environment as a career; 2) why they chose that field of study; 3) why they should be selected as a recipient of this scholarship; 4) how this scholarship will help them achieve their educational/career goals; and 5) the positive impact they hope to have on society and/or the environment. They must also submit Tweets on why diversity is important in education, what Powerful Together means to them, and why living sustainably is so important to them.

Financial Data Stipends are $10,000, $6,000, or $4,000.

Duration 1 year.

Additional data This program, which began in 2013, is sponsored by Liberty Power of Fort Lauderdale, Florida.

Number awarded 1 at $10,000, 1 at $6,000, and 1 at $4,000 each year.

Deadline July of each year.

[857]
LIBRARY AND INFORMATION TECHNOLOGY ASSOCIATION MINORITY SCHOLARSHIPS

American Library Association
Attn: Library and Information Technology Association
50 East Huron Street
Chicago, IL 60611-2795
(312) 280-4270   Toll Free: (800) 545-2433, ext. 4270
Fax: (312) 280-3257   TDD: (888) 814-7692
E-mail: lita@ala.org
Web: www.ala.org/lita/awards

Summary To provide financial assistance to Hispanic and other minority graduate students interested in preparing for a career in library automation.

Eligibility This program is open to U.S. or Canadian citizens who are interested in working on a master's degree in library/information science and preparing for a career in the field of library and automated systems. Applicants must be a member of 1 of the following ethnic groups: Hispanic, American Indian, Alaskan Native, Asian, Pacific Islander, or African American. They may not have completed more than 12 credit hours of course work for their degree. Selection is based on academic excellence, leadership potential, evidence of a commitment to a career in library automation and information technology, and prior activity and experience in those fields. Financial need is considered when all other factors are equal.

Financial Data Stipends are $3,000 or $2,500. Funds are paid directly to the recipient.

Duration 1 year.

Additional data This program includes scholarships funded by Online Computer Library Center (OCLC) and by Library Systems & Services, Inc. (LSSI).

Number awarded 2 each year: 1 at $3,000 (funded by OCLC) and 1 at $2,500 (funded by LSSI).

Deadline February of each year.

[858]
LILLIAN MARRERO SCHOLARSHIP AWARD

REFORMA-Northeast Chapter
c/o Louis Muñoz, Scholarship Committee Chair
Morristown and Morris Township Library
1 Miller Road
Morristown, NJ 07960
(973) 538-6161   Fax: (973) 267-4064
E-mail: louismunoz@yahoo.com
Web: www.reformanortheast.org

Summary To provide financial assistance to members of the Northeast Chapter of REFORMA who are working on a graduate degree in library science and are committed to serving the Spanish-speaking community.

Eligibility This program is open to members of the Northeast Chapter of REFORMA, an association committed to serving the Latino community in Connecticut, Massachusetts, New Jersey, New York, Pennsylvania, and Rhode Island. Applicants must be working on a master's or doctoral degree in library science and be able to demonstrate an understanding of and desire to serve the Spanish-speaking community. They are not required to be enrolled full time, but they must be U.S. citizens or permanent residents. In the selection process, special attention is paid to participation in chapter activities.

Financial Data The stipend is $1,000.

Duration 1 year.

Number awarded 1 each year.

Deadline March of each year.

[859]
LIONEL C. BARROW MINORITY DOCTORAL STUDENT SCHOLARSHIP

Association for Education in Journalism and Mass Communication
Attn: Communication Theory and Methodology Division
234 Outlet Pointe Boulevard, Suite A
Columbia, SC 29210-5667
(803) 798-0271   Fax: (803) 772-3509
E-mail: aejmc@aejmc.org
Web: www.aejmc.us

Summary To provide financial assistance to Hispanics and other minorities who are interested in working on a doctorate in mass communication.

Eligibility This program is open to minority students enrolled in a Ph.D. program in journalism and/or mass communication. Applicants must submit 2 letters of recommendation, a resume, and a brief letter outlining their research interests and career plans. Membership in the association is not required, but applicants must be U.S. citizens or permanent residents. Selection is based on the likelihood that the applicant's work will contribute to communication theory and/or methodology.

Financial Data The stipend is $2,000.

Duration 1 year.

Additional data This program began in 1972.

Number awarded 1 each year.

Deadline May of each year.

[860]
LMSA SCHOLARSHIP FOR U.S. MEDICAL STUDENTS

Latino Medical Student Association
113 South Monroe Street, First Floor
Tallahassee, FL 32301
E-mail: scholarship@lmsa.net
Web: lmsa.site-ym.com/?Scholarships

Summary To provide financial assistance to members of the Latino Medical Student Association (LMSA) who are currently enrolled at a medical school in any state.

Eligibility This program is open to LMSA members who are entering or enrolled at an accredited medical school in any state. Applicants should be able to demonstrate a desire to advance the state of health care and education in Latino communities through extracurricular activities and/or membership in civic organizations. There are no citizenship requirements. Along with their application, they must submit a 1-page personal statement describing their family and personal background, educational objectives, community involvement, and how they would assist the sponsoring organization in its mission to provide health care to the Latino and underserved communities. Selection is based on personal qualities, academic and extracurricular achievement, and financial need.

Financial Data A stipend is awarded (amount not specified).

Duration 1 year.

Additional data This program began in 2009.

Number awarded Varies each year; recently, 6 were awarded.

Deadline January of each year.

[861]
LTK ENGINEERING SCHOLARSHIP

Conference of Minority Transportation Officials
Attn: National Scholarship Program
100 M Street, S.E., Suite 917
Washington, DC 20003
(202) 506-2917   E-mail: info@comto.org
Web: www.comto.org/page/scholarships

Summary To provide financial assistance to Hispanic and other minority upper-division and graduate students in engineering or other field related to transportation.

Eligibility This program is open to full-time minority juniors, seniors, and graduate students in engineering or other technical transportation-related disciplines. Applicants must have a GPA of 3.0 or higher. Along with their application they must submit a cover letter on their transportation-related career goals and life aspirations. Financial need is not considered in the selection process.

Financial Data The stipend is $6,000. Funds are paid directly to the recipient's college or university.

Duration 1 year.

Additional data This program is sponsored by LTK Engineering Services.

Number awarded 1 each year.

Deadline April of each year.

[862]
LTK ENGINEERING TRANSPORTATION PLANNING SCHOLARSHIP

Conference of Minority Transportation Officials
Attn: National Scholarship Program
100 M Street, S.E., Suite 917
Washington, DC 20003
(202) 506-2917   E-mail: info@comto.org
Web: www.comto.org/page/scholarships

Summary To provide financial assistance to Hispanic and other minority upper-division and graduate students in planning or other field related to transportation.

Eligibility This program is open to full-time minority juniors, seniors, and graduate students in planning of other technical transportation-related disciplines. Applicants must have a GPA of 3.0 or higher. Along with their application they must submit a cover letter on their transportation-related career goals and life aspirations. Financial need is not considered in the selection process.

Financial Data The stipend is $5,000. Funds are paid directly to the recipient's college or university.

Duration 1 year.

Additional data This program is sponsored by LTK Engineering Services.

Number awarded 1 each year.

Deadline April of each year.

[863]
LULAC GENERAL AWARDS

League of United Latin American Citizens
Attn: LULAC National Education Service Centers
1133 19th Street, N.W., Suite 1000
Washington, DC 20036
(202) 835-9646   Fax: (202) 835-9685
E-mail: scholarships@lnesc.org
Web: www.lnesc.org/#!lnsf/c17bl

Summary To provide financial assistance to Hispanic American undergraduate and graduate students.

Eligibility This program is open to Hispanic Americans who are U.S. citizens, permanent residents, or Deferred Action for Childhood Arrivals (DACA) students currently enrolled or planning to enroll at an accredited college or university as a graduate or undergraduate student. Although grades are considered in the selection process, emphasis is placed on the applicant's motivation, sincerity, and integrity, as revealed through a personal interview and in a 300-word essay on their personal and professional goals. Need, community involvement, and leadership activities are also considered. Candidates must live near a participating local council of the League of United Latin American Citizens (LULAC) and must apply directly to that council.

Financial Data The stipend ranges from $250 to $1,000 per year, depending on the need of the recipient.

Duration 1 year.

Additional data This program represents an attempt to forge a partnership between the corporate world and the community. Under its fundsharing concept, LULAC's National Education Service Center gathers contributions nationally from corporations, while LULAC councils raise money locally. The total corporate donations are then apportioned back to the councils according to effort. Applications must be obtained directly from participating LULAC councils; for a list, contact the sponsor.

Number awarded   Varies; approximately 500 each year.

Deadline   March of each year.

[864]
LULAC HONORS AWARDS

League of United Latin American Citizens
Attn: LULAC National Education Service Centers
1133 19th Street, N.W., Suite 1000
Washington, DC 20036
(202) 835-9646   Fax: (202) 835-9685
E-mail: scholarships@lnesc.org
Web: www.lnesc.org/#!lnsf/c17bl

Summary   To provide financial assistance to Hispanic American undergraduate and graduate students who are doing well in school.

Eligibility   This program is open to Hispanic Americans who are U.S. citizens, permanent residents, or Deferred Action for Childhood Arrivals (DACA) students currently enrolled or planning to enroll at an accredited college or university as a graduate or undergraduate student. Applicants who are already in college must have a GPA of 3.0 or higher. Entering freshmen must have ACT scores of 23 or higher or SAT scores of 1100 or higher. In addition, applicants must demonstrate motivation, sincerity, and integrity through a personal interview and in a 300-word essay on their personal and professional goals. Need, community involvement, and leadership activities are also considered. Candidates must live near a participating local council of the League of United Latin American Citizens (LULAC) and must apply directly to that council.

Financial Data   The stipend ranges from $500 to $2,000 per year, depending on the need of the recipient.

Duration   1 year.

Additional data   This program represents an attempt to forge a partnership between the corporate world and the community. Under its fundsharing concept, LULAC's National Education Service Center gathers contributions nationally from corporations, while LULAC councils raise money locally. The total corporate donations are then apportioned back to the councils according to effort. Applications must be obtained directly from participating LULAC councils; for a list, send a self-addressed stamped envelope to the sponsor.

Number awarded   Varies each year.

Deadline   March of each year.

[865]
LULAC NATIONAL SCHOLASTIC ACHIEVEMENT AWARDS

League of United Latin American Citizens
Attn: LULAC National Education Service Centers
1133 19th Street, N.W., Suite 1000
Washington, DC 20036
(202) 835-9646   Fax: (202) 835-9685
E-mail: scholarships@lnesc.org
Web: www.lnesc.org/#!lnsf/c17bl

Summary   To provide financial assistance to academically outstanding Hispanic American undergraduate and graduate students.

Eligibility   This program is open to Hispanic Americans who are U.S. citizens, permanent residents, or Deferred Action for Childhood Arrivals (DACA) students currently enrolled or planning to enroll at an accredited college or university as a graduate or undergraduate student. Applicants who are already in college must have a GPA of 3.5 or higher. Entering freshmen must have ACT scores of 29 or higher or SAT scores of 1350 or higher. In addition, applicants must demonstrate motivation, sincerity, and community involvement through a personal interview and in a 300-word essay on their personal and professional goals. Need, community involvement, and leadership activities are also considered. Candidates must live near a participating local council of the League of United Latin American Citizens (LULAC) and must apply directly to that council.

Financial Data   Stipends are at least $2,000 per year.

Duration   1 year.

Additional data   This program represents an attempt to forge a partnership between the corporate world and the community. Under its fundsharing concept, LULAC's National Education Service Center gathers contributions nationally from corporations, while LULAC councils raise money locally. The total corporate donations are then apportioned back to the councils according to effort. Applications must be obtained directly from participating LULAC councils; for a list, send a self-addressed stamped envelope to the sponsor.

Number awarded   Varies each year.

Deadline   March of each year.

[866]
MALDEF LAW SCHOOL SCHOLARSHIP PROGRAM

Mexican American Legal Defense and Educational Fund
634 South Spring Street, 11th Floor
Los Angeles, CA 90014-1974
(213) 629-2512   Fax: (213) 629-0266
E-mail: lawscholarships@maldef.org
Web: www.maldef.org/leadership/scholarships/index.html

Summary   To provide financial assistance to Latino students who are attending or interested in attending law school.

Eligibility   This program is open to Latino students entering their first, second, or third year of law school. Applicants must be enrolled full time. Along with their application, they must submit a 750-word personal statement detailing their personal background, academic and extracurricular achievement, record of service to the Latino community, future plans and financial need. Selection is based on personal background; academic and extracurricular achievement; demonstrated commitment to serving the Latino community, shown through record of service to the Latino community and future plans for service; and financial need.

Financial Data   Stipends range up to $5,000.

Duration   1 year.

Number awarded   Varies each year; recently, 15 were awarded.

Deadline   January of each year.

[867]
MARILYN A. JACKSON MEMORIAL AWARD

Omaha Presbyterian Seminary Foundation
7101 Mercy Road, Suite 216
Omaha, NE 68106-2616
(402) 397-5138   Toll Free: (888) 244-6714
Fax: (402) 397-4944   E-mail: opsf@opsf-omaha.org
Web: www.omahapresbyterianseminaryfoundation.org

Summary To provide financial assistance to students at Presbyterian theological seminaries who are willing to serve in designated states, especially Hispanics and members of other ethnic minority groups.

Eligibility This program is open to members of a Presbyterian Church, under the care of a presbytery as a candidate/inquirer, and accepted or enrolled to work on a master's degree in divinity at 1 of the following 10 Presbyterian theological institutions: Austin Presbyterian Theological Seminary (Austin, Texas); Columbia Theological Seminary (Decatur, Georgia); University of Dubuque Theological Seminary (Dubuque, Iowa); Johnson C. Smith Theological Seminary (Atlanta, Georgia); Louisville Presbyterian Theological Seminary (Louisville, Kentucky); McCormick Theological Seminary (Chicago, Illinois); Pittsburgh Theological Seminary (Pittsburgh, Pennsylvania); Princeton Theological Seminary (Princeton, New Jersey); San Francisco Theological Seminary (San Anselmo, California); or Union Theological Seminary and Presbyterian School of Christian Education (Richmond, Virginia). Applicants must be willing to serve in a small Presbyterian church for 5 years in Colorado, Iowa, Kansas, Minnesota, Missouri, Montana, Nebraska, North Dakota, Oklahoma, South Dakota, Utah, Wisconsin, or Wyoming. Along with their application, they must submit answers to 7 questions about themselves and their commitment to pastoral service. Preference is given to members of ethnic minority groups from the following synods: Lakes and Prairies (Iowa, Minnesota, Nebraska, North Dakota, South Dakota, Wisconsin), Mid-America (Delaware, Maryland, North Carolina, Virginia, Washington, D.C.), Rocky Mountains (Colorado, Montana, Utah, Wyoming), and Sun (Arkansas, Louisiana, Oklahoma, Texas). Financial need is considered in the selection process.

Financial Data The stipend is $7,500.

Duration 1 year.

Number awarded 1 each year.

Deadline April of each year.

[868]
MARIO G. OBLEDO MEMORIAL SCHOLARSHIP

Hispanic National Bar Association
Attn: HNBA Legal Education Fund
1020 19th Street, N.W., Suite 505
Washington, DC 20036
(202) 223-4777   Fax: (202) 503-3403
E-mail: ovargas@hnbafund.org
Web: www.hnbafund.org

Summary To provide financial assistance to Hispanic law students.

Eligibility This program is open to Hispanic students enrolled at an ABA-accredited law school. Applicants must exemplify the life, aspirations, and commitments of Mario Obledo, who founded the Hispanic National Bar Association (HNBA) and Mexican American Legal Defense and Educational Fund (MALDEF).

Financial Data The stipend is $10,000.

Duration 1 year.

Additional data This program was established in 2010 and the scholarship was first offered in 2014.

Number awarded 1 each year.

Deadline October of each year.

[869]
MARJORIE BOWENS-WHEATLEY SCHOLARSHIPS

Unitarian Universalist Association
Attn: UU Women's Federation
258 Harvard Street
Brookline, MA 02446
(617) 838-6989   E-mail: uuwf@uua.org
Web: www.uuwf.org

Summary To provide financial assistance to Hispanic and other women of color who are working on an undergraduate or graduate degree to prepare for Unitarian Universalist ministry or service.

Eligibility This program is open to women of color who are either 1) aspirants or candidates for the Unitarian Universalist ministry; or 2) candidates in the Unitarian Universalist Association's professional religious education or music leadership credentialing programs. Applicants must submit a 1- to 2-page narrative that covers their call to UU ministry, religious education, or music leadership; their passions; how their racial/ethnic/cultural background influences their goals for their calling; and how the work of the program's namesake relates to their dreams and plans for their UU service.

Financial Data The stipend is $1,500.

Duration 1 year.

Additional data This program began in 2009.

Number awarded Varies each year; recently, 2 were awarded.

Deadline March of each year.

[870]
MARK T. BANNER SCHOLARSHIP FOR LAW STUDENTS

Richard Linn American Inn of Court
c/o Amy Ziegler, Scholarship Chair
Green Burns & Crain
300 South Wacker Drive, Suite 2500
Chicago, IL 60606
(312) 987-2926   Fax: (312) 360-9315
E-mail: marktbannerscholarship@linninn.org
Web: www.linninn.org/Pages/scholarship.shtml

Summary To provide financial assistance to law students who are Hispanics or members of other groups historically underrepresented in intellectual property law.

Eligibility This program is open to students at ABA-accredited law schools in the United States who are members of groups historically underrepresented (by race, sex, ethnicity, sexual orientation, or disability) in intellectual property law. Applicants must submit a 3-page statement on how ethics, civility, and professionalism have been their focus; how diversity has impacted them; and their commitment to a career in intellectual property law. Selection is based on academic merit; written and oral communication skills; leadership qualities; community involvement; commitment, qualities and actions toward ethics, civility and professionalism; and commitment to a career in IP law.

Financial Data The stipend is $5,000.

Duration 1 year.

Number awarded 1 each year.

Deadline November of each year.

[871]
MARTHA AND ROBERT ATHERTON MINISTERIAL SCHOLARSHIP

Unitarian Universalist Association
Attn: Ministerial Credentialing Office
24 Farnsworth Street
Boston, MA 02210-1409
(617) 948-6403   Fax: (617) 742-2875
E-mail: mcoadministrator@uua.org
Web: www.uua.org

Summary To provide financial assistance to seminary students, especially Hispanics and other persons of color, who are preparing for the Unitarian Universalist (UU) ministry.

Eligibility This program is open to second- or third-year seminary students currently enrolled full or at least half time in a UU ministerial training program with aspirant or candidate status. Applicants must respect hard work as a foundation of a full life and appreciate the freedom, political system, and philosophical underpinnings of our country. They should be citizens of the United States or Canada. Priority is given first to those who have demonstrated outstanding ministerial ability and secondarily to students with the greatest financial need (especially persons of color).

Financial Data The stipend ranges from $1,000 to $15,000 per year.

Duration 1 year.

Additional data This program began in 1997.

Number awarded 1 or 2 each year.

Deadline April of each year.

[872]
MARTIN LUTHER KING, JR. MEMORIAL SCHOLARSHIP FUND

California Teachers Association
Attn: CTA Foundation for Teaching and Learning
1705 Murchison Drive
P.O. Box 921
Burlingame, CA 94011-0921
(650) 697-1400   E-mail: scholarships@cta.org
Web: www.cta.org

Summary To provide financial assistance for college or graduate school to Hispanic and other racial and ethnic minorities who are members of the California Teachers Association (CTA), children of members, or members of the Student CTA.

Eligibility This program is open to members of racial or ethnic minority groups (Hispanics, African Americans, American Indians/Alaska Natives, and Asians/Pacific Islanders) who are 1) active CTA members; 2) dependent children of active, retired, or deceased CTA members; or 3) members of Student CTA. Applicants must be interested in preparing for a teaching career in public education or already engaged in such a career.

Financial Data Stipends vary each year; recently, they ranged up to $6,000.

Duration 1 year.

Number awarded Varies each year; recently, 24 were awarded: 1 to a CTA member, 10 to children of CTA members, and 13 to Student CTA members.

Deadline February of each year.

[873]
MARTIN LUTHER KING JR. SCHOLARSHIP AWARDS

American Correctional Association
Attn: Scholarship Award Committee
206 North Washington Street, Suite 200
Alexandria, VA 22314
(703) 224-0000   Toll Free: (800) ACA-JOIN
Fax: (703) 224-0179   E-mail: execoffice@aca.org
Web: www.aca.org

Summary To provide financial assistance for undergraduate or graduate study to Hispanics and other minorities interested in a career in the criminal justice field.

Eligibility Members of the American Correctional Association (ACA) may nominate a minority person for these awards. Nominees do not need to be ACA members, but they must have been accepted to or be enrolled in an undergraduate or graduate program in criminal justice at a 4-year college or university. Along with the nomination package, they must submit a 250-word essay describing their reflections on the ideals and philosophies of Dr. Martin Luther King and how they have attempted to emulate those qualities in their lives. They must provide documentation of financial need, academic achievement, and commitment to the principles of Dr. King.

Financial Data A stipend is awarded (amount not specified). Funds are paid directly to the recipient's college or university.

Duration 1 year.

Number awarded 1 each year.

Deadline May of each year.

[874]
MARY MUNSON RUNGE SCHOLARSHIP

American Pharmacists Association
Attn: APhA Foundation
2215 Constitution Avenue, N.W.
Washington, DC 20037-2985
(202) 429-7503   Toll Free: (800) 237-APhA
Fax: (202) 638-3793   E-mail: bwall@aphanet.org
Web: www.aphafoundation.org

Summary To provide financial assistance to members of the Academy of Student Pharmacists of the American Pharmacists Association (APhA-ASP), especially Hispanics and members of other underrepresented minority groups.

Eligibility This program is open to full-time pharmacy students who have been actively involved in their school's APhA-ASP chapter. Applicants must have completed at least 1 year in the professional sequence of courses with a GPA of 2.75 or higher. Preference is given to members of underrepresented minority groups (Hispanics or Latinos, American Indians or Alaska Natives, Blacks or African Americans, Native Hawaiians or other Pacific Islanders). Along with their application, they must submit a 500-word essay on a topic that changes annually but relates to the future of the pharmacy profession, 2 letters of recommendation, a current resume or curriculum vitae, and a list of pharmacy and non-pharmacy related activities. Selection is based on the essay (20 points), academic performance (10 points), pharmacy-related activities (25 points), non-pharmacy/community activities (25 points), and letters of recommendation (20 points).

Financial Data The stipend is $1,000.

Duration 1 year; recipients may reapply.

Number awarded 1 each year.

Deadline November of each year.

[875]
MARY WOLFSKILL TRUST FUND INTERNSHIP

Library of Congress
Library Services
Attn: Junior Fellows Program Coordinator
101 Independence Avenue, S.E., Room LM-642
Washington, DC 20540-4600
(202) 707-9929   Fax: (202) 707-6269
E-mail: jfla@loc.gov
Web: www.loc.gov

Summary To provide summer work experience in the Manuscript Division of the Library of Congress (LC) to upper-division and graduate students, especially Hispanics and other minorities.

Eligibility This program is open to undergraduate and graduate students who have expertise in library science or collections conservation and preservation. Applicants must be interested in gaining an introductory knowledge of the principles, concepts, and techniques of archival management through a summer internship in the LC Manuscript Division. They should be able to demonstrate an ability to communicate effectively in writing and have knowledge of integrated library systems, basic library applications, and other information technologies. Knowledge of American history is beneficial. Applications from minorities and students at smaller and lesser-known schools are particularly encouraged. U.S. citizenship is required.

Financial Data The stipend is $3,000.

Duration 10 weeks during the summer. Fellows work a 40-hour week.

Number awarded 1 each year.

Deadline January of each year.

[876]
MATHEMATICA SUMMER FELLOWSHIPS

Mathematica Policy Research, Inc.
Attn: Human Resources
600 Alexander Park
P.O. Box 2393
Princeton, NJ 08543-2393
(609) 799-3535   Fax: (609) 799-0005
E-mail: humanresources@mathematica-mpr.com
Web: www.mathematica-mpr.com

Summary To provide an opportunity for graduate students in social policy fields, especially Hispanics and members of other underrepresented groups, to work on an independent summer research project at an office of Mathematica Policy Research, Inc.

Eligibility This program is open to students enrolled in a master's or Ph.D. program in public policy or a social science. Applicants must be interested in conducting independent research on a policy issue of relevance to the economic and social problems of minority groups or individuals with disabilities. They are placed with a mentor in 1 of the following divisions: health research, human services research, or survey research. The proposed research must relate to the work of Mathematica, but fellows do not work on Mathematica projects. Qualified minority students and students with disabilities are encouraged to apply.

Financial Data The stipend is $10,000. Fellows also receive $500 for project-related expenses.

Duration 3 months during the summer.

Additional data Mathematica offices are located in Ann Arbor (Michigan), Cambridge (Massachusetts), Chicago (Illinois), Oakland (California), Princeton (New Jersey), and Washington, D.C. Fellows may indicate their choice of location, but they are assigned to the office where the work of the research staff meshes best with their topic and interests.

Number awarded Up to 5 each year.

Deadline March of each year.

[877]
MCKINNEY FAMILY FUND SCHOLARSHIP

Cleveland Foundation
Attn: Scholarship Processing
1422 Euclid Avenue, Suite 1300
Cleveland, OH 44115-2001
(216) 861-3810   Fax: (216) 861-1729
E-mail: mbaker@clevefdn.org
Web: www.clevelandfoundation.org

Summary To provide financial assistance to residents of Ohio, especially Hispanics and members of other minority groups, who are interested in attending college or graduate school in any state.

Eligibility This program is open to U.S. citizens who have been residents of Ohio for at least 2 years. Applicants must be high school seniors or graduate students and interested in working full or part time on an associate, bachelor's, master's, or doctoral degree at an accredited college or university in any state. They must have a GPA of 2.5 or higher. Preference is given to applicants of minority descent. Selection is based on evidence of sincerity toward obtaining an academic credential. Financial need may be used as a tiebreaker.

Financial Data The stipend is $2,000 per year. Funds are paid directly to the school and must be applied to tuition, fees, books, supplies, and equipment required for course work.

Duration 1 year; may be renewed up to 3 additional.

Number awarded 1 or more each year.

Deadline March of each year.

[878]
MCKNIGHT DOCTORAL FELLOWSHIP PROGRAM

Florida Education Fund
201 East Kennedy Boulevard, Suite 1525
Tampa, FL 33602
(813) 272-2772   Fax: (813) 272-2784
E-mail: mdf@fefonline.org
Web: www.fefonline.org/mdf.html

Summary   To provide financial assistance to doctoral students from any state who are working on a degree in designated fields at selected universities in Florida and preparing for an academic career in that state.

Eligibility   This program is open to Hispanics and African Americans from any state who are working on a Ph.D. degree at 1 of 9 universities in Florida. Fellowships may be given in any discipline in the arts and sciences, business, engineering, health sciences, nursing, or the visual and performing arts; preference is given to the following fields of study: agriculture, biology, business administration, chemistry, computer science, engineering, marine biology, mathematics, physics, or psychology. Academic programs that lead to professional degrees (such as the M.D., D.B.A., D.D.S., J.D., or D.V.M.) are not covered by the fellowship. Graduate study in education, whether leading to an Ed.D. or a Ph.D., is generally not supported. Because this program is intended to increase African American and Hispanic graduate enrollment at the 9 participating universities, currently-enrolled doctoral students at those universities are not eligible to apply. U.S. citizenship is required.

Financial Data   Each award provides annual tuition up to $5,000 and an annual stipend of $12,000. Recipients are also eligible for the Fellows Travel Fund, which supports recipients who wish to attend and present papers at professional conferences.

Duration   3 years; an additional 2 years of support may be provided by the university if the recipient maintains satisfactory performance and normal progress toward the Ph.D. degree.

Additional data   This program began in 1984. The participating universities are Florida Agricultural and Mechanical University, Florida Atlantic University, Florida Institute of Technology, Florida International University, Florida State University, University of Central Florida, University of Florida, University of Miami, and University of South Florida.

Number awarded   Up to 50 each year.

Deadline   January of each year.

[879]
MEDICAL RESEARCH FELLOWS PROGRAM

Howard Hughes Medical Institute
Attn: Department of Science Education
4000 Jones Bridge Road
Chevy Chase, MD 20815-6789
(301) 951-6708   Toll Free: (800) 448-4882, ext. 8889
Fax: (301) 215-8888   E-mail: medfellows@hhmi.org
Web: www.hhmi.org

Summary   To provide financial assistance to medical, dental, and veterinary students, especially Hispanics and other underrepresented minorities, who are interested in pursuing research training.

Eligibility   Applicants must be enrolled in a medical, dental, or veterinary school in the United States, although they may be citizens of any country with a visa authorizing them to work in this country. They must describe a proposed research project to be conducted at an academic or nonprofit research institution in the United States (other than a facility of the National Institutes of Health or other federal agency) or at the sponsor's Janelia Research Campus in Ashburn, Virginia. Research proposals should reflect the interests of the Howard Hughes Medical Institute (HHMI), especially in biochemistry, bioinformatics, biomedical engineering, biophysics, biostatistics, cell biology, developmental biology, epidemiology, genetics, immunology, mathematical and computational biology, microbiology, molecular biology, neuroscience, pharmacology, physiology, structural biology, or virology. Applications from women and minorities underrepresented in the sciences (Blacks or African Americans, Hispanics, American Indians, Native Alaskans, and Native Pacific Islanders) are especially encouraged. Students enrolled in M.D./Ph.D., Ph.D., or Sc.D. programs and those who have completed a Ph.D. or Sc.D. in a laboratory-based science are not eligible. Selection is based on the applicant's ability and promise for a research career as a physician-scientist and the quality of training that will be provided.

Financial Data   Fellows receive a stipend of $33,000 per year, an allowance of $5,500 for research-related enrichment activities, and an allowance of $5,500 for health, dental, and vision insurance and education and moving expenses.

Duration   12 months, beginning any time between June and August.

Additional data   HHMI has entered into partnership agreements with designated sponsors to support fellows in certain areas; those include the Burroughs Wellcome Fund for veterinary students, the Foundation Fighting Blindness for ophthalmology research (particularly in the area of inherited retinal degenerative diseases), the Duchenne Research Fund for research in a field related to Duchenne Muscular Dystrophy, Citizens United for Research in Epilepsy for epilepsy research, the American Society of Human Genetics for genetics research, the Orthopaedic Research and Education Foundation for orthopaedic research, the Parkinson's Disease Foundation for Parkinson's Disease research, and the Society of Interventional Radiology Foundation for preclinical research in interventional radiology.

Number awarded   Up to 60 each year.

Deadline   January of each year.

[880]
MEDICAL STUDENT ELECTIVE IN HIV PSYCHIATRY

American Psychiatric Association
Attn: Office of HIV Psychiatry
1000 Wilson Boulevard, Suite 1825
Arlington, VA 22209-3901
(703) 907-8668   Toll Free: (888) 357-7849
Fax: (703) 907-1087   E-mail: aids@psych.org
Web: www.psychiatry.org

Summary   To provide an opportunity for Hispanic and other minority medical students to spend an elective residency learning about HIV psychiatry.

Eligibility   This program is open to medical students entering their fourth year at an accredited M.D. or D.O. degree-granting institution. Preference is given to minority candidates and those who have primary interests in services related to HIV/AIDS and substance abuse and its relationship to the mental health or the psychological well-being of ethnic minorities. Applicants should be interested in a psychiatry, internal medicine, pediatrics, or research career. They must be interested in participating in a program that includes intense training in HIV mental health (including neuropsychiatry), a clinical and/or research experience working with a mentor, and participation in the Committee on AIDS of the American Psychiatric Association (APA). U.S. citizenship is required.

Financial Data A small stipend is provided (amount not specified).

Duration 1 month.

Additional data The heart of the program is in establishing a mentor relationship at 1 of several sites, becoming involved with a cohort of medical students interested in HIV medicine/psychiatry, participating in an interactive didactic/experimental learning program, and developing expertise in areas related to ethnic minority mental health research or psychiatric services. Students selected for the program who are not APA members automatically receive membership.

Number awarded Varies each year.

Deadline March of each year.

[881]
MEDICAL STUDENT TRAINING IN AGING RESEARCH PROGRAM

American Federation for Aging Research
Attn: Executive Director
55 West 39th Street, 16th Floor
New York, NY 10018
(212) 703-9977   Toll Free: (888) 582-2327
Fax: (212) 997-0330   E-mail: grants@afar.org
Web: www.afar.org/research/funding/mstar

Summary To enable medical students, especially Hispanics and other diverse students, who have completed at least 1 year at an American medical school to attend a short training session in clinical geriatrics and aging research at selected training centers.

Eligibility This program is open to allopathic and osteopathic medical students in good standing who have completed at least 1 year of medical school and are citizens, nationals, or permanent residents of the United States. Applicants must be interested in a summer experience in aging-related research and geriatrics either at a National Training Center supported by the National Institute on Aging (NIA) or at their home institution. Selection is based on academic excellence, interest in geriatrics, and potential for success. Applications are especially encouraged from students who are members of ethnic or racial groups underrepresented in aging and geriatric research, students with disabilities, and students whose background and experience are likely to diversify the research or medical questions being addressed.

Financial Data The stipend is $1,980 per month.

Duration 8 to 12 weeks during the summer.

Additional data This program began in 1994. Major funding is provided by the NIA, the John A. Hartford Foundation, the MetLife Foundation, and the Jean and Louis Dreyfus Foundation. It is administered by the American Federation for Aging Research (AFAR) and NIA. Scholars attend training sessions with top experts in geriatrics and/or gerontology and other disciplines (e.g., physiology, molecular biology, neurology, and epidemiology). The training sessions are conducted at designated National Training Centers; for a complete list, including all partnership institutions, contact AFAR.

Number awarded Approximately 130 each year.

Deadline January of each year.

[882]
MENTAL HEALTH AND SUBSTANCE ABUSE FELLOWSHIP PROGRAM

Council on Social Work Education
Attn: Minority Fellowship Program
1701 Duke Street, Suite 200
Alexandria, VA 22314-3457
(703) 683-2050   Fax: (703) 683-8099
E-mail: mfpy@cswe.org
Web: www.cswe.org

Summary To provide financial assistance to Hispanic and other racial minority members interested in preparing for a clinical career in the mental health fields.

Eligibility This program is open to U.S. citizens, noncitizen nationals, and permanent residents who have been underrepresented in the field of social work. These include but are not limited to the following groups: Hispanics (e.g., Mexicans/Chicanos, Puerto Ricans, Cubans, Central or South Americans), American Indians/Alaskan Natives, Asian/Pacific Islanders (e.g., Chinese, East Indians, South Asians, Filipinos, Hawaiians, Japanese, Koreans, and Samoans), and Blacks. Applicants must be interested in and committed to a career in mental health and/or substance abuse with specialization in the delivery of services of ethnic and racial minority groups. They must have a degree in social work and be accepted to or enrolled in a full-time master's or doctoral degree program. Selection is based on evidence of strong fit with and commitment to behavioral health services for underserved racial/ethnic populations; life experiences relevant to and/or volunteer or work experience with racial/ethnic populations; high quality scholarly writing showing ability to think and write at the doctoral level; academic evidence of ability to achieve timely degree completion; and fit of the sponsor's mission with the applicant's behavioral health services or research agenda.

Financial Data The program provides a monthly stipend (amount not specified), specialized training, and support for professional development.

Duration 1 academic year; renewable for 2 additional years if funds are available and the recipient makes satisfactory progress toward the degree objectives.

Additional data The program has been funded since 1978 by the Center for Mental Health Services (CMHS), the Center for Substance Abuse Prevention (CSAP), and the Center for Substance Abuse Treatment (CSAT) within the Substance Abuse and Mental Health Services Administration. The master's degree program was added in 2014.

Number awarded Varies each year; recently, 40 master's degree students, 12 new doctoral fellows and 12 returning doctoral fellows were appointed.

Deadline February of each year.

[883]
MENTAL HEALTH RESEARCH DISSERTATION GRANT TO INCREASE WORKFORCE DIVERSITY

National Institute of Mental Health
Attn: Division of Extramural Activities
6001 Executive Boulevard, Room 6138
Bethesda, MD 20892-9609
(301) 443-3534   Fax: (301) 443-4720
TDD: (301) 451-0088   E-mail: armstrda@mail.nih.gov
Web: www.grants.nih.gov

Summary To provide research funding to Hispanic and other doctoral candidates from underrepresented groups planning to prepare for a research career in any area relevant to mental health and/or mental disorders.

Eligibility This program is open to doctoral candidates conducting dissertation research in a field related to mental health and/or mental disorders at a university, college, or professional school with an accredited doctoral degree granting program. Applicants must be 1) members of an ethnic or racial group that has been determined by the National Science Foundation to be underrepresented in health-related sciences (i.e., Hispanic Americans, African Americans, Alaska Natives, American Indians, Native Hawaiians, and other Pacific Islanders); 2) individuals with disabilities; or 3) individuals from socially, culturally, economically, or educationally disadvantaged backgrounds that have inhibited their ability to prepare for a career in health-related research. They must be U.S. citizens, nationals, or permanent residents.

Financial Data The stipend is $23,376. An additional grant up to $15,000 is provided for additional research expenses, fringe benefits (including health insurance), travel to scientific meetings, and research costs of the dissertation. Facilities and administrative costs are limited to 8% of modified total direct costs.

Duration Up to 2 years; nonrenewable.

Number awarded Varies each year.

Deadline Applications must be submitted by February, June, or October of each year.

[884]
MEXICAN AMERICAN ENGINEERS AND SCIENTISTS SCHOLARSHIP PROGRAM

Society of Mexican American Engineers and Scientists
Attn: Scholarship Program
2437 Bay Area Boulevard, Suite 100
Houston, TX 77058
(281) 557-3677   Fax: (281) 715-5100
E-mail: questions@mymaes.org
Web: www.mymaes.org/student

Summary To provide financial assistance to undergraduate and graduate student members of the Society of Mexican American Engineers and Scientists (MAES).

Eligibility This program is open to MAES student members who are full-time undergraduate or graduate students at a college or university in the United States and have a GPA of 2.0 or higher. Community college students must be enrolled in majors that can transfer to a 4-year institution offering a baccalaureate degree. All applicants must be majoring in a field of science, technology, engineering, or mathematics (STEM). U.S. citizenship or permanent resident status is required. Along with their application, they must submit a personal statement that includes information on their family background, involvement in school and community activities, MAES involvement, and financial need.

Financial Data Stipends range from $1,000 to $4,000.

Duration 1 year.

Additional data This program includes Padrino/Madrina Scholarships at $4,000, the Founder's Scholarship at $2,500, the Presidential Scholarship at $2,500, and general scholarships at $1,000 or $2,000. The Padrino/Madrina Scholarships are sponsored by ExxonMobil and Lockheed Martin; the Presidential Scholarship is sponsored by ExxonMobil; other scholarships are sponsored by Applied Materials, General Motors, Lockheed Martin, and various professional chapters of MAES. Recipients must attend the MAES International Symposium's Medalla de Oro Banquet in December.

Number awarded Varies each year; recently, available scholarships included 2 Padrino/Madrina Scholarships, 1 Founder's Scholarship, 1 Presidential Scholarship, and 13 general scholarships.

Deadline September of each year.

[885]
MEXICAN FIESTA SCHOLARSHIPS

Wisconsin Hispanic Scholarship Foundation, Inc.
2997 South 20th Street
Milwaukee, WI 53215
(414) 383-7066   Fax: (414) 383-6677
E-mail: info@mexicanfiesta.org
Web: www.mexicanfiesta.org/scholarships.php

Summary To provide financial assistance to Hispanic American students in Wisconsin who are interested in attending college or graduate school in the state.

Eligibility This program is open to Wisconsin residents who are of at least 25% Hispanic descent and entering or enrolled at a 2- or 4-year college or university or graduate school in the state. Applicants must complete at least 20 hours of volunteer service during the Mexican Fiesta festival in Milwaukee during August of each year. They must have a GPA of 2.5 or higher. Along with their application, they must submit an essay on how they plan to assist or help the Hispanic community after their receive their degree. U.S. citizenship or permanent resident status is required.

Financial Data Stipends range from $250 to $2,000.

Duration 1 year; recipients may reapply.

Additional data The sponsor is an affiliate of the League of United Latin American Citizens (LULAC) Wisconsin Councils 319 and 322.

Number awarded More than 100 each year.

Deadline March of each year.

[886]
MICHIGAN ACCOUNTANCY FOUNDATION FIFTH/ GRADUATE YEAR SCHOLARSHIP PROGRAM

Michigan Association of Certified Public Accountants
Attn: Michigan Accountancy Foundation
5480 Corporate Drive, Suite 200
P.O. Box 5068
Troy, MI 48007-5068
(248) 267-3680   Toll Free: (888) 877-4CPE (within MI)
Fax: (248) 267-3737   E-mail: MAF@micpa.org
Web: www.mafonline.org/?page_id=35

Summary To provide financial assistance to students at Michigan colleges and universities, especially Hispanics and members of other underrepresented groups, who are working on a degree in accounting.

Eligibility This program is open to students enrolled full time at accredited Michigan colleges and universities with a declared concentration in accounting. Applicants must be seniors planning to enter the fifth or graduate year of their school's program. They must intend to or have successfully passed the Michigan C.P.A. examination and intend to practice public accounting in the state. Along with their application, they must submit 500-word statements about 1) examples of their leadership roles and extracurricular activities, community involvement and volunteerism, how they are financing their education, and the accomplishments of which they are most proud; and 2) their professional goals for the next 5 years and any special circumstances they wish to have considered. Special consideration is given to applicants who are single parents, physically challenged, minority, or self-supporting. U.S. citizenship or eligibility for permanent employment in the United States is required.

Financial Data The stipend is $3,000; funds are disbursed directly to the recipient's college or university.

Duration 1 year.

Additional data This program includes the William E. Balhoff Leadership Scholarship, the Jeff Bergeron Leadership Scholarship, the Robert A. Bogan Scholarship (limited to a student from the metropolitan Detroit area), the Kenneth Bouyer Leadership Scholarship, the Peggy A. Dzierzawski Leadership Scholarship, the George Johnson Leadership Scholarship, the Thomas McTavish Leadership Scholarship, the Randy Paschke Leadership Scholarship, and the Governor Rick Snyder Leadership Scholarship.

Number awarded 15 to 20 each year.

Deadline January of each year.

[887]
MICHIGAN AUTO LAW DIVERSITY SCHOLARSHIP

Michigan Auto Law
Attn: Natalie Lombardo
30101 Northwestern Highway
Farmington Hills, MI 48334
(248) 353-7575 Fax: (248) 353-4504
E-mail: bwarner@ michiganautolaw.com
Web: www.michiganautolaw.com

Summary To provide financial assistance to Hispanics and other law students who will contribute to diversity of their school's student body.

Eligibility This program is open to students entering their first, second, or third year at an accredited law school in the United States. Applicants must be a member of an ethnic or racial minority or demonstrate a defined commitment to issues of diversity within their academic career. They must be U.S. citizens and have a GPA of 3.0 or higher. Selection is based on transcripts and an essay describing their efforts to encourage greater racial or ethnic diversity within the student body of their law school and/or undergraduate program.

Financial Data The stipend is $2,000.

Duration 1 year.

Number awarded 1 each year.

Deadline April of each year.

[888]
MICKEY LELAND ENERGY FELLOWSHIPS

Oak Ridge Institute for Science and Education
Attn: MLEF Fellowship Program
1299 Bethel Valley Road, Building SC-200
P.O. Box 117, MS 36
Oak Ridge, TN 37831-0117
(865) 574-6440 Fax: (865) 576-0734
E-mail: barbara.dunkin@orau.org
Web: orise.orau.gov/mlef/index.html

Summary To provide summer work experience at fossil energy sites of the Department of Energy (DOE) to Hispanic and other underrepresented minority and female students or postdoctorates.

Eligibility This program is open to U.S. citizens currently enrolled full time at an accredited college or university. Applicants must be undergraduate, graduate, or postdoctoral students in fields of science, technology (IT), engineering, or mathematics (STEM) and have a GPA of 3.0 or higher. They must be interested in a summer work experience at a DOE fossil energy research facility. Along with their application, they must submit a 100-word statement on why they want to participate in this program. A goal of the program is to recruit women and underrepresented minorities into careers related to fossil energy, although all qualified students are encouraged to apply.

Financial Data Weekly stipends are $600 for undergraduates, $750 for master's degree students, or $850 for doctoral and postdoctoral students. Travel costs for a round trip to and from the site and for a trip to a designated place for technical presentations are also paid.

Duration 10 weeks during the summer.

Additional data This program began as 3 separate activities: the Historically Black Colleges and Universities Internship Program established in 1995, the Hispanic Internship Program established in 1998, and the Tribal Colleges and Universities Internship Program, established in 2000. Those 3 programs were merged into the Fossil Energy Minority Education Initiative, renamed the Mickey Leland Energy Fellowship Program in 2000. Sites to which interns may be assigned include the National Energy Technology Laboratory (Morgantown, West Virginia, Albany, Oregon and Pittsburgh, Pennsylvania), Pacific Northwest National Laboratory (Richland, Washington), Sandia National Laboratory (Livermore, California), Lawrence Berkeley National Laboratory (Berkeley, California), Los Alamos National Laboratory (Los Alamos, New Mexico), Strategic Petroleum Reserve Project Management Office (New Orleans, Louisiana), or U.S. Department of Energy Headquarters (Washington, D.C.).

Number awarded Varies each year; recently, 30 students participated in this program.

Deadline December of each year.

[889]
MIDWIVES OF COLOR-WATSON MIDWIFERY STUDENT SCHOLARSHIP

American College of Nurse-Midwives
Attn: ACNM Foundation, Inc.
8403 Colesville Road, Suite 1550
Silver Spring, MD 20910-6374
(240) 485-1850   Fax: (240) 485-1818
E-mail: foundation@acnmf.org
Web: www.midwife.org

Summary To provide financial assistance for midwifery education to Hispanic and other students of color who belong to the American College of Nurse-Midwives (ACNM).

Eligibility This program is open to ACNM members of color who are currently enrolled in an accredited basic midwife education program and have successfully completed 1 academic or clinical semester/quarter or clinical module. Applicants must submit they must submit a 150-word essay on their 5-year midwifery career plans; a 150-word essay on their intended future participation in the local, regional, and/or national activities of the ACNM; a 150-word essay on their need for financial assistance; and a 100-word statement on how they would use the funds if they receive the scholarship. Selection is based on academic excellence, leadership potential, and financial need.

Financial Data The stipend is $3,000.

Duration 1 year.

Number awarded Varies each year; recently, 3 were awarded.

Deadline February of each year.

[890]
MIGRANT HEALTH SCHOLARSHIPS

National Center for Farmworker Health, Inc.
Attn: Migrant Health Scholarship
1770 FM 967
Buda, TX 78610
(512) 312-2700   Toll Free: (800) 531-5120
Fax: (512) 312-2600   E-mail: favre@ncfh.org
Web: www.ncfh.org/scholarships.html

Summary To provide financial assistance to people working in the migrant health field, especially those with a farmworker background, who are interested in additional education.

Eligibility This program is open to staff in clinical, administrative, and support positions at community and migrant health centers who are interested in obtaining additional education at the undergraduate or graduate level. Applicants must submit a 1-page personal statement discussing such issues as why they are interested in migrant health, personal experiences and achievements, future career goals, commitment to migrant health, and financial need. Preference is given to applicants with a farmworker background.

Financial Data The stipend is $1,000.

Duration 1 year.

Additional data This program began in 1984.

Number awarded Varies each year; recently, 6 were awarded. Since the program was established, it has awarded 210 of these scholarships.

Deadline March of each year.

[891]
MIGUEL CONTRERAS FELLOWSHIPS

Labor Council for Latin American Advancement
Attn: Communication Manager
815 16th Street, N.W., Third Floor
Washington, DC 20006
(202) 508-6919   Fax: (202) 508-6922
E-mail: headquarters@lclaa.org
Web: www.lclaa.org/about-lclaa/partnership-opportunities

Summary To provide work experience at designated Latino-related labor organizations to college seniors and recent graduates who are planning to enter graduate school.

Eligibility This program is open to college seniors and recent graduates who are planning to work on a law, master's, or doctoral degree in labor studies at an accredited institution. Applicants must be interested in working at the national headquarters (housed within the AFL-CIO) of the Labor Council for Latin American Advancement (LCLAA) in Washington, D.C. Their field of study may include public service, legal studies, international relations, government relations, or public policy; other areas may be considered, but applicants must demonstrate a clear interest in labor issues. U.S. citizenship is not required. Financial need is considered in the selection process.

Financial Data The stipend ranges from $15,000 to $35,000, depending on the need of the fellow. Funds are intended to cover housing and living expenses.

Duration 1 year.

Additional data LCLAA is a national organization for Latino/a trade unionists throughout the United States and Puerto Rico. Fellows work to facilitate and enhance ongoing research to help increase the knowledge and tools that strengthen the labor movement.

Number awarded 1 or 2 each year.

Deadline June of each year.

[892]
MILDRED COLODNY DIVERSITY SCHOLARSHIP FOR GRADUATE STUDY IN HISTORIC PRESERVATION

National Trust for Historic Preservation
Attn: Scholarship Coordinator
2600 Virginia Avenue, N.W., Suite 1000
Washington, DC 20037
(202) 588-6124   Toll Free: (800) 944-NTHP, ext. 6124
Fax: (202) 588-6038   E-mail: david_field@nthp.org
Web: www.preservationnation.org

Summary To provide financial assistance for study, conference attendance, and summer work experience to Hispanic and other graduate students from diverse backgrounds who are interested in working on a degree in a field related to historic preservation.

Eligibility This program is open to students in their final year of undergraduate study intending to enroll in a graduate program in historic preservation and graduate students enrolled in or intending to enroll in historic preservation programs; these programs may be in a department of history, architecture, American studies, urban planning, museum studies, or a related field with a primary emphasis on historic preservation. The program of study must be at a U.S. college, university, or other institution and students must be eligible to work in the United States. Applications are especially encouraged from people who will contribute to diversity in the field of historic preservation. The sponsor defines diversity to include people of all races, creeds, genders, ages, sexual orientations, religions, physical characteristics and abilities, veteran status, and economic or social backgrounds. Selection is based on financial need, undergraduate academic performance, promise shown for future achievement, commitment to working in preservation in the United States following graduation, and potential to help increase diversity within the preservation movement.

Financial Data The program provides a stipend of up to $15,000 that covers graduate school tuition, a summer internship with the sponsor following the student's first year of study, and the student's attendance at a National Preservation Conference.

Duration 1 year; nonrenewable.

Additional data Internships may be completed at 1) the sponsor's Washington, D.C. office; 2) a regional office or historic museum site; or 3) the offices of 1 of the sponsor's partner organizations.

Number awarded 1 each year.

Deadline February of each year.

[893]
MILLER JOHNSON WEST MICHIGAN DIVERSITY LAW SCHOOL SCHOLARSHIP

Grand Rapids Community Foundation
Attn: Education Program Officer
185 Oakes Street S.W.
Grand Rapids, MI 49503-4008
(616) 454-1751, ext. 103   Fax: (616) 454-6455
E-mail: rbishop@grfoundation.org
Web: www.grfoundation.org/scholarshipslist

Summary To provide financial assistance to Hispanic and other minorities from Michigan who are attending law school in any state.

Eligibility This program is open to U.S. citizens who are students of color (Hispanic, African American, Asian, Native American, Pacific Islander) and residents of Michigan. Applicants must be attending an accredited law school in any state. They must have a GPA of 3.0 or higher and be able to demonstrate financial need.

Financial Data The stipend is $5,000. Funds are paid directly to the recipient's institution.

Duration 1 year.

Number awarded 1 each year.

Deadline March of each year.

[894]
MINORITIES IN GOVERNMENT FINANCE SCHOLARSHIP

Government Finance Officers Association
Attn: Scholarship Committee
203 North LaSalle Street, Suite 2700
Chicago, IL 60601-1210
(312) 977-9700   Fax: (312) 977-4806
Web: www.gfoa.org

Summary To provide financial assistance to Hispanic and other minority upper-division and graduate students who are preparing for a career in state and local government finance.

Eligibility This program is open to upper-division and graduate students who are preparing for a career in public finance by working on a degree in public administration, accounting, finance, political science, economics, or business administration (with a specific focus on government or nonprofit management). Applicants must be members of a minority group, citizens or permanent residents of the United States or Canada, and able to provide a letter of recommendation from a representative of their school. The program defines minorities as Hispanics or Latinos, Blacks or African Americans, American Indians or Alaskan Natives, Native Hawaiians or other Pacific Islanders, or Asians. Selection is based on career plans, academic record, plan of study, letters of recommendation, and GPA. Financial need is not considered.

Financial Data The stipend is $6,000.

Duration 1 year.

Number awarded 1 each year.

Deadline February of each year.

[895]
MINORITY AND UNDERREPRESENTED ENVIRONMENTAL LITERACY PROGRAM

Missouri Department of Higher Education
Attn: Student Financial Assistance
205 Jefferson Street
P.O. Box 1469
Jefferson City, MO 65102-1469
(573) 751-2361   Toll Free: (800) 473-6757
Fax: (573) 751-6635   E-mail: info@dhe.mo.gov
Web: www.dhe.mo.gov/ppc/grants/muelp_0310_final.php

Summary To provide financial assistance to Hispanic and other underrepresented and minority students from Missouri who are or will be working on a bachelor's or master's degree in an environmental field.

Eligibility This program is open to residents of Missouri who are high school seniors or current undergraduate or graduate students enrolled or planning to enroll full time at a college or university in the state. Priority is given to members of the following underrepresented minority ethnic groups: Hispanic or Latino Americans, African Americans, Native Americans and Alaska Natives, and Native Hawaiians and Pacific Islanders. Applicants must be working on or planning to work on a bachelor's or master's degree in 1) engineering (civil, chemical, environmental, mechanical, or agricultural); 2) environmental studies (geology, biology, wildlife management, natural resource planning, natural resources, or a closely-related course of study); 3) environmental chemistry; or 4) environmental law enforcement. They must be U.S. citizens or permanent residents or otherwise lawfully present in the United States. Graduating high school seniors must have a GPA of 3.0 or higher; students currently enrolled in college or graduate school must have a GPA of 2.5 or higher. Along with their application, they must submit a 1-page essay on why they are applying for this scholarship, 3 letters of recommendation, a resume of school and community activities, and transcripts that include SAT or ACT scores. Financial need is not considered in the selection process.

Financial Data Stipends vary each year; recently, they averaged approximately $3,045 per year.

Duration 1 year; may be renewed if the recipient maintains a GPA of 2.5 or higher and full-time enrollment.

Additional data This program was established by the Missouri Department of Natural Resources but transferred to the Department of Higher Education in 2009.

Number awarded Varies each year.

Deadline May of each year.

[896]
MINORITY FACULTY DEVELOPMENT SCHOLARSHIP AWARD IN PHYSICAL THERAPY

American Physical Therapy Association
Attn: Honors and Awards Program
1111 North Fairfax Street
Alexandria, VA 22314-1488
(703) 684-APTA   Toll Free: (800) 999-APTA, ext. 8082
Fax: (703) 684-7343   TDD: (703) 683-6748
E-mail: honorsandawards@apta.org
Web: www.apta.org

Summary To provide financial assistance to Hispanic and other minority faculty members in physical therapy who are interested in working on a post-professional doctoral degree.

Eligibility This program is open to U.S. citizens and permanent residents who are members of the following minority groups: Hispanic/Latino, African American or Black, Asian, Native Hawaiian or other Pacific Islander, or American Indian or Alaska Native. Applicants must be full-time faculty members, teaching in an accredited or developing professional physical therapist education program, who will have completed the equivalent of 2 full semesters of post-professional doctoral course work. They must possess a license to practice physical therapy in a U.S. jurisdiction and be enrolled as a student in an accredited post-professional doctoral program whose content has a demonstrated relationship to physical therapy. Along with their application, they must submit a personal essay on their professional goals, including their plans to contribute to the profession and minority services. Selection is based on contributions in the area of minority affairs and services and contributions to the profession of physical therapy. Preference is given to members of the American Physical Therapy Association (APTA).

Financial Data A stipend is awarded (amount not specified).

Duration 1 year.

Additional data This program began in 1999.

Number awarded 1 or more each year.

Deadline November of each year.

[897]
MINORITY FELLOWSHIPS IN ENVIRONMENTAL LAW

New York State Bar Association
Attn: Environmental Law Section
One Elk Street
Albany, NY 12207
(518) 463-3200   Fax: (518) 487-5517
E-mail: lbataille@nysba.org
Web: www.nysba.org

Summary To provide an opportunity for Latino and other minority law students from New York to gain summer work experience in environmental law.

Eligibility This program is open to law students who are Latino, African American, Native American, Alaskan Native, Asian, or Pacific Islander. Applicants must be residents of New York or attending law school in that state. They must be interested in a summer internship working on legal matters for a government environmental agency or public interest environmental organization in New York State. Selection is based on interest in environmental issues, academic record (undergraduate and/or law school), personal qualities, leadership abilities, and financial need.

Financial Data The stipend is $6,000.

Duration At least 10 weeks during the summer.

Additional data This program began in 1992.

Number awarded 1 each year.

Deadline December of each year.

[898]
MINORITY MEDICAL STUDENT AWARD PROGRAM OF THE AMERICAN SOCIETY OF HEMATOLOGY

American Society of Hematology
Attn: Awards Manager
2021 L Street, N.W., Suite 900
Washington, DC 20036
(202) 776-0544   Fax: (202) 776-0545
E-mail: awards@hematology.org
Web: www.hematology.org

Summary To provide an opportunity for Hispanic and other underrepresented minority medical students to conduct a research project in hematology.

Eligibility This program is open to medical students enrolled in D.O., M.D., or M.D./Ph.D. programs in the United States or Canada who are members of minority groups. For purposes of this program, minority is defined as a member of a racial or ethnic group that has been shown to be underrepresented in health-related sciences in the United States and Canada, including Hispanics or Latinos, American Indians, Alaska Natives, Blacks or African Americans, Native Hawaiians, other Pacific Islanders, African Canadians, Inuit, and First Nation Peoples. Applicants must be interested in conducting a research project in hematology at their home institution or at another institution that has agreed to host them. They must work with 2 mentors who are members of the American Society of Hematology (ASH): a research mentor who oversees the participant's work and progress and a career development mentor (who is from the same minority group as the student) who participates for the duration of the program. U.S. or Canadian citizenship or permanent resident status is required.

Financial Data The grant includes $5,000 for research support, an additional $1,000 to support travel to the annual meeting of the ASH, and another $1,000 for making a short presentation about the research experience at a special reception at the ASH annual meeting. Research mentors receive an allowance of $2,000 for supplies and $1,000 for attendance at the ASH annual meeting. Career development mentors receives $1,000 as a travel allowance each time they accompany the student to an ASH annual meeting during their remaining years of medical school and residency.

Duration 8 to 12 weeks.

Additional data This program is supported by Amgen, Celgene Corporation, Cephalon Oncology, and Genentech BioOncology.

Number awarded Up to 10 each year.

Deadline March of each year.

[899]
MINORITY MEDICAL STUDENT SUMMER EXTERNSHIP IN ADDICTION PSYCHIATRY

American Psychiatric Association
Attn: Division of Diversity and Health Equity
1000 Wilson Boulevard, Suite 1825
Arlington, VA 22209-3901
(703) 907-8653   Toll Free: (888) 35-PSYCH
Fax: (703) 907-7852   E-mail: mking@psych.org
Web: www.psychiatry.org/minority-fellowship

Summary To provide funding to Hispanic and othr minority medical students who are interested in working on a research externship during the summer with a mentor who specializes in addiction psychiatry.

Eligibility This program is open to minority medical students who have a specific interest in services related to substance abuse treatment and prevention. Minorities include Hispanics/Latinos, American Indians, Alaska Natives, Native Hawaiians, Asian Americans, and African Americans. Applicants must be interested in working with a mentor who specializes in addiction psychiatry. Work settings provide an emphasis on working clinically with or studying underserved minority populations and issues of co-occurring disorders, substance abuse treatment, and mental health disparity. Most of them are in inner-city or rural settings.

Financial Data Externships provide $1,500 for travel expenses to go to the work setting of the mentor and up to another $1,500 for out-of-pocket expenses directly related to the conduct of the externship.

Duration 1 month during the summer.

Additional data Funding for this program is provided by the Substance Abuse and Mental Health Services Administration (SAMHSA).

Number awarded 10 each year.

Deadline March of each year.

[900]
MINORITY TEACHERS OF ILLINOIS SCHOLARSHIP PROGRAM

Illinois Student Assistance Commission
Attn: Scholarship and Grant Services
1755 Lake Cook Road
Deerfield, IL 60015-5209
(847) 948-8550   Toll Free: (800) 899-ISAC
Fax: (847) 831-8549   TDD: (800) 526-0844
E-mail: isac.studentservices@isac.illinois.gov
Web: www.isac.org

Summary To provide scholarship/loans to Hispanic and other minority students in Illinois who plan to become teachers at the preschool, elementary, or secondary level.

Eligibility Applicants must be Illinois residents, U.S. citizens or eligible noncitizens, members of a minority group (Hispanic American, African American/Black, Asian American, or Native American), and high school graduates or holders of a General Educational Development (GED) certificate. They must be enrolled at least half time as an undergraduate or graduate student, have a GPA of 2.5 or higher, not be in default on any student loan, and be enrolled or accepted for enrollment in a teacher education program.

Financial Data Grants up to $5,000 per year are awarded. This is a scholarship/loan program. Recipients must agree to teach full time 1 year for each year of support received. The teaching agreement may be fulfilled at a public, private, or parochial preschool, elementary school, or secondary school in Illinois; at least 30% of the student body at those schools must be minority. It must be fulfilled within the 5-year period following the completion of the undergraduate program for which the scholarship was awarded. The time period may be extended if the recipient serves in the U.S. armed forces, enrolls full time in a graduate program related to teaching, becomes temporarily disabled, is unable to find employment as a teacher at a qualifying school, or takes additional courses on at least a half-time basis to obtain certification as a teacher in Illinois. Recipients who fail to honor this work obligation must repay the award with 5% interest.

Duration 1 year; may be renewed for a total of 8 semesters or 12 quarters.

Number awarded Varies each year.

Deadline Priority consideration is given to applications received by February of each year.

[901]
MIRIAM WEINSTEIN PEACE AND JUSTICE EDUCATION AWARD

Philanthrofund Foundation
Attn: Scholarship Committee
1409 Willow Street, Suite 109
Minneapolis, MN 55403-2241
(612) 870-1806   Toll Free: (800) 435-1402
Fax: (612) 871-6587   E-mail: info@PfundOnline.org
Web: www.pfundonline.org/scholarships.html

Summary To provide financial assistance to Hispanic and other minority students from Minnesota who have supported gay, lesbian, bisexual, and transgender (GLBT) activities and are interested in working on a degree in education.

Eligibility This program is open to residents of Minnesota and students attending a Minnesota educational institution who are members of a religious, racial, or ethnic minority. Applicants must be self-identified as GLBT or from a GLBT family and have demonstrated a commitment to peace and justice issues. They may be attending or planning to attend trade school, technical college, college, or university (as an undergraduate or graduate student). Preference is given to students who have completed at least 2 years of college and are working on a degree in education. Selection is based on the applicant's 1) affirmation of GLBT or allied identity; 2) evidence of experience and skills in service and leadership; and 3) evidence of service, leading, and working for change in GLBT communities, including serving as a role model, mentor, and/or adviser.

Financial Data The stipend is $3,000. Funds must be used for tuition, books, fees, or dissertation expenses.

Duration 1 year.

Number awarded 1 each year.

Deadline January of each year.

[902]
MLA/NLM SPECTRUM SCHOLARSHIPS

Medical Library Association
Attn: Grants Coordinator
65 East Wacker Place, Suite 1900
Chicago, IL 60601-7246
(312) 419-9094, ext. 15   Fax: (312) 419-8950
E-mail: awards@mail.mlahq.org
Web: www.mlanet.org/p/cm/ld/fid=449

Summary To provide financial assistance to Hispanics and members of other minority groups interested in preparing for a career as a medical librarian.

Eligibility This program is open to members of minority groups (Hispanics, African Americans, Asians, Native Americans, and Pacific Islanders) who are attending library schools accredited by the American Library Association (ALA). Applicants must be interested in preparing for a career as a health sciences information professional.

Financial Data The stipend is $3,250.

Duration 1 year.

Additional data This program, established in 2001, is jointly sponsored by the Medical Library Association (MLA) and the National Library of Medicine (NLM) of the U.S. National Institutes of Health (NIH). It operates as a component of the Spectrum Initiative Scholarship program of the ALA.

Number awarded 2 each year.

Deadline February of each year.

[903]
MLA SCHOLARSHIP FOR MINORITY STUDENTS

Medical Library Association
Attn: Grants Coordinator
65 East Wacker Place, Suite 1900
Chicago, IL 60601-7246
(312) 419-9094, ext. 15   Fax: (312) 419-8950
E-mail: awards@mail.mlahq.org
Web: www.mlanet.org/p/cm/ld/fid=304

Summary To assist Hispanic and other minority students interested in preparing for a career in medical librarianship.

Eligibility This program is open to racial minority students (Hispanics or Latinos, Asians, Blacks or African Americans, Aboriginals, North American Indians or Alaskan Natives, Native Hawaiians, or other Pacific Islanders) who are entering an ALA-accredited graduate program in librarianship or who have completed less than half of their academic requirements for a master's degree in library science. They must be interested in preparing for a career in medical librarianship. Selection is based on academic record, letters of reference, professional potential, and the applicant's statement of career objectives. U.S. or Canadian citizenship or permanent resident status is required.

Financial Data The stipend is $5,000.

Duration 1 year.

Additional data This program began in 1973.

Number awarded 1 each year.

Deadline November of each year.

[904]
MORENO/RANGEL LEGISLATIVE LEADERSHIP PROGRAM

Mexican American Legislative Leadership Foundation
Attn: Legislative Leadership Program
202 West 13th Street
Austin, TX 78701
(512) 499-0804   Fax: (512) 480-8313
E-mail: director@mallfoundation.org
Web: mallfoundation.org

Summary To provide an opportunity for undergraduate and graduate students in Texas to gain work experience on the staff of members of the Mexican American Legislative Caucus of the Texas state legislature.

Eligibility This program is open to undergraduate and graduate students who are enrolled at 2- and 4-year colleges and universities in Texas and have completed at least 60 credit hours of work; recent graduates are also welcome to apply. Applicants must be interested in working full time on the staff of a Latino member of the Texas House of Representatives. They must be at least 21 years of age, have a record of community and extracurricular involvement, be able to demonstrate excellent composition and communication skills, and have a GPA of 2.5 or higher. Along with their application, they must submit an essay of 500 to 750 words in which they describe the family, work, educational, and community experiences that led them to apply for this program; they should also explain how those experiences relate to their long-term personal goals and how this legislative experience will contribute to their future leadership within the Latino community.

Financial Data Participants receive a monthly stipend (amount not specified) to assist with living expenses.

Duration 5 months, beginning in January.

Additional data This program is named after Paul C. Moreno (the longest-serving Hispanic member of the Texas House of Representatives) and Irma Rangel (the first Mexican American woman to serve in the Texas Legislature).

Number awarded Varies each year; recently, 6 of these internships/fellowships were awarded.

Deadline November of each year.

[905]
MORGAN STANLEY MBA FELLOWSHIP

Morgan Stanley
Attn: Diversity Recruiting
1585 Broadway
New York, NY 10036
(212) 762-0211   Toll Free: (888) 454-3965
Fax: (212) 507-4972
E-mail: mbafellowship@morganstanley.com
Web: www.morganstanley.com

Summary To provide financial assistance and work experience to Hispanics and members of other underrepresented groups who are working on an M.B.A. degree.

Eligibility This program is open to full-time M.B.A. students who are Hispanics, African Americans, Native Americans, women, or lesbian/gay/bisexual/transgender. Selection is based on assigned essays, academic achievement, recommendations, extracurricular activities, leadership qualities, and on-site interviews.

Financial Data The program provides full payment of tuition and fees and a paid summer internship.

Duration 1 year; may be renewed for a second year, providing the student remains enrolled full time in good academic standing and completes the summer internship following the first year.

Additional data The paid summer internship is offered within Morgan Stanley institutional securities (equity research, fixed income, institutional equity, investment banking), investment management, or private wealth management. This program was established in 1999.

Number awarded 1 or more each year.

Deadline December of each year.

[906]
MOSS ADAMS FOUNDATION SCHOLARSHIP

Educational Foundation for Women in Accounting
Attn: Foundation Administrator
136 South Keowee Street
Dayton, OH 45402
(937) 424-3391   Fax: (937) 222-5749
E-mail: info@efwa.org
Web: www.efwa.org/scholarships_graduate.php

Summary To provide financial support to women, including Hispanic and other minority women, who are working on an accounting degree.

Eligibility This program is open to women who are enrolled in an accounting degree program at an accredited college or university. Applicants must meet 1 of the following criteria: 1) women pursuing a fifth-year requirement either through general studies or within a graduate program; 2) women returning to school as current or reentry juniors or seniors; or 3) minority women. Selection is based on aptitude for accounting and business, commitment to the goal of working on a degree in accounting (including evidence of continued commitment after receiving this award), clear evidence that the candidate has established goals and a plan for achieving those goals (both personal and professional), financial need, and a demonstration of how the scholarship will impact her life. U.S. citizenship is required.

Financial Data The stipend is $1,000.

Duration 1 year.

Additional data This program was established by Rowling, Dold & Associates LLP, a woman-owned C.P.A. firm based in San Diego. It was renamed when that firm merged with Moss Adams LLP.

Number awarded 2 each year: 1 to an undergraduate and 1 to a graduate student.

Deadline April of each year.

[907]
MSCPA MINORITY SCHOLARSHIPS

Missouri Society of Certified Public Accountants
Attn: MSCPA Educational Foundation
540 Maryville Centre Drive, Suite 200
P.O. Box 958868
St. Louis, MO 63195-8868
(314) 997-7966   Toll Free: (800) 264-7966 (within MO)
Fax: (314) 997-2592   E-mail: dhull@mocpa.org
Web: www.mocpa.org/students/scholarships

Summary To provide financial assistance to Hispanic and other minority residents of Missouri who are working on an undergraduate or graduate degree in accounting at a university in the state.

Eligibility This program is open to members of minority groups underrepresented in the accounting profession (Hispanic/Latino, Black/African American, Native American, Asian American) who are currently working full time on an undergraduate or graduate degree in accounting at a college or university in Missouri. Applicants must either be residents of Missouri or the children of members of the Missouri Society of Certified Public Accountants (MSCPA). They must be U.S. citizens, have completed at least 30 semester hours of college work, have a GPA of 3.3 or higher, and be student members of the MSCPA. Selection is based on the GPA, involvement in MSCPA, educator recommendations, and leadership potential. Financial need is not considered.

Financial Data The stipend is $1,250 per year.

Duration 1 year; may be renewed.

Number awarded Varies each year; recently, 3 were awarded.

Deadline February of each year.

[908]
MSIPP INTERNSHIPS

Department of Energy
Office of Environmental Management
Savannah River National Laboratory
Attn: MSIPP Program Manager
Building 773-41A, 232
Aiken, SC 29808
(803) 725-9032   E-mail: connie.yung@srnl.doe.gov
Web: srnl.doe.gov/msipp/internships.htm

Summary To provide an opportunity for undergraduate and graduate students at Hispanic and other Minority Serving Institutions (MSIs) to work on a summer research project at designated National Laboratories of the U.S. Department of Energy (DOE).

Eligibility This program is open to full-time undergraduate and graduate students enrolled at an accredited MSI. Applicants must be interested in working during the summer on a research project at a participating DOE National Laboratory. They must be working on a degree in a field of science, technology, engineering, or mathematics (STEM); the specific field depends on the particular project on which they wish to work. Their GPA must be 3.0 or higher. U.S. citizenship is required.

Financial Data The stipend depends on the cost of living at the location of the host laboratory.

Duration 10 weeks during the summer.

Additional data This program is administered at the Savannah River National Laboratory (SRNL) in Aiken, South Carolina, which serves as the National Laboratory for the DOE Office of Environmental Management. The other participating National Laboratories are Argonne National Laboratory (ANL) in Argonne, Illinois, Idaho National Laboratory (INL) in Idaho Falls, Idaho, Los Alamos National Laboratory (LANL) in Los Alamos, New Mexico, Oak Ridge National Laboratory (ORNL) in Oak Ridge, Tennessee, and Pacific Northwest National Laboratory (PNNL) in Richland, Washington. The program began in 2016.

Number awarded Varies each year. Recently, the program offered 11 research projects at SRNL, 12 at ANL, 1 at INL, 7 at LANL, 4 at ORNL, and 7 at PNNL.

Deadline March of each year.

[909]
MULTICULTURAL AUDIENCE DEVELOPMENT INITIATIVE INTERNSHIPS

Metropolitan Museum of Art
Attn: Internship Programs
1000 Fifth Avenue
New York, NY 10028-0198
(212) 570-3710   Fax: (212) 570-3782
E-mail: mmainterns@metmuseum.org
Web: www.metmuseum.org

Summary To provide summer work experience at the Metropolitan Museum of Art to Hispanic and other college undergraduates, graduate students, and recent graduates from diverse backgrounds.

Eligibility This program is open to members of diverse groups who are undergraduate juniors and seniors, students currently working on a master's degree, or individuals who completed a bachelor's or master's degree within the past year. Ph.D. students may be eligible to apply during the first 12 months of their program, provided they have not yet achieved candidacy. Students from various academic backgrounds are encouraged to apply, but they must be interested in preparing for a career in the arts and museum fields. Freshmen and sophomores are not eligible.

Financial Data The stipend is $3,750.

Duration 10 weeks, beginning in June.

Additional data Interns are assigned to departmental projects (curatorial, administration, or education) at the Metropolitan Museum of Art; other assignments may include giving gallery talks and working at the Visitor Information Center. The assignment is for 35 hours a week. The internships are funded by the Multicultural Audience Initiative at the museum.

Number awarded 1 or more each year.

Deadline January of each year.

[910]
NAHN PAST PRESIDENTS SCHOLARSHIP FUND

National Association of Hispanic Nurses
Attn: Scholarships
1500 Sunday Drive, Suite 102
Raleigh, NC 27607
(919) 787-5181, ext. 1255   Fax: (919) 787-4916
E-mail: director@thehispanicnurses.org
Web: www.nahnnet.org/NAHNScholarships.html

Summary To provide financial assistance for nursing education to members of the National Association of Hispanic Nurses (NAHN).

Eligibility Eligible are members of the association enrolled in associate, diploma, baccalaureate, graduate, or practical/vocational nursing programs at NLN-accredited schools of nursing. Applicants must have a GPA of 3.0 or higher. Along with their application, they must submit a letter of recommendation; a 300-word essay that reflects their qualifications and potential for leadership in nursing in the Hispanic community; a resume that includes earned certificates, awards, and special honors; information on their financial status; and an offi-

cial transcript. U.S. citizenship or permanent resident status is required.

Financial Data Stipends recently averaged $1,125.

Duration 1 year.

Number awarded Varies each year; recently, 4 were awarded.

Deadline June of each year.

[911]
NASA EARTH AND SPACE SCIENCE FELLOWSHIP PROGRAM

National Aeronautics and Space Administration
Attn: Science Mission Directorate
NASA Headquarters
300 E Street, S.W., Suite 200
Washington, DC 20546-0001
(202) 358-0734   E-mail: hq-nessf-Space@nasa.gov
Web: nspires.nasaprs.com

Summary To provide financial assistance to graduate students, especially Hispanics and other underrepresented minorities, in earth and space system sciences.

Eligibility This program is open to students accepted or enrolled in a full-time M.Sc. and/or Ph.D. program at accredited U.S. universities. Applicants must be interested in conducting interdisciplinary research relevant to the 4 science divisions of the Science Mission Directorate of the U.S. National Aeronautics and Space Administration (NASA): earth science (climate variability and change, atmospheric composition, carbon cycle and ecosystems, water and energy cycle, weather and earth surface and interior), heliophysics (the scientific analysis of phenomena or the variable, magnetic Sun, its effects on the Earth and the other planets of the solar system, and its interaction with the interstellar medium), planetary science (research that enables, and is enabled by, the robotic exploration of the solar system), and astrophysics (the study of the universe beyond our solar system). U.S. citizens and permanent residents are given preference, although the program is not restricted to them. Students with disabilities and from underrepresented minority groups (African Americans, Native Americans, Alaskan Natives, Mexican Americans, Puerto Ricans, and Native Pacific Islanders) are especially urged to apply. Selection is based on quality of the proposed research, relevance of the proposed research to NASA's objectives in earth or space science, and academic excellence (based on transcripts and a letter of reference from the student's academic adviser).

Financial Data The grant is $45,000 per year, including the recipient's stipend of $35,000 and a university allowance of up to $10,000 for tuition, fees, and other expenses.

Duration 1 year; may be renewed for up to 2 additional years.

Additional data This program began in 1990.

Number awarded Approximately 84 to 90 each year: 50 in earth science, 3 to 5 in heliophysics, 25 in planetary science, and 6 to 10 in astrophysics.

Deadline January of each year.

[912]
NASA EDUCATION AERONAUTICS SCHOLARSHIP AND ADVANCED STEM TRAINING AND RESEARCH FELLOWSHIP

National Aeronautics and Space Administration
Attn: National Scholarship Deputy Program Manager
Office of Education and Public Outreach
Ames Research Center
Moffett Field, CA 94035
(650) 604-6958   E-mail: elizabeth.a.cartier@nasa.gov
Web: nspires.nasaprs.com

Summary To provide financial assistance to Hispanics and members of other underrepresented groups interested in working on a graduate degree in fields of science, technology, engineering, and mathematics (STEM) of interest to the U.S. National Aeronautics and Space Administration (NASA).

Eligibility This program (identified as AS&ASTAR) is open to students who have a bachelor's degree and have historically been underrepresented in NASA-related fields (women, minorities, persons with disabilities, and veterans). Applicants must be working on a research-based master's or doctoral degree in a NASA-related field of STEM, including chemistry, computer and information science and engineering, geosciences (e.g., geophysics, hydrology, oceanography, paleontology, planetary science), engineering (e.g., aeronautical, aerospace, biomedical, chemical, civil, computer, electrical, electronic, environmental, industrial, materials, mechanical, nuclear, ocean, optical, systems), life sciences (e.g., biochemistry, cell biology, environmental biology, genetics, neurosciences, physiology), materials research, mathematical sciences, or physics and astronomy). They must arrange with a researcher at a NASA Center to serve as a technical adviser in collaboration with the student's faculty adviser. Research must be conducted at a NASA Center as a team project involving the student, the faculty adviser, and the NASA technical adviser. In the selection process, consideration is given to the proposed use of NASA facilities, content, and people. Applications must include a plan for a Center-Based Research Experience (CBRE) to be conducted during the summer at the NASA facility. Students must be U.S. citizens and have a GPA of 3.0 or higher.

Financial Data Grants provide a stipend of $25,000 for master's degree students or $30,000 for doctoral candidates, $10,000 for tuition offset and fees, $8,000 as a CBRE allowance, $1,000 as a health insurance allowance, $4,500 as a faculty adviser allowance, and $1,500 as a fellow professional development allowance.

Duration 1 year; may be renewed up to 2 additional years.

Additional data The participating NASA facilities are Ames Research Center (Moffett Field, California), Armstrong Flight Research Center (Edwards, California), Glenn Research Center (Cleveland, Ohio), Goddard Space Flight Center (Greenbelt, Maryland), Jet Propulsion Laboratory (Pasadena, California), Johnson Space Center (Houston, Texas), Kennedy Space Center (Kennedy Space Center, Florida), Langley Research Center (Hampton, Virginia), Marshall Space Flight Center (Marshall Space Flight Center, Alabama), and Stennis Space Center (Stennis Space Center, Mississippi).

Number awarded At least 13 each year.

Deadline June of each year.

[913]
NASP-ERT MINORITY SCHOLARSHIP PROGRAM

National Association of School Psychologists
Attn: Education and Research Trust
4340 East-West Highway, Suite 402
Bethesda, MD 20814
(301) 657-0270   Toll Free: (866) 331-NASP
Fax: (301) 657-0275   TDD: (301) 657-4155
E-mail: kbritton@naspweb.org
Web: www.nasponline.org

Summary To provide financial assistance to Hispanic and other minority graduate students who are members of the National Association of School Psychologists (NASP) and enrolled in a school psychology program.

Eligibility This program is open to minority students who are NASP members enrolled full or part time in a regionally-accredited school psychology program in the United States. Applicants must have a GPA of 3.0 or higher. Doctoral candidates are not eligible. Applications must be accompanied by 1) a resume that includes undergraduate and/or graduate schools attended, awards and honors, student and professional activities, work and volunteer experiences, research and publications, workshops or other presentations, and any special skills, training, or experience, such as bilingualism, teaching experience, or mental health experience; and 2) a statement, up to 1,000 words, of professional goals. Selection is based on adherence to instructions; completeness of the application; applicant's experience, interests and growth as reflected on their resume; applicant's professional goals statement; recommendations; financial standing; and degree of scholarship. U.S. citizenship is required.

Financial Data The stipend is $5,000 per year.

Duration 1 year; may be renewed up to 2 additional years.

Additional data This program, which began in 1995, includes the Deborah Peek Crockett Minority Scholarship Award, the Wayne Gressett Memorial Minority Scholarship Award, and the Pearson Minority Scholarship Award.

Number awarded Varies each year; recently, 4 were awarded.

Deadline November of each year.

[914]
NATIONAL ASSOCIATION OF HISPANIC JOURNALISTS SCHOLARSHIPS

National Association of Hispanic Journalists
Attn: Scholarship Committee
1050 Connecticut Avenue, N.W., Fifth Floor
Washington, DC 20036
(202) 853-7760   E-mail: nahj@nahj.org
Web: www.nahj.org/nahj-scholarships

Summary To provide financial assistance to undergraduate and graduate student members of the National Association of Hispanic Journalists (NAHJ) who are interested in preparing for careers in the media.

Eligibility This program is open to Hispanic American high school seniors, undergraduates, and graduate students who are interested in preparing for a career in English- or Spanish-language print, broadcast (radio or television), online, or photojournalism; students majoring in other fields must be able to demonstrate a strong interest in preparing for a career in journalism. Applicants must be enrolled full time at a college or university in the United States or Puerto Rico. They must be NAHJ members. Along with their application, they must submit transcripts, a 1-page resume, 2 letters of recommendation, work samples, and a 1,000-word autobiographical essay that includes why they are interested in a career in journalism, what inspired them to prepare for a career in the field, what hardships or obstacles they have experienced while trying to realize their goal of becoming a journalist, and the role Latino journalists play in the news industry. Selection is based on commitment to the field of journalism, academic achievement, awareness of the Latino community, and financial need.

Financial Data   Stipends range from $2,000 to $5,000.

Duration   1 year.

Additional data   This program consists of the Rubén Salazar Scholarships (established in 1986), the Maria Elena Salinas Scholarships (established in 2002), and the Hortencia Zavala Scholarship (established in 2016).

Number awarded   Varies each year.

Deadline   February of each year.

[915]
NATIONAL ASSOCIATION OF HISPANIC NURSES MICHIGAN CHAPTER SCHOLARSHIPS

National Association of Hispanic Nurses-Michigan
    Chapter
c/o Dottie Rodriquez, Scholarship Committee
769 Fox River Drive
Bloomfield Township, MI 48304
(313) 282-8471   E-mail: dottierodr@aol.com
Web: michiganhispanicnurses.org/scholarships.html

Summary   To provide financial assistance to undergraduate and graduate nursing students who are members of the National Association of Hispanic Nurses (NAHN) enrolled in a program in Michigan or Ohio.

Eligibility   This program is open to members of NAHN and its Michigan chapter who have completed at least 1 semester of a generic nursing degree or certificate (L.P.N., A.D.N., B.S.N., M.S., M.S.N., Ph.D., or D.N.P.) at a school in Michigan or Ohio; R.N. to B.S.N. students are not eligible. Undergraduates must have a GPA of 2.75 or higher and graduate students 3.0 or higher. Applicants must submit a 2-page essay that includes personal background information, school involvement, community service, goals after graduation, and how they plan to serve the NAHN Michigan chapter. Financial need is not considered in the selection process.

Financial Data   The stipend is $1,000.

Duration   1 year; nonrenewable.

Additional data   Recipients must agree to perform 10 to 20 hours of volunteer service to the sponsor within 1 year of receipt of this scholarship.

Number awarded   Varies each year; recently, 4 were awarded.

Deadline   October of each year.

[916]
NATIONAL DEFENSE SCIENCE AND ENGINEERING GRADUATE FELLOWSHIP PROGRAM

American Society for Engineering Education
Attn: NDSEG Fellowship Program
1818 N Street, N.W., Suite 600
Washington, DC 20036-2479
(202) 649-3831   Fax: (202) 265-8504
E-mail: ndseg@asee.org
Web: ndseg.asee.org/about_ndseg

Summary   To provide financial assistance to doctoral students in areas of science and engineering that are of potential military importance, especially Hispanics and other minorities.

Eligibility   This program is open to U.S. citizens and nationals entering or enrolled in the early stages of a doctoral program in aeronautical and astronautical engineering; biosciences, including toxicology; chemical engineering; chemistry; civil engineering; cognitive, neural, and behavioral sciences; computer and computational sciences; electrical engineering; geosciences, including terrain, water, and air; materials science and engineering; mathematics; mechanical engineering; naval architecture and ocean engineering; oceanography; or physics, including optics. Applicants must be enrolled or planning to enroll as full-time students. Applications are particularly encouraged from women, members of ethnic minority groups (American Indians, African Americans, Hispanics or Latinos, Native Hawaiians and other Pacific Islanders, Alaska Natives, and Asians), and persons with disabilities. Selection is based on all available evidence of ability, including academic records, letters of recommendation, and GRE scores.

Financial Data   The annual stipend is $30,500 for the first year, $31,000 for the second year; and $31,500 for the third year; the program also pays the recipient's institution full tuition and required fees (not to include room and board). Medical insurance is covered up to $1,000 per year.

Duration   3 years, as long as satisfactory academic progress is maintained.

Additional data   This program is sponsored by the High Performance Computing Modernization Program within the Department of Defense, the Army Research Office, the Air Force Office of Scientific Research, and the Office of Naval Research. Recipients do not incur any military or other service obligation.

Number awarded   Approximately 200 each year.

Deadline   December of each year.

[917]
NATIONAL HISPANIC FOUNDATION FOR THE ARTS SCHOLARSHIP PROGRAM

National Hispanic Foundation for the Arts
Attn: Scholarship Selection Committee
1050 Connecticut Avenue, N.W., Tenth Floor
Washington, DC 20007
(202) 293-8330   Fax: (202) 722-3101
E-mail: info@hispanicarts.org
Web: www.hispanicarts.org/rules

Summary To provide financial assistance to Hispanic students working on a graduate degree in fields related to the performing arts at designated universities.

Eligibility This program is open to U.S. citizens and permanent residents who are of Hispanic heritage (1 parent fully Hispanic or each parent half Hispanic). Applicants must be enrolled full time at a designated university and working on a graduate degree in drama/theater, set design/costume design, lighting design, film (writing/directing/producing), broadcast communications, entertainment law, or business administration with an emphasis on entertainment management. They must have a GPA of 3.0 or higher. Selection is based on academic record, academic plans and career goals, financial need, community service, essays, a letter of recommendation, and a portfolio.

Financial Data A stipend is awarded (amount not specified).

Duration 1 year.

Additional data The designated universities are Columbia University, Harvard University, New York University, Northwestern, University of California at Los Angeles, University of Southern California, University of Texas at Austin, and Yale University.

Number awarded Varies each year; since its founding in 1997, this foundation has awarded more than 350 scholarships worth more than $1 million.

Deadline July of each year.

[918]
NATIONAL HISPANIC HEALTH PROFESSIONAL SCHOLARSHIPS

National Hispanic Medical Association
Attn: National Hispanic Health Foundation
1216 Fifth Avenue, Room 457
New York, NY 10029
(212) 419-3686   Toll Free: (866) 628-6462
E-mail: scholarship@nhmafoundation.org
Web: www.nhmafoundation.org

Summary To provide financial assistance to Hispanic students working on a health-related degree at the graduate level.

Eligibility This program is open to U.S. citizens, permanent residents, and Deferred Action for Childhood Arrivals (DACA) students. Applicants must be currently enrolled full time at a graduate dental, medical (allopathic or osteopathic), nursing, pharmacy, public health, or health policy school in any state and have a GPA of 3.0 or higher. They are not required to be Hispanic, but they must be able to demonstrate an affinity for the health of Hispanic communities. Along with their application, they must submit a letter of recommendation, transcripts, a personal statement that includes their career goals, and a current curriculum vitae. Students in pre-health professional program are not eligible. The only eligible undergraduates are nursing students who have completed at least 60 sememster hours of a B.S.N. program. Selection is based on academic performance, leadership, and commitment to their Hispanic community.

Financial Data Stipends are $5,000 or $2,000.

Duration 1 year; the $5,000 awards may be renewed 1 additional year.

Additional data This program began in 2005 in affiliation with the Robert F. Wagner Graduate School of Public Service at New York University.

Number awarded Varies each year; recently, 21 were awarded: 11 at $5,000 per year for 2 years and 10 for 1 year at $2,000.

Deadline September of each year.

[919]
NATIONAL MEDICAL FELLOWSHIPS EMERGENCY SCHOLARSHIP FUND

National Medical Fellowships, Inc.
Attn: Scholarship Program
347 Fifth Avenue, Suite 510
New York, NY 10016
(212) 483-8880   Toll Free: (877) NMF-1DOC
Fax: (212) 483-8897 E-mail: scholarships@nmfonline.org
Web: www.nmfonline.org

Summary To provide financial assistance to Latinos and other minority medical students who are facing financial emergencies.

Eligibility This program is open to U.S. citizens who are enrolled in the third or fourth year of an accredited M.D. or D.O. degree-granting program in the United States and are facing extreme financial difficulties because of unforeseen training-related expenses. The emergency must be sudden, unexpected, and unbudgeted. Applicants must be Latinos, African Americans, Native Hawaiians, Alaska Natives, American Indians, Pacific Islanders, Vietnamese, or Cambodians who permanently reside in the United States. They must be interested in primary care practice in underserved communities.

Financial Data Assistance ranges up to $5,000.

Duration 1 year; nonrenewable.

Additional data This program began in 2008.

Number awarded Varies each year; recently, 3 were awarded.

Deadline Applications may be submitted at any time.

[920]
NATIONAL PHYSICAL SCIENCE CONSORTIUM GRADUATE FELLOWSHIPS

National Physical Science Consortium
c/o University of Southern California
3716 South Hope Street, Suite 348
Los Angeles, CA 90007-4344
(213) 821-2409   Toll Free: (800) 854-NPSC
Fax: (213) 821-6329   E-mail: npsc@npsc.org
Web: www.npsc.org

Summary To provide financial assistance and summer work experience to Hispanics and other underrepresented minorities who are interested in working on a Ph.D. in designated science and engineering fields.

Eligibility This program is open to U.S. citizens who are seniors graduating from college with a GPA of 3.0 or higher, enrolled in the first year of a doctoral program, completing a terminal master's degree, or returning from the workforce and holding no more than a master's degree. Students currently in the third or subsequent year of a Ph.D. program or who already have a doctoral degree in any field (Ph.D., M.D., J.D., Ed.D.) are ineligible. Applicants must be interested in working on a Ph.D. in fields that vary but emphasize astronomy, chemistry, computer science, engineering (chemical, computer, electrical, environmental, or mechanical), geology, materials science, mathematical sciences, or physics. The program welcomes applications from all qualified students and continues to emphasize the recruitment of underrepresented minority (Hispanic, African American, Native American Indian, Eskimo, Aleut, and Pacific Islander) and women physical science and engineering students. Fellowships are provided to students at more than 100 universities that are members of the consortium. Selection is based on academic standing (GPA), course work taken in preparation for graduate school, university and/or industry research experience, letters of recommendation, and GRE scores.

Financial Data The fellowship pays tuition and fees plus an annual stipend of $20,000. It also provides on-site paid summer employment to enhance technical experience. The exact value of the fellowship depends on academic standing, summer employment, and graduate school attended; the total amount generally exceeds $200,000.

Duration Support is initially provided for 2 or 3 years, depending on the employer-sponsor. If the fellow makes satisfactory progress and continues to meet the conditions of the award, support may continue for a total of up to 6 years or completion of the Ph.D., whichever comes first.

Additional data This program began in 1989. Tuition and fees are provided by the participating universities. Stipends and summer internships are provided by sponsoring organizations. Students must submit separate applications for internships, which may have additional eligibility requirements. Internships are currently available at Lawrence Livermore National Laboratory in Livermore, California (astronomy, chemistry, computer science, geology, materials science, mathematics, and physics); National Institute of Standards and Technology in Gaithersburg, Maryland (various fields of STEM); National Security Agency in Fort Meade, Maryland (astronomy, chemistry, computer science, geology, materials science, mathematics, and physics); Sandia National Laboratory in Livermore, California (biology, chemistry, computer science, environmental science, geology, materials science, mathematics, and physics); and Sandia National Laboratory in Albuquerque, New Mexico (chemical engineering, chemistry, computer science, materials science, mathematics, mechanical engineering, and physics). Fellows must submit a separate application for dissertation support in the year prior to the beginning of their dissertation research program, but not until they can describe their intended research in general terms.

Number awarded Varies each year; recently, 11 were awarded.

Deadline November of each year.

[921]
NATIONAL SPACE GRANT COLLEGE AND FELLOWSHIP PROGRAM

National Aeronautics and Space Administration
Attn: Office of Education
300 E Street, S.W.
Mail Suite 6M35
Washington, DC 20546-0001
(202) 358-1069   Fax: (202) 358-7097
E-mail: aleksandra.korobov@nasa.gov
Web: www.nasa.gov

Summary To provide financial assistance to undergraduate and graduate students, especially Hispanics and members of other underrepresented groups, who are interested in preparing for a career in a space-related field.

Eligibility This program is open to undergraduate and graduate students at colleges and universities that participate in the National Space Grant program of the U.S. National Aeronautics and Space Administration (NASA) through their state consortium. Applicants must be interested in a program of study and/or research in a field of science, technology, engineering, or mathematics (STEM) related to space. A specific goal of the program is to recruit and train U.S. citizens, especially underrepresented minorities, women, and persons with disabilities, for careers in aerospace science and technology. Financial need is not considered in the selection process.

Financial Data Each consortium establishes the terms of the fellowship program in its state.

Additional data NASA established the Space Grant program in 1989. It operates through 52 consortia in each state, the District of Columbia, and Puerto Rico. Each consortium includes selected colleges and universities in that state as well as other affiliates from industry, museums, science centers, and state and local agencies.

Number awarded Varies each year.

Deadline Each consortium sets its own deadlines.

[922]
NATIONAL URBAN FELLOWS PROGRAM

National Urban Fellows, Inc.
Attn: Program Director
1120 Avenue of the Americas, Fourth Floor
New York, NY 10036
(212) 730-1700   Fax: (212) 730-1823
E-mail: info@nuf.org
Web: www.nuf.org/fellows-overview

Summary To provide mid-career public sector professionals, especially Hispanics and other people of color, with an opportunity to strengthen leadership skills through a master's degree program coupled with a mentorship.

Eligibility This program is open to U.S. citizens who have a bachelor's degree, have at 5 to 7 years of professional work experience with 2 years in a management capacity, have demonstrated leadership capacity with potential for further growth, have a GPA of 3.0 or higher, and can demonstrate a commitment to public service. Applicants must submit a 1-page autobiographical statement, a 2-page personal statement, and a 2-page statement on their career goals. They may be of any racial or ethnic background, but the program's goal is to increase the number of competent administrators from underrepresented ethnic and cultural groups at all levels of public and private urban management organizations. Semifinalists are interviewed.

Financial Data The stipend is $25,000. Fellows are required to pay a $500 registration fee and a $7,500 co-investment tuition payment upon acceptance and enrollment in the program.

Duration 14 months.

Additional data The program begins with a summer semester of study at Bernard M. Baruch College of the City University of New York. Following this, fellows spend 9 months in mentorship assignments with a senior administrator in a government agency, a major nonprofit, or a foundation. The final summer is spent in another semester of study at Baruch College. Fellows who successfully complete all requirements are granted a master's of public administration from that college. A $150 processing fee must accompany each application.

Number awarded Approximately 40 to 50 each year.

Deadline December of each year.

[923]
NBCC MINORITY FELLOWSHIP PROGRAM

National Board for Certified Counselors
Attn: NBCC Foundation
3 Terrace Way
Greensboro, NC 27403
(336) 232-0376   Fax: (336) 232-0010
E-mail: foundation@nbcc.org
Web: nbccf-mfpdr.applicantstack.com/x/detail/a2b3qvixcgjm

Summary To provide financial assistance to doctoral candidates, especially Hispanics and those from other racially and ethnically diverse populations, who are interested in working on a degree in mental health and/or substance abuse counseling.

Eligibility This program is open to U.S. citizens and permanent residents who are enrolled full time in an accredited doctoral degree mental health and/or substance abuse and addictions counseling program. Applicants must have a National Certified Counselor or equivalent credential. They must commit to provide mental health and substance abuse services to racially and ethnically diverse populations. Hispanics/Latinos, African Americans, Alaska Natives, American Indians, Asian Americans, Native Hawaiians, and Pacific Islanders are especially encouraged to apply. Applicants must be able to commit to providing substance abuse and addictions counseling services to underserved minority populations for at least 2 years after graduation.

Financial Data The stipend is $20,000.

Duration 1 year.

Additional data This program began in 2012 with support from the Substance Abuse and Mental Health Services Administration.

Number awarded 23 each year.

Deadline June of each year.

[924]
NBCC MINORITY FELLOWSHIP PROGRAM (MASTER'S ADDICTIONS)

National Board for Certified Counselors
Attn: NBCC Foundation
3 Terrace Way
Greensboro, NC 27403
(336) 232-0376   Fax: (336) 232-0010
E-mail: foundation@nbcc.org
Web: nbccf-mfp.applicantstack.com/x/detail/a2hlw8mozup7

Summary To provide financial assistance to students, especially Hispanics and members of other racially and ethnically diverse populations, who are interested in working on a master's degree in substance abuse and addictions counseling.

Eligibility This program is open to U.S. citizens and permanent residents who are enrolled full time in an accredited master's degree substance abuse and addictions counseling program. Applicants must demonstrate knowledge of and experience with racially and ethnically diverse populations. They must be able to commit to applying for the National Certified Counselor credential prior to graduation and to providing substance abuse and addictions counseling services to underserved minority transition-age youth populations (16-25 years of age) for at least 2 years after graduation. Hispanics/Latinos, African Americans, Alaska Natives, American Indians, Asian Americans, Native Hawaiians, and Pacific Islanders are especially encouraged to apply.

Financial Data The stipend is $11,000.

Duration 1 year.

Additional data This program began in 2012 with support from the Substance Abuse and Mental Health Services Administration.

Number awarded 40 each year.

Deadline June of each year.

[925]
NBCC MINORITY FELLOWSHIP PROGRAM (MASTER'S MENTAL HEALTH)

National Board for Certified Counselors
Attn: NBCC Foundation
3 Terrace Way
Greensboro, NC 27403
(336) 232-0376   Fax: (336) 232-0010
E-mail: foundation@nbcc.org
Web: nbccf-mfp.applicantstack.com/x/detail/a2hlw8m1394v

Summary To provide financial assistance to students who have knowledge of and experience with Hispanics and other racially and ethnically diverse populations and are interested in working on a master's degree in mental health counseling.

Eligibility This program is open to U.S. citizens and permanent residents who are enrolled full time in an accredited master's degree mental health counseling program. Applicants must demonstrate knowledge of and experience with racially and ethnically diverse populations. They must be able to commit to applying for the National Certified Counselor credential prior to graduation and to providing mental health counseling services to underserved minority transition-age youth populations (16-25 years of age) for at least 2 years after graduation. Hispanics/Latinos, African Americans, Alaska Natives, American Indians, Asian Americans, Native

Hawaiians, and Pacific Islanders are especially encouraged to apply.

Financial Data   The stipend is $5,000.

Duration   1 year.

Additional data   This program is supported by the Substance Abuse and Mental Health Services Administration.

Number awarded   40 each year.

Deadline   June of each year.

[926]
NCAA ETHNIC MINORITY ENHANCEMENT POSTGRADUATE SCHOLARSHIP FOR CAREERS IN ATHLETICS

National Collegiate Athletic Association
Attn: Office for Diversity and Inclusion
700 West Washington Street
P.O. Box 6222
Indianapolis, IN 46206-6222
(317) 917-6683   Fax: (317) 917-6888
E-mail: lthomas@ncaa.org
Web: www.ncaa.org

Summary   To provide funding to Hispanic and other ethnic minority graduate students who are interested in preparing for a career in intercollegiate athletics.

Eligibility   This program is open to members of minority groups who have been accepted into a program at a National Collegiate Athletic Association (NCAA) member institution that will prepare them for a career in intercollegiate athletics (athletics administrator, coach, athletic trainer, or other career that provides a direct service to intercollegiate athletics). Applicants must be U.S. citizens, have performed with distinction as a student body member at their respective undergraduate institution, have a cumulative undergraduate GPA of 3.2 or higher, and be entering the first semester or term of full-time postgraduate study. Selection is based on the applicant's involvement in extracurricular activities, course work, commitment to preparing for a career in intercollegiate athletics, and promise for success in that career. Financial need is not considered.

Financial Data   The stipend is $7,500; funds are paid to the college or university of the recipient's choice.

Duration   1 year; nonrenewable.

Number awarded   13 each year.

Deadline   February of each year.

[927]
NEIGHBORHOOD DIABETES EDUCATION PROGRAM

National Medical Fellowships, Inc.
Attn: Scholarship Program
347 Fifth Avenue, Suite 510
New York, NY 10016
(212) 483-8880   Toll Free: (877) NMF-1DOC
Fax: (212) 483-8897 E-mail: scholarships@nmfonline.org
Web: www.nmfonline.org

Summary   To provide funding to Hispanic and other underrepresented medical and nursing students who wish to participate in a neighborhood diabetes education project in New York City.

Eligibility   This program is open to members of underrepresented minority groups (Hispanic/Latino, African American, Native American, Vietnamese, or Cambodian) who are U.S. citizens. Applicants must be currently enrolled in an accredited medical school or graduate-level nursing degree program in Connecticut, New Jersey, New York, or Pennsylvania. They must be interested in a mentored service-learning experience that provides 200 hours of proactive diabetes education at a variety of community sites and health care settings in New York City. Selection is based on demonstrated leadership early in career and commitment to serving medically underserved communities.

Financial Data   The stipend is $5,000.

Additional data   Funding for this program, which began in 2015 and is administered by National Medical Fellowships (NMF), is provided by the Empire BlueCross BlueShield Foundation.

Number awarded   10 each year.

Deadline   March of each year.

[928]
NELLIE STONE JOHNSON SCHOLARSHIP

Nellie Stone Johnson Scholarship Program
P.O. Box 40309
St. Paul, MN 55104
(651) 738-1404   Toll Free: (866) 738-5238
E-mail: info@nelliestone.org
Web: www.nelliestone.org/scholarship-program

Summary   To provide financial assistance to Hispanic and other racial minority union members and their families who are interested in working on an undergraduate or graduate degree in any field at a Minnesota state college or university.

Eligibility   This program is open to students in undergraduate and graduate programs at a 2- or 4-year institution that is a component of Minnesota State Colleges and Universities (MnSCU). Applicants must be a minority (Chicano(a) or Latino(a), Asian, American Indian, Alaska Native, Black/African American, Native Hawaiian, or Pacific Islander) and a union member or the child, grandchild, or spouse of a minority union member. They must submit a 2-page essay about their background, educational goals, career goals, and commitment to the causes of human or civil rights. Undergraduates must have a GPA of 2.0 or higher; graduate students must have a GPA of 3.0 or higher. Preference is given to Minnesota residents. Selection is based on the essay, commitment to human or civil rights, extracurricular activities, volunteer activities, community involvement, academic standing, and union verification.

Financial Data   Stipends are $1,200 per year for full-time students or $500 per year for part-time students.

Duration   1 year; may be renewed up to 3 additional years for students working on a bachelor's degree, 1 additional year for students working on a master's degree, or 1 additional year for students in a community or technical college program.

Number awarded   Varies each year; recently, 18 were awarded.

Deadline   May of each year.

[929]
NEW MEXICO ALLIANCE FOR HISPANIC EDUCATION SCHOLARSHIPS

New Mexico Alliance for Hispanic Education
Attn: Program Director
P.O. Box 25806
Albuquerque, NM 87125
(505) 342-3504
Web: www.nmalliance.org/home/scholarships

Summary To provide financial assistance to Hispanic residents of New Mexico who are interested in attending college or graduate school in any state.

Eligibility This program is open to residents of New Mexico who are of Hispanic heritage and interested enrolling full time at an accredited 2- or 4-year college or university in the United States, Puerto Rico, the U.S. Virgin Islands, or Guam. Applicants must have a GPA of 3.0 or higher and be working on or planning to work on an undergraduate or graduate degree. They must be U.S. citizens, permanent residents, or visitors with a passport stamped I-551. In addition to submitting the application, they must apply for federal financial aid by completing the Free Application for Federal Student Aid (FAFSA).

Financial Data Stipends range from $1,000 to $2,500.

Duration 1 year.

Number awarded Varies each year.

Deadline February of each year.

[930]
NEW MEXICO MINORITY DOCTORAL LOAN-FOR-SERVICE PROGRAM

New Mexico Higher Education Department
Attn: Financial Aid Division
2048 Galisteo Street
Santa Fe, NM 87505-2100
(505) 476-8460   Toll Free: (800) 279-9777
Fax: (505) 476-8454   E-mail: fin.aid@state.nm.us
Web: www.hed.state.nm.us/students/minoritydoc.aspx

Summary To provide loans-for-service to Hispanic and other underrepresented minorities who reside in New Mexico and are interested in working on a doctoral degree in selected fields.

Eligibility This program is open to ethnic minorities and women who are residents of New Mexico and have received a baccalaureate degree from a public 4-year college or university in the state in mathematics, engineering, the physical or life sciences, or any other academic discipline in which ethnic minorities and women are demonstrably underrepresented in New Mexico academic institutions. Applicants must have been admitted as a full-time doctoral student at an approved university in any state. They must be sponsored by a New Mexico institution of higher education which has agreed to employ them in a tenure-track faculty position after they obtain their degree. U.S. citizenship is required.

Financial Data Loans average $15,000. This is a loan-for-service program; for every year of service as a college faculty member in New Mexico, a portion of the loan is forgiven. If the entire service agreement is fulfilled, 100% of the loan is eligible for forgiveness. Penalties may be assessed if the service agreement is not satisfied.

Duration 1 year; may be renewed up to 3 additional years.

Number awarded Up to 12 each year.

Deadline March of each year.

[931]
NEW YORK CITY DEPARTMENT OF EDUCATION GRADUATE SCHOLARSHIP PROGRAM

New York City Department of Education
Attn: Scholarships, Incentives, and Special Programs
65 Court Street, Room 508
Brooklyn, NY 11201
(718) 935-2449
Web: www.teachnycprograms.net

Summary To provide scholarship/loans to bilingual and other college graduates who are interested in working on a master's degree in a designated critical shortage area and subsequently working in that field in the New York City public schools.

Eligibility This program is open to college graduates who have a bachelor's degree from a college or university in any state. Applicants must be interested in working on a master's degree in 1 of the following areas: monolingual or bilingual speech language pathology, monolingual visually impaired, bilingual special education, or bilingual school psychology. They must have a GPA of 3.0 or higher. For the bilingual programs, applicants must be proficient in both English and a language other than English. U.S. citizenship or permanent resident status is required. For each critical subject shortage area, specified colleges or universities in the New York City region are designated where the degree may be obtained.

Financial Data This is a scholarship/loan program. Recipients are reimbursed for the full cost of tuition for their approved master's degree. They must serve as New York State certified professionals for the New York City public schools in the area in which they earn a master's degree for 2 years per year of support.

Duration Until completion of a master's degree.

Additional data Applications must be filed in person. There is a non-refundable $75 application fee. Recipients must complete at least 18 credits per year with a grade of "B" or better.

Number awarded Varies each year.

Deadline April of each year.

[932]
NEW YORK COMMUNITY TRUST/NMF MEDICAL EDUCATION AND POLICY SCHOLARSHIP

National Medical Fellowships, Inc.
Attn: Scholarship Program
347 Fifth Avenue, Suite 510
New York, NY 10016
(212) 483-8880   Toll Free: (877) NMF-1DOC
Fax: (212) 483-8897 E-mail: scholarships@nmfonline.org
Web: www.nmfonline.org

Summary To provide funding for medical education or health policy research to Hispanics and other underrepresented minority students at designated medical schools in New York City.

Eligibility This program is open to Hispanics/Latinos, African Americans, Native Americans, Vietnamese, Cambodians, and Pacific Islanders who are enrolled at Montefiore Medical Center, Icahn School of Medicine at Mount Sinai, or

Columbia University's College of Physicians and Surgeons. Applicants must be interested in conducting medical education or health policy research. They must be U.S. citizens or DACA students. Selection is based on leadership, commitment to serving medically underserved communities, and financial need.

Financial Data   The stipend is $6,000.

Duration   1 year.

Additional data   This program is sponsored by the New York Community Trust.

Number awarded   1 each year.

Deadline   September of each year.

[933]
NEW YORK COMMUNITY TRUST/NMF MEDICAL RESEARCH SCHOLARSHIPS

National Medical Fellowships, Inc.
Attn: Scholarship Program
347 Fifth Avenue, Suite 510
New York, NY 10016
(212) 483-8880   Toll Free: (877) NMF-1DOC
Fax: (212) 483-8897 E-mail: scholarships@nmfonline.org
Web: www.nmfonline.org

Summary   To provide funding for community health research to Hispanic and other underrepresented minority students at medical schools in New York City.

Eligibility   This program is open to Hispanics/Latinos, African Americans, Native Americans, Vietnamese, Cambodians, and Pacific Islanders who are entering their second through fourth year at a medical school in New York City. Applicants must be interested in conducting community health research that addresses health inequities in the city. They must be U.S. citizens or DACA students. Selection is based on leadership, commitment to serving medically underserved communities, and financial need.

Financial Data   The stipend is $6,000.

Duration   1 year.

Additional data   This program was established by the New York Community Trust in 2013.

Number awarded   2 each year.

Deadline   September of each year.

[934]
NEW YORK EXCEPTIONAL UNDERGRADUATE/ GRADUATE STUDENT SCHOLARSHIP

Conference of Minority Transportation Officials
Attn: National Scholarship Program
100 M Street, S.E., Suite 917
Washington, DC 20003
(202) 506-2917   E-mail: info@comto.org
Web: www.comto.org/page/scholarships

Summary   To provide financial assistance to Hispanic and other minority students who are members or relatives of members of the Conference of Minority Transportation Officials (COMTO) in New York and working on an undergraduate or graduate degree in transportation.

Eligibility   This program is open to minorities who have been members or relatives of members of COMTO in New York for at least 1 year. Applicants must be enrolled full time at an accredited college, university, or vocational/technical institute and working on an undergraduate or graduate degree in a transportation-related discipline. They must have a GPA of 3.5 or higher. Along with their application they must submit a cover letter on their transportation-related career goals and life aspirations. Financial need is not considered in the selection process.

Financial Data   The stipend is $5,000. Funds are paid directly to the recipient's college or university.

Duration   1 year.

Number awarded   1 each year.

Deadline   April of each year.

[935]
NMF NATIONAL ALUMNI COUNCIL SCHOLARSHIP PROGRAM

National Medical Fellowships, Inc.
Attn: Scholarship Program
347 Fifth Avenue, Suite 510
New York, NY 10016
(212) 483-8880   Toll Free: (877) NMF-1DOC
Fax: (212) 483-8897 E-mail: scholarships@nmfonline.org
Web: www.nmfonline.org

Summary   To provide financial assistance to Hispanic and other underrepresented minority medical students who are committed to the health of underserved communities.

Eligibility   This program is open to Hispanics/Latinos, African Americans, Native Americans, Vietnamese, Cambodians, and Pacific Islanders who are entering their fourth year of medical school. Applicants must have demonstrated commitment to the health of underserved communities through community service and leadership potential at an early stage in their professional careers. They must be U.S. citizens or DACA students. Financial need is considered in the selection process.

Financial Data   The stipend is $5,000.

Duration   1 year.

Number awarded   8 each year.

Deadline   September of each year.

[936]
NOAA EDUCATIONAL PARTNERSHIP PROGRAM WITH MINORITY SERVING INSTITUTIONS GRADUATE RESEARCH AND TRAINING SCHOLARSHIP PROGRAM

National Oceanic and Atmospheric Administration
Attn: Office of Education
1315 East-West Highway
SSMC3, Room 10600
Silver Spring, MD 20910-6233
(301) 628-2900   E-mail: gsp@noaa.gov
Web: www.noaa.gov/office-education/epp-msi/grtsp

Summary   To provide financial assistance and summer research experience to graduate students at Hispanic and other Minority Serving Institutions who are majoring in scientific fields of interest to the National Oceanic and Atmospheric Administration (NOAA).

Eligibility   This program is open to full-time graduate students working on master's or doctoral degrees at Minority Serving Institutions, including Hispanic Serving Institutions (HSIs), Alaska Native Serving Institutions (ANSIs), Historically Black Colleges and Universities (HBCUs), Native Hawaiian Serving Institutions (NHSIs), and Tribal Colleges and Universities (TCUs). Applicants must be working on a degree in biology, chemistry, computer science, economics, engineering, environmental law, geography, geology, mathematics, physical science, physics, or social science. They must have a GPA of 3.5 or higher. The program includes a training program during the summer at a NOAA research facility. Selection is based on academic records, a statement of career interests and goals, and compatibility of applicant's background with the interests of NOAA. U.S. citizenship is required.

Financial Data Doctoral candidates receive a stipend of $45,000 to support tuition and fees and up to $10,000 to support research travel and to present findings at conferences; master's degree candidates receive $36,000 to support tuition and fees and up to $7,000 to support research travel and to present findings at conferences.

Duration 1 year; may be renewed 1 additional year for doctoral students, provided the recipient maintains a GPA of 3.5 or higher.

Number awarded Varies each year; recently, 9 were awarded.

Deadline January of each year.

[937]
NORTH TEXAS EXCEPTIONAL UNDERGRADUATE/GRADUATE STUDENT SCHOLARSHIP

Conference of Minority Transportation Officials
Attn: National Scholarship Program
100 M Street, S.E., Suite 917
Washington, DC 20003
(202) 506-2917   E-mail: info@comto.org
Web: www.comto.org/page/scholarships

Summary To provide financial assistance to Hispanic and other minority residents of Texas who are working on an undergraduate or graduate degree in transportation.

Eligibility This program is open to minorities who are residents of Texas enrolled at an accredited college, university, or vocational/technical institute and working on an undergraduate or graduate degree in a transportation-related discipline. Applicants must have a GPA of 2.5 or higher. Along with their application they must submit a cover letter on their transportation-related career goals and life aspirations. Financial need is not considered in the selection process. Membership in the Conference of Minority Transportation Officials (COMTO) is considered a plus but is not required.

Financial Data The stipend is $4,500. Funds are paid directly to the recipient's college or university.

Duration 1 year.

Number awarded 1 each year.

Deadline April of each year.

[938]
NOTRE DAME INSTITUTE FOR ADVANCED STUDY GRADUATE STUDENT FELLOWSHIPS

University of Notre Dame
Institute for Advanced Study
Attn: Programs Administrator
1124 Flanner Hall
Notre Dame, IN 46556
(574) 631-1305   Fax: (574) 631-8997
E-mail: csherman@nd.edu
Web: ndias.nd.edu/fellowships/graduate-student

Summary To provide funding to graduate students, especially Hispanics and members of other underrepresented groups, who are interested in conducting research on topics of interest to the Notre Dame Institute for Advanced Study (NDIAS) while in residence at the institute.

Eligibility This program is open to graduate students in all disciplines, including the arts, engineering, the humanities, law, and the natural, social, and physical sciences. Applicants must be interested in conducting research that furthers the work of the NDIAS, defined as cultivating "the contemplative ideal that is an essential factor in the Catholic intellectual tradition and vital for the progression of scholarship." They must be able to demonstrate excellent records of scholarly, artistic, or research accomplishment in their field; ability to interact with other fellows and to engage in collegial discussions of research presentations; a willingness to contribute to a cooperative community of scholars; and projects that touch on normative, integrative, or ultimate questions, especially as they involve the Catholic intellectual tradition. Applications are especially encouraged from traditionally underrepresented groups. There are no citizenship requirements; non-U.S. nationals are welcome to apply.

Financial Data The grant is $25,000, including a $1,000 research account, office facilities, a computer and printer, access to libraries and other facilities, and twice-weekly institute seminars and events.

Duration 1 academic year.

Number awarded Varies each year; recently, 2 were awarded.

Deadline October of each year.

[939]
NPM LA BECA JUAN XXIII

National Association of Pastoral Musicians
Attn: NPM Scholarships
962 Wayne Avenue, Suite 210
Silver Spring, MD 20910-4461
(240) 247-3000   Toll Free: (855) 207-0293
Fax: (240) 247-3001   E-mail: npmsing@npm.org
Web: www.npm.org/Membership/scholarship.htm

Summary To provide financial assistance to Latino/a undergraduate or graduate student members of the National Association of Pastoral Musicians.

Eligibility This program is open to Latino/a members of the association who are enrolled part or full time in an undergraduate or graduate degree program. They must be studying in a field related to pastoral music, be able to demonstrate financial need, and be intending to work for at least 2 years in the field of pastoral music following graduation. Applicants must submit 1) documentation of financial need; and 2) a 5-minute performance CD of themselves or the choir-ensemble they direct.

Financial Data The stipend is $3,000 per year. Funds must be used to pay for tuition, registration, fees, or books.

Duration 1 year; recipients may reapply.

Number awarded 1 each year.

Deadline April of each year.

[940]
NSCA MINORITY SCHOLARSHIPS

National Strength and Conditioning Association
Attn: NSCA Foundation
1885 Bob Johnson Drive
Colorado Springs, CO 80906-4000
(719) 632-6722, ext. 152   Toll Free: (800) 815-6826
Fax: (719) 632-6367   E-mail: foundation@nsca.org
Web: www.nsca.com/foundation/nsca-scholarships

Summary To provide financial assistance to Hispanics and other minorities who are interested in working on an undergraduate or graduate degree in strength training and conditioning.

Eligibility This program is open to Hispanics, Blacks, Asian Americans, and Native Americans who are 17 years of age and older. Applicants must have been accepted into an accredited postsecondary institution to work on an undergraduate or graduate degree in the strength and conditioning field. Along with their application, they must submit a 500-word essay on their personal and professional goals and how receiving this scholarship will assist them in achieving those goals. Selection is based on that essay, academic achievement, strength and conditioning experience, honors and awards, community involvement, letters of recommendation, and involvement in the National Strength and Conditioning Association (NSCA).

Financial Data The stipend is $1,500.

Duration 1 year.

Additional data The NSCA is a nonprofit organization of strength and conditioning professionals, including coaches, athletic trainers, physical therapists, educators, researchers, and physicians. This program was first offered in 2003.

Number awarded Varies each year; recently, 5 were awarded.

Deadline March of each year.

[941]
OACTA LAW STUDENT DIVERSITY SCHOLARSHIPS

Ohio Association of Civil Trial Attorneys
17 South High Street, Suite 200
Columbus, OH 43215
(614) 228-4727   E-mail: oacta@assnoffices.com
Web: www.oacta.org/About/diversity_scholarship.aspx

Summary To provide financial assistance to Hispanics and other minorities who are enrolled at law schools in Ohio.

Eligibility This program is open to students entering their second or third year at a law school in Ohio. Applicants must be women or members of minority ethnic or racial groups (Hispanic, African American, Asian, Pan Asian, or Native American). Along with their application, they must submit a law school transcript and a cover letter that addresses their academic, personal, and professional accomplishments and

why they should be selected as a recipient of this scholarship. Selection is based on academic achievement in law school, professional interest in civil defense practice, service to community, and service to the cause of diversity.

Financial Data The stipend is $1,250.

Duration 1 year.

Number awarded Up to 3 each year.

Deadline April of each year.

[942]
OHIO SOCIETY OF CPAS COLLEGE SCHOLARSHIP PROGRAM

Ohio Society of CPAs
Attn: Ohio CPA Foundation
535 Metro Place South
P.O. Box 1810
Dublin, OH 43017-7810
(614) 764-2727, ext. 344
Toll Free: (800) 686-2727, ext. 344
Fax: (614) 764-5880   E-mail: oscpa@ohio-cpa.com
Web: www.ohiocpa.com

Summary To provide financial assistance to undergraduate and graduate student members of the Ohio Society of CPAs, especially Hispanics and members of other underrepresented groups, who are working on a degree in accounting at colleges and universities in the state.

Eligibility This program is open to U.S. citizens who are Ohio residents working on undergraduate or graduate degrees in accounting at colleges and universities in the state in order to complete the 150 hours required for the C.P.A. examination. Applicants must have completed at least 30 hours of college credit and have a GPA of 3.0 or higher. Awards are available to 3 categories of students: 1) 2-year awards, for students at community colleges or other 2-year institutions; 2) 4-year awards, for students at 4-year colleges and universities; and 3) diversity awards, for students from underrepresented ethnic, racial, or cultural groups.

Financial Data The stipend is $2,000.

Duration 1 year; nonrenewable.

Number awarded Varies each year; recently, 20 were awarded.

Deadline November of each year.

[943]
OKLAHOMA CAREERTECH FOUNDATION TEACHER RECRUITMENT/RETENTION SCHOLARSHIP FOR TEACHERS

Oklahoma CareerTech Foundation
Attn: Administrator
1500 West Seventh Avenue
Stillwater, OK 74074-4364
(405) 743-5453   Fax: (405) 743-5541
E-mail: leden@careertech.ok.gov
Web: www.okcareertech.org

Summary To provide financial assistance to residents of Oklahoma who are Hispanics or reflect the diversity of the state in other ways and are interested in attending a college or university in the state to earn a credential or certification for a career in the Oklahoma CareerTech system.

Eligibility This program is open to residents of Oklahoma who are incumbent CareerTech teachers working toward a

CareerTech credential or certification at an institution of higher education in the state. Applicants must reflect the ethnic diversity of the state. Along with their application, they must submit brief statements on their interest and commitment to the CareerTech teaching profession and their financial need.

Financial Data The stipend ranges from $500 per semester to $1,500 per year.

Duration 1 semester; may be renewed, provided the recipient maintains a GPA of 2.5 or higher.

Number awarded 1 or more each year.

Deadline May of each year.

[944]
OLIVER GOLDSMITH, M.D. SCHOLARSHIP

Kaiser Permanente Southern California
Attn: Residency Administration and Recruitment
393 East Walnut Street, Fifth Floor
Pasadena, CA 91188
Toll Free: (877) 574-0002   Fax: (626) 405-6581
E-mail: socal.residency@kp.org
Web: residency-scal-kaiserpermanente.org

Summary To provide financial assistance to medical students, especially Hispanics and members of other groups that will help bring diversity to the profession.

Eligibility This program is open to students entering their third or fourth year of allopathic or osteopathic medical school. Members of all ethnic and racial groups are encouraged to apply, but applicants must have demonstrated their commitment to diversity through community service, clinical volunteering, or research. They may be attending medical school in any state, but they must intend to practice in southern California and they must be available to participate in a mentoring program and a clerkship at a Kaiser Permanente facility in that region.

Financial Data The stipend is $5,000.

Duration 1 year.

Additional data This program began in 2004.

Number awarded 12 each year.

Deadline January of each year.

[945]
OLYMPIA BROWN AND MAX KAPP AWARD

Unitarian Universalist Association
Attn: Ministerial Credentialing Office
24 Farnsworth Street
Boston, MA 02210-1409
(617) 948-6403   Fax: (617) 742-2875
E-mail: mcoadministrator@uua.org
Web: www.uua.org

Summary To provide financial assistance to Unitarian Universalist (UU) candidates for the ministry, especially Hispanics and other persons of color, who submit a project on an aspect of Universalism.

Eligibility This program is open to students currently enrolled full or at least half time in a UU ministerial training program with candidate status. Applicants are primarily citizens of the United States or Canada. Along with their application, they may submit a paper, sermon, or a special project on an aspect of Unitarian Universalism. Priority is given first to those who have demonstrated outstanding ministerial ability

and secondarily to students with the greatest financial need (especially persons of color).

Financial Data The stipend is $2,500.

Duration 1 year.

Number awarded 1 each year.

Deadline April of each year.

[946]
OPERATION JUMP START III SCHOLARSHIPS

American Association of Advertising Agencies
Attn: AAAA Foundation
1065 Avenue of the Americas, 16th Floor
New York, NY 10018
(212) 262-2500   E-mail: ameadows@aaaa.org
Web: www.aaaa.org

Summary To provide financial assistance to Hispanic and other multicultural art directors and copywriters interested in working on an undergraduate or graduate degree in advertising.

Eligibility This program is open to Hispanic Americans, African Americans, Asian Americans, and Native Americans who are U.S. citizens or permanent residents. Applicants must be incoming graduate students at 1 of 6 designated portfolio schools or full-time juniors at 1 of 2 designated colleges. They must be able to demonstrate extreme financial need, creative talent, and promise. Along with their application, they must submit 10 samples of creative work in their respective field of expertise.

Financial Data The stipend is $5,000 per year.

Duration Most awards are for 2 years.

Additional data Operation Jump Start began in 1997 and was followed by Operation Jump Start II in 2002. The current program began in 2006. The 6 designated portfolio schools are the AdCenter at Virginia Commonwealth University, the Creative Circus in Atlanta, the Portfolio Center in Atlanta, the Miami Ad School, the University of Texas at Austin, and Pratt Institute. The 2 designated colleges are the Minneapolis College of Art and Design and the Art Center College of Design at Pasadena, California.

Number awarded 20 each year.

Deadline Deadline not specified.

[947]
OREGON STATE BAR SCHOLARSHIPS

Oregon State Bar
Attn: Diversity and Inclusion Department
16037 S.W. Upper Boones Ferry Road
P.O. Box 231935
Tigard, OR 97281-1935
(503) 620-0222
Toll Free: (800) 452-8260, ext. 338 (within OR)
Fax: (503) 684-1366   TDD: (503) 684-7416
E-mail: cling@osbar.org
Web: www.osbar.org/diversity/programs.html#scholar

Summary To provide financial assistance to entering and continuing students from any state enrolled at law schools in Oregon, especially Hispanics or others who will help the Oregon State Bar achieve its diversity and inclusion objectives.

Eligibility This program is open to students entering or continuing at 1 of the law schools in Oregon (Willamette, University of Oregon, and Lewis and Clark). Preference is given to students who will contribute to the Oregon State Bar's diversity and inclusion program, defined to include age, culture, disability, ethnicity, gender and gender identity or expression, geographic location, national origin, race, religion, sex, sexual orientation, and socio-economic status. Along with their application, they must submit a 500-word personal statement on either 1) how their status as a person of diversity has influenced their decision to become a lawyer and how will it influence them throughout their legal professional career; or 2) a challenge they have faced, how they met the challenge, and how that experience will affect the decisions they will make as a legal professional. They must also submit a sample of their legal writing. Selection is based on the personal statement (35%), legal writing ability (25%), academic achievement (15%), work experience and honors (10%), and financial need (15%).

Financial Data   The stipend is $2,000 per year. Funds are credited to the recipient's law school tuition account.

Duration   1 year; recipients may reapply.

Number awarded   10 each year.

Deadline   March of each year.

[948]
ORGANIC CHEMISTRY GRADUATE STUDENT FELLOWSHIPS

American Chemical Society
Division of Organic Chemistry
1155 16th Street, N.W.
Washington, DC 20036
(202) 872-4401   Toll Free: (800) 227-5558, ext. 4401
E-mail: division@acs.org
Web: www.organicdivision.org/?nd=graduate_fellowship

Summary   To provide funding for research to members of the Division of Organic Chemistry of the American Chemical Society (ACS), especially Hispanics other other minorities, who are working on a doctoral degree in organic chemistry.

Eligibility   This program is open to members of the division who are entering the third or fourth year of a Ph.D. program in organic chemistry. Applicants must submit 3 letters of recommendation, a resume, and a short essay on a research area of their choice. U.S. citizenship or permanent resident status is required. Selection is based primarily on evidence of research accomplishment. Applications from women and minorities are especially encouraged.

Financial Data   The stipend is $26,000; that includes $750 for travel support to present a poster of their work at the National Organic Symposium.

Duration   1 year.

Additional data   This program began in 1982. It includes the Emmanuil Troyansky Fellowship. Current corporate sponsors include Organic Syntheses, Boehringer Ingelheim, and Amgen.

Number awarded   Varies each year; recently, 5 were awarded.

Deadline   May of each year.

[949]
PA STUDENT SCHOLARSHIPS

American Academy of Physician Assistants
Attn: Physician Assistant Foundation
2318 Mill Road, Suite 1300
Alexandria, VA 22314-6868
(703) 836-2272   Fax: (703) 684-1924
E-mail: pafoundation@aapa.org
Web: www.pa-foundation.org

Summary   To provide financial assistance to student members of the American Academy of Physician Assistants (AAPA) who are Hispanics, other underrepresented minorities, or economically and/or educationally disadvantaged.

Eligibility   This program is open to AAPA student members attending a physician assistant program accredited by the Commission on Accreditation of Allied Health Education Programs. Applicants must qualify as 1) an underrepresented minority (American Indian, Alaska Native, Black or African American, Hispanic or Latino, Native Hawaiian or other Pacific Islander, or Asian other than Chinese, Filipino, Japanese, Korean, Asian Indian, or Thai); 2) economically disadvantaged (with income below a specified level); or 3) educationally disadvantaged (from a high school with low SAT scores, from a school district in which less than half of graduates go on to college, has a diagnosed physical or mental impairment, English is not their primary language, the first member of their family to attend college). They must have completed at least 1 semester of PA studies.

Financial Data   Stipends are $2,500, $2,000, or $1,000.

Duration   1 year; nonrenewable.

Additional data   This program includes the AAPA Past Presidents Scholarship, the Bristol-Myers Squibb Endowed Scholarship, the National Commission on Certification of Physician Assistants Endowed Scholarships, the Procter & Gamble Endowed Scholarship, and the PA Foundation Scholarships.

Number awarded   Varies each year; recently, 32 were awarded: 3 at $2,500, 27 at $2,000, and 2 at $1,000.

Deadline   January of each year.

[950]
PATRICIA G. ARCHBOLD PREDOCTORAL SCHOLAR AWARD

National Hartford Center of Gerontological Nursing
   Excellence
Attn: Hartford Institute for Geriatric Nursing
NYU Rory Myers College of Nursing
433 First Avenue, Fifth Floor
New York, NY 10010
(202) 779-1439   E-mail: nhcgne@nyu.edu
Web: www.nhcgne.org

Summary   To provide funding to nurses who are Hispanics or other underrepresented minority groups and interested in working on a doctoral degree in gerontological nursing.

Eligibility   This program is open to registered nurses who are members of underrepresented minority groups (American Indians, Alaska Natives, Asians, Blacks or African Americans, Hispanics or Latinos/Latinas, Native Hawaiians or other Pacific Islanders) and have been admitted to a doctoral program as a full-time student. The institution they plan to attend must be a member of the National Hartford Center of Gerontological Nursing Excellence (NHCGNE). Applicants must plan an academic research career in geriatric nursing. They must identify a mentor/adviser with whom they will work and whose program of research in geriatric nursing is a good match with their own research interest area. Selection is based on potential for substantial long-term contributions to the knowledge base in geriatric nursing; leadership potential; evidence of commitment to a career in academic geriatric nursing; and evidence of involvement in educational, research, and professional activities. U.S. citizenship or permanent resident status is required.

Financial Data   The stipend is $50,000 per year. An additional stipend of $5,000 is available to fellows whose research includes the study of pain in the elderly.

Duration   2 years.

Additional data   This program began in 2001 with funding from the John A. Hartford Foundation. In 2004, the Mayday Fund added support to scholars who focus on the study of pain in the elderly. Until 2013 it was known as the Building Academic Geriatric Nursing Capacity Program.

Number awarded   1 or more each year.

Deadline   January of each year.

[951]
PATRICIA M. LOWRIE DIVERSITY LEADERSHIP SCHOLARSHIP

Association of American Veterinary Medical Colleges
Attn: Diversity Committee
1101 Vermont Avenue, N.W., Suite 301
Washington, DC 20005-3536
(202) 371-9195, ext. 147   Toll Free: (877) 862-2740
Fax: (202) 842-0773   E-mail: lgreenhill@aavmc.org
Web: www.aavmc.org

Summary   To provide financial assistance to Hispanic and other veterinary students who have promoted diversity in the profession.

Eligibility   This program is open to second-, third-, and fourth-year students at veterinary colleges in the United States. Applicants must have a demonstrated record of contributing to enhancing diversity and inclusion through course projects, co-curricular activities, outreach, domestic and community engagement, research, and/or an early reputation for influencing others to be inclusive. Along with their application, they must submit a 3-page personal statement that describes 1) why diversity and inclusion are important to them personally and professionally; 2) how they intend to continue contributing to diversity and inclusion efforts in the veterinary profession after graduation; and 3) what it might mean to be honored as a recipient of this scholarship. They must also indicate how they express their race and/or ethnicity (Hispanic, American Indian or Alaskan, Asian, Black or African American, Native Hawaiian or Pacific Islander, or White) and how they express their gender (male, female, transgender spectrum, or other). Selection is based primarily on documentation of a demonstrated commitment to promoting diversity in academic veterinary medicine; consideration is also given to academic achievement, the student's broader community service record, and financial need.

Financial Data   The stipend is $6,000.

Duration   1 year; nonrenewable.

Additional data   This program began in 2013.

Number awarded   1 each odd-numbered year.

Deadline   October of each even-numbered year.

[952]
PEERMUSIC LATIN SCHOLARSHIP

Broadcast Music Inc.
Attn: BMI Foundation, Inc.
7 World Trade Center
250 Greenwich Street
New York, NY 10007-0030
(212) 220-3103   E-mail: info@bmifoundation.org
Web: www.bmifoundation.org

Summary   To recognize and reward students at colleges and universities who submit outstanding songs or instrumental works in a Latin genre.

Eligibility   This competition is open to students between 16 and 24 years of age enrolled at colleges and universities in the United States and Puerto Rico. Applicants may not have had any musical work commercially recorded or distributed. They must submit an original song or instrumental work in a Latin genre. The entry must be submitted as an MP3 or MP4a, accompanied by a typed copy of the lyric as a PDF.

Financial Data   The award is $5,000.

Duration   The award is presented annually.

Additional data   This award, first presented in 2003, is sponsored by peermusic Companies.

Number awarded   1 each year.

Deadline   January of each year.

[953]
PEGGY PETERMAN SCHOLARSHIP

Tampa Bay Times
Attn: Director of Corporate Giving
490 First Avenue South
St. Petersburg, FL 33701
(727) 893-8780   Toll Free: (800) 333-7505, ext. 8780
Fax: (727) 892-2257   E-mail: waclawek@tampabay.com
Web: www.tampabay.com

Summary   To provide financial assistance to Hispanic and other minority undergraduate and graduate students who are interested in preparing for a career in the newspaper industry and who accept an internship at the *Tampa Bay Times*.

Eligibility   This program is open to minority college sophomores, juniors, seniors, and graduate students from any state who are interested in preparing for a career in the newspaper industry. Applicants must be interested in an internship at the *Tampa Bay Times* and must apply for that at the same time as they apply for this scholarship. They should have experience working on a college publication and at least 1 professional internship.

Financial Data   The stipend is $5,000.

Duration   Internships are for 12 weeks during the summer. Scholarships are for 1 year.

Number awarded   1 each year.

Deadline   October of each year.

[954]
PFATS-NFL CHARITIES MINORITY SCHOLARSHIPS

Professional Football Athletic Trainers Society
c/o Britt Brown, ATC, Associate Athletic Trainer
Dallas Cowboys
One Cowboys Parkway
Irving, TX 75063
(972) 497-4992   E-mail: bbrown@dallascowboys.net
Web: www.pfats.com/about/scholarships

Summary To provide financial assistance to Hispanic and other ethnic minority undergraduate and graduate students working on a degree in athletic training.

Eligibility This program is open to ethnic minority students who are working on an undergraduate or graduate degree in athletic training. Applicants must have a GPA of 2.5 or higher. Along with their application, they must submit a cover letter, a curriculum vitae, and a letter of recommendation from their supervising athletic trainer. Female athletic training students are encouraged to apply.

Financial Data A stipend is awarded (amount not specified).

Duration 1 year.

Additional data Recipients also have an opportunity to work at summer training camp of a National Football League (NFL) team. Support for this program, which began in 1993, is provided by NFL Charities.

Number awarded 1 or more each year.

Deadline March of each year.

[955]
PHILLIPS EXETER ACADEMY DISSERTATION YEAR FELLOWSHIP

Phillips Exeter Academy
Attn: Dean of Multicultural Affairs
20 Main Street
Exeter, NH 03833-2460
(603) 772-4311   Fax: (603) 777-4393
E-mail: teaching_opportunities@exeter.edu
Web: www.exeter.edu

Summary To provide an opportunity for doctoral candidates who are Hispanics or from other diverse backgrounds to work on their dissertation during a residency at Phillips Exeter Academy in Exeter, New Hampshire.

Eligibility This program is open to Ph.D. candidates in any discipline who are in the completion stage of their dissertation. Applicants must be prepared to devote full time to their writing during a residency at the academy. Along with their application, they must submit a curriculum vitae, 2 letters of reference, a 2- to 3-page synopsis of the dissertation, and a 500-word statement of purpose testifying to the appropriateness of the fellowship. Candidates who are interested in potentially teaching in an independent school setting and who are underrepresented in higher education are particularly encouraged to apply.

Financial Data This program provides a stipend ($14,310), research and travel funds up to $1,000, room and board, benefits, access to facilities and resources of the school, and professional development opportunities.

Duration 1 academic year.

Additional data Fellows do not have any regular or prescribed duties. During the tenure of the program, fellows may not have any other full- or part-time job.

Number awarded 1 each year.

Deadline March of each year.

[956]
PORTER PHYSIOLOGY DEVELOPMENT AWARDS

American Physiological Society
Attn: Education Office
9650 Rockville Pike, Room 3111
Bethesda, MD 20814-3991
(301) 634-7132   Fax: (301) 634-7098
E-mail: education@the-aps.org
Web: www.the-aps.org

Summary To provide financial assistance to Hispanics and other minorities who are members of the American Physiological Society (APS) interested in working on a doctoral degree in physiology.

Eligibility This program is open to U.S. citizens and permanent residents who are members of racial or ethnic minority groups (Hispanic or Latino, American Indian or Alaska Native, Asian, Black or African American, or Native Hawaiian or other Pacific Islander). Applicants must be currently enrolled in or accepted to a doctoral program in physiology at a university as full-time students. They must be APS members and have actively participated in its work. Selection is based on the applicant's potential for success (academic record, statement of interest, previous awards and experiences, letters of recommendation); applicant's proposed training environment (including quality of preceptor); and applicant's research and training plan (clarity and quality).

Financial Data The stipend is $28,300 per year. No provision is made for a dependency allowance or tuition and fees.

Duration 1 year; may be renewed for 1 additional year and, in exceptional cases, for a third year.

Additional data This program is supported by the William Townsend Porter Foundation (formerly the Harvard Apparatus Foundation). The first Porter Fellowship was awarded in 1920. In 1966 and 1967, the American Physiological Society established the Porter Physiology Development Committee to award fellowships to minority students engaged in graduate study in physiology. The highest ranked applicant for these fellowships is designated the Eleanor Ison Franklin Fellow.

Number awarded Varies each year; recently, 6 were awarded.

Deadline January of each year.

[957]
POST-BACCALAUREATE INTERNSHIP PROGRAM IN BIOSTATISTICS AND COMPUTATIONAL BIOLOGY

Harvard T.H. Chan School of Public Health
Department of Biostatistics
Attn: Diversity Coordinator
677 Huntington Avenue, SPH2, Fourth Floor
Boston, MA 02115
(617) 432-3175   Fax: (617) 432-5619
E-mail: biostat_diversity@hsph.harvard.edu
Web: www.hsph.harvard.edu

Summary To enable Hispanic and other underrepresented minority or disadvantaged science post-baccalaureates to participate in a summer research internship at Harvard T.H. Chan School of Public Health that focuses on biostatistics and epidemiology.

Eligibility This program is open to students who have received a bachelor's degree and are interested in or planning to attend a graduate degree program in biostatistics or epidemiology. Applicants must be U.S. citizens or permanent residents who are 1) members of ethnic groups underrepresented in graduate education (Hispanic/Latinos, African Americans, Native Americans, Pacific Islanders, biracial/multiracial); 2) first-generation college students; 3) low-income students; or 4) individuals with a disability. They must have a strong GPA, including course work in calculus, and a strong interest in mathematics, statistics, computer science, and other quantitative subjects.

Financial Data Interns receive a salary (amount not specified) and support for travel.

Duration 2 to 3 months, starting in June.

Additional data Interns conduct biostatistical or epidemiologic research alongside a Harvard faculty mentor and graduate student mentor, participate in collaborative research projects, attend regular seminars, and receive directed mentoring and support for graduate school applications and selection.

Number awarded 2 each year.

Deadline January of each year.

[958]
POSTDOCTORAL RESEARCH FELLOWSHIPS IN BIOLOGY

National Science Foundation
Directorate for Biological Sciences
Attn: Division of Biological Infrastructure
4201 Wilson Boulevard, Room 615N
Arlington, VA 22230
(703) 292-2299   Fax: (703) 292-9063
TDD: (800) 281-8749   E-mail: bio-dbi-prfb@nsf.gov
Web: www.nsf.gov

Summary To provide funding for research and training in specified areas related to biology to junior doctoral-level scientists, especially Hispanics and other underrepresented minorities, at sites in the United States or abroad.

Eligibility This program is open to citizens, nationals, and permanent residents of the United States who are graduate students completing a Ph.D. or who have earned the degree no earlier than 12 months preceding the deadline date. Applicants must be interested in a program of research and training in any of 3 competitive areas: 1) Broadening Participation of Groups Underrepresented in Biology, designed to increase the diversity of scientists by providing support for research and training to biologists with disabilities and underrepresented minority (Hispanic, Native American, Native Pacific Islander, Alaskan Native, and African American) biologists; 2) Research Using Biological Collections, to address key questions in biology and potentially develop applications that extend biology to physical, mathematical, engineering, and social sciences by the use of biological research collections in museums and archives in the United States and abroad; and 3) National Plant Genome Initiative (NPGI) Postdoctoral Research Fellowships, for postdoctoral training in plant improvement and associated sciences such as physiology and pathology, quantitative genetics, or computational biology. They must identify a sponsor at a host institution who will serve as a mentor for their training program.

Financial Data Grants are $69,000 per year, including $54,000 as a stipend for the fellow and $15,000 as a fellowship allowance that is intended to cover direct research expenses, facilities and other institutional resources, and fringe benefits. An extra allowance of $10,000 is provided to fellows who go overseas.

Duration Fellowships are 24 to 36 months for Broadening Participation, 24 months for Research Using Biological Collections, or 36 months for NPGI Postdoctoral Research Fellowships.

Number awarded Approximately 40 each year in each competitive area.

Deadline October of each year.

[959]
PREDOCTORAL FELLOWSHIP IN MENTAL HEALTH AND SUBSTANCE ABUSE SERVICES

American Psychological Association
Attn: Minority Fellowship Program
750 First Street, N.E.
Washington, DC 20002-4242
(202) 336-6127   Fax: (202) 336-6012
TDD: (202) 336-6123   E-mail: mfp@apa.org
Web: www.apa.org

Summary To provide financial assistance to doctoral students, especially Hispanics and other minorities, who are committed to providing mental health and substance abuse services to ethnic minority populations.

Eligibility Applicants must be U.S. citizens, nationals, or permanent residents, enrolled full time in an accredited doctoral program, and committed to a career in psychology related to ethnic minority mental health and substance abuse services. Members of ethnic minority groups (African Americans, Hispanics/Latinos, American Indians, Alaskan Natives, Asian Americans, Native Hawaiians, and other Pacific Islanders) are especially encouraged to apply. Preference is given to students specializing in clinical, school, and counseling psychology. Selection is based on commitment to ethnic minority behavioral health services or policy, knowledge of ethnic minority behavioral health services, the fit between career goals and training environment selected, potential as a future leader in ethnic minority psychology as demonstrated through accomplishments and goals, scholarship and grades, and letters of recommendation.

Financial Data The stipend varies but is based on the amount established by the National Institutes of Health for predoctoral students; recently that was $23,376 per year.

Duration 1 academic or calendar year; may be renewed for up to 2 additional years.

Additional data Funding is provided by the U.S. Substance Abuse and Mental Health Services Administration.

Number awarded Varies each year.

Deadline January of each year.

[960]
PREDOCTORAL FELLOWSHIPS OF THE FORD FOUNDATION DIVERSITY FELLOWSHIP PROGRAM

The National Academies of Sciences, Engineering, and Medicine
Attn: Fellowships Office
500 Fifth Street, N.W.
Washington, DC 20001
(202) 334-2872　　　　　Fax: (202) 334-3419
E-mail: FordApplications@nas.edu
Web: sites.nationalacademies.org

Summary　To provide financial assistance for graduate school to Hispanice and other students whose success will increase the racial and ethnic diversity of U.S. colleges and universities.

Eligibility　This program is open to citizens, permanent residents, and nationals of the United States who are enrolled or planning to enroll full time in a Ph.D. or Sc.D. degree program and are committed to a career in teaching and research at the college or university level. Applicants may be undergraduates in their senior year, individuals who have completed undergraduate study or some graduate study, or current Ph.D. or Sc.D. students who can demonstrate that they can fully utilize a 3-year fellowship award. They must be working on or planning to work on a degree in 1 of the following fields: American studies, anthropology, archaeology, art and theater history, astronomy, chemistry, communications, computer science, cultural studies, earth sciences, economics, education, engineering, ethnic studies, ethnomusicology, geography, history, international relations, language, life sciences, linguistics, literature, mathematics, performance study, philosophy, physics, political science, psychology, religious studies, sociology, urban planning, and women's studies. Also eligible are interdisciplinary programs such as African American studies, Native American studies, area studies, peace studies, and social justice. Students in practice-oriented areas, terminal master's degrees, other doctoral degrees (e.g., Ed.D., D.F.A., Psy.D.), professional degrees (e.g., medicine, law, public health), or joint degrees (e.g., M.D./Ph.D., J.D./Ph.D., M.F.A./Ph.D.) are not eligible. The following are considered as positive factors in the selection process: evidence of superior academic achievement; promise of continuing achievement as scholars and teachers; membership in a group whose underrepresentation in the American professoriate has been severe and longstanding, including Puerto Ricans, Mexican Americans/Chicanos/Chicanas, Black/African Americans, Native American Indians, Alaska Natives (Eskimos, Aleuts, and other indigenous people of Alaska), and Native Pacific Islanders (Hawaiians, Micronesians, or Polynesians); capacity to respond in pedagogically productive ways to the learning needs of students from diverse backgrounds; sustained personal engagement with communities that are underrepresented in the academy and an ability to bring this asset to learning, teaching, and scholarship at the college and university level; and likelihood of using the diversity of human experience as an educational resource in teaching and scholarship.

Financial Data　The program provides a stipend to the student of $24,000 per year and an award to the host institution of $2,000 per year in lieu of tuition and fees.

Duration　3 years of support is provided, to be used within a 5-year period.

Additional data　The competition for this program is conducted by the National Research Council on behalf of the Ford Foundation. Applicants who merit receiving the fellowship but to whom awards cannot be made because of insufficient funds are given Honorable Mentions; this recognition does not carry with it a monetary award but honors applicants who have demonstrated substantial academic achievement. The National Research Council publishes a list of those Honorable Mentions who wish their names publicized. Fellows may not accept remuneration from another fellowship or similar external award while on this program; however, supplementation from institutional funds, educational benefits from the Department of Veterans Affairs, or educational incentive funds may be received concurrently with Ford Foundation support. Predoctoral fellows are required to submit an interim progress report 6 months after the start of the fellowship and a final report at the end of the 12 month tenure.

Number awarded　Approximately 60 each year.

Deadline　November of each year.

[961]
PRESBYTERIAN WOMEN OF COLOR GRANTS

Presbyterian Church (USA)
Attn: Office of Financial Aid for Service
100 Witherspoon Street
Louisville, KY 40202-1396
(502) 569-5224　　　　Toll Free: (888) 728-7228, ext. 5224
Fax: (502) 569-8766　　　　TDD: (800) 833-5955
E-mail: finaid@pcusa.org
Web: www.presbyterianmission.org

Summary　To provide financial assistance to graduate students who are Hispanics or othr women of color and Presbyterian Church (USA) members interested in preparing for church occupations.

Eligibility　This program is open to women of color who are full-time graduate students at a PCUSA seminary or accredited theological institution approved by their Committee on Preparation for Ministry. Applicants must be working on 1) an M.Div. degree and enrolled as an inquirer or candidate by a PCUSA presbytery; or 2) an M.A.C.E. degree and preparing for a church occupation. They must be PCUSA members, U.S. citizens or permanent residents, able to demonstrate financial need, and recommended by the financial aid officer at their theological institution. Along with their application, they must submit a 1,000-word essay on what they believe God is calling them to do in ministry.

Financial Data　Stipends range from $1,000 to $3,000 per year. Funds are intended as supplements to students who have been awarded a Presbyterian Study Grant but still demonstrate remaining financial need.

Duration　1 year; may be renewed up to 2 additional years.

Number awarded　Varies each year; the sponsor awards approximately 130 grants for this and 3 related programs each year.

Deadline　June of each year.

[962]
PRESIDENT WILLIAM G. SINKFORD SCHOLARSHIP

Unitarian Universalist Association
Attn: Ministerial Credentialing Office
24 Farnsworth Street
Boston, MA 02210-1409
(617) 948-6403   Fax: (617) 742-2875
E-mail: mcoadministrator@uua.org
Web: www.uua.org

Summary To provide financial assistance to Hispanic seminary students preparing for the Unitarian Universalist (UU) ministry.

Eligibility This program is open to seminary students who identify as people of color, Latino/a, Hispanic, or multi-racial. Applicants must have achieved candidate status for UU ministry.

Financial Data The stipend ranges from $1,000 to $15,000 per year.

Duration 1 year.

Additional data This program began in 2008.

Number awarded Varies each year.

Deadline April of each year.

[963]
PROCTER & GAMBLE DENTAL AND DENTAL AUXILIARY SCHOLARSHIPS

Hispanic Dental Association
Attn: HDA Foundation
3910 South IH-35, Suite 245
Austin, TX 78704
(512) 904-0252   E-mail: jessicac@hdassoc.org
Web: www.hdassoc.org

Summary To provide financial assistance to members of the Hispanic Dental Association (HDA) interested in preparing for a career in a dental profession.

Eligibility This program is open to HDA members who are entering their first through fourth year of dental school or first or second year at an accredited dental hygiene, dental assisting, or dental technician program in the United States or Puerto Rico. Applicants must have a GPA of 3.0 or higher, an interest in improving the health of the Hispanic community, and a demonstrated commitment and dedication to serving the Hispanic community. They must be enrolled full time Along with their application, they must submit a 250-word essay on their career goals, including how they were inspired to become a dentist, dental hygienist, dental assistant, or dental technician. Selection is based on academic achievement, leadership skills, community service, and commitment and dedication to improving the oral health of the Hispanic community.

Financial Data The stipend is $2,000 for dental students or $1,000 for dental hygiene, dental assisting, or dental technician students. An additional grant of $500 is provided for travel reimbursement and complimentary registration to the HDA annual meeting.

Duration 1 year.

Additional data This program, which began in 1994, is sponsored by Procter & Gamble Company.

Number awarded 6 each year.

Deadline May of each year.

[964]
PUBLIC HONORS FELLOWSHIPS OF THE OREGON STATE BAR

Oregon State Bar
Attn: Diversity and Inclusion Department
16037 S.W. Upper Boones Ferry Road
P.O. Box 231935
Tigard, OR 97281-1935
(503) 620-0222
Toll Free: (800) 452-8260, ext. 338 (within OR)
Fax: (503) 684-1366   TDD: (503) 684-7416
E-mail: cling@osbar.org
Web: www.osbar.org/diversity/programs.html#honors

Summary To provide law students in Oregon with summer work experience in public interest law, especially Hispanics and others who will help the Oregon State Bar achieve its diversity and inclusion objectives.

Eligibility This program is open to students at law schools in Oregon who are not in the first or final year of study. Each school may nominate up to 5 students. Nominees must have demonstrated a career goal in public interest or public sector law. Preference is given to students who will contribute to the Oregon State Bar's diversity and inclusion program, defined to include age, culture, disability, ethnicity, gender and gender identity or expression, geographic location, national origin, race, religion, sex, sexual orientation, and socio-economic status. They must be interested in working in a law office during the summer; the employment should be in Oregon, although exceptions will be made if the job offers the student special experience not available within the state. Along with their application, they must submit a 500-word personal statement on either 1) how their status as a person of diversity has influenced their decision to become a lawyer and how will it influence them throughout their legal professional career; or 2) a challenge they have faced, how they met the challenge, and how that experience will affect the decisions they will make as a legal professional. They must also submit a sample of their legal writing. Selection is based on the personal statement (35%), legal writing ability (25%), academic achievement (15%), work experience and honors (10%), and financial need (15%). The information on those students is forwarded to prospective employers in Oregon and they arrange to interview the selectees.

Financial Data Fellows receive a stipend of $5,000.

Duration 3 months during the summer.

Additional data There is no guarantee that all students selected by the sponsoring organization will receive fellowships at Oregon law firms.

Number awarded 6 each year: 2 from each of the law schools.

Deadline Each law school sets its own deadline.

[965]
PUBLIC POLICY AND INTERNATIONAL AFFAIRS FELLOWSHIPS

Public Policy and International Affairs Fellowship Program
c/o University of Minnesota
Humphrey School of Public Affairs
130 Humphrey School
301 19th Avenue South
Minneapolis, MN 55455
Toll Free: (877) 774-2001   E-mail: hadd0029@umn.edu
Web: www.ppiaprogram.org/ppia

Summary   To provide financial assistance to Hispanic and other students from underrepresented groups who have completed a specified summer institute and are interested in preparing for graduate study in the fields of public policy and/or international affairs.

Eligibility   This program is open to people of color historically underrepresented in public policy and international affairs. Applicants must be U.S. citizens or permanent residents interested in a summer institute in public policy and international affairs. They must first apply directly to the summer institute. Following participation in that institute, they apply for graduate study in fields of their choice at 41 designated universities. For a list of participating institutions, contact the sponsor.

Financial Data   The participating programs in public policy and/or international affairs have agreed to waive application fees and grant fellowships of at least $5,000 to students who have participated in the summer institutes.

Duration   1 summer and 1 academic year.

Additional data   This program was established in 1981 when the Alfred P. Sloan Foundation provided a grant to the Association for Public Policy Analysis and Management (APPAM). From 1981 through 1988, participants were known as Sloan Fellows. From 1889 through 1995, the program was supported by the Ford Foundation and administered by the Woodrow Wilson National Fellowship Administration, so participants were known as Woodrow Wilson Fellows in Public Policy and International Affairs. Beginning in 1995, the program's name was shortened to the Public Policy and International Affairs Fellowship Program (PPIA) and the Association of Professional Schools of International Affairs (APSIA) also became an institutional sponsor. In 1999, the Ford Foundation ended its support for PPIA effective with the student cohort that participated in summer institutes in 1999. The APPAM and APSIA incorporated PPIA as an independent organization and have continued to sponsor it. Since summer of 2001, summer institutes have been held at 5 universities: the Summer Program in Public Policy and International Affairs at the Gerald R. Ford School of Public Policy at the University of Michigan, the Humphrey School Junior Institute at the Humphrey School of Public Affairs at the University of Minnesota (which serves as host of the program), the UCP-PIA Junior Summer Institute at the Richard and Rhoda Goldman School of Public Policy at the University of California at Berkeley, the PPIA Junior Summer Institute at the Woodrow Wilson School of Public and International Affairs at Princeton University, and the PPIA Junior Summer Institute at the Heinz School of Public Policy and Management at Carnegie Mellon University. For information on those institutes, contact the respective school. Additional support is currently provided by the Foundation for Child Development and the William T. Grant Foundation.

Number awarded   Varies each year.

Deadline   Each of the 5 participating universities that offer summer institutes and each of the 41 universities that accept students for graduate study sets its own deadline.

[966]
PUERTO RICAN BAR ASSOCIATION SCHOLARSHIP PROGRAM

Puerto Rican Bar Association
c/o Carmen A. Pacheco, PRBA Scholarship Fund Chair
Pacheco & Lugo, PLLC
340 Atlantic Avenue
Brooklyn, NY 11201
(718) 855-3000   E-mail: puertoricanbarny@gmail.com
Web: www.prbany.com/scolarship-fund/application

Summary   To provide financial assistance to Latino law students who are residents of New York or attending law school in the state.

Eligibility   This program is open to Latino law students who are enrolled at law schools in New York or are permanent residents of that state. Applicants may be first- or second-year students or third-year evening students. Along with their application, they must submit a 2-page personal statement discussing their career goals, school and community activities, and any activities demonstrating their commitment to serve the Latino community. They must also submit a 2,500-word legal commentary on a topic that changes annually but relates to Puerto Ricans and law. Candidates for an LL.M. degree are not eligible. Selection is based on academic achievement, community involvement, dedication to the advancement of minorities through the legal process, commitment to diversity and inclusion in the profession, and financial need.

Financial Data   Stipends range from $2,500 to $5,000.

Duration   1 year.

Number awarded   Varies each year; recently, 4 were awarded.

Deadline   June of each year.

[967]
PUERTO RICAN BAR FOUNDATION SCHOLARSHIP

Puerto Rican Bar Association of Illinois
2332 North Milwaukee Avenue, Suite 104
Chicago, IL 60647
(773) 278-8140   E-mail: prbalawscholarship@gmail.com
Web: www.prbalawil.com/foundation

Summary   To provide financial assistance to law students from any state who have demonstrated a commitment to the Hispanic community.

Eligibility   This program is open to students who have completed 1 year of law school. Applicants must have distinguished themselves academically, have demonstrated a commitment to the advancement of the Hispanic community, and have financial need. Special consideration is given to students who plan to practice law in Illinois after graduation from law school.

Financial Data   A stipend is awarded (amount not specified).

Duration 1 year; nonrenewable.

Additional data This program began in 2004.

Number awarded 3 each year.

Deadline September of each year.

[968]
RACE RELATIONS MULTIRACIAL STUDENT SCHOLARSHIP

Christian Reformed Church
Attn: Office of Race Relations
1700 28th Street, S.E.
Grand Rapids, MI 49508
(616) 224-5883   Toll Free: (877) 864-3977
Fax: (616) 224-0834   E-mail: elugo@crcna.org
Web: www.crcna.org/race/scholarships

Summary To provide financial assistance to Hispanic and other minority undergraduate and graduate students interested in attending colleges related to the Christian Reformed Church in North America (CRCNA).

Eligibility This program is open to students of color in the United States and Canada. Normally, applicants are expected to be members of CRCNA congregations who plan to pursue their educational goals at Calvin Theological Seminary or any of the colleges affiliated with the CRCNA. They must be interested in training for the ministry of racial reconciliation in church and/or in society. Along with their application, they must submit paragraphs about their personal history and family, Christian faith, and Christian leadership goals. Students who have no prior history with the CRCNA must attend a CRCNA-related college or seminary for a full academic year before they are eligible to apply for this program. Students entering their sophomore year must have earned a GPA of 2.0 or higher as freshmen; students entering their junior year must have earned a GPA of 2.3 or higher as sophomores; students entering their senior year must have earned a GPA of 2.6 or higher as juniors.

Financial Data First-year students receive $500 per semester. Other levels of students may receive up to $2,000 per academic year.

Duration 1 year.

Additional data This program was first established in 1971 and revised in 1991. Recipients are expected to train to engage actively in the ministry of racial reconciliation in church and in society. They must be able to work in the United States or Canada upon graduating and must consider working for 1 of the agencies of the CRCNA.

Number awarded Varies each year; recently, 31 students received a total of $21,000 in support.

Deadline March of each year.

[969]
RACIAL ETHNIC PASTORAL LEADERSHIP PROGRAM

Synod of Southern California and Hawaii
Attn: Racial Ethnic Pastoral Leadership Program
14225 Roscoe Boulevard
Panorama, CA 91402
(213) 483-3840, ext. 112   Fax: (818) 891-0212
E-mail: ntucker@synod.org
Web: www.synod.org/#repl

Summary To provide financial assistance to Hispanics and other members of racial minority groups in the Presbyterian Church (USA) Synod of Southern California and Hawaii who are preparing for a career as a pastor or other church vocation.

Eligibility Applicants must be under care of their church's Session and enrolled with a Presbytery within the Synod of Southern California and Hawaii. They must be members of racial ethnic groups interested in becoming a Presbyterian pastor or other church worker (e.g., commissioned ruling elder, certified Christian educator) and serving in a racial ethnic ministry within the PCUSA. Racial ethnic persons who already have an M.Div. degree, are from another denomination in correspondence with the PCUSA, and are seeking to meet PCUSA requirements for ordination or transfer may also be eligible if they plan to serve in a racial ethnic congregation or an approved specialized ministry. Applicants must submit documentation of financial need, recommendations from the appropriate presbytery committee or session, a current transcript, and essays on their goals and objectives. They must be enrolled full or part time in a PCUSA seminary or other seminary approved by the Committee on Preparation for Ministry of their Presbytery.

Financial Data The stipend is $5,000 per year.

Duration 1 year; may be renewed.

Additional data This program began in 1984.

Number awarded Varies each year; recently, 5 students were receiving support from this program. Since the program began, it has awarded $372,375 to approximately 335 seminarians.

Deadline April of each year.

[970]
RACIAL ETHNIC SUPPLEMENTAL GRANTS

Presbyterian Church (USA)
Attn: Office of Financial Aid for Service
100 Witherspoon Street
Louisville, KY 40202-1396
(502) 569-5224   Toll Free: (888) 728-7228, ext. 5224
Fax: (502) 569-8766   TDD: (800) 833-5955
E-mail: finaid@pcusa.org
Web: www.presbyterianmission.org

Summary To provide financial assistance to Hispanic and other minority graduate students who are Presbyterian Church (USA) members interested in preparing for church occupations.

Eligibility This program is open to racial/ethnic graduate students (Hispanic American, Asian American, African American, Native American, or Alaska Native) who are enrolled full time at a PCUSA seminary or accredited theological institution approved by their Committee on Preparation for Ministry. Applicants must be working on 1) an M.Div. degree and enrolled as an inquirer or candidate by a PCUSA presbytery; or 2) an M.A.C.E. degree and preparing for a church occupation. They must be PCUSA members, U.S. citizens or permanent residents, able to demonstrate financial need, and recommended by the financial aid officer at their theological institution. Along with their application, they must submit a 1,000-word essay on what they believe God is calling them to do in ministry.

Financial Data Stipends range from $500 to $1,000 per year. Funds are intended as supplements to students who have been awarded a Presbyterian Study Grant but still demonstrate remaining financial need.

Duration   1 year; may be renewed up to 2 additional years.

Number awarded   Varies each year; the sponsor awards approximately 130 grants for this and 3 related programs each year.

Deadline   June of each year.

[971]
RALPH W. SHRADER GRADUATE DIVERSITY SCHOLARSHIP

Armed Forces Communications and Electronics
  Association
Attn: AFCEA Educational Foundation
4400 Fair Lakes Court
Fairfax, VA 22033-3899
(703) 631-6147   Toll Free: (800) 336-4583, ext. 6147
Fax: (703) 631-4693   E-mail: edfoundation@afcea.org
Web: www.afcea.org

Summary   To provide financial assistance to Hispanic and other minorities working on a master's degree in fields related to communications and electronics.

Eligibility   This program is open to women and minorities working full time on a graduate degree at an accredited college or university in the United States. Applicants must be studying biometrics, computer science, cybersecurity, engineering (computer, electrical, electronics, network, robotics, telecommunications), geospatial science, information technology, information resources management, mathematics, network security, operations research, physics, robotics, statistics, strategic intelligence, or telecommunications. They must have a GPA of 3.5 or higher. U.S. citizenship is required.

Financial Data   The stipend is $3,000. Funds are paid directly to the recipient.

Duration   1 year.

Additional data   This program is sponsored by Booz Allen Hamilton.

Number awarded   1 or more each year.

Deadline   April of each year.

[972]
RAMSEY COUNTY BAR FOUNDATION LAW STUDENT SCHOLARSHIP

Ramsey County Bar Foundation
Attn: Diversity Committee
E-1401 First National Bank Building
332 Minnesota Street
St. Paul, MN 55101
(651) 222-0846   Fax: (651) 223-8344
E-mail: Cheryl@ramseybar.org
Web: www.ramseybar.org/news/law-student-scholarship

Summary   To provide financial assistance to Hispanics and members of other groups traditionally underrepresented in the legal profession who are attending law school in Minnesota.

Eligibility   This program is open to residents of any state who are currently enrolled at a Minnesota law school. Applicants must be a member of a group traditionally underrepresented in the legal profession, including race, sex, ethnicity, sexual orientation, or disability. They must contribute meaningfully to diversity in their community, have a record of aca-

demic or professional achievement, and display leadership qualities through past work experience, community involvement, or student activities.

Financial Data   The stipend ranges up to $6,000.

Duration   1 year.

Number awarded   1 each year.

Deadline   February of each year.

[973]
RAY AND CARMELLA MELLADO SCHOLARSHIP

Great Minds in STEM
Attn: HENAAC Scholars Program
602 Monterey Pass Road
Monterey Park, CA 91754
(323) 262-0997   Fax: (323) 262-0946
E-mail: scholars@greatmindsinstem.org
Web: www.greatmindsinstem.org

Summary   To provide financial assistance to Hispanic undergraduate and graduate students who are enrolled at a university in any state and working on a degree in a field of science, technology, engineering, or mathematics (STEM).

Eligibility   This program is open to undergraduate and graduate students who are working on a degree in a field of STEM at colleges and universities in any state. Applicants must be of Hispanic origin and/or must significantly participate in and promote organizations and activities in the Hispanic community. They must have a GPA of 3.0 or higher. There is no citizenship requirement. Along with their application, they must submit a 700-word essay on a topic that changes annually. Selection is based on leadership, academic achievements, and campus and community activities; financial need is not considered.

Financial Data   Stipends range from $500 to $10,000.

Duration   1 year; recipients may reapply.

Additional data   The Hispanic Engineer National Achievement Awards Conference (HENAAC) was established in 1989 and initiated a scholarship program in 2000. In 2010, the sponsoring organization officially adopted its current name, but it continues to hold the annual HENAAC conference, at which the scholarships are presented. Recipients must attend the conference to accept their scholarship. The sponsor subsidizes the cost of travel, 3 nights of lodging, and meals.

Number awarded   4 each year: 2 to undergraduates and 2 to graduate students.

Deadline   April of each year.

[974]
RDW GROUP, INC. MINORITY SCHOLARSHIP FOR COMMUNICATIONS

Rhode Island Foundation
Attn: Donor Services Administrator
One Union Station
Providence, RI 02903
(401) 427-4011   Fax: (401) 331-8085
E-mail: rbogert@rifoundation.org
Web: www.rifoundation.org

Summary   To provide financial assistance to Hispanic and other undergraduate and graduate students of color from Rhode Island who are interested in preparing for a career in communications at a school in any state.

Eligibility This program is open to undergraduate and graduate students at colleges and universities in any state who are Rhode Island residents of color. Applicants must intend to work on a degree in communications (including computer graphics, art, cinematography, or other fields that would prepare them for a career in advertising). They must be able to demonstrate financial need and a commitment to a career in communications. Along with their application, they must submit an essay (up to 300 words) on the impact they would like to have on the communications field.

Financial Data The stipend is approximately $2,000 per year.

Duration 1 year; recipients may reapply.

Additional data This program is sponsored by the RDW Group, Inc.

Number awarded 1 each year.

Deadline April of each year.

[975]
REFORMA SCHOLARSHIP

REFORMA (National Association to Promote Library and
    Information Services to Latinos and the Spanish
    Speaking)
P.O. Box 832
Anaheim, CA 92815-0832
(209) 379-5637   E-mail: officemgr@reforma.org
Web: www.reforma.org

Summary To provide financial assistance to Spanish-speaking students interested in preparing for a career in library or information science.

Eligibility The program is open to citizens and permanent residents of the United States who are Spanish-speaking students enrolled or entering a master's or Ph.D. program in library and information science. While eligibility is not restricted by age, sex, creed, national origin, or minority group/association membership, it is required that those who apply have an understanding of and desire to serve the Spanish-speaking community. Applicants must show evidence of commitment to a career in librarianship and the potential for high academic achievement. Along with their application, they must submit a personal statements on how they plan to serve Latinos and Spanish-speakers if they are awarded this scholarship.

Financial Data The stipend is $1,500.

Duration 1 year.

Number awarded Varies each year; recently, 5 were awarded.

Deadline March of each year.

[976]
RENE MATOS SCHOLARSHIP

National Hispanic Coalition of Federal Aviation
    Employees
Attn: Scholarship Selection Committee
P.O. Box 23276
Washington, DC 20026-3276
E-mail: doe@nhcfae.org
Web: www.nhcfae.org/rene-matos-scholarship-program

Summary To provide financial assistance to students of Hispanic descent who are working on an undergraduate or graduate degree.

Eligibility This program is open to U.S. citizens and permanent residents of Hispanic descent who reside in the United States or Puerto Rico. Applicants must be accepted to or attending an accredited college, university, or vocational/trade school as an undergraduate or graduate student. Selection is based on academic achievement, community involvement, honors and awards, leadership, personal qualities and strengths, student activities, and financial need.

Financial Data A stipend is awarded (amount not specified).

Duration 1 year; may be renewed.

Additional data The National Hispanic Coalition of Federal Aviation Employees, established in 1978, is a nonprofit organization comprised mainly of Hispanics who are employed at the Federal Aviation Administration.

Number awarded 1 or more each year.

Deadline April of each year.

[977]
RESOURCES FOR THE FUTURE SUMMER INTERNSHIPS

Resources for the Future
Attn: Internship Coordinator
1616 P Street, N.W., Suite 600
Washington, DC 20036-1400
(202) 328-5020   Fax: (202) 939-3460
E-mail: IC@rff.org
Web: www.rff.org

Summary To provide internships to undergraduate and graduate students, especially Hispanics and other minorities, who are interested in working on research projects in public policy during the summer.

Eligibility This program is open to undergraduate and graduate students (with priority to graduate students) interested in an internship at Resources for the Future (RFF). Applicants must be working on a degree in the social and natural sciences and have training in economics and quantitative methods or an interest in public policy. They should display strong writing skills and a desire to analyze complex environmental policy problems amenable to interdisciplinary methods. The ability to work without supervision in a careful and conscientious manner is essential. Women and minority candidates are strongly encouraged to apply. Both U.S. and non-U.S. citizens are eligible, if the latter have proper work and residency documentation.

Financial Data The stipend is $375 per week for graduate students or $350 per week for undergraduates. Housing assistance is not provided.

Duration 10 weeks during the summer; beginning and ending dates can be adjusted to meet particular student needs.

Number awarded Varies each year.

Deadline March of each year.

[978]
RETAIL REAL ESTATE DIVERSITY SCHOLARSHIP

International Council of Shopping Centers
Attn: ICSC Foundation
1221 Avenue of the Americas, 41st Floor
New York, NY 10020-1099
(646) 728-3628   Fax: (732) 694-1690
E-mail: foundation@icsc.org
Web: www.icsc.org

Summary To provide financial assistance to Hispanic and other minority graduate students who are members of the International Council of Shopping Centers (ICSC) and preparing for a career as a retail real estate professional.

Eligibility This program is open to U.S. citizens who are graduate student members of ICSC and working on a degree related to the retail real estate profession. Applicants must be a member of an underrepresented ethnic minority group (Hispanic, Caribbean, American Indian or Alaskan Native, Asian or Pacific Islander, African American). They must have a GPA of 3.0 or higher and be enrolled full time or enrolled part time while working.

Financial Data The stipend is $2,500.

Duration 1 year.

Number awarded 1 or more each year.

Deadline January of each year.

[979]
RICHARD D. HAILEY SCHOLARSHIP

American Association for Justice
Attn: AAJ Education
777 Sixth Street, N.W., Suite 200
Washington, DC 20001
(202) 684-9563   Toll Free: (800) 424-2725
Fax: (202) 965-0355   E-mail: education@justice.org
Web: www.justice.org

Summary To provide financial assistance for law school to Hispanic and other minority student members of the American Association for Justice (AAJ).

Eligibility This program is open to Hispanic, African American, Asian American, Native American, and biracial members of the association who are entering the first, second, or third year of law school. Applicants must submit a 500-word essay on how they meet the selection criteria: commitment to the association, involvement in student chapter and minority caucus activities, desire to represent victims, interest and proficiency of skills in trial advocacy, and financial need.

Financial Data The stipend is $1,000.

Duration 1 year.

Additional data The American Association for Justice was formerly the Association of Trial Lawyers of America.

Number awarded Up to 6 each year.

Deadline May of each year.

[980]
RISA MARI OTTO SCHOLARSHIP

Wisconsin Speech-Language Pathology and Audiology
   Association
Attn: WSHA Foundation
344 Evergreen Lane
Pewaukee, WI 53072
E-mail: CSEasterling@aol.com
Web: www.wisha.org/?page=Scholarships

Summary To provide financial assistance to Spanish-speaking students at colleges in Wisconsin who are working on a graduate degree in speech-language pathology.

Eligibility This program is open to residents of any state who are working on a graduate degree in speech-language pathology at a college or university in Wisconsin. Applicants must be able to demonstrate ability in spoken Spanish and have completed at least 20 undergraduate units in study of that language. Preference is given to those who intend to seek employment in facilities that serve the Hispanic community. Along with their application, they must submit brief statements on their career plans and goals, the strengths they bring to their intended profession, their Spanish language skill level, who or what inspired or motivated them to join the profession, and why they should be selected to receive this scholarship.

Financial Data The stipend is $2,000.

Duration 1 year.

Number awarded 1 each year.

Deadline June of each year.

[981]
RIXIO MEDINA & ASSOCIATES HISPANICS IN SAFETY GRADUATE SCHOLARSHIP

American Society of Safety Engineers
Attn: ASSE Foundation
Scholarship Award Program
520 North Northwest Highway
Park Ridge, IL 60068-2538
(847) 699-2929   Fax: (847) 296-3769
E-mail: assefoundation@asse.org
Web: foundation.asse.org/scholarships-and-grants

Summary To provide financial assistance to Hispanic graduate students working on a degree related to occupational safety.

Eligibility This program is open to students who are working on a graduate degree in occupational safety, health, environment, industrial hygiene, occupational health nursing, or a closely-related field (e.g., industrial or environmental engineering). Applicants must be bilingual (Spanish-English); Hispanic ethnicity is preferred. Students enrolled in an ASAC/ABET-accredited safety program also receive preference. They must be full- or part-time students who have completed at least 9 semester hours and have a GPA of 3.5 or higher. U.S. citizenship is not required. Membership in the American Society of Safety Engineers (ASSE) is not required, but preference is given to members.

Financial Data The stipend is $4,000 per year.

Duration 1 year; recipients may reapply.

Additional data This program began in 2005.

Number awarded 1 each year.

Deadline November of each year.

[982]
ROBERT D. WATKINS GRADUATE RESEARCH FELLOWSHIP

American Society for Microbiology
Attn: Education Board
1752 N Street, N.W.
Washington, DC 20036-2904
(202) 942-9283   Fax: (202) 942-9329
E-mail: fellowships@asmusa.org
Web: www.asm.org

Summary To provide funding for research in microbiology to Hispanic and other underrepresented minority doctoral students who are members of the American Society for Microbiology (ASM).

Eligibility This program is open to Hispanics, African Americans, Native Americans, Alaskan Natives, and Pacific Islanders enrolled as full-time graduate students who have completed their first year of doctoral study and who are members of the society. Applicants must propose a joint research plan in collaboration with a society member scientist. They must have completed all graduate course work requirements for the doctoral degree by the date of the activation of the fellowship. U.S. citizenship or permanent resident status is required. Selection is based on academic achievement, evidence of a successful research plan developed in collaboration with a research adviser/mentor, relevant career goals in the microbiological sciences, and involvement in activities that serve the needs of underrepresented groups.

Financial Data Students receive $21,000 per year as a stipend; funds may not be used for tuition or fees.

Duration 3 years.

Number awarded Varies each year.

Deadline April of each year.

[983]
ROBERT TOIGO FOUNDATION FELLOWSHIPS

Robert Toigo Foundation
Attn: Fellowship Program Administrator
180 Grand Avenue, Suite 450
Oakland, CA 94612
(510) 763-5771   Fax: (510) 763-5778
E-mail: info@toigofoundation.org
Web: www.toigofoundation.org

Summary To provide financial assistance to Hispanic and other minority students working on a master's degree in business administration or a related field.

Eligibility This program is open to members of minority groups (Hispanic/Latino, African American, Native American/Alaskan Native, South Asian American, or Asian American/Pacific Islander) who are entering or enrolled in a program for an M.B.A., J.D./M.B.A., master's in real estate, or master's in finance. Applicants must be preparing for a career in finance, including (but not limited to) investment management, investment banking, corporate finance, real estate, private equity, venture capital, business development, pension fund investment, or financial services consulting. U.S. citizenship or permanent resident status is required.

Financial Data The stipend is $2,500 per year.

Duration Up to 2 years.

Additional data The application fee is $50.

Number awarded Approximately 50 to 60 each year.

Deadline March of each year.

[984]
RONALD M. DAVIS SCHOLARSHIP

American Medical Association
Attn: AMA Foundation
330 North Wabash Avenue, Suite 39300
Chicago, IL 60611-5885
(312) 464-4193   Fax: (312) 464-4142
E-mail: amafoundation@ama-assn.org
Web: www.ama-assn.org

Summary To provide financial assistance to medical school students who are Hispanics or members of other underrepresented minority groups and are planning to become a primary care physician.

Eligibility This program is open to first- and second-year medical students who are members of the following minority groups: Hispanic/Latino, African American/Black, American Indian, Native Hawaiian, or Alaska Native. Candidates must have an interest in becoming a primary care physician. Only nominations are accepted. Each medical school is invited to submit 2 nominees. U.S. citizenship or permanent resident status is required.

Financial Data The stipend is $10,000.

Duration 1 year.

Additional data This program is offered by the AMA Foundation of the American Medical Association as a component of its Minority Scholars Awards. Support is provided by the National Business Group on Health.

Number awarded 1 each year.

Deadline March of each year.

[985]
ROSA L. PARKS COLLEGE SCHOLARSHIP

Conference of Minority Transportation Officials
Attn: National Scholarship Program
100 M Street, S.E., Suite 917
Washington, DC 20003
(202) 506-2917   E-mail: info@comto.org
Web: www.comto.org/page/scholarships

Summary To provide financial assistance to Hispanic and other students who have a tie to the Conference of Minority Transportation Officials (COMTO) and are interested in working on an undergraduate or master's degree in transportation.

Eligibility This program is open to 1) undergraduates who have completed at least 60 semester credit hours in a transportation discipline; and 2) students working on a master's degree in transportation who have completed at least 15 credits. Applicants must be or have a parent, guardian, or grandparent who has been a COMTO member for at least 1 year. They must have a GPA of 3.0 or higher. Along with their application they must submit a cover letter on their transportation-related career goals and life aspirations. Financial need is not considered in the selection process.

Financial Data The stipend is $4,500. Funds are paid directly to the recipient's college or university.

Duration 1 year.

Number awarded 1 each year.

Deadline April of each year.

[986]
ROSE TREVINO MEMORIAL SCHOLARSHIP

REFORMA (National Association to Promote Library and
Information Services to Latinos and the Spanish
Speaking)
P.O. Box 832
Anaheim, CA 92815-0832
(209) 379-5637   E-mail: officemgr@reforma.org
Web: www.reforma.org

Summary To provide financial assistance to Spanish-speaking students interested in preparing for a career in children and young adult librarianship.

Eligibility The program is open to citizens and permanent residents of the United States who are Spanish-speaking students enrolled or entering a master's or Ph.D. program in library and information science. While eligibility is not restricted by age, sex, creed, national origin, or minority group/association membership, it is required that those who apply have an understanding of and desire to serve the Spanish-speaking community. Applicants must show evidence of commitment to a career in children and young adult librarianship and the potential for high academic achievement. Along with their application, they must submit a personal statements on how they plan to serve Latinos and Spanish-speakers if they are awarded this scholarship.

Financial Data The stipend is $1,500.

Duration 1 year.

Number awarded 1 each year.

Deadline March of each year.

[987]
ROY H. POLLACK SCHOLARSHIP

Unitarian Universalist Association
Attn: Ministerial Credentialing Office
24 Farnsworth Street
Boston, MA 02210-1409
(617) 948-6403   Fax: (617) 742-2875
E-mail: mcoadministrator@uua.org
Web: www.uua.org

Summary To provide financial assistance to seminary students, especially Hispanics and other persons of color, who are preparing for the Unitarian Universalist (UU) ministry.

Eligibility This program is open to seminary students who are enrolled full or at least half time in their second or third year in a UU ministerial training program with candidate status. Applicants must be citizens of the United States or Canada. Priority is given first to those who have demonstrated outstanding ministerial ability and secondarily to students with the greatest financial need (especially persons of color).

Financial Data The stipend ranges from $1,000 to $15,000 per year.

Duration 1 year.

Additional data This program began in 1998.

Number awarded Varies each year; recently, 2 were awarded.

Deadline April of each year.

[988]
RUBINOS-MESIA SCHOLARSHIP

Structural Engineers Association of Illinois
Attn: Structural Engineers Foundation
134 North LaSalle Street, Suite 1910
Chicago, IL 60602
(312) 726-4165   Fax: (312) 277-1991
E-mail: eoconnor@seaol.org
Web: www.seaoi.org/sef.htm

Summary To provide financial assistance to upper-division and graduate students of Hispanic descent interested in a career in structural engineering.

Eligibility This program is open to students of Hispanic descent who are 1) entering their third or higher year of an undergraduate program; or 2) entering or continuing a graduate program. Applicants must be enrolled in a civil or architectural engineering program and planning to continue with a structural engineering specialization. Students enrolled in structural engineering technology programs are also eligible if they are qualified to take the Fundamentals of Engineering and Principles and Practice licensure examinations in their home state upon graduation. U.S. citizenship or permanent resident status is required. Students enrolled in military academies or ROTC programs are not eligible. Selection is based on a statement giving reasons why the applicant should receive the award (including plans for continued formal education), academic performance, and potential for development and leadership. Financial need is not considered.

Financial Data The stipend is $2,000.

Duration 1 year; nonrenewable.

Number awarded 1 each year.

Deadline April of each year.

[989]
RURAL OPPORTUNITY FELLOWSHIPS OF THE OREGON STATE BAR

Oregon State Bar
Attn: Diversity and Inclusion Department
16037 S.W. Upper Boones Ferry Road
P.O. Box 231935
Tigard, OR 97281-1935
(503) 620-0222
Toll Free: (800) 452-8260, ext. 338 (within OR)
Fax: (503) 684-1366   TDD: (503) 684-7416
E-mail: cling@osbar.org
Web: www.osbar.org/diversity/programs.html#rural

Summary To provide summer work experience in rural areas to law students in Oregon who are Hispanics or will help the Oregon State Bar achieve its diversity and inclusion objectives in other ways.

Eligibility This program is open to students at law schools in Oregon who are interested in working for a public employer or nonprofit organization in rural areas of the state during the summer. The program defines rural areas as anywhere along the Oregon coast, anywhere east of the Cascade Mountains, or anywhere south of Roseburg. Applicants must contribute to the Oregon State Bar's diversity and inclusion program, defined to include age, culture, disability, ethnicity, gender and gender identity or expression, geographic location, national origin, race, religion, sex, sexual orientation, and socio-economic status. They must be planning to practice in

Oregon. Along with their application, they must submit a 500-word personal statement on either 1) how their status as a person of diversity has influenced their decision to become a lawyer and how will it influence them throughout their legal professional career; or 2) a challenge they have faced, how they met the challenge, and how that experience will affect the decisions they will make as a legal professional. They must also submit a sample of their legal writing. Selection is based on the personal statement (35%), legal writing ability (25%), academic achievement (15%), work experience and honors (10%), and financial need (15%).

Financial Data Fellows receive a stipend of $8,360.

Duration 3 months during the summer.

Number awarded 2 each year.

Deadline January of each year.

[990]
RUTH D. PETERSON FELLOWSHIPS FOR RACIAL AND ETHNIC DIVERSITY

American Society of Criminology
Attn: Awards Committee
1314 Kinnear Road, Suite 212
Columbus, OH 43212-1156
(614) 292-9207   Fax: (614) 292-6767
E-mail: asc@asc41.com
Web: www.asc41.com

Summary To provide financial assistance to Latinos and other ethnic minority doctoral students in criminology and criminal justice.

Eligibility This program is open to students of color, especially members of ethnic groups underrepresented in the field of criminology and criminal justice, including (but not limited to) Latina/os, Asians, Blacks, and Indigenous peoples. Applicants must have been accepted into a doctoral program in the field. Along with their application, they must submit an up-to-date curriculum vitae; a personal statement on their race or ethnicity; copies of undergraduate and graduate transcripts; a statement of need and prospects for other financial assistance; a letter describing career plans, salient experiences, and nature of interest in criminology and criminal justice; and 3 letters of reference.

Financial Data The stipend is $6,000.

Duration 1 year.

Additional data This program began in 1988 as the American Society of Criminology Graduate Fellowships for Ethnic Minorities. Its current name was adopted in 2016.

Number awarded 3 each year.

Deadline February of each year.

[991]
RUTH L. KIRSCHSTEIN NATIONAL RESEARCH SERVICE AWARDS FOR INDIVIDUAL PREDOCTORAL FELLOWSHIPS TO PROMOTE DIVERSITY IN HEALTH-RELATED RESEARCH

National Institutes of Health
Office of Extramural Research
Attn: Grants Information
6705 Rockledge Drive, Suite 4090
Bethesda, MD 20892-7983
(301) 435-0714   Fax: (301) 480-0525
TDD: (301) 451-5936   E-mail: grantsinfo@nih.gov
Web: www.grants.nih.gov

Summary To provide financial assistance to Hispanic students and those from other underrepresented groups interested in working on a doctoral degree and preparing for a career in biomedical and behavioral research.

Eligibility This program is open to students enrolled or accepted for enrollment in a Ph.D. or equivalent research degree program; a formally combined M.D./Ph.D. program; or other combined professional doctoral/research Ph.D. program in the biomedical, behavioral, or clinical sciences. Students in health professional degree programs (e.g., M.D., D.O., D.D.S., D.V.M.) are not eligible. Applicants must be 1) members of an ethnic or racial group underrepresented in biomedical or behavioral research; 2) individuals with disabilities; or 3) individuals from socially, culturally, economically, or educationally disadvantaged backgrounds that have inhibited their ability to prepare for a career in health-related research. They must be U.S. citizens, nationals, or permanent residents.

Financial Data The fellowship provides an annual stipend of $23,376, a tuition and fee allowance (60% of costs up to $16,000 or 60% of costs up to $21,000 for dual degrees), and an institutional allowance of $4,200 ($3,100 at for-profit and federal institutions) for travel to scientific meetings, health insurance, and laboratory and other training expenses.

Duration Up to 5 years for Ph.D. students or up to 6 years for M.D./Ph.D. or other combined research degree programs.

Additional data These fellowships are offered by most components of the National Institutes of Health (NIH). Contact the NIH for a list of names and telephone numbers of responsible officers at each component.

Number awarded Varies each year.

Deadline April, August, or December of each year.

[992]
RUTH WEBB MINORITY SCHOLARSHIP

California Academy of Physician Assistants
2318 South Fairview Street
Santa Ana, CA 92704-4938
(714) 427-0321   Fax: (714) 427-0324
E-mail: capa@capanet.org
Web: www.capanet.org

Summary To provide financial assistance to Hispanic and other minority student members of the California Academy of Physician Assistants (CAPA) enrolled in physician assistant programs in California.

Eligibility This program is open to student members of CAPA enrolled in primary care physician assistant programs in California. Applicants must be members of a minority group

(Hispanic, African American, Asian/Pacific Islander, or Native American/Alaskan Native). They must have maintained good academic standing and conducted activities to promote the physician assistant profession. Along with their application, they must submit an essay describing the activities they have performed to promote the physician assistant profession, the importance of representing minorities in their community, and why they should be awarded this scholarship. Financial need is considered in the selection process.

Financial Data   The stipend is $2,000.

Duration   1 year.

Number awarded   1 each year.

Deadline   December of each year.

[993]
SAN FRANCISCO LA RAZA LAWYERS PUBLIC INTEREST LAW FELLOWSHIP

San Francisco La Raza Lawyers Association
Attn: Bay Area Latino Lawyers Fund
P.O. Box 192241
San Francisco, CA 94119-2241
(415) 983-1082   Fax: (415) 983-1200
E-mail: laura.hurtado@gmail.com
Web: www.larazalawyers.org/students

Summary   To provide summer work experience to law students at nonprofit organizations serving the Latino community in the San Francisco Bay area.

Eligibility   This program is open to law students from any state who are interested in summer employment with San Francisco Bay area nonprofit organizations serving the Latino community. Applicants must submit 1) the name, address, and telephone number of the community-based legal services provider where they plan to work; 2) a description of legal services to be provided, anticipated length of the project, population to be served, and project objective; 3) a narrative describing their qualifications and financial need; and 4) letters in support of their project. Proposals should address at least 1 of the following objectives: projects to develop or expand legal services in the areas of housing, employment, discrimination, immigration, and naturalization; projects to develop materials and training to educate the Latino community about its legal rights and to facilitate its access to the justice system and the courts; projects to provide training, referral, recruitment, and mentoring to law students; or other creative projects. Personal interviews are conducted.

Financial Data   The stipend depends on the need of the recipient, to a maximum of $5,000.

Duration   Summer months.

Number awarded   4 to 6 each year.

Deadline   February of each year.

[994]
SARASOTA COUNTY BAR ASSOCIATION DIVERSITY SCHOLARSHIP

Community Foundation of Sarasota County
Attn: Grants and Scholarships Coordinator
2635 Fruitville Road
P.O. Box 49587
Sarasota, FL 34230-6587
(941) 556-7114   Fax: (941) 952-7115
E-mail: eyoung@cfsarasota.org
Web: www.cfsarasota.org

Summary   To provide financial assistance and work experience in Sarasota County, Florida to law students from any state who are Hispanics or will add to the diversity of the legal profession in other ways.

Eligibility   This program is open to first- through third-year law students of traditionally underrepresented backgrounds (e.g., race, color, religion, national origin, ethnicity, age, gender, sexual orientation, physical disability, socioeconomic background). Applicants must be interested in practicing law after graduation and in obtaining summer placement in private law firms or government agencies in Sarasota County. They may be attending law school in any state but they should have or have had family, school, or community ties to the county. Along with their application, they must submit a 250-word essay describing how their particular background would help the Sarasota County Bar Association achieve its goal of making the local legal community more diverse.

Financial Data   Students receive a salary for their summer employment and a stipend of $5,000, sent directly to their law school, upon completion of their employment.

Duration   1 summer for employment and 1 year for law school enrollment.

Additional data   This program, also known as the Richard R. Garland Diversity Scholarship, is sponsored by the Sarasota County Bar Association.

Number awarded   1 or more each year.

Deadline   February of each year.

[995]
SASP ADVANCED STUDENT DIVERSITY SCHOLARSHIPS

American Psychological Association
Attn: Division 16 (School Psychology)
750 First Street, N.E.
Washington, DC 20002-4242
(202) 336-6165   Fax: (202) 218-3599
TDD: (202) 336-6123   E-mail: cchambers@apa.org
Web: www.apadivisions.org/division-16/awards/sasp.aspx

Summary   To provide financial assistance to continuing graduate student members of the Student Affiliates in School Psychology (SASP) of Division 16 (School Psychology) of the American Psychological Association (APA) who are Hispanics or from other underrepresented cultural backgrounds.

Eligibility   This program is open to SASP members who come from underrepresented cultural backgrounds. Applicants must be working on a graduate degree to prepare for a career as a school psychologist. They must be entering their third, fourth, or fifth year of graduate study.

Financial Data   The stipend is $1,000.

Duration   1 year; nonrenewable.

Number awarded 1 each year.

Deadline April of each year.

[996]
SCHOLARSHIP FOR A THEOLOGICAL LIBRARIANSHIP COURSE

American Theological Library Association
Attn: Diversity Committee
300 South Wacker Drive, Suite 2100
Chicago, IL 60606-6701
(312) 454-5100   Toll Free: (888) 665-ATLA
Fax: (312) 454-5505   E-mail: memberrep@atla.com
Web: www.atla.com

Summary To provide funding to Hispanic library students and those from other underrepresented groups who are members of the American Theological Library Association (ATLA) and interested in taking a course in theological librarianship.

Eligibility This program is open to ATLA members from underrepresented groups (religious, racial, ethnic, or gender) who wish to attend a theological librarianship course at an ALA-accredited master's program in library and information studies. Applicants must submit personal statements on what diversity means to them, why their voice has not yet been heard, how their voice will add diversity to the theological librarianship course, how they will increase diversity in their immediate context, and how they plan to increase diversity and participate fully in the ATLA.

Financial Data The stipend is $1,200.

Duration Up to 1 year.

Number awarded 1 each year.

Deadline April of each year.

[997]
SCIENCE, TECHNOLOGY, AND PUBLIC POLICY FELLOWSHIPS

Harvard University
John F. Kennedy School of Government
Belfer Center for Science and International Affairs
Attn: STPP Fellowship Coordinator
79 John F. Kennedy Street, Mailbox 53
Cambridge, MA 02138
(617) 495-1498   Fax: (617) 495-8963
E-mail: patricia_mclaughlin@hks.harvard.edu
Web: belfercenter.ksg.harvard.edu

Summary To provide funding to professionals, postdoctorates, and doctoral students, especially Hispanics and other minorities, who are interested in conducting research in science, technology, and public policy areas of concern to the Belfer Center for Science and International Affairs at Harvard University in Cambridge, Massachusetts.

Eligibility The postdoctoral fellowship is open to recent recipients of the Ph.D. or equivalent degree, university faculty members, and employees of government, military, international, humanitarian, and private research institutions who have appropriate professional experience. Applicants for predoctoral fellowships must have passed their general examinations. Scholars from a wide range of disciplinary and multi-disciplinary fields and those holding a Ph.D. in engineering or in the natural sciences are strongly encouraged to apply. The program especially encourages applications from women, minorities, and citizens of all countries. All applicants must be interested in conducting research on projects of the Science, Technology, and Public Policy (STPP) Program. Recently, those included projects on Internet policy and regulatory reform, energy technology innovation, water and energy resources, sustainable energy development in China, technology and innovation, solar geoengineering and climate policy, technological innovation and globalization, agricultural innovation in Africa, managing the atom, and the geopolitics of energy.

Financial Data The stipend is $37,500 for postdoctoral research fellows or $25,000 for predoctoral research fellows. Fellows who renew their grant receive a monthly stipend of $3,750 for postdoctoral fellows or $2,500 for predoctoral fellows. Stipends for advanced research fellows vary. Health insurance is also provided.

Duration 10 months; may be renewed on a month-by-month basis.

Additional data Fellows are expected to devoted some portion of their time to collaborative endeavors, as arranged by the appropriate program or project director. Predoctoral fellows are expected to contribute to the program's research activities, as well as work on (and ideally complete) their dissertations. Postdoctoral research fellows are also expected to complete a book, monograph, or other significant publication during their period of residence.

Number awarded A limited number each year.

Deadline January of each year.

[998]
SECTION OF BUSINESS LAW DIVERSITY CLERKSHIP PROGRAM

American Bar Association
Attn: Section of Business Law
321 North Clark Street
Chicago, IL 60654-7598
(312) 988-5588   Fax: (312) 988-5578
E-mail: businesslaw@americanbar.org
Web: www.americanbar.org

Summary To provide summer work experience in business law to student members of the American Bar Association (ABA) and its Section of Business Law who are Hispanics or will help the section to fulfill its goal of promoting diversity in other ways.

Eligibility This program is open to first- and second-year students at ABA-accredited law schools who are interested in a summer business court clerkship. Applicants must 1) be a member of an underrepresented group (student of color, woman, student with disabilities, gay, lesbian, bisexual, or transgender); or 2) have overcome social or economic disadvantages, such as a physical disability, financial constraints, or cultural impediments to becoming a law student. They must be able to demonstrate financial need. Along with their application, they must submit a 500-word essay that covers why they are interested in this clerkship program, what they would gain from the program, how it would positively influence their future professional goals as a business lawyer, and how they meet the program's criteria. Membership in the ABA and its Section of Business Law are required.

Financial Data The stipend is $6,000.

Duration Summer months.

Additional data This program began in 2008. Assignments vary, but have included business courts in Delaware, Illinois, Maryland, Pennsylvania, and South Carolina.

Number awarded 9 each year.

Deadline January of each year.

[999]
SELECTED PROFESSIONS FELLOWSHIPS FOR WOMEN OF COLOR

American Association of University Women
Attn: AAUW Educational Foundation
1111 16th Street, N.W.
Washington, DC 20036-4873
(202) 785-7700   Toll Free: (800) 326-AAUW
Fax: (202) 872-1425   TDD: (202) 785-7777
E-mail: aauw@applyists.com
Web: www.aauw.org

Summary To aid Hispanic and other women of color who are in their final year of graduate training in the fields of business administration, law, or medicine.

Eligibility This program is open to women who are working full time on a degree in fields in which women of color have been historically underrepresented: business administration (M.B.A.), law (J.D.), or medicine (M.D., D.O.). They must be Mexican Americans, Puerto Ricans, other Hispanics, African Americans, Native Americans, Alaska Natives, Asian Americans, or Pacific Islanders. U.S. citizenship or permanent resident status is required. Applicants in business administration must be entering their second year of study; applicants in law must be entering their third year of study; applicants in medicine may be entering their third or fourth year of study. Special consideration is given to applicants who 1) demonstrate their intent to enter professional practice in disciplines in which women are underrepresented, to serve underserved populations and communities, or to pursue public interest areas; and 2) are nontraditional students. Selection is based on professional promise and personal attributes (50%), academic excellence and related academic success indicators (40%), and financial need (10%).

Financial Data Stipends range from $5,000 to $18,000.

Duration 1 year, beginning in July.

Additional data The filing fee is $35.

Number awarded Varies each year; recently, a total of 25 Selected Professions Fellowships were awarded.

Deadline January of each year.

[1000]
SEMICONDUCTOR RESEARCH CORPORATION MASTER'S SCHOLARSHIP PROGRAM

Semiconductor Research Corporation
Attn: Global Research Collaboration
1101 Slater Road, Suite 120
P.O. Box 12053
Research Triangle Park, NC 27709-2053
(919) 941-9400   Fax: (919) 941-9450
E-mail: students@src.org
Web: www.src.org/student-center/fellowship/#tab2

Summary To provide financial assistance to Hispanics and other minorities who are interested in working on a master's degree in a field of microelectronics relevant to the interests of the Semiconductor Research Corporation (SRC).

Eligibility This program is open to women and members of underrepresented minority groups (Hispanics, African Americans, and Native Americans). Applicants must be U.S. citizens or have permanent resident, refugee, or political asylum status in the United States. They must be admitted to an SRC participating university to work on a master's degree in a field relevant to microelectronics under the guidance of an SRC-sponsored faculty member and under an SRC-funded contract. Selection is based on academic achievement.

Financial Data The fellowship provides full tuition and fee support, a competitive stipend (recently, $2,536 per month), an annual grant of $2,000 to the university department with which the student recipient is associated, and travel expenses to the Graduate Fellowship Program Annual Conference.

Duration Up to 2 years.

Additional data This program began in 1997 for underrepresented minorities and expanded to include women in 1999.

Number awarded Approximately 12 each year.

Deadline January of each year.

[1001]
SENATOR GREGORY LUNA LEGISLATIVE SCHOLARS AND FELLOWS PROGRAM

Senate Hispanic Research Council, Inc.
Attn: Executive Director
1001 Congress Avenue, Suite 100
Austin, TX 78701
(512) 499-8606   Fax: (512) 499-8607
E-mail: sarah@tshrc.org
Web: www.tshrc.org/luna-scholars-fellows-program

Summary To provide Hispanic undergraduate and graduate students at colleges and universities in Texas with an opportunity to gain work experience at the Texas Senate.

Eligibility This program is open to undergraduate and graduate students who have completed at least 60 semester hours at an accredited 2- or 4-year educational institution in Texas; recent graduates are also eligible. Applicants must demonstrate academic achievement; leadership qualities; potential for further growth; exceptional writing, comprehension, and analytical skills; and an interest in government and public policy through active participation in community service activities. Along with their application, they must submit a personal statement on the experiences or activities that led to their interest in government and this internship program, a sample of their writing of a policy analysis on an issue affecting the state of Texas, and 2 letters of recommendation.

Financial Data Interns receive a stipend of $2,000 per month to help cover the expense of living and working in Austin.

Duration Approximately 5 months, during the term of the Texas Senate, beginning in mid-January of odd-numbered years.

Additional data This program began in 2001. Interns are assigned to the office of a state senator to perform a variety of legislative tasks, including drafting legislation, floor statements, articles, press releases, legislative research summaries, and hearing agendas. The Senate Hispanic Research Council was established in 1993 to provide educational and leadership opportunities to all segments of the Hispanic community in Texas.

Number awarded Up to 16 each odd-numbered year.

Deadline November of each even-numbered year.

[1002]
SEO CAREER LAW PROGRAM

Sponsors for Educational Opportunity
Attn: Career Program
55 Exchange Place
New York, NY 10005
(212) 979-2040   Toll Free: (800) 462-2332
Fax: (646) 706-7113
E-mail: careerprogram@seo-usa.org
Web: www.seo-usa.org/Career/Corporate_Law

Summary To provide summer work experience to Hispanics and other students of color interested in studying law.

Eligibility This program is open to students of color who are college seniors or recent graduates planning to attend law school in the United States. Applicants must be interested in a summer internship at a participating law firm that specializes in corporate law, including initial public offerings of stock, mergers and acquisitions, joint ventures, corporate reorganizations, cross-border financing, including securities, tax, bankruptcy, antitrust, real estate and white-collar crime. They must have a cumulative GPA of 3.0 or higher. Personal interviews are required.

Financial Data Interns receive a competitive stipend of up to $1,300 per week.

Duration 10 weeks during the summer.

Additional data This program began in 1980. Internships are available in New York City, Washington, D.C., Houston, Los Angeles, San Francisco, Menlo Park, Palo Alto, or Atlanta.

Number awarded Varies each year.

Deadline February of each year.

[1003]
SHERRY R. ARNSTEIN MINORITY STUDENT SCHOLARSHIP

American Association of Colleges of Osteopathic
  Medicine
Attn: Scholarships
5550 Friendship Boulevard, Suite 310
Chevy Chase, MD 20815-7231
(301) 968-4142   Fax: (301) 968-4101
E-mail: jshepperd@aacom.org
Web: www.aacom.org

Summary To provide financial assistance to Hispanic and other underrepresented minority students entering or enrolled in osteopathic medical school.

Eligibility This program is open to mainland Puerto Rican, Hispanic, African American, Native American, Native Hawaiian, and Alaska Native students who are entering or currently enrolled in good standing in their first, second, or third year of osteopathic medical school. Applicants must submit a 4-page essay on what osteopathic medical schools can do to recruit and retain more underrepresented minority students, what they personally plan to do as a student and as a future D.O. to help increase minority student enrollment at a college of osteopathic medicine, and how and why they were drawn to osteopathic medicine.

Financial Data The stipend is $2,500.

Duration 1 year; nonrenewable.

Number awarded 2 each year: 1 entering and 1 continuing student.

Deadline March of each year.

[1004]
SHPE DISSERTATION SCHOLARSHIP

Society of Hispanic Professional Engineers
Attn: Scholarships
13181 Crossroads Parkway North, Suite 450
City of Industry, CA 91715
(323) 725-3970, ext. 108   Fax: (323) 725-0316
E-mail: scholarships@shpe.org
Web: shpe.awardspring.com

Summary To provide funding for dissertation research to doctoral candidates of Hispanic descent who are preparing for a career in science, technology, engineering, mathematics (STEM), or a related field.

Eligibility This program is open to doctoral candidates of Hispanic descent who are enrolled full time at an accredited university in the United States or Puerto Rico and are members of the Society of Hispanic Professional Engineers (SHPE). Applicants must be working on a Ph.D. or Eng.D. degree in a STEM or related field and have completed all work except the dissertation. They must have a GPA of 2.75 or higher and be able to demonstrate financial need. Along with their application, they must submit a 500-word personal statement covering their community involvement, leadership, academic achievements, research internship and co-op experiences, and short-term and long-term goals and aspirations.

Financial Data The grant is $5,000.

Duration 1 year.

Number awarded 1 or more each year.

Deadline July of each year.

[1005]
SHPE GRADUATE SCHOLARSHIP

Society of Hispanic Professional Engineers
Attn: Scholarships
13181 Crossroads Parkway North, Suite 450
City of Industry, CA 91715
(323) 725-3970, ext. 108   Fax: (323) 725-0316
E-mail: scholarships@shpe.org
Web: shpe.awardspring.com

Summary To provide financial assistance to graduate students of Hispanic descent who are preparing for a career in science, technology, engineering, mathematics (STEM), or a related field.

Eligibility This program is open to students of Hispanic descent who are accepted into or attending an accredited college or university in the United States or Puerto Rico and are members of the Society of Hispanic Professional Engineers (SHPE). Applicants must be working or planning to work full time on a graduate degree in a STEM or related field. They must have a GPA of 2.75 or higher and be able to demonstrate financial need. Along with their application, they must submit a 500-word personal statement covering their community involvement, leadership, academic achievements, research internship and co-op experiences, and short-term and long-term goals and aspirations.

Financial Data   The stipend is $3,000.
Duration   1 year.
Number awarded   1 or more each year.
Deadline   July of each year.

[1006]
SHPE PROFESSIONAL SCHOLARSHIP

Society of Hispanic Professional Engineers
Attn: Scholarships
13181 Crossroads Parkway North, Suite 450
City of Industry, CA 91715
(323) 725-3970, ext. 108   Fax: (323) 725-0316
E-mail: scholarships@shpe.org
Web: shpe.awardspring.com

Summary   To provide financial assistance to Hispanic professionals working on a graduate degree in science, technology, engineering, or mathematics.

Eligibility   This program is open to members of the Society of Hispanic Professional Engineers (SHPE) who are employed full time in the United States or Puerto Rico in a technical career field. Applicants must be enrolled at least half time in a science, technology, engineering, or mathematics (STEM) degree program in the United States or Puerto Rico. They must have a GPA of 2.75 or higher and be able to demonstrate financial need. Along with their application, they must submit a 500-word personal statement covering their community involvement, leadership, academic achievements, research internship and co-op experiences, and short-term and long-term goals and aspirations.

Financial Data   The stipend is $2,000.
Duration   1 year.
Number awarded   1 or more each year.
Deadline   July of each year.

[1007]
SIDNEY B. WILLIAMS, JR. INTELLECTUAL PROPERTY LAW SCHOOL SCHOLARSHIPS

Thurgood Marshall College Fund
Attn: Senior Manager of Scholarship Programs
1770 St. James Place, Suite 414
Houston, TX 77056
(713) 955-1073   Fax: (202) 448-1017
E-mail: deshuandra.walker@tmcf.org
Web: tmcf.org

Summary   To provide financial assistance to Hispanic and other underrepresented minority law school students who are interested in preparing for a career in intellectual property law.

Eligibility   This program is open to members of underrepresented minority groups currently enrolled in or accepted to an ABA-accredited law school. Applicants must be U.S. citizens with a demonstrated intent to engage in the full-time practice of intellectual property law. Along with their application, they must submit a 250-word essay on how this scholarship will make a difference to them in meeting their goal of engaging in the full-time practice of intellectual property law and why they intend to do so. Selection is based on 1) demonstrated commitment to developing a career in intellectual property law; 2) academic performance at the undergraduate, graduate, and law school levels (as applicable); 3) general factors, such as

leadership skills, community activities, or special accomplishments; and 4) financial need.

Financial Data   The stipend is $10,000 per year. Funds may be used for tuition, fees, books, supplies, room, board, and a patent bar review course.
Duration   1 year; may be renewed up to 2 additional years if the recipient maintains a GPA of 2.0 or higher.
Additional data   This program, which began in 2002, is administered by the Thurgood Marshall College Fund with support from the American Intellectual Property Law Education Foundation.
Number awarded   Varies each year; recently, 12 were awarded.
Deadline   March of each year.

[1008]
SLA NEW ENGLAND DIVERSITY LEADERSHIP DEVELOPMENT SCHOLARSHIP

SLA New England
c/o Khalilah Gambrell, Diversity Chair
EBSCO Information Services
10 Estes Street
Ipswich, MA 01938
(978) 356-6500   Toll Free: (800) 653-2726
Fax: (978) 356-6565   E-mail: gambrell9899@gmail.com
Web: newengland.sla.org/member-benefits/stipends

Summary   To provide financial assistance for library science tuition or attendance at the annual conference of the Special Libraries Association (SLA) to members of SLA New England who are Hispanics or represent another diverse population.

Eligibility   This program is open to SLA New England members who are of Hispanic, Black (African American), Asian American, Pacific Islander American, Native Alaskan, or Native Hawaiian heritage. Applicants must be seeking funding for SLA annual meeting attendance, tuition reimbursement for a library science program, or tuition reimbursement for a course directly related to the library and information science field. Along with their application, they must submit a 500-word essay on how they will encourage and celebrate diversity within the SLA New England community.

Financial Data   The award covers actual expenses up to $1,500.
Duration   This is a 1-time award.
Number awarded   1 each year.
Deadline   April of each year.

[1009]
SMITHSONIAN MINORITY AWARDS PROGRAM

Smithsonian Institution
Attn: Office of Fellowships and Internships
470 L'Enfant Plaza, Suite 7102
P.O. Box 37012, MRC 902
Washington, DC 20013-7012
(202) 633-7070   Fax: (202) 633-7069
E-mail: siofi@si.edu
Web: www.smithsonianofi.com

Summary   To provide funding to Hispanic and other minority undergraduate and graduate students interested in conducting research at the Smithsonian Institution.

Eligibility This program is open to members of U.S. minority groups underrepresented in the Smithsonian's scholarly programs. Applicants must be undergraduates or beginning graduate students interested in conducting research in the Institution's disciplines and in the museum field. They must be U.S. citizens or permanent residents and have a GPA of 3.0 or higher.

Financial Data Students receive a grant of $600 per week.

Duration Up to 10 weeks.

Additional data Recipients must carry out independent research projects in association with the Smithsonian's research staff. Eligible fields of study currently include animal behavior, ecology, and environmental science (including an emphasis on the tropics); anthropology (including archaeology); astrophysics and astronomy; earth sciences and paleobiology; evolutionary and systematic biology; history of science and technology; history of art (especially American, contemporary, African, Asian, and 20th-century art); American crafts and decorative arts; social and cultural history of the United States; and folklife. Students are required to be in residence at the Smithsonian for the duration of the fellowship.

Number awarded Varies each year; recently, 25 were granted: 2 for fall, 19 for summer, and 4 for spring.

Deadline January of each year for summer and fall residency; September of each year for spring residency.

[1010]
SOCIETY FOR THE STUDY OF SOCIAL PROBLEMS RACIAL/ETHNIC MINORITY GRADUATE SCHOLARSHIP

Society for the Study of Social Problems
Attn: Executive Officer
University of Tennessee
901 McClung Tower
Knoxville, TN 37996-0490
(865) 689-1531   Fax: (865) 689-1534
E-mail: sssp@utk.edu
Web: www.sssp1.org

Summary To provide funding to Hispanic and other ethnic and racial minority members of the Society for the Study of Social Problems (SSSP) who are interested in conducting research for their doctoral dissertation.

Eligibility This program is open to SSSP members who are Black or African American, Hispanic or Latino, Asian or Asian American, Native Hawaiian or other Pacific Islander, or American Indian or Alaska Native. Applicants must have completed all requirements for a Ph.D. (course work, examinations, and approval of a dissertation prospectus) except the dissertation. They must have a GPA of 3.25 or higher and be able to demonstrate financial need. Their field of study may be any of the social and/or behavioral sciences that will enable them to expand their perspectives in the investigation into social problems. U.S. citizenship or permanent resident status is required.

Financial Data The stipend is $15,000. Additional grants provide $500 for the recipient to 1) attend the SSSP annual meeting prior to the year of the work to receive the award; and 2) attend the meeting after the year of the award to present a report on the work completed.

Duration 1 year.

Number awarded 1 each year.

Deadline January of each year.

[1011]
SOUTHERN REGIONAL EDUCATION BOARD DISSERTATION AWARDS

Southern Regional Education Board
Attn: Coordinator, Institute and Scholar Services
592 Tenth Street N.W.
Atlanta, GA 30318-5776
(404) 879-5516   Fax: (404) 872-1477
E-mail: tammy.wright@sreb.org
Web: www.sreb.org/types-awards

Summary To provide funding to Hispanic and other minority students who wish to complete a Ph.D. dissertation, especially in fields of science, technology, engineering, or mathematics (STEM), while in residence at a university in the southern states.

Eligibility This program is open to U.S. citizens and permanent residents who are members of racial/ethnic minority groups (Hispanic Americans, Native Americans, Asian Americans, and African Americans) and have completed all requirements for a Ph.D. except the dissertation. Applicants must be enrolled at a designated college or university in the following 11 states: Alabama, Arkansas, Georgia, Kentucky, Louisiana, Maryland, Mississippi, South Carolina, Tennessee, Virginia, or West Virginia. Enrollment at a graduate school in 5 of those states (Georgia, Mississippi, South Carolina, Tennessee, and Virginia) is available only to residents of those states. Residents of any state in the country may attend a university in the other 5 states. Preference is given to students in STEM disciplines with particularly low minority representation, although all academic fields are eligible. Applicants must be in a position to write full time and must expect to complete their dissertation within the year of the fellowship. Eligibility is limited to individuals who plan to become full-time faculty members at a college or university upon completion of their doctoral degree. The program is not open to students working on other doctoral degrees (e.g., M.D., D.B.A., D.D.S., J.D., D.V.M., Ed.D., Pharm.D., D.N.P., D.P.T.).

Financial Data Fellows receive waiver of tuition and fees (in or out of state), a stipend of $20,000, a $500 research allowance, and reimbursement of expenses for attending the Compact for Faculty Diversity's annual Institute on Teaching and Mentoring.

Duration 1 year; nonrenewable.

Additional data This program began in 1993 as part of the Compact for Faculty Diversity, supported by the Pew Charitable Trusts and the Ford Foundation. It currently operates at universities in 10 of the member states of the Southern Regional Education Board (SREB): Alabama, Arkansas, Georgia, Kentucky, Louisiana, Mississippi, South Carolina, Tennessee, Virginia, and West Virginia; the other 6 member states (Delaware, Florida, Maryland, North Carolina, Oklahoma, and Texas) do not participate.

Number awarded Varies each year.

Deadline March of each year.

[1012]
SPANISH BAPTIST CONVENTION OF NEW MEXICO SCHOLARSHIP

Baptist Convention of New Mexico
Attn: Missions Mobilization Team
5325 Wyoming Boulevard, N.E.
P.O. Box 94485
Albuquerque, NM 87199-4485
(505) 924-2315   Toll Free: (800) 898-8544
Fax: (505) 924-2320   E-mail: cpairett@bcnm.com
Web: www.bcnm.com/scholarships

Summary To provide financial assistance to Hispanic Baptist students from New Mexico interested in attending college or seminary in any state.

Eligibility This program is open to college and seminary students who are active members of churches affiliated with the Baptist Convention of New Mexico. Applicants must be of Hispanic background and committed to full-time Christian service. They must be attending college or seminary in any state.

Financial Data A stipend is awarded (amount not specified).

Duration 1 year; may be renewed.

Number awarded 1 or more each year.

Deadline April of each year.

[1013]
SPECTRUM SCHOLARSHIP PROGRAM

American Library Association
Attn: Office for Diversity
50 East Huron Street
Chicago, IL 60611-2795
(312) 280-5048   Toll Free: (800) 545-2433, ext. 5048
Fax: (312) 280-3256   TDD: (888) 814-7692
E-mail: spectrum@ala.org
Web: www.ala.org/offices/diversity/spectrum

Summary To provide financial assistance to Hispanic and other minority students interested in working on a degree in librarianship.

Eligibility This program is open to ethnic minority students (Latino or Hispanic, African American or Black, Asian, Native Hawaiian or other Pacific Islander, and American Indian or Alaska Native). Applicants must be U.S. or Canadian citizens or permanent residents who have completed no more than a third of the requirements for a master's or school library media degree. They must be enrolled full or part time at an ALA-accredited school of library and information studies or an ALA-recognized NCATE school library media program. Selection is based on academic leadership, outstanding service, commitment to a career in librarianship, statements indicating the nature of the applicant's library and other work experience, letters of reference, and personal presentation.

Financial Data The stipend is $5,000.

Duration 1 year; nonrenewable.

Additional data This program began in 1998. It is administered by a joint committee of the American Library Association (ALA).

Number awarded Varies each year; recently, 69 were awarded.

Deadline February of each year.

[1014]
SREB DOCTORAL AWARDS

Southern Regional Education Board
Attn: Coordinator, Institute and Scholar Services
592 Tenth Street N.W.
Atlanta, GA 30318-5776
(404) 879-5516   Fax: (404) 872-1477
E-mail: tammy.wright@sreb.org
Web: www.sreb.org/types-awards

Summary To provide financial assistance to Hispanic and other minority students who wish to work on a doctoral degree, especially in fields of science, technology, engineering, or mathematics (STEM), at designated universities in the southern states.

Eligibility This program is open to U.S. citizens and permanent residents who are members of racial/ethnic minority groups (Hispanic Americans, Native Americans, Asian Americans, and African Americans) and have or will receive a bachelor's or master's degree. Applicants must be entering or enrolled in the first year of a Ph.D. program at a designated college or university in the following 11 states: Alabama, Arkansas, Georgia, Kentucky, Louisiana, Maryland, Mississippi, South Carolina, Tennessee, Virginia, West Virginia. Enrollment at a graduate school in 5 of those states (Georgia, Mississippi, South Carolina, Tennessee, and Virginia) is available only to residents of those states. Residents of any state in the country may attend a university in the other 5 states. Applicants must indicate an interest in becoming a full-time college or university professor. The program does not support students working on other doctoral degrees (e.g., M.D., D.B.A., D.D.S., J.D., D.V.M., Ed.D., Pharm.D., D.N.P., D.P.T.). Preference is given to applicants in STEM disciplines with particularly low minority representation, although all academic fields are eligible.

Financial Data Scholars receive a waiver of tuition and fees (in or out of state) for up to 5 years, an annual stipend of $20,000 for 3 years, an annual allowance of $500 for research and professional development activities, and reimbursement of travel expenses to attend the Compact for Faculty Diversity's annual Institute on Teaching and Mentoring.

Duration Up to 5 years.

Additional data This program began in 1993 as part of the Compact for Faculty Diversity, supported by the Pew Charitable Trusts and the Ford Foundation.

Number awarded Varies each year; recently, the program was supporting more than 300 scholars.

Deadline March of each year.

[1015]
STANTON NUCLEAR SECURITY FELLOWSHIP

Stanford University
Center for International Security and Cooperation
Attn: Fellowships Coordinator
Encina Hall, Room C206-10
616 Serra Street
Stanford, CA 94305-6165
(650) 723-9625   Fax: (650) 724-5683
E-mail: CISACfellowship@stanford.edu
Web: cisac.fsi.stanford.edu/docs/cisac_fellowship_program

Summary To provide funding to doctoral candidates and junior scholars, especially Hispanics and other mnorities, who are interested in conducting research on nuclear security issues at Stanford University's Center for International Security and Cooperation.

Eligibility This program is open to doctoral candidates, recent postdoctorates, and junior faculty. Applicants must be interested in conducting research on nuclear security issues while in residence at the center. The sponsor welcomes applications from women, minorities, and citizens of all countries.

Financial Data The stipend ranges from $25,000 to $28,000 for doctoral candidates or from $48,000 to $66,000 for postdoctorates, depending on experience. Medical insurance is available for those who do not have coverage.

Duration 9 to 11 months.

Additional data Fellows are expected to write a dissertation chapter or chapters, publishable article or articles, and/or make significant progress on turning a thesis into a book manuscript. They should not plan to spend any time conducting research abroad or in other parts of the country.

Number awarded Varies each year; recently, 3 were awarded: 1 doctoral candidate, 1 recent postdoctorate, and 1 junior faculty member.

Deadline January of each year.

[1016]
SUMMER INTERNSHIPS IN NUCLEAR FORENSICS AND ENVIRONMENTAL RADIOCHEMISTRY

Lawrence Livermore National Laboratory
Physical and Life Sciences Directorate
Attn: Director of Student Programs
7000 East Avenue, L-452
Livermore, CA 94550
(925) 422-6351   E-mail: kulp2@llnl.gov
Web: www-pls.llnl.gov

Summary To provide an opportunity for graduate students, especially Hispanics and other minorities, to work on summer research projects on nuclear forensics and environmental radiochemistry at Lawrence Livermore National Laboratory (LLNL).

Eligibility This program is open to full-time master's and doctoral students who are interested in working on research projects at LLNL involving nuclear forensics, nuclear chemistry, and environmental radiochemistry. Applicants must be U.S. citizens. Selection is based on academic record, aptitude, research interests, and recommendations of instructors. Strong preference is given to students with exceptional academic records and potential for making outstanding contributions to applied science. Women and minorities are encouraged to apply.

Financial Data The stipend ranges from $4,100 to $4,900 per month, depending on number of school years completed. Living accommodations and arrangements are the responsibility of the intern.

Duration 8 weeks, during the summer.

Number awarded 10 to 15 each year.

Deadline February of each year.

[1017]
SUMMER RESEARCH OPPORTUNITY PROGRAM IN PATHOLOGY

American Society for Investigative Pathology
Attn: Executive Officer
9650 Rockville Pike, Suite E133
Bethesda, MD 20814-3993
(301) 634-7130   Fax: (301) 634-7990
E-mail: asip@asip.org
Web: www.asip.org/awards/sropp.cfm

Summary To provide an opportunity for Hispanics and members of other underrepresented minority groups to participate in a summer research program in pathology.

Eligibility This program is open to students who are members of underrepresented minority groups. Applicants must be interested in visiting prominent research laboratories and institutions during the summer to learn and participate in new research in the mechanisms of disease.

Financial Data The program provides housing at the host laboratory and a grant of $2,800 to cover travel costs to and from the site, living expenses, and a stipend.

Duration 10 weeks during the summer.

Additional data This program operates in partnership with the Intersociety Council for Pathology Information.

Number awarded Varies each year; recently, 2 laboratories were selected and 1 student was assigned to each.

Deadline March of each year.

[1018]
SUMMER TRANSPORTATION INTERNSHIP PROGRAM FOR DIVERSE GROUPS

Department of Transportation
Attn: Summer Transportation Internship Program for Diverse Groups
Eighth Floor E81-105
1200 New Jersey Avenue, S.E.
Washington, DC 20590
(202) 366-2907   E-mail: Crystal.Taylor@dot.gov
Web: www.fhwa.dot.gov/education/stipdg.cfm

Summary To enable Hispanic and other undergraduate, graduate, and law students from diverse groups to gain work experience during the summer at facilities of the U.S. Department of Transportation (DOT).

Eligibility This program is open to all qualified applicants, but it is designed to provide women, persons with disabilities, and members of diverse social and ethnic groups with summer opportunities in transportation. Applicants must be U.S. citizens currently enrolled in a degree-granting program of study at an accredited institution of higher learning at the undergraduate (community or junior college, university, college, or Tribal College or University) or graduate level. Undergraduates must be entering their junior or senior year; students attending a Tribal or community college must have completed their first year of school; law students must be entering their second or third year of school. Students who will graduate during the spring or summer are not eligible unless they have been accepted for enrollment in graduate school. The program accepts applications from students in all majors who are interested in working on transportation-related topics and issues. Preference is given to students with a GPA of 3.0 or higher. Undergraduates must submit a 1-page essay on their transportation interests and how participation in this program will enhance their educational and career plans and goals. Graduate students must submit a writing sample representing their educational and career plans and goals. Law students must submit a legal writing sample.

Financial Data   The stipend is $4,000 for undergraduates or $5,000 for graduate and law students. The program also provides housing and reimbursement of travel expenses from interns' homes to their assignment location.

Duration   10 weeks during the summer.

Additional data   Assignments are at the DOT headquarters in Washington, D.C., a selected modal administration, or selected field offices around the country.

Number awarded   80 to 100 each year.

Deadline   January of each year.

[1019]
SUNY GRADUATE DIVERSITY FELLOWSHIP PROGRAM

State University of New York
Attn: Office of Diversity, Equity and Inclusion
State University Plaza, T1000A
353 Broadway
Albany, NY 12246
(518) 320-1189   E-mail: carlos.medina@suny.edu
Web: system.suny.edu/odei/diversity-programs

Summary   To provide financial assistance to graduate students at campuses of the State University of New York (SUNY) who are Hispanics or will contribute to the diversity of the student body in other ways.

Eligibility   This program is open to U.S. citizens and permanent residents who are entering or enrolled full-time graduate or professional students at any of the participating SUNY colleges. Applicants must be able to demonstrate how they will contribute to the diversity of the student body for the program for which they are applying, including having overcome a disadvantage or other impediment to success in higher education. Economic disadvantage, although not a requirement, may be the basis for eligibility. Membership in a racial or ethnic group that is underrepresented in the graduate or professional program involved may serve as a plus factor in making awards, but may not form the sole basis of selection. Awards are granted in the following priority order: 1) new graduate students who are being recruited but have not yet accepted admission to a graduate program; 2) Graduate Opportunity Waiver Program students who can be awarded a stipend to supplement their waiver to tuition; 3) currently-enrolled doctoral candidates who have completed all degree requirements except the dissertation; and 4) graduate assistants and teaching assistants who can receive a supplement to their current stipends to enhance their retention in graduate studies.

Financial Data   Stipends range from $7,500 to $10,000.

Duration   1 year; renewable.

Number awarded   Varies each year; recently, this program awarded nearly $6 million in fellowships to 511 graduate students on 24 SUNY campuses. Of the recipients 32% were Latinos, 34% African Americans, 17% Whites, 5% Asians, and 5% Native Americans.

Deadline   Deadline not specified.

[1020]
SUSAN M. JACKSON MINISTERIAL SCHOLARS FUND

Unitarian Universalist Association
Attn: Ministerial Credentialing Office
24 Farnsworth Street
Boston, MA 02210-1409
(617) 948-6403   Fax: (617) 742-2875
E-mail: mcoadministrator@uua.org
Web: www.uua.org

Summary   To provide financial assistance to seminary students, especially Hispanics and other persons of color, who are preparing for the Unitarian Universalist (UU) ministry and demonstrate enthusiasm about their faith.

Eligibility   This program is open to seminary students who are enrolled full or at least half time in a UU ministerial training program with candidate status. Applicants must be citizens of the United States or Canada. They must be able to demonstrate their enthusiasm about Unitarian Universalist ideas and conclusions, drawn from their faith, that influence their lives. Priority is given first to those who have demonstrated outstanding ministerial ability and secondarily to students with the greatest financial need (especially persons of color).

Financial Data   The stipend ranges from $1,000 to $15,000 per year.

Duration   1 year.

Number awarded   1 each year.

Deadline   April of each year.

[1021]
SYNOD OF LAKES AND PRAIRIES RACIAL ETHNIC SCHOLARSHIPS

Synod of Lakes and Prairies
Attn: Committee on Racial Ethnic Ministry
2115 Cliff Drive
Eagen, MN 55122-3327
(651) 357-1140   Toll Free: (800) 328-1880, ext. 202
Fax: (651) 357-1141   E-mail: mkes@lakesandprairies.org
Web: www.lakesandprairies.org

Summary   To provide financial assistance to Hispanic and other minority residents of the Presbyterian Church (USA) Synod of Lakes and Prairies who are working on an undergraduate or graduate degree at a college or seminary in any state as preparation for service to the church.

Eligibility   This program is open to members of Presbyterian churches who reside within the Synod of Lakes and Prairies (Iowa, Minnesota, Nebraska, North Dakota, South Dakota, and Wisconsin). Applicants must be members of ethnic minority groups studying at least half time for service in the Presbyterian Church (USA) as a teaching elder, ordained minister, commissioned ruling elder, lay professional, or volunteer. They must be in good academic standing, making progress toward an undergraduate or graduate degree, and able to demonstrate financial need. Along with their application, they must submit essays of 200 to 500 words on 1) what the church needs to do to be faithful to its mission in the world today; and 2) the people, practices, or events that influence their commitment to Christ in ways that renew their fair and strengthen their service.

Financial Data   Stipends range from $850 to $3,500.

Duration 1 year.

Number awarded Varies each year; recently, 9 were awarded.

Deadline September of each year.

[1022]
TEXAS ASSOCIATION OF CHICANOS IN HIGHER EDUCATION GRADUATE FELLOWSHIP AWARDS

Texas Association of Chicanos in Higher Education
c/o Maria Aguirre, Awards Committee Chair
Texas State Technical College West Texas
1420 Edgewood
Sweetwater, TX 79556
E-mail: maria.aguirre@tstc.edu
Web: www.tache.org/Awards.aspx

Summary To provide financial assistance to Hispanic residents of Texas who are enrolled in a graduate program in any state to prepare for a career in higher education.

Eligibility This program is open to residents of Texas who are of Chicano/Latino heritage (1 parent fully Hispanic or both parents half Hispanic). Applicants must be enrolled full time in a U.S. graduate or professional school in a degree program to prepare for a career in higher education or administration. They must have a cumulative GPA of 3.0 or higher. Along with their application, they must submit a 2-page personal statement that describes any obstacles they have faced in attaining graduate studies, how this award will be used to support educational career goals, and plans for future contributions to the educational advancement of Latinos in Texas. They must also submit a resume that includes their contributions, achievements, awards, honors, and service activities related to the Chicano/Latino culture and community in Texas.

Financial Data The stipend is $2,000 per year.

Duration 1 year.

Additional data Recipients are required to become members of the Texas Association of Chicanos in Higher Education.

Number awarded 4 each year: 2 to students whose career emphasis is in community college education and 2 to students whose study emphasis is in university or postgraduate education.

Deadline December of each year.

[1023]
TEXAS MEDICAL ASSOCIATION MINORITY SCHOLARSHIP PROGRAM

Texas Medical Association
Attn: Director, Educational Loans, Scholarships and Awards
401 West 15th Street, Suite 100
Austin, TX 78701-1680
(512) 370-1600   Toll Free: (800) 880-1300, ext. 1600
Fax: (512) 370-1693
E-mail: gail.schatte@tmaloanfunds.com
Web: www.tmaloanfunds.com/Content/Template.aspx?id=9

Summary To provide financial assistance to Mexican Amricans and members of other underrepresented minority groups from any state who are entering medical school in Texas.

Eligibility This program is open to members of minority groups that are underrepresented in the medical profession

(Mexican American, African American, Native American). Applicants must have been accepted at a medical school in Texas; students currently enrolled are not eligible. Along with their application, they must submit a 750-word essay on how they, as a physician, would improve the health of all Texans.

Financial Data The stipend is $2,500 per year.

Duration 4 years.

Additional data This program began in 1999.

Number awarded 12 each year: 1 at each of the medical schools in Texas.

Deadline February of each year.

[1024]
TEXAS YOUNG LAWYERS ASSOCIATION DIVERSITY SCHOLARSHIP PROGRAM

Texas Young Lawyers Association
Attn: Diversity Committee
1414 Colorado, Fourth Floor
P.O. Box 12487
Austin, TX 78711-2487
(512) 427-1529   Toll Free: (800) 204-2222, ext. 1529
Fax: (512) 427-4117   E-mail: btrevino@texasbar.com
Web: www.tyla.org

Summary To provide financial assistance to residents of any state who are Hispanics or members of other diverse groups attending law school in Texas.

Eligibility This program is open to members of recognized diverse groups, including diversity based on gender, national origin, race, ethnicity, sexual orientation, gender identity, disability, socioeconomic status, and geography. Applicants must be attending an ABA-accredited law school in Texas. Along with their application, they must submit a brief essay on 1) why they believe diversity is important to the practice of law; and 2) what the Texas Young Lawyers Association and the State Bar of Texas can do to promote and support diversity in the legal profession. Selection is based on those essays, academic performance, demonstrated commitment to diversity, letters of recommendation, and financial need.

Financial Data The stipend is $1,000.

Duration 1 year.

Number awarded At least 9 each year: at least 1 at each accredited law school in Texas.

Deadline October of each year.

[1025]
THE LEADERSHIP INSTITUTE SCHOLARSHIPS

The Leadership Institute for Women of Color Attorneys, Inc.
Attn: Scholarship Chair
1266 West Paces Ferry Road, N.W., Suite 263
Atlanta, GA 30327
(404) 443-5715   E-mail: hhorton@mcguirewoods.com
Web: www.leadingwomenofcolor.org

Summary To provide financial assistance to Hispanics and other women of color who are attending law school.

Eligibility This program is open to women of color who have completed at least 1 year at an accredited law school and have a GPA of 3.0 or higher. Applicants must be U.S. citizens who can demonstrate a commitment to the legal profession. Along with their application, they must submit brief statements on their work experience, extracurricular activities, why they think it is important for women of color to serve in the legal profession, what they believe is necessary for success in the legal profession, and what they plan to do with their law degree.

Financial Data   The stipend is $3,000.

Duration   1 year.

Number awarded   5 each year.

Deadline   December of each year.

[1026]
THE REV. DR. HECTOR E. LOPEZ SCHOLARSHIP

United Church of Christ
Attn: Associate Director, Grant and Scholarship
  Administration
700 Prospect Avenue East
Cleveland, OH 44115-1100
(216) 736-2166   Toll Free: (866) 822-8224, ext. 2166
Fax: (216) 736-3783   E-mail: scholarships@ucc.org
Web: www.ucc.org/lopez_scholarship

Summary   To provide financial assistance to Latino/a students at seminaries of the United Church of Christ (UCC).

Eligibility   This program is open to Latino/a students working on a master's degree at any of the 6 seminaries of the UCC. Applicants must 1) have a GPA of 3.0 or higher; 2) be a member in discernment of a UCC congregation; and 3) be planning to return from seminary to lead vital congregations and minister to Latino constituencies, multi-cultural communities, and the whole church.

Financial Data   Stipends range from $1,500 to $2,500 per year. Funds are paid directly to the seminary, to be applied toward tuition.

Duration   1 year.

Additional data   This program began in 2006. The UCC seminaries are Andover Newton Theological School (Newton Centre, Massachusetts), Chicago Theological Seminary (Chicago, Illinois), Eden Theological Seminary (St. Louis, Missouri), Lancaster Theological Seminary (Lancaster, Pennsylvania), Pacific School of Religion (Berkeley, California), and United Theological Seminary of the Twin Cities (New Brighton, Minnesota).

Number awarded   Varies each year; recently, 3 were awarded.

Deadline   February of each year.

[1027]
THOMAS G. NEUSOM SCHOLARSHIPS

Conference of Minority Transportation Officials
Attn: National Scholarship Program
100 M Street, S.E., Suite 917
Washington, DC 20003
(202) 506-2917   E-mail: info@comto.org
Web: www.comto.org/page/scholarships

Summary   To provide financial assistance for college or graduate school to Hispanic and other minority members of the Conference of Minority Transportation Officials (COMTO) and their families.

Eligibility   This program is open to undergraduate and graduate students who have been members of COMTO or whose parents, guardians, or grandparents have been members for at least 1 year. Applicants must be working (either full or part time) on a degree in a field related to transportation and have a GPA of 2.5 or higher. Along with their application they must submit a cover letter on their transportation-related career goals and life aspirations. Financial need is not considered in the selection process.

Financial Data   The stipend is $5,500. Funds are paid directly to the recipient's college or university.

Duration   1 year.

Number awarded   1 each year.

Deadline   April of each year.

[1028]
TRAILBLAZER SCHOLARSHIP

Conference of Minority Transportation Officials
Attn: National Scholarship Program
100 M Street, S.E., Suite 917
Washington, DC 20003
(202) 506-2917   E-mail: info@comto.org
Web: www.comto.org/page/scholarships

Summary   To provide financial assistance for college or graduate school to Hispanic and other minority members of the Conference of Minority Transportation Officials (COMTO) and their families.

Eligibility   This program is open to undergraduate and graduate students who have been members of COMTO or whose parents, guardians, or grandparents have been members for at least 1 year. Applicants must be working (either full or part time) on a degree in a field related to transportation and have a GPA of 2.5 or higher. Along with their application they must submit a cover letter on their transportation-related career goals and life aspirations. Financial need is not considered in the selection process.

Financial Data   The stipend is $2,500. Funds are paid directly to the recipient's college or university.

Duration   1 year.

Number awarded   1 each year.

Deadline   April of each year.

[1029]
TRANSAMERICA RETIREMENT SOLUTIONS LEADERS IN HEALTH CARE SCHOLARSHIP

Institute for Diversity in Health Management
Attn: Membership and Education Specialist
155 North Wacker Avenue
Chicago, IL 60606
(312) 422-2658   E-mail: cbiddle@aha.org
Web: www.diversityconnection.org

Summary   To provide financial assistance to graduate students in health care management who are Hispanics or will contribute to ethnic diversity in the profession in other ways.

Eligibility   This program is open to U.S. citizens who represent ethnically diverse cultural backgrounds. Applicants must be enrolled in the second year of a master's degree program in health administration or a comparable program and have a GPA of 3.0 or higher. Along with their application, they must submit 1) a personal statement of 1 to 2 pages on their interest in health care management and their career goals; 2) an essay on what they see as the most challenging issue facing America's hospitals and health systems; and 3) a 500-word essay on their interest and background in health care finance. Selection is based on academic achievement, commitment to community service, and financial need.

Financial Data The stipend is $5,000.

Duration 1 year.

Additional data This program began in 2007 as the Diversified Investment Advisors Leaders in Healthcare Scholarship. Its current name became effective in 2013 when Transamerica Retirement Solutions assumed sponsorship.

Number awarded 2 each year.

Deadline January of each year.

[1030]
UNDERREPRESENTED MINORITY DENTAL STUDENT SCHOLARSHIP

American Dental Association
Attn: ADA Foundation
211 East Chicago Avenue
Chicago, IL 60611
(312) 440-2547   Fax: (312) 440-3526
E-mail: adaf@ada.org
Web: www.adafoundation.org/en/how-to-apply/education

Summary To provide financial assistance to Hispanics and other underrepresented minorities who wish to enter the field of dentistry.

Eligibility This program is open to U.S. citizens from a minority group that is currently underrepresented in the dental profession: Hispanic, Native American, or African American. Applicants must have a GPA of 3.25 or higher and be entering their second year of full-time study at a dental school in the United States accredited by the Commission on Dental Accreditation. Selection is based upon academic achievement, a written summary of personal and professional goals, letters of reference, and demonstrated financial need.

Financial Data The maximum stipend is $2,500. Funds are sent directly to the student's financial aid office to be used to cover tuition, fees, books, supplies, and living expenses.

Duration 1 year.

Additional data This program, established in 1991, is supported by the Harry J. Bosworth Company, Colgate-Palmolive, Sunstar Americas, and Procter & Gamble Company. Students receiving a full scholarship from any other source are ineligible to receive this scholarship.

Number awarded Approximately 25 each year.

Deadline November of each year.

[1031]
UNITED HEALTH FOUNDATION NATIONAL ASSOCIATION OF HISPANIC NURSES SCHOLARSHIP AWARDS

National Association of Hispanic Nurses
Attn: Scholarships
1500 Sunday Drive, Suite 102
Raleigh, NC 27607
(919) 787-5181, ext. 1255   Fax: (919) 787-4916
E-mail: director@thehispanicnurses.org
Web: www.nahnnet.org/NAHNScholarships.html

Summary To provide financial assistance for nursing education to members of the National Association of Hispanic Nurses (NAHN).

Eligibility Eligible are members of the association enrolled in associate, diploma, baccalaureate, graduate, or practical/vocational nursing programs at NLN-accredited schools of nursing. Applicants must have a GPA of 3.0 or higher. Along with their application, they must submit a letter of recommendation; a 300-word essay that reflects their qualifications and potential for leadership in nursing in the Hispanic community; a resume that includes earned certificates, awards, and special honors; information on their financial status; and an official transcript. U.S. citizenship or permanent resident status is required.

Financial Data The stipend is $5,000.

Duration 1 year; may be renewed.

Additional data This program is sponsored by United Health Foundation as part of its Latino Health Scholars Program.

Number awarded Varies each year; recently, 8 new and 8 renewal scholarships were awarded.

Deadline June of each year.

[1032]
UNITED HEALTH FOUNDATION/NMF DIVERSE MEDICAL SCHOLARS PROGRAM

National Medical Fellowships, Inc.
Attn: Scholarship Program
347 Fifth Avenue, Suite 510
New York, NY 10016
(212) 483-8880   Toll Free: (877) NMF-1DOC
Fax: (212) 483-8897 E-mail: scholarships@nmfonline.org
Web: www.nmfonline.org

Summary To provide financial assistance to Hispanic and other underrepresented minority students at medical schools in designated areas who are interested in conducting a community health project.

Eligibility This program is open to Hispanics/Latinos, African Americans, Native Americans, Vietnamese, Cambodians, and Pacific Islanders who are currently enrolled at an accredited medical school in the greater New York City metropolitan area (including Connecticut, New Jersey, New York, and Pennsylvania), Florida (Orlando, Tampa, and greater Miami), Arizona (Phoenix), New Mexico (Albuquerque), Tennessee (Nashville), Texas (San Antonio), Wisconsin (Milwaukee), or Georgia (Atlanta). Applicants must have demonstrated leadership and a commitment to serving medically underserved communities. They must be interested in conducting a self-directed health project of 200 hours at a site of choice in an underserved community in the same area as their medical school. U.S. citizenship or DACA status is required.

Financial Data The grant is $7,000.

Duration 1 year; recipients may apply for a second year of funding.

Additional data This program, sponsored by United Health Foundation, began in 2007.

Number awarded 30 each year.

Deadline October of each year.

[1033]
UNITED HEALTHCARE/LAWYERS COLLABORATIVE FOR DIVERSITY CLERKSHIP

Lawyers Collaborative for Diversity
Attn: Program Coordinator
P.O. Box 230637
Hartford, CT 06123-0637
(860) 275-0668
E-mail: kdavis@lawyerscollaborativefordiversity.org
Web: www.lcdiversity.com/scholarships.htm

Summary To provide summer work experience at United Healthcare Services in Hartford, Connecticut to Hispanic and other underrepresented students at law schools in Connecticut and western Massachusetts.

Eligibility This program is open to women and students of color in their first year at law schools in Connecticut or western Massachusetts. Applicants must be interested in a summer internship at United Healthcare Services in Harford, Connecticut. Along with their application, they must submit 500-word essays on 1) why they should be selected for this opportunity; and 2) their thoughts about diversity in Connecticut's legal community.

Financial Data The stipend is $5,000.

Duration 8 weeks during the summer.

Additional data This program is sponsored by United HealthCare Services, Inc.

Number awarded 1 each year.

Deadline February of each year.

[1034]
UNITED METHODIST FOUNDATION THEOLOGICAL AND PROFESSIONAL SCHOOL MERIT SCHOLARS PROGRAM

United Methodist Higher Education Foundation
Attn: Scholarships Administrator
60 Music Square East, Suite 350
P.O. Box 340005
Nashville, TN 37203-0005
(615) 649-3974   Toll Free: (800) 811-8110
Fax: (615) 649-3980
E-mail: umhefscholarships@umhef.org
Web: www.umhef.org

Summary To provide financial assistance to students, especially Hispanics and other minorities, who are preparing for ordination at seminaries affiliated with the United Methodist Church.

Eligibility This program is open to first- through third-year students working on a master's degree at the 14 United Methodist-related theological and professional schools. Applicants must be U.S. citizens or permanent residents and active members of the United Methodist Church for at least 1 year prior to application. They must be planning to enroll full time and have a GPA of 3.0 or higher. Preference is given to ethnic minority and first generation college students. Financial need is considered in the selection process.

Financial Data The stipend is $3,000.

Duration 1 year; nonrenewable.

Additional data Students may obtain applications from their school.

Number awarded 42 each year: 1 to a member of each class at each school.

Deadline Nominations from schools must be received by September of each year.

[1035]
UNITED METHODIST WOMEN OF COLOR SCHOLARS PROGRAM

United Methodist Church
Attn: General Board of Higher Education and Ministry
Office of Loans and Scholarships
1001 19th Avenue South
P.O. Box 340007
Nashville, TN 37203-0007
(615) 340-7342   Fax: (615) 340-7367
E-mail: umscholar@gbhem.org
Web: www.gbhem.org

Summary To provide financial assistance to Methodist Hispanic and other women of color who are working on a doctoral degree to prepare for a career as an educator at a United Methodist seminary.

Eligibility This program is open to women of color (have at least 1 parent who is Hispanic, African American, African, Asian, Native American, Alaska Native, or Pacific Islander) who have an M.Div. degree. Applicants must have been active, full members of a United Methodist Church for at least 3 years prior to applying. They must be enrolled full time in a degree program at the Ph.D. or Th.D. level to prepare for a career teaching at a United Methodist seminary.

Financial Data The maximum stipend is $10,000 per year.

Duration 1 year; may be renewed up to 3 additional years.

Number awarded Varies each year; recently, 10 were awarded.

Deadline January of each year.

[1036]
UTC/LCD DIVERSITY SCHOLARS PROGRAM

Lawyers Collaborative for Diversity
Attn: Program Coordinator
P.O. Box 230637
Hartford, CT 06123-0637
(860) 275-0668
E-mail: kdavis@lawyerscollaborativefordiversity.org
Web: www.lcdiversity.com/scholarships.htm

Summary To provide financial assistance and summer work experience to Hispanic and other underrepresented students at law schools in Connecticut and western Massachusetts.

Eligibility This program is open to women and people of color from any state who are currently enrolled in the first year at a law school in Connecticut or western Massachusetts. Applicants must be available to work as an intern during the summer following their first year. Along with their application, they must submit 500-word essays on 1) why diversity is important to them and how the Connecticut legal community can improve diversity in the legal profession; and 2) why they should be selected for this program.

Financial Data The program provides a stipend of $2,000 per year for the second and third years of law school, a paid internship during the summer after the first year at a member firm of the Lawyers Collaborative for Diversity (LCD), and an unpaid internship with a legal department of United Technologies Corporation during that same summer.

Duration The scholarship is for 2 years; the paid internship is for 5 weeks during the summer; the unpaid internship is for 3 weeks during the summer.

Additional data This program is sponsored by United Technologies Corporation (UTC).

Number awarded 2 each year.

Deadline January of each year.

[1037]
UVALDO HERRERA NATIONAL MOOT COURT COMPETITION

Hispanic National Bar Association
Attn: HNBA Legal Education Fund
1020 19th Street, N.W., Suite 505
Washington, DC 20036
(202) 223-4777   Fax: (202) 503-3403
E-mail: ovargas@hnbafund.org
Web: www.hnbafund.org/Scholarships.aspx

Summary To recognize and reward student members of the Hispanic National Bar Association (HNBA) who participate in a moot court competition.

Eligibility This competition is open to HNBA members who are also members of the HNBA Law Student Division. Applicants must be enrolled as full- or part-time students at any law school. They must apply to participate in the moot court competition on a team of 2 or 3 students. Teams are selected by the local Hispanic/Latino law student organization at the school (if it exists).

Financial Data Awards are $8,000 for the national champion team, $6,000 for the runner-up team, $4,000 for the third-place team, and $2,000 for the fourth-place team.

Duration The competition is held annually.

Additional data The participation fee is $495.

Number awarded 4 winning teams are selected each year.

Deadline January of each year.

[1038]
VICTOR GRIFOLS ROURA SCHOLARSHIP

National Medical Fellowships, Inc.
Attn: Scholarship Program
347 Fifth Avenue, Suite 510
New York, NY 10016
(212) 483-8880   Toll Free: (877) NMF-1DOC
Fax: (212) 483-8897 E-mail: scholarships@nmfonline.org
Web: www.nmfonline.org

Summary To provide financial assistance to Hispanic and other underrepresented minority students at medical schools in the Los Angeles metropolitan area.

Eligibility This program is open to Hispanics/Latinos, African Americans, Native Americans, Vietnamese, Cambodians, and Pacific Islanders who are entering their second or third year at a medical school in the Los Angeles metropolitan area. Applicants must demonstrate an interest in hematology (diseases of the blood). They must be U.S. citizens or DACA students. Selection is based on leadership, commitment to serving medically underserved communities, and financial need.

Financial Data The stipend is $7,500.

Duration 1 year.

Additional data This program began in 2013.

Number awarded 1 each year.

Deadline September of each year.

[1039]
VIRGINIA TEACHING SCHOLARSHIP LOAN PROGRAM

Virginia Department of Education
Division of Teacher Education and Licensure
Attn: Director of Teacher Education
P.O. Box 2120
Richmond, VA 23218-2120
(804) 371-2475   Toll Free: (800) 292-3820
Fax: (804) 786-6759
E-mail: JoAnne.Carver@doe.virginia.gov
Web: www.doe.virginia.gov

Summary To provide scholarship/loans to Hispanic and other minority undergraduate and graduate students in Virginia who are interested in a career in teaching.

Eligibility This program is open to Virginia residents who are enrolled full or part time as a sophomore, junior, senior, or graduate student in a state-approved teacher preparation program in Virginia, who were in the top 10% of their high school class, and have a GPA of 2.7 or higher. Applicants must meet 1 or more of the following criteria: 1) are enrolled in a program leading to endorsement in a critical shortage area; 2) are a male in an elementary or middle school education program; 3) are a minority teaching candidate in any endorsement area; or 4) are a student in an approved teacher education program leading to an endorsement in career and technical education. They must agree to engage in full-time teaching following graduation in 1) designated teacher shortage areas within Virginia; 2) a school with a high concentration of students eligible for free or reduced lunch; 3) within a school division with a shortage of teachers; or 4) in a rural or urban region of the state with a teacher shortage.

Financial Data The maximum scholarship/loan is $10,000 per year for full-time students or a prorated amount for part-time students. Loans are forgiven by qualified teaching of 1 year for each year of support received. If the recipient fails to fulfill the teaching service requirement, the loan must be repaid with interest.

Duration 1 year; may be renewed.

Additional data Critical shortage teaching areas in Virginia are currently identified as special education, career and technical education (including technology education, trade and industrial education, business education, and family and consumer sciences), mathematics (6-12), foreign language (preK-12), English, middle school (6-8), elementary education (preK-6), history and social sciences, health and physical education (preK-12), and school counselor (preK-12).

Number awarded Varies each year.

Deadline Deadline not specified.

[1040]
VISITING RESEARCH INTERNSHIP PROGRAM

Harvard Medical School
Office for Diversity Inclusion and Community Partnership
Attn: Program for Faculty Development and Diversity
  Inclusion
164 Longwood Avenue, Second Floor
Boston, MA 02115-5810
(617) 432-1892   Fax: (617) 432-3834
E-mail: pfdd_dcp@hms.harvard.edu
Web: mfdp.med.harvard.edu

Summary   To provide an opportunity for medical students, especially Hispanics and other underrepresented minorities, to conduct a mentored research project at Harvard Medical School during the summer.

Eligibility   This program is open to first- and second-year medical students, particularly underrepresented minority and/or disadvantaged individuals, in good standing at accredited U.S. medical schools. Applicants must be interested in conducting a summer research project at Harvard Medical School under the mentorship of a faculty advisor. They must be interested in a research and health-related career, especially in clinical or translational research or research that transforms scientific discoveries arising from laboratory, clinical, or population studies into clinical or population-based applications to improve health. U.S. citizenship, nationality, or permanent resident status is required.

Financial Data   Participants receive a stipend (amount not specified), housing, and reimbursement of transportation costs to Boston up to $400.

Duration   8 weeks during the summer.

Additional data   This program, established in 2008, is funded by the National Center for Research Resources of the National Institutes of Health NIH). It is a joint enterprise of Harvard University, its 10 schools, its 17 Academic Healthcare Centers, Boston College School of Nursing, MIT, the Cambridge Health Alliance, and other community partners. Interns attend weekly seminars with Harvard faculty focusing on such topics as research methodology, health disparities, ethics, and career paths. They also have the opportunity to participate in offerings of other Harvard Medical School programs, such a career development seminars and networking dinners.

Number awarded   Varies each year; recently, 6 medical students were admitted to this program.

Deadline   December of each year.

[1041]
WARNER NORCROSS & JUDD LAW SCHOOL SCHOLARSHIP

Grand Rapids Community Foundation
Attn: Education Program Officer
185 Oakes Street S.W.
Grand Rapids, MI 49503-4008
(616) 454-1751, ext. 103   Fax: (616) 454-6455
E-mail: rbishop@grfoundation.org
Web: www.grfoundation.org/scholarshipslist

Summary   To provide financial assistance to Hispanic and other minorities from Michigan who are attending law school.

Eligibility   This program is open to students of color who are attending or planning to attend an accredited law school.

Applicants must be residents of Michigan or attending law school in the state. They must be U.S. citizens or permanent residents and have a GPA of 2.5 or higher. Financial need is considered in the selection process.

Financial Data   The stipend is $5,000. Funds are paid directly to the recipient's institution.

Duration   1 year.

Additional data   Funding for this program is provided by the law firm Warner Norcross & Judd LLP.

Number awarded   1 each year.

Deadline   March of each year.

[1042]
WAYNE ANTHONY BUTTS SCHOLARSHIP

National Medical Fellowships, Inc.
Attn: Scholarship Program
347 Fifth Avenue, Suite 510
New York, NY 10016
(212) 483-8880   Toll Free: (877) NMF-1DOC
Fax: (212) 483-8897   E-mail: scholarships@nmfonline.org
Web: www.nmfonline.org

Summary   To provide financial assistance to Hispanic and other underrepresented minority students at medical schools in the New York City metropolitan area.

Eligibility   This program is open to Hispanics/Latinos, African Americans, Native Americans, Vietnamese, Cambodians, and Pacific Islanders who are entering their first or second year of medical school. Applicants must be enrolled at a school in the New York City metropolitan area. They must be U.S. citizens or DACA students. Selection is based on leadership, commitment to serving medically underserved communities, and financial need.

Financial Data   The stipend is $3,000.

Duration   1 year.

Additional data   This program began in 2013.

Number awarded   1 each year.

Deadline   September of each year.

[1043]
WILLIAM AND CHARLOTTE CADBURY AWARD

National Medical Fellowships, Inc.
Attn: Scholarship Program
347 Fifth Avenue, Suite 510
New York, NY 10016
(212) 483-8880   Toll Free: (877) NMF-1DOC
Fax: (212) 483-8897   E-mail: scholarships@nmfonline.org
Web: www.nmfonline.org

Summary   To provide financial assistance to Hispanic and other underrepresented minority medical students who demonstrate academic achievement.

Eligibility   This program is open to Hispanics/Latinos, African Americans, Native Americans, Vietnamese, Cambodians, and Pacific Islanders who are entering their senior year of medical school. They must be U.S. citizens or DACA students. Selection is based on academic achievement, leadership, and community service.

Financial Data   The stipend is $5,000.

Duration   1 year.

Additional data   This program began in 1977.

Number awarded 1 each year.

Deadline September of each year.

[1044]
WILLIAM G. ANDERSON, D.O. MINORITY SCHOLARSHIP

American Osteopathic Foundation
Attn: Director, Internal and External Affairs
142 East Ontario Street
Chicago, IL 60611-2864
(312) 202-8235   Toll Free: (866) 455-9383
Fax: (312) 202-8216   E-mail: ehart@aof-foundation.org
Web: www.aof.org

Summary To provide financial assistance to Hispanic and other minority students enrolled at colleges of osteopathic medicine.

Eligibility This program is open to minority (Hispanic, African American, Native American, Asian American, or Pacific Islander) students entering their second, third, or fourth year at an accredited college of osteopathic medicine. Applicants must demonstrate 1) interest in osteopathic medicine, its philosophy, and its principles; 2) academic achievement; 3) leadership efforts in addressing the educational, societal, and health needs of minorities; 4) leadership efforts in addressing inequities in medical education and health care; 5) accomplishments, awards and honors, special projects, and extracurricular activities that demonstrate the applicant's ability to be a leader.

Financial Data The stipend is $7,500.

Duration 1 year.

Additional data This program began in 1998.

Number awarded 1 each year.

Deadline April of each year.

[1045]
WILLIAM K. SCHUBERT M.D. MINORITY NURSING SCHOLARSHIP

Cincinnati Children's Hospital Medical Center
Attn: Office of Diversity and Inclusion, MLC 9008
3333 Burnet Avenue
Cincinnati, OH 45229-3026
(513) 803-6416   Toll Free: (800) 344-2462
Fax: (513) 636-5643   TDD: (513) 636-4900
E-mail: diversity@cchmc.org
Web: www.cincinnatichildrens.org

Summary To provide financial assistance to Hispanics and members of other underrepresented groups interested in working on a bachelor's or master's degree in nursing to prepare for licensure in Ohio.

Eligibility This program is open to members of groups underrepresented in the nursing profession (males, American Indians or Alaska Natives, Blacks or African Americans, Hawaiian Natives or other Pacific Islanders, Hispanics or Latinos, or Asians). Applicants must be enrolled or accepted in a professional bachelor's or master's registered nurse program at an accredited school of nursing to prepare for initial licensure in Ohio. They must have a GPA of 2.75 or higher. Along with their application, they must submit a 750-word essay that covers 1) their long-range personal, educational, and professional goals; 2) why they chose nursing as a profession; 3) how their experience as a member of an underrepresented

group has influenced a major professional and/or personal decision in their life; 4) any unique qualifications, experiences, or special talents that demonstrate their creativity; and 5) how their work experience has contributed to their personal development.

Financial Data The stipend is $2,750 per year.

Duration 1 year. May be renewed up to 3 additional years for students working on a bachelor's degree or 1 additional year for students working on a master's degree; renewal requires that students maintain a GPA of 2.75 or higher.

Number awarded 1 or more each year.

Deadline April of each year.

[1046]
WILLIAM RUCKER GREENWOOD SCHOLARSHIP

Association for Women Geoscientists-Potomac Chapter
Attn: Scholarships
P.O. Box 6644
Arlington, VA 22206-0644
E-mail: awgpotomacschol@hotmail.com
Web: www.awg.org/members/po_scholarships.htm

Summary To provide financial assistance to Hispanic and other minority women from any state working on an undergraduate or graduate degree in the geosciences at a college in the Potomac Bay region.

Eligibility This program is open to minority women who are residents of any state and currently enrolled as full-time undergraduate or graduate geoscience majors at an accredited, degree-granting college or university in Delaware, the District of Columbia, Maryland, Virginia, or West Virginia. Selection is based on the applicant's 1) participation in geoscience or earth science educational activities; and 2) potential for leadership as a future geoscience professional.

Financial Data The stipend is $1,000. The recipient also is granted a 1-year membership in the Association for Women Geoscientists (AWG).

Duration 1 year.

Number awarded 1 each year.

Deadline April of each year.

[1047]
WOMAN WHO MOVES THE NATION SCHOLARSHIP

Conference of Minority Transportation Officials
Attn: National Scholarship Program
100 M Street, S.E., Suite 917
Washington, DC 20003
(202) 506-2917   E-mail: info@comto.org
Web: www.comto.org/page/scholarships

Summary To provide financial assistance to Hispanic and other minority women who are working on an undergraduate or graduate degree in specified fields to prepare for a management career in a transportation-related organization.

Eligibility This program is open to minority women who are working on an undergraduate or graduate degree with intent to lead in some capacity as a supervisor, manager, director, or other position in transit or a transportation-related organization. Applicants may be studying business, entrepreneurship, political science, or other specialized area. They must have a GPA of 3.0 or higher. Along with their application they must submit a cover letter on their transportation-related career goals and life aspirations. Financial need is not considered in the selection process.

Financial Data   The stipend is $5,000. Funds are paid directly to the recipient's college or university.

Duration   1 year.

Number awarded   1 each year.

Deadline   April of each year.

[1048]
WORLD COMMUNION NATIONAL SCHOLARSHIPS

United Methodist Church
General Board of Global Ministries
Attn: Scholarship/Leadership Development Office
475 Riverside Drive, Room 1479
New York, NY 10115
(212) 870-3787   Toll Free: (800) UMC-GBGM
Fax: (212) 870-3654   E-mail: scholars@umcmission.org
Web: www.umcor.org/explore-our-work/Scholarships

Summary   To provide financial assistance to U.S. Hispanics and other students of color who are interested in attending graduate school to prepare for leadership in promoting the mission goals of the United Methodist Church.

Eligibility   This program is open to U.S. citizens and permanent residents who are members of a community of color. Applicants must have applied to or been admitted to a master's, doctoral, or professional program at an institution of higher education in the United States. They must indicate a willingness to provide 5 years of Christian service after graduation in the areas of elimination of poverty, expansion of global health, leadership development, or congregational development. High priority is given to members of the United Methodist Church. Financial need is considered in the selection process.

Financial Data   The stipend ranges from $1,000 to $12,500, depending on the recipient's related needs and school expenses.

Duration   1 year.

Additional data   These awards are funded by the World Communion Offering received in United Methodist Churches on the first Sunday in October.

Number awarded   5 to 10 each year.

Deadline   November of each year.

[1049]
WORLDSTUDIO AIGA SCHOLARSHIPS

AIGA, the professional association for design
Attn: Scholarships
233 Broadway, 17th floor
New York, NY 10279
(212) 710-3111   E-mail: scholarship@aiga.org
Web: www.aiga.org/worldstudio-scholarship

Summary   To provide financial assistance to Hispanic and other minority or economically disadvantaged students who are interested in working on an undergraduate or graduate degree in specified fields of the arts.

Eligibility   This program is open to undergraduate and graduate students who are currently enrolled or planning to enroll full time at an accredited college or university and work on a degree in 1 of the following areas: fine art, graphic design (including visual design), illustration (including anima-

tion), interactive design (including UI/UX, motion, digital, and web design), or photography. Other fields of the arts, (e.g., industrial design, interior design, film, architecture, landscape design, theater design, fashion design) are not eligible. Although not required, minority status is a significant factor in the selection process. U.S. citizenship or permanent resident status is required. Applicants must have a GPA of 2.0 or higher. Along with their application, they must submit a 600-word statement of purpose that includes a brief autobiography, an explanation of how their experiences have influenced their creative work and/or their career plans, and how they see themselves contributing to the community at large in the future. Selection is based on that statement, the quality of submitted work, financial need, minority status, recommendations, and academic record.

Financial Data   Basic stipends range from $2,000 to $3,000, but awards up to $5,000 are also presented at the discretion of the jury. Honorable mentions are $500. Funds are paid directly to the recipient's school.

Duration   1 academic year. Recipients may reapply.

Additional data   This program is offered by AIGA, founded in 1914 as the American Institute of Graphic Arts, in cooperation with the Worldstudio Foundation.

Number awarded   Varies each year; recently, 16 scholarships and 2 honorable mentions were awarded.

Deadline   April of each year.

[1050]
WRITING COMPETITION TO PROMOTE DIVERSITY IN LAW SCHOOLS AND IN THE LEGAL PROFESSION

Law School Admission Council
Attn: Office of Diversity Initiatives
662 Penn Street
P.O. Box 40
Newtown, PA 18940-0040
(215) 968-1338   TDD: (215) 968-1169
E-mail: DiversityOffice@lsac.org
Web: www.lsac.org

Summary   To recognize and reward law students who submit outstanding essays on what law schools can do to promote diversity.

Eligibility   This competition is open to J.D. candidates in each year of study at law schools in the United States and Canada that are members of the Law School Admission Council (LSAC). Applicants must submit articles, up to 20 pages in length, on the techniques, resources and strategies law schools can utilize to recruit and retain students of color, students living with a disability, LGBTQ students, and other students who are from groups underrepresented in law schools and the legal profession. Selection is based on research and use of relevant sources and authorities; quality and clarity of legal analysis, persuasion, and writing; understanding, interpretations, and conclusions regarding diversity and the implications of diversity in this context; and compliance with all competition procedures.

Financial Data   The prize is $5,000.

Duration   The prize is awarded annually.

Number awarded   3 each year: 1 to a student in each year of law school.

Deadline   April of each year.

[1051]
WSP/PARSONS BRINCKERHOFF WOMEN IN LEADERSHIP SCHOLARSHIP

Conference of Minority Transportation Officials
Attn: National Scholarship Program
100 M Street, S.E., Suite 917
Washington, DC 20003
(202) 506-2917   E-mail: info@comto.org
Web: www.comto.org/page/scholarships

Summary   To provide financial assistance to Hispanic and other minority women who are working on a master's degree in civil engineering or other transportation-related field.

Eligibility   This program is open to minority women who are working full time on a master's degree in civil engineering with intent to prepare for a leadership role in transportation. They must have a GPA of 3.0 or higher. Along with their application they must submit a cover letter on their transportation-related career goals and life aspirations. Financial need is not considered in the selection process.

Financial Data   The stipend is $3,000. Funds are paid directly to the recipient's college or university.

Duration   1 year.

Additional data   This program is sponsored by WSP USA, formerly Parsons Brinckerhoff, Inc.

Number awarded   1 each year.

Deadline   April of each year.

[1052]
XEROX TECHNICAL MINORITY SCHOLARSHIP PROGRAM

Xerox Corporation
Attn: Technical Minority Scholarship Program
150 State Street, Fourth Floor
Rochester, NY 14614
Toll Free: (877) 747-3625   E-mail: xtmsp@rballiance.com
Web: www.xerox.com/jobs/minority-scholarships/enus.html

Summary   To provide financial assistance to Hispanics and other minorities interested in undergraduate or graduate education in the sciences and/or engineering.

Eligibility   This program is open to minorities (people of Hispanic, African American, Asian, Pacific Islander, Native American, or Native Alaskan descent) working full time on a bachelor's, master's, or doctoral degree in chemistry, computing and software systems, engineering (chemical, computer, electrical, imaging, manufacturing, mechanical, optical, or software), information management, laser optics, materials science, physics, or printing management science. Applicants must be U.S. citizens or permanent residents with a GPA of 3.0 or higher and attending a 4-year college or university.

Financial Data   Stipends range from $1,000 to $10,000.

Duration   1 year.

Number awarded   Varies each year, recently, 128 were awarded.

Deadline   September of each year.

[1053]
ZOETIS/AAVMC VETERINARY STUDENT SCHOLARSHIP PROGRAM

Association of American Veterinary Medical Colleges
Attn: Associate Executive Director for Academic and
   Research Affairs
1101 Vermont Avenue, N.W., Suite 301
Washington, DC 20005-3536
(202) 371-9195, ext. 118   Toll Free: (877) 862-2740
Fax: (202) 842-0773   E-mail: tmashima@aavmc.org
Web: www.aavmc.org

Summary   To provide financial assistance to veterinary students in all areas of professional interest, especially Hispanics and members of other underrepresented groups.

Eligibility   This program is open to second- and third-year students at veterinary colleges in the United States. Applicants may have a professional interest in any area, including food animal medicine, small animal clinical medicine, research, government services, public health, or organized veterinary medicine. Along with their application, they must submit a 3-page personal statement that describes 1) why diversity and inclusion are important to them personally and professionally; 2) how they intend to continue contributing to diversity and inclusion efforts in the veterinary profession after graduation; and 3) what it might mean to be honored as a recipient of this scholarship. They must also indicate how they express their race and/or ethnicity (Hispanic, American Indian or Alaskan, Asian, Black or African American, Native Hawaiian or Pacific Islander, or White) and how they express their gender (male, female, transgender spectrum, or other). Selection is based primarily on documentation of a demonstrated commitment to promoting diversity in academic veterinary medicine; consideration is also given to academic achievement, the student's broader community service record, and financial need.

Financial Data   The stipend is $2,000.

Duration   1 year; nonrenewable.

Additional data   This program was established by Zoetis in 2010. That firm partnered with the Association of American Veterinary Medical Colleges (AAVMC) in 2014 to administer the program.

Number awarded   Varies each year; recently, 452 were awarded.

Deadline   November of each year.

Professionals/ Postdoctorates

Listed alphabetically by program title and described in detail here are 162 grants, awards, educational support programs, residencies, and other sources of "free money" available to Hispanic American professionals and postdoctorates. This funding is available to support research, creative activities, professional projects, training courses, and/or residencies in the United States.

[1054]
AAHE AND ETS OUTSTANDING DISSERTATIONS COMPETITION

American Association of Hispanics in Higher Education
Attn: Dissertation Chair
1120 South Cady Mall, First Floor, Suite B-159
Tempe, AZ 85287-6303
E-mail: edu_rar@shsu.edu
Web: www.aahhe.org

Summary To recognize and reward authors of outstanding doctoral dissertations who either are Hispanics in the social sciences or wrote about Hispanics in higher education in their dissertation.

Eligibility This competition is open to anyone who has completed a doctoral dissertation during the preceding period of approximately 30 months. The author of the dissertation must be an Hispanic working in the social sciences (broadly defined) or an individual who wrote about Hispanics in higher education. Eligible fields are those that relate to the corporate mission of the Educational Testing Service (ETS), including education, linguistics, psychology, statistics, and testing; dissertations in the humanities, basic sciences, technology, engineering, and mathematics are not eligible. Dissertations may use any research approach (e.g., historical, experimental, qualitative, survey). Applicants must submit an abstract, up to 25 pages in length, of their dissertation. Judging is based on the appropriateness of the research approach used, the impact the dissertation will have on the field, the creativity and innovation of the study, the scholarly quality of the dissertation, and significance of contribution to knowledge in the field. Based on the abstracts, 10 semifinalists are selected and asked to submit their complete dissertation. From among those, 3 finalists are invited to present their dissertations at the national conference of the American Association of Hispanics in Higher Education (AAHHE), where winners are selected.

Financial Data Awards are $1,000 for first place, $500 for second, and $250 for third. All travel expenses of finalists to attend the AAHHE national conference are paid.

Duration The awards are presented annually.

Additional data This program began in 2010 as a joint undertaking of AAHHE and ETS.

Number awarded 3 cash awards are presented each year.

Deadline August of each year.

[1055]
AAUW CAREER DEVELOPMENT GRANTS

American Association of University Women
Attn: AAUW Educational Foundation
1111 16th Street, N.W.
Washington, DC 20036-4873
(202) 785-7700   Toll Free: (800) 326-AAUW
Fax: (202) 872-1425   TDD: (202) 785-7777
E-mail: aauw@applyists.com
Web: www.aauw.org

Summary To provide financial assistance to women who are seeking career advancement, career change, or reentry into the workforce, especially Hispanics and other women of color.

Eligibility This program is open to women who are U.S. citizens or permanent residents, have earned a bachelor's degree, received their most recent degree more than 4 years ago, and are making career changes, seeking to advance in current careers, or reentering the workforce. Applicants must be interested in working toward a master's degree, second bachelor's or associate degree, professional degree (e.g., M.D., J.D.), certification program, or technical school certificate. They must be planning to undertake course work at an accredited 2- or 4-year college or university (or a technical school that is licensed, accredited, or approved by the U.S. Department of Education). Primary consideration is given to women of color and women pursuing their first advanced degree or credentials in nontraditional fields. Support is not provided for prerequisite course work or for Ph.D. course work or dissertations. Selection is based on demonstrated commitment to education and equity for women and girls, reason for seeking higher education or technical training, degree to which study plan is consistent with career objectives, potential for success in chosen field, documentation of opportunities in chosen field, feasibility of study plans and proposed time schedule, validity of proposed budget and budget narrative (including sufficient outside support), and quality of written proposal.

Financial Data Grants range from $2,000 to $12,000. Funds may be used for tuition, fees, books, supplies, local transportation, dependent child care, or purchase of a computer required for the study program.

Duration 1 year, beginning in July; nonrenewable.

Additional data The filing fee is $35.

Number awarded Varies each year; recently, 63 of these grants, with a value of $670,000, were awarded.

Deadline December of each year.

[1056]
ACADEMY OF NUTRITION AND DIETETICS GRADUATE SCHOLARSHIPS

Academy of Nutrition and Dietetics
Attn: Foundation
120 South Riverside Plaza, Suite 2000
Chicago, IL 60606-6995
(312) 899-4821   Toll Free: (800) 877-1600, ext. 4821
Fax: (312) 899-4796   E-mail: scholarship@eatright.org
Web: www.eatrightacend.org

Summary To provide financial assistance to graduate student members of the Academy of Nutrition and Dietetics, especially Hispanics and members of other underrepresented groups.

Eligibility This program is open to members of the academy who are enrolled in the second year of a master's or doctoral degree program in dietetics. Applicants who are currently completing a dietetic internship or pre-professional practice program that is combined with a graduate program may also apply. The graduate scholarships are available only to U.S. citizens and permanent residents. Applicants should intend to practice in the field of dietetics. Some scholarships require specific areas of study (e.g., public health nutrition, food service administration) and status as a registered dietitian. Others may require membership in a specific dietetic practice group, residency in a specific state, or underrepresented minority group status. The same application form can be used for all categories.

Financial Data Stipends range from $500 to $10,000.

Duration 1 year.

Additional data The Academy of Nutrition and Dietetics was formerly the American Dietetic Association.

Number awarded Approximately 60 each year.

Deadline February of each year.

[1057]
AERA FELLOWSHIP PROGRAM ON THE STUDY OF DEEPER LEARNING

American Educational Research Association
Attn: Fellowships Program
1430 K Street, N.W., Suite 1200
Washington, DC 20005
(202) 238-3200   Fax: (202) 238-3250
E-mail: fellowships@aera.net
Web: www.aera.net

Summary To provide an opportunity for early-career scholars in the field of education, especially Hispanic and other underrepresented minorities, to conduct research using the Deeper Learning dataset.

Eligibility This program is open to scholars who received a Ph.D. or Ed.D. degree within the past 7 years in a field of education or related social or behavioral science field (e.g., economics, political science, psychology, psychometrics, sociology). Applicants must be proposing a program of research utilizing the Study of Deeper Learning (SDL) dataset collected by the American Institutes for Research (AIR). Selection is based on potential for the study to advance knowledge and understanding with the discipline and/or the education field; what is already known on the issue; appropriateness of the SDL dataset to address the research questions; qualifications of the applicant to carry out the proposed study; and alignment of the research procedures, methods, and approaches with the study objectives. Underrepresented racial and ethnic minority researchers and women and strongly encouraged to apply. U.S. citizenship or permanent resident status is required.

Financial Data Fellows receive a stipend of $20,000 plus full payment of expenses to attend a study overview and data training session in Washington, D.C. at the beginning of the fellowship and the fall research conference of the American Educational Research Association (AERA), also in Washington, D.C.

Duration 1 year.

Additional data This program is jointly administered by the AERA and the AIR with funding provided by the William and Flora Hewlett Foundation.

Number awarded Up to 8 each year.

Deadline June of each year.

[1058]
AIR FORCE SUMMER FACULTY FELLOWSHIP PROGRAM

Systems Plus, Inc.
Attn: AFSFF Program
One Research Court, Suite 360
Rockville, MD 20850
(301) 948-4232   Fax: (301) 948-3918
E-mail: afsffp.pmo@sysplus.com
Web: afsffp.sysplus.com

Summary To provide funding to science and engineering faculty and graduate students interested in conducting summer research at Air Force facilities, especially those teaching at Hispanic and other minority institutions.

Eligibility This program is open to U.S. citizens and permanent residents who have a full-time faculty appointment at a U.S. college or university in a field of engineering, mathematics, or science of interest to the Air Force. Applicants must be interested in conducting a research project, under the direction of an Air Force research adviser, at an Air Force Research Laboratory, Air Force Test Center, the U.S. Air Force Academy, or the Air Force Institute of Technology. A graduate student may accompany the faculty member. Faculty and students at Historically Black Colleges and Universities ((HBCUs), Minority Institutions (MIs), American Indian Tribal Colleges and Universities (TCUs), and Hispanic Serving Institutions (HSIs) are especially encouraged to apply.

Financial Data Stipends depend on academic rank or position. Relocation reimbursement and a weekly expense allowance of $350 (for fellows with a commute distance greater than 50 miles) are also available.

Duration 8 to 12 weeks during the summer. May be renewed for a second and third summer, but recipients may not reapply for 2 years after completing a third summer.

Additional data This program first operated in 2005. Research must be conducted in residence at an Air Force facility.

Number awarded Approximately 100 each year.

Deadline December of each year.

[1059]
ALONZO DAVIS FELLOWSHIP

Virginia Center for the Creative Arts
Attn: Admissions Committee
154 San Angelo Drive
Amherst, VA 24521
(434) 946-7236   Fax: (434) 946-7239
E-mail: vcca@vcca.com
Web: www.vcca.com

Summary To provide support to writers, visual artists, and composers who are of Latino or African descent and interested in a residency at the Virginia Center for the Creative Arts in Sweet Briar, Virginia.

Eligibility This program is open to writers, visual artists, and composers who are interested in a residency at the center so they can concentrate solely on their creative work. Applicants must be U.S citizens of Latino or African descent. They must submit samples of their work completed within the past 4 years.

Financial Data The fellowship provides payment of all residency costs, including a private bedroom, separate studio, and 3 prepared meals a day.

Duration Up to 1 month.

Additional data This fellowship was established in 2004. The application fee is $40.

Number awarded 1 each year.

Deadline January of each year for June to September residencies; May of each year for October to January residencies; September of each year for February to May residencies.

[1060]
ALZHEIMER'S ASSOCIATION CLINICAL FELLOWSHIPS TO PROMOTE DIVERSITY

Alzheimer's Association
Attn: Medical and Scientific Affairs
225 North Michigan Avenue, 17th Floor
Chicago, IL 60601-7633
(312) 335-5747   Toll Free: (800) 272-3900
Fax: (866) 699-1246   TDD: (312) 335-5886
E-mail: grantsapp@alz.org
Web: www.alz.org

Summary To provide funding for clinical research training on Alzheimer's Disease to Hispanic and other recent postdoctorates who will contribute to diversity in the field.

Eligibility This program is open to junior faculty members at recognized academic institutions who completed residency for an M.D. or D.O. or a postdoctoral fellowship (Ph.D.) or both within the past 5 years. Applicants must be proposing to conduct clinical research training in Alzheimer's and related dementias. Proposals are strongly encouraged from individuals training with a focus on dementia or cognitive disorders in behavioral neurology and neuropathy, geriatrics, geriatric psychiatry, or neuropsychology. Eligibility is restricted to investigators who will contribute to diversity in the field of biomedical research, including 1) members of underrepresented racial and ethnic minority groups (Hispanic Americans, African Americans, American Indians, Alaska Natives, Native Hawaiians, and Pacific Islanders); 2) individuals with disabilities; and 3) individuals from disadvantaged backgrounds. Selection is based on applicant's ability and promise as a clinician scientist (30%), quality and nature of the training to be provided and the institutional, departmental, and mentor-specific training environment (30%), and quality and originality of the research plan (40%).

Financial Data Grants up to $60,000 per year, including direct expenses and up to 10% for overhead costs, are available. The total award for the life of the grant may not exceed $175,000, including $155,000 for costs related to the proposed research, $10,000 to the fellow upon successful completion of the program, and $10,000 to the primary mentor upon successful completion of the program.

Duration 2 to 3 years.

Number awarded 1 or 2 each year.

Deadline Letters of intent must be submitted by the end of September of each year. Final applications are due in November.

[1061]
ALZHEIMER'S ASSOCIATION RESEARCH FELLOWSHIPS TO PROMOTE DIVERSITY

Alzheimer's Association
Attn: Medical and Scientific Affairs
225 North Michigan Avenue, 17th Floor
Chicago, IL 60601-7633
(312) 335-5747   Toll Free: (800) 272-3900
Fax: (866) 699-1246   TDD: (312) 335-5886
E-mail: grantsapp@alz.org
Web: www.alz.org

Summary To provide funding for research training on Alzheimer's Disease to Hispanic and other postdoctoral fellows who will contribute to diversity in the field.

Eligibility This program is open to postdoctoral fellows who have not received their first independent faculty position. Applicants must be proposing to conduct research related to Alzheimer's Disease. They must identify a mentor who is experienced in conducting Alzheimer's and related dementia research and in mentoring junior investigators. Eligibility is restricted to investigators who will contribute to diversity in the field of biomedical research, including 1) members of underrepresented racial and ethnic minority groups (Hispanic Americans, African Americans, American Indians, Alaska Natives, Native Hawaiians, and Pacific Islanders); 2) individuals with disabilities; and 3) individuals from disadvantaged backgrounds. Selection is based on quality and nature of the training to be provided and the institutional, departmental, and mentor-specific training environment (30%), quality and emphasis of the applicant and originality of the research plan (40%), and significance of the question being studied, quality of the work plan, and impact-risk of the proposal (30%).

Financial Data Grants up to $60,000 per year, including direct expenses and up to 10% for overhead costs, are available. The total award for the life of the grant may not exceed $175,000, including $155,000 for costs related to the proposed research, $10,000 to the fellow upon successful completion of the program, and $10,000 to the mentor upon successful completion of the program.

Duration Up to 3 years.

Number awarded 1 or 2 each year.

Deadline Letters of intent must be submitted by the end of September of each year. Final applications are due in November.

[1062]
ALZHEIMER'S ASSOCIATION RESEARCH GRANTS TO PROMOTE DIVERSITY

Alzheimer's Association
Attn: Medical and Scientific Affairs
225 North Michigan Avenue, 17th Floor
Chicago, IL 60601-7633
(312) 335-5747   Toll Free: (800) 272-3900
Fax: (866) 699-1246   TDD: (312) 335-5886
E-mail: grantsapp@alz.org
Web: www.alz.org

Summary To provide funding for preliminary research on Alzheimer's Disease to Hispanic and other junior investigators who will contribute to diversity in the field.

Eligibility This program is open to investigators who are less than 10 years past their doctoral or post-residency (M.D. or D.O.) or who are new to Alzheimer's and related dementia research. Applicants must be seeking funding that will allow them to develop preliminary or pilot data, to test procedures, and to develop hypotheses that will lay the groundwork for future grant applications to major governmental or private funding agencies. Eligibility is restricted to investigators who will contribute to diversity in the field of biomedical research, including 1) members of underrepresented racial and ethnic minority groups (Hispanic Americans, African Americans, American Indians, Alaska Natives, Native Hawaiians, and Pacific Islanders); 2) individuals with disabilities; and 3) individuals from disadvantaged backgrounds.

Financial Data Grants up to $60,000 per year, including direct expenses and up to 10% for overhead costs, are available. The total award for the life of the grant may not exceed $150,000.

Duration 2 or 3 years.

Number awarded 1 or 2 each year.

Deadline Letters of intent must be submitted by the end of September of each year. Final applications are due in November.

[1063]
AMERICAN GEOGRAPHICAL SOCIETY LIBRARY FELLOWSHIP FOR MSI SCHOLARS

University of Wisconsin at Milwaukee
Attn: Libraries
American Geographical Society Library
2311 East Hartford Avenue
P.O. Box 399,
Milwaukee, WI 53201-0399
(414) 229-6282   Toll Free: (800) 558-8993
Fax: (414) 229-3624   E-mail: agsl@uwm.edu
Web: www.uwm.edu/libraries/agsl/fellowshipdescriptions

Summary To provide funding to pre- and postdoctoral scholars at Minority Serving Institutions (MSIs) interested in conducting research at the American Geographical Society Library (AGSL) of the University of Wisconsin at Milwaukee (UWM) Libraries.

Eligibility This program is open to established scholars and doctoral students who are affiliated with an MSI. Doctoral students must have completed their course work and be writing their dissertations. Individuals with a record of publication relevant to this program and those with government or business ties who could use the library's resources to further policy studies are also eligible. Applicants' research must benefit from extensive use of the AGSL, including (but not limited to) area studies, history of cartography, history of geographic thought, discovery and exploration, historical geography, other geographic themes with a significant historical component, or any topic that has policy, business, or similar applications.

Financial Data The grant is $600 per week. Funds must be used to help pay travel and living expenses related to the residency.

Duration Up to 4 weeks.

Additional data Funding for this program is provided by a U.S. Department of Education National Resource Center grant.

Number awarded 1 or more each year.

Deadline November of each year.

[1064]
AMERICAN NURSES ASSOCIATION MINORITY FELLOWSHIP PROGRAM

American Nurses Association
Attn: SAMHSA Minority Fellowship Programs
8515 Georgia Avenue, Suite 400
Silver Spring, MD 20910-3492
(301) 628-5247   Toll Free: (800) 274-4ANA
Fax: (301) 628-5339   E-mail: janet.jackson@ana.org
Web: www.emfp.org

Summary To provide financial assistance to Hispanic and other minority nurses who are doctoral candidates interested

in psychiatric, mental health, and substance abuse issues that impact the lives of ethnic minority people.

Eligibility This program is open to nurses who have a master's degree and are members of an ethnic or racial minority group, including but not limited to Hispanics or Latinos, Blacks or African Americans, American Indians and Alaska Natives, Asians and Asian Americans, and Native Hawaiians and other Pacific Islanders. Applicants must be enrolled full time in an accredited doctoral nursing program. They must be certified as a Mental Health Nurse Practitioner, Mental Health Clinical Nurse Specialist, or Mental Health Nurse. U.S. citizenship or permanent resident status and membership in the American Nurses Association are required. Selection is based on commitment to a career in substance abuse in psychiatric/mental health issues affecting minority populations.

Financial Data The program provides an annual stipend of $22,476 and tuition assistance up to $5,000.

Duration 3 to 5 years.

Additional data Funds for this program are provided by the Substance Abuse and Mental Health Services Administration (SAMHSA).

Number awarded 1 or more each year.

Deadline March of each year.

[1065]
AMERICAN SOCIETY FOR CELL BIOLOGY MINORITIES AFFAIRS COMMITTEE VISITING PROFESSOR AWARDS

American Society for Cell Biology
Attn: Minority Affairs Committee
8120 Woodmont Avenue, Suite 750
Bethesda, MD 20814-2762
(301) 347-9323   Fax: (301) 347-9310
E-mail: dmccall@ascb.org
Web: ascb.org/mac-visiting-professorship-awards

Summary To provide funding for summer research to faculty members at primarily teaching institutions that serve Hispanic and other minority students and scientists.

Eligibility Eligible to apply for this support are professors at primarily teaching institutions. They must be interested in working in the laboratories of members of the American Society for Cell Biology during the summer. Hosts and visitor scientists are asked to submit their applications together as a proposed team. Minority professors and professors at Minority Serving Institutions are especially encouraged to apply for this award. Minorities are defined as U.S. citizens of Chicano/Hispanic, Black, Native American, or Pacific Islands background.

Financial Data The stipend for the summer is $13,500 plus $700 for travel expenses and $4,000 to the host institution for supplies.

Duration From 8 to 10 weeks during the summer.

Additional data Funds for this program, established in 1997, are provided by the Minorities Access to Research Careers (MARC) program of the National Institutes of Health.

Number awarded Varies each year; recently, 3 were awarded.

Deadline March of each year.

[1066]
ANAC STUDENT DIVERSITY MENTORSHIP SCHOLARSHIP

Association of Nurses in AIDS Care
Attn: Awards Committee
3538 Ridgewood Road
Akron, OH 44333-3122
(330) 670-0101   Toll Free: (800) 260-6780
Fax: (330) 670-0109   E-mail: anac@anacnet.org
Web: www.nursesinaidscare.org

Summary To provide financial assistance to student nurses from Hispanic and other minority groups who are interested in HIV/AIDS nursing and in attending the national conference of the Association of Nurses in AIDS Care (ANAC).

Eligibility This program is open to student nurses from a diverse racial or ethnic background, defined to include Hispanics/Latinos, African Americans, Asians/Pacific Islanders, and American Indians/Alaskan Natives. Candidates must have a genuine interest in HIV/AIDS nursing, be interested in attending the ANAC national conference, and desire to develop a mentorship relationship with a member of the ANAC Diversity Specialty Committee. They may be 1) pre-licensure students enrolled in an initial R.N. or L.P.N./L.V.N. program (i.e. L.P.N./L.V.N., A.D.N., diploma, B.S./B.S.N.); or 2) current licensed R.N. students with an associate or diploma degree who are enrolled in a bachelor's degree program. Nominees may be recommended by themselves, nursing faculty members, or ANAC members, but their nomination must be supported by an ANAC member. Along with their nomination form, they must submit a 2,000-character essay describing their interest or experience in HIV/AIDS care and why they want to attend the ANAC conference.

Financial Data Recipients are awarded a $1,000 scholarship (paid directly to the school), up to $599 in reimbursement of travel expenses to attend the ANAC annual conference, free conference registration, an award plaque, a free ticket to the awards ceremony at the conference, and a 2-year ANAC membership.

Duration 1 year.

Additional data The mentor will be assigned at the conference and will maintain contact during the period of study.

Number awarded 1 each year.

Deadline August of each year.

[1067]
ANDRÉS MONTOYA POETRY PRIZE

University of Notre Dame
Attn: Institute for Latino Studies
230 McKenna Hall
Notre Dame, IN 46556
(574) 631-4440   Toll Free: (866) 460-5586
Fax: (574) 631-3522
Web: latinostudies.nd.edu

Summary To recognize and reward Latino/a poets who submit examples of their work.

Eligibility This competition is open to Latino/a poets who have not had a book professionally published and are U.S. citizens or permanent residents. Applicants must submit manuscripts of 50 to 100 pages of poetry, in English, in any style or on any subject. Authors of chapbooks and self-published

works are eligible, but the manuscript submitted may not have been published as a whole in any form.

Financial Data The prize is $1,000 and publication by the University of Notre Dame Press.

Duration The prize is awarded biennially, in even-numbered years.

Additional data This prize was first awarded in 2004.

Number awarded 1 each even-numbered year.

Deadline January of each even-numbered year.

[1068]
ANDREW W. MELLON FELLOWSHIP IN LATINO STUDIES

School for Advanced Research
Attn: Director of Scholar Programs
660 Garcia Street
P.O. Box 2188
Santa Fe, NM 87504-2188
(505) 954-7201   E-mail: scholar@sarsf.org
Web: www.sarweb.org

Summary To provide funding to scholars interested in conducting research in Latino studies while in residence at the School for Advanced Research (SAR) in Santa Fe, New Mexico.

Eligibility This program is open to scholars at the assistant professor level who have a doctorate in the fields of anthropology, history, religious studies, sociology, Latino/Chicano studies, cultural studies, or an interdisciplinary field that combines 2 or more of those. Applicants must be planning to complete a book-length study. Along with their application, they must submit a 150-word abstract describing the purpose, goals, and objectives of their research project; a 4-page proposal; a bibliography; a curriculum vitae; and 3 letters of recommendation. Underrepresented scholars are especially encouraged to apply.

Financial Data The fellowship provides an apartment and office on the school's campus, a stipend of $50,000, library assistance, and other benefits.

Duration 9 months.

Additional data This program is sponsored by the Andrew W. Mellon Foundation. Recipients are expected to reside at the school, in Santa Fe, for the tenure of the fellowship.

Number awarded 1 each year.

Deadline October of each year.

[1069]
APA/SAMHSA MINORITY FELLOWSHIP PROGRAM

American Psychiatric Association
Attn: Division of Diversity and Health Equity
1000 Wilson Boulevard, Suite 1825
Arlington, VA 22209-3901
(703) 907-8653   Toll Free: (888) 35-PSYCH
Fax: (703) 907-7852   E-mail: mking@psych.org
Web: www.psychiatry.org/minority-fellowship

Summary To provide educational enrichment to psychiatrists-in-training who are interested in providing quality and effective services to minorities and the underserved.

Eligibility This program is open to residents who are in at least their second year of psychiatric training, members of the American Psychiatric Association (APA), and U.S. citizens or permanent residents. A goal of the program is to develop leadership to improve the quality of mental health care for members of ethnic minority groups (Hispanics/Latinos, American Indians, Native Alaskans, Asian Americans, Native Hawaiians, Native Pacific Islanders, and African Americans). Applicants must be interested in working with a component of the APA that is of interest to them and relevant to their career goals. Along with their application, they must submit a 2-page essay on how the fellowship would be utilized to alter their present training and ultimately assist them in achieving their career goals. Selection is based on commitment to serve ethnic minority populations, demonstrated leadership abilities, awareness of the importance of culture in mental health, and interest in the interrelationship between mental health/illness and transcultural factors.

Financial Data Fellows receive a monthly stipend (amount not specified) and reimbursement of transportation, lodging, meals, and incidentals in connection with attendance at program-related activities. They are expected to use the funds to enhance their own professional development, improve training in cultural competence at their training institution, improve awareness of culturally relevant issues in psychiatry at their institution, expand research in areas relevant to minorities and underserved populations, enhance the current treatment modalities for minority patients and underserved individuals at their institution, and improve awareness in the surrounding community about mental health issues (particularly with regard to minority populations).

Duration 1 year; may be renewed 1 additional year.

Additional data Funding for this program is provided by the Substance Abuse and Mental Health Services Administration (SAMHSA). As part of their assignment to an APA component, fellows must attend the fall component meetings in September and the APA annual meeting in May. At those meeting, they can share their experiences as residents and minorities and discuss issues that impact on minority populations. This program is an outgrowth of the fellowships that were established in 1974 under a grant from the National Institute of Mental Health in answer to concerns about the underrepresentation of minorities in psychiatry.

Number awarded Varies each year; recently, 21 were awarded.

Deadline January of each year.

[1070]
ARNULFO D. TREJO LIBRARIAN OF THE YEAR AWARD

REFORMA (National Association to Promote Library and
  Information Services to Latinos and the Spanish
  Speaking)
P.O. Box 832
Anaheim, CA 92815-0832
(209) 379-5637   E-mail: officemgr@reforma.org
Web: www.reforma.org

Summary To recognize and reward members of REFORMA, the National Association to Promote Library Services to the Spanish Speaking, who have made significant contributions to Latino librarianship.

Eligibility This award is available to members of the association who are early to mid-career librarians. Letters of nomination should describe 1) the degree to which the nominee's work filled any unmet library or other needs in the Latino and

Spanish-speaking community, including work in administration, instruction, technical services, or computer-oriented activities; and 2) the contributions the nominee has made to REFORMA. Nominations may be submitted by individual members or chapters of the association.

Financial Data The award is $1,000.

Duration The award is presented annually.

Additional data This program began in 1992.

Number awarded 1 each year.

Deadline April of each year.

[1071]
ARTTABLE MENTORED INTERNSHIPS FOR DIVERSITY IN THE VISUAL ARTS PROFESSIONS

ArtTable Inc.
1 East 53rd Street, Fifth Floor
New York, NY 10022
(212) 343-1735   Fax: (866) 363-4188
E-mail: info@arttable.org
Web: www.arttable.org/summermentoredinternship

Summary To provide an opportunity for women who are Hispanics or from other diverse backgrounds to gain mentored work experience during the summer and to prepare for a career as an art professional.

Eligibility This program is open to women who are college seniors, recent graduates, or graduate students and interested in preparing for a career as a visual arts professional (including administrative director, art adviser, art appraiser, art critic, art dealer, art librarian, arts funder, arts lawyer, conservator, curator, editor, educator, fundraiser, management consultant, public relations consultant, writer). Applicants must be from a cultural or ethnic background that is underrepresented in the field. They must be interested in working during the summer with a mentor at an art museum or similar facility. U.S. citizenship or permanent resident status is required.

Financial Data The stipend is $3,000. The hosting institution or mentor receives $500 for administrative and other costs.

Duration 8 weeks during the summer.

Additional data This program began in 2000. Support is provided by the Samuel H. Kress Foundation.

Number awarded Varies each year; recently, 5 of these internships were awarded.

Deadline February of each year.

[1072]
ASH-AMFDP AWARDS

American Society of Hematology
Attn: Awards Manager
2021 L Street, N.W., Suite 900
Washington, DC 20036
(202) 776-0544   Fax: (202) 776-0545
E-mail: awards@hematology.org
Web: www.hematology.org

Summary To provide an opportunity for Hispanic and other historically disadvantaged postdoctoral physicians to conduct a research project in hematology.

Eligibility This program is open to postdoctoral physicians who are members of historically disadvantaged groups, defined as individuals who face challenges because of their race, ethnicity, socioeconomic status, or other similar factors. Applicants must be committed to a career in academic medicine in hematology and to serving as a role model for students and faculty of similar backgrounds. They must identify a mentor at their institution to work with them and give them research and career guidance. Selection is based on excellence in educational career; willingness to devote 4 consecutive years to research; and commitment to an academic career, improving the health status of the underserved, and decreasing health disparities. U.S. citizenship or permanent resident status is required.

Financial Data The grant includes a stipend of up to $75,000 per year, a grant of $30,000 per year for support of research activities, complimentary membership in the American Society of Hematology (ASH), and travel support to attend the ASH annual meeting.

Duration 4 years.

Additional data This program, first offered in 2006, is a partnership between the ASH and the Robert Wood Johnson Foundation, whose Minority Medical Faculty Development Program (MMFDP) was renamed the Harold Amos Medical Faculty Development Program (AMFDP) in honor of the first African American to chair a department at the Harvard Medical School. Scholars must spend at least 70% of their time in research activities.

Number awarded At least 1 each year.

Deadline March of each year.

[1073]
ASTRONOMY AND ASTROPHYSICS POSTDOCTORAL FELLOWSHIPS

National Science Foundation
Directorate for Mathematical and Physical Sciences
Attn: Division of Astronomical Sciences
4201 Wilson Boulevard, Room 1080n
Arlington, VA 22230
(703) 292-5039   Fax: (703) 292-9034
TDD: (800) 281-8749   E-mail: hgupta@nsf.gov
Web: www.nsf.gov

Summary To provide funding to recent doctoral recipients in astronomy or astrophysics, especially Hispanics and other underrepresented minorities, who are interested in pursuing a program of research and education in the United States or at eligible foreign sites.

Eligibility This program is open to U.S. citizens, nationals, and permanent residents who completed a Ph.D. in astronomy or astrophysics during the previous 5 years. Applicants must be interested in a program of research of an observational, instrumental, or theoretical nature, especially research that is facilitated or enabled by new ground-based capability in radio, optical/IR, or solar astrophysics. Research may be conducted at a U.S. institution of higher education; a national center, facility, or institute funded by the National Science Foundation (NSF), such as the Kavli Institute for Theoretical Physics; a U.S. nonprofit organization with research and educational missions; and/or an international site operated by a U.S. organization eligible for NSF funding, such as Cerro Tololo InterAmerican Observatory. The proposal must include a coherent program of educational activities, such as teaching a course each year at the host institution or an academic institution with ties to the host institution, developing educational materials, or engaging in a significant program of out-

reach or general education. In the selection process, consideration is given to the achievement of societally relevant outcomes, including full participation of women, persons with disabilities, and underrepresented minorities.

Financial Data Grants up to $100,000 per year are available, including a stipend of $69,000 per year paid directly to the fellow and an allowance of $31,000 per year to cover expenses directly related to the research, facilities and other institutional resources, and fringe benefits.

Duration Up to 3 years.

Number awarded 8 to 9 each year.

Deadline October of each year.

[1074]
ATMOSPHERIC AND GEOSPACE SCIENCES POSTDOCTORAL RESEARCH FELLOWSHIPS

National Science Foundation
Directorate for Geosciences
Attn: Division of Atmospheric and Geospace Sciences
4201 Wilson Boulevard, Room 775S
Arlington, VA 22230
(703) 292-8520   Fax: (703) 292-9022
TDD: (800) 281-8749   E-mail: amadams@nsf.gov
Web: www.nsf.gov

Summary To provide funding to postdoctoral scientists, especially Hispanics and other underrepresented minorities, who are interested in conducting research in the United States or any other country related to activities of the National Science Foundation (NSF) Division of Atmospheric and Geospace Sciences.

Eligibility This program is open to U.S. citizens, nationals, and permanent residents who received a Ph.D. within the past 3 years. Applicants must be interested in conducting a research project that is relevant to the activities of NSF Division of Atmospheric and Geospace Sciences: studies of the physics, chemistry, and dynamics of Earth's upper and lower atmosphere and its space environment; research on climate processes and variations; or studies to understand the natural global cycles of gases and particles in Earth's atmosphere. The project should be conducted at an institution (college or university, private nonprofit institute or museum, government installation, or laboratory) in the United States or abroad other than the applicant's Ph.D.-granting institution. In the selection process, consideration is given to the achievement of societally relevant outcomes, including full participation of women, persons with disabilities, and underrepresented minorities.

Financial Data Grants are $86,000 per year, including a stipend of $58,000 per year, a research allowance of $19,000 per year, and a fringe benefit allowance of $9,000 per year. For fellows who wish to conduct research abroad, an additional supplement of $10,000 is provided.

Duration 2 years.

Number awarded 10 each year.

Deadline January of each year.

[1075]
ATMOSPHERIC SCIENCES ASCENT AWARD

American Geophysical Union
Attn: Atmospheric Sciences Section
2000 Florida Avenue, N.W.
Washington, DC 20009-1277
(202) 462-6900   Toll Free: (800) 966-2481
Fax: (202) 328-0566   E-mail: leadership@agu.org
Web: atmospheres.agu.org/awards/ascent-award

Summary To recognize and reward mid-career members of the American Geophysical Union (AGU), especially Hispanics and other minorities, who have conducted outstanding research in atmospheric sciences.

Eligibility This award is available to AGU members who completed their Ph.D. between 8 and 20 years previously and are employed in academic, government, or the private sector. Nominees must demonstrate excellence in research and leadership in the field of atmospheric sciences. Nominations of women and underrepresented minorities are encouraged.

Financial Data The award consists of $1,000, a certificate, and dinner during the annual meeting of the Atmospheric Sciences Section of the AGU.

Duration The award is presented annually.

Additional data These awards were first presented in 2012.

Number awarded Up to 4 each year.

Deadline April of each year.

[1076]
AWARDS FOR FACULTY AT HISPANIC SERVING INSTITUTIONS

National Endowment for the Humanities
Attn: Division of Research Programs
400 Seventh Street, S.W.
Washington, DC 20506
(202) 606-8200   Toll Free: (800) NEH-1121
Fax: (202) 606-8204   TDD: (866) 372-2930
E-mail: FacultyAwards@neh.gov
Web: www.neh.gov

Summary To provide funding for research to faculty at colleges and universities designated as Hispanic Serving Institutions (HSIs).

Eligibility This program is open to faculty members at HSIs who are interested in conducting research of value to humanities scholars, students, or general audiences. Eligible projects include conducting research in primary and secondary sources; producing articles, monographs, books, digital materials, archaeological site reports, translations, editions, or other scholarly resources; or conducting basic research leading to the improvement of an existing undergraduate course or the achievement or institutional or community research goals. Applicants must be U.S. citizens or foreign nationals who have lived in the United States for at least 3 years. They are not required to have advanced degrees, but individuals enrolled in a degree-granting program are ineligible.

Financial Data The grant is $4,200 per month, to a maximum of $50,400 for 12 months.

Duration 2 to 12 months.

Number awarded Approximately 3 each year.

Deadline April of each year.

[1077]
BERNARD MAJEWSKI FELLOWSHIP

University of Wyoming
Attn: American Heritage Center
1000 East University Avenue
P.O. Box 3924
Laramie, WY 82071-3924
(307) 766-4114   Fax: (307) 766-5511
E-mail: ahc@uwyo.edu
Web: www.uwyo.edu/ahc/grants/majewski.html

Summary To provide funding to scholars, including Hispanics and other underrepresented minorities, who are interested in using the resources at the University of Wyoming's American Heritage Center to conduct research in economic geology.

Eligibility This program is open to scholars who are interested in conducting research at the center in the history of economic geology. For purposes of the fellowship, economic geology is defined as the activities of exploration and development of petroleum and base, precious, and industrial minerals, including basic geological research. Acceptable related fields include history; oral history; historical archaeology pertaining to economic geology, environmental, and natural resources history; and business or economic history related to economic geology. Applicants must be recognized scholars in 1 of those fields of research. They should have a record of publication in the field or show significant potential for publication. Young scholars, minorities, and multi-disciplinary researchers are encouraged to apply.

Financial Data The grant is $2,500.

Duration 1 calendar year.

Number awarded 1 each year.

Deadline February of each year.

[1078]
BRANDON FRADD FELLOWSHIP IN MUSIC COMPOSITION

Cintas Foundation, Inc.
c/o Laurie Escobar, Cintas Administrator
MDC Museum of Art + Design
Freedom Tower at Miami Dade College
600 Biscayne Boulevard
Miami, FL 33132
(305) 237-7901   E-mail: lescobar@mdc.edu
Web: www.cintasfoundation.org

Summary To provide funding for creative activities in composing to Cubans who are living outside of Cuba.

Eligibility This program is open to composers of Cuban citizenship or lineage (having a Cuban parent or grandparent) but living in the United States or any other country except Cuba. Applicants must be interested in completing a project in the field of musical composition. Submissions should include from 3 to 5 recordings, of which 2 should be of recent works. Scores must accompany the recordings. Applicants must also include 2 narrative statements in English or Spanish: 1) a record of their personal history, their development as an artist, and their plans for the future; and 2) a description of the project or activity that they would undertake if awarded a fellowship. Fellowships are not awarded for academic study, research, or writing; performing artists are not eligible.

Financial Data Grants are $10,000.

Duration 1 year.

Additional data This program began in 1963.

Number awarded 1 or more each year. Since this program began, it has awarded more than 24 fellowships.

Deadline June of each year.

[1079]
BRONSON T.J. TREMBLAY MEMORIAL SCHOLARSHIP

Colorado Nurses Foundation
Attn: Scholarships
P.O. Box 3406
Englewood, CO 80155
(303) 694-4728   Toll Free: (800) 205-6655
Fax: (303) 200-7099   E-mail: mail@cnfound.org
Web: www.coloradonursesfoundation.com/?page_id=1087

Summary To provide financial assistance to Hispanic and other non-white male undergraduate and graduate nursing students in Colorado.

Eligibility This program is open to non-white male Colorado residents who have been accepted as a student in an approved nursing program in the state. Applicants may be 1) second-year students in an associate degree program; 2) junior or senior level B.S.N. undergraduate students; 3) R.N.s enrolled in a baccalaureate or higher degree program in a school of nursing; 4) R.N.s with a master's degree in nursing, currently practicing in Colorado and enrolled in a doctoral program; or 5) students in the second or third year of a Doctorate Nursing Practice (D.N.P.) or Ph.D. program. Undergraduates must have a GPA of 3.25 or higher and graduate students must have a GPA of 3.5 or higher. Selection is based on professional philosophy and goals, dedication to the improvement of patient care in Colorado, demonstrated commitment to nursing, potential for leadership, involvement in community and professional organizations, recommendations, GPA, and financial need.

Financial Data The stipend is $1,000.

Duration 1 year.

Number awarded 1 each year.

Deadline October of each year.

[1080]
BYRD FELLOWSHIP PROGRAM

Ohio State University
Byrd Polar and Climate Research Center
Attn: Fellowship Committee
Scott Hall Room 108
1090 Carmack Road
Columbus, OH 43210-1002
(614) 292-6531   Fax: (614) 292-4697
E-mail: contact@bpcrc.osu.edu
Web: bpcrc.osu.edu/byrdfellow

Summary To provide funding to postdoctorates, especially Hispanics and other underrepresented minorities, who are interested in conducting research on the Arctic or Antarctic areas at Ohio State University.

Eligibility This program is open to postdoctorates of superior academic background who are interested in conducting advanced research on either Arctic or Antarctic problems at the Byrd Polar and Climate Research Center at Ohio State University. Applicants must have received their doctorates within the past 5 years. Along with their application, they must submit a description of the specific research to be conducted during the fellowship and a curriculum vitae. Women, minorities, Vietnam-era veterans, disabled veterans, and individuals with disabilities are particularly encouraged to apply.

Financial Data The stipend is $44,000 per year; an allowance of $5,000 for research and travel is also provided.

Duration 18 months.

Additional data This program was established by a major gift from the Byrd Foundation in memory of Rear Admiral Richard Evelyn Byrd and Marie Ames Byrd, his wife. Except for field work or other research activities requiring absence from campus, fellows are expected to be in residence at the university for the duration of the program.

Number awarded 1 each year.

Deadline March of each year.

[1081]
CAMINOS THESIS COMPETITION IN FOOD AND AGRICULTURAL SCIENCE

American Association of Hispanics in Higher Education
Attn: Thesis Competition Chair
1120 South Cady Mall, First Floor, Suite B-159
Tempe, AZ 85287-6303
E-mail: tc03@txstate.edu
Web: www.aahhe.org

Summary To recognize and reward Hispanic authors of outstanding master's theses on topics related to priority areas of the United States Department of Agriculture (USDA).

Eligibility This competition is open to Hispanic U.S. citizens and permanent residents who have completed a thesis during the preceding 2 years. The topic of the thesis must be related to a food and agricultural science topic in a USDA priority area, including food safety, climate change, sustainable energy, childhood obesity, or global food security and hunger. Theses may use any research approach (e.g., historical, experimental, qualitative, survey). Applicants must submit a 150-word summary of their thesis. Judging is based on the appropriateness of the research design, approach, and data analysis; the conceptualization of inquiry and focus; the discussion of findings focused on comprehension and integration; the scholarly quality of the thesis; and significance of contribution to knowledge in the field. Based on the abstracts, 5 semifinalists are selected and asked to submit their complete thesis. From among those, 3 finalists are invited to present their theses at the national conference of the American Association of Hispanics in Higher Education (AAHHE), where winners are selected.

Financial Data Awards are $1,500 for first place, $1,000 for second, and $500 for third. All travel expenses of finalists to attend the AAHHE national conference are paid.

Duration The awards are presented annually.

Additional data This program is managed by the AAHHE in partnership with Texas A&M University at Corpus Christi. Funding is provided by the USDA National Institute of Food and Agriculture.

Number awarded 3 cash awards are presented each year.

Deadline September of each year.

[1082]
CARLOS M. CASTANEDA JOURNALISM SCHOLARSHIP

Carlos M. Castañeda Educational Foundation
Attn: FECMC Journalism Scholarship
1925 Brickell Avenue, Suite D-1108
Miami, FL 33129
(305) 283-4963   E-mail: fecmc@me.com
Web: fecmc.tripod.com

Summary To provide financial assistance to Spanish-speaking graduate students and journalists working on a master's degree in journalism.

Eligibility This program is open to Spanish-speaking students and journalists from any country (including the United States) who have been accepted into a graduate program in journalism at a university in the United States. Applicants must have completed a 4-year undergraduate degree with a GPA of 3.0 or higher. They are not required to have majored in journalism as an undergraduate, but their curriculum must have included courses in history and liberal arts. A knowledge of and interest in Hispanic culture and an awareness of current events in Latin America are also required. Along with their application, they must submit a curriculum vitae, a cover letter, 3 reference letters, a portfolio with 3 stories published by professional or school publications in Spanish, and a 2,000-word essay (in Spanish) on the work of Carlos M. Castañeda as a champion of freedom of the press and human rights. Financial need is considered in the selection process.

Financial Data The stipend is $7,000.

Duration 1 year; may be renewed 1 additional year if the recipient maintains a GPA of 3.0 or higher.

Additional data This program began in 2005.

Number awarded 1 or more each year.

Deadline April of each year.

[1083]
CARRINGTON-HSIA-NIEVES SCHOLARSHIP FOR MIDWIVES OF COLOR

American College of Nurse-Midwives
Attn: ACNM Foundation, Inc.
8403 Colesville Road, Suite 1550
Silver Spring, MD 20910-6374
(240) 485-1850   Fax: (240) 485-1818
E-mail: foundation@acnmf.org
Web: www.midwife.org

Summary To provide financial assistance to Hispanic and other midwives of color who are members of the American College of Nurse-Midwives (ACNM) and engaged in doctoral or postdoctoral study.

Eligibility This program is open to ACNM members of color who are certified nurse midwives (CNM) or certified midwives (CM). Applicants must be enrolled in a program of doctoral or postdoctoral education. Along with their application, they must submit brief statements on their 5-year academic career plans, their intended use of the funds, and their intended future participation in the local, regional, and/or national activities of the ACNM and in activities that otherwise contribute substantially to midwifery research, education, or practice.

Financial Data The stipend is $5,000.

Duration 1 year.

Number awarded 1 each year.

Deadline October of each year.

[1084]
CENTER FOR ADVANCED STUDY IN THE BEHAVIORAL SCIENCES FELLOWSHIPS

Center for Advanced Study in the Behavioral Sciences
Attn: Secretary and Program Coordinator
75 Alta Road
Stanford, CA 94305-8090
(650) 736-0100   Fax: (650) 736-0221
E-mail: casbs-info@casbs.org
Web: casbs.stanford.edu/fellowships

Summary To provide funding to behavioral scientists, especially Hispanics and members of other underrepresented groups, who are interested in conducting research at Stanford University's Center for Advanced Study in the Behavioral Sciences.

Eligibility Eligible to be nominated for this fellowship are scientists and scholars from this country or abroad who show exceptional accomplishment or promise in the core social and behavioral disciplines: anthropology, economics, history, political science, psychology, or sociology; applications are also accepted from scholars in a wide range of humanistic disciplines, communications, education, linguistics, and the biological, computer, health, and natural sciences. Selection is based on standing in the field rather than on the merit of a particular project under way at a given time. A special effort is made to promote diversity among the scholars by encouraging participation from groups that often have been overlooked in academia: women, minorities, international scholars, and scholars from a wide variety of colleges and universities.

Financial Data The stipend is based on the fellow's regular salary for the preceding year, with a cap of $73,000. In most cases, the fellow contributes to the cost of the stipend with support from sabbatical or other funding source.

Duration From 9 to 11 months.

Additional data This program partners with the Berggruen Institute to select fellows whose work focuses on understanding technological, social, and cultural changes that may radically transform humanity; the American Council of Learned Societies to participate in the Frederick Burkhardt Residential Fellowship Program; the William T. Grant Foundation to select scholars whose work emphasizes reducing inequality; the Mindset Scholars Network which hosts a fellow who is interested in interdisciplinary scholarship on mindsets and serving in a leadership role in the Mindset research community; the Presence-CASBS Fellowship that addresses focus areas of harnessing technology for the human experience in medicine, studying and advocating for the patient-physician relationship, and reducing medical errors; the Stanford Cyber Initiative which selects a fellow who will be engaged in producing policy-relevant research on the integration of cyber technologies in our ways of life and informing debate about urgent cyber issues; and the National Applied Research Laboratories of Taiwan which selects a fellow in the behavioral and social sciences from Taiwan. Fellows must be in residence in a community within 10 miles of the center for the duration of the program (that requirement excludes San Francisco, Berkeley, and San Jose, for example).

Number awarded Approximately 45 each year.

Deadline November of each year.

[1085]
CESAR CHAVEZ POSTDOCTORAL FELLOWSHIP

Dartmouth College
Attn: Program in Latin American, Latino, and Caribbean
   Studies
Raven 202
HB 6026
Hanover, NH 03755
(603) 646-3530
Web: lalacs.dartmouth.edu

Summary To provide funding to postdoctoral scholars who are interested in conducting research related to Latino studies at Dartmouth College.

Eligibility This program is open to postdoctoral scholars whose research addresses aspects of Latino/a experience and culture. Preference is given to applicants who work in comparative literature; English; Latin American, Latino, and Caribbean studies; Spanish; women's, gender, or sexuality studies; or an interdisciplinary field that incorporates 1 or more of those disciplines.

Financial Data The stipend is $55,200 per year. In addition, fellows receive health benefits and a grant of $4,000 to support computing, travel, and other research needs.

Duration 2 years, beginning in September.

Number awarded 1 each year.

Deadline January of each year.

[1086]
CHEST DIVERSITY COMMITTEE MINORITY INVESTIGATOR RESEARCH GRANT

American College of Chest Physicians
Attn: The CHEST Foundation
2595 Patriot Boulevard
Glenview, IL 60026
(224) 521-9527   Toll Free: (800) 343-2227
Fax: (224) 521-9801   E-mail: grants@chestnet.org
Web: www.chestnet.org

Summary To provide funding to Hispanic and other minority physicians who are interested in conducting clinical or translational research on topics of interest to the American College of Chest Physicians (ACCP).

Eligibility This program is open to members of the ACCP who are members of an underrepresented group (Hispanic American, African American, Latin American, Asian/Pacific Island American, Native American, women). Applicants must be interested in conducting a clinical or translational research project that contributes to the understanding of the pathophysiology or treatment of conditions or diseases related to pulmonary, cardiovascular, critical care, or sleep medicine. They may be at later career stages, but special consideration is given to those within 5 years of completing an advanced training program.

Financial Data The grant is $25,000.

Duration 1 year, beginning in July.

Additional data This program is supported in part by AstraZeneca.

Number awarded 1 each year.

Deadline April of each year.

[1087]
CHICANO STUDIES VISITING SCHOLAR AND VISITING RESEARCHER PROGRAM

University of California at Los Angeles
Institute of American Cultures
Attn: Chicano Studies Research Center
193 Haines Hall
P.O. Box 951544
Los Angeles, CA 90095-1544
(310) 825-2363   Fax: (310) 206-1784
E-mail: repstein@chicano.ucla.edu
Web: www.iac.ucla.edu/fellowships_visitingscholar.html

Summary To provide funding to scholars interested in conducting research in Chicano studies at UCLA's Chicano Studies Research Center.

Eligibility Applicants must have completed a doctoral degree in Chicano or related studies. They must be interested in teaching or conducting research at UCLA's Chicano Studies Research Center. Visiting Scholar appointments are available to people who currently hold permanent academic appointments; Visiting Researcher appointments are available to postdoctorates who recently received their degree. UCLA faculty, students, and staff are not eligible. U.S. citizenship or permanent resident status is required.

Financial Data Fellows receive a stipend of $35,000, health benefits, and up to $4,000 in research support. Visiting Scholars are paid through their home institution; Visiting Researchers receive their funds directly from UCLA.

Duration 9 months, beginning in October.

Additional data Fellows must teach or do research in the programs of the center. The award is offered in conjunction with UCLA's Institute of American Cultures (IAC).

Number awarded 1 each year.

Deadline January of each year.

[1088]
CHIPS QUINN SCHOLARS PROGRAM

Newseum Institute
Attn: Chips Quinn Scholars Program
555 Pennsylvania Avenue, N.W.
Washington, DC 20001
(202) 292-6271   Fax: (202) 292-6275
E-mail: kcatone@freedomforum.org
Web: www.newseuminstitute.org

Summary To provide work experience to Hispanic and other minority college students and recent graduates who are majoring in journalism.

Eligibility This program is open to students of color who are college juniors, seniors, graduate students, or recent graduates with journalism majors or career goals in newspapers. Candidates must be nominated or endorsed by journalism faculty, campus media advisers, editors of newspapers, or leaders of minority journalism associations. Along with their application, they must submit a resume, transcripts, 2 letters of recommendation, and an essay of 200 to 400 words on why they want to be a Chips Quinn Scholar. Reporters and copy editors must also submit 6 samples of published articles they have written; photographers must submit 15 to 25 photographs on a DVD; multimedia journalists and graphic designers should submit 6 to 10 samples of their work on a DVD. Applicants must have a car and be available to work as a full-time intern during the spring or summer. U.S. citizenship or permanent resident status is required. Campus newspaper experience is strongly encouraged.

Financial Data   Students chosen for this program receive a travel stipend to attend a Multimedia training program in Nashville, Tennessee prior to reporting for their internship, a $500 housing allowance from the Freedom Forum, and a competitive salary during their internship.

Duration   Internships are for 10 to 12 weeks, in spring or summer.

Additional data   This program began in 1991 in memory of the late John D. Quinn Jr., managing editor of the *Poughkeepsie Journal*. Funding is provided by the Freedom Forum, formerly the Gannett Foundation. After graduating from college and obtaining employment with a newspaper, alumni of this program are eligible to apply for fellowship support to attend professional journalism development activities.

Number awarded   Approximately 70 each year. Since the program began, more than 1,300 scholars have been selected.

Deadline   September of each year.

[1089]
CINTAS FOUNDATION FELLOWSHIP IN ARCHITECTURE

Cintas Foundation, Inc.
c/o Laurie Escobar, Cintas Administrator
MDC Museum of Art + Design
Freedom Tower at Miami Dade College
600 Biscayne Boulevard
Miami, FL 33132
(305) 237-7901   E-mail: lescobar@mdc.edu
Web: www.cintasfoundation.org

Summary   To provide funding for creative activities in architecture to Cubans who are living outside of Cuba.

Eligibility   This program is open to architects of Cuban citizenship or lineage (having a Cuban parent or grandparent) but living in the United States or any other country except Cuba. Applicants must be interested in completing a project in the field of architectural design. They must include 2 narrative statements in English or Spanish: 1) a record of their personal history, their development as an artist, and their plans for the future; and 2) a description of the project or activity that they would undertake if awarded a fellowship. Fellowships are not awarded for academic study, research, or writing.

Financial Data   Grants are $10,000.

Duration   1 year.

Additional data   This program began in 1963.

Number awarded   Up to 1 each odd-numbered year. Since this program began, it has awarded more than 21 fellowships.

Deadline   June of odd-numbered years.

[1090]
CINTAS FOUNDATION FELLOWSHIP IN CREATIVE WRITING

Cintas Foundation, Inc.
c/o Laurie Escobar, Cintas Administrator
MDC Museum of Art + Design
Freedom Tower at Miami Dade College
600 Biscayne Boulevard
Miami, FL 33132
(305) 237-7901   E-mail: lescobar@mdc.edu
Web: www.cintasfoundation.org

Summary   To provide funding for creative activities in writing to Cubans who are living outside of Cuba.

Eligibility   This program is open to writers of Cuban citizenship or lineage (having a Cuban parent or grandparent) but living in the United States or any other country except Cuba. Applicants must be interested in completing a project in the field of creative writing. Submissions must be original manuscripts up to 25 pages in length. They must include 2 narrative statements in English or Spanish: 1) a record of their personal history, their development as an artist, and their plans for the future; and 2) a description of the project or activity that they would undertake if awarded a fellowship. Fellowships are not awarded for academic study, research, or writing.

Financial Data   Grants are $10,000.

Duration   1 year.

Additional data   This program began in 1963.

Number awarded   1 or more each odd-numbered year. Since this program began, it has awarded more than 81 fellowships.

Deadline   June of odd-numbered years.

[1091]
CINTAS-KNIGHT FELLOWSHIP IN VISUAL ARTS

Cintas Foundation, Inc.
c/o Laurie Escobar, Cintas Administrator
MDC Museum of Art + Design
Freedom Tower at Miami Dade College
600 Biscayne Boulevard
Miami, FL 33132
(305) 237-7901   E-mail: lescobar@mdc.edu
Web: www.cintasfoundation.org

Summary   To provide funding for creative activities in visual arts to Cubans who are living outside of Cuba.

Eligibility   This program is open to artists of Cuban citizenship or lineage (having a Cuban parent or grandparent) but living in the United States or any other country except Cuba. Applicants must be interested in completing a project in the field of visual arts, including painting, sculpture, installation art, photography, video, and the media arts. Submissions may consist of up to 10 digital images. They must include 2 narrative statements in English or Spanish: 1) a record of their personal history, their development as an artist, and their plans for the future; and 2) a description of the project or activity that they would undertake if awarded a fellowship. Fellowships are not awarded for academic study, research, or writing.

Financial Data   Grants are $10,000.

Duration   1 year.

Additional data   This program began in 1963.

Number awarded Varies each year. Since this program began, it has awarded more than 185 fellowships.

Deadline June of each year.

[1092]
CIVIL SOCIETY INSTITUTE FELLOWSHIPS

Vermont Studio Center
80 Pearl Street
P.O. Box 613
Johnson, VT 05656
(802) 635-2727 Fax: (802) 635-2730
E-mail: info@vermontstudiocenter.org
Web: www.vermontstudiocenter.org/fellowships

Summary To provide funding to Hispanic and other minority artists from the East Coast who are interested in a residency at the Vermont Studio Center in Johnson, Vermont.

Eligibility Eligible to apply for this support are painters, sculptors, printmakers, new and mixed-media artists, and photographers who are members of a minority group and residents of the East Coast. Preference is given to applicants from New Haven (Connecticut), Jersey City (New Jersey), or Baltimore (Maryland). Applicants must be interested in a residency at the center in Johnson, Vermont. Visual artists must submit up to 20 slides or visual images of their work, poets must submit up to 10 pages, and other writers must submit 10 to 15 pages. Selection is based on artistic merit and financial need.

Financial Data The residency fee of $3,950 covers studio space, room, board, lectures, and studio visits. The fellowship pays all residency fees plus a $500 travel stipend.

Duration 4 weeks.

Additional data This program is sponsored by the Institute for Civil Society.

Number awarded 3 each year (1 for each term).

Deadline February, June, or September of each year.

[1093]
COLGATE-PALMOLIVE DENTAL RESIDENCY OR SPECIALTY PROGRAM SCHOLARSHIPS

Hispanic Dental Association
Attn: HDA Foundation
3910 South IH-35, Suite 245
Austin, TX 78704
(512) 904-0252 E-mail: jessicac@hdassoc.org
Web: www.hdassoc.org

Summary To provide financial assistance to members of the Hispanic Dental Association (HDA) interested in enrolling in a dental residency or a dental specialty program.

Eligibility This program is open to HDA members who are accepted or enrolled full time in a dental program in the United States or Puerto Rico. Applicants must be seeking support for training in an accredited dental residency or dental specialty program, including dental public health, oral surgery, orthodontics, endodontics, pediatric dentistry, prosthodontics, periodontics, pathology, or radiology. They must have a GPA of 3.0 or higher, an interest in improving the health of the Hispanic community, and a demonstrated commitment and dedication to serving the Hispanic community. Along with their application, they must submit a 250-word essay on their career goals, including how they were inspired to become a dentist. Selection is based on academic

achievement, leadership skills, community service, and commitment and dedication to improving the oral health of the Hispanic community.

Financial Data The stipend is $4,000. An additional grant of $500 is provided for travel reimbursement and complimentary registration to the HDA annual meeting.

Duration 1 year.

Additional data This program, which began in 2005, is sponsored by the Colgate-Palmolive Company.

Number awarded Varies each year; recently, 4 were awarded.

Deadline May of each year.

[1094]
CONGRESSIONAL HISPANIC CAUCUS INSTITUTE GRADUATE FELLOWSHIPS

Congressional Hispanic Caucus Institute, Inc.
911 Second Street, N.E.
Washington, DC 20002
(202) 543-1771 Toll Free: (800) EXCEL-DC
Fax: (202) 546-2143 E-mail: chci@chci.org
Web: www.chci.org

Summary To provide Latinos who recently completed a graduate degree in specified fields with the opportunity to apply their academic expertise during a work experience program in Washington, D.C.

Eligibility This program is open to U.S. citizens, asylees, valid visa holders, and permanent residents who are of Hispanic descent who completed a master's degree or higher within the past 3 years. Applicants must be interested in gaining experience in the following areas: higher education, secondary education, health, housing, law, or STEM (science, technology, engineering, and mathematics). They must be able to demonstrate high academic achievement (GPA of 3.0 or higher), evidence of leadership skills, potential for leadership growth, commitment to public service-oriented activities, and superior analytical and communication skills (oral and written). Students registered in the DACA program must possess an Employment Authorization Document.

Financial Data This program provides transportation to and from Washington, D.C., a monthly stipend of $2,900, and health insurance.

Duration 8 months, beginning in late August.

Additional data Placements are available in Congressional offices or committees and federal agencies. Fellows select the placement that best matches their interests.

Number awarded Varies each year; recently, 9 were awarded.

Deadline February of each year.

[1095]
CONGRESSIONAL HISPANIC CAUCUS INSTITUTE PUBLIC POLICY FELLOWSHIP

Congressional Hispanic Caucus Institute, Inc.
911 Second Street, N.E.
Washington, DC 20002
(202) 543-1771 Toll Free: (800) EXCEL-DC
Fax: (202) 546-2143 E-mail: chci@chci.org
Web: www.chci.org

Summary To provide Latino recent college graduates with the opportunity to apply their academic expertise in the area of public policy during a work experience program in Washington, D.C.

Eligibility This program is open to U.S. citizens, asylees, valid visa holders, and permanent residents who earned a bachelor's degree within the past 2 years and have not received credit towards an advanced degree. Applicants must be interested in gaining experience in the area of public policy. They must be able to demonstrate high academic achievement (preference is given to those with a GPA of 3.0 or higher), evidence of leadership skills, potential for leadership growth, and superior analytical and communication skills (oral and written). Students registered in the DACA program must possess an Employment Authorization Document.

Financial Data This program provides transportation to and from Washington, D.C., a monthly stipend of $2,400, and health insurance.

Duration 9 months, beginning in late August.

Additional data Placements are available in Congressional offices and federal agencies, advocacy groups, media groups, and a broad range of policy-related organizations. Fellows select the placement that best matches their interests.

Number awarded Varies each year; recently, 10 were awarded.

Deadline February of each year.

[1096]
DEEP CARBON OBSERVATORY DIVERSITY GRANTS

American Geosciences Institute
Attn: Grant Coordinator
4220 King Street
Alexandria, VA 22302-1502
(703) 379-2480　　　　　　Fax: (703) 379-7563
E-mail: hrhp@agiweb.org
Web: www.americangeosciences.org

Summary To provide funding to geoscientists who are Hispanics or members of other underrepresented ethnic groups and interested in participating in research and other activities of the Deep Carbon Observatory (DCO) project.

Eligibility This program is open to traditionally underrepresented geoscientists (e.g., African Americans, Native Americans, Native Alaskans, Hispanics, Latinos, Latinas, Native Hawaiians, Native Pacific Islanders, Filipinos, of mixed racial/ethnic backgrounds) who are U.S. citizens or permanent residents. Applicants must be interested in participating in the DCO, a global research program focused on understanding carbon in Earth, and must have research interests that are aligned with its mission. They may be doctoral students, postdoctoral researchers, or early-career faculty members or research staff.

Financial Data Grants average $5,000.

Duration 1 year.

Additional data This program is funded by the Alfred P. Sloan Foundation.

Number awarded 4 or 5 each year.

Deadline April of each year.

[1097]
DIETETIC INTERNSHIP SCHOLARSHIPS

Academy of Nutrition and Dietetics
Attn: Foundation
120 South Riverside Plaza, Suite 2000
Chicago, IL 60606-6995
(312) 899-4821　　　　Toll Free: (800) 877-1600, ext. 4821
Fax: (312) 899-4796　　　E-mail: scholarship@eatright.org
Web: www.eatrightacend.org

Summary To provide financial assistance to student members of the Academy of Nutrition and Dietetics who have applied for a dietetic internship, especially Hispanics and other underrepresented minorities.

Eligibility This program is open to student members who have applied for an accredited dietetic internship. Applicants must be participating in the computer-matching process, be U.S. citizens or permanent residents, and show promise of being a valuable, contributing member of the profession. Some scholarships require membership in a specific dietetic practice group, residency in a specific state, or underrepresented minority group status. The same application form can be used for all categories. Students who are currently completing the internship component of a combined graduate/dietetic internship should apply for the Academy of Nutrition and Dietetics' Graduate Scholarship.

Financial Data Stipends range from $500 to $10,000 but most are for $1,000.

Duration 1 year.

Additional data The Academy of Nutrition and Dietetics was formerly the American Dietetic Association.

Number awarded Approximately 40 each year.

Deadline February of each year.

[1098]
DISSERTATION AWARD IN LATIN AMERICAN POLITICS

Harvard University
David Rockefeller Center for Latin American Studies
Attn: Thesis Prize Committee
CGIS South Building
1730 Cambridge Street
Cambridge, MA 02138
(617) 495-3366　　　　　　Fax: (617) 496-2802
E-mail: ned_strong@fas.harvard.edu
Web: www.drclas.harvard.edu

Summary To recognize and reward authors of outstanding doctoral dissertations in Latin American politics.

Eligibility This award is available to doctoral students at universities in the United States or abroad who passed their thesis defense for the Ph.D. during the preceding 2 calendar years. The dissertation must present outstanding original research on a Latin American and Caribbean political topic undertaken in any of the social sciences or history. Authors must be nominated by their thesis adviser. Nominations of qualified women, members of underrepresented minority groups, and scholars from outside the United States are especially encouraged.

Financial Data The award is $4,000.

Duration The award is presented annually.

Number awarded 1 each year.

Deadline May of each year.

[1099]
DOCTORAL/POST-DOCTORAL FELLOWSHIP PROGRAM IN LAW AND SOCIAL SCIENCE

American Bar Foundation
Attn: Administrative Assistant for Academic Affairs and
    Research Administration
750 North Lake Shore Drive
Chicago, IL 60611-4403
(312) 988-6517   Fax: (312) 988-6579
E-mail: aehrhardt@abfn.org
Web: www.americanbarfoundation.org

Summary To provide research funding to scholars, especially Hispanics and other minorities, who are completing or have completed doctoral degrees in fields related to law, the legal profession, and legal institutions.

Eligibility This program is open to Ph.D. candidates in the social sciences who have completed all doctoral requirements except the dissertation. Applicants who have completed the dissertation are also eligible. Doctoral and proposed research must be in the general area of sociolegal studies or in social scientific approaches to law, the legal profession, or legal institutions and legal processes. Applications must include 1) a dissertation abstract or proposal with an outline of the substance and methods of the research; 2) 2 letters of recommendation; and 3) a curriculum vitae. Minority candidates are especially encouraged to apply.

Financial Data The stipend is $30,000. Fellows may request up to $1,500 to reimburse expenses associated with research, travel to meet with advisers, or travel to conferences at which papers are presented. Relocation expenses of up to $2,500 may be reimbursed on application.

Duration 12 months, beginning in September.

Additional data Fellows are offered access to the computing and word processing facilities of the American Bar Foundation and the libraries of Northwestern University and the University of Chicago. This program was established in 1996. Fellowships must be held in residence at the American Bar Foundation. Appointments to the fellowship are full time; fellows are not permitted to undertake other work.

Number awarded 1 or more each year.

Deadline December of each year.

[1100]
DOROTHY BRACY/JANICE JOSEPH MINORITY AND WOMEN NEW SCHOLAR AWARD

Academy of Criminal Justice Sciences
7339A Hanover Parkway
P.O. Box 960
Greenbelt, MD 20768-0960
(301) 446-6300   Toll Free: (800) 757-ACJS
Fax: (301) 446-2819   E-mail: info@acjs.org
Web: www.acjs.org/Awards

Summary To recognize and reward Hispanic and other minority junior scholars who have made outstanding contributions to the field of criminal justice.

Eligibility This award is available to members of the Academy of Criminal Justice Sciences (ACJS) who are members of a group that has experienced historical discrimination, including minorities and women. Applicants must have obtained a Ph.D. in a field of criminal justice within the past 7 years and be able to demonstrate a strong record as a new scholar in the areas of research, teaching, and service.

Financial Data The award is $1,000.

Duration The award is presented annually.

Number awarded 1 each year.

Deadline October of each year.

[1101]
DR. DAVID MONASH/HARRY LLOYD AND ELIZABETH PAWLETTE MARSHALL RESIDENCY SCHOLARSHIPS

National Medical Fellowships, Inc.
Attn: Scholarship Program
347 Fifth Avenue, Suite 510
New York, NY 10016
(212) 483-8880   Toll Free: (877) NMF-1DOC
Fax: (212) 483-8897 E-mail: scholarships@nmfonline.org
Web: www.nmfonline.org

Summary To provide funding for repayment of student loans and other expenses to Hispanic and other underrepresented medical residents in Chicago who are committed to remaining in the area and working to reduce health disparities.

Eligibility This program is open to residents of any state who graduated from a medical school in Chicago and are currently engaged in a clinical residency program in the area in primary care, community/family medicine, or a related field. U.S. citizenship is required. Applicants must be seeking funding for repayment of student loans and other residency-related expenses. They must identify as an underrepresented minority student in health care (defined as African American, Hispanic/Latino, American Indian, Alaska Native, Native Hawaiian, Vietnamese, Cambodian, or Pacific Islander) and/or socioeconomically disadvantaged student. Along with their application, they must submit documentation of financial status; a short biography; a resume; 2 letters of recommendation; a personal statement of 500 to 1,000 words on their personal and professional motivation for a medical career, their commitment to primary care and service in a health and/or community setting, their motivation for working to reduce health disparities, and their commitment to improving health care; a personal statement of 500 to 1,000 words on the experiences that are preparing them to practice in an underserved community; and a copy of a residency contract from a Chicago clinical residency program. Selection is based on demonstrated leadership early in career and commitment to serving medically underserved communities in Chicago.

Financial Data The grant is $25,000, of which 80% must be used to decrease medical school debt.

Duration 1 year.

Additional data This program began in 2010 with support from the Chicago Community Trust.

Number awarded 4 each year.

Deadline May of each year.

[1102]
DUPONT MINORITIES IN ENGINEERING AWARD

American Society for Engineering Education
Attn: Awards Administration
1818 N Street, N.W., Suite 600
Washington, DC 20036-2479
(202) 331-3550   Fax: (202) 265-8504
E-mail: board@asee.org
Web: www.asee.org

Summary To recognize and reward outstanding achievements by engineering educators to increase diversity by ethnicity and gender in science, engineering, and technology.

Eligibility Eligible for nomination are engineering or engineering technology educators who, as part of their educational activity, either assume or are charged with the responsibility of motivating underrepresented students to enter and continue in engineering or engineering technology curricula at the college or university level, graduate or undergraduate. Nominees must demonstrate leadership in the conception, organization, and operation of pre-college and college activities designed to increase participation by underrepresented students in engineering and engineering technology.

Financial Data The award consists of $1,500, a certificate, and a grant of $500 for travel expenses to the ASEE annual conference.

Duration The award is granted annually.

Additional data Funding for this award is provided by DuPont. It was originally established in 1956 as the Vincent Bendix Minorities in Engineering Award.

Number awarded 1 each year.

Deadline January of each year.

[1103]
EARTH SCIENCES POSTDOCTORAL FELLOWSHIPS

National Science Foundation
Directorate for Geosciences
Attn: Division of Earth Sciences
4201 Wilson Boulevard, Room 785S
Arlington, VA 22230
(703) 292-5047   Fax: (703) 292-9025
TDD: (800) 281-8749   E-mail: lpatino@nsf.gov
Web: www.nsf.gov

Summary To provide funding to postdoctoral scientists, especially Hispanics and members of other underrepresented groups, who are interested in participating in a program of research training and education, in the United States or abroad, in a field relevant to the work of the Division of Earth Sciences of the National Science Foundation (NSF).

Eligibility This program is open to U.S. citizens, nationals, and permanent residents who received a Ph.D. within the past 18 months. Applicants must be interested in a program of research training in any of the disciplines supported by the NSF Division of Earth Sciences: geobiology and low temperature geochemistry, geomorphology and land use dynamics, geophysics, hydrologic sciences, petrology and geochemistry, sedimentary geology and paleobiology, and tectonics. The project should be conducted at an institution in the United States or abroad other than the applicant's Ph.D.-granting institution. The application must include a plan to broaden the participation of groups underrepresented in earth sciences (women, persons with disabilities, Hispanics,

African Americans, Native Americans, Alaska Natives, and Pacific Islanders).

Financial Data Grants are $87,000 per year, including a stipend of $62,000 per year and an annual fellowship allowance of $25,000 that is intended to cover direct research expenses, facilities and other institutional resources, and fringe benefits. For fellows who wish to conduct research abroad, an additional supplement of $10,000 is provided.

Duration 2 years.

Number awarded 10 each year.

Deadline January of each year.

[1104]
EDWARD A. BOUCHET AWARD

American Physical Society
Attn: Honors Program
One Physics Ellipse
College Park, MD 20740-3844
(301) 209-3268   Fax: (301) 209-0865
E-mail: honors@aps.org
Web: www.aps.org/programs/honors/awards/bouchet.cfm

Summary To recognize and reward outstanding research in physics by Hispanics or members of other underrepresented minority groups.

Eligibility Nominees for this award must be Hispanics or Latinos, African Americans, or Native Americans who have made significant contributions to physics research and are effective communicators.

Financial Data The award consists of a grant of $3,500 to the recipient, a travel allowance for the recipient to visit 3 academic institutions to deliver lectures, and an allowance for travel expenses to the meeting of the American Physical Society (APS) at which the prize is presented.

Duration The award is presented annually.

Additional data This award was established in 1994 by a grant from the Research Corporation and is currently funded by institutional and individual donations. As part of the award, the recipient visits 3 academic institutions where the impact of the visit on minority students will be significant. The purpose of those visits is to deliver technical lectures on the recipient's field of specialization, to visit classrooms where appropriate, to assist the institution with precollege outreach efforts where appropriate, and to talk informally with faculty and students about research and teaching careers in physics.

Number awarded 1 each year.

Deadline June of each year.

[1105]
EINSTEIN POSTDOCTORAL FELLOWSHIP PROGRAM

Smithsonian Astrophysical Observatory
Attn: Chandra X-Ray Center
Einstein Fellowship Program Office
60 Garden Street, MS4
Cambridge, MA 02138
(617) 496-7941   Fax: (617) 495-7356
E-mail: fellows@head.cfa.harvard.edu
Web: cxc.harvard.edu/fellows

Summary To provide funding to recent postdoctoral scientists, especially Hispanics and other minorities, who are interested in conducting research related to high energy astrophysics missions of the National Aeronautics and Space Administration (NASA).

Eligibility This program is open to postdoctoral scientists who completed their Ph.D., Sc.D., or equivalent doctoral degree within the past 3 years in astronomy, physics, or related disciplines. Applicants must be interested in conducting research related to NASA Physics of the Cosmos program missions: Chandra, Fermi, XMM-Newton and International X-Ray Observatory, cosmological investigations relevant to the Planck and JDEM missions, and gravitational astrophysics relevant to the LISA mission. They must be citizens of the United States or English-speaking citizens of other countries who have valid visas. Women and minorities are strongly encouraged to apply.

Financial Data Stipends are approximately $66,500 per year. Fellows may also receive health insurance, relocation costs, and moderate support (up to $16,000 per year) for research-related travel, computing services, publications, and other direct costs.

Duration 3 years (depending on a review of scientific activity).

Additional data This program, which began in 2009 with funding from NASA, incorporates the former Chandra and GLAST Fellowship programs.

Number awarded Varies each year; recently, 13 were awarded.

Deadline November of each year.

[1106]
ENVIRONMENT AND NATURAL RESOURCES FELLOWSHIPS

Harvard University
John F. Kennedy School of Government
Belfer Center for Science and International Affairs
Attn: STPP Fellowship Coordinator
79 John F. Kennedy Street, Mailbox 53
Cambridge, MA 02138
(617) 495-1498   Fax: (617) 495-8963
E-mail: patricia_mclaughlin@hks.harvard.edu
Web: belfercenter.ksg.harvard.edu

Summary To provide funding to professionals, postdoctorates, and doctoral students, especially Hispanics and other minorities, who are interested in conducting research on environmental and natural resource issues at the Belfer Center for Science and International Affairs at Harvard University in Cambridge, Massachusetts.

Eligibility The postdoctoral fellowship is open to recent recipients of the Ph.D. or equivalent degree, university faculty members, and employees of government, military, international, humanitarian, and private research institutions who have appropriate professional experience. Applicants for predoctoral fellowships must have passed their general examinations. Scholars from a wide range of disciplinary and multi-disciplinary fields and those holding a Ph.D. in engineering or in the natural sciences are strongly encouraged to apply. The program especially encourages applications from women, minorities, and citizens of all countries. All applicants must be interested in conducting research on projects of the Environment and Natural Resources (ENRP) Program. Recently, those included projects on energy technology innovation, sustainable energy development in China, managing the atom, and the geopolitics of energy.

Financial Data The stipend is $37,500 for postdoctoral research fellows or $25,000 for predoctoral research fellows. Fellows who renew their grant receive a monthly stipend of $3,750 for postdoctoral fellows or $2,500 for predoctoral fellows. Stipends for advanced research fellows vary. Health insurance is also provided.

Duration 10 months; may be renewed on a month-by-month basis.

Additional data Fellows are expected to devote some portion of their time to collaborative endeavors, as arranged by the appropriate program or project director. Predoctoral fellows are expected to contribute to the program's research activities, as well as work on (and ideally complete) their dissertations. Postdoctoral research fellows are also expected to complete a book, monograph, or other significant publication during their period of residence.

Number awarded A limited number each year.

Deadline January of each year.

[1107]
ETHNIC IN-SERVICE TRAINING FUND FOR CLINICAL PASTORAL EDUCATION (EIST-CPE)

United Methodist Church
Attn: General Board of Higher Education and Ministry
Office of Loans and Scholarships
1001 19th Avenue South
P.O. Box 340007
Nashville, TN 37203-0007
(615) 340-7342   Fax: (615) 340-7367
E-mail: umscholar@gbhem.org
Web: www.gbhem.org

Summary To provide financial assistance to United Methodist Church clergy and candidates for ministry who are Hispanics or members of other minority groups interested in preparing for a career as a clinical pastor.

Eligibility This program is open to U.S. citizens and permanent residents who are members of ethnic or racial minority groups and have been active, full members of a United Methodist Church for at least 1 year prior to applying. Applicants must be United Methodist clergy, certified candidates for ministry, or seminary students accepted into an accredited Clinical Pastor Education (CPE) or an accredited American Association of Pastoral Counselors (AAPC) program. They must be preparing for a career as a chaplain, pastoral counselor, or in pastoral care.

Financial Data Grants range up to $2,000.

Duration 1 year.

Number awarded 1 each year.

Deadline February of each year.

[1108]
EVA KING KILLAM RESEARCH AWARD

American College of Neuropsychopharmacology
Attn: Executive Office
5034-A Thoroughbred Lane
Brentwood, TN 37027
(615) 324-2360   Fax: (615) 523-1715
E-mail: acnp@acnp.org
Web: www.acnp.org/programs/awards.aspx

Summary To recognize and reward young scientists, especially Hispanics and other minorites, who have contributed outstanding translational research to neuropsychopharmacology.

Eligibility This award is available to scientists who are no more than 12 years past their terminal degree. Nominees must have made an outstanding translational research contribution to neuropsychopharmacology. The contributions should focus on translating advances from basic science to human investigations. Selection is based on the quality of the contribution and its impact in advancing neuropsychopharmacology. Neither membership in the American College of Neuropsychopharmacology (ACNP) nor U.S. citizenship are required. Nomination of women and minorities is highly encouraged.

Financial Data The award consists of an expense-paid trip to the ACNP annual meeting, a monetary honorarium, and a plaque.

Duration The award is presented annually.

Additional data This award was first presented in 2011.

Number awarded 1 each year.

Deadline Nominations must be submitted by June of each year.

[1109]
FACULTY EARLY CAREER DEVELOPMENT PROGRAM

National Science Foundation
Directorate for Education and Human Resources
Senior Staff Associate for Cross Directorate Programs
4201 Wilson Boulevard, Room 805
Arlington, VA 22230
(703) 292-8600   TDD: (800) 281-8749
E-mail: info@nsf.gov
Web: www.nsf.gov

Summary To provide funding to outstanding new faculty in science and engineering fields of interest to the National Science Foundation (NSF), especially Hispanics and other underrepresented minorities, who intend to develop academic careers involving both research and education.

Eligibility This program, identified as the CAREER program, is open to faculty members who meet all of the following requirements: 1) be employed in a tenure-track (or equivalent) position at an institution in the United States, its territories or possessions, or the Commonwealth of Puerto Rico that awards degrees in a field supported by NSF or that is a nonprofit, non-degree granting organization, such as a museum, observatory, or research laboratory; 2) have a doctoral degree in a field of science or engineering supported by NSF: 3) not have competed more than 3 times in this program; 4) be untenured; and 5) not be a current or former recipient of a Presidential Early Career Award for Scientists and Engineers (PECASE) or CAREER award. Applicants are not required to be U.S. citizens or permanent residents. They must submit a career development plan that indicates a description of the proposed research project, including preliminary supporting data (if appropriate), specific objectives, methods, procedures to be used, and expected significance of the results; a description of the proposed educational activities, including plans to evaluate their impact; a description of how the research and educational activities are integrated with each other; and results of prior NSF support (if applicable). Proposals from women, underrepresented minorities, and persons with disabilities are especially encouraged.

Financial Data The grant is at least $80,000 per year (or $100,000 per year for the Directorate of Biological Sciences or the Office of Polar Programs), including indirect costs or overhead.

Duration 5 years.

Additional data This program is operated by various disciplinary divisions within the NSF; for a list of the participating divisions and their telephone numbers, contact the sponsor. Outstanding recipients of these grants are nominated for the NSF component of the PECASE awards, which are awarded to 20 recipients of these grants as an honorary award.

Number awarded Approximately 400, with a value of $222,000,000, are awarded each year.

Deadline July of each year.

[1110]
FELLOWSHIPS FOR ADVANCED SOCIAL SCIENCE RESEARCH ON JAPAN

National Endowment for the Humanities
Attn: Division of Research Programs
400 Seventh Street, S.W.
Washington, DC 20506
(202) 606-8200   Toll Free: (800) NEH-1121
Fax: (202) 606-8204   TDD: (866) 372-2930
E-mail: fellowships@neh.gov
Web: www.neh.gov

Summary To provide funding to scholars and faculty members, especially those at Hispanic and other Minority Serving Institutions, who wish to conduct social science research related to Japan.

Eligibility This program is open to faculty and staff of colleges, universities, primary schools, and secondary schools, as well as independent scholars and writers. Applicants must be U.S. citizens or foreign nationals who have resided in the United States or its jurisdictions for at least 3 years. The proposed research should relate to modern Japanese society and political economy, Japan's international relations, and U.S.-Japan relations. Disciplines include anthropology, economics, geography, history, international relations, linguistics, political science, psychology, public administration, or sociology. The fellowships are designed for researchers with advanced language skills whose research will require use of data, sources, and documents in their original languages or whose research requires interviews onsite in direct one-on-one contact. Fellows may conduct their projects in Japan, the United States, or both, and may include work in other countries for comparative purposes. Selection is based on 1) the intellectual significance of the project, including its value to scholars and general audiences; 2) the quality or promise of quality of the applicant's work as an interpreter of the social sciences; 3) the quality of the conception, definition, organization, and description of the project; and 4) the feasibility of the proposed plan of work; and 5) the likelihood that the applicant will complete the project. The program encourages submission of applications from faculty at Historically Black Colleges and Universities, Hispanic Serving Institutions, and Tribal Colleges and Universities.

Financial Data The grant is $4,200 per month, to a maximum of $50,400 for 12 months.

Duration 6 to 12 months.

Additional data This program is sponsored jointly by the Japan-US Friendship Commission (JUSFC) and the National Endowment for the Humanities (NEH).

Number awarded Approximately 2 each year.

Deadline April of each year.

[1111]
FIRST BOOK GRANT PROGRAM FOR MINORITY SCHOLARS

Louisville Institute
Attn: Executive Director
1044 Alta Vista Road
Louisville, KY 40205-1798
(502) 992-5432   Fax: (502) 894-2286
E-mail: info@louisville-institute.org
Web: www.louisville-institute.org

Summary To provide funding to Hispanic and other scholars of color interested in completing a major research and book project that focuses on an aspect of Christianity in North America.

Eligibility This program is open to members of racial/ethnic minority groups (African Americans, Hispanics, Native Americans, Asian Americans, Arab Americans, and Pacific Islanders) who have an earned doctoral degree (normally the Ph.D. or Th.D.). Applicants must be a non-tenured faculty member in a full-time, tenure-track position at an accredited institution of higher education (college, university, or seminary) in North America. They must be able to negotiate a full academic year free from teaching and committee responsibilities in order to engage in a scholarly research project leading to the publication of their first (or second) book focusing on an aspect of Christianity in North America. Selection is based on the intellectual quality of the research and writing project, its potential to contribute to scholarship in religion, and the potential contribution of the research to the vitality of North American Christianity.

Financial Data The grant is $40,000. Awards are intended to make possible a full academic year of sabbatical research and writing by providing up to half of the grantee's salary and benefits for that year. Funds are paid directly to the grantee's institution, but no indirect costs are allowed.

Duration 1 academic year; nonrenewable.

Additional data The Louisville Institute is located at Louisville Presbyterian Theological Seminary and is supported by the Lilly Endowment. These grants were first awarded in 2003. Grantees may not accept other awards that provide a stipend during the tenure of this award, and they must be released from all teaching and committee responsibilities during the award year.

Number awarded Varies each year; recently, 3 were awarded.

Deadline January of each year.

[1112]
FIU-AEJMC LATINO/LATIN AMERICAN COMMUNICATION RESEARCH AWARD

Association for Education in Journalism and Mass Communication
Attn: International Communication Division
234 Outlet Pointe Boulevard, Suite A
Columbia, SC 29210-5667
(803) 798-0271   Fax: (803) 772-3509
E-mail: aejmc@aejmc.org
Web: www.aejmc.us/icd

Summary To recognize and reward Latino and Latin American student and faculty members who submit outstanding research papers relevant to journalism and mass media in their communities for presentation at the annual conference of the Association for Education in Journalism and Mass Communication (AEJMC).

Eligibility This competition is open to AEJMC members and non-members, students, and faculty who regard themselves as members of the Latino, Hispanic, or Latin American community. Applicants must submit papers for presentation at the AEJMC annual conference either for the International Communication Division or the Minorities in Communication Division. Eligible topics include matters of Inter-American or Iberian-American communication, new media flow, media theory, media technology or new media, communication for development and social change, media law and ethics, media education, ethnic or gender media and integration, media economics, media and the environment, political communication, critical media studies, popular culture, or cultural studies. All research methodologies are welcome.

Financial Data Cash prizes are awarded.

Duration The prizes are presented annually.

Additional data This program began in 2014 with support from Florida International University's School of Journalism and Mass Communications.

Number awarded 1 each year.

Deadline March of each year.

[1113]
FRAMELINE COMPLETION FUND

Frameline
Attn: Completion Fund
145 Ninth Street, Suite 300
San Francisco, CA 94103
(415) 703-8650   Fax: (415) 861-1404
E-mail: info@frameline.org
Web: frameline.org

Summary To provide funding to lesbian, gay, bisexual, and transgender (LGBT) film/video artists, including Hispanics and other people of color.

Eligibility This program is open to LGBT artists who are in the last stages of the production of documentary, educational, narrative, animated, or experimental projects about or of interest to LGBT people and their communities. Applicants may be independent artists, students, producers, or nonprofit corporations. They must be interested in completion work and must have 90% of the production completed; projects in development, script-development, pre-production, or production are not eligible. Student projects are eligible only if the student maintains artistic and financial control of the project.

Women and people of color are especially encouraged to apply. Selection is based on financial need, the contribution the grant will make to completing the project, assurances that the project will be completed, and the statement the project makes about LGBT people and/or issues of concern to them and their communities.

Financial Data   Grants range from $1,000 to $5,000.

Duration   These are 1-time grants.

Additional data   This program began in 1990.

Number awarded   Varies each year; recently, 5 were awarded. Since this program was established, it has provided $464,200 in support to 136 films.

Deadline   October of each year.

[1114]
FRAMELINE40 AT&T AUDIENCE AWARDS

Frameline
Attn: Festival
145 Ninth Street, Suite 300
San Francisco, CA 94103
(415) 703-8650   Fax: (415) 861-1404
E-mail: info@frameline.org
Web: ticketing.frameline.org/festival/about/awards.aspx

Summary   To recognize and reward outstanding films of interest to the lesbian, gay, bisexual, and transgender (LGBT) audience, including those created by Hispanics and other people of color.

Eligibility   This competition is open to directors of films by, about, and of interest to LGBT people. Applicants must submit previews of their work on DVD or VHS in the following categories: narrative feature films (40 minutes and longer), documentary feature films (40 minutes and longer), and shorts (all films less than 40 minutes in length). The program actively seeks out work by women and people of color. Recently, awards have been presented for best feature film, best documentary film, and best short film.

Financial Data   Awards are $1,000 for best feature and best documentary and $500 for best short film.

Duration   The awards are presented annually.

Additional data   No fees are charged for the early deadline. Standard fees are $35 for the regular deadline, $50 for the late deadline, or $55 for the extended deadline. Student fees are $15 for regular, late, and extended deadlines. Fees are waived for youth up to 18 years of age.

Number awarded   3 each year.

Deadline   December of each year for the early deadline; January of each year for the regular deadline; mid-February for the late deadline; and the end of February for the extended deadline.

[1115]
FRONTIERS IN PHYSIOLOGY RESEARCH TEACHER FELLOWSHIPS

American Physiological Society
Attn: Education Office
9650 Rockville Pike, Room 3111
Bethesda, MD 20814-3991
(301) 634-7132   Fax: (301) 634-7098
E-mail: education@the-aps.org
Web: www.the-aps.org

Summary   To provide an opportunity for middle/high school life science teachers, especially Hispanics and other underrepresented minorities, to participate in a summer research project in physiology.

Eligibility   This program is open to science teachers at middle schools (grades 6-9) and high schools (grades 9-12) who do not have recent (within 10 years) laboratory experience in physiology or the life sciences, do not have an advanced degree in laboratory science, and are not a candidate for an advanced degree in a laboratory science. Applicants must be able to demonstrate a commitment to excellence in science teaching, a desire to learn new teaching methods, and a desire to learn about research first-hand. Teachers who are members of minority groups underrepresented in science (Hispanics, African Americans, Native Americans, and Pacific Islanders) or who teach in schools with a predominance of underrepresented minority students are especially encouraged to apply. Teachers must apply jointly with a member of the American Physiological Society (APS) at a research institution in the same geographic area as their home and school. Selection is based on the quality of the summer research experience and potential long-term impact on teaching and on students.

Financial Data   For all activities, teachers receive a stipend of $5,700. They also receive $1,200 for reimbursement of travel costs to attend the Experimental Biology meeting.

Duration   1 year, including 7 to 8 weeks during the summer for participation in the research experience.

Additional data   This program enables teachers to work on a summer research project in the laboratory of their APS sponsor, use the Internet to expand their repertory of teaching methods and their network of colleagues, and develop an inquiry-based classroom activity or laboratory, along with a corresponding web page. They also take a break from their summer research to attend a 1-week Science Teaching Forum in Washington D.C. where they work with APS staff, physiologists, and mentors to explore and practice effective teaching methods focused on how to integrate inquiry, equity, and the Internet into their classrooms. This program is supported by the National Center for Research Resources (NCRR) and the National Institute of Diabetes and Digestive and Kidney Diseases (NIDDK), both components of the National Institutes of Health (NIH).

Number awarded   Varies each year; recently 17 were awarded.

Deadline   January of each year.

[1116]
FUND FOR LATINO SCHOLARSHIP

American Political Science Association
Attn: Diversity and Inclusion Programs
1527 New Hampshire Avenue, N.W.
Washington, DC 20036-1206
(202) 349-9362   Fax: (202) 483-2657
E-mail: kmealy@apsanet.org
Web: www.apsanet.org

Summary   To provide funding for travel or research to members of the American Political Science Association (APSA) and other students and scholars who are involved with Latinos.

Eligibility   Applications for this assistance should involve activities that 1) provide professional opportunities and financial assistance to Latino/a graduate students in political science programs; 2) support the teaching, research, and publishing activities of junior-level, tenure-track Latino/a political science faculty; or 3) support activities that advance our knowledge of Latino/a politics. Latino/a scholars (whatever their research field) and all scholars (including non-Latinos/as) who are studying Latino politics in the United States are eligible.

Financial Data Travel grants and most research grants are $500. Under exceptional circumstances, a grant of up to $1,000 may be awarded. Funding is intended for travel assistance to attend the APSA annual meeting, conduct field research, attend another scholarly conference, or participate in a program at the APSA Centennial Center for Political Science and Public Affairs.

Duration These are 1-time grants.

Number awarded 1 or more each year.

Deadline June of each year.

[1117]
GAIUS CHARLES BOLIN DISSERTATION AND POST-MFA FELLOWSHIPS

Williams College
Attn: Dean of the Faculty
880 Main Street
Hopkins Hall, Third Floor
P.O. Box 141
Williamstown, MA 01267
(413) 597-4351   Fax: (413) 597-3553
E-mail: gburda@williams.edu
Web: faculty.williams.edu

Summary To provide financial assistance to Hispanics and members of other underrepresented groups who are interested in teaching courses at Williams College while working on their doctoral dissertation or building their post-M.F.A. professional portfolio.

Eligibility This program is open to members of underrepresented groups, including ethnic minorities, first-generation college students, women in predominantly male fields, and scholars with disabilities. Applicants must be 1) doctoral candidates in any field who have completed all work for a Ph.D. except for the dissertation; or 2) artists who completed an M.F.A. degree within the past 2 years and are building their professional portfolio. They must be willing to teach a course at Williams College. Along with their application, they must submit a full curriculum vitae, a graduate school transcript, 3 letters of recommendation, a copy of their dissertation prospectus or samples of their artistic work, and a description of their teaching interests within a department or program at Williams College. U.S. citizenship or permanent resident status is required.

Financial Data Fellows receive $38,000 for the academic year, plus housing assistance, office space, computer and library privileges, and a research allowance of up to $4,000.

Duration 2 years.

Additional data Bolin fellows are assigned a faculty adviser in the appropriate department. This program was established in 1985. Fellows are expected to teach a 1-semester course each year. They must be in residence at Williams College for the duration of the fellowship.

Number awarded 2 each year.

Deadline November of each year.

[1118]
GEORGE A. STRAIT MINORITY SCHOLARSHIP ENDOWMENT

American Association of Law Libraries
Attn: Chair, Scholarships Committee
105 West Adams Street, Suite 3300
Chicago, IL 60603
(312) 939-4764   Fax: (312) 431-1097
E-mail: scholarships@aall.org
Web: www.aallnet.org

Summary To provide financial assistance to Hispanic and other minority college seniors or college graduates who are interested in becoming law librarians.

Eligibility This program is open to college graduates with meaningful law library experience who are members of minority groups and intend to have a career in law librarianship. Applicants must be degree candidates at an ALA-accredited library school or an ABA-accredited law school. Along with their application, they must submit a personal statement that discusses their interest in law librarianship, reason for applying for this scholarship, career goals as a law librarian, and any other pertinent information.

Financial Data The stipend is $3,500.

Duration 1 year.

Additional data This program, established in 1990, is currently supported by Thomson Reuters.

Number awarded Varies each year; recently, 6 were awarded.

Deadline March of each year.

[1119]
GERALD OSHITA MEMORIAL FELLOWSHIP

Djerassi Resident Artists Program
Attn: Admissions
2325 Bear Gulch Road
Woodside, CA 94062-4405
(650) 747-1250   Fax: (650) 747-0105
E-mail: drap@djerassi.org
Web: www.djerassi.org/oshita.html

Summary To provide an opportunity for Latino and other composers of color to participate in the Djerassi Resident Artists Program.

Eligibility This program is open to composers of Latino, Asian, African, or Native American ethnic background. Applicants must be interested in utilizing a residency to compose, study, rehearse, and otherwise advance their own creative projects.

Financial Data The fellow is offered housing, meals, studio space, and a stipend of $2,500.

Duration 1 month, from late March through mid-November.

Additional data This fellowship was established in 1994. The program is located in northern California, 45 miles south of San Francisco, on 600 acres of rangeland, redwood forests, and hiking trails. There is a $45 non-refundable application fee.

Number awarded 1 each year.

Deadline February of each year.

[1120]
GERTRUDE AND MAURICE GOLDHABER DISTINGUISHED FELLOWSHIPS

Brookhaven National Laboratory
Attn: Bill Bookless
Building 460
40 Brookhaven Avenue
Upton, NY 11973
(631) 344-5734   E-mail: barkigia@bnl.gov
Web: www.bnl.gov/HR/goldhaber

Summary To provide funding to postdoctoral scientists, especially Hispanics and other minorities, who are interested in conducting research at Brookhaven National Laboratory (BNL).

Eligibility This program is open to scholars who are no more than 3 years past receipt of the Ph.D. and are interested in working at BNL. Candidates must be interested in working in close collaboration with a member of the BNL scientific staff and qualifying for a scientific staff position at BNL upon completion of the appointment. The sponsoring scientist must have an opening and be able to support the candidate at the standard starting salary for postdoctoral research associates. The program especially encourages applications from minorities and women.

Financial Data The program provides additional funds to bring the salary to $81,200 per year.

Duration 3 years.

Additional data This program is funded by Battelle Memorial Institute and the State University of New York at Stony Brook.

Number awarded Up to 2 each year.

Deadline June of each year.

[1121]
GLOBAL AMERICAN STUDIES POSTDOCTORAL FELLOWSHIPS

Harvard University
Charles Warren Center for Studies in American History
Emerson Hall, Fourth Floor
Cambridge, MA 02138
(617) 495-3591   Fax: (617) 496-2111
E-mail: cwc@fas.harvard.edu
Web: warrencenter.fas.harvard.edu/postdoc-fellowship

Summary To provide funding to recent postdoctoral scholars, especially Hispanics and other minorities who are interested in conducting research in the Boston area on the history of the United States in the world.

Eligibility This program is open to scholars who completed a Ph.D. within the past 4 years. Applicants must be interested in conducting research in residence at Harvard on the history of the United States in the world and the world in the United States. Applications are welcomed from scholars with a variety of disciplinary backgrounds who bring a historical perspective to topics such as empire, migration, race, indigeneity, and ethnicity, and whose work investigates and/or interprets the history and experience in the United States of native peoples, or peoples of Hispanic, African, or Asian descent. The program especially welcomes applications from scholars who can contribute, through their research, teaching, and service, to the diversity and excellence of Harvard's academic community.

Financial Data The maximum grant is $53,600.

Duration 1 year; may be renewed 1 additional year.

Additional data This program began in 2013. Fellows must remain in residence at the center for the duration of the program and teach 1 course per year.

Number awarded 2 each year.

Deadline December of each year.

[1122]
GLORIA E. ANZALDUA BOOK PRIZE

National Women's Studies Association
Attn: Book Prizes
11 East Mount Royal Avenue, Suite 100
Baltimore, MD 21202
(410) 528-0355   Fax: (410) 528-0357
E-mail: awards@nwsa.org
Web: www.nwsa.org

Summary To recognize and reward members of the National Women's Studies Association (NWSA) who have written outstanding books on women of color and transnational issues.

Eligibility This award is available to NWSA members who submit a book that was published during the preceding year. Entries must present groundbreaking scholarship in women's studies and make a significant multicultural feminist contribution to women of color and/or transnational studies.

Financial Data The award provides an honorarium of $1,000 and lifetime membership in NWSA.

Duration The award is presented annually.

Additional data This award was first presented in 2008.

Number awarded 1 each year.

Deadline April of each year.

[1123]
GREENWALL FACULTY SCHOLARS PROGRAM

Greenwall Foundation
Attn: Faculty Scholars Program Coordinator
One Penn Plaza, 47th Floor
New York, NY 10019
(212) 679-7266   E-mail: rboxt@greenwall.org
Web: www.greenwall.org/faculty-scholars-program.php

Summary To provide funding to junior faculty members, especially Hispanics and members of other underrepresented groups, who are interested in conducting innovative bioethics research.

Eligibility This program is open to junior faculty who have a least a 60% appointment in a tenure series at a university or nonprofit research institute. Applicants must be interested in conducting research on an important bioethics issue. Priority is given to applicants who have not yet been considered for tenure, who have not received a comparable career development award, and whose work will have an impact on public policy, biomedical research, or clinical practice. Applications are especially encouraged from applicants whose backgrounds are underrepresented in bioethics and academia. Selection is based on applicants' achievements, the strength of their research project, their commitment to the field of bioethics, and support from their home institution.

Financial Data The award supports 50% of the scholar's salary plus benefits (up to 1.5 times the NIH salary cap) and

10% institutional costs. An additional $5,000 per year for limited project support and travel is also provided.

Duration 3 years.

Number awarded 3 to 5 each year.

Deadline Letters of intent must be submitted by early October of each year; final proposals are due in January.

[1124]
HARVARD MEDICAL SCHOOL DEAN'S POSTDOCTORAL FELLOWSHIP

Harvard Medical School
Office for Diversity Inclusion and Community Partnership
Attn: Program Manager, Dean's Postdoctoral Fellowship
164 Longwood Avenue, Second Floor
Boston, MA 02115-5818
(617) 432-1083   Fax: (617) 432-3834
E-mail: brian_anderson@hms.harvard.edu
Web: www.hms.harvard.edu/dcp/deanspdfellowship

Summary To provide an opportunity for postdoctoral scholars, especially Hispanics and others who will contribute to diversity in the social and basic sciences, to obtain research training at Harvard Medical School.

Eligibility This program is open to U.S. citizens and permanent residents who have completed an M.D., Ph.D., Sc.D., or equivalent degree in the basic or social sciences and have less than 4 years of relevant postdoctoral research experience. Applicants must be interested in a program of research training under the mentorship of a professor in 1 of the departments of Harvard Medical School: biological chemistry and molecular pharmacology, biomedical informatics, cell biology, genetics, global health and social medicine, health care policy, microbiology and immunobiology, neurobiology, stem cell and regenerative biology, or systems biology. Scientists from minority and disadvantaged backgrounds are especially encouraged to apply. Selection is based on academic achievement, scholarly promise, potential to add to the diversity of the Harvard Medical School community, and the likelihood that the application will become an independent scientist and societal leader.

Financial Data Fellows receive a professional development allowance of $1,250 per year and a stipend that depends on the years of postdoctoral experience, ranging from $40,992 for zero to $47,820 for 4 years.

Duration 2 years.

Number awarded 2 each year.

Deadline Applications may be submitted at any time.

[1125]
HAZEL D. COLE FELLOWSHIP

University of Washington
Attn: Stroum Center for Jewish Studies
Henry M. Jackson School of International Studies
Thomson Hall
Box 353650
Seattle, WA 98195-3650
(206) 543-0138   Fax: (206) 685-0668
E-mail: jewishst@uw.edu
Web: www.jewishstudies.washington.edu

Summary To provide funding to pre- and postdoctoral scholars in Jewish studies, including Hispanics and other underrepresented minorities, who are interested in conducting research at the University of Washington.

Eligibility This program is open to postdoctoral scholars who completed their Ph.D. within the past 3 years and to doctoral candidates working on a dissertation. Applicants must be interested in conducting research in a field of Jewish studies while in residence at the University of Washington for the tenure of their fellowship. They may be from any American or foreign university. Along with their application, they must submit a current curriculum vitae, a description of their scholarly interests and their proposed research project, a proposal for a course they would like to teach (including a prospective syllabus), 2 letters of recommendation, and an academic writing sample. The program encourages applications from women, minorities, individuals with disabilities, and covered veterans.

Financial Data The fellowship provides a stipend of $50,000 plus benefits.

Duration 1 year.

Additional data The fellow also offers an undergraduate seminar or lecture course and makes a public presentation.

Number awarded 1 each year.

Deadline October of each year.

[1126]
HIGH-RISK RESEARCH IN BIOLOGICAL ANTHROPOLOGY AND ARCHAEOLOGY GRANTS

National Science Foundation
Social, Behavioral, and Economic Sciences
Attn: Division of Behavioral and Cognitive Sciences
4201 Wilson Boulevard, Room 995 N
Arlington, VA 22230
(703) 292-8759   Fax: (703) 292-9068
TDD: (800) 281-8749   E-mail: jyellen@nsf.gov
Web: www.nsf.gov

Summary To provide funding to scholars, especially Hispanics and other underrepresented minorities, who are interested in conducting high-risk research in anthropology or archaeology.

Eligibility This program is open to scholars interested in conducting research projects in cultural anthropology, archaeology, or physical anthropology that might be considered too risky for normal review procedures. A project is considered risky if the data may not be obtainable in spite of all reasonable preparation on the researcher's part. Proposals for extremely urgent research where access to the data may not be available in the normal review schedule, even with all reasonable preparation by the researcher, are also appropriate for this program. Graduate students are not eligible. Applications are encouraged from all citizens, including women and men, underrepresented minorities, and persons with disabilities.

Financial Data Grants up to $35,000, including indirect costs, are available.

Duration 1 year.

Number awarded Generally, 5 of these grants are awarded each year.

Deadline Applications may be submitted at any time.

[1127]
HISPANIC HEALTH SERVICES RESEARCH GRANT PROGRAM

Centers for Medicare & Medicaid Services
Attn: Center for Medicare and Medicaid Innovation
Mail Stop WB-06-05
7500 Security Boulevard
Baltimore, MD 21244-1850
(410) 786-7250   Toll Free: (877) 267-2323
TDD: (877) 486-2048   E-mail: Richard.bragg@cms.hhs.
  gov
Web: www.cms.gov

Summary To provide funding to scholars at Hispanic Serving Institutions (HSIs) who are interested in carrying out health services research activities.

Eligibility This program is open to scholars at an HSI that meets 1 of the following requirements: 1) offers a Ph.D. or master's degree in 1 or more of the following disciplines: allied health, gerontology, health care administration, nursing, pharmacology, public health, or social work; 2) is a member of a community-based health association with a Hispanic health services research component; or 3) is a member of a professional association focusing on Hispanic health services and health disparities issues. Applicants must be interested in conducting small research projects that address health care issues such as financing, delivery, access, quality, and barriers affecting the Hispanic community.

Financial Data Grants range up to $100,000 per year.

Duration Up to 2 years.

Additional data This program began in 1999. Until 2001, the Centers for Medicare & Medicaid Services was known as the Health Care Financing Administration.

Number awarded 1 each year.

Deadline Letters of intent must be submitted by June of each year. Final applications are due in July.

[1128]
HISPANIC ORGANIZATION OF TOXICOLOGISTS DISTINGUISHED TOXICOLOGIST AWARD

Society of Toxicology
Attn: Hispanic Organization of Toxicologists
1821 Michael Faraday Drive, Suite 300
Reston, VA 20190-5348
(703) 438-3115   Fax: (703) 438-3113
E-mail: sothq@toxicology.org
Web: www.toxicology.org/ai/af/awards_details.aspx?id=211

Summary To recognize and reward members of the Hispanic Organization of Toxicologists (HOT) who make significant contributions to the field of toxicology.

Eligibility This award recognizes scientific accomplishments, regulatory accomplishments, and/or community services related to the field of toxicology. Nominees must be HOT members; nominators must be members of HOT and/or the Society of Toxicology.

Financial Data The award includes a plaque and a stipend.

Duration The award is presented annually.

Number awarded 1 each year.

Deadline January of each year.

[1129]
HUBBLE FELLOWSHIPS

Space Telescope Science Institute
Attn: Hubble Fellowship Program Office
3700 San Martin Drive
Baltimore, MD 21218
(410) 338-2474   Fax: (410) 338-4211
E-mail: hfinquiry@stsci.edu
Web: www.stsci.edu

Summary To provide funding to recent postdoctoral scientists, especially Hispanics and other minorities, who are interested in conducting research related to the Hubble Space Telescope or related missions of the National Aeronautics and Space Administration (NASA).

Eligibility This program is open to postdoctoral scientists who completed their doctoral degree within the past 3 years in astronomy, physics, or related disciplines. Applicants must be interested in conducting research related to NASA Cosmic Origins missions: the Hubble Space Telescope, Herschel Space Observatory, James Webb Space Telescope, Stratospheric Observatory for Infrared Astronomy, or the Spitzer Space Telescope. They may U.S. citizens or English-speaking citizens of other countries with valid visas. Research may be theoretical, observational, or instrumental. Women and members of minority groups are strongly encouraged to apply.

Financial Data Stipends are approximately $66,500 per year. Other benefits may include health insurance, relocation costs, and support for travel, equipment, and other direct costs of research.

Duration 3 years: an initial 1-year appointment and 2 annual renewals, contingent on satisfactory performance and availability of funds.

Additional data This program, funded by NASA, began in 1990 and was limited to work with the Hubble Space Telescope. A parallel program, called the Spitzer Fellowship, began in 2002 and was limited to work with the Spitzer Space Telescope. In 2009, those programs were combined into this single program, which was also broadened to include the other NASA Cosmic Origins missions. Fellows are required to be in residence at their host institution engaged in full-time research for the duration of the grant.

Number awarded Varies each year; recently, 17 were awarded.

Deadline October of each year.

[1130]
IDAHO FOLK AND TRADITIONAL ARTS APPRENTICESHIP AWARDS

Idaho Commission on the Arts
Attn: Traditional Arts
2410 North Old Penitentiary Road
P.O. Box 83720
Boise, ID 83720-0008
(208) 334-2119   Toll Free: (800) 278-3863
Fax: (208) 334-2488   E-mail: info@arts.idaho.gov
Web: www.arts.idaho.gov/grants/trap.aspx

Summary To provide funding to masters of traditional art forms in Idaho and apprentices who wish to learn from them.

Eligibility This program is open to traditional arts masters and apprentices who have been residents of Idaho for at least

1 year. Applicants must be interested in establishing a partnership in which the apprentice will learn by observation and practice within the family, tribe, occupational, or other group. Master artists should have learned skills informally and have received peer recognition for achieving the highest level of artistry according to community standards. Apprentices should have some background in the proposed art form, wish to learn from a recognized master, and be committed to continue practicing after the apprenticeship has ended. Art forms must represent shared cultural traditions of both applicants. Priority is given to art forms with few practitioners. In-family apprenticeships are encouraged. Selection is based on quality (master is recognized by peers and by community standards, the apprentice will benefit from working with the master at this time, the apprentice is committed to advancing his or her skills in the art form and carrying on the tradition); community (master and apprentice share the same cultural background, the art form is significant to their community, the art form is endangered within the particular traditional culture or there are few artists practicing it); and feasibility (the goals for the apprenticeship are clear, the budget is appropriate, the work plan provides appropriate time for interaction to achieve meaningful results).

Financial Data The maximum grant is $3,000.

Duration From 4 to 10 months, depending on the particular art form and on the proposed work plan.

Number awarded Varies each year; recently, 7 of these fellowships were awarded.

Deadline January of each year.

[1131]
INTERNATIONAL SECURITY AND COOPERATION POSTDOCTORAL FELLOWSHIPS

Stanford University
Center for International Security and Cooperation
Attn: Fellowships Coordinator
Encina Hall, Room C206-10
616 Serra Street
Stanford, CA 94305-6165
(650) 723-9625   Fax: (650) 724-5683
E-mail: CISACfellowship@stanford.edu
Web: cisac.fsi.stanford.edu/docs/cisac_fellowship_program

Summary To provide funding to postdoctorates, especially Hispanics and other minorities, who are interested in conducting research on international security problems at Stanford University's Center for International Security and Cooperation.

Eligibility This program is open to scholars who have a Ph.D. or equivalent degree from the United States or abroad and would benefit from using the resources of the center. Applicants may be working in any discipline of the social sciences, humanities, natural sciences, law, or engineering that relates to international security problems. Relevant topics include nuclear weapons policy and nonproliferation; nuclear energy; cybersecurity, cyberwarfare, and the future of the Internet; war and civil conflict; global governance, migration and transnational flows, from norms to criminal trafficking; biosecurity and global health; implications of geostrategic shifts; insurgency, terrorism, and homeland security; and consolidating peace after conflict. The sponsor welcomes applications from women, minorities, and citizens of all countries.

Financial Data The stipend ranges from $48,000 to $66,000, depending on experience. Medical insurance is available for those who do not have coverage.

Duration 9 to 11 months.

Additional data Fellows are expected to write a publishable article or articles and/or make significant progress on turning a thesis into a book manuscript. They should not plan to spend any time conducting research abroad or in other parts of the country.

Number awarded Varies each year; recently, 7 were awarded.

Deadline January of each year.

[1132]
INTERNATIONAL SECURITY AND COOPERATION PROFESSIONAL FELLOWSHIPS

Stanford University
Center for International Security and Cooperation
Attn: Fellowships Coordinator
Encina Hall, Room C206-10
616 Serra Street
Stanford, CA 94305-6165
(650) 723-9625   Fax: (650) 724-5683
E-mail: CISACfellowship@stanford.edu
Web: cisac.fsi.stanford.edu/docs/cisac_fellowship_program

Summary To provide funding to professionals, especially Hispanics and other minorities, who are interested in conducting research in residence on topics of interest to Stanford University's Center for International Security and Cooperation.

Eligibility This program is open to mid-career professionals in journalism, law, the military, government, or international organizations, either from the United States or abroad. Applicants must be interested in conducting research in any discipline of the social sciences, humanities, natural sciences, law, or engineering that relates to international security problems. Relevant topics include nuclear weapons policy and nonproliferation; nuclear energy; cybersecurity, cyberwarfare, and the future of the Internet; war and civil conflict; global governance, migration and transnational flows, from norms to criminal trafficking; biosecurity and global health; implications of geostrategic shifts; insurgency, terrorism, and homeland security; and consolidating peace after conflict. The sponsor welcomes applications from women, minorities, and citizens of all countries.

Financial Data The stipend depends on experience and is determined on a case-by-case basis. Additional funds may be available for dependents and travel.

Duration 9 to 11 months.

Additional data Fellows are expected to write a publishable article during their fellowship. They should not plan to spend any time conducting research abroad or in other parts of the country.

Number awarded Varies each year; recently, 2 were awarded.

Deadline January of each year.

[1133]
JOHN C. DANFORTH CENTER ON RELIGION AND POLITICS POSTDOCTORAL RESEARCH ASSOCIATE FELLOWSHIP

Washington University
Attn: John C. Danforth Center on Religion and Politics
118 Umrath Hall
Campus Box 1066
One Brookings Drive
St. Louis, MO 63130
(314) 935-9545   Fax: (314) 935-5755
E-mail: rap@wustl.edu
Web: rap.wustl.edu/postdoctoral-research-associate

Summary To provide funding to recent postdoctorates, especially Hispanics and members of other underrepresented groups, who are interested in conducting research while in residence at the John C. Danforth Center on Religion and Politics of Washington University in St. Louis.

Eligibility This program is open to scholars who completed a Ph.D. within the past 5 years in religious studies, politics, anthropology, American studies, history, Jewish studies, sociology, or other relevant field. They must be engaged in projects centrally concerned with religion and politics in the United States, historically or in the present day. Members of underrepresented groups are encouraged to apply.

Financial Data Fellows receive a stipend commensurate with their experience.

Duration 1 year; may be renewed 1 additional year.

Number awarded Up to 3 each year.

Deadline January of each year.

[1134]
JOHN MCLENDON MEMORIAL MINORITY POSTGRADUATE SCHOLARSHIP AWARD

National Association of Collegiate Directors of Athletics
Attn: NACDA Foundation
24651 Detroit Road
Westlake, OH 44145
(440) 788-7474   Fax: (440) 892-4007
E-mail: knewman@nacda.com
Web: www.nacda.com/mclendon/scholarship.html

Summary To provide financial assistance to Hispanic and other minority college seniors who are interested in working on a graduate degree in athletics administration.

Eligibility This program is open to minority college students who are seniors, are attending school on a full-time basis, have a GPA of 3.2 or higher, intend to attend graduate school to earn a degree in athletics administration, and are involved in college or community activities. Also eligible are college graduates who have at least 2 years' experience in an athletics administration position. Candidates must be nominated by an official of a member institution of the National Association of Collegiate Directors of Athletics (NACDA) or (for college graduates) a supervisor.

Financial Data The stipend is $10,000.

Duration 1 year.

Additional data Recipients must maintain full-time status during the senior year to retain their eligibility. They must attend NACDA-member institutions.

Number awarded 5 each year.

Deadline Nominations must be submitted by April of each year.

[1135]
JONATHAN REICHERT AND BARBARA WOLFF-REICHERT AWARD FOR EXCELLENCE IN ADVANCED LABORATORY INSTRUCTION

American Physical Society
Attn: Honors Program
One Physics Ellipse
College Park, MD 20740-3844
(301) 209-3268   Fax: (301) 209-0865
E-mail: honors@aps.org
Web: www.aps.org/programs/honors/awards/lab.cfm

Summary To recognize and reward physicists, especially Hispanics and other underrepresented minorities, who have made outstanding achievements in teaching undergraduate laboratory courses.

Eligibility This award is available to individuals or teams of individuals who have taught, developed, and sustained advanced undergraduate physics laboratory courses for at least 4 years at an institution in the United States. Nominations should present evidence of the dissemination of the laboratory work to the broader physics community. Nominations of qualified women and members of underrepresented minority groups are especially encouraged.

Financial Data The award consists of $5,000 as an honorarium, a certificate citing the accomplishments of the recipient, and an allowance up to $2,000 for travel expenses to the meeting where the award is presented.

Duration The award is presented annually.

Additional data This award was established in 2012.

Number awarded 1 each year.

Deadline June of each year.

[1136]
KING-CHAVEZ-PARKS VISITING PROFESSORS PROGRAM

University of Michigan
Attn: Office of the Provost and Executive Vice President
  for Academic Affairs
503 Thompson Street
3084 Fleming Administration Building
Ann Arbor, MI 48109-1340
(734) 764-3982   Fax: (734) 764-4546
E-mail: provost@umich.edu
Web: www.provost.umich.edu

Summary To provide an opportunity for Hispanic and other minority scholars to visit and teach at the University of Michigan.

Eligibility Outstanding minority (Latino/a-Hispanic American, African American, Asian/Pacific American, and Native American) scholars, performers, or practitioners are eligible to be nominated by University of Michigan faculty members to visit and lecture there. Nominations that include collaborations with other educational institutions in Michigan are of high priority.

Financial Data Visiting Professors receive round-trip transportation and an appropriate honorarium.

Duration Visits range from 1 to 5 days.

Additional data This program was established in 1986. Visiting Professors are expected to lecture or teach at the university, offer at least 1 event open to the general public, and meet with minority campus/community groups, including local K-12 schools.

Number awarded Varies each year.

Deadline Nominations may be submitted at any time, but they must be received at least 30 days before a funding decision is required.

[1137]
LABORATORY ASTROPHYSICS PRIZE

American Astronomical Society
Attn: Laboratory Astrophysics Division
2000 Florida Avenue, N.W., Suite 400
Washington, DC 20009-1231
(202) 328-2010   Fax: (202) 234-2560
E-mail: aas@aas.org
Web: lad.aas.org/prizes/lab_astro_prize

Summary To recognize and reward outstanding contributions to laboratory astrophysics, including those by Hispanics and other underrepresented minorities.

Eligibility Nominees for this award must have made outstanding contributions to laboratory physics over an extended period of time. Full consideration is given to qualified women, members of underrepresented minority groups, and scientists from outside the United States.

Financial Data The prize includes a cash award, a framed certificate, and reimbursement of travel expenses to attend a meeting where an invited is presented.

Duration The prize is presented annually.

Additional data This prize was first presented in 2015.

Number awarded 1 each year.

Deadline September of each year.

[1138]
LAD EARLY CAREER AWARD

American Astronomical Society
Attn: Laboratory Astrophysics Division
2000 Florida Avenue, N.W., Suite 400
Washington, DC 20009-1231
(202) 328-2010   Fax: (202) 234-2560
E-mail: aas@aas.org
Web: lad.aas.org/prizes/lab_astro_prize

Summary To recognize and reward outstanding contributions to laboratory astrophysics by early-career scientists, including those by Hispanics and other underrepresented minorities.

Eligibility Nominees for this award must have made outstanding contributions to laboratory physics early in their professional career. They must have no more than 10 years of professional experience since their Ph.D. or equivalent degree. Full consideration is given to qualified women, members of underrepresented minority groups, and scientists from outside the United States.

Financial Data The prize includes a cash award, a framed certificate, and reimbursement of travel expenses to attend a meeting where an invited is presented.

Duration The prize is presented annually.

Additional data This prize was first presented in 2016.

Number awarded 1 each year.

Deadline September of each year.

[1139]
LATINA LAWYERS BAR ASSOCIATION SCHOLARSHIPS

Latina Lawyers Bar Association
Attn: Scholarship Committee
P.O. Box 86488
Los Angeles, CA 90086
E-mail: scholarships@llbalaw.org
Web: www.llbalaw.org/content/scholarship

Summary To provide financial assistance for tuition or bar review courses to students, especially Latinas, currently enrolled at law schools in California or preparing for the state bar examination.

Eligibility This program is open to students currently enrolled at California law schools and current candidates for the California State Bar examination. Preference is given to Latina law students. Applicants must be able to demonstrate community service, commitment to the Latina community, potential to succeed, and financial need. Along with their application, they must submit a 1,000-word statement that includes information regarding their background, reasons for pursuing further education, challenges they face outside of school, legal field of interest, career goals, special circumstances, and financial need.

Financial Data A stipend is awarded (amount not specified).

Duration Funds provide 1 year of support at a California law school or a 1-time grant for bar examination assistance.

Number awarded 1 or more each year.

Deadline July of each year.

[1140]
LATINO PUBLIC BROADCASTING PUBLIC MEDIA CONTENT FUND

Latino Public Broadcasting
2550 North Hollywood Way, Suite 301
Burbank, CA 91505
(818) 847-9656   Fax: (818) 847-9663
E-mail: info@lpbp.org
Web: www.lpbp.org/fundingguidelines.php

Summary To provide funding to film and video producers interested in developing projects for broadcast on public television that relate to the Latino experience in America.

Eligibility This program is open to independent producers and production entities that are creating programs on the Latino experience. The programs must be independent of the support of a film studio or commercial broadcast entity. The producer or production entity must retain the copyright and have artistic, budgetary, and editorial control over the proposed project. Applicants must be at least 18 years of age, be citizens or legal residents of the United States or its territories, and have previous film or television experience that can be documented by detailed personnel resumes and by sample tapes upon request. Projects that are ineligible include thesis projects and student films; producers or production entities that are foreign based, owned, or controlled; industrial or promotional projects; projects for which the exclusive domestic television rights are not available; projects with a primarily commercial interest; and proposals by current recipients of these grants who have not yet completed delivery. The project genres may include drama, documentary, narrative, performance, mixed genre, or new media. The project may be at any stage of production. Priority is given too programs that address Latino arts and culture.

Financial Data Grants range from $5,000 to $20,000 for research and development, $25,000 to $100,000 for production, $25,000 to $100,000 for post-production, or $5,000 to $20,000 for new media.

Additional data Funding for these grants is provided by the Corporation for Public Broadcasting. Producers must agree to complete the program according to the proposed schedule, project description, and budget, and to certain oversight rights and accountability obligations to the sponsor. The producer also agrees to royalty participation by the sponsor in a percentage of net revenues from ancillary distribution.

Number awarded Varies each year; recently, 9 were awarded, of which 7 were for post-production and 2 for new media.

Deadline May of each year.

[1141]
LAURENCE R. FOSTER MEMORIAL SCHOLARSHIPS

Oregon Office of Student Access and Completion
Attn: Scholarship Processing Coordinator
1500 Valley River Drive, Suite 100
Eugene, OR 97401-2146
(541) 687-7422   Toll Free: (800) 452-8807, ext. 7422
Fax: (541) 687-7414   TDD: (800) 735-2900
E-mail: cheryl.a.connolly@state.or.us
Web: app.oregonstudentaid.gov/Catalog/Default.aspx

Summary To provide financial assistance to residents of Oregon, especially Hispanics and members of other diverse groups, who are enrolled at a college or graduate school in any state to prepare for a public health career.

Eligibility This program is open to residents of Oregon who are enrolled at least half time at a 4-year college or university in any state to prepare for a career in public health (not private practice). Preference is given first to applicants from diverse environments; second to persons employed in, or graduate students working on a degree in, public health; and third to juniors and seniors majoring in a health program (e.g., nursing, medical technology, physician assistant). Applicants must be able to demonstrate financial need. Along with their application, they must submit essays of 250 to 350 words on 1) what public health means to them; 2) the public health aspect they intend to practice and the health and population issues impacted by that aspect; and 3) their experience living or working in diverse environments.

Financial Data Stipends for scholarships offered by the Oregon Office of Student Access and Completion (OSAC) range from $1,000 to $10,000 but recently averaged $4,368.

Duration 1 year.

Additional data This program is administered by the OSAC with funds provided by the Oregon Community Foundation.

Number awarded Varies each year; recently, 6 were awarded.

Deadline February of each year.

[1142]
LEE & LOW BOOKS NEW VISIONS AWARD

Lee & Low Books
95 Madison Avenue, Suite 1205
New York, NY 10016
(212) 779-4400   Fax: (212) 683-1894
E-mail: general@leeandlow.com
Web: www.leeandlow.com

Summary To recognize and reward outstanding unpublished fantasy or mystery books for young readers by Hispanics and other writers of color.

Eligibility The contest is open to writers of color who are residents of the United States. Applicants must submit a manuscript of a fantasy, science fiction, or mystery book directed to readers at the middle grade or young adult level. They may not previously have published a middle grade or young adult novel published.

Financial Data The award is a $1,000 cash grant plus the standard publication contract, including the standard advance and royalties. The Honor Award winner receives a cash grant of $500.

Duration The competition is held annually.

Additional data This program began in 2012. Manuscripts may not be sent to any other publishers while under consideration for this award.

Number awarded 2 each year.

Deadline October of each year.

[1143]
LEE & LOW BOOKS NEW VOICES AWARD

Lee & Low Books
95 Madison Avenue, Suite 1205
New York, NY 10016
(212) 779-4400   Fax: (212) 683-1894
E-mail: general@leeandlow.com
Web: www.leeandlow.com

Summary To recognize and reward outstanding unpublished children's picture books by Hispanics and other writers of color.

Eligibility The contest is open to writers of color who are residents of the United States and who have not previously published a children's picture book. Writers who have published in other venues, (e.g., children's magazines, young adult fiction and nonfiction) are eligible. Manuscripts previously submitted to the sponsor are not eligible. Submissions should be no more than 1,500 words and must address the needs of children of color by providing stories with which they can identify and relate and that promote a greater understanding of each other. Submissions may be fiction or nonfiction for children between the ages of 5 and 12. Folklore and animal stories are not considered. Up to 2 submissions may be submitted per entrant.

Financial Data The award is a $1,000 cash grant plus the standard publication contract, including the standard advance and royalties. The Honor Award winner receives a cash grant of $500.

Duration The competition is held annually.

Additional data This program began in 2000. Manuscripts may not be sent to any other publishers while under consideration for this award.

Number awarded 2 each year.
Deadline September of each year.

[1144]
LEON BRADLEY SCHOLARSHIPS

American Association of School Personnel Administrators
Attn: Scholarship Program
11863 West 112th Street, Suite 100
Overland Park, KS 66210
(913) 327-1222   Fax: (913) 327-1223
E-mail: aaspa@aaspa.org
Web: www.aaspa.org/leon-bradley-scholarship

Summary To provide financial assistance to Hispanic and other minority undergraduates, paraprofessionals, and graduate students preparing for a career in teaching and school leadership at colleges in designated southeastern states.

Eligibility This program is open to members of minority groups (Hispanic, American Indian, Alaskan Native, Asian, Pacific Islander, Black, Middle Easterner) currently enrolled full time at a college or university in Alabama, Florida, Georgia, Kentucky, North Carolina, South Carolina, Tennessee, or Virginia. Applicants must be 1) undergraduates in their final year (including student teaching) of an initial teaching certification program; 2) paraprofessional career-changers in their final year (including student teaching) of an initial teaching certification program; or 3) graduate students who have served as a licensed teacher and are working on a school administrator credential. They must have an overall GPA of 3.0 or higher. Priority is given to applicants who 1) can demonstrate work experience that has been applied to college expenses; 2) have received other scholarship or financial aid support; or 3) are seeking initial certification and/or endorsement in a state-identified critical area.

Financial Data Stipends are $2,500 for undergraduates in their final year, $1,500 for paraprofessionals in their final year, and $1,500 for graduate students.

Duration 1 year.

Number awarded 4 each year: 1 undergraduate, 1 paraprofessional, and 2 graduate students.

Deadline May of each year.

[1145]
LETRAS LATINAS/RED HEN POETRY PRIZE

Red Hen Press
Attn: Production Coordinator
1335 North Lake Avenue, Suite 200
P.O. Box 40820
Pasadena, CA 91114
(626) 356-4760   Fax: (626) 356-9974
E-mail: productioncoordinator@redhen.org
Web: www.redhen.org

Summary To recognize and reward outstanding second or third collections of poems by Latino or Latina poets.

Eligibility This competition is open to Latino and Latina poets who have had 1 or 2 full-length books of poetry professionally published. Manuscripts must be 50 to 100 pages in length, in English; there are no restrictions on the style of poetry or subject matter.

Financial Data The award is $1,000, publication by Red Hen Press, and support for travel costs associated with further promotion of the winning book through readings in Los Angeles, Chicago, New York, and Washington, D.C.

Duration The competition is held biennially, in odd-numbered years.

Additional data This competition began in 2012, with the first 2 winners selected in that year and published in 2013 and 2015. The program is sponsored by Red Hen Press in partnership with the Institute for Latino Studies at the University of Notre Dame.

Number awarded 1 each even-numbered year.

Deadline January of each even-numbered year.

[1146]
LILLA JEWEL AWARD FOR WOMEN ARTISTS

McKenzie River Gathering Foundation
Attn: Office Manager
1235 S.E. Morrison Street, Suite A
Portland, OR 97214
(503) 289-1517   Toll Free: (800) 489-6743
Fax: (503) 232-1731   E-mail: info@mrgfoundation.org
Web: www.mrgfoundation.org

Summary To recognize and reward Hispanic and other women of color performance artists in Oregon who utilize the spoken word.

Eligibility Eligible to apply for this award are women artists in Oregon whose work relies on the spoken word and performance. Applicants must have demonstrated success as a spoken word artist and experience performing spoken word in front of a large audience. They must be interested in developing a work for presentation at the sponsoring organization's annual fundraising party. The performance may include music and mixed media. It should address progressive social, racial, economic, and/or environmental justice issues. Priority is given to women of color and those who identify as LGBT.

Financial Data The award is $2,500.

Duration The award is presented annually.

Number awarded 1 each year.

Deadline November of each year.

[1147]
LOFT SPOKEN WORD IMMERSION GRANTS

The Loft Literary Center
Attn: Immersion Grant Program Director
1011 Washington Avenue South, Suite 200
Minneapolis, MN 55415
(612) 215-2585   Fax: (612) 215-2576
E-mail: bphi@loft.org
Web: www.loft.org/programs__awards/grants__awards

Summary To provide funding to Hispanic and other spoken word poets of color who are interested in developing and implementing community learning and enrichment projects of their own design.

Eligibility This program is open to spoken word poets of color currently residing in the United States; the program definesnclude Latino/as, Chicano/as, Native Americans, Pacific Islanders, Africans, African Americans, Asians, South Asians, Asian Americans, Arabs, Middle Easterners, and mixed race. Applicants must proposed to develop and implement a project that enriches their art as well as the community's. Proposal objectives and activities may include, but are not limited to, personal artistic growth; developing and teaching workshops or open mics in a non-traditional space; research and immersion into community-specific art forms; multidisciplinary and cross-community spoken word projects; ELL, bilingual, and multilingual immersion; or improving speaking, performance, and presentation skills. Tuition for non-degree granting programs (e.g., writers' conferences, community-based education) may be approved, but tuition for classes leading to a degree is not eligible. Selection is based on quality of a work sample; merit of the project design (originality, feasibility, clarity of the stated objectives, community immersion and enrichment, artistic growth of the artist); and the applicant's potential ability to complete the project.

Financial Data The grant is $7,500.

Duration Projects must conclude within a year and a half.

Additional data Funding for this program comes from the Surdna Foundation.

Number awarded 4 each year, of whom 1 must be a resident of Minnesota.

Deadline October of each year.

[1148]
LYMAN T. JOHNSON POSTDOCTORAL FELLOWSHIP

University of Kentucky
Attn: Vice President for Research
311 Main Building, 0032
Lexington, KY 40506-0032
(859) 257-5090   Fax: (859) 323-2800
E-mail: vprgrants@uky.edu
Web: www.research.uky.edu

Summary To provide an opportunity for recent postdoctorates, especially Hispanics and other minorities, to conduct research at the University of Kentucky (U.K.).

Eligibility This program is open to U.S. citizens and permanent residents who have completed a doctoral degree within the past 2 years. Applicants must be interested in conducting an individualized research program under the mentorship of a U.K. professor. They should indicate, in their letter of application, how their participation in this program would contribute to the compelling interest of diversity at U.K. Race, ethnicity, and national origin are among the factors that contribute to diversity. Selection is based on evidence of scholarship with competitive potential for a tenure-track faculty appointment at a research university, compatibility of specific research interests with those in doctorate-granting units at U.K., quality of the research proposal, support from mentor and references, and effect of the appointment on the educational benefit of diversity within the research or professional area.

Financial Data The fellowship provides a stipend of $35,000 plus $5,000 for support of research activities.

Duration Up to 2 years.

Additional data In addition to conducting an individualized research program under the mentorship of a U.K. professor, fellows actively participate in research, teaching, and service to the university, their profession, and the community. This program began in 1992.

Number awarded 2 each year.

Deadline October of each year.

[1149]
MANY VOICES FELLOWSHIPS

Playwrights' Center
Attn: Artistic Programs Administrator
2301 East Franklin Avenue
Minneapolis, MN 55406-1024
(612) 332-7481, ext. 115   Fax: (612) 332-6037
E-mail: julia@pwcenter.org
Web: www.pwcenter.org/programs/many-voices-fellowships

Summary To provide funding to Hispanic and other playwrights of color from Minnesota and other states so they can spend a year in residence at the Playwrights' Center in Minneapolis.

Eligibility This program is open to playwrights of color who are citizens or permanent residents of the United States; residents of Minnesota and of other states are eligible. Applicants must be interested in playwriting and creating theater in a supportive artist community at the Playwrights' Center.

Financial Data Fellows receive a $10,000 stipend, $2,500 for living expenses, and $1,500 in play development funds.

Duration 9 months, beginning in October.

Additional data This program, which began in 1994, is funded by the Jerome Foundation. Fellows must be in residence at the Playwrights' Center for the duration of the program.

Number awarded 2 each year: 1 to a resident of Minnesota and 1 to a resident of any state.

Deadline November of each year.

[1150]
MARIAM K. CHAMBERLAIN FELLOWSHIP IN WOMEN AND PUBLIC POLICY

Institute for Women's Policy Research
Attn: Fellowship Coordinator
1200 18th Street, N.W., Suite 301
Washington, DC 20036
(202) 785-5100   Fax: (202) 833-4362
E-mail: MKCfellowship@iwpr.org
Web: www.iwpr.org/about/fellowships

Summary To provide work experience at the Institute for Women's Policy Research (IWPR) to Hispanic and other college graduates and graduate students who are from underrepresented groups and interested in economic justice for women.

Eligibility This program is open to scholars interested in conducting research projects on policies that affect women. Current topics of interest include the quality of women's jobs, including wages, paid sick leave, paid family leave, and workplace flexibility; increasing access to higher education and non-traditional jobs for low-income women and women with children; examining socioeconomic supports for women in job training programs, and for college students with children; the economic status of women and girls, women of color, and immigrant women across the United States. Applicants should have at least a bachelor's degree in social science (e.g., psychology, education, sociology, public policy), statistics, economics, mathematics, or women's studies. Graduate work is desirable but not required. They should have strong quantitative and library research skills and knowledge of women's issues. Familiarity with Microsoft Word and Excel is required; knowledge of STATA, SPSS, SAS, or graphics software is a plus. Members of underrepresented groups, based on race, color, religion, gender, national origin, age, disability, marital or veteran status, sexual orientation, or any other legally protected status, are especially encouraged to apply.

Financial Data The stipend is $31,000 and includes health insurance and a public transportation stipend.

Duration 9 months, beginning in September.

Additional data The institute is a nonprofit, scientific research organization that works primarily on issues related to equal opportunity and economic and social justice for women. Research topics vary each year but relate to women and public policy.

Number awarded 1 each year.

Deadline February of each year.

[1151]
MARTIN LUTHER KING, JR. MEMORIAL SCHOLARSHIP FUND

California Teachers Association
Attn: CTA Foundation for Teaching and Learning
1705 Murchison Drive
P.O. Box 921
Burlingame, CA 94011-0921
(650) 697-1400   E-mail: scholarships@cta.org
Web: www.cta.org

Summary To provide financial assistance for college or graduate school to Hispanic and other racial and ethnic minorities who are members of the California Teachers Association (CTA), children of members, or members of the Student CTA.

Eligibility This program is open to members of racial or ethnic minority groups (Hispanics, African Americans, American Indians/Alaska Natives, and Asians/Pacific Islanders) who are 1) active CTA members; 2) dependent children of active, retired, or deceased CTA members; or 3) members of Student CTA. Applicants must be interested in preparing for a teaching career in public education or already engaged in such a career.

Financial Data Stipends vary each year; recently, they ranged up to $6,000.

Duration 1 year.

Number awarded Varies each year; recently, 24 were awarded: 1 to a CTA member, 10 to children of CTA members, and 13 to Student CTA members.

Deadline February of each year.

[1152]
MATHEMATICAL SCIENCES POSTDOCTORAL RESEARCH FELLOWSHIPS

National Science Foundation
Directorate for Mathematical and Physical Sciences
Attn: Division of Mathematical Sciences
4201 Wilson Boulevard, Room 1025N
Arlington, VA 22230
(703) 292-4856   Fax: (703) 292-9032
TDD: (800) 281-8749   E-mail: bpalka@nsf.gov
Web: www.nsf.gov

Summary To provide financial assistance to postdoctorates, especially Hispanics and other underrepresented minorities, who are interested in pursuing research training in mathematics in the United States or any other country.

Eligibility Applicants for these fellowships must 1) be U.S. citizens, nationals, or permanent residents; 2) have earned a Ph.D. in a mathematical science or have had equivalent research training and experience; 3) have held the Ph.D. for no more than 2 years; and 4) have not previously held any other postdoctoral fellowship from the National Science Foundation (NSF) or been offered an award from this program. They must be proposing to conduct a program of postdoctoral research training at an appropriate nonprofit U.S. institution, including government laboratories, national laboratories, and privately sponsored nonprofit institutes, as well as institutions of higher education in any country. A senior scientist at the institution must indicate availability for consultation and agreement to work with the fellow. In the selection process, consideration is given to the achievement of societally relevant outcomes, including full participation of women, persons with disabilities, and underrepresented minorities.

Financial Data The total grant is $150,000, consisting of 3 components: 1) a monthly stipend of $5,000 for full-time support or $2,500 for half-time support, paid directly to the fellow; 2) a research allowance of $12,000, also paid directly to the fellow; and 3) an institutional allowance of $9,000, paid to the host institution for fringe benefits (including health insurance payments for the fellow) and expenses incurred in support of the fellow, such as space, equipment, and general purpose supplies. Fellows who wish to conduct their training at an international host institution may apply for an additional allowance of up to $10,000.

Duration Fellows may select either of 2 options: the research fellowship option provides full-time support for any 18 academic-year months in a 3-year period, in intervals not shorter than 3 consecutive months; the research instructorship option provides a combination of full-time and half-time support over a period of 3 academic years. Both options include 6 summer months.

Number awarded 30 to 33 each year. A total of $5.0 million is available for this program annually.

Deadline October of each year.

[1153]
MICKEY LELAND ENERGY FELLOWSHIPS

Oak Ridge Institute for Science and Education
Attn: MLEF Fellowship Program
1299 Bethel Valley Road, Building SC-200
P.O. Box 117, MS 36
Oak Ridge, TN 37831-0117
(865) 574-6440   Fax: (865) 576-0734
E-mail: barbara.dunkin@orau.org
Web: orise.orau.gov/mlef/index.html

Summary To provide summer work experience at fossil energy sites of the Department of Energy (DOE) to Hispanic and other underrepresented minority and female students or postdoctorates.

Eligibility This program is open to U.S. citizens currently enrolled full time at an accredited college or university. Applicants must be undergraduate, graduate, or postdoctoral students in fields of science, technology (IT), engineering, or mathematics (STEM) and have a GPA of 3.0 or higher. They must be interested in a summer work experience at a DOE fossil energy research facility. Along with their application, they must submit a 100-word statement on why they want to participate in this program. A goal of the program is to recruit women and underrepresented minorities into careers related to fossil energy, although all qualified students are encouraged to apply.

Financial Data Weekly stipends are $600 for undergraduates, $750 for master's degree students, or $850 for doctoral and postdoctoral students. Travel costs for a round trip to and from the site and for a trip to a designated place for technical presentations are also paid.

Duration 10 weeks during the summer.

Additional data This program began as 3 separate activities: the Historically Black Colleges and Universities Internship Program established in 1995, the Hispanic Internship Program established in 1998, and the Tribal Colleges and Universities Internship Program, established in 2000. Those 3 programs were merged into the Fossil Energy Minority Education Initiative, renamed the Mickey Leland Energy Fellowship Program in 2000. Sites to which interns may be assigned include the National Energy Technology Laboratory (Morgantown, West Virginia, Albany, Oregon and Pittsburgh, Pennsylvania), Pacific Northwest National Laboratory (Richland, Washington), Sandia National Laboratory (Livermore, California), Lawrence Berkeley National Laboratory (Berkeley, California), Los Alamos National Laboratory (Los Alamos, New Mexico), Strategic Petroleum Reserve Project Management Office (New Orleans, Louisiana), or U.S. Department of Energy Headquarters (Washington, D.C.).

Number awarded Varies each year; recently, 30 students participated in this program.

Deadline December of each year.

[1154]
MIGRANT HEALTH SCHOLARSHIPS

National Center for Farmworker Health, Inc.
Attn: Migrant Health Scholarship
1770 FM 967
Buda, TX 78610
(512) 312-2700   Toll Free: (800) 531-5120
Fax: (512) 312-2600   E-mail: favre@ncfh.org
Web: www.ncfh.org/scholarships.html

Summary To provide financial assistance to people working in the migrant health field, especially those with a farmworker background, who are interested in additional education.

Eligibility This program is open to staff in clinical, administrative, and support positions at community and migrant health centers who are interested in obtaining additional education at the undergraduate or graduate level. Applicants must submit a 1-page personal statement discussing such issues as why they are interested in migrant health, personal experiences and achievements, future career goals, commitment to migrant health, and financial need. Preference is given to applicants with a farmworker background.

Financial Data The stipend is $1,000.

Duration 1 year.

Additional data This program began in 1984.

Number awarded Varies each year; recently, 6 were awarded. Since the program was established, it has awarded 210 of these scholarships.

Deadline March of each year.

[1155]
MINORITY FACULTY DEVELOPMENT SCHOLARSHIP AWARD IN PHYSICAL THERAPY

American Physical Therapy Association
Attn: Honors and Awards Program
1111 North Fairfax Street
Alexandria, VA 22314-1488
(703) 684-APTA   Toll Free: (800) 999-APTA, ext. 8082
Fax: (703) 684-7343   TDD: (703) 683-6748
E-mail: honorsandawards@apta.org
Web: www.apta.org

Summary To provide financial assistance to Hispanic and other minority faculty members in physical therapy who are interested in working on a post-professional doctoral degree.

Eligibility This program is open to U.S. citizens and permanent residents who are members of the following minority groups: Hispanic/Latino, African American or Black, Asian, Native Hawaiian or other Pacific Islander, or American Indian or Alaska Native. Applicants must be full-time faculty members, teaching in an accredited or developing professional physical therapist education program, who will have completed the equivalent of 2 full semesters of post-professional doctoral course work. They must possess a license to practice physical therapy in a U.S. jurisdiction and be enrolled as a student in an accredited post-professional doctoral program whose content has a demonstrated relationship to physical therapy. Along with their application, they must submit a personal essay on their professional goals, including their plans to contribute to the profession and minority services. Selection is based on contributions in the area of minority affairs and services and contributions to the profession of physical therapy. Preference is given to members of the American Physical Therapy Association (APTA).

Financial Data A stipend is awarded (amount not specified).

Duration 1 year.

Additional data This program began in 1999.

Number awarded 1 or more each year.

Deadline November of each year.

[1156]
MINORITY POSTDOCTORAL FELLOWSHIP AWARDS IN DIABETES

American Diabetes Association
Attn: Research Programs
1701 North Beauregard Street
Alexandria, VA 22311
(703) 549-1500, ext. 2362   Toll Free: (800) DIABETES
Fax: (703) 549-1715
E-mail: grantquestions@diabetes.org
Web: professional.diabetes.org

Summary To provide financial assistance to Hispanic and other minority postdoctoral fellows for additional research training in diabetes.

Eligibility This program is open to members of underrepresented minority groups (Hispanic or Latino, African American, American Indian or Alaskan Native, Native Hawaiian or Pacific Islander) who have an M.D., Ph.D., D.O., D.P.M., or Pharm.D. degree and less than 10 years of postdoctoral experience. Applicants must be authorized to work in the United States or its territories. They must be interested in a program of research (basic, clinical, or translational) training related to diabetes under the supervision of a mentor. Selection is based on the potential of the project and investigator to significantly impact the field of diabetes research and/or advance the prevention, cure or treatment of diabetes; applicant's scientific potential and potential for establishing a successful and independent career in diabetes-related research; quality and originality of the research proposal and experimental approach, and its relevance to diabetes; tangible evidence of the applicant's performance in research in the form of peer-reviewed scientific publications or equivalent; and evidence of a strong commitment from the mentor toward providing quality training and support in preparation for an independent career in diabetes research.

Financial Data The investigator's stipend ranges from $42,000 to $55,272 per year, depending on the number of years of postdoctoral experience. Other support includes a $5,000 training allowance (travel to diabetes-related scientific meetings, computer, books, publication costs, equipment, training courses/workshops, reagents, laboratory supplies) and a $5,000 fringe benefits allowance. Indirect costs are not covered.

Duration Up to 3 years.

Number awarded Varies each year.

Deadline April of each year.

[1157]
MLA PRIZE IN UNITED STATES LATINA AND LATINO AND CHICANA AND CHICANO LITERARY AND CULTURAL STUDIES

Modern Language Association of America
Attn: Office of Programs
85 Broad Street, Suite 500
New York, NY 10004-2434
(646) 576-5141   Fax: (646) 458-0030
E-mail: awards@mla.org
Web: www.mla.org

Summary To recognize and reward members of the Modern Language Association (MLA) who have written outstanding books on Latina, Latino, Chicana, or Chicano literature.

Eligibility This award is presented to authors of outstanding scholarly studies in any language of Latina and Latino and Chicana and Chicano literature or culture published the previous year. Books that are primarily translations are not eligible. Authors must be members of MLA.

Financial Data The prize is $1,000 and a certificate.

Duration The prize is awarded biennially.

Additional data This prize was first awarded in 2002.

Number awarded 1 each odd-numbered year.

Deadline April of each odd-numbered year.

[1158]
MORENO/RANGEL LEGISLATIVE LEADERSHIP PROGRAM

Mexican American Legislative Leadership Foundation
Attn: Legislative Leadership Program
202 West 13th Street
Austin, TX 78701
(512) 499-0804   Fax: (512) 480-8313
E-mail: director@mallfoundation.org
Web: mallfoundation.org

Summary To provide an opportunity for undergraduate and graduate students in Texas to gain work experience on the staff of members of the Mexican American Legislative Caucus of the Texas state legislature.

Eligibility This program is open to undergraduate and graduate students who are enrolled at 2- and 4-year colleges and universities in Texas and have completed at least 60 credit hours of work; recent graduates are also welcome to apply. Applicants must be interested in working full time on the staff of a Latino member of the Texas House of Representatives. They must be at least 21 years of age, have a record of community and extracurricular involvement, be able to demonstrate excellent composition and communication skills, and have a GPA of 2.5 or higher. Along with their application, they must submit an essay of 500 to 750 words in which they describe the family, work, educational, and community experiences that led them to apply for this program; they should also explain how those experiences relate to their long-term personal goals and how this legislative experience will contribute to their future leadership within the Latino community.

Financial Data Participants receive a monthly stipend (amount not specified) to assist with living expenses.

Duration 5 months, beginning in January.

Additional data This program is named after Paul C. Moreno (the longest-serving Hispanic member of the Texas House of Representatives) and Irma Rangel (the first Mexican American woman to serve in the Texas Legislature).

Number awarded Varies each year; recently, 6 of these internships/fellowships were awarded.

Deadline November of each year.

[1159]
MULTICULTURAL AUDIENCE DEVELOPMENT INITIATIVE INTERNSHIPS

Metropolitan Museum of Art
Attn: Internship Programs
1000 Fifth Avenue
New York, NY 10028-0198
(212) 570-3710   Fax: (212) 570-3782
E-mail: mmainterns@metmuseum.org
Web: www.metmuseum.org

Summary To provide summer work experience at the Metropolitan Museum of Art to Hispanic and other college undergraduates, graduate students, and recent graduates from diverse backgrounds.

Eligibility This program is open to members of diverse groups who are undergraduate juniors and seniors, students currently working on a master's degree, or individuals who completed a bachelor's or master's degree within the past year. Ph.D. students may be eligible to apply during the first 12 months of their program, provided they have not yet achieved candidacy. Students from various academic backgrounds are encouraged to apply, but they must be interested in preparing for a career in the arts and museum fields. Freshmen and sophomores are not eligible.

Financial Data The stipend is $3,750.

Duration 10 weeks, beginning in June.

Additional data Interns are assigned to departmental projects (curatorial, administration, or education) at the Metropolitan Museum of Art; other assignments may include giving gallery talks and working at the Visitor Information Center.

The assignment is for 35 hours a week. The internships are funded by the Multicultural Audience Initiative at the museum.

Number awarded 1 or more each year.

Deadline January of each year.

[1160]
NATIONAL ALUMNI CHAPTER GRANTS

Kappa Omicron Nu
Attn: Awards Committee
1749 Hamilton Road, Suite 106
Okemos, MI 48864
(517) 351-8335   Fax: (517) 351-8336
E-mail: info@kon.org
Web: www.kon.org/awards/grants.html

Summary To provide financial assistance to members, especially Hispanics and other underrepresented minorities, of Kappa Omicron Nu, an honor society in the human sciences, who are interested in conducting research.

Eligibility This program is open to 1) individual scholars who are members of the society; and 2) research teams where the leader is a member of the society. Applicants must be interested in conducting research in family and consumer sciences or any of its related specializations. The research approach should be integrative in nature and shall make connections across specializations to pursue problems or questions. Special consideration is given to research that studies the cultural and religious differences affecting leadership, especially Hispanic, Asian, and Native American. Another topic of interest is the exploration of how minority students "strike out on their own" in career development.

Financial Data The grant is $1,000.

Duration 1 year; multi-year funding may be accomplished by including a multi-year management plan in the initial proposal and reporting successful accomplishment of previous objectives annually.

Additional data The sponsor defines the "human sciences" to include athletic training, design, education, exercise science, family and consumer sciences, financial planning, food science and human nutrition, gerontology, health sciences, hotel/restaurant management, human development, interior design and human environment, kinesiology, leadership, merchandising management, policy analysis and management, social work, textiles and apparel, and wellness. Funding for these grants is provided by the National Alumni Chapter of Kappa Omicron Nu.

Number awarded 1 or more each year.

Deadline February of each year.

[1161]
NATIONAL CENTER FOR ATMOSPHERIC RESEARCH POSTDOCTORAL FELLOWSHIPS

National Center for Atmospheric Research
Attn: Advanced Study Program
3090 Center Green Drive
P.O. Box 3000
Boulder, CO 80307-3000
(303) 497-1601   Fax: (303) 497-1646
E-mail: asp-apply@asp.ucar.edu
Web: www.asp.ucar.edu/pdfp/pd_announcement.php

Summary To provide funding to recent doctorates, especially Hispanics and other minorities, who wish to conduct research at the National Center for Atmospheric Research (NCAR) in Boulder, Colorado.

Eligibility This program is open to recent Ph.D.s and Sc.D.s in atmospheric sciences as well as specialists from such disciplines as applied mathematics, biology, chemistry, computer science, economics, engineering, geography, geology, physics, and science education. Applicants must be interested in conducting research at the center in atmospheric sciences and global change. Selection is based on the applicant's scientific capability and potential, originality and independence, and the match between their interests and the research opportunities at the center. Applications from women and minorities are encouraged.

Financial Data The stipend is $60,500 in the first year and $62,000 in the second year. Fellows also receive life and health insurance, a relocation allowance, an allowance of $750 for moving and storing personal belongings, and scientific travel and registration fee reimbursement up to $3,500 per year.

Duration 2 years.

Additional data NCAR is operated by the University Corporation for Atmospheric Research (a consortium of universities and research institutes) and sponsored by the National Science Foundation.

Number awarded Varies; currently, up to 9 each year.

Deadline January of each year.

[1162]
NATIONAL ENDOWMENT FOR THE HUMANITIES COLLABORATIVE RESEARCH GRANTS

National Endowment for the Humanities
Attn: Division of Research Programs
400 Seventh Street, S.W.
Washington, DC 20506
(202) 606-8200   Toll Free: (800) NEH-1121
Fax: (202) 606-8204   TDD: (866) 372-2930
E-mail: collaborative@neh.gov
Web: www.neh.gov

Summary To provide funding to teams of scholars, especially faculty at Hispanic and other Minority Serving Institutions, who wish to conduct research in the humanities.

Eligibility This program is open to 1) U.S. citizens and foreign nationals who have been living in the United States or its jurisdictions for at least 3 years; 2) state and local governmental agencies; and 3) nonprofit, tax-exempt institutions and organizations in the United States. It supports original research undertaken by a team of 2 or more scholars or research coordinated by an individual scholar that, because of its scope or complexity, requires additional staff or resources beyond the individual's salary. Eligible projects include research that significantly adds to knowledge and understanding in the humanities; archaeology projects that include the interpretation and dissemination of results; and conferences on topics of major importance in the humanities that will benefit scholarly research. Selection is based on 1) the intellectual significance of the project, including its potential contribution to scholarship in the humanities, the likelihood that it will stimulate new research, its relationship to larger themes in the humanities, and the significance of the material on which the project is based; 2) the pertinence of the research questions being posed, the appropriateness of research methods or conference design, the feasibility of the work plan, the quality of samples, and the appropriateness of the field work, the archival or source materials, and the research site; 3) the qualifications, expertise, and levels of commitment to the project of the project director and key project staff or contributors, and the appropriateness of the staff to the goals of the project; 4) soundness of the dissemination and access plans; and 5) the potential for success, including the likelihood that the project will be successfully completed within the projected time frame. The program encourages submission of applications from faculty at Hispanic Serving Institutions, Historically Black Colleges and Universities, and Tribal Colleges and Universities.

Financial Data Grants range from $25,000 to $100,000 per year. Awards for conferences range from $15,000 t0 $65,000. The use of federal matching funds in encouraged. Normally, support does not exceed 80% of total costs.

Duration 1 to 3 years.

Additional data All grantees are expected to publish or in other ways to disseminate the results of their work.

Number awarded Approximately 10 each year.

Deadline December of each year.

[1163]
NATIONAL ENDOWMENT FOR THE HUMANITIES FELLOWSHIPS

National Endowment for the Humanities
Attn: Division of Research Programs
400 Seventh Street, S.W.
Washington, DC 20506
(202) 606-8200   Toll Free: (800) NEH-1121
Fax: (202) 606-8204   TDD: (866) 372-2930
E-mail: fellowships@neh.gov
Web: www.neh.gov/grants/research/fellowships

Summary To provide funding to scholars and faculty members, especially faculty at Hispanic and other Minority Serving Institutions, who wish to conduct research in the humanities.

Eligibility This program is open to faculty and staff of colleges, universities, primary schools, and secondary schools, as well as independent scholars and writers. Applicants must be U.S. citizens or foreign nationals who have resided in the United States or its jurisdictions for at least 3 years. The proposed project should contribute to scholarly knowledge or to the public's understanding of the humanities, usually in the form of scholarly articles, monographs on specialized subjects, books on broad topics, archaeological site reports, translations, editions, or other scholarly tools. Applicants do not need to have advanced degrees, but students currently enrolled in a degree-granting program are ineligible. Grants are not provided for curriculum development; empirical social science research, unless part of a larger humanities project; specific policy studies; the development of pedagogical tools; educational or technical impact assessments; the creation or enhancement of databases, unless part of a larger interpretive project; inventories of collections; the writing of autobiographies or memoirs; the writing of guide books, how-to books, or self-help books; preparation or revision of textbooks; works in the creative or performing arts; projects that seek to promote a particular political, philosophical, religious, or ideological point of view; projects that advocate a particular program of social action; works in the creative or performing arts; or doctoral dissertations or theses. Selection is based on 1) the intellectual significance of the project to the humanities,

including its value to scholars and general audiences in the humanities; 2) the quality or promise of quality of the applicant's work as an interpreter of the humanities; 3) the quality of the conception, definition, organization, and description of the project; 4) the feasibility of the proposed plan of work; and 5) the likelihood that the applicant will complete the project. The program encourages submission of applications from faculty at Hispanic Serving Institutions, Historically Black Colleges and Universities, and Tribal Colleges and Universities.

Financial Data The grant is $4,200 per month, to a maximum of $50,400 for 12 months.

Duration 6 to 12 months.

Additional data Fellows may hold other fellowships or grants in support of the same project during their tenure, including sabbaticals and grants from their own institutions.

Number awarded Approximately 80 each year.

Deadline April of each year.

[1164]
NATIONAL ENDOWMENT FOR THE HUMANITIES SUMMER STIPENDS

National Endowment for the Humanities
Attn: Division of Research Programs
400 Seventh Street, S.W.
Washington, DC 20506
(202) 606-8200   Toll Free: (800) NEH-1121
Fax: (202) 606-8204   TDD: (866) 372-2930
E-mail: stipends@neh.gov
Web: www.neh.gov/grants/research/summer-stipends

Summary To provide funding to scholars and other professionals, especially faculty at Hispanic and other Minority Serving Institutions, who are interested in conducting research in the humanities during the summer.

Eligibility Faculty members teaching full time in U.S. colleges and universities may be nominated by their schools for these awards. Each school may nominate 2 candidates. Also eligible are independent scholars not affiliated with a college or university, non-faculty college and university staff members who will not be teaching during the academic year preceding the grant tenure, and adjunct and part-time faculty with academic appointments that terminate by the summer of the grant tenure; such applicants do not require nomination. All applicants must be U.S. citizens or foreign nationals who have lived in the United States or its territories for 3 years prior to the application deadline. They must be proposing to pursue research in the humanities that contributes to scholarly knowledge or to the public's understanding of the humanities, normally through scholarly articles, a monograph on a specialized subject, a book on a broad topic, an archaeological site report, a translation, an edition, a database, or other scholarly tools. Support is not provided for research for doctoral dissertations or theses by students enrolled in a degree program; specific policy studies or educational or technical impact assessments; preparation or publication of textbooks; studying teaching methods or theories, surveys of courses and programs, or curriculum development; works in the creative or performing arts; projects that seek to promote a particular political, philosophical, religious, or ideological point of view; projects that advocate a particular program of social action; or creating inventories of collections. Persons who have held a major fellowship or research grant or its equivalent during any of the preceding 3 academic years are ineligible. Selection is based on the intellectual significance of the proposed project, including its value to humanities scholars, general audiences, or both; the quality or promise of quality of the applicant's work as an interpreter of the humanities; the quality of the conception, definition, organization, and description of the proposed project; the feasibility of the proposed plan of work; and the likelihood that the applicant will complete the project. The program encourages submission of applications from faculty at Hispanic Serving Institutions, Historically Black Colleges and Universities, and Tribal Colleges and Universities.

Financial Data The stipend is $6,000.

Duration 2 months during the summer.

Additional data Previous recipients may reapply after 5 years. Recipients may hold other research grants during the tenure of their awards, and they must devote full time to their projects for the 2 months of their tenure.

Number awarded Approximately 81 each year.

Deadline September of each year.

[1165]
NATIONAL LATINO PLAYWRITING AWARD

Arizona Theatre Company
Attn: Literary Manager
343 South Scott Avenue
Tucson, AZ 85701
(520) 884-8210, ext. 7508   Fax: (520) 628-9129
E-mail: info@arizonatheatre.org
Web: www.arizonatheatre.org

Summary To recognize and reward outstanding unpublished, unproduced plays written by Latino/Latinas in the United States or Mexico.

Eligibility This program is open to all Latino playwrights currently residing in the United States, its territories, or Mexico. Applicants may submit scripts in English, Spanish and English, or solely in Spanish; scripts in Spanish must be accompanied by an English translation. Only unpublished, unproduced plays are eligible. Full-length and 1-act plays (at least 50 pages in length) are accepted.

Financial Data The prize is $1,000 and possible inclusion in Cafe Bohemia, the Arizona Theatre Company's play reading series.

Duration The competition is held annually.

Additional data Previously, this award was known as the National Hispanic Playwriting Contest.

Number awarded 1 each year.

Deadline December of each year.

[1166]
NATIONAL URBAN FELLOWS PROGRAM

National Urban Fellows, Inc.
Attn: Program Director
1120 Avenue of the Americas, Fourth Floor
New York, NY 10036
(212) 730-1700   Fax: (212) 730-1823
E-mail: info@nuf.org
Web: www.nuf.org/fellows-overview

Summary To provide mid-career public sector professionals, especially Hispanics and other people of color, with an opportunity to strengthen leadership skills through a master's degree program coupled with a mentorship.

Eligibility This program is open to U.S. citizens who have a bachelor's degree, have at 5 to 7 years of professional work experience with 2 years in a management capacity, have demonstrated leadership capacity with potential for further growth, have a GPA of 3.0 or higher, and can demonstrate a commitment to public service. Applicants must submit a 1-page autobiographical statement, a 2-page personal statement, and a 2-page statement on their career goals. They may be of any racial or ethnic background, but the program's goal is to increase the number of competent administrators from underrepresented ethnic and cultural groups at all levels of public and private urban management organizations. Semifinalists are interviewed.

Financial Data The stipend is $25,000. Fellows are required to pay a $500 registration fee and a $7,500 co-investment tuition payment upon acceptance and enrollment in the program.

Duration 14 months.

Additional data The program begins with a summer semester of study at Bernard M. Baruch College of the City University of New York. Following this, fellows spend 9 months in mentorship assignments with a senior administrator in a government agency, a major nonprofit, or a foundation. The final summer is spent in another semester of study at Baruch College. Fellows who successfully complete all requirements are granted a master's of public administration from that college. A $150 processing fee must accompany each application.

Number awarded Approximately 40 to 50 each year.

Deadline December of each year.

[1167]
NBCC MINORITY FELLOWSHIP PROGRAM

National Board for Certified Counselors
Attn: NBCC Foundation
3 Terrace Way
Greensboro, NC 27403
(336) 232-0376   Fax: (336) 232-0010
E-mail: foundation@nbcc.org
Web: nbccf-mfpdr.applicantstack.com/x/detail/a2b3qvixcgjm

Summary To provide financial assistance to doctoral candidates, especially Hispanics and those from other racially and ethnically diverse populations, who are interested in working on a degree in mental health and/or substance abuse counseling.

Eligibility This program is open to U.S. citizens and permanent residents who are enrolled full time in an accredited doctoral degree mental health and/or substance abuse and addictions counseling program. Applicants must have a National Certified Counselor or equivalent credential. They must commit to provide mental health and substance abuse services to racially and ethnically diverse populations. Hispanics/Latinos, African Americans, Alaska Natives, American Indians, Asian Americans, Native Hawaiians, and Pacific Islanders are especially encouraged to apply. Applicants must be able to commit to providing substance abuse and addictions counseling services to underserved minority populations for at least 2 years after graduation.

Financial Data The stipend is $20,000.

Duration 1 year.

Additional data This program began in 2012 with support from the Substance Abuse and Mental Health Services Administration.

Number awarded 23 each year.

Deadline June of each year.

[1168]
NEH-MELLON FELLOWSHIPS FOR DIGITAL PUBLICATION

National Endowment for the Humanities
Attn: Division of Research Programs
400 Seventh Street, S.W.
Washington, DC 20506
(202) 606-8200   Toll Free: (800) NEH-1121
Fax: (202) 606-8204   TDD: (866) 372-2930
E-mail: fellowships@neh.gov
Web: www.neh.gov

Summary To provide funding to scholars and faculty members, especially those at Hispanic and other Minority Serving Institutions, who wish to conduct research in the humanities that requires digital expression and digital publication.

Eligibility This program is open to faculty and staff of colleges, universities, primary schools, and secondary schools, as well as independent scholars and writers. Applicants must be U.S. citizens or foreign nationals who have resided in the United States or its jurisdictions for at least 3 years. The proposed project should require digital publication as essential to the project's research goals. The projects must be conceived as digital because the nature of the research and the topics being addressed demand presentation beyond traditional print publication. They should incorporate visual, audio, and/or other multimedia materials or flexible reading pathways that could not be included in traditional published books. Applicants do not need to have advanced degrees, but students currently enrolled in a degree-granting program are ineligible. Grants are not provided for curriculum development; empirical social science research, unless part of a larger humanities project; specific policy studies; the development of pedagogical tools; educational or technical impact assessments; the creation or enhancement of databases, unless part of a larger interpretive project; inventories of collections; the writing of autobiographies or memoirs; the writing of guide books, how-to books, or self-help books; preparation or revision of textbooks; works in the creative or performing arts; projects that seek to promote a particular political, philosophical, religious, or ideological point of view; projects that advocate a particular program of social action; works in the creative or performing arts; or doctoral dissertations or theses. Selection is based on 1) the intellectual significance of the project to the humanities, including its value to scholars and general audiences in the humanities; 2) the quality or promise of quality of the applicant's work as an interpreter of the humanities; 3) the quality of the conception, definition, organization, and description of the project; 4) the feasibility of the proposed plan of work; and 5) the likelihood that the applicant will complete the project. The program encourages submission of applications from faculty at Hispanic Serving Institutions, Historically Black Colleges and Universities, and Tribal Colleges and Universities.

Financial Data The grant is $4,200 per month, to a maximum of $50,400 for 12 months.

Duration 6 to 12 months.

Additional data Fellows may hold other fellowships or grants in support of the same project during their tenure, including sabbaticals and grants from their own institutions. This program is a collaboration between the National Endowment for the Humanities (NEH) and the Andrew W. Mellon Foundation.

Number awarded 1 or more each year.

Deadline April of each year.

[1169]
NEW INITIATIVES GRANTS

Kappa Omicron Nu
Attn: Awards Committee
1749 Hamilton Road, Suite 106
Okemos, MI 48864
(517) 351-8335   Fax: (517) 351-8336
E-mail: info@kon.org
Web: www.kon.org/awards/grants.html

Summary To provide financial assistance to members, especially Hispanic and other minorities, of Kappa Omicron Nu, an honor society in the human sciences, who are interested in conducting research.

Eligibility This program is open to 1) individual members of the society; and 2) research teams where the leader is a member of the society. Applicants must be interested in conducting research in family and consumer sciences or any of its related specializations. The research approach should be integrative in nature and must make connections across specializations to pursue problems or questions. Special consideration is given to research that studies the cultural and religious differences that affect leadership, especially Hispanic, Asian, and Native American. Another topic of interest is the exploration of how minority students "strike out on their own" in career development.

Financial Data The maximum grant is $3,000.

Duration 1 year; multi-year funding may be accomplished by including a multi-year management plan in the initial proposal and reporting successful accomplishment of previous objectives annually.

Additional data The sponsor defines the "human sciences" to include athletic training, design, education, exercise science, family and consumer sciences, financial planning, food science and human nutrition, gerontology, health sciences, hotel/restaurant management, human development, interior design and human environment, kinesiology, leadership, merchandising management, policy analysis and management, social work, textiles and apparel, and wellness. Funding for these grants is provided by the New Initiatives Fund of Kappa Omicron Nu.

Number awarded 1 or more each year.

Deadline February of each year.

[1170]
NEW YORK FOUNDATION FOR THE ARTS ARTISTS' FELLOWSHIPS

New York Foundation for the Arts
20 Jay Street, Seventh Floor
Brooklyn, NY 11202
(212) 366-6900   Fax: (212) 366-1778
E-mail: fellowships@nyfa.org
Web: www.nyfa.org/Content/Show/Artists'%20Fellowships

Summary   To provide funding for career development to creative artists living and working in the state of New York, especially Hispanics and members of other diverse groups.
Eligibility   Artists in New York who are more than 18 years of age are eligible to apply for this program if they are not currently enrolled in a degree program. Applicants must have lived in the state for at least 2 years at the time of application. They are required to submit, along with the application form, samples of current work. Awards are presented in a 3-year cycle with 5 fields each year: crafts/sculpture, printmaking/drawing/book arts, nonfiction literature, poetry, and digital/electronic arts (2017); fiction, folk/traditional arts, interdisciplinary work, painting, and video/film (2018); and architecture/environmental structures/design, choreography, music/sound, photography, and playwriting/screenwriting (2019). Selection is based on artistic excellence. The program is committed to supporting artists of diverse cultural, sexual, and ethnic backgrounds.
Financial Data   The grant is $7,000. Some special awards are larger.
Duration   1 year.
Additional data   Since this program began in 1985, the sponsor has awarded more than $27 million to more than 4,000 artists. Named awards include the Geri Ashur Screenwriting Award (for $10,000), the Gregory Millard Fellowships (supported by the New York City Department of Cultural Affairs for artists in several categories), the Lily Auchincloss Foundation Fellow (painting), the Deutsche Bank Americas Foundation Fellow (painting), and the Basil H. Alkazzi Award for Excellence (which awards $40,000 to 2 painters). Major funding for this program is provided by the New York State Council on the Arts and the New York City Department of Cultural Affairs. Other support is provided by the Lily Auchincloss Foundation, Deutsche Bank Americas Foundation, and the Milton & Sally Avery Arts Foundation. Recipients must perform a public service activity coordinated by the Artists and Audiences Exchange.
Number awarded   Varies each year; recently, 91 of these fellowships, worth $642,000, were awarded.
Deadline   January of each year.

[1171]
NOTRE DAME INSTITUTE FOR ADVANCED STUDY RESIDENTIAL FELLOWSHIPS

University of Notre Dame
Institute for Advanced Study
Attn: Programs Administrator
1124 Flanner Hall
Notre Dame, IN 46556
(574) 631-1305   Fax: (574) 631-8997
E-mail: csherman@nd.edu
Web: ndias.nd.edu/fellowships/residential

Summary   To provide funding to scholars, especially Hispanics and members of other underrepresented groups at all levels, who are interested in conducting research on topics of interest to the Notre Dame Institute for Advanced Study (NDIAS) while in residence at the institute.
Eligibility   This program is open to faculty, scholars, public intellectuals, fellows from other institutes, and professional researchers in all disciplines, including the arts, engineering, the humanities, law, and the natural, social, and physical sciences. Applicants must be interested in conducting research that aligns with the intellectual orientation of the NDIAS, which asks scholars "to include questions of values in their analyses, to integrate diverse disciplines, and to ask how their findings advance civilization." They must be able to demonstrate excellent records of scholarly, artistic, or research accomplishment in their field; ability to interact with other fellows and to engage in collegial discussions of research presentations; a willingness to contribute to a cooperative community of scholars; and projects that touch on normative, integrative, or ultimate questions, especially as the involve the Catholic intellectual tradition. Applications are especially encouraged from traditionally underrepresented groups. There are no citizenship requirements; non-U.S. nationals are welcome to apply.
Financial Data   The grant is $60,000 for a full academic year or prorated amounts for shorter periods. Other benefits include subsidized visiting faculty housing, research support up to $1,000, a private office at the institute, a computer and printer, access to university libraries and other facilities, and weekly institute seminars and events.
Duration   Up to 1 academic year.
Number awarded   Varies each year; recently, 14 were awarded.
Deadline   October of each year.

[1172]
NSF STANDARD AND CONTINUING GRANTS

National Science Foundation
4201 Wilson Boulevard
Arlington, VA 22230
(703) 292-5111   TDD: (800) 281-8749
E-mail: info@nsf.gov
Web: www.nsf.gov/funding/aboutfunding.jsp

Summary   To provide financial support to students, engineers, and educators, especially Hispanics and members of other underrepresented groups, for research in broad areas of science and engineering.
Eligibility   The National Science Foundation (NSF) supports research through its Directorates of Biological Sciences; Computer and Information Science and Engineering; Education and Human Resources; Engineering; Geosciences; Mathematical and Physical Sciences; and Social, Behavioral, and Economic Sciences. Within those general areas of science and engineering, NSF awards 2 types of grants: 1) standard grants, in which NSF agrees to provide a specific level of support for a specified period of time with no statement of NSF intent to provide additional future support without submission of another proposal; and 2) continuing grants, in which NSF agrees to provide a specific level of support for an initial specified period of time with a statement of intent to provide additional support of the project for additional periods, provided funds are available and the results achieved warrant further support. Although NSF often solicits proposals for support of targeted areas through issuance of specific program solicitations, it also accepts unsolicited proposals. Scientists, engineers, and educators usually act as the principal investigator and initiate proposals that are officially submitted by their employing organization. Most employing organizations are universities, colleges, and non-profit non-academic organizations (such as museums, observatories, research laboratories, and professional societies). Certain programs are open to for-profit organizations, state

and local governments, or unaffiliated individuals. Principal investigators usually must be U.S. citizens, nationals, or permanent residents. In the selection process, consideration is given to the achievement of societally relevant outcomes, including full participation of women, persons with disabilities, and underrepresented minorities.

Financial Data Funding levels vary, depending on the nature of the project and the availability of funds. Awards resulting from unsolicited research proposals are subject to statutory cost-sharing.

Duration Standard grants specify the period of time, usually up to 1 year; continuing grants normally specify 1 year as the initial period of time, with support to continue for additional periods.

Additional data Researchers interested in support from NSF should contact the address above to obtain further information on areas of support and programs operating within the respective directorates. They should consult with a program officer before submitting an application. Information on programs is available on the NSF home page. NSF does not normally support technical assistance, pilot plant efforts, research requiring security classification, the development of products for commercial marketing, or market research for a particular project or invention. Bioscience research with disease-related goals, including work on the etiology, diagnosis, or treatment of physical or mental disease, abnormality, or malfunction in human beings or animals, is normally not supported.

Number awarded Approximately 11,000 new grants are awarded each year.

Deadline Many programs accept proposals at any time. Other programs establish target dates or deadlines; those target dates and deadlines are published in the *NSF Bulletin* and in specific program announcements/solicitations.

[1173]
OKLAHOMA CAREERTECH FOUNDATION TEACHER RECRUITMENT/RETENTION SCHOLARSHIP FOR TEACHERS

Oklahoma CareerTech Foundation
Attn: Administrator
1500 West Seventh Avenue
Stillwater, OK 74074-4364
(405) 743-5453   Fax: (405) 743-5541
E-mail: leden@careertech.ok.gov
Web: www.okcareertech.org

Summary To provide financial assistance to residents of Oklahoma who are Hispanics or reflect the diversity of the state in other ways and are interested in attending a college or university in the state to earn a credential or certification for a career in the Oklahoma CareerTech system.

Eligibility This program is open to residents of Oklahoma who are incumbent CareerTech teachers working toward a CareerTech credential or certification at an institution of higher education in the state. Applicants must reflect the ethnic diversity of the state. Along with their application, they must submit brief statements on their interest and commitment to the CareerTech teaching profession and their financial need.

Financial Data The stipend ranges from $500 per semester to $1,500 per year.

Duration 1 semester; may be renewed, provided the recipient maintains a GPA of 2.5 or higher.

Number awarded 1 or more each year.

Deadline May of each year.

[1174]
OMOHUNDRO INSTITUTE NEH POSTDOCTORAL FELLOWSHIP

Omohundro Institute of Early American History and
  Culture
1 Landrum Drive
P.O. Box 8781
Williamsburg, VA 23187-8781
(757) 221-1115   Fax: (757) 221-1047
E-mail: oieahc@wm.edu
Web: oieahc.wm.edu/fellowship/submission/index.cfm

Summary To provide funding to scholars in American studies, especially Hispanics and other underrepresented minorities, who wish to revise their dissertation or other manuscript in residence at the Omohundro Institute of Early American History and Culture in Williamsburg, Virginia.

Eligibility Applicants must have completed a Ph.D. in a field that encompasses all aspects of the lives of North America's indigenous and immigrant peoples during the colonial, Revolutionary, and early national periods of the United States and the related histories of Canada, the Caribbean, Latin America, the British Isles, Europe, and Africa, from the 16th century to approximately 1820. They must be U.S. citizens or have lived in the United States for the 3 previous years. The proposed fellowship project must not be under contract to another publisher. The revisions must be made at the Omohundro Institute. Applicants may not have previously published a book or have entered into a contract for the publication of a scholarly monograph. Selection is based on the potential of the candidate's dissertation or other manuscript to make a distinguished, book-length contribution to scholarship. The Institute encourages applications from women, minorities, protected veterans, and individuals with disabilities.

Financial Data The fellowship includes a stipend of $50,400 per year, funds for travel to conferences and research centers, and access to office, research, and computer facilities at the institute.

Duration 2 years.

Additional data Funding for this program is provided by the National Endowment for the Humanities (NEH) for the first year and by the Omohundro Institute for the second year. Fellows have an option to teach at the College of William and Mary during the second year.

Number awarded 1 each year.

Deadline October of each year.

[1175]
ONLINE BIBLIOGRAPHIC SERVICES/ TECHNICAL SERVICES JOINT RESEARCH GRANT

American Association of Law Libraries
Attn: Online Bibliographic Services Special Interest
  Section
105 West Adams Street, Suite 3300
Chicago, IL 60603
(312) 939-4764   Fax: (312) 431-1097
E-mail: aallhq@aall.org
Web: www.aallnet.org

Summary To provide funding to members of the American Association of Law Libraries (AALL), especially Hispanics and other minorities, who are interested in conducting a research project related to technical services in the United States, Canada, or any other country.

Eligibility This program is open to AALL members who are technical services law librarians. Preference is given to members of the Online Bibliographic Services and Technical Services Special Interest Sections, although members of other special interest sections are eligible if their work relates to technical services law librarianship. Applicants must be interested in conducting research that will enhance technical services law librarianship. Women and minorities are especially encouraged to apply. Preference is given to projects that can be completed in the United States or Canada, although foreign research projects are given consideration.

Financial Data Grants range up to $1,000.

Duration 1 year.

Number awarded 1 or more each year.

Deadline March or September of each year.

[1176]
PARKER B. FRANCIS FELLOWSHIPS

Parker B. Francis Fellowship Program
Attn: Program Specialist
800 West 47th Street, Suite 717
Kansas City, MO 64112
(816) 531-0077   Fax: (816) 531-8810
E-mail: shari@francisfoundation.org
Web: www.francisfellowships.org

Summary To provide financial support to postdoctorates, especially Hispanics and members of other underrepresented groups, who are interested in research training in pulmonary or related disease.

Eligibility This program is open to citizens and permanent residents of the United States or Canada who have a doctoral degree (M.D., Ph.D., Sc.D., D.V.M., Dr.P.H.) and show evidence of aptitude and proficiency in research. Applicants must be interested in a program of research training in pulmonary, critical care, or sleep medicine. They should not be more than 7 years beyond receipt of their doctoral degree. Sponsorship of the fellow by an established pulmonary investigator is required. Members of underrepresented groups are particularly encouraged to apply. Selection is based on the qualifications and career trajectory of the candidate, the scientific merits of the research project proposal, and an assessment of the mentor's credentials and the institution as resources for training in research.

Financial Data Grants are $50,000 for the first year, $52,000 for the second year, and $54,000 for the third year; those amounts are to cover the stipend, fringe benefits, and a travel allowance of up to $2,000. No direct research project costs or indirect costs are allowed.

Duration 3 years.

Additional data These fellowships are supported by the Francis Families Foundation, the result of the merger in 1989 of the Parker B. Francis Foundation and the Parker B. Francis III Foundation. The former foundation began awarding the research fellowships in 1975. Fellows must be able to devote at least 75% of their time to research.

Number awarded Varies each year; recently, 13 were awarded.

Deadline October of each year.

[1177]
PATRICIA M. LOWRIE DIVERSITY LEADERSHIP SCHOLARSHIP

Association of American Veterinary Medical Colleges
Attn: Diversity Committee
1101 Vermont Avenue, N.W., Suite 301
Washington, DC 20005-3536
(202) 371-9195, ext. 147   Toll Free: (877) 862-2740
Fax: (202) 842-0773   E-mail: lgreenhill@aavmc.org
Web: www.aavmc.org

Summary To provide financial assistance to Hispanic and other veterinary students who have promoted diversity in the profession.

Eligibility This program is open to second-, third-, and fourth-year students at veterinary colleges in the United States. Applicants must have a demonstrated record of contributing to enhancing diversity and inclusion through course projects, co-curricular activities, outreach, domestic and community engagement, research, and/or an early reputation for influencing others to be inclusive. Along with their application, they must submit a 3-page personal statement that describes 1) why diversity and inclusion are important to them personally and professionally; 2) how they intend to continue contributing to diversity and inclusion efforts in the veterinary profession after graduation; and 3) what it might mean to be honored as a recipient of this scholarship. They must also indicate how they express their race and/or ethnicity (Hispanic, American Indian or Alaskan, Asian, Black or African American, Native Hawaiian or Pacific Islander, or White) and how they express their gender (male, female, transgender spectrum, or other). Selection is based primarily on documentation of a demonstrated commitment to promoting diversity in academic veterinary medicine; consideration is also given to academic achievement, the student's broader community service record, and financial need.

Financial Data The stipend is $6,000.

Duration 1 year; nonrenewable.

Additional data This program began in 2013.

Number awarded 1 each odd-numbered year.

Deadline October of each even-numbered year.

[1178]
PAUL B. BEESON EMERGING LEADERS CAREER DEVELOPMENT AWARDS IN AGING

American Federation for Aging Research
Attn: Executive Director
55 West 39th Street, 16th Floor
New York, NY 10018
(212) 703-9977   Toll Free: (888) 582-2327
Fax: (212) 997-0330   E-mail: grants@afar.org
Web: www.afar.org/research/funding/beeson

Summary To provide funding for additional training to Hispanic and other underrepresented physicians interested in conducting aging research.

Eligibility Applicants must have a clinical doctoral degree (e.g., M.D., D.O., D.D.S, D.M.D., D.V.M., Pharm.D.) or a Ph.D. in a clinical discipline (e.g., clinical psychology, nursing, clinical genetics, speech-language pathology, audiology, rehabilitation). Applicants must be interested in preparing for an independent research career through a mentored program of medical, academic, and scientific training relative to caring for older people. The sponsoring institution must be a domestic public or private institution, such as a university, college, hospital, or laboratory, that has a well-established research and clinical career development program, faculty experienced in research on aging and geriatrics to serve as mentors, and a commitment to the applicant's development and emergence as a productive, independent investigator. U.S. citizenship, national status, or permanent resident status is required. Members of underrepresented racial and ethnic groups and individuals with disabilities are especially encouraged to apply for programs of the National Institutes of Health (NIH).

Financial Data The maximum grant is $225,000 per year. Salaries are paid according to the established structure at the host institution. Facilities and administrative costs are reimbursed at 8% of modified total direct costs.

Duration 5 years.

Additional data The program is sponsored by the John A. Hartford Foundation and 2 components of the NIH: the National Institute on Aging (NIA) and the National Institute of Neurological Disorders and Strokes (NINDS).

Number awarded 7 to 10 each year.

Deadline Letters of intent must be submitted by mid-October of each year. Complete applications are due in mid-November.

[1179]
PAULA DE MERIEUX RHEUMATOLOGY FELLOWSHIP AWARD

American College of Rheumatology
Attn: Rheumatology Research Foundation
2200 Lake Boulevard N.E.
Atlanta, GA 30319
(404) 633-3777   Fax: (404) 633-1870
E-mail: foundation@rheumatology.org
Web: rheumresearch.org/Awards/Education_Training

Summary To provide funding to Hispanic and other underrepresented minorities interested in a program of training for a career providing clinical care to people affected by rheumatic diseases.

Eligibility This program is open to trainees at ACGME-accredited institutions. Applications must be submitted by the training program director at the institution who is responsible for selection and appointment of trainees. The program must train and prepare fellows to provide clinical care to those affected by rheumatic diseases. Trainees must be women or members of underrepresented minority groups, defined as Hispanics, Black Americans, and Native Americans (Native Hawaiians, Alaska Natives, and American Indians). They must be U.S. citizens, nationals, or permanent residents. Selection is based on the institution's pass rate of rheumatology fellows, publication history of staff and previous fellows, current positions of previous fellows, and status of clinical faculty.

Financial Data The grant is $50,000, to be used as salary for the trainee. Other trainee costs (e.g., fees, health insurance, travel, attendance at scientific meetings) are to be incurred by the recipient's institutional program. Supplemental or additional support to offset the cost of living may be provided by the grantee institution.

Duration Up to 1 year.

Additional data This fellowship was first awarded in 2005.

Number awarded 1 each year.

Deadline July of each year.

[1180]
PEN OPEN BOOK AWARD

PEN American Center
Attn: Literary Awards Associate
588 Broadway, Suite 303
New York, NY 10012
(212) 334-1660, ext. 4813   Fax: (212) 334-2181
E-mail: awards@pen.org
Web: www.pen.org/content/pen-open-book-award-5000

Summary To recognize and reward outstanding Latino and other authors of color from any country.

Eligibility This award is presented to an author of color (Latino, African, Arab, Asian, Caribbean, and Native American) whose book-length writings were published in the United States during the current calendar year. Works of fiction, literary nonfiction, biography/memoir, poetry, and other works of literary character are strongly preferred. U.S. citizenship or residency is not required. Nominations must be submitted by publishers or literary agents. Self-published books are not eligible.

Financial Data The prize is $5,000.

Duration The prizes are awarded annually.

Additional data This prize was formerly known as the Beyond Margins Award. The entry fee is $75.

Number awarded 1 or 2 each year.

Deadline August of each year.

[1181]
POSTDOCTORAL FELLOWSHIP IN MENTAL HEALTH AND SUBSTANCE ABUSE SERVICES

American Psychological Association
Attn: Minority Fellowship Program
750 First Street, N.E.
Washington, DC 20002-4242
(202) 336-6127   Fax: (202) 336-6012
TDD: (202) 336-6123   E-mail: mfp@apa.org
Web: www.apa.org/pi/mfp/psychology/postdoc/index.aspx

Summary To provide financial assistance to postdoctoral scholars, especially Hispanics and other minorities, who are interested in a program of research training related to providing mental health and substance abuse services to ethnic minority populations.

Eligibility This program is open to U.S. citizens, nationals, and permanent residents who received a doctoral degree in psychology in the last 5 years. Applicants must be interested in participating in a program of training under a qualified sponsor for research and have a strong commitment to a career in ethnic minority behavioral health services or policy. Members of ethnic minority groups (African Americans, Hispanics/Latinos, American Indians, Alaskan Natives, Asian Americans, Native Hawaiians, and other Pacific Islanders) are especially encouraged to apply. Selection is based on commitment to a career in ethnic minority mental health service delivery or public policy; qualifications of the sponsor; the fit between career goals and training environment selected; merit of the training proposal; potential as a future leader in ethnic minority psychology, demonstrated through accomplishments and goals; consistency between the applicant's work and the goals of the program; and letters of recommendation.

Financial Data The stipend depends on the number of years of research experience and is equivalent to the standard postdoctoral stipend level of the National Institutes of Health (recently ranging from $47,484 for no years of experience to $58,510 for 7 or more years of experience).

Duration 1 academic or calendar year; may be renewed for 1 additional year.

Additional data Funding is provided by the U.S. Substance Abuse and Mental Health Services Administration.

Number awarded Varies each year.

Deadline January of each year.

[1182]
POSTDOCTORAL FELLOWSHIPS OF THE FORD FOUNDATION DIVERSITY FELLOWSHIP PROGRAM

The National Academies of Sciences, Engineering, and
  Medicine
Attn: Fellowships Office
500 Fifth Street, N.W.
Washington, DC 20001
(202) 334-2872   Fax: (202) 334-3419
E-mail: FordApplications@nas.edu
Web: sites.nationalacademies.org

Summary To provide funding for postdoctoral research to be conducted in the United States or any other country to Hispanic and other scholars whose success will increase the racial and ethnic diversity of U.S. colleges and universities.

Eligibility This program is open to U.S. citizens, permanent residents, and nationals who earned a Ph.D. or Sc.D. degree within the past 7 years and are committed to a career in teaching and research at the college or university level. The following are considered as positive factors in the selection process: evidence of superior academic achievement; promise of continuing achievement as scholars and teachers; membership in a group whose underrepresentation in the American professoriate has been severe and longstanding, including Black/African Americans, Puerto Ricans, Mexican Americans/Chicanos/Chicanas, Native American Indians, Alaska Natives (Eskimos, Aleuts, and other indigenous people of Alaska), and Native Pacific Islanders (Hawaiians, Micronesians, or Polynesians); capacity to respond in pedagogically productive ways to the learning needs of students from diverse backgrounds; sustained personal engagement with communities that are underrepresented in the academy and an ability to bring this asset to learning, teaching, and scholarship at the college and university level; and likelihood of using the diversity of human experience as an educational resource in teaching and scholarship. Eligible areas of study include American studies, anthropology, archaeology, art and theater history, astronomy, chemistry, communications, computer science, cultural studies, earth sciences, economics, education, engineering, ethnic studies, ethnomusicology, geography, history, international relations, language, life sciences, linguistics, literature, mathematics, performance study, philosophy, physics, political science, psychology, religious studies, sociology, urban planning, and women's studies. Also eligible are interdisciplinary programs such as African American studies, Native American studies, area studies, peace studies, and social justice. Awards are not available for practice-oriented programs or professional programs such as medicine, law, or public health. Research may be conducted at an appropriate institution of higher education in the United States (normally) or abroad, including universities, museums, libraries, government or national laboratories, privately sponsored nonprofit institutes, government chartered nonprofit research organizations, or centers for advanced study. Applicants should designate a faculty member or other scholar to serve as host at the proposed fellowship institution. They are encouraged to choose a host institution other than that where they are affiliated at the time of application.

Financial Data The stipend is $45,000. Funds may be supplemented by sabbatical leave pay or other sources of support that do not carry with them teaching or other responsibilities. The employing institution receives an allowance of $1,500, paid after fellowship tenure is completed; the employing institution is expected to match the grant and to use the allowance and the match to assist with the fellow's continuing research expenditures.

Duration 9 to 12 months.

Additional data Fellows may not accept another major fellowship while they are being supported by this program.

Number awarded Approximately 24 each year.

Deadline November of each year.

[1183]
POSTDOCTORAL RESEARCH FELLOWSHIPS IN BIOLOGY

National Science Foundation
Directorate for Biological Sciences
Attn: Division of Biological Infrastructure
4201 Wilson Boulevard, Room 615N
Arlington, VA 22230
(703) 292-2299   Fax: (703) 292-9063
TDD: (800) 281-8749   E-mail: bio-dbi-prfb@nsf.gov
Web: www.nsf.gov

Summary To provide funding for research and training in specified areas related to biology to junior doctoral-level scientists, especially Hispanics and other underrepresented minorities, at sites in the United States or abroad.

Eligibility This program is open to citizens, nationals, and permanent residents of the United States who are graduate students completing a Ph.D. or who have earned the degree no earlier than 12 months preceding the deadline date. Applicants must be interested in a program of research and training in any of 3 competitive areas: 1) Broadening Participation of Groups Underrepresented in Biology, designed to increase the diversity of scientists by providing support for research and training to biologists with disabilities and underrepresented minority (Hispanic, Native American, Native Pacific Islander, Alaskan Native, and African American) biologists; 2) Research Using Biological Collections, to address key questions in biology and potentially develop applications that extend biology to physical, mathematical, engineering, and social sciences by the use of biological research collections in museums and archives in the United States and abroad; and 3) National Plant Genome Initiative (NPGI) Postdoctoral Research Fellowships, for postdoctoral training in plant improvement and associated sciences such as physiology and pathology, quantitative genetics, or computational biology. They must identify a sponsor at a host institution who will serve as a mentor for their training program.

Financial Data Grants are $69,000 per year, including $54,000 as a stipend for the fellow and $15,000 as a fellowship allowance that is intended to cover direct research expenses, facilities and other institutional resources, and fringe benefits. An extra allowance of $10,000 is provided to fellows who go overseas.

Duration Fellowships are 24 to 36 months for Broadening Participation, 24 months for Research Using Biological Collections, or 36 months for NPGI Postdoctoral Research Fellowships.

Number awarded Approximately 40 each year in each competitive area.

Deadline October of each year.

[1184]
PRESIDIO LA BAHIA AWARD
Sons of the Republic of Texas
Attn: Administrative Assistant
1717 Eighth Street
Bay City, TX 77414
(979) 245-6644   Fax: (979) 244-3819
E-mail: srttexas@srttexas.org
Web: www.srttexas.org/community.html

Summary To recognize and reward the most outstanding works that demonstrate the impact and influence of the Spanish colonial heritage on the laws, customs, language, religion, architecture, and art of Texas.

Eligibility The competition is open to any person interested in Spanish colonial influence on Texas culture. Eligible to be considered are books, published papers, articles published in periodicals, and non-literary projects (such as art, architecture, and archaeological discovery).

Financial Data A total of $2,000 is available annually as awards. The prize for the best book is at least $1,200; the organization may award a second-place book prize. The amounts of prizes for best published paper, article published in a periodical, and non-literary project vary each year.

Duration The competition is held annually.

Additional data This award was established in 1968.

Number awarded From 1 to 5 each year.
Deadline September of each year.

[1185]
REGINALD F. LEWIS FELLOWSHIP FOR LAW TEACHING
Harvard Law School
Attn: Lewis Committee
Griswold Two South
1525 Massachusetts Avenue
Cambridge, MA 02138
(617) 495-3109
E-mail: LewisFellowship@law.harvard.edu
Web: hls.harvard.edu

Summary To provide funding to law school graduates, especially Hispanics and others of color, who are preparing for a career in law teaching and are interested in a program of research and training at Harvard Law School.

Eligibility This program is open to recent graduates of law school who have demonstrated an interest in law scholarship and teaching. Applicants must be interested in spending time in residence at Harvard Law School where they will audit courses, attend workshops, and follow a schedule of research under the sponsorship of the committee. The program encourages the training of prospective law teachers who will enhance the diversity of the profession and especially encourages applications from candidates of color.

Financial Data The stipend is $50,000 per year.
Duration 2 years.
Number awarded 1 each year.
Deadline January of each year.

[1186]
RESEARCH AND TRAINING PROGRAM ON POVERTY AND PUBLIC POLICY POSTDOCTORAL FELLOWSHIPS
University of Michigan
Gerald R. Ford School of Public Policy
Attn: National Poverty Center
Joan and Sanford Weill Hall
735 South State Street, Room 5100
Ann Arbor, MI 48109-3091
(734) 764-3490   Fax: (734) 763-9181
E-mail: npcinfo@umich.edu
Web: npc.umich.edu/opportunities/visiting

Summary To provide funding to Hispanic and other minority postdoctorates interested in conducting research and pursuing intensive training on poverty-related public policy issues at the University of Michigan.

Eligibility This program is open to U.S. citizens and permanent residents who are members of a minority group that is underrepresented in the social sciences. Applicants must have received the Ph.D. degree within the past 5 years and be engaged in research on poverty and public policy. Along with their application, they must submit a research proposal that represents either a significant extension upon previous work or a new poverty research project; a 1- to 2-page statement that specifies the ways in which residence at the University of Michigan will foster their career development and research goals and provides information about how their racial/ethnic/regional/economic background qualifies them as a members of a group that is underrepresented in the social sciences; a curriculum vitae; and a sample of their scholarly writing. Preference is given to proposals that would benefit from resources available at the University of Michigan and from interactions with affiliated faculty.

Financial Data   The stipend is $50,000 per calendar year.

Duration   1 or 2 years.

Additional data   This program is funded by the Ford Foundation. Fellows spend the year participating in a seminar on poverty and public policy and conducting their own research. Topics currently pursued include the effects of the recession and the American Recovery and Reinvestment Act of 2009 on workers, families, and children; evolution of the social safety net; longitudinal analyses of youth development; family formation and healthy marriages; immigration and poverty; investing in low-income families: the accumulation of financial assets and human capital; and qualitative and mixed-methods research on poverty. Fellows must be in residence at the University of Michigan for the duration of the program.

Number awarded   1 or more each year.

Deadline   January of each year.

[1187]
ROBERT WOOD JOHNSON HEALTH POLICY FELLOWSHIPS

National Academy of Medicine
Attn: Health Policy Fellowships Program
500 Fifth Street, N.W.
Washington, DC 20001
(202) 334-1506   Fax: (202) 334-3862
E-mail: info@healthpolicyfellows.org
Web: www.healthpolicyfellows.org/apply

Summary   To provide an opportunity to health professionals and behavioral and social scientists, especially Hispanics and members of other diverse groups, who have an interest in health to participate in the formulation of national health policies while in residence at the National Academy of Medicine (NAM) in Washington, D.C.

Eligibility   This program is open to mid-career professionals from academic faculties and nonprofit health care organizations who are interested in experiencing health policy processes at the federal level. Applicants must have a background in allied health professions, biomedical sciences, dentistry, economics or other social sciences, health services organization and administration, medicine, nursing, public health, social and behavioral health, or health law. They must be sponsored by the chief executive officer of an eligible nonprofit health care organization or academic institution. Selection is based on potential for leadership in health policy, potential for future growth and career advancement, professional achievements, interpersonal and communication skills, potential for significant contributions to building a Culture of Health, and individual plans for incorporating the fellowship experience into specific career goals. U.S. citizenship or permanent resident status is required. Applications are especially encouraged from candidates with diverse backgrounds of race, ethnicity, gender, age, disability, and socioeconomic status.

Financial Data   Total support for the Washington stay and continuing activities may not exceed $165,000. Grant funds may cover salary support at a level of up to $104,000 plus fringe benefits. Fellows are reimbursed for relocation expenses to and from Washington, D.C. No indirect costs are paid.

Duration   The program lasts 1 year and includes an orientation in September and October; meetings in November and December with members of Congress, journalists, policy analysts, and other experts on the national political and governmental process; and working assignments from January through August. Fellows then return to their home institutions, but they receive up to 2 years of continued support for further development of health policy leadership skills.

Additional data   This program, initiated in 1973, is funded by the Robert Wood Johnson Foundation.

Number awarded   Up to 6 each year.

Deadline   November of each year.

[1188]
SBE POSTDOCTORAL RESEARCH FELLOWSHIPS

National Science Foundation
Directorate for Social, Behavioral, and Economic
  Sciences
Attn: Office of Multidisciplinary Activities
4201 Wilson Boulevard, Room 907.09
Arlington, VA 22230
(703) 292-7376   Fax: (703) 292-9083
TDD: (800) 281-8749   E-mail: jwelkom@nsf.gov
Web: www.nsf.gov

Summary   To provide financial assistance for postdoctoral research training in the United States or any other country to Hispanic and other underrepresented minority scientists in fields of interest to the Directorate for Social, Behavioral, and Economic Sciences (SBE) of the National Science Foundation (NSF) and to others interested in interdisciplinary research.

Eligibility   This program is open to U.S. citizens, nationals, and permanent residents who completed a doctorate within the past 36 months but are not already in a full-time tenure-track faculty position. Applicants may be interested in either of 2 tracks offered by this program: 1) Broadening Participation, to increase involvement in social, behavioral, and economic research by persons with disabilities and members of ethnic groups that are currently underrepresented, including Hispanics, Native Americans (Alaska Natives and American Indians), African Americans, and Native Pacific Islanders; and/or 2) Fundamental Research in which at least 1 of the disciplines is an SBE science. Proposals must involve research training to be conducted at any appropriate U.S. or foreign nonprofit institution (government laboratory, institution of higher education, national laboratory, or public or private research institute), but not at the same institution where the doctorate was obtained. For the first track, applications must include a statement on how the fellowship will help broaden the participation of scientists from currently underrepresented groups in the United States. For the second track, applications must include a statement on why the project requires interdisciplinary training beyond the core doctoral experiences.

Financial Data   Grants include an annual stipend of $54,000 and $15,000 per year for fellowship expenses.

Duration   2 years.

Number awarded   15 to 20 each year.

Deadline   October of each year.

[1189]
SCHOLARLY EDITIONS AND TRANSLATIONS GRANTS

National Endowment for the Humanities
Attn: Division of Research Programs
400 Seventh Street, S.W.
Washington, DC 20506
(202) 606-8200   Toll Free: (800) NEH-1121
Fax: (202) 606-8204   TDD: (866) 372-2930
E-mail: editions@neh.gov
Web: www.neh.gov

Summary To provide funding to scholars and organizations, especially those affiliated with Hispanic and other Minority Serving Institutions, who are interested in preparing texts and documents in the humanities.

Eligibility This program is open to 1) U.S. citizens and foreign nationals who have been living in the United States or its jurisdictions for at least 3 years; 2) state and local governmental agencies; and 3) nonprofit, tax-exempt institutions and organizations in the United States. It supports the preparation of editions and translations of pre-existing texts and documents of value to the humanities that are currently inaccessible or available in inadequate editions. Projects must be undertaken by a team of at least 1 editor or translator and 1 other staff member. Grants typically support editions and translations of significant literary, philosophical, and historical materials, but other types of work, such as the editing of musical notation, are also eligible. Selection is based on 1) the intellectual significance of the project, including its potential contribution to scholarship in the humanities, the likelihood that it will stimulate new research, its relationship to larger themes in the humanities, and the significance of the material on which the project is based; 2) the appropriateness of the research methods, critical apparatus, and editorial policies; the appropriateness of selection criteria; the thoroughness and feasibility of the work plan; and the quality of the samples; 3) the qualifications, expertise, and levels of commitment of the project director and key project staff or contributors, and the appropriateness of the staff to the goals of the project; 4) the promise of quality, usefulness, and impact on scholarship of any resulting publication or other product; and 5) the potential for success, including the likelihood that the project will be successfully completed within the projected time frame. The program encourages submission of applications from faculty at Hispanic Serving Institutions, Historically Black Colleges and Universities, and Tribal Colleges and Universities.

Financial Data Grants range from $50,000 to $100,000 per year. The use of federal matching funds in encouraged. Normally, support does not exceed 80% of total costs.

Duration 1 to 3 years.

Number awarded Approximately 26 each year.

Deadline December of each year.

[1190]
SCIENCE, TECHNOLOGY, AND PUBLIC POLICY FELLOWSHIPS

Harvard University
John F. Kennedy School of Government
Belfer Center for Science and International Affairs
Attn: STPP Fellowship Coordinator
79 John F. Kennedy Street, Mailbox 53
Cambridge, MA 02138
(617) 495-1498   Fax: (617) 495-8963
E-mail: patricia_mclaughlin@hks.harvard.edu
Web: belfercenter.ksg.harvard.edu

Summary To provide funding to professionals, postdoctorates, and doctoral students, especially Hispanics and other minorities, who are interested in conducting research in science, technology, and public policy areas of concern to the Belfer Center for Science and International Affairs at Harvard University in Cambridge, Massachusetts.

Eligibility The postdoctoral fellowship is open to recent recipients of the Ph.D. or equivalent degree, university faculty members, and employees of government, military, international, humanitarian, and private research institutions who have appropriate professional experience. Applicants for predoctoral fellowships must have passed their general examinations. Scholars from a wide range of disciplinary and multi-disciplinary fields and those holding a Ph.D. in engineering or in the natural sciences are strongly encouraged to apply. The program especially encourages applications from women, minorities, and citizens of all countries. All applicants must be interested in conducting research on projects of the Science, Technology, and Public Policy (STPP) Program. Recently, those included projects on Internet policy and regulatory reform, energy technology innovation, water and energy resources, sustainable energy development in China, technology and innovation, solar geoengineering and climate policy, technological innovation and globalization, agricultural innovation in Africa, managing the atom, and the geopolitics of energy.

Financial Data The stipend is $37,500 for postdoctoral research fellows or $25,000 for predoctoral research fellows. Fellows who renew their grant receive a monthly stipend of $3,750 for postdoctoral fellows or $2,500 for predoctoral fellows. Stipends for advanced research fellows vary. Health insurance is also provided.

Duration 10 months; may be renewed on a month-by-month basis.

Additional data Fellows are expected to devoted some portion of their time to collaborative endeavors, as arranged by the appropriate program or project director. Predoctoral fellows are expected to contribute to the program's research activities, as well as work on (and ideally complete) their dissertations. Postdoctoral research fellows are also expected to complete a book, monograph, or other significant publication during their period of residence.

Number awarded A limited number each year.

Deadline January of each year.

[1191]
SENATOR GREGORY LUNA LEGISLATIVE SCHOLARS AND FELLOWS PROGRAM

Senate Hispanic Research Council, Inc.
Attn: Executive Director
1001 Congress Avenue, Suite 100
Austin, TX 78701
(512) 499-8606   Fax: (512) 499-8607
E-mail: sarah@tshrc.org
Web: www.tshrc.org/luna-scholars-fellows-program

Summary To provide Hispanic undergraduate and graduate students at colleges and universities in Texas with an opportunity to gain work experience at the Texas Senate.

Eligibility This program is open to undergraduate and graduate students who have completed at least 60 semester hours at an accredited 2- or 4-year educational institution in Texas; recent graduates are also eligible. Applicants must demonstrate academic achievement; leadership qualities; potential for further growth; exceptional writing, comprehension, and analytical skills; and an interest in government and public policy through active participation in community service activities. Along with their application, they must submit a personal statement on the experiences or activities that led to their interest in government and this internship program, a sample of their writing of a policy analysis on an issue affecting the state of Texas, and 2 letters of recommendation.

Financial Data Interns receive a stipend of $2,000 per month to help cover the expense of living and working in Austin.

Duration Approximately 5 months, during the term of the Texas Senate, beginning in mid-January of odd-numbered years.

Additional data This program began in 2001. Interns are assigned to the office of a state senator to perform a variety of legislative tasks, including drafting legislation, floor statements, articles, press releases, legislative research summaries, and hearing agendas. The Senate Hispanic Research Council was established in 1993 to provide educational and leadership opportunities to all segments of the Hispanic community in Texas.

Number awarded Up to 16 each odd-numbered year.

Deadline November of each even-numbered year.

[1192]
SHPE PROFESSIONAL SCHOLARSHIP

Society of Hispanic Professional Engineers
Attn: Scholarships
13181 Crossroads Parkway North, Suite 450
City of Industry, CA 91715
(323) 725-3970, ext. 108   Fax: (323) 725-0316
E-mail: scholarships@shpe.org
Web: shpe.awardspring.com

Summary To provide financial assistance to Hispanic professionals working on a graduate degree in science, technology, engineering, or mathematics.

Eligibility This program is open to members of the Society of Hispanic Professional Engineers (SHPE) who are employed full time in the United States or Puerto Rico in a technical career field. Applicants must be enrolled at least half time in a science, technology, engineering, or mathematics (STEM) degree program in the United States or Puerto Rico. They must have a GPA of 2.75 or higher and be able to demonstrate financial need. Along with their application, they must submit a 500-word personal statement covering their community involvement, leadership, academic achievements, research internship and co-op experiences, and short-term and long-term goals and aspirations.

Financial Data The stipend is $2,000.

Duration 1 year.

Number awarded 1 or more each year.

Deadline July of each year.

[1193]
SLA NEW ENGLAND DIVERSITY LEADERSHIP DEVELOPMENT SCHOLARSHIP

SLA New England
c/o Khalilah Gambrell, Diversity Chair
EBSCO Information Services
10 Estes Street
Ipswich, MA 01938
(978) 356-6500   Toll Free: (800) 653-2726
Fax: (978) 356-6565   E-mail: gambrell9899@gmail.com
Web: newengland.sla.org/member-benefits/stipends

Summary To provide financial assistance for library science tuition or attendance at the annual conference of the Special Libraries Association (SLA) to members of SLA New England who are Hispanics or represent another diverse population.

Eligibility This program is open to SLA New England members who are of Hispanic, Black (African American), Asian American, Pacific Islander American, Native Alaskan, or Native Hawaiian heritage. Applicants must be seeking funding for SLA annual meeting attendance, tuition reimbursement for a library science program, or tuition reimbursement for a course directly related to the library and information science field. Along with their application, they must submit a 500-word essay on how they will encourage and celebrate diversity within the SLA New England community.

Financial Data The award covers actual expenses up to $1,500.

Duration This is a 1-time award.

Number awarded 1 each year.

Deadline April of each year.

[1194]
STANFORD HUMANITIES CENTER EXTERNAL FACULTY FELLOWSHIPS

Stanford Humanities Center
Attn: Fellowship Administrator
424 Santa Teresa Street
Stanford, CA 94305-4015
(650) 723-3054   Fax: (650) 723-1895
E-mail: pterraza@stanford.edu
Web: shc.stanford.edu/fellowships/non-stanford-faculty

Summary To offer scholars in the humanities, especially Hispanics and other underrepresented minorities, with an opportunity to conduct research and teach at Stanford University.

Eligibility External fellowships at Stanford University fall into 2 categories: 1) senior fellowships for scholars who are more than 10 years beyond receipt of the Ph.D.; and 2) junior fellowships for scholars who at the time of application are at least 3 but normally no more than 10 years beyond receipt of the Ph.D. The fields of study should be the humanities as defined in the act that established the National Foundation for the Arts and Humanities. There are no citizenship requirements; non-U.S. nationals are eligible. Scholars who are members of traditionally underrepresented groups are encouraged to apply. Applications are judged on 1) the promise of the specific research project being proposed; 2) the originality and intellectual distinction of the candidate's previous work; 3) the research project's potential interest to scholars in different fields of the humanities; and 4) the applicant's ability to engage in collegial interaction and to contribute to the discussion of presentations.

Financial Data The annual stipend is up to $70,000. In addition, a housing/travel subsidy of up to $30,000, depending on size of family, is offered.

Duration 1 academic year.

Additional data Fellows are expected to make an intellectual contribution not only within the center but to humanistic studies in general at Stanford. Normally, this requirement is fulfilled by teaching an undergraduate or graduate course or seminar for 1 quarter within a particular department or program. Fellows should live within 10 miles of Stanford University. Regular attendance at center events is expected and fellows are expected to be present during the fall, winter, and spring quarters and to attend weekday lunches on a regular basis.

Number awarded 6 to 8 each year.

Deadline October of each year.

[1195]
STANTON NUCLEAR SECURITY FELLOWSHIP

Stanford University
Center for International Security and Cooperation
Attn: Fellowships Coordinator
Encina Hall, Room C20G-10
616 Serra Street
Stanford, CA 94305-6165
(650) 723-9625   Fax: (650) 724-5683
E-mail: CISACfellowship@stanford.edu
Web: cisac.fsi.stanford.edu/docs/cisac_fellowship_program

Summary To provide funding to doctoral candidates and junior scholars, especially Hispanics and other minorities, who are interested in conducting research on nuclear security issues at Stanford University's Center for International Security and Cooperation.

Eligibility This program is open to doctoral candidates, recent postdoctorates, and junior faculty. Applicants must be interested in conducting research on nuclear security issues while in residence at the center. The sponsor welcomes applications from women, minorities, and citizens of all countries.

Financial Data The stipend ranges from $25,000 to $28,000 for doctoral candidates or from $48,000 to $66,000 for postdoctorates, depending on experience. Medical insurance is available for those who do not have coverage.

Duration 9 to 11 months.

Additional data Fellows are expected to write a dissertation chapter or chapters, publishable article or articles, and/or make significant progress on turning a thesis into a book manuscript. They should not plan to spend any time conducting research abroad or in other parts of the country.

Number awarded Varies each year; recently, 3 were awarded: 1 doctoral candidate, 1 recent postdoctorate, and 1 junior faculty member.

Deadline January of each year.

[1196]
STUDIO MUSEUM IN HARLEM ARTIST-IN-RESIDENCE PROGRAM

Studio Museum in Harlem
Attn: Education and Public Programs Department
144 West 125th Street
New York, NY 10027
(212) 864-4500, ext. 230   Fax: (212) 864-4800
Web: www.studiomuseum.org/learn/artist-in-residence

Summary To support visual artists of Latino and African descent who are interested in a residency at the Studio Museum in Harlem.

Eligibility This program is open to artists of Latino and African descent locally, nationally, or internationally. Applicants may be working in sculpture, painting, photography, printmaking, film and video, digital art, or mixed media. They must be professional artists with at least 3 years of professional commitment and currently engaged in studio work; high school, college, and graduate students are not considered. Selection is based on quality of the work, a record of exhibition and critical review, demonstration of a serious and consistent dedication to the professional practice of fine arts, evidence that the applicant is at a critical juncture in development that will be advanced by a residency, and letters of recommendation.

Financial Data This fellowship provides non-residential studio space, a stipend of $20,000, and a $1,000 material grant.

Duration 11 months.

Additional data Support for this program is provided by the Robert Lehman Foundation, the Jerome Foundation, and the Milton and Sally Avery Arts Foundation. Additional support is provided by the Andrew W. Mellon Foundation, New York City Department of Cultural Affairs, New York State Council on the Arts, and the New York City Council. Artists must spend at least 20 hours per week in their studios, exhibit their works in the museum, and conduct 2 public presentations/workshops.

Number awarded 3 each year.

Deadline March of each year.

[1197]
SUBSTANCE ABUSE FELLOWSHIP PROGRAM

American Psychiatric Association
Attn: Division of Diversity and Health Equity
1000 Wilson Boulevard, Suite 1825
Arlington, VA 22209-3901
(703) 907-8653   Toll Free: (888) 35-PSYCH
Fax: (703) 907-7852   E-mail: mking@psych.org
Web: www.psychiatry.org/minority-fellowship

Summary To provide educational enrichment to Hispanic and other minority psychiatrists-in-training and stimulate their interest in providing quality and effective services related to substance abuse to minorities and the underserved.

Eligibility This program is open to psychiatric residents who are members of the American Psychiatric Association (APA) and U.S. citizens or permanent residents. A goal of the program is to develop leadership to improve the quality of mental health care for members of ethnic minority groups (Hispanics/Latinos, American Indians, Native Alaskans, Asian Americans, Native Hawaiians, Native Pacific Islanders, and African Americans). Applicants must be in at least their fifth year of a substance abuse training program approved by an affiliated medical school or agency where a significant number of substance abuse patients are from minority and underserved groups. They must also be interested in working with a component of the APA that is of interest to them and relevant to their career goals. Along with their application, they must submit a 2-page essay on how the fellowship would be utilized to alter their present training and ultimately assist them in achieving their career goals. Selection is based on commitment to serve ethnic minority populations, demonstrated leadership abilities, awareness of the importance of culture in mental health, and interest in the interrelationship between mental health/illness and transcultural factors.

Financial Data   Fellows receive a monthly stipend (amount not specified) and reimbursement of transportation, lodging, meals, and incidentals in connection with attendance at program-related activities. They are expected to use the funds to enhance their own professional development, improve training in cultural competence at their training institution, improve awareness of culturally relevant issues in psychiatry at their institution, expand research in areas relevant to minorities and underserved populations, enhance the current treatment modalities for minority patients and underserved individuals at their institution, and improve awareness in the surrounding community about mental health issues (particularly with regard to minority populations).

Duration   1 year; may be renewed 1 additional year.

Additional data   Funding for this program is provided by the Substance Abuse and Mental Health Services Administration (SAMHSA). As part of their assignment to an APA component, fellows must attend the fall component meetings in September and the APA annual meeting in May. At those meeting, they can share their experiences as residents and minorities and discuss issues that impact minority populations. This program is an outgrowth of the fellowships that were established in 1974 under a grant from the National Institute of Mental Health in answer to concerns about the underrepresentation of minorities in psychiatry.

Number awarded   Varies each year; recently, 3 were awarded.

Deadline   January of each year.

[1198]
SUMMER RESEARCH PROGRAM IN ECOLOGY

Harvard University
Harvard Forest
324 North Main Street
Petersham, MA 01366
(978) 724-3302   Fax: (978) 724-3595
E-mail: hfapps@fas.harvard.edu
Web: harvardforest.fas.harvard.edu/other-tags/reu

Summary   To provide an opportunity for undergraduate students and recent graduates, especially Hispanics and members of other diverse groups, to participate in a summer ecological research project at Harvard Forest in Petersham, Massachusetts.

Eligibility   This program is open to undergraduate students and recent graduates interested in participating in a mentored research project at the Forest. The research may relate to the effects of natural and human disturbances on forest ecosystems, including global climate change, hurricanes, forest harvest, changing wildlife dynamics, or invasive species. Investigators come from many disciplines, and specific projects center on population and community ecology, paleoecology, land use history, aquatic ecology, biochemistry, soil science, ecophysiology, and atmosphere-biosphere exchanges. Students from diverse backgrounds are strongly encouraged to apply.

Financial Data   The stipend is $5,775. Free housing, meals, and travel reimbursement for 1 round trip are also provided.

Duration   11 weeks during the summer.

Additional data   Funding for this program is provided by the National Science Foundation (as part of its Research Experience for Undergraduates program).

Number awarded   Up to 25 each year.

Deadline   February of each year.

[1199]
TACHE DISTINGUISHED COMMUNITY COLLEGE FACULTY AWARD

Texas Association of Chicanos in Higher Education
c/o Maria Aguirre, Awards Committee Chair
Texas State Technical College West Texas
1420 Edgewood
Sweetwater, TX 79556
E-mail: maria.aguirre@tstc.edu
Web: www.tache.org/Awards.aspx

Summary   To recognize and reward outstanding community college faculty members in Texas who are members of the Texas Association of Chicanos in Higher Education (TACHE).

Eligibility   Eligible to be nominated for this award are active TACHE members who have taught for at least the last 5 years at a Texas community college. Nominees must have demonstrated a consistent pattern of teaching excellence, innovation in teaching, contributions to discipline-specific scholarship, a consistent pattern of service to the community, a consistent pattern of support of Chicano/Latino programs and students, support for and promotion of postsecondary education, and a consistent pattern of mentoring other faculty and/or students. Self-nominations are accepted.

Financial Data   The award is $1,000.

Duration   The award is presented annually.

Number awarded   1 each year.

Deadline   December of each year.

[1200]
TACHE DISTINGUISHED UNIVERSITY FACULTY AWARD

Texas Association of Chicanos in Higher Education
c/o Maria Aguirre, Awards Committee Chair
Texas State Technical College West Texas
1420 Edgewood
Sweetwater, TX 79556
E-mail: maria.aguirre@tstc.edu
Web: www.tache.org/Awards.aspx

Summary To recognize and reward outstanding university faculty members in Texas who are members of the Texas Association of Chicanos in Higher Education (TACHE).

Eligibility Eligible to be nominated for this award are active TACHE members who have taught for at least the last 5 years at a Texas university. Nominees must have demonstrated a consistent pattern of excellence in teaching, innovation in teaching, a record of scholarly publications or other contributions to the profession or academic discipline, a consistent pattern of service to the community, a consistent pattern of support of Chicano/Latino programs and students, support for and promotion of postsecondary and graduate education, and a consistent pattern of mentoring other faculty and/or students. Self-nominations are accepted.

Financial Data The award is $1,000.

Duration The award is presented annually.

Number awarded 1 each year.

Deadline December of each year.

[1201]
TOMAS RIVERA MEXICAN AMERICAN CHILDREN'S BOOK AWARD

Texas State University at San Marcos
Attn: Department of Curriculum and Instruction
601 University Drive
San Marcos, TX 78666-4616
(512) 245-2157   Fax: (512) 245-3158
E-mail: riverabookaward@txstate.edu
Web: www.education.txstate.edu

Summary To recognize and reward outstanding children's books that reflect the culture of Mexican Americans in the United States.

Eligibility Eligible to be nominated for this award are books for children and young adults that authentically reflect the lives and experiences of Mexican Americans in the United States. Entries may be fiction or nonfiction. Entries are accepted in 2 categories: works for younger children (grades preK-5) and works for older children (grades 6-12). Nominations may be submitted by authors, illustrators, published, and the public at large.

Financial Data The award is $3,000.

Duration The award is presented annually, during Hispanic Heritage month at Texas State University at San Marcos.

Additional data The award was first presented in 1995.

Number awarded 2 each year: 1 in each category.

Deadline October of each year.

[1202]
UC BERKELEY'S CHANCELLOR'S POSTDOCTORAL FELLOWSHIP PROGRAM FOR ACADEMIC DIVERSITY

University of California at Berkeley
Attn: Division of Equity and Inclusion
402 Sproul Hall
Berkeley, CA 94720-5920
(510) 643-8235   E-mail: ppfpinfo@berkeley.edu
Web: diversity.berkeley.edu

Summary To provide an opportunity for recent postdoctorates who are Hispanics or will increase diversity in other ways at the University of California at Berkeley to conduct research on the campus.

Eligibility This program is open to U.S. citizens and permanent residents who received a doctorate within 3 years of the start of the fellowship. The program solicits applications from scholars whose research, teaching, and service will contribute to diversity and equal opportunity at the university. The contributions to diversity may include public service towards increasing equitable access in fields where women and minorities are underrepresented or research focusing on underserved populations or understanding inequalities related to race, gender, disability, or LGBT issues. Applicants should have the potential to bring to their academic and research careers the perspective that comes from their non-traditional educational background or understanding of the experiences of members of groups historically underrepresented in higher education.

Financial Data The stipend is $44,500 per year (11 months, plus 1 month vacation). The award also includes health insurance, vision and dental benefits, and up to $5,000 for research-related and program travel expenses.

Duration 1 year; may be renewed 1 additional year.

Additional data This program operates in addition to the University of California President's Postdoctoral Fellowship Program for Academic Diversity. Interested candidates may apply to either program.

Number awarded Varies each year; recently, 3 were awarded.

Deadline October of each year.

[1203]
UC DAVIS CHANCELLOR'S POSTDOCTORAL FELLOWSHIP PROGRAM

University of California at Davis
Attn: Office of Graduate Studies
250 Mrak Hall
One Shields Avenue
Davis, CA 95616
(530) 752-0650   Fax: (530) 752-6222
E-mail: gradservices@ucdavis.edu
Web: gradstudies.ucdavis.edu

Summary To provide an opportunity for Hispanics and other recent postdoctorates who will increase diversity at the University of California at Davis to conduct research at the university.

Eligibility This program is open to scholars who have a Ph.D. in any field from an accredited university. Applicants must be interested in conducting research at UC Davis under the mentorship of an established scholar in their field. The program particularly solicits applications from scholars whose research, teaching, and service will contribute to the diversity and equal opportunity at the university. Those contributions may include public service addressing the needs of our increasingly diverse society, efforts to improve equitable access to higher education, or research focusing on underserved populations or understanding inequities related to race, gender, disability, or LGBT status. They must be able to demonstrate that they are legally authorized to work in the United States without restrictions or limitations; individuals granted deferred action status under the Deferred Action for Childhood Arrivals (DACA) program are encouraged to apply. Selection is based on academic accomplishments, strength of research proposal, and potential for faculty careers that will contribute to diversity through their teaching, research, and service.

Financial Data   The stipend is at least $44,500 per year (11 months, plus 1 month vacation). The award also includes health insurance, vision and dental benefits, and up to $5,000 for research-related and program travel expenses.

Duration   1 year; may be renewed 1 additional year.

Additional data   This program, which began in 2012, operates in addition to the University of California President's Postdoctoral Fellowship Program for Academic Diversity. Interested candidates may apply to either program.

Number awarded   Varies each year; recently, 7 were appointed.

Deadline   October of each year.

[1204]
UC SAN DIEGO CHANCELLOR'S POSTDOCTORAL FELLOWSHIP PROGRAM FOR ACADEMIC DIVERSITY

University of California at San Diego
Attn: Office of the Vice Chancellor for Equity, Diversity and
   Inclusion
302 University Center, Room 102
La Jolla, CA 92093-0029
(858) 246-1923   E-mail: mcg005@ucsd.edu
Web: facultyexcellence.ucsd.edu/funding/cpfp1/index.html

Summary   To provide an opportunity for Hispanics and other recent postdoctorates who will increase diversity at the University of California at San Diego to conduct research at the university.

Eligibility   This program is open to U.S. citizens and permanent residents who received a doctorate within 3 years of the start of the fellowship and are interested in conducting research at UCSD. The program particularly solicits applications from scholars whose research, teaching, and service will contribute to the diversity and equal opportunity at the university. Those contributions may include public service towards increasing equitable access in fields where women and minorities are under-represented. In some fields, the contributions may include research focusing on underserved populations or understanding inequalities related to race, gender, disability, or LGBT. The program is seeking applicants with the potential to bring to their academic and research careers the critical perspective that comes from their nontraditional educational background or understanding of the experiences of members of groups historically underrepresented in higher education in the United States.

Financial Data   The stipend is $44,500 per year (11 months, plus 1 month vacation). The award also includes health insurance, vision and dental benefits, and up to $5,000 for research-related and program travel expenses.

Duration   1 year; may be renewed 1 additional year.

Additional data   This program operates in addition to the University of California President's Postdoctoral Fellowship Program for Academic Diversity. Interested candidates may apply to either program.

Number awarded   2 each year.

Deadline   October of each year.

[1205]
UCAR VISITING SCIENTIST PROGRAMS

University Corporation for Atmospheric Research
Attn: Visiting Scientist Programs
3090 Center Green Drive
P.O. Box 3000
Boulder, CO 80307-3000
(303) 497-1605   Fax: (303) 497-8668
E-mail: vspapply@ucar.edu
Web: www.vsp.ucar.edu

Summary   To provide funding to recent postdoctorates in atmospheric sciences, especially Hispanics and other minorities, who wish to participate in designated research programs.

Eligibility   This program is open to postdoctorates (preferably those who received their Ph.D. within the preceding 3 years) who wish to conduct research with experienced scientists at designated facilities. Applicants must submit a cover letter stating the name of the program, potential host and institution, and where they learned of this opportunity; their curriculum vitae; names and addresses of at least 4 professional references; an abstract of their Ph.D. dissertation; and a description of the research they wish to conduct at the relevant facility. Women and minorities are encouraged to apply. U.S. citizenship is not required, although the research must be conducted at a U.S. institution.

Financial Data   The salary is $60,000 for the first year and $62,000 for the second year. A moving allowance of $750, an allowance of $5,000 per year for scientific travel, and a $3,000 publication allowance for the term of the award are also provided. Benefits include health and dental insurance, sick and annual leave, paid holidays, participation in a retirement fund, and life insurance.

Duration   2 years.

Additional data   Recently, positions were available through 3 programs: 1) the NOAA Climate and Global Change Postdoctoral Fellowship Program (sponsored by the National Oceanic and Atmospheric Administration; 2) the Postdocs Applying Climate Expertise (PACE) Fellowship Program; and 3) the Jack Eddy Postdoctoral Program in heliophysics (defined as all science common to the field of Sun-Earth connections).

Number awarded   Recently, 8 fellowships for the NOAA Climate and Global Change Postdoctoral Fellowship Program, 2 for the PACE Fellowship Program, and 4 for the Jack Eddy Postdoctoral Program were awarded.

Deadline   January of each year for the NOAA Climate and Global Change Postdoctoral Fellowship Program and the Jack Eddy Postdoctoral Program; May of each year for the PACE Fellowship Program.

[1206]
UCLA CHANCELLOR'S POSTDOCTORAL FELLOWSHIP PROGRAM

University of California at Los Angeles
Attn: Office for Diversity and Faculty Development
3109 Murphy Hall
P.O. Box 951407
Los Angeles, CA 90095-1407
(310) 206-7411   Fax: (310) 206-8427
E-mail: facdiversity@conet.ucla.edu
Web: faculty.diversity.ucla.edu

Summary To provide an opportunity for Hispanic and other recent postdoctorates who will increase diversity at the University of California at Los Angeles to conduct research at the university.

Eligibility This program is open to U.S. citizens and permanent residents who received a doctorate within 3 years of the start of the fellowship. Applicants must be interested in conducting research at UCLA. The program particularly solicits applications from scholars whose research, teaching, and service will contribute to the diversity and equal opportunity at the university. Those contributions may include public service addressing the needs of our increasingly diverse society, efforts to improve equitable access to higher education, or research focusing on underserved populations or understanding inequities related to race, gender, disability, or LGBT status.

Financial Data The stipend is at least $44,500 per year (11 months, plus 1 month vacation). The award also includes health insurance, vision and dental benefits, and up to $5,000 for research-related and program travel expenses.

Duration 1 year; may be renewed 1 additional year.

Additional data This program operates in addition to the University of California President's Postdoctoral Fellowship Program for Academic Diversity. Interested candidates may apply to either program.

Number awarded 2 each year.

Deadline October of each year.

[1207]
UNIVERSITY OF CALIFORNIA PRESIDENT'S POSTDOCTORAL FELLOWSHIP PROGRAM FOR ACADEMIC DIVERSITY

University of California at Berkeley
Attn: Office of Equity and Inclusion
402 Sproul Hall
Berkeley, CA 94720-5920
(510) 643-8235   E-mail: ppfpinfo@berkeley.edu
Web: ppfp.ucop.edu/info

Summary To provide an opportunity to conduct research at campuses of the University of California to recent postdoctorates who are committed to careers in university teaching and research and are Hispanics or other underrepresented minorities who will contribute to diversity.

Eligibility This program is open to U.S. citizens or permanent residents who have a Ph.D. from an accredited university. Applicants must be proposing to conduct research at a branch of the university under the mentorship of a faculty or laboratory sponsor. They must have the potential to contribute to higher education through their understanding of the barriers facing women, domestic minorities, LGBTQ individuals, students with disabilities, and other domestic groups in fields where they are underrepresented. Along with their application, they must submit an Education Background Statement that includes their potential to contribute to higher education through their understanding of the barriers facing members of groups underrepresented in higher education careers as evidenced by their life experiences and educational background.

Financial Data The stipend is $44,500 or higher, depending on the field and level of experience. The program also offers health benefits and up to $5,000 for supplemental and research-related expenses.

Duration Appointments are for 1 academic year, with possible renewal for a second year.

Additional data Research may be conducted at any of the University of California's 10 campuses (Berkeley, Davis, Irvine, Los Angeles, Merced, Riverside, San Diego, San Francisco, Santa Barbara, or Santa Cruz). The program provides mentoring and guidance in preparing for an academic career. This program was established in 1984 to encourage applications from minority and women scholars in fields where they were severely underrepresented; it is now open to all qualified candidates whose research, teaching, and service will contribute to diversity and equal opportunity at the University of California. In addition to this program for UC campuses in general, the Universities of California at Berkeley, Davis, Irvine, Los Angeles, Merced, Riverside, and San Diego offer separate Chancellor's Postdoctoral Fellowship programs for their institutions. Interested candidates may apply to those programs and/or this system-wide program.

Number awarded Varies each year; recently, 33 were selected.

Deadline October of each year.

[1208]
UNIVERSITY OF NORTH CAROLINA POSTDOCTORAL PROGRAM FOR FACULTY DIVERSITY

University of North Carolina at Chapel Hill
Attn: Office of Postdoctoral Affairs
301 Bynum Hall, CB 4100
Chapel Hill, NC 27599-4100
(919) 843-4793   Fax: (919) 962-6769
E-mail: jennifer_pruitt@unc.edu
Web: www.research.unc.edu/carolina-postdocs/applicants

Summary To support Hispanic and other minority scholars who are interested in teaching and conducting research at the University of North Carolina (UNC).

Eligibility This program is open to scholars, especially members of underrepresented groups (Hispanic Americans, African Americans, Native Americans) who have completed their doctoral degree within the past 5 years. Applicants must be interested in teaching and conducting research at UNC. Preference is given to U.S. citizens and permanent residents. Selection is based on the evidence of scholarship potential and ability to compete for tenure-track appointments at UNC and other research universities.

Financial Data Fellows receive $47,476 per year, plus an allowance of $2,000 for research and travel. Health benefits are also available.

Duration Up to 2 years.

Additional data Fellows must be in residence at the Chapel Hill campus for the duration of the program. They teach 1 course per year and spend the rest of the time in research. This program began in 1983.

Number awarded 4 or 5 each year.

Deadline November of each year.

[1209]
WARREN G. MAGNUSON EDUCATIONAL SUPPORT PERSONNEL SCHOLARSHIP GRANT

Washington Education Association
32032 Weyerhaeuser Way South
P.O. Box 9100
Federal Way, WA 98063-9100
(253) 765-7056   Toll Free: (800) 622-3393, ext. 7056
E-mail: Janna.Connor@Washingtonea.org
Web: www.washingtonea.org

Summary To provide funding to Educational Support Personnel (ESP) members of the Washington Education Association (WEA), especially Hispanics and other minorities, who are interested in taking classes to obtain an initial teaching certificate.

Eligibility This program is open to WEA/ESP members who are engaged in course work related to obtaining an initial teaching certificate. Applicants must submit a plan for obtaining an initial certificate, a letter describing their passion to become a teacher, evidence of activities and/or leadership in the association, and 3 to 5 letters of reference. Minority members of the association are especially encouraged to apply; 1 of the scholarships is reserved for them.

Financial Data The stipend is $1,500.

Duration These are 1-time grants.

Number awarded 3 each year, including 1 reserved for a minority member.

Deadline June of each year.

[1210]
W.E.B. DUBOIS FELLOWSHIP FOR RESEARCH ON RACE AND CRIME

Department of Justice
National Institute of Justice
Attn: W.E.B. DuBois Fellowship Program
810 Seventh Street, N.W.
Washington, DC 20531
Toll Free: (800) 851-3420   Fax: (301) 240-5830
TDD: (301) 240-6310   E-mail: grants@ncjrs.gov
Web: www.nij.gov

Summary To provide funding to junior investigators, especially Hispanics and other minorities, who are interested in conducting research on "crime, justice, and culture in various societal contexts."

Eligibility This program is open to investigators who have a Ph.D. or other doctoral-level degree (including a legal degree of J.D. or higher). Applicants should be early in their careers and not have been awarded tenure. They must be interested in conducting research that relates to specific areas that change annually but relate to criminal justice policy and practice in the United States. The sponsor strongly encourages applications from women and minorities. Selection is based on understanding of the problem and its importance (10%); quality and technical merit (40%); potential for a significant scientific or technical advance that will improve criminal/juvenile justice in the United states (20%); capabilities, demonstrated productivity, and experience of the principal investigator and the institution (15%); and dissemination strategy to broader audiences (15%).

Financial Data Grants range up to $100,000 for fellows who propose to conduct secondary data analysis or up to $150,000 for fellows who proposed to conduct primary data collection. Funds may be used for salary, fringe benefits, reasonable costs of relocation, travel essential to the project, and office expenses not provided by the sponsor. Indirect costs are limited to 20%.

Duration Up to 24 months; residency at the National Institute of Justice (NIJ) is not required but it is available.

Number awarded Up to 3 each year.

Deadline May of each year.

[1211]
W.E.B. DUBOIS SCHOLARS

Department of Justice
National Institute of Justice
Attn: W.E.B. DuBois Fellowship Program
810 Seventh Street, N.W.
Washington, DC 20531
Toll Free: (800) 851-3420   Fax: (301) 240-5830
TDD: (301) 240-6310   E-mail: grants@ncjrs.gov
Web: www.nij.gov

Summary To provide funding to advanced investigators, especially Hispanics and other minorities, who are interested in conducting research on "crime, justice, and culture in various societal contexts."

Eligibility This program is open to investigators who received their terminal degree in their field more than 5 years previously. Applicants must be interested in conducting primary research that relates to specific areas that change annually but relate to criminal justice policy and practice in the United States. The sponsor strongly encourages applications from women and minorities. Selection is based on understanding of the problem and its importance (10%); quality and technical merit (40%); potential for a significant scientific or technical advance that will improve criminal/juvenile justice in the United states (20%); capabilities, demonstrated productivity, and experience of the principal investigator and the institution (15%); and dissemination strategy to broader audiences (15%).

Financial Data Grants range up to $500,000. Funds may be used for salary, fringe benefits, reasonable costs of relocation, travel essential to the project, and office expenses not provided by the sponsor.

Duration Up to 36 months; residency at the National Institute of Justice (NIJ) is not required but it is available.

Number awarded Up to 4 each year.

Deadline May of each year.

[1212]
WILLIAM J. PERRY FELLOWSHIP IN INTERNATIONAL SECURITY

Stanford University
Center for International Security and Cooperation
Attn: Fellowships Coordinator
Encina Hall, Room C206-10
616 Serra Street
Stanford, CA 94305-6165
(650) 723-9625   Fax: (650) 724-5683
E-mail: perryfellows@stanford.edu
Web: cisac.fsi.stanford.edu/fellowships/perry_fellowship

Summary To provide funding to Hispanice and other minority professionals who are interested in conducting policy-relevant research on international security issues while in residence at Stanford University's Center for International Security and Cooperation.

Eligibility This program is open to early and mid-career professionals from academia, the public and private sectors, national laboratories, and the military, either from the United States or abroad. Applicants must have a record of outstanding work in natural science, engineering, or mathematics and a genuine interest in and dedication to solving international security problems. Their proposed research may involve interlapping issues of nuclear weapons policy and nuclear proliferation, regional tensions, biosecurity, homeland security, and effective global engagement. The sponsor welcomes applications from women, minorities, and citizens of all countries.

Financial Data The stipend depends on experience and is determined on a case-by-case basis. Health care and other benefits are also provided.

Duration 9 to 11 months.

Additional data Fellows are expected to produce a publishable manuscript based on their research. They should not plan to spend any time conducting research abroad or in other parts of the country.

Number awarded Varies each year; recently, 3 of these fellows were in residence.

Deadline January of each year.

[1213]
WRITERS OF COLOR FELLOWSHIPS OF OREGON LITERARY FELLOWSHIPS

Literary Arts, Inc.
Attn: Oregon Book Awards and Fellowships Program
  Coordinator
925 S.W. Washington Street
Portland, OR 97205
(503) 227-2583 Fax: (503) 243-1167
E-mail: susan@literary-arts.org
Web: www.literary-arts.org

Summary To provide funding to Hispanic and other writers of color in Oregon who are interested in working on a literary project.

Eligibility This program is open to writers of color who have been residents of Oregon for at least 1 year and are interested in initiating, developing, or completing a literary project in the areas of poetry, fiction, literary nonfiction, drama, or young readers' literature. Priority is given to writers whose work promotes perspectives from a variety of cultural, ethnic, and racial backgrounds. Writers in the early stages of their careers are especially encouraged to apply. Selection is based primarily on literary merit.

Financial Data Grants are at least $2,500.

Duration The grants are presented annually.

Additional data This program began in 2016.

Number awarded 1 each year.

Deadline June of each year.

[1214]
YERBY POSTDOCTORAL FELLOWSHIP PROGRAM

Harvard T.H. Chan School of Public Health
Attn: Office of Faculty Affairs
90 Smith Street, First Floor
Boston, MA 02120
(617) 432-1047 Fax: (617) 432-4711
E-mail: cburkot@hsph.harvard.edu
Web: www.hsph.harvard.edu

Summary To provide Hispanics and other postdoctorates who will contribute to diversity with an opportunity to pursue a program of research training at Harvard School of Public Health.

Eligibility This program is open to postdoctorates who are interested in preparing for a career in public health. The program emphasizes applicants who will contribute to academic diversity, meaning 1) members of minority groups underrepresented in public health (American Indians or Alaska Natives, Blacks or African Americans, Hispanics or Latinos, and Native Hawaiians or other Pacific Islanders); and 2) individuals with disabilities.

Financial Data Fellows receive a competitive salary.

Duration 1 year; may be renewed 1 additional year.

Number awarded Up to 5 each year.

Deadline November of each year.

[1215]
ZENITH FELLOWS AWARD PROGRAM

Alzheimer's Association
Attn: Medical and Scientific Affairs
225 North Michigan Avenue, 17th Floor
Chicago, IL 60601-7633
(312) 335-5747 Toll Free: (800) 272-3900
Fax: (866) 699-1246 TDD: (312) 335-5886
E-mail: grantsapp@alz.org
Web: www.alz.org

Summary To provide funding to established investigators, especially Hispanics and other underrepresented minorities, who are interested in conducting advanced research on Alzheimer's Disease.

Eligibility Eligible are scientists who have already contributed significantly to the field of Alzheimer's Disease research and are likely to continue to make significant contributions for many years to come. The proposed research must be "on the cutting edge" of basic, biomedical research and may not fit current conventional scientific wisdom or may challenge the prevailing orthodoxy. It should address fundamental problems related to early detection, etiology, pathogenesis, treatment, and/or prevention of Alzheimer's Disease. Scientists from underrepresented groups are especially encouraged to apply.

Financial Data Grants up to $250,000 per year, including direct expenses and up to 10% for overhead costs, are available. The total award for the life of the grant may not exceed $450,000.

Duration 2 or 3 years.

Additional data This program began in 1991.

Number awarded Up to 4 each year.

Deadline Letters of intent must be submitted by the end of March of each year. Final applications are due in May.

Indexes

Program Title Index

If you know the name of a particular funding program open to Hispanic Americans and want to find out where it is covered in the directory, use the Program Title Index. Here, program titles are arranged alphabetically, word by word. To assist you in your search, every program is listed by all its known names or abbreviations. In addition, we've used an alphabetical code (within parentheses) to help you determine if the program is aimed at you: U = Undergraduates; G = Graduate Students; P = Professionals/Postdoctorates. Here's how the code works: if a program is followed by (U) 241, the program is described in the Undergraduates chapter, in entry 241. If the same program title is followed by another entry number—for example, (P) 901—the program is also described in the Professionals/Postdoctorates chapter, in entry 901. Remember: the numbers cited here refer to program entry numbers, not to page numbers in the book.

U–Undergraduates   **G–Graduate Students**   **P–Professionals/Postdoctorates**

U–Undergraduates　　　　**G–Graduate Students**　　　　**P–Professionals/Postdoctorates**

ASME Graduate Teaching Fellowship, (G) 644

ASP Graduate Student Visitor Program, (G) 645

ASSE Diversity Committee Graduate Scholarship, (G) 646

ASSE Diversity Committee Undergraduate Scholarship, (U) 47

Associated Food and Petroleum Dealers Minority Scholarships, (U) 48

Association for Computing Machinery/IEEE-CS George Michael Memorial HPC Fellowships. See ACM/IEEE-CS George Michael Memorial HPC Fellowships, entry (G) 598

Association for Computing Machinery Special Interest Group on High Performance Computing Intel Computational and Data Science Fellowships. See ACM SIGHPC/Intel Computational and Data Science Fellowships, entry (G) 599

Association for Education in Journalism and Mass Communication Latino/Latin American Communication Research Award. See FIU-AEJMC Latino/Latin American Communication Research Award, entries (U) 185, (G) 739, (P) 1112

Association for Women Geoscientists Minority Scholarship, (U) 49

Association for Women in Science Seattle Scholarships. See Seattle Chapter AWIS Scholarships, entry (U) 499

Association of American Veterinary Medical Colleges Veterinary Student Scholarship Program. See Zoetis/AAVMC Veterinary Student Scholarship Program, entry (G) 1053

Association of Cuban Engineers Scholarships, (U) 50, (G) 647

Association of Latino Administrators & Superintendents/ Houghton Mifflin Scholarship. See ALAS/Houghton Mifflin Harcourt Scholarship, entry (G) 613

Association of Latino Professionals For America Scholarship Program, (U) 51, (G) 648

Association of Latino Professionals in Finance and Accounting Scholarship Program. See Association of Latino Professionals For America Scholarship Program, entries (U) 51, (G) 648

Association of National Advertisers Multicultural Excellence Scholarship. See ANA Multicultural Excellence Scholarship, entry (U) 32, 144

Association of Nurses in AIDS Care Student Diversity Mentorship Scholarship. See ANAC Student Diversity Mentorship Scholarship, entries (U) 33, (P) 1066

Association of Peruvian American Professionals Scholarship. See APAPRO Scholarship, entry (U) 38

Association of Research Libraries Career Enhancement Program. See ARL Career Enhancement Program, entry (G) 637

Association of Research Libraries Initiative to Recruit a Diverse Workforce. See ARL Initiative to Recruit a Diverse Workforce, entry (G) 638

Association of Research Libraries/Society of American Archivists Mosaic Scholarships. See ARL/SAA Mosaic Scholarships, entry (G) 639

Astronomy and Astrophysics Postdoctoral Fellowships, (P) 1073

Atherton Ministerial Scholarship. See Martha and Robert Atherton Ministerial Scholarship, entry (G) 871

Atkins North America Achievement College Scholarship, (U) 52

Atkins North America Achievement High School Scholarship, (U) 53

Atkins North America Leadership Scholarship, (U) 54, (G) 649

Atlanta Chapter AABE Scholarships, (U) 55

Atmospheric and Geospace Sciences Postdoctoral Research Fellowships, (P) 1074

Atmospheric Sciences Ascent Award, (P) 1075

Auchincloss Foundation Fellow. See New York Foundation for the Arts Artists' Fellowships, entry (P) 1170

Aurelio "Larry" Jazo Migrant Scholarship, (U) 56

Auzenne Fellowship for Graduate Study. See Delores A. Auzenne Fellowship for Graduate Study, entry (G) 700

Aviation and Professional Development Scholarship, (U) 57

Awards for Faculty at Hispanic Serving Institutions, (P) 1076

AWS Fox Valley Section Scholarship, (U) 58

AWS Tidewater Virginia Section Scholarship, (U) 59

AZALAS High School Senior Scholarships, (U) 60

B

Baker Scholarship for Diversity in Engineering. See Michael Baker Scholarship for Diversity in Engineering, entry (U) 355

Balfour Phi Delta Phi Minority Scholarship Award, (G) 650

Balhoff Leadership Scholarship. See Michigan Accountancy Foundation Fifth/Graduate Year Scholarship Program, entries (U) 356, (G) 886

Baltimore Chapter AABE Scholarships, (U) 61

Banks Memorial Undergraduate Scholarship. See Sharon D. Banks Memorial Undergraduate Scholarship, entry (U) 502

Banner Scholarship for Law Students. See Mark T. Banner Scholarship for Law Students, entry (G) 870

Barbara Wolff-Reichert Award for Excellence in Advanced Laboratory Instruction. See Jonathan Reichert and Barbara Wolff-Reichert Award for Excellence in Advanced Laboratory Instruction, entry (P) 1135

Barrientos Scholarship. See Lucy Mora Barrientos Scholarship, entry (U) 326

Barrientos Scholarship Foundation Arts Scholarships, (U) 62

Barrientos Scholarship Foundation Education Scholarships, (U) 63

Barrientos Scholarship Foundation Engineering/Technology Scholarships, (U) 64

Barrientos Scholarship Foundation Health Scholarships, (U) 65

Barrow Minority Doctoral Student Scholarship. See Lionel C. Barrow Minority Doctoral Student Scholarship, entry (G) 859

Basic Psychological Science Research Grant, (G) 651

Basil H. Alkazzi Award for Excellence. See New York Foundation for the Arts Artists' Fellowships, entry (P) 1170

Bayer Scholarships, (U) 66

Beautiful Minds Scholarship, (U) 67

Becas Univision Scholarship Program, (U) 68, (G) 652

Bechtel Undergraduate Fellowship Award, (U) 69

Beeson Emerging Leaders Career Development Awards in Aging. See Paul B. Beeson Emerging Leaders Career Development Awards in Aging, entry (P) 1178

Ben and Delia Sifuentes Scholarships, (U) 70

Bendix Minorities in Engineering Award. See DuPont Minorities in Engineering Award, entry (P) 1102

Benjamin Schneider Scholarship. See Goldstein and Schneider Scholarships by the Macey Fund, entry (G) 760

Benjamin Webber Trust Scholarships. See Josephine and Benjamin Webber Trust Scholarships, entries (U) 284, (G) 827

Bergeron Leadership Scholarship. See Michigan Accountancy Foundation Fifth/Graduate Year Scholarship Program, entries (U) 356, (G) 886

Bernard Harris Math and Science Scholarships. See ExxonMobil Bernard Harris Math and Science Scholarships, entry (U) 180

Bernard Majewski Fellowship, (P) 1077

Bernbach Diversity Scholarships. See Bill Bernbach Diversity Scholarships, entries (U) 71, (G) 654

Betancourt Award. See Association of Cuban Engineers Scholarships, entries (U) 50, (G) 647

Betty Lea Stone Research Fellowship, (G) 653

U–Undergraduates   **G–Graduate Students**   **P–Professionals/Postdoctorates**

U–Undergraduates   G–Graduate Students   P–Professionals/Postdoctorates

U–Undergraduates   **G–Graduate Students**   **P–Professionals/Postdoctorates**

U–Undergraduates G–Graduate Students P–Professionals/Postdoctorates

U–Undergraduates   **G–Graduate Students**   **P–Professionals/Postdoctorates**

U–Undergraduates   **G–Graduate Students**   **P–Professionals/Postdoctorates**

U–Undergraduates   **G–Graduate Students**   **P–Professionals/Postdoctorates**

U–Undergraduates   **G–Graduate Students**   **P–Professionals/Postdoctorates**

U–Undergraduates   **G–Graduate Students**   **P–Professionals/Postdoctorates**

U–Undergraduates   **G–Graduate Students**   **P–Professionals/Postdoctorates**

Society of Hispanic Professional Engineers Graduate Scholarship. *See* SHPE Graduate Scholarship, entry (G) 1005

Society of Hispanic Professional Engineers Graduating High School Senior Scholarship. *See* SHPE Graduating High School Senior Scholarship, entry (U) 507

Society of Hispanic Professional Engineers Northrop Grumman Scholarship. *See* SHPE Northrop Grumman Scholarship, entry (U) 508

Society of Hispanic Professional Engineers Professional Scholarship. *See* SHPE Professional Scholarship, entries (G) 1006, (P) 1192

Society of Hispanic Professional Engineers Undergraduate Scholarship. *See* SHPE Undergraduate Scholarship, entry (U) 509

Society of Hispanic Professional Engineers-Twin Cities Scholarships. *See* SHPE-TC Scholarships, entry (U) 510

Solar, Stellar, and Planetary Solar Summer Intern Program. *See* CfA HEA/SSP Solar Summer Intern Program, entry (U) 101

Solar Summer Intern Program. *See* CfA HEA/SSP Solar Summer Intern Program, entry (U) 101

Somos Scholarships, (U) 515

Soto Scholarship. *See* Cuban American Bar Association Scholarships, entry (G) 690

South Carolina Professional Association for Access and Equity Scholarships. *See* SC-PAAE Scholarships, entry (U) 497

Southern Regional Education Board Dissertation Awards, (G) 1011

Southern Regional Education Board Doctoral Awards. *See* SREB Doctoral Awards, entry (G) 1014

Spanish Baptist Convention of New Mexico Scholarship, (U) 516, (G) 1012

Special Libraries Association New England Diversity Leadership Development Scholarship. *See* SLA New England Diversity Leadership Development Scholarship, entries (G) 1008, (P) 1193

Spectrum Scholarship Program, (G) 1013

Sphinx Competition Awards, (U) 517

Spielberger Scholarship. *See* APF Graduate Student Scholarships, entry (G) 635

Spitzer Fellowship. *See* Hubble Fellowships, entry (P) 1129

Sponsors for Educational Opportunity Career Law Program. *See* SEO Career Law Program, entry (G) 1002

Sponsors for Educational Opportunity Career Program. *See* SEO Undergraduate Career Program, entry (U) 501

Spurlock Research Fellowship in Substance Abuse and Addiction for Minority Medical Students. *See* Jeanne Spurlock Research Fellowship in Substance Abuse and Addiction for Minority Medical Students, entry (G) 816

SREB Doctoral Awards, (G) 1014

SRO MUREP. *See* NASA Scholarship and Research Opportunities (SRO) Minority University Research and Education Project (MUREP) Scholarships, entry (U) 402

SSP Solar Summer Intern Program. *See* CfA HEA/SSP Solar Summer Intern Program, entry (U) 101

SSRP-Amgen Scholars Program, (U) 518

Stafford Scholarship in Architecture. *See* Gordon Stafford Scholarship in Architecture, entries (U) 212, (G) 761

Stanford Humanities Center External Faculty Fellowships, (P) 1194

Stanford Memorial WLMA Scholarship. *See* John Stanford Memorial WLMA Scholarship, entry (G) 824

Stanford Summer Research Program/Amgen Scholars Program. *See* SSRP-Amgen Scholars Program, entry (U) 518

Stanley Minority and International Scholarship. *See* Alan Compton and Bob Stanley Minority and International Scholarship, entry (U) 19

Stanton Nuclear Security Fellowship, (G) 1015, (P) 1195

State Council on Adapted Physical Education Cultural Diversity Student Scholarship, (U) 519

State Representative Irma Rangel Memorial Scholarships, (U) 520

Stephens Graduate Scholarship. *See* Jack L. Stephens Graduate Scholarship, entry (G) 808

Steps to Success-The Doug Paul Scholarship Program, (U) 521

Stone Research Fellowship. *See* Betty Lea Stone Research Fellowship, entry (G) 653

Stoudt Scholarships. *See* James W. Stoudt Scholarships, entry (G) 814

Strait Minority Scholarship Endowment. *See* George A. Strait Minority Scholarship Endowment, entries (G) 755, (P) 1118

Student Affiliates in School Psychology Advanced Student Diversity Scholarships. *See* SASP Advanced Student Diversity Scholarships, entry (G) 995

Student Opportunity Scholarships of the Presbyterian Church (USA), (U) 522

Studio Museum in Harlem Artist-in-Residence Program, (P) 1196

Stulman Endowed Scholars Grants. *See* Leonard and Helen R. Stulman Endowed Scholars Grants, entry (G) 855

Substance Abuse and Mental Health Services Minority Fellowship Program. *See* APA/SAMHSA Minority Fellowship Program, entry (P) 1069

Substance Abuse Fellowship Program, (P) 1197

Summer Clinical and Translational Research Program, (U) 523

Summer Honors Undergraduate Research Program, (U) 524

Summer Internships in Nuclear Forensics and Environmental Radiochemistry, (G) 1016

Summer Judicial Internship Program. *See* JTBF Summer Judicial Internship Program, entry (G) 831

Summer Program in Biostatistics and Computational Biology, (U) 525

Summer Program in Epidemiology, (U) 526

Summer Research Opportunities Program (SROP), (U) 527

Summer Research Opportunity Program in Pathology, (G) 1017

Summer Research Program in Ecology, (U) 528, (P) 1198

Summer Transportation Internship Program for Diverse Groups, (U) 529, (G) 1018

Summer Undergraduate Research Fellow (SURF) Individual Awards, (U) 530

Summer Undergraduate Research Fellowships in Organic Chemistry, (U) 531

Sumner M. Redstone Fellowship. *See* IRTS Summer Fellowship Program, entries (U) 265, (G) 806

SUNY Graduate Diversity Fellowship Program, (G) 1019

Surety and Fidelity Industry Scholarship Program, (U) 532

Susan M. Jackson Ministerial Scholars Fund, (G) 1020

Susie Revels Cayton Scholarship. *See* Horace and Susie Revels Cayton Scholarship, entry (U) 244

Synod of Lakes and Prairies Racial Ethnic Scholarships, (U) 533, (G) 1021

T

TACHE Distinguished Community College Faculty Award, (P) 1199

TACHE Distinguished University Faculty Award, (P) 1200

Taylor Memorial Summer Minority Policy Fellowship. *See* Dalmas A. Taylor Memorial Summer Minority Policy Fellowship, entry (G) 692

U–Undergraduates   **G–Graduate Students**   **P–Professionals/Postdoctorates**

U–Undergraduates   G–Graduate Students   P–Professionals/Postdoctorates

U–Undergraduates　　　　**G–Graduate Students**　　　　**P–Professionals/Postdoctorates**

Sponsoring Organization Index

The Sponsoring Organization Index makes it easy to identify agencies that offer financial aid to Hispanic Americans. In this index, the sponsoring organizations are listed alphabetically, word by word. In addition, we've used an alphabetical code (within parentheses) to help you identify the intended recipients of the funding offered by the organizations: U = Undergraduates; G = Graduate Students; P = Professionals/Postdoctorates. For example, if the name of a sponsoring organization is followed by (U) 241, a program sponsored by that organization is described in the Undergraduate chapter, in entry 241. If that sponsoring organization's name is followed by another entry number—for example, (G) 915—the same or a different program sponsored by that organization is described in the Professionals/Postdoctorates chapter, in entry 915. Remember: the numbers cited here refer to program entry numbers, not to page numbers in the book.

A

ABC National Television Sales, (U) 265, (G) 806
Academic Library Association of Ohio, (G) 593
Academy of Applied Science, (U) 472
Academy of Criminal Justice Sciences, (P) 1100
Academy of Nutrition and Dietetics, (U) 5, 122, 143, (G) 594, 682, 701, (P) 1056, 1097
Accountancy Board of Ohio, (U) 7
Accounting and Financial Women's Alliance, (U) 313
Acoustical Society of America, (G) 600
Act Six, (U) 8
Actuarial Foundation, (U) 9
Acxiom Corporation, (U) 10, (G) 601
A-dec Inc., (G) 603
Adelante, (U) 467
¡Adelante! U.S. Education Leadership Fund, (U) 207, 365-368
Advanced Laboratory Physics Association, (U) 2
AIGA, the professional association for design, (U) 586, (G) 1049
Airport Minority Advisory Council, (U) 23, 57
Alabama Society of Certified Public Accountants, (U) 45
Albuquerque Hispano Chamber of Commerce, (U) 21
Alfred P. Sloan Foundation, (G) 698, (P) 1096
Allina Health System, (U) 174
Alpha Kappa Delta, (G) 642
Alzheimer's Association, (P) 1060-1062, 1215
American Academy of Child and Adolescent Psychiatry, (G) 816
American Academy of Physician Assistants, (U) 443, (G) 949
American Anthropological Association, (G) 618
American Association for Justice, (G) 979
American Association for Respiratory Care, (U) 276
American Association of Advertising Agencies, (U) 32, 71, 144, 440, (G) 654, 946
American Association of Blacks in Energy, (U) 25
American Association of Blacks in Energy. Atlanta Chapter, (U) 55, 479

American Association of Blacks in Energy. Baltimore Chapter, (U) 61
American Association of Blacks in Energy. Birmingham Chapter, (U) 73
American Association of Blacks in Energy. Connecticut Chapter, (U) 129
American Association of Blacks in Energy. Denver Area Chapter, (U) 113
American Association of Blacks in Energy. East Tennessee Chapter, (U) 163, 581
American Association of Blacks in Energy. Florida Chapter, (U) 187
American Association of Blacks in Energy. Houston Chapter, (U) 245
American Association of Blacks in Energy. Indiana Chapter, (U) 259
American Association of Blacks in Energy. Michigan Chapter, (U) 357
American Association of Blacks in Energy. Mississippi Chapter, (U) 383
American Association of Blacks in Energy. New Jersey Chapter, (U) 415
American Association of Blacks in Energy. North Carolina Chapter, (U) 422
American Association of Blacks in Energy. Philadelphia Chapter, (U) 452
American Association of Blacks in Energy. South Carolina Chapter, (U) 285
American Association of Blacks in Energy. Virginia Chapter, (U) 562
American Association of Blacks in Energy. Washington DC Metropolitan Area Chapter, (U) 570
American Association of Colleges of Nursing, (G) 825
American Association of Colleges of Osteopathic Medicine, (G) 1003
American Association of Critical-Care Nurses, (U) 78, (G) 656

U–Undergraduates　　　　**G–Graduate Students**　　　　**P–Professionals/Postdoctorates**

U–Undergraduates   G–Graduate Students   P–Professionals/Postdoctorates

U–Undergraduates   G–Graduate Students   P–Professionals/Postdoctorates

Massachusetts Society of Certified Public Accountants, (U) 392
Mathematica Policy Research, Inc., (G) 876
Mayday Fund, (G) 950
Mayo Clinic, (U) 78, (G) 656
McKenzie River Gathering Foundation, (P) 1146
McNair Scholars Program, (U) 474
Mecklenburg County Bar, (G) 673
Media General, (U) 350
Medical College of Wisconsin, (U) 147
Medical Library Association, (G) 902-903
Medtronic, Inc., (U) 510
Merck Research Laboratories, (U) 474
MetLife Foundation, (G) 881
Metropolitan Museum of Art, (U) 395, (G) 909, (P) 1159
Mexican American Legal Defense and Educational Fund, (G) 866
Mexican American Legislative Leadership Foundation, (U) 389, (G) 904, (P) 1158
Michael Baker Corporation, (U) 355
Michigan Association of Certified Public Accountants, (U) 356, (G) 886
Michigan Auto Law, (G) 887
Midwest Sociological Society, (G) 642
Migrant Students Foundation, (U) 90
MillerCoors LLC, (U) 365-368
Milton & Sally Avery Arts Foundation, (P) 1170
Mindset Scholars Network, (P) 1084
Minnesota Association of Administrators of State and Federal Education Programs, (U) 229
Minnesota Association of Counselors of Color, (U) 386
Minnesota Broadcasters Association, (U) 274
Minnesota Social Service Association, (U) 369
Minority Corporate Counsel Association, (G) 596
Minority Educational Foundation of the United States of America, (U) 108
Missouri Department of Higher Education, (U) 372, 384, (G) 895
Missouri Society of Certified Public Accountants, (U) 393, (G) 907
Modern Language Association of America, (P) 1157
Montgomery County Executive Hispanic Gala, (U) 344
Morgan Stanley, (U) 477, (G) 905
Mortenson, (U) 510
Moss Adams LLP, (U) 390, (G) 906
Museum of Fine Arts, Houston, (U) 351
Mutual of Omaha, (U) 396
MV Transportation, Inc., (U) 397-398

N

The National Academies of Sciences, Engineering, and Medicine, (G) 703, 960, (P) 1182
National Academy of Medicine, (P) 1187
National Academy of Television Arts & Sciences, (U) 265, (G) 806
National Action Council for Minorities in Engineering, (U) 69, 204, 455, 578
National Applied Research Laboratories of Taiwan, (P) 1084
National Association of Broadcasters, (U) 171
National Association of Collegiate Directors of Athletics, (G) 823, (P) 1134
National Association of Health Services Executives. Memphis Chapter, (U) 75
National Association of Hispanic Journalists, (U) 403, (G) 914
National Association of Hispanic Journalists. Seattle Chapter, (U) 429

National Association of Hispanic Nurses, (U) 109, 401, 551, (G) 677, 910, 1031
National Association of Hispanic Nurses. Michigan Chapter, (U) 404, (G) 915
National Association of Pastoral Musicians, (U) 430, (G) 939
National Association of School Psychologists, (G) 913
National Association of Social Workers, (G) 687
National Association of State Directors of Migrant Education, (U) 20
National Association of Teacher Educators for Family and Consumer Sciences, (G) 735
National Athletic Trainers' Association, (G) 819
National Board for Certified Counselors, (G) 923-925, (P) 1167
National Business Group on Health, (G) 984
National Center for Atmospheric Research, (U) 473, 511, (G) 645, (P) 1161
National Center for Farmworker Health, Inc., (U) 362, (G) 890, (P) 1154
National Collegiate Athletic Association, (G) 817, 926
National Conference of Puerto Rican Women. Miami Chapter, (U) 400
National Conference of Puerto Rican Women. New York Chapter, (U) 399
National Consortium for Graduate Degrees for Minorities in Engineering and Science (GEM), (G) 747-749
National Hispanic Caucus of State Legislators, (U) 281
National Hispanic Coalition of Federal Aviation Employees, (U) 139, 471, (G) 976
National Hispanic Foundation for the Arts, (G) 917
National Hispanic Medical Association, (U) 406, (G) 918
National Lesbian & Gay Journalists Association, (U) 294, (G) 837
National Medical Fellowships, Inc., (G) 662, 712-713, 744, 751, 756, 795, 829, 919, 927, 932-933, 935, 1032, 1038, 1042-1043, (P) 1101
National Minority Junior Golf Scholarship Association, (U) 72
National Naval Officers Association. Washington, D.C. Chapter, (U) 94, 134, 309, 391, 568-569
National Organization of Professional Hispanic Natural Resources Conservation Service Employees, (U) 338, 409
National Physical Science Consortium, (G) 920
National Press Club, (U) 410
National Science Foundation, (U) 74, 83, 98, 101, 116, 133, 145, 148, 323, 345, 466, 473-474, 478, 492, 511, 528, 557, 585, (G) 645, (P) 1161, 1172, 1198
National Science Foundation. Directorate for Biological Sciences, (G) 707, 958, (P) 1183
National Science Foundation. Directorate for Education and Human Resources, (G) 763, (P) 1109
National Science Foundation. Directorate for Geosciences, (P) 1074, 1103
National Science Foundation. Directorate for Mathematical and Physical Sciences, (P) 1073, 1152
National Science Foundation. Directorate for Social, Behavioral, and Economic Sciences, (G) 753, 851, (P) 1126, 1188
National Society of Professional Engineers, (U) 348
National Strength and Conditioning Association, (U) 431, (G) 940
National Student Nurses' Association, (U) 78, (G) 656
National Trust for Historic Preservation, (G) 892
National Urban Fellows, Inc., (G) 922, (P) 1166
National Weather Association, (U) 140, (G) 697
National Women's Studies Association, (P) 1122
Native American Journalists Association. Seattle Chapter, (U) 429

U–Undergraduates   **G–Graduate Students**   **P–Professionals/Postdoctorates**

U–Undergraduates   G–Graduate Students   P–Professionals/Postdoctorates

U–Undergraduates   **G–Graduate Students**   **P–Professionals/Postdoctorates**

U.S. National Institutes of Health, (U) 221, (G) 991
U.S. National Institutes of Health. National Cancer Institute, (U) 91
U.S. National Institutes of Health. National Center for Research Resources, (U) 523, (G) 1040, (P) 1115
U.S. National Institutes of Health. National Heart, Lung, and Blood Institute, (U) 147, 550
U.S. National Institutes of Health. National Institute of Diabetes and Digestive and Kidney Diseases, (U) 14, (G) 607, (P) 1115
U.S. National Institutes of Health. National Institute of General Medical Sciences, (P) 1065
U.S. National Institutes of Health. National Institute of Mental Health, (G) 883
U.S. National Institutes of Health. National Institute of Neurological Disorders and Stroke, (P) 1178
U.S. National Institutes of Health. National Institute on Aging, (G) 608, 881, (P) 1178
U.S. National Institutes of Health. National Institute on Drug Abuse, (G) 719, 816
U.S. National Institutes of Health. National Library of Medicine, (G) 902
U.S. National Institutes of Health. Office of Intramural Training and Education, (U) 30, 407
U.S. National Park Service, (U) 202, (G) 752
U.S. National Security Agency, (G) 920
U.S. Navy. Naval Sea Systems Command, (U) 560
U.S. Navy. Naval Service Training Command Officer Development, (U) 199, 378
U.S. Navy. Office of Naval Research, (G) 916
U.S. Substance Abuse and Mental Health Services Administration, (G) 624-625, 633, 882, 899, 923-925, 959, (P) 1064, 1069, 1167, 1181, 1197
USA Funds, (U) 490

V

Vermont Studio Center, (P) 1092
Virgin Islands Society of Certified Public Accountants, (U) 17, (G) 611
Virginia Center for the Creative Arts, (P) 1059
Virginia Department of Education, (U) 564, (G) 1039
Virginia Latino Higher Education Network, (U) 563
Virginia Society of Certified Public Accountants, (U) 565

W

Warner Norcross & Judd LLP, (U) 566, (G) 1041
Washington Apple Education Foundation, (U) 363, 439
Washington Education Association, (U) 567, (P) 1209
Washington Library Association. School Library Division, (G) 824
Washington Science Teachers Association, (U) 571
Washington University. Division of Biology and Biomedical Sciences, (U) 572
Washington University. John C. Danforth Center on Religion and Politics, (P) 1133
Weber Shandwick, (U) 438
Wells Fargo Bank, (U) 441
Western Union Foundation, (U) 575
William and Flora Hewlett Foundation, (P) 1057
William Randolph Hearst Foundation, (U) 578
William T. Grant Foundation, (G) 965, (P) 1084
William Townsend Porter Foundation, (G) 956
Williams College. Dean of the Faculty, (G) 746, (P) 1117
Williams Companies, Inc., (U) 135

Wisconsin Association of Independent Colleges and Universities, (U) 558
Wisconsin Education Association Council, (U) 293
Wisconsin Higher Educational Aids Board, (U) 582
Wisconsin Hispanic Scholarship Foundation, Inc., (U) 353, (G) 885
Wisconsin Institute of Certified Public Accountants, (U) 317
Wisconsin League for Nursing, (U) 37, (G) 632
Wisconsin Speech-Language Pathology and Audiology Association, (G) 980
Wisconsin Women of Color Network, Inc., (U) 89, 222, 331
Wishes for Elliott, (G) 621
Women of the Evangelical Lutheran Church in America, (U) 24, (G) 617
Women's Transportation Seminar, (U) 321, 502, 584, 589, (G) 671, 778, 853
Woods Hole Oceanographic Institution, (U) 585
World Association for Cooperative Education (WACE), (U) 405
Worldstudio Foundation, (U) 586, (G) 1049
WSP USA, (U) 587-588, (G) 1051
Wyndham Worldwide, (U) 106, (G) 676

X

Xcel Energy, (U) 510
Xerox Corporation, (U) 590, (G) 1052

Z

ZGS Communications, (U) 107
Zoetis, Inc., (G) 1053
ZymoGenetics, Inc., (U) 499
3M Company, (U) 510

Residency Index

Some programs listed in this book are set aside for Hispanic Americans who are residents of a particular state or region. Others are open to applicants wherever they may live. The Residency Index will help you pinpoint programs available in your area as well as programs that have no residency restrictions at all (these are listed under the term "United States"). To use this index, look up the geographic areas that apply to you (always check the listings under "United States"), jot down the entry numbers listed for the recipient level that applies to you (Undergraduates, Graduate Students, or Professionals/Postdoctorates), and use those numbers to find the program descriptions in the directory. To help you in your search, we've provided some "see" and "see also" references in the index entries. Remember: the numbers cited here refer to program entry numbers, not to page numbers in the book.

A

Alabama: **Undergraduates,** 73. *See also* United States

Alaska: **Undergraduates,** 138, 543. *See also* United States

Albuquerque, New Mexico: **Undergraduates,** 181. *See also* New Mexico

Arizona: **Undergraduates,** 43, 60, 112, 153, 243, 284; **Graduate Students,** 827. *See also* United States

Arkansas: **Undergraduates,** 42, 543; **Graduate Students,** 636, 867. *See also* United States

Atlanta, Georgia: **Undergraduates,** 234. *See also* Georgia

Austin, Texas: **Undergraduates,** 534-539; **Graduate Students,** 694. *See also* Texas

B

Baldwin Park, California: **Undergraduates,** 534-539; **Graduate Students,** 694. *See also* California

Baltimore, Maryland: **Professionals/Postdoctorates,** 1092. *See also* Maryland

Bell Gardens, California: **Undergraduates,** 534-539; **Graduate Students,** 694. *See also* California

Burnett County, Wisconsin: **Undergraduates,** 174. *See also* Wisconsin

C

California: **Undergraduates,** 43, 84-87, 92-93, 99, 111-112, 153, 212, 237, 243, 258, 273, 304, 310, 339, 459, 489, 519; **Graduate Students,** 663-665, 679, 761, 789, 813, 846, 852, 872, 992; **Professionals/Postdoctorates,** 1139, 1151. *See also* United States

California, southern: **Graduate Students,** 683, 969. *See also* California

Campbellsville, Kentucky. *See* Kentucky

Chicago, Illinois: **Undergraduates,** 234. *See also* Illinois

Clark County, Washington: **Undergraduates,** 235, 458; **Graduate Students,** 787. *See also* Washington

Colorado: **Undergraduates,** 79, 100, 113, 119-120, 125, 167, 231, 289, 305, 335, 364; **Graduate Students,** 657, 723, 836, 867; **Professionals/Postdoctorates,** 1079. *See also* United States

Colorado Springs, Colorado: **Undergraduates,** 181. *See also* Colorado

Commerce, California: **Undergraduates,** 534-539; **Graduate Students,** 694. *See also* California

Connecticut: **Undergraduates,** 22, 38, 128-130, 132, 178, 183, 264; **Graduate Students,** 730, 736, 858. *See also* New England states; Northeastern states; United States

Cook County, Illinois: **Undergraduates,** 534-539; **Graduate Students,** 694. *See also* Illinois

Corpus Christi, Texas: **Undergraduates,** 181. *See also* Texas

D

Dallas, Texas: **Undergraduates,** 181, 234. *See also* Texas

Delaware: **Undergraduates,** 142, 452; **Graduate Students,** 699, 867. *See also* Northeastern states; Southeastern states; United States

Detroit, Michigan: **Undergraduates,** 356; **Graduate Students,** 886. *See also* Michigan

District of Columbia. *See* Washington, D.C.

E

Edinburg, Texas: **Undergraduates,** 534-539; **Graduate Students,** 694. *See also* Texas

El Paso, Texas: **Undergraduates,** 181. *See also* Texas

F

Florida: **Undergraduates,** 114, 187, 243, 283, 373, 379; **Graduate Students,** 700, 741, 826. *See also* Southeastern states; United States

G

Georgia: **Undergraduates,** 55, 205, 210, 479, 543. *See also* Southeastern states; United States

Tenability Index

Some programs listed in this book can be used only in specific cities, counties, states, or regions. Others may be used anywhere in the United States. The Tenability Index will help you locate funding that is restricted to a specific area as well as funding that has no tenability restrictions (these are listed under the term "United States"). To use this index, look up the geographic areas where you'd like to go (always check the listings under "United States"), jot down the entry numbers listed for the recipient group that represents you (Undergraduates, Graduate Students, Professionals/Postdoctorates), and use those numbers to find the program descriptions in the directory. To help you in your search, we've provided some "see" and "see also" references in the index entries. Remember: the numbers cited here refer to program entry numbers, not to page numbers in the book.

A

Aberdeen Proving Ground, Maryland: **Undergraduates,** 495. *See also* Maryland

Adelphi, Maryland: **Undergraduates,** 495. *See also* Maryland

Aiken, South Carolina: **Undergraduates,** 394; **Graduate Students,** 908. *See also* South Carolina

Alabama: **Undergraduates,** 45, 314; **Graduate Students,** 854, 1011, 1014; **Professionals/Postdoctorates,** 1144. *See also* United States; names of specific cities and counties

Alaska: **Undergraduates,** 428. *See also* United States; names of specific cities

Albany, Oregon: **Undergraduates,** 359; **Graduate Students,** 888; **Professionals/Postdoctorates,** 1153. *See also* Oregon

Albuquerque, New Mexico: **Undergraduates,** 199, 378; **Graduate Students,** 920, 1032. *See also* New Mexico

Alexandria, Virginia: **Undergraduates,** 495. *See also* Virginia

Allentown, Pennsylvania: **Graduate Students,** 702. *See also* Pennsylvania

Ames, Iowa: **Undergraduates,** 40. *See also* Iowa

Amherst, Massachusetts: **Undergraduates,** 168; **Graduate Students,** 702, 724. *See also* Massachusetts

Ann Arbor, Michigan: **Undergraduates,** 527; **Graduate Students,** 686, 876; **Professionals/Postdoctorates,** 1136, 1186. *See also* Michigan

Appleton, Wisconsin: **Graduate Students,** 702. *See also* Wisconsin

Argonne, Illinois: **Undergraduates,** 394; **Graduate Students,** 631, 908. *See also* Illinois

Arizona: **Undergraduates,** 41, 90, 243, 263, 284, 311, 544; **Graduate Students,** 803, 827. *See also* United States; names of specific cities and counties

Arkansas: **Graduate Students,** 1011, 1014. *See also* United States; names of specific cities and counties

Arlington, Virginia: **Undergraduates,** 495. *See also* Virginia

Armonk, New York: **Undergraduates,** 83. *See also* New York

Ashburn, Virginia: **Graduate Students,** 879. *See also* Virginia

Ashland, Wisconsin: **Undergraduates,** 493-494. *See also* Wisconsin

Atlanta, Georgia: **Undergraduates,** 71, 266, 351, 378, 440; **Graduate Students,** 654, 686, 751, 867, 946, 1002, 1032. *See also* Georgia

Austin, Texas: **Undergraduates,** 10, 39, 71, 332, 378, 389, 440, 500, 506, 561; **Graduate Students,** 601, 654, 686, 867, 904, 917, 946, 1001; **Professionals/Postdoctorates,** 1158, 1191. *See also* Texas

B

Baltimore County, Maryland: **Undergraduates,** 179. *See also* Maryland

Baton Rouge, Louisiana: **Undergraduates,** 378. *See also* Louisiana

Berkeley, California: **Undergraduates,** 359, 555-556; **Graduate Students,** 686, 888, 1026; **Professionals/Postdoctorates,** 1153, 1202, 1207. *See also* California

Bethesda, Maryland: **Undergraduates,** 30, 407. *See also* Maryland

Big Rapids, Michigan: **Undergraduates,** 451. *See also* Michigan

Bloomington, Indiana: **Undergraduates,** 40; **Graduate Students,** 686. *See also* Indiana

Boston, Massachusetts: **Undergraduates,** 168, 221, 523-526; **Graduate Students,** 724, 751, 957, 1040; **Professionals/Postdoctorates,** 1121, 1124, 1214. *See also* Massachusetts

Boulder, Colorado: **Undergraduates,** 473, 511; **Graduate Students,** 645; **Professionals/Postdoctorates,** 1161. *See also* Colorado

Brunswick, Maine: **Graduate Students,** 702. *See also* Maine

Bryn Mawr, Pennsylvania: **Graduate Students,** 702. *See also* Pennsylvania

Buies Creek, North Carolina: **Undergraduates,** 451. *See also* North Carolina

Burlington County, New Jersey: **Graduate Students,** 773. *See also* New Jersey

Subject Index

There are hundreds of specific subject fields covered in this directory. Use the Subject Index to identify these topics, as well as the recipient level supported (Undergraduates, Graduate Students, or Professionals/Postdoctorates) by the available funding programs. To help you pinpoint your search, we've included many "see" and "see also" references. Since a large number of programs are not restricted by subject, be sure to check the references listed under the "General programs" heading in the subject index (in addition to the specific terms that directly relate to your interest areas); hundreds of funding opportunities are listed there that can be used to support activities in any subject area   although the programs may be restricted in other ways. Remember: the numbers cited in this index refer to program entry numbers, not to page numbers in the book.

A

Academic librarianship. *See* Libraries and librarianship, academic

Accounting: **Undergraduates,** 7, 17, 23, 45, 51, 57, 106, 114, 135, 167, 187, 262, 272, 313, 317, 356, 365-366, 368, 370, 390, 392-393, 423, 428, 436, 501, 532, 565; **Graduate Students,** 610-611, 648, 676, 723, 812, 843, 886, 894, 906-907, 942. *See also* Finance; General programs

Acoustical engineering. *See* Engineering, acoustical

Acoustics: **Graduate Students,** 600. *See also* General programs; Physics

Acquired Immunodeficiency Syndrome. *See* AIDS

Acting. *See* Performing arts

Actuarial sciences: **Undergraduates,** 9, 347, 396, 532. *See also* General programs; Statistics

Addiction. *See* Alcohol use and abuse; Drug use and abuse

Administration. *See* Business administration; Education, administration; Management; Nurses and nursing, administration; Personnel administration; Public administration

Adolescents: **Graduate Students,** 816. *See also* Child development; General programs

Advertising: **Undergraduates,** 32, 71, 123, 144, 178, 237, 264, 287, 302, 434, 440, 469; **Graduate Students,** 616, 654, 730, 789, 834, 845, 946, 974. *See also* Communications; General programs; Marketing; Public relations

Aeronautical engineering. *See* Engineering, aeronautical

Aeronautics: **Graduate Students,** 912. *See also* Aviation; Engineering, aeronautical; General programs; Physical sciences

Aerospace engineering. *See* Engineering, aerospace

Aerospace sciences. *See* Space sciences

Affirmative action: **Undergraduates,** 260. *See also* Equal opportunity; General programs

African American studies: **Graduate Students,** 703, 960; **Professionals/Postdoctorates,** 1182. *See also* General programs; Minority studies

African history. *See* History, African

Aged and aging: **Graduate Students,** 608, 881; **Professionals/ Postdoctorates,** 1127, 1160, 1169, 1178. *See also* General programs; Social sciences

Agribusiness: **Undergraduates,** 183, 428; **Graduate Students,** 736. *See also* Agriculture and agricultural sciences; Business administration; General programs

Agricultural economics. *See* Economics, agricultural

Agricultural engineering. *See* Engineering, agricultural

Agriculture and agricultural sciences: **Undergraduates,** 183, 409; **Graduate Students,** 736, 878, 997; **Professionals/ Postdoctorates,** 1081, 1190. *See also* Biological sciences; General programs

Agrimarketing and sales. *See* Agribusiness

AIDS: **Undergraduates,** 33, 221; **Graduate Students,** 880; **Professionals/Postdoctorates,** 1066. *See also* Disabilities; General programs; Immunology; Medical sciences

Air conditioning industry. *See* Cooling industry

Alcohol use and abuse: **Graduate Students,** 733, 882, 924; **Professionals/Postdoctorates,** 1197. *See also* Drug use and abuse; General programs; Health and health care

Alzheimer's Disease: **Graduate Students,** 608; **Professionals/ Postdoctorates,** 1060-1062, 1215. *See also* Aged and aging; Disabilities; General programs; Medical sciences

American history. *See* History, American

American Indian language. *See* Language, Native American

American Indian studies. *See* Native American studies

American literature. *See* Literature, American

American studies: **Graduate Students,** 703, 892, 960; **Professionals/Postdoctorates,** 1133, 1182. *See also* General programs; Humanities

Animal science: **Undergraduates,** 514; **Graduate Students,** 600, 1009. *See also* General programs; Sciences; names of specific animal sciences

Animation: **Undergraduates,** 586; **Graduate Students,** 1049. *See also* Cartoonists and cartoons; Filmmaking; General programs

Business education. *See* Education, business

Business enterprises. *See* Entrepreneurship

Business law: **Graduate Students,** 998. *See also* General programs; Law, general

C

Cable TV journalism. *See* Journalism, cable

Canadian history. *See* History, Canadian

Cancer: **Undergraduates,** 91, 221, 518; **Graduate Students,** 643, 653. *See also* Disabilities; General programs; Health and health care; Medical sciences

Cardiology: **Undergraduates,** 221. *See also* General programs; Medical sciences

Caribbean history. *See* History, Caribbean

Caribbean studies: **Professionals/Postdoctorates,** 1085, 1098. *See also* General programs; Humanities; Latin American studies

Cars. *See* Engineering, automotive

Cartoonists and cartoons: **Undergraduates,** 177. *See also* Art; General programs; Illustrators and illustrations

Cell biology: **Undergraduates,** 121, 402, 555, 557, 572; **Graduate Students,** 879, 912; **Professionals/Postdoctorates,** 1065, 1124. *See also* Biological sciences; General programs

Chemical engineering. *See* Engineering, chemical

Chemistry: **Undergraduates,** 28, 39, 49, 88, 129, 182, 186-187, 202, 345, 372, 385, 402, 419, 496, 499, 511, 513, 530-531, 555-557, 572, 590; **Graduate Students,** 684, 698, 703, 734, 740, 749, 752, 763, 797, 878, 895, 912, 916, 920, 936, 948, 960, 1016, 1052; **Professionals/Postdoctorates,** 1096, 1161, 1182. *See also* Engineering, chemical; General programs; Physical sciences

Chicano affairs. *See* Hispanic American affairs

Chicano studies. *See* Hispanic American studies

Child development: **Graduate Students,** 816. *See also* Adolescents; General programs

Children's literature. *See* Literature, children's

Choreography: **Professionals/Postdoctorates,** 1170. *See also* Dance; General programs; Performing arts

Church music. *See* Music, church

Cinema: **Professionals/Postdoctorates,** 1170. *See also* Filmmaking; General programs; Literature

City and regional planning. *See* Urban and regional planning

Civil engineering. *See* Engineering, civil

Classical studies: **Undergraduates,** 377. *See also* General programs; Literature

Clerical skills. *See* Secretarial sciences

Climatology: **Graduate Students,** 645, 911; **Professionals/Postdoctorates,** 1074, 1080-1081, 1205. *See also* Atmospheric sciences; General programs; Physical sciences

Clothing: **Undergraduates,** 284; **Graduate Students,** 827. *See also* General programs

Colleges and universities. *See* Education, higher; Libraries and librarianship, academic

Commerce. *See* Business administration

Communications: **Undergraduates,** 19, 106-107, 123, 178, 237, 265, 287, 315, 338, 346, 350, 365-366, 368, 434, 463, 469, 545; **Graduate Students,** 600, 672, 676, 703, 730, 789, 805-806, 817, 834, 859, 960, 974; **Professionals/Postdoctorates,** 1084, 1182. *See also* General programs; Humanities

Community colleges. *See* Education, higher; Libraries and librarianship, academic

Community services. *See* Social services

Composers and compositions: **Undergraduates,** 447; **Graduate Students,** 952; **Professionals/Postdoctorates,** 1078, 1119, 1170. *See also* General programs; Music

Computer engineering. *See* Engineering, computer

Computer sciences: **Undergraduates,** 10, 39-40, 66, 106, 116, 125, 136, 145, 177, 179, 187, 196, 200-202, 204, 242-243, 262, 266, 280, 365-366, 368, 402, 408, 419, 455, 457, 491, 496, 506, 508, 511, 578, 590; **Graduate Students,** 598-599, 601, 631, 645, 676, 684, 703, 747, 749-750, 752, 763, 797, 800, 821-822, 878, 912, 916, 920, 936, 960, 971, 1000, 1052; **Professionals/Postdoctorates,** 1084, 1161, 1182. *See also* General programs; Mathematics; Technology

Computers. *See* Computer sciences

Conflict resolution. *See* Peace studies

Conservation. *See* Art conservation; Environmental sciences; Preservation

Construction. *See* Building trades; Housing

Construction engineering. *See* Engineering, construction

Construction industry: **Undergraduates,** 125. *See also* General programs

Consumer and family studies education. *See* Education, family and consumer studies

Cooking. *See* Culinary arts

Cooling industry: **Undergraduates,** 125. *See also* General programs

Copyright law. *See* Intellectual property law

Corporate law: **Graduate Students,** 595-596, 1002. *See also* General programs; Law, general

Costume: **Graduate Students,** 917. *See also* Art; General programs

Counseling: **Graduate Students,** 923-925; **Professionals/Postdoctorates,** 1167. *See also* Behavioral sciences; General programs; Psychiatry; Psychology

Counselors and counseling, school: **Undergraduates,** 63, 564; **Graduate Students,** 959, 1039. *See also* Counseling; Education; General programs

Counter-intelligence service. *See* Intelligence service

Crafts. *See* Arts and crafts

Criminal justice: **Undergraduates,** 218-219, 340, 372; **Graduate Students,** 769, 851, 873, 895, 990; **Professionals/Postdoctorates,** 1100, 1210-1211. *See also* General programs; Law, general

Criminal law: **Graduate Students,** 851. *See also* General programs; Law, general

Culinary arts: **Undergraduates,** 92-93, 284; **Graduate Students,** 827. *See also* Food service industry; General programs

D

Dance: **Undergraduates,** 62, 273, 534; **Graduate Students,** 813. *See also* Choreography; General programs; Performing arts

Data entry. *See* Computer sciences; Secretarial sciences

Deafness. *See* Hearing impairments

Dental assisting: **Undergraduates,** 223, 289, 461; **Graduate Students,** 774, 836, 963. *See also* General programs; Health and health care

Dental hygiene: **Undergraduates,** 115, 156, 223, 289, 461; **Graduate Students,** 715, 774, 836, 963. *See also* General programs; Health and health care

Calendar Index

Since most funding programs have specific deadline dates, some may have already closed by the time you begin to look for money. You can use the Calendar Index to identify which programs are still open. To do that, go to the recipient category (Undergraduates, Graduate Students, or Professionals/Postdoctorates) that interests you, think about when you'll be able to complete your application forms, go to the appropriate months, jot down the entry numbers listed there, and use those numbers to find the program descriptions in the directory. Keep in mind that the numbers cited here refer to program entry numbers, not to page numbers in the book.

August: 627, 683, 690, 765, 789

September: 609, 613, 678, 685, 705, 712, 735, 744, 756, 762, 773, 795, 829, 852, 884, 918, 932-933, 935, 967, 1021, 1034, 1038, 1042-1043, 1052

October: 620-621, 637, 645, 650, 657, 668, 702, 707, 742, 760, 763, 770, 772, 797, 849, 868, 883, 915, 938, 951, 953, 958, 1024, 1032

November: 622, 634, 646-647, 651, 671, 689, 703, 723, 746-749, 759, 778, 794, 803, 806, 813-814, 838, 853, 870, 874, 896, 903-904, 913, 920, 942, 960, 981, 1001, 1030, 1048, 1053

December: 591, 601, 606, 612, 676, 706, 709, 716, 758, 793, 888, 897, 905, 916, 922, 992, 1022, 1025, 1040

Any time: 631, 781, 919

Deadline not specified: 700, 840, 921, 946, 964-965, 1019, 1039

Professionals/Postdoctorates:

January: 1059, 1067, 1069, 1074, 1085, 1087, 1102-1103, 1106, 1111, 1115, 1128, 1130-1133, 1145, 1159, 1161, 1170, 1181, 1185-1186, 1190, 1195, 1197, 1205, 1212

February: 1056, 1071, 1077, 1092, 1094-1095, 1097, 1107, 1119, 1141, 1150-1151, 1160, 1169, 1198

March: 1064-1065, 1072, 1080, 1112, 1118, 1154, 1175, 1196, 1215

April: 1070, 1075-1076, 1082, 1086, 1096, 1110, 1122, 1134, 1156-1157, 1163, 1168, 1193

May: 1093, 1098, 1101, 1140, 1144, 1173, 1210-1211

June: 1057, 1078, 1089-1091, 1104, 1108, 1116, 1120, 1127, 1135, 1167, 1209, 1213

July: 1109, 1139, 1179, 1192

August: 1054, 1066, 1180

September: 1060-1062, 1081, 1088, 1137-1138, 1143, 1164, 1184

October: 1068, 1073, 1079, 1083, 1100, 1113, 1123, 1125, 1129, 1142, 1147-1148, 1152, 1171, 1174, 1176-1178, 1183, 1188, 1194, 1201-1204, 1206-1207

November: 1063, 1084, 1105, 1117, 1146, 1149, 1155, 1158, 1182, 1187, 1191, 1208, 1214

December: 1055, 1058, 1099, 1114, 1121, 1153, 1162, 1165-1166, 1189, 1199-1200

Any time: 1124, 1126, 1136

Deadline not specified: 1172

76969881R20254

Made in the USA
Middletown, DE
16 June 2018